Getting Started is as EASY as 1, 2,

1. Sign Up
Instructors register with myBusinessCourse.com

2. Setup Your Course
Add your class details and additional materials.

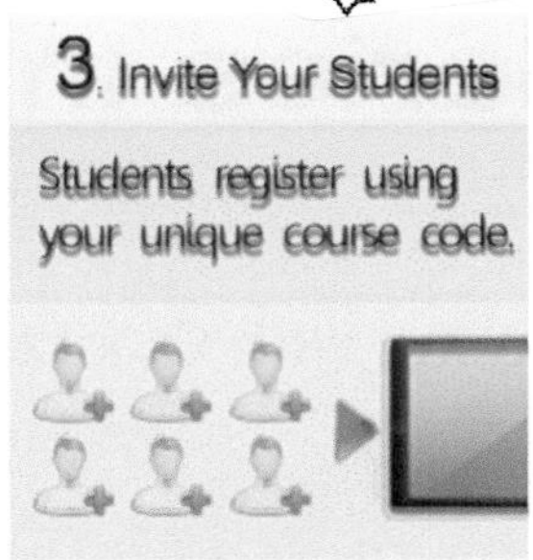
3. Invite Your Students
Students register using your unique course code.

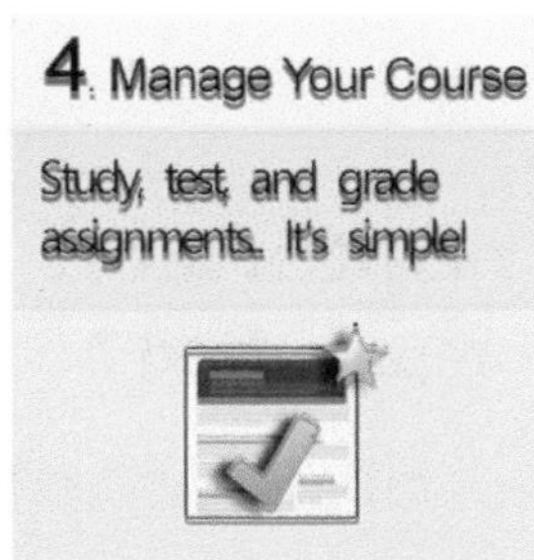
4. Manage Your Course
Study, test, and grade assignments. It's simple!

Provide Instruction and Practice 24/7

- Assign homework from your Cambridge Business Publishers textbook and have myBusinessCourse grade it for you automatically.
- With our eLectures, your students can revisit accounting topics as often as they like or until they master the topic.
- Guided Examples show students how to solve select problems.
- Make homework due before class to ensure students enter your classroom prepared.
- For an additional fee, upgrade MBC to include the eBook and you have all the tools needed for an online course.

STUDENT SELF-STUDY OPTION

Not all instructors choose to incorporate **myBusinessCourse** into their course. In such cases, students can access the Self-Study option for MBC. The Self-Study option provides most of the learning tools available in the Instructor-Led courses, including:

- eLectures
- Guided Examples
- Practice Quizzes

The Self-Study option does not include homework assignments from the textbook. Only the Instructor-Led option includes homework assignments.

Want to learn more about myBusinessCourse?

Contact your sales representative or visit www.mybusinesscourse.com.

STUDENTS: Find your access code on the myBusinessCourse insert on the following pages. If you have a used copy of this textbook, you can purchase access online at www.mybusinesscourse.com.

Cambridge Business Publishers Series in Accounting

Computerized Accounting

- **Computerized Accounting with QuickBooks® 2015**, by Williams

Financial Accounting

- **Financial Accounting for Undergraduates, 3e** by Wallace, Nelson, Christensen, and Ferris
- **Financial Accounting, 5e** by Dyckman, Hanlon, Magee, and Pfeiffer
- **Financial Accounting for MBAs, 6e** by Easton, Wild, Halsey, and McAnally
- **Financial Accounting for Executives & MBAs, 4e** by Simko, Ferris, and Wallace
- **Cases in Financial Reporting, 8e** by Drake, Engel, Hirst, and McAnally

Financial Accounting Using IFRS

- **Financial Accounting, 2e** by Wong, Dyckman, Hanlon, Magee, and Pfeiffer

Managerial Accounting

- **Managerial Accounting for Undergraduates, 1e** by Christensen, Hobson, and Wallace
- **Managerial Accounting, 7e** by Hartgraves & Morse
- **Cases in Managerial and Cost Accounting, 1e** by Allen, Brownlee, Haskins, and Lynch

Combined Financial & Managerial Accounting

- **Financial & Managerial Accounting for Decision Makers, 2e** by Dyckman, Magee, Pfeiffer, Hartgraves, and Morse
- **Financial & Managerial Accounting for MBAs, 4e** by Easton, Halsey, McAnally, Hartgraves, and Morse

Intermediate Accounting

- **Cases in Financial Reporting, 8e** by Drake, Engel, Hirst, and McAnally

Cost Accounting

- **Cases in Managerial and Cost Accounting, 1e** by Allen, Brownlee, Haskins, and Lynch

Financial Statement Analysis & Valuation

- **Financial Statement Analysis & Valuation, 4e** by Easton, McAnally, Sommers, and Zhang
- **Corporate Valuation, 1e** by Holthausen & Zmijewski
- **Cases in Financial Reporting, 8e** by Drake, Engel, Hirst, and McAnally

Advanced Accounting

- **Advanced Accounting, 3e** by Hamlen, Huefner, and Largay
- **Advanced Accounting, 3e** by Halsey & Hopkins

FASB Codification and eIFRS

- **Skills for Accounting Research: Text & Cases, 3e** by Collins

my BusinessCourse

FREE WITH NEW COPIES OF THIS TEXTBOOK

Scratch here for access code

Scratch here for access code

cctfyzErUjKpntbP

Start using myBusinessCourse Today: www.mybusinesscourse.com

myBusinessCourse is a web-based learning and assessment program intended to complement your textbook and faculty instruction.

Student Benefits

- eLectures
- Guided examples
- Immediate feedback with auto graded homework from the textbook **(with Instructor-Led courses ONLY)**
- Opportunities for additional practice and exam preparation
- For additional fee, can be upgraded to include eBook

Instructor Benefits

- Easy-to-use course management system
- Homework automatically graded **(with Instructor-Led courses ONLY)**
- Provide students with additional help when you are not available
- Detailed diagnostic tools to assess class performance
- Resources for a complete online course
- Integrates with other CMS platforms, such as Canvas, Blackboard, and Moodle

Interactive content that runs on any device.

Built for PCs, iPads, Laptops, Tablets, Smartphones

You can access myBusinessCourse 24/7 from any web-enabled device, including iPads, smartphones, laptops, and tablets.

If you purchased a used book and the protective coating that covers the access code has been removed, your code may be invalid.

Access to myBusinessCourse is free ONLY with the purchase of a new textbook.

FIFTH EDITION

Financial Accounting

THOMAS R. DYCKMAN
Cornell University

MICHELLE L. HANLON
Massachusetts Institute of Technology

ROBERT P. MAGEE
Northwestern University

GLENN M. PFEIFFER
Chapman University

To my wife, Ann, and children, Daniel, James, Linda, and David; and to Pete Dukes, a friend who is always there.

—TRD

To my husband, Chris, and to our children, Clark and Josie.

—MLH

To my wife, Peggy, and our family, Paul and Teisha, Michael and Heather, and grandchildren Sage, Caillean, Rhiannon, Corin, Connor, and Harrison.

—RPM

To my wife, Kathie, and my daughter, Jaclyn.

—GMP

Cambridge Business Publishers

FINANCIAL ACCOUNTING, Fifth Edition, by Thomas R. Dyckman, Michelle L. Hanlon, Robert P. Magee, and Glenn M. Pfeiffer.

Student Edition ISBN: 978-1-61853-165-0

Bookstores & Faculty: To order this book, contact the company via email **customerservice@cambridgepub.com** or call 800-619-6473.

Students: To order this book, please visit the book's website and order directly online.

Printed in the United States of America.
10 9 8 7 6 5 4 3 2 1

About the Authors

The combined skills and expertise of Tom Dyckman, Michelle Hanlon, Bob Magee, and Glenn Pfeiffer create the ideal team to author this exciting financial accounting textbook. Their combined experience in award-winning teaching, consulting, and research in the area of financial accounting and analysis provides a powerful foundation for this pioneering textbook.

Thomas R. Dyckman is Ann Whitney Olin Professor Emeritus of Accounting and Quantitative Analysis at Cornell University's Johnson Graduate School of Management. In addition to teaching accounting and quantitative analysis, he has taught in Cornell's Executive Development Program. He earned his doctorate degree from the University of Michigan. He is a former member of the Financial Accounting Standards Board Advisory Committee and the Financial Accounting Foundation, which oversees the FASB. He was president of the American Accounting Association in 1982 and received the association's *Outstanding Educator* Award for the year 1987. He also received the AICPA's *Notable Contributions to Accounting Literature Award* in 1966 and 1978.

Professor Dyckman has extensive industrial experience that includes work with the U.S. Navy and IBM. He has conducted seminars for Cornell Executive Development Program and Managing the Next Generation of Technology, as well as for Ocean Spray, Goodyear, Morgan Guaranty, GTE, Southern New England Telephone, and Goulds Pumps. Professor Dyckman was elected to The Accounting Hall of Fame in 2009.

Professor Dyckman has coauthored eleven books and written over 50 journal articles on topics from financial markets to the application of quantitative and behavioral theory to administrative decision making. He has been a member of the editorial boards of *The Accounting Review, The Journal of Finance and Quantitative Analysis, The Journal of Accounting and Economics, The Journal of Management Accounting Research,* and *The Journal of Accounting Education*.

Michelle L. Hanlon is the Howard W. Johnson Professor at the MIT Sloan School of Management. She earned her doctorate degree at the University of Washington. Prior to joining MIT, she was a faculty member at the University of Michigan. Professor Hanlon has taught financial accounting to undergraduates, MBA students, Executive MBA students, and Masters of Finance students. Professor Hanlon also teaches Taxes and Business Strategy to MBA students. She is the winner of the 2013 Jamieson Prize for Excellence in Teaching at MIT Sloan.

Professor Hanlon's research focuses primarily on the intersection of taxation and financial accounting. Her recent work examines the capital market effects of the accounting for income tax, the reputational effects of corporate tax avoidance, and the economic consequences of U.S. international tax policies for multinational corporations. She has published research studies in the *Journal of Accounting and Economics*, the *Journal of Accounting Research*, *The Accounting Review*, the *Review of Accounting Studies*, the *Journal of Finance*, the *Journal of Financial Economics*, the *Journal of Public Economics*, and others. She has won several awards for her research and has presented her work at numerous universities and conferences. Professor Hanlon has served on several editorial boards and currently serves as an editor at the *Journal of Accounting and Economics*.

Professor Hanlon is a co-author on another textbook, *Taxes and Business Strategy*. She has testified in front of the U.S. Senate Committee on Finance and the U.S. House of Representatives Committee on Ways and Means about the interaction of financial accounting and tax policy. She served as a U.S. delegate to the American-Swiss Young Leaders Conference in 2010 and worked as an Academic Fellow at the U.S. House Ways and Means Committee in 2015.

Robert P. Magee is Keith I. DeLashmutt Professor of Accounting Information and Management at the Kellogg School of Management at Northwestern University. He received his A.B., M.S. and Ph.D. from Cornell University. Prior to joining the Kellogg faculty in 1976, he was a faculty member at the University of Chicago's Graduate School of Business. For academic year 1980-81, he was a visiting faculty member at IMEDE (now IMD) in Lausanne, Switzerland.

Professor Magee's research focuses on the use of accounting information to facilitate decision-making and control within organizations. He has published articles in *The Accounting Review,* the *Journal of Accounting Research*, the *Journal of Accounting and Economics*, and a variety of other journals. He is the author of *Advanced Managerial Accounting* and co-author (with Thomas R. Dyckman and David H. Downes) of *Efficient Capital Markets and Accounting: A Critical Analysis*. The latter book received the Notable Contribution to the Accounting Literature Award from the AICPA in 1978. Professor Magee has served on the editorial boards of *The Accounting Review,* the *Journal of Accounting Research*, the *Journal of Accounting and Economics* and the *Journal of Accounting, Auditing and*

Finance. From 1994–96, he served as Editor of *The Accounting Review*, the quarterly research journal of the American Accounting Association. He received the American Accounting Association's Outstanding Accounting Educator Award in 1999 and the Illinois CPA Society Outstanding Educator Award in 2000.

Professor Magee teaches financial accounting to MBA and Executive MBA students. He has received several teaching awards at the Kellogg School, including the Alumni Choice Outstanding Professor Award in 2003.

Glenn M. Pfeiffer is the Warren and Doris Uehlinger Professor of Business at the George L. Argyros School of Business and Economics at Chapman University. He received his M.S. and Ph.D. from Cornell University after he earned a bachelors degree from Hope College. Prior to joining the faculty at the Argyros School, he held appointments at the University of Washington, Cornell University, the University of Chicago, the University of Arizona, and San Diego State University.

Professor Pfeiffer's research focuses on accounting and capital markets. He has investigated issues relating to lease accounting, LIFO inventory liquidation, earnings per share, management compensation, corporate reorganization, and technology investments. He has published articles in *The Accounting Review*, *Accounting Horizons*, the *Financial Analysts Journal*, the *International Journal of Accounting Information Systems*, the *Journal of High Technology Management Research*, the *Journal of Economics*, the *Journal of Accounting Education*, and several other academic journals. In addition, he has published numerous case studies in financial accounting and reporting.

Professor Pfeiffer teaches financial accounting and financial analysis to undergraduate, MBA, and Law students. He has also taught managerial accounting for MBAs. He has won several teaching awards at both the undergraduate and graduate levels.

Preface

Welcome to the fifth edition of *Financial Accounting* and, to adopters of the first four editions, thank you for the great success those editions have enjoyed. We wrote this book to equip students with the accounting techniques and insights necessary to succeed in today's business environment. It reflects our combined experience in teaching financial accounting to college students at all levels. For anyone who pursues a career in business, the ability to read, analyze, and interpret published financial reports is an essential skill. *Financial Accounting* is written for future business leaders who want to understand how financial statements are prepared and how the information in published financial reports is used by investors, creditors, financial analysts, and managers. Our goal is to provide the most engaging, relevant, and accessible textbook available.

TARGET AUDIENCE

Financial Accounting is intended for use in the first financial accounting course at either the undergraduate or graduate level; one that balances the preparation of financial statements with their analysis and interpretation. This book accommodates mini-courses lasting only a few days as well as extended courses lasting a full semester.

Financial Accounting is real-world oriented and focuses on the most salient aspects of accounting. It teaches students how to read, analyze, and interpret financial accounting data to make informed business decisions. To that end, it consistently incorporates **real company data**, both in the body of each chapter and throughout the assignment material.

REAL DATA INCORPORATED THROUGHOUT

Today's business students must be skilled in using real financial statements to make business decisions. We feel strongly that the more exposure students get to real financial statements, the more comfortable they become with the variety in financial statements that exists across companies and industries. Through their exposure to various financial statements, students will learn that, while financial statements do not all look the same, they can readily understand and interpret them to make business decisions. Furthermore, today's students must have the skills to go beyond basic financial statements to interpret and apply nonfinancial disclosures, such as footnotes and supplementary reports. We expose students to the analysis and interpretation of real company data and nonfinancial disclosures through the use of focus companies in each chapter, the generous incorporation of footnotes, financial analysis discussions in nearly every chapter, and an abundance of assignments that draw on real company data and disclosures.

Focus Companies for Each Chapter

Each chapter's content is explained through the accounting and reporting activities of real companies. Each chapter incorporates a "focus company" for special emphasis and demonstration. The enhanced instructional value of focus companies comes from the way they engage students in real analysis and interpretation. Focus companies were selected based on student appeal and the diversity of industries.

Chapter 1	**Nike**	**Chapter 7**	**Home Depot**
Chapter 2	**Walgreens**	**Chapter 8**	**Procter & Gamble**
Chapter 3	**Walgreens**	**Chapter 9**	**Verizon**
Chapter 4	**Golden Enterprises**	**Chapter 10**	**Delta Air Lines**
Chapter 5	**PepsiCo**	**Chapter 11**	**Pfizer**
Chapter 6	**Cisco**	**Chapter 12**	**Google**

Footnotes and Management Disclosures

We incorporate footnote and other management disclosures, where appropriate, throughout the book. We explain the significance of the footnote and then demonstrate how to use the disclosed information to make managerial inferences and decisions. A representative sample follows.

Footnote Disclosures and Interpretations

In its balance sheets, Cisco reports Accounts receivables, net of allowance for doubtful accounts of $5,157 million at July 26, 2014, and $5,470 at July 27, 2013. In its MD&A (Management Discussion and Analysis), the company provides the following information.

Allowances for Receivables and Sales Returns

The allowances for receivables were as follows (in millions, except percentages):

	July 26, 2014	July 27, 2013
Allowance for doubtful accounts	$265	$228
Percentage of gross accounts receivable	4.9%	4.0%

The allowance for doubtful accounts is based on our assessment of the collectability of customer accounts. We regularly review the allowances to ensure their adequacy by considering internal factors such as historical experience, credit quality, age of the receivable balances as well as external factors such as economic conditions that may affect a customer's ability to pay. . . . We also consider the concentration of receivables outstanding with a particular customer in assessing the adequacy of our allowances . . .

Financial Analysis Discussions

Each chapter includes a financial analysis discussion that introduces key ratios and applies them to the financial statements of the chapter's focus company. By weaving some analysis into each chapter, we try to instill in students a deeper appreciation for the significance of the accounting methods being discussed. One such analysis discussion follows.

ANALYZING FINANCIAL STATEMENTS

LO5 Define and interpret gross profit margin and inventory turnover ratios. Use inventory footnote information to make appropriate adjustments to ratios.

Analysis Objective

We are trying to determine whether Home Depot's sales provide sufficient revenues to cover its operation costs, primarily selling and administrative expenses, after allowing for the costs of manufacturing.

Analysis Tool Gross Profit Margin (GPM) Ratio

$$\textbf{Gross profit margin} = \frac{\textbf{Sales revenue} - \textbf{Cost of goods sold}}{\textbf{Sales revenue}}$$

Applying the Gross Profit Margin Ratio to Home Depot

$$\textbf{2012:}\ \frac{(\$74{,}754 - \$48{,}912)}{\$74{,}754} = 0.346 \text{ or } 34.6\%$$

$$\textbf{2013:}\ \frac{(\$78{,}812 - \$51{,}422)}{\$78{,}812} = 0.348 \text{ or } 34.8\%$$

$$\textbf{2014:}\ \frac{(\$83{,}176 - \$54{,}222)}{\$83{,}176} = 0.348 \text{ or } 34.8\%$$

Assignments that Draw on Real Data

It is essential for students to be able to apply what they have learned to real financial statements. Therefore, we have included an abundance of assignments in each chapter that draw on recent, real data and disclosures. These assignments are readily identified by an icon in the margin that usually includes the company's ticker symbol and the exchange on which the company's stock trades. A representative example follows.

P5-45. Comparing Profitability Ratios for Competitors

LO3

Abbott Laboratories NYSE :: ABT
Bristol-Myers Squibb Company NYSE :: BMY
Johnson & Johnson NYSE :: JNJ
GlaxoSmithKline plc (ADR) NYSE :: GSK
Pfizer Inc. NYSE :: PFE

Selected income statement data for **Abbott Laboratories**, **Bristol-Myers Squibb Company**, **Johnson & Johnson**, **GlaxoSmithKline plc**, and **Pfizer, Inc.** is presented in the following table:

($ millions)	Abbott Laboratories	Bristol-Myers Squibb	Johnson & Johnson	Glaxo Smith Kline plc	Pfizer
Sales revenue	$20,247	$11,660	$74,331	$35,872	$49,605
Cost of sales	9,218	3,932	22,746	11,418	9,577
SG&A expense	6,530	4,822	21,954	13,466	14,097
R&D expense	1,345	4,534	8,494	5,379	8,393
Interest expense	150	203	533	1,134	1,360
Net income	2,284	2,029	16,323	4,297	9,168

REQUIRED

a. Compute the profit margin (PM) and gross profit margin (GPM) ratios for each company. (As a British company, GlaxoSmithKline plc has a statutory tax rate of 26.5% in 2014.)

b. Compute the research and development (R&D) expense to sales ratio and the selling, general and administrative (SG&A) expense to sales ratio for each company.

c. Compare the relative profitability of these pharmaceutical companies.

BALANCED APPROACH

As instructors of introductory financial accounting, we recognize that the first financial accounting course serves the general business students as well as potential accounting majors. *Financial Accounting* embraces this reality. This book **balances financial reporting, analysis**, **interpretation**, and **decision making** with the more standard aspects of accounting such as **journal entries**, **T-accounts**, and the **preparation of financial statements**.

3-Step Process: Analyze, Journalize, Post

One technique we use throughout the book to maintain a balanced approach is the incorporation of a 3-step process to analyze and record transactions. **Step 1** analyzes the impact of various transactions on the financial statements using the financial statement effects template. **Step 2** records the transaction using journal entries, and **Step 3** requires students to post the journal entries to T-accounts.

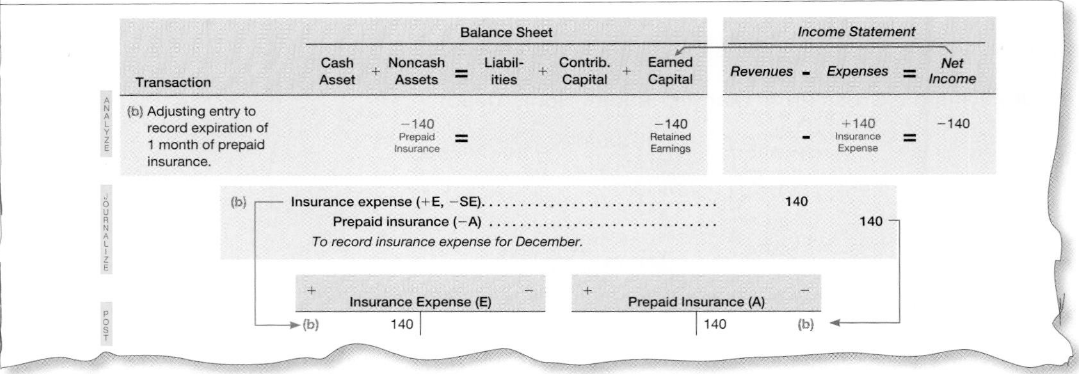

The template captures each transaction's effects on the four financial statements: the balance sheet, income statement, statement of stockholders' equity, and statement of cash flows. For the balance sheet, we differentiate between cash and noncash assets to identify the cash effects of transactions. Likewise, equity is separated into the contributed and earned capital components (the latter includes retained earnings as its major element). Finally, income statement effects are separated into revenues, expenses, and net income (the updating of retained earnings is denoted with an arrow line running from net income to earned capital). This template provides a convenient means to represent financial accounting transactions and events in a simple, concise manner for assessing their effects on financial statements.

INTERNATIONAL FINANCIAL REPORTING STANDARDS (IFRS)

The convergence of U.S. GAAP and International Financial Reporting Standards (IFRS) is in process. Our introductory students should be prepared for this eventuality with a basic understanding of the similarities and differences in the current reporting requirements and methods under U.S. GAAP and IFRS. Consequently, we incorporate discussions that examine these similarities and differences where appropriate throughout the book in Global Perspective boxes, as illustrated here:

A GLOBAL PERSPECTIVE

Under U.S. GAAP, inventory that has been written down cannot be revalued later at higher levels even if the market value of that inventory increases. IFRS, on the other hand, does allow companies to reverse the write-down of the inventory up to the acquisition cost if market values warrant. The revaluation results in a debit to Inventory and a credit to Cost of Goods Sold. The option to revalue inventory after a write-down differs across countries.

We also include exercises and problems throughout the text, where appropriate, to stimulate a discussion of international reporting differences. Our approach is conceptual—we purposefully avoid the detailed mechanics that are more appropriate for an intermediate level accounting course at either the undergraduate or graduate level. We feel strongly that our IFRS coverage exposes students to the similarities and differences without overwhelming them.

INNOVATIVE PEDAGOGY

Business Insights

Students appreciate and become more engaged when they can see the real world relevance of what they are learning in the classroom. We have included a generous number of current, real world examples throughout each chapter in Business Insight boxes. The following is a representative example:

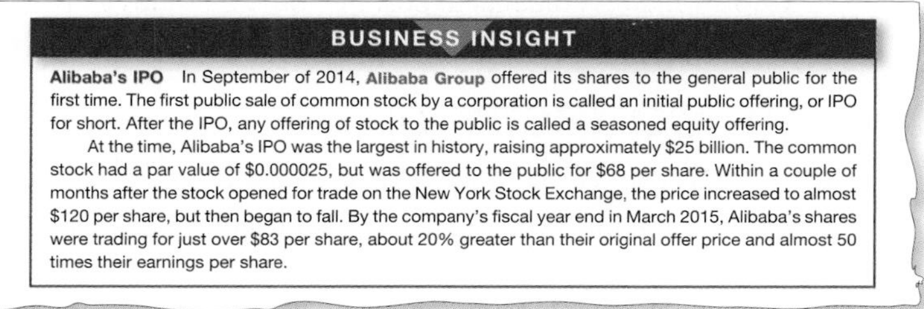

BUSINESS INSIGHT

Alibaba's IPO In September of 2014, **Alibaba Group** offered its shares to the general public for the first time. The first public sale of common stock by a corporation is called an initial public offering, or IPO for short. After the IPO, any offering of stock to the public is called a seasoned equity offering.

At the time, Alibaba's IPO was the largest in history, raising approximately $25 billion. The common stock had a par value of $0.000025, but was offered to the public for $68 per share. Within a couple of months after the stock opened for trade on the New York Stock Exchange, the price increased to almost $120 per share, but then began to fall. By the company's fiscal year end in March 2015, Alibaba's shares were trading for just over $83 per share, about 20% greater than their original offer price and almost 50 times their earnings per share.

Decision Making Orientation

One primary goal of a financial accounting course is to teach students the skills needed to apply their accounting knowledge to solving real business problems. With that goal in mind, **You Make the Call** boxes in each chapter encourage students to apply the material presented to solving actual business scenarios.

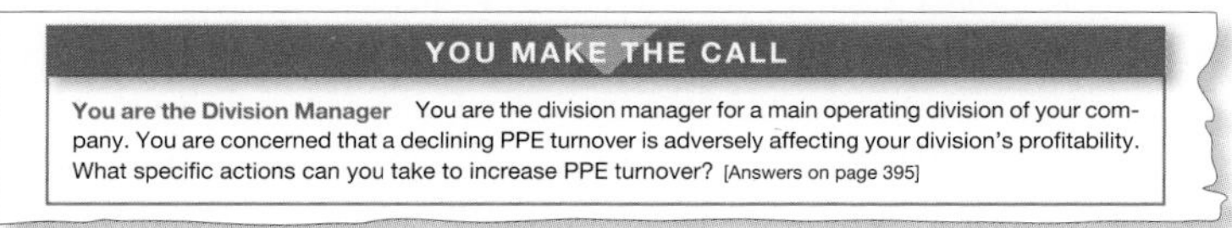

YOU MAKE THE CALL

You are the Division Manager You are the division manager for a main operating division of your company. You are concerned that a declining PPE turnover is adversely affecting your division's profitability. What specific actions can you take to increase PPE turnover? [Answers on page 395]

Mid-Chapter and Chapter-End Reviews

Financial accounting can be challenging—especially for students lacking business experience or previous exposure to business courses. To reinforce concepts presented in each chapter and to ensure student comprehension, we include mid-chapter and chapter-end reviews that require students to recall and apply the financial accounting techniques and concepts described in each chapter.

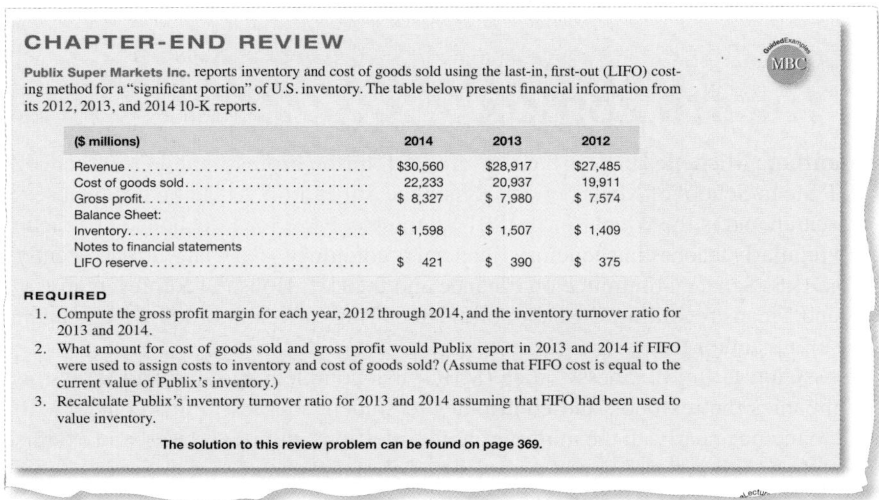

CHAPTER-END REVIEW

Publix Super Markets Inc. reports inventory and cost of goods sold using the last-in, first-out (LIFO) costing method for a "significant portion" of U.S. inventory. The table below presents financial information from its 2012, 2013, and 2014 10-K reports.

($ millions)	2014	2013	2012
Revenue	$30,560	$28,917	$27,485
Cost of goods sold	22,233	20,937	19,911
Gross profit	$ 8,327	$ 7,980	$ 7,574
Balance Sheet:			
Inventory	$ 1,598	$ 1,507	$ 1,409
Notes to financial statements			
LIFO reserve	$ 421	$ 390	$ 375

REQUIRED

1. Compute the gross profit margin for each year, 2012 through 2014, and the inventory turnover ratio for 2013 and 2014.
2. What amount for cost of goods sold and gross profit would Publix report in 2013 and 2014 if FIFO were used to assign costs to inventory and cost of goods sold? (Assume that FIFO cost is equal to the current value of Publix's inventory.)
3. Recalculate Publix's inventory turnover ratio for 2013 and 2014 assuming that FIFO had been used to value inventory.

The solution to this review problem can be found on page 369.

Research Insights for Business Students

Academic research plays an important role in the way business is conducted, accounting is performed, and students are taught. It is important for students to recognize how modern research and modern business practice interact. Therefore, we periodically incorporate relevant research to help students understand the important relation between research and modern business.

> **RESEARCH INSIGHT**
>
> **Accounting Conservatism and Cost of Debt** Research indicates that companies applying more conservative accounting methods incur a lower cost of debt. Research also suggests that while accounting conservatism can lead to lower-quality accounting income (because such income does not fully reflect economic reality), creditors are more confident in the numbers and view them as more credible. Evidence also implies that companies can lower the required return demanded by creditors (the risk premium) by issuing high-quality financial reports that include enhanced footnote disclosures and detailed supplemental reports.

FLEXIBILITY FOR COURSES OF VARYING LENGTHS

Many instructors have approached us to ask about suggested chapter coverage based on courses of varying length. To that end, we provide the following table of possible course designs:

	15 Week Semester-Course	10 Week Quarter-Course	6 Week Mini-Course	1 Week Intensive-Course
Chapter 1	Week 1	Week 1	Week 1	Day 1
Chapter 2	Week 2 & 3	Week 2	Week 1 & 2	
Chapter 3	Week 3 & 4	Week 3 & 4	Week 2 & 3	Day 2
Chapter 4	Week 5 & 6	Week 4 & 5	Optional	Optional
Chapter 5	Week 6 & 7	Optional	Optional	Optional
Chapter 6	Week 7 & 8	Week 6	Week 3	Day 3
Chapter 7	Week 9	Week 7	Week 4	Day 4
Chapter 8	Week 10	Week 8	Week 5	
Chapter 9	Week 11 & 12	Week 9	Week 6	Day 5
Chapter 10	Week 12 & 13	Week 10	Week 6 (optional)	Skim
Chapter 11	Week 14	Optional	Optional	Optional
Chapter 12	Week 15	Optional	Optional	Optional

NEW IN THE 5TH EDITION

- **New Co-author:** Michelle Hanlon, the Howard W. Johnson Professor and Professor of Accounting at the MIT Sloan School of Management, joined the 5th edition. Michelle has won several awards for her research and is the winner of the 2013 Jamieson Prize for Excellence in Teaching at Sloan where she regularly teaches introductory financial accounting to MBAs. Hanlon recently testified in front of the U.S. Senate Committee on Finance and the U.S. House of Representatives Committee on Ways and Means regarding U.S. tax policy. She brings a wealth of knowledge and expertise to this best-selling author team.
- **myBusinessCourse:** myBusinessCourse (MBC) is a complete learning and assessment program that accompanies the textbook and contributes to student success in this course. MBC has been expanded to include nearly all the multiple choice questions, mini-exercises, and exercises from the 5th edition. In addition, the Guided Examples and eLectures have been revised and improved. The 5th edition will also feature Flashcards and other tools that help students master concepts.

- **Updated Standards:** As appropriate, the text and assignments have been updated to reflect the latest standards. A brief discussion of the pending Revenue Recognition standard is included in Chapter 6 and the chapter-end appendix contains more detailed coverage of the new standard. The text and assignments have also been revised to reflect the change in accounting standards related to Extraordinary Items. Chapter 10 now includes a discussion of the new lease standard.

In addition to the chapter specific changes, there have been several changes that span the entire book. Some of these global changes include: updated numbers for examples, illustrations, and assignments that use real data; updated footnotes and other nonfinancial disclosures; updated excerpts from the business and popular press; numerous assignments in each chapter have been revised or replaced with new assignments; and a new, accessible design was created for the 5th edition.

SUPPLEMENT PACKAGE

Fundamentals of Financial Accounting Tutorial

This interactive tutorial is intended for use in programs that either require or would like to offer a pre-term tutorial that creates a baseline of accounting knowledge for students with little to no prior exposure to financial accounting. Initially developed as a pre-term tutorial for first year MBA students, this product can be used as a warm-up for any introductory level financial accounting course. It is designed as an asynchronous, interactive, self-paced experience for students.

Available Learning Modules (You Select)

1. Introducing Financial Accounting (approximate completion time 2 hours)
2. Constructing Financial Statements (approximate completion time 4 hours)
3. Adjusting Entries and Completing the Accounting Cycle (approximate completion time 4 hours)
4. Reporting and Analyzing Cash Flows (approximate completion time 3.5 hours)
5. Analyzing and Interpreting Financial Statements (approximate completion time 3.5 hours)

This is a separate, saleable item. Contact your sales representative to receive more information or email customerservice@cambridgepub.com.

Companion Casebook

Cases in Financial Reporting, 8th edition by Michael Drake (Brigham Young University), Ellen Engel (University of Chicago), D. Eric Hirst (University of Texas – Austin), and Mary Lea McAnally (Texas A&M University). This book comprises 27 cases and is a perfect companion book for faculty interested in exposing students to a wide range of real financial statements. The cases are current and cover companies from Canada, France, Austria, the Netherlands, the UK, India, as well as from the U.S. Many of the U.S. companies are major multinationals. Each case deals with a specific financial accounting topic within the context of one (or more) company's financial statements. Each case contains financial statement information and a set of directed questions pertaining to one or two specific financial accounting issues. This is a separate, saleable casebook (**ISBN 978-1-61853-122-3**). Contact your sales representative to receive a desk copy or email customerservice@cambridgepub.com.

For Instructors

Instructor CD-ROM: This convenient supplement provides the text's ancillary materials on a portable CD-ROM. All the faculty supplements that accompany the textbook are available, including PowerPoint, Solutions Manual, Test Bank, and Computerized Test Bank.

Solutions Manual: Created by the authors, the *Solutions Manual* contains complete solutions to all the assignment material in the text.

PowerPoint: The PowerPoint slides outline key elements of each chapter.

Test Bank: The Test Bank includes multiple-choice items, matching questions, short essay questions, and problems.

Website: All instructor materials are accessible via the book's Website (password protected) along with other useful links and marketing information. **www.cambridgepub.com**

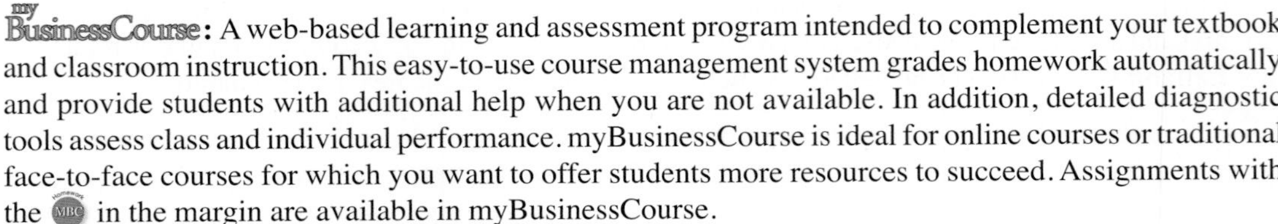

myBusinessCourse: A web-based learning and assessment program intended to complement your textbook and classroom instruction. This easy-to-use course management system grades homework automatically and provide students with additional help when you are not available. In addition, detailed diagnostic tools assess class and individual performance. myBusinessCourse is ideal for online courses or traditional face-to-face courses for which you want to offer students more resources to succeed. Assignments with the MBC in the margin are available in myBusinessCourse.

For Students

Student Solutions Manual: Created by the authors, the student Solutions Manual contains solutions to the even numbered assignments in the textbook. This is a **restricted** item that is only available to students after their instructor has authorized its purchase.

Website: Practice quizzes and other useful links are available to students free of charge on the book's Website.

myBusinessCourse: A web-based learning and assessment program intended to complement your textbook and faculty instruction. This easy-to-use program grades homework automatically and provides the sutdent with additional help when the instructor is not available. Assignments with the MBC in the margin are available in myBusinessCourse. Access is free with new copies of this textbook (look for page containing the access code towards the front of the book). If you buy a used copy of the book, you can purchase access at **www.mybusinesscourse.com**.

ACKNOWLEDGMENTS

This book has benefited greatly from the valuable feedback of focus group attendees, reviewers, students, and colleagues. We are extremely grateful to them for their help in making this project a success.

Ajay Adhikari, *American University*
Hank Adler, *Chapman University*
Kris Allee, *University of Wisconsin*
Bob Allen, *University of Utah*
Beverley Alleyne, *Belmont University*
Elizabeth Arnold, *Citadel*
Frances Ayres, *University of Oklahoma*
Paul Bahnson, *Boise State University*
Jan Barton, *Emory University*
Progyan Basu, *University of Maryland*
James Benjamin, *Texas A&M University*
Anne Beyer, *Stanford University*
Robert Bowen, *University of San Diego*
Kimberly Brickler-Ulrich, *Lindenwood University*
Rada Brooks, *University of California, Berkeley*
Helen Brubeck, *San Jose State University*
Jacqueline Burke, *Hofstra University*
Richard J. Campbell, *University of Rio Grande*
Judson Caskey, *UCLA*
Sumantra Chakravarty, *California State University, Fullerton*
Paul Chaney, *Vanderbilt University*
Craig Chapman, *Northwestern University*
Sean Chen, *Furman University*
Hans Christensen, *University of Chicago*
Daniel Cohen, *University of Texas, Dallas*
John Core, *MIT*
Steve Crawford, *Rice University*
Somnath Das, *University of Illinois, Chicago*
Angela Davis, *University of Oregon*
Mark Dawkins, *University of Georgia*
David DeBoskey, *San Diego State University*
Mark DeFond, *University of Southern California*
Bruce Dehning, *Chapman University*
Timothy Dimond, *Northern Illinois University*
Joe Dulin, *University of Oklahoma*
Reed Easton, *Seton Hall University*
Tom Fields, *Washington University*
Mark Finn, *Northwestern University*
Linda Flaming, *Monmouth University*
Elizabeth Foster, *College of William & Mary*
Micah Frankel, *California State University, East Bay*
George Geis, *University of California, Los Angeles*
Hubert Glover, *Drexel University*
Nancy Goble, *University of Southern California*
Rajul Gokarn, *Clark Atlanta University*
Jeff Gramlich, *University of Southern Maine*
Wayne Guay, *University of Pennsylvania*
Umit Gurun, *University of Texas, Dallas*
Rebecca Hann, *University of Maryland*
David Harvey, *University of Georgia*
Rayford Harwell, *California State University, East Bay*
Susan Hass, *Simmons College*

Joseph Hatch, *Lewis University*
Haihong He, *California State University, Los Angeles*
Kenneth Henry, *Florida International University*
Eric Hirst, *University of Texas, Austin*
Robert Hoskin, *University of Connecticut*
Marsha Huber, *Otterbein College*
Richard E. Hurley, *University of Connecticut*
Robert L. Hurt, *California State University, Pomona*
Marianne L. James, *California State University, LA*
Ross Jennings, *University of Texas*
Chris Jones, *George Washington University*
Jane Kennedy, *University of San Diego*
Irene Kim, *George Washington University*
Michael Kimbrough, *University of Maryland*
Kalin Kolev, *Yale University*
Gopal Krishnan, *George Mason University*
Benjamin Lansford, *Rice University*
Xu Li, *University of Texas, Dallas*
Thomas Lin, *University of Southern California*
Jiangxia Liu, *Valparaiso University*
Annette Leps, *Johns Hopkins University*
Alina Lerman, *Yale University*
Frank Longo, *Centenary College*
Barbara Lougee, *University of San Diego*
Luann Lynch, *University of Virginia, Darden*
Bill Magrogan, *University of South Carolina*
Cathy Margolin, *Brandman University*
Maureen Mascha, *University of Wisconsin, Oshkosh*
Katie Maxwell, *University of Arizona*
Bruce McClain, *Cleveland State University*
Harvey McCown, *California State University, Bakersfield*
Jeff McMillan, *Clemson University*
John McCauley, *San Diego State University*
Marc McIntosh, *Augsburg College*
Greg Miller, *University of Michigan*
Jeffrey Miller, *University of Notre Dame*
Marilyn Misch, *Pepperdine University, Malibu*
Stephen Moehrle, *University of Missouri, Kansas City*
Matt Munson, *Chapman University*
Mark Myring, *Ball State University*
Sandeep Nabar, *Oklahoma State University*
James Naughton, *Northwestern University*
Karen Nelson, *Rice University*
Christopher Noe, *MIT*
Walter O'Connor, *Fordham University*
Jose Oaks, *University of Connecticut*
Shailendra Pandit, *University of Illinois, Chicago*
Simon Pearlman, *California State University, Long Beach*
Marietta Peytcheva, *Lehigh University*
Brandis Phillips, *North Carolina A&T State University*
Richard Price, *Utah State University*
S.E.C. Purvis, *University of Nevada, Reno*
Kathleen Rankin, *Chatham University*
Lynn Rees, *Texas A&M University*
Susan Riffe, *Southern Methodist University*
Leslie Robinson, *Dartmouth College*
Darren Roulstone, *Ohio State University*
Anwar Y. Salimi, *California State University, Pomona*
Haresh Sapra, *University of Chicago*
Robert Scharlach, *University of Southern California*
Nemit Shroff, *MIT*
Steve Sefcik, *University of Washington*
Timothy Shields, *Chapman University*
Andreas Simon, *California Polytechnic*
Robert Singer, *Lindenwood University*
Parveen Sinha, *Chapman University*
Kathleen Sobieralski, *University of Maryland*
Gregory Sommers, *Southern Methodist University*
David Smith, *University of Nebraska Lincoln*
Sri Sridharan, *Northwestern University*
Vic Stanton, *University of California, Berkeley*
Jack Stecher, *Carnegie Mellon University*
Doug Stevens, *Georgia State University*
Toby Stock, *Ohio University*
William Stout, *University of Louisville*
Shyam Sunder, *University of Arizona*
Robert J. Swieringa, *Cornell University*
Mary Tarling, *Aurora University*
Thomas Tallerico, *Dowling College*
Robin Tarpley, *George Washington University*
Nicole Thibodeau, *Willamette University*
Rick Warne, *George Mason University*
Catherine Weber, *University of Houston*
Lourdes White, *University of Baltimore*
Donna Whitten, *Purdue University North Central*
Rahnl Wood, *Northwest Missouri State University*
Jia Wu, *University of Massachusetts, Dartmouth*
Jennifer Yin, *University of Texas, San Antonio*
Stephen Zeff, *Rice University*
Yuping Zhao, *University of Houston*

In addition, we are extremely grateful to George Werthman, Lorraine Gleeson, Jocelyn Mousel, Pat Evett, Jill Sternard, Marnee Fieldman, Debbie McQuade, Terry McQuade, and the entire team at Cambridge Business Publishers for their encouragement, enthusiasm, and guidance.

Thomas R. Dyckman — *Ithaca, NY*
Michelle L. Hanlon — *Cambridge, MA*
Robert P. Magee — *Evanston, IL*
Glenn M. Pfeiffer — *Orange, CA*

December 2015

Brief Contents

Contents

Walgreens

pepsi

Chapter 6 Reporting and Analyzing Revenues, Receivables, and Operating Income 270

Chapter 7 Reporting and Analyzing Inventory 326

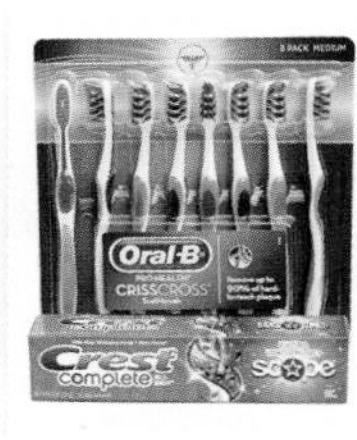

Chapter 8 Reporting and Analyzing Long-Term Operating Assets 372

DELTA
DELTA

Chapter 11 Reporting and Analyzing Stockholders' Equity 516

Chapter 12 Reporting and Analyzing Financial Investments 562

Appendix A Compound Interest and the Time-Value of Money 618

Introducing Financial Accounting

Learning Objectives *identify the key learning goals of the chapter.*

A **Focus Company** *introduces each chapter and illustrates the relevance of accounting in everyday business.*

LEARNING OBJECTIVES

1. Identify the users of accounting information and discuss the costs and benefits of disclosure. (p. 4)
2. Describe a company's business activities and explain how these activities are represented by the accounting equation. (p. 7)
3. Introduce the four key financial statements including the balance sheet, income statement, statement of stockholders' equity, and statement of cash flows. (p. 11)
4. Describe the institutions that regulate financial accounting and their role in establishing generally accepted accounting principles. (p. 17)
5. Compute two key ratios that are commonly used to assess profitability and risk—return on equity and the debt-to-equity ratio. (p. 21)
6. Appendix 1A: Explain the conceptual framework for financial reporting. (p. 25)

NIKE
www.Nike.com

Phil Knight majored in accounting and was a member of the track team at the University of Oregon. Today he is the chairman of the board of **Nike, Inc.**, the largest sports and fitness company in the world.

A few years after graduation, Knight teamed up with his former track coach, Bill Bowerman, to form a business called Blue Ribbon Sports to import, sell, and distribute running shoes from Japan. Blue Ribbon Sports, or BRS as it came to be known, was started on a shoestring—Knight and Bowerman each contributed $500 to start the business. A few years later, BRS introduced its own line of running shoes called Nike. It also unveiled a new logo, the now familiar Nike swoosh. Following the overwhelming success of the Nike shoe line, BRS officially changed its company name to Nike, Inc. Today, the company is worth more than $60 billion.

By 2014, Nike, Inc. products were marketed on six continents with total company sales of $28 billion and income of almost $2.7 billion. Nike owes much of its success to marketing prowess and innovative design and development of new products. The swoosh, along with advertising campaigns featuring taglines such as "just do it," have made the company and its products instantly recognizable to consumers all over the world. Endorsements by the most recognizable icons in sports, including Michael Jordan, Tiger Woods, Maria Sharapova, Tom Brady, LeBron James, and Mike Trout, add to Nike's brand recognition.

In recent years, Nike has expanded its product lines beyond the traditional offerings of athletic shoes, athletic apparel and sports equipment to include eyewear, watches such as the *Nike+ Sportwatch GPS*, and *Fuelband*, a wearable wristband which tracks energy output. In recent years, Nike further expanded its product offering by acquiring other companies such as Converse, an established athletic shoe company; Hurley International, a leading designer and distributor of surf, skate, and snowboarding apparel and footwear; and Umbro, specializing in soccer equipment, footwear, and apparel.

But as CEO Mark Parker recognizes, Nike needs to stay on its toes as newcomers **Under Armour** and **Quiksilver** challenge for customers. Nike also cannot ignore **Adidas**. As Nike's main competitor, it is more than two-thirds of Nike's size in terms of sales. Perhaps this situation, along with new product developments, explains Nike's major new marketing commitment that reached $2.3 billion in 2014 and continues to grow.

How does someone take a $1,000 investment and turn it into a company whose stock is worth more than $60 billion? Well, Nike's success is not an accident. Along the way, Nike management made countless decisions that ultimately led the company to where it is today. Each of these decisions involved identifying alternative courses of action and weighing their costs, benefits, and risks in light of the available information.

Accounting is the process of identifying, measuring, and communicating financial information to help people make *economic* decisions. People use accounting information to facilitate a wide variety of transactions, including assessing whether, and on what terms, they should invest in a firm, seek employment in a business, or continue purchasing its products. Accounting information is crucial to any successful business, and without it, most businesses would not even exist.

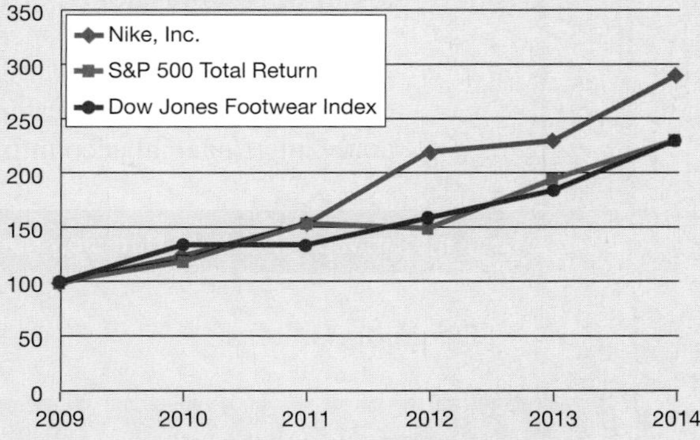

Comparison of 5-Year Cumulative Total Return for Nike, Inc., The S&P 500 Index, and The Dow Jones U.S. Footwear Index (Assumes an investment of $100 on May 31, 2009)

This book explains how to create and analyze financial statements, an important source of accounting information prepared by companies to communicate with a variety of users. We begin by introducing transactions between the firm and its investors, creditors, suppliers, employees, and customers. We continue by demonstrating how accounting principles are applied to these transactions to create the financial statements. Then, we "invert" the process and learn how to analyze the firm's financial statements to assess the firm's underlying economic performance. Our philosophy is simple—we believe it is crucial to have a deep understanding of financial accounting to become critical readers and users of financial statements. Financial statements tell a story—a business story. Our goal is to understand that story, and apply the knowledge gleaned from financial statements to make good business decisions.

Sources: Nike.com; Nike, Inc. 2014 10-K Report; *Business Week* (October 2007, August 2009); *Portland Business Journal* (October 2007); *Fortune* (February 2012).

CHAPTER ORGANIZATION

Chapter Organization *Charts visually depict the key topics and their sequence within the chapter.*

Introducing Financial Accounting

Demand for Accounting Information	Business Activities	Financial Statements	Financial Reporting Environment	Financial Statement Analysis
• Who Uses Financial Accounting Information? • Costs and Benefits of Disclosure	• Planning Activities • Investing Activities • Financing Activities • Operating Activities	• Balance Sheet • Income Statement • Statement of Stockholders' Equity • Statement of Cash Flows • Financial Statement Linkages	• Generally Accepted Accounting Principles • Regulation and Oversight • Role of the Auditor • A Global Perspective • Conceptual Framework (Appendix 1A)	• Profitability Analysis • Credit Risk Analysis

eLecture *icons identify topics for which there are instructional videos in* **myBusinessCourse** *(MBC). See the Preface for more information on MBC.*

1

LO1 Identify the users of accounting information and discuss the costs and benefits of disclosure.

DEMAND FOR ACCOUNTING INFORMATION

Accounting can be defined as the process of recording, summarizing, and analyzing financial transactions. While accounting information attempts to satisfy the needs of a diverse set of users, the accounting information a company produces can be classified into two categories (see **Exhibit 1.1**):

- **Financial accounting**—designed primarily for decision makers outside of the company
- **Managerial accounting**—designed primarily for decision makers within the company

Financial accounting reports include information about company profitability and financial health. This information is useful to various economic actors who wish to engage in contracts with the firm, including investors, creditors, employees, customers, and governments. Managerial accounting information is not reported outside of the company because it includes proprietary information about the profitability of specific products, divisions, or customers. Company managers use managerial accounting reports to make decisions such as whether to drop or add products or divisions, or whether to continue serving different types of customers. This text focuses on understanding and analyzing financial accounting information.

EXHIBIT 1.1 Information Needs of Decision Makers Who Use Financial and Managerial Accounting

	Decision Makers	Decisions	Information
Financial Accounting	• Investors and analysts • Creditors • Suppliers and customers	• Buy or sell stock? • Lend or not? • Purchase/sell goods or not?	• Sales and costs • Cash in and out • Assets and liabilities
Managerial Accounting	• Top management • Marketing teams • Production and operations	• Develop new strategy? • Launch a new product or not? • Manage operations	• Product sales and costs • Department performance reports • Budgets and quality reports

Who Uses Financial Accounting Information?

Demand for financial accounting information derives from numerous users including:

- Shareholders and potential shareholders
- Creditors and suppliers
- Managers and directors
- Financial analysts
- Other users

FYI *features provide additional information that complements the text.*

Shareholders and Potential Shareholders Corporations are the dominant form of business organization for large companies around the world, and corporate shareholders are one important group of decision makers that have an interest in financial accounting information. A **corporation** is a form of business organization that is characterized by a large number of owners who are not involved in managing the day-to-day operations of the company.[1] A corporation exists as a legal entity that issues **shares of stock** to its owners in exchange for cash and, therefore, the owners of a corporation are referred to as *shareholders* or **stockholders**.

FYI Shareholders of a corporation are its owners; although managers can own stock in the corporation, most shareholders are not managers.

Because the shareholders are not involved in the day-to-day operations of the business, they rely on the information in financial statements to evaluate management performance and assess the company's financial condition.

In addition to corporations, sole proprietorships and partnerships are also common forms of business ownership. A **sole proprietorship** has a single owner who typically manages the daily operations. Small family-run businesses, such as corner grocery stores, are commonly organized as sole proprietorships. A **partnership** has two or more owners who are also usually involved in managing the business. Many professionals, such as lawyers and CPAs, organize their businesses as partnerships.

Most corporations begin as small, privately held businesses (sole proprietorships or partnerships). As their operations expand, however, they require additional capital to finance their growth. One of the principle advantages of a corporation over sole proprietorships and partnerships is the ability to raise large amounts of cash by issuing (selling) stock. For example, as Nike grew from a small business with only two owners into a larger company, it raised the funds needed for expansion by selling shares of Nike stock to new shareholders. In the United States, large corporations can raise funds by issuing stock on organized exchanges, such as the **New York Stock Exchange (NYSE)** or **NASDAQ** (which is an acronym for the National Association of Securities Dealers Automated Quotations system). Corporations with stock that is traded on public exchanges are known as *publicly traded corporations* or simply *public corporations*.

Financial statements and the accompanying footnotes provide information on the risk and return associated with owning shares of stock in the corporation, and they reveal how well management has performed. Financial statements also provide valuable insights into future performance by revealing management's plans for new products, new operating procedures, and new strategic directions for the company as well as for their implementation. Corporate management provides this information because the information reduces uncertainty about the company's future prospects which, in turn, increases the market price of its shares and helps the company raise the funds it needs to grow.

Creditors and Suppliers Few businesses rely solely on shareholders for the cash needed to operate the company. Instead, most companies borrow from banks or other lenders known as **creditors**. Creditors are interested in the potential borrower's ability to repay. They use financial accounting information to help determine loan terms, loan amounts, interest rates, and collateral. In addition, creditors' loans often include contractual requirements based on information found in the financial statements.

FYI Financial statements are typically required when a business requests a bank loan.

[1] Most countries have business forms that are similar in structure to those of a U.S. corporation, though they are referred to by different names. For example, while firms that are incorporated in the United States have the extension, "Inc." appended to their names, similar firms in the United Kingdom are referred to as a Public Limited Company, which has the extension "PLC."

Suppliers use financial information to establish credit sales terms and to determine their long-term commitment to supply-chain relationships. Supplier companies often justify an expansion of *their* businesses based on the growth and financial health of their customers. Both creditors and suppliers rely on information in the financial statements to monitor and adjust their contracts and commitments with a company.

Managers and Directors Financial statements can be thought of as a financial report card for management. A well-managed company earns a good return for its shareholders, and this is reflected in the financial statements. In most companies, management is compensated, at least in part, based on the financial performance of the company. That is, managers often receive cash bonuses, shares of stock, or other *incentive compensation* that is linked directly to the information in the financial statements.

FYI The Sarbanes-Oxley Act requires issuers of securities to disclose whether they have a code of ethics for the senior officers.

Publicly traded corporations are required by law to have a **board of directors**. Directors are elected by the shareholders to represent shareholder interests and oversee management. The board hires executive management and regularly reviews company operations. Directors use financial accounting information to review the results of operations, evaluate future strategy, and assess management performance.

Both managers and directors use the published financial statements of *other companies* to perform comparative analyses and establish performance benchmarks. For example, managers in some companies are paid a bonus for financial performance that exceeds the industry average.

BUSINESS INSIGHT

Recent court cases involving corporations such as **Enron**, **Tyco**, and **WorldCom** (now **MCI**) have found executives, including several CEOs, guilty of issuing fraudulent financial statements. These executives have received substantial fines and, in some cases, long jail sentences. These trials have resulted in widespread loss of reputation and credibility among corporate boards.

Financial Analysts Many decision makers lack the time, resources, or expertise to efficiently and effectively analyze financial statements. Instead, they rely on professional financial analysts, such as credit rating agencies like **Moody's** investment services, portfolio managers, and security analysts. Financial analysts play an important role in the dissemination of financial information and often specialize in specific industries. Their analysis helps to identify and assess risk, forecast performance, establish prices for new issues of stock, and make buy-or-sell recommendations to investors.

Other Users of Financial Accounting Information External decision makers include many users of accounting information in addition to those listed above. For example, ***prospective employees*** often examine the financial statements of an employer to learn about the company before interviewing for or accepting a new job.

Labor unions examine financial statements in order to assess the financial health of firms prior to negotiating labor contracts on behalf of the firms' employees. ***Customers*** use accounting information to assess the ability of a company to deliver products or services and to assess the company's long-term reliability.

Government agencies rely on accounting information to develop and enforce regulations, including public protection, price setting, import-export, taxation, and various other policies.[2] Timely and reliable information is crucial to effective regulatory policy. Moreover, accounting information is often used to assess penalties for companies that violate various regulations.

Costs and Benefits of Disclosure

The act of providing financial information to external users is called **disclosure**. As with every decision, the benefits of disclosure must be weighed against the costs of providing the information.

[2] A company's tax returns are distinctly different from its financial statements. Tax returns are prepared for tax authorities in order to comply with income tax rules. The financial statements are prepared to provide information to investors, creditors and other decision makers outside of the business.

One reason companies are motivated to disclose financial information to external decision makers is that it often lowers financing and operating costs. For example, when a company applies for a loan, the bank uses the company's financial statements to help determine the appropriate interest rate. Without adequate financial disclosures in its financial statements, the bank is likely to demand a higher interest rate or perhaps not make the loan at all. Thus, in this setting, a benefit of financial disclosure is that it reduces the company's cost of borrowing.

While there are benefits from disclosing financial information, there are also costs. Besides the obvious cost of hiring accountants and preparing the financial statements, financial disclosures can also result in costs being imposed by competitors. It is common practice for managers to scrutinize the financial statements of competitors to learn about successful products, new strategies, innovative technologies, and changing market conditions. Thus, disclosing too much information can place a company at a competitive disadvantage. Disclosure can also raise investors' expectations about a company's future profitability. If those expectations are not met, they may bring litigation against the managers.

There are also political costs that are potentially associated with accounting disclosure. Highly visible companies, such as defense contractors and oil companies, are often the target of scrutiny by the public and by government officials. When these companies report unusually large accounting profits, they are often the target of additional regulation or increased taxes.

Stock market regulators impose disclosure standards for publicly traded corporations, but the nature and extent of the required disclosures vary substantially across countries. Further, because the requirements only set the minimum level of disclosure, the quantity and quality of information provided by firms will vary. This variation in disclosure ultimately reflects differences among companies in the benefits and costs of disclosing information to the public.

You Make The Call *requires you to assume various roles within a business and use your accounting knowledge to address an issue. Solutions are at the end of the chapter.*

YOU MAKE THE CALL

You are a Product Manager There is often friction between investors' needs for information and a company's desire to safeguard competitive advantages. Assume that you are the product manager for a key department at your company and you are asked for advice on the extent of information to disclose in the annual report on a potentially lucrative new product that your department has test marketed. What considerations affect the advice you provide and why? [Answer on page 29]

BUSINESS ACTIVITIES

LO2 Describe a company's business activities and explain how these activities are represented by the accounting equation.

2

Businesses produce accounting information to help develop strategies, attract financing, evaluate investment opportunities, manage operations, and measure performance. Before we can attempt to understand the information provided in financial statements, we must understand these business activities. That is, what does a business actually do? For example:

- Where does a company such as Nike find the resources to develop new products and open new retail stores?
- What new products should Nike bring to market?
- How much should Nike spend on product development? On advertising? On executive compensation?
- How does Nike's management determine if a product is a success?

Questions such as these define the activities of Nike and other companies.

Exhibit 1.2 illustrates the activities of a typical business. All businesses *plan* business activities, *finance* those activities, *invest* resources in those activities, and then engage in *operating* activities. Companies conduct all these activities while confronting a variety of *external forces,* including competition from other businesses, government regulation, economic conditions and market forces, and changing preferences of customers. The financial statements provide information that helps us understand and evaluate each of these activities.

EXHIBIT 1.2 Business Activities

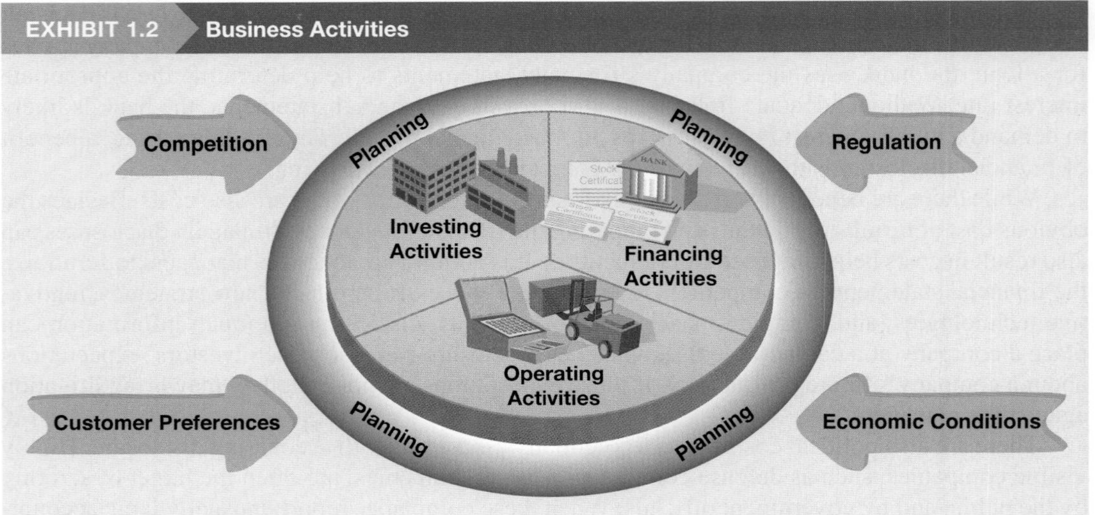

Planning Activities

Excerpts from recent financial statements are used to illustrate and reinforce concepts.

A company's goals, and the strategies adopted to reach those goals, are the product of its **planning activities**. Nike, for example, states that its mission is "To bring inspiration and innovation to every athlete in the world" adding "If you have a body, you are an athlete." However, in its 2014 annual report to shareholders, Nike management suggests another goal that focuses on financial success and earning a return for the shareholders.

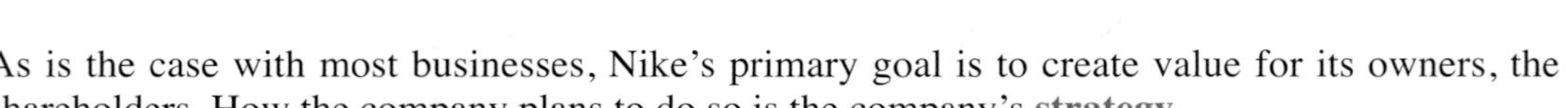
Our goal is to deliver value to our shareholders by building a profitable global portfolio of branded footwear, apparel, equipment, and accessories businesses.

As is the case with most businesses, Nike's primary goal is to create value for its owners, the shareholders. How the company plans to do so is the company's **strategy**.

A company's *strategic* (or *business*) *plan* describes how it plans to achieve its goals. The plan's success depends on an effective review of market conditions. Specifically, the company must assess both the demand for its products and services, and the supply of its inputs (both labor and capital). The plan must also include competitive analyses, opportunity assessments, and consideration of business threats. The strategic plan specifies both broad management designs that generate company value and tactics to achieve those designs.

Most information in a strategic plan is proprietary and guarded closely by management. However, outsiders can gain insight into planning activities through various channels, including newspapers, magazines, and company publications. Understanding a company's planning activities helps focus accounting analysis and place it in context.

Investing Activities

Key Terms are highlighted in bold, red font.

Investing activities consist of acquiring and disposing of the resources needed to produce and sell a company's products and services. These resources, called **assets**, provide future benefits to the company. Companies differ on the amount and mix of these resources. Some companies require buildings and equipment while others have abandoned "bricks and mortar" to conduct business through the Internet.

Some assets that a company invests in are used quickly. For instance, a retail clothing store hopes to sell its spring and summer merchandise before purchasing more inventory for the fall and winter. Other assets are acquired for long-term use. Buildings are typically used for several decades. The relative proportion of short-term and long-term investments depends on the type of business and the strategic plan that the company adopts. For example, Nike has relatively few long-term assets because it outsources most of the production of its products to other companies.

The graph in **Exhibit 1.3** compares the relative proportion of short-term and long-term assets held by Nike and seven other companies, several of which are featured in later chapters. Nike has adopted a business model that requires very little investment in long-term resources. A majority of its investments are short-term assets. In contrast, **Verizon**, **PepsiCo**, and **Procter & Gamble** all rely heavily on long-term investments. These companies hold relatively small proportions of short-term assets. This mix of long-term and short-term assets is described in more detail in Chapter 2.

Real Companies *and* **Institutions** *are highlighted in bold, blue font.*

EXHIBIT 1.3 Relative Proportion of Short-Term and Long-Term Assets

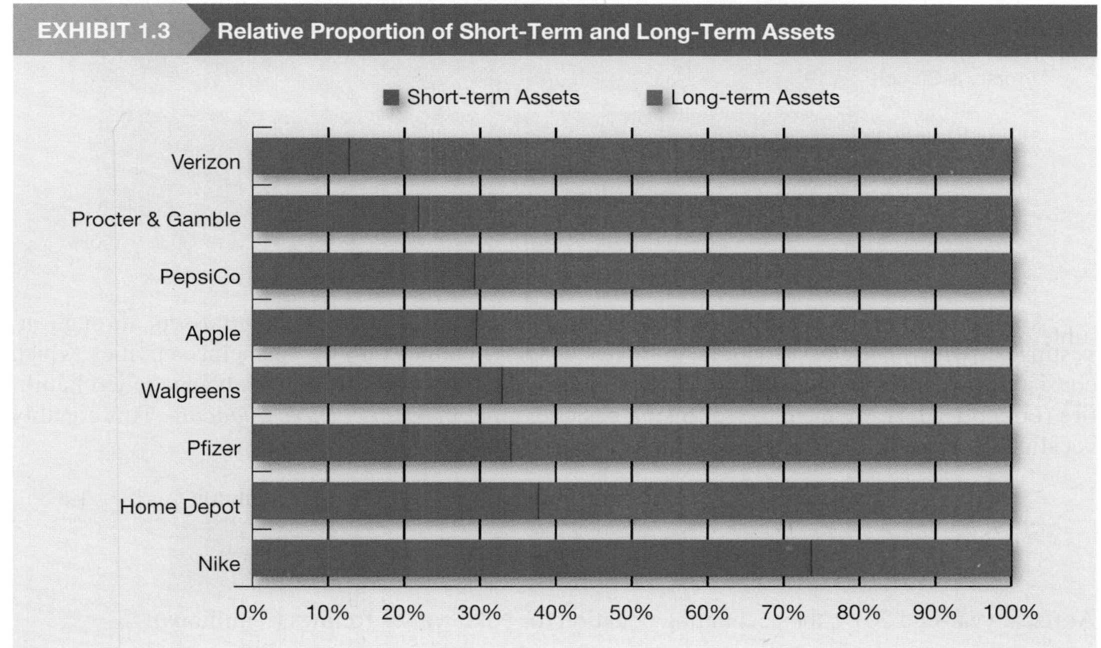

Financing Activities

Investments in resources require funding, and **financing activities** refer to the methods companies use to fund those investments. *Financial management* is the planning of resource needs, including the proper mix of financing sources.

Companies obtain financing from two sources: equity (owner) financing and creditor (nonowner) financing. *Equity financing* refers to the funds contributed to the company by its owners along with any income retained by the company. One form of equity financing is the cash raised from the sale (or issuance) of stock by a corporation. *Creditor* (or debt) *financing* is funds contributed by nonowners, which create *liabilities*. **Liabilities** are obligations the company must repay in the future. One example of a liability is a bank loan. We draw a distinction between equity and creditor financing for an important reason: creditor financing imposes a legal obligation to repay, usually with interest, and failure to repay amounts borrowed can result in adverse legal consequences such as bankruptcy. In contrast, equity financing does not impose an obligation for repayment.

Exhibit 1.4 compares the relative proportion of creditor and equity financing for Nike and other companies. PepsiCo uses liabilities to finance 75% of its resources. In contrast, **Walgreen Co.** relies more heavily on its equity financing, receiving 45% of its financing from creditors. Nike has the lowest proportion of creditor financing in this sample of companies with just 42% of its assets financed by nonowners.

EXHIBIT 1.4 Relative Proportion of Credit and Equity Financing

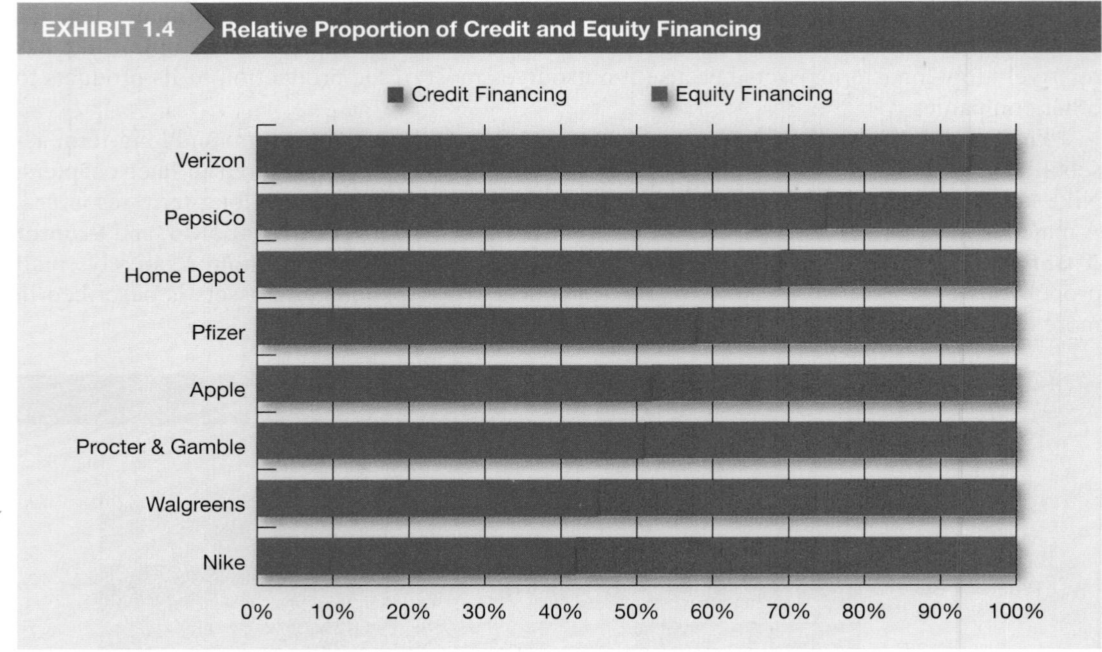

Infographics *are used to convey difficult concepts and procedures.*

As discussed in the previous section, companies acquire resources, called assets, through investing activities. The cash to acquire these resources is obtained through financing activities, which consist of owner financing, called equity, and creditor financing, called liabilities (or debt). Thus, we have the following basic relation: *investing equals financing*. This equality is called the **accounting equation**, which is expressed as:

Investing = Creditor Financing + Owner Financing

Assets = **Liabilities** + **Equity**

At fiscal year-end 2014, the accounting equation for Nike was as follows ($ millions):

$$\$18{,}594 = \$7{,}770 + \$10{,}824$$

By definition, the accounting equation holds for all companies at all times. This relation is a very powerful tool for analyzing and understanding companies, and we will use it often throughout the text.

Operating Activities

Operating activities refer to the production, promotion, and selling of a company's products and services. These activities extend from a company's input markets, involving its suppliers, and to its output markets, involving its customers. Input markets generate *operating expenses* (or *costs*) such as inventory, salaries, materials, and logistics. Output markets generate *operating revenues* (or *sales*) from customers. Output markets also generate some operating expenses such as for marketing and distributing products and services to customers. When operating revenues exceed operating expenses, companies report *operating income*, also called *operating profit* or *operating earnings*. When operating expenses exceed operating revenues, companies report operating losses.

Revenue is the increase in equity resulting from the sale of goods and services to customers. The amount of revenue is determined *before* deducting expenses. An **expense** is the cost incurred to generate revenue, including the cost of the goods and services sold to customers as well as the cost of carrying out other business activities. **Income**, also called *net income*, equals revenues minus expenses, and is the net increase in equity from the company's operating activities.

Income = **Revenues** − **Expenses**

For fiscal year 2014, Nike reported revenues of almost $28 billion, yet its reported income was a fraction of that amount—just under $2.7 billion.

Business Insights offer recent examples from the business news and popular press.

BUSINESS INSIGHT

Each year, *Fortune* magazine ranks the 500 largest corporations in the United States based on total revenues. For 2013, which is based on fiscal 2012 financial results, Nike ranked 126th on the *Fortune 500* list with revenues of just over $24 billion. The company also ranked 97th in profits, with net income of approximately $2.2 billion. For comparison, the largest corporation was **Wal-Mart Stores**, with revenues of $469.1 billion and $17 billion in net income. (Source: http://fortune.com/fortune500/2013/)

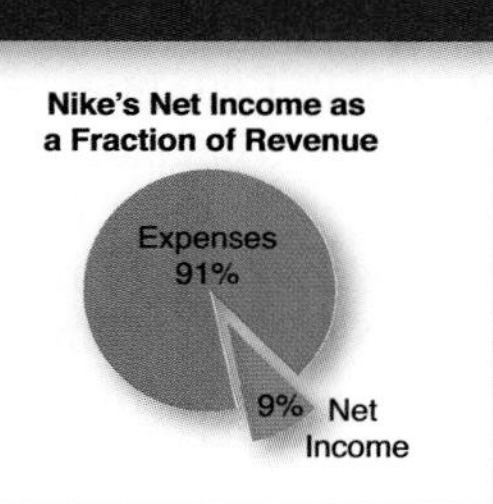

FINANCIAL STATEMENTS

LO3 Introduce the four key financial statements including the balance sheet, income statement, statement of stockholders' equity, and statement of cash flows.

3

Four financial statements are used to periodically report on a company's business activities. These statements are:

- **balance sheet**, which lists the company's investments and sources of financing using the accounting equation;
- **income statement**, which reports the results of operations;
- **statement of stockholders' equity**, which details changes in owner financing;
- **statement of cash flows**, which details the sources and uses of cash.

Exhibit 1.5 shows how these statements are linked across time. A balance sheet reports on a company's position at a point in time. The income statement, statement of stockholders' equity, and the statement of cash flows report on performance over a period of time. The three statements in the middle of **Exhibit 1.5** (period-of-time statements) link the balance sheet from the beginning of a period to the balance sheet at the end of a period.

EXHIBIT 1.5 Financial Statement Links Across Time

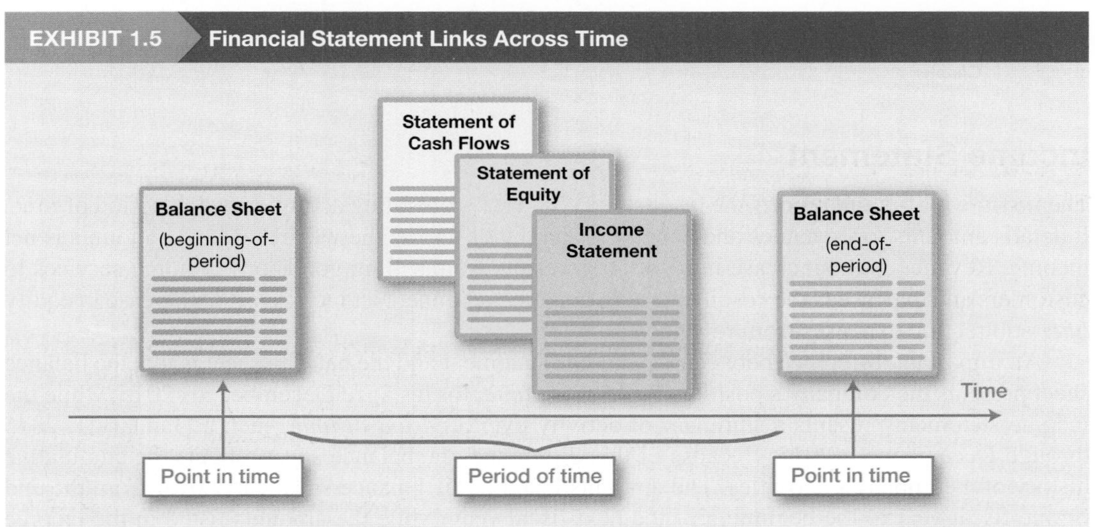

A one-year, or annual, reporting period is common, which is called the *accounting*, or *fiscal year*. Semiannual, quarterly, and monthly reporting periods are also common. *Calendar-year* companies have a reporting period that begins on January 1 and ends on December 31. **Pfizer**, **Google**, and **Verizon** are examples of calendar-year companies. Some companies choose a fiscal year ending on a date other than December 31. Seasonal businesses, such as retail stores, often choose a fiscal year that ends when sales and inventories are at their lowest level. For example, **Home Depot**, the retail home improvement store chain, ends its fiscal year on the Sunday closest to February 1, after the busy holiday season. Nike has a May 31 fiscal year. The heading of each statement identifies the: (1) company name, (2) statement title, and (3) date or time period of the statement.

FYI The heading of each financial statement includes who, what, and when.

Balance Sheet

FYI The balance sheet is also known as the statement of financial position and the statement of financial condition.

A **balance sheet** reports a company's financial position at a point in time. It summarizes the result of the company's investing and financing activities by listing amounts for assets, liabilities, and equity. The balance sheet is based on the accounting equation, also called the *balance sheet equation*: Assets = Liabilities + Equity.

Nike's balance sheet for fiscal year 2014, which ended May 31, 2014, is reproduced in a reduced format in **Exhibit 1.6** and reports that assets are $18,594 million, liabilities are $7,770 million, and equity is $10,824 million, where owner financing is the sum of contributed capital of $5,868 million, retained earnings of $4,871 million, and other equity of $85 million. Thus, the balance sheet equation holds true for Nike's balance sheet: assets equal liabilities plus equity.

Real financial data *for focus companies illustrate key concepts of each chapter.*

EXHIBIT 1.6 Balance Sheet ($ millions)

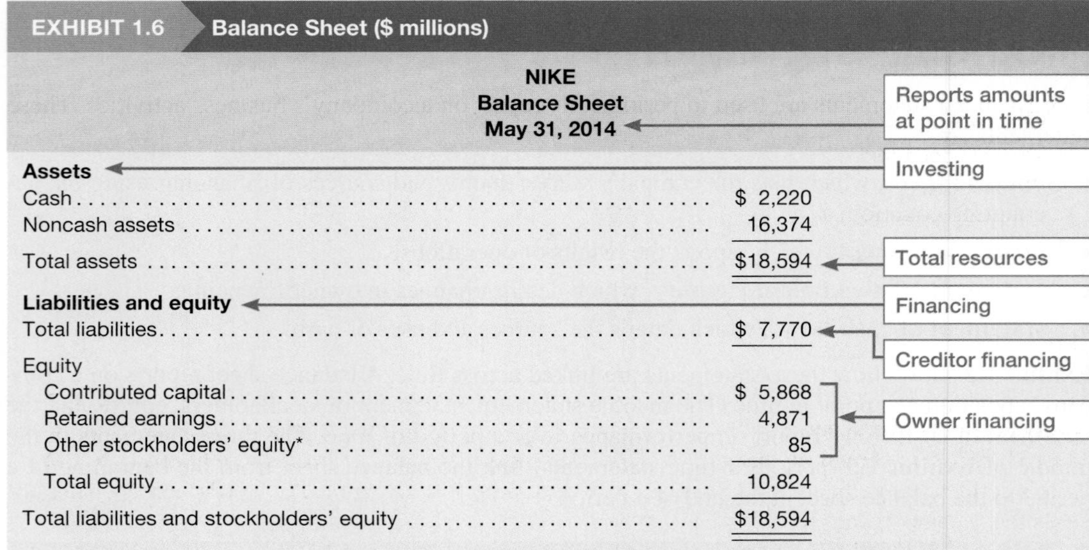

NIKE Balance Sheet May 31, 2014	
Assets	
Cash	$ 2,220
Noncash assets	16,374
Total assets	$18,594
Liabilities and equity	
Total liabilities	$ 7,770
Equity	
Contributed capital	$ 5,868
Retained earnings	4,871
Other stockholders' equity*	85
Total equity	10,824
Total liabilities and stockholders' equity	$18,594

* Other stockholders' equity includes accumulated other comprehensive income. Other components of stockholders' equity are discussed in Chapter 11.

FYI The income statement is also known as statement of income, statement of earnings, statement of operations, and statement of profit and loss.

Income Statement

The **income statement** reports the results of a company's operating activities over a period of time. It details amounts for revenues and expenses, and the difference between these two amounts is net income. Revenue is the increase in equity that results from selling goods or providing services to customers and expense is the cost incurred to generate revenue. Net income is the increase in equity *after* subtracting expenses from revenues.

FYI The term "gross" refers to an amount before subtractions, such as Gross Sales. An exception is made for the term Gross Profit (Gross Margin), defined as Sales less Cost of Goods Sold (Cost of Sales). When items are subtracted from a gross amount, the term "net" is generally used, as in the case of Net Sales (Gross Sales less returns and other items) or Net Income (Sales less all expenses).

An important difference between the income statement and the balance sheet is that the balance sheet presents the company's position at a *point in time*, for instance December 31, 2015, while the income statement presents a summary of activity over a *period of time*, such as January 1, 2015 through December 31, 2015. Because of this difference, the balance sheet reflects the cumulative history of a company's activities. The amounts listed in the balance sheet carry over from the end of one fiscal year to the beginning of the next fiscal year, while the amounts listed in the income statement do not carry over from one year to the next.

Refer to Nike's income statement for the fiscal year ended May 31, 2014, shown in reduced format as **Exhibit 1.7**. It reports that revenues = $27,799 million, expenses = $25,106 million, and net income = $2,693 million. Thus, revenues minus expenses equals net income for Nike.

For manufacturing and merchandising companies, the **cost of goods sold** is an important expense that is typically disclosed separately in the income statement immediately following revenues. It is also common to report a subtotal for gross profit (also called gross margin), which is revenues less the cost of goods sold. The company's remaining expenses are then reported below gross profit. Nike's income statement is presented in this reduced format in **Exhibit 1.8**:

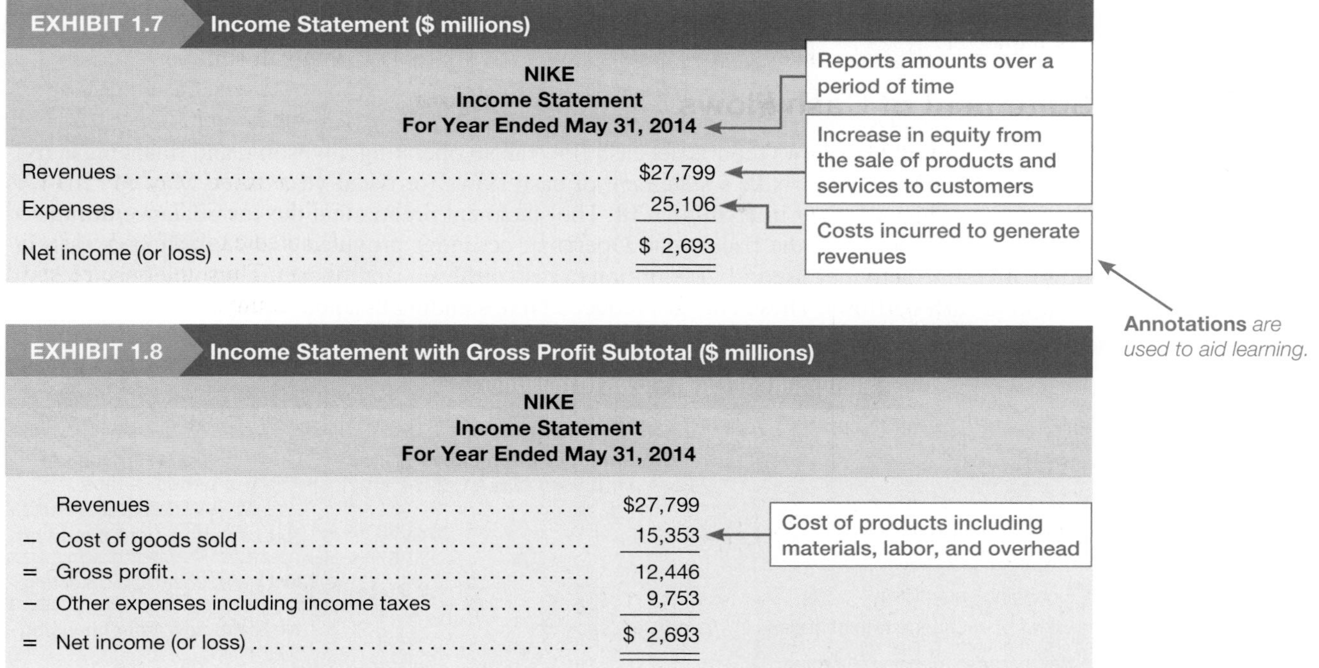

EXHIBIT 1.7 Income Statement ($ millions)

NIKE
Income Statement
For Year Ended May 31, 2014

Revenues	$27,799
Expenses	25,106
Net income (or loss)	$ 2,693

EXHIBIT 1.8 Income Statement with Gross Profit Subtotal ($ millions)

NIKE
Income Statement
For Year Ended May 31, 2014

	Revenues	$27,799
−	Cost of goods sold	15,353
=	Gross profit	12,446
−	Other expenses including income taxes	9,753
=	Net income (or loss)	$ 2,693

Annotations *are used to aid learning.*

Statement of Stockholders' Equity

The **statement of stockholders' equity**, or simply *statement of equity*, reports the changes in the equity accounts over a period of time. Nike's statement of stockholders' equity for fiscal year ended May 31, 2014, is shown in reduced format as **Exhibit 1.9**. During the year ended May 31, 2014, Nike's equity changed due to share issuance and income reinvestment. The exhibit details and classifies these changes into three categories:

- Contributed capital (includes common stock, and additional paid-in capital)
- Retained earnings (includes cumulative net income or loss, and deducts dividends)
- Other stockholders' equity

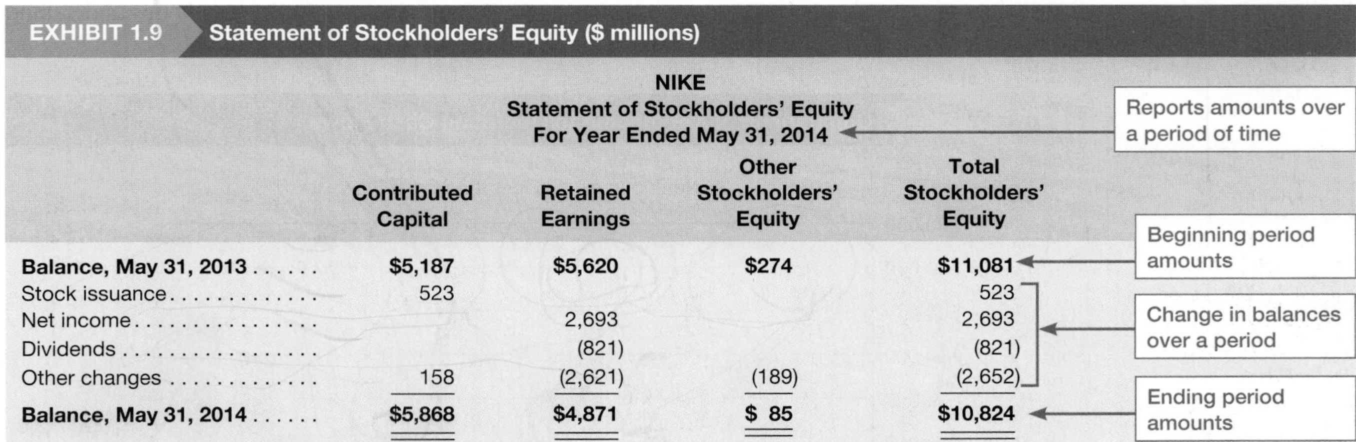

EXHIBIT 1.9 Statement of Stockholders' Equity ($ millions)

NIKE
Statement of Stockholders' Equity
For Year Ended May 31, 2014

	Contributed Capital	Retained Earnings	Other Stockholders' Equity	Total Stockholders' Equity
Balance, May 31, 2013	**$5,187**	**$5,620**	**$274**	**$11,081**
Stock issuance	523			523
Net income		2,693		2,693
Dividends		(821)		(821)
Other changes	158	(2,621)	(189)	(2,652)
Balance, May 31, 2014	**$5,868**	**$4,871**	**$ 85**	**$10,824**

Contributed capital represents the net amount received from issuing stock to shareholders (owners). **Retained earnings** (also called *earned capital*) represents the income the company has earned since its inception, minus the dividends it has paid out to shareholders. Thus, retained earnings equals the amount of income retained in the company. The change in retained earnings links consecutive balance sheets through the income statement. Nike's retained earnings decreased from $5,620 million at May 31, 2013 to $4,871 million at May 31, 2014. This decrease is explained by net income of $2,693 million, less dividends of $821 million and other reductions of $2,621 million. The category

FYI Dividends are reported in the statement of equity, and not in the income statement.

titled “other changes” refers to changes in equity that are not recorded in income and is discussed in Chapter 11.

Statement of Cash Flows

FYI Cash is critical to operations because it is necessary for purchasing resources and paying bills.

The **statement of cash flows** reports net cash flows from operating, investing, and financing activities over a period of time. Nike’s statement of cash flows for fiscal year ended May 31, 2014, is shown in a reduced format in **Exhibit 1.10**. The statement reports that the cash balance decreased by $1,117 million during the fiscal year. Operating activities provided $3,003 million (a cash inflow), investing activities used $1,207 million (a cash outflow), and financing activities used $2,914 million (a cash outflow). These changes reduced Nike’s ending balance of cash to $2,220 million.

EXHIBIT 1.10 Statement of Cash Flows ($ millions)

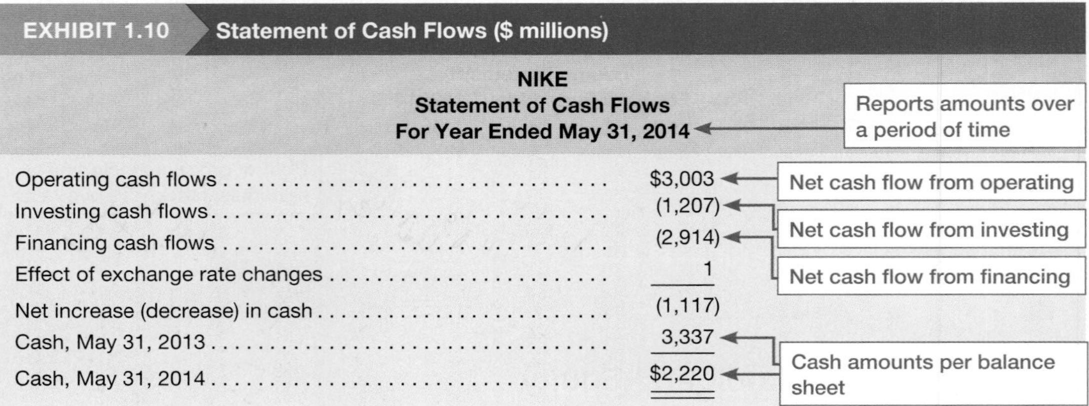

NIKE
Statement of Cash Flows
For Year Ended May 31, 2014

Operating cash flows	$3,003
Investing cash flows	(1,207)
Financing cash flows	(2,914)
Effect of exchange rate changes	1
Net increase (decrease) in cash	(1,117)
Cash, May 31, 2013	3,337
Cash, May 31, 2014	$2,220

FYI Common formatting for U.S. financial statements includes:

- Dollar sign next to first and last amount listed in a column
- Single underline before a subtraction or addition; double underline after a major total
- Assets listed in order of liquidity, which is nearness to cash
- Liabilities listed in order of due dates

Operating cash flow is the amount of cash generated from operating activities. This amount usually differs from net income due to differences between the time that revenues and expenses are recorded, and the time that the related cash receipts and disbursements occur. For example, a company may report revenues for goods sold to customers this period, but not collect the payment until next period. Consistent with most companies, Nike’s operating cash flows of $3,003 million do not equal its net income of $2,693 million. **Exhibit 1.11** compares net income and operating cash flows for Nike and several other companies. The exhibit shows that there is large variation across companies in the amount of net income and operating cash flows.

Both cash flow and net income are important for making business decisions. They each capture different aspects of firm performance and together help financial statement users better understand and assess a company’s past, present, and future business activities.

EXHIBIT 1.11 Comparison of Net Income to Operating Cash Flows

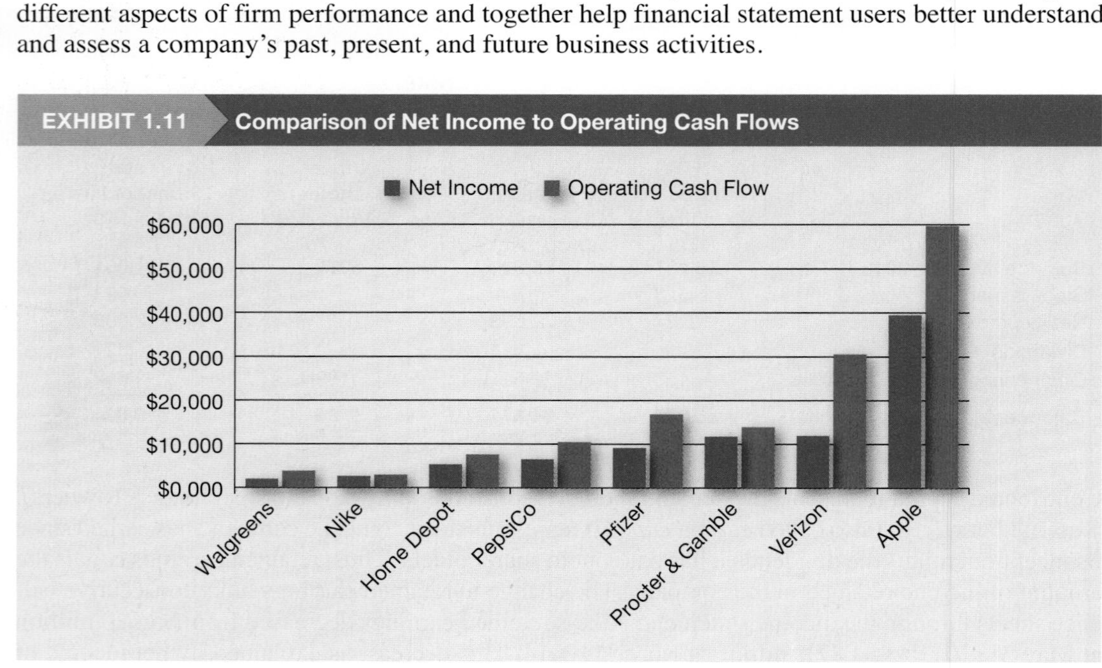

Financial Statement Linkages

A central feature of the accounting system is the linkage among the four primary statements, referred to as the *articulation* of the financial statements. Three of the key linkages are:

- The statement of cash flows links the beginning and ending cash in the balance sheet.
- The income statement links the beginning and ending retained earnings in the statement of stockholders' equity.
- The statement of stockholders' equity links the beginning and ending equity in the balance sheet.

Exhibit 1.12 demonstrates these links using Nike's financial statements from **Exhibits 1.6** through **1.10**. The left side of **Exhibit 1.12** presents Nike's beginning-year balance sheet for fiscal year 2014 (which is the same as the balance sheet for the end of fiscal year 2013) and the right side presents Nike's year-end balance sheet for fiscal year 2014. These balance sheets report Nike's investing and financing activities at the beginning and end of the fiscal year, two distinct points in time. The middle column of **Exhibit 1.12** presents the three financial statements

EXHIBIT 1.12 Articulation of Nike Financial Statements ($ millions)

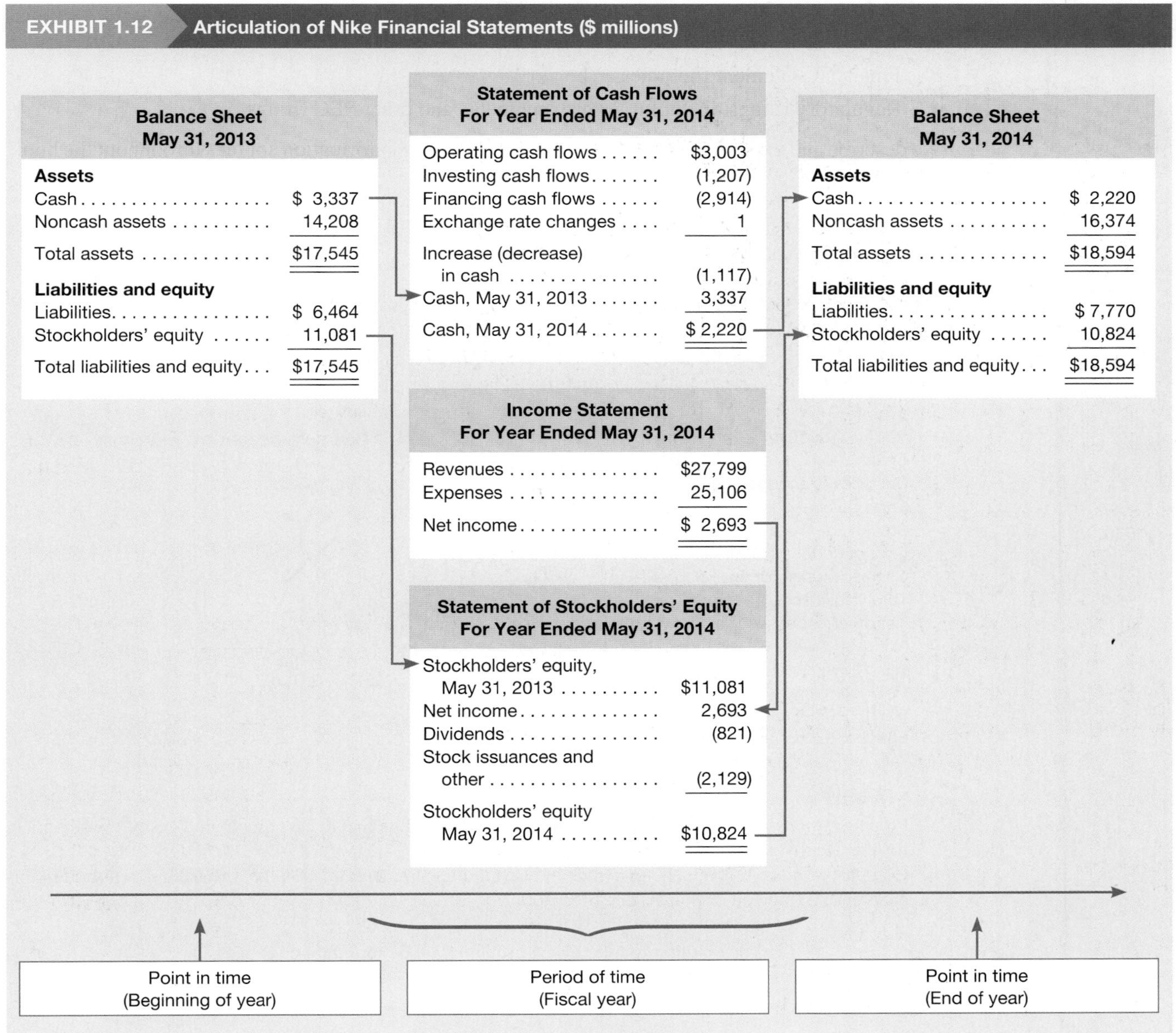

Balance Sheet May 31, 2013

Assets	
Cash	$ 3,337
Noncash assets	14,208
Total assets	$17,545
Liabilities and equity	
Liabilities	$ 6,464
Stockholders' equity	11,081
Total liabilities and equity	$17,545

Statement of Cash Flows For Year Ended May 31, 2014

Operating cash flows	$3,003
Investing cash flows	(1,207)
Financing cash flows	(2,914)
Exchange rate changes	1
Increase (decrease) in cash	(1,117)
Cash, May 31, 2013	3,337
Cash, May 31, 2014	$ 2,220

Income Statement For Year Ended May 31, 2014

Revenues	$27,799
Expenses	25,106
Net income	$ 2,693

Statement of Stockholders' Equity For Year Ended May 31, 2014

Stockholders' equity, May 31, 2013	$11,081
Net income	2,693
Dividends	(821)
Stock issuances and other	(2,129)
Stockholders' equity May 31, 2014	$10,824

Balance Sheet May 31, 2014

Assets	
Cash	$ 2,220
Noncash assets	16,374
Total assets	$18,594
Liabilities and equity	
Liabilities	$ 7,770
Stockholders' equity	10,824
Total liabilities and equity	$18,594

that report Nike's fiscal year 2014 business activities over time: the statement of cash flows, the income statement, and the statement of stockholders' equity. The three key linkages shown in **Exhibit 1.12** are:

- The statement of cash flows explains how operating, financing, and investing activities decreased the cash balance by $1,117 million, from the $3,337 million reported in the beginning-year balance sheet, to the $2,220 million reported in the year-end balance sheet.
- The net income of $2,693 million reported in the income statement is added to retained earnings in the statement of stockholders' equity.
- The statement of stockholders' equity explains how total equity of $11,081 million, reported in the beginning-year balance sheet, becomes total equity of $10,824 million, reported in the year-end balance sheet.

Information Beyond Financial Statements

FYI An analysis of a firm's activities requires extensive study of its footnotes and the MD&A.

Important information about a company is communicated to various decision makers through reports other than financial statements. These reports include the following:

- Management Discussion and Analysis (MD&A)
- Independent Auditor Report
- Financial statement footnotes
- Regulatory filings, including proxy statements and other SEC filings

We describe and explain the usefulness of these additional information sources throughout the book.

Review Problems *are self-study tools that require the application of accounting. To aid learning, solutions are provided at the end of the chapter.*

Guided Example *icons denote the availability of a demonstration video in* **myBusinessCourse** *(MBC)—see the Preface for more on MBC.*

MID-CHAPTER REVIEW

Based in Germany, **Adidas** is one of **Nike**'s primary competitors. It markets athletic shoes and apparel under the Adidas and Reebok brands. It also sells Solomon ski equipment as well as TaylorMade and Adams golf equipment. Adidas' financial statements are reported in Euros, the currency of the European Union. The following information is from the company's December 31, 2013, financial statements (€ millions):

	2013
Cash	€ 1,587
Cash flow from operations	634
Sales revenue	14,492
Stockholders' equity	5,481
Cost of goods sold	7,352
Cash flow used for financing	(439)
Total liabilities	6,118
Net other expenses	6,350
Noncash assets	10,012
Cash flow used for investing	(243)
Net income	790
Cash, beginning of year	1,670
Effect of exchange rates on cash	(35)

REQUIRED

a. Prepare Adidas' balance sheet at December 31, 2013, and its income statement and cash flow statement for the fiscal year ended December 31, 2013.

b. Compare Adidas' revenue, net income, and cash flow from operations to that of Nike (as reported in this chapter). Assume an exchange rate of €1.00 = $1.35.

The solution to this review problem can be found on pages 39–40.

FINANCIAL REPORTING ENVIRONMENT

LO4 Describe the institutions that regulate financial accounting and their role in establishing generally accepted accounting principles.

Learning Objectives *are repeated at the start of the section covering that topic.*

4

Information presented in financial statements is of critical importance to external decision makers. Financial statements affect the prices paid for equity securities and interest rates attached to debt securities. To the extent that financial performance and condition are accurately communicated to business decision makers, debt and equity securities are more accurately priced. By extension, financial reporting plays a crucial role in efficient resource allocation within and across economies. Accounting information contributes to the efficient operation of securities markets, labor markets, commodity markets, and other markets.

To illustrate, imagine the consequences of a breakdown in the integrity of financial reporting. The Enron scandal provides a case in point. At the beginning of 2001, **Enron** was one of the more, if not the most, innovative and respected companies in the United States. With revenues of over $100 billion and total company value of over $60 billion, it was the fifth largest U.S. corporation based on market value. In October 2001, the company released its third quarter earnings report to the public. Although operating earnings were higher than in previous years, the income statement contained a $1 billion "special charge." Financial analysts began investigating the cause of this charge and discovered that it was linked to related-party transactions and questionable accounting practices. Once it became clear to the capital markets that Enron had not faithfully and accurately reported its financial condition and performance, people became unwilling to purchase its securities. The value of its debt and equity securities dropped precipitously and the company was unable to obtain the cash needed for operating activities. By the end of 2001, Enron was bankrupt!

The Enron case illustrates the importance of reliable financial reporting. Accountants recognize the importance of the information that they produce and, as a profession, they agree to follow a set of standards for the presentation of financial statements and the disclosure of related financial information. In the following paragraphs, we discuss these standards, or *principles*, as well as the institutional and regulatory environment in which accountants operate.

Generally Accepted Accounting Principles

Decision makers who rely on audited financial statements expect that all companies follow similar procedures in preparing their statements. In response to these expectations, U.S. accountants have developed a set of standards and procedures called **generally accepted accounting principles (GAAP)**. GAAP is not a set of immutable laws. Instead, it is a set of standards and accepted practices, based on underlying principles, that are designed to guide the preparation of the financial statements. GAAP is subject to change as conditions warrant. As a result, specific rules are altered or new practices are formulated to fit changes in underlying economic circumstances or business transactions.

Some people mistakenly assume that financial accounting is an exact discipline—that is, companies select the proper standard to account for a transaction and then follow the rules. The reality is that GAAP allows companies considerable discretion in preparing financial statements. The choice of methods often yields financial statements that are markedly different from one company to another in terms of reported income, assets, liabilities, and equity amounts. In addition, financial statements depend on numerous estimates. Consequently, even though two companies may engage in the same transactions and choose the same accounting methods, their financial statements will differ because their managements have made different estimates about such things as the amount to be collected from customers who buy on credit, the length of time that buildings and equipment will be in use, and the future costs for product warranties.

Accounting standard setters walk a fine line regarding choice in accounting. On one hand, they are concerned that management discretion in preparing financial statements will lead to abuse by those seeking to influence the decisions of those who rely on the statements. On the other hand, they are concerned that companies are too diverse for a "one size fits all" financial accounting system. Ultimately, GAAP attempts to strike a balance by imposing constraints on the choice of accounting procedures, while allowing companies some flexibility within those constraints.

YOU MAKE THE CALL

You are a Financial Analyst Accountants, business leaders, and politicians have long debated the importance of considering the **economic consequences** of accounting standards (GAAP). Should accounting standards be designed to influence behavior and affect social or economic change considered by, say, a government body or other interested group? Alternatively, should such standards be designed simply to provide relevant and reliable information on which economic decisions can be made by others with a reasonable degree of confidence? What do you believe the objectives of financial reporting should be? [Answers on page 29.]

Regulation and Oversight

Following the U.S. stock market crash of 1929, the United States Congress passed the Securities Acts of 1933 and 1934. These acts were passed to require disclosure of financial and other information about securities being offered for public sale and to prohibit deceit, misrepresentations, and other fraud in the sale of securities. The 1934 Act created the **Securities and Exchange Commission (SEC)** and gave it broad powers to regulate the issuance and trading of securities. The act also provided that companies with more than $10 million in assets and whose securities are held by more than 500 owners must file annual and other periodic reports, including a complete set of financial statements.

While the SEC has ultimate authority over financial reporting by companies in the United States, it has ceded the task of setting accounting standards to a professional body, the **American Institute of Certified Public Accountants (AICPA)**. Over the years, this process has resulted in three standard-setting organizations.

Currently, accounting standards are established by the **Financial Accounting Standards Board (FASB)**. The FASB is a seven-member board that has the primary responsibility for setting financial accounting standards in the United States. It has published over 160 accounting statements governing the preparation of financial reports. These, along with numerous bulletins, interpretations, opinions, and earlier standards form the body of GAAP.

BUSINESS INSIGHT

Accounting can be complicated—but rule-makers are trying to make it a little simpler.
The Financial Accounting Standards Board, which sets accounting rules for U.S. companies, is expanding its effort to simplify some areas of accounting to make financial reporting a little less complex and reduce costs for companies and their accountants. The FASB has added five more projects it plans to tackle as part of that initiative, covering areas like how companies report their debt and when they record taxes on certain transactions.

The projects are low-hanging fruit—relatively narrow, straightforward changes in accounting that clearly would help reduce complexity and that the board expects to be able to make relatively quickly, without the years of work that often accompany major revisions in accounting rules.

"Complexity in accounting can be costly to both investors and companies," FASB Chairman Russ Golden said. The simplification initiative, which FASB began in June 2014, "is focused on identifying areas that we can address quickly and effectively, without compromising the quality of information provided to investors."

Besides setting standards for financial accounting, the FASB has developed a framework to form the basis for future discussion of proposed standards and serve as a guide to accountants for reporting information that is not governed by specific standards. A summary of this *Conceptual Framework* is presented in Appendix 1A at the end of this chapter.

In the wake of the Enron, Tyco, AOL, Global Crossing, Halliburton, Xerox, Adelphia, Bristol-Myers Squibb, and WorldCom scandals, concerns over the quality of corporate financial reporting led Congress to pass the **Sarbanes-Oxley Act** in 2002. The goal of this Act—sometimes referred to as SOX—was to increase the level of confidence that external users, particularly investors, have in the financial statements. To accomplish this objective, SOX imposed a number of requirements to strengthen audit committees and improve deficient **internal controls** by:

- increasing management's responsibility for accounting information,
- increasing the independence of the auditors,
- increasing the accountability of the board of directors,
- establishing adequate internal controls to prevent fraud.

SOX requires that the chief executive officer (CEO) and the chief financial officer (CFO) of a publicly traded corporation personally sign a statement attesting to the accuracy and completeness of financial statements. The prospect of severe penalties is designed to make these managers more vigilant in monitoring the financial accounting process. In addition, SOX established the **Public Company Accounting Oversight Board (PCAOB)** to approve auditing standards and monitor the quality of financial statements and audits.

SOX has had an impact on financial disclosures. A report by Glass, Lewis and Co. indicates that the number of publicly traded companies restating their financial reports increased to 1,295 in 2005, which is one restatement for every 12 reporting companies. That's triple the total in 2002 when SOX was passed.

The Sarbanes-Oxley Act is not without critics. Many small companies complain that the additional reporting and auditing requirements established in the act are prohibitively costly. In response to this criticism, the JOBS Act of 2012 relaxed the SOX reporting requirements for companies with less than one billion dollars in sales. Of even greater concern is the criticism that the penalties imposed on management for misstatements or errors are too severe. Some argue that managers have become less forthcoming in their disclosures and more conservative in choosing accounting methods and making accrual estimates to avoid the possibility of heavy fines or criminal charges.

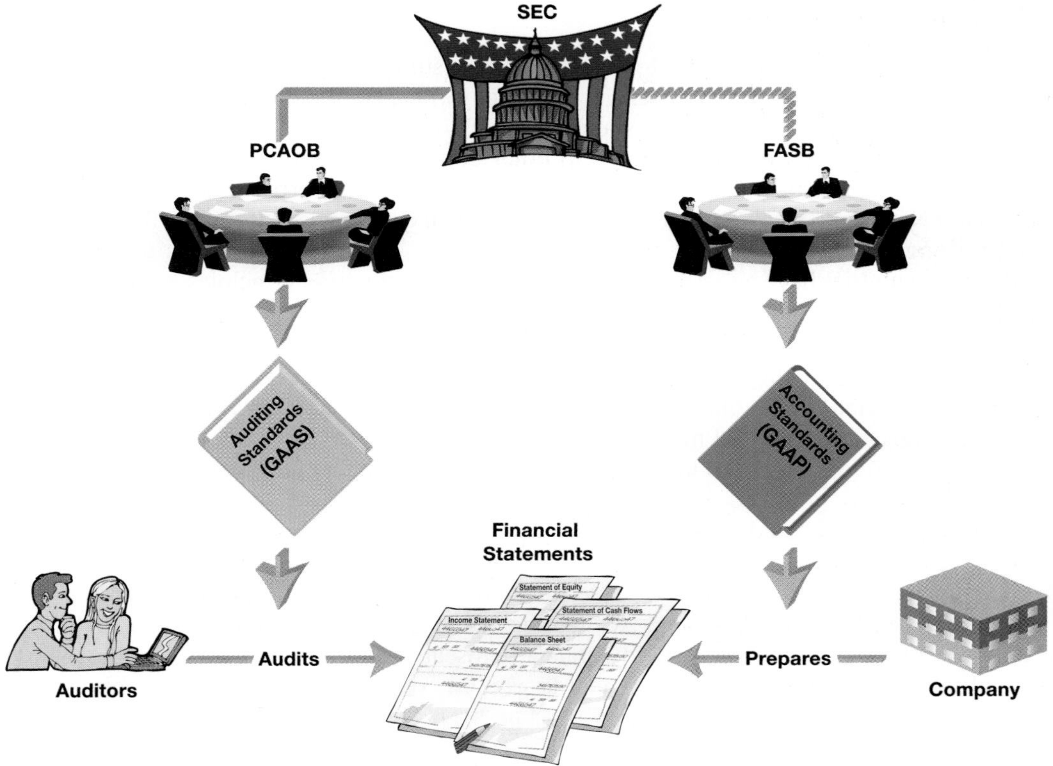

Role of the Auditor

What prevents a company from disclosing false or misleading information? For one thing, the financial statements are prepared by management, and management must take responsibility for what is disclosed. Management's reputation can be severely damaged by false disclosures when subsequent events unfold to refute the information. This situation can adversely affect the firm's ability to compete in capital, labor, and consumer markets. It can also lead to litigation and even criminal charges against management.

Even though management must personally attest to the accuracy and completeness of the financial statements, markets also demand assurances from independent parties. Therefore, the financial statements of publicly traded corporations must be **audited** by an *independent audit firm*. The auditors provide an opinion as to whether the statements *present fairly* and *in all material respects* a company's financial condition and the results of its operations.

The audit opinion is not a guarantee. Auditors only provide reasonable assurance that the financial statements are free of material misstatements. Even so, auditors provide a valuable service. Auditors effectively ensure that the information contained in the financial statements is reliable, thus increasing the confidence of outside decision makers in the information they use to make investment, credit, and other decisions. Therefore, creditors and shareholders of privately held corporations often demand that the financial statements be audited as well.

Public corporations are required to establish audit committees whose purpose is not to audit but, rather, to appoint the audit firm and assure that what is learned in the audit is disclosed to the firm's directors and shareholders.

YOU MAKE THE CALL

You are a Member of the Board of Directors Until recently accounting firms were permitted to earn money for consulting activities performed for clients they audited. Do you see any reason why this might not be an acceptable practice? Do you see any advantage to your firm from allowing such activity? [Answer on page 29.]

A Global Perspective

Businesses increasingly operate in global markets. Consumers and businesses with access to the Internet can purchase products and services from anywhere in the world. Products produced in one country are often made with parts and materials imported from many different countries. Businesses outsource parts of operations to other countries to take advantage of better labor markets in those countries. Capital markets are global as well. Corporations whose securities trade on the New York Stock Exchange may also trade on exchanges in London, Toronto, Tokyo, or Hong Kong.

Because countries have a variety of laws and customs, accounting principles and practices vary considerably from one country to the next. Many companies based in countries other than the United States choose to present financial statements that conform to U.S. GAAP because they believe that doing so provides them better access to investors in the U.S. capital markets. Many other companies prepare financial statements following GAAP of the country in which they are based.

The globalization of capital markets, combined with the diversity of international accounting principles, has led to an effort to increase comparability of financial information across countries. The **International Accounting Standards Board (IASB)** oversees the development of accounting standards outside the United States. Over 100 countries, including those in the European Union, require the use of **International Financial Reporting Standards (IFRS)** developed by the IASB. The intention is to unify all public companies under one global set of reporting standards.

Early in the 2000s, the Financial Accounting Standards Board (FASB) and the IASB committed to developing the highest-quality standards useable for both domestic and cross-border financial reporting and to assure the standards would (a) be fully compatible as soon as practicable and (b) maintain that compatibility. In May 2011, the SEC proposed a transition method to incorporate IFRS into the U.S. reporting system but did not delineate a definitive time for implementation. A number of large international companies now issue IFRS-compliant financial statements, however without reconciling them with U.S. GAAP as previously required. Statements prepared under IFRS and U.S. GAAP are quite similar, yet important differences remain. For example, balance sheets prepared under IFRS often classify assets in reverse order of liquidity to those prepared under GAAP. Thus, intangible assets are listed first and cash last on the balance sheet. Both approaches require the same basic set of four financial statements, with explanatory footnotes. We shall examine some of the more important differences under a Global Perspective heading as they arise in future chapters. Websites maintained by the larger accounting firms as well as both the FASB and IASB provide considerable information.

Because it is international in its scope, the IASB has no legal authority to impose accounting standards on any country. However, by working with standard setters within countries, such as the FASB within the United States, the IASB is working to reduce diversity in financial reporting practice. Despite the push for comparability, not everyone is convinced that IFRS will improve the usefulness of accounting information. As one observer put it, "There is a real risk of a veneer of comparability that hides a lot of differences." A number of countries—over 30 at last count—have reserved the right to adopt exceptions to IFRS when they deem them to be appropriate. Perhaps this helps explain why the SEC on July 13, 2012, declined to recommend IFRS for adoption by the United States.

Global Perspectives *examine issues related to similarities and differences in accounting practices of the U.S. and other countries.*

A GLOBAL PERSPECTIVE

Prior to 2007, foreign-based companies wishing to sell securities in the United States were required to reconcile their financial statements to be consistent with U.S. GAAP. However, in June 2007, the SEC adopted a rule that allows foreign companies using international accounting standards to stop reconciling their financial statements to American rules. While this change made it easier for U.S. investors to purchase securities from around the world, a *New York Times* article referred to a "Tower of Babel in Accounting." The article raises concerns about the difficulty of comparing companies when their financial statements are based on diverse reporting standards. The situation is complicated by the fact that a number of developing countries have reserved the right to adopt exceptions to IFRS when deemed appropriate.

Each chapter includes a section on **Analyzing Financial Statements** *to emphasize the use of accounting information in making business decisions.*

ANALYZING FINANCIAL STATEMENTS

LO5 Compute two key ratios that are commonly used to assess profitability and risk—return on equity and the debt-to-equity ratio.

The financial statements provide insights into the financial health and performance of a company. However, the accounting data presented in these statements are difficult to interpret in raw form. For example, knowing that Nike's net income was $2,693 million in 2014 is, by itself, not very useful. Similarly, knowing the dollar amount of liabilities does not tell us whether or not Nike relies too heavily on creditor financing.

Financial analysts use a number of tools to help interpret the information found in the financial statements. They look at trends over time and compare one company to another. They calculate ratios using financial statement information to summarize the data in a form that is easier to interpret. Ratios also allow us to compare the performance and condition of different companies even if the companies being compared are dramatically different in size. Ratios also help analysts spot trends or changes in performance over time.

Throughout the book, we introduce ratios that are commonly used by financial analysts and other users who rely on the financial statements. Our goal is to develop an understanding of how to effectively use the information in the financial statements, as well as to demonstrate how these statements are prepared. In this chapter we introduce one important measure of **profitability** and one measure of financial **risk**.

Profitability Analysis

Profitability reveals whether or not a company is able to bring its product or service to the market in an efficient manner, and whether the market values that product or service. Companies that are consistently unprofitable are unlikely to succeed in the long run.

A key profitability metric for stockholders and other decision makers is company return on equity. This metric compares the level of net income with the amount of equity financing used to generate that income.

Analysis Objective

We are trying to determine Nike's ability to earn a return for its stockholders.

Analysis Tool Return on Equity

$$\textbf{Return on equity} = \frac{\textbf{Net income}}{\textbf{Average stockholders' equity}}$$

Applying the Return on Equity Ratio to Nike

$$\textbf{2012:}\ \frac{\$2{,}211}{[(\$10{,}381+\$9{,}843)/2]}=0.219\text{ or }21.9\%$$

$$\textbf{2013:}\ \frac{\$2{,}472}{[(\$11{,}081+\$10{,}381)/2]}=0.230\text{ or }23.0\%$$

$$\textbf{2014:}\ \frac{\$2{,}693}{[(\$10{,}824+\$11{,}081)/2]}=0.246\text{ or }24.6\%$$

Guidance Taken over time, ROE ratios that are over 10% and preferably increasing suggest the company is earning reasonable returns. For firms that are in more risky businesses, such as renewable power, even larger returns on equity would be appropriate, while firms in less risky endeavors, such as large food chains, would not be expected to generate as large returns.

Nike in Context

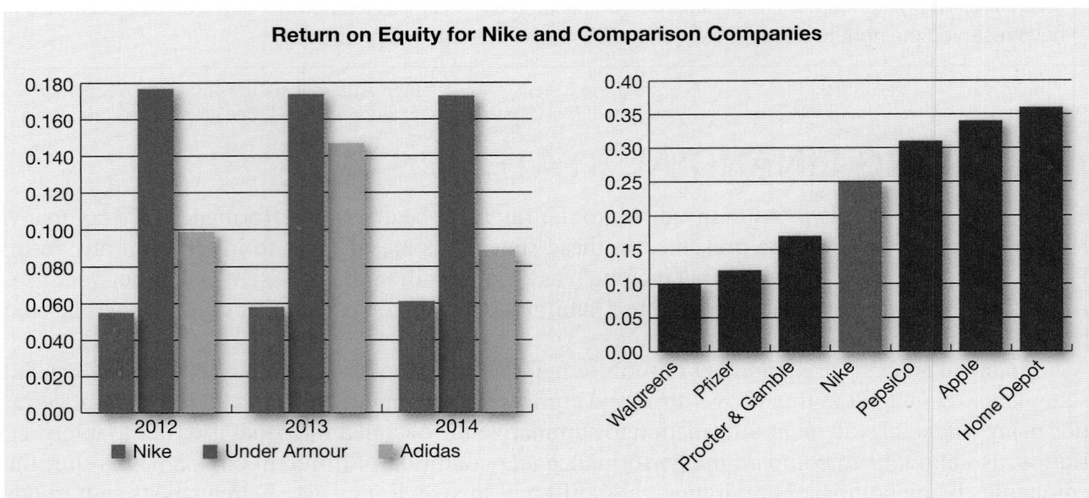

Takeaways Over the time period covered by our calculations and by the graph, it is clear that Nike has done very well earning returns for its stockholders. Not only have returns been over 20% but the trend is one of increasing profitability. Whether Nike can continue to do so is less clear. Several new companies have entered the market and Nike will need to continue developing new products to preserve its market leadership.

Other Considerations As with all ratios, care in their interpretation is essential. First, we need to be careful about comparing companies that operate in different product markets.

Second, firms with different customer or supplier demographics can also produce different conclusions. Furthermore, different management policies toward assets and liabilities have their own unique effect on ratios across firms. For example, the conversion of inventories to sales can be subject to slowdowns that affect companies differently, within the same industry.

Third, these measures can be altered by management decisions designed solely for cosmetic effects such as improving current earnings or an important ratio. Thus, delaying inventory orders or filling sales orders early can lead to increasing net income and ROE in current periods to the detriment of future periods.

Finally, differences in the fiscal year-end of companies can influence a comparison of ROE ratios. If one company's fiscal year ends in May and another company's fiscal year ends in December, economic conditions may change between May and December, creating differences in ROE that are not due to differences in the operations of the two companies. Among the companies compared above, fiscal year ends range from January 2014 (Home Depot) to December 2014 (Adidas and others).

Credit Risk Analysis

In addition to measuring profitability, analysts also frequently analyze the level of risk associated with investing in or lending to a given company. The riskier an investment is, the greater the return demanded by investors. For example, a low-risk borrower is likely to be able to borrow money at a lower interest rate than would a high-risk borrower. Similarly, there is a risk-return trade-off in equity returns. Investments in risky stocks are expected to earn higher returns than investments in low-risk stocks, and stocks are priced accordingly. The higher expected rate of return is compensation for accepting greater uncertainty in returns.

FYI Return cannot be evaluated without considering risk; the greater the risk of any decision, the greater the expected return.

Many factors contribute to the risk a company faces. One important factor is a company's *long-term solvency*. **Solvency** refers to the ability of a company to remain in business and avoid bankruptcy or financial distress. One such measure is the **debt-to-equity (D/E) ratio**.

Analysis Objective

We are interested in determining the ability of a company to make the necessary interest and principal payments on its debt.

Analysis Tool Debt-to-Equity

$$\textbf{Debt-to-equity ratio} = \frac{\textbf{Total liabilities}}{\textbf{Total stockholders' equity}}$$

Applying the Debt-to-Equity Ratio to Nike

$$\textbf{2012:}\ \frac{\$5,084}{\$10,381} = 0.49$$

$$\textbf{2013:}\ \frac{\$6,464}{\$11,081} = 0.58$$

$$\textbf{2014:}\ \frac{\$7,770}{\$10,824} = 0.72$$

Guidance Solvency is closely related to the extent a company relies on creditor financing. As the amount of creditor financing increases, the possibility of bankruptcy also increases. Short of bankruptcy, a company that has borrowed too much will occasionally find that the required interest payments are hurting the company's cash flow. The debt-to equity ratio is an important measure used by analysts and others to assess a company's ability to make the necessary interest and principal payments on its debt.

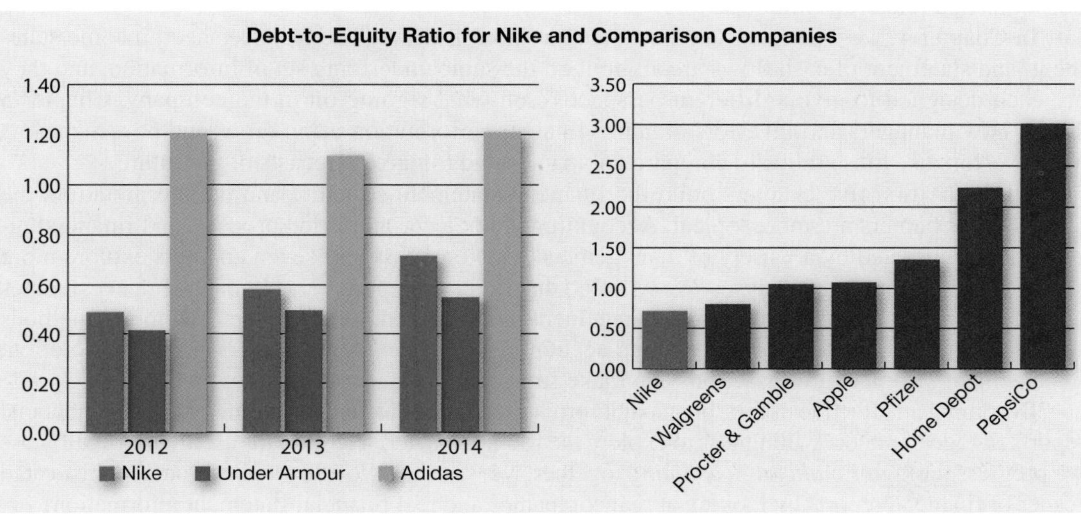

A debt-to equity ratio of one indicates that the company is using equal parts of debt and equity financing. Nike's borrowing has consistently been less than half its assets, resulting in a ratio substantially below one.

The appropriate D/E ratio level depends on the nature of the business and will differ appreciably as can be seen in the chart below. Typically, firms with large long-term commitments often reflected in fixed assets will find it appropriate to raise more capital through borrowing. The amount of debt relative to equity will also mirror the risk tolerance of the firm's management. If management believes it can earn a return above the debt interest cost, borrowing will increase the expected return to the owners.

Takeaways Nike's D/E ratio has increased slightly over the three years presented. Nike's liabilities have been steadily increasing. Yet, stockholders' equity has not increased at the same pace, and in fact it declined in 2014. Nevertheless, Nike's D/E ratio remains low, which is reasonable given nearly all its production is carried out overseas.

Other Considerations Comparisons with other companies in similar lines of business, such as Under Armour and Adidas, are always appropriate. New competitors, such as Quiksilver, could also prove insightful to examine in regards to strategic decisions. In Chapter 9, we will explore the accounting for liabilities in more depth. Balance sheets do not always recognize all obligations of a firm, and a careful reader will examine the footnotes to get a more complete picture of financial health in such comparisons. Nike might also consider increasing its debt level if profitable opportunities exist. The company has been, and remains, very successful, but new entrants are emerging indicating there is additional business to be had.

The graph shows that Nike had the lowest debt-to-equity ratio among this group of firms, followed closely by Walgreens. In contrast, PepsiCo had a debt-to-equity ratio of approximately 3.0. PepsiCo financed 75% of its assets with debt.

There are other measures of profitability and risk that will be introduced in later chapters. Collectively, these ratios, when placed in the context of the company's business activities, help to provide a clear picture of the *drivers* of a company's financial performance and the factors affecting its financial condition. Understanding these performance drivers and their impact on the financial health of a company is key to effectively using the information presented in the financial statements.

ORGANIZATION OF THE BOOK

In the pages that follow Chapter 1, we will explore the financial accounting model and how it reflects an organization's activities and events. Chapters 2 and 3 are focused on building the balance sheet and the income statement from transactions and a set of required adjustments. This process requires a structure for "bookkeeping" and also an understanding of the basic rules of the accounting language. When do we recognize revenue? When do we recognize an asset? We will look at these questions in a relatively simple setting.

In Chapter 4, we will construct the statement of cash flows. The balance sheet, income statement, and statement of cash flows are all built on the same underlying set of information, and they are each designed to give a different perspective on what's going on in the company. Chapter 5 shows how managers and investors organize financial information using ratios and how managers and investors use those ratios to compare companies and to make forecasts of the future.

While the first five chapters build the financial statement structure and its interpretation, the latter seven chapters are more topical. Accounting is not a cut-and-dried process, and financial reports can be affected by a variety of management decisions. So these seven chapters explore more sophisticated settings and analyses. We will find that financial reports rely on management estimates of future events, and that sometimes management has the freedom to choose accounting methods that affect income and assets. And, when accounting practices don't allow reporting discretion, management's choice of transactions can make financial reports look more favorable.

Becoming an effective user of financial information requires an understanding of how the financial reports fit together and a willingness to explore the footnote material to look for useful information. As we progress through *Financial Accounting* together, we will show you how to become a sophisticated reader of financial reports by looking at real companies and real financial statement information.

CHAPTER-END REVIEW

Adidas, a major competitor of Nike, markets athletic shoes and apparel under the Adidas and Reebok brands. It also sells Solomon ski equipment and TaylorMade golf equipment. The following information is from Adidas' 2013 financial statements (Adidas' financial statements are reported in Euros, the currency of the European Union):

(millions)	Adidas
Net income (loss) (2013)	€ 790
Stockholders' equity (2013 year-end)	5,481
Stockholders' equity (2012 year-end)	5,291
Total liabilities (2013 year-end)	6,118

REQUIRED

a. Calculate the 2013 return on equity (ROE) ratio for Adidas.
b. Calculate the 2013 debt-to-equity ratio for Adidas.
c. Compare the profitability and risk of Adidas to that of Nike.

The solution to this review problem can be found on page 40.

APPENDIX 1A: Conceptual Framework for Financial Reporting

LO6 Explain the conceptual framework for financial reporting.

Accountants establish GAAP to ensure that the financial statements published by a company reflect its economic condition and performance. To meet this objective, the FASB sets accounting standards that reduce management discretion for reporting much of the information in the financial statements. To provide a structure for considering future standards, as well as to guide accountants in areas where standards do not currently exist, the FASB has developed a **conceptual framework**. This conceptual framework includes, among other things, a statement of the *objectives* of financial reporting along with a discussion of the *qualitative characteristics* of accounting information that are important to users. We discuss these objectives and characteristics in this appendix, along with some of the important assumptions underlying the preparation of financial statements.

Objectives of Financial Reporting

A fundamental goal of financial accounting is to provide information that promotes the efficient allocation and use of economic resources. To this end, the FASB established several objectives of financial reporting which are summarized here.

- Financial accounting should provide information that is useful to investors, creditors, and other decision makers who possess a reasonable knowledge of business activities and accounting.
- Financial accounting should provide information to help investors and creditors assess the amount, timing, and uncertainty of cash flows. This includes the information presented in the cash flow statement as well as other information that might help investors and creditors assess future dividend and debt payments.
- Financial accounting should provide information about economic resources and financial claims on those resources. This includes the information in the balance sheet and any supporting information that might help the user assess the value of the company's assets and future obligations.
- Financial accounting should provide information about a company's financial performance, including net income and its components (i.e., revenues and expenses).
- Financial accounting should provide information that allows decision makers to monitor company management to evaluate their effective, efficient, and ethical stewardship of company resources.

FYI The FASB and the IASB are currently working to create a common conceptual framework that will guide firms reporting under International Financial Reporting Standards (IFRS).

Qualitative Characteristics of Accounting Information

Qualitative characteristics of useful accounting information were developed to help managers, accountants, auditors, and standard setters make reasonable choices among accounting alternatives. These qualitative characteristics are depicted in **Exhibit 1A.1** and discussed below.

EXHIBIT 1A.1 Qualitative Characteristics of Accounting Information

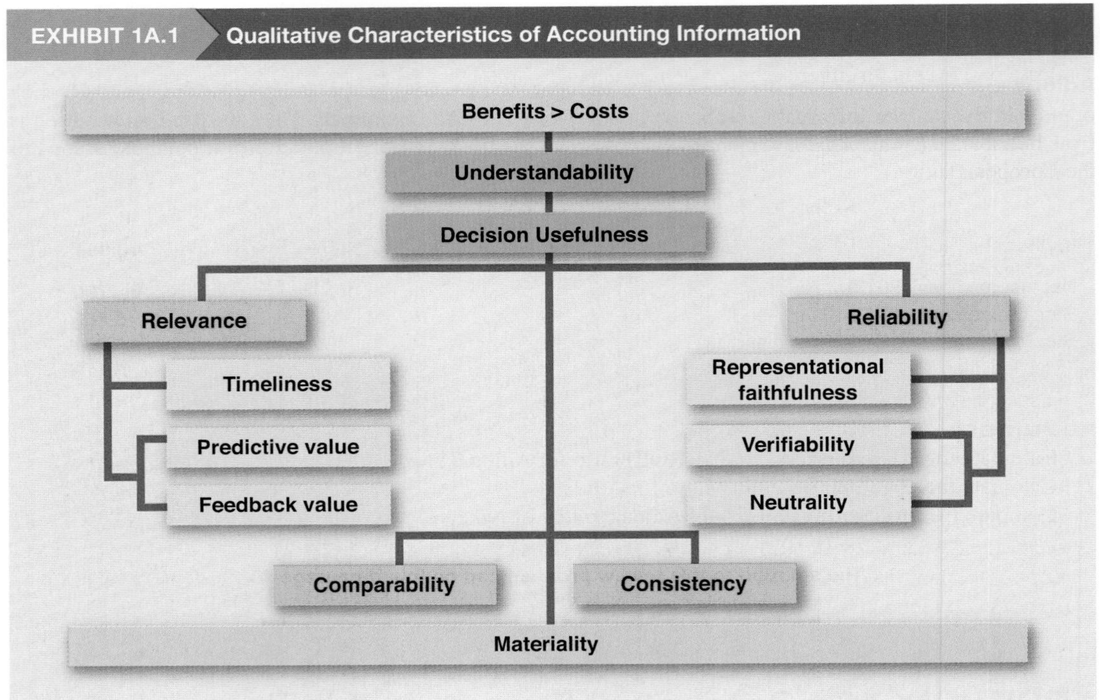

Exhibit 1A.1 neither distinguishes between primary and secondary qualities nor does it assign priorities among the qualities. It is an explanatory device and must be applied with consideration of the specific application intended. Each of the qualities is essential in some degree, but that degree will differ depending on the circumstances. We now expand briefly on each of the qualities delineated in the exhibit.

Benefits > Costs Reported accounting information must be cost-effective. This characteristic implies that if the benefit to the economy does not exceed the cost, the information does not meet the test of usefulness. The operational difficulty with this information quality is that while the reporting cost can usually be ascertained, the benefit to information users is often difficult to quantify. Nevertheless, the need to weigh costs and benefits is seen as an overriding constraint on the financial reporting process.

Materiality Materiality refers to whether or not a particular amount is large enough to affect a decision. Some items are not reported based on this constraint because they are considered *not material* in that the magnitude of the omission would not influence the judgment of a reasonable decision maker. In practice, materiality is typically judged by the relative size of an item related to a major reported variable such as total assets, sales revenues, or net income. However, some items are required to meet a lower threshold of materiality. The more critical an item is to understanding the condition and performance of the company, the finer the screen that should be used to determine whether or not it is material.

Understandability and Decision Usefulness Accounting information should be presented so that a knowledgeable reader can understand how it relates to the decision problem at hand. Because different users will require different information, suppliers (standard setters) must tread a fine line between reporting (requiring) too much or too little information.

BUSINESS INSIGHT

What Is Material? *The Wall Street Journal* recently reported that the SEC initiated an informal inquiry into **Pixar Animation Studios** concerning its disclosure of "heavier than expected returns of its *The Incredibles* DVD that forced the Emeryville, California-based studio to miss its second quarter earnings forecast." This inquiry follows an informal SEC investigation of **DreamWorks Animation**, the filmmaker that twice reduced earnings forecasts after substantial returns of its *Shrek 2* DVD. The issue in these two cases is whether companies are under obligation to inform market participants of material events affecting earnings. The *Journal* points out that "in the wave of recent corporate scandals, some companies have been more conservative in assessing what constitutes a material event."

Relevance Accounting information must have the ability to make a difference in a decision. Such information may be useful in making *predictions* about future performance of the company or in providing *feedback* to evaluate past events. In either case, the *timeliness* of the disclosure is paramount to its relevance.

- **Timeliness**: The information must be available to decision makers before it loses its capacity to influence decisions. That is, information that is reported *after* a decision is made is not relevant to that decision.
- **Predictive value**: Refers to the ability of the information to increase the accuracy of a forecast.
- **Feedback value**: Refers to the quality of information that enables users to confirm or correct prior expectations.

RESEARCH INSIGHT

Research has documented a decline in the value relevance of accounting information, particularly earnings, over the past few decades. The decline has been attributed by some to conservatism in reporting. However, recent research has not been able to establish an association between this decrease in value relevance and conservatism despite using several alternative measures of conservative accounting. One explanation offered for the research finding is that conservatism favors more objective measures while avoiding additional estimation, thereby increasing reliability. If true, conservative accounting measurement could lead to greater relevance. The issue remains unresolved at this time and conservatism in reporting continues.

Research Insights *introduce relevant research findings on the topics presented.*

Reliability Accounting information should be accurate and free of misstatement or bias. It must be reasonably *neutral*, *verifiable*, and possess *representational faithfulness*.

- **Representational faithfulness**: Accounting information should reflect the underlying economic events it purports to measure.
- **Verifiability**: This characteristic implies that consensus among measures assures that the information is free of error. An independent auditor should be able to examine the economic events and transactions underlying the financial statements and reach conclusions that are similar to those of management concerning how these events are measured and reported.
- **Neutrality**: Information must be free of any bias intended to attain a predetermined result or to induce a particular mode of behavior.

Comparability Accounting information should enable users to identify similarities and differences between sets of economic phenomena. For instance, the financial statements of different companies should be presented in a way that allows users to make comparisons across companies concerning their activities, financial condition, and performance. Although management has the flexibility to choose how events are measured and reported, this discretion should not be used to obscure the underlying economic substance of the event. One of the consequences of comparability is that firms in the same business (industry) should use the same, or similar, reporting techniques.

Consistency The information supplied to decision makers should exhibit conformity from one reporting period to the next with unchanging policies and procedures. Companies can choose to change accounting methods, and sometimes they are required to do so by standard setters. However, such changes make it difficult to evaluate financial performance over time. Accounting changes should be rare and supported as the better means of reporting the organization's financial condition and performance. Whenever possible, using the same accounting methods from one period to the next increases the quality of accounting information.

Underlying Assumptions

Four assumptions underlie the preparation of financial statements. Knowing these assumptions is helpful in understanding how the statements are prepared and in interpreting the information reported therein. These assumptions include:

Separate Economic Entity For accounting purposes, the activities of a company are considered independent, distinct, and separate from the activities of its stockholders and from other companies.

Going Concern Companies are assumed to have continuity in that they can be expected to continue in operation over time. This assumption is essential for valuing assets (future benefits) and liabilities (future obligations).

Accounting Period While continuity is assumed, company operations must be reported periodically, normally each fiscal year. Interim reporting periods, such as quarterly or monthly reports, allow companies to supplement the annual financial statements with more timely information.

Measuring Unit The unit of measure is the monetary unit of the country in which the firm's accounting reports are issued. The dollar is the monetary unit in the United States.

YOU MAKE THE CALL

You are the Bank Loan Officer **Hertz**, the rental car firm, has a fleet of relatively new automobiles that it rents to customers for usually short periods. Suppose that Hertz applied to your bank for a loan and offered their fleet of cars as collateral. Would you, as the loan officer, be satisfied with the value shown on Hertz's balance sheet as a measure of the fleet's value? If not, what value would you prefer and how might you estimate that value? [Answers on page 30.]

Summary *offers key bullet point takeaways for each Learning Objective.*

SUMMARY

LO1 Identify the users of accounting information and discuss the costs and benefits of disclosure. (p. 4)

- There are many diverse decision makers who use financial information.
- The benefits of disclosure of credible financial information must exceed the costs of providing the information.

LO2 Describe a company's business activities and explain how these activities are represented by the accounting equation. (p. 7)

- To effectively manage a company or infer whether it is well managed, we must understand its activities as well as the competitive and regulatory environment in which it operates.
- All corporations *plan* business activities, *finance* and *invest* in them, and then engage in *operations*.
- Financing is obtained partly from stockholders and partly from creditors, including suppliers and lenders.
- Investing activities involve the acquisition and disposition of the company's productive resources called assets.
- Operating activities include the production of goods or services that create operating revenues (sales) and expenses (costs). Operating profit (income) arises when operating revenues exceed operating expenses.

LO3 Introduce the four key financial statements including the balance sheet, income statement, statement of stockholders' equity, and statement of cash flows. (p. 11)

- The four basic financial statements used to periodically report the company's progress are the balance sheet, the income statement, the statement of stockholders' equity, and the statement of cash flows. These statements articulate with one another.
- The balance sheet reports the company's financial position *at a point* in time. It lists the company's asset, liability, and equity items, and it typically aggregates similar items.
- The income statement reports the firm's operating activities to determine income earned, and thereby the firm's performance *over a period* of time.
- The stockholders' equity statement reports the changes in the key equity accounts *over a period* of time.
- The statement of cash flows reports the cash flows into and out of the firm from its operating, investing, and financing sources *over a period* of time.

LO4 Describe the institutions that regulate financial accounting and their role in establishing generally accepted accounting principles. (p. 17)

- Generally Accepted Accounting Principles (GAAP) are established standards and accepted practices designed to guide the preparation of the financial statements.
- While the Securities and Exchange Commission (SEC) has ultimate authority over financial reporting by companies in the United States, it has ceded the task of setting accounting standards to the accounting profession.

- The Financial Accounting Standards Board (FASB) has the primary responsibility for setting financial accounting standards in the United States.
- The Sarbanes-Oxley Act established the Public Company Accounting Oversight Board (PCAOB) to approve auditing standards and monitor the quality of financial statements and audits.
- International Financial Reporting Standards (IFRS) are set by the International Accounting Standards Board (IASB).
- IFRS are an attempt to achieve a greater degree of commonality in financial reporting across different countries.

Compute two key ratios that are commonly used to assess profitability and risk—return on equity and the debt-to-equity ratio. (p. 21) LO5

- **Return on equity (ROE)**—a measure of profitability that assesses the performance of the firm relative to the investment made by stockholders (equity financing)
- Return on equity (ROE) is an important profitability metric for stockholders.

$$\text{ROE} = \frac{\text{Net income}}{\text{Average stockholders' equity}}$$

- **Debt-to-equity ratio (D/E)**—a measure of long-term solvency that relates the amount of creditor financing to the amount of equity financing
- The debt-to-equity ratio is an important measure of long-term solvency, a determinant of overall company risk.

$$\text{D/E} = \frac{\text{Total liabilities}}{\text{Total stockholders' equity}}$$

Appendix 1A: Explain the conceptual framework for financial reporting. (p. 25) LO6

- The conceptual framework includes, among other things, a statement of the *objectives* of financial reporting along with a discussion of the *qualitative characteristics* of accounting information that are important to users.

GUIDANCE ANSWERS . . . YOU MAKE THE CALL

You are a Product Manager There are at least two considerations that must be balanced—namely, the disclosure requirements and your company's need to protect its competitive advantages. You must comply with all minimum required disclosures. The extent to which you offer additional disclosures depends on the sensitivity of the information; that is, how beneficial it is to your existing and potential competitors. Another consideration is how the information disclosed will impact your existing and potential investors. Disclosures such as this can be beneficial in that they convey the positive investments that are available to your company. Still, there are many stakeholders impacted by your decision and each must be given due consideration.

You are a Financial Analyst This question has received a lot of discussion from both sides under the title "Economic Consequences." On one side are those who maintain that accounting rules should not only reflect a rule's economic consequences but should be designed to facilitate the attainment of a specific economic goal. One example is the case where the oil industry lobbied for an accounting rule that they and others believed would increase the incentive to explore and develop new oil deposits.

Those on the other side of the argument believe that accounting should try to provide data that is objective, reliable, and free from bias without considering the economic consequences of the decisions to be made. They believe that accounting rule makers have neither the insight nor the public mandate to attempt forecasts of the economic effects of financial reporting. Decisions that will affect the allocation of resources or that affect society's social structure should be made only by our elected representatives. While there are substantive points on both sides, we believe that it is the job of accounting rule makers to work toward the objective of financial reporting that reflects economic reality, subject to practical measurement limitations.

You are a Member of the Board of Directors In order to perform a thorough audit, a company's auditors must gain an intimate knowledge of its operations, its internal controls, and its accounting system. Because of this familiarity, the accounting firm is in a position to provide insights and recommendations that another consulting firm might not be able to provide. However, the independence of the auditor is critical to the credibility of the audit and there is some concern that the desire to retain a profitable consulting engagement might lead the auditors to tailor their audit opinions to "satisfy the customer." Contrary to this concern, however, research finds that there is no evidence that auditors provide more optimistic audit reports for the companies they consult for. Rather, it appears that litigation and/or reputation concerns are reasonably effective in keeping auditors honest. Nevertheless, recent legislation in the United States now prohibits auditors from performing consulting services for their audit clients.

You are the Bank Loan Officer The value shown on Hertz's books will be the purchase price, though perhaps reduced for the time the fleet has been in use. However, the bank would want to know the current market value of the fleet, not its book value, and the bank would then adjust this market value. The current market value of a single car can be found in used-car market quotes. If the bank ultimately becomes the owner of the fleet, it will need to sell the cars, probably a few at a time through wholesalers. Therefore, the adjusted market value and the book value are likely to differ for several reasons, including:

1. Hertz would have been able to buy the fleet at a reduced value due to buying in large volume regularly (market value lower than used-car quotes).
2. Hertz is likely to have kept the cars in better condition than would the average buyer (market value higher than used-car quotes).
3. The bank would reduce the value by some percentage due to the costs associated with disposing of the fleet (including the wholesaler's discount) and the length of the bank loan (reduction to the value as otherwise determined).

KEY RATIOS

$$\text{Return on equity (ROE)} = \frac{\text{Net income}}{\text{Average stockholders' equity}} \qquad \text{Debt-to-equity (D/E)} = \frac{\text{Total liabilities}}{\text{Total stockholders' equity}}$$

Key Terms *are listed for each chapter with references to page numbers within the chapter.*

KEY TERMS

Accounting (p. 4)
Accounting equation (p. 10)
American Institute of Certified Public Accountants (AICPA) (p. 18)
Assets (p. 8)
Audited (p. 20)
Balance sheet (p. 11, 12)
Board of directors (p. 6)
Conceptual framework (p. 25)
Corporation (p. 5)
Cost of goods sold (p. 12)
Creditors (p. 5)
Debt-to-equity (D/E) ratio (p. 23)
Disclosure (p. 6)
Economic consequences (p. 18)
Expense (p. 10)
Feedback value (p. 27)
Financial accounting (p. 4)
Financial Accounting Standards Board (FASB) (p. 18)
Financing activities (p. 9)
Generally accepted accounting principles (GAAP) (p. 17)
Income (p. 10)
Income statement (p. 11, 12)
Internal controls (p. 18)
International Accounting Standards Board (IASB) (p. 20)
International Financial Reporting Standards (IFRS) (p. 20)
Investing activities (p. 8)
Liabilities (p. 9)
Managerial accounting (p. 4)
Neutrality (p. 27)
Operating activities (p. 10)
Partnership (p. 5)
Planning activities (p. 8)
Predictive value (p. 27)
Profitability (p. 21)
Public Company Accounting Oversight Board (PCAOB) (p. 19)
Representational faithfulness (p. 27)
Retained earnings (p. 13)
Revenue (p. 10)
Risk (p. 21)
Sarbanes-Oxley Act (p. 18)
Securities and Exchange Commission (SEC) (p. 18)
Shares of stock (p. 5)
Sole proprietorship (p. 5)
Solvency (p. 23)
Statement of cash flows (p. 11, 14)
Statement of stockholders equity (p. 11, 13)
Stockholders (p. 5)
Strategy (p. 8)
Suppliers (p. 6)
Timeliness (p. 27)
Verifiability (p. 27)

Assignments with the MBC logo in the margin are available in myBusinessCourse. See the Preface of the book for details.

Multiple Choice questions with answers are provided for each chapter.

MULTIPLE CHOICE

1. Which of the following is a potential cost of the public disclosure of accounting information?
   a. Loss of competitive advantage caused by revealing information to competitors.
   b. Potential increased regulation and taxes due to reporting excessive profits in politically sensitive industries.
   c. Raising and then failing to meet the expectations of investors.
   d. All of the above are potential costs of disclosure.

2. Banks that lend money to corporations are considered
   a. creditors.
   b. stockholders.
   c. both *a* and *b* above.
   d. neither *a* nor *b* above.

3. Which of the following financial statements reports the financial condition of a company at a point in time?
   a. the balance sheet
   b. the income statement
   c. the statement of cash flows
   d. the statement of stockholders' equity

4. Which of the following is *not* one of the four basic financial reports?
   a. the balance sheet
   b. the income statement
   c. the statement of stockholders' equity
   d. the notes to the financial statements

5. Which of the following expressions is a correct statement of the accounting equation?
   a. Equity + Assets = Liability
   b. Assets − (Liabilities + Equity) = 0
   c. Liabilities − Equity = Assets
   d. Liabilities + Assets = Equity

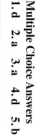

Multiple Choice Answers
1.d 2.a 3.a 4.d 5.b

Homework icons indicate which assignments are available in myBusinessCourse (MBC). This feature is only available when the instructor incorporates MBC in the course.

Superscript A denotes assignments based on Appendix 1A.

QUESTIONS

Q1-1. What are the three major business activities of a company that are motivated and shaped by planning activities? Explain each activity.

Q1-2. The accounting equation (Assets = Liabilities + Equity) is a fundamental business concept. Explain what this equation reveals about a company's sources and uses of funds and the claims on company resources.

Q1-3. Companies prepare four primary financial statements. What are those financial statements and what information is typically conveyed in each?

Q1-4. Does a balance sheet report on a period of time or at a point in time? Also, explain the information conveyed in that report. Does an income statement report on a period of time or at a point in time? Also, explain the information conveyed in that report.

Q1-5. Warren Buffett, CEO of Berkshire Hathaway, and known as the "Sage of Omaha" for his investment success, has stated that his firm is not interested in investing in a company whose business model he does not understand through reading its financial statements. Would you agree? Name several information items (3 or 4) reported in financial statements that corporate finance officers would find particularly relevant in considering whether to invest in a firm.

Q1-6. Does a statement of cash flows report on a period of time or at a point in time? Also, explain the information and activities conveyed in that report.

Q1-7. Explain what is meant by the articulation of financial statements.

Q1-8. The trade-off between risk and return is a fundamental business concept. Briefly describe both risk and return and their trade-off. Provide some examples that demonstrate investments of varying risk and the approximate returns that you might expect to earn on those investments.

Q1-9. Why might a company voluntarily disclose more information than is required by GAAP?

Q1-10. Financial statements are used by several interested stakeholders. Develop a listing of three or more potential external users of financial statements and their applications.

Q1-11. What ethical issues might managers face in dealing with confidential information?

Q1-12. Return on equity (ROE) is an important summary measure of financial performance. How is it computed? Describe what this metric reveals about company performance.

Q1-13. Business decision makers external to the company increasingly demand more financial information on business activities of companies. Discuss the reasons why companies have traditionally opposed the efforts of regulatory agencies like the SEC to require more disclosure.

Q1-14. What are generally accepted accounting principles and what organization presently establishes them?

Q1-15. What are International Financial Reporting Standards (IFRS)? Why are IFRS needed? What potential issues can you see with requiring all public companies to prepare financial statements using IFRS?

Q1-16. What is the primary function of the auditor? To what does the auditor attest in its opinion?

Q1-17.[A] What are the objectives of financial accounting? Which of the financial statements satisfies each of these objectives?

Q1-18.[A] What are the four qualitative characteristics of accounting information? Explain how each characteristic improves the quality of accounting disclosures.

MINI EXERCISES

LO2 Homework MBC

WhiteWave Foods, Inc.
NYSE :: WWAV

M1-19. Financing and Investing Relations, and Financing Sources

Total assets of **WhiteWave Foods** equals \$2,283.2 million and its equity is \$961.4 million. What is the amount of its liabilities? Does WhiteWave Foods receive more financing from its owners or nonowners, and what percentage of financing is provided by its owners?

LO2 Homework MBC

Coca-Cola Company
NYSE :: KO

M1-20. Financing and Investing Relations, and Financing Sources

Total assets of **The Coca-Cola Company** equals \$90,055 million and its liabilities equal \$56,615 million. What is the amount of its equity? Does Coke receive more financing from its owners or nonowners, and what percentage of financing is provided by its owners?

LO2 Homework MBC

M1-21. Applying the Accounting Equation and Computing Financing Proportions

Use the accounting equation to compute the missing financial amounts (a), (b), and (c). Which of these companies is more owner-financed? Which of these companies is more nonowner-financed?

Hewlett-Packard
NYSE :: HPQ
General Mills
NYSE :: GIS
Harley-Davidson
NYSE :: HOG

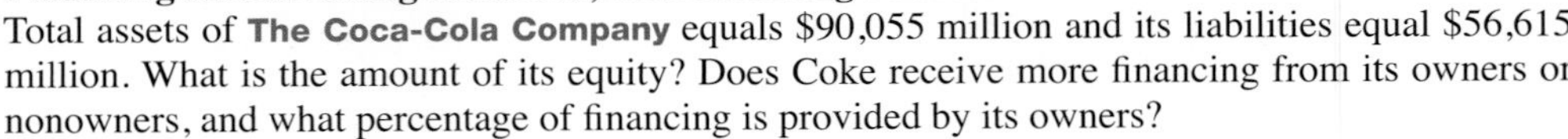

(\$ millions)	Assets	=	Liabilities	+	Equity
Hewlett-Packard	\$ 105,676		\$ 78,020		\$ (a)
General Mills	23,145.7		(b)		7,005.4
Harley-Davidson	(c)		6,395.5		3,009.5

LO3 Homework MBC

Apple Inc.
NASDAQ :: AAPL

M1-22. Identifying Key Numbers from Financial Statements

Access the most recent 10-K for **Apple Inc.**, at the SEC's EDGAR database for financial reports (www.sec.gov). What are Apple's dollar amounts for assets, liabilities, and equity at September 27, 2014? Confirm that the accounting equation holds in this case. What percent of Apple's assets is financed from creditor financing sources?

LO3

Nike
NYSE :: NKE

M1-23. Verifying Articulation of Financial Statements

Access the 2014 10-K for **Nike** at the SEC's EDGAR database of financial reports (www.sec.gov). Using its consolidated statement of stockholders' equity, prepare a table similar to **Exhibit 1.9** showing the articulation of its retained (reinvested) earnings for the year ended May 31, 2013. Was Nike more or less profitable in 2014 compared to 2013?

LO3

M1-24. Identifying Financial Statement Line Items and Accounts

Several line items and account titles are listed below. For each, indicate in which of the following financial statement(s) you would likely find the item or account: income statement (IS), balance sheet (BS), statement of stockholders' equity (SE), or statement of cash flows (SCF).

a. Cash asset
b. Expenses
c. Noncash assets
d. Contributed capital
e. Cash outflow for land
f. Retained earnings
g. Cash inflow for stock issued
h. Cash outflow for dividends
i. Net income

M1-25. Ethical Issues and Accounting Choices

LO1

Assume that you are a technology services provider and you must decide whether to record revenue from the installation of computer software for one of your clients. Your contract calls for acceptance of the software by the client within six months of installation before payment is due. Although you have not yet received formal acceptance, you are confident that it is forthcoming. Failure to record these revenues will cause your company to miss Wall Street's earnings estimates. What stakeholders will be affected by your decision and how might they be affected?

LOs *link assignments to the Learning Objectives of each chapter.*

M1-26. Internal Controls and Their Importance

LO4

The Sarbanes-Oxley legislation requires companies to report on the effectiveness of their internal controls. What are internal controls and their purpose? Why do you think Congress felt it to be such an important area to monitor and report?

EXERCISES

E1-27. Applying the Accounting Equation and Assessing Financing Contributions

LO2

Motorola Solutions NYSE :: MSI
Kraft Foods NASDAQ :: KRFT
Merck & Co. NYSE :: MRK

Determine the missing amount from each of the separate situations (a), (b), and (c) below. Which of these companies is more owner-financed? Which of these companies is more creditor-financed?

($ millions)	Assets	=	Liabilities	+	Equity
a. **Motorola Solutions, Inc.**	$ 11,851		$?		$3,689
b. **Kraft Foods Group, Inc.**	?		17,961		5,187
c. **Merck & Co., Inc.**	105,645		53,319		?

E1-28. Financial Information Users and Uses

LO1

Financial statements have a wide audience of interested stakeholders. Identify two or more financial statement users that are external to the company. Specify two questions for each user identified that could be addressed or aided by use of financial statements.

E1-29. Applying the Accounting Equation and Financial Statement Articulation

LO2, 3

Intel NASDAQ :: INTC
JetBlue Airways NASDAQ :: JBLU
Walt Disney Company NYSE :: DIS

Answer the following questions. (*Hint*: Apply the accounting equation.)

a. **Intel Corporation** had assets equal to $92,358 million and liabilities equal to $34,102 million for a recent year-end. What was the total equity for Intel's business at year-end?

b. At the beginning of a recent year, **JetBlue Airways Corporation**'s assets were $7,070 million and its equity was $1,888 million. During the year, assets increased $280 million and liabilities increased $34 million. What was its equity at the end of the year?

c. At the beginning of a recent year, **The Walt Disney Company**'s liabilities equaled $32,940 million. During the year, assets increased by $6,343 million, and year-end assets equaled $81,241 million. Liabilities increased $151 million during the year. What were its beginning and ending amounts for equity?

E1-30. Financial Statement Relations to Compute Dividends

LO3

Colgate-Palmolive NYSE :: CL

Ticker *symbols are provided for companies so one can easily obtain additional information.*

Colgate-Palmolive Company reports the following balances in its retained earnings.

($ millions)	2013	2012
Retained earnings	$17,952	$16,953

During 2013, Colgate-Palmolive reported net income of $2,410 million.

a. Assume that the only changes affecting retained earnings were net income and dividends. What amount of dividends did Colgate-Palmolive pay to its shareholders in 2013?

b. This dividend amount constituted what percent of its net income?

LO3

Colgate-Palmolive
NYSE :: CL

E1-31. Calculating Gross Profit and Preparing an Income Statement
In 2013, **Colgate-Palmolive Company** reported sales revenue of $17,420 million and cost of goods sold of $7,219 million. Its net income was $2,410 million. Calculate gross profit and prepare an income statement using the format illustrated in **Exhibit 1.8**.

LO2, 5
Colgate-Palmolive
NYSE :: CL

E1-32. Applying the Accounting Equation and Calculating Return on Equity and Debt-to-Equity Ratio
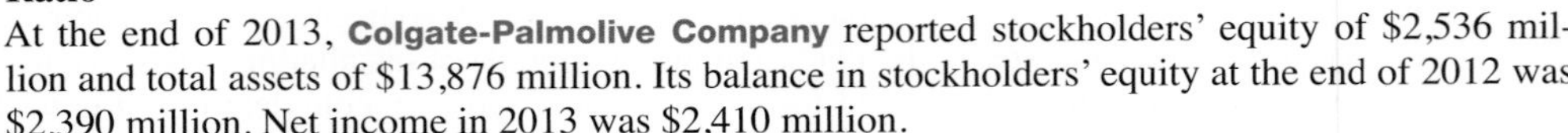
At the end of 2013, **Colgate-Palmolive Company** reported stockholders' equity of $2,536 million and total assets of $13,876 million. Its balance in stockholders' equity at the end of 2012 was $2,390 million. Net income in 2013 was $2,410 million.

a. Calculate Colgate-Palmolive's return on equity ratio for 2013.
b. Calculate its debt-to-equity ratio as of December 31, 2013. (*Hint:* Apply the accounting equation to determine total liabilities.)

LO2, 5
Daimler AG
OTC :: DDAIF

E1-33. Applying the Accounting Equation and Computing Return on Equity and Debt-to-Equity Ratio
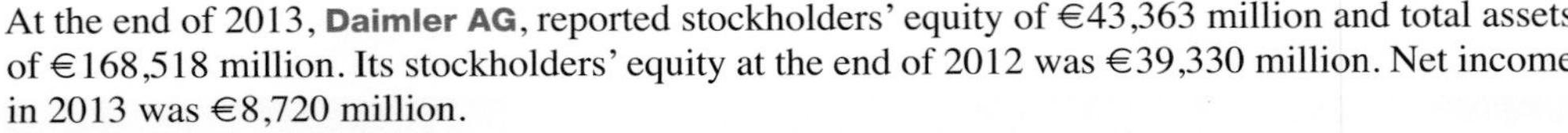
At the end of 2013, **Daimler AG**, reported stockholders' equity of €43,363 million and total assets of €168,518 million. Its stockholders' equity at the end of 2012 was €39,330 million. Net income in 2013 was €8,720 million.

a. Calculate Daimler's return on equity ratio for 2013.
b. Calculate Daimler's debt-to-equity ratio as of December 31, 2013.

LO1, 4

E1-34. Accounting in Society
Financial accounting plays an important role in modern society and business.

a. What role does financial accounting play in the allocation of society's financial resources?
b. What are three aspects of the accounting environment that can create ethical pressure on management?

LO6

E1-35.[A] Basic Assumptions, Principles, and Terminology in the Conceptual Framework
Match each item in the left column with the correct description in the right column.

_____ 1. Relevance
_____ 2. Verifiability
_____ 3. Going concern
_____ 4. Materiality
_____ 5. Measuring unit
_____ 6. Representational faithfulness
_____ 7. Accounting period
_____ 8. Consistency
_____ 9. Reliability
_____ 10. Economic entity

a. Refers to whether or not a particular amount is large enough to affect a decision.
b. The activities of a business are considered to be independent and distinct from those of its owners or from other companies.
c. Whenever possible, information in concurrent periods should be presented without changes to policies and procedures
d. Accounting information should be accurate and free of misstatement or bias.
e. Information is useful if it has the ability to influence decisions.
f. Consensus among measures assures that the information is free of error.
g. Accounting information should reflect the underlying economic events that it purports to measure.
h. The financial reports are presented in one consistent monetary unit, such as U.S. dollars.
i. A business is expected to have continuity in that it is expected to continue to operate indefinitely.
j. The life of a business can be divided into discrete accounting periods such as a year or quarter.

PROBLEMS

LO2, 5
Procter & Gamble
NYSE :: PG

P1-36. Applying the Accounting Equation and Calculating Ratios
The following table contains financial statement information for **The Procter & Gamble Company** ($ millions):

Year	Assets	Liabilities	Equity	Net Income
2011	$138,354	$70,353	$?	$11,927
2012	?	68,209	64,035	10,904
2013	139,263	?	68,709	11,402

REQUIRED

a. Compute the missing amounts for assets, liabilities, and equity for each year.

b. Compute return on equity for 2012 and 2013. The median ROE for Fortune 500 companies is about 15%. How does P&G compare with this median?

c. Compute the debt-to-equity ratio for 2012 and 2013. The median debt-to-equity ratio for the Fortune 500 companies is 1.8. How does P&G compare to this median?

P1-37. Formulating Financial Statements from Raw Data

LO2, 3

General Mills
NYSE :: GIS

Following is selected financial information from **General Mills, Inc.**, for its fiscal year ended May 25, 2014 ($ millions):

Cash and cash equivalents	$ 867.3
Net cash from operations.	2,541.0
Sales.	17,909.6
Stockholders' equity	7,005.4
Cost of goods sold.	11,539.8
Net cash from financing	(1,824.1)
Total liabilities.	16,140.3
Other expenses, including income taxes	4,508.5
Noncash assets	22,278.4
Net cash from investing	(561.8)
Net income.	1,861.3
Effect of exchange rate changes on cash	(29.2)
Cash, beginning year	741.4

REQUIRED

a. Prepare an income statement, balance sheet, and statement of cash flows for General Mills, Inc.

b. What portion of the financing is contributed by owners?

P1-38. Formulating Financial Statements from Raw Data

LO2, 3

Abercrombie & Fitch
NYSE :: ANF

Following is selected financial information from **Abercrombie & Fitch** for its fiscal year ended February 1, 2014 ($ millions):

Cash asset	$ 600.1
Cash flows from operations.	175.5
Sales.	4,116.9
Stockholders' equity	1,729.5
Cost of goods sold.	1,541.5
Cash flows from financing	(40.8)
Total liabilities.	1,121.5
Other expenses, including income taxes.	2,520.8
Noncash assets	2,250.9
Cash flows from investing	(173.9)
Net income.	54.6
Effect of exchange rate changes on cash	(4.2)
Cash, beginning year	643.5

REQUIRED

a. Prepare an income statement, balance sheet, and statement of cash flows for Abercrombie & Fitch.

b. Determine the owner and creditor financing levels.

P1-39. Preparing Comparative Financial Statements from Raw Data

LO3

Tilly's, Inc.
NYSE :: TLYS

Following is selected financial information for **Tilly's, Inc.**

($ thousands)	Feb. 1, 2014	Feb. 2, 2013
Cash and cash equivalents	$ 25,412	$ 17,314
Cash flow from operations	43,794	41,730
Cost of goods sold	343,542	317,096
Total liabilities	91,484	88,085
Total assets	232,407	205,381
Cash flow from financing	1,834	22,819
Sales revenue	495,837	467,291
Cash flow from investing	(37,530)	(72,326)
Other expenses, including income taxes	134,158	126,302

REQUIRED

Prepare balance sheets, income statements and cash flow statements for the years ended February 1, 2014 and February 2, 2013.

LO3 **P1-40. Preparing Comparative Financial Statements from Raw Data**

Tesla Motors, Inc.
NASDAQ :: TSLA

Following is selected financial information for **Tesla Motors, Inc.**

($ thousands)	Dec. 31, 2013	Dec. 31, 2012
Cash and cash equivalents	$ 845,889	$ 201,890
Cash flow from operations	257,994	(266,081)
Cost of goods sold	1,557,234	383,189
Total liabilities	1,749,810	989,490
Total assets	2,416,930	1,114,190
Cash flow from financing	635,422	419,635
Sales revenue	2,013,496	413,256
Cash flow from investing	(249,417)	(206,930)
Other expenses, including income taxes	530,276	426,280

REQUIRED

Prepare balance sheets, income statements and cash flow statements for the years ended December 31, 2013 and 2012.

LO3 **P1-41. Formulating a Statement of Stockholders' Equity from Raw Data**

Crocker Corporation began calendar-year 2016 with stockholders' equity of $100,000, consisting of contributed capital of $70,000 and retained earnings of $30,000. During 2016, it issued additional stock for total cash proceeds of $30,000. It also reported $50,000 of net income, of which $25,000 was paid as a cash dividend to shareholders.

REQUIRED

Prepare the December 31, 2016 statement of stockholders' equity for Crocker Corporation.

LO3 **P1-42. Formulating a Statement of Stockholders' Equity from Raw Data**

DP Systems, Inc., reports the following selected information at December 31, 2016 ($ millions):

Contributed capital, December 31, 2015 and 2016	$ 550
Retained earnings, December 31, 2015	2,437
Cash dividends, 2016	281
Net income, 2016	859

REQUIRED

Use this information to prepare its statement of stockholders' equity for 2016.

LO3, 5 **P1-43. Analyzing and Interpreting Return on Equity**

Nokia
NYSE :: NOK

Nokia Corp. manufactures, markets, and sells phones and other electronics. Stockholders' equity for Nokia are €6,660 million in 2013 and €9,239 million in 2012. In 2013, Nokia reported a loss of €739 million on sales of €12,709 million.

REQUIRED

a. What is Nokia's return on equity for 2013?

b. Nokia's total assets were €25,191 million at the end of 2013. Compute its debt-to-equity ratio.

c. What are total expenses for Nokia in 2013?

P1-44. Presenting an Income Statement and Computing Key Ratios

LO3, 5

Best Buy
NYSE :: BBY

Best Buy Co., Inc., reported the following amounts in its February 1, 2014, and February 2, 2013, financial statements.

($ millions)	2014	2013
Sales revenue	$42,410	$39,827
Cost of sales	32,720	30,528
Net income (loss)	523	(420)
Total assets	14,013	16,787
Stockholders' equity	3,989	3,715

REQUIRED

a. Prepare an income statement for Best Buy for the year ended February 1, 2014, using the format illustrated in **Exhibit 1.8**.

b. Calculate Best Buy's return on equity for the year ended February 1, 2014.

c. Compute Best Buy's debt-to-equity ratio as of February 1, 2014.

P1-45. Preparing Income Statements and Computing Key Ratios

LO3, 5

Facebook, Inc.
NASDAQ :: FB

Facebook, Inc. reported the following amounts in its 2012 and 2013 financial statements.

($ millions)	Dec. 31, 2013	Dec. 31, 2012
Total assets	$17,895	$15,103
Total liabilities	2,425	3,348
Retained earnings	3,159	1,659
Revenue	7,872	5,089
Operating expenses	5,068	4,551
Other expenses, including income taxes	1,304	485

REQUIRED

a. Prepare income statements for Facebook for 2013 and 2012. Use the format illustrated in **Exhibit 1.8**.

b. Compute Facebook's return on equity ratio for 2013 and 2012. Facebook's stockholders' equity at the end of 2011 was $4,899 million.

c. Compute Facebook's debt-to-equity ratio for 2013 and 2012.

d. What amount of dividends did Facebook pay to its shareholders in 2013?

CASES AND PROJECTS

C1-46. Preparing Comparative Income Statements and Computing Key Ratios

LO3, 5

Starbucks Corporation
NASDAQ :: SBUX

Starbucks Corporation reported the following data in its 2013 and 2012 10-K reports.

($ millions)	Sep. 29, 2013	Sep. 30, 2012
Total assets	$11,516.7	$ 8,219.2
Total liabilities	7,034.4	3,104.7
Sales revenue	14,892.2	13,299.5
Cost of goods sold	6,382.3	5,813.3
Other expenses, including income taxes	8,501.1	6,101.5

REQUIRED

a. Prepare income statements for Starbucks for the years ended September 29, 2013 and September 30, 2012. Use the format illustrated in **Exhibit 1.8**.

b. Compute Starbucks' return on equity ratio for 2013 and 2012. Starbucks stockholders' equity at October 2, 2011 was $4,387.3 million.

c. Compute Starbucks' debt-to-equity ratio for 2013 and 2012.

d. Starbucks' net income and return on equity were considerably lower in 2013 than in 2012. In 2013, Starbucks reported a litigation charge of $2,784.1 million, which is included above in other expenses. What effect did this one-time charge have on the company's return on equity ratio? (*Hint:* Compute the ratio excluding the litigation charge from other expenses and compare to the ratio computed in *b*.)

e. Starbucks disclosed information about the pending litigation in the footnotes to its 2012 financial statements (before the case was settled). Discuss the costs and benefits of disclosing this information in its 2012 annual report.

LO2, 3, 5
The Gap
NYSE :: GPS
Nordstrom
NYSE :: JWN

C1-47. Computing and Interpreting Key Ratios and Formulating an Income Statement

Data from the financial statements of **The Gap, Inc.**, and **Nordstrom, Inc.**, are presented below.

($ millions)	The Gap	Nordstrom
Stockholders' equity, 2013	$ 3,062	$ 2,080
Stockholders' equity, 2012	2,894	1,913
Total assets, 2013	7,849	8,574
Total assets, 2012	7,470	8,089
Revenue, 2013	16,148	12,540
Cost of goods sold, 2013	9,855	7,737
Net income, 2013	1,280	734

REQUIRED

a. Compute the return on equity ratio for The Gap and Nordstrom for 2013. Which company earned the higher return for its shareholders?

b. Compute the debt-to-equity ratio for each company as of 2013. Which company relies more on creditor financing?

c. Prepare a 2013 income statement for each company using the format in **Exhibit 1.8**. For each firm, compute gross profit as a percentage of sales revenue.

d. Based on your answers to questions *a*, *b*, and *c*, compare these two retail companies. What might be the cause of any differences in the ratios that you computed?

LO5

JetBlue Airways
NASDAQ :: JBLU
Southwest Airlines
NYSE :: LUV

C1-48. Computing and Interpreting Key Ratios

Data from the financial statements of **JetBlue Airways** and **Southwest Airlines** are presented below.

($ millions)	JetBlue Airways	Southwest Airlines
Total liabilities, 2013	$5,216	$12,009
Total liabilities, 2012	5,182	11,604
Total assets, 2013	7,350	19,345
Total assets, 2012	7,070	18,596
Revenue, 2013	5,441	17,699
Net income, 2013	168	754

REQUIRED

a. Compute the return on equity ratio for JetBlue and Southwest for 2013. Which company earned the higher return for its shareholders?

b. Compute the debt-to-equity ratio for each company as of December 31, 2013. Which company relies more on creditor financing?

c. For each firm, compute net income as a percentage of revenue in 2013.

d. Based on your answers to questions *a*, *b*, and *c*, compare these two competitors. What might be the cause of any differences in the ratios that you computed?

LO1, 3, 5

C1-49. Interpreting Financial Statement Information

Paula Seale is negotiating the purchase of an extermination firm called Total Pest Control. Seale has been employed by a national pest control service and knows the technical side of the business. However, she knows little about accounting data and financial statements. The sole owner of the firm, Meg Krey, has provided Seale with income statements for the past three years, which show an average net income of $72,000 per year. The latest balance sheet shows total assets of $285,000 and liabilities of $45,000. Seale brings the following matters to your attention and requests advice.

1. Krey is asking $300,000 for the firm. She has told Seale that because the firm has been earning 30% on its investment, the price should be higher than the net assets on the balance sheet (net assets equals total assets minus total liabilities).
2. Seale has noticed no salary for Krey on the income statements, even though she worked half-time in the business. Krey explained that because she had other income, the firm only paid $18,000 in cash dividends to Krey (the sole shareholder). If she purchases the firm, Seale will hire a full-time manager for the firm at an annual salary of $36,000.
3. Krey's tax returns for the past 3 years report a lower net income for the firm than the amounts shown in the financial statements. Seale is skeptical about the accounting principles used in preparing the financial statements.

REQUIRED

a. How did Krey arrive at the 30% return figure in point 1? If Seale accepts Krey's average annual net income figure of $72,000, what would Seale's percentage return be, assuming that the net income remained at the same level and that the firm was purchased for $300,000?

b. Should the dividend to Krey affect the net income reported in the financial statements? What will Seale's percentage return be if she takes into consideration the $36,000 salary she plans to pay a full-time manager?

c. Could there be legitimate reasons for the difference between net income shown in the financial statements and net income reported on the tax returns, as mentioned in point 3? How might Seale obtain additional assurance about the propriety of the financial statements?

C1-50. Management, Auditing, and Ethical Behavior LO1, 4

Jackie Hardy, CPA, has a brother, Ted, in the retail clothing business. Ted ran the business as its sole owner for 10 years. During this 10-year period, Jackie helped Ted with various accounting matters. For example, Jackie designed the accounting system for the company, prepared Ted's personal income tax returns (which included financial data about the clothing business), and recommended various cost control procedures. Ted paid Jackie for all these services. A year ago, Ted markedly expanded the business; Ted is president of the corporation and also chairs the corporation's board of directors. The board of directors has overall responsibility for corporate affairs. When the corporation was formed, Ted asked Jackie to serve on its board of directors. Jackie accepted. In addition, Jackie now prepares the corporation's income tax returns and continues to advise her brother on accounting matters.

Recently, the corporation applied for a large bank loan. The bank wants audited financial statements for the corporation before it will decide on the loan request. Ted asked Jackie to perform the audit. Jackie replied that she cannot do the audit because the code of ethics for CPAs requires that she be independent when providing audit services.

REQUIRED

a. Why is it important that a CPA be independent when providing audit services?

b. Which of Jackie's activities or relationships impair her independence?

SOLUTIONS TO REVIEW PROBLEMS

Mid-Chapter Review

SOLUTION

a.

ADIDAS
Balance Sheet (€ millions)
December 31, 2013

Cash	€ 1,587	Total liabilities.	€ 6,118
Noncash assets	10,012	Stockholders' equity	5,481
Total assets	€11,599	Total liabilities and stockholders' equity	€11,599

ADIDAS
Income Statement (€ millions)
For Year Ended December 31, 2013

Sales revenue	€14,492
Cost of goods sold	7,352
Gross profit	7,140
Other expenses	6,350
Net income (loss)	€ 790

ADIDAS
Statement of Cash Flows (€ millions)
For Year Ended December 31, 2013

Cash flow from operations	€ 634
Cash flow from investing	(243)
Cash flow from financing	(439)
Effect of exchange rates on cash	(35)
Net increase (decrease) in cash	(83)
Cash, beginning of year	1,670
Cash, end of year	€ 1,587

b. Adidas reported revenues of €14,492 million (which is approximately equivalent to $19,564 million) compared to Nike's $27,799 million. Adidas reported net income of €790 million ($1,067 million) compared to Nike's $2,693 million. Adidas' operations produced cash flow of €634 million ($856 million) while Nike's cash flow from operations was $3,003 million. Hence, based on revenues, Nike is a larger company indicated by its substantially larger sales revenue. Its total assets of $18,594 million are also greater than Adidas' (€11,599 million or $15,659 million). Consistent with its larger size, Nike's operating cash flows and income are also larger than those of Adidas.

Chapter-End Review

SOLUTION

a. $$\text{ROE} = \frac{€790}{[(€5{,}481 + €5{,}291)/2]} = 0.147 \text{ or } 14.7\%$$

b. $$\text{Debt-to-equity} = \frac{€6{,}118}{€5{,}481} = 1.12$$

c. One additional benefit to using ratios to analyze financial information is that ratios can be computed for amounts denominated in any currency. Thus, we can compare Adidas and Nike without translating Euros into Dollars. Adidas' ROE of 14.7% is lower than Nike's of 24.6%. This means that Nike is more profitable in that it earned a higher return for its stockholders in 2014.

Adidas' debt-to-equity ratio is 1.12 compared to Nike's 0.72. This means that Adidas relies more on debt financing than does Nike. The higher debt-to-equity ratio indicates a higher level of risk associated with an investment in Adidas than with an investment in Nike.

Constructing Financial Statements

LEARNING OBJECTIVES

1. Describe and construct the balance sheet and understand how it can be used for analysis. (p. 44)
2. Use the financial statement effects template (FSET) to analyze transactions. (p. 49)
3. Describe and construct the income statement and discuss how it can be used to evaluate management performance. (p. 53)
4. Explain revenue recognition, accrual accounting, and their effects on retained earnings. (p. 54)
5. Illustrate equity transactions and the statement of stockholders' equity. (p. 60)
6. Use journal entries and T-accounts to analyze and record transactions. (p. 62)
7. Compute net working capital, the current ratio, and the quick ratio, and explain how they reflect liquidity. (p. 71)

WALGREENS

www.walgreens.com

More than a hundred years have passed since Charles R. Walgreen, Sr. purchased his first pharmacy in 1901. In that time, the company that bears his name has grown remarkably. As of August 31, 2014, **Walgreen Co.** operated 8,309 locations in 50 states, the District of Columbia, Puerto Rico, and the U.S. Virgin Islands; it had 251,000 employees; and it filled 19% of the retail prescriptions in the United States.

Even with the company's recent success, Walgreens faces a number of challenges. The economic changes of the recent past have made consumers more cautious and cost-conscious. Pharmacy sales constitute two-thirds of Walgreens' sales, and almost all of those are paid for by a third party. The success of that business depends significantly on factors like the growth of generic pharmaceuticals, legislative changes such as the Affordable Care Act, and the relationships with Pharmacy Benefit Managers. Furthermore, Walgreens faces rising costs for pharmaceuticals and increasing competition from other drugstore chains like **CVS Health Corp.** and discount retailers like **Wal-Mart Stores, Inc.**

These factors, however, have not prevented Walgreens from reporting profits continuously for the last five years. Chief Executive Officer, Gregory D. Wasson, seems to have found a strategy for profitable growth by slowing the rate of new store openings and turning its focus to cost control and operating efficiencies.

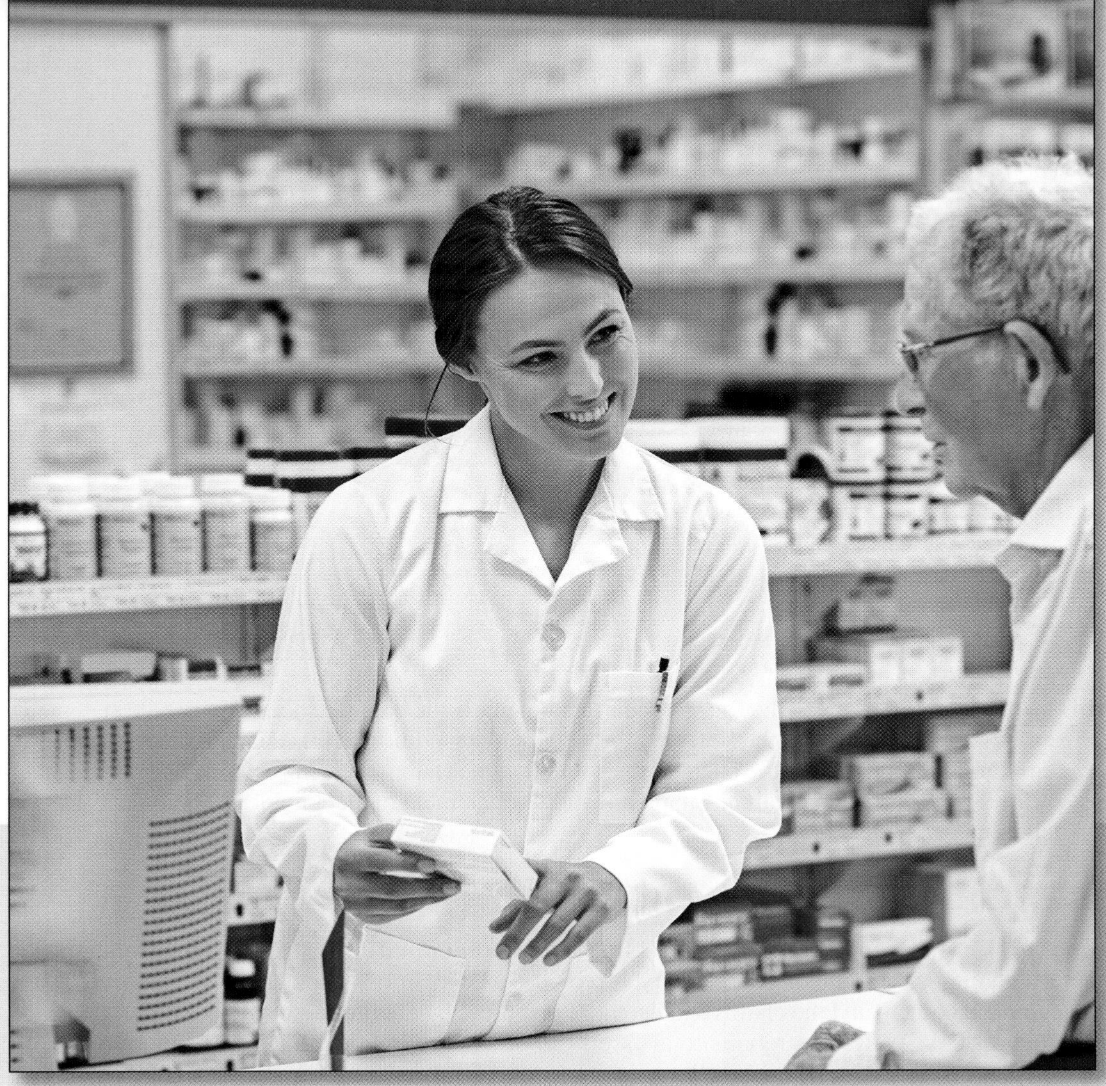

Walgreens is poised to increase sales substantially and increase its geographic footprint with its recent decision to acquire **Alliance Boots GmbH**, an international health and beauty group. Subsequent to August 31, 2014, the merged companies have reorganized into Walgreens Boots Alliance, Inc.

As we discovered in Chapter 1, companies like Walgreens prepare financial statements annually. These financial statements allow investors and creditors to assess the impact of changing economic conditions on the company's financial health and performance.

This chapter will introduce and explain financial statements using Walgreens as its prime example. The chapter also introduces some key accounting procedures such as transaction analysis, journal entries, and posting. The general ledger, key accounting assumptions, and basic accounting definitions are also introduced.

Sources: "In the beginning…" Walgreens history on the corporate Web site; Walgreen Co. and Subsidiaries 2014 10-K annual report; *Fortune* magazine Web site.

CHAPTER ORGANIZATION

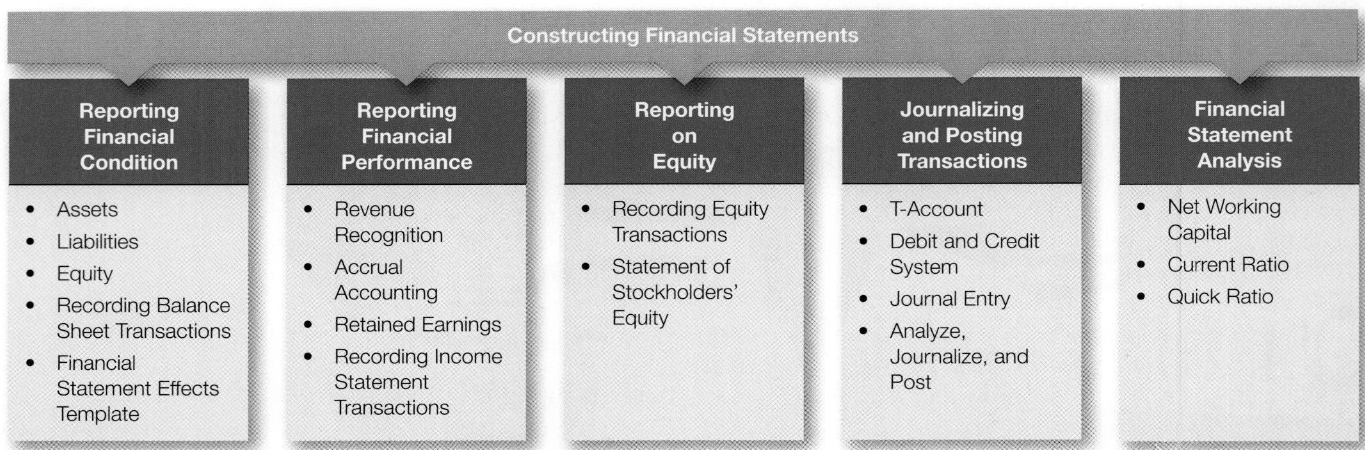

In Chapter 1, we introduced the four financial statements—the balance sheet, the income statement, the cash flow statement, and the statement of stockholders' equity. In this chapter and in Chapter 3, we turn our attention to how the balance sheet and income statement are prepared. The statement of cash flows is discussed in detail in Chapter 4, and the statement of stockholders' equity is discussed in detail in Chapter 11.

REPORTING FINANCIAL CONDITION

1 **LO1** Describe and construct the balance sheet and understand how it can be used for analysis.

The balance sheet reports on a company's financial condition and is divided into three components: assets, liabilities, and stockholders' equity. It provides us with information about the resources available to management and the claims against those resources by creditors and shareholders. At the end of August 2014, Walgreens reports total assets of $37,182 million, total liabilities of $16,621 million, and equity of $20,561 million. Drawing on the **accounting equation**, Walgreens' balance sheet is summarized as follows ($ millions).

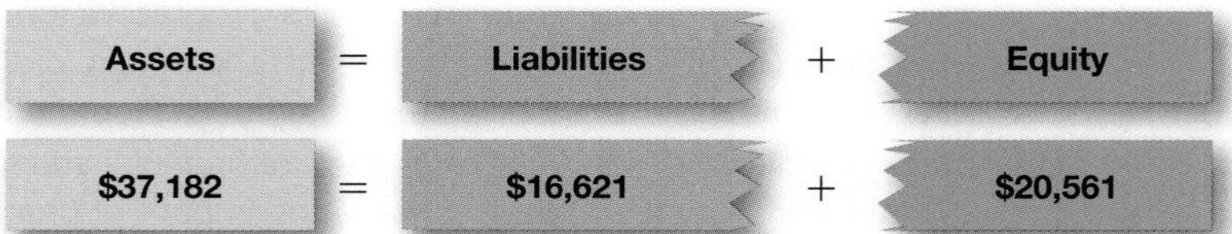

The balance sheet is prepared at a *point in time*. It is a snapshot of the financial condition of the company at that instant. For Walgreens, the above balance sheet amounts were reported at the close of business on August 31, 2014. Balance sheet accounts carry over from one period to the next; that is, the ending balance from one period becomes the beginning balance for the next period.

Walgreens' summarized 2014 and 2013 balance sheets are shown in **Exhibit 2.1**. These balance sheets report the assets and the liabilities and shareholders' equity amounts as of August 31, the company's fiscal year-end. Walgreens had $37,182 million in assets at the end of August 31, 2014, with the same amount reported in liabilities and shareholders' equity. Companies report their audited financial results on a yearly basis.[1] Many companies use the calendar year as their fiscal year. Other companies prefer to prepare their yearly report at a time when business activity is at a low level. Walgreens is an example of the latter reporting choice.

Assets

An **asset** is a resource owned or controlled by a company and expected to provide the company with future economic benefits. When a company incurs a cost to acquire future benefits, we say that cost is capitalized and an asset is recorded. An asset must possess two characteristics to be reported on the balance sheet:

[1] Companies also report quarterly financial statements, and these are reviewed by the independent accountant, but not audited.

1. It must be owned or controlled by the company.
2. It must possess probable future benefits that can be measured in monetary units.

The first requirement, that the asset must be owned or controlled by the company, implies that the company has legal title to the asset or has the unrestricted right to use the asset. This requirement presumes that the cost to acquire the asset has been incurred, either by paying cash, by trading other assets, or by assuming an obligation to make future payments.

The second requirement indicates that the company expects to receive some future benefit from ownership of the asset. Benefits can be the expected cash receipts from selling the asset or from selling products or services produced by the asset. Benefits can also refer to the receipt of other noncash assets, such as accounts receivable or the reduction of a liability (e.g., when assets are given up to settle debts). It also requires that a monetary value can be assigned to the asset.

Companies acquire assets to yield a return for their shareholders. Assets are expected to produce revenues, either directly (e.g., inventory that is sold) or indirectly (e.g., a manufacturing plant that produces inventories for sale). To create shareholder value, assets must yield resources that are in excess of the cost of the funds utilized to acquire the assets.

EXHIBIT 2.1 Walgreens' Balance Sheet

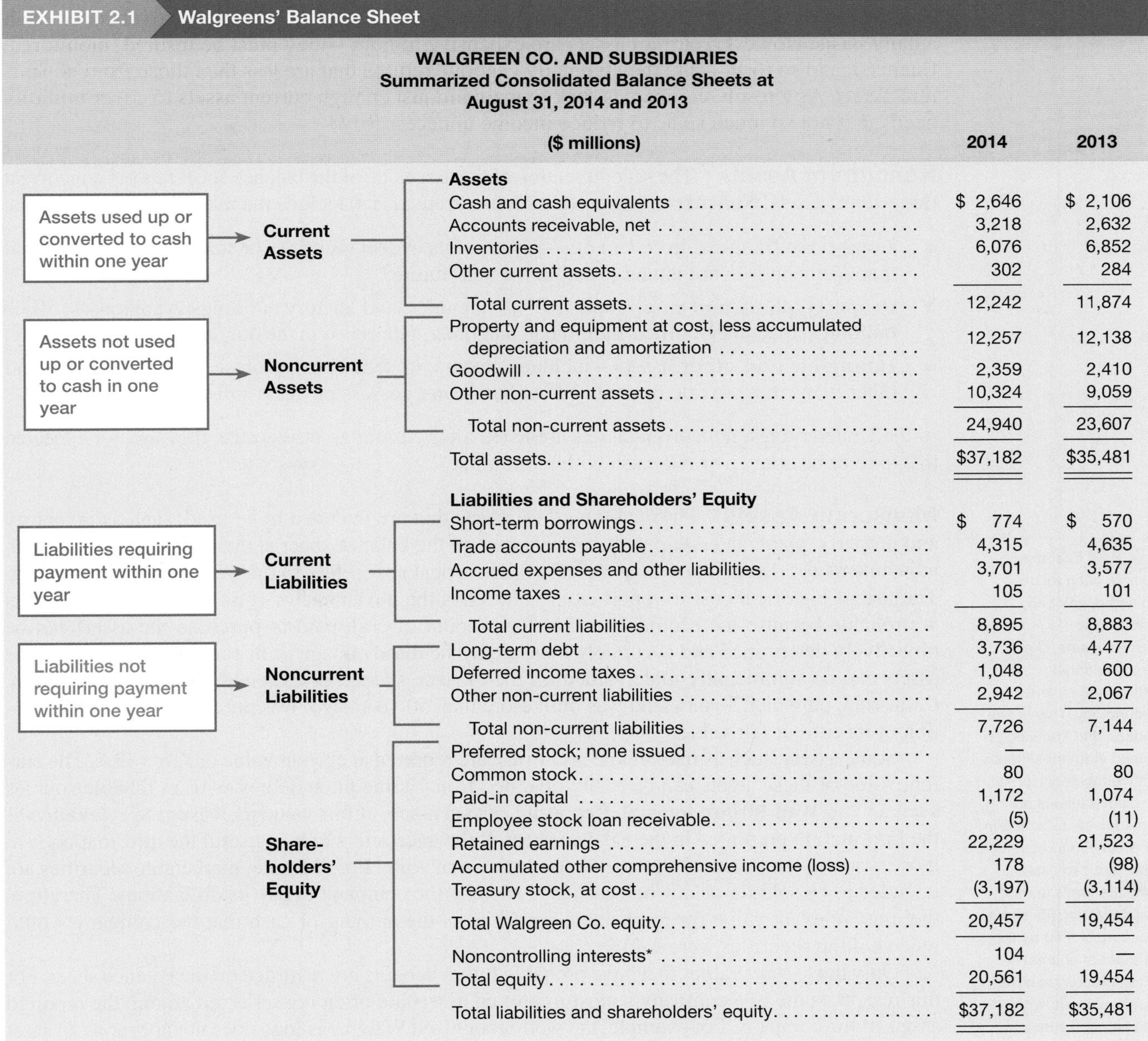

WALGREEN CO. AND SUBSIDIARIES
Summarized Consolidated Balance Sheets at August 31, 2014 and 2013

($ millions)	2014	2013
Assets		
Cash and cash equivalents	$ 2,646	$ 2,106
Accounts receivable, net	3,218	2,632
Inventories	6,076	6,852
Other current assets	302	284
Total current assets	12,242	11,874
Property and equipment at cost, less accumulated depreciation and amortization	12,257	12,138
Goodwill	2,359	2,410
Other non-current assets	10,324	9,059
Total non-current assets	24,940	23,607
Total assets	$37,182	$35,481
Liabilities and Shareholders' Equity		
Short-term borrowings	$ 774	$ 570
Trade accounts payable	4,315	4,635
Accrued expenses and other liabilities	3,701	3,577
Income taxes	105	101
Total current liabilities	8,895	8,883
Long-term debt	3,736	4,477
Deferred income taxes	1,048	600
Other non-current liabilities	2,942	2,067
Total non-current liabilities	7,726	7,144
Preferred stock; none issued	—	—
Common stock	80	80
Paid-in capital	1,172	1,074
Employee stock loan receivable	(5)	(11)
Retained earnings	22,229	21,523
Accumulated other comprehensive income (loss)	178	(98)
Treasury stock, at cost	(3,197)	(3,114)
Total Walgreen Co. equity	20,457	19,454
Noncontrolling interests*	104	—
Total equity	20,561	19,454
Total liabilities and shareholders' equity	$37,182	$35,481

*** Noncontrolling interests arise from the practice of consolidating subsidiaries that are controlled, but not wholly owned. Chapters 11 and 12 provide a brief introduction to this topic.**

Current Assets In the United States, the assets section of a balance sheet is presented in order of **liquidity**, which refers to the ease of converting noncash assets into cash. The most liquid assets are called **current assets**. Current assets are assets expected to be converted into cash or used in operations within the next year, or within the next operating cycle. Some typical examples of current assets include the following accounts, which are listed in order of their liquidity:

FYI Cash equivalents are short-term, highly liquid investments that mature in three months or less and can be easily converted to cash.

- **Cash** and **cash equivalents**—currency, bank deposits, certificates of deposit, and other cash equivalents;
- **Marketable securities**—short-term investments that can be quickly sold to raise cash;
- **Accounts receivable**—amounts due to the company from customers arising from the past sale of products or services on credit;
- **Inventory**—goods purchased or produced for sale to customers, and supplies used in operating activities;
- **Prepaid expenses**—costs paid in advance for rent, insurance, or other services.

The amount of current assets is an important component of liquidity (the ability to meet obligations when they come due). Companies require a degree of liquidity to effectively operate on a daily basis. However, current assets are expensive to hold—they must be insured, monitored, financed, and so forth—and they typically generate returns that are less than those from noncurrent assets. As a result, companies seek to maintain just enough current assets to cover liquidity needs, but not so much so as to reduce income unnecessarily.

Noncurrent Assets The second section of the asset side of the balance sheet reports noncurrent (long-term) assets. **Noncurrent assets** (also non-current assets) include the following asset accounts:

- **Long-term financial investments**—investments in debt securities or shares of other firms that management does not intend to sell in the near future;
- **Property, plant, and equipment (PPE)**—includes land, factory buildings, warehouses, office buildings, machinery, office equipment, and other items used in the operations of the company;
- **Intangible and other assets**—includes patents, trademarks, franchise rights, goodwill, and other items that provide future benefits, but do not possess physical substance.

In the United States, noncurrent assets are listed after current assets because they are not expected to expire or be converted into cash within one year.

Measuring Assets Physical (tangible) assets that are intended to be used, such as inventory and property, plant, and equipment, are reported on the balance sheet at their **historical cost** (with adjustments for depreciation in some cases). Historical cost refers to the original acquisition cost. The use of historical cost to report asset values has the advantage of **reliability**. Historical costs are reliable because the acquisition cost (the amount of cash paid to purchase the asset) can be objectively determined and accurately measured. The disadvantage of historical costs is that some assets can be significantly undervalued on the balance sheet. For example, the land in Anaheim, California, on which Disneyland was built more than 50 years ago, was purchased for a mere fraction of its current fair value.

FYI Excluded assets often relate to self-developed, knowledge-based assets, like organizational effectiveness and technology. This is one reason that knowledge-based industries are so difficult to analyze. Yet, excluded assets are presumably reflected in company market values. This fact can explain why the firm's market capitalization (its share price multiplied by the number of shares) is often greater than the book value shown on the balance sheet.

Some assets, such as marketable securities, are reported at current value or **fair value**. The current value of these assets can be easily obtained from online price quotes or from reliable sources such as **The Wall Street Journal**. Reporting certain assets at fair value increases the **relevance** of the information presented in the balance sheet. Relevance refers to how useful the information is to those who use the financial statements for decision making. For example, marketable securities are intended to be sold for cash when cash is needed by the company to pay its obligations. Therefore, the most relevant value for marketable securities is the amount of cash that the company would receive if the securities were sold.

Only those asset values that have probable future benefits are recorded on the balance sheet. For this reason, some of a company's most important assets are often not reflected among the reported assets of the company. For example, the well-recognized Walgreens logo does not appear as an asset on the company's balance sheet. The image of Mickey Mouse and that of the Aflac Duck are also absent from **The Walt Disney Company**'s and **Aflac Incorporated**'s balance sheets. Each of these items is referred to as an unrecognized intangible asset. These intangible assets and the Coke bottle silhouette, the Kleenex name, or a well-designed supply chain, are measured and reported on the balance sheet only when they are purchased from a third party (usually in a merger). As a result, *internally created* intangible assets, such as the Mickey Mouse image, are not reported on a balance sheet, even though many of these internally created intangible assets are of enormous value.

Liabilities and Equity

Liabilities and equity represent the sources of capital to the company that are used to finance the acquisition of assets. **Liabilities** represent the firm's obligations for borrowed funds from lenders or bond investors, as well as obligations to pay suppliers, employees, tax authorities, and other parties. These obligations can be interest-bearing or non-interest-bearing. **Equity** represents capital that has been invested by the shareholders, either directly via the purchase of stock (when issued by the company), or indirectly in the form of earnings that are reinvested in the business and not paid out as dividends (retained earnings). We discuss liabilities and equity in this section.

The liabilities and equity sections of Walgreens' balance sheets for 2014 and 2013 are reproduced in the lower section of **Exhibit 2.1**. Walgreens reports $16,621 million of total liabilities and $20,561 million of equity as of its 2014 fiscal year-end. The total of liabilities and equity equals $37,182—the same as the total assets—because the shareholders have the residual claim on the company.

A liability is a probable future economic sacrifice resulting from a current or past event. The economic sacrifice can be a future cash payment to a creditor, or it can be an obligation to deliver goods or services to a customer at a future date. A liability must be reported in the balance sheet when each of the following three conditions is met:

1. The future sacrifice is probable.
2. The amount of the obligation is known or can be reasonably estimated.
3. The transaction or event that caused the obligation has occurred.

When conditions 1 and 2 are satisfied, but the transaction that caused the obligation has not occurred, the obligation is called an **executory contract** and no liability is reported. An example of such an obligation is a purchase order. When a company signs an agreement to purchase materials from a supplier, it commits to making a future cash payment of a known amount. However, the obligation to pay for the materials is not considered a liability until the materials are delivered. Therefore, even though the company is contractually obligated to make the cash payment to the supplier, a liability is not recorded on the balance sheet. However, information about purchase commitments and other executory contracts is useful to investors and creditors, and the obligations, if material, should be disclosed in the footnotes to the financial statements. In its annual report, Walgreens reports open inventory purchase orders of $1,537 million at the end of fiscal year 2014.

Current Liabilities Liabilities on the balance sheet are listed according to maturity. Obligations that are due within one year or within one operating cycle are called **current liabilities**. Some examples of common current liabilities include:

- **Accounts payable**—amounts owed to suppliers for goods and services purchased on credit. Walgreens uses another common name for this account—trade accounts payable.
- **Accrued liabilities**—obligations for expenses that have been recorded but not yet paid. Examples include accrued compensation payable (wages earned by employees but not yet paid), accrued interest payable (interest on debt that has not been paid), and accrued taxes (taxes due).
- **Short-term borrowings**—short-term debt payable to banks or other creditors.
- **Deferred (unearned) revenues**—an obligation created when the company accepts payment in advance for goods or services it will deliver in the future. Sometimes also called advances from customers or customer deposits.
- **Current maturities of long-term debt**—the current portion of long-term debt that is due to be paid within one year.

Noncurrent Liabilities **Noncurrent liabilities** (also non-current liabilities) are obligations to be paid after one year. Examples of noncurrent liabilities include:

FYI Borrowings are often titled **Notes Payable**. When a company borrows money it normally signs a promissory note agreeing to pay the money back (including interest)—hence, the title notes payable.

- **Long-term debt**—amounts borrowed from creditors that are scheduled to be repaid more than one year in the future. Any portion of long-term debt that is due within one year is reclassified as a current liability called *current maturities of long-term debt*.
- **Other long-term liabilities**—various obligations, such as warranty and deferred compensation liabilities and long-term tax liabilities, that will be satisfied at least a year in the future. These items are discussed in later chapters.

Detailed information about a company's noncurrent liabilities, such as payment schedules, interest rates, and restrictive covenants, are provided in the footnotes to the financial statements.

BUSINESS INSIGHT

How Much Debt Is Reasonable? In August 2014, Walgreens reports total assets of $37,182 million, liabilities of $16,621 ($8,895 current + $7,726 non-current) million, and equity of $20,561 million. This means that Walgreens finances 45% of its assets with borrowed funds and 55% with shareholder investment. Liabilities represent claims for fixed amounts, while shareholders' equity represents a flexible claim (because shareholders have a residual claim). Companies must monitor their financing sources and amounts because borrowing too much increases risk, and investors must recognize that companies may have substantial obligations (like Walgreens' inventory purchase commitment) that do not appear on the balance sheet.

Stockholders' Equity Equity reflects capital provided by the shareholders of the company. It is often referred to as a *residual interest*. That is, stockholders have a claim on any assets that are not needed to meet the company's obligations to creditors. The following are examples of items that are typically included in stockholders' equity:

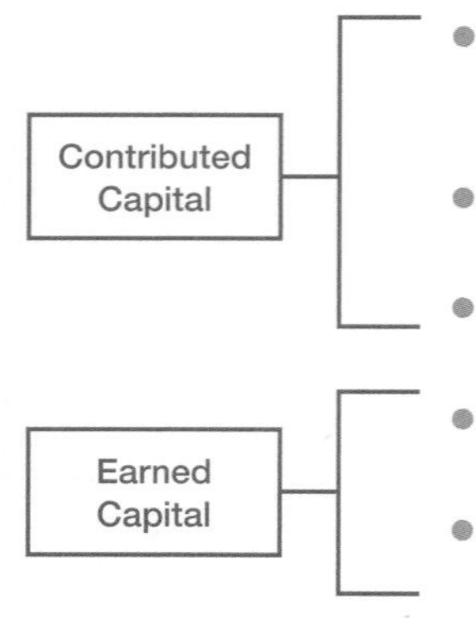

- **Common stock**—the capital received from the primary owners of the company. Total common stock is divided into shares. One share of common stock represents the smallest fractional unit of ownership of a company.[2]
- **Additional paid-in capital**—amounts received from the common shareholders in addition to the par value or stated value of the common stock.
- **Treasury stock**—the amount paid for its own common stock that the company has reacquired, which reduces contributed capital.
- **Retained earnings**—the accumulated earnings that have not been distributed to stockholders as dividends.
- **Accumulated other comprehensive income or loss**—accumulated changes in equity that are not reported in the income statement; discussed in Chapters 11 and 12.

The equity section of a balance sheet consists of two basic components: contributed capital and earned capital. **Contributed capital** is the net funding that a company has received from issuing and reacquiring its equity shares. That is, the funds received from issuing shares less any funds paid to repurchase such shares. In 2014, Walgreens' equity section reports $20,561 million in equity. Its contributed capital is a negative $1,950 million ($80 million in common stock plus $1,172 million in [additional] paid-in capital minus $5 million in an employee stock loan receivable and minus $3,197 million in treasury stock). The negative balance indicates that Walgreens has returned more

[2] Many companies' common shares have a par value, but that value has little economic significance. For instance, Walgreens' shares have a par value of $.078125 per share, while the market price of the stock is about $76 at the time of this writing. In most cases, the sum of common stock (at par) and additional paid-in capital represents the value of stockholders' contributions to the business in exchange for shares.

cash to its shareholders (by buying its own stock) than it has received in cash from its shareholder capital contributions.

Earned capital is the cumulative net income (and losses) retained by the company (not paid out to shareholders as dividends). Earned capital typically includes retained earnings and accumulated other comprehensive income or loss. Walgreens' earned capital is $22,407 million ($22,229 million in retained earnings plus $178 million in accumulated other comprehensive income). Other comprehensive income is discussed in Chapters 11 and 12.

RETAINED EARNINGS There is an important relation for retained earnings that reconciles its beginning and ending balances as follows:

Beginning retained earnings
+ Net income (or − Net loss)
− Dividends
= Ending retained earnings

This relation is useful to remember, even though there are other items that sometimes impact retained earnings. We revisit this relation after our discussion of the income statement and show how it links the balance sheet and income statement.

FYI **Equity** is a term used to describe owners' claims on the company. For corporations, the terms **shareholders' equity** and **stockholders' equity** are also used to describe owners' claims. We use all three terms interchangeably.

MID-CHAPTER REVIEW 1

GuidedExamples MBC

Assume Schaefer's Pharmacy, Inc. has the following detailed accounts as part of its accounting system. Enter the letter of the balance sheet category A through E in the space next to the balance sheet items numbered 1 through 20. Enter an **X** in the space if the item is not reported on the balance sheet.

A. Current assets
B. Noncurrent assets
C. Current liabilities
D. Noncurrent liabilities
E. Equity

_____ 1. Accounts receivable
_____ 2. Short-term notes payable
_____ 3. Land
_____ 4. Retained earnings
_____ 5. Intangible assets
_____ 6. Common stock
_____ 7. Repairs expense
_____ 8. Equipment
_____ 9. Treasury stock
_____ 10. Investments (noncurrent)
_____ 11. Rent expense
_____ 12. Cash
_____ 13. Buildings
_____ 14. Accounts payable
_____ 15. Prepaid rent
_____ 16. Borrowings (due in 25 years)
_____ 17. Marketable securities
_____ 18. Inventories
_____ 19. Additional paid-in capital
_____ 20. Unearned revenue

The solution to this review problem can be found on page 93.

eLectures MBC

Analyzing and Recording Transactions for the Balance Sheet

LO2 Use the financial statement effects template (FSET) to analyze transactions.

The balance sheet is the foundation of the accounting system. Every event, or transaction, that is recorded in the accounting system must be recorded so that the following accounting equation is maintained:

Assets = Liabilities + Equity

We use this fundamental relation throughout the book to help us assess the financial impact of transactions. This is our "step 1" when we encounter a transaction. Our "steps 2 and 3" are to journalize those financial impacts and then post them to individual accounts to emphasize the linkage from entries to accounts (steps 2 and 3 are explained later in this chapter).

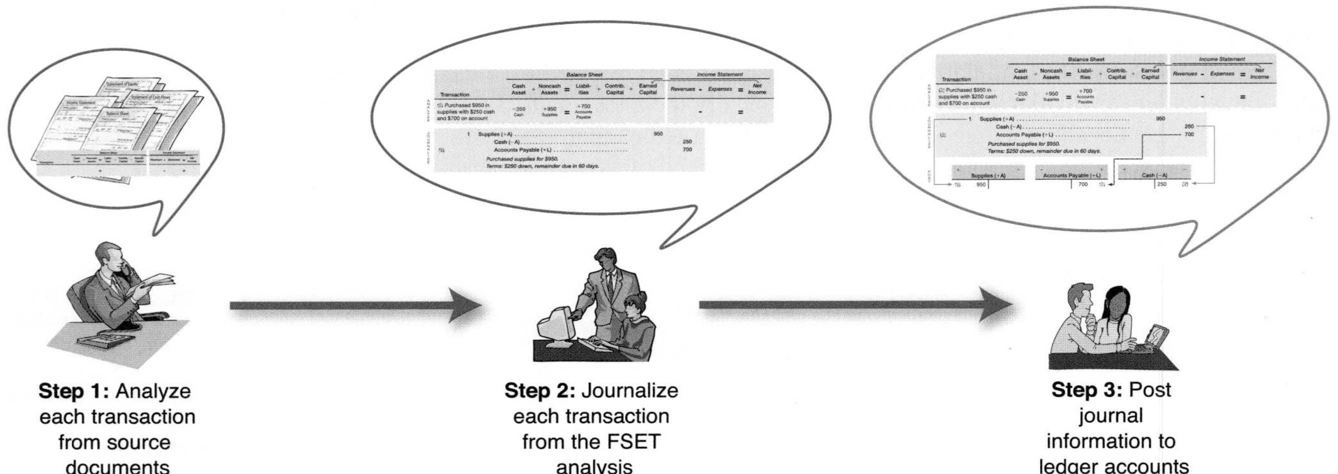
Step 1: Analyze each transaction from source documents
Step 2: Journalize each transaction from the FSET analysis
Step 3: Post journal information to ledger accounts

Financial Statement Effects Template To analyze the financial impacts of transactions, we employ the following **financial statement effects template (FSET)**.

	Balance Sheet									*Income Statement*				
Transaction	Cash Asset	+	Noncash Assets	=	Liabil-ities	+	Contrib. Capital	+	Earned Capital	*Revenues*	-	*Expenses*	=	*Net Income*
				=							-		=	

The template accomplishes several things. First and foremost, it captures the transaction that must be recorded in the accounting system. That "recording" function is our focus for the next several pages. But accounting is not just recording financial data; it is also the reporting of information that is useful to financial statement readers. So, the template also depicts the effects of the transaction on the four financial statements: balance sheet, income statement, statement of stockholders' equity, and statement of cash flows. For the balance sheet, we differentiate between cash and noncash assets so as to identify the cash effects of transactions. Likewise, equity is separated into the contributed and earned capital components (the latter includes retained earnings as its major element). Finally, income statement effects are separated into revenues, expenses, and net income (the updating of retained earnings is denoted with an arrow line running from net income to earned capital). This template provides a convenient means to demonstrate the relationships among the four financial statements and of representing financial accounting transactions and events in a simple, concise manner for analyzing, journalizing, and posting.

The Account An **account** is a mechanism for accumulating the effects of an organization's transactions and events. For instance, an account labeled "Merchandise Inventory" allows a retailer's accounting system to accumulate information about the receipts of inventory from suppliers and the delivery of inventory to customers.

Before a transaction is recorded, we first analyze the effect of the transaction on the accounting equation by asking the following questions:

- What accounts are affected by the transaction?
- What is the direction and magnitude of each effect?

To maintain the equality of the accounting equation, each transaction must affect (at least) two accounts. For example, a transaction might increase assets and increase equity by equal amounts. Another transaction might increase one asset and decrease another asset, while yet another might decrease an asset and decrease a liability. These *dual effects* are what constitute the **double-entry accounting system**.

The account is a record of increases and decreases for each important asset, liability, equity, revenue, or expense item. The **chart of accounts** is a listing of the titles (and identification codes) of all accounts for a company.[3] Account titles are commonly grouped into five categories: assets, liabilities, equity, revenues, and expenses. The accounts for Natural Beauty Supply, Inc. (introduced below), follow:

Assets	Equity
110 Cash	310 Common Stock
120 Accounts Receivable	320 Retained Earnings
130 Other Receivables	**Revenues and Income**
140 Inventory	410 Sales Revenue
150 Prepaid Insurance	420 Interest Revenue
160 Security Deposit	**Expenses**
170 Fixtures and Equipment	510 Cost of Goods Sold
175 Accumulated Depreciation—Fixtures and Equipment	520 Wages Expense
Liabilities	530 Rent Expense
210 Accounts Payable	540 Advertising Expense
220 Interest Payable	550 Depreciation Expense—Fixtures and Equipment
230 Wages Payable	560 Insurance Expense
240 Taxes Payable	570 Interest Expense
250 Unearned Revenue	580 Tax Expense
260 Notes Payable	

Each transaction entered in the template must maintain the equality of the accounting equation, and the accounts cited must correspond to those in its chart of accounts.

Transaction Analysis Using FSET To illustrate the effect of transactions on the accounting equation and, correspondingly, the financial statements, we consider the business activities of Natural Beauty Supply, Inc. Natural Beauty Supply was established to operate as a retailer of organic beauty and health care products, though the owners hoped that they also would become a wholesale provider of such products to local salons. The company began business on November 1, 2015. The following transactions occurred on the first day of business:

(1) Nov. 1 Investors contributed $20,000 cash to launch Natural Beauty Supply, Inc. (NBS), in exchange for 10,000 shares of NBS stock.

(2) Nov. 1 NBS borrowed $5,000 cash from a family member of the company's founders by signing a note. The $5,000 must be paid back on November 30 with interest of $50.

(3) Nov. 1 NBS arranged to rent a storefront location and began to use the property. The landlord requires payment of $1,500 at the end of each month. NBS paid a $2,000 security deposit that will be returned at the end of the lease.

(4) Nov. 1 NBS purchased, on account (i.e., to be paid later), and received $17,000 of inventory consisting of natural soaps and beauty products.

Let's begin by analyzing the financial statement effects of the first transaction. At the beginning of its life, Natural Beauty Supply has accounts that show no balances, so the financial statements would be filled with zeroes. In the company's very first transaction, shareholders invested $20,000 cash in Natural Beauty Supply, and the company issued 10,000 shares of common stock, which increased equity (contributed capital). This transaction is reflected in the following financial statements effects template.

---

[3] Accounting systems at large organizations have much more detail in their account structures than we use here. The account structure's detail allows management to accumulate information by responsibility center or by product line or by customer.

	Balance Sheet					Income Statement		
Transaction	Cash Asset +	Noncash Assets =	Liabil-ities +	Contrib. Capital +	Earned Capital	Revenues −	Expenses =	Net Income
(1) Issue stock for $20,000 cash.	+20,000 Cash	=		+20,000 Common Stock			−	=

Assets (cash) and equity (common stock) increased by the same amount, and the accounting equation remains in balance (as it always must).

In the second transaction, Natural Beauty Supply borrowed cash by signing a note (loan agreement) with a family member. This transaction increased cash (an asset) and increased notes payable (a liability) by the same amount. The notes payable liability recognizes the obligation to repay the family member.

Transaction	Cash Asset	Noncash Assets	Liabilities	Contrib. Capital	Earned Capital	Revenues	Expenses	Net Income
(2) Sign a note and receive $5,000 cash.	+5,000 Cash	=	+5,000 Notes Payable				−	=

At this point, Natural Beauty Supply would not record anything for the interest that will eventually be paid. Interest expense occurs with the passage of time, and at the moment of borrowing on November 1, there is no interest obligation to be recognized.

Also on November 1, 2015, Natural Beauty Supply arranged for rental of a location and paid a security deposit which it expects to be returned at a future date. This transaction decreased cash (an asset) and increased security deposits (another asset). We'll assume that Natural Beauty Supply hopes to move to a more upscale location within a year, so the security deposit is considered a current asset.

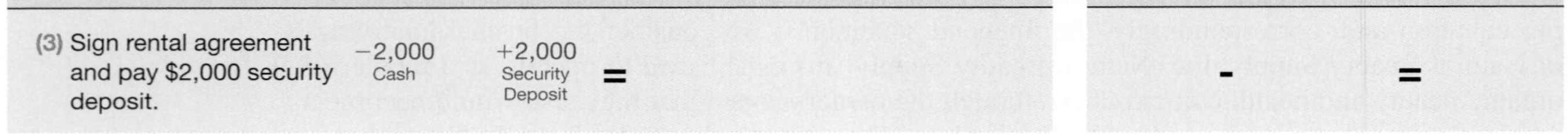

Transaction	Cash Asset	Noncash Assets	Liabilities	Contrib. Capital	Earned Capital	Revenues	Expenses	Net Income
(3) Sign rental agreement and pay $2,000 security deposit.	−2,000 Cash	+2,000 Security Deposit =					−	=

Like the case of interest expense, Natural Beauty Supply would make no entry for rent expense on November 1, because the obligation to pay for the use of the location occurs with the passage of time.

Finally, Natural Beauty Supply purchased and received $17,000 of inventory on credit. This transaction increased inventory (an asset) by $17,000 and increased accounts payable (a liability) by $17,000, recognizing the obligation to the supplier. This transaction is recorded as follows:

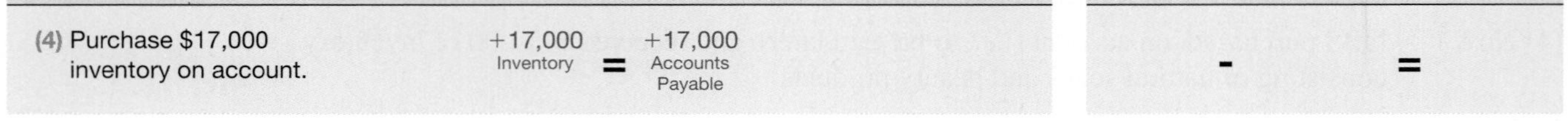

Transaction	Cash Asset	Noncash Assets	Liabilities	Contrib. Capital	Earned Capital	Revenues	Expenses	Net Income
(4) Purchase $17,000 inventory on account.		+17,000 Inventory =	+17,000 Accounts Payable				−	=

To summarize, the description of each transaction appears in the first column of the template. Then the financial statement effects of that transaction are recorded with a + or a – in the appropriate columns of the template. Under each number, the account title within that column of the balance sheet or income statement is entered. So far, Natural Beauty Supply's activities have not affected the revenue or expense accounts of the income statement.

After each transaction, the equality of the accounting equation is maintained. If we so choose, we can prepare a balance sheet at any time, reflecting the transactions up to that point in time. At the end of the day on November 1, 2015, Natural Beauty Supply's balance sheet appears as follows:

NATURAL BEAUTY SUPPLY, INC. Balance Sheet November 1, 2015			
Assets		**Liabilities and Equity**	
Cash	$23,000	Notes payable	$ 5,000
Inventory	17,000	Accounts payable	17,000
Security deposit	2,000	Total current liabilities	22,000
Total current assets	42,000	**Equity**	
		Common stock	20,000
Total assets	$42,000	Total liabilities and equity	$42,000

MID-CHAPTER REVIEW 2

Assume that Schaefer's Pharmacy, Inc. enters into the following transactions. Record each of the following transactions in the financial statement effects template.

a. Issued common stock for $20,000 cash.
b. Purchased inventory costing $8,000 on credit.
c. Purchased equipment costing $10,000 for cash.
d. Paid suppliers $3,000 cash for part of the inventory purchased in *b*.

The solution to this review problem can be found on page 94.

REPORTING FINANCIAL PERFORMANCE

LO3 Describe and construct the income statement and discuss how it can be used to evaluate management performance.

While balance sheets provide useful information about the structure of a company's resources and the claims on those resources at a point in time, they provide little sense of recent movement or trajectory. The retained earnings balance represents the amount earned (but not paid out in dividends) over the entire life of the company. Looking at the difference between points in time doesn't give a clear picture about what happened between those points in time. For that perspective, we need the income statement to see whether our business activities generated more resources than they used. For instance, Walgreens' retained earnings increased by $706 million over fiscal year 2014, but that amount does not convey the volume of activity that occurred to accomplish it.

Walgreens' fiscal year summarized 2014 Statement of Earnings is shown in **Exhibit 2.2**. Walgreens reported net earnings of $2,031 million on revenues of $76,392 million, or about $0.027 of each revenue dollar ($2,031 million/$76,392 million). The remaining $0.973 of that revenue dollar relates to costs incurred to generate the revenues, such as the costs of products sold and equipment used, wages, advertising and promotion, interest and taxes. Interpretation of this $0.027 amount requires further analysis, as shown in Chapter 5, but we can compare it to previous amounts of $0.034 in fiscal year 2013, and $0.030 in fiscal year 2012.

FYI The income statement is also called the statement of earnings or the statement of operations or the profit and loss statement. Walgreens uses all three terms (profit, income and earnings) in **Exhibit 2.2**.

To analyze an income statement, we need to understand some terminology. **Revenues** result in increases in **net assets** (assets minus liabilities) that are caused by the company's transferring goods or services to customers. **Expenses** result from decreases in net assets (assets minus liabilities) that are caused by the company's revenue-generating activities, including costs of products and services sold, operating costs like depreciation, wages and advertising, nonoperating costs like interest on debt and, finally, taxes on income. The difference between revenues and expenses is **net income** when revenues exceed expenses, or **net loss** when expenses exceed revenues. The connection to the balance sheet can be seen in that reporting net income means that revenues exceeded expenses, which in turn means that the company's business activities increased its net assets.

Operating expenses are the usual and customary costs that a company incurs to support its main business activities. These include cost of goods sold expense, selling expenses, depreciation expense, amortization expense, and research and development expense. Not all of these expenses are recognized in the period in which cash is disbursed. For example, depreciation expense is recognized in the time period during which the asset is used, not in the period when it was first acquired in exchange for cash. In contrast, other expenses, such as compensation expense, are recognized in

FYI The terms revenues and sales are often used interchangeably.

EXHIBIT 2.2 Walgreens' Income Statement

WALGREEN CO. AND SUBSIDIARIES Summarized Consolidated Statement of Earnings Year ended August 31, 2014 ($ millions)	
Net sales	$76,392
Cost of sales	54,823
Gross profit	21,569
Selling, general and administrative expenses	17,992
Equity earnings in Alliance Boots	617
Operating income	4,194
Interest (expense) income, net	(156)
Other (expense) income	(481)
Earnings before income tax provision	3,557
Income tax provision	1,526
Net earnings	2,031
Net earnings attributable to non-controlling interests*	(99)
Net earnings attributable to Walgreen Co	$ 1,932

*Noncontrolling interests arise from the practice of consolidating subsidiaries that are controlled, but not wholly owned. Chapters 11 and 12 provide a brief introduction to this topic.

the period when the services are performed, which is often before cash is actually paid to employees. Walgreens' operating expenses in 2014 were $72,815 million ($54,823 million + $17,992 million).[4]

Nonoperating revenues and expenses relate to the company's financing and investing activities, and include interest revenue and interest expense. Business decision makers and analysts usually segregate operating and nonoperating activities as they offer different insights into company performance and condition. Walgreens' income statement reports net nonoperating expenses in 2014 of $637 million ($156 million + $481 million), followed by tax expense of $1,526 million.

It is helpful to distinguish income from continuing operations from nonrecurring items. Many readers of financial statements are interested in forecasting future company performance and focus their analysis on sources of operating income that are expected to *persist* into the future. Nonrecurring revenues and expenses are unlikely to arise in the future and are largely irrelevant to predictions of future performance. Consequently, many decision makers identify transactions and events that are unlikely to recur and separate them from operating income in the income statement. These nonrecurring items are described in greater detail in Chapter 6.

Accrual Accounting for Revenues and Expenses

4 **LO4** Explain revenue recognition, accrual accounting, and their effects on retained earnings.

The income statement's ability to measure a company's periodic performance depends on the proper timing of revenues and expenses. Revenue should be recorded when the company has transferred goods or services to customers, in an amount that reflects how much the company expects to be entitled from the transfer—even if there is not an immediate increase in cash. This is called **revenue recognition**, a topic that receives more detailed attention in Chapter 6. Expenses are recognized when assets are diminished (or liabilities increased) as a result of earning revenue or supporting operations, even if there is no immediate decrease in cash. This is called **expense recognition**. **Accrual accounting** refers to this practice of recognizing revenues when earned through the company's operations and recognizing expenses as the assets used and obligations incurred in carrying out those operations.

An important consequence of accrual accounting for revenues and expenses is that the balance sheet depicts the resources of the company (in addition to cash) and the obligations which the company must fulfill in the future. Accrual accounting is required under U.S. GAAP and IFRS because it is considered to be the most useful information for making business decisions and evaluating business performance. (That is not to say that information on cash flows is not important—but it is conveyed by the statement of cash flows discussed in Chapter 4.)

[4] Walgreens also reports $617 million in Equity earnings in Alliance Boots, a company in which Walgreens invested. The operations of Alliance Boots are similar enough to Walgreens' operations that they include this as a component of operating income.

Walgreens' net sales in 2014 were $76,392 million. **Cost of goods sold** (cost of sales) is an expense item in the income statements of manufacturing and merchandising companies. It represents the cost of products that are delivered to customers during the period. The difference between revenues (at selling prices) and cost of goods sold (at purchase price or manufacturing cost) is called **gross profit**. Gross profit for merchandisers and manufacturers is an important number as it represents the remaining income available to cover all of the company's overhead and other expenses (selling, general and administrative expenses, research and development, interest, and so on). Walgreens' gross profit in 2014 is calculated as total net revenues less cost of sales, which equals $21,569 million ($76,392 million − $54,823 million).

The principles of revenue and expense recognition are crucial to income statement reporting. To illustrate, assume a company purchases inventories for $100,000 cash, which it sells later in that same period for $150,000 cash. The company would record $150,000 in revenue when the inventory is delivered to the customer, because at that point, the company has fulfilled its responsibilities in the exchange with the customer. Also assume that the company pays $20,000 cash for sales employee wages during the period. The income statement is designed to tell how effective the company was at generating more resources than it used, and it would appear as follows (ignoring income taxes for the moment):

Revenues	$150,000
Cost of goods sold.	100,000
Gross profit.	50,000
Wages expense	20,000
Net income (earnings) . .	$ 30,000

FYI Purchase of inventories on credit or on account means that the buyer does not pay the seller at the time of purchase. The buyer reports a liability (accounts payable) on its balance sheet that is later removed when payment is made. The seller reports an asset (accounts receivable) on its balance sheet until it is removed when the buyer pays.

In this illustration, there is a correspondence between each of the revenues/expenses and a cash inflow/outflow within the accounting period. Net income was $30,000 and the increase in cash was $30,000.

However, that need not be the case under accrual accounting. Suppose that the company sells its product on **credit** (also referred to as *on account*) rather than for cash. Does the seller still report sales revenue? The answer is yes. Under GAAP, revenues are reported when a company has earned those sales at delivery. Earned means that the company has done everything required under the sales agreement—no material contingencies remain. The seller reports an accounts receivable asset on its balance sheet, and revenue can be recognized before cash collection.

Credit sales mean that companies can report substantial sales revenue and assets without receiving cash. When such receivables are ultimately collected, no further revenue is recorded because it was recorded earlier when the revenue recognition criteria were met. The collection of a receivable merely involves the decrease of one asset (accounts receivable) and the increase of another asset (cash), with no resulting increase in net assets.

FYI Sales on credit will not always be collected. The potential for uncollectable accounts introduces additional risk to the firm.

Next, consider a different situation. Assume that the company sells gift cards to customers for $9,500. Should the $9,500 received in cash be recognized as revenue? No. Even though the gift cards were sold and cash was collected, there has been no transfer of goods or services to the customer. The revenue from gift cards is recognized when the product or service is provided. For example, revenue can be recognized when a customer purchases an item of merchandise using the gift card for payment. Hence, the $9,500 is then recorded as an increase in cash and an increase in *unearned revenue*, a liability, with no resulting increase in net assets.

FYI **Cash accounting** recognizes revenues only when received in cash and expenses only when paid in cash. This approach is not acceptable under GAAP.

The proper timing of revenue recognition suggests that the expenses incurred in earning that revenue be recognized in the same fiscal period. Thus, if merchandise inventory is purchased in one period and sold in another, the cost of the merchandise should be retained as an asset until the items are sold. It would not be proper to recognize expense when the inventory was purchased or the cash was paid. Accurate income determination requires the proper timing of revenue and expense recognition, and the exchange of cash is *not* the essential ingredient.

We have already seen that when a company incurs a cost to acquire a resource that produces benefits in the future (for example, merchandise inventory for future sale), it recognizes an asset. That asset represents costs that are waiting to be recognized as expenses in the future, when these assets are used to produce revenue or to support operations. When inventory is delivered to a customer, we recognize that the asset no longer belongs to the selling company. The inventory asset is decreased, and cost of goods sold is recognized as an expense.

The same principle applies when employees earn wages for work in one period, but are paid in the next period. Wages expense must be recognized when the liability (obligation) is *incurred*, regardless of when they are paid. If the company in the illustration doesn't pay its employees until the following reporting period, it recognizes a wages payable liability of $20,000 and, because this decreases net assets, it would recognize a wage expense of the same amount.

When wages are paid in the next reporting period, both cash and the wages payable liability are decreased. No expense is reported when the wages are paid, because the expense is recognized when the employees worked to generate sales in the prior period.

Accrual accounting principles are crucial for reporting the income statement revenues and expenses in the proper period, and these revenues and expenses provide a more complete view of the inflows and outflows of resources (including cash) for the firm. Was an outflow of cash supposed to produce benefits in the current period or in a future period? Was an inflow of cash the result of past operations or current operations? The accrual accounting model uses the balance sheet and income statement to answer such questions and to enable users of financial statements to make more timely assessments of the firm's economic performance.

However, accrual accounting's timeliness requires management to estimate future events in determining the amount of expenses incurred and revenue earned. The precise amount of cash to be received or disbursed may not be known until a later date. In the case of wages, the amount of the accrual is known with certainty. In other cases (e.g., incentive bonuses), it may not and thus require an estimate.

Retained Earnings

Net income for the period is added to the company's retained earnings, which, in turn, is part of stockholders' equity. The linkage between the income statement and the beginning- and end-of-period balance sheets, which we called articulation in Chapter 1, is achieved by tying net income to retained earnings because net income is, by definition, the *change* in retained earnings resulting from business activities during an accounting period. This link is highlighted by the red arrow at the top of the financial statement effects template (FSET).[5] There are typically other adjustments to retained earnings. The most common adjustment is for dividend payments to stockholders. **Exhibit 2.3** provides the annual adjustments to retained earnings for Walgreens.

EXHIBIT 2.3 Walgreens' Retained Earnings Reconciliation

WALGREEN CO. AND SUBSIDIARIES
Year Ended August 31, 2014
($ millions)

Retained earnings, August 31, 2013	$21,523
Add: Net earnings attributable to Walgreen Co.	1,932
	23,455
Less: Cash dividends declared	1,226
Retained earnings, August 31, 2014	$22,229

Analyzing and Recording Transactions for the Income Statement

Earlier, we introduced the financial statement effects template as a tool to illustrate the effects of transactions on the balance sheet. In this section, we show how this template is used to analyze transactions that may affect the current period's income statement. To do so, we extend our illustration of Natural Beauty Supply (NBS) to reflect the following events in 2015:

(5) Nov. 2 NBS paid $670 to advertise in the local newspaper for November.

(6) Nov. 18 NBS paid $13,300 cash to its suppliers in partial payment for the earlier delivery of inventory.

[5] In the FSET, we show that each transaction that affects the income statement also impacts retained earnings. This approach is useful for *analyzing* the effect of the transaction on both the income statement and balance sheet. However, the impact of net income on retained earnings is *recorded* only once each accounting period, after all of the revenues and expenses have been recorded. This recording procedure is explained later in this chapter and in Chapter 3.

(7) Nov. — During the month of November, NBS sold and delivered products to retail customers. The customers paid $7,000 cash for products that had cost NBS $4,000.

(8) Nov. — During the month of November, sales and deliveries to wholesale customers totaled $2,400 for merchandise that had cost $1,700. Instead of paying cash, wholesale customers are required to pay for the merchandise within ten working days.

(9) Nov. — NBS employed a salesperson who earned $1,400 for the month of November and was paid that amount in cash.

(10) Nov. 24 NBS received an order from a wholesale customer to deliver products in December. The agreed price of the products to be delivered is $700 and the cost is $450.

(11) Nov. 25 NBS introduced holiday gift certificates, which entitle the recipient to a one-hour consultation on the use of NBS's products. $300 of gift certificates were sold for cash, but none were redeemed before the end of November.

(12) Nov. 30 NBS received $1,450 in partial payment from customers billed in (8).

(13) Nov. 30 NBS repaid the loan and interest in (2).

(14) Nov. 30 NBS paid $1,680 for a twelve-month fire insurance policy. Coverage begins on December 1.

(15) Nov. 30 NBS paid $1,500 to the landlord for November rent.

In the fifth transaction, Natural Beauty Supply gave cash in return for advertising for the month of November. This payment does not create a benefit for future periods, so it does not create an asset. Nor does the payment discharge an existing obligation. Therefore, it decreases NBS's net assets (assets minus liabilities). The purpose of this decrease in net assets is to generate revenues for the company, so it is reported as an expense in the income statement.

We begin by entering the decrease in cash and an increase in expenses. (The minus sign in front of expenses insures that the accounting equation still holds.) Recording the expense allows the income statement to keep track of the flows of assets and liabilities that result from the company's operations.

	Balance Sheet					Income Statement		
Transaction	Cash Asset +	Noncash Assets =	Liabilities +	Contrib. Capital +	Earned Capital	*Revenues* −	*Expenses* =	*Net Income*
(5) Pay $670 cash for November advertising.	−670 Cash	=				−	+670 Advertising Expense	=

However, the FSET goes further than recording the accounting entry. It also depicts the effects of the expense on net income and of net income on retained earnings. So, the complete FSET description of transaction (5) is as follows. The FSET uses color to differentiate between the accounting entry (in blue) and the resulting effect on income and retained earnings (in black).

Transaction	Cash Asset +	Noncash Assets =	Liabilities +	Contrib. Capital +	Earned Capital	Revenues −	Expenses =	Net Income
(5) Pay $670 cash for November advertising.	−670 Cash	=			−670 Retained Earnings	−	+670 Advertising Expense	= −670

In the sixth transaction, Natural Beauty Supply made a partial payment of $13,300 in cash to the suppliers who delivered inventory on November 1. This transaction decreases cash by $13,300 and decreases the accounts payable liability by $13,300. The income statement is not affected by this payment. The cost of merchandise is reflected in the income statement when the merchandise is sold, not when it is paid for (as we will see shortly).

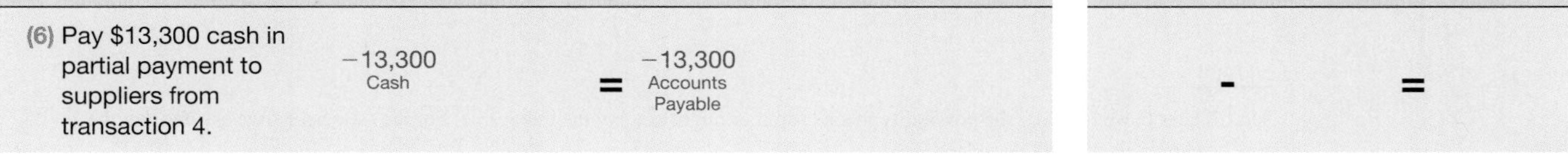

Transaction	Cash Asset +	Noncash Assets =	Liabilities +	Contrib. Capital +	Earned Capital	Revenues −	Expenses =	Net Income
(6) Pay $13,300 cash in partial payment to suppliers from transaction 4.	−13,300 Cash	=	−13,300 Accounts Payable			−	=	

In transaction seven, Natural Beauty Supply sold and delivered products to customers who paid \$7,000 in cash. NBS's transfer of products to customers results in the recognition of revenue in the income statement and an increase in net assets (cash) on the balance sheet. As in transaction 5, the FSET also depicts the impact of these sales on net income and on the retained earnings balance.

	Balance Sheet					Income Statement		
Transaction	Cash Asset +	Noncash Assets =	Liabil-ities +	Contrib. Capital +	Earned Capital	Revenues −	Expenses =	Net Income
(7a) Sell \$7,000 of products for cash.	+7,000 Cash				+7,000 Retained Earnings	+7,000 Sales Revenue		+7,000

At the same time, NBS must recognize that these sales transactions involved an exchange, and cash was received while inventory costing \$4,000 was delivered. Transaction (7b) recognizes that NBS no longer has this inventory and that this decrease in net assets produces an expense called cost of goods sold. In this way, the income statement portrays the increases in net assets (revenues) and the decreases in net assets (expenses like cost of goods sold and advertising) from the company's operating activities. (Again, the minus sign in front of all expenses insures that the accounting equation remains balanced.)

Transaction	Cash Asset	Noncash Assets	Liabilities	Contrib. Capital	Earned Capital	Revenues	Expenses	Net Income
(7b) Record \$4,000 for the cost of merchandise sold in transaction 7a.		−4,000 Inventory			−4,000 Retained Earnings		+4,000 Cost of Goods Sold	−4,000

The eighth transaction is very similar to the previous one, except that Natural Beauty Supply's customers will pay for the products ten days after they were delivered. Should NBS recognize revenue on these sales? The products have been delivered, so the revenue has been earned.[6] Therefore, NBS should recognize that it has a new asset—accounts receivable—equal to \$2,400, and that it has earned revenue in the same amount. As above, NBS would also record cost of goods sold to recognize the cost of inventory delivered to the customers.

Transaction	Cash Asset	Noncash Assets	Liabilities	Contrib. Capital	Earned Capital	Revenues	Expenses	Net Income
(8a) Sell \$2,400 of products on account.		+2,400 Accounts Receivable			+2,400 Retained Earnings	+2,400 Sales Revenue		+2,400
(8b) Record \$1,700 for the cost of merchandise sold in transaction 8a.		−1,700 Inventory			−1,700 Retained Earnings		+1,700 Cost of Goods Sold	−1,700

The ninth entry records wage expense. In this case, wages were paid in cash. Cash is decreased by \$1,400, and this decrease in net assets results in a recognition of wages expense in the income statement (with resulting decreases in net income and retained earnings).

Transaction	Cash Asset	Noncash Assets	Liabilities	Contrib. Capital	Earned Capital	Revenues	Expenses	Net Income
(9) Record \$1,400 in wages to employees.	−1,400 Cash				−1,400 Retained Earnings		+1,400 Wages Expense	−1,400

Transaction ten involves a customer order for products to be delivered in December. This transaction is an example of an *executory contract*, which does not require a journal entry (just like Walgreens' open purchase orders for inventory described earlier). NBS has not earned revenue, because it has not yet delivered the products.

[6] In Chapter 6, we consider the possibility that a customer might not pay the receivable. For the time being, we assume that the receivables' collectability is assured.

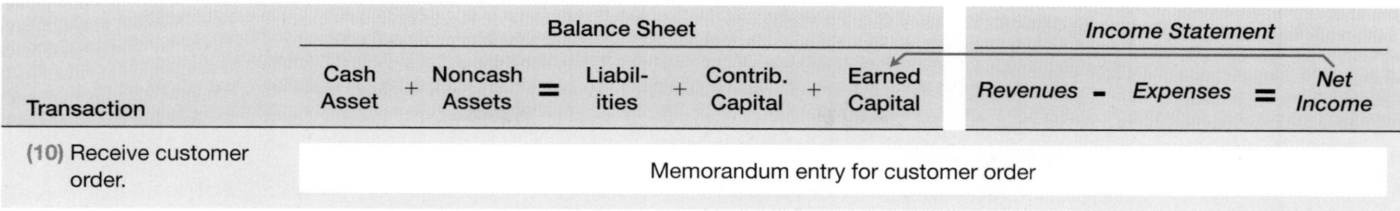

Transaction	Cash Asset	+	Noncash Assets	=	Liabilities	+	Contrib. Capital	+	Earned Capital	Revenues	−	Expenses	=	Net Income
(10) Receive customer order.	Memorandum entry for customer order													

In transaction eleven, Natural Beauty Supply sold gift certificates for $300 cash, but none were redeemed. In this case, NBS has received cash, but revenue cannot be recognized because no goods or services have been transferred to the customers. Rather, NBS has accepted an obligation to provide services in the future when the gift certificates are redeemed. This obligation is recognized as a liability titled unearned revenue.

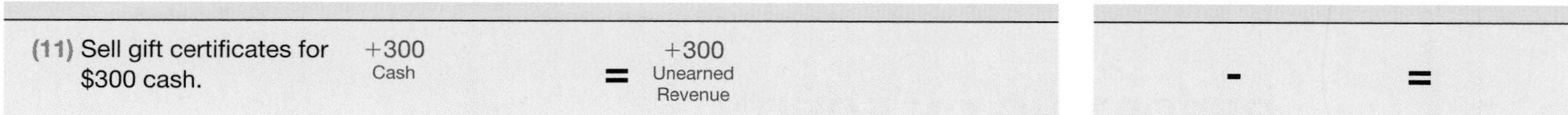

Transaction	Cash Asset	+	Noncash Assets	=	Liabilities	+	Contrib. Capital	+	Earned Capital	Revenues	−	Expenses	=	Net Income
(11) Sell gift certificates for $300 cash.	+300 Cash			=	+300 Unearned Revenue						−		=	

In transaction twelve, NBS received $1,450 cash as partial payment from customers billed in transaction eight. Cash increases by $1,450 and accounts receivable decreases by $1,450. Recall that revenues are recorded when earned (transaction 8), not when cash is received.

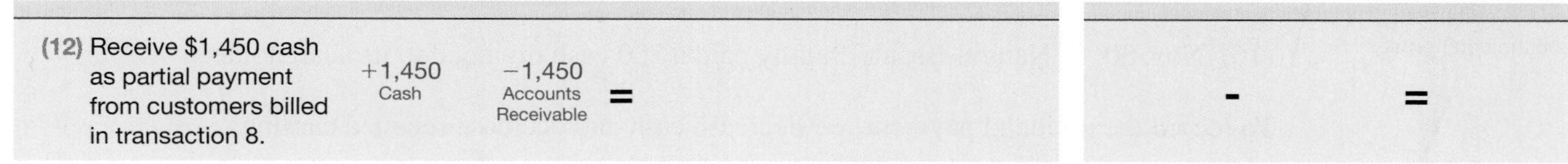

Transaction	Cash Asset	+	Noncash Assets	=	Liabilities	+	Contrib. Capital	+	Earned Capital	Revenues	−	Expenses	=	Net Income
(12) Receive $1,450 cash as partial payment from customers billed in transaction 8.	+1,450 Cash		−1,450 Accounts Receivable	=							−		=	

In transaction thirteen on November 30, Natural Beauty Supply paid back the family member who had loaned money to the business. The cash payment was the agreed-upon $5,050 ($5,000 principal and $50 interest). The repayment of the principal does not change the net assets of NBS; cash goes down by $5,000 and the note payable liability goes down an equal amount. However, the payment of $50 interest does cause the net assets to decrease, and this net asset decrease creates an interest expense in the income statement.

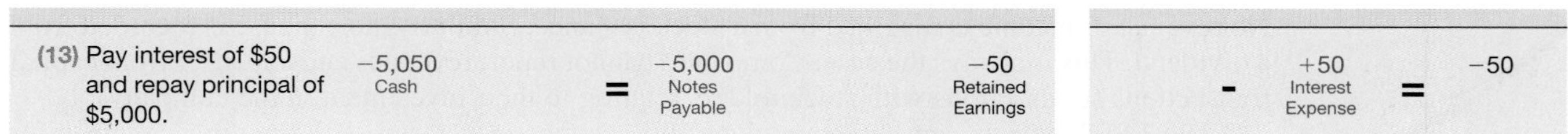

Transaction	Cash Asset	+	Noncash Assets	=	Liabilities	+	Contrib. Capital	+	Earned Capital	Revenues	−	Expenses	=	Net Income
(13) Pay interest of $50 and repay principal of $5,000.	−5,050 Cash			=	−5,000 Notes Payable				−50 Retained Earnings		−	+50 Interest Expense	=	−50

In the fourteenth transaction, NBS paid an annual insurance premium of $1,680 for coverage beginning December 1. NBS will receive the benefits of the insurance coverage in the future, so insurance expense will be recognized in those future periods. At this time, a noncash asset titled prepaid insurance is increased by $1,680, and cash is decreased by the same amount.

Transaction	Cash Asset	+	Noncash Assets	=	Liabilities	+	Contrib. Capital	+	Earned Capital	Revenues	−	Expenses	=	Net Income
(14) Pay $1,680 for one-year insurance policy.	−1,680 Cash		+1,680 Prepaid Insurance	=							−		=	

In the last transaction of the month of November, Natural Beauty Supply paid $1,500 cash to the landlord for November's rent. This $1,500 reduction of net assets is balanced by rent expense in the income statement.

Transaction	Cash Asset	+	Noncash Assets	=	Liabilities	+	Contrib. Capital	+	Earned Capital	Revenues	−	Expenses	=	Net Income
(15) Pay $1,500 rent for November.	−1,500 Cash			=					−1,500 Retained Earnings		−	+1,500 Rent Expense	=	−1,500

We can summarize the revenue and expense entries of these transactions to prepare an income statement for Natural Beauty Supply for the month ended November 30, 2015.

NATURAL BEAUTY SUPPLY, INC. Income Statement For Month Ended November 30, 2015	
Sales revenue	$ 9,400
Cost of goods sold	5,700
Gross profit	3,700
Wages expense	1,400
Rent expense	1,500
Advertising expense	670
Operating income	130
Interest expense	50
Net income	$ 80

REPORTING ON EQUITY

Analyzing and Recording Equity Transactions

5

LO5 Illustrate equity transactions and the statement of stockholders' equity.

Earlier we recorded the effect of issuing common stock on the balance sheet of Natural Beauty Supply. To complete our illustration, we illustrate one final equity transaction—a dividend payment.

(16) Nov. 30 Natural Beauty Supply paid a $50 cash dividend to its shareholders.

To record the dividend payment, we decrease cash and decrease retained earnings.

Transaction	Cash Asset	+	Noncash Assets	=	Liabil-ities	+	Contrib. Capital	+	Earned Capital	Revenues	-	Expenses	=	Net Income
	Balance Sheet									Income Statement				
(16) Pay $50 cash dividend to shareholders.	−50 Cash			=					−50 Retained Earnings		-		=	

No revenue or income is recorded from a stock issuance. Similarly, no expense is recorded from a dividend. This is always the case. Companies cannot report revenues and expenses from capital transactions (transactions with stockholders relating to their investment in the company).

The FSET entries can be accumulated by account to determine the ending balances for assets, liabilities and equity. Natural Beauty Supply's balance sheet for November 30, 2015, appears in **Exhibit 2.4**. The balance in retained earnings is $30 (net income of $80 less the cash dividend of $50).

EXHIBIT 2.4 Natural Beauty Supply's Balance Sheet

NATURAL BEAUTY SUPPLY, INC. Balance Sheet November 30, 2015			
Assets		Liabilities	
Cash	$ 8,100	Accounts payable	$ 3,700
Accounts receivable	950	Unearned revenue	300
Inventory	11,300	Total current liabilities	4,000
Prepaid insurance	1,680	Equity	
Security deposit	2,000	Common stock	20,000
Total current assets	24,030	Retained earnings	30
		Total equity	20,030
Total assets	$24,030	Total liabilities and equity	$24,030

Statement of Stockholders' Equity

The statement of stockholders' equity is a reconciliation of the beginning and ending balances of selected stockholders' equity accounts. The statement of stockholders' equity for Natural Beauty Supply for the month of November is in **Exhibit 2.5**.

EXHIBIT 2.5 Natural Beauty Supply's Statement of Stockholders' Equity

NATURAL BEAUTY SUPPLY, INC.
Statement of Stockholders' Equity
For Month Ended November 30, 2015

	Contributed Capital	Earned Capital	Total Equity
Balance, November 1, 2015	**$ 0**	**$ 0**	**$ 0**
Common stock issued	20,000	—	20,000
Net income	—	80	80
Cash dividends	—	(50)	(50)
Balance, November 30, 2015	**$20,000**	**$30**	**$20,030**

This statement highlights three main changes to Natural Beauty Supply's equity during November.

1. Natural Beauty raised $20,000 in equity capital during the month.
2. Natural Beauty Supply earned net income of $80. That is, its business activities increased the company's net assets by $80 during the month.
3. Natural Beauty Supply declared a $50 cash dividend.

At this point, we can make the important observation that the various financial statements are not the result of independent processes. That is, the process of constructing the income statement is intimately tied to the process of constructing the balance sheet. When we think about the fact that revenues reflect how much the company expects to receive from its delivery of goods to customers, while expenses measure the outflow of assets and increases in liabilities resulting from earning revenues and supporting operations, it should be apparent that an error on the income statement will, in all likelihood, lead to an error in the balance sheet. Understanding the connections among the various statements is a key step in becoming an effective reader of financial information.

YOU MAKE THE CALL

You are an Analyst Walgreens reported a balance in retained earnings of $22,229 million at August 31, 2014. This amount compares to $21,523 million one year earlier at the end of 2013. In 2014, Walgreens reported net income of $1,932 million. Why did the company's retained earnings go up by less than reported net income? [Answer on page 74.]

MID-CHAPTER REVIEW 3

Part 1. Assume that Schaefer's Pharmacy, Inc.'s records show the following amounts at December 31, 2015. Use this information, as necessary, to prepare its 2015 income statement (ignore income taxes).

Cash	$ 3,000	Cash dividends	$ 1,000
Accounts receivable	12,000	Revenues	45,000
Office equipment	32,250	Cost of goods sold	20,000
Inventory	26,000	Rent expense	5,000
Land	10,000	Wages expense	8,000
Accounts payable	7,500	Utilities expense	2,000
Common stock	45,750	Other expenses	4,000

Part 2. Assume that Schaefer's Pharmacy, Inc. reports the following selected financial information for the year ended December 31, 2015.

Retained earnings, Dec. 31, 2015 . . .	$30,000	Dividends	$ 1,000
Net income	$ 6,000	Retained earnings, Dec. 31, 2014 . . .	$25,000

Prepare the 2015 calendar-year retained earnings reconciliation for this company.

Part 3. Use the listing of accounts and figures reported in part 1 along with the ending retained earnings from part 2 to prepare the December 31, 2015, balance sheet for Schaefer's Pharmacy, Inc.

The solution to this review problem can be found on pages 94–95.

JOURNALIZING AND POSTING TRANSACTIONS

6

LO6 Use journal entries and T-accounts to analyze and record transactions.

The financial statement effects template is a useful tool for illustrating the effects of a transaction on the balance sheet, income statement, statement of stockholders' equity, and statement of cash flows. However, when representing individual transactions or analyzing individual accounts, the accounting system records information in journal entries (step 2) that are collected in individual accounts. This section introduces the basics of that system. It also introduces the T-account as a useful tool for learning debits and credits and for representing accounts in the ledger (step 3).

T-Account

Accountants commonly use a graphic representation of an account called a **T-account**, so named because it looks like a large T. The typical form of a T-account is:

Account Title	
Debits	Credits
(Dr.)	(Cr.)
Always the left side	Always the right side

FYI Recall that an account is a record of increases and decreases in asset, liability, equity, revenue or expense items.

One side of the T-account is used to record increases to the account and the other side is used to record decreases.

Accountants record individual transactions using the journal entry. A **journal entry** is an accounting entry in the financial records (journals) of a company. The journal entry is the *bookkeeping* aspect of accounting. Even if we never make a journal entry for a company, we still interact with accounting and finance professionals who do, and who will use this language. Further, journal entries and T-accounts can help in reconstructing transactions and interpreting their financial effects.

Debit and Credit System

FYI Debit and credit are accounting terms meaning left and right, respectively.

Accountants describe increases and decreases in accounts using the terms **debit** and **credit**. The left side of each account is the debit side (abbreviated Dr.) and the right side of each account is the credit side (abbreviated Cr.). In some accounts, increases are recorded on the debit (left) side of the account and decreases are recorded on the credit (right) side of the account. In other accounts, just the opposite is true—increases are credits and decreases are debits. An easy way to remember what the words debit and credit reflect is to visualize a balance sheet in "T" account form with assets on the left and liabilities and equity on the right as follows:

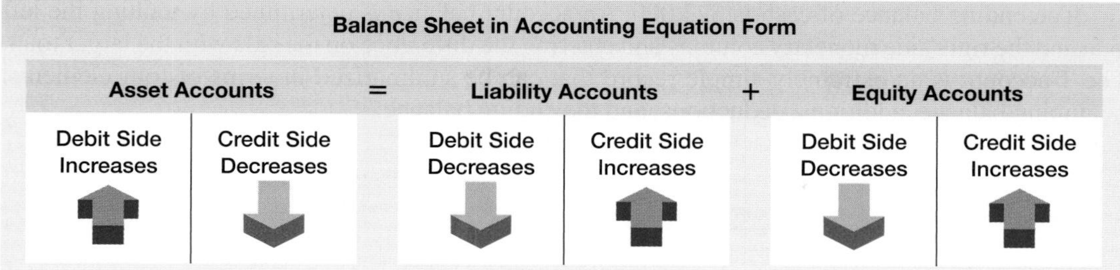

FYI In our everyday speech, the words "debit" and "credit" are often imbued with value connotations. For example, "To her credit, she took responsibility for the incident." But there are no value connotations within the accounting system. Every good event is recorded with both a debit and a credit, and the same is true for every bad event.

Thus, assets are assigned a *normal debit balance* because they are on the left side. Liabilities and equity are assigned a *normal credit balance* because they are on the right side. So, to reflect an increase in an asset, we debit the asset account. To reflect an increase in a liability or equity account we credit the account. Conversely, to reflect a decrease in an asset account, we credit it. To reflect a decrease in a liability or equity account we debit it. (There are exceptions to these normal balances; one case is accumulated depreciation, which is explained in Chapter 3.)

The balance sheet must always balance (assets = liabilities + equity). So too must total debits equal total credits in each journal entry. There can, however, be more than one debit and one credit in an entry. These so-called **compound entries** still adhere to the rule: *total debits equal total credits for each entry*. This important relation is extended below to show the *expanded accounting equation* in T-account form with the inclusion of debit (Dr.) and credit (Cr.) rules. Equity is expanded to reflect increases from stock issuances and revenues, and to reflect decreases from dividends and expenses.

FYI The rule that total debits equal total credits for each entry is known as double-entry accounting, or the duality of accounting.

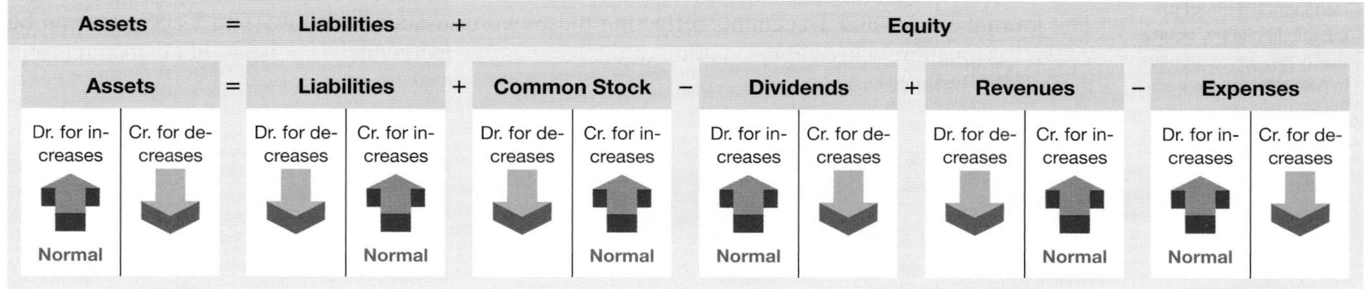

Income (revenues less expenses) feeds directly into retained earnings. Also, anything that increases equity is a credit and anything that decreases equity is a debit. So, to reflect an increase in revenues (which increases retained earnings and, therefore, equity), we credit the revenue account, and to reflect an increase in an expense account (which reduces retained earnings and, therefore, equity), we debit it.

FYI The **normal balance** of any account is on the side on which increases are recorded.

To summarize, the following table reflects the use of the terms debit and credit to reflect increases and decreases to the usual balance sheet and the income statement relations.

Accounting Relation		Debit	Credit
Balance sheet	Assets (A)	Increase	Decrease
	Liabilities (L)	Decrease	Increase
	Equity (SE)	Decrease	Increase
Income statement	Revenue (R)	Decrease	Increase
	Expense (E)	Increase	Decrease

T-Account with Debits and Credits

To illustrate use of debits and credits with a T-account, we use the Cash T-account for NBS transactions 1, 2, 3, and 4 (see page 51). There is a beginning balance of $0 on the left side (which is also the ending balance of the previous period). Increases in cash have been placed on the left side of the Cash T-account and the decreases have been placed on the right side. Transactions (1) and (2) increased the cash balance, while transaction (3), decreased it. Transaction (4) does not involve cash.

The ending balance of cash is $23,000. An account balance is determined by totaling the left side and the right side monetary columns and entering the difference on the side with the larger total. The T-account is an extremely simple record that can be summarized in terms of four elements: beginning balance, additions, deductions, and the ending balance.

+	Cash (A)		−
Beg. bal.	0		
(1)	20,000	2,000	(3)
(2)	5,000		
End. bal.	23,000		

Dates and other related data are usually omitted in T-accounts, but it is customary to *key* entries with a number or a letter to identify the similarly coded transaction. The number or letter is keyed to the journal entry (discussed next) that identifies the transaction involved. The type and number of accounts used by a business depend on the complexity of its operations and the degree of detail demanded by managers.

The Journal Entry

FYI We denote the transaction's effect on assets, liabilities, equity, revenues, and expenses in parentheses for each journal entry.

The journal entry records each transaction (step 2) by summarizing the debits and credits. To illustrate the use of journal entries and T-accounts (step 3), assume that Walgreens: (1) Paid employees $1,200 cash wages, recognizing that amount as an expense, and (2) Paid $9,500 cash to acquire equipment. The journal entries and T-accounts reflecting these two transactions follow. The T-accounts can be viewed as an abbreviated representation of the company *ledger,* which is a listing of all accounts and their dollar balances.

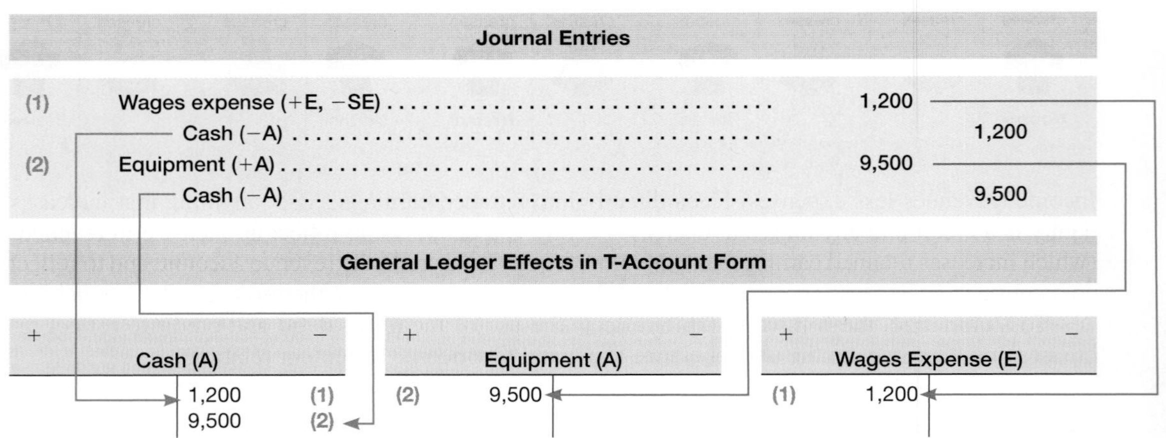

For journal entries, debits are recorded first followed by the credits. Credits are commonly indented. The dollar amounts are entered in both the debit (left) column and credit (right) column. In practice, recordkeepers also enter the date. An alternative presentation is to utilize the abbreviation *Dr* to denote debits and *Cr* to denote credits that precede the account title. We use the first approach in this book.

Analyze, Journalize, and Post

To illustrate the use of journal entries and T-accounts to record transactions, we return to Natural Beauty Supply and reexamine the same transactions recorded earlier in the financial statement effects template. The following layout illustrates our 3-step accounting process of analyzing, journalizing, and posting.

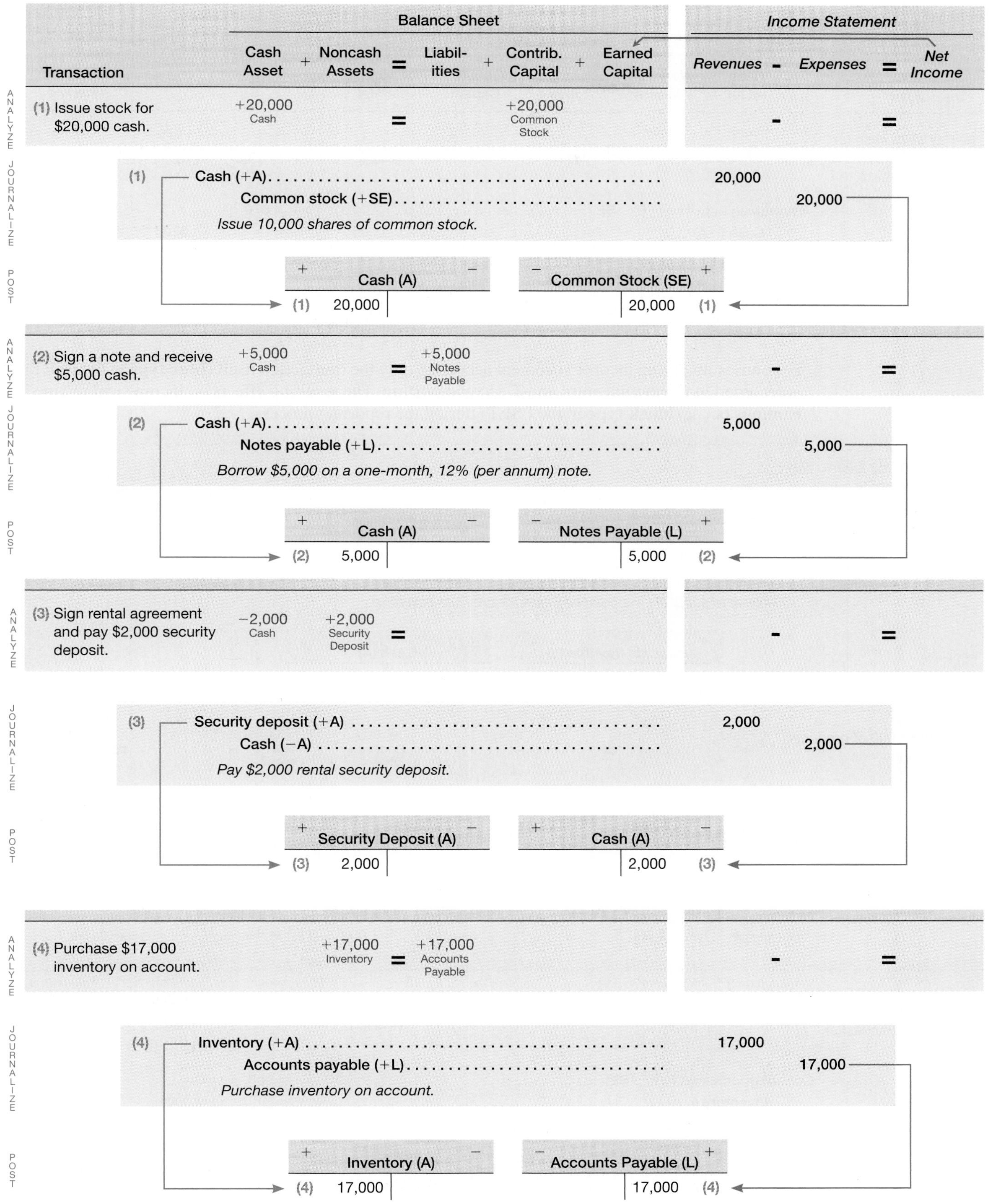

Transaction	Cash Asset	+ Noncash Assets	=	Liabil-ities	+ Contrib. Capital	+ Earned Capital	Revenues	- Expenses	= Net Income
(1) Issue stock for $20,000 cash.	+20,000 Cash		=		+20,000 Common Stock			-	=
(2) Sign a note and receive $5,000 cash.	+5,000 Cash		=	+5,000 Notes Payable				-	=
(3) Sign rental agreement and pay $2,000 security deposit.	−2,000 Cash	+2,000 Security Deposit	=					-	=
(4) Purchase $17,000 inventory on account.		+17,000 Inventory	=	+17,000 Accounts Payable				-	=

(1) Cash (+A) 20,000
Common stock (+SE) 20,000
Issue 10,000 shares of common stock.

Cash (A): + (1) 20,000 | −
Common Stock (SE): − | 20,000 (1) +

(2) Cash (+A) 5,000
Notes payable (+L) 5,000
Borrow $5,000 on a one-month, 12% (per annum) note.

Cash (A): + (2) 5,000 | −
Notes Payable (L): − | 5,000 (2) +

(3) Security deposit (+A) 2,000
Cash (−A) 2,000
Pay $2,000 rental security deposit.

Security Deposit (A): + (3) 2,000 | −
Cash (A): + | 2,000 (3) −

(4) Inventory (+A) 17,000
Accounts payable (+L) 17,000
Purchase inventory on account.

Inventory (A): + (4) 17,000 | −
Accounts Payable (L): − | 17,000 (4) +

continued

continued from previous page

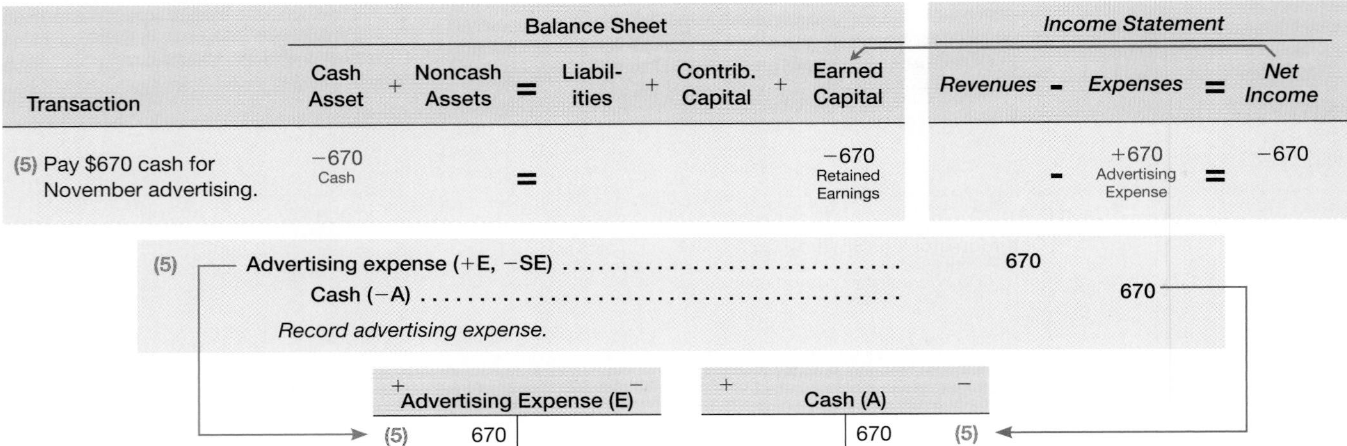

	Balance Sheet									Income Statement				
Transaction	Cash Asset	+	Noncash Assets	=	Liabil-ities	+	Contrib. Capital	+	Earned Capital	Revenues	−	Expenses	=	Net Income
(5) Pay $670 cash for November advertising.	−670 Cash			=					−670 Retained Earnings		−	+670 Advertising Expense	=	−670

ANALYZE / JOURNALIZE / POST

(5) Advertising expense (+E, −SE) 670
  Cash (−A) 670
Record advertising expense.

+ Advertising Expense (E) −	
(5) 670	

+ Cash (A) −	
	670 (5)

For entries involving income statement accounts, only the transaction itself (**blue type** in the FSET) is recorded in the journal entry and T-account posting. The resulting effects on income and retained earnings occur (**black type** in the FSET) during the reporting process.

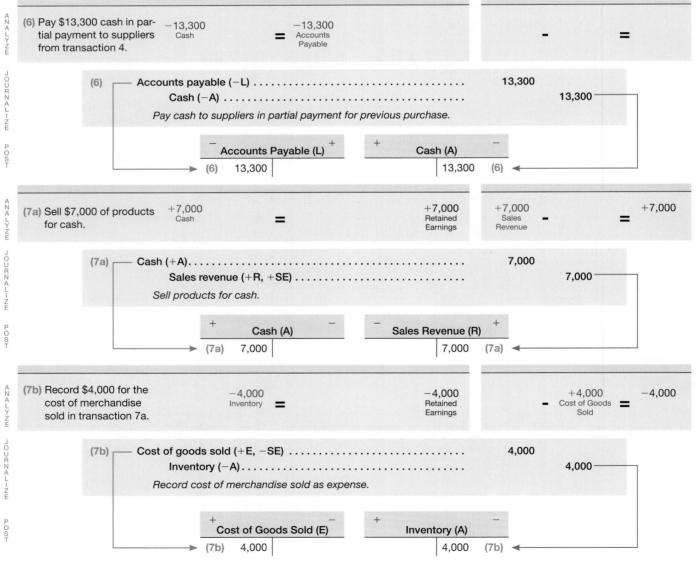

Transaction	Cash Asset	+	Noncash Assets	=	Liabil-ities	+	Contrib. Capital	+	Earned Capital	Revenues	−	Expenses	=	Net Income
(6) Pay $13,300 cash in partial payment to suppliers from transaction 4.	−13,300 Cash			=	−13,300 Accounts Payable						−		=	
(7a) Sell $7,000 of products for cash.	+7,000 Cash			=					+7,000 Retained Earnings	+7,000 Sales Revenue	−		=	+7,000
(7b) Record $4,000 for the cost of merchandise sold in transaction 7a.			−4,000 Inventory	=					−4,000 Retained Earnings		−	+4,000 Cost of Goods Sold	=	−4,000

ANALYZE / JOURNALIZE / POST

(6) Accounts payable (−L) 13,300
  Cash (−A) 13,300
Pay cash to suppliers in partial payment for previous purchase.

− Accounts Payable (L) +	
(6) 13,300	

+ Cash (A) −	
	13,300 (6)

ANALYZE / JOURNALIZE / POST

(7a) Cash (+A) 7,000
  Sales revenue (+R, +SE) 7,000
Sell products for cash.

+ Cash (A) −	
(7a) 7,000	

− Sales Revenue (R) +	
	7,000 (7a)

ANALYZE / JOURNALIZE / POST

(7b) Cost of goods sold (+E, −SE) 4,000
  Inventory (−A) 4,000
Record cost of merchandise sold as expense.

+ Cost of Goods Sold (E) −	
(7b) 4,000	

+ Inventory (A) −	
	4,000 (7b)

continued

continued from previous page

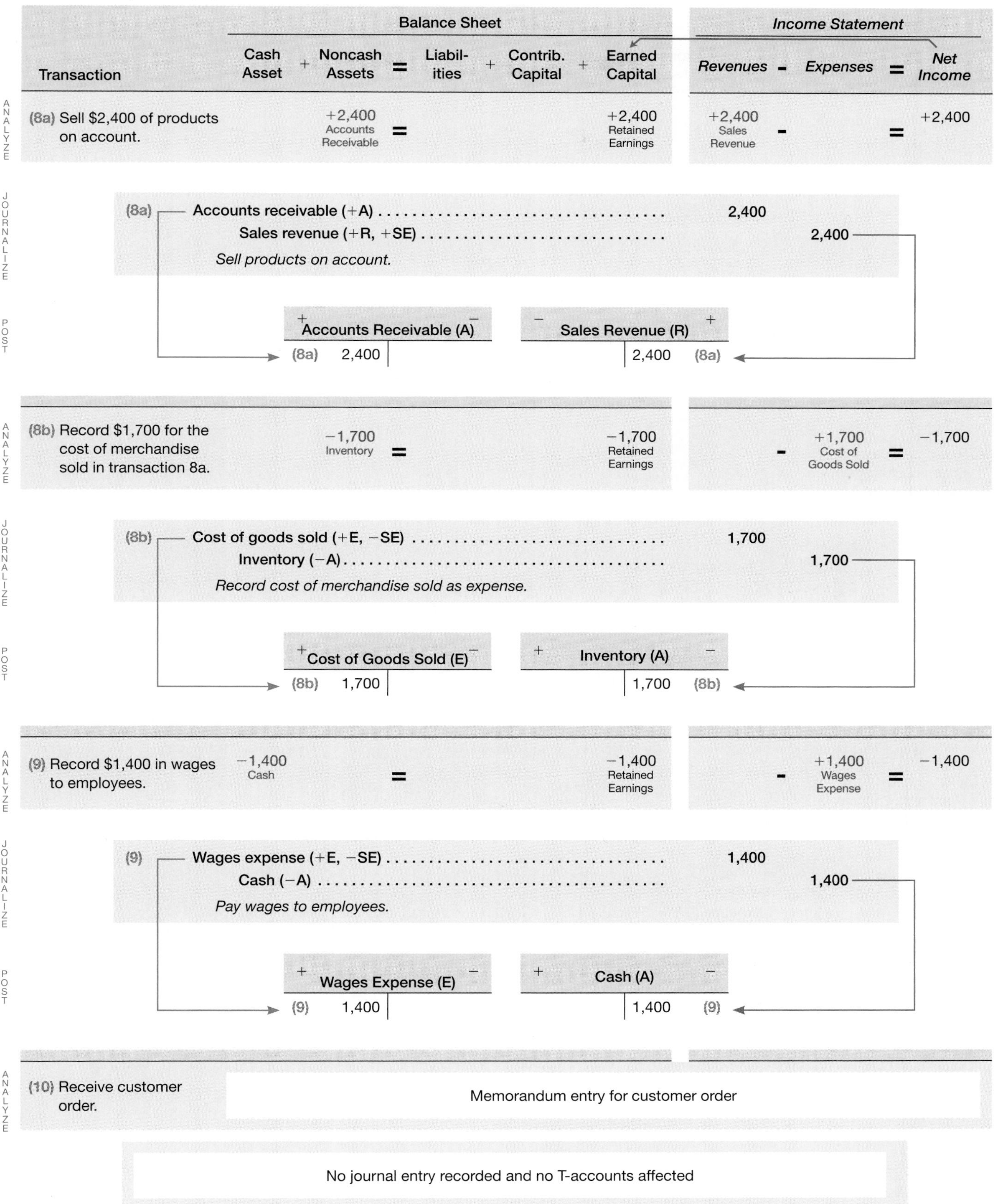

	Balance Sheet									Income Statement				
Transaction	Cash Asset	+	Noncash Assets	=	Liabil-ities	+	Contrib. Capital	+	Earned Capital	*Revenues*	-	*Expenses*	=	*Net Income*
ANALYZE (8a) Sell $2,400 of products on account.			+2,400 Accounts Receivable	=					+2,400 Retained Earnings	+2,400 Sales Revenue	-		=	+2,400

JOURNALIZE

		Debit	Credit
(8a)	Accounts receivable (+A)	2,400	
	Sales revenue (+R, +SE)		2,400
	Sell products on account.		

POST

+ Accounts Receivable (A) −	
(8a) 2,400	

− Sales Revenue (R) +	
	2,400 (8a)

Transaction	Cash Asset	+	Noncash Assets	=	Liabil-ities	+	Contrib. Capital	+	Earned Capital	*Revenues*	-	*Expenses*	=	*Net Income*
ANALYZE (8b) Record $1,700 for the cost of merchandise sold in transaction 8a.			−1,700 Inventory	=					−1,700 Retained Earnings		-	+1,700 Cost of Goods Sold	=	−1,700

JOURNALIZE

		Debit	Credit
(8b)	Cost of goods sold (+E, −SE)	1,700	
	Inventory (−A)		1,700
	Record cost of merchandise sold as expense.		

POST

+ Cost of Goods Sold (E) −	
(8b) 1,700	

+ Inventory (A) −	
	1,700 (8b)

Transaction	Cash Asset	+	Noncash Assets	=	Liabil-ities	+	Contrib. Capital	+	Earned Capital	*Revenues*	-	*Expenses*	=	*Net Income*
ANALYZE (9) Record $1,400 in wages to employees.	−1,400 Cash			=					−1,400 Retained Earnings		-	+1,400 Wages Expense	=	−1,400

JOURNALIZE

		Debit	Credit
(9)	Wages expense (+E, −SE)	1,400	
	Cash (−A)		1,400
	Pay wages to employees.		

POST

+ Wages Expense (E) −	
(9) 1,400	

+ Cash (A) −	
	1,400 (9)

ANALYZE (10) Receive customer order.

Memorandum entry for customer order

No journal entry recorded and no T-accounts affected

continued

continued from previous page

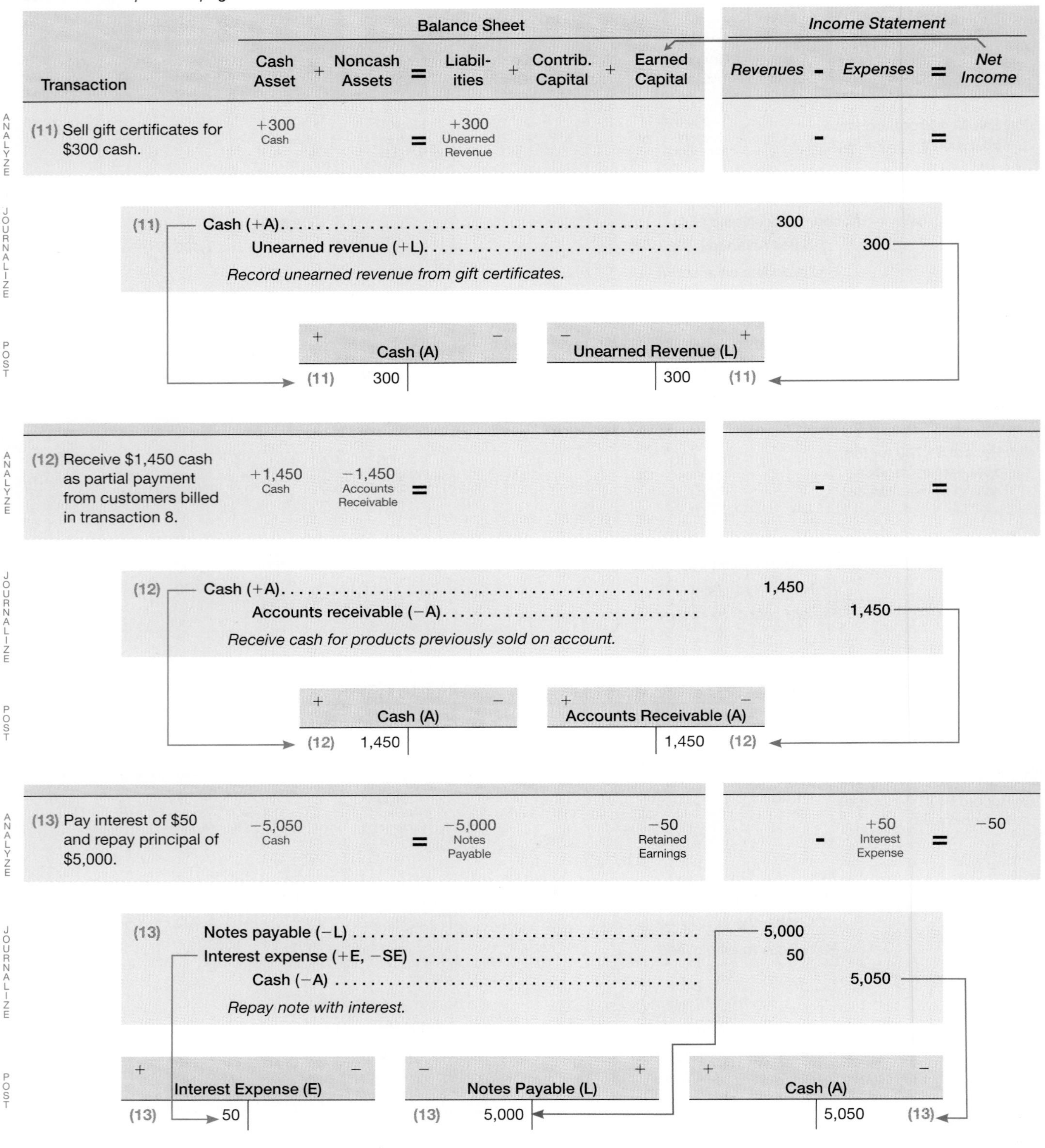

Transaction	Cash Asset	+	Noncash Assets	=	Liabil-ities	+	Contrib. Capital	+	Earned Capital	Revenues	-	Expenses	=	Net Income
(11) Sell gift certificates for $300 cash.	+300 Cash			=	+300 Unearned Revenue						-		=	
(12) Receive $1,450 cash as partial payment from customers billed in transaction 8.	+1,450 Cash		−1,450 Accounts Receivable	=							-		=	
(13) Pay interest of $50 and repay principal of $5,000.	−5,050 Cash			=	−5,000 Notes Payable				−50 Retained Earnings		-	+50 Interest Expense	=	−50

(11)

	Debit	Credit
Cash (+A)	300	
Unearned revenue (+L)		300

Record unearned revenue from gift certificates.

POST: Cash (A): (11) 300 (debit). Unearned Revenue (L): 300 (11) (credit).

(12)

	Debit	Credit
Cash (+A)	1,450	
Accounts receivable (−A)		1,450

Receive cash for products previously sold on account.

POST: Cash (A): (12) 1,450 (debit). Accounts Receivable (A): 1,450 (12) (credit).

(13)

	Debit	Credit
Notes payable (−L)	5,000	
Interest expense (+E, −SE)	50	
Cash (−A)		5,050

Repay note with interest.

POST: Interest Expense (E): (13) 50 (debit). Notes Payable (L): (13) 5,000 (debit). Cash (A): 5,050 (13) (credit).

continued

continued from previous page

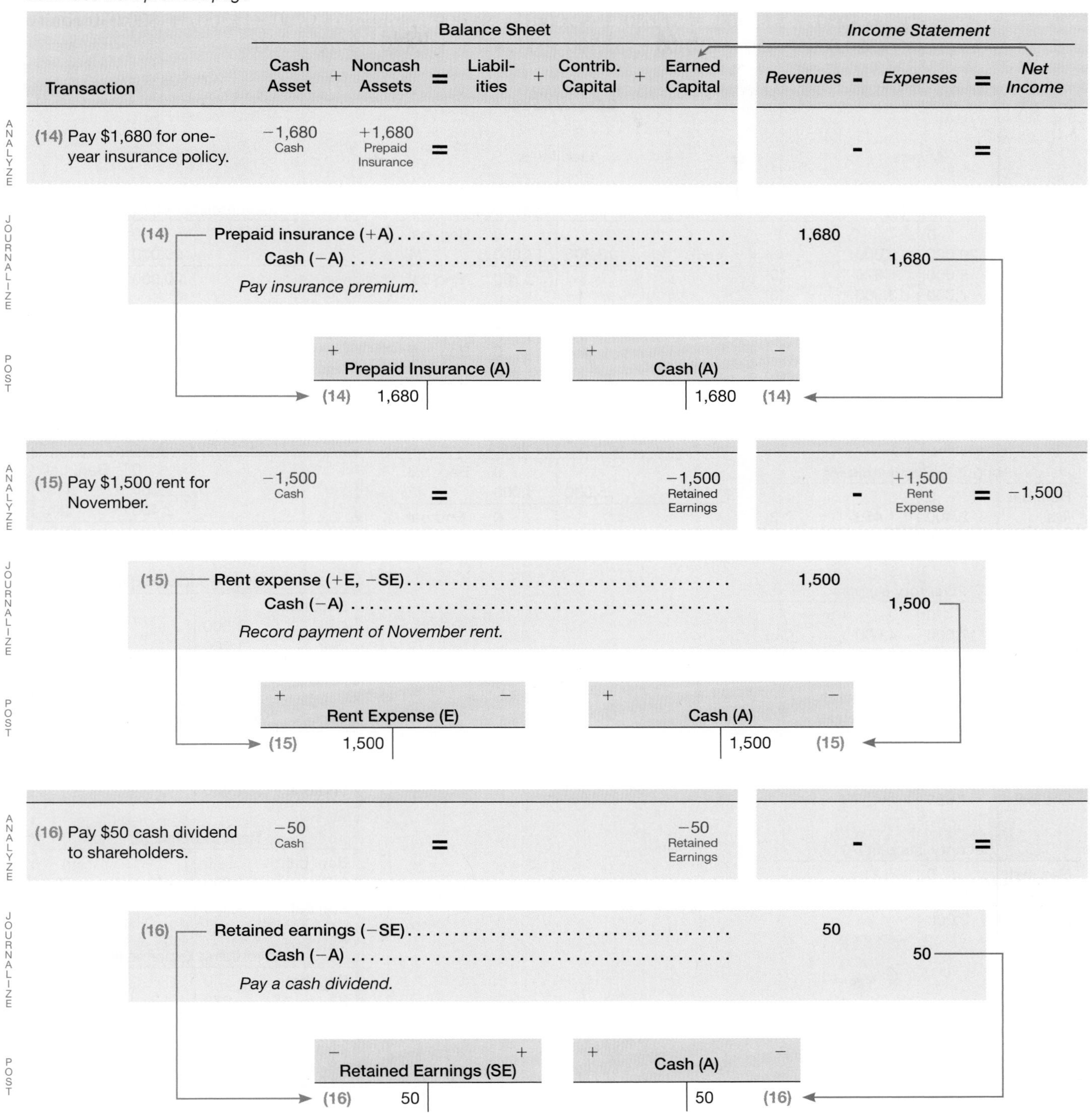

Balance Sheet
Income Statement
Transaction
Cash Asset + Noncash Assets = Liabil-ities + Contrib. Capital + Earned Capital
Revenues - Expenses = Net Income
ANALYZE
(14) Pay $1,680 for one-year insurance policy.
−1,680 Cash
+1,680 Prepaid Insurance
JOURNALIZE
(14) Prepaid insurance (+A) 1,680
Cash (−A) 1,680
Pay insurance premium.
POST
Prepaid Insurance (A)
(14) 1,680
Cash (A)
1,680 (14)
ANALYZE
(15) Pay $1,500 rent for November.
−1,500 Cash
−1,500 Retained Earnings
+1,500 Rent Expense
−1,500
JOURNALIZE
(15) Rent expense (+E, −SE) 1,500
Cash (−A) 1,500
Record payment of November rent.
POST
Rent Expense (E)
(15) 1,500
Cash (A)
1,500 (15)
ANALYZE
(16) Pay $50 cash dividend to shareholders.
−50 Cash
−50 Retained Earnings
JOURNALIZE
(16) Retained earnings (−SE) 50
Cash (−A) 50
Pay a cash dividend.
POST
Retained Earnings (SE)
(16) 50
Cash (A)
50 (16)

As shown above, each of the journal entries is posted to the appropriate T-accounts, which represent the general ledger. The complete general ledger reflecting each of these sixteen transactions follows, reflecting how the balance sheet and income statement are produced by the same underlying process. The dashed line around the six equity accounts indicates those that are reported in the income statement before becoming part of retained earnings. Each balance sheet T-account starts with an opening balance on November 1 (zero in this case), and the ending balances are the starting balances for December. Income statement T-accounts do not have an opening balance, for reasons we explore in Chapter 3.

As always, we see that: Assets = Liabilities + Equity. Specifically, $24,030 assets ($8,100 + $950 + $11,300 + $1,680 + $2,000) = $4,000 liabilities ($3,700 + $300) + $20,030 equity ($20,000 − $50 + $9,400 − $5,700 − $1,400 − $1,500 − $670 − $50).

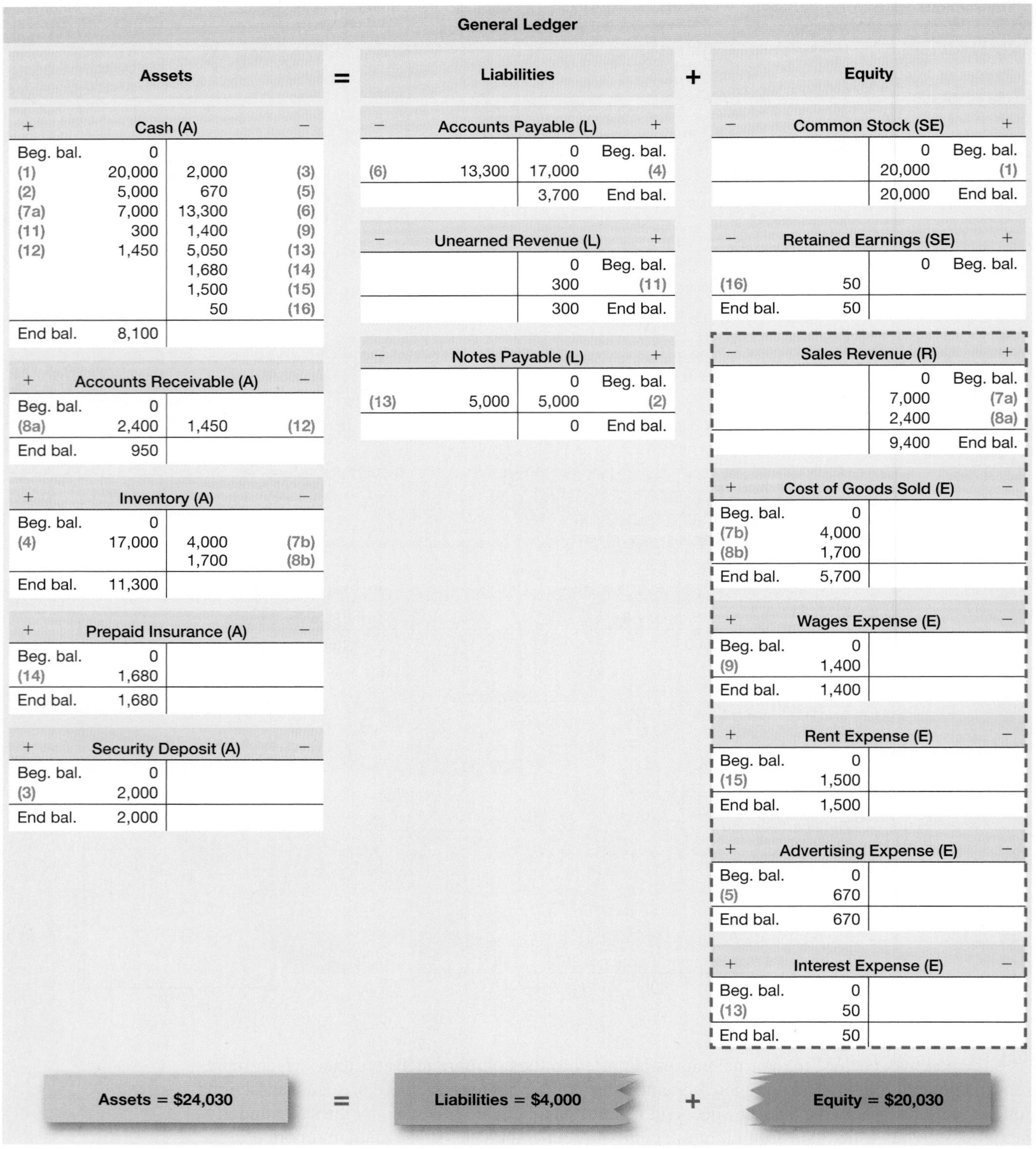

General Ledger

Assets = Liabilities + Equity

Assets

+	Cash (A)		−
Beg. bal.	0		
(1)	20,000	2,000	(3)
(2)	5,000	670	(5)
(7a)	7,000	13,300	(6)
(11)	300	1,400	(9)
(12)	1,450	5,050	(13)
		1,680	(14)
		1,500	(15)
		50	(16)
End bal.	8,100		

+	Accounts Receivable (A)		−
Beg. bal.	0		
(8a)	2,400	1,450	(12)
End bal.	950		

+	Inventory (A)		−
Beg. bal.	0		
(4)	17,000	4,000	(7b)
		1,700	(8b)
End bal.	11,300		

+	Prepaid Insurance (A)		−
Beg. bal.	0		
(14)	1,680		
End bal.	1,680		

+	Security Deposit (A)		−
Beg. bal.	0		
(3)	2,000		
End bal.	2,000		

Liabilities

−	Accounts Payable (L)		+
		0	Beg. bal.
(6)	13,300	17,000	(4)
		3,700	End bal.

−	Unearned Revenue (L)		+
		0	Beg. bal.
		300	(11)
		300	End bal.

−	Notes Payable (L)		+
		0	Beg. bal.
(13)	5,000	5,000	(2)
		0	End bal.

Equity

−	Common Stock (SE)		+
		0	Beg. bal.
		20,000	(1)
		20,000	End bal.

−	Retained Earnings (SE)		+
		0	Beg. bal.
(16)	50		
End bal.	50		

−	Sales Revenue (R)		+
		0	Beg. bal.
		7,000	(7a)
		2,400	(8a)
		9,400	End bal.

+	Cost of Goods Sold (E)		−
Beg. bal.	0		
(7b)	4,000		
(8b)	1,700		
End bal.	5,700		

+	Wages Expense (E)		−
Beg. bal.	0		
(9)	1,400		
End bal.	1,400		

+	Rent Expense (E)		−
Beg. bal.	0		
(15)	1,500		
End bal.	1,500		

+	Advertising Expense (E)		−
Beg. bal.	0		
(5)	670		
End bal.	670		

+	Interest Expense (E)		−
Beg. bal.	0		
(13)	50		
End bal.	50		

Assets = $24,030 = Liabilities = $4,000 + Equity = $20,030

ANALYZING FINANCIAL STATEMENTS

LO7 Compute net working capital, the current ratio, and the quick ratio, and explain how they reflect liquidity.

7

Analysis Objective

We are trying to determine if Walgreens has sufficient funds to pay their short-term debts as they come due. To accomplish this task, we employ several measures of liquidity. We introduce three such measures below to assess liquidity.

Analysis Tool Net Working Capital

Net working capital = Current assets − Current liabilities

Applying Net Working Capital to Walgreens

2012: \$10,760 − \$8,722 = \$2,038
2013: \$11,874 − \$8,883 = \$2,991
2014: \$12,242 − \$8,895 = \$3,347

Guidance A company's net working capital is determined primarily by the time between paying for goods and employee services and the receipt of cash from sales for cash or on credit. This cycle is referred to as the firm's **cash operating cycle** (see **Exhibit 2.6**). The cash operating cycle can provide additional resources through trade credit financing. For example, inventory is typically bought on credit with terms that allow payment to be deferred for 30 to 90 days without penalty. The delay in payment allows the cash to be invested, thereby increasing the cash to be used in the following operating cycle. Of course, the reluctant supplier of the credit strives to reduce this payment delay, for example, through discounts for early payment.

A company's net working capital is a broad measure including all current assets even though some of them—inventories for one—require time to turn them into cash. Later in the book, we will discover that the accounting for some components of working capital, like inventory, needs to be adjusted with information found in the footnotes.

EXHIBIT 2.6 Operating Cycle

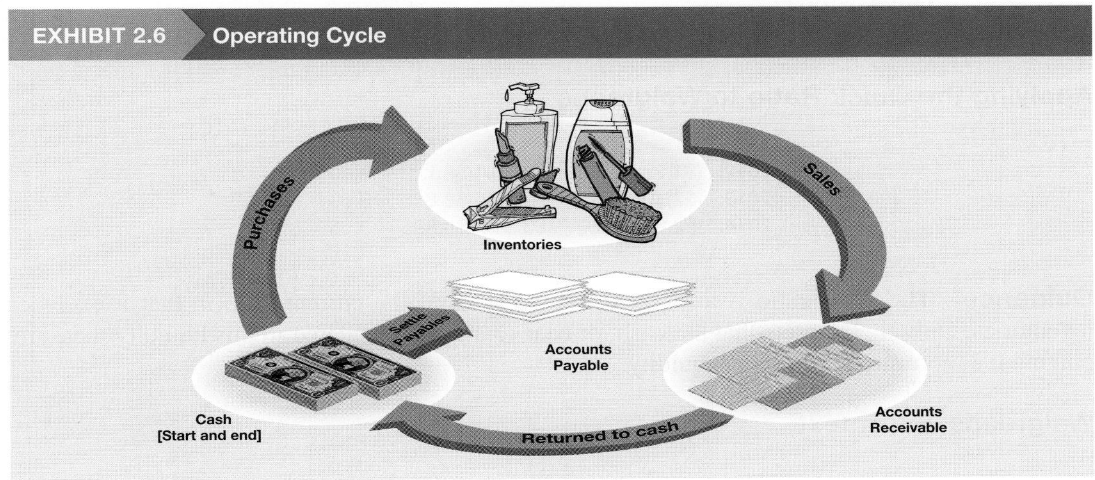

Analysis Tool Current Ratio

$$\textbf{Current ratio} = \frac{\textbf{Current assets}}{\textbf{Current liabilities}}$$

Applying the Current Ratio to Walgreens

2012: \$10,760/\$8,722 = 1.23
2013: \$11,874/\$8,883 = 1.34
2014: \$12,242/\$8,895 = 1.38

Guidance The current ratio is just a different form of net working capital and as such simply provides a different viewpoint. Current ratios exceeding one indicate a positive net working capital. However, for firms that find difficulty in predicting sales and collections, a higher current ratio is desirable, as discussed in Chapter 5. Companies generally prefer a current ratio greater than one but less than two. The ratio allows us to discern whether the company is likely to have difficulty meeting its short-term obligations. The current ratio has additional value as a ratio because net working capital depends on the size of the company. This is useful when comparing companies as below.

Walgreens in Context

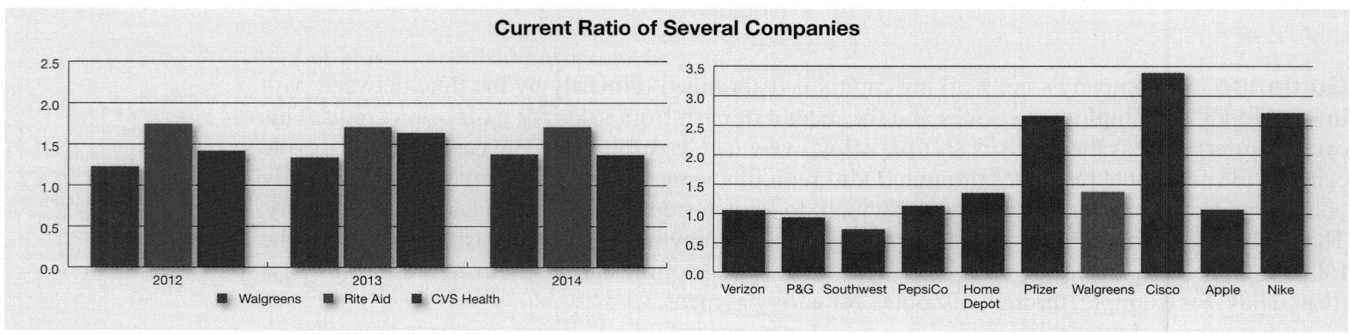

Analysis Tool Quick Ratio

$$\textbf{Quick ratio} = \frac{\textbf{Cash + Short-term securities + Accounts receivable}}{\textbf{Current liabilities}}$$

Applying the Quick Ratio to Walgreens

2012: (\$1,297 + \$0 + \$2,167)/\$8,722 = 0.40
2013: (\$2,106 + \$0 + \$2,632)/\$8,883 = 0.53
2014: (\$2,646 + \$0 + \$3,218)/\$8,895 = 0.66

Guidance The quick ratio is a more restrictive form of the current ratio in that it excludes inventories. Only those assets that are cash, or near cash, are considered in this liquidity measure, making it a more stringent test of liquidity.

Walgreens in Context

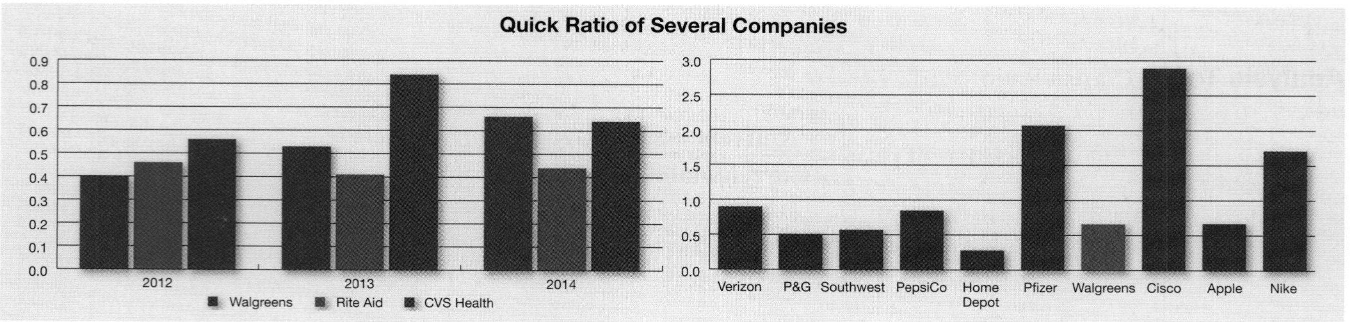

Takeaways Over the three-year period covered by our calculations, we can conclude that Walgreens is in a strong position with respect to liquidity. Its net working capital, while declining slightly over the last several years has remained positive and is currently one-and-one-half times its liabilities. Our conclusions are bolstered by comparing Walgreens with two of its major competitors, CVS Health Corp. and **Rite Aid Corporation**. All three companies are quite similar on liquidity measures even though quite different in size. CVS is about 1.8 the size of Walgreens while Rite Aid is about one-third the size based on revenues.

Other Considerations While the ratios above tell us about retail pharmacy chains, other companies with different operating cycles are likely to exhibit different values at optimal levels of activity. Thus grocery stores will have few current assets but consistent large operating cash inflows that ensure sufficient liquidity despite current ratios less than one. Additionally, companies that efficiently manage inventories, receivables and payables can also operate with current ratios below one. **Wal-Mart**, for example, uses its strong market power to extract extended credit terms from suppliers while simultaneously enforcing short payment periods on customers. In Chapter 10, we explore how many technology and pharmaceutical companies have adopted tax strategies that accumulate large amounts of assets that appear to be liquid, but which could be significantly reduced if brought back to the United States.

CHAPTER-END REVIEW

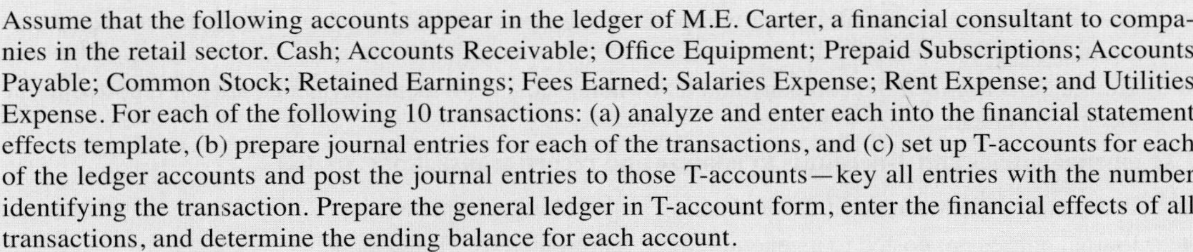

Assume that the following accounts appear in the ledger of M.E. Carter, a financial consultant to companies in the retail sector. Cash; Accounts Receivable; Office Equipment; Prepaid Subscriptions; Accounts Payable; Common Stock; Retained Earnings; Fees Earned; Salaries Expense; Rent Expense; and Utilities Expense. For each of the following 10 transactions: (a) analyze and enter each into the financial statement effects template, (b) prepare journal entries for each of the transactions, and (c) set up T-accounts for each of the ledger accounts and post the journal entries to those T-accounts—key all entries with the number identifying the transaction. Prepare the general ledger in T-account form, enter the financial effects of all transactions, and determine the ending balance for each account.

(1) M.E. Carter started the firm by contributing $19,500 cash to the business in exchange for common stock.
(2) The firm purchased $10,400 in office equipment on account.
(3) Paid $700 cash for this period's office rent.
(4) Paid $9,600 cash for subscriptions to online financial databases covering the next three periods.
(5) Billed clients $11,300 for services rendered.
(6) Made $6,000 cash payment on account for the equipment purchased in transaction 2.
(7) Paid $2,800 cash for assistant's salary for this period.
(8) Collected $9,400 cash from clients previously billed in transaction 5.
(9) Received $180 invoice for this period's utilities; it is paid early in the next period.
(10) Paid $1,500 cash for dividends to shareholders.

The solution to this review problem can be found on pages 95–98.

SUMMARY

Describe and construct the balance sheet and understand how it can be used for analysis. (p. 44) LO1

- Assets, which reflect investment activities, are reported (in order of their liquidity) as current assets (expected to be used typically within a year) and noncurrent (or plant) assets.
- Assets are reported at their historical cost and not at market values (with a few exceptions) and are restricted to those that can be reliably measured.
- Not all assets are reported on the balance sheet; a company's self-developed intellectual capital, often one of its more valuable assets, is one example.

- For an asset to be recorded, it must be owned or controlled by the company and carry future economic benefits.
- Liabilities and equity are the sources of company financing; ordered by maturity dates.

LO2 Use the financial statement effects template (FSET) to analyze transactions. (p. 49)

- The FSET captures the effects of transactions on the balance sheet, income statement, statement of stockholders' equity, and the statement of cash flows.
- Income statement effects are separated into revenues, expenses, and net income. The updating of retained earnings is denoted with an arrow line running from net income to earned capital.

LO3 Describe and construct the income statement and discuss how it can be used to evaluate management performance. (p. 53)

- The income statement presents the revenues, expenses, and net income recognized by the company during the accounting period.
- Net income (or loss) is the increase (decrease) in net assets that results from business activities.
- Net income is determined based on the use of accrual accounting.

LO4 Explain revenue recognition, accrual accounting, and their effects on retained earnings. (p. 54)

- Revenues must be recognized only when goods or services have been transferred to the customer.
- Expenses should be recognized as assets are used or liabilities incurred in order to earn revenues or carry out other operating activities.

LO5 Illustrate equity transactions and the statement of stockholders' equity. (p. 60)

- The statement of stockholders' equity reports transactions resulting in changes in equity accounts during the accounting period.
- Transactions between the company and its owners, such as dividend payments, are not reported in the income statement.

LO6 Use journal entries and T-accounts to analyze and record transactions. (p. 62)

- Transactions are recorded in the accounting system using journal entries.
- Journal entries are posted to a general ledger, represented by "T-accounts."
- Accountants use "debits" and "credits" to record transactions in the accounts.

LO7 Compute net working capital, the current ratio, and the quick ratio, and explain how they reflect liquidity. (p. 71)

- Net working capital: an indicator of a firm's ability to pay its short-term debts computed as the difference between current assets and current liabilities.
- Current ratio (CR): A measure of liquidity indicating the degree of coverage of current liabilities by current assets.
- Quick ratio (QR): A measure of the ability to cover current liabilities using only cash and cash equivalents (such as money market accounts), short-term securities, and accounts receivable.

GUIDANCE ANSWERS . . . YOU MAKE THE CALL

You are an Analyst In 2014, Walgreens paid cash dividends of $1,226 million. The net income and dividend payments account for the change in retained earnings ($22,229 million − $21,523 million = $1,932 million − $1,226 million). On occasion, companies pay dividends in excess of their earnings (or pay dividends even when earning losses), resulting in a decrease in retained earnings over the period.

KEY RATIOS

Net working capital = Current assets − Current liabilities

$$\text{Current ratio} = \frac{\text{Current assets}}{\text{Current liabilities}} \qquad \text{Quick ratio} = \frac{\text{Cash} + \text{Short-term securities} + \text{Accounts receivable}}{\text{Current liabilities}}$$

KEY TERMS

Account (p. 50)
Accounting equation (p. 44)
Accounts payable (p. 47)
Accounts receivable (p. 46)
Accrual accounting (p. 54)
Accrued liabilities (p. 47)
Accumulated other comprehensive income or loss (p. 48)
Additional paid-in capital (p. 48)
Asset (p. 44)
Cash (p. 46)
Cash accounting (p. 55)
Cash equivalents (p. 46)
Cash operating cycle (p. 71)
Chart of accounts (p. 51)
Common stock (p. 48)
Compound entries (p. 63)
Contributed capital (p. 48)
Cost of goods sold (p. 55)
Credit (p. 55, 62)
Current assets (p. 46)
Current liabilities (p. 47)
Current maturities of long-term debt (p. 47)
Debit (p. 62)
Deferred (unearned) revenues (p. 47)
Double-entry accounting system (p. 50)
Earned capital (p. 49)
Equity (p. 47, 49)
Executory contract (p. 47)
Expense recognition (p. 54)
Expenses (p. 53)
Fair value (p. 46)
Financial statement effects template (FSET) (p. 50)
Gross profit (p. 55)
Historical cost (p. 46)
Intangible and other assets (p. 46)
Inventory (p. 46)
Journal entry (p. 62)
Liabilities (p. 47)
Liquidity (p. 46)
Long-term debt (p. 48)
Long-term financial investments (p. 46)
Marketable securities (p. 46)
Net assets (p. 53)
Net income (p. 53)
Net loss (p. 53)
Noncurrent assets (p. 46)
Noncurrent liabilities (p. 48)
Nonoperating revenues and expenses (p. 54)
Normal balance (p. 63)
Notes payable (p. 48)
Operating expenses (p. 53)
Other long-term liabilities (p. 48)
Prepaid expenses (p. 46)
Property, plant, and equipment (PPE) (p. 46)
Relevance (p. 46)
Reliability (p. 46)
Retained earnings (p. 48)
Revenue recognition (p. 54)
Revenues (p. 53)
Shareholders' equity (p. 49)
Short-term borrowings (p. 47)
Stockholders' equity (p. 49)
T-account (p. 62)
Treasury stock (p. 48)

Assignments with the MBC logo in the margin are available in myBusinessCourse. See the Preface of the book for details.

MULTIPLE CHOICE

Multiple Choice Answers
1. d 2. a 3. c 4. b 5. d

1. Which of the following conditions must exist for an item to be recorded as an asset?
   a. Item is not owned or controlled by the company.
   b. Future benefits from the item cannot be reliably measured.
   c. Item must be a tangible asset.
   d. Item must be expected to yield future benefits.

2. Company assets that are excluded from the company financial statements
   a. are presumably reflected in the company's stock price.
   b. include all of the company's intangible assets.
   c. are known as intangible assets.
   d. include investments in other companies.

3. If an asset declines in value, which of the following must be true?
   a. A liability also declines.
   b. Equity also declines.
   c. Either a liability or equity also declines or another asset increases in value.
   d. Neither *a* nor *b* can occur.

4. Which of the following is true about accrual accounting?
   a. Accrual accounting requires that expenses always be recognized when cash is paid out.
   b. Accrual accounting is required under GAAP.
   c. Accrual accounting recognizes revenue only when cash is received.
   d. Recognition of a prepaid asset (e.g., prepaid rent) is not an example of accrual accounting.

5. Which of the following options accurately identifies the effects a cash sale of an iPhone has on Apple's accounts?

a. Accounts receivable increases, sales revenue increases, cost of goods sold increases, and inventory decreases.

b. Cash increases, sales revenue increases, cost of goods sold decreases, and inventory decreases.

c. Accounts receivable increases, sales revenue increases, cost of goods sold decreases, and inventory decreases.

d. Cash increases, sales revenue increases, cost of goods sold increases, and inventory decreases.

QUESTIONS

Q2-1. The balance sheet consists of assets, liabilities, and equity. Define each category and provide two examples of accounts reported within each category.

Q2-2. Two important concepts that guide income statement reporting are the revenue recognition principle and the expense recognition principle. Define and explain each of these two guiding principles.

Q2-3. GAAP is based on the concept of accrual accounting. Define and describe accrual accounting.

Q2-4. What is the statement of stockholders' equity? What information is conveyed in that statement?

Q2-5. What are the two essential characteristics of an asset?

Q2-6. What does the concept of liquidity refer to? Explain.

Q2-7. What does the term *current* denote when referring to assets?

Q2-8. Assets are recorded at historical costs even though current market values might, arguably, be more relevant to financial statement readers. Describe the reasoning behind historical cost usage.

Q2-9. Identify three intangible assets that are likely to be excluded from the balance sheet because they cannot be reliably measured.

Q2-10. How does the quick ratio differ from the current ratio?

Q2-11. What three conditions must be satisfied to require reporting of a liability on the balance sheet?

Q2-12. Define net working capital. Explain how increasing the amount of trade credit can reduce the net working capital for a company.

Q2-13. On December 31, 2015, Miller Company had $700,000 in total assets and owed $220,000 to creditors. If this corporation's common stock totaled $300,000, what amount of retained earnings is reported on its December 31, 2015, balance sheet?

MINI EXERCISES

LO1 **M2-14. Determining Retained Earnings and Net Income Using the Balance Sheet**

The following information is reported for Kinney Corporation at the end of 2015.

Accounts receivable	$ 23,000	Retained earnings	$?
Accounts payable	11,000	Supplies inventory	9,000
Cash	8,000	Equipment	138,000
Common stock	110,000		

a. Compute the amount of retained earnings at the end of 2015.

b. If the amount of retained earnings at the beginning of 2015 was $30,000, and $12,000 in cash dividends were declared and paid during 2015, what was its net income for 2015?

LO1 **M2-15. Applying the Accounting Equation to the Balance Sheet**

Determine the missing amount in each of the following separate company cases.

	Assets	Liabilities	Equity
a.	$200,000	$85,000	$?
b.	?	32,000	28,000
c.	93,000	?	52,000

M2-16. Applying the Accounting Equation to the Balance Sheet

LO1

Determine the missing amount in each of the following separate company cases.

	Assets	Liabilities	Equity
a.	$375,000	$105,000	$?
b.	?	43,000	11,000
c.	878,000	?	422,000

M2-17. Applying the Accounting Equation to Determine Unknown Values

LO1

Determine the following for each separate company case:

a. The stockholders' equity of Jensen Corporation, which has assets of $450,000 and liabilities of $326,000.

b. The liabilities of Sloan & Dechow, Inc., which has assets of $618,000 and stockholders' equity of $165,000.

c. The assets of Clem Corporation, which has liabilities of $400,000, common stock of $200,000, and retained earnings of $185,000.

M2-18. Analyzing Transaction Effects on Equity

LO2, 4, 5

Would each of the following transactions increase, decrease, or have no effect on equity?

a. Paid cash to acquire supplies.

b. Paid cash for dividends to shareholders.

c. Paid cash for salaries.

d. Purchased equipment for cash.

e. Shareholders invested cash in business in exchange for common stock.

f. Rendered service to customers on account.

g. Rendered service to customers for cash.

M2-19. Identifying and Classifying Financial Statement Items

LO1, 3, 4

For each of the following items, identify whether they would most likely be reported in the balance sheet (B) or income statement (I).

a.	Machinery	_____	*e.*	Common stock	_____	*i.*	Taxes expense	_____
b.	Supplies expense	_____	*f.*	Factory buildings	_____	*j.*	Cost of goods sold	_____
c.	Prepaid advertising	_____	*g.*	Receivables	_____	*k.*	Long-term debt	_____
d.	Advertising expense	_____	*h.*	Taxes payable	_____	*l.*	Treasury stock	_____

M2-20. Computing Net Income

LO3, 4

Healy Corporation recorded service revenues of $100,000 in 2015, of which $70,000 were for credit and $30,000 were for cash. Moreover, of the $70,000 credit sales for 2015, it collected $20,000 cash on those receivables before year-end 2015. The company also paid $60,000 cash for 2015 wages.

a. Compute the company's net income for 2015.

b. Suppose you discover that employees had earned an additional $10,000 in wages in 2015, but this amount had not been paid. Would 2015 net income change? If so, by how much?

M2-21. Classifying Items in Financial Statements

LO1, 3, 5

Next to each item, indicate whether it would most likely be reported on the balance sheet (B), the income statement (I), or the statement of stockholders' equity (SE).

a.	Liabilities	_____	*d.*	Revenues	_____	*g.*	Assets	_____
b.	Net income	_____	*e.*	Stock issuance	_____	*h.*	Expenses	_____
c.	Cash	_____	*f.*	Dividends	_____	*i.*	Equity	_____

M2-22. Classifying Items in Financial Statements

LO1, 3, 4, 5

For each of the following items, indicate whether it is most likely reported on the balance sheet (B), the income statement (I), or the statement of stockholders' equity (SE).

a. Accounts receivable	_____	*e.* Notes payable	_____
b. Prepaid rent	_____	*f.* Supplies expense	_____
c. Net income	_____	*g.* Land	_____
d. Stockholders' equity	_____	*h.* Supplies	_____

LO1, 3, 4, 5

M2-23. Classifying Items in Financial Statements

For each of the following items, indicate whether it is most likely reported on the balance sheet (B), the income statement (I), or the statement of stockholders' equity (SE).

a. Cash (year-end balance)	_____	*e.* Dividends	_____
b. Advertising expense	_____	*f.* Accounts payable	_____
c. Common stock	_____	*g.* Inventory	_____
d. Printing fees earned	_____	*h.* Equipment	_____

LO1, 5

L Brands, Inc.
NYSE :: LB

M2-24. Determining Company Performance and Retained Earnings Using the Accounting Equation

Use your knowledge of accounting relations to complete the following table for **L Brands, Inc.** (All amounts in $ millions.)

Fiscal year ending	February 2, 2013	February 1, 2014
Beginning retained earnings (deficit)	$ 24	$(672)
Net income (loss)	?	903
Dividends paid	(1,449)	?
Ending retained earnings (deficit)	$?	$(118)

LO1, 4

M2-25. Analyzing the Effect of Transactions on the Balance Sheet

Following the example in *a* below, indicate the effects of transactions *b* through *i* on assets, liabilities, and equity, including identifying the individual accounts affected.

a. Rendered legal services to clients for cash
ANSWER: Increase assets (Cash)
Increase equity (Service Revenues)

b. Purchased office supplies on account
c. Issued additional common stock in exchange for cash
d. Paid amount due on account for office supplies purchased in *b*
e. Borrowed cash (and signed a six-month note) from bank
f. Rendered legal services and billed clients
g. Paid cash to acquire a desk lamp for the office
h. Paid cash to cover interest on note payable to bank
i. Received invoice for this period's utilities

LO1, 4

M2-26. Analyzing the Effect of Transactions on the Balance Sheet

Following the example in *a* below, indicate the effects of transactions *b* through *i* on assets, liabilities, and equity, including identifying the individual accounts affected.

a. Paid cash to acquire a computer for use in office
ANSWER: Increase assets (Office Equipment)
Decrease assets (Cash)

b. Rendered services and billed client
c. Paid cash to cover rent for this period
d. Rendered services to client for cash
e. Received amount due from client in *b*
f. Purchased an office desk on account
g. Paid cash to cover this period's employee salaries
h. Paid cash to cover desk purchased in *f*
i. Declared and paid a cash dividend

M2-27. Constructing a Retained Earnings Reconciliation from Financial Data LO1, 5

Johnson & Johnson
NYSE :: JNJ

Following is financial information from **Johnson & Johnson** for the year ended December 28, 2014. Prepare the 2014 fiscal-year retained earnings reconciliation for Johnson & Johnson ($ millions).

Retained earnings, Dec. 29, 2013	$89,493	Dividends	$7,768
Net earnings	16,323	Retained earnings, Dec. 28, 2014	?
Other retained earnings changes	$ (803)		

M2-28. Analyzing Transactions to Compute Net Income LO3, 4

Guay Corp., a start-up company, provided services that were acceptable to its customers and billed those customers for $350,000 in 2015. However, Guay collected only $280,000 cash in 2015, and the remaining $70,000 of 2015 revenues were collected in 2016. Guay employees earned $200,000 in 2015 wages that were not paid until the first week of 2016. How much net income does Guay report for 2015? For 2016 (assuming no new transactions)?

M2-29. Analyzing Transactions Using the Financial Statement Effects Template LO1, 2

Report the effects for each of the following independent transactions using the financial statement effects template. If no entry should be made, answer "No entry."

	Balance Sheet									*Income Statement*				
Transaction	Cash Asset	+	Noncash Assets	=	Liabil-ities	+	Contrib. Capital	+	Earned Capital	*Revenues*	-	*Expenses*	=	*Net Income*
a. Issue common stock for $20,000 cash.				=							-		=	
b. Pay $2,000 rent in advance.				=							-		=	
c. Purchase computer equipment for $7,000 cash.				=							-		=	
d. Purchase and receive $13,000 of inventory on account (i.e., pay supplier later)				=							-		=	
e. Pay supplier of inventory in part (d)				=							-		=	

M2-30. Analyzing Transactions Using the Financial Statement Effects Template LO1, 2

Report the effects for each of the following independent transactions using the financial statement effects template. If no entry should be made, answer "No entry."

	Balance Sheet									*Income Statement*				
Transaction	Cash Asset	+	Noncash Assets	=	Liabil-ities	+	Contrib. Capital	+	Earned Capital	*Revenues*	-	*Expenses*	=	*Net Income*
a. Borrow €19,000 from local bank.				=							-		=	
b. Pay €3,000 insurance premium for coverage for following year.				=							-		=	
c. Purchase vehicle for €32,000 cash.				=							-		=	

continued

continued from previous page

Transaction	Cash Asset	+	Noncash Assets	=	Liabil-ities	+	Contrib. Capital	+	Earned Capital	Revenues	-	Expenses	=	Net Income
d. Purchase and receive €2,500 of office supplies on account (i.e., pay supplier later).				=							-		=	
e. Place order for €1,000 of additional supplies to be delivered next month.				=							-		=	

LO1, 2, 3, 4 **M2-31. Analyzing Transactions Using the Financial Statement Effects Template**

Report the effects for each of the following independent transactions using the financial statement effects template. If no entry should be made, answer "No entry."

Transaction	Cash Asset	+	Noncash Assets	=	Liabil-ities	+	Contrib. Capital	+	Earned Capital	Revenues	-	Expenses	=	Net Income
a. Receive merchandise inventory costing $9,000, purchased with cash.				=							-		=	
b. Sell half of inventory in (a) for $7,500 on credit.				=							-		=	
c. Place order for $5,000 of additional merchandise inventory to be delivered next month.				=							-		=	
d. Pay employee $4,000 for compensation earned during the month.				=							-		=	
e. Pay $7,000 rent for use of premises during the month.				=							-		=	
f. Receive full payment from customer in part (b).				=							-		=	

(Balance Sheet: Cash Asset through Earned Capital; Income Statement: Revenues through Net Income)

LO6 **M2-32. Journalizing Business Transactions**

Refer to the transactions in M2-31. Prepare journal entries for each of the transactions (*a*) through (*f*).

LO6 **M2-33. Posting to T-Accounts**

Refer to the transactions in M2-31. Set up T-accounts for each of the accounts referenced by the transactions and post the amounts for each transaction to those T-accounts.

EXERCISES

LO1, 7 **E2-34. Constructing Balance Sheets and Computing Working Capital**

The following balance sheet data are reported for Beaver, Inc., at May 31, 2015.

Accounts receivable	$18,300	Accounts payable	$ 5,200
Notes payable	20,000	Cash	12,200
Equipment	55,000	Common stock	42,500
Supplies	16,400	Retained earnings	?

Assume that on June 1, 2015, only the following two transactions occurred.

June 1 Purchased additional equipment costing \$15,000, giving \$2,000 cash and a \$13,000 note payable.
Declared and paid a \$7,000 cash dividend.

a. Prepare its balance sheet at May 31, 2015.
b. Prepare its balance sheet at June 1, 2015.
c. Calculate its net working capital at June 1, 2015. (Assume that Notes Payable are noncurrent.)

E2-35. Applying the Accounting Equation to Determine Missing Data LO1, 3, 5

For each of the four separate situations *1* through *4* below, compute the unknown amounts referenced by the letters *a* through *d* shown.

	1	2	3	4
Beginning				
Assets	\$28,000	\$12,000	\$28,000	\$ (d)
Liabilities	18,600	5,000	19,000	9,000
Ending				
Assets	30,000	26,000	34,000	40,000
Liabilities	17,300	(b)	15,000	19,000
During Year				
Common Stock Issued	2,000	4,500	(c)	3,500
Revenues	(a)	28,000	18,000	24,000
Expenses	8,500	21,000	11,000	17,000
Cash Dividends Paid	5,000	1,500	1,000	6,500

E2-36. Preparing Balance Sheets, Computing Income, and Applying the Current and Quick Ratios LO1, 5, 7

Balance sheet information for Lang Services at the end of 2014 and 2015 is:

	December 31, 2015	December 31, 2014
Accounts receivable	\$22,800	\$17,500
Notes payable	1,800	1,600
Cash	10,000	8,000
Equipment	32,000	27,000
Supplies	4,700	4,200
Accounts payable	25,000	25,000
Stockholders' equity	?	?

a. Prepare its balance sheet for December 31 of each year.
b. Lang Services raised \$5,000 cash through issuing additional common stock early in 2015, and it declared and paid a \$17,000 cash dividend in December 2015. Compute its net income or loss for 2015.
c. Calculate the current ratio and quick ratio for 2015.
d. Assume the industry average is 1.5 for the current ratio and 1.0 for the quick ratio. Comment on Lang's current and quick ratios relative to the industry.

E2-37. Constructing Balance Sheets and Determining Income LO1, 3, 5

Following is balance sheet information for Lynch Services at the end of 2014 and 2015.

	December 31, 2015	December 31, 2014
Accounts payable	\$ 6,000	\$ 9,000
Cash	23,000	20,000
Accounts receivable	42,000	33,000
Land	40,000	40,000
Building	250,000	260,000
Equipment	43,000	45,000
Mortgage payable	90,000	100,000
Supplies	20,000	18,000
Common stock	220,000	220,000
Retained earnings	?	?

a. Prepare balance sheets at December 31 of each year.

b. The firm declared and paid a cash dividend of $10,000 in December 2015. Compute its net income for 2015.

LO1, 7 Homework MBC

E2-38. Constructing Balance Sheets and Applying the Current and Quick Ratios

The following balance sheet data are reported for Brownlee Catering at September 30, 2015.

Accounts receivable	$17,000	Accounts payable	$24,000
Notes payable	12,000	Cash	10,000
Equipment	34,000	Common stock	27,500
Supplies inventory	9,000	Retained earnings	?

Assume that on October 1, 2015, only the following two transactions occurred:

October 1 Purchased additional equipment costing $11,000, giving $3,000 cash and signing an $8,000 note payable.
Declared and paid a cash dividend of $3,000.

REQUIRED

a. Prepare Brownlee Catering's balance sheet at September 30, 2015.

b. Prepare the company's balance sheet at the close of business on October 1, 2015.

c. Calculate Brownlee's current and quick ratios on September 30 and October 1. (Assume that Notes Payable are noncurrent.)

d. The October 1, 2015 transactions have decreased Brownlee's current and quick ratios, reflecting a decline in liquidity. Identify two transactions that would increase the company's liquidity.

LO1, 3, 4 

E2-39. Constructing Financial Statements from Transaction Data

Baiman Corporation commences operations at the beginning of January. It provides its services on credit and bills its customers $30,000 for January sales to be collected in February. Its employees also earn January wages of $12,000 that are not paid until the first of February. Complete the following statements for the month-end of January.

Income Statement		Balance Sheet	
Sales	$	Cash	$ 8,000
Wages expense		Accounts receivable	
Net income (loss)	$	Total assets	$
		Wages payable	$
		Common stock	8,000
		Retained earnings	
		Total liabilities and equity	$

LO1, 3 

Procter & Gamble
NYSE :: PG

E2-40. Classifying Balance Sheet and Income Statement Accounts

Following are selected accounts for **The Procter & Gamble Company** for June 30, 2014.

($ millions)	Amount	Classification
Net sales	$83,062	
Income tax expense	3,178	
Retained earnings	84,990	
Net earnings	11,785	
Property, plant & equipment (net)	22,304	
Selling, general & administrative expense	25,314	
Accounts receivable	6,386	
Total liabilities	74,290	
Stockholders' equity	69,976	
Net earnings from continuing operations	11,707	

a. Indicate the appropriate classification of each account as appearing in either its balance sheet (B) or its income statement (I).

b. Using the data, compute its amount for total assets.

E2-41. Classifying Balance Sheet and Income Statement Accounts and Computing Current Ratio LO1, 3, 7

Shoprite Holdings Ltd
JSE :: SHP

Shoprite Holdings Ltd is an African food retailer listed on the Johannesburg Stock Exchange. The following accounts are selected from its annual report for the fiscal year ended June 30, 2014. The amounts below are in millions of South African Rand.

(Rand millions)	Amount	Classification
Sales of merchandise	R 102,204	
Depreciation and amortisation	1,730	
Reserves (Retained earnings)	13,218	
Property, plant and equipment	13,576	
Cost of goods and services	86,444	
Trade and other payables	16,332	
Total equity and liabilities	40,533	
Total equity	17,283	
Salaries, wages and service benefits	8,373	
Total non-current assets	15,730	
Total non-current liabilities	5,531	

a. Indicate the appropriate classification of each account as appearing in either its balance sheet (B) or its income statement (I). (Note: Shoprite presents a "Value-added Statement" in lieu of an income statement, but it provides the same information as an income statement.)

b. Using the data, compute Shoprite's total assets at June 30, 2014.

c. Calculate Shoprite's current ratio as of June 30, 2014.

E2-42. Classifying Balance Sheet and Income Statement Accounts and Computing Quick Ratio LO1, 3, 7

El Puerto de Liverpool
OTCMKTS :: ELPQF

El Puerto de Liverpool (Liverpool) is a large retailer in Mexico. The following accounts are selected from its annual report for the fiscal year ended December 31, 2013. The amounts below are in thousands of Mexican pesos.

(Pesos thousands)	Amount	Classification
Total revenue	$74,105,444	
Retained earnings	50,347,782	
Inventory	11,421,969	
Administration expenses	19,397,781	
Total assets	94,936,904	
Long-term loans from financial institutions	921,456	
Financing costs	1,088,892	
Total current assets	37,556,611	
Total stockholders' equity	54,827,332	
Prepaid expenses	617,387	
Total non-current liabilities	14,483,101	

a. Indicate the appropriate classification of each account as appearing in either its balance sheet (B) or its income statement (I).

b. Determine Liverpool's total liabilities and current liabilities as of December 31, 2013.

c. Calculate Liverpool's quick ratio as of December 31, 2013. (Assume that Liverpool only has five types of current assets—cash, marketable securities, accounts receivable, inventory and prepaid expenses.)

E2-43. Classifying Balance Sheet and Income Statement Accounts and Computing Debt-to-Equity LO1, 3

Kimberly-Clark
NYSE :: KMB

Following are selected accounts for **Kimberly-Clark Corporation** for 2014.

($ millions)	Amount	Classification
Net sales	$19,724	
Cost of goods sold	13,041	
Retained earnings	8,470	
Net income	1,595	
Property, plant & equipment, net	7,359	
Marketing research and general expenses	3,709	
Accounts receivable, net	2,223	
Total liabilities	14,527	
Total stockholders' equity	999	

a. Indicate the appropriate classification of each account as appearing in either its balance sheet (B) or its income statement (I).

b. Using the data, compute its amounts for total assets and for total expenses.

c. Compute Kimberly-Clark's debt-to-equity ratio. (Debt-to-equity was defined in Chapter 1.)

LO1, 2, 3, 4

E2-44. Analyzing Transactions Using the Financial Statement Effects Template
Record the effect of each of the following independent transactions using the financial statements effects template provided. Confirm that Assets = Liabilities + Equity for each transaction.

Transaction	Balance Sheet: Cash Asset	+	Noncash Assets	=	Liabil-ities	+	Contrib. Capital	+	Earned Capital	Income Statement: Revenues	−	Expenses	=	Net Income
(1) Receive €50,000 in exchange for common stock.				=							−		=	
(2) Borrow €10,000 from bank.				=							−		=	
(3) Purchase €2,000 of supplies inventory on credit.				=							−		=	
(4) Receive €15,000 cash from customers for services provided.				=							−		=	
(5) Pay €2,000 cash to supplier in transaction 3.				=							−		=	
(6) Receive order for future services with €3,500 advance payment.				=							−		=	
(7) Pay €5,000 cash dividend to shareholders.				=							−		=	
(8) Pay employees €6,000 cash for compensation earned.				=							−		=	
(9) Pay €500 cash for interest on loan in transaction 2.				=							−		=	
Totals				=							−		=	

LO6

E2-45. Recording Transactions Using Journal Entries and T-Accounts
Use the information in Exercise 2-44 to complete the following.

a. Prepare journal entries for each of the transactions (1) through (9).

b. Set up T-accounts for each of the accounts used in part *a* and post the journal entries to those T-accounts. (The T-accounts will not have opening balances.)

LO1, 7

E2-46. Constructing Balance Sheets and Intrepreting Liquidity Measures
The following balance sheet data are reported for Bettis Contractors at June 30, 2015.

Accounts payable.	$ 8,900	Common stock.	$100,000
Cash	14,700	Retained earnings	?
Supplies	30,500	Notes payable	30,000
Equipment	98,000	Accounts receivable.	9,200
Land	25,000		

Assume that during the next two days only the following three transactions occurred:

July 1 Paid $5,000 cash toward the notes payable owed.
2 Purchased equipment for $10,000, paying $2,000 cash and an $8,000 note payable for the remaining balance.
2 Declared and paid a $5,500 cash dividend.

a. Prepare a balance sheet at June 30, 2015.
b. Prepare a balance sheet at July 2, 2015.
c. Calculate its current and quick ratios at June 30, 2015. (Notes Payable is a noncurrent liability.)
d. Assume the industry average is 3.0 for the current ratio and 2.0 for the quick ratio. Comment on Bettis's current and quick ratios relative to the industry.

E2-47. Analyzing Transactions Using the Financial Statement Effects Template LO1, 2, 3, 4

Record the effect of each of the following independent transactions using the financial statement effects template provided. Confirm that Assets = Liabilities + Equity.

	Balance Sheet									Income Statement				
Transaction	Cash Asset	+	Noncash Assets	=	Liabil-ities	+	Contrib. Capital	+	Earned Capital	Revenues	-	Expenses	=	Net Income
(1) Receive $20,000 cash in exchange for common stock.				=							-		=	
(2) Purchase $2,000 of inventory on credit.				=							-		=	
(3) Sell inventory for $3,000 on credit.				=							-		=	
(4) Record $2,000 for cost of inventory sold in 3.				=							-		=	
(5) Collect $3,000 cash from transaction 3.				=							-		=	
(6) Acquire $5,000 of equipment by signing a note.				=							-		=	
(7) Pay wages of $1,000 in cash.				=							-		=	
(8) Pay $5,000 on a note payable that came due.				=							-		=	
(9) Pay $2,000 cash dividend.				=							-		=	
Totals				=							-		=	

E2-48. Recording Transactions Using Journal Entries and T-Accounts LO6

Use the information in Exercise 2-47 to complete the following.

a. Prepare journal entries for each of the transactions 1 through 9.
b. Set up T-accounts for each of the accounts used in part *a* and post the journal entries to those T-accounts. (The T-accounts will not have opening balances.)

PROBLEMS

LO1, 3

Comcast Corporation
NASDAQ :: CMCSA
Apple Inc.
NASDAQ :: AAPL
Nike, Inc.
NYSE :: NKE
Target Corporation
NYSE :: TGT
Harley-Davidson, Inc.
NYSE :: HOG

P2-49. Comparing Operating Characteristics Across Industries

Review the following selected income statement and balance sheet data for fiscal years ending in 2014.

($ millions)	Sales	Cost of Sales	Gross Profit	Net Income	Assets	Liabilities	Equity
Comcast Corporation . . .	$ 68,775	$ 20,912	$47,863	$ 8,592	$159,339	$106,628	$ 52,711
Apple Inc.	182,795	112,258	70,537	39,510	231,839	120,292	111,547
Nike Inc.	27,799	15,353	12,446	2,693	18,594	7,770	10,824
Target Corporation	72,618	51,278	21,340	(1,636)	41,404	27,407	13,997
Harley-Davidson Inc. . . .	6,229	3,707	2,522	845	9,528	6,619	2,909

REQUIRED

a. Compare and discuss how these companies finance their operations.
b. Which companies report the highest ratio of income to assets (net income/total assets)? Suggest a reason for this result.
c. Which companies have the highest estimated ROE? Is this result a surprise? Explain.

LO1, 3

Hewlett-Packard Company
NYSE :: HPQ

P2-50. Comparing Operating Characteristics Within an Industry

Selected data from **Hewlett-Packard Company** at October 31, 2014, follow.

($ millions)	Sales	Cost of Sales	Gross Profit	Net Income	Assets	Liabilities	Equity
Hewlett-Packard.	$111,454	$84,839	$26,615	$5,013	$103,206	$76,475	$26,731

REQUIRED

Apple inc.
NASDAQ :: AAPL

a. Using the data for **Apple Inc.** in P2-49, compare and discuss the two companies on the basis of how they finance their operations.
b. Which company reports the higher ratio of income to assets (net income/total assets)? Suggest a reason for this result.
c. Which firm has the higher gross margin (gross profit as a percentage of sales)? What factors might account for the difference?

LO1, 3

Verizon Communications Inc.
NYSE :: VZ

P2-51. Comparing Operating Characteristics Within an Industry

Review the following selected income statement and balance sheet data for **Verizon Communications Inc.** as of December 31, 2014.

($ millions)	Sales	Cost of Sales	Gross Profit	Net Income	Assets	Liabilities	Equity
Verizon Communications Inc. . . .	$127,079	$49,931	$77,148	$9,625	$232,708	$220,410	$12,298

REQUIRED

Comcast Corporation
NASDAQ :: CMCSA

a. Using the data for **Comcast Corporation** in P2-49, compare and discuss how Verizon and Comcast finance their operations.
b. Which company reports the higher ratio of income to assets (net income/total assets)? Suggest a reason for this result.
c. Which company is likely better able to raise capital? Explain.

LO1, 7

P2-52. Comparing Operating Structure Across Industries

Review the following selected income statement and balance sheet data from the fiscal years ending in 2014 and 2015.

($ millions)	Current Assets	Non-current Assets	Total Assets	Current Liab.	Non-current Liab.	Total Liab.	Equity
3M*	$11,765	$ 19,504	$ 31,269	$ 5,998	$12,162	$ 18,160	$ 13,109
Abercrombie & Fitch**	1,165	1,340	2,505	486	629	1,115	1,390
Apple†	68,531	163,308	231,839	63,448	56,844	120,292	111,547

* Manufacturer of consumer and business products
** Retailer of name-brand apparel at premium prices
† Computer company

3M Company
NYSE :: MMM
Abercrombie & Fitch Co.
NYSE :: ANF
Apple Inc.
NYSE :: AAPL

REQUIRED

a. Compare and discuss how these companies finance their operations.

b. Which company has the greatest net working capital? Which company has the highest current ratio? Do you have any concerns about any firm's net working capital position? Explain.

P2-53. Preparing a Balance Sheet, Computing Net Income, and Understanding Equity Transactions

LO1, 5

At the beginning of 2015, Barth Company reported the following balance sheet.

Assets		Liabilities	
Cash	$ 4,800	Accounts payable	$12,000
Accounts receivable	14,700	Equity	
Equipment	10,000	Common stock	47,500
Land	50,000	Retained earnings	20,000
Total assets	$79,500	Total liabilities and equity	$79,500

REQUIRED

a. At the end of 2015, Barth Company reported the following assets and liabilities: Cash, $8,800; Accounts Receivable, $18,400; Equipment, $9,000; Land, $50,000; and Accounts Payable, $7,500. Prepare a year-end balance sheet for Barth. (*Hint:* Report equity as a single total.)

b. Assuming that Barth did not issue any common stock during the year but paid $12,000 cash in dividends, what was its net income or net loss for 2015?

c. Assuming that Barth issued an additional $13,500 common stock early in the year but paid $21,000 cash in dividends before the end of the year, what was its net income or net loss for 2015?

P2-54. Analyzing and Interpreting the Financial Performance of Competitors

LO1, 3

Abercrombie & Fitch Co.
NYSE :: ANF
Nordstrom, Inc.
NYSE :: JWN

Abercrombie & Fitch Co. and **Nordstrom, Inc.**, are major retailers that concentrate in the higher-end clothing lines. Following are selected data from their 2014 fiscal-year ended January 31, 2015, financial statements:

($ millions)	ANF	JWN
Total liabilities and equity	$2,505	$ 9,245
Net income	52	720
Net sales	3,744	13,506
Total liabilities	1,115	6,805

REQUIRED

a. What is the total amount of assets invested in (1) ANF and (2) JWN? What are the total expenses for each company (1) in dollars and (2) as a percentage of sales?

b. What is the return on equity (ROE) for (1) ANF and (2) JWN? ANF's total equity at the beginning of 2014 is $1,729 million and JWN's beginning 2014 equity is $2,080 million. (ROE was defined in Chapter 1.)

P2-55. Analyzing Balance Sheet Numbers from Incomplete Data and Interpreting Liquidity Measures

LO1, 7
Kimberly-Clark Corp
NYSE :: KMB

Selected balance sheet amounts for **Kimberly-Clark Corp**, a consumer products company, for four recent years follow:

($ millions)	Current Assets	Non-current Assets	Total Assets	Current Liabilities	Non-current Liabilities	Total Liabilities	Equity
2011	$?	$13,090	$19,373	$5,397	$8,727	$14,124	$?
2012	6,589	13,284	?	?	8,797	?	4,985
2013	6,550	?	18,919	5,848	?	?	4,856
2014	?	9,967	15,526	6,226	?	14,797	?

REQUIRED

a. Compute the missing balance sheet amounts for each of the four years shown.
b. What types of accounts would you expect to be included in current assets? In noncurrent assets?
c. Calculate Kimberly-Clark's working capital and current ratio for 2011 and 2014.
d. Assume that the industry average is 2.0 for the current ratio. Comment on Kimberly-Clark's liquidity measures relative to the industry.

LO1, 7
Sears Holdings Corp.
NASDAQ :: SHLD

P2-56. Analyzing and Interpreting Balance Sheet Data and Interpreting Liquidity Measures
Selected balance sheet amounts for **Sears Holdings Corp.**, a retail company, for four recent fiscal years follow:

($ millions)	Current Assets	Non-current Assets	Total Assets	Current Liabilities	Non-current Liabilities	Total Liabilities	Equity
2011	$10,244	$11,137	$?	$9,212	$7,888	$17,100	$?
2012	?	10,075	19,340	?	8,171	16,585	?
2013	8,959	?	18,261	8,185	?	16,522	1,739
2014	5,863	7,346	?	6,076	?	14,160	?

REQUIRED

a. Compute the missing balance sheet amounts for each of the four years shown.
b. What asset category do you expect to constitute the majority of the company's current assets?
c. Calculate SHLD's current ratio for fiscal years 2011 and 2014.
d. Recent popular press articles have described SHLD's declining sales and deteriorating financial condition. What indications of financial deterioration do you see in the balance sheet numbers?

LO1, 2, 3, 4
Homework MBC

P2-57. Analyzing Transactions Using the Financial Statement Effects Template and Preparing an Income Statement
On December 1, 2015, R. Lambert formed Lambert Services, which provides career and vocational counseling services to graduating college students. The following transactions took place during December, and company accounts include the following: Cash, Accounts Receivable, Land, Accounts Payable, Notes Payable, Common Stock, Retained Earnings, Counseling Services Revenue, Rent Expense, Advertising Expense, Interest Expense, Salary Expense, and Utilities Expense.

1. Raised $7,000 cash through common stock issuance.
2. Paid $750 cash for December rent on its furnished office space.
3. Received $500 invoice for December advertising expenses.
4. Borrowed $15,000 cash from bank and signed note payable for that amount.
5. Received $1,200 cash for counseling services rendered.
6. Billed clients $6,800 for counseling services rendered.
7. Paid $2,200 cash for secretary salary.
8. Paid $370 cash for December utilities.
9. Declared and paid a $900 cash dividend.
10. Purchased land for $13,000 cash to use for its own facilities.
11. Paid $100 cash to bank as December interest expense on note payable.

REQUIRED

a. Report the effects for each of the separate transactions 1 through 11 using the financial statement effects template. Total all columns and prove that (1) assets equal liabilities plus equity at December 31, and (2) revenues less expenses equal net income for December.
b. Prepare an income statement for the month of December.

P2-58. Recording Transactions in Journal Entries and T-Accounts LO6

Homework MBC

Use the information in Problem 2-57 to complete the following requirements.

REQUIRED

a. Prepare journal entries for each of the transactions 1 through 11.

b. Set up T-accounts for each of the accounts used in part *a* and post the journal entries to those T-accounts.

P2-59. Analyzing and Interpreting Balance Sheet Data and Interpreting Liquidity Measures LO1, 7

Apple Inc.
NYSE :: AAPL

Selected balance sheet amounts for **Apple Inc.**, a retail company, for four recent fiscal years follow:

($ millions)	Current Assets	Non-current Assets	Total Assets	Current Liabilities	Non-current Liabilities	Total Liabilities	Stockholders' Equity
2011	$44,988	$?	$116,371	$?	$11,786	$ 39,756	$ 76,615
2012	57,653	118,411	?	38,542	?	57,854	118,210
2013	73,286	133,714	?	?	39,793	83,451	?
2014	?	163,308	231,839	63,448	?	120,292	111,547

REQUIRED

a. Compute the missing balance sheet amounts for each of the four years shown.

b. What asset category would you expect to constitute the majority of Apple's current assets? Of its long-term assets?

c. Is the company conservatively financed; that is, is it financed by a greater proportion of equity than of debt?

d. Calculate the current ratio for 2011 and 2014.

e. Assume the industry average is 2.0 for the current ratio. Comment on Apple's current ratio relative to the industry.

P2-60. Analyzing Balance Sheet Numbers from Incomplete Data and Interpreting Liquidity Measures LO1, 7

Alibaba Group Holding Ltd
NYSE :: BABA

Selected balance sheet amounts for **Alibaba Group Holding Ltd**, a China-based online and mobile commerce company, for three recent fiscal years follow:

(millions of RMB)	Current Assets	Non-current Assets	Total Assets	Current Liabilities	Non-current Liabilities	Total Liabilities	Equity
2012	$27,899	$?	$?	$11,751	$?	$15,692	$31,518
2013	?	20,624	63,786	?	29,282	53,277	10,509
2014	?	43,716	111,549	37,384	34,426	?	?

REQUIRED

a. Compute the missing balance sheet amounts for each of the three years shown.

b. What asset category do you expect to constitute the majority of the company's current assets?

c. Calculate Alibaba's current ratio for fiscal years 2012 and 2014.

d. Calculate net working capital for 2012 and 2014.

P2-61. Analyzing and Interpreting Income Statement Data LO3

Nike, Inc.
NYSE :: NKE

Selected income statement information for **Nike, Inc.**, a manufacturer of athletic footwear, for four recent fiscal years follows.

($ millions)	Revenues	Cost of Goods Sold	Gross Profit	Operating Expenses	Operating Income	Other Expenses	Net Income
2011	$20,117	$10,915	$?	$6,361	$2,841	$708	$?
2012	23,331	?	10,148	7,079	3,069	?	2,211
2013	?	14,279	11,034	7,796	3,238	766	?
2014	27,799	15,353	12,446	?	3,680	?	2,693

REQUIRED

a. Compute the missing amounts for each of the four years shown.

b. Compute the gross profit margin (gross profit/sales) for each of the four years and comment on its level and any trends that are evident.

c. What would you expect to be the major cost categories constituting its operating expenses?

LO1, 2, 3, 4 **P2-62. Analyzing Transactions Using the Financial Statement Effects Template and Preparing an Income Statement**

On June 1, 2015, a group of pilots in Melbourne, Australia, formed Outback Flights by issuing common stock for $50,000 cash. The group then leased several amphibious aircraft and docking facilities, equipping them to transport campers and hunters to outpost camps owned by various resorts in remote parts of Australia. The following transactions occurred during June 2015, and company accounts include the following: Cash, Accounts Receivable, Prepaid Insurance, Accounts Payable, Common Stock, Retained Earnings, Flight Services Revenue, Rent Expense, Entertainment Expense, Advertising Expense, Insurance Expense, Wages Expense, and Fuel Expense.

1. Issued common stock for $50,000 cash.
2. Paid $4,800 cash for June rent of aircraft, dockage, and dockside office.
3. Received $1,600 invoice for the cost of a reception to entertain resort owners in June.
4. Paid $900 cash for June advertising in various sport magazines.
5. Paid $1,800 cash for insurance premium for July.
6. Rendered flight services for various groups for $22,700 cash.
7. Billed client $2,900 for transporting personnel, and billed various firms for $13,000 in flight services.
8. Paid $1,500 cash to cover accounts payable.
9. Received $13,200 on account from clients in transaction 7.
10. Paid $16,000 cash to cover June wages.
11. Received $3,500 invoice for the cost of fuel used during June.
12. Declared and paid a $3,000 cash dividend.

REQUIRED

a. Report the effects for each of the separate transactions 1 through 12 using the financial statement effects template. Total all columns and prove that (1) assets equal liabilities plus equity at June 30, 2015, and (2) revenues less expenses equal net income for June.

b. Prepare an income statement for the month of June.

LO6 **P2-63. Recording Transactions in Journal Entries and T-Accounts**

Use the information in Problem 2-62 to complete the following requirements.

REQUIRED

a. Prepare journal entries for each of the transactions 1 through 12.

b. Set up T-accounts for each of the accounts used in part *a* and post the journal entries to those T-accounts.

LO3 Homework MBC **P2-64. Analyzing and Interpreting Income Statement Numbers from Incomplete Data**

Starbucks Corporation
NASDAQ :: SBUX

Selected income statement information for **Starbucks Corporation**, a coffee-related restaurant chain, for four recent fiscal years follows.

($ millions)	Revenues	Cost of Revenues	Gross Profit	Operating Expenses	Operating Income	Other Expenses	Net Income
2011	$?	$ 8,510	$3,190	$?	$1,729	$ 483	$?
2012	13,277	?	3,545	?	?	614	1,384
2013	14,867	10,668	?	4,400	(201)	?	9
2014	?	11,497	4,951	1,870	3,081	1,013	?

REQUIRED

a. Compute the missing amounts for each of the four years shown.

b. Compute the gross profit margin (gross profit/sales) for each of the four years and comment on its level and any trends that are evident.

c. What would you expect to be the major cost categories constituting its operating expenses?

LO3 **P2-65. Analyzing, Reconstructing, and Interpreting Income Statement Data**

Siemens AG
OTCMKTS :: SIEGY

Selected income statement information for **Siemens AG**, a global technology company, for four fiscal years follows:

($ millions)	Revenues	Cost of Goods Sold	Gross Profit	Operating Expenses	Operating Income	Other Expense	Net Income
2011	€73,275	€51,046	€ ?	€ ?	€8,217	€ ?	€6,145
2012	?	55,470	21,925	15,210	6,715	2,565	?
2013	73,445	?	20,135	?	5,177	?	4,284
2014	71,920	51,165	?	14,038	?	1,344	5,373

REQUIRED

a. Compute the missing amounts for each of the four years shown.

b. Compute the gross profit margin (gross profit/sales) for each of the four years and comment on its level and any trends that are evident.

c. What would we expect to be the major cost categories constituting Siemens' operating expenses?

P2-66. Preparing the Income Statement, Statement of Stockholders' Equity, and the Balance Sheet LO1, 3, 5

The records of Geyer, Inc., show the following information after all transactions are recorded for 2015.

Notes payable	$ 4,000	Supplies	$ 6,100
Service fees earned	67,600	Cash	14,800
Supplies expense..............	9,700	Advertising expense...........	1,700
Insurance expense.............	1,500	Salaries expense	30,000
Miscellaneous expense	200	Rent expense.................	7,500
Common stock (beg. year).......	4,000	Retained earnings (beg. year).....	6,200
Accounts payable..............	1,800		

Geyer, Inc., raised $1,400 cash through the issuance of additional common stock during this year and it declared and paid a $13,500 cash dividend near year-end.

REQUIRED

a. Prepare its income statement for 2015.

b. Prepare its statement of stockholders' equity for 2015.

c. Prepare its balance sheet at December 31, 2015.

P2-67. Analyzing Transactions Using the Financial Statement Effects Template and Preparing Financial Statements LO1, 2, 3, 4, 5

Schrand Aerobics, Inc., rents studio space (including a sound system) and specializes in offering aerobics classes. On January 1, 2015, its beginning account balances are as follows: Cash, $5,000; Accounts Receivable, $5,200; Equipment, $0; Notes Payable, $2,500; Accounts Payable, $1,000; Common Stock, $5,500; Retained Earnings, $1,200; Services Revenue, $0; Rent Expense, $0; Advertising Expense, $0; Wages Expense, $0; Utilities Expense, $0; Interest Expense, $0. The following transactions occurred during January.

1. Paid $600 cash toward accounts payable.
2. Paid $3,600 cash for January rent.
3. Billed clients $11,500 for January classes.
4. Received $500 invoice from supplier for T-shirts given to January class members as an advertising promotion.
5. Collected $10,000 cash from clients previously billed for services rendered.
6. Paid $2,400 cash for employee wages.
7. Received $680 invoice for January utilities expense.
8. Paid $20 cash to bank as January interest on notes payable.
9. Declared and paid $900 cash dividend to stockholders.
10. Paid $4,000 cash on January 31 to purchase sound equipment to replace the rental system.

REQUIRED

a. Using the financial statement effects template, enter January 1 beginning amounts in the appropriate columns of the first row. (*Hint:* Beginning balances for columns can include amounts from more than one account.)

b. Report the effects for each of the separate transactions *1* through *10* in the financial statement effects template set up in part *a*. Total all columns and prove that (1) assets equal liabilities plus equity at January 31, and (2) revenues less expenses equal net income for January.

c. Prepare its income statement for January 2015.

d. Prepare its statement of stockholders' equity for January 2015.

e. Prepare its balance sheet at January 31, 2015.

LO6 Homework MBC **P2-68. Recording Transactions in Journal Entries and T-Accounts**

Use the information in Problem 2-67 to complete the following requirements.

REQUIRED

a. Prepare journal entries for each of the transactions 1 through 10.

b. Set up T-accounts, including beginning balances, for each of the accounts used in part *a*. Post the journal entries to those T-accounts.

LO1, 2, 3, 4, 5 **P2-69. Analyzing Transactions Using the Financial Statement Effects Template and Preparing Financial Statements**

Kross, Inc., provides appraisals and feasibility studies. On January 1, 2015, its beginning account balances are as follows: Cash, $6,700; Accounts Receivable, $14,800; Notes Payable, $2,500; Accounts Payable, $600; Retained Earnings, $12,400; and Common Stock, $6,000. The following transactions occurred during January, and company accounts include the following: Cash, Accounts Receivable, Vehicles, Accounts Payable, Notes Payable, Services Revenue, Rent Expense, Interest Expense, Salary Expense, Utilities Expense, Common Stock, and Retained Earnings.

1. Paid $950 cash for January rent.
2. Received $8,800 cash on customers' accounts.
3. Paid $500 cash toward accounts payable.
4. Received $1,600 cash for services performed for customers.
5. Borrowed $5,000 cash from bank and signed note payable for that amount.
6. Billed the city $6,200 for services performed, and billed other credit customers for $1,900 in services.
7. Paid $4,000 cash for salary of assistant.
8. Received $410 invoice for January utilities expense.
9. Declared and paid a $6,000 cash dividend.
10. Paid $9,800 cash to acquire a vehicle (on January 31) for business use.
11. Paid $50 cash to bank for January interest on notes payable.

REQUIRED

a. Using the financial statement effects template, enter January 1 beginning amounts in the appropriate columns of the first row. (*Hint:* Beginning balances for columns can include amounts from more than one account.)

b. Report the effects for each of the separate transactions 1 through 11 in the financial statement effects template set up in part *a*. Total all columns and prove that (1) assets equal liabilities plus equity at January 31, and (2) revenues less expenses equal net income for January.

c. Prepare its income statement for January 2015.

d. Prepare its statement of stockholders' equity for January 2015.

e. Prepare its balance sheet at January 31, 2015.

LO6 **P2-70. Recording Transactions in Journal Entries and T-Accounts**

Use the information in Problem 2-69 to complete the following requirements.

REQUIRED

a. Prepare journal entries for each of the transactions 1 through 11.

b. Set up T-accounts, including beginning balances, for each of the accounts used in part *a*. Post the journal entries to those T-accounts.

CASES AND PROJECTS

LO1, 3, 4, 5 **C2-71. Constructing Financial Statements from Cash Data**

Sarah Penney operates the Wildlife Picture Gallery, selling original art and signed prints received on consignment (rather than purchased) from recognized wildlife artists throughout the country.

The firm receives a 30% commission on all art sold and remits 70% of the sales price to the artists. All art is sold on a strictly cash basis.

Sarah began the business on March 1, 2015. The business received a $10,000 loan from a relative of Sarah to help her get started; it took on a note payable agreeing to pay the loan back in one year. No interest is being charged on the loan, but the relative does want to receive a set of financial statements each month. On April 1, 2015, Sarah asks for your help in preparing the statements for the first month.

Sarah has carefully kept the firm's checking account up to date and provides you with the following complete listing of the cash receipts and cash disbursements for March 2015.

Cash Receipts	
Original investment by Sarah Penney	$ 6,500
Loan from relative	10,000
Sales of art	95,000
Total cash receipts	111,500
Cash Disbursements	
Payments to artists for sales made	54,000
Payment of March rent for gallery space	900
Payment of March wages to staff	4,900
Payment of airfare for personal vacation of Sarah (vacation will be in April)	500
Total cash disbursements	60,300
Cash balance, March 31, 2015	$ 51,200

Sarah also gives you the following documents she has received:

1. A $350 invoice for March utilities; payment is due by April 15, 2015.
2. A $1,700 invoice from Careful Express for the shipping of artwork sold in March; payment is due by April 10, 2015.
3. Sarah signed a one-year lease for the gallery space; as an incentive to sign the lease, the landlord reduced the first month's rent by 25%; the monthly rent starting in April is $1,200.

In your discussions with Sarah, she tells you that she has been so busy that she is behind in sending artists their share of the sales proceeds. She plans to catch up within the next week.

REQUIRED

From the above information, prepare the following financial statements for Wildlife Picture Gallery: (*a*) income statement for the month of March 2015; (*b*) statement of stockholders' equity for the month of March 2015; and (*c*) balance sheet as of March 31, 2015.

C2-72. Financial Records and Ethical Behavior LO3

Andrea Frame and her supervisor are sent on an out-of-town assignment by their employer. At the supervisor's suggestion, they stay at the Spartan Inn (across the street from the Luxury Inn). After three days of work, they settle their lodging bills and leave. On the return trip, the supervisor gives Andrea what appears to be a copy of a receipt from the Luxury Inn for three nights of lodging. Actually, the supervisor indicates that he prepared the Luxury Inn receipt on his office computer and plans to complete his expense reimbursement request using the higher lodging costs from the Luxury Inn.

REQUIRED

What are the ethical considerations that Andrea faces when she prepares her expense reimbursement request?

SOLUTIONS TO REVIEW PROBLEMS

Mid-Chapter Review 1

SOLUTION

1. A	2. C	3. B	4. E	5. B	6. E	7. X	8. B	9. E	10. B
11. X	12. A	13. B	14. C	15. A	16. D	17. A	18. A	19. E	20. C

Mid-Chapter Review 2

SOLUTION

Transaction	Cash Asset	+	Noncash Assets	=	Liabil-ities	+	Contrib. Capital	+	Earned Capital	Revenues	-	Expenses	=	Net Income
(a) Issue common stock for $20,000.	+20,000 Cash			=			+20,000 Common Stock				-		=	
(b) Purchase $8,000 of inventory on credit.			+8,000 Inventory	=	+8,000 Accounts Payable						-		=	
(c) Purchase equipment for $10,000 cash.	−10,000 Cash		+10,000 Equipment	=							-		=	
(d) Pay suppliers $3,000 cash.	−3,000 Cash			=	−3,000 Accounts Payable						-		=	
Totals	+7,000		+18,000	=	+5,000		+20,000							
	Assets			=	Liabilities	+	Equity							

Mid-Chapter Review 3

SOLUTION TO PART 1

SCHAEFER'S PHARMACY, INC.
Income Statement
For Year Ended December 31, 2015

Revenues		$45,000
Expenses		
Cost of goods sold	$20,000	
Wages expense	8,000	
Rent expense	5,000	
Utilities expense	2,000	
Other expenses	4,000	
Total expenses		39,000
Net income		$ 6,000

SOLUTION TO PART 2

SCHAEFER'S PHARMACY, INC.
Retained Earnings Reconciliation
For Year Ended December 31, 2015

Retained earnings, Dec. 31, 2014	$25,000
Add: Net income	6,000
Less: Dividends	(1,000)
Retained earnings, Dec. 31, 2015	$30,000

SOLUTION TO PART 3

SCHAEFER'S PHARMACY, INC. Balance Sheet December 31, 2015			
Cash	$ 3,000	Accounts payable	$ 7,500
Accounts receivable	12,000		
Inventory	26,000		
Office equipment	32,250	Common stock	45,750
Land	10,000	Retained earnings	30,000
Total assets	$83,250	Total liabilities and equity	$83,250

Chapter-End Review

SOLUTION

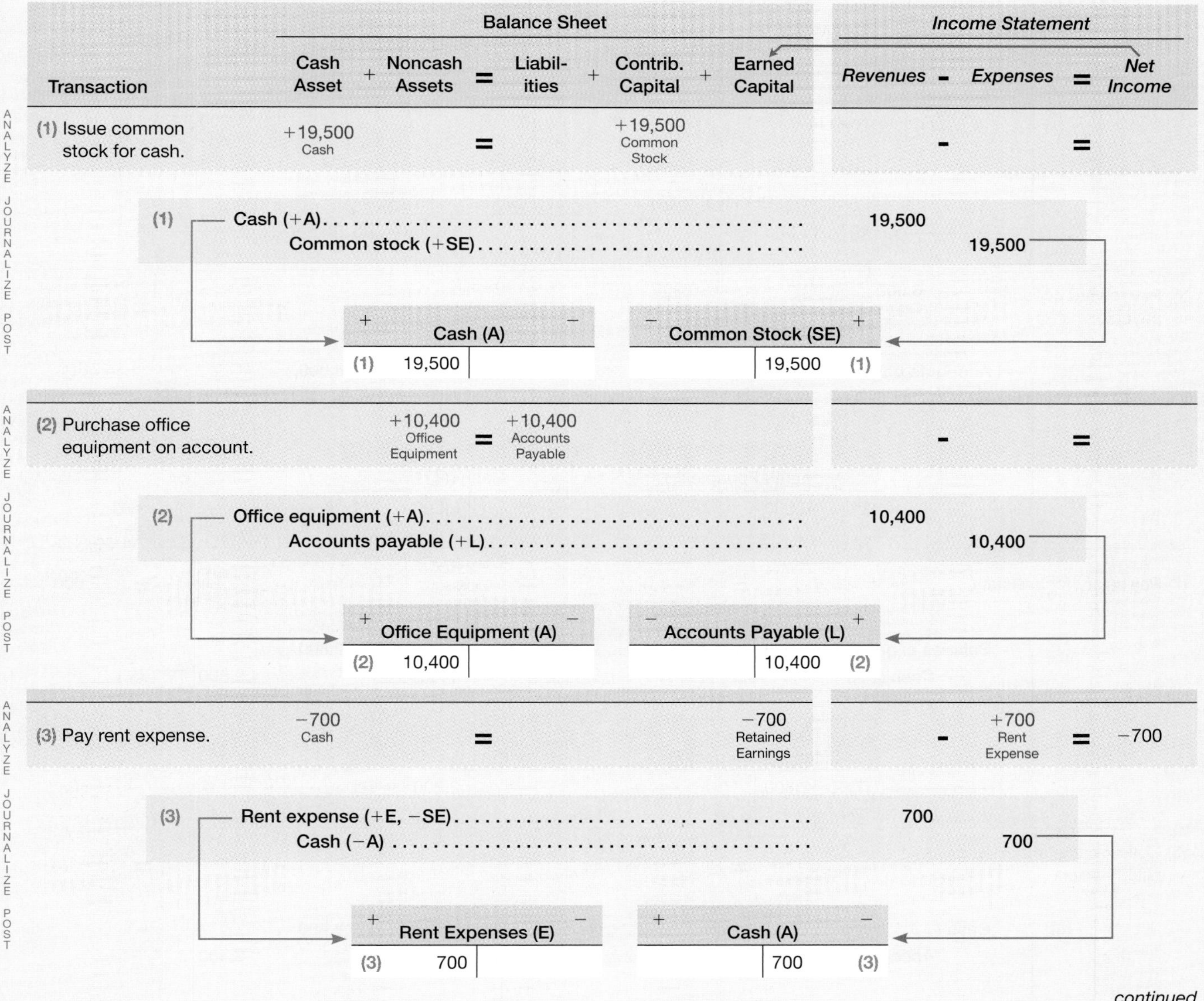

Transaction	Cash Asset	+	Noncash Assets	=	Liabil-ities	+	Contrib. Capital	+	Earned Capital	Revenues	−	Expenses	=	Net Income
(1) Issue common stock for cash.	+19,500 Cash			=			+19,500 Common Stock				−		=	
(2) Purchase office equipment on account.			+10,400 Office Equipment	=	+10,400 Accounts Payable						−		=	
(3) Pay rent expense.	−700 Cash			=					−700 Retained Earnings		−	+700 Rent Expense	=	−700

(1) Cash (+A) 19,500
  Common stock (+SE) 19,500

+ Cash (A) −	
(1) 19,500	

− Common Stock (SE) +	
	19,500 (1)

(2) Office equipment (+A) 10,400
  Accounts payable (+L) 10,400

+ Office Equipment (A) −	
(2) 10,400	

− Accounts Payable (L) +	
	10,400 (2)

(3) Rent expense (+E, −SE) 700
  Cash (−A) 700

+ Rent Expenses (E) −	
(3) 700	

+ Cash (A) −	
	700 (3)

continued

continued from previous page

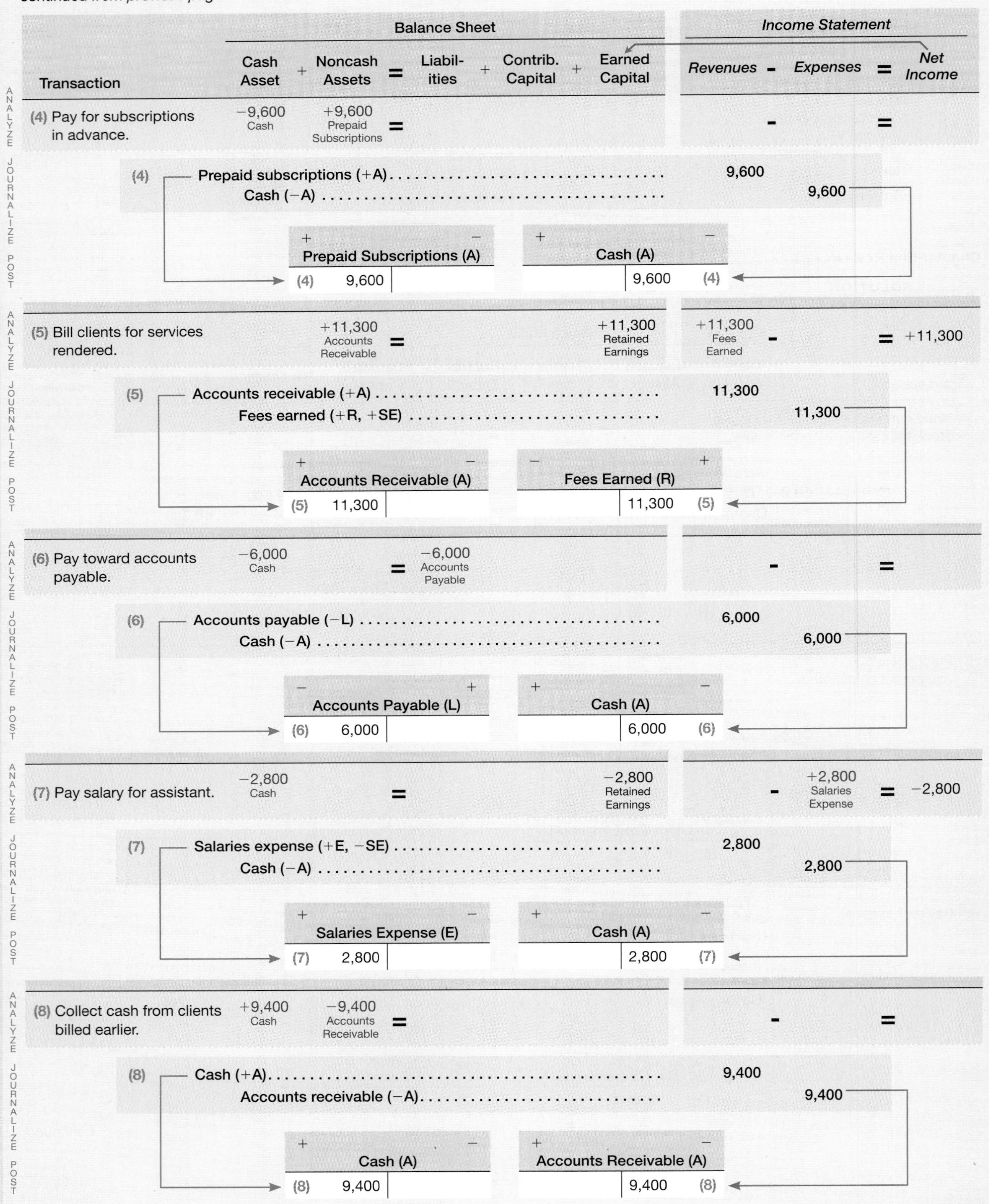

Transaction	Cash Asset	+ Noncash Assets	=	Liabil-ities	+ Contrib. Capital	+ Earned Capital	Revenues	− Expenses	=	Net Income
(4) Pay for subscriptions in advance.	−9,600 Cash	+9,600 Prepaid Subscriptions	=					−	=	
(5) Bill clients for services rendered.		+11,300 Accounts Receivable	=			+11,300 Retained Earnings	+11,300 Fees Earned	−	=	+11,300
(6) Pay toward accounts payable.	−6,000 Cash		=	−6,000 Accounts Payable				−	=	
(7) Pay salary for assistant.	−2,800 Cash		=			−2,800 Retained Earnings		− +2,800 Salaries Expense	=	−2,800
(8) Collect cash from clients billed earlier.	+9,400 Cash	−9,400 Accounts Receivable	=					−	=	

(4) Prepaid subscriptions (+A) 9,600
  Cash (−A) 9,600

+ Prepaid Subscriptions (A) −	
(4) 9,600	

+ Cash (A) −	
	9,600 (4)

(5) Accounts receivable (+A) 11,300
  Fees earned (+R, +SE) 11,300

+ Accounts Receivable (A) −	
(5) 11,300	

− Fees Earned (R) +	
	11,300 (5)

(6) Accounts payable (−L) 6,000
  Cash (−A) 6,000

− Accounts Payable (L) +	
(6) 6,000	

+ Cash (A) −	
	6,000 (6)

(7) Salaries expense (+E, −SE) 2,800
  Cash (−A) 2,800

+ Salaries Expense (E) −	
(7) 2,800	

+ Cash (A) −	
	2,800 (7)

(8) Cash (+A) 9,400
  Accounts receivable (−A) 9,400

+ Cash (A) −	
(8) 9,400	

+ Accounts Receivable (A) −	
	9,400 (8)

continued

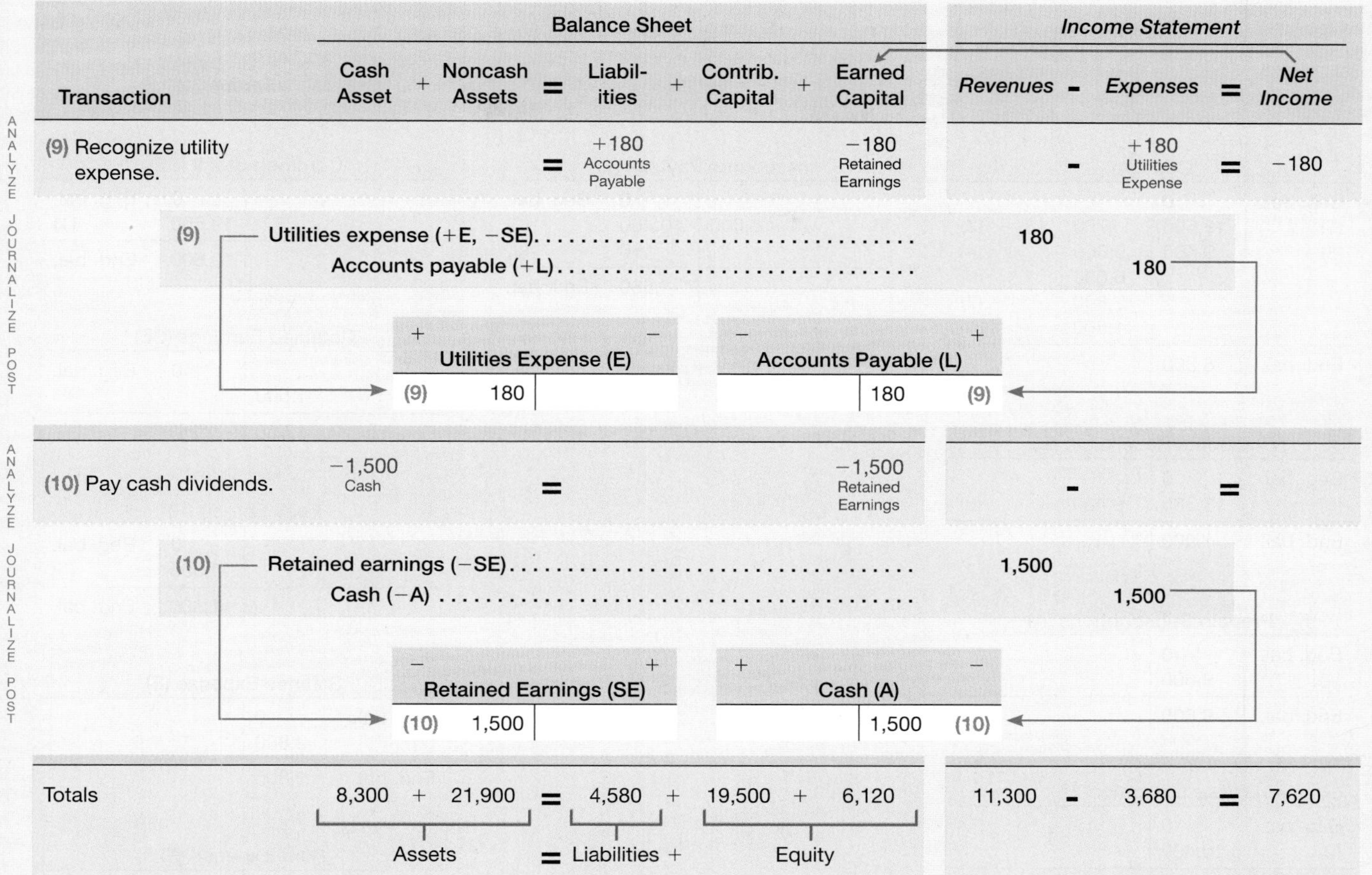

Transaction	Cash Asset	+	Noncash Assets	=	Liabil-ities	+	Contrib. Capital	+	Earned Capital	Revenues	-	Expenses	=	Net Income
(9) Recognize utility expense.				=	+180 Accounts Payable				−180 Retained Earnings		-	+180 Utilities Expense	=	−180
(10) Pay cash dividends.	−1,500 Cash			=					−1,500 Retained Earnings		-		=	
Totals	8,300	+	21,900	=	4,580	+	19,500	+	6,120	11,300	-	3,680	=	7,620
	Assets			=	Liabilities	+	Equity							

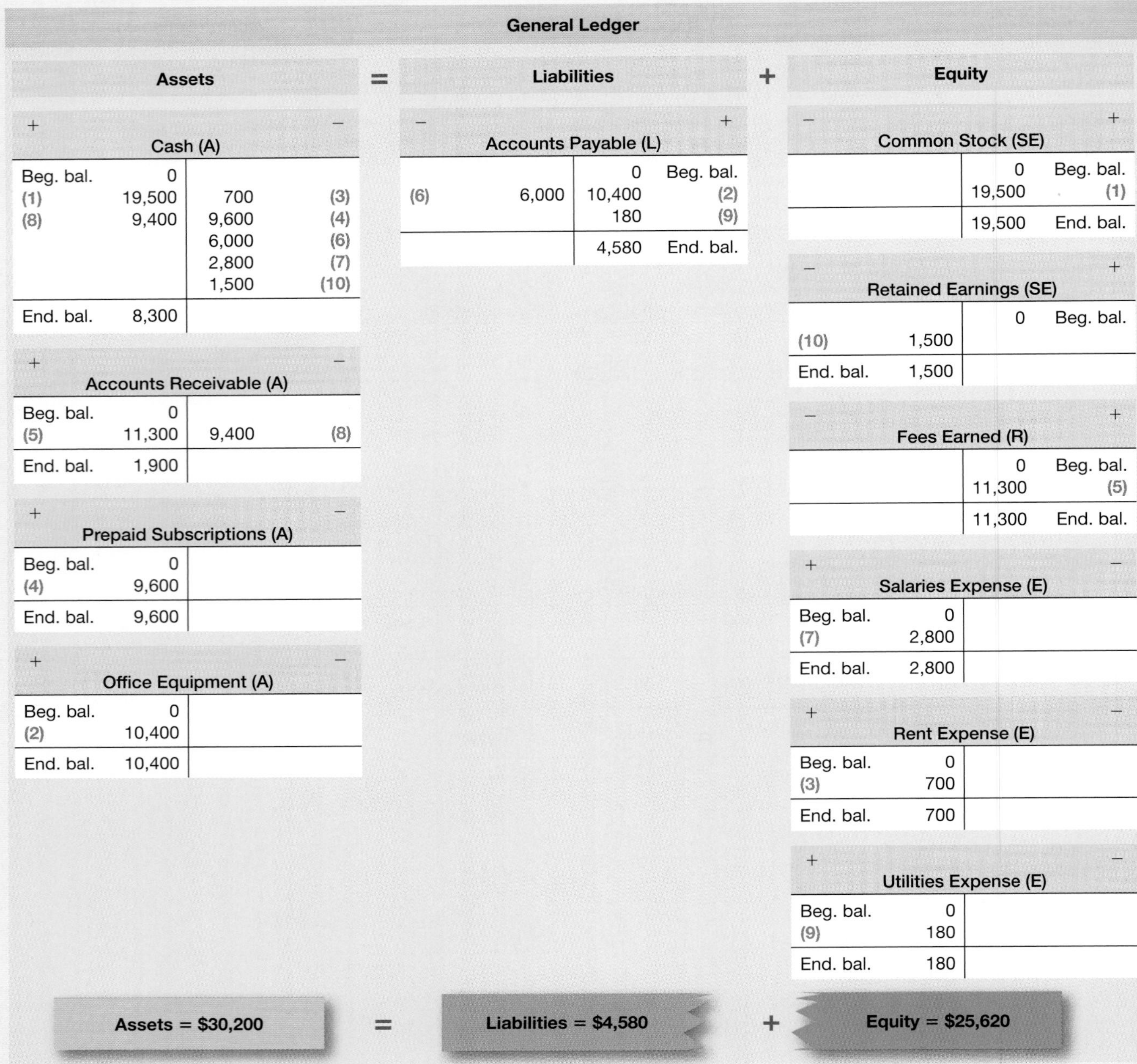
General Ledger
Assets
=
Liabilities
+
Equity
+ Cash (A) −
Beg. bal. 0
(1) 19,500 | 700 (3)
(8) 9,400 | 9,600 (4)
6,000 (6)
2,800 (7)
1,500 (10)
End. bal. 8,300
+ Accounts Receivable (A) −
Beg. bal. 0
(5) 11,300 | 9,400 (8)
End. bal. 1,900
+ Prepaid Subscriptions (A) −
Beg. bal. 0
(4) 9,600
End. bal. 9,600
+ Office Equipment (A) −
Beg. bal. 0
(2) 10,400
End. bal. 10,400
− Accounts Payable (L) +
0 Beg. bal.
(6) 6,000 | 10,400 (2)
180 (9)
4,580 End. bal.
− Common Stock (SE) +
0 Beg. bal.
19,500 (1)
19,500 End. bal.
− Retained Earnings (SE) +
0 Beg. bal.
(10) 1,500
End. bal. 1,500
− Fees Earned (R) +
0 Beg. bal.
11,300 (5)
11,300 End. bal.
+ Salaries Expense (E) −
Beg. bal. 0
(7) 2,800
End. bal. 2,800
+ Rent Expense (E) −
Beg. bal. 0
(3) 700
End. bal. 700
+ Utilities Expense (E) −
Beg. bal. 0
(9) 180
End. bal. 180
Assets = $30,200
=
Liabilities = $4,580
+
Equity = $25,620

Adjusting Accounts for Financial Statements

LEARNING OBJECTIVES

WALGREENS

www.walgreens.com

Walgreen Co.'s strategy for growth has three principal components. Within its network of more than 8,300 stores, it strives to create a "Well Experience" for customers, by store design and layout, by employee training and by digital applications. Their goal is to give the customer the "Three Ws"—What they want. Where they want it. When they want it. In fiscal year 2014, Walgreens reported an increase of 4.9% in same-store sales.

Pharmacy sales represent almost two-thirds of Walgreens' revenue, and the aging U.S. population will cause this to grow. In 2014, Walgreens completed multi-year agreements with major insurance companies, bringing greater stability to their pharmacy business. Finally, Walgreens made a significant international investment by purchasing 45% of the outstanding shares of **Alliance Boots GmbH**, plus an option to purchase the remaining 55% (which Walgreens exercised in late 2014). This acquisition creates the world's "leading pharmacy-led health and well-being enterprise," and provides the companies with a global platform for growth.

Because the financial statements should reflect the firm's underlying economic reality, Walgreens' management will need to "adjust" or "update" its financial statements to reflect the changes in its strategy and performance.

Accounting adjustments are a key part of creating the financial statements, and they are central to the difference between accrual and cash accounting. While cash accounting only records transactions that involve cash receipts and disbursements,

accrual accounting records revenues when they are earned (even if cash has not yet been received) and expenses as they are incurred (regardless of when the cash disbursement associated with that expense is made). The quality, or lack thereof, of the financial statements often hinges on the quality of those adjustments. Thus, understanding how and why accounting adjustments occur is fundamentally important to those who wish to analyze and interpret the financial statements.

This chapter describes the need for adjustments, how they are prepared, their financial statement effect, and the need for ethics and oversight in this process. We illustrate how financial statements are prepared from those adjusted accounts. Then, we end the chapter with the closing process for the financial statements. Such "closing of the books" enables firms to report their performance for the year and then "open the books" anew for the next period.

Sources: Walgreen Co. and Subsidiaries 2013 Annual Report and 2014 10-K.

CHAPTER ORGANIZATION

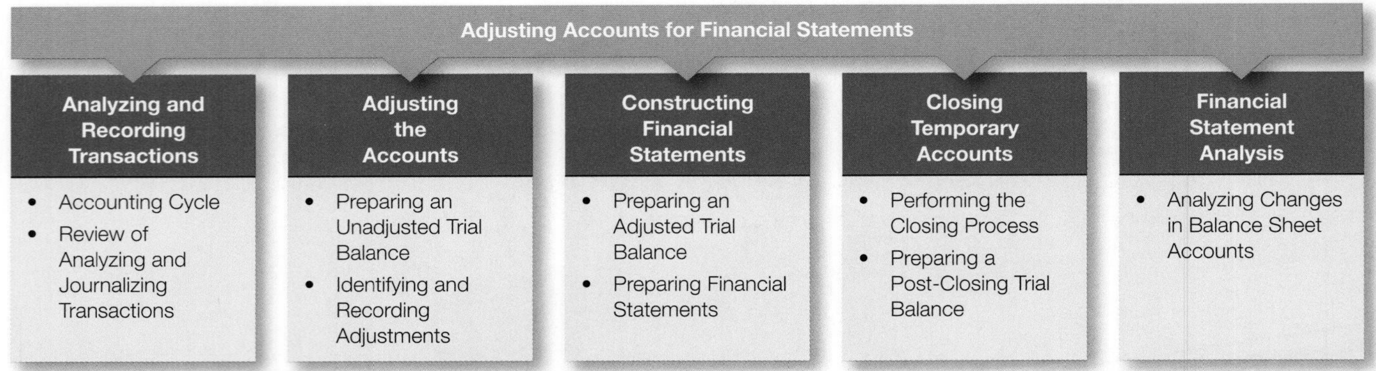

Adjusting Accounts for Financial Statements
Analyzing and Recording Transactions
• Accounting Cycle
• Review of Analyzing and Journalizing Transactions
Adjusting the Accounts
• Preparing an Unadjusted Trial Balance
• Identifying and Recording Adjustments
Constructing Financial Statements
• Preparing an Adjusted Trial Balance
• Preparing Financial Statements
Closing Temporary Accounts
• Performing the Closing Process
• Preparing a Post-Closing Trial Balance
Financial Statement Analysis
• Analyzing Changes in Balance Sheet Accounts

The double-entry accounting system introduced in Chapter 2 provides us with a framework for the analysis of business activities, and we use that framework to record transactions and create financial reports. This chapter describes more fully the procedures companies use to account for the operations of a business during a specific time period. All companies, regardless of size or complexity, perform accounting steps, known as the *accounting cycle*, to accumulate and report their financial information. An important step in the accounting cycle is the *adjusting* process that occurs at the end of every reporting period. This chapter focuses on the accounting cycle with emphasis on the adjusting process.

1 **LO1** Identify the major steps in the accounting cycle.

ACCOUNTING CYCLE

Companies engage in business activities. These activities are analyzed for their financial impact, and the results from that analysis are entered into the accounting information system. When management and others want to know where the company stands financially, and what its recent performance tells about future prospects, the financial data often require adjustment prior to financial statements being prepared. At the end of this adjustment process, the company *closes the books*. This closing process prepares accounts for the next accounting period.

The process described constitutes the major steps in the **accounting cycle**—a sequence of activities to accumulate and report financial statements. The steps are: analyze, record, adjust, report, and close. **Exhibit 3.1** shows the sequence of major steps in the accounting cycle.

EXHIBIT 3.1 Accounting Cycle—Abbreviated

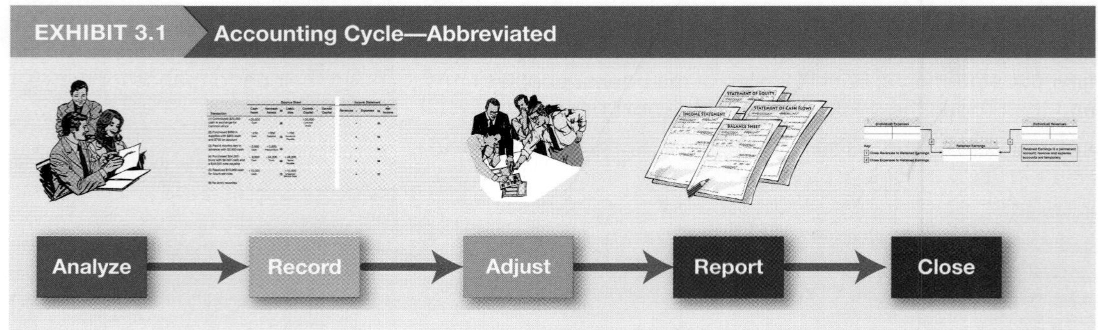

The steps in the accounting cycle do not occur with equal frequency. That is, companies analyze and record daily transactions throughout the accounting period, but they adjust and report only when management requires financial statements, often monthly or quarterly, but at least annually. Closing occurs once during the accounting cycle, at the period-end.

The annual (one-year) accounting period adopted by a company is known as its **fiscal year**. Companies with fiscal year-ends on December 31 are said to be on a **calendar year**. About 60% of U.S. companies are on a calendar-year basis. Many companies prefer to have their accounting year coincide with their "natural" year; that is, the fiscal year ends when business is slow. For example,

L Brands, Inc., a specialty retailer, ends its fiscal year on the Saturday nearest January 31. **Starbucks Corporation** ends its fiscal year on the Sunday nearest to September 30. The **Manchester United Ltd.**, a professional soccer team, ends its fiscal year on June 30, during its off-season.

ANALYZING AND RECORDING TRANSACTIONS

LO2 Review the process of journalizing and posting transactions.

The purpose of this section is to (1) review the analysis and recording of transactions as described in Chapter 2, and (2) to extend the Natural Beauty Supply example to illustrate the process of adjusting and closing accounts in the following sections. Natural Beauty Supply's fiscal year-end is December 31.

Review of Accounting Procedures

The **chart of accounts** for Natural Beauty Supply is in **Exhibit 3.2**, and lists the titles and numbers of all accounts found in its general ledger. The account titles are grouped into the five major sections of the general ledger (assets, liabilities, equity, revenues, and expenses). We saw in Chapter 2 that the recording process involves analyzing, journalizing, and posting. The **general journal**, or *book of original entry*, is a tabular record where business activities are captured in debits and credits and recorded in chronological order before they are posted to the general ledger. The word *journalize* means to record a transaction in a **journal**. Each transaction entered in the journal must be stated in terms of equal dollar amounts of debits and credits—the double-entry system at work. The account titles cited must correspond to those in the general ledger (per the chart of accounts).

EXHIBIT 3.2 Chart of Accounts for Natural Beauty Supply

Assets	**Equity**
110 Cash	310 Common Stock
120 Accounts Receivable	320 Retained Earnings
130 Other Receivables	
140 Inventory	**Revenues and Income**
150 Prepaid Insurance	410 Sales Revenue
160 Security Deposit	420 Interest Income
170 Fixtures and Equipment	
175 Accumulated Depreciation—Fixtures and Equipment	**Expenses**
	510 Cost of Goods Sold
	520 Wages Expense
Liabilities	530 Rent Expense
210 Accounts Payable	540 Advertising Expense
220 Interest Payable	550 Depreciation Expense—Fixtures and Equipment
230 Wages Payable	
240 Taxes Payable	560 Insurance Expense
250 Unearned Revenue	570 Interest Expense
260 Notes Payable	580 Tax Expense

After transactions are journalized, the debits and credits in each journal entry are transferred to their related general ledger accounts. This transcribing process is called posting to the general ledger, or simply **posting**. Journalizing and posting occur simultaneously when recordkeeping is automated.

Review of Recording Transactions

In Chapter 2, we recorded the November activities of Natural Beauty Supply (NBS) and created the end-of-November financial statements. As NBS continues its activities into the next month, the end-of-November balance sheet provides the starting point for December. **Exhibit 3.3** provides a summary of Natural Beauty Supply's December 2015 transactions.

EXHIBIT 3.3 Transactions for Natural Beauty Supply for December 2015

Event	Date	Description
(17)	Dec. 1	NBS signed a three-year note to borrow $11,000 cash from a financial institution. NBS will pay interest on the first business day of every month (starting in January) at the rate of 12% per year or 1% per month. The $11,000 principal is due at the end of three years.
(18)	Dec. 1	NBS purchased and installed improved fixtures and equipment for $18,000 cash.
(19)	Dec. 10	NBS paid $700 to advertise in the local newspaper for December.
(20)	Dec. 20	NBS paid $3,300 cash to its suppliers in partial payment for the delivery of inventory in November.
(21)	Dec. —	During the month of December, NBS sold products costing $5,000 to retail customers for $8,500 cash.
(22)	Dec. —	During the month of December, sales to wholesale customers totaled $4,500 for merchandise that had cost $3,000. Instead of paying cash, wholesale customers are required to pay for the merchandise within ten business days.
(23)	Dec. —	$1,200 of gift certificates were sold during the month of December. Each gift certificate entitles the recipient to a one-hour consultation on the use of NBS' products.
(24)	Dec. —	NBS employed salespersons who were paid $1,625 in cash in December.
(25)	Dec. —	During the month of December, NBS received $3,200 in cash from wholesale customers for products that had been delivered earlier.
(26)	Dec. 28	NBS purchased and received $4,000 of inventory on account.
(27)	Dec. 31	NBS paid $1,500 to the landlord for December rent.
(28)	Dec. 31	NBS paid $50 cash dividend to its shareholders.

Most of these transactions are similar to those that we analyzed in Chapter 2. Each of the transactions involves an exchange of some kind. Suppliers provide inventory and employees provide labor services in exchange for cash or the promise of future cash payments. Customers receive products in exchange for cash or a promise to pay cash in the future. For each of these items, we analyze, journalize, and post as shown in Chapter 2.

NBS has the opportunity to secure long-term financing from a financial institution, and signs a note that must be paid back at the end of three years. Cash increases, and a noncurrent liability increases. Interest payments are made at the start of every month, beginning on January 2, 2016, but no entry is made for interest until time passes and an interest obligation is created.

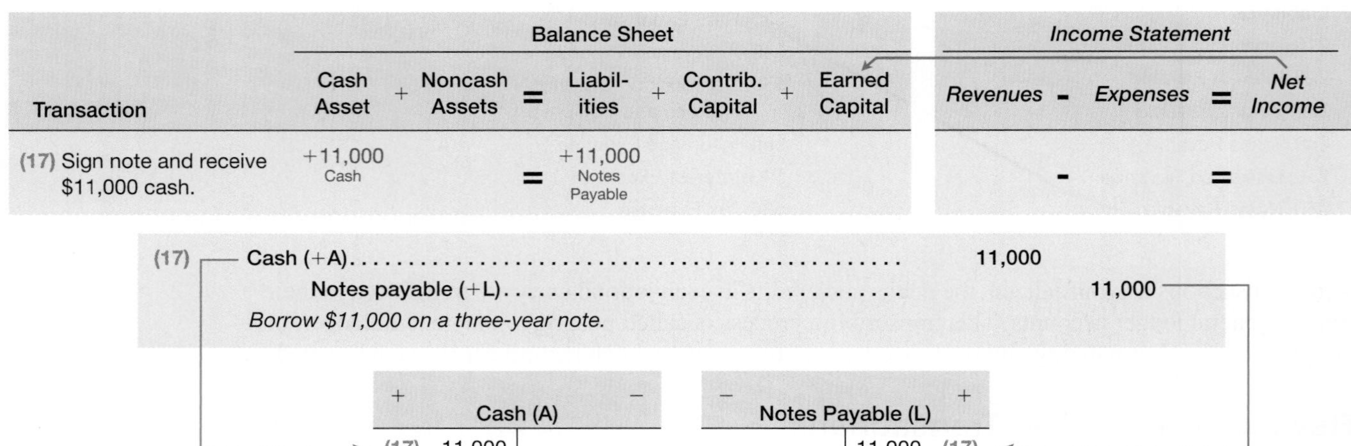

NBS pays $18,000 cash to purchase improved fixtures and equipment for its store location. One asset (cash) decreases, while a noncurrent asset (fixtures and equipment) is increased.

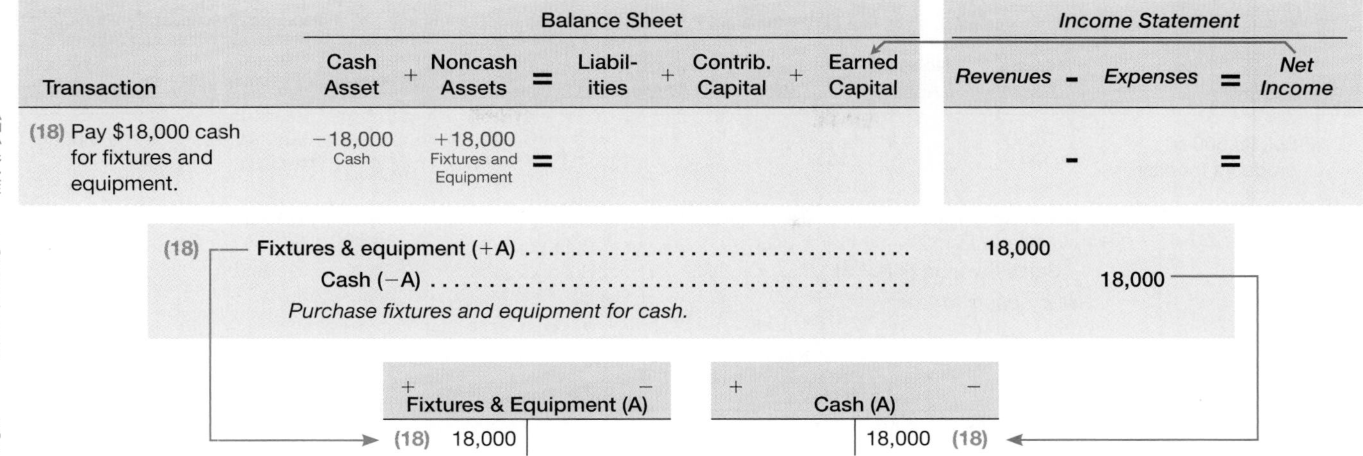

Transactions (19) and (20) are similar to ones that we saw in Chapter 2. The expenditure for advertising results in an expense that decreases net income and ultimately, retained earnings. The payment to suppliers fulfills (in part) an obligation that appeared in the November 30 balance sheet.

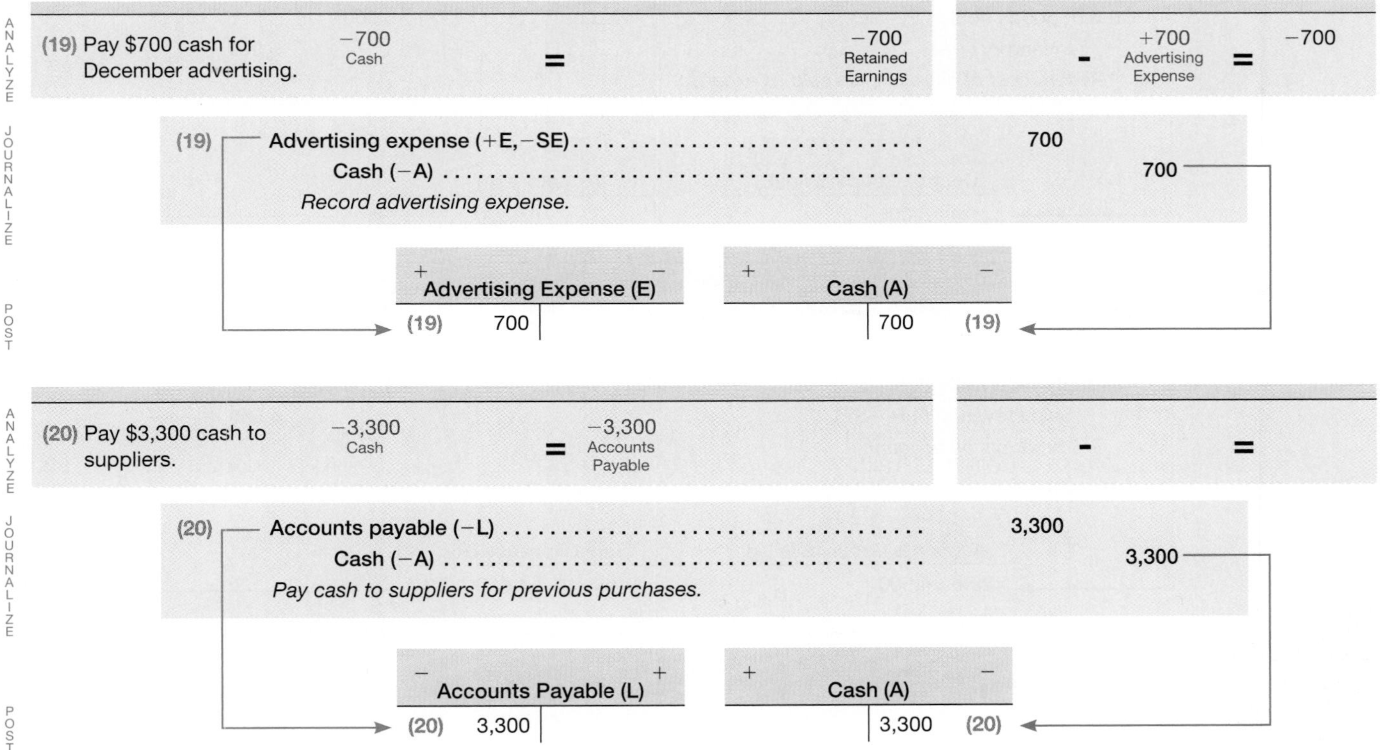

Sales to customers in (21), (22), and (23) are also similar to transactions in Chapter 2, and they are accounted for in similar fashion. Revenue is recognized when products are delivered to customers, rather than when cash is received. When cash is received after delivery, an accounts receivable asset is recognized; when cash is received before delivery, an unearned revenue liability is recognized. Cost of goods sold expense is recognized when the associated revenue is recognized.

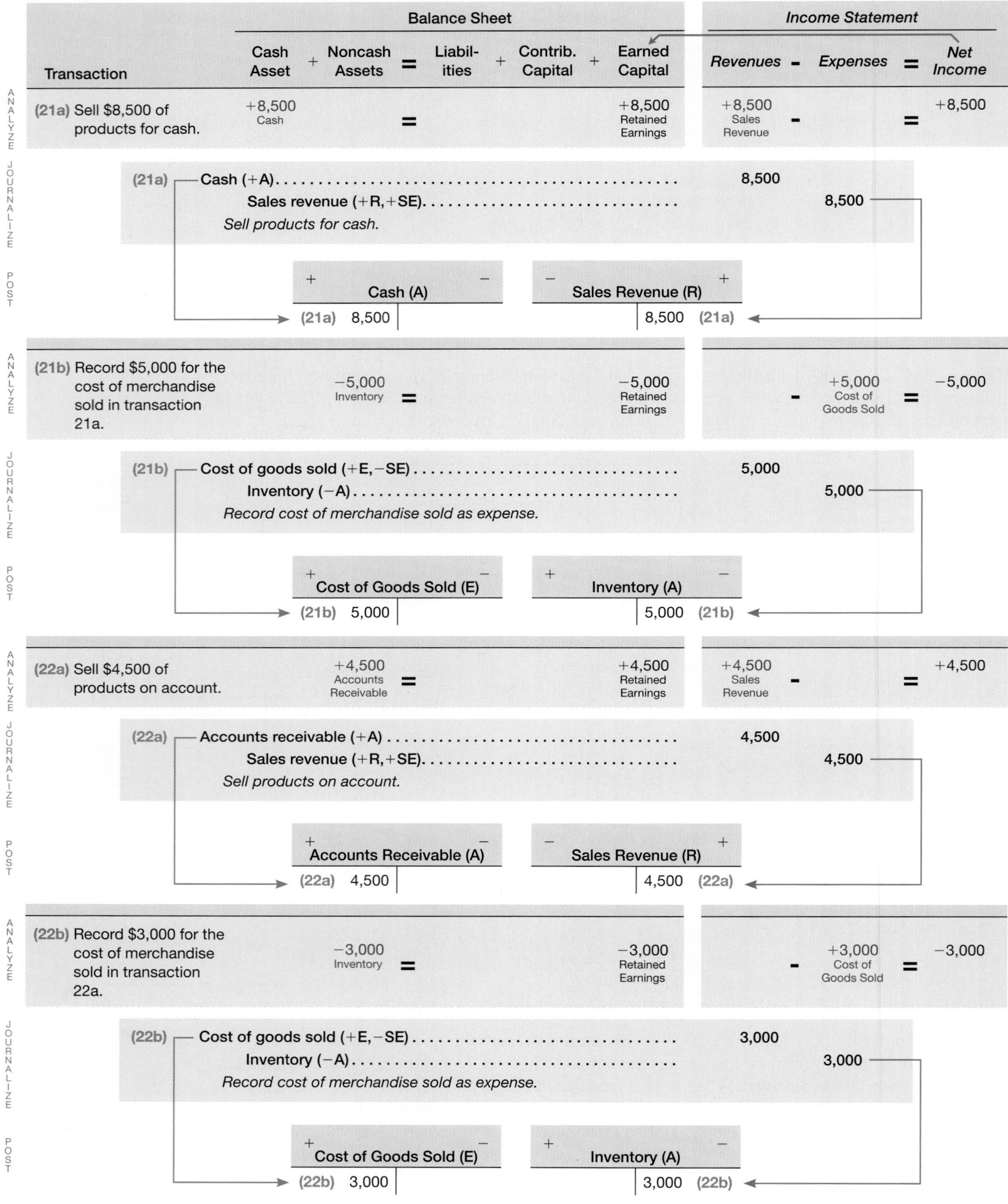

Balance Sheet
Income Statement
Transaction
Cash Asset + Noncash Assets = Liabilities + Contrib. Capital + Earned Capital
Revenues - Expenses = Net Income
ANALYZE
(21a) Sell $8,500 of products for cash.
+8,500 Cash = +8,500 Retained Earnings
+8,500 Sales Revenue - = +8,500
JOURNALIZE
(21a) Cash (+A) 8,500
Sales revenue (+R, +SE) 8,500
Sell products for cash.
POST
+ Cash (A) −
(21a) 8,500
− Sales Revenue (R) +
8,500 (21a)
ANALYZE
(21b) Record $5,000 for the cost of merchandise sold in transaction 21a.
−5,000 Inventory = −5,000 Retained Earnings
- +5,000 Cost of Goods Sold = −5,000
JOURNALIZE
(21b) Cost of goods sold (+E, −SE) 5,000
Inventory (−A) 5,000
Record cost of merchandise sold as expense.
POST
+ Cost of Goods Sold (E) −
(21b) 5,000
+ Inventory (A) −
5,000 (21b)
ANALYZE
(22a) Sell $4,500 of products on account.
+4,500 Accounts Receivable = +4,500 Retained Earnings
+4,500 Sales Revenue - = +4,500
JOURNALIZE
(22a) Accounts receivable (+A) 4,500
Sales revenue (+R, +SE) 4,500
Sell products on account.
POST
+ Accounts Receivable (A) −
(22a) 4,500
− Sales Revenue (R) +
4,500 (22a)
ANALYZE
(22b) Record $3,000 for the cost of merchandise sold in transaction 22a.
−3,000 Inventory = −3,000 Retained Earnings
- +3,000 Cost of Goods Sold = −3,000
JOURNALIZE
(22b) Cost of goods sold (+E, −SE) 3,000
Inventory (−A) 3,000
Record cost of merchandise sold as expense.
POST
+ Cost of Goods Sold (E) −
(22b) 3,000
+ Inventory (A) −
3,000 (22b)

continued

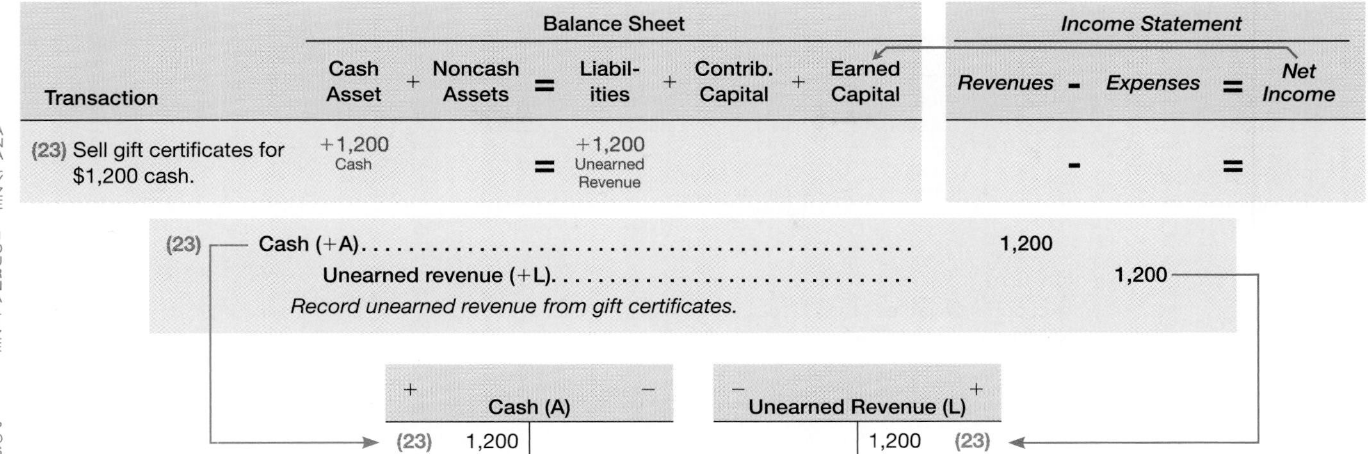

The final five transactions in December also are similar to transactions that NBS had in November. Payment of wages to the employee is reflected in a wage expense. Cash received from wholesale (credit) customers does not cause revenue; rather the increase in cash is balanced by a decrease in accounts receivable. Purchase of inventory on account does not create an expense—the cost of the inventory is held in the inventory asset account until it is purchased by a customer. Payments to the landlord are balanced by a rent expense in the income statement. The cash dividend to shareholders decreases an asset (cash) and shareholders' equity (retained earnings), but does not affect the income statement.

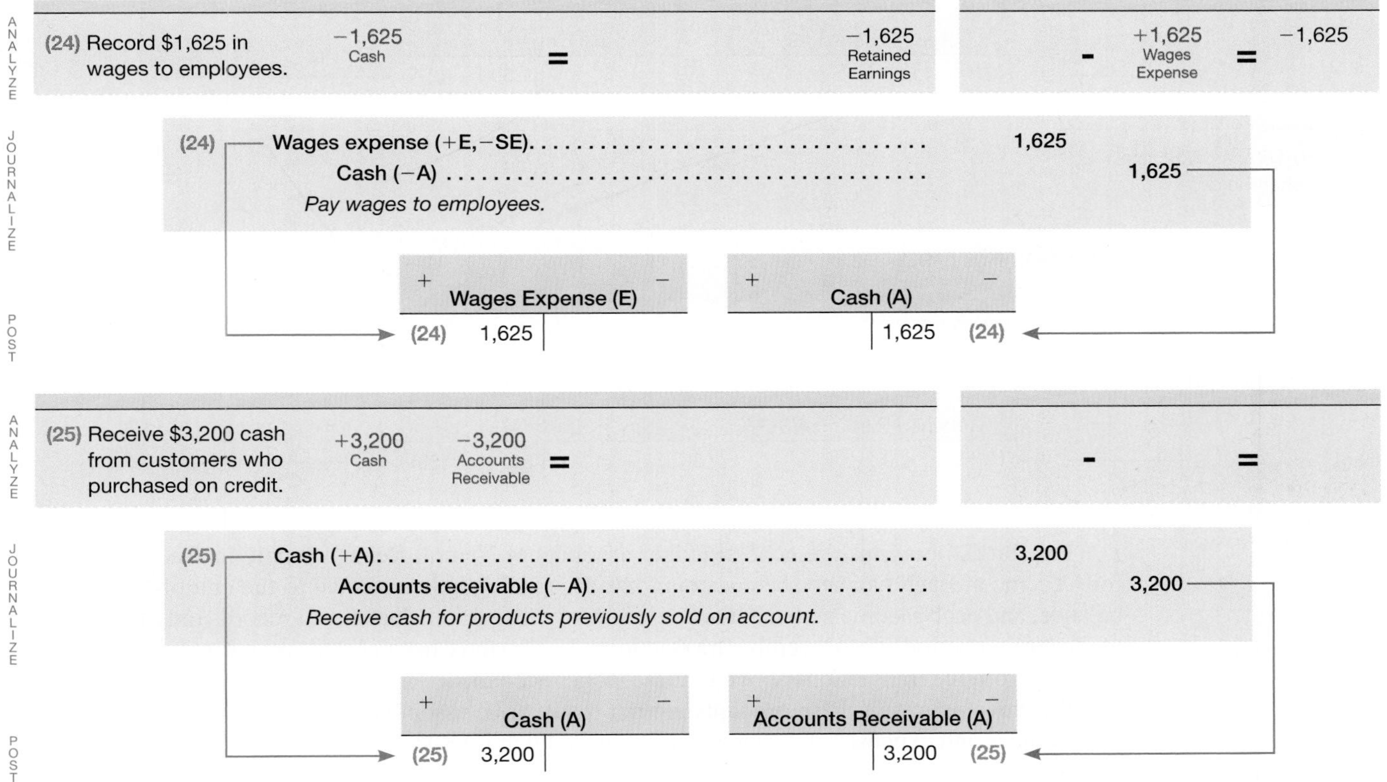

continued

continued from previous page

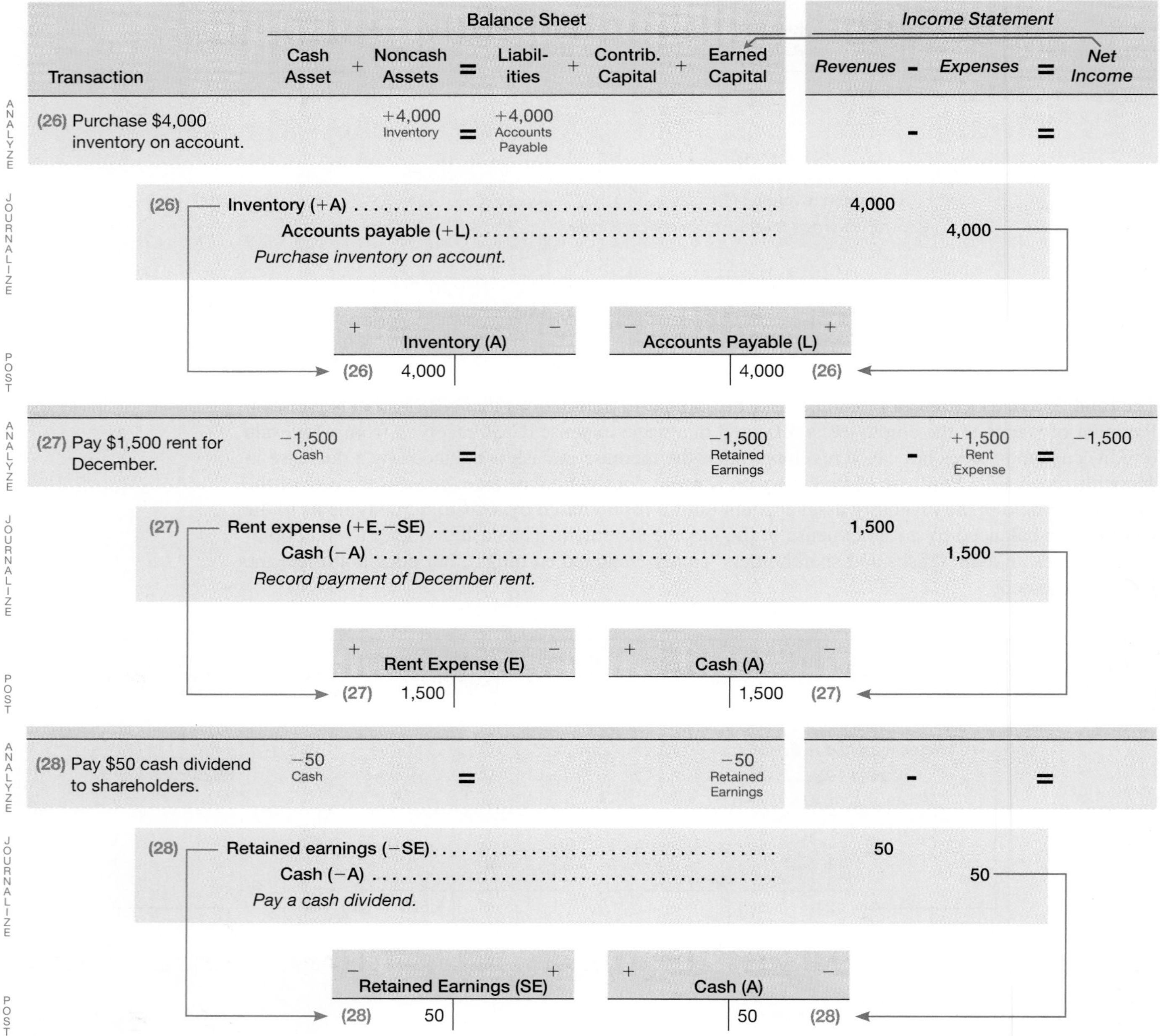

Exhibit 3.4 presents the general ledger accounts of Natural Beauty Supply in T-account form for December. Each balance sheet account has an opening balance equal to the end-of-November balance, and each income statement account starts with a zero balance so it records only the events of the current period. The December transactions (17–28) have been posted. We can trace each of the postings from the transactions above to these ledger accounts.

But the amounts in these accounts are not ready to be assembled into financial reports. There are revenues and expenses and changes in assets and liabilities that occur with the passage of time.[1] Accounting for these items is essential for us to determine how well a company has performed in an accounting period and to assess its financial standing.

[1] Natural Beauty Supply's November activities in Chapter 2 were carefully chosen so we could produce financial statements without adjusting entries. But, as **Exhibit 3.1** depicts, the adjusting process is an essential part of the accounting cycle.

EXHIBIT 3.4 General Ledger for Natural Beauty Supply before Adjustments

General Ledger

Assets = Liabilities + Equity

Assets

+	Cash (A)		−
Beg. bal.	8,100		
(17)	11,000	18,000	(18)
(21a)	8,500	700	(19)
(23)	1,200	3,300	(20)
(25)	3,200	1,625	(24)
		1,500	(27)
		50	(28)
Unadj. bal.	6,825		

+	Accounts Receivable (A)		−
Beg. bal.	950		
(22a)	4,500	3,200	(25)
Unadj. bal.	2,250		

+	Inventory (A)		−
Beg. bal.	11,300		
(26)	4,000	5,000	(21b)
		3,000	(22b)
Unadj. bal.	7,300		

+	Prepaid Insurance (A)		−
Beg. bal.	1,680		
Unadj. bal.	1,680		

+	Security Deposit (A)		−
Beg. bal.	2,000		
Unadj. bal.	2,000		

+	Fixtures and Equipment (A)		−
Beg. bal.	0		
(18)	18,000		
Unadj. bal.	18,000		

Liabilities

−	Accounts Payable (L)		+
		3,700	Beg. bal.
(20)	3,300	4,000	(26)
		4,400	Unadj. bal.

−	Unearned Revenue (L)		+
		300	Beg. bal.
		1,200	(23)
		1,500	Unadj. bal.

−	Notes Payable (L)		+
		0	Beg. bal.
		11,000	(17)
		11,000	Unadj. bal.

Equity

−	Common Stock (SE)		+
		20,000	Beg. bal.
		20,000	Unadj. bal.

−	Retained Earnings (SE)		+
		30	Beg. bal.
(28)	50		
Unadj. bal.	20		

−	Sales Revenue (R)		+
		0	Beg. bal.
		8,500	(21a)
		4,500	(22a)
		13,000	Unadj. bal.

+	Cost of Goods Sold (E)		−
Beg. bal.	0		
(21b)	5,000		
(22b)	3,000		
Unadj. bal.	8,000		

+	Wages Expense (E)		−
Beg. bal.	0		
(24)	1,625		
Unadj. bal.	1,625		

+	Rent Expense (E)		−
Beg. bal.	0		
(27)	1,500		
Unadj. bal.	1,500		

+	Advertising Expense (E)		−
Beg. bal.	0		
(19)	700		
Unadj. bal.	700		

Assets = $38,055 = Liabilities = $16,900 + Equity = $21,155

ADJUSTING THE ACCOUNTS

LO3 Describe the adjusting process and illustrate adjusting entries.

It is important that accounts in financial statements be properly reported. For many accounts, the balances shown in the general ledger after all transactions are posted are not the proper balances for financial statements. So, when it is time to prepare financial statements, management must review account balances and make proper adjustments to these balances. The adjustments required are based on accrual accounting and generally accepted accounting principles. This section focuses on this adjustment process.

Preparing an Unadjusted Trial Balance

The T-accounts in **Exhibit 3.4** show balances for each account after recording all transactions. This set of balances is called an **unadjusted trial balance** because it shows account balances before any adjustments are made. The purpose of an unadjusted trial balance is to be sure the general ledger is in balance before management adjusts the accounts. Showing all general ledger account balances in one place also makes it easier to review accounts and determine which account balances require adjusting. Natural Beauty Supply's unadjusted trial balance at December 31 is shown in **Exhibit 3.5**.

FYI Even if the unadjusted trial balance shows an equal amount of debits and credits, this does not mean that the general ledger is correct. Journal entries could have been omitted or falsified, or the accounts used or the amounts involved may have been wrong. Thus, the equality of debits and credits is a necessary, but not a sufficient condition for the financial statements to be correct.

EXHIBIT 3.5 Unadjusted Trial Balance

NATURAL BEAUTY SUPPLY
Unadjusted Trial Balance
December 31, 2015

	Debit	Credit
Cash	$ 6,825	
Accounts receivable	2,250	
Inventory	7,300	
Prepaid insurance	1,680	
Security deposit	2,000	
Fixtures & equipment	18,000	
Accounts payable		$ 4,400
Unearned revenue		1,500
Notes payable		11,000
Common stock		20,000
Retained earnings	20	
Sales revenue		13,000
Cost of goods sold	8,000	
Wages expense	1,625	
Rent expense	1,500	
Advertising expense	700	
Totals	$49,900	$49,900

Types of Adjustments

Accrual adjustments are caused by a variety of accounting practices. There are some revenues and expenses that arise with the passage of time, rather than in a transaction. There are asset and liability values that change over time or that require estimation based on recent events. All of these require adjustments before proper financial statements can be produced.

Adjusting entries have two common characteristics. First, they occur at the end of a reporting period, just before the construction of financial statements. Second, they (almost) never involve cash. Changes in cash require a transaction, and adjusting entries are not transactions.

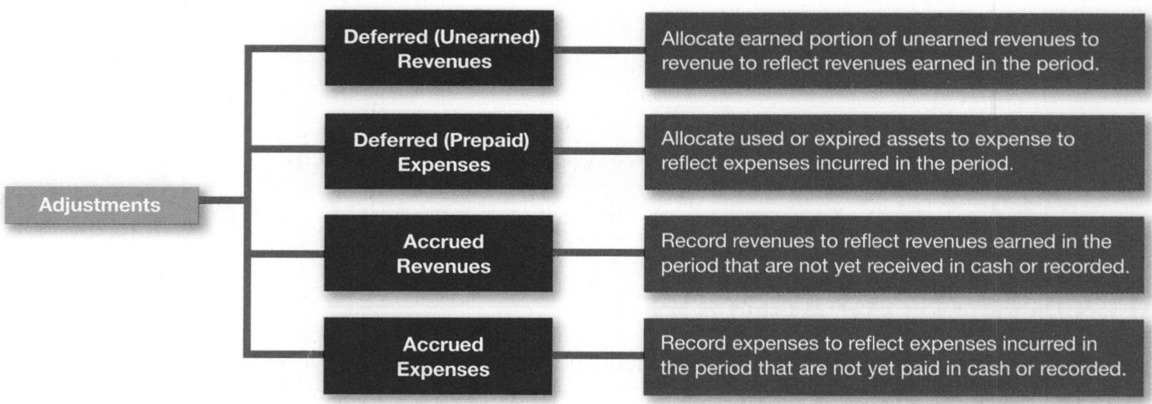

Through the course of this book, we will encounter quite a few required adjusting entries, but we will start with four general types of adjustments made at the end of an accounting period.

Journal entries made to reflect these adjustments are known as **adjusting entries**. Each adjusting entry usually affects a balance sheet account (an asset or liability account) and an income statement account (an expense or revenue account). The first two types of adjustments—allocating assets to expense and allocating unearned revenues to revenue—are often referred to as **deferrals**. The distinguishing characteristic of a deferral is that the adjustment deals with an amount previously recorded in a balance sheet account; the adjusting entry decreases the balance sheet account and increases an income statement account. The last two types of adjustments—accruing expenses and accruing revenues—are often referred to as **accruals**. The unique characteristic of an accrual is that the adjustment deals with an amount not previously recorded in any account; this type of adjusting entry increases both a balance sheet account and an income statement account. Both accruals and deferrals allow revenue to be recognized when it is earned and the expenses of the period to reflect asset decreases and liability increases from generating revenues or supporting that period's operations. Let's consider each of these adjustments in more detail.

Type 1: Deferred Revenue—Allocating Unearned Revenue to Revenue Companies often receive fees for products or services before those products or services are rendered. Such transactions are recorded by debiting Cash and crediting a liability account for the **unearned revenue**—also referred to as **deferred revenue**. This account reflects the obligation for performing future services or delivering a product in the future. As services are performed or the product delivered, revenue is earned. At period-end, an adjusting entry records the revenue that was earned in the current accounting period and the liability amount that was reduced.

FYI Chapter 2 explained that revenue recognition is key to determining net income under accrual accounting, which recognizes revenues when services are performed or when goods are sold and recognizes expenses in the period that they help to generate the recorded revenues.

DEFERRED REVENUE During November and December, Natural Beauty Supply sold gift certificates that entitled the recipient to a one-hour consultation with a salesperson on the use of natural and organic health and beauty products. When the gift certificates were purchased, NBS recognized an unearned revenue liability that reflected the obligation to provide these services. During the month of December, gift certificates totaling $900 were redeemed. On December 31, Natural Beauty Supply made the adjustment (a) in the following template, journal entry, and T-accounts to recognize the (partial) fulfillment of the obligation and to recognize the $900 of revenue to which it is now entitled. The $900 increase in sales revenue is reflected in net income and carried over to retained earnings.

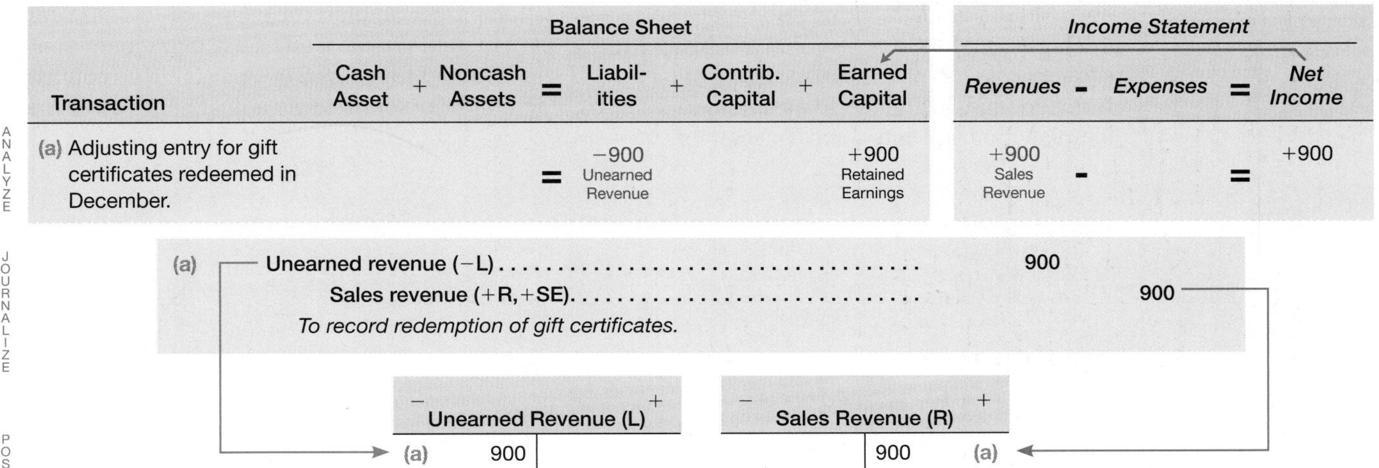

ANALYZE

Transaction	Cash Asset	+	Noncash Assets	=	Liabilities	+	Contrib. Capital	+	Earned Capital	Revenues	−	Expenses	=	Net Income
(a) Adjusting entry for gift certificates redeemed in December.				=	−900 Unearned Revenue				+900 Retained Earnings	+900 Sales Revenue	−		=	+900

JOURNALIZE

		Debit	Credit
(a)	Unearned revenue (−L)	900	
	Sales revenue (+R, +SE)		900
	To record redemption of gift certificates.		

POST

− Unearned Revenue (L) +		− Sales Revenue (R) +	
(a) 900			900 (a)

After this entry (a) is posted, the Unearned Revenue liability account has a balance of $600 for the remaining gift certificates outstanding, and the Sales Revenue account reflects the $900 earned in December.

In this case, the cost of the salesperson's time has already been recognized as an expense. If Natural Beauty Supply's gift certificates had been redeemable for products, then we would have recognized a Cost of Goods Sold expense for the items purchased with the redeemed certificates.

Other examples of revenues received in advance include gift cards, rental payments received in advance by real estate management companies, insurance premiums received in advance by insurance companies, subscription revenues received in advance by magazine and newspaper publishers, and membership fees received in advance by health clubs. In each case, a liability account is set up when the advance payment is received. Later, an adjusting entry is made to reflect the revenues earned from the services provided or products delivered during the period.

YOU MAKE THE CALL

You are the Chief Accountant REI requires customers of its travel-vacation business to make an initial deposit equal to $400 when the trip is reserved and to make full payment two months before departure. REI's refunding policy is to return the entire deposit if the customer informs REI of the trip's cancellation three or more months in advance of the trip. REI will refund all but $400 of the deposit if the customer cancels between 60 and 90 days prior to the trip or 50% of the deposit if a customer cancels between 30 and 60 days prior to the trip. There is no refund if notification occurs within 30 days of the trip. REI's cancellation rate is very low. How should you account for deposits, and when should revenue be recorded? [Answers on page 128]

Type 2: Prepaid Expenses—Allocating Assets to Expenses Many cash outlays benefit several accounting periods. Examples are purchases of buildings, equipment, and supplies; prepayments of rent and advertising; and payments of insurance premiums covering several periods. These outlays are added to (debited to) an asset account when the expenditure occurs. Then at the end of each accounting period, the estimated portion of the outlay that has expired in that period or has benefited that period, is transferred to an expense account.

We can usually see when adjustments of this type are needed by inspecting the unadjusted trial balance for costs that benefit several periods. Looking at the December 31 trial balance of Natural Beauty Supply (**Exhibit 3.5**), for example, adjustments are required to record the costs of prepaid insurance and the fixtures and equipment for the month of December.

FYI Many transactions reflected in ledger accounts affect net income of more than one period. Likewise, other events that are not yet recorded in accounts affect the current period's income. The adjusting process identifies these situations to record the proper revenues and expenses in the current period.

PREPAID INSURANCE On November 30, Natural Beauty Supply paid one year's insurance premium in advance and debited the $1,680 payment to Prepaid Insurance, an asset account. As each day passes and the insurance coverage is being used, insurance expense is being incurred, and the Prepaid Insurance asset is decreasing. It is not necessary to record insurance expense on a daily basis because financial statements are not prepared daily. At the end of an accounting period, however, an adjustment must be made to recognize the proper amount of Insurance Expense for the period and to decrease Prepaid Insurance by that amount. On December 31, one month's insurance coverage has been used up, so Natural Beauty Supply transfers $140 ($1,680/12 months) from Prepaid Insurance to Insurance Expense. This entry is identified as adjustment (b) in the template, journal entry, and T-accounts.

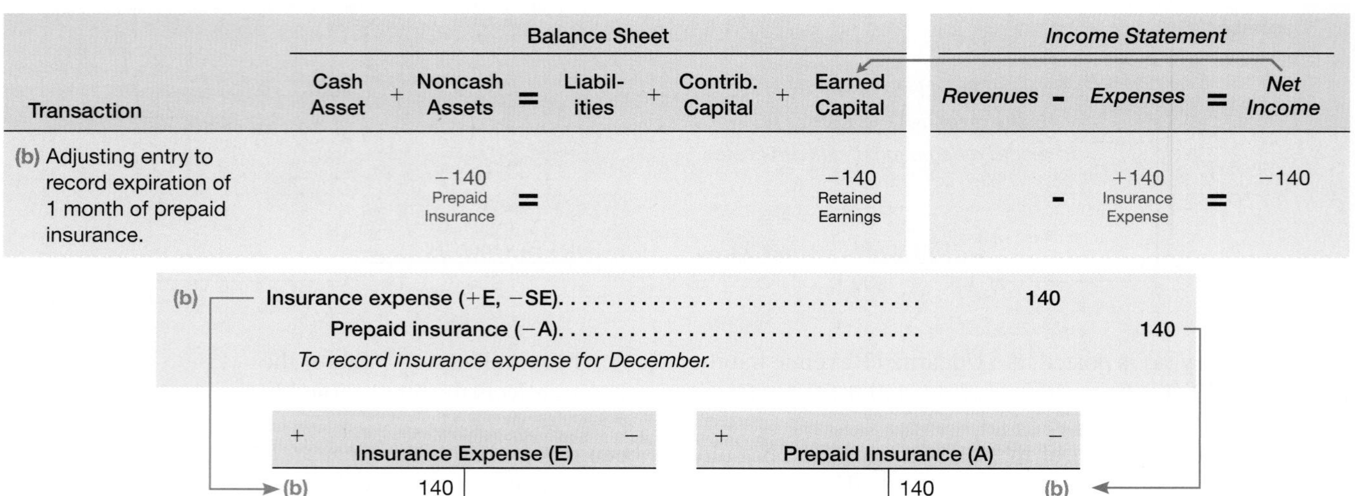

The posting of this adjusting entry creates the proper Insurance Expense of $140 for December in the Insurance Expense ledger account and reduces the Prepaid Insurance balance to the (eleven-month) amount that is prepaid as of December 31, which is $1,540.

Examples of other prepaid expenses for which similar adjustments are made include prepaid rent and prepaid advertising. When rent payments are made in advance, the amount is added to (debited to) a Prepaid Rent asset. At the end of an accounting period, an adjusting entry is made to record the portion of occupancy or usage that expired during the period. Rent Expense is debited (increased) and Prepaid Rent is credited (decreased). Similarly, when advertising services are purchased in advance, the payment is debited to Prepaid Advertising. At the end of an accounting period, an adjustment is needed to recognize the cost of any of the prepaid advertising used during the period. The adjusting entry debits (increases) Advertising Expense and credits (decreases) Prepaid Advertising.

DEPRECIATION The process of allocating the costs of equipment, vehicles, and buildings to the periods benefiting from their use is called **depreciation**. Each accounting period in which such assets are used must reflect a portion of their cost as expense because these assets helped generate revenue or support operations for those periods. This periodic expense is known as *depreciation expense*. Periodic depreciation expense is an estimate. The procedure we use here estimates the annual amount of depreciation expense by dividing the asset cost by its estimated useful life. (We assume that the entire asset cost is depreciated—so-called zero salvage value; later in the book we consider salvage values other than zero.) This method is called **straight-line depreciation** and is used by the great majority of companies in their financial reports.

FYI Contra accounts are used to provide more information to users of financial statements. For example, Accumulated Depreciation is a contra asset reported in the balance sheet, which enables users to estimate asset age. For Natural Beauty Supply, the December 31 balance sheet reveals that its Fixtures and Equipment is nearly new as its accumulated depreciation is only \$375, which is 1/48th of the \$18,000 original cost.

Expenses are recorded when business activities reduce net assets. But when we record depreciation expense, the asset amount is not reduced directly. Instead, the reduction is recorded in a **contra asset** account (labeled XA in the journal entries and T-accounts) called *Accumulated Depreciation*. **Contra accounts** are so named because they are used to record reductions in or offsets against a related account. The Accumulated Depreciation account normally has a credit balance and appears in the balance sheet as a deduction from the related asset amount. Use of the *contra asset* Accumulated Depreciation allows the original cost of the asset to be reported in the balance sheet, followed (and reduced) by the accumulated depreciation. Let's consider an example.

The fixtures and equipment purchased by Natural Beauty Supply for \$18,000 are expected to last for four years. Straight-line depreciation recorded on the equipment is \$4,500 per year (\$18,000/4 years), or \$375 per month (\$18,000/48 months). At December 31, Natural Beauty Supply makes adjustment (c), as shown in the following template, journal entry, and T-accounts.

The introduction of contra assets requires a new column in the FSET for these accounts.[2] Increases in a contra asset decrease the net balance of the company's long-term assets. The new column is preceded by a minus sign to indicate that increases in contra assets create a decrease in the asset side of the accounting equation.

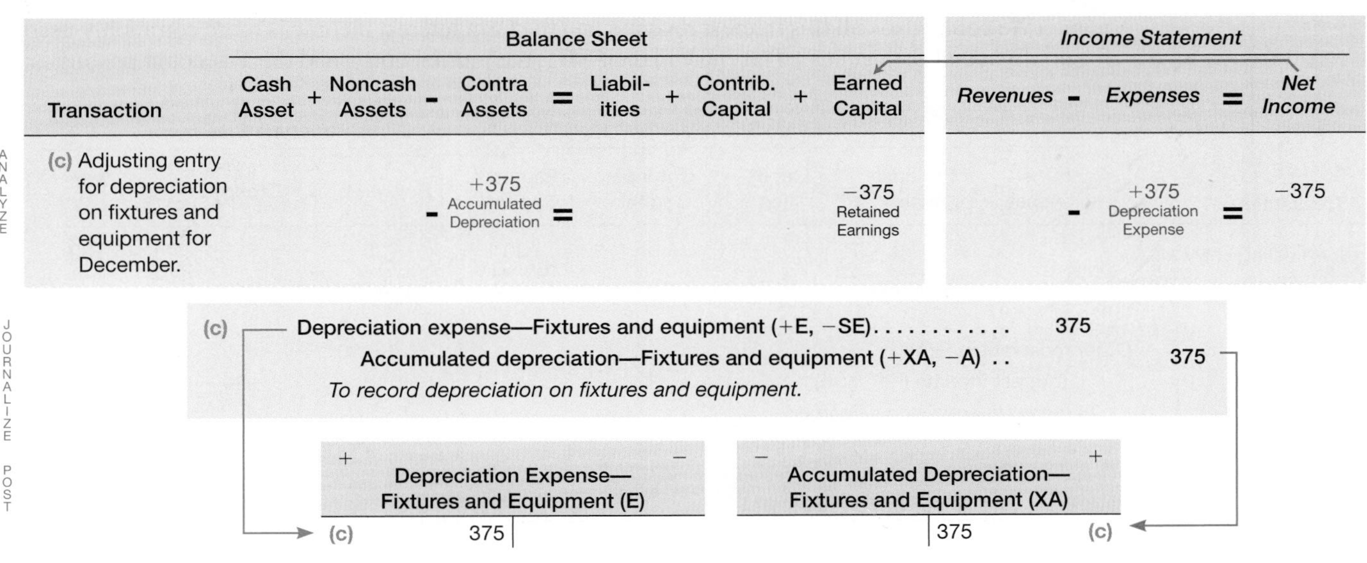

[2] Our practice is to include a separate FSET column where contra assets are required, but not to do so all the time. As we progress through the topics in this text, we will also see examples of contra liability accounts and contra equity accounts.

When this entry is posted, it properly reflects the cost of using this asset during December, and the $375 depreciation expense appears in the December income statement. On the balance sheet, the accumulated depreciation is an offset to the asset amount. The resulting balance (cost less accumulated depreciation), which is the asset's **book value**, represents the unexpired asset cost to be allocated as an expense in future periods. For example, the December 31, 2015, balance sheet reports the equipment with a book value of $17,625, as follows.

FYI An increase in the contra asset account Accumulated Depreciation reduces the book value of the asset.

Fixtures and equipment	$18,000	
Less: Accumulated depreciation	375	
Fixtures and equipment, net	$17,625	(book value)

In each subsequent month, $375 is recognized as depreciation expense, and the Accumulated Depreciation contra asset is increased by the same amount (from $375 to $750 to $1,125 and so on). As a result, the book value of the fixtures and equipment is decreased by $375 each month. In Chapter 8, we will see the same principles applied to certain intangible assets.

Type 3: Accrued Revenues Revenue should be recognized when the company has transferred goods or services to customers, and in an amount that reflects the amount to which the company expects to be entitled from the transfer. Yet, a company often provides services or earns income during a period that is neither paid for by clients or customers nor billed before the end of the period. Such values should be included in the firm's current period income statement, reflecting the company's fulfillment of its agreement with the customer. To properly account for such situations, end-of-period adjusting entries are made to reflect any revenues or income earned, but not yet billed or received. Such accumulated revenue is often called **accrued revenue** or **accrued income**.

ACCRUED SALES REVENUE/INCOME At the end of December, Natural Beauty Supply learns that its bank has decided to provide interest on checking accounts for small businesses like NBS. Each month, NBS earns interest income based on the average balance in its checking account. The interest is paid into NBS's checking account on the fifth business day of the following month. Based on its average daily balance, NBS earned $30 in interest during December.

In this instance, Natural Beauty Supply does not receive the interest payment until January. Nevertheless, the company earned interest during the month of December. Therefore, it should recognize an interest receivable (or "other receivables") asset and interest income in the income statement. (We could also call this interest revenue, but the term interest income is more commonly used for nonfinancial companies.) The entry in the FSET, the journal entry, and the T-account posting is:

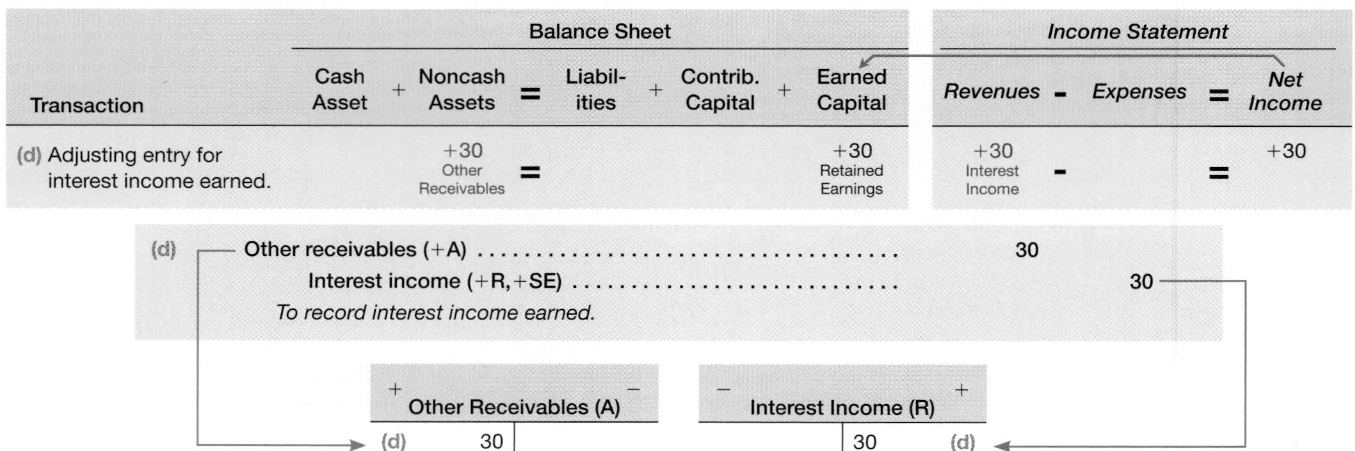

Transaction	Cash Asset	+	Noncash Assets	=	Liabilities	+	Contrib. Capital	+	Earned Capital	Revenues	−	Expenses	=	Net Income
(d) Adjusting entry for interest income earned.			+30 Other Receivables	=					+30 Retained Earnings	+30 Interest Income	−		=	+30

ANALYZE

JOURNALIZE

		Dr.	Cr.
(d)	Other receivables (+A)	30	
	Interest income (+R, +SE)		30
	To record interest income earned.		

POST

+ Other Receivables (A) −	
(d) 30	

− Interest Income (R) +	
	30 (d)

Revenue accruals also occur for landlords who receive rent payments after they are earned. In these cases, revenue has been earned over time as the customer receives and consumes the benefits of the services provided on a continuous basis. We look into these issues more closely in Chapter 6.

Type 4: Accrued Expenses Companies often incur expenses before paying for them. Wages, interest, utilities, and taxes are examples of expenses that are incurred before cash payment is made. Usually the payments are made at regular intervals of time, such as weekly, monthly, quarterly, or annually. If the accounting period ends on a date that does not coincide with a scheduled cash payment date, an adjusting entry is required to reflect the expense incurred since the last cash payment. Such an expense is referred to as an **accrued expense**. Natural Beauty Supply has three such required adjustments for December 31; one for wages, one for interest and one for income tax.

ACCRUED WAGES Natural Beauty Supply employees are paid on a weekly basis. Recall that wages of $1,625 were paid during December in transaction 24. However, as of December 31, the company's employees have earned wages of $480 that will be paid in January. Wages expense of $480 must be recorded in the income statement for December because there is now an obligation to compensate employees, who helped generate revenues for December.

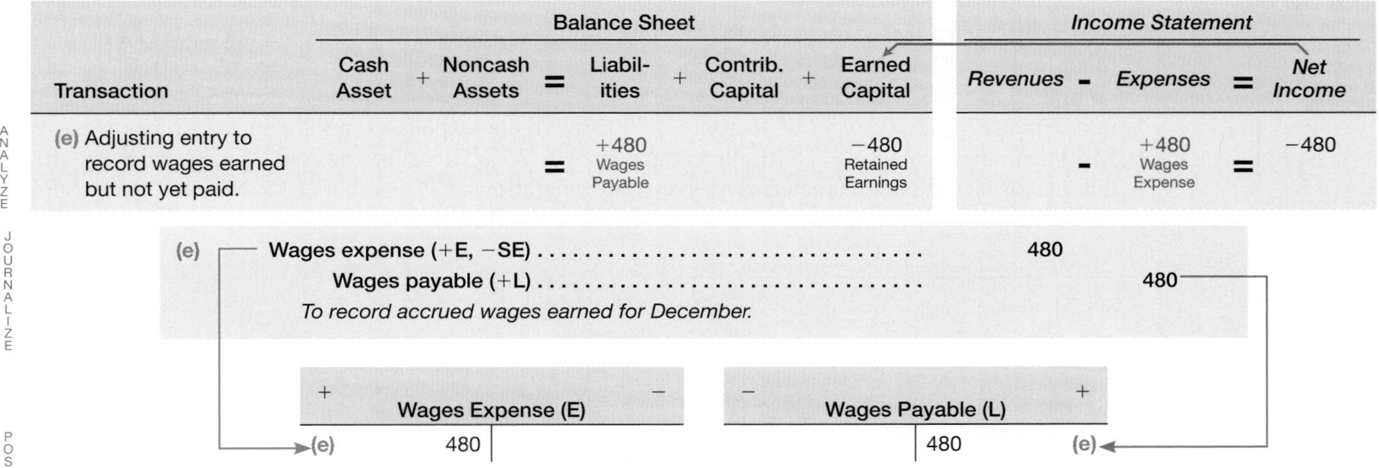

ANALYZE

Transaction	Cash Asset	+	Noncash Assets	=	Liabilities	+	Contrib. Capital	+	Earned Capital	Revenues	−	Expenses	=	Net Income
(e) Adjusting entry to record wages earned but not yet paid.				=	+480 Wages Payable				−480 Retained Earnings		−	+480 Wages Expense	=	−480

JOURNALIZE

		Dr.	Cr.
(e)	Wages expense (+E, −SE)	480	
	Wages payable (+L)		480
	To record accrued wages earned for December.		

POST

+ Wages Expense (E) −		− Wages Payable (L) +	
(e) 480			480 (e)

This adjustment enables the firm to reflect as December expense the cost of all wages *incurred* during the month rather than just the wages *paid*. In addition, the balance sheet shows the liability for unpaid wages at the end of the period.

When the employees are paid in January, the following entry is made.

		Dr.	Cr.
Jan.	Wages payable (−L)	480	
	Cash (−A)		480

This entry eliminates the liability recorded in Wages Payable at the end of December and reduces Cash for the wages paid.

ACCRUED INTEREST On December 1, 2015, Natural Beauty Supply signed a three-year note payable for $11,000. This note has a 12% annual interest rate and requires monthly (interest-only) payments (1% per month), payable on the first business day of the following month. (The interest payment for the month of December is due on January 2.) The $11,000 principal on the note is due at the end of three years. An adjusting entry is required at December 31, 2015, to record interest expense for December and to recognize a liability. December's interest is $110 [$11,000 × (12%/12 months)], and at December 31, NBS makes adjustment (f) in the following template, journal entry, and T-accounts.

	Balance Sheet									*Income Statement*				
Transaction	Cash Asset	+	Noncash Assets	=	Liabil-ities	+	Contrib. Capital	+	Earned Capital	*Revenues*	-	*Expenses*	=	*Net Income*
ANALYZE (f) Adjusting entry to record interest owed but not yet paid.				=	+110 Interest Payable				−110 Retained Earnings		-	+110 Interest Expense	=	−110

JOURNALIZE

		Debit	Credit
(f)	Interest expense (+E, −SE)	110	
	Interest payable (+L)		110
	To record December interest on note payable.		

POST

+ Interest Expense (E) −		− Interest Payable (L) +	
(f) 110			110 (f)

When these entries are posted to the general ledger, the accounts show the correct interest expense for December and the interest liability for one month's interest on the note that has accrued by December 31.

ACCRUED INCOME TAX Natural Beauty Supply is required to pay income taxes based on how much it earns. Using an estimated 35% tax rate, income tax expense for December 2015 is \$350, computed as (\$13,900 sales revenue + \$30 interest income − \$8,000 cost of goods sold − \$1,500 rent expense − \$2,105 wages expense − \$700 advertising expense − \$375 depreciation expense − \$140 insurance expense − \$110 interest expense) × 35%. Taxes are not paid until April 15, 2016, but there is an obligation created as a result of the operations in December 2015. Natural Beauty Supply makes adjustment (g) for taxes in the following template, journal entry, and T-accounts.

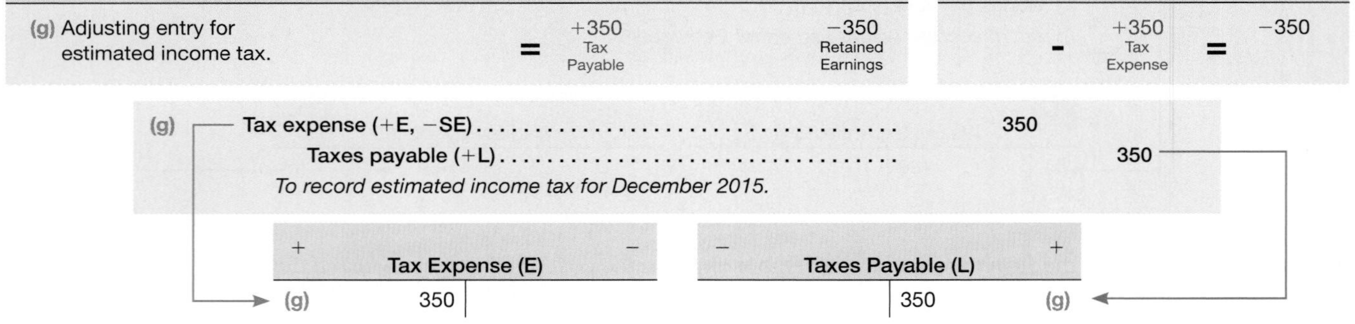

ANALYZE
(g) Adjusting entry for estimated income tax.
=
+350 Tax Payable
−350 Retained Earnings
-
+350 Tax Expense
=
−350
JOURNALIZE
(g) Tax expense (+E, −SE) 350
Taxes payable (+L) 350
To record estimated income tax for December 2015.
POST
+ Tax Expense (E) −
(g) 350
− Taxes Payable (L) +
350 (g)

Exhibit 3.6 summarizes the four types of accounting adjustments, the usual journal entries required for each, and their financial impacts on the balance sheet and income statements.

EXHIBIT 3.6 Summary of Accounting Adjustments

Accounting Adjustment	Examples	Adjusting Entry	Financial Effects if *Not* Adjusted: Balance Sheet	Financial Effects if *Not* Adjusted: Income Statement
Deferrals:				
Unearned revenues	Delivery on advances from clients, gift cards, and subscribers	Dr. Liability Cr. Revenue	Liability overstated Equity understated	Revenue understated
Prepaid expenses	Expiration of prepaid rent, insurance, and advertising; depreciation of buildings and equipment	Dr. Expense Cr. Asset (or Contra asset)	Asset overstated Equity overstated	Expense understated
Accruals:				
Accrued revenues	Earned but not received service, sales, and interest revenues	Dr. Asset Cr. Revenue	Asset understated Equity understated	Revenue understated
Accrued expenses	Incurred but unpaid wages, interest, and tax expenses	Dr. Expense Cr. Liability	Liabilty understated Equity overstated	Expense understated

Ethics and Adjusting Entries

When companies engage in transactions, there is some evidence of the exchange. Cash increases or decreases; asset and liability levels change. Adjusting entries are much more dependent on estimation processes. What was the value of service provided to customers? What obligations have arisen in the past period without a transaction? What is their value? What is the expected useful life of our depreciable assets?

The usefulness of financial performance measures such as net income depends on these questions being answered to the best of management's ability. However, there often are pressures not to provide the most accurate information. For instance, an estimate might convey information about management's strategy that could be used by competitors. Or, the financial community may have set expectations for performance that management cannot meet by executing its current business plan. In these circumstances, managers are sometimes pressured to use the discretion inherent in the reporting process to meet analysts' expectations or to disguise a planned course of action.

The financial reporting environment described in Chapter 1 imposes significant controls on financial reporting, because that reporting process is important to the health of the economy. Managers who do not report accurately and completely are potentially subject to severe penalties. Moreover, adjusting entry estimates have a "self-correcting" character. Underestimating expenses today means greater expenses tomorrow; overestimating revenues today means lower revenues tomorrow.

MID-CHAPTER REVIEW

The following transactions relate to Lundholm Transport Company.

a. The Supplies and Parts balance on September 30, 2015, the company's accounting year-end, reveals $100,000 available. This amount reflects its beginning-year balance and all purchases for the year. A physical inventory indicates that much of this balance has been used in service operations, leaving supplies valued at $9,000 remaining at year-end September 30, 2015.

b. A $5,000 bill for September and October rent on the warehouse was received on September 29, but has not yet been paid or recorded.

c. A building holding its offices was purchased for $400,000 five years ago. The building's life was estimated at 8 years. Assume the entire asset cost is depreciated over its useful life. No depreciation has been recorded for this fiscal year.

d. An executive was hired on September 15 with a $120,000 annual salary. Payment and work are to start on October 15. No entry has yet been made to record this event.

e. A services contract is signed with the local university on September 1. Lundholm Transport Company received $1,200 cash on September 1 as a retainer for the months of September and October, but it has not yet been recorded. Lundholm Transport Company retains the money whether the university requires its services or not.

f. Employees are paid on the first day of the month following the month in which work is performed. Wages earned in September, but not yet paid or recorded as of September 30, amount to $25,000.

Lundholm Transport's ledger includes the following ledger accounts and unadjusted normal balances at September 30: Cash $80,000; Accounts Receivable $95,000; Supplies and Parts $100,000; Building $400,000; Accumulated Depreciation—Building $200,000; Land $257,500; Accounts Payable $20,000; Wages Payable $0; Unearned Revenue $0; Common Stock $80,000; Retained Earnings $380,000; Services Revenue $720,000; Rent Expense $27,500; Depreciation Expense $0; Wages Expense $440,000; Supplies and Parts Expense $0.

Required

1. For each of the six items described above, enter their effects in the financial statement effects template.
2. For each of the six items described above, enter their effects in journal entry form.
3. Set up T-accounts for all ledger accounts and enter the beginning unadjusted balance, the adjustments from part 2, and the adjusted ending balance.

The solution to this review problem can be found on pages 147–149.

CONSTRUCTING FINANCIAL STATEMENTS FROM ADJUSTED ACCOUNTS

4

LO4 Prepare financial statements from adjusted accounts.

This section explains the preparation of financial statements from the adjusted financial accounts.

Preparing an Adjusted Trial Balance

After adjustments are recorded and posted, the company prepares an adjusted trial balance. The **adjusted trial balance** lists all the general ledger account balances after adjustments. Much of the content for company financial statements is taken from an adjusted trial balance. **Exhibit 3.7** shows the general ledger accounts for Natural Beauty Supply after adjustments, in T-account form.

The adjusted trial balance at December 31 for Natural Beauty Supply is prepared from its general ledger accounts and is in the right-hand two columns of **Exhibit 3.8**. We show the unadjusted balances along with the adjustments to highlight the adjustment process.

Preparing Financial Statements

A company prepares its financial statements from the adjusted trial balance (and sometimes other supporting information). The set of financial statements consists of (and is prepared in the order of) the income statement, statement of stockholders' equity, balance sheet, and statement of cash flows. The following diagram summarizes this process.

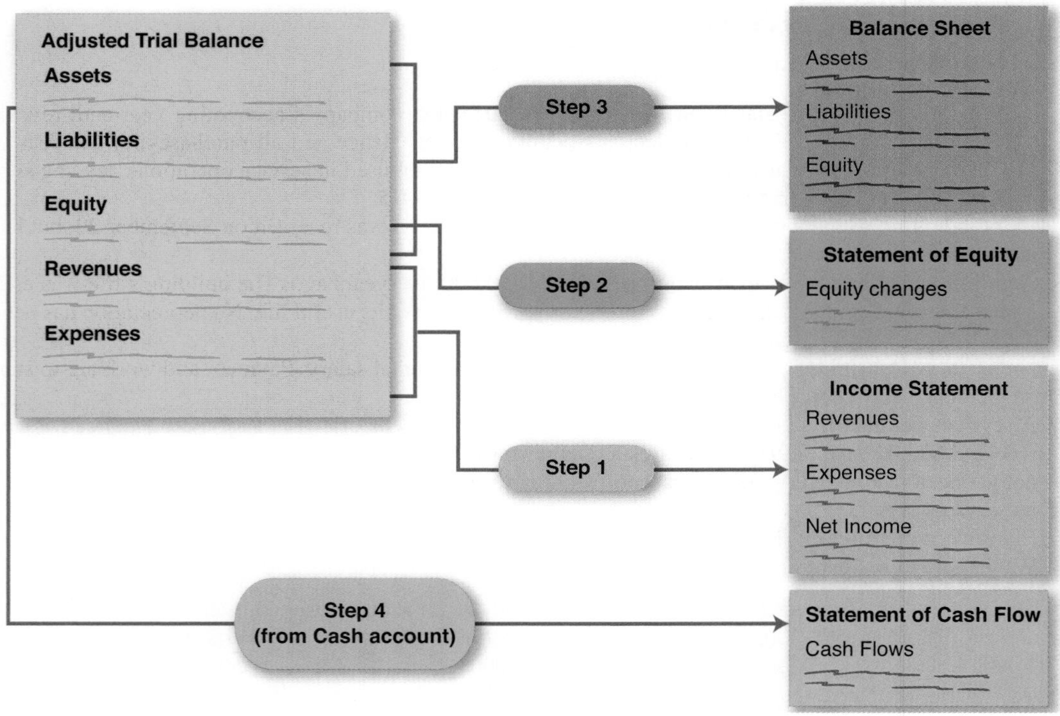

Income Statement The income statement reports a company's revenues and expenses. Natural Beauty Supply's adjusted trial balance contains two revenue/income accounts and eight expense accounts. The revenues and expenses are reported in Natural Beauty Supply's income statement for December as shown in **Exhibit 3.9**. Its net income for December is $650.

EXHIBIT 3.7 General Ledger for Natural Beauty Supply after Adjustments

General Ledger

Assets

Cash (A) (+ / −)

Beg. bal.	8,100		
(17)	11,000	18,000	(18)
(21a)	8,500	700	(19)
(23)	1,200	3,300	(20)
(25)	3,200	1,625	(24)
		1,500	(27)
		50	(28)
Adj. bal.	6,825		

Accounts Receivable (A) (+ / −)

Beg. bal. 950		3,200	(25)
(22a)	4,500		
Adj. bal.	2,250		

Other Receivables (A) (+ / −)

Beg. bal.	0		
(d)	30		
Adj. bal.	30		

Inventory (A) (+ / −)

Beg. bal.	11,300		
(26)	4,000	5,000	(21b)
		3,000	(22b)
Adj. bal.	7,300		

Prepaid Insurance (A) (+ / −)

Beg. bal.	1,680		
		140	(b)
Adj. bal.	1,540		

Security Deposit (A) (+ / −)

Beg. bal.	2,000		
Adj. bal.	2,000		

Fixtures and Equipment (A) (+ / −)

Beg. bal.	0		
(18)	18,000		
Adj. bal.	18,000		

Accumulated Depreciation—Fixtures and Equipment (XA) (− / +)

		0	Beg. bal.
		375	(c)
		375	Adj. bal.

=

Liabilities

Accounts Payable (L) (− / +)

		3,700	Beg. bal.
(20)	3,300	4,000	(26)
		4,400	Adj. bal.

Interest Payable (L) (− / +)

		0	Beg. bal.
		110	(f)
		110	Adj. bal.

Wages Payable (L) (− / +)

		0	Beg. bal.
		480	(e)
		480	Adj. bal.

Taxes Payable (L) (− / +)

		0	Beg. bal.
		350	(g)
		350	Adj. bal.

Unearned Revenue (L) (− / +)

		300	Beg. bal.
(a)	900	1,200	(23)
		600	Adj. bal.

Notes Payable (L) (− / +)

		0	Beg. bal.
		11,000	(17)
		11,000	Adj. bal.

+

Equity

Common Stock (SE) (− / +)

		20,000	Beg. bal.
		20,000	Adj. bal.

Retained Earnings (SE) (− / +)

		30	Beg. bal.
(28)	50		
Adj. bal.	20		

Sales Revenue (R) (− / +)

		0	Beg. bal.
		8,500	(21a)
		4,500	(22a)
		900	(a)
		13,900	Adj. bal.

Interest Income (R) (− / +)

		0	Beg. bal.
		30	(d)
		30	Adj. bal.

Cost of Goods Sold (E) (+ / −)

Beg. bal.	0		
(21b)	5,000		
(22b)	3,000		
Adj. bal.	8,000		

Wages Expense (E) (+ / −)

Beg. bal.	0		
(24)	1,625		
(e)	480		
Adj. bal.	2,105		

Rent Expense (E) (+ / −)

Beg. bal.	0		
(27)	1,500		
Adj. bal.	1,500		

Advertising Expense (E) (+ / −)

Beg. bal.	0		
(19)	700		
Adj. bal.	700		

Depreciation Expense—Fixtures and Equipment (E) (+ / −)

Beg. bal.	0		
(c)	375		
Adj. bal.	375		

Insurance Expense (E) (+ / −)

Beg. bal.	0		
(b)	140		
Adj. bal.	140		

Interest Expense (E) (+ / −)

Beg. bal.	0		
(f)	110		
Adj. bal.	110		

Tax Expense (E) (+ / −)

Beg. bal.	0		
(g)	350		
Adj. bal.	350		

Assets = $37,570 = **Liabilities = $16,940** + **Equity = $20,630**

EXHIBIT 3.8 Unadjusted and Adjusted Trial Balances

NATURAL BEAUTY SUPPLY, INC.
Trial Balance
December 31, 2015

	Unadjusted Trial Balance		Adjustments		Adjusted Trial Balance	
	Debit	Credit	Debit	Credit	Debit	Credit
Cash	$ 6,825				$ 6,825	
Accounts receivable	2,250				2,250	
Other receivables			(d) $ 30		30	
Inventory	7,300				7,300	
Prepaid insurance	1,680			(b) $ 140	1,540	
Security deposit	2,000				2,000	
Fixtures and equipment	18,000				18,000	
Accumulated depreciation				(c) 375		$ 375
Accounts payable		$ 4,400				4,400
Interest payable				(f) 110		110
Wages payable				(e) 480		480
Taxes payable				(g) 350		350
Unearned revenue		1,500	(a) 900			600
Notes payable		11,000				11,000
Common stock		20,000				20,000
Retained earnings	20				20	
Sales revenue		13,000		(a) 900		13,900
Interest income				(d) 30		30
Cost of goods sold	8,000				8,000	
Wages expense	1,625		(e) 480		2,105	
Rent expense	1,500				1,500	
Advertising expense	700				700	
Depreciation expense			(c) 375		375	
Insurance expense			(b) 140		140	
Interest expense			(f) 110		110	
Tax expense			(g) 350		350	
Totals	$49,900	$49,900	$2,385	$2,385	$51,245	$51,245

EXHIBIT 3.9 Income Statement

NATURAL BEAUTY SUPPLY, INC.
Income Statement
For Month Ended December 31, 2015

Sales revenue	$13,900
Cost of goods sold	8,000
Gross profit	5,900
Wages expense	2,105
Rent expense	1,500
Advertising expense	700
Depreciation expense	375
Insurance expense	140
Operating income	1,080
Interest income	30
Interest expense	(110)
Income before tax expense	1,000
Tax expense	350
Net income	$ 650

Statement of Stockholders' Equity The statement of stockholders' equity reports the events causing the major equity components to change during the accounting period. **Exhibit 3.10** shows Natural Beauty Supply's statement of stockholders' equity for December. A review of its common stock account in the general ledger provides some of the information for this statement; namely, its balance at the beginning of the period and stock issuances during the period. The net income (or net loss) amount comes from the income statement. Dividends during the period are reflected in the retained earnings balance from the adjusted trial balance.

EXHIBIT 3.10 Statement of Stockholders' Equity

NATURAL BEAUTY SUPPLY, INC.
Statement of Stockholders' Equity
For Month Ended December 31, 2015

	Contributed Capital	Earned Capital	Total Equity
Balance, November 30, 2015	$20,000	$ 30	$20,030
Net income	—	650	650
Common stock issued	—	—	—
Cash dividends	—	(50)	(50)
Balances, December 31, 2015	$20,000	$630	$20,630

Balance Sheet The balance sheet reports a company's assets, liabilities, and equity. The assets and liabilities for Natural Beauty Supply's balance sheet at December 31, 2015, shown in **Exhibit 3.11**, come from the adjusted trial balance in **Exhibit 3.8**. The amounts reported for Common Stock and Retained Earnings in the balance sheet are taken from the statement of stockholders' equity for December (**Exhibit 3.10**).

FYI Financial statements are most commonly prepared for annual and quarterly accounting periods. A request for a bank loan is an example of a situation that can lead to financial statement preparation for a non-accounting period.

EXHIBIT 3.11 Balance Sheet

NATURAL BEAUTY SUPPLY, INC.
Balance Sheet
December 31, 2015

Assets			**Liabilities**	
Cash		$ 6,825	Accounts payable	$ 4,400
Accounts receivable		2,250	Interest payable	110
Other receivables		30	Wages payable	480
Inventory		7,300	Taxes payable	350
Prepaid insurance		1,540	Unearned revenue	600
Security deposit		2,000	Current liabilities	5,940
Current assets		19,945	Notes payable	11,000
Fixtures and equipment	$18,000		Total liabilities	16,940
Less: Accumulated depreciation	375		**Equity**	
Fixtures and equipment, net		17,625	Common stock	20,000
			Retained earnings	630
Total assets		$37,570	Total liabilities and equity	$37,570

Statement of Cash Flows The statement of cash flows is formatted to report cash inflows and outflows by the three primary business activities:

- *Cash flows from operating activities* Cash flows from the company's transactions and events that relate to its primary operations.
- *Cash flows from investing activities* Cash flows from acquisitions and divestitures of investments and long-term assets.
- *Cash flows from financing activities* Cash flows from issuances of and payments toward equity, borrowings, and long-term liabilities.

The net cash flows from these three sections yield the change in cash for the period.

In analyzing the statement of cash flows, we should not necessarily conclude that the company is better off if cash increases and worse off if cash decreases. It is not the cash change that is most important, but the reasons for the change. For example, what are the sources of the cash inflows?

FYI The income statement, statement of stockholders' equity, and statement of cash flows report on periods of time. These statements illustrate the accounting period concept—the concept that useful statements can be prepared for arbitrary time periods within a company's life span. The purpose of adjusting entries is to obtain useful statements for specific time periods.

Are these sources mainly from operating activities? To what uses have cash inflows been put? Such questions (and their answers) are key to properly using the statement of cash flows. In Chapter 4, we examine the statement of cash flows more closely and answer these questions. The procedures for preparing a statement of cash flows are discussed in the next chapter. For completeness, we present Natural Beauty Supply's statement of cash flows for December in **Exhibit 3.12**.

EXHIBIT 3.12 Statement of Cash Flows

NATURAL BEAUTY SUPPLY, INC.
Statement of Cash Flows
For Month Ended December 31, 2015

Cash Flows from Operating Activities	
Cash received from customers	$12,900
Cash paid for inventory	(3,300)
Cash paid for wages	(1,625)
Cash paid for rent	(1,500)
Cash paid for advertising	(700)
Net cash provided by operating activities	5,775
Cash Flows from Investing Activities	
Cash paid for fixtures and equipment	(18,000)
Net cash used for investing activities	(18,000)
Cash Flows from Financing Activities	
Cash received from loans	11,000
Cash paid for dividends	(50)
Net cash provided by financing activities	10,950
Net change in cash	(1,275)
Cash balance, November 30, 2015	8,100
Cash balance, December 31, 2015	$ 6,825

5 **LO5** Describe the process of closing temporary accounts.

CLOSING TEMPORARY ACCOUNTS

The chart of accounts contains two different types of accounts. Income statement accounts (revenues, expenses, etc.) are used to measure the net assets generated and used in a specific accounting period. As such, their end-of-period balances are reported in the income statement for that period. We use those balances to construct the statements of stockholders' equity and cash flows. But then these account balances have served their purpose, and we must get them ready to do the same thing for the following accounting period. Specifically, we must set their balances to zero so they can accumulate the revenues and expenses for that following period. For this reason, income statement accounts are called **temporary accounts**. Their end-of-period values do not carry over to the next reporting period.

In contrast, balance sheet account balances do carry over to the next reporting period. For example, the end-of-period balance in accounts receivable is the beginning-of-period balance for the next period. Therefore, balance sheet accounts are referred to as **permanent accounts**.

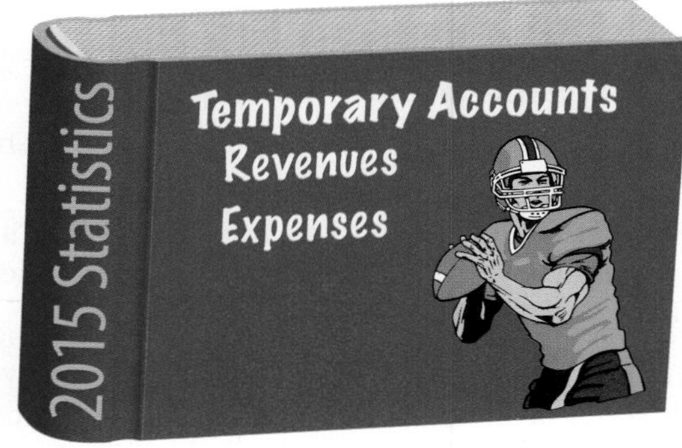

The **closing process** takes the end-of-period balances in the temporary accounts and moves them to a permanent account—the Retained Earnings account. A temporary account is *closed* when an entry is made that changes its balance to zero. The entry is equal in amount to the account's balance but is opposite to the balance as a debit or credit. An account that is closed is said to be closed *to* the account that receives the offsetting debit or credit. Thus, a closing entry simply transfers the balance of one account to another account. When closing entries bring temporary account balances to zero, the temporary accounts are then ready to accumulate data for the next accounting period.

Closing Process

The Retained Earnings account can be used to close the temporary revenue and expense accounts.[3] The entries to close temporary accounts are:

1. **Close revenue accounts.** Debit each revenue account for an amount equal to its balance, and credit Retained Earnings for the total of revenues.
2. **Close expense accounts.** Credit each expense account for an amount equal to its balance, and debit Retained Earnings for the total of expenses.

After these temporary accounts are closed, the difference equals the period's net income (if revenues exceed expenses) or net loss (if expenses exceed revenues) and that difference is now included in Retained Earnings. The closing process is graphically portrayed as follows.

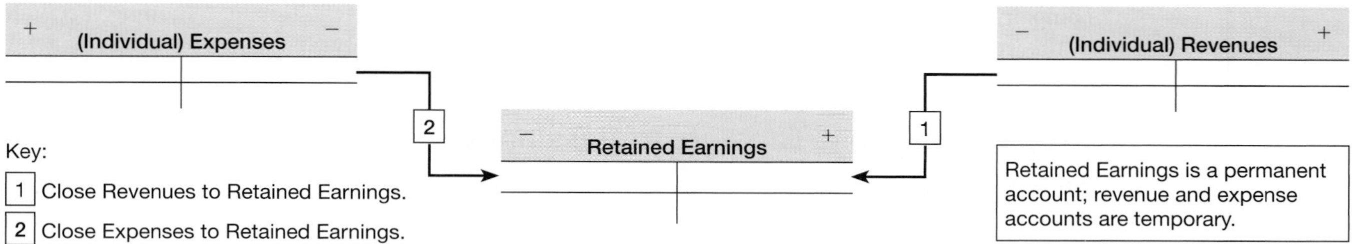

Closing Steps Illustrated

Exhibit 3.13 illustrates the entries for closing revenues and expenses for Natural Beauty Supply. The effects of these entries in T-accounts are shown after the journal entries. (We do not show the financial statement effects template for closing entries because the template automatically closes revenues and expenses to the Retained Earnings account as they occur—see earlier transactions for examples.)

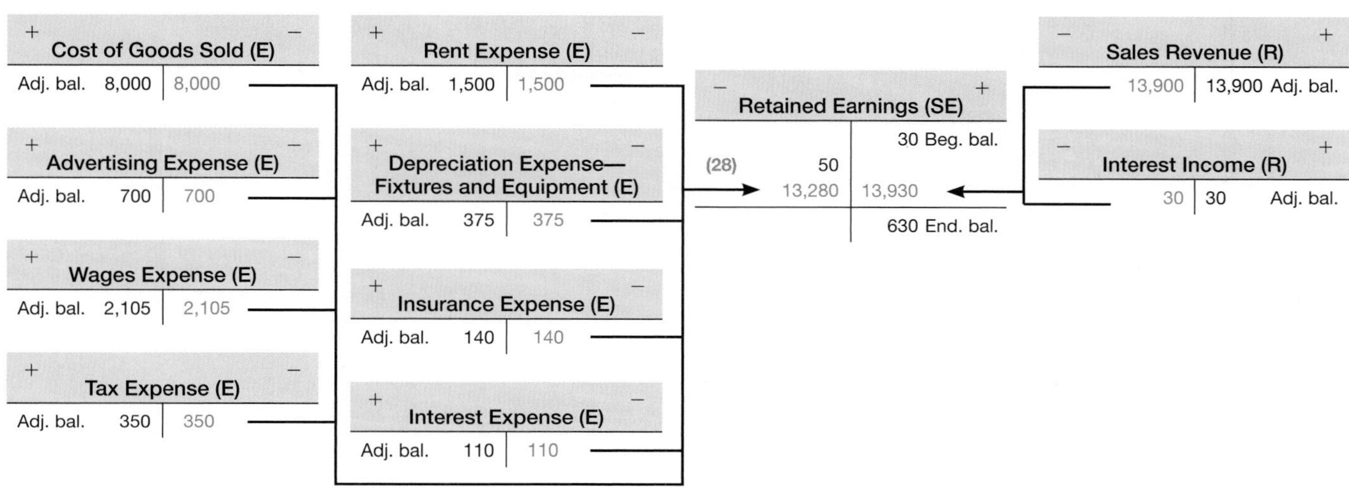

[3] *All* revenue and expense accounts are temporary accounts, so all revenue and expense accounts are closed to retained earnings at the end of the reporting period. In addition, companies often use a temporary account entitled Dividends Declared to record the amount of shareholder dividends declared during a reporting period. This account would accumulate a debit balance (because it reduces equity), and is closed to retained earnings at the end of the reporting period.

EXHIBIT 3.13 Closing Revenues and Expenses*

			Debit	Credit
1	Dec. 31	Sales revenue (−R)	13,900	
		Interest income (−R)	30	
		Retained earnings (+SE)		13,930
2	Dec. 31	Retained earnings (−SE)	13,280	
		Cost of goods sold (−E)		8,000
		Wages expense (−E)		2,105
		Rent expense (−E)		1,500
		Advertising expense (−E)		700
		Depreciation expense (−E)		375
		Insurance expense (−E)		140
		Interest expense (−E)		110
		Tax expense (−E)		350

* The two entries in this exhibit can be combined into a single entry where the credit (debit) to retained earnings would be net income (loss).

After these two steps, the net adjustment to the Retained Earnings account is a credit equal to the company's net income of $650, computed as $13,930 less $13,280. The Retained Earnings account in this case is increased by $650. We also recall that Natural Beauty Supply paid a cash dividend of $50 (transaction 28), which reduces retained earnings and results in the ending balance of $630.

Preparing a Post-Closing Trial Balance

After closing entries are recorded and posted to the general ledger, all temporary accounts have zero balances. At this point, a **post-closing trial balance** is prepared. A balancing of this trial balance is evidence that an equality of debits and credits has been maintained in the general ledger throughout the adjusting and closing process and that the general ledger is in balance to start the next accounting period. Only balance sheet accounts appear in a post-closing trial balance because all income statement accounts have balances of zero. The post-closing trial balance for Natural Beauty Supply is shown in **Exhibit 3.14**.

EXHIBIT 3.14 Post-Closing Trial Balance

NATURAL BEAUTY SUPPLY, INC.
Post-Closing Trial Balance
December 31, 2015

	Debit	Credit
Cash	$ 6,825	
Accounts receivable	2,250	
Other receivables	30	
Inventory	7,300	
Prepaid insurance	1,540	
Security deposit	2,000	
Fixtures and equipment	18,000	
Accumulated depreciation		$ 375
Accounts payable		4,400
Interest payable		110
Wages payable		480
Taxes payable		350
Unearned revenue		600
Notes payable		11,000
Common stock		20,000
Retained earnings		630
Totals	$37,945	$37,945

Subsequent Events

There is usually a few weeks' delay between the end of the fiscal reporting period and the issuing of the financial reports for that period. What happens if a significant event occurs (e.g., a fire at a production facility, an acquisition, etc.) during that interim? Should the previous period's financial statements be changed to reflect the event?

If the event doesn't provide information about the company's condition on the balance sheet date, then the answer is no. So, neither the fire nor the acquisition would be reported in the previous period's financial statements. Such events should be disclosed in a footnote, if they are material.

SUMMARIZING THE ACCOUNTING CYCLE

The sequence of accounting procedures known as the accounting cycle occurs each fiscal year (period) and represents a systematic process for accumulating and reporting financial data of a company. **Exhibit 3.15** expands on **Exhibit 3.1** to include descriptions of the five major steps in the accounting cycle.

EXHIBIT 3.15 Accounting Cycle

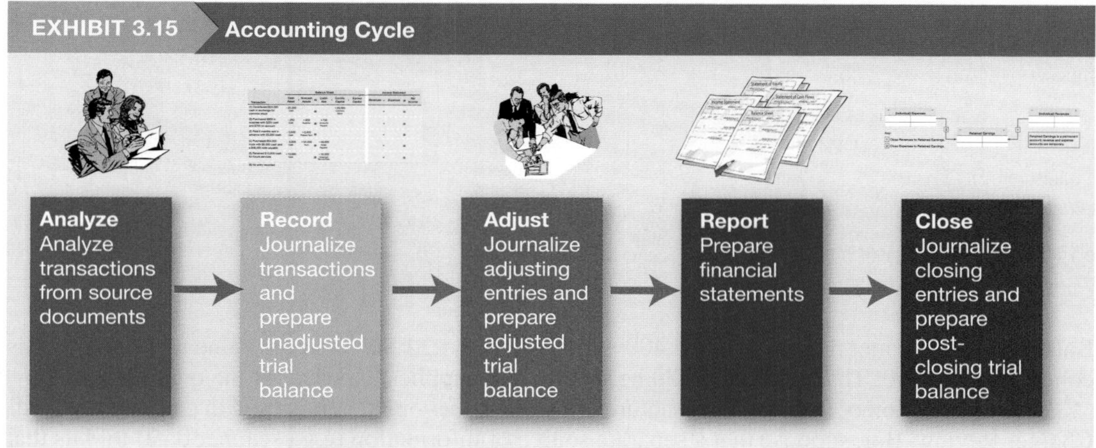
Analyze
Analyze transactions from source documents
Record
Journalize transactions and prepare unadjusted trial balance
Adjust
Journalize adjusting entries and prepare adjusted trial balance
Report
Prepare financial statements
Close
Journalize closing entries and prepare post-closing trial balance

FINANCIAL STATEMENT ANALYSIS

Using Information on Levels and Flows

eLectures
MBC

LO6 Analyze changes in balance sheet accounts.

A careful reader of financial statements must differentiate between those things that depict *levels* and those that depict *flows* or *changes*. The balance sheet portrays levels of resources and claims on those resources at a point in time, and the income statement portrays changes in those levels over a period of time. Knowing how the levels and flows relate to each other can be a very useful tool for analysis.

For instance, suppose that a service business has an inventory of office supplies. On July 1, an inventory count determined that the business has $2,400 of supplies inventory on hand. During the third calendar quarter, there were deliveries of office supplies with a cost of $5,700. And, at the end of the third quarter—on September 30—an inventory count finds $1,900 of supplies on hand. What amount of supplies expense should be recognized for the quarter?

Finding the answer to this question is easier if we recall the transactions that can affect the supplies inventory account, and that these transactions (changes) must lead from the beginning inventory level to the ending inventory level. At present, we know of two such transactions: the purchase of supplies inventory and the usage of supplies inventory.

(a)	Supplies inventory (+A)	5,700	
	Cash (−A) or Accounts payable (+L)		5,700
	Purchase supplies inventory.		
(b)	Supplies expense (+E, −SE)	?	
	Supplies inventory (−A)		?
	Record expense for supplies used.		

The supplies inventory T-account must look like the following:

+	Supplies Inventory (A)		−
Beg. bal.	2,400		
(a)	5,700	?	(b)
End. bal.	1,900		

An FSET version of this analysis would look like the following, with the only noncash account being supplies inventory, and assuming that the inventory purchase was made with cash.

	Balance Sheet					Income Statement		
Transaction	Cash Asset +	Supplies Inventory =	Liabil-ities +	Contrib. Capital +	Earned Capital	*Revenues* −	*Expenses* =	*Net Income*
Beginning balance		$2,400						
(a) Purchase office supplies	−5,700	+5,700						
(b) Office supplies taken for use in client service activities		−?			−? Retained Earnings		+? Supplies Expense	−?
Ending balance		$1,900						

Balancing the account requires that \$2,400 + \$5,700 − ? = \$1,900, and the value that satisfies this condition is \$6,200. That amount would be recorded as supplies expense for the quarter.

This application of the account structure is a simple one—in fact, it is used in part *a* of the Mid-Chapter Review. But, suppose that a separate source of information (e.g., scanner data) told us that \$5,900 in supplies had been taken from inventory for client service activities. When put into the FSET/T-account analysis above, this new fact would imply an additional \$300 in supplies had been removed for reasons such as breakage, obsolescence, or pilferage.

As we progress through the topics in future chapters, we will find that accounting reports do not always provide the information that is most useful for assessment of a company's current performance or standing. In those cases, we can often use T-accounts and journal entries or the FSET to analyze levels and changes and to develop the numbers that do a better job of answering important questions.

CHAPTER-END REVIEW

Assume that Atwell Laboratories, Inc., operates with an accounting fiscal year ending June 30. The company's accounts are adjusted annually and closed on that date. Its unadjusted trial balance as of June 30, 2015, is as follows.

ATWELL LABORATORIES, INC.
Unadjusted Trial Balance
June 30, 2015

	Debit	Credit
Cash	$ 1,000	
Accounts receivable	9,200	
Prepaid insurance	6,000	
Supplies	31,300	
Equipment	270,000	
Accumulated depreciation—equipment		$ 60,000
Accounts payable		3,100
Unearned fees		4,000
Fees revenue		150,000
Wages expense	58,000	
Rent expense	22,000	
Common stock		120,400
Retained earnings		60,000
Totals	$397,500	$397,500

Additional Information

1. Atwell acquired a two-year insurance policy on January 1, 2015. The policy covers fire and casualty; Atwell had no coverage prior to January 1, 2015.
2. An inventory of supplies was taken on June 30 and the amount available was $6,300.
3. All equipment was purchased on July 1, 2012, for $270,000. The equipment's life is estimated at 9 years. Assume the entire asset cost is depreciated over its useful life.
4. Atwell received a $4,000 cash payment on April 1, 2015, from Beave Clinic for diagnostic work to be provided uniformly over the next 4 months, beginning April 1, 2015. The amount was credited to Unearned Fees. The service was provided per the agreement.
5. Unpaid and unrecorded wages at June 30, 2015, were $600.
6. Atwell rents facilities for $2,000 per month. Atwell has not yet made or recorded the payment for June 2015.

In addition to the unadjusted accounts listed above, Atwell's ledger includes the following accounts, all with zero balances: Insurance Expense; Depreciation Expense; Supplies Expense; Wages Payable; and Rent Payable.

Required

1. Show the impact of the necessary adjusting entries using the FSET.
2. Show the impact of the necessary adjusting entries using journal entries.
3. Prepare T-accounts with the unadjusted balances as beginning balances and enter the adjusting entries from part 2. Prepare Atwell's June 30, 2015 adjusted trial balance by entering the adjusting journal entries into the T-accounts.
4. Prepare Atwell's closing journal entries and post them to the T-accounts (key the entries).
5. Prepare the company's June 30, 2015 balance sheet and its income statement and statement of stockholders equity for the year ended June 30, 2015.

The solution to this review problem can be found on pages 150–155.

SUMMARY

LO1 Identify the major steps in the accounting cycle. (p. 102)

- The major steps in the accounting cycle are
  a. Analyze *b.* Record *c.* Adjust *d.* Report *e.* Close

LO2 Review the process of journalizing and posting transactions. (p. 103)

- Transactions are initially recorded in a journal; the entries are in chronological order, and the journal shows the total effect of each transaction or adjustment.
- Posting is the transfer of information from a journal to the general ledger accounts.

LO3 Describe the adjusting process and illustrate adjusting entries. (p. 109)

- Adjusting entries achieve the proper recognition of revenues and the proper matching of expenses with those revenues; adjustments are summarized as follows.

Adjustment	Adjusting Entry
Adjusting prepaid (deferred) expenses	Increase expense Decrease asset
Adjusting unearned (deferred) revenues	Decrease liability Increase revenue
Accruing expenses	Increase expense Increase liability
Accruing revenues	Increase asset Increase revenue

LO4 Prepare financial statements from adjusted accounts. (p. 118)

- An income statement, statement of stockholders' equity, balance sheet, and statement of cash flows are prepared from an adjusted trial balance and other information.

LO5 Describe the process of closing temporary accounts. (p. 122)

- *Closing the books* means closing (yielding zero balances) revenues and expenses—that is, all temporary accounts. Revenue and expense account balances are transferred (closed) to the Retained Earnings account.

LO6 Analyze changes in balance sheet accounts. (p. 125)

- The combination of balance sheet levels and income statement flows allows a financial statement reader to infer the effects of transactions and adjustments that are not disclosed directly.

GUIDANCE ANSWERS . . . YOU MAKE THE CALL

You are the Chief Accountant Deposits represent a liability and should be included in REI's current liabilities at the time the cash or check is received. The account that would be used may have several names, including advances, trip deposits, and unearned revenues. Revenue should not be recognized until the trip has been completed. It is not unusual for events to occur that result in a refund of some portion or even all of the traveler's total payment. In the present case involving a low cancellation rate, waiting until the trip is over is not only conservative reporting, but is likely more efficient bookkeeping as well.

KEY TERMS

Accounting cycle (p. 102)
Accruals (p. 111)
Accrued expense (p. 115)
Accrued income (p. 114)
Accrued revenue (p. 114)
Adjusted trial balance (p. 118)
Adjusting entries (p. 111)
Book value (p. 114)
Calendar year (p. 102)
Chart of accounts (p. 103)
Close expense accounts (p. 123)
Close revenue accounts (p. 123)
Closing process (p. 123)
Contra accounts (p. 113)
Contra asset (p. 113)
Deferrals (p. 111)
Deferred revenue (p. 111)
Depreciation (p. 113)
Fiscal year (p. 102)
General journal (p. 103)
Journal (p. 103)
Permanent accounts (p. 122)
Post-closing trial balance (p. 124)
Posting (p. 103)
Straight-line depreciation (p. 113)
Temporary accounts (p. 122)
Unadjusted trial balance (p. 110)
Unearned revenue (p. 111)

Assignments with the MBC logo in the margin are available in myBusinessCourse. See the Preface of the book for details.

MULTIPLE CHOICE

1. An end-of-period journal entry made to reflect accrual accounting is called
a. a posted journal entry.
b. an adjusting journal entry.
c. an erroneous journal entry.
d. a compound journal entry.

2. Posting refers to the process whereby journal entry information is transferred from 
a. journal to general ledger accounts.
b. general ledger accounts to a journal.
c. source documents to a journal.
d. a journal to source documents.

3. Which of the following is an example of an adjusting entry?
a. Recording the purchase of supplies on account
b. Recording depreciation expense on a truck
c. Recording cash received from customers for services rendered
d. Recording the cash payment of wages to employees

4. A piece of equipment was placed in service on January 1, 2013. The cost of the equipment was $20,000, and it is expected to have no value at the end of its eight-year life. Using straight-line depreciation, what amounts will be seen for depreciation expense and accumulated depreciation for fiscal (and calendar) year 2015? 

	Fiscal Year 2015 Depreciation Expense	Fiscal Year-End 2015 Accumulated Depreciation
a.	$2,500	$ 2,000
b.	–0–	$20,000
c.	$2,500	$ 7,500
d.	$7,500	$ 7,500

5. When a customer places an order, Custom Cakes requires a deposit equal to the full purchase price. However, Custom Cakes does not recognize revenue until the completed cake is delivered. During the month of November 2015, Custom Cakes received $24,000 in customer deposits. The balance in its unearned revenue liability was $4,000 at the beginning of November and $6,000 at the end of November. How much revenue did Custom Cakes recognize during the month of November? 
a. $26,000
b. $24,000
c. $22,000
d. $4,000

Multiple Choice Answers
1. b 2. a 3. b 4. c 5. c

QUESTIONS

Q3-1. What are the five major steps in the accounting cycle? List them in their proper order.

Q3-2. What does the term *fiscal year* mean?

Q3-3. What are three examples of source documents that underlie business transactions?

Q3-4. What is the nature and purpose of a general journal?

Q3-5. Explain the process of posting.

Q3-6. What is an adjusting journal entry?

Q3-7. What is a chart of accounts? Give an example of a coding system for identifying different types of accounts.

Q3-8. Why is the adjusting step of the accounting cycle necessary?

Q3-9. What four different types of adjustments are frequently necessary at the close of an accounting period? Give examples of each type.

Q3-10. On January 1, Prepaid Insurance was debited with the cost of a two-year premium, $1,872. What adjusting entry should be made on January 31 before financial statements are prepared for the month?

Q3-11. What is a contra account? What contra account is used in reporting the book value of a depreciable asset?

Q3-12. A building was acquired on January 1, 2011, at a cost of $4,000,000, and its depreciation is calculated using the straight-line method. At the end of 2015, the accumulated depreciation contra asset for the building is $800,000. What will be the balance in the building's accumulated depreciation contra asset at the end of 2022? What is the building's book value at that date?

Q3-13. The publisher of *International View*, a monthly magazine, received two-year subscriptions totaling $9,720 on January 1. (a) What entry should be made to record the receipt of the $9,720? (b) What entry should be made at the end of January before financial statements are prepared for the month?

Q3-14. Globe Travel Agency pays an employee $475 in wages each Friday for the five-day workweek ending on that day. The last Friday of January falls on January 27. What adjusting entry should be made on January 31, the fiscal year-end?

Q3-15. The Bayou Company earns interest amounting to $360 per month on its investments. The company receives the interest every six months, on December 31 and June 30. Monthly financial statements are prepared. What adjusting entry should be made on January 31?

Q3-16. Which groups of accounts are closed at the end of the accounting year?

Q3-17. What are the two major steps in the closing process?

Q3-18. What is the purpose of a post-closing trial balance? Which of the following accounts should *not* appear in the post-closing trial balance: Cash; Unearned Revenue; Prepaid Rent; Depreciation Expense; Utilities Payable; Supplies Expense; and Retained Earnings?

Q3-19. Dehning Corporation is an international manufacturer of films and industrial identification products. Included among its prepaid expenses is an account titled Prepaid Catalog Costs; in recent years, this account's size has ranged between $2,500,000 and $4,000,000. The company states that catalog costs are initially capitalized and then written off over the estimated useful lives of the publications (generally eight months). Identify and briefly discuss the accounting principles that support Dehning Corporation's handling of its catalog costs.

Q3-20. At the beginning of January, the first month of the accounting year, the supplies account had a debit balance of $825. During January, purchases of $260 worth of supplies were debited to the account. Although only $630 of supplies were still available at the end of January, the necessary adjusting entry was omitted. How will the omission affect (a) the income statement for January, and (b) the balance sheet prepared at January 31?

MINI EXERCISES

LO2

M3-21. Journalizing Transactions in Template, Journal Entry Form, and T-Accounts

Creative Designs, a firm providing art services for advertisers, began business on June 1, 2015. The following transactions occurred during the month of June.

June 1 Anne Clem invested $12,000 cash to begin the business in exchange for common stock.
2 Paid $950 cash for June rent.

June 3 Purchased $6,400 of office equipment on account.
6 Purchased $3,800 of art materials and other supplies; paid $1,800 cash with the remainder due within 30 days.
11 Billed clients $4,700 for services rendered.
17 Collected $3,250 cash from clients on their accounts.
19 Paid $3,000 cash toward the account for office equipment suppliers (see June 3).
25 Paid $900 cash for dividends.
30 Paid $350 cash for June utilities.
30 Paid $2,500 cash for June salaries.

REQUIRED

a. Record the above transactions for June using the financial statement effects template.

b. The following accounts in its general ledger are needed to record the transactions for June: Cash; Accounts Receivable; Supplies; Office Equipment; Accounts Payable; Common Stock; Retained Earnings; Service Fees Earned; Rent Expense; Utilities Expense; and Salaries Expense. Record the above transactions for June in journal entry form.

c. Set up T-accounts for each of the ledger accounts and post the entries to them (key the numbers in T-accounts by date).

M3-22. Journalizing Transactions in Template, Journal Entry Form, and T-Accounts LO2

Minute Maid, a firm providing housecleaning services, began business on April 1, 2015. The following transactions occurred during the month of April.

April 1 A. Falcon invested $9,000 cash to begin the business in exchange for common stock.
2 Paid $2,850 cash for six months' lease on van for the business.
3 Borrowed $10,000 cash from bank and signed note payable agreeing to repay it in 1 year plus 10% interest.
3 Purchased $5,500 of cleaning equipment; paid $2,500 cash with the remainder due within 30 days.
4 Paid $4,300 cash for cleaning supplies.
7 Paid $350 cash for advertisements to run in newspaper during April.
21 Billed customers $3,500 for services performed.
23 Paid $3,000 cash on account to cleaning equipment suppliers (see April 3).
28 Collected $2,300 cash from customers on their accounts.
29 Paid $1,000 cash for dividends.
30 Paid $1,750 cash for April wages.
30 Paid $995 cash to service station for gasoline used during April.

REQUIRED

a. Record the above transactions for April using the financial statement effects template.

b. The following accounts in its general ledger are needed to record the transactions for April: Cash; Accounts Receivable; Supplies; Prepaid Van Lease; Equipment; Accounts Payable; Notes Payable; Common Stock; Retained Earnings; Cleaning Fees Earned; Van Fuel Expense; Advertising Expense; and Wages Expense. Record the above transactions for April in journal entry form.

c. Set up T-accounts for each of the ledger accounts and post the entries to them (key the numbers in T-accounts by date).

M3-23. Journalizing Transactions and Adjusting Accounts LO2, 3

Deluxe Building Services offers custodial services on both a contract basis and an hourly basis. On January 1, 2015, Deluxe collected $20,100 in advance on a six-month contract for work to be performed evenly during the next six months. Assume that Deluxe closes its books and issues financial reports on a monthly basis.

a. Prepare the entry on January 1 to record the receipt of $20,100 cash for contract work (1) using the financial statements effect template and (2) in journal entry form.

b. Prepare the adjusting entry to be made on January 31, 2015, for the contract work done during January (1) using the financial statements effect template and (2) in journal entry form.

c. At January 31, a total of 30 hours of hourly rate custodial work was unbilled. The billing rate is $19 per hour. Prepare the adjusting entry needed on January 31, 2015, (1) using the financial statements effect template and (2) in journal entry form. (The firm uses the account Fees Receivable to reflect amounts due but not yet billed.)

LO3, 6

M3-24. Adjusting Accounts

Selected accounts of Ideal Properties, a real estate management firm, are shown below as of January 31, 2015, before any adjusting entries have been made.

Unadjusted Account Balances	Debits	Credits
Prepaid insurance	$6,660	
Supplies inventory	1,930	
Office equipment	5,952	
Unearned rent revenue		$ 5,250
Salaries expense	3,100	
Rent revenue		15,000

Monthly financial statements are prepared. Using the following information, record the adjusting entries necessary on January 31 (a) using the financial statements effect template and (b) in journal entry form.

1. Prepaid Insurance represents a three-year premium paid on January 1, 2015.
2. Supplies of $850 were still available on January 31.
3. Office equipment—purchased on January 1, 2015—is expected to last eight years.
4. On January 1, 2015, Ideal Properties collected six months' rent in advance from a tenant renting space for $875 per month.
5. Accrued employee salaries of $490 have not been recorded as of January 31.

LO2, 3, 6

El Puerto de Liverpool
OTCMKTS :: ELPQF

M3-25. Inferring Transactions from Financial Statements

El Puerto de Liverpool (Liverpool) is a large retailer in Mexico. The following accounts are selected from its annual report for the fiscal year ended December 31, 2013. For the fiscal year ended December 31, 2013, Liverpool purchased merchandise inventory costing 44,998,092 thousand Mexican pesos. Assume that all purchases were made on account. The following T-accounts reflect information contained in the company's 2013 and 2012 balance sheets (in thousands of Mexican pesos).

+ Inventories (A)	−
12/31/2012 Bal. 10,558,247	
12/31/2013 Bal. 11,421,969	

− Suppliers (Accounts Payable)	+
	10,288,069 12/31/2012 Bal.
	11,454,374 12/31/2013 Bal.

a. Prepare the entry, using the financial statement effects template and in journal entry form, to record Liverpool's purchases for the 2013 fiscal year.

b. What amount did Liverpool pay in cash to its suppliers for the fiscal year ended December 31, 2013? Explain. Assume that Suppliers (Accounts payable) is affected only by transactions related to inventory.

c. Prepare the entry, using the financial statement effects template and in journal entry form, to record cost of goods sold for the year ended December 31, 2013.

LO4

M3-26. Preparing a Statement of Stockholders' Equity

On December 31, 2014, the credit balances of the Common Stock and Retained Earnings accounts were $30,000 and $18,000, respectively, for Architect Services Company. Its stock issuances for 2015 totaled $6,000, and it paid $9,700 cash toward dividends in 2015. For the year ended December 31, 2015, the company had net income of $29,900. Prepare a 2015 statement of stockholders' equity for Architect Services.

LO5

M3-27. Applying Closing Procedures

Assume you are in the process of closing procedures for Echo Corporation. You have already closed all revenue and expense accounts to the Retained Earnings account. The total debits to Retained Earnings equal $308,800 and total credits to Retained Earnings equal $347,400. The Retained Earnings account had a credit balance of $99,000 at the start of this current year. What is the post-closing ending balance of Retained Earnings at the end of this current year?

LO5

M3-28. Preparing Closing Entries Using Journal Entries and T-Accounts

The adjusted trial balance at December 31, 2015, for Smith Company includes the following selected accounts.

Adjusted Account Balances	Debit	Credit
Commissions revenue		$84,900
Wages expense	$36,000	
Insurance expense	1,900	
Utilities expense	8,200	
Depreciation expense	9,800	
Retained earnings		72,100

a. Prepare entries to close these accounts in journal entry form.

b. Set up T-accounts for each of these ledger accounts, enter the balances above, and post the closing entries to them. After these entries are posted, what is the post-closing balance of the Retained Earnings account?

M3-29. Inferring Transactions from Financial Statements

LO2, 3, 6

Amazon.com Inc.
NASDAQ :: AMZN

Amazon.com Inc. is one of the world's leading e-commerce companies, with almost $90 billion in revenues for the fiscal year ended December 31, 2014. For the year ended December 31, 2014, Amazon's cost of goods sold was $62,752 million. Assume that all purchases were made on account. The following T-accounts reflect information contained in the company's 2014 and 2013 balance sheets (in millions).

+ Inventories		−
12/31/2013 Bal.	$7,411	
12/31/2014 Bal.	$8,299	

− Accounts Payable		+
	$15,133	12/31/2013 Bal.
	$16,459	12/31/2014 Bal.

a. Prepare the entry, using the financial statement effects template and in journal entry form, to record cost of goods sold for the year ended December 31, 2014.

b. Prepare the entry, using the financial statement effects template and in journal entry form, to record Amazon's inventory purchases for the year ended December 31, 2014. (Assume all purchases are made on account.)

c. What amount did Amazon pay in cash to its suppliers for the year ended December 31, 2014?

M3-30. Preparing Entries Across Two Periods

LO2, 3, 5

Homework MBC

Hatcher Company closes its accounts on December 31 each year. On December 31, 2015, Hatcher accrued $600 of interest income that was earned on an investment but not yet received or recorded (the investment will pay interest of $900 cash on January 31, 2016). On January 31, 2016, the company received the $900 cash as interest on the investment. Prepare journal entries to:

a. Accrue the interest earned on December 31;

b. Close the Interest Income account on December 31 (the account has a year-end balance of $2,400 after adjustments); and

c. Record the cash receipt of interest on January 31, 2016.

EXERCISES

E3-31. Journalizing and Posting Closing Entries

LO5

Homework MBC

The adjusted trial balance as of December 31, 2015, for Brooks Consulting Company contains the following selected accounts.

Adjusted Account Balances	Debit	Credit
Service fees earned		€80,300
Rent expense	€20,800	
Salaries expense	45,700	
Supplies expense	5,600	
Depreciation expense	10,200	
Retained earnings		67,000

a. Prepare entries to close these accounts in journal entry form.

b. Set up T-accounts for each of the ledger accounts, enter the balances above, and post the closing entries to them. After these entries are posted, what is the post-closing balance of the Retained Earnings account?

LO3 

Hartford Financial Services Group
NYSE :: HIG

E3-32. Preparing and Journalizing Adjusting Entries

For each of the following separate situations, prepare the necessary adjustments (a) using the financial statement effects template, and (b) in journal entry form.

1. Unrecorded depreciation on equipment is $610.
2. On the date for preparing financial statements, an estimated utilities expense of $390 has been incurred, but no utility bill has yet been received or paid.
3. On the first day of the current period, rent for four periods was paid and recorded as a $2,800 debit to Prepaid Rent and a $2,800 credit to Cash.
4. Nine months ago, the **Hartford Financial Services Group** sold a one-year policy to a customer and recorded the receipt of the premium by debiting Cash for $624 and crediting Unearned Premium Revenue for $624. No adjusting entries have been prepared during the nine-month period. Hartford's annual financial statements are now being prepared.
5. At the end of the period, employee wages of $965 have been incurred but not yet paid or recorded.
6. At the end of the period, $300 of interest income has been earned but not yet received or recorded.

LO2, 3, 5 

E3-33. Preparing Adjusting and Closing Entries Across Two Periods

Norton Company closes its accounts on December 31 each year. The company works a five-day work week and pays its employees every two weeks. On December 31, 2015, Norton accrued $4,700 of salaries payable. On January 7, 2016, the company paid salaries of $12,000 cash to employees. Prepare journal entries to:

a. Accrue the salaries payable on December 31;

b. Close the Salaries Expense account on December 31 (the account has a year-end balance of $250,000 after adjustments); and

c. Record the salary payment on January 7.

LO3, 6 

E3-34. Analyzing Accounts Using Adjusted Data

Selected T-account balances for Fields Company are shown below as of January 31, 2016; adjusting entries have already been posted. The firm uses a calendar-year accounting period but prepares *monthly* adjustments.

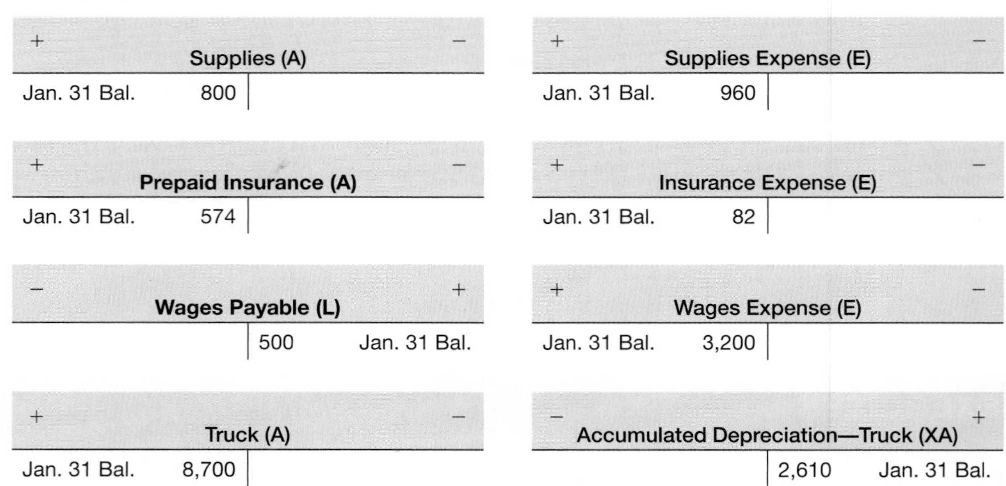

a. If the amount in Supplies Expense represents the January 31 adjustment for the supplies used in January, and $620 worth of supplies were purchased during January, what was the January 1 beginning balance of Supplies?

b. The amount in the Insurance Expense account represents the adjustment made at January 31 for January insurance expense. If the original insurance premium was for one year, what was the amount of the premium and on what date did the insurance policy start?

c. If we assume that no beginning balance existed in wages payable or wages expense on January 1, how much cash was paid as wages during January?

d. If the truck has a useful life of five years, what is the monthly amount of depreciation expense and how many months has Fields owned the truck?

E3-35. Preparing Adjusting Entries

LO2, 3, 6

Jake Thomas began Thomas Refinishing Service on July 1, 2015. Selected accounts are shown below as of July 31, before any adjusting entries have been made.

Unadjusted Account Balances	Debit	Credit
Prepaid rent	$5,700	
Prepaid advertising	630	
Supplies inventory	3,000	
Unearned refinishing fees		$ 600
Refinishing fees revenue		2,500

Using the following information, prepare the adjusting entries necessary on July 31 (a) using the financial statement effects template and (b) in journal entry form. (c) Set up T-accounts for each of the ledger accounts, enter the balances above, and post the adjusting entries to them.

1. On July 1, the firm paid one year's advance rent of $5,700 in cash.
2. On July 1, $630 cash was paid to the local newspaper for an advertisement to run daily for the months of July, August, and September.
3. Supplies still available at July 31 total $1,100.
4. At July 31, refinishing services of $800 have been performed but not yet recorded or billed to customers. The firm uses the account Fees Receivable to reflect amounts due but not yet billed.
5. A customer paid $600 in advance for a refinishing project. At July 31, the project is one-half complete.

E3-36. Inferring Transactions from Financial Statements

LO2, 3, 6

Abercrombie & Fitch Co.
NYSE :: ANF

Abercrombie & Fitch Co. (ANF) is a specialty retailer of casual apparel. The following information is taken from ANF's fiscal 10-K report for the fiscal year 2013, which ended February 1, 2014. (All amounts in $ thousands.)

Selected Balance Sheet Data	February 1, 2014	February 2, 2013
Inventory	$530,192	$426,962
Accrued compensation	49,878	74,747

a. ANF reported Cost of Goods Sold of $1,541,462 (thousand) for its fiscal year 2013. What was the cost that ANF incurred to acquire inventory for its fiscal year 2013?

b. Assume that ANF reported Compensation Expense of $650,000 (thousand) for its fiscal year 2013. What amount of compensation was paid to its employees for fiscal year 2013?

c. Where would you expect ANF to report its balance of Accrued Compensation?

E3-37. Preparing Closing Procedures

LO5

The adjusted trial balance of Parker Corporation, prepared December 31, 2015, contains the following selected accounts.

Adjusted Account Balances	Debit	Credit
Service fees earned		$92,500
Interest income		2,200
Salaries expense	$41,800	
Advertising expense	4,300	
Depreciation expense	8,700	
Income tax expense	9,900	
Retained earnings		42,700

a. Prepare entries to close these accounts in journal entry form.

b. Set up T-accounts for each of the ledger accounts, enter the balances above, and post the closing entries to them. After these entries are posted, what is the post-closing balance of the Retained Earnings account?

E3-38. Inferring Transactions from Financial Statements

LO2, 3, 6

Ethan Allen Interiors Inc.
NYSE :: ETH

Ethan Allen Interiors Inc., a leading manufacturer and retailer of home furnishings and accessories, sells products through an exclusive network of approximately 300 design centers. All of Ethan Allen's products are sold by special order. Customers generally place a deposit equal to 25%

to 50% of the purchase price when ordering. Orders take 4 to 12 weeks to be delivered. Selected fiscal-year information from the company's balance sheets is as follows ($ thousands):

Selected Balance Sheet Data	2014	2013
Inventories	$146,275	$137,256
Customer deposits	59,684	59,098

a. In fiscal 2014, Ethan Allen reported total sales revenue of $746,659 (thousand). Assume that the company collected customer deposits equal to $200,000 (thousand) over the year. Prepare entries, using the financial statement effects template and in journal entry form, to record customer deposits and its sales revenue for fiscal year 2014.

b. Ethan Allen's cost of goods sold for 2014 was $340,163 (thousand). Prepare the adjusting entry, using the financial statement effects template and in journal entry form, that it made to record inventory acquisitions.

c. Where would you expect Ethan Allen to report its Customer Deposits?

LO4, 5

E3-39. Preparing Financial Statements and Closing Procedures

Solomon Corporation's adjusted trial balance for the year ending December 31, 2015, is:

SOLOMON CORPORATION Adjusted Trial Balance December 31, 2015	Debit	Credit
Cash	$ 4,000	
Accounts receivable	6,500	
Equipment	78,000	
Accumulated depreciation		$ 14,000
Notes payable		10,000
Common stock		43,000
Retained earnings		12,600
Service fees earned		71,000
Rent expense	18,000	
Salaries expense	37,100	
Depreciation expense	7,000	
Totals	$150,600	$150,600

a. Prepare its income statement and statement of stockholders' equity for the current year, and its balance sheet for the current year-end. Cash dividends were $8,000 and there were no stock issuances or repurchases.

b. Prepare entries to close its temporary accounts in journal entry form.

c. Set up T-accounts for each of the ledger accounts, enter the balances above, and post the closing entries to them. After these entries are posted, what is the post-closing balance of the Retained Earnings account?

PROBLEMS

LO2, 3, 6

P3-40. Journalizing and Posting Transactions, and Preparing a Trial Balance and Adjustments

B. Lougee opened Lougee Roofing Service on April 1, 2015. Transactions for April are as follows:

Apr. 1 Lougee contributed $11,500 cash to the business in exchange for common stock.
1 Paid $2,880 cash for two-year premium toward liability insurance effective immediately.
2 Paid $6,100 cash for the purchase of a used truck.
2 Purchased $3,100 of ladders and other equipment; paid $1,000 cash, with the balance due in 30 days.
5 Purchased $1,200 of supplies on account.
5 Received an advance of $1,800 cash from a customer for roof repairs to be done during April and May.
12 Billed customers $5,500 for roofing services performed.

Apr 18 Collected $4,900 cash from customers on their accounts.
29 Paid $675 cash for truck fuel used in April.
30 Paid $100 cash for April newspaper advertising.
30 Paid $2,500 cash for assistants' wages.
30 Billed customers $4,000 for roofing services performed.

REQUIRED

a. Set up a general ledger in T-account form for the following accounts: Cash; Accounts Receivable; Supplies; Prepaid Insurance; Trucks; Accumulated Depreciation—Trucks; Equipment; Accumulated Depreciation—Equipment; Accounts Payable; Unearned Roofing Fees; Common Stock; Roofing Fees Earned; Fuel Expense; Advertising Expense; Wages Expense; Insurance Expense; Supplies Expense; Depreciation Expense—Trucks; and Depreciation Expense—Equipment.

b. Record these transactions for April (1) using the financial statement effects template and (2) in journal entry form. (3) Post these entries to their T-accounts (key numbers in T-accounts by date).

c. Prepare an unadjusted trial balance as of April 30, 2015.

d. Supplies still available on April 30 amount to $400; and depreciation for April was $125 on the truck and $35 on equipment; and one-fourth of the roofing fee received in advance was earned by April 30. Prepare entries to adjust the books for Insurance Expense, Supplies Expense, Depreciation Expense—Trucks, Depreciation Expense—Equipment, and Roofing Fees Earned (1) using the financial statement effects template and (2) in journal entry form. (3) Post adjusting entries to their T-accounts.

P3-41. Preparing an Unadjusted Trial Balance and Adjustments **LO2, 3**

SnapShot Company, a commercial photography studio, has just completed its first full year of operations on December 31, 2015. General ledger account balances *before* year-end adjustments follow; no adjusting entries have been made to the accounts at any time during the year. Assume that all balances are normal.

Cash	$ 2,150	Accounts payable	$ 1,910
Accounts receivable	3,800	Unearned photography fees	2,600
Prepaid rent	12,600	Common stock	24,000
Prepaid insurance	2,970	Photography fees earned	34,480
Supplies	4,250	Wages expense	11,000
Equipment	22,800	Utilities expense	3,420

An analysis of the firm's records discloses the following.

1. Photography services of $925 have been rendered, but customers have not yet paid or been billed. The firm uses the account Fees Receivable to reflect amounts due but not yet billed.
2. Equipment, purchased January 1, 2015, has an estimated life of 10 years.
3. Utilities expense for December is estimated to be $400, but the bill will not arrive or be paid until January of next year.
4. The balance in Prepaid Rent represents the amount paid on January 1, 2015, for a 2-year lease on the studio.
5. In November, customers paid $2,600 cash in advance for photos to be taken for the holiday season. When received, these fees were credited to Unearned Photography Fees. By December 31, all of these fees are earned.
6. A 3-year insurance premium paid on January 1, 2015, was debited to Prepaid Insurance.
7. Supplies available at December 31 are $1,520.
8. At December 31, wages expense of $375 has been incurred but not paid or recorded.

REQUIRED

a. Prove that debits equal credits for SnapShot's unadjusted account balances by preparing its unadjusted trial balance at December 31, 2015.

b. Prepare its adjusting entries using the financial statement effects template.

c. Prepare its adjusting entries in journal entry form.

d. Set up T-accounts, enter the balances above, and post the adjusting entries to them.

P3-42. Preparing Adjusting Entries, Financial Statements, and Closing Entries **LO2, 3, 4, 5, 6**

Murdock Carpet Cleaners ended its first month of operations on June 30, 2015. Monthly financial statements will be prepared. The unadjusted account balances are as follows.

MURDOCK CARPET CLEANERS Unadjusted Trial Balance June 30, 2015	Debit	Credit
Cash	$ 1,180	
Accounts receivable	450	
Prepaid rent	3,100	
Supplies	2,520	
Equipment	4,440	
Accounts payable		$ 760
Common stock		2,000
Retained earnings		5,300
Service fees earned		4,650
Wages expense	1,020	
	$12,710	$12,710

The following information is available.

1. The balance in Prepaid Rent was the amount paid on June 1 for the first four months' rent.
2. Supplies available at June 30 were $820.
3. Equipment, purchased June 1, has an estimated life of five years.
4. Unpaid and unrecorded employee wages at June 30 were $210.
5. Utility services used during June were estimated at $300. A bill is expected early in July.
6. Fees earned for services performed but not yet billed on June 30 were $380. The company uses the account Accounts Receivable to reflect amounts due but not yet billed.

REQUIRED

a. Prepare its adjusting entries at June 30, 2015 using the financial statement effects template.
b. Prepare its adjusting entries at June 30, 2015 in journal entry form.
c. Set up T-accounts, enter the balances above, and post the adjusting entries to them.
d. Prepare its income statement for June and its balance sheet at June 30, 2015.
e. Prepare entries to close its temporary accounts in journal entry form and post the closing entries to the T-accounts.

LO3 **P3-43. Preparing Adjusting Entries**

The following information relates to the December 31 adjustments for Kwik Print Company. The firm's fiscal year ends on December 31.

1. Weekly employee salaries for a five-day week total $1,800, payable on Fridays. December 31 of the current year is a Tuesday.
2. Kwik Print has $20,000 of notes payable outstanding at December 31. Interest of $200 has accrued on these notes by December 31, but will not be paid until the notes mature next year.
3. During December, Kwik Print provided $900 of printing services to clients who will be billed on January 2. The firm uses the account Fees Receivable to reflect amounts due but not yet billed.
4. Starting December 1, all maintenance work on Kwik Print's equipment is handled by Richardson Repair Company under an agreement whereby Kwik Print pays a fixed monthly charge of $400. Kwik Print paid six months' service charge in advance on December 1, debiting Prepaid Maintenance for $2,400.
5. The firm paid $900 cash on December 15 for a series of radio commercials to run during December and January. One-third of the commercials have aired by December 31. The $900 payment was debited to Prepaid Advertising.
6. Starting December 16, Kwik Print rented 400 square feet of storage space from a neighboring business. The monthly rent of $0.80 per square foot is due in advance on the first of each month. Nothing was paid in December, however, because the neighbor agreed to add the rent for the one-half of December to the January 1 payment.
7. Kwik Print invested $5,000 cash in securities on December 1 and earned interest of $38 on these securities by December 31. No interest payment will be received until January, and the end-of-December market value of the securities remains at $5,000.
8. Annual depreciation on the firm's equipment is $2,175. No depreciation has been recorded during the year.

REQUIRED

Prepare its adjusting entries required at December 31:

a. using the financial statement effects template, and
b. in journal entry form.

P3-44. Preparing Financial Statements and Closing Entries LO4, 5

The following adjusted trial balance is for Trueman Consulting Inc. at December 31, 2015. The company had no stock issuances or repurchases during 2015.

	Debit	Credit
Cash	$ 2,700	
Accounts receivable	3,270	
Supplies	3,060	
Prepaid insurance	1,500	
Equipment	6,400	
Accumulated depreciation—equipment		$ 1,080
Accounts payable		845
Long-term notes payable		7,000
Common stock		1,000
Retained earnings		3,305
Service fees earned		58,400
Rent expense	12,000	
Salaries expense	33,400	
Supplies expense	4,700	
Insurance expense	3,250	
Depreciation expense—equipment	720	
Interest expense	630	
	$71,630	$71,630

REQUIRED

a. Prepare its income statement and statement of stockholders' equity for 2015 and its balance sheet at December 31, 2015.
b. Prepare entries to close its accounts in journal entry form.

P3-45. Preparing Closing Entries LO5

The following adjusted trial balance is for Wilson Company at December 31, 2015.

	Debit	Credit
Cash	$ 8,500	
Accounts receivable	8,000	
Prepaid insurance	3,600	
Equipment	72,000	
Accumulated depreciation		$ 12,000
Accounts payable		600
Common stock		25,000
Retained earnings		19,100
Service fees earned		97,200
Miscellaneous income		4,200
Salaries expense	42,800	
Rent expense	13,400	
Insurance expense	1,800	
Depreciation expense	8,000	
Income tax expense	8,800	
Income tax payable		8,800
	$166,900	$166,900

REQUIRED

a. Prepare closing entries in journal entry form.
b. After the firm's closing entries are posted, what is the post-closing balance for the Retained Earnings account?
c. Prepare its post-closing trial balance.

LO2, 3, 6 **P3-46. Preparing Entries Across Two Periods**

The following selected accounts appear in Shaw Company's unadjusted trial balance at December 31, 2015, the end of its fiscal year (all accounts have normal balances).

Prepaid advertising.	$ 1,200	Unearned service fees	$ 5,400
Wages expense	43,800	Service fees earned	87,000
Prepaid insurance.	3,420	Rental income	4,900

REQUIRED

a. Prepare its adjusting entries at December 31, 2015, (1) using the financial statement effects template, and (2) in journal entry form using the following additional information.
   1. Prepaid advertising at December 31 is $800.
   2. Unpaid and unrecorded wages earned by employees in December are $1,300.
   3. Prepaid insurance at December 31 is $2,280.
   4. Unearned service fees at December 31 are $3,000.
   5. Rent revenue of $1,000 owed by a tenant is not recorded at December 31.

b. Prepare entries on January 4, 2016, using the financial statement effects template and in journal entry form, to record (1) payment of $2,400 cash in wages, which includes the $1,300 accrued at December 31 and (2) cash receipt of the $1,000 rent revenue owed from the tenant.

LO2, 3, 6 **P3-47. Journalizing and Posting Transactions, and Preparing a Trial Balance and Adjustments**

Market-Probe, a market research firm, had the following transactions in June 2015, its first month of operations.

June 1 B. May invested $24,000 cash in the firm in exchange for common stock.
1 The firm purchased the following: office equipment, $11,040; office supplies, $2,840. Terms are $4,400 cash with the remainder due in 60 days. (Make a compound entry requiring two credits.)
2 Paid $875 cash for June rent owed to the landlord.
2 Contracted for 3 months' advertising in a local newspaper at $310 per month and paid for the advertising in advance.
2 Signed a 6-month contract with a customer to provide research consulting services at a rate of $3,200 per month. Received two months' fees in advance. Work on the contract started immediately.
10 Billed various customers $5,800 for services rendered.
12 Paid $3,600 cash for two weeks' salaries (5-day week) to employees.
15 Paid $1,240 cash to employee for travel expenses to conference.
18 Paid $520 cash to post office for bulk mailing of research questionnaire (postage expense).
26 Paid $3,600 cash for two weeks' salaries to employees.
28 Billed various customers $5,200 for services rendered.
30 Collected $7,800 cash from customers on their accounts.
30 Paid $1,500 cash for dividends.

REQUIRED

a. Set up a general ledger in T-account form for the following accounts: Cash; Accounts Receivable; Office Supplies; Prepaid Advertising; Office Equipment; Accumulated Depreciation—Office Equipment; Accounts Payable; Salaries Payable; Unearned Service Fees; Common Stock; Retained Earnings; Service Fees Earned; Salaries Expense; Advertising Expense; Supplies Expense; Rent Expense; Travel Expense; Depreciation Expense—Office Equipment; and Postage Expense.

b. Record these transactions (1) using the financial statement effects template, and (2) in journal entry form. (3) Post these entries to their T-accounts (key numbers in T-accounts by date).

c. Prepare an unadjusted trial balance at June 30, 2015.

d. Prepare adjusting entries (1) using the financial statement effects template and (2) in journal entry form, that reflect the following information at June 30, 2015:

- Office supplies available, $1,530
- Accrued employee salaries, $725
- Estimated life of office equipment is 8 years

Adjusting entries must also be prepared for advertising and service fees per information in the June transactions. (3) Post all adjusting entries to their T-accounts.

P3-48. Preparing an Unadjusted Trial Balance and Adjusting Entries LO3

DeliverAll, a mailing service, has just completed its first full year of operations on December 31, 2015. Its general ledger account balances *before* year-end adjustments follow; no adjusting entries have been made to the accounts at any time during the year. Assume that all balances are normal.

Cash	$ 2,300	Accounts payable	$ 2,700
Accounts receivable	5,120	Common stock	9,530
Prepaid advertising	1,680	Mailing fees earned	86,000
Supplies	6,270	Wages expense	38,800
Equipment	42,240	Rent expense	6,300
Notes payable	7,500	Utilities expense	3,020

An analysis of the firm's records reveals the following.

1. The balance in Prepaid Advertising represents the amount paid for newspaper advertising for one year. The agreement, which calls for the same amount of space and cost each month, covers the period from February 1, 2015, to January 31, 2016. DeliverAll did not advertise during its first month of operations.
2. Equipment, purchased January 1, has an estimated life of eight years.
3. Utilities expense does not include expense for December, estimated at $325. The bill will not arrive until January 2016.
4. At year-end, employees have earned an additional $1,200 in wages that will not be paid or recorded until January.
5. Supplies available at year-end amount to $1,520.
6. At year-end, unpaid interest of $450 has accrued on the notes payable.
7. The firm's lease calls for rent of $525 per month payable on the first of each month, plus an amount equal to 1/2% of annual mailing fees earned. The rental percentage is payable within 15 days after the end of the year.

REQUIRED

a. Prove that debits equal credits for its unadjusted account balances by preparing its unadjusted trial balance at December 31, 2015.

b. Prepare its adjusting entries: (1) using the financial statement effects template, and (2) in journal entry form.

c. Set up T-accounts, enter the balances above, and post the adjusting entries to them.

P3-49. Preparing Adjusting Entries LO3, 4, 5, 6

Wheel Place Company began operations on March 1, 2016, to provide automotive wheel alignment and balancing services. On March 31, 2016, the unadjusted balances of the firm's accounts are as follows.

WHEEL PLACE COMPANY
Unadjusted Trial Balance
March 31, 2016

	Debit	Credit
Cash	$ 1,900	
Accounts receivable	3,820	
Prepaid rent	4,770	
Supplies	3,700	
Equipment	36,180	
Accounts payable		$ 2,510
Unearned service revenue		1,000
Common stock		38,400
Service revenue		12,360
Wages expense	3,900	
Totals	$54,270	$54,270

The following information is available.

1. The balance in Prepaid Rent was the amount paid on March 1 to cover the first 6 months' rent.
2. Supplies available on March 31 amount to $1,720.
3. Equipment has an estimated life of nine years and a zero salvage value.
4. Unpaid and unrecorded wages at March 31 were $560.

5. Utility services used during March were estimated at $390; a bill is expected early in April.
6. The balance in Unearned Service Revenue was the amount received on March 1 from a car dealer to cover alignment and balancing services on cars sold by the dealer in March and April. The Wheel Place agreed to provide the services at a fixed fee of $500 each month.

REQUIRED

a. Prepare its adjusting entries at March 31, 2016, (1) using the financial statement effects template, and (2) in journal entry form.

b. Set up T-accounts, enter the balances above, and post the adjusting entries to them.

c. Prepare its income statement for March and its balance sheet at March 31, 2016.

d. Prepare entries to close its temporary accounts in journal entry form and post the closing entries to the T-accounts.

LO4, 5 **P3-50. Preparing Financial Statements and Closing Entries**

Trails, Inc., publishes magazines for skiers and hikers. The company's adjusted trial balance for the year ending December 31, 2015 is:

TRAILS, INC.
Adjusted Trial Balance
December 31, 2015

	Debit	Credit
Cash	$ 3,400	
Accounts receivable	8,600	
Supplies	4,200	
Prepaid insurance	930	
Office equipment	66,000	
Accumulated depreciation		$ 11,000
Accounts payable		2,100
Unearned subscription revenue		10,000
Salaries payable		3,500
Common stock		25,000
Retained earnings		23,220
Subscription revenue		168,300
Advertising revenue		49,700
Salaries expense	100,230	
Printing and mailing expense	85,600	
Rent expense	8,800	
Supplies expense	6,100	
Insurance expense	1,860	
Depreciation expense	5,500	
Income tax expense	1,600	
Totals	$292,820	$292,820

REQUIRED

a. Prepare its income statement and statement of stockholders' equity for 2015, and its balance sheet at December 31, 2015. There were no cash dividends and no stock issuances or repurchases during the year.

b. Prepare entries to close its accounts in journal entry form.

LO5 **P3-51. Preparing Closing Entries**

The following adjusted trial balance is for Mayflower Moving Service at December 31, 2015.

MAYFLOWER MOVING SERVICE Adjusted Trial Balance December 31, 2015	Debit	Credit
Cash	$ 3,800	
Accounts receivable	5,250	
Supplies	2,300	
Prepaid advertising	3,000	
Trucks	28,300	
Accumulated depreciation—trucks		$ 10,000
Equipment	7,600	
Accumulated depreciation—equipment		2,100
Accounts payable		1,200
Unearned service fees		2,700
Common stock		5,000
Retained earnings		15,550
Service fees earned		72,500
Wages expense	29,800	
Rent expense	10,200	
Insurance expense	2,900	
Supplies expense	5,100	
Advertising expense	6,000	
Depreciation expense—trucks	4,000	
Depreciation expense—equipment	800	
Totals	$109,050	$109,050

REQUIRED

a. Prepare closing entries in journal entry form.

b. After its closing entries are posted, what is the post-closing balance for the Retained Earnings account?

c. Prepare Mayflower's post-closing trial balance.

P3-52. Preparing Entries Across Two Periods LO2, 3, 5, 6

The following selected accounts appear in Zimmerman Company's unadjusted trial balance at December 31, 2015, the end of its fiscal year (all accounts have normal balances).

Prepaid maintenance	$2,700	Commission fees earned	$84,000
Supplies	8,400	Rent expense	10,800
Unearned commission fees	8,500		

Additional information is as follows.

1. On September 1, 2015, the company entered into a prepaid equipment maintenance contract. Zimmerman Company paid $2,700 to cover maintenance service for 6 months, beginning September 1, 2015. The $2,700 payment was debited to Prepaid Maintenance.
2. Supplies available on December 31 are $3,200.
3. Unearned commission fees at December 31 are $4,000.
4. Commission fees earned but not yet billed at December 31 are $2,800. (*Hint:* Debit Fees Receivable.)
5. Zimmerman Company's lease calls for rent of $900 per month payable on the first of each month, plus an annual amount equal to 1% of annual commissions earned. This additional rent is payable on January 10 of the following year. (*Hint:* Use the adjusted amount of commissions earned in computing the additional rent.)

REQUIRED

a. Prepare Zimmerman Company's adjusting entries at December 31, 2015 using the financial statement effects template.

b. Prepare entries on January 10, 2016, using the financial statement effects template to record (1) the billing of $4,600 in commissions earned (which includes the $2,800 of commissions earned but not billed at December 31) and (2) the cash payment of the additional rent owed for 2015. (*Hint for part (1)*: Zimmerman Company has two receivable accounts—Fees Receivable is used for amounts earned, but not yet billed, and Accounts Receivable for amounts that are earned and billed to the customer.)

c. Prepare the adjusting entries from part *a* and the transactions in part *b* in journal entry form.

LO2, 3, 4, 5, 6 **P3-53. Preparing Adjusting Entries, Financial Statements, and Closing Entries**

Fischer Card Shop is a small retail shop. Fischer's balance sheet at year-end 2014 is as follows. The following information details transactions and adjustments that occurred during 2015.

1. Sales total $145,850 in 2015; all sales were cash sales.
2. Inventory purchases total $76,200 in 2015; at December 31, 2015, inventory totals $14,500. Assume all purchases were made on account.
3. Accounts payable totals $4,100 at December 31, 2015.
4. Annual store rent of $24,000 was paid on March 1, 2015, covering the next 12 months. The balance in prepaid rent at December 31, 2014, was the balance remaining from the advance rent payment in 2014.
5. Wages are paid every other week on Friday; during 2015, Fischer paid $12,500 cash for wages. At December 31, 2015, Fischer owed employees unpaid and unrecorded wages of $350.
6. Depreciation on equipment totals $1,700 in 2015.

FISCHER CARD SHOP
Balance Sheet
December 31, 2014

Cash		$ 8,500	Accounts payable	$ 5,200
Inventories		12,000	Wages payable	100
Prepaid rent		3,800	Total current liabilities	5,300
Total current assets		24,300	Total equity (includes retained earnings)	23,500
Equipment	$7,500		Total liabilities and equity	$28,800
Less accumulated depreciation	3,000			
Equipment, net		4,500		
Total assets		$28,800		

REQUIRED

a. Prepare any necessary transaction entries for 2015 and adjusting entries at December 31, 2015, using the financial statement effects template.

b. Prepare any necessary transaction entries for 2015 and adjusting entries at December 31, 2015, in journal entry form.

c. Set up T-accounts, enter the balances above, and post the transactions and adjusting entries to them.

d. Prepare its income statement for 2015, and its balance sheet at December 31, 2015.

e. Prepare entries to close its temporary accounts in journal entry form and post the closing entries to the T-accounts.

LO2, 3, 4, 5, 6 **P3-54. Applying the Entire Accounting Cycle**

Rhoades Tax Services began business on December 1, 2015. Its December transactions are as follows.

Dec.	1	Rhoades invested $20,000 in the business in exchange for common stock.
	2	Paid $1,200 cash for December rent to Bomba Realty.
	2	Purchased $1,080 of supplies on account.
	3	Purchased $9,500 of office equipment; paying $4,700 cash with the balance due in 30 days.
	8	Paid $1,080 cash on account for supplies purchased December 2.
	14	Paid $900 cash for assistant's wages for 2 weeks' work.
	20	Performed consulting services for $3,000 cash.
	28	Paid $900 cash for assistant's wages for 2 weeks' work.
	30	Billed clients $7,200 for December consulting services.
	31	Paid $1,800 cash for dividends.

Additional information:

1. Supplies available at December 31 are $710.
2. Accrued wages payable at December 31 are $270.
3. Depreciation for December is $120.
4. Rhoades has spent 30 hours on an involved tax fraud case during December. When completed in January, his work will be billed at $75 per hour. (The account Fees Receivable is used to reflect amounts earned but not yet billed.)

REQUIRED

a. Record these transactions and any necessary adjusting entries using the financial statement effects template.

b. Set up a general ledger in T-account form for the following accounts: Cash; Fees Receivable; Supplies; Office Equipment; Accumulated Depreciation—Office Equipment; Accounts Payable; Wages Payable; Common Stock; Retained Earnings; Consulting Revenue; Supplies Expense; Wages Expense; Rent Expense; and Depreciation Expense.

c. Record the above transactions in journal entry form and post these entries to their T-accounts (key numbers in T-accounts by date).

d. Prepare an unadjusted trial balance at December 31, 2015.

e. Journalize the adjusting entries at December 31 in journal entry form, drawing on the information above. Then post adjusting entries to their T-accounts and prepare an adjusted trial balance at December 31, 2015.

f. Prepare a December 2015 income statement and statement of stockholders' equity, and a December 31, 2015, balance sheet.

g. Record its closing entries in journal entry form. Post these entries to their T-accounts.

h. Prepare a post-closing trial balance at December 31, 2015.

CASES AND PROJECTS

C3-55. Preparing Adjusting Entries, Financial Statements, and Closing Entries LO2, 3, 4, 5, 6

Seaside Surf Shop began operations on July 1, 2015, with an initial investment of $50,000. During the initial 3 months of operations, the following cash transactions were recorded in the firm's checking account.

Cash receipts		Cash payments	
Initial investment by owner........	$ 50,000	Rent	$ 24,000
Collected from customers	81,000	Fixtures and equipment	25,000
Borrowed from bank 7/1/2015.....	10,000	Merchandise inventory...........	62,000
Total cash receipts	$141,000	Salaries........................	6,000
		Other expenses	13,000
		Total cash payments	$130,000

Additional information

1. Most sales were for cash, however, the store accepted a limited amount of credit sales; at September 30, 2015, customers owed the store $9,000.
2. Rent was paid on July 1 for six months.
3. Salaries of $3,000 per month are paid on the 1st of each month for salaries earned in the month prior.
4. Inventories are purchased for cash; at September 30, 2015, inventory worth $21,000 was available.
5. Fixtures and equipment were expected to last five years with zero salvage value.
6. The bank charges 12% annual interest (1% per month) on its bank loan.

REQUIRED

a. Prepare any necessary adjusting entries at September 30, 2015, (1) using the financial statement effects template, and (2) in journal entry form.

b. Set up T-accounts and post the adjusting entries to them.

c. Prepare its initial three-month income statement for 2015 and its balance sheet at September 30, 2015. (Ignore taxes.)

d. Analyze the statements from part *c* and assess the company's performance over its initial 3 months.

C3-56. Analyzing Transactions, Impacts on Financial Ratios, and Loan Covenants LO2, 3, 6

Wyland Consulting, a firm started three years ago by Reyna Wyland, offers consulting services for material handling and plant layout. Its balance sheet at the close of 2015 is as follows.

WYLAND CONSULTING
Balance Sheet
December 31, 2015

Assets			**Liabilities**	
Cash		$ 3,400	Notes payable	$30,000
Accounts receivable		22,875	Accounts payable	4,200
Supplies		13,200	Unearned consulting fees	11,300
Prepaid insurance		4,500	Wages payable	400
Equipment	$68,500		Total liabilities	45,900
Less: accumulated depreciation	23,975	44,525	**Equity**	
			Common stock	8,000
			Retained earnings	34,600
Total assets		$88,500	Total liabilities and equity	$88,500

Earlier in the year Wyland obtained a bank loan of $30,000 cash for the firm. One of the provisions of the loan is that the year-end debt-to-equity ratio (ratio of total liabilities to total equity) cannot exceed 1.0. Based on the above balance sheet, the ratio at the end of 2015 is 1.08. Wyland is concerned about being in violation of the loan agreement and requests assistance in reviewing the situation. Wyland believes that she might have overlooked some items at year-end. Discussions with Wyland reveal the following.

1. On January 1, 2015, the firm paid a $4,500 insurance premium for 2 years of coverage; the amount in Prepaid Insurance has not yet been adjusted.
2. Depreciation on the equipment should be 10% of cost per year; the company inadvertently recorded 15% for 2015.
3. Interest on the bank loan has been paid through the end of 2015.
4. The firm concluded a major consulting engagement in December, doing a plant layout analysis for a new factory. The $6,000 fee has not been billed or recorded in the accounts.
5. On December 1, 2015, the firm received an $11,300 advance payment from Croy Corporation for consulting services to be rendered over a 2-month period. This payment was credited to the Unearned Consulting Fees account. One-half of this fee was earned by December 31, 2015.
6. Supplies costing $4,800 were available on December 31; the company has made no entry in the accounts.

REQUIRED

a. What portion of the company is financed by debt versus equity (called the debt-to-equity ratio and defined in Chapter 1) at December 31, 2015?

b. Is the firm in violation of its loan agreement? Prepare computations to support the correct total liabilities and total equity figures at December 31, 2015.

LO2, 3 **C3-57. Ethics, Accounting Adjustments, and Auditors**

It is the end of the accounting year for Juliet Javetz, controller of a medium-sized, publicly held corporation specializing in toxic waste cleanup. Within the corporation, only Javetz and the president know that the firm has been negotiating for several months to land a large contract for waste cleanup in Western Europe. The president has hired another firm with excellent contacts in Western Europe to help with negotiations. The outside firm will charge an hourly fee plus expenses, but has agreed not to submit a bill until the negotiations are in their final stages (expected to occur in another 3 to 4 months). Even if the contract falls through, the outside firm is entitled to receive payment for its services. Based upon her discussion with a member of the outside firm, Javetz knows that its charge for services provided to date will be $150,000. This is a material amount for the company.

Javetz knows that the president wants negotiations to remain as secret as possible so that competitors will not learn of the contract the company is pursuing in Europe. In fact, the president recently stated to her, "Now is not the time to reveal our actions in Western Europe to other staff members, our auditors, or the readers of our financial statements; securing this contract is crucial to our future growth." No entry has been made in the accounting records for the cost of contract negotiations. Javetz now faces an uncomfortable situation. The company's outside auditor has just asked her if she knows of any year-end adjustments that have not yet been recorded.

REQUIRED

a. What are the ethical considerations that Javetz faces in answering the auditor's question?

b. How should Javetz respond to the auditor's question?

C3-58. Inferring Adjusting Entries from Financial Statements LO2, 3, 4, 6

Lady G's Fashions, a specialty retailer of women's apparel, markets its products through retail stores and catalogs. Selected information from its 2015 and 2014 balance sheets is as follows.

Selected Balance Sheet Data ($ thousands)	2014	2015
Prepaid catalog expenses (asset)	$3,894	$4,306
Advertising credits receivable	21	534
Customer deposits	6,108	7,053

The following excerpts are from Lady G's Fashions accompanying footnotes:

- Catalog costs in the direct segment are considered direct response advertising and as such are capitalized as incurred and amortized over the expected sales life of each catalog, which is generally a period not exceeding six months.
- The Company periodically enters into arrangements with certain national magazine publishers whereby the Company includes magazine subscription cards in its catalog mailings in exchange for advertising credits or discounts on advertising.

REQUIRED

a. Assume that Lady G's Fashions spent $62,550 to design, print, and mail catalogs in 2015. Also assume that it received advertising credits of $849. Prepare the entry, using the financial statement effects template and in journal entry form, that Lady G's Fashions would have recorded when these costs were incurred.

b. Prepare the adjusting entry, using the financial statement effects template and in journal entry form, that would be necessary to record its amortization of prepaid catalog costs.

c. How do advertising credits expire? Prepare the adjusting entry, using both the financial statement effects template and in journal entry form, that Lady G's Fashions would record to reflect the change in advertising credits.

d. Assume that Lady G's Fashions sold gift certificates valued at $19,175 in 2015. Prepare the entry, using the financial statement effects template and in journal entry form, that Lady G's Fashions would make to record these sales. Next, prepare the entry, using the financial statement effects template and in journal entry form, that it makes to record merchandise sales to customers who pay with gift certificates.

SOLUTIONS TO REVIEW PROBLEMS

Mid-Chapter Review

SOLUTION TO PARTS 1 AND 2

a.

	Balance Sheet											Income Statement				
Transaction	Cash Asset	+	Noncash Assets	−	Contra Assets	=	Liabil-ities	+	Contrib. Capital	+	Earned Capital	Revenues	−	Expenses	=	Net Income
(a) Adjusting entry to record supplies and parts used.			−91,000 Supplies and Parts	−		=					−91,000 Retained Earnings		−	+91,000 Supplies and Parts Expenses	=	−91,000

(a)	Supplies and parts expense (+E, −SE)	91,000	
	Supplies and parts (−A)		91,000

b.

	Balance Sheet						Income Statement		
Transaction	Cash Asset +	Noncash Assets −	Contra Assets =	Liabil-ities +	Contrib. Capital +	Earned Capital	*Revenues* −	*Expenses* =	*Net Income*
(b) Adjusting entry to record rent expense accrued but not yet paid.				+2,500 Accounts Payable		−2,500 Retained Earnings		+2,500 Rent Expense	−2,500

(b)	Rent expense (+E, −SE)	2,500	
	Accounts payable (+L)		2,500

The $2,500 expense for October is not recorded because it is not yet incurred as of September 30.

c.

Transaction	Cash Asset +	Noncash Assets −	Contra Assets =	Liabil-ities +	Contrib. Capital +	Earned Capital	*Revenues* −	*Expenses* =	*Net Income*
(c) Adjusting entry to record depreciation on building.			+50,000 Accumulated Depreciation —Building			−50,000 Retained Earnings		+50,000 Depreciation Expense	−50,000

(c)	Depreciation expense (+E, −SE)	50,000	
	Accumulated depreciation—Building (+XA, −A)		50,000

d. No entry required; the executive has not yet begun work and thus, no expense is incurred.

e.

Transaction	Cash Asset +	Noncash Assets −	Contra Assets =	Liabil-ities +	Contrib. Capital +	Earned Capital	*Revenues* −	*Expenses* =	*Net Income*
(e) Adjusting entry to record cash advance, of which a part is earned.	+1,200 Cash			+600 Unearned Revenue		+600 Retained Earnings	+600 Services Revenue		+600

(e)	Cash (+A)	1,200	
	Unearned revenue (+L)		600
	Services revenue (+R, +SE)		600

f.

Transaction	Cash Asset +	Noncash Assets −	Contra Assets =	Liabil-ities +	Contrib. Capital +	Earned Capital	*Revenues* −	*Expenses* =	*Net Income*
(f) Adjusting entry to record wages earned but not yet paid.				+25,000 Wages Payable		−25,000 Retained Earnings		+25,000 Wages Expense	−25,000

(f)	Wages expense (+E, −SE)	25,000	
	Wages payable (+L)		25,000

SOLUTION TO PART 3

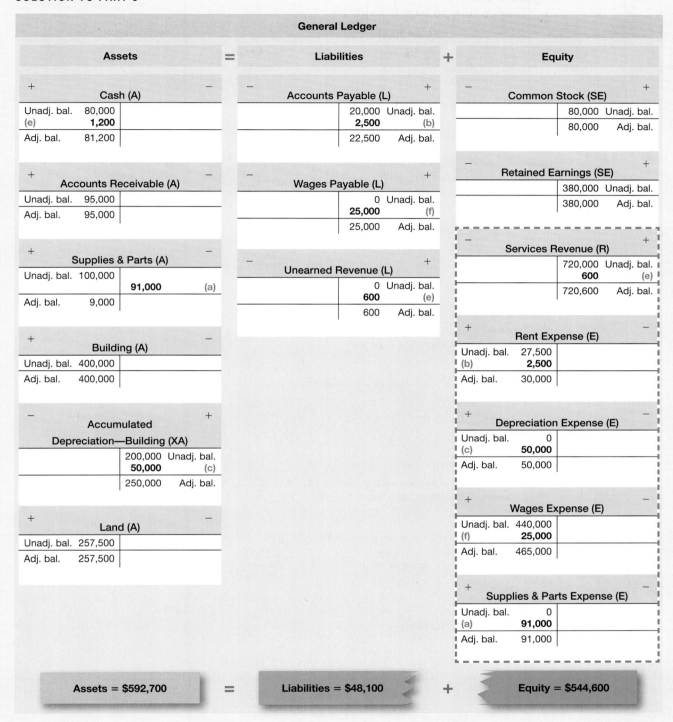

General Ledger

Assets

Cash (A) (+ / −)

+		−	
Unadj. bal.	80,000		
(e)	**1,200**		
Adj. bal.	81,200		

Accounts Receivable (A) (+ / −)

+		−	
Unadj. bal.	95,000		
Adj. bal.	95,000		

Supplies & Parts (A) (+ / −)

+		−	
Unadj. bal.	100,000		
		91,000	(a)
Adj. bal.	9,000		

Building (A) (+ / −)

+		−	
Unadj. bal.	400,000		
Adj. bal.	400,000		

Accumulated Depreciation—Building (XA) (− / +)

−		+	
		200,000	Unadj. bal.
		50,000	(c)
		250,000	Adj. bal.

Land (A) (+ / −)

+		−	
Unadj. bal.	257,500		
Adj. bal.	257,500		

=

Liabilities

Accounts Payable (L) (− / +)

−		+	
		20,000	Unadj. bal.
		2,500	(b)
		22,500	Adj. bal.

Wages Payable (L) (− / +)

−		+	
		0	Unadj. bal.
		25,000	(f)
		25,000	Adj. bal.

Unearned Revenue (L) (− / +)

−		+	
		0	Unadj. bal.
		600	(e)
		600	Adj. bal.

+

Equity

Common Stock (SE) (− / +)

−		+	
		80,000	Unadj. bal.
		80,000	Adj. bal.

Retained Earnings (SE) (− / +)

−		+	
		380,000	Unadj. bal.
		380,000	Adj. bal.

Services Revenue (R) (− / +)

−		+	
		720,000	Unadj. bal.
		600	(e)
		720,600	Adj. bal.

Rent Expense (E) (+ / −)

+		−	
Unadj. bal.	27,500		
(b)	**2,500**		
Adj. bal.	30,000		

Depreciation Expense (E) (+ / −)

+		−	
Unadj. bal.	0		
(c)	**50,000**		
Adj. bal.	50,000		

Wages Expense (E) (+ / −)

+		−	
Unadj. bal.	440,000		
(f)	**25,000**		
Adj. bal.	465,000		

Supplies & Parts Expense (E) (+ / −)

+		−	
Unadj. bal.	0		
(a)	**91,000**		
Adj. bal.	91,000		

Assets = $592,700 = **Liabilities = $48,100** + **Equity = $544,600**

Chapter-End Review

SOLUTION TO PARTS 1 AND 2

Transaction	Cash Asset	+	Noncash Assets	-	Contra Assets	=	Liabil-ities	+	Contrib. Capital	+	Earned Capital	Revenues	-	Expenses	=	Net Income
	Balance Sheet											Income Statement				
(1) Adjustment to record insurance expense.			−1,500 Prepaid Insurance	-		=					−1,500 Retained Earnings		-	+1,500 Insurance Expense	=	−1,500

		Dr.	Cr.
(1)	Insurance expense (+E, −SE)	1,500	
	Prepaid insurance (−A)		1,500
	Record insurance expired $6,000 × (6 months/24 months).		

Transaction	Cash Asset	+	Noncash Assets	-	Contra Assets	=	Liabil-ities	+	Contrib. Capital	+	Earned Capital	Revenues	-	Expenses	=	Net Income
(2) Adjustment to record supplies expense.			−25,000 Supplies	-		=					−25,000 Retained Earnings		-	+25,000 Supplies Expense	=	−25,000

		Dr.	Cr.
(2)	Supplies expense (+E, −SE)	25,000	
	Supplies (−A)		25,000
	Record supplies used ($31,300 − $6,300).		

Transaction	Cash Asset	+	Noncash Assets	-	Contra Assets	=	Liabil-ities	+	Contrib. Capital	+	Earned Capital	Revenues	-	Expenses	=	Net Income
(3) Adjustment to record depreciation expense.				-	+30,000 Accumulated Depreciation —Equipment	=					−30,000 Retained Earnings		-	+30,000 Depreciation Expense	=	−30,000

		Dr.	Cr.
(3)	Depreciation expense (+E, −SE)	30,000	
	Accumulated depreciation—Equipment (+XA, −A)		30,000
	Record depreciation [($270,000 − $0) ÷ 9 years].		

Transaction	Cash Asset	+	Noncash Assets	-	Contra Assets	=	Liabil-ities	+	Contrib. Capital	+	Earned Capital	Revenues	-	Expenses	=	Net Income
(4) Adjustment to record fees revenue.				-		=	−3,000 Unearned Fees				+3,000 Retained Earnings	+3,000 Fees Revenue	-		=	+3,000

		Dr.	Cr.
(4)	Unearned fees (−L)	3,000	
	Fees revenue (+R, +SE)		3,000
	Record fees earned.		

Transaction	Cash Asset	+	Noncash Assets	-	Contra Assets	=	Liabil-ities	+	Contrib. Capital	+	Earned Capital	Revenues	-	Expenses	=	Net Income
(5) Adjustment to record wages expense.				-		=	+600 Wages Payable				−600 Retained Earnings		-	+600 Wages Expense	=	−600

		Dr.	Cr.
(5)	Wages expense (+E, −SE)	600	
	Wages payable (+L)		600
	Record employee wages incurred.		

	Balance Sheet										Income Statement				
Transaction	Cash Asset	+	Noncash Assets	-	Contra Assets	=	Liabil-ities	+	Contrib. Capital	+	Earned Capital	Revenues	-	Expenses	=	Net Income
(6) Adjustment to record rent expense.				-		=	+2,000 Rent Payable				−2,000 Retained Earnings		-	+2,000 Rent Expense	=	−2,000

(6)	Rent expense (+E, −SE)	2,000	
	Rent payable (+L)		2,000
	Record rent owed.		

SOLUTION TO PART 3

General Ledger

Assets

+	Cash (A)		–
Unadj. bal.	1,000		
Adj. bal.	1,000		

+	Accounts Receivable (A)		–
Unadj. bal.	9,200		
Adj. bal.	9,200		

+	Prepaid Insurance (A)		–
Unadj. bal.	6,000		
		1,500	(1)
Adj. bal.	4,500		

+	Supplies (A)		–
Unadj. bal.	31,300		
		25,000	(2)
Adj. bal.	6,300		

+	Equipment (A)		–
Unadj. bal.	270,000		
Adj. bal.	270,000		

–	Accumulated Depreciation—Equipment (XA)		+
		60,000	Unadj. bal.
		30,000	(3)
		90,000	Adj. bal.

=

Liabilities

–	Accounts Payable (L)		+
		3,100	Unadj. bal.
		3,100	Adj. bal.

–	Unearned Fees (L)		+
		4,000	Unadj. bal.
(4)	3,000		
		1,000	Adj. bal.

–	Wages Payable (L)		+
		0	Unadj. bal.
		600	(5)
		600	Adj. bal.

–	Rent Payable (L)		+
		0	Unadj. bal.
		2,000	(6)
		2,000	Adj. bal.

+

Equity

–	Common Stock (SE)		+
		120,400	Unadj. bal.
		120,400	Adj. bal.

–	Retained Earnings (SE)		+
		60,000	Unadj. bal.
		60,000	Adj. bal.

–	Fees Revenue (R)		+
		150,000	Unadj. bal.
		3,000	(4)
		153,000	Adj. bal.

+	Insurance Expense (E)		–
Unadj. bal.	0		
(1)	1,500		
Adj. bal.	1,500		

+	Supplies Expenses (E)		–
Unadj. bal.	0		
(2)	25,000		
Adj. bal.	25,000		

+	Depreciation Expense (E)		–
Unadj. bal.	0		
(3)	30,000		
Adj. bal.	30,000		

+	Rent Expense (E)		–
Unadj. bal.	22,000		
(6)	2,000		
Adj. bal.	24,000		

+	Wages Expense (E)		–
Unadj. bal.	58,000		
(5)	600		
Adj. bal.	58,600		

Assets = $201,000 = **Liabilities = $6,700** + **Equity = $194,300**

ATWELL LABORATORIES, INC. Adjusted Trial Balance June 30, 2015	Debits	Credits
Cash	$ 1,000	
Accounts receivable	9,200	
Prepaid insurance	4,500	
Supplies	6,300	
Equipment	270,000	
Accumulated depreciation—equipment		$ 90,000
Accounts payable		3,100
Rent payable		2,000
Wages payable		600
Unearned fees		1,000
Fees revenue		153,000
Wages expense	58,600	
Rent expense	24,000	
Insurance expense	1,500	
Supplies expense	25,000	
Depreciation expense	30,000	
Common stock		120,400
Retained earnings		60,000
Totals	$430,100	$430,100

SOLUTION TO PART 4

		Debit	Credit
a.	Retained earnings (−SE)	139,100	
	Insurance expense (−E)		1,500
	Supplies expense (−E)		25,000
	Depreciation expense (−E)		30,000
	Rent expense (−E)		24,000
	Wages expense (−E)		58,600

		Debit	Credit
b.	Fees revenue (−R)	153,000	
	Retained earnings (+SE)		153,000

General Ledger

Assets = Liabilities + Equity

Assets

+ Cash (A)		−	
Unadj. bal.	1,000		
Adj. bal.	1,000		

+ Accounts Receivable (A)		−	
Unadj. bal.	9,200		
Adj. bal.	9,200		

+ Prepaid Insurance (A)		−	
Unadj. bal.	6,000		
		1,500	(1)
Adj. bal.	4,500		

+ Supplies (A)		−	
Unadj. bal.	31,300		
		25,000	(2)
Adj. bal.	6,300		

+ Equipment (A)		−	
Unadj. bal.	270,000		
Adj. bal.	270,000		

− Accumulated Depreciation—Equipment (XA)		+	
		60,000	Unadj. bal.
		30,000	(3)
		90,000	Adj. bal.

Liabilities

− Accounts Payable (L)		+	
		3,100	Unadj. bal.
		3,100	Adj. bal.

− Unearned Fees (L)		+	
		4,000	Unadj. bal.
(4)	3,000		
		1,000	Adj. bal.

− Wages Payable (L)		+	
		0	Unadj. bal.
		600	(5)
		600	Adj. bal.

− Rent Payable (L)		+	
		0	Unadj. bal.
		2,000	(6)
		2,000	Adj. bal.

Equity

− Common Stock (SE)		+	
		120,400	Unadj. bal.
		120,400	Adj. bal.

− Retained Earnings (SE)		+	
		60,000	Unadj. bal.
(a)	139,100	153,000	(b)
		73,900	Adj. bal.

− Fees Revenue (R)		+	
		150,000	Unadj. bal.
(b)	153,000	3,000	(4)
		0	Adj. bal.

+ Insurance Expense (E)		−	
Unadj. bal.	0		
(1)	1,500	1,500	(a)
Adj. bal.	0		

+ Supplies Expenses (E)		−	
Unadj. bal.	0		
(2)	25,000	25,000	(a)
Adj. bal.	0		

+ Depreciation Expense (E)		−	
Unadj. bal.	0		
(3)	30,000	30,000	(a)
Adj. bal.	0		

+ Rent Expense (E)		−	
Unadj. bal.	22,000		
(6)	2,000	24,000	(a)
Adj. bal.	0		

+ Wages Expense (E)		−	
Unadj. bal.	58,000		
(5)	600	58,600	(a)
Adj. bal.	0		

Assets = \$201,000 = Liabilities = \$6,700 + Equity = \$194,300

SOLUTION TO PART 5

ATWELL LABORATORIES, INC.
Balance Sheet
June 30, 2015

Assets			Liabilities	
Cash		$ 1,000	Accounts payable	$ 3,100
Accounts receivable		9,200	Unearned fees	1,000
Prepaid insurance		4,500	Wages payable	600
Supplies		6,300	Rent payable	2,000
Total current assets		21,000	Total current liabilities	6,700
Equipment, original cost	$270,000			
Less accumulated depreciation	90,000	180,000	**Equity**	
			Common stock	120,400
			Retained earnings	73,900
Total assets		$201,000	Totals liabilities and equity	$201,000

ATWELL LABORATORIES, INC.
Income Statement
For Year Ended June 30, 2015

Fees revenue		$153,000
Expenses		
Insurance expense	$ 1,500	
Supplies expense	25,000	
Depreciation expense	30,000	
Rent expense	24,000	
Wages expense	58,600	
Total expense		139,100
Net income		$ 13,900

ATWELL LABORATORIES, INC.
Statement of Stockholders' Equity
For Year Ended June 30, 2015

	Common Stock	Retained Earnings	Total
Balance at June 30, 2014	$120,400	$60,000	$180,400
Net Income	—	13,900	13,900
Balance at June 30, 2015	$120,400	$73,900	$194,300

Atwell's statement of stockholders' equity is much simpler than the usual statement because we have focused on the adjustment and closing process. In doing so, we did not consider additional activities in which corporations commonly engage, such as paying dividends, issuing stock, and repurchasing stock. (Requirements did not ask for a statement of cash flows. The next chapter is devoted to the statement of cash flows.)

Reporting and Analyzing Cash Flows

LEARNING OBJECTIVES

1. Explain the purpose of the statement of cash flows and classify cash transactions by type of business activity: operating, investing, or financing. (p. 158)
2. Construct the operating activities section of the statement of cash flows using the direct method. (p. 162)
3. Reconcile cash flows from operations to net income and use the indirect method to compute operating cash flows. (p. 171)
4. Construct the investing and financing activities sections of the statement of cash flows. (p. 174)
5. Compute and interpret ratios that reflect a company's liquidity and solvency using information reported in the statement of cash flows. (p. 181)
6. Appendix 4A: Use a spreadsheet to construct the statement of cash flows. (p. 185)

GOLDEN ENTERPRISES
www.goldenflake.com

In the southeastern United States, Golden Flake Snack Foods, Inc. is well-known for its tasty products. Founded in 1923 as Magic City Foods, it now operates as a wholly-owned subsidiary of **Golden Enterprises, Inc.** The company distributes potato chips, pork skins, tortilla chips, and many more products in fifteen states from Florida to Kentucky to Texas.

In 2014, sales at Golden Enterprises declined for the first time in five years from $137.3 million in fiscal 2013 to $135.9 million in fiscal 2014. Mark McCutcheon (Chairman and CEO) announced a restructuring of Golden Enterprises' operations in 2014, resulting in a $1 million charge against income in that fiscal year. As a consequence, net income declined for the fourth consecutive year to $921,829. The snack food market is highly competitive with large companies (Frito-Lay, Kraft Foods) competing with smaller firms like Golden Enterprises for market share. Small profit margins leave little leeway for increases in fuel or commodity costs, or significant shifts in consumer preferences. The graph below compares revenues for Golden Enterprises and three of its smaller competitors—**Snyder's-Lance** (LNCE: Snyder's of Hanover pretzels, Cape Cod potato chips), **J & J Snack Foods** (JJSF: Bavarian pretzels, ICEE beverages), and **Diamond Foods** (DMND: Diamond nuts, Pop Secret popcorn).

Golden Flake's headquarters and main production facilities are located in Birmingham, Alabama, and a second manufacturing plant is located in Florida. In addition to these properties, Golden Flake owns 20 warehouses and a fleet of delivery vehicles. The company's recent investments include improvements to its waste water treatment and a significant investment in an Enterprise Resource Planning (ERP) system that will improve the company's operating efficiency. Both of these investments should improve the company's margins in the future. Golden Flake spent almost $2.4 million in fiscal 2014 on additions to property, plant, and equipment. These costs are listed in Golden Flake's cash flow statement under *investing activities*.

In addition to making investments to improve operations, Golden Flake regularly returns about $1.5 million cash to its shareholders in the form of dividends or repurchases of its own stock (treasury shares). These cash outflows are reported in Golden Flake's statement of cash flows under *financing activities*.

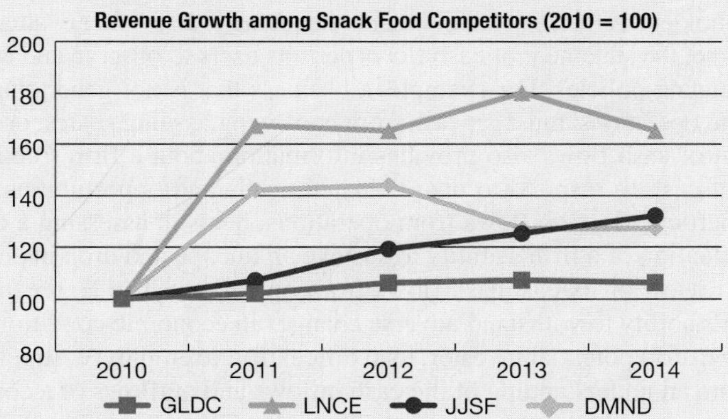

How does a company with income of less than $1 million spend almost $4 million in investments and dividends? To accomplish its objectives, Golden Flake must generate positive cash flow from *operating activities*, and its operating activities produced cash flows of almost $3.3 million in the fiscal year ended May 30, 2014. The company's operations are the engine that produces cash that can be used to grow the business and to provide a return to shareholders.

As we will discover in this chapter, a business must make sure that its cash inflows are adequate to fund new investments, meet obligations to creditors as they come due, and pay dividends to shareholders. Even a profitable company can fail if it does not have a healthy cash flow. We will also discover why it is important to look at the cash flow statement along with the income statement and balance sheet when trying to assess the financial health of a company.

Sources: Golden Enterprises, Inc. Form 10-K 2010–2014; Golden Enterprises, Inc. Annual Report 2010–2014.

CHAPTER ORGANIZATION

Reporting and Analyzing Cash Flows

Purpose of the Statement of Cash Flows	Framework for the Statement of Cash Flows	Preparing the Statement of Cash Flows	Analysis of Cash Flows
• What Do We Mean by Cash? • What Does a Statement of Cash Flows Look Like?	• Operating Activities • Investing Activities • Financing Activities • Usefulness of Classifications	• Cash Flows from Operating Activities • Cash Flows from Investing and Financing Activities • Additional Detail in the Statement of Cash Flows • Preparing the Statement of Cash Flows Using a Spreadsheet (Appendix 4A)	• Operating Cash Flow to Current Liabilities • Operating Cash Flow to Capital Expenditures • Free Cash Flow

PURPOSE OF THE STATEMENT OF CASH FLOWS

1 **LO1** Explain the purpose of the statement of cash flows and classify cash transactions by type of business activity: operating, investing or financing.

In addition to the balance sheet and the income statement, corporations are required to report a statement of cash flows. The **statement of cash flows** tells us how a company generated cash (cash inflows) and how it used cash (cash outflows). The statement of cash flows complements the income statement and the balance sheet by providing information that neither the income statement nor the balance sheet can provide. For instance, slower collection of receivables doesn't affect income, but it does reduce the amount of cash coming into the company.

Understanding the statement of cash flows helps us understand trends in a firm's **liquidity** (ability to pay near-term liabilities and take advantage of investment opportunities), and it helps us assess a firm's **solvency** (ability to pay long-term liabilities). With information about how cash was generated or used, creditors and investors are better able to assess a firm's ability to settle its liabilities and pay dividends to shareholders. A firm's need for outside financing is also better evaluated when using cash flow data. Over time, the statement of cash flows permits users to observe and assess management's investing and financing policies. For example, a business that is not generating enough cash flow internally, i.e., from operations, must get cash from borrowing, issuing shares, or selling off its assets.

The statement of cash flows also provides information about a firm's ability to generate sufficient amounts of cash to respond to unanticipated needs and opportunities. Information about past cash flows, particularly cash flows from operations, helps in assessing a company's financial flexibility. An evaluation of a firm's ability to survive an unexpected drop in demand, for example, should include a review of its past cash flows from operations. The larger these cash flows, the greater is the firm's ability to withstand adverse changes in economic conditions.

So, whether we are a potential investor, loan officer, future employee, supplier, or customer, we greatly benefit from an understanding of the cash inflows and outflows of a company.

What Do We Mean by "CASH"?

FYI A cash equivalent is a short-term, highly liquid investment that is easily converted to cash and is close enough to maturity that its market value is not sensitive to interest rate changes.

The statement of cash flows explains the change in a firm's cash *and* cash equivalents. **Cash equivalents** are short-term, highly liquid investments that are (1) easily convertible into a known cash amount and (2) close enough to maturity that their market value is not sensitive to interest rate changes (generally, investments with remaining maturities of three months or less). Treasury bills, commercial paper (short-term notes issued by corporations), and money market funds are typical examples of cash equivalents.

When preparing a statement of cash flows, the cash and cash equivalents are added together and treated as a single sum. The addition is done because the purchase and sale of investments in cash equivalents are considered to be part of a firm's overall management of cash rather than a source or use of cash. As statement users evaluate and project cash flows, for example, it should not matter whether the cash is readily available in a cash register or safe, deposited in a bank account, or invested in cash equivalents. Consequently, transfers back and forth between a firm's cash on hand, its bank accounts, and its investments in cash equivalents, are not treated as cash inflows and cash outflows in its statement of cash flows. When discussing the statement of cash flows, managers generally use the word *cash* rather than the phrase *cash and cash equivalents*. We will follow the same practice.

What Does a Statement of Cash Flows Look Like?

Exhibit 4.1 reproduces Golden Enterprises' cash flow statement for the fiscal year ended on May 30, 2014. During this fiscal year, Golden Enterprises generated $3,263,728 in cash from its operations. Investing activities used $2,332,162 in cash, and financing activities used another $528,047 of cash. Over the entire year, the company's cash balance increased by $757,111 and ended the year at $1,160,630 on May 30, 2014.

EXHIBIT 4.1 Golden Enterprises Cash Flow Statement

GOLDEN ENTERPRISES, INC. AND SUBSIDIARY
Consolidated Statement of Cash Flows
For the Fiscal Year Ended May 30, 2014

	2014
Cash Flows from Operating Activities	
Cash received from customers	$135,015,577
Interest income	1,956
Rental income	29,783
Other operating cash payments/receipts	67,133
Cash paid to suppliers and employees for cost of goods sold	(68,774,050)
Cash paid for suppliers and employees for selling general and administrative	(62,094,737)
Income taxes	(645,342)
Interest expense	(336,592)
Net cash provided by operating activities	3,263,728
Cash Flows from Investing Activities	
Purchase of property, plant and equipment	(2,380,287)
Proceeds from sale of property, plant and equipment	48,125
Net cash used in investing activities	(2,332,162)
Cash Flows from Financing Activities	
Debt proceeds	35,726,909
Debt repayments	(35,316,537)
Change in checks outstanding in excess of bank balances*	528,162
Cash dividends paid	(1,466,581)
Net cash used in financing activities	(528,047)
Net increase (decrease) in cash and cash equivalents	403,519
Cash and cash equivalents at beginning of year	757,111
Cash and cash equivalents at end of year	$1,160,630

* Golden Enterprises has an overdraft arrangement at one or more of its banks that allows it to write checks in excess of its balance. This negative balance creates a financial liability (essentially a loan) that must be settled according to its arrangement with the bank.

FRAMEWORK FOR THE STATEMENT OF CASH FLOWS

The statement of cash flows classifies cash receipts and payments into one of three categories: operating activities, investing activities, or financing activities. Classifying cash flows into these categories identifies the effects on cash of each of the major activities of a firm. The combined effects on cash of all three categories explain the net change in cash for the period. The period's net change in cash is then reconciled with the beginning and ending amounts of cash.

Operating Activities

A company's income statement mainly reflects the transactions and events that constitute its operating activities. The cash effects of these operating transactions and events determine the net cash

FYI Cash flows from operating activities (cash flows from operations) refer to cash inflows and outflows directly related to the firm's primary day-to-day business activities.

flow from operating activities. The usual focus of a firm's **operating activities** is on selling goods or rendering services, but the activities are defined broadly enough to include any cash receipts or payments that are not classified as investing or financing activities. For example, Golden Enterprises reports cash received from customers and renters and borrowers. The company paid cash to suppliers and employees and tax authorities and to lenders for interest. The following are examples of cash inflows and outflows relating to operating activities.

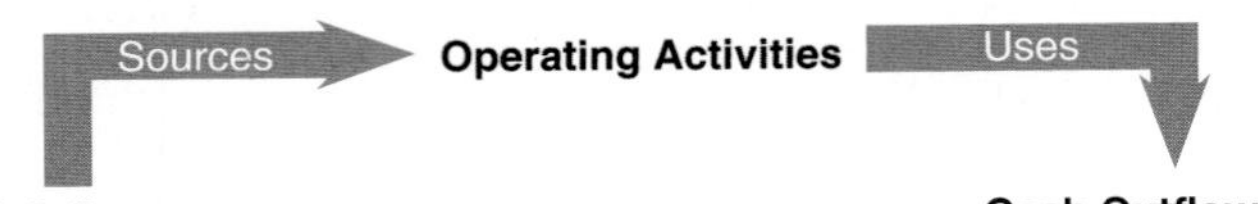

Cash Inflows	Cash Outflows
1. Cash receipts from customers for sales made or services rendered (or in anticipation of future deliveries of goods or services).	1. Cash payments to employees or suppliers.
2. Cash receipts of interest and dividends.[1]	2. Cash payments to purchase inventories.
3. Other cash receipts that are not related to investing or financing activities, such as rentals, lawsuit settlements, and refunds received from suppliers.	3. Cash payments of interest to creditors.[1]
	4. Cash payments of taxes to government.
	5. Other cash payments that are not related to investing or financing activities, such as contributions to charity and lawsuit settlements.

Investing Activities

FYI Cash flows from investing activities are cash inflows and outflows related to acquiring or selling productive assets and the investments in securities of other entities.

A firm's transactions involving (1) the acquisition and disposal of property, plant, and equipment (PPE) assets and intangible assets, (2) the purchase and sale of government securities and securities of other companies, including stocks, bonds, and other securities that are not classified as cash equivalents, and (3) the lending and subsequent collection of money constitute the basic components of its **investing activities**. The related cash receipts and payments appear in the investing activities section of the statement of cash flows and, if material in amount, inflows and outflows should be reported separately (not as a net amount). Examples of these cash flows follow:

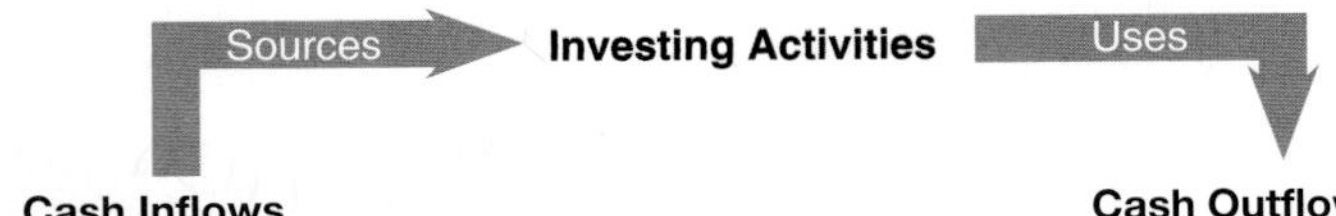

Cash Inflows	Cash Outflows
1. Cash receipts from sales of property, plant, and equipment (PPE) assets and intangible assets.	1. Cash payments to purchase property, plant, and equipment (PPE) assets and intangible assets.
2. Cash receipts from sales of investments in government securities and securities of other companies (including divestitures).	2. Cash payments to purchase government securities and securities of other companies (including acquisitions).
3. Cash receipts from repayments of loans by borrowers.	3. Cash payments made to lend money to borrowers.

Financing Activities

FYI Cash flows from financing activities are cash inflows and outflows related to external sources of financing (owners and nonowners).

A firm engages in **financing activities** when it receives cash from shareholders, returns cash to shareholders, borrows from creditors, and repays amounts borrowed. Cash flows related to these transactions are reported in the financing activities section of the statement of cash flows and again, inflows and outflows should be reported separately (not as a net amount) if material. For instance, Golden Enterprises reports proceeds from new debt and debt repayments separately, rather than as a net amount. Examples of these cash flows follow:

[1] Many financial statement readers believe that interest and dividends received should be considered cash inflows from investing activities and that interest payments should be considered cash outflows from financing activities. In fact, when the reporting standard was passed by the Financial Accounting Standards Board, three of the seven members dissented from the standard for this reason (among others). The majority based their decision on "the view that, in general, cash flows from operating activities should reflect the cash effects of transactions and other events that enter into the determination of net income." (Statement of Financial Accounting Standards No. 95, paragraph 88.)

Cash Inflows

1. Cash receipts from issuances of common stock and preferred stock and from sales of treasury stock.
2. Cash receipts from issuances of bonds payable, mortgage notes payable, and other notes payable.

Cash Outflows

1. Cash payments to acquire treasury stock.
2. Cash payments of dividends.
3. Cash payments to settle outstanding bonds payable, mortgage notes payable, and other notes payable.

Paying cash to settle such obligations as accounts payable, wages payable, interest payable, and income tax payable are operating activities, not financing activities because they are related to the daily operations of the company such as buying and selling inventory. Also, cash received as interest and dividends and cash paid as interest (not dividends) are classified as cash flows from operating activities. However, cash paid to shareholders as dividends is classified as cash flows from financing activities.

FYI Treasury stock refers to the amount paid by a company to purchase its own common stock.

A GLOBAL PERSPECTIVE

Under U.S. accounting principles, payments for interest expense and receipts for interest and dividend income are considered part of cash from operations. International Financial Reporting Standards allow companies to report interest payments as part of either operating activities or financing activities and to report interest and dividend receipts as part of either operating activities or investing activities.

Usefulness of Classifications

The classification of cash flows into three categories of activities helps financial statement users interpret cash flow data. To illustrate, assume that Faultless, Inc., Peerless Co. and Dauntless Ltd. each reports a $100,000 cash increase during the current year. Information from their current-year statements of cash flows is summarized in **Exhibit 4.2**.

EXHIBIT 4.2 Summary Information for Three Competitors

	Faultless	Peerless	Dauntless
Net cash provided by operating activities	$100,000	$ 0	$ 0
Cash flows from investing activities			
Sale of property, plant, and equipment	0	100,000	0
Cash flows from financing activities			
Issuance of notes payable	0	0	100,000
Net increase in cash	$100,000	$100,000	$100,000

One of the keys to evaluating a company's worth is estimating its future cash flows based on the information available. Companies that can generate a stream of future cash flows are worth more than a company with a single cash flow. In **Exhibit 4.2**, each company's net cash increase was the same, but the source of the increase varied by company. This variation affects the analysis of the cash flow data, particularly for potential creditors who must evaluate the likelihood of obtaining repayment in the future for any funds loaned to the company. Based only on these cash flow data, a potential creditor would feel more comfortable lending money to Faultless than to either Peerless or Dauntless. This choice is because Faultless's cash increase came from its operating activities, and operations tend to be continuing. Both Peerless and Dauntless could only break even on their cash flows from operations. Also, Peerless's cash increase came from the sale of property, plant, and equipment (PPE) assets—a source of cash that is not likely to recur regularly. Dauntless's cash increase came entirely from borrowed funds. This means Dauntless faces additional cash burdens in the future when the interest and principal payments on the note payable become due.

BUSINESS INSIGHT

Objectivity of Cash Usefulness of financial statements is enhanced when the underlying data are objective and verifiable. Measuring cash and the changes in cash are among the most objective measurements that accountants make. Thus, the statement of cash flows is arguably the most objective financial statement. This characteristic of the statement of cash flows is welcomed by those investors and creditors interested in evaluating the quality of a firm's income.

MID-CHAPTER REVIEW 1

Assume **Golden Enterprises** executed the following transactions during 2015. Indicate whether the transaction creates a cash inflow (In) or outflow (Out). Next, determine how each item should be classified in the statement of cash flows: an operating activity (O), an investing activity (I), or a financing activity (F). For example: $50,000 cash received for the sale of snack foods. Answer: In/O

1. ____ $250,000 cash paid to purchase a warehouse
2. ____ $120,000 cash paid for interest on a loan
3. ____ $850,000 cash paid to employees as wages
4. ____ $20,000,000 cash raised through the issuance of stock
5. ____ $450,000 cash paid to the government for taxes
6. ____ $350,000 cash received as part of a settlement of a legal case
7. ____ $630,000 cash received from the sale of long-term securities
8. ____ $75,000 cash received from the sale of used office equipment
9. ____ $500,000 cash dividend paid to shareholders
10. ____ $90,000 cash received as interest earned on a government bond

The solution to this review problem can be found on page 214.

PREPARING THE STATEMENT OF CASH FLOWS—OPERATING ACTIVITIES

2

LO2 Construct the operating activities section of the statement of cash flows using the direct method.

In Chapter 3's **Exhibit 3.12**, we presented a statement of cash flows for Natural Beauty Supply (hereafter, NBS) for the month of December, 2015. This statement is reproduced in **Exhibit 4.3**. The statement details how NBS' cash balance decreases by $1,275 in December, from $8,100 to $6,825. The statement was prepared by examining all of the cash transactions that occurred during the month, and then grouping them according to the type of activity each represents—operating, investing, or financing. Transaction (17) was the loan, so that was a financing activity, transaction (18) was the purchase of fixtures and equipment, an investing activity, and so on. These cash transactions can be taken directly from the cash T-account, which is reproduced here:

+	Cash (A)		−
Beg. bal.	8,100		
(17)	11,000	18,000	(18)
(21)	8,500	700	(19)
(23)	1,200	3,300	(20)
(25)	3,200	1,625	(24)
		1,500	(27)
		50	(28)
End. bal.	6,825		

This approach to preparing the statement of cash flows is straightforward and doesn't require any additional bookkeeping steps, other than those introduced in Chapters 2 and 3.

EXHIBIT 4.3 NBS Statement of Cash Flows (Direct Method)

NATURAL BEAUTY SUPPLY, INC. Statement of Cash Flows For the Month Ended December 31, 2015		
Cash Flows from Operating Activities		
Cash received from customers (entries 21, 23, 25)	$12,900	
Cash paid for inventory (entry 20)	(3,300)	
Cash paid for wages (entry 24)	(1,625)	
Cash paid for rent (entry 27)	(1,500)	
Cash paid for advertising (entry 19)	(700)	
Net cash provided by operating activities		$ 5,775
Cash Flows from Investing Activities		
Cash paid for fixtures and equipment (entry 18)	(18,000)	
Net cash used for investing activities		(18,000)
Cash Flows from Financing Activities		
Cash received from loans (entry 17)	11,000	
Cash paid for dividends (entry 28)	(50)	
Net cash provided by financing activities		10,950
Net change in cash		(1,275)
Cash balance, November 30, 2015		8,100
Cash balance, December 31, 2015		$ 6,825

However, for many companies, the number and variety of cash transactions that occur each period are so large that such an approach is often impractical. A company with revenues and assets and liabilities in the billions of dollars, like Walgreens for example, has thousands of cash transactions each day. It has accounts with several different banks in numerous locations, and regularly transfers cash from one account to another or back and forth between cash accounts and cash equivalents, as needed. For such a company, simply listing the cash transactions is not practical.

An alternative to this approach of compiling a list of cash flows is to reconcile the information in the income statement and balance sheet to prepare the cash flow statement. The statement of cash flows complements the balance sheet and the income statement. The balance sheet details the financial position of the company at a given point in time. Comparing two balance sheets prepared at the beginning and at the end of a period reveals changes that transpired during the accounting period. These changes are explained by the income statement and the statement of cash flows. Both the income statement and the cash flow statement summarize the events and transactions of the business during the accounting period, and as such, provide complementary descriptions of a company's activities. While the cash flow statement provides information that is not explicitly found in either of the other two statements, it must articulate with the balance sheet and income statement to present a complete picture of company activities.

One of the characteristics of the accounting system is that when an entry changes Net Income without a change in Cash, then it must change another account on the balance sheet. And, when an operating cash flow occurs without a change in Net Income, then there must be a change in some other balance sheet account. Therefore, we can start with information from the income statement and then use the balance sheet (and some additional information) to prepare the statement of cash flows. **Exhibit 4.4** presents the income statement and comparative balance sheets for NBS. We will use the data from these financial statements to prepare NBS' reconciliation of Net Income to Cash from Operating Activities.

Converting Revenues and Expenses to Cash Flows from Operating Activities

We know from Chapter 3 that net income consists of revenues and expenses. We also know that these are often not cash transactions. For example, sales on account will be considered revenue but are not cash inflows until collected. Depreciation is an expense, but is not a current-period cash outflow (the cash outflow presumably occurred when the underlying asset was acquired). We can compute cash flow from operating activities by making adjustments to the

EXHIBIT 4.4 NBS Income Statement and Comparative Balance Sheet

NATURAL BEAUTY SUPPLY
Income Statement
For the Month Ended December 31, 2015

Sales revenue		$13,900
Cost of goods sold		8,000
Gross profit		5,900
Operating expenses:		
Rent	$1,500	
Wages	2,105	
Advertising	700	
Depreciation	375	
Insurance	140	
Total operating expenses		4,820
Operating income		1,080
Interest income		30
Interest expense		(110)
Income before taxes		1,000
Income tax expense		350
Net income		$ 650

NATURAL BEAUTY SUPPLY
Comparative Balance Sheets

	12/31/15	11/30/15
Assets:		
Cash	$ 6,825	$ 8,100
Interest receivable	30	
Accounts receivable	2,250	950
Inventory	7,300	11,300
Prepaid insurance	1,540	1,680
Security deposit	2,000	2,000
Fixtures and equipment	18,000	
Accumulated depreciation	(375)	
Total assets	$37,570	$24,030
Liabilities:		
Accounts payable	$ 4,400	$ 3,700
Unearned revenue	600	300
Wages payable	480	
Interest payable	110	
Income taxes payable	350	
Notes payable	11,000	
Stockholders' equity:		
Common stock	20,000	20,000
Retained earnings	630	30
Total liabilities and equity	$37,570	$24,030

revenues and expenses presented in the income statement. The adjustment amounts represent differences between revenues, expenses, gains, and losses recorded under accrual accounting and the related operating cash inflows and outflows. The adjustments are added to or subtracted from net income, depending on whether the related cash flow is more or less than the accrual amount.

Convert Sales Revenues to Cash Received from Customers To illustrate this adjustment procedure for revenues and cash receipts from customers, consider the Chapter 3 transactions and adjusting entry that occurred for NBS in December 2015:

(21) Dec. During the month of December, NBS sold products costing $5,000 to retail customers for $8,500 cash.

(22) Dec. During the month of December, sales to wholesale customers totaled $4,500 for merchandise that had cost $3,000. Instead of paying cash, wholesale customers are required to pay for the merchandise within ten working days.

(23) Dec. $1,200 of gift certificates were sold during the month of December. Each gift certificate entitles the recipient to a one-hour consultation on the use of NBS' products.

(25) Dec. During the month of December, NBS received $3,200 in cash from wholesale customers for products that had been delivered earlier.

(a) Dec. Gift certificates worth $900 were redeemed during the month.

We enter the revenue and cash receipts implications of each of these into the Financial Statement Effects Template (FSET) on the following page. Whenever there is a difference between the revenue recognized and the cash received, that difference affects an operating asset (accounts receivable) or an operating liability (unearned revenue). For instance, in transaction (22a), NBS recognizes credit sales revenue. That is, revenue increases, but cash does not, and the accounting equation is kept by increasing accounts receivable, an operating asset. When NBS received cash in advance of revenue recognition, as in transaction (23), the balancing entry is in unearned revenue, an operating liability. We will find that when an operating transaction affects cash or income—but not both—the operating assets and operating liabilities serve as a temporary buffer between the two.

The total of each of these columns is given in the last row, and because each individual entry is balanced, the totals are balanced.

Transaction	Cash Asset	+	Noncash Assets	=	Liabil-ities	+	Contrib. Capital	+	Earned Capital	Revenues	-	Expenses	=	Net Income
	Balance Sheet									Income Statement				
(21a) Sell $8,500 of products for cash.	+8,500 Cash			=					+8,500 Retained Earnings	+8,500 Sales Revenue	-		=	+8,500
(22a) Sell $4,500 of products on account.			+4,500 Accounts Receivable	=					+4,500 Retained Earnings	+4,500 Sales Revenue	-		=	+4,500
(23) Sell gift certificates for $1,200 cash.	+1,200 Cash			=	+1,200 Unearned Revenue						-		=	
(25) Receive $3,200 cash from customers who purchased on credit.	+3,200 Cash		−3,200 Accounts Receivable	=							-		=	
(a) Adjusting entry for gift certificates redeemed in December.				=	−900 Unearned Revenue				+900 Retained Earnings	+900 Sales Revenue	-		=	+900
Total changes	+12,900 Cash	+	+1,300 Accounts Receivable	=	+300 Unearned Revenue	+	0	+	+13,900 Retained Earnings	+13,900 Sales Revenue	-	0	=	+13,900

We can see that December's revenue was $13,900, and NBS collected $12,900 from customers during the month. Accounts receivable increased by $1,300 over the month, and unearned revenue increased by $300. The FSET maintains the accounting equation at every entry, so we know that the equality will hold for the totals in the last row.

$$\text{Cash flow (receipts)} + \text{Change in accounts receivable} = \text{Change in unearned revenue} + \text{Net income (Sales revenue)}$$

$$\$12{,}900 + \$1{,}300 = \$300 + \$13{,}900$$

And this relationship can be rewritten as the following:

$$\text{Cash flow} = \text{Net income} - \text{Change in accounts receivable} + \text{Change in unearned revenue}$$

$$\$12{,}900 = \$13{,}900 - \$1{,}300 + \$300$$

So, when we start with net income and then subtract the change in accounts receivable and add the change in unearned revenue, we convert the revenues in net income into the cash receipts from customers needed for cash from operations.

Convert Cost of Goods Sold to Cash Paid for Merchandise Purchased As a second illustration, let's examine the December 2015 transactions involving NBS' inventory and its suppliers (**Exhibit 3.3** in Chapter 3).

(20) Dec. 20 NBS paid $3,300 cash to its suppliers in partial payment for the delivery of inventory in November.

(21) Dec. During the month of December, NBS sold products costing $5,000 to retail customers for $8,500 cash.

(22) Dec. During the month of December, sales to wholesale customers totaled $4,500 for merchandise that had cost $3,000. Instead of paying cash, wholesale customers are required to pay for the merchandise within ten working days.

(26) Dec. 28 NBS purchased and received $4,000 of inventory on account.

When a company like NBS purchases inventory for future sale, we know that the purchase will be followed by two events in the normal course of business. One event is that NBS will have to pay the supplier in cash according to the terms of the purchase, resulting in a cash outflow. The other event is the sale of that inventory to a customer of NBS, resulting in a cost of goods sold expense on the income statement. But these two events do not necessarily occur at the same point in time.

As we enter these events into the FSET, we see that the differences between cash payments for inventory and cost of goods sold expense are buffered by inventory, an operating asset, and accounts payable, an operating liability.

	Balance Sheet									Income Statement				
Transaction	Cash Asset	+	Noncash Assets	=	Liabil-ities	+	Contrib. Capital	+	Earned Capital	Revenues	-	Expenses	=	Net Income
(20) Pay $3,300 cash to suppliers.	−3,300 Cash			=	−3,300 Accounts Payable						-		=	
(21b) Record $5,000 for the cost of merchandise sold in transaction 21a.			−5,000 Inventory	=					−5,000 Retained Earnings		-	+5,000 Cost of Goods Sold	=	−5,000
(22b) Record $3,000 for the cost of merchandise sold in transaction 22a.			−3,000 Inventory	=					−3,000 Retained Earnings		-	+3,000 Cost of Goods Sold	=	−3,000
(26) Purchase $4,000 inventory on account.			+4,000 Inventory	=	+4,000 Accounts Payable						-		=	
Total changes	−3,300 Cash	+	−4,000 Inventory	=	+700 Accounts Payable	+	0	+	−8,000 Retained Earnings	0	-	+8,000 Cost of Goods Sold	=	−8,000

Again, the FSET keeps the accounting equation with every entry, so we know that the total changes in the last row must also conform to the accounting equation.

$$\underset{\textbf{(payments)}}{\textbf{Cash flow}} + \underset{\textbf{inventory}}{\textbf{Change in}} = \underset{\textbf{accounts payable}}{\textbf{Change in}} + \underset{\textbf{(COGS expense)}}{\textbf{Net income}}$$

$$-\$3{,}300 + -\$4{,}000 = \$700 + -\$8{,}000$$

And this relationship can be written as the following:

$$\underset{\textbf{flow}}{\textbf{Cash}} = \underset{\textbf{income}}{\textbf{Net}} - \underset{\textbf{inventory}}{\textbf{Change in}} + \underset{\textbf{accounts payable}}{\textbf{Change in}}$$

$$-\$3{,}300 = -\$8{,}000 - (-\$4{,}000) + \$700$$

The change in inventory is negative for NBS during December 2015, so when we subtract the change in inventory above, we must subtract a negative number, making a positive adjustment. (That is, −(−$4,000) = +$4,000.) And, when we subtract the change in inventory from net income and add the change in accounts payable to net income, we convert the (minus) cost of goods sold expense to the (minus) payments to suppliers we need for the cash from operations.

Stepping back to look at the big picture, we begin to see a pattern. The cash flow effect of an item is equal to its income statement effect, minus the change in any associated operating asset(s) plus the change in any associated operating liability(ies). That pattern can be confirmed as we look at the remaining necessary adjustments.

Convert Wages Expense to Cash Paid to Employees To determine the adjustment needed for transactions involving employees, we look at the two entries from Chapter 3 related to the wages earned and paid during the month of December 2015.

Transaction	Cash Asset	+	Noncash Assets	=	Liabil-ities	+	Contrib. Capital	+	Earned Capital	Revenues	-	Expenses	=	Net Income
(24) Record $1,625 in wages to employees.	−1,625 Cash			=					−1,625 Retained Earnings		-	+1,625 Wages Expense	=	−1,625
(e) Adjusting entry to record wages earned but not yet paid.				=	+480 Wages Payable				−480 Retained Earnings		-	+480 Wages Expense	=	−480
Total changes	−1,625 Cash	+	0	=	+480 Wages Payable	+	0	+	−2,105 Retained Earnings	0	-	+2,105 Wages Expense	=	−2,105

Using the same approach as above, the FSET tells us the following about the totals:

$$\textbf{Cash flow (payments)} = \textbf{Change in wages payable} + \textbf{Net income (wage expense)},$$

which can be rewritten as

Cash flow = Net income + Change in wages payable
−$1,625 = −$2,105 + $480

NBS recorded more wage expense than it paid to its employees, and that additional expense goes into an operating liability, wages payable. If wages payable had decreased over the period, it would imply that NBS had paid more to its employees than they had earned during the period (perhaps because they were owed compensation from a prior period).

Convert Rent Expense to Cash Paid for Rent and Advertising Expense to Cash Paid for Advertising The December 2015 entries for rent and advertising are presented in the FSET below.

	Balance Sheet									Income Statement				
Transaction	Cash Asset	+	Noncash Assets	=	Liabil-ities	+	Contrib. Capital	+	Earned Capital	*Revenues*	−	*Expenses*	=	*Net Income*
(19) Pay $700 cash for December advertising.	−700 Cash			=					−700 Retained Earnings		−	+700 Advertising Expense	=	−700
(27) Pay $1,500 rent for December.	−1,500 Cash			=					−1,500 Retained Earnings		−	+1,500 Rent Expense	=	−1,500
Total changes	−2,200 Cash	+	0	=	0	+	0	+	−2,200 Retained Earnings	0	−	+2,200 Advertising and Rent Expense	=	−2,200

For these items, the amount paid is exactly equal to the amount recorded as expense, so no adjustment is necessary. The amounts included for advertising and rent in the determination of net income are exactly what we want in the cash from operations. If NBS had paid rent in advance or promised to pay later for its advertising, then operating assets and/or liabilities would have been created, and an adjustment would have been necessary (as we see in the case immediately following).

Other Adjustments There are five more items in NBS' income statement that require adjustment to arrive at the amount of cash from operations for the month of December. Four of these items are insurance expense, interest income, interest expense and income tax expense. These items involved only adjusting entries during the month of December, so there were no cash flows involved, and we present the adjustments in an abbreviated fashion below.

Transaction	Cash Asset	+	Noncash Assets	=	Liabilities	+	Contrib. Capital	+	Earned Capital	Revenues	−	Expenses	=	Net Income
(b) Adjusting entry to record expiration of 1 month of prepaid insurance.			−140 Prepaid insurance	=					−140 Retained Earnings		−	+140 Insurance Expense	=	−140
Total changes	0 Cash	+	−140 Prepaid Insurance	=	0	+	0	+	−140 Retained Earnings	0	−	+140 Insurance Expense	=	−140

Cash flow + Change in prepaid insurance = Net income, or

Cash flow = Net income − Change in prepaid insurance, or
$0 (zero) = −$140 − (−$140)

Transaction	Balance Sheet: Cash Asset +	Noncash Assets =	Liabil-ities +	Contrib. Capital +	Earned Capital	Income Statement: Revenues −	Expenses =	Net Income
(d) Adjusting entry for interest income earned.		+30 Other Receivables =			+30 Retained Earnings	+30 Interest Income −		= +30
Total changes	0 Cash +	+30 Other Receivables =	0 +	0 +	+30 Retained Earnings	+30 Interest Income −	0	= +30

Cash flow + Change in other receivables = Net income, or

Cash flow = Net income − Change in other receivables, or
\$0 (zero) = \$30 − \$30

Transaction	Cash Asset +	Noncash Assets =	Liabil-ities +	Contrib. Capital +	Earned Capital	Revenues −	Expenses =	Net Income
(f) Adjusting entry to record interest owed but not yet paid.		=	+110 Interest Payable		−110 Retained Earnings	−	+110 Interest Expense	= −110
Total changes	0 Cash +	0 =	+110 Interest Payable +	0 +	−110 Retained Earnings	0 −	+110 Interest Expense	= −110

Cash flow = Change in interest payable + Net income, or

Cash flow = Net income + Change in interest payable, or
\$0 (zero) = −\$110 + \$110

Transaction	Cash Asset +	Noncash Assets =	Liabil-ities +	Contrib. Capital +	Earned Capital	Revenues −	Expenses =	Net Income
(g) Adjusting entry for estimated income tax.		=	+350 Tax Payable		−350 Retained Earnings	−	+350 Tax Expense	= −350
Total changes	0 Cash +	0 =	+350 Tax Payable +	0 +	−350 Retained Earnings	0 −	+350 Tax Expense	= −350

Cash flow = Change in tax payable + Net income, or

Cash flow = Net income + Change in tax payable, or
\$0 (zero) = −\$350 + \$350

Each of the above four items involved only an adjusting entry (i.e., an entry at the end of the fiscal period). Adjusting entries rarely involve cash, so the adjustment simply cancels out the item in the income statement. We will see more examples in later chapters (e.g., write-downs of physical or intangible assets, restructuring charges, etc.).

Eliminate Depreciation Expense and Other Noncash Operating Expenses NBS recorded an adjusting entry for depreciation at the end of December 2015 for \$375. That entry into the FSET was the following.

Transaction	Cash Asset +	Noncash Assets =	Liabil-ities +	Contrib. Capital +	Earned Capital	Revenues −	Expenses =	Net Income
(c) Adjusting entry for depreciation on fixtures and equipment for December.		+375 Accumulated Depreciation =			−375 Retained Earnings	−	+375 Depreciation Expense	= −375
Total changes	0 +	0 − +375 Accumulated Depreciation =	0 +	0 +	−375 Retained Earnings	0 −	+375 Depreciation Expense	= −375

We can see that this entry reduced net income by $375, but it had no effect on cash. When we look at the total impact of this entry on the FSET (in the last row), its effect can be written in the following way.

$$\textbf{Cash flow} - \textbf{Change in accumulated depreciation (for depreciation expense)} = \textbf{Net income,}$$

or

$$\textbf{Cash flow} = \textbf{Net income} + \textbf{Depreciation expense}$$
$$\$0\ (\text{zero}) = -\$375 + \$375$$

So, NBS' net income of $650 for December includes a depreciation expense of $375 that did not involve any cash outflow. When we add back depreciation expense (and similar items like amortization expense), we move the net income number one step closer to cash from operations.

Would increasing depreciation expense increase the cash flows from operations? That question is more complex than it initially appears. In Chapter 8, we will find that companies use different depreciation methods for tax reporting and financial reporting, and in Chapter 10 we will see how differences between tax and financial reporting are reconciled. Increasing the tax depreciation expense reduces taxable income and the amount of tax that has to be paid. Increasing depreciation expense in financial reports to shareholders has no effect on the amount of taxes paid and, therefore, no effect on the amount of cash generated.

A General Rule . . . with a Note of Caution The relationships illustrated in the above examples suggest a general rule that we can use to prepare the cash flow statement:

> The difference between a revenue or an expense reported in the income statement and a related cash receipt or expenditure reported in the statement of cash flows will be reflected in the balance sheet as a change in one or more balance sheet accounts.

More specifically, all the above reconciliation adjustments for NBS can be summarized in a pattern:

$$\textbf{Net income} \pm \textbf{Adjustments} = \textbf{Cash from operations}$$

Or, more particularly

$$\textbf{Net income} + \textbf{Depreciation expense} - \textbf{Change in operating assets} + \textbf{Change in operating liabilities} = \textbf{Cash from operations}$$

By "operating assets," we mean receivables, inventories, prepaid expenses and similar assets. "Operating liabilities" refers to accounts and wages payable, accrued expenses, unearned revenues, taxes payable, interest payable and similar items. Investing assets (like investment securities and property, plant, and equipment) and financing liabilities (like notes payable and long-term debt) would not be included in these adjustments.

Exhibit 4.5 summarizes the basic adjustments needed to convert the revenues, expenses, gains and losses presented in the income statement to cash receipts and payments presented in the statement of cash flows from operating activities. (The adjustments for non-operating gains and losses will be discussed shortly.)

We have now applied the adjustments to convert each accrual revenue and expense to the corresponding operating cash flow. We use these individual cash inflows and outflows to prepare the operating activities section of the statement of cash flows. The adjustments to convert revenues and expenses to operating cash flows are summarized in **Exhibit 4.6**, and this information can be used to produce NBS' cash from operating activities by using the information in the income statement and balance sheet.

Like all general rules, this one provides useful insights, but it also has limitations. As we learn more and more about business activities and the accounting for them, we find the need for refinements of this general rule. For instance, in Chapter 12, we will see that operating assets and liabilities can increase from acquisitions (an investing activity) as well as from operations. But for the time-being, the general rule is a useful way to approach the calculation of operating cash flow.

EXHIBIT 4.5 Adjustments to Convert Income Statement Items to Cash Flows From Operating Activities

	Net income	= Sales revenue	− Cost of goods sold	− Operating expenses	− Depreciation expense	+ Dividend and Interest income	− Interest expense	+ Gains	− Losses	− Income tax expense
Adjustments:										
Add back depreciation expense					⊕ Depreciation expense					
Subtract (add) non-operating gains (losses)								⊖ Gains	⊕ Losses	
Subtract the change in operating assets (operating investments)		⊖ Change in accounts receivable	⊖ Change in inventory	⊖ Change in related prepaid expenses		⊖ Change in dividend and interest receivable				
Add the change in operating liabilities (operating financing)		⊕ Change in unearned revenue	⊕ Change in accounts payable	⊕ Change in related accrued liabilities			⊕ Change in interest payable			⊕ Change in income tax payable
Cash from operations		= Receipts from customers	− Payments for merchandise	− Payments for expenses	− 0	+ Receipts from dividends and interest	− Payments for interest	+ 0	− 0	− Payments for income tax

EXHIBIT 4.6 Converting Revenues and Expenses to Cash Inflows and Outflows from Operating Activity (Natural Beauty Supply)

	Net income	= Sales revenue	+ Interest income	− Cost of goods sold	− Wages expense	− Rent expense	− Advertising expense	− Insurance expense	− Interest expense	− Depreciation expense	− Income tax expense
	$ 650	= $13,900	+ 30	− 8,000	− 2,105	− 1,500	− 700	− 140	− 110	− 375	− 350
Adjustments:											
Add back depreciation expense										⊕ 375 Depreciation expense	
Subtract the change in operating assets (operating investments)		⊖ 1,300 Change in accounts receivable	⊖ 30 Change in interest receivable	⊖ (−4,000)* Change in inventory				⊖ (−140)* Change in prepaid insurance			
Add the change in operating liabilities (operating financing)		⊕ 300 Change in unearned revenue		⊕ 700 Change in accounts payable	⊕ 480 Change in wages payable				⊕ 110 Change in interest payable		⊕ 350 Change in income tax payable
	$5,775	= $12,900	+ 0	− 3,300	− 1,625	− 1,500	− 700	− 0	− 0	− 0	− 0
Cash from operations		= Receipts from customers	+ Receipts for interest	− Payments for merchandise	− Payments to employees	− Payments for rent	− Payments for advertising	− Payments for insurance	− Payments for interest	− 0	− Payments for income tax

* When the change in an operating asset is negative, subtracting that negative amount results in a positive adjustment.

MID-CHAPTER REVIEW 2

The income statement and comparative balance sheets for Mug Shots, Inc., (a photography studio) are presented below. Use the information in these financial statements and the frameworks in **Exhibits 4.5** and **4.6** to compute Mug Shots' cash flow from operating activities using the direct method.

MUG SHOTS, INC. Income Statement For Month Ended December 31, 2015		
Revenue		
Sales revenue		$31,000
Expenses		
Cost of goods sold	$16,700	
Wages expense	4,700	
Interest expense	300	
Advertising expense	1,800	
Rent expense	1,500	
Depreciation expense	700	
Total expenses		25,700
Income before taxes		5,300
Income tax expense		1,855
Net income		$ 3,445

MUG SHOTS, INC. Comparative Balance Sheets	12/31/15	11/30/15
Assets		
Cash	$10,700	$ 5,000
Accounts receivable	2,500	
Inventory	32,300	24,000
Prepaid rent	7,500	9,000
Equipment	30,000	18,000
Accumulated depreciation	(700)	
Total assets	$82,300	$56,000
Liabilities		
Accounts payable	$25,000	$24,000
Interest payable	300	
Wages payable	2,200	
Income tax payable	1,855	
Unearned revenue	500	
Notes payable	30,000	12,000
Equity		
Common stock	20,000	20,000
Retained earnings	2,445	
Total liabilities and equity	$82,300	$56,000

The solution to this review problem can be found on page 214.

eLectures MBC

Reconciling Net Income and Cash Flow from Operating Activities

LO3 Reconcile cash flows from operations to net income and use the indirect method to compute operating cash flows.

We now have two metrics to consider when examining the operations of a company over a period of time—net income and cash from operations. For December 2015, NBS reported net income of $650 and cash from operations of $5,775. For its fiscal year ended May 30, 2014, Golden Enterprises reported net income of $921,829 and cash from operations of $3,263,728. While both net income and cash from operations measure aspects of operations over the same time period, they can sometimes be very far apart, as seen in the following table.

	2013 ($ millions)	
	Net Income	**Cash from Operations**
Snyder's-Lance, Inc.	$ 79	$ 141
Diamond Foods, Inc.	(165)	(102)
Verizon Communications, Inc.	23,547	38,818
Sprint Communications	(4,326)	2,999
Ford Motor Company	7,155	10,444
Daimler AG	10,139	3,285
Tesla Motors, Inc.	(74)	258
CarMax, Inc.	493	(613)
Starbucks Corp.	2,068	608
Keurig Green Mountain, Inc.	597	719
Delta Air Lines, Inc.	10,540	4,504
American Airlines Group, Inc.	(1,876)	1,279

It would be natural for a financial statement reader to want to understand the source(s) of the differences between net income and cash from operations. So, companies that present their statement of cash flows like Golden Enterprises must also present a reconciliation of net income to cash from operations. The reconciliation for Golden Enterprises' fiscal year ending May 30, 2014 is in **Exhibit 4.7**.

3

EXHIBIT 4.7 Golden Enterprises Income to Operating Cash Flows Reconciliation

GOLDEN ENTERPRISES, INC. AND SUBSIDIARY
CONSOLIDATED STATEMENT OF CASH FLOWS
For the Fiscal Year Ended May 30, 2014
RECONCILIATION OF NET INCOME TO NET CASH PROVIDED BY OPERATING ACTIVITIES

	2014
Net income	$ 921,829
Adjustments to reconcile net income to net cash provided by operating activities:	
Depreciation	3,778,563
Deferred income taxes	(298,467)
Gain on sale of property and equipment	(22,693)
Subtract:	
Change in receivables—net	(881,318)
Change in inventories	(703,826)
Change in prepaid expenses	276,876
Change in cash surrender value of insurance	93,408
Change in other assets—other	434,287
Add:	
Change in accounts payable	(1,089,964)
Change in accrued expenses	526,154
Change in salary continuation plan	(96,305)
Change in accrued income taxes	325,184
Net cash provided by operating activities	$3,263,728

This reconciliation leads to exactly the same number that was presented in the operating section of **Exhibit 4.1**, but in a very different format. How is it produced? It is constructed using exactly the same adjustment process depicted in **Exhibits 4.5** and **4.6**.

Golden Enterprises' reconciliation contains a couple of entries that we did not see for Natural Beauty Supply. A company's income statement may contain gains and losses related to investing or financing activities. Examples include gains and losses from the sale of plant assets and gains and losses from the retirement of bonds payable. Golden Enterprises reported a $22,693 gain on sale of assets in its income statement. Because these gains and losses are not related to operating activities, **Exhibit 4.5** shows that we omit them as we convert income statement items to various cash flows from operating activities. The cash flows relating to these gains and losses are reported in the investing activities or financing activities sections of the statement of cash flows. NBS had no gains or losses in December, but Golden Enterprises made an adjustment for an investing activity gain in its reconciliation in **Exhibit 4.7**, and we will see an example of this type of adjustment in a later section.

Golden Enterprises also makes a $298,467 adjustment for deferred income taxes. Deferred income taxes occur when companies use different accounting methods for tax and financial reporting and are beyond our scope for the moment. It will be covered later in Chapter 10.

Cash Flow from Operating Activities Using the Indirect Method

Two alternative formats may be used to report the net cash flow from operating activities: the direct method and the indirect method. *Both methods report the same amount of net cash flow from operating activities*. Net cash flows from investing and financing activities are prepared in the same manner under both the indirect and direct methods; only the format for cash flows from operating activities differs.

For Natural Beauty Supply, we computed cash flow from operating activities using the direct method. The **direct method** presents the components of cash flow from operating activities as a list of gross cash receipts and gross cash payments. This format is illustrated in **Exhibit 4.3** and by Golden Enterprises' statement in **Exhibit 4.1**.

The direct method is logical and relatively easy to follow. In practice, however, nearly all statements of cash flows are presented using what is called the **indirect method**. Under this method, the reconciliation of net income to operating cash flow (e.g., **Exhibit 4.7**) is used for the presentation of cash flow from operations. The cash flow from operations section begins with net income and applies a series of adjustments to net income to convert it to net cash flow from operating activities. However, the adjustments to net income are not cash flows themselves, so the indirect method does not report any detail concerning individual operating cash inflows and outflows. In fact, there are no cash flows in the indirect method operating section of the cash flow statement, except the subtotal—cash flow from operations. The **Apple Inc.** statement of cash flows on page 206 is an example.

While accounting standard-setters prefer the direct method presentation, the AICPA's *Accounting Trends & Techniques 2011*, a survey of large U.S. companies, found that *more than 98% of companies preparing the statement of cash flows use the indirect method*, so the Golden Enterprises presentation is unusual. The indirect method is popular because (1) it is easier and less expensive to prepare than the direct method and (2) companies that use the direct method are required to present a supplemental disclosure showing the reconciliation of net income to cash from operations (thus, essentially requiring the company to report both methods for cash from operations). The same phenomenon occurs internationally. International standard-setters have stated a preference for the direct method, but the AICPA's *IFRS Accounting Trends & Techniques 2011*, a survey of large firms reporting under IFRS, found that only 23 (13.5%) used the direct method for cash from operations.

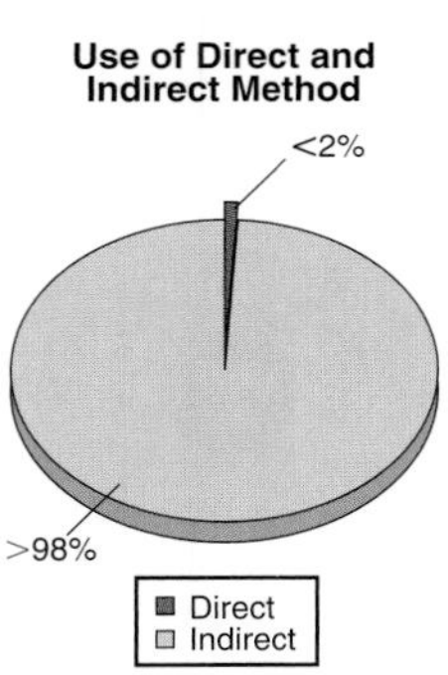

The procedure for presenting indirect method cash flows from operations uses the same approach that we applied above to convert income statement items to operating cash flows. In fact, the indirect method can be viewed as a "short-cut" calculation of the process shown in **Exhibit 4.5**. That is:

Net income ± Adjustments = Cash flow from operating activities

In **Exhibit 4.5**, revenue and expense components of the income statement are presented in the orange row that totals to net income. The yellow rows list the adjustments, and cash receipts and payments are listed in the green row at the bottom. The total of the green row is cash flow from operating activities. The indirect method skips the listing of individual revenues and expenses and starts with net income. After adjustments, we have total cash flow from operating activities, but not individual receipts and payments.

FYI Managers can boost declining sales by lengthening credit periods or by lowering credit standards. The resulting increase in accounts receivable can cause net income to outpace operating cash flow. Consequently, many view a large receivables increase as a warning sign.

Cash flow from operating activities for NBS is presented using the indirect method in **Exhibit 4.8**. The calculation begins with the December net income of $650 and ends with cash flow from operating activities, $5,775. The total cash flow from operating activities is the same amount as was computed in **Exhibit 4.6** using the direct method. If we compare **Exhibit 4.6** and **Exhibit 4.8**, we see that the two exhibits are very similar. The only difference is that all of the revenues and expenses are listed in the orange row at the top of **Exhibit 4.6**, while **Exhibit 4.8** lists only the total—net income. Similarly, the green row at the bottom of **Exhibit 4.6** lists all of the cash inflows and outflows, while the bottom line of **Exhibit 4.8** lists only the net cash flow from operating activities. In both exhibits, the center rows list the adjustments.

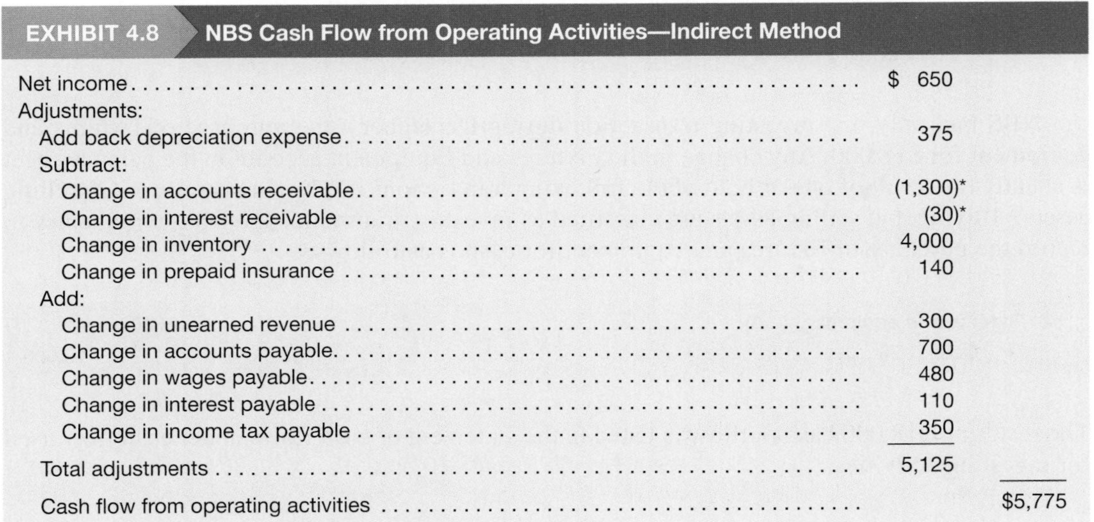

EXHIBIT 4.8 NBS Cash Flow from Operating Activities—Indirect Method

Net income	$ 650	
Adjustments:		
Add back depreciation expense	375	
Subtract:		
Change in accounts receivable	(1,300)*	
Change in interest receivable	(30)*	
Change in inventory	4,000	
Change in prepaid insurance	140	
Add:		
Change in unearned revenue	300	
Change in accounts payable	700	
Change in wages payable	480	
Change in interest payable	110	
Change in income tax payable	350	
Total adjustments	5,125	
Cash flow from operating activities		$5,775

* When the change in an operating asset is negative, subtracting that negative amount results in a positive adjustment.

MID-CHAPTER REVIEW 3

Refer to the financial statements for Mug Shots, Inc. presented in Mid-Chapter Review 2. Compute cash flows from operating activities for Mug Shots, Inc. using the indirect method.

The solution to this review problem can be found on page 215.

PREPARING THE STATEMENT OF CASH FLOWS—INVESTING AND FINANCING ACTIVITIES

4 **LO4** Construct the investing and financing activities sections of the statement of cash flows.

The remaining sections of the statement of cash flows focus on investing and financing activities. Investing activities are concerned with transactions affecting noncurrent (and some current) noncash assets. Financing activities are concerned with raising capital from owners and creditors. The presentation of the cash effects of investing and financing transactions is not affected by the method of presentation (direct or indirect) of cash flows from operating activities.

Accounting standard-setters (both in the United States and International) require that financing and investing items be presented in the statement of cash flows using gross amounts instead of net amounts. In **Exhibit 4.1**, Golden Enterprises reports that it spent $2,380,287 cash to acquire property, plant, and equipment in 2014, and it received $48,125 in cash from the sale of property, plant, and equipment. It would *not* be acceptable to show the net amount—an outflow of $2,332,162—as a single item unless one of the components is consistently immaterial.

Cash Flows from Investing Activities

Investing activities cause changes in noncash asset accounts. Usually the accounts affected (other than cash) are noncurrent operating asset accounts such as property, plant, and equipment assets and investing assets like marketable securities and long-term financial investments. Cash paid for acquisitions of other companies would be included as well. To determine the cash flows from investing activities, *we analyze changes in all noncash asset accounts not used in computing net cash flow from operating activities*. Our objective is to identify any investing cash flows related to these changes.

Purchases of noncash assets cause cash outflow. Conversely, a sale of a noncash asset results in cash inflow. This relationship is highlighted in the following decision guide:

Cash flows increase due to:	Cash flows decrease due to:
Sales of assets	Purchases of assets

NBS had only one investing transaction during December—the purchase of fixtures and equipment for $18,000. Any change in the Fixtures and Equipment account in the balance sheet is usually the result of one or both of the following transactions: (1) buying assets, or (2) selling assets.[2] Buying and selling assets are classified as investing transactions. NBS' journal entry to record the purchase of fixtures and equipment for cash is as follows:

		Debit	Credit
(18)	Fixtures and equipment (+A)	18,000	
	Cash (−A)		18,000

The resulting $18,000 cash outflow is listed in the statement of cash flows under cash flow used for investing activities.

[2] The Accumulated Depreciation—Fixtures and Equipment contra-asset account is affected by depreciation expense and selling assets.

Cash Flows from Financing Activities

Financing activities cause changes in financial liabilities and stockholders' equity accounts. Financial liabilities include current liability items like seasonal bank borrowing and the current portion of long-term debt due within the next year, plus noncurrent items like long-term debt issues and longer term borrowing from financial institutions. Cash receipts from the issuance of these liabilities and cash payments to settle outstanding principal balances are considered cash flows from financing activities. Stockholders' equity accounts include contributed capital (common stock, additional paid-in-capital and treasury stock) and retained earnings. Transactions with shareholders are always considered part of a company's financing activities. This relationship is highlighted in the following decision guide:

Cash flows increase due to:	Cash flows decrease due to:
Taking on a financial liability or issuing shares	Repaying principal on a financial liability or paying dividends to shareholders or making share repurchases

NBS had two financing transactions during December. It borrowed $11,000 on a three-year note, resulting in an increase in cash, and it paid $50 in cash dividends to shareholders. The journal entry to record the $11,000 note is illustrated as:

		Debit	Credit
(17)	Cash (+A).	11,000	
	Notes payable (+L)		11,000

The resulting $11,000 cash inflow is listed in the statement of cash flows under cash flow from financing activities.

The journal entry to record dividends is illustrated as follows:

		Debit	Credit
(28)	Retained earnings (−SE).	50	
	Cash (−A)		50

This dividend payment is a financing cash outflow and would be deducted from cash flow from financing activities.

When using the indirect method for the cash flow from operating activities, we should remember that there are some balance sheet accounts that will be affected by more than one type of activity. For instance, the balance in retained earnings will be affected by net income (which is going to appear in the operations section) and shareholder dividends (which will appear in the financing section).

The statement of cash flows lists cash flows from operating activities first (using either the direct or the indirect method), followed by cash flows from investing activities, then cash flows from financing activities. Once all three categories of cash flows have been listed, we total the three amounts to arrive at net cash flow for the period. The final step is to reconcile the cash balance from the beginning of the period to the ending balance. The completed statement of cash flows for NBS using the indirect method for operating cash flows is presented in **Exhibit 4.9**. We see from this statement that operating activities produced a cash inflow of $5,775, while investing activities resulted in a cash outflow of $18,000, and financing activities resulted in a cash inflow of $10,950. The sum of these three amounts ($5,775 − $18,000 + $10,950) equals the change in cash for December of −$1,275 ($6,825 − $8,100).

YOU MAKE THE CALL

You are the Chief Accountant The February 24, 2012, *Wall Street Journal* reported that **Sears Holdings Corp.** "will unload more than 1,200 stores in an effort to raise up to $770 million of much-needed cash." How would the proceeds from the sales of Sears' stores be reflected in its cash flow statement? [Answer on page 189.]

EXHIBIT 4.9 NBS Statement of Cash Flows—Indirect Method

NATURAL BEAUTY SUPPLY Statement of Cash Flows For the Month Ended December 31, 2015		
Operating activities:		
Net income	$ 650	
Adjustments:		
Add back Depreciation expense	375	
Subtract:		
Change in accounts receivable	(1,300)	
Change in interest receivable	(30)	
Change in inventory	4,000*	
Change in prepaid insurance	140*	
Add:		
Change in unearned revenue	300	
Change in accounts payable	700	
Change in wages payable	480	
Change in interest payable	110	
Change in income tax payable	350	
Total adjustments	5,125	
Cash flow from operating activities		$5,775
Investing activities:		
Purchase of fixtures and equipment	(18,000)	
Cash flow used for investing activities		(18,000)
Financing activities:		
Bank note	11,000	
Dividends paid	(50)	
Cash flow from financing activities		10,950
Net decrease in cash		(1,275)
Cash, November 30, 2015		8,100
Cash, December 31, 2015		$ 6,825

* When the change in an operating asset is negative, subtracting that negative amount results in a positive adjustment.

FYI The net cash inflow or outflow for the period is the same amount as the increase or decrease in cash and cash equivalents for the period from the balance sheet.

MID-CHAPTER REVIEW 4

Refer to the financial statements for Mug Shots, Inc. in Mid-Chapter Review 2. Prepare a complete statement of cash flows for December using the indirect method for cash flows from operating activities. Follow the format used in **Exhibit 4.9**.

The solution to this review problem can be found on page 215.

ADDITIONAL DETAIL IN THE STATEMENT OF CASH FLOWS

There are two additional types of transactions that we must explore to understand the statement of cash flows. The first of these is the sale of investing assets like equipment or an investment security. The transaction itself isn't very complicated, but the use of the indirect method for operating cash flows makes it seem so. And, companies often engage in investing and financing activities that do not involve cash (e.g., acquiring another company through an exchange of stock). This section explores the accounting for these two types of transactions and their effect on the statement of cash flows.

Case Illustration Natural Beauty Supply did not have any disposals of assets or repayments of debt in December 2015, so there is no adjustment to make in this case. However, let's consider the financial statements of One World Café, a coffee shop that is located next door to NBS. The income statement and comparative balance sheet for One World Café are presented in **Exhibit 4.10**. The cash flow statement is presented in **Exhibit 4.11**.

EXHIBIT 4.10 One World Café Income Statement and Comparative Balance Sheets

ONE WORLD CAFÉ, INC.
Income Statement
For Year Ended December 31, 2015

Revenue		
Sales revenue		$390,000
Expenses		
Cost of goods sold	$227,000	
Wages expense	82,000	
Advertising expense	9,800	
Depreciation expense	17,000	
Interest expense	200	
Loss on sale of plant assets	2,000	
Total expenses		338,000
Income before taxes		52,000
Income tax expense		17,000
Net income		$ 35,000

ONE WORLD CAFÉ, INC.
Comparative Balance Sheets
At December 31

	2015	2014
Assets		
Cash	$ 8,000	$ 12,000
Accounts receivable	22,000	28,000
Inventory	94,000	66,000
Prepaid advertising	12,000	9,000
Plant assets, at cost	208,000	170,000
Less accumulated depreciation	(72,000)	(61,000)
Total assets	$272,000	$224,000
Liabilities		
Accounts payable	$ 27,000	$ 14,000
Wages payable	6,000	2,500
Income tax payable	3,000	4,500
Notes payable	5,000	—
Equity		
Common stock	134,000	125,000
Retained earnings	97,000	78,000
Total liabilities and equity	$272,000	$224,000

EXHIBIT 4.11 Cash Flow Statement for One World Café

ONE WORLD CAFÉ, INC.
Statement of Cash Flows
For Year Ended December 31, 2015

Cash flows from operating activities		
Net income	$35,000	
Add (deduct) items to convert net income to cash basis		
Add back depreciation	17,000	
Add back loss on sale of plant assets	2,000	
Subtract change in:		
Accounts receivable	6,000*	
Inventory	(28,000)	
Prepaid advertising	(3,000)	
Add change in:		
Accounts payable	13,000	
Wages payable	3,500	
Income tax payable	(1,500)	
Net cash provided by operating activities		$44,000
Cash flows from investing activities		
Purchase of plant assets	(45,000)	
Proceeds from sale of plant assets	4,000	
Net cash used for investing activities		(41,000)
Cash flows from financing activities		
Issuance of common stock	9,000	
Payment of dividends	(16,000)	
Net cash flows used for financing activities		(7,000)
Net cash decrease		(4,000)
Cash at beginning of year		12,000
Cash at end of year		$ 8,000

* When the change in an operating asset is negative, subtracting that negative amount results in a positive adjustment.

For One World Café, creation of the statement of cash flows requires information that cannot be discerned from the income statement and balance sheet. (After all, the statement of cash flows is *supposed* to provide additional information!) In particular, the following events occurred during the year.

- Plant assets were purchased for cash.
- Obsolete plant assets, with original cost of \$12,000 and accumulated depreciation of \$6,000, were sold for \$4,000 cash, resulting in a \$2,000 loss.
- Additional common stock was issued for cash.
- Cash dividends of \$16,000 were declared and paid during the year.
- One World Café acquired \$5,000 of plant assets by issuing notes payable.

Reviewing One World Café's comparative balance sheet, we see that plant assets at cost increased from \$170,000 to \$208,000, an increase of \$38,000. In addition, the accumulated depreciation contra-asset increased by \$11,000 from \$61,000 to \$72,000. However, these are *net* increases, and we need information on the individual components of the increases. Consequently, we need to determine the gross amounts to ensure the statement of cash flows we create properly presents the gross amounts in the investing activities section.

In addition to the changes in plant assets and accumulated depreciation, notes payable increased by \$5,000 in 2015. The best way to fully understand what happened to cause the changes in balance sheet accounts during the year, and the impact of these changes on cash flows, is to "work backwards" to reconstruct the investing and financing transactions using journal entries and T-accounts, especially the plant assets and accumulated depreciation accounts.

Gains and Losses on Investing and Financing Activities

The focus of the income statement is on the revenues and expenses that are generated by a company's transactions with customers, suppliers, employees, and other operating activities. But the income statement also contains gains and losses that result from investing or financing transactions. Gains and losses from the sale of investments, property, plant, and equipment, or intangible assets result from investing activities, not operating activities. A gain or loss from the retirement of bonds payable is an example of a financing gain or loss. When these transactions occur, the income statement does not show a revenue and an expense, but rather shows only the net amount as a gain or loss.

The full cash flow effect from these types of events is reported in the investing or financing sections of the statement of cash flows. To illustrate, we record the sale of Old World Café's obsolete plant assets at a loss with the following journal entry:

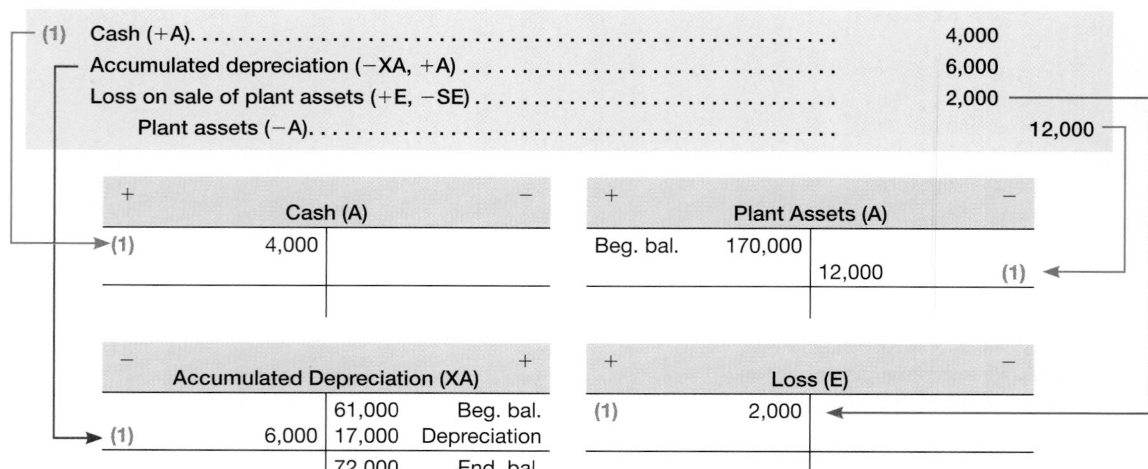

		Debit	Credit
(1)	Cash (+A)	4,000	
	Accumulated depreciation (−XA, +A)	6,000	
	Loss on sale of plant assets (+E, −SE)	2,000	
	Plant assets (−A)		12,000

The \$4,000 of cash received from this sale should be listed as a cash inflow under cash flows from investing activities, and it can be seen in **Exhibit 4.11**. The \$4,000 cash flow is equal to the \$6,000 net book value of the plant assets that were sold (\$12,000 − \$6,000) less the \$2,000 loss on the sale.

If we were using the direct method to report the cash flows from operating activities, we wouldn't need to take any additional steps. But an indirect method operating cash flows starts with net income, and Old World Café's net income includes a $2,000 loss from this investing transaction (**Exhibit 4.10**). So, when we add back the investing loss to net income (or subtract an investing gain), we remove the effect of this investing transaction from the determination of cash flows from operating activities. It's one more step in the adjustments that are needed to reconcile net income to the cash flows from operating activities.

In Chapter 9, we will find that companies can experience financing gains (losses) from the early retirement of their debt. These gains and losses appear in the income statement, but they result from financing activities. In an indirect method statement of cash flows, the financing gains (losses) must be subtracted from (added to) net income to determine cash flows from operating activities.

We also see that the accumulated depreciation account started with a credit balance of $61,000, and the obsolete asset sale reduced this by $6,000 to $55,000. But the balance sheet in **Exhibit 4.10** tells us that the ending (credit) balance is $72,000. The difference is due to $17,000 depreciation expense for the year.

YOU MAKE THE CALL

You are the Securities Analyst You are analyzing a company's statement of cash flows. The company has two items relating to its accounts receivable. First, the company finances the sale of its products to some customers with notes receivable; the increase to notes receivable is classified as an investing activity. Second, the company sells its accounts receivable to another company. As a result, the sale of receivables is reported as an asset sale, which reduces receivables and yields a gain or loss on sale. This action increases its operating cash flows. How should you interpret these items in the cash flow statement? [Answer on p. 189.]

Noncash Investing and Financing Activities

In addition to reporting how cash changed from one balance sheet to the next, cash flow reporting is intended to present summary information about a firm's investing and financing activities. Many of these activities affect cash and are therefore already included in the investing and financing sections of the statement of cash flows. Some significant investing and financing events, however, do not affect current cash flows. Examples of **noncash investing and financing activities** are the issuance of stocks, bonds, or leases in exchange for property, plant, and equipment (PPE) assets or intangible assets; the exchange of long-term assets for other long-term assets; and the conversion of long-term debt into common stock.

To illustrate the effect of noncash transactions on the preparation of the cash flow statement, consider One World Café's purchase of $5,000 of plant assets that was financed with notes payable. The journal entry to record the purchase is as follows:

	Account	Debit	Credit
(2)	Plant assets (+A)	5,000	
	Notes payable (+L)		5,000

Plant Assets (A)

	+	−	
Beg. bal.	170,000		
		12,000	(1)
(2)	5,000		

Notes Payable (L)

−	+	
	0	Beg. bal.
	5,000	(2)
	5,000	End. bal.

Because this purchase did not use any cash, it is not presented in the statement of cash flows. Only those capital expenditures that use cash are listed as cash flows from investing activities. That is, cash flows from investing activities should reflect the actual amount of cash spent to purchase plant assets or investment assets.

Noncash investing and financing transactions generally do affect *future* cash flows. Issuing notes payable to acquire equipment, for example, requires future cash payments for interest and principal on the notes, and should produce future operating cash flows from the equipment. Alternatively, converting bonds payable into common stock eliminates future cash payments related to the bonds, but may carry the expectation of future cash dividends. Knowledge of these types of events, therefore, is helpful to users of cash flow data who wish to assess a firm's future cash flows.

Information on noncash investing and financing transactions is disclosed in a schedule that is separate from the statement of cash flows. The separate schedule is reported either immediately below the statement of cash flows or among the notes to the financial statements.

Solving for Purchases of Plant Assets The remaining entry affecting plant assets is the purchase of plant assets for cash. The amount of plant assets purchased can be determined by solving for the missing amount in the Plant Assets T-account:

+	Plant Assets (A)		−
Beg. bal.	170,000		
		12,000	(1)
(2)	5,000		
(3)	X		
End. bal.	208,000		

Balancing the account requires that we solve for the unknown amount:

$$\$170{,}000 + \$5{,}000 + X - \$12{,}000 = \$208{,}000$$
$$X = \$45{,}000$$

Thus, plant assets costing $45,000 were purchased for cash. This amount is listed as a cash outflow under cash flows for investing activities.

Examining the cash flow statement for One World Café in **Exhibit 4.11**, we see that two cash flows are listed under investing activities: (1) a $45,000 cash outflow for the purchase of plant assets, and (2) a $4,000 cash inflow from the sale of plant assets. The purchase of plant assets costing $5,000 by issuing notes payable is not listed; nor is the increase in notes payable listed under financing activities.

Appendix 4A at the end of this chapter introduces a spreadsheet approach that can be used to prepare the statement of cash flows. The appendix uses the One World Café financial statements as the illustration.

MID-CHAPTER REVIEW 5

The balance sheet of Jack's Snacks, Inc. reports the following amounts:

	End-of-year	Beginning-of-year
Property, plant & equipment at cost.	$670,000	$600,000
Accumulated depreciation	(150,000)	(140,000)
Property, plant & equipment, net	$520,000	$460,000

Additional information:

During the year, Jack's Snacks disposed of a used piece of equipment. The original cost of the equipment was $80,000 and, at the time of disposal, the accumulated depreciation on the equipment was $60,000. The purchaser of the used piece of equipment paid in cash, and Jack's Snacks reported a gain of $35,000 on the disposal.

All acquisitions of new property, plant, and equipment were paid for in cash.

Questions:

1. How much cash did Jack's Snacks receive from the used equipment disposal?
2. How much cash did Jack's Snacks spend to acquire new property, plant, and equipment during the year?
3. How much depreciation expense did Jack's Snacks record during the year?

The solution to this review problem can be found on pages 215–216.

The Effects of Foreign Currencies on the Cash Flow Statement

Multinational companies often engage in transactions that involve currencies other than U.S. dollars and may hold assets that were acquired with foreign currencies or liabilities that must be repaid in foreign currencies. Also, part of a company's cash balance may be held in a currency other than dollars. If the company prepares its financial statements in U.S. dollars, these foreign currency amounts must be converted, or *translated*, into dollars before preparing the financial statements. The process of translating transactions based in many currencies into one common currency for financial statement presentation is beyond the scope of an introductory text. However, foreign exchange rates fluctuate and these fluctuations can have an effect on the cash flow statement.

The statement of cash flows explains the change in the cash balance during the fiscal year, but part of this change may be due to changes in the dollar value of foreign currencies. This amount is typically small and it is not a cash flow, but it is included in the cash flow statement so that we can accurately reconcile the beginning balance in cash to the ending balance. The statement of cash flows for **Nike, Inc.** was summarized in Chapter 1 in **Exhibit 1.10** and is repeated here for illustration.

NIKE
Statement of Cash Flows
For the Year Ended May 31, 2014
($ millions)

Operating cash flows	$3,003
Investing cash flows	(1,207)
Financing cash flows	(2,914)
Effect of exchange rate changes	1
Net decrease in cash and cash equivalents	(1,117)
Cash and equivalents, beginning of year	3,337
Cash and equivalents, end of year	$2,220

Supplemental Disclosures

When the indirect method is used in the statement of cash flows, three separate supplemental disclosures are required: (1) two specific operating cash outflows—cash paid for interest and cash paid for income taxes, (2) a schedule or description of all noncash investing and financing transactions, and (3) the firm's policy for determining which highly liquid, short-term investments are treated as cash equivalents. If the direct method is used, a reconciliation of net income to cash flows from operating activities is also required. A firm's policy regarding cash equivalents is placed in the financial statement notes. The other disclosures are reported either in the notes or at the bottom of the statement of cash flows.

One World Café Case Illustration One World Café incurred $200 of interest expense which was paid in cash. It also reported income tax expense of $17,000 and reported a decrease in income taxes payable of $1,500 ($4,500 − $3,000). Thus, One World Café paid $18,500 ($17,000 + $1,500) in income taxes during 2015. It also had the noncash investment in plant assets costing $5,000, which was financed with notes payable. One World Café would provide the following disclosure:

Supplemental cash flow information	
Cash payments for interest	$ 200
Cash payments for income taxes	18,500
Noncash transaction—investment in plant assets financed with notes payable	5,000

ANALYZING FINANCIAL STATEMENTS

LO5 Compute and interpret ratios that reflect a company's liquidity and solvency using information reported in the statement of cash flows.

Cash is a special resource for companies because of its flexibility. At short notice, it can be used to fulfill obligations and to take advantage of investment opportunities. When companies run short of cash, their suppliers may be reluctant to deliver and lenders may be able to take over control of decision making. In Chapter 2, we introduced the current ratio, which compares the level of current

5

assets to the level of current liabilities at a point in time. But the statement of cash flows gives us the opportunity to compare a company's ongoing cash generating activities to its obligations and to its investment opportunities.

Interpreting Indirect Method Cash from Operations

We want to interpret the cash flows from operations presented using the indirect method.

When companies use the indirect method to present their cash flows from operating activities, it is difficult to interpret the numbers presented to adjust net income to cash from operating activities. For instance, in **Exhibit 4.11**, One World Café reports \$6,000 for the change in accounts receivable. Does that mean that the company received cash payments of \$6,000 from its customers? It does not! Every item in the reconciliation has to be interpreted relative to the net income at the top. Net income includes revenue of \$390,000, and the adjustment addition of \$6,000 means that One World Café received payments of \$390,000 + \$6,000 = \$396,000 from its customers.

The \$3,500 adjustment for wages payable does not mean that One World Café received payments of \$3,500 from its employees. Rather, the company paid its employees \$3,500 less than it recognized as wage expense in determining net income. The adjustment for income tax payable was \$(1,500), but that doesn't mean that One World Café's tax payments totaled \$1,500 for the year. Rather, the \$35,000 net income already reflects a charge for tax expense of \$17,000, so the adjustment means that One World's payments for income tax totaled \$17,000 + \$1,500 = \$18,500. Depreciation expense is added back not because it increases cash, but because it is an expense that doesn't require a cash outflow.

How should we interpret the changes in operating assets and liabilities? These assets and liabilities are a function of both the scale of the business and the practices of the business. If we're selling to 10% more customers this year, then we would expect an increase in receivables of about 10% over the previous year. If the increase is substantially more than that amount, then there must have been some other change as well. Perhaps increasing sales required that we give more favorable payment terms and customers are taking longer to pay. Such a development could cause an investor to question the "quality" of the company's earnings. If sales are constant and accounts payable are increasing, that may imply that the company is taking longer to pay its suppliers. That change would appear as a positive adjustment in the indirect method cash from operations, but it may indicate an unfavorable development for the company.

The indirect method may also alert us to gains and losses from non-operating transactions. These gains and losses are often in "other income" in the income statement, and therefore it's easy for a financial statement reader to miss them. The fact that gains must be subtracted and losses must be added back in the indirect cash from operations, gives them a prominence that they don't have in the income statement.

Analysis Objective

We are trying to gauge Golden Enterprises' generation of cash from its operating activities relative to its average short-term obligations found in the balance sheet.

Analysis Tool Operating Cash Flow to Current Liabilities (OCFCL)

$$\textbf{Operating cash flow to current liabilities} = \frac{\textbf{Operating cash flow}}{\textbf{Average current liabilities}}$$

Applying the Operating Cash Flow to Current Liabilities Ratio to Golden Enterprises

$$\textbf{2012:}\ \frac{\$5.747}{\$14.129} = 0.41 \text{ or } 41\%$$

$$\textbf{2013:}\ \frac{\$4.607}{\$14.044} = 0.33 \text{ or } 33\%$$

$$\textbf{2014:}\ \frac{\$3.264}{\$14.590} = 0.22 \text{ or } 22\%$$

Guidance Golden Enterprise's OCFCL is lower than the food industry average. Golden Enterprises' business is relatively low-margin, which means that it requires a large flow of resources to generate profits and cash from operations, and that large volume of activity results in high levels of current liabilities relative to the cash generated. The OCFCL ratio complements the current ratio and quick ratio introduced in Chapter 2. Golden Enterprises' current ratio is 1.32, also lower than average for the food industry, but its quick ratio of 0.95 is right at the industry average.

Golden Enterprises in Context

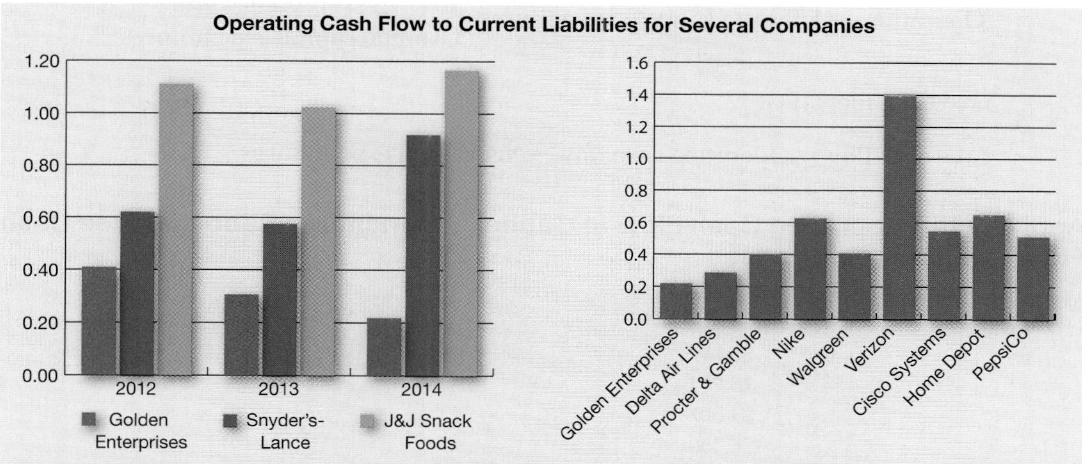

Golden Enterprises' fiscal year ends at the end of May each year. J&J Snack Foods' fiscal year ends at the end of September and Snyder's-Lance's year ends at the end of December. In the graph on the left, Golden Enterprises' end-of-May ratio is compared with J&J's end of September ratio and Snyder's-Lance's most recent December ratio.

Takeaways Over the past three years, Golden Enterprises' OCFCL ratio is consistently lower than the two competitors that are included in the graph on the left. Snyder's-Lance's ratio is near the industry average for 2012 and 2013 but increases in 2014. J&J Snack Foods' ratio is well above the industry average all three years. There is also variation in the ratio from one year to the next. This is largely due to the fluctuation in operating cash flows. The comparison of focus companies' OCFCLs in the right-hand graph shows a range from 0.33 for Delta Air Lines to a high of over 1.40 for Verizon. Golden Enterprises is lower than any of these companies.

Other Considerations There are some transactions that change both the numerator and the denominator, like using cash to pay current operating liabilities. Such a transaction would decrease both the numerator and the denominator, and these changes have an indeterminate effect on the ratio. Paying $100 to a creditor decreases operating cash flow and ending current liabilities by $100, with the average current liabilities decreasing by $50. If the OCFCL is below 2.0 prior to the transaction, it will be even lower after the transaction. If the OCFCL is greater than 2.0 prior to the transaction, it will be even higher after the transaction. Delaying a payment to the creditor would have the opposite effect.

It is also important to take a look at the components of current liabilities. Sometimes there is a large portion of long-term debt that comes due and increases current liabilities for one year. Or, in the case of Delta Air Lines, more than 25% of their current liabilities represent unearned revenue from customers who have purchased tickets in advance of travel (like the gift certificates at NBS). For this liability, Delta doesn't have to pay someone, they just need to keep flying.

Analysis Objective

We wish to determine Golden Enterprises' ability to fund the capital expenditures needed to maintain and grow its operations.

Does Golden Enterprises generate enough cash from its operations to make its capital investments? If it does not, then the company will have to finance those investments by selling other investments, by borrowing (resulting in future interest costs), by getting cash from shareholders or by reducing cash balances. If it generates more cash than needed for capital expenditures, then the additional cash can be used to grow the business (e.g., by acquisition) or to distribute cash to investors. Two measures may be used in making this assessment. The first of these measures, operating cash flow to capital expenditures, is a ratio that facilitates comparisons with other companies. The second, free cash flow,[3] is a monetary amount that reflects the funds available for investing in new ventures, buying back stock, paying down debt, or returning funds to stockholders in the form of dividends. The concept is also used in mergers and acquisitions to indicate cash that would be available to the acquirer for investment.

Analysis Tools Operating Cash Flow to Capital Expenditures (OCFCX)

$$\textbf{Operating cash flow to capital expenditures} = \frac{\textbf{Operating cash flow}}{\textbf{Annual capital expenditures}}$$

Free Cash Flow (FCF)

$$\textbf{Free cash flow} = \textbf{Operating cash flow} - \textbf{Net capital expenditures}$$

Applying the Operating Cash Flow to Capital Expenditures Ratio and Free Cash Flow to Golden Enterprises

	OCFCX	FCF
2012:	$\frac{\$5.747}{\$5.214} = 1.10$ or 110%	$5.747 – $4.992 = $0.755
2013:	$\frac{\$4.607}{\$4.150} = 1.11$ or 111%	$4.607 – $4.075 = $0.532
2014:	$\frac{\$3.264}{\$2.380} = 1.37$ or 137%	$3.264 – $2.332 = $0.932

Guidance Operating cash flows to capital expenditures ratios that exceed 1.0 (or free cash flows that are positive) mean that the company can make its capital investments without obtaining additional financing or reducing its cash balances. The excess cash could be used to reduce borrowing, or it could be returned to shareholders. In both 2012 and 2013, Golden Enterprises' cash from operations exceeded its capital expenditures, though not by a large margin. The ratio increased in 2014 despite a drop in operating cash flows. In 2013, the company completed a major investment in an enterprise resource planning system and capital expenditures subsequently declined.

Golden Enterprises in Context

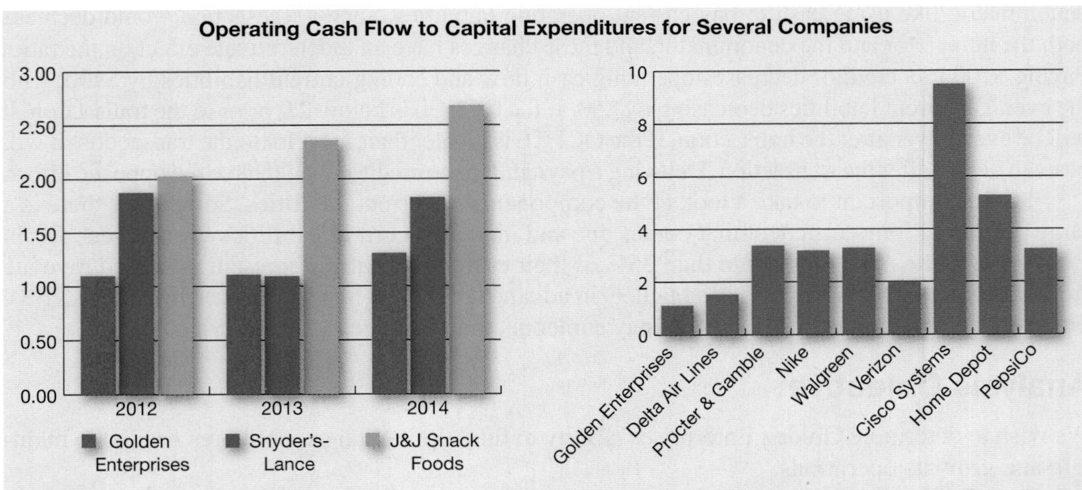

Golden Enterprises' fiscal year ends at the end of May each year. J&J Snack Foods' fiscal year ends at the end of September and Snyder's-Lance's year ends at the end of December. In the graph on the left, Golden Enterprises' end-of-May ratio is compared with J&J's end of September ratio and Snyder's-Lance's most recent December ratio.

[3] Free cash flow can be defined in several ways, but it always includes a measure of the cash resources generated by the company's current operations minus a measure of the cash required to sustain those operations. One of the simpler, more common definitions is presented here.

Takeaways OCFCX increased over the last three years for Golden Enterprises, but its OCFCX is substantially lower than either of the two comparison companies from the same industry. Snyder's-Lance and J&J Snack Foods have used the additional cash flow to acquire other businesses, pay dividends and repay long-term debt. We can see that all of the focus companies have OCFCX well above the levels of Golden Enterprises. These companies can use the cash in excess of capital expenditures to make acquisitions or to return cash to shareholders in the form of dividends or common stock repurchases.

Other Considerations Measurement of cash flows is regarded as more objective than measures of income and less dependent on management judgments and estimates. But it may be subject to "lumpy" behavior from management's decisions, particularly for a smaller company. Capital expenditures may differ significantly from year to year if management takes on large, but infrequent, projects. A series of high values of OCFCX followed by a low value might mean deterioration in cash generating performance, but it might also mean that management has been accumulating cash in anticipation of a major project.

RESEARCH INSIGHT

Is the Cash Flow Statement Useful? Some analysts rely on cash flow forecasts to value common stock. Research shows that both net income and operating cash flows are correlated with stock prices, but that stock prices are more highly correlated with net income than with cash flows. So, do we need both statements? Evidence suggests that by using *both* net income and cash flow information, we can improve our forecasts of *future* cash flows. Also, net income and cash flow together are more highly correlated with stock prices than either net income or cash flow alone. This result suggests that, for purposes of stock valuation, information from the cash flow statement complements information from the income statement.

CHAPTER-END REVIEW

Refer to One World Café's statement of cash flows and comparative balance sheets from **Exhibits 4.10** and **4.11** to complete the following.

Required

1. Calculate the operating cash flow to current liabilities (OCFCL) ratio for One World Café and interpret your findings. Assume that the notes payable are due within the year and are a current liability.
2. Calculate One World Café's operating cash flow to capital expenditures (OCFCX) ratio. What observations can you make about your findings?
3. Calculate the free cash flow (FCF) for One World Café.

The solution to this review problem can be found on page 216.

APPENDIX 4A: A Spreadsheet Approach to Preparing the Statement of Cash Flows

LO6 Use a spreadsheet to construct the statement of cash flows.

Preparing the statement of cash flows is aided by the use of a spreadsheet. The procedure is somewhat mechanical and is quite easy once someone has mastered the material in the chapter. We illustrate this procedure using the data for One World Café presented in the chapter in **Exhibit 4.10**. By following the steps presented below, we are able to readily prepare One World Café's cash flow statement for 2015.

To set up the spreadsheet, we list all of the accounts in the balance sheet in the first column of the spreadsheet. We list depreciable assets net of accumulated depreciation. In column C, we list the most recent balance sheet (the ending balances) followed by the earlier balance sheet (beginning balances) in column D. There is no need to list totals such as total assets or total current liabilities. See **Exhibit 4A.1**. We will build the statement of cash flows in columns F, G and H.

Step 1: Classify the balance sheet accounts. For each of the accounts (other than cash), classify them in column B as Operating (O), Investing (I) or Financing (F) according to where the effect of changes in that account will appear in the statement of cash flows. There are two accounts that have a

6

EXHIBIT 4A.1 Cash Flow Spreadsheet for One World Café

	A	B	C	D	E	F	G	H	I	J
1		O, I or F?	2015	2014	Change	Effect of change on cash flow: Operating	Investing	Financing	No effect on cash	Total F,G,H,I
2										
3	**Assets**									
4	Cash		8,000	12,000	(4,000)					
5										
6	Accounts receivable	O	22,000	28,000	(6,000)	6,000				6,000
7	Inventory	O	94,000	66,000	28,000	(28,000)				(28,000)
8	Prepaid advertising	O	12,000	9,000	3,000	(3,000)				(3,000)
9	Plant assets, net	O,I	136,000	109,000	27,000					
10	Depreciation expense					17,000				
11	Plant assets purchased						(45,000)		(5,000)	(27,000)
12	Plant assets sold					2,000	4,000			
13										
14	**Liabilities**									
15	Accounts payable	O	27,000	14,000	13,000	13,000				13,000
16	Wages payable	O	6,000	2,500	3,500	3,500				3,500
17	Income tax payable	O	3,000	4,500	(1,500)	(1,500)				(1,500)
18	Notes payable	F	5,000	—	5,000					
19	New borrowing								5,000	5,000
20	Borrowing repayments									
21										
22	**Shareholders' Equity**									
23	Common stock	F	134,000	125,000	9,000					
24	New issue of common stock							9,000		9,000
25	Repurchase of common stock									
26	Retained earnings	O,F	97,000	78,000	19,000					
27	Net income					35,000				19,000
28	Dividends							(16,000)		
29										
30	**Totals**					44,000	(41,000)	(7,000)	—	(4,000)

double classification. Changes in the plant assets, net account can be caused by depreciation expense (which will appear in the indirect method cash from operations) and by investing activities, so we label it as (O, I). Changes in the retained earnings account are caused by net income (which appears in the indirect method cash from operations) and dividends, so we label it as (O, F).

For those rows labeled I or F, insert two rows below: one for increases in the account and one for decreases in the account because we must report increases and decreases separately. For plant assets, net, insert three rows below: one for depreciation expense, one for plant asset acquisitions and one for plant asset sales. For retained earnings, insert two rows below: one for net income and one for dividends.

Step 2: Compute the changes in the balance sheet accounts. Subtract the beginning balances in each account from the ending balances and record these in column E. We highlight the change in the cash balance, because this is the amount that we are trying to explain. At this point it is useful to verify that the change in cash is equal to the changes in liabilities plus the changes in stockholders' equity minus the changes in noncash assets:

$$\Delta \textbf{ Cash} = \Delta \textbf{ Liabilities} + \Delta \textbf{ Stockholders' Equity} - \Delta \textbf{ Noncash Assets}$$

In effect, we're going to use changes on the right-hand side of this equation to explain the changes in cash on the left-hand side.

Step 3: Handle the accounts that have single classifications. For those accounts that are operating-only assets (accounts receivable, inventory, prepaid expenses, etc.), we enter in column F the *negative* of the value in column E. The $28,000 increase in inventories in column E results in $(28,000) for the operating cash flows in column F. Changes in assets have the opposite effect on cash. Increases in assets have a negative effect on cash, while decreases in assets lead to positive adjustments to cash.

For those accounts that are operating only liabilities (accounts payable, wages payable, taxes payables, etc.), we enter in column F the value in column E. The $13,000 increase in accounts payable produces a $13,000 entry in column F.

For those accounts that are financing only (notes payable, common stock), we enter in column H the cash effect(s) of the change in column E. For example, we must be aware that the common stock account could have changed due to both issuing stock for cash and repurchasing stock for cash. For One World Café, there was only a $9,000 inflow due to a new stock issue in column H. (We will deal with the notes payable changes in the next step.)

One World Café has no assets that are investing only, but for such accounts (marketable securities, investments, etc.), we would again make entries for increases and decreases separately. And, since these are assets, the change in the balance sheet has the opposite sign of the entry in the cash flow columns. For instance, if One World Café had invested $10,000 in a financial security, its investments asset would increase, and we would put an entry of $(10,000) in column G.

Step 4: Enter the effect of investing/financing transactions that do not involve cash. We know from the information provided about One World Café that it arranged the purchase of $5,000 of plant assets by signing a note payable for the same amount. This transaction affected an investing asset and a financing liability at the same time, and we put the effects into column I. $5,000 is put in the new borrowing row (19), and $(5,000) is put in the plant assets purchased row (11). This transaction will not appear in the cash flow statement in columns F, G and H, but it does explain some of the changes in the company's assets and liabilities.

Step 5: Analyze the change in retained earnings. Some accounts require special attention because the change in the account balance involves two types of cash flow effects. For example, the change in retained earnings is actually two changes—net income, which is related to operations, and dividends, which is a financing cash outflow.

One World Café's retained earnings increased by $19,000. It reported net income of $35,000, which is listed as an operating item (because we're using the indirect method), and paid dividends of $16,000, a cash outflow listed under financing activities. For clarity, it is helpful to list each of these changes on a separate line. Thus, we have inserted two lines into the spreadsheet immediately below retained earnings—the first for net income and the second for dividends. The $35,000 inflow and the $16,000 outflow net to $19,000.

Step 6: Analyze the change in plant assets. A change in depreciable assets is actually the result of both operating and investing items. The change in plant assets can be explained by looking at the individual transactions that caused the change. As was the case with retained earnings, it is helpful to list each of these transactions in a separate row in the spreadsheet. Thus, we have inserted three rows into the spreadsheet immediately below the change in plant assets. First, we recall that One World Café reported depreciation expense of $17,000, which reduced its plant assets, net. This is listed in the first row under plant assets as a positive adjustment to cash flow from operations because cash flow effects on the asset side have the opposite sign.

In the next row, we list purchases of plant assets. One World Café purchased plant assets for $45,000 in cash, which is listed under investing as a cash outflow in column F. There was also the $5,000 purchase of plant assets that was financed with notes payable. This transaction did not affect cash so it's in column I.

In the third row below plant assets, we list the sale of plant assets. One World Café sold plant assets for $4,000 cash, recognizing a loss of $2,000. The loss is listed in the operations column (as a positive adjustment to operating cash flow) and the proceeds from the sale are listed under investing as a cash inflow in column F.

When all of the balance sheet changes have been analyzed, the change for each account should add up to the sum of the effect on operating, investing, and financing cash flows, plus the amount in the "no effect" column. That is, for each change listed in the spreadsheet in column E, we can add columns F, G, H and I to get the change in the balance sheet account in column J. For retained earnings: $35,000 − $16,000 = $19,000. For assets, the total will be the *negative* of the change. Adding up entries for plant assets: $17,000 − $45,000 − $5,000 + $2,000 + $4,000 = −$27,000, which is minus the amount in column E, row 9.

Step 7: Total the columns. We add up the effects listed in columns F, G, H and I to get the cash flow subtotals. One World Café had cash flow from operations of $44,000, investing cash flows of −$41,000 and financing cash flows of −$7,000. The total for the "no effect" column (column I) should be $0, because the entries in this column had no effect on cash flow. Finally, we add up these totals to make sure that the cash flow effects equal the change in cash: $44,000 − $41,000 − $7,000 − $0 = −$4,000. If the totals do not add up to the change in cash, then there must be an error in analyzing one or more of the balance sheet changes. For example, if we had forgotten to subtract dividends, then the cash flow effects in columns F, G and H would not add up to the change in retained earnings listed in column E. Likewise, if we had mistakenly omitted the sale of plant assets, then the change in plant assets would not add up correctly. Totaling the columns and rows is a check to verify that our analysis is complete and correct.

Step 8: Prepare the cash flow statement. Starting with operating cash flows (column F), we list each of the items in the statement of cash flows. We start with net income, and then add depreciation and the loss on the sale of plant assets, then we list the remaining adjustments, starting with the change in accounts receivable and working down the column. Next, we do the same for the items listed in the investing (column G) and financing (column H) sections of the cash flow statement. The resulting statement is identical to the statement presented in **Exhibit 4.11**.

APPENDIX 4A REVIEW

The comparative balance sheets and income statement for Rocky Road Bicycles, Inc., are as follows.

ROCKY ROAD BICYCLES, INC. Comparative Balance Sheets		
At December 31	2015	2014
Assets		
Cash	$ 106,000	$ 96,000
Accounts receivable	156,000	224,000
Inventory	752,000	528,000
Prepaid rent	68,000	72,000
Plant assets	1,692,000	1,360,000
Less accumulated depreciation	(562,000)	(488,000)
Total assets	$2,212,000	$1,792,000
Liabilities		
Accounts payable	$ 216,000	$ 112,000
Wages payable	18,000	20,000
Income tax payable	44,000	36,000
Equity		
Common stock	1,142,000	1,000,000
Retained earnings	792,000	624,000
Total liabilities and equity	$2,212,000	$1,792,000

Additional Information:

- Rocky Road reported net income of $326,000 in 2015.
- Depreciation expense was $122,000 in 2015.
- Rocky Road sold plant assets during 2015. The plant assets originally cost $88,000, with accumulated depreciation of $48,000, and were sold for a gain of $16,000.
- Rocky Road declared and paid a $158,000 cash dividend in 2015.

REQUIRED

Use a spreadsheet to create a statement of cash flows for Rocky Road Bicycles, Inc.

The solution to this review problem can be found on page 217.

SUMMARY

LO1 Explain the purpose of the statement of cash flows and classify cash transactions by type of business activity: operating, investing or financing. (p. 158)

- The statement of cash flows summarizes information about the flow of cash into and out of the business.
- Operating cash flow includes any cash transactions related to selling goods or rendering services, as well as interest payments and receipts, tax payments and any transaction not specifically classified as investing or financing.
- Investing cash flow includes acquiring and disposing of plant assets, buying and selling securities, including securities of other companies, and lending and subsequently collecting funds from a borrower.
- Financing cash flow includes all cash received or paid to shareholders, including stock issued or repurchased and dividends paid. In addition, it includes amounts borrowed and repaid to creditors.

LO2 Construct the operating activities section of the statement of cash flows using the direct method. (p. 162)

- The direct method presents net cash flow from operating activities by showing the major categories of operating cash receipts and payments.
- The operating cash receipts and payments are usually determined by converting the accrual revenues and expenses to corresponding cash amounts.

Reconcile cash flows from operations to net income and use the indirect method to compute operating cash flows. (p. 171) LO3

- Because operating cash flow differs from net income, a reconciliation of these two amounts helps financial statement users understand the sources of this difference.
- The indirect method reconciles net income and operating cash flows by making adjustments for noncash revenues and expenses and changes in balance sheet accounts related to operations.

Construct the investing and financing activities sections of the statement of cash flows. (p. 174) LO4

- Cash investment outlays are captured in the investing section along with any cash receipts from asset disposals. Because cash receipts include any gain on sale (or reflect any loss), the gain (loss) must be subtracted from (added to) net income in the operating section to avoid double-counting.
- Cash obtained from the issuance of securities or borrowings, and any repayments of debt, are disclosed in the financing section. Cash dividends are also included in this section. Interest payments are included in the operating section of the statement.
- Some events, for example assets donated to the firm, provide resources to the business that are important but which do not involve cash outlays. These events are disclosed separately, along with the statement of cash flows, as supplementary disclosures or in the notes.

Compute and interpret ratios that reflect a company's liquidity and solvency using information reported in the statement of cash flows. (p. 181) LO5

- Interpreting indirect method cash from operations requires reference to those items that comprise net income. Each adjustment is intended to modify an income statement item to bring it to cash from operations.
- Two ratios of importance that are based on cash flows include:
  - Operating cash flow to current liabilities—a measure of the adequacy of current operations to cover current liability payments.
  - Operating cash flow to capital expenditures—a reflection of a company's ability to replace or expand its activities based on the level of current operations.
- Free cash flow is defined as: Cash flow from operations − Net capital expenditures.
- Free cash flow is a measure of a company's ability to apply its resources to new endeavors.

Appendix 4A: Use a spreadsheet to construct the statement of cash flows. (p. 185) LO6

- A spreadsheet helps to prepare the statement of cash flows by classifying the effect of each change in the balance sheet as operating, investing, financing, or not affecting cash.
- The spreadsheet approach relies on the key relationship:

$$\text{Cash} = \text{Liabilities} + \text{Stockholders' equity} - \text{Noncash assets}$$

GUIDANCE ANSWERS . . . YOU MAKE THE CALL

You are the Chief Accountant The transaction's effect will appear in the investing section of the cash flow statement in the amount of a positive $770 million.

You are the Securities Analyst Many companies, but not all, treat customers' notes receivable as an investing activity. In 2005, the SEC became concerned with this practice and issued letters to a number of companies objecting to this accounting classification. "Presenting cash receipts from receivables generated by the sale of inventory as investing activities in the company's consolidated statements of cash flows is not in accordance with GAAP," wrote the chief accountant for the SEC's division of corporation finance, in her letter to the companies ("Little Campus Lab Shakes Big Firms—Georgia Tech Crew's Report Spurs Change in Accounting for Operating Cash Flow," March 1, 2005, *The Wall Street Journal*). The SEC's position is that these notes receivable are an operating activity and analysts are certainly justified in treating them likewise. Concerning the sale of receivables, the transaction can be treated as a sale with a consequent reduction in receivables and a gain or loss on the sale recorded in the income statement. Many analysts treat this as a financing activity and argue that the cash inflow should not be regarded as an increase in operating cash flows. Bottom line: many argue that operating cash flows do not increase as a result of these two transactions and analysts should adjust the statement of cash flows to properly classify the financing of notes receivable as an operating activity and the sale of receivables as a financing activity.

KEY RATIOS

$$\text{Operating cash flow to current liabilities} = \frac{\text{Operating cash flow}}{\text{Average current liabilities}}$$

$$\text{Operating cash flow to capital expenditures} = \frac{\text{Operating cash flow}}{\text{Annual capital expenditures}}$$

$$\text{Free cash flow} = \text{Operating cash flow} - \text{Net capital expenditures}$$

KEY TERMS

Cash equivalents (p. 158)
Direct method (p. 172)
Financing activities (p. 160)
Indirect method (p. 172)
Investing activities (p. 160)
Liquidity (p. 158)
Noncash investing and financing activities (p. 179)
Operating activities (p. 160)
Solvency (p. 158)
Statement of cash flows (p. 158)
Treasury stock (p. 161)

Assignments with the logo in the margin are available in myBusinessCourse. See the Preface of the book for details.

MULTIPLE CHOICE

Multiple Choice Answers
1. a 2. c 3. d 4. c 5. c

1. Which of the following is not disclosed in a statement of cash flows?
a. A transfer of cash to a cash equivalent investment
b. The amount of cash at year-end
c. Cash outflows from investing activities during the period
d. Cash inflows from financing activities during the period

2. Which of the following events appears in the cash flows from investing activities section of the statement of cash flows?
a. Cash received from customers
b. Cash received from issuance of common stock
c. Cash purchase of equipment
d. Cash payment of dividends

3. Which of the following events appears in the cash flows from financing activities section of the statement of cash flows?
a. Cash purchase of equipment
b. Cash purchase of bonds issued by another company
c. Cash received as repayment for funds loaned
d. Cash purchase of treasury stock

4. Tyler Company has a net income of $49,000 and the following related items:

Depreciation expense	$ 5,000
Accounts receivable increase	2,000
Inventory decrease	10,000
Accounts payable decrease	4,000

Using the indirect method, what is Tyler's net cash flow from operations?
a. $42,000
b. $46,000
c. $58,000
d. $38,000

5. Refer to information in Mid-Chapter Review 2. Assume that notes payable are not due within the coming year and are classified as a noncurrent liability. The operating cash flow to current liabilities ratio for Mug Shots, Inc. in December is 
   a. 6.4%.
   b. 2.9%.
   c. 2.6%.
   d. impossible to determine from the data provided.

Superscript A denotes assignments based on Appendix 4A.

QUESTIONS

Q4-1. What is the definition of *cash equivalents*? Give three examples of cash equivalents.

Q4-2. Why are cash equivalents included with cash in a statement of cash flows?

Q4-3. What are the three major types of activities classified on a statement of cash flows? Give an example of a cash inflow and a cash outflow in each classification.

Q4-4. In which of the three activity categories of a statement of cash flows would each of the following items appear? Indicate for each item whether it represents a cash inflow or a cash outflow:
   a. Cash purchase of equipment.
   b. Cash collection on loans.
   c. Cash dividends paid.
   d. Cash dividends received.
   e. Cash proceeds from issuing stock.
   f. Cash receipts from customers.
   g. Cash interest paid.
   h. Cash interest received.

Q4-5. Traverse Company acquired a $3,000,000 building by issuing $3,000,000 worth of bonds payable. In terms of cash flow reporting, what type of transaction is this? What special disclosure requirements apply to a transaction of this type?

Q4-6. Why are noncash investing and financing transactions disclosed as supplemental information to a statement of cash flows?

Q4-7. Why is a statement of cash flows a useful financial statement?

Q4-8. What is the difference between the direct method and the indirect method of presenting net cash flow from operating activities?

Q4-9. In determining net cash flow from operating activities using the indirect method, why must we add depreciation back to net income? Give an example of another item that is added back to net income under the indirect method.

Q4-10. Vista Company sold for $98,000 cash land originally costing $70,000. The company recorded a gain on the sale of $28,000. How is this event reported in a statement of cash flows using the indirect method?

Q4-11. A firm uses the indirect method. Using the following information, what is its net cash flow from operating activities?

Net income	$88,000
Accounts receivable decrease	13,000
Inventory increase	9,000
Accounts payable decrease	3,500
Income tax payable increase	1,500
Depreciation expense	6,000

Q4-12. What separate disclosures are required for a company that reports a statement of cash flows using the indirect method?

Q4-13. If a business had a net loss for the year, under what circumstances would the statement of cash flows show a positive net cash flow from operating activities?

Q4-14. A firm is converting its accrual revenues to corresponding cash amounts using the direct method. Sales on the income statement are $925,000. Beginning and ending accounts receivable on the balance sheet are $58,000 and $44,000, respectively. What is the amount of cash received from customers?

Q4-15. A firm reports $86,000 wages expense in its income statement. If beginning and ending wages payable are $3,900 and $2,800, respectively, what is the amount of cash paid to employees?

Q4-16. A firm reports $43,000 advertising expense in its income statement. If beginning and ending prepaid advertising are $6,000 and $7,600, respectively, what is the amount of cash paid for advertising?

Q4-17. Rusk Company sold equipment for $5,100 cash that had cost $35,000 and had $29,000 of accumulated depreciation. How is this event reported in a statement of cash flows using the direct method?

Q4-18. What separate disclosures are required for a company that reports a statement of cash flows using the direct method?

Q4-19. How is the operating cash flow to current liabilities ratio calculated? Explain its use.

Q4-20. How is the operating cash flow to capital expenditures ratio calculated? Explain its use.

MINI EXERCISES

LO1, 3

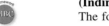

Target
NYSE :: TGT

M4-21. Identifying the Impact of Account Changes on Cash Flow from Operating Activities (Indirect Method)
The following account information was presented as adjustments to net income in a recent statement of cash flows for **Target Corporation**. Determine whether each item would be a positive adjustment or a negative adjustment to net income in determining cash from operations. ($ millions).

a. Operating activities increased accounts payable by $625.
b. Operating activities increased inventories by $885.
c. Operating activities decreased other noncurrent liabilities by $50.
d. Depreciation and amortization expense was $2,223.
e. Operating activities decreased other noncurrent assets by $19.

LO1

M4-22. Classifying Cash Flows
For each of the items below, indicate whether the cash flow relates to an operating activity, an investing activity, or a financing activity.

a. Cash receipts from customers for services rendered.
b. Sale of long-term investments for cash.
c. Acquisition of plant assets for cash.
d. Payment of income taxes.
e. Bonds payable issued for cash.
f. Payment of cash dividends declared in previous year.
g. Purchase of short-term investments (not cash equivalents) for cash.

LO1, 3

Dole Food Company, Inc.
NYSE :: DOLE

M4-23. Classifying Cash Flow Statement Components
The following table presents selected items from a recent cash flow statement of **Dole Food Company, Inc.** For each item, determine whether the amount would be disclosed in the cash flow statement under operating activities, investing activities, or financing activities. (Dole uses the indirect method of reporting cash flows from operating activities.)

DOLE FOOD COMPANY, INC. Selected Items from its Cash Flow Statement	
1	Long-term debt repayments
2	Change in receivables
3	Depreciation and amortization
4	Change in accrued liabilities
5	Dividends paid
6	Change in income taxes payable
7	Cash received from sales of assets and businesses
8	Net income
9	Change in accounts payable
10	Short-term debt borrowings
11	Capital expenditures

LO1, 4

M4-24. Classifying Cash Flows
For each of the items below, indicate whether it is (1) a cash flow from an operating activity, (2) a cash flow from an investing activity, (3) a cash flow from a financing activity, (4) a noncash investing and financing activity, or (5) none of the above.

a. Paid cash to retire bonds payable at a loss.
b. Received cash as settlement of a lawsuit.
c. Acquired a patent in exchange for common stock.
d. Received advance payments from customers on orders for custom-made goods.
e. Gave large cash contribution to local university.
f. Invested cash in 60-day commercial paper (a cash equivalent).

M4-25. Reconciling Net Income and Cash Flow from Operations Using FSET LO2, 3

For fiscal year 2015, Beyer GMBH had the following summary information available concerning its operating activities. The company had no investing or financing activities this year.

1.	Sales of merchandise to customers on credit	€507,400
2.	Sales of merchandise to customers for cash	91,500
3.	Cost of merchandise sold on credit	320,100
4.	Cost of merchandise sold for cash	63,400
5.	Purchases of merchandise from suppliers on credit	351,600
6.	Purchases of merchandise from suppliers for cash	47,700
7.	Collections from customers on accounts receivable	483,400
8.	Cash payments to suppliers on accounts payable	340,200
9.	Operating expenses (all paid in cash)	172,300

REQUIRED

a. Enter the items above into the Financial Statement Effects Template. Under noncash assets, use two separate columns for accounts receivable and inventories. Calculate the totals for each column.

b. What was the company's net income for the year? What was the cash flow from operating activities? (Use the direct method.)

c. Indicate the direction and amounts by which each of the following accounts changed during the year.

1. Accounts receivable
2. Merchandise inventory
3. Accounts payable

d. Using your results above, prepare the operating activities section of the statement of cash flows using the indirect format.

M4-26. Calculating Net Cash Flow from Operating Activities (Indirect Method) LO3

The following information was obtained from Galena Company's comparative balance sheets. Assume that Galena Company's 2016 income statement showed depreciation expense of $8,000, a gain on sale of investments of $9,000, and net income of $45,000. Calculate the net cash flow from operating activities using the indirect method.

	Dec. 31, 2016	Dec. 31, 2015
Cash	$ 19,000	$ 9,000
Accounts receivable	44,000	35,000
Inventory	55,000	49,000
Prepaid rent	6,000	8,000
Long-term investments	21,000	34,000
Plant assets	150,000	106,000
Accumulated depreciation	40,000	32,000
Accounts payable	24,000	20,000
Income tax payable	4,000	6,000
Common stock	121,000	92,000
Retained earnings	106,000	91,000

M4-27. Reconciling Net Income and Cash Flow from Operations Using FSET LO2, 3

For fiscal year 2016, Riffe Enterprises had the following summary information available concerning its operating activities. The company had no investing or financing activities this year.

1.	Sales of services to customers on credit	$769,200
2.	Sales of services to customers for cash	46,200
3.	Employee compensation earned	526,700
4.	Cash payment in advance to landlord for offices	149,100
5.	Cash paid to employees for compensation	521,600
6.	Rental expense for offices used over the year	117,900
7.	Collections from customers on accounts receivable	724,100
8.	Operating expenses (all paid in cash)	122,800
9.	Depreciation expense	23,000

REQUIRED

a. Enter the items above into the Financial Statement Effects Template. Under noncash assets, use three separate columns for accounts receivable and prepaid rent and the accumulated depreciation contra-asset. Calculate the totals for each column.

b. What was the company's net income for the year? What was the cash flow from operating activities? (Use the direct method.)

c. Indicate the direction and amounts by which each of the following accounts changed during the year.
1. Accounts receivable
2. Prepaid rent
3. Accumulated depreciation
4. Wages payable

d. Using your results above, prepare the operating activities section of the statement of cash flows using the indirect format.

LO3

M4-28. Calculating Net Cash Flow from Operating Activities (Indirect Method)

Weber Company had a $21,000 net loss from operations for 2016. Depreciation expense for 2016 was $8,600 and a 2016 cash dividend of $6,000 was declared and paid. Balances of the current asset and current liability accounts at the beginning and end of 2016 follow. Did Weber Company's 2016 operating activities provide or use cash? Use the indirect method to determine your answer.

	Ending	Beginning
Cash	$ 3,500	$ 7,000
Accounts receivable	16,000	25,000
Inventory	50,000	53,000
Prepaid expenses	6,000	9,000
Accounts payable	12,000	8,000
Accrued liabilities	5,000	7,600

LO1

Nordstrom, Inc.
NYSE :: JWN

M4-29. Classifying Cash Flow Statement Components and Determining Their Effects

The following table presents selected items from a recent cash flow statement of **Nordstrom, Inc.**

a. For each item, determine whether the amount would be disclosed in the cash flow statement under operating activities, investing activities, or financing activities. (Nordstrom uses the indirect method of reporting.)

b. For each item, determine whether it will appear as a positive or negative in determining the net increase in cash and cash equivalents.

NORDSTROM, INC. Consolidated Statement of Cash Flows—Selected Items	
1	Increase in accounts receivable
2	Capital expenditures
3	Proceeds from long-term borrowings
4	Increase in deferred income tax net liability
5	Principal payments on long-term borrowings
6	Increase in merchandise inventories
7	Decrease in prepaid expenses and other assets
8	Proceeds from issuances under stock compensation plans
9	Increase in accounts payable
10	Net earnings
11	Payments for repurchase of common stock
12	Increase in accrued salaries, wages and related benefits
13	Cash dividends paid
14	Depreciation and amortization expenses

M4-30. Calculating Operating Cash Flows (Direct Method)

LO2

Calculate the cash flow for each of the following cases.

a. Cash paid for rent:

Rent expense	$60,000
Prepaid rent, beginning year	10,000
Prepaid rent, end of year	8,000

b. Cash received as interest:

Interest income	$16,000
Interest receivable, beginning year	3,000
Interest receivable, end of year	3,700

c. Cash paid for merchandise purchased:

Cost of goods sold	$98,000
Inventory, beginning year	19,000
Inventory, end of year	22,000
Accounts payable, beginning year	11,000
Accounts payable, end of year	7,000

M4-31. Calculating Operating Cash Flows (Direct Method)

LO2

Chakravarthy Company's current year income statement reports the following:

Sales	$825,000
Cost of goods sold	550,000
Gross profit	$275,000

Chakravarthy's comparative balance sheets show the following (accounts payable relate to merchandise purchases):

	End of Year	Beginning of Year
Accounts receivable	$ 71,000	$60,000
Inventory	109,000	96,000
Accounts payable	31,000	37,000

Compute Chakravarthy's current-year cash received from customers and cash paid for merchandise purchased.

EXERCISES

LO5 **E4-32. Comparing Firms Using Ratio Analysis**

Consider the following 2013 data for several pharmaceutical firms ($ millions):

Merck & Co. NYSE :: MRK
Pfizer Inc. NYSE :: PFE
Abbott Laboratories NYSE :: ABT
Johnson & Johnson NYSE :: JNJ

	Average current liabilities	Cash from operations	Expenditures on PPE	Proceeds from the sale of PPE
Merck & Co., Inc.	$18,108	$11,654	$1,548	$ 0
Pfizer Inc.	26,276	17,765	1,206	0
Abbott Laboratories	11,394	3,324	1,145	0
Johnson & Johnson	24,969	17,414	3,595	458

a. Compute the operating cash flow to current liabilities (OCFCL) ratio for each firm.
b. Compute the free cash flow for each firm.
c. Comment on the results of your computations.

LO5 **E4-33. Comparing Firms Using Ratio Analysis**

Consider the following data for several firms from 2013 ($ millions):

Wal-Mart NYSE :: WMT
The Coca-Cola Company NYSE :: KO
Exxon Mobil Corp. NYSE :: XOM

	Average current liabilities	Cash from operations	Expenditures on PPE	Proceeds from the sale of PPE
Wal-Mart Stores, Inc.	$70,582	$23,257	$13,115	$ 727
The Coca-Cola Company	27,816	10,542	2,550	111
Exxon Mobil Corporation	67,932	44,914	33,669	2,707

a. Compute the operating cash flow to current liabilities (OCFCL) ratio for each firm.
b. Compute the free cash flow for each firm.
c. Comment on the results of your computations.

LO2 **E4-34. Preparing a Statement of Cash Flows (Direct Method)**

Use the following information about the 2016 cash flows of Mason Corporation to prepare a statement of cash flows under the direct method. Refer to **Exhibit 4.3** for the appropriate format.

Cash balance, end of 2016	$ 12,000
Cash paid to employees and suppliers	148,000
Cash received from sale of land	40,000
Cash paid to acquire treasury stock	10,000
Cash balance, beginning of 2016	16,000
Cash received as interest	6,000
Cash paid as income taxes	11,000
Cash paid to purchase equipment	89,000
Cash received from customers	194,000
Cash received from issuing bonds payable	30,000
Cash paid as dividends	16,000

LO3, 5 **E4-35. Calculating Net Cash Flow from Operating Activities (Indirect Method)**

Lincoln Company owns no plant assets and reported the following income statement for the current year:

Sales		$750,000
Cost of goods sold	$470,000	
Wages expense	110,000	
Rent expense	42,000	
Insurance expense	15,000	637,000
Net income		$113,000

Additional balance sheet information about the company follows:

	End of Year	Beginning of Year
Accounts receivable	$54,000	$49,000
Inventory	60,000	66,000
Prepaid insurance	8,000	7,000
Accounts payable	22,000	18,000
Wages payable	9,000	11,000

Use the information to

a. calculate the net cash flow from operating activities under the indirect method.

b. compute its operating cash flow to current liabilities (OCFCL) ratio. (Assume current liabilities consist of accounts payable and wages payable.)

E4-36. Accounting Sleuth: Reconstructing Entries LO4

Meubles Fischer SA had the following balances for its property, plant, and equipment accounts (in thousands of euros):

	September 30, 2015	September 30, 2016
Property, plant, and equipment at cost	€1,000	€1,200
Accumulated depreciation	(350)	(390)
Property, plant, and equipment, net	€ 650	€ 810

During fiscal year 2016, Meubles Fischer acquired €100 thousand in property by signing a mortgage, plus another €300 thousand in equipment for cash. The company also received €100 thousand in cash from the sale of used equipment, and its income statement reveals a €20 thousand gain from this transaction.

a. What was the original cost of the used equipment that Meubles Fischer SA sold during fiscal year 2016?

b. How much depreciation had been accumulated on the used equipment at the time it was sold?

c. How much depreciation expense did Meubles Fischer SA recognize in its fiscal year 2016 income statement?

E4-37. Accounting Sleuth: Reconstructing Entries LO4

Kasznik Ltd. had the following balances for its property, plant, and equipment accounts (in millions of pounds):

	December 31, 2015	December 31, 2016
Property, plant, and equipment at cost	£175	£183
Accumulated depreciation	(78)	(83)
Property, plant, and equipment, net	£ 97	£100

During 2016, Kasznik Ltd. paid £28 million in cash to acquire property and equipment, and this amount represents all the acquisitions of property, plant, and equipment for the period. The company's income statement reveals depreciation expense of £17 million and a £5 million loss from the disposal of used equipment.

a. What was the original cost of the used equipment that Kasznik Ltd. sold during 2016?

b. How much depreciation had been accumulated on the used equipment at the time it was sold?

c. How much cash did Kasznik Ltd. receive from its disposal of used equipment?

E4-38. Reconciling Changes in Balance Sheet Accounts LO2, 4

The following table presents selected items from the 2014 and 2013 balance sheets and 2014 income statement of **Walgreen Company**.

Walgreen Company
NYSE :: WAG

WALGREEN CO. AND SUBSIDIARIES ($ millions)				
Selected Balance Sheet Data			**Selected Income Statement Data**	
	2014	**2013**		**2014**
Inventories	$ 6,076	$ 6,852	Cost of merchandise sold	$54,823
Property and equipment, less accumulated depreciation	12,257	12,138	Depreciation expense	1,316
Trade accounts payable	4,315	4,635	Net earnings	2,031
Retained earnings	22,229	21,523		

a. Compute the cash paid for merchandise inventories in 2014. Assume that trade accounts payable is only for merchandise purchases.
b. Compute the net cost of property acquired in 2014.
c. Compute the cash dividends paid in 2014.

LO4 

E4-39. Analyzing Investing and Financing Cash Flows
During 2016, Paxon Corporation's long-term investments account (at cost) increased $15,000, which was the net result of purchasing stocks costing $80,000 and selling stocks costing $65,000 at a $6,000 loss. Also, its bonds payable account decreased $10,000, the net result of issuing $130,000 of bonds and retiring bonds with a book value of $140,000 at a $9,000 gain. What items and amounts appear in the (a) cash flows from investing activities and (b) cash flows from financing activities sections of its 2016 statement of cash flows?

LO4 

E4-40. Reconciling Changes in Balance Sheet Accounts
The following table presents selected items from the 2014 and 2013 balance sheets and 2014 income statement of **Golden Enterprises, Inc.**

Golden Enterprises, Inc.
NASDAQ :: GLDC

GOLDEN ENTERPRISES, INC.				
Selected Balance Sheet Data			**Selected Income Statement Data**	
	2014	**2013**		**2014**
Property and equipment, cost	$95,174,198	$93,022,443	Depreciation expense	$3,778,563
Accumulated depreciation	69,502,854	65,927,389	Gain on sale of property and equipment	22,693
Retained earnings	18,728,462	19,273,214	Net income	921,829

Golden Enterprises reported expenditures for property and equipment of $2,380,287 in 2014.
a. What was the original cost of the property and equipment that Golden Enterprises sold during 2014? What was the accumulated depreciation on that property and equipment at the time of sale?
b. Compute the cash proceeds from the sale of property and equipment in 2014.
c. Prepare the journal entry to describe the sale of property and equipment.
d. Determine the cash dividends paid in 2014.

LO2 

E4-41. Calculating Operating Cash Flows (Direct Method)
Calculate the cash flow for each of the following cases.
a. Cash paid for advertising:

Advertising expense	$62,000
Prepaid advertising, beginning of year	11,000
Prepaid advertising, end of year	15,000

b. Cash paid for income taxes:

Income tax expense	$29,000
Income tax payable, beginning of year	7,100
Income tax payable, end of year	4,900

c. Cash paid for merchandise purchased:

Cost of goods sold	$180,000
Inventory, beginning of year	30,000
Inventory, end of year	25,000
Accounts payable, beginning of year	10,000
Accounts payable, end of year	12,000

E4-42. Preparing a Statement of Cash Flows (Indirect Method) LO3, 4

The following financial statements were issued by Hoskins Corporation for the fiscal year ended December 31, 2016. All amounts are in millions of U.S. dollars.

Balance Sheets	December 31, 2015		December 31, 2016	
Assets				
Cash		$ 300		$ 550
Accounts receivable		600		1,500
Inventory		400		500
Prepaid expenses		400		150
Current assets		1,700		2,700
Property, plant, and equipment at cost	6,200		6,100	
Less accumulated depreciation	(2,100)		(1,750)	
Property, plant, and equipment, net		4,100		4,350
Total assets		$5,800		$7,050
Liabilities and Shareholders' Equity				
Accounts payable		$ 400		$ 800
Income tax payable		200		100
Short-term debt		1,200		2,700
Current liabilities		1,800		3,600
Long-term debt		1,000		0
Total liabilities		2,800		3,600
Contributed capital		800		800
Retained earnings		2,200		2,650
Total shareholders' equity		3,000		3,450
Total liabilities and shareholders' equity		$5,800		$7,050

Income Statement	Fiscal year 2016
Sales revenues	$6,500
Cost of goods sold	3,400
Gross profit	3,100
Selling, general and administrative expenses	1,450
Depreciation expense	350
Operating income	1,300
Interest expense	350
Income before income tax expense	950
Income tax expense	250
Net income	$ 700

Additional information:

1. During fiscal year 2016, Hoskins Corporation acquired new equipment for $1,200 in cash. In addition, the company disposed of used equipment that had original cost of $1,300 and accumulated depreciation of $700, receiving $600 in cash from the buyer.
2. During fiscal year 2016, Hoskins Corporation arranged short-term bank financing and borrowed $1,500, using a portion of the cash to repay all of its outstanding long-term debt.

3. During fiscal year 2016, Hoskins Corporation engaged in no transactions involving its common stock, though it did declare and pay in cash a common stock dividend of $250.

REQUIRED

Prepare a statement of cash flows (all three sections) for Hoskins Corporation's fiscal year 2016, using the indirect method for the cash from operations section.

LO2, 5 **E4-43. Analyzing Operating Cash Flows (Direct Method)**

Refer to the information in Exercise 4-35. Calculate the net cash flow from operating activities using the direct method. Show a related cash flow for each revenue and expense. Also, compute its operating cash flow to current liabilities (OCFCL) ratio. (Assume current liabilities consist of accounts payable and wages payable.)

LO2, 3 **E4-44. Interpreting Cash Flow from Operating Activities**

Carter Company's income statement and cash flow from operating activities (indirect method) are provided as follows ($ thousands):

Income statement	
Revenue	$400
Cost of goods sold	215
Gross profit	185
Operating expenses	110
Operating income	75
Interest expense	25
Income before taxes	50
Income tax expense	15
Net income	$ 35

Cash flow from operating activities	
Net income	$35
Plus depreciation expense	70
Operating asset adjustments	
Less increase in accounts receivable	(25)
Less increase in inventories	(50)
Less increase in prepaid rent	(5)
Plus increase in accounts payable	65
Plus increase in income tax payable	5
Cash flow from operating activities	$95

a. For each of the four statements below, determine whether the statement is true or false.

b. If the statement is false, provide the (underlined) dollar amount that would make it true.

1. Carter collected <u>$375</u> from customers in the current period.
2. Carter paid <u>$0</u> interest in the current period.
3. Carter paid <u>$20</u> in income taxes in the current period.
4. If Carter increased the depreciation expense by $50, it would increase its cash from operations by <u>$50</u>.

PROBLEMS

LO3 **P4-45. Reconciling and Computing Operating Cash Flows from Net Income**

Petroni Company reports the following selected results for its calendar year 2016.

Net income	$135,000
Depreciation expense	25,000
Gain on sale of assets	5,000
Accounts receivable increase	10,000
Accounts payable increase	6,000
Prepaid expenses decrease	3,000
Wages payable decrease	4,000

REQUIRED

Prepare the operating section only of Petroni Company's statement of cash flows for 2016 under the indirect method of reporting.

P4-46. Preparing a Statement of Cash Flows (Indirect Method) LO3, 4

Wolff Company's income statement and comparative balance sheets follow.

WOLFF COMPANY Income Statement For Year Ended December 31, 2016		
Sales		$635,000
Cost of goods sold	$430,000	
Wages expense	86,000	
Insurance expense	8,000	
Depreciation expense	17,000	
Interest expense	9,000	
Income tax expense	29,000	579,000
Net income		$ 56,000

WOLFF COMPANY Balance Sheets	Dec. 31, 2016	Dec. 31, 2015
Assets		
Cash	$ 11,000	$ 5,000
Accounts receivable	41,000	32,000
Inventory	90,000	60,000
Prepaid insurance	5,000	7,000
Plant assets	250,000	195,000
Accumulated depreciation	(68,000)	(51,000)
Total assets	$329,000	$248,000
Liabilities and Stockholders' Equity		
Accounts payable	$ 7,000	$ 10,000
Wages payable	9,000	6,000
Income tax payable	7,000	8,000
Bonds payable	130,000	75,000
Common stock	90,000	90,000
Retained earnings	86,000	59,000
Total liabilities and equity	$329,000	$248,000

Cash dividends of $29,000 were declared and paid during 2016. Also in 2016, plant assets were purchased for cash, and bonds payable were issued for cash. Bond interest is paid semiannually on June 30 and December 31. Accounts payable relate to merchandise purchases.

REQUIRED

a. Compute the change in cash that occurred during 2016.

b. Prepare a 2016 statement of cash flows using the indirect method.

c. Compute and interpret Wolff's
   (1) operating cash flow to current liabilities ratio, and
   (2) operating cash flow to capital expenditures ratio.

P4-47. Computing Cash Flow from Operating Activities (Direct Method) LO2

Refer to the income statement and comparative balance sheets for Wolff Company presented in P4-46.

REQUIRED

a. Compute Wolff Company's cash flow from operating activities using the direct method. Use the format illustrated in **Exhibit 4.5** in the chapter.

b. What can we learn from the direct method that may not be readily apparent when reviewing a cash flow statement prepared using the indirect method?

LO3, 4 **P4-48. Preparing a Statement of Cash Flows (Indirect Method)**
Arctic Company's income statement and comparative balance sheets follow.

ARCTIC COMPANY
Income Statement
For Year Ended December 31, 2016

Sales		$728,000
Cost of goods sold	$534,000	
Wages expense	190,000	
Advertising expense	31,000	
Depreciation expense	22,000	
Interest expense	18,000	
Gain on sale of land	(25,000)	770,000
Net loss		$ (42,000)

ARCTIC COMPANY
Balance Sheets

	Dec. 31, 2016	Dec. 31, 2015
Assets		
Cash	$ 49,000	$ 28,000
Accounts receivable	42,000	50,000
Inventory	107,000	113,000
Prepaid advertising	10,000	13,000
Plant assets	360,000	222,000
Accumulated depreciation	(78,000)	(56,000)
Total assets	$490,000	$370,000
Liabilities and Stockholders' Equity		
Accounts payable	$ 17,000	$ 31,000
Interest payable	6,000	—
Bonds payable	200,000	—
Common stock	245,000	245,000
Retained earnings	52,000	94,000
Treasury stock	(30,000)	—
Total liabilities and equity	$490,000	$370,000

During 2016, Arctic sold land for $70,000 cash that had originally cost $45,000. Arctic also purchased equipment for cash, acquired treasury stock for cash, and issued bonds payable for cash in 2016. Accounts payable relate to merchandise purchases.

REQUIRED

a. Compute the change in cash that occurred during 2016.

b. Prepare a 2016 statement of cash flows using the indirect method.

c. Compute and interpret Arctic's
(1) operating cash flow to current liabilities ratio, and
(2) operating cash flow to capital expenditures ratio.

LO2 **P4-49. Computing Cash Flow from Operating Activities (Direct Method)**
Refer to the income statement and comparative balance sheets for Arctic Company presented in P4-48.

REQUIRED

a. Compute Arctic Company's cash flow from operating activities using the direct method. Use the format illustrated in **Exhibit 4.5** in the chapter.

b. What can we learn from the direct method that may not be readily apparent when reviewing a cash flow statement prepared using the indirect method?

P4-50. Preparing a Statement of Cash Flows (Indirect Method) **LO3, 4, 5**

Dair Company's income statement and comparative balance sheets follow.

DAIR COMPANY
Income Statement
For Year Ended December 31, 2016

Sales		$700,000
Cost of goods sold	$440,000	
Wages and other operating expenses	95,000	
Depreciation expense	22,000	
Amortization expense	7,000	
Interest expense	10,000	
Income tax expense	36,000	
Loss on bond retirement	5,000	615,000
Net income		$ 85,000

DAIR COMPANY
Balance Sheets

	Dec. 31, 2016	Dec. 31, 2015
Assets		
Cash	$ 27,000	$ 18,000
Accounts receivable	53,000	48,000
Inventory	103,000	109,000
Prepaid expenses	12,000	10,000
Plant assets	360,000	336,000
Accumulated depreciation	(87,000)	(84,000)
Intangible assets	43,000	50,000
Total assets	$511,000	$487,000
Liabilities and Shareholders' Equity		
Accounts payable	$ 32,000	$ 26,000
Interest payable	4,000	7,000
Income tax payable	6,000	8,000
Bonds payable	60,000	120,000
Common stock	252,000	228,000
Retained earnings	157,000	98,000
Total liabilities and equity	$511,000	$487,000

During 2016, the company sold for $17,000 cash old equipment that had cost $36,000 and had $19,000 accumulated depreciation. Also in 2016, new equipment worth $60,000 was acquired in exchange for $60,000 of bonds payable, and bonds payable of $120,000 were retired for cash at a loss. A $26,000 cash dividend was declared and paid in 2016. Any stock issuances were for cash.

REQUIRED

a. Compute the change in cash that occurred in 2016.

b. Prepare a 2016 statement of cash flows using the indirect method.

c. Prepare separate schedules showing
(1) cash paid for interest and for income taxes and
(2) noncash investing and financing transactions.

d. Compute its
(1) operating cash flow to current liabilities ratio,
(2) operating cash flow to capital expenditures ratio, and
(3) free cash flow.

LO2, 3, 4 **P4-51. Interpreting the Statement of Cash Flows**

CVS Health Corp.
NYSE :: CVS

Following is the statement of cash flows of **CVS Health Corp.**

CVS HEALTH CORP. **Consolidated Statement of Cash Flows** **Year Ended December 31, 2013 ($ millions)**	
Cash flows from operating activities:	
Cash receipts from customers	$114,993
Cash paid for inventory and prescriptions dispensed by retail network pharmacies	(91,178)
Cash paid to other suppliers and employees	(14,295)
Interest received	8
Interest paid	(534)
Income taxes paid	(3,211)
Net cash provided by operating activities	5,783
Cash flows from investing activities:	
Purchases of property and equipment	(1,984)
Proceeds from sale-leaseback transactions	600
Proceeds from sale of property and equipment and other assets	54
Acquisitions (net of cash acquired) and other investments	(415)
Purchase of available-for-sale investments	(226)
Maturity of available-for-sale investments	136
Net cash used in investing activities	(1,835)
Cash flows from financing activities:	
Increase (decrease) in short-term debt	(690)
Proceeds from issuance of long-term debt	3,964
Dividends paid	(1,097)
Proceeds from exercise of stock options	500
Excess tax benefits from stock-based compensation	62
Repurchase of common stock	(3,976)
Net cash used in financing activities	(1,237)
Effect of exchange rate changes on cash and cash equivalents	3
Net increase (decrease) in cash and cash equivalents	2,714
Cash and cash equivalents at the beginning of the year	1,375
Cash and cash equivalents at the end of the year	$ 4,089
Reconciliation of net income to net cash provided by operating activities:	
Net income	$ 4,592
Adjustments to reconcile net income to net cash provided by operating activities:	
Depreciation and amortization	1,870
Stock-based compensation	141
Deferred income taxes and other noncash items	(86)
Change in operating assets and liabilities, net of effects from acquisitions:	
Accounts receivable, net	(2,210)
Inventories	12
Other current assets	105
Other assets	(135)
Accounts payable and claims and discounts payable	1,024
Accrued expenses	471
Other long-term liabilities	(1)
Net cash provided by operating activities	$ 5,783

REQUIRED

a. Does CVS use the direct method or the indirect method to present its statement of cash flows? Explain.

b. Based on the information presented in its statement of cash flows, what amount of revenues should CVS report in its income statement?

c. CVS reported retained earnings of $24,998 million at the end of 2012. What amount of retained earnings did the company report in its 2013 balance sheet?

d. Why is "stock-based compensation" listed under "adjustments to reconcile net income to net cash provided by operating activities"?

e. Why does CVS list the "effect of exchange rate changes on cash and cash equivalents" in its statement of cash flows? What does this amount represent?

f. Using three bullet points, explain what CVS did with the $5.8 billion in cash that was provided by operating activities in 2013.

P4-52. Preparing a Statement of Cash Flows (Indirect Method) LO3, 4, 5

Rainbow Company's income statement and comparative balance sheets follow.

RAINBOW COMPANY
Income Statement
For Year Ended December 31, 2016

Sales		$750,000
Dividend income		15,000
Total revenue		765,000
Cost of goods sold	$440,000	
Wages and other operating expenses	130,000	
Depreciation expense	39,000	
Patent amortization expense	7,000	
Interest expense	13,000	
Income tax expense	44,000	
Loss on sale of equipment	5,000	
Gain on sale of investments	(3,000)	675,000
Net income		$ 90,000

RAINBOW COMPANY
Balance Sheets

	Dec. 31, 2016	Dec. 31, 2015
Assets		
Cash and cash equivalents	$ 19,000	$ 25,000
Accounts receivable	40,000	30,000
Inventory	103,000	77,000
Prepaid expenses	10,000	6,000
Long-term investments	—	57,000
Land	190,000	100,000
Buildings	445,000	350,000
Accumulated depreciation—buildings	(91,000)	(75,000)
Equipment	179,000	225,000
Accumulated depreciation—equipment	(42,000)	(46,000)
Patents	50,000	32,000
Total assets	$903,000	$781,000
Liabilities and Stockholders' Equity		
Accounts payable	$ 20,000	$ 16,000
Interest payable	6,000	5,000
Income tax payable	8,000	10,000
Bonds payable	155,000	125,000
Preferred stock ($100 par value)	100,000	75,000
Common stock ($5 par value)	379,000	364,000
Paid-in capital in excess of par value—common	133,000	124,000
Retained earnings	102,000	62,000
Total liabilities and equity	$903,000	$781,000

During 2016, the following transactions and events occurred:

1. Sold long-term investments costing $57,000 for $60,000 cash.
2. Purchased land for cash.
3. Capitalized an expenditure made to improve the building.

4. Sold equipment for $14,000 cash that originally cost $46,000 and had $27,000 accumulated depreciation.
5. Issued bonds payable at face value for cash.
6. Acquired a patent with a fair value of $25,000 by issuing 250 shares of preferred stock at par value.
7. Declared and paid a $50,000 cash dividend.
8. Issued 3,000 shares of common stock for cash at $8 per share.
9. Recorded depreciation of $16,000 on buildings and $23,000 on equipment.

REQUIRED

a. Compute the change in cash and cash equivalents that occurred during 2016.
b. Prepare a 2016 statement of cash flows using the indirect method.
c. Prepare separate schedules showing (1) cash paid for interest and for income taxes and (2) noncash investing and financing transactions.
d. Compute its (1) operating cash flow to current liabilities ratio, (2) operating cash flow to capital expenditures ratio, and (3) free cash flow.

LO2, 3, 4 Homework MBC

P4-53. Preparing a Statement of Cash Flows (Direct Method)
Refer to the data for Rainbow Company in Problem 4-52.

REQUIRED

a. Compute the change in cash that occurred in 2016.
b. Prepare a 2016 statement of cash flows using the direct method. Use one cash outflow for "cash paid for wages and other operating expenses." Accounts payable relate to inventory purchases only.
c. Prepare separate schedules showing (1) a reconciliation of net income to net cash flow from operating activities and (2) noncash investing and financing transactions.

LO3, 4
Apple Inc.
NASDAQ :: AAPL

P4-54. Interpreting Cash Flow Information
The 2014 cash flow statement for **Apple Inc.** is presented below (all $ amounts in millions):

APPLE INC.
Consolidated Statement of Cash Flows
Year Ended September 27, 2014

Cash and cash equivalents, beginning of the year	$ 14,259
Operating activities	
Net income	39,510
Adjustments to reconcile net income to cash generated by operating activities:	
Depreciation, and amortization	7,946
Share-based compensation expense	2,863
Deferred income tax expense	2,347
Changes in operating assets and liabilities:	
Accounts receivable, net	(4,232)
Inventories	(76)
Vendor non-trade receivables	(2,220)
Other current and non-current assets	167
Accounts payable	5,938
Deferred revenue	1,460
Other current and non-current liabilities	6,010
Cash generated by operating activities	59,713
Investing activities	
Purchases of marketable securities	(217,128)
Proceeds from maturities of marketable securities	18,810
Proceeds from sales of marketable securities	189,301
Payments made in connection with business acquisitions, net of cash acquired	(3,765)
Payments for acquisition of property, plant and equipment	(9,571)
Payments made for acquisitions of intangible assets	(242)
Other	16
Cash used in investing activities	(22,579)

continued

Financing activities	
Proceeds from issuance of common stock	730
Excess tax benefits from equity awards	739
Taxes paid related to net share settlement of equity awards	(1,158)
Dividends and dividend equivalents paid	(11,126)
Repurchase of common stock	(45,000)
Proceeds from issuance of long-term debt, net	11,960
Proceeds from issuance of commercial paper, net	6,306
Cash used in financing activities	(37,549)
Increase (decrease) in cash and cash equivalents	(415)
Cash and cash equivalents, end of the year	$13,844
Supplemental cash flow disclosure:	
Cash paid for income taxes, net	$10,026
Cash paid for interest	$ 339

REQUIRED

a. Did Apple's accounts receivable go up or down in 2014? Explain. Apple reported net sales of $182,795 million in its fiscal 2014 income statement. What amount of cash did Apple collect from customers during the year? (Ignore the Vendor non-trade receivables account, which relates to Apple's suppliers.)

b. Apple's cost of goods sold was $112,258 million in 2014. Assuming that accounts payable applies only to the purchase of inventory, what amount did Apple pay to purchase inventory in 2014?

c. At September 27, 2014, Apple reported a balance of $20.6 billion in property, plant, and equipment, net of accumulated depreciation, and its footnotes revealed that depreciation expense for fiscal 2014 was $6.9 billion. What was the balance in property, plant, and equipment, net of accumulated depreciation at the end of fiscal 2013?

d. Apple lists stock based compensation as a positive amount—$2,863 million—under cash flow from operating activities. Why is this amount listed here? Explain how this amount increases cash flow from operating activities.

P4-55.[A] Preparing the Statement of Cash Flows Using a Spreadsheet

LO5, 6

Golden Enterprises, Inc.
NASDAQ :: GLDC

The table below provides the balance sheets for **Golden Enterprises, Inc.** for the fiscal years ended May 30, 2014 and May 31, 2013.

	Year Ended	
Consolidated Balance Sheets	**May 30, 2014**	**May 31, 2013**
Assets		
Cash and cash equivalents	$ 1,160,630	$ 757,111
Receivables, net	11,341,024	10,459,706
Inventories	5,659,639	4,955,813
Prepaid expenses	1,277,861	1,554,737
Deferred income taxes	559,672	596,267
Total current assets	19,998,826	18,323,634
Property, plant and equipment at cost	95,174,198	93,022,443
Accumulated depreciation	(69,502,854)	(65,927,389)
Property, plant and equipment, net	25,671,344	27,095,054
Cash surrender of life insurance	602,353	695,761
Other	1,207,743	1,642,030
Total assets	$47,480,266	$47,756,479

continued

continued from previous page

	May 30, 2014	May 31, 2013
Liabilities & stockholders' equity		
Checks outstanding in excess of bank balances	$ 1,971,076	$ 1,442,915
Accounts payable	3,719,102	4,809,066
Accrued income taxes	378,659	53,475
Current portion of long-term debt	369,979	392,850
Line of credit outstanding	2,528,511	1,725,289
Other accrued expenses	5,953,171	5,427,017
Salary continuation plan	212,970	196,649
Total current liabilities	15,133,468	14,047,261
Note payable to bank, non-current	4,944,233	5,314,213
Salary continuation plan	920,184	1,032,810
Deferred income taxes	2,969,389	3,304,451
Total liabilities	23,967,274	23,698,735
Common stock at par	9,219,195	9,219,195
Additional paid-in capital	6,497,954	6,497,954
Retained earnings	18,728,462	19,273,214
Treasury shares, at cost	(10,932,619)	(10,932,619)
Total stockholders' equity	23,512,992	24,057,744
Total liabilities and stockholders' equity	$47,480,266	$47,756,479

Additional information:

1. Net income for the year ended May 30, 2014 was $921,829.
2. Depreciation expense for the year ended May 30, 2014 was $3,778,563.
3. Accounts for the life insurance asset and salary continuation liabilities are operating.
4. Checks outstanding in excess of bank balances should be treated as a financing liability.
5. During the year ended May 30, 2014, Golden Enterprises sold used property, plant, and equipment, receiving $48,125 in cash and recognizing a gain of $22,693.
6. For the year ended May 30, 2014, debt proceeds (encompassing the liabilities for current portion of long-term debt, line of credit outstanding and note payable to bank, non-current) were $35,726,909 and debt repayments were $35,316,538.

REQUIRED

a. Set up a spreadsheet to analyze the changes in Golden Enterprises' comparative balance sheets. Use the format illustrated in **Exhibit 4A.1**.

b. Prepare a statement of cash flows (including operations, investing and financing) for Golden Enterprises for the year ended May 30, 2014 using the indirect method for the operating section.

c. Using information in the statement of cash flows prepared in part *b*, compute (1) the operating cash flow to current liabilities ratio and (2) the operating cash flow to capital expenditures ratio.

LO3, 4, 5 **P4-56. Interpreting the Statement of Cash Flows**

Groupon, Inc.
NASDAQ :: GRPN

Groupon, Inc. provides an electronic marketplace to connect local merchants to consumers. Merchants offer discounts which customers purchase through Groupon, and Groupon makes payments (keeping approximately 40%) to the merchants over the next few weeks. Its growth prior to the company's initial public offering in November 2011 can only be described as meteoric. The company's revenues grew from $5 thousand in 2008 to $312,941 thousand in 2010 to $1,118,266 thousand in the first nine months of 2011. The sales growth did not translate into profitability, and Groupon reported net losses of $1,542 thousand in 2008, $413,386 thousand in 2010 and $238,083 thousand in the first nine months of 2011. However, the company generated positive cash flow from operating activity as can be seen in the accompanying nine-month statement of cash flows issued just prior to its initial public offering (Page F-52 of Form S-1/A filed with the Securities and Exchange Commission on November 1, 2011). While Groupon's net loss was $238,083 thousand for the period, its cash from operating activities was $129,511.

REQUIRED

a. Groupon uses the indirect method to present its cash from operating activities. The largest single positive adjustment is $314,872 for Accrued Merchant Payable. Explain the causes of this adjustment and its magnitude. Is this adjustment likely to recur in future periods? Explain.

b. How much of Groupon's investing cash flows are being spent on property and equipment? Calculate the company's operating cash flow to capital expenditures ratio.

c. What are the significant items in the financing cash flows section? Groupon raised $509,692 thousand through the issuing of shares. What did the company do with most of those funds?

GROUPON, INC.
CONDENSED CONSOLIDATED STATEMENTS OF CASH FLOWS (UNAUDITED)

	Nine Months Ended September 30,	
(in thousands)	**2010**	**2011**
Operating activities		
Net loss	$(77,783)	$(238,083)
Adjustments to reconcile net loss to net cash provided by operating activities:		
Depreciation and amortization	6,908	22,754
Stock-based compensation	8,739	60,922
Deferred income taxes	(4,615)	602
Excess tax benefit on stock-based compensation	—	(11,323)
Losses in equity interests	—	19,974
Non cash interest expense	106	—
Acquisition-related	37,844	(4,793)
Gain on return of common stock	—	(4,916)
Change in assets and liabilities, net of acquisitions:		
Accounts receivable	(16,071)	(69,690)
Prepaid expenses and other current assets	1,916	(41,023)
Accounts payable	12,178	(21,924)
Accrued merchant payable	47,518	314,872
Accrued expenses and other current liabilities	23,690	108,963
Due to related parties	682	361
Other	(6,146)	(7,185)
Net cash provided by operating activities	34,966	129,511
Investing activities		
Purchases of property and equipment	(6,092)	(29,825)
Acquisitions of businesses, net of acquired cash	6,495	(12,553)
Purchases of intangible assets	(707)	(15,072)
Changes in restricted cash	200	(8,141)
Purchases of investments in subsidiaries	—	(34,887)
Purchases of equity investments	—	(20,189)
Net cash used in investing activities	(104)	(120,667)
Financing activities		
Issuance of shares, net of issuance costs	134,932	509,692
Excess tax benefit on stock-based compensation	—	11,323
Loans from related parties	5,035	—
Repayments of loans to related parties	—	(14,358)
Repurchase of common stock	(119,891)	(353,550)
Proceeds from exercise of stock options	68	2,269
Proceeds from sale of common stock	—	137
Redemption of preferred stock	—	(35,221)
Net cash provided by financing activities	20,144	120,292
Effect of exchange rate changes on cash and cash equivalents	1,316	(4,034)
Net increase in cash and cash equivalents	56,322	125,102
Cash and cash equivalents, beginning of period	12,313	118,833
Cash and cash equivalents, end of period	$ 68,635	$ 243,935

CASES AND PROJECTS

LO3, 4 **C4-57. Analyzing a Projected Statement of Cash Flows and Loan Covenants**
The President and CFO of Lambert Co. will be meeting with their bankers next week to discuss the short-term financing needs of the company for the next six months. Lambert's controller has provided a projected income statement for the next six-month period, and a current balance sheet along with a projected balance sheet for the end of that six-month period. These statements are presented below ($ millions).

LAMBERT CO. Projected Six-Month Income Statement	
Revenues	$400
Cost of goods sold	200
Gross profit	200
Selling and administrative expense	50
Depreciation expense	120
Income before income taxes	30
Income taxes	12
Net income	$ 18

LAMBERT CO. Current and Projected Six-Month Balance Sheets	Current	6-month projected
Cash	$ 50	$???
Accounts receivable	180	220
Inventory	200	180
Total current assets	430	???
Property, plant & equipment, cost	400	500
Less accumulated depreciation	(150)	(220)
Property, plant & equipment, net	250	280
Total assets	$680	???
Accounts payable	$150	$180
Income taxes payable	20	10
Short-term borrowing	50	???
Long-term debt	200	180
Total liabilities	420	???
Common stock at par	100	125
Retained earnings	160	148
Total liabilities and shareholders' equity	$680	???

Additional Information (already reflected in the projected income statement and balance sheet):

- Lambert's current long-term debt includes $100 that is due within the next six months. During the next six months, the company plans to take advantage of lower interest rates by issuing new long-term debt that will provide $80 in cash proceeds.
- During the next six months, the company plans to dispose of equipment with an original cost of $125 and accumulated depreciation of $50. An appraisal by an equipment broker indicates that Lambert should be able to get $75 in cash for the equipment. In addition, Lambert plans to acquire new equipment at a cost of $225.
- A small issue of common stock for cash ($25) and a cash dividend to shareholders ($30) are planned in the next six months.
- Lambert's outstanding long-term debt imposes a restrictive loan covenant on the company that requires Lambert to maintain a debt-to-equity ratio below 1.75.

REQUIRED

The CFO says, "I would like a clear estimate of the amount of short-term borrowing that we will need six months from now. I want you to prepare a forecasted statement of cash flows that we can take to the meeting next week."

Prepare the required statement of cash flows, using the indirect method to compute cash flow from operating activities. The forecasted statement should include the needed amount of short-term borrowing and should be consistent with the projected balance sheet and income statement, as well as the loan covenant restriction.

C4-58. Reconstructing Journal Entries and T-Accounts from Completed Financial Statements LO1, 3, 4

Lundholm Company's comparative balance sheets, income statement, and statement of cash flows for July are presented below:

LUNDHOLM COMPANY Comparative Balance Sheets	July 1	July 31
Cash	$ 600	$ 1,184
Accounts receivable	6,500	6,800
Inventory	2,400	1,800
Prepaid rent	—	400
Current assets	9,500	10,184
Fixtures and equipment at cost	1,900	2,620
Accumulated depreciation	(800)	(880)
Plant and equipment, net	1,100	1,740
Total assets	$10,600	$11,924
Accounts payable	$ 3,000	$ 3,100
Salaries and wages payable	100	70
Taxes payable	—	374
Bank loan payable	1,600	—
Current liabilities	4,700	3,544
Long-term loan	—	2,000
Common stock	4,600	4,600
Retained earnings	1,300	1,780
Total liabilities and shareholders' equity	$10,600	$11,924

LUNDHOLM COMPANY Income Statement Month Ended July 31		
Revenue		$3,800
Operating expenses:		
Cost of goods sold	$1,800	
Salaries and wages	700	
Rent	200	
Depreciation	150	
Total operating expenses		2,850
Operating income		950
Interest expense		16
Income before taxes		934
Income taxes		374
Net income		$ 560

LUNDHOLM COMPANY Statement of Cash Flows Month Ended July 31	
Operating activities:	
Net income	$ 560
Adjustments:	
Depreciation	150
Increase in accounts receivable	(300)
Decrease in inventory	600
Increase in prepaid rent	(400)
Increase in accounts payable	100
Decrease in salaries and wages payable	(30)
Increase in taxes payable	374
Total adjustments	494
Cash flow from operating activities	1,054
Investing activities:	
Proceeds from disposal of fixtures and equipment	10
Purchases of fixtures and equipment	(800)
Cash flow used for investing activities	(790)
Financing activities:	
Loan repayment	(1,600)
Proceeds from new loan	2,000
Dividends paid to shareholders	(80)
Cash flow from financing activities	320
Net increase in cash	584
Cash balance, July 1	600
Cash balance, July 31	$1,184

REQUIRED

a. Set up T-accounts and enter beginning and ending balances for each account in Lundholm Company's balance sheet.

b. Provide a set of *summary journal entries* for July that would produce the financial statements presented above. For simplicity, you may assume that all of Lundholm Company's sales are made on account and that all of its purchases are made on account. One such entry is provided as an example.

		Debit	Credit
(1)	Accounts receivable (+A)	3,800	
	Sales revenue (+R, +SE)		3,800

c. Post the journal entries from part *b* to T-accounts and verify ending balances.

C4-59. Interpreting the Statement of Cash Flows

LO1, 2, 3, 4, 5
Daimler AG
ETR :: DAI

The statement of cash flows for **Daimler AG** follows:

DAIMLER AG Consolidated Statement of Cash Flows Year Ended December 31, 2013 (€ millions)	
Profit before income taxes	€10,139
Depreciation and amortization	4,368
Other non-cash expense and income	(3,345)
(Gains)/losses on disposals of assets	193
Change in operating assets and liabilities	
Inventories	(592)
Trade receivables	(695)
Trade payables	610
Receivables from financial services	(5,334)
Vehicles on operating leases	(2,990)
Other operating assets and liabilities	2,240
Income taxes paid	(1,309)
Cash provided by/used for operating activities	3,285
Additions to property, plant and equipment	(4,975)
Additions to intangible assets	(1,932)
Proceeds from disposals of property, plant and equipment and intangible assets	180
Investments in share property	(969)
Proceeds from disposals of share property	2,414
Acquisition of marketable debt securities	(6,566)
Proceeds from sales of marketable debt securities	4,991
Other	28
Cash used for investing activities	(6,829)
Change in short-term financing liabilities	845
Additions to long-term financing liabilities	37,602
Repayment of long-term financing liabilities	(31,987)
Dividend paid to shareholders of Daimler AG	(2,349)
Dividends paid to non-controlling interests	(269)
Proceeds from issuance of share capital	101
Acquisition of treasury shares	(24)
Acquisition of non-controlling interests in subsidiaries	(73)
Proceeds from disposals of interests in subsidiaries without loss of control	9
Cash provided by/used for financing activities	3,855
Effect of foreign exchange rate changes on cash and cash equivalents	(254)
Net increase/decrease in cash and cash equivalents	57
Cash and cash equivalents at the beginning of the period	10,996
Cash and cash equivalents at the end of the period	€11,053

REQUIRED

a. Daimler begins its cash flow statement with net income of €10,139 million, then adds €4,368 million for depreciation and amortization. Why is Daimler adding depreciation and amortization to net income in this computation?

b. Why does Daimler add €193 million of losses on disposals of assets in its indirect method cash flows from operating activities? If these losses are all created by disposals of property, plant, and equipment and intangible assets, what was the book value of the assets Daimler disposed of during fiscal year 2013?

c. Daimler shows a negative €592 million for inventories in the statement of cash flows. Does this mean that Daimler paid €592 million for inventories in 2013? Explain.

d. Compute Daimler's free cash flow for 2013. How did the company finance its investing activities?

e. Daimler reports a cash flow from operating activities of only €3,285 million, despite reporting net income of €10,139 million. What principal activities account for this difference? Does this raise concerns about the health of Daimler AG?

f. Why does Daimler list the "effect of foreign exchange rate changes on cash and cash equivalents" in its statement of cash flows? What does this amount represent?

SOLUTIONS TO REVIEW PROBLEMS

Mid-Chapter Review 1

SOLUTION

1. Out/I; 2. Out/O; 3. Out/O; 4. In/F; 5. Out/O; 6. In/O; 7. In/I; 8. In/I; 9. Out/F; 10. In/O

Mid-Chapter Review 2

SOLUTION

MUG SHOTS, INC.
Computation of Cash Flow from Operating Activities
For Month Ended December 31, 2015

Net income	=	Sales revenue	−	Cost of goods sold	−	Wage expenses	−	Interest expense	−	Advertising expense	−	Rent expense	−	Depreciation expense	−	Income tax expense
$3,445		$31,000		16,700		4,700		300		1,800		1,500		700		1,855
Adjustments:																
Add back depreciation expense														⊕ 700 Depreciation expense		
Subtract (add) non-operating gains (losses)																
Subtract the change in operating assets (operating investments)		⊖ 2,500 Change in accounts receivable		⊖ 8,300 Change in inventory								⊖ (−1,500) Change in prepaid rent				
Add the change in operating liabilities (operating financing)		⊕ 500 Change in unearned revenue		⊕ 1,000 Change in accounts payable		⊕ 2,200 Change in wages payable		⊕ 300 Change in interest payable								⊕ 1,855 Change in income tax payable
$700	=	$29,000	−	24,000	−	2,500	−	0	−	1,800	−	0	−	0	−	0
Cash from operations	=	Receipts from customers	−	Payments for merchandise	−	Payments for wages	−	Payments for interest	−	Payments for advertising	−	Payments for rent	−		−	Payments for income tax

Mid-Chapter Review 3

SOLUTION

MUG SHOTS, INC. Cash Flow from Operating Activities—Indirect Method		
Net income		$3,445
Adjustments:		
Add back depreciation expense	$ 700	
Subtract changes in:		
Accounts receivable	(2,500)	
Inventory	(8,300)	
Prepaid rent	1,500	
Add changes in:		
Unearned revenue	500	
Accounts payable	1,000	
Wages payable	2,200	
Interest payable	300	
Income tax payable	1,855	
Total adjustments		(2,745)
Cash flow from operating activities		$700

Mid-Chapter Review 4

SOLUTION

MUG SHOTS, INC. Statement of Cash Flows For Month Ended December 31, 2015		
Cash flow from operating activities		
Net income	$ 3,445	
Add back depreciation	700	
Subtract changes in:		
Accounts receivable	(2,500)	
Inventory	(8,300)	
Prepaid rent	1,500	
Add changes in:		
Accounts payable	1,000	
Unearned revenue	500	
Income tax payable	1,855	
Wages payable	2,200	
Interest payable	300	
Net cash provided by operating activities		$700
Cash flow from investing activities		
Purchase of equipment	(12,000)	
Net cash used by investing activities		(12,000)
Cash flow from financing activities		
Bank loan	18,000	
Payment of dividend	(1,000)	
Net cash provided by financing activities		17,000
		5,700
Cash, beginning of period		5,000
Cash, end of period		$10,700

Mid-Chapter Review 5

SOLUTION

There are three entries that affected the balance sheet accounts of Property, Plant, and Equipment at cost and Accumulated Depreciation. We know some of the amounts involved, but not all. Let P be the proceeds on the sale of used equipment, let A be the cash spent to acquire new property, plant, and equipment, and let D be the year's depreciation expense. Here are the entries:

1. Disposal:

DR Cash (+A)	P	
DR Accumulated depreciation (−XA, +A)	60,000	
CR Property, plant, and equipment at cost (−A)		80,000
CR Gain on equipment disposal (+R, +SE)		35,000

The value of P must be \$55,000, because Jack's Snacks reported a gain of \$35,000 on selling an asset with book value of \$20,000 (= \$80,000 − \$60,000).

2. Acquisition:

DR Property, plant, and equipment at cost (+A)	A	
CR Cash (−A)		A

We can determine the cost of acquired assets by looking at the T-account for Property, Plant, and Equipment at Cost.

+	Property, Plant, and Equipment at Cost		−
Beg. bal.	600,000		
Purchases	A	80,000	Disposal
End. bal.	670,000		

The value of A, i.e., the amount spent on acquiring PPE, must have been \$150,000.

3. Depreciation expense:

DR Depreciation expense (+E, −SE)	D	
CR Accumulated depreciation (+XA, −A)		D

We can determine the depreciation expense by looking at the T-account for the Accumulated Depreciation contra-asset.

+	Accumulated Depreciation		−
		140,000	Beg. bal.
Disposal	60,000	D	Deprec. Exp.
		150,000	End. bal.

The depreciation expense for the year, D, must have been \$70,000, because the contra-asset increased by \$10,000 even though the disposal decreased it by \$60,000.

Chapter-End Review

SOLUTION

1. We assume that One World Café's notes payable are classified as current liabilities. If so, current liabilities are \$41,000 (\$27,000+\$6,000+\$3,000+\$5,000) in 2015 and \$21,000 (\$14,000+\$2,500+\$4,500) in 2014.
   \$44,000 / [(\$41,000 + \$21,000)/2] = 1.42
   One World Café is generating cash flows from operations in excess of its current liabilities. Assuming that this continues, it should have no difficulty meeting its obligations.
2. \$44,000 / \$45,000 = 0.98
   One World Café spent a little more on plant capacity than it generated through operations. However, for a small business, capital expenditures are often irregular. Thus, this ratio is not alarmingly low.
3. \$44,000 – (\$45,000 − \$4,000) = \$3,000.

Appendix 4A Review

SOLUTION

Cash Flow Spreadsheet for Rocky Road Bicycles, Inc.

	A	B	C	D	E	F	G	H	I	J
1						Effect of change on cash flow				
2		O, I, or F?	2015	2014	Change	Operating	Investing	Financing	No effect on cash	Total F, G, H, I
3	**Assets**									
4	Cash		106,000	96,000	10,000					
5										
6	Accounts receivable	O	156,000	224,000	(68,000)	68,000				68,000
7	Inventory	O	752,000	528,000	224,000	(224,000)				(224,000)
8	Prepaid rent	O	68,000	72,000	(4,000)	4,000				4,000
9	Plant assets, net	O, I	1,130,000	872,000	258,000					
10	Depreciation expense					122,000				
10	Plant assets purchased						(420,000)			(258,000)
12	Plant assets sold					(16,000)	56,000			
13										
14	**Liabilities**									
15	Accounts payable	O	216,000	112,000	104,000	104,000				104,000
16	Wages payable	O	18,000	20,000	(2,000)	(2,000)				(2,000)
17	Income tax payable	O	44,000	36,000	8,000	8,000				8,000
18	Notes payable	F								
19	New borrowing									—
20	Borrowing repayments									
21										
22	**Shareholders' Equity**									
23	Common stock	F	1,142,000	1,000,000	142,000					
24	New issue of common stock							142,000		142,000
25	Repurchase of common stock									
26	Retained earnings	O, F	792,000	624,000	168,000					
27	Net income					326,000				168,000
28	Dividends							(158,000)		
29										
30	Totals					390,000	(364,000)	(16,000)	—	10,000

$\$390{,}000 - \$364{,}000 - \$16{,}000 = \$10{,}000.$

ROCKY ROAD BICYCLES, INC.
Statement of Cash Flows
For Year Ended December 31, 2015

Cash flows from operating activities		
Net income	$326,000	
Add (deduct) items to convert net income to cash basis		
Depreciation	122,000	
Gain on sale of plant assets	(16,000)	
Accounts receivable	68,000	
Inventory	(224,000)	
Prepaid rent	4,000	
Accounts payable	104,000	
Wages payable	(2,000)	
Income tax payable	8,000	
Net cash provided by operating activities		$390,000
Cash flows from investing activities		
Purchase of plant assets	(420,000)	
Proceeds from sale of plant assets	56,000	
Net cash used for investing activities		(364,000)
Cash flows from financing activities		
Issuance of common stock	142,000	
Payment of dividends	(158,000)	
Net cash used for financing activities		(16,000)
Net cash increase		10,000
Cash at beginning of year		96,000
Cash at end of year		$106,000

5 Analyzing and Interpreting Financial Statements

LEARNING OBJECTIVES

1. Prepare and analyze common-size financial statements. (p. 221)
2. Compute and interpret measures of return on investment, including return on equity (ROE), return on assets (ROA), and return on financial leverage (ROFL). (p. 224)
3. Disaggregate ROA into profitability (profit margin) and efficiency (asset turnover) components. (p. 227)
4. Compute and interpret measures of liquidity and solvency. (p. 232)
5. Appendix 5A: Measure and analyze the effect of operating activities on ROE. (p. 240)
6. Appendix 5B: Prepare *pro forma* financial statements. (p. 242)

PEPSICO
www.pepsico.com

In recent years, **PepsiCo** CEO Indra K. Nooyi faced increasing pressure from shareholders. Its flagship soft drink—Pepsi-Cola—was unseated as the second best-selling brand in the U.S. by Diet Coke in 2010, and revenue at its principal beverage unit has increased only marginally. The company's North American snack foods unit has experienced solid growth, accounting for 22% of PepsiCo's revenue and 36% of its operating profit in 2014. This disparity in performance has activist shareholders calling for a split-up of the company. Ms. Nooyi maintains that PepsiCo will do better keeping all its business units and has taken several steps to improve performance.

PepsiCo was created by the merger of Pepsi-Cola and the Frito-Lay Company in 1965. Since then, the company has grown through selective acquisitions and creative marketing of its products to become the largest food and beverage company in the United States. By 2014, its sales topped $66.6 billion, and the company ranked 44th in the Fortune 500 ranking of the largest companies based on revenues. Yet, between 2008 and 2014, PepsiCo's stock price has performed below the level of the S&P 500 index, and below that of its chief competitor, Coca-Cola, as well.

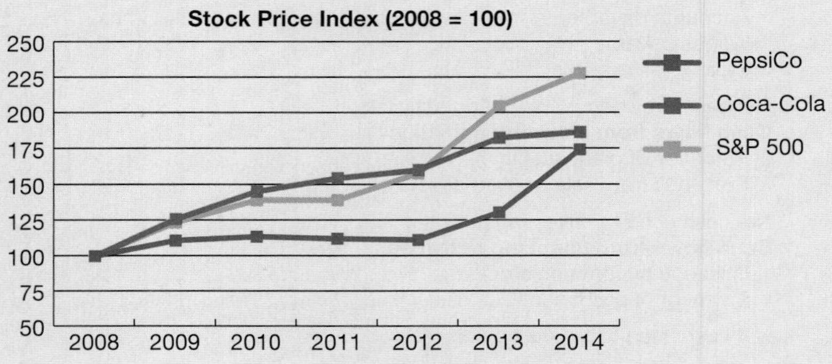

As is the case in most companies, PepsiCo's management employs a number of financial measures to assess the performance and financial condition of its operating units. These measures include ratios related to profitability and asset

utilization as well as return on investment. Investors, creditors and financial analysts use similar measures to evaluate company performance, assess credit risk, and estimate share value.

This chapter focuses on the analysis of information reported in the financial statements. We discuss a variety of measures that provide insights into a company's performance to answer questions such as: Is it managed efficiently and profitably? Does it use assets efficiently? Is the performance achieved with an optimal amount of debt? We pay especially close attention to measures of return. In Chapter 1, we introduced one such return metric, namely return on equity (ROE). In this chapter, we review ROE and add another return metric—return on assets (ROA).

ROE and ROA differ by the use of debt financing, or financial leverage. Companies can increase ROE by borrowing money and using these funds to finance investment in operating assets. However, debt financing can increase company risk and, if not used judiciously, can have a detrimental effect on ROE and even lead to financial distress. In the latter part of this chapter, we examine metrics that measure liquidity and solvency that allow us to assess that risk.

PepsiCo tackled its sluggish beverage sales by launching a major "rebranding" program for all of its beverage product lines, including Pepsi, Gatorade, Tropicana, SoBe Lifewater, Sierra Mist, and others. Rebranding requires creating new product logos, new packaging, new slogans and, most importantly, new advertising campaigns. PepsiCo's most recent efforts include reducing headcount by almost 9,000, modifying products to make them more appealing to health-conscious consumers, and investing an additional $600 million in marketing to maintain its brand equity and ability to charge premium prices. It is too soon to tell whether these efforts will produce the growth that investors desire. Ultimately, we will be able to assess the success of this initiative by looking at specific measures of PepsiCo's performance. In doing so, we seek the answer to the root question: Can the company achieve a high return on investment and, if so, is that return sustainable?

Sources: PepsiCo annual report 2014; *New York Times*, April 26, 2012; *Wall Street Journal*, May 15, 2012, July 25, 2012. *The New Yorker*, May 16, 2011, *USA Today*, April 24, 2015

CHAPTER ORGANIZATION

Analyzing and Interpreting Financial Statements

Common-Size Statements	Return on Investment	Liquidity and Solvency	Appendices
• Vertical Analysis • Horizontal Analysis	• Return on Equity • Return on Assets • Return on Financial Leverage • Disaggregating ROA into Profit Margin and Asset Turnover	• Short-term Liquidity: Current Ratio and Quick Ratio • Long-term Solvency: Debt-to-Equity and Times Interest Earned • Limitations of Ratio Analysis	• Analyzing Core Operating Activities • Pro Forma Financial Statements

INTRODUCTION

Companies prepare financial statements to be used. These statements are used by investors who rely on financial statement information to assess investment risk, forecast income and dividends, and estimate value. They are used by creditors to assess credit risk and monitor outstanding loans for compliance with debt covenants. And, as the PepsiCo example illustrates, they are used by management to evaluate the performance of operating units. **Financial statement analysis** identifies relationships between numbers within the financial statements and trends in these relationships from one period to the next. The goal is to help users such as investors, creditors, and managers interpret the information presented in the financial statements.

Financial statement analysis is all about making comparisons. Accounting information is difficult to interpret when the numbers are viewed in isolation. For example, a company that reports net income of $7 million may have had a good year or a bad year. However, if we know that total sales were $100 million, assets total $90 million, and that the previous year's net income was $6 million, we have a better idea about how well the company performed. If we go a step further and compare these numbers to those of a competing company or to an industry average, we begin to make an assessment about the relative quality of management, the prospects for future growth, overall company risk, and the potential to earn sustainable returns.

Assessing the Business Environment

Financial statement analysis cannot be undertaken in a vacuum. A meaningful interpretation of financial information requires an understanding of the business, its operations, and the environment in which it operates. That is, before we begin crunching the numbers, we must consider the broader business context in which the company operates. This approach requires starting with the Management's Discussion and Analysis section of the financial reports and asking questions about the company and its business environment, including:

- *Life cycle*—At what stage in its life is this company? Is it a start-up, experiencing the growing pains that often result from rapid growth? Is it a mature company, reaping the benefits of its competitive advantages? Is it in decline?
- *Outputs*—What products does it sell? Are its products new, established, or dated? Do its products have substitutes? Are its products protected by patents? How complicated are its products to produce?
- *Customers*—Who are its customers? How often do customers purchase the company's products? What demographic trends are likely to have an effect on future sales?
- *Competition*—Who are the company's competitors? How is it positioned in the market relative to its competition? Is it easy for new competitors to enter the market for its products? Are its products differentiated from competitors' products? Does it have any cost advantages over its competitors?
- *Inputs*—Who are the company's suppliers? Are there multiple supply sources? Does the company depend on one (or a few) key supply sources creating the potential for high input costs?

- *Labor*—Who are the company's managers? How effective are they? Is the company unionized? Does it depend on a skilled or educated workforce?
- *Technology*—What technology does the company employ to produce its products? Does the company outsource production? What transport systems does the company rely on to deliver its products?
- *Capital*—To what extent does the company rely on public markets to raise needed capital? Has it recently gone public? Does it have expansion plans that require large sums of cash to carry out? Is it planning to acquire another company? Is it in danger of defaulting on its debt?
- *Political*—How does the company interact with the communities, states, and countries in which it operates? What government regulations affect the company's operations? Are any proposed regulations likely to have a significant impact on the company?

These are just a few of the questions that we should ask before we begin analyzing a company's financial statements. Ultimately, the answers will help us place our numerical analysis in the proper context, so that we can effectively interpret the accounting numbers.

In this chapter, we introduce the tools that are used to analyze and interpret financial statements. These tools include common-size financial statements that are used in vertical and horizontal analysis and ratios that measure return on investment and help to assess liquidity and solvency.

VERTICAL AND HORIZONTAL ANALYSIS

LO1 Prepare and analyze common-size financial statements. 1

Companies come in all sizes, a fact that presents difficulties when making comparisons between firms and over time. **Vertical analysis** is a method that attempts to overcome this obstacle by restating financial statement information in ratio (or percentage) form. Specifically, it is common to express components of the income statement as a percent of net sales, and balance sheet items as a percent of total assets. This restatement is often referred to as **common-size financial statements** and it facilitates comparisons across companies of different sizes as well as comparisons of accounts within a set of financial statements.

Exhibit 5.1 presents PepsiCo's summarized comparative balance sheets for 2014 and 2013. Next to the comparative balance sheets are common-size balance sheets for the same two years. Vertical analysis helps us interpret the composition of the balance sheet. For example, as of the end of 2014, 29.3% of PepsiCo's assets were current assets and 24.5% were property, plant, and equipment. Intangible assets made up a greater share of the company's total assets. In addition, 75.1% of PepsiCo's total assets were financed with liabilities—up from 68.5% in 2013 (and 56.2% in 2009). Long-term debt obligations were 33.8% of total assets in 2014, but as recent as 2009, long-term liabilities were 18.6% of total assets. This significant change in liabilities is largely due to the acquisition of Pepsi Bottling Group, Inc. (PBG) and PepsiAmericas, Inc. (PAS) in February 2010. Financial statement analysts should be aware of changes in a company's organization that produce significant changes in financial statement relationships. It is not uncommon for companies to use lower-cost debt financing to finance expansion, especially if management believes that low stock prices prevent them from issuing common stock. However, increasing debt levels are a concern if profits and cash flows are not growing fast enough to cover the rising interest and principal payments.

In **Exhibit 5.2**, we present PepsiCo's summarized comparative income statements for 2014 and 2013, along with common-size income statements for the same years. Vertical analysis reveals that cost of sales is 46.3% of net revenue, down from 47.0% in 2013, while the increased percentage for selling, general and administrative expenses left operating profit slightly lower as a percentage of revenue compared to the year before. An increase in selling, general and administrative expenses could be due to higher marketing and advertising costs, supply chain or distribution problems, or increased management costs. PepsiCo's management noted that the increased cost of international operations was a significant contributor to the lower operating profit as a percentage of sales in 2014. While further analysis would be necessary to determine the exact causes of any fluctuation, common size financial statements highlight important changes and help to reveal the factors that may contribute to these changes.

EXHIBIT 5.1 **PepsiCo Comparative Balance Sheets**

PEPSICO, INC.
Balance Sheets and Common-Size Balance Sheets
December 27, 2014 and December 28, 2013

	As reported ($ millions)		As a percentage of Total Assets	
	2014	**2013**	**2014**	**2013**
Assets				
Current assets				
Cash and cash equivalents	$ 6,134	$ 9,375	8.7%	12.1%
Short-term investments	2,592	303	3.7	0.4
Accounts and notes receivable, net	6,651	6,954	9.4	9.0
Inventories	3,143	3,409	4.5	4.4
Prepaid expenses and other current assets	2,143	2,162	3.0	2.8
Total current assets	20,663	22,203	29.3	28.7
Property, plant, and equipment, net	17,244	18,575	24.5	24.0
Amortizable intangible assets, net	1,449	1,638	2.1	2.1
Goodwill	14,965	16,613	21.2	21.4
Other nonamortizable intangible assets	12,639	14,401	17.9	18.6
Investments in noncontrolled affiliates	2,689	2,623	3.8	3.4
Other assets	860	1,425	1.2	1.8
Total assets	$70,509	$77,478	100.0%	100.0%
Liabilities and equity				
Current liabilities				
Short-term obligations	$ 5,076	$ 5,306	7.2%	6.8%
Accounts payable and other current liabilities	13,016	12,533	18.5	16.2
Total current liabilities	18,092	17,839	25.7	23.0
Long-term debt obligations	23,821	24,333	33.8	31.4
Other liabilities	5,744	4,931	8.1	6.4
Deferrred income taxes	5,304	5,986	7.5	7.7
Total liabilities	52,961	53,089	75.1	68.5
Total equity	17,548	24,389	24.9	31.5
Total liabilities and equity	$70,509	$77,478	100.0%	100.0%

EXHIBIT 5.2 **PepsiCo Comparative Income Statements**

PEPSICO, INC.
Income Statements and Common-Size Income Statements
Fiscal years ended December 27, 2014 and December 28, 2013

	As reported ($ millions)		As a percentage of Net Revenue	
	2014	**2013**	**2014**	**2013**
Net revenue	$66,683	$66,415	100.0%	100.0%
Cost of sales	30,884	31,243	46.3	47.0
Gross profit	35,799	35,172	53.7	53.0
Selling, general and administrative expenses	26,126	25,357	39.2	38.2
Amortization of intangible assets	92	110	0.1	0.2
Operating profit	9,581	9,705	14.4	14.6
Interest expense	(909)	(911)	(1.4)	(1.4)
Interest income and other	85	97	0.1	0.1
Income before income taxes	8,757	8,891	13.1	13.4
Provision for income taxes	2,199	2,104	3.3	3.2
Net income	$ 6,558	$ 6,787	9.8%	10.2%

Horizontal analysis examines changes in financial data across time. Comparing data across two or more consecutive periods is helpful in analyzing company performance and in predicting future performance. **Exhibit 5.3** presents a horizontal analysis of a few selected items from PepsiCo's income statement—revenue, operating income, and net income. The dollar amounts reported in each year from 2010 through 2014 are shown for each item along with a percentage change for each item. The amount of the change for a given year is computed by subtracting the amount for the prior year from the amount for the current year. The change is then divided by the reported amount for the prior year to get the percentage change. For example, PepsiCo's percentage change in net revenue was 0.4% in 2014, computed as follows:

$$0.4\% = \frac{\$66{,}683 \text{ million} - \$66{,}415 \text{ million}}{\$66{,}415 \text{ million}}$$

Exhibit 5.3 highlights some important changes in PepsiCo's income statement. The table shows that, since 2011 both revenue and net income have increased by a very small amount and operating profit has actually decreased. In 2014, revenues increased by only 0.4% and net income decreased by 3.4%. The decline in net income is largely due to the increase in operating expenses as well as higher income taxes.

EXHIBIT 5.3 **Horizontal Analysis of Selected Income Statement Items**

PEPSICO, INC.
Revenue, Operating Income and Net Income
($ millions and percent changes)

	2014	2013	2012	2011	2010
Revenue	$66,683	$66,415	$65,492	$66,504	$57,838
	0.4%	1.4%	−1.5%	15.0%	
Operating profit	$ 9,581	$ 9,705	$ 9,112	$ 9,633	$ 8,332
	−1.3%	6.5%	−5.4%	15.6%	
Net income	$ 6,558	$ 6,787	$ 6,214	$ 6,462	$ 6,338
	−3.4%	9.2%	−3.8%	2.0%	

Horizontal analysis is useful in identifying unusual changes that might not be obvious when looking at the reported numbers alone. At the same time, it is important to look at both the percentage change and the reported dollar amount. If a reported amount is close to $0 in one year, the percentage change will likely be very large the following year, even if the amount reported in that year is small. Similarly, if reported earnings is negative one year and positive the next, the percentage change will be negative even though the earnings increased. Horizontal analysis that is based on a denominator that is negative or zero is not meaningful.

MID-CHAPTER REVIEW 1

Following are summarized 2014 and 2013 income statements and balance sheets for **The Coca-Cola Company**.

Required

Prepare common-size income statements and balance sheets for Coca-Cola. Comment on any noteworthy relationships that you observe.

THE COCA-COLA COMPANY AND SUBSIDIARIES
Consolidated Statements of Income
($ millions)

Year ended December 31	2014	2013
Net operating revenues	$45,998	$46,854
Cost of goods sold	17,889	18,421
Gross profit	28,109	28,433
Selling, general and administrative expenses	17,218	17,310
Other operating charges	1,183	895
Operating income	9,708	10,228
Interest income	594	534
Interest expense	(483)	(463)
Other income (loss)—net	(494)	1,178
Income before income taxes	9,325	11,477
Income taxes	2,201	2,851
Consolidated net income	$ 7,124	$ 8,626

THE COCA-COLA COMPANY AND SUBSIDIARIES
Consolidated Balance Sheets
($ millions)

December 31,	2014	2013
ASSETS		
Cash and cash equivalents	$ 8,958	$10,414
Short-term investments and marketable securities	12,717	9,854
Trade accounts receivable	4,466	4,873
Inventories	3,100	3,277
Prepaid expenses and other assets	3,745	2,886
Total current assets	32,986	31,304
Equity method investments	9,947	10,393
Other investments	3,678	1,119
Property, plant, and equipment, net	14,633	14,967
Goodwill and other intangible assets	26,372	27,611
Other assets	4,407	4,661
Total assets	$92,023	$90,055
LIABILITIES AND EQUITY		
Accounts payable and accrued expenses	$ 9,234	$ 9,577
Loans and notes payable	19,188	16,901
Current maturities of long-term debt	3,552	1,024
Accrued income taxes	400	309
Total current liabilities	32,374	27,811
Long-term debt	19,063	19,154
Other liabilities	4,389	3,498
Deferred income taxes	5,636	6,152
Total liabilities	61,462	56,615
Total equity	30,561	33,440
Total liabilities and equity	$92,023	$90,055

The solution to this review problem can be found on page 265.

RETURN ON INVESTMENT

2 **LO2** Compute and interpret measures of return on investment, including return on equity (ROE), return on assets (ROA), and return on financial leverage (ROFL).

Common-size financial statements and percentage changes are useful, but there is a limit to what we can learn from this type of analysis. While vertical and horizontal analysis focuses on relationships within a particular financial statement, either the income statement or the balance sheet, many of the questions that we might ask about a company can be answered only by comparing amounts between statements. For example, return on investment measures are ratios that divide some measure of performance—typically reported in the income statement—by the average amount of investment as reported in the balance sheet.

In this section, we discuss three important return metrics—return on equity (ROE), return on assets (ROA), and return on financial leverage (ROFL). We also examine return on investment in detail by disaggregating ROA into performance drivers that capture profitability and efficiency.

Return on Equity (ROE)

Return on equity (ROE) is the primary summary measure of company performance and is defined as:

$$\textbf{ROE} = \frac{\textbf{Net income}}{\textbf{Average stockholders' equity}}$$

ROE relates net income to the average investment by shareholders as measured by total stockholders' equity from the balance sheet. The net income number in the numerator measures the performance of the firm for a specific period (typically a fiscal year). Therefore, in order to accurately capture the return for that period, we use the average level of stockholders' equity for the same period as the denominator. The average is computed by adding the beginning and ending stockholders' equity balances and then dividing by two.

FYI Whenever we compare an income statement amount with a balance sheet amount, the balance sheet amount should be the *average* balance for the period (beginning balance plus ending balance divided by 2) rather than the year-end balance.

PepsiCo's ROE was 31.3% in 2014. This return is computed as \$6,558 million/[(\$17,548 million + \$24,389 million)/2]. PepsiCo's ROE has been consistently high over the past 5 years, ranging from a low of 28.7% in 2012 to a high of 32.6% in 2010.

ROE is widely used by analysts, investors, and managers as a key overall measure of company performance. Billionaire investor Warren Buffett highlights ROE as part of his acquisition criteria: "businesses earning good returns on equity while employing little or no debt." Companies can use debt to increase their return on equity, but too much debt increases risk as the failure to make required debt payments is likely to yield many legal consequences, including bankruptcy. This is one reason why many analysts focus on returns generated by assets used in operations, rather than on returns produced by increasing the amount of debt financing. Next, we discuss each of these sources of return in more detail.

Return on Assets (ROA)

ROE measures the return on the investment made by the firm's stockholders. In contrast, **return on assets (ROA)** measures the return earned on each dollar that the firm invests in assets. By focusing on the asset side of the balance sheet, ROA captures the returns generated by the firm's operating and investing activities, without regard for how those activities are financed. ROA is defined as:

$$\textbf{Return on assets (ROA)} = \frac{\textbf{Earnings without interest expense (EWI)}}{\textbf{Average total assets}}$$

Average total assets is computed in much the same way that we calculated average stockholders' equity for ROE. We add the beginning and ending balances in total assets and then divide by two. The numerator in this ratio, **earnings without interest expense (EWI)**, is defined to be:

Earnings without interest expense (EWI) =
Net income + [Interest expense × (1 − Statutory tax rate)]

EWI measures the income generated by the firm before taking into account any of its financing costs. Interest costs should be excluded from the ROA calculation so that return is measured without the effect of debt financing. Because interest expense is subtracted when net income is calculated, it must be added back to net income when we compute EWI. However, interest expense is tax deductible and, as such, it reduces the firm's tax obligation. That is, interest expense produces a tax *savings* for the firm. This tax savings is equal to the interest expense times the statutory tax rate. In order to eliminate the full effect of interest cost on EWI, we must add back the interest expense *net* of the resulting tax savings. To accomplish this, we multiply the interest expense by (1 − the statutory tax rate). This amount is then added to net income to get EWI. Thus, we can compute ROA as follows:

$$\textbf{Return on assets (ROA)} = \frac{\textbf{Net income} + [\textbf{Interest expense} \times (1 - \textbf{Statutory tax rate})]}{(\textbf{Beginning total assets} + \textbf{Ending total assets}) / 2}$$

ROA is an important measure of how well a company's management has utilized assets to earn a profit. If ROA is high, the firm can pay its interest costs to creditors and still have sufficient resources left over to distribute to stockholders as a dividend or to reinvest in the firm.

PepsiCo's ROA was 9.7% in 2014. PepsiCo's return is computed as follows: [1]

$$\text{ROA} = \frac{\$6{,}558 \text{ million} + [\$909 \text{ million} \times (1 - 35\%)]}{(\$77{,}478 \text{ million} + \$70{,}509 \text{ million}) / 2} = 9.7\%$$

PepsiCo's return on assets has fluctuated over the past 5 years from a high of 12.8% in 2010 to a low of 9.2% in 2012.

Return on Financial Leverage (ROFL)

The principal difference between ROE and ROA is the effect that liabilities (including debt financing) have on the return measure. ROA is calculated so that it is independent of financing costs, whereas ROE is computed net of the cost of debt financing. **Financial leverage** refers to the effect that liabilities (including debt financing) have on ROE. A firm's management can increase the return to shareholders (ROE) by effectively using financial leverage. On the other hand, too much financial leverage can be risky. To help gauge the effect that financial leverage has on a firm, the **return on financial leverage (ROFL)** is defined as:

ROFL = ROE − ROA

This return metric captures the amount of ROE that can be attributed to financial leverage. In the case of PepsiCo, the ROFL is 21.6% (31.3% − 9.7%). Over the past 5 years, financial leverage has had a significant impact on PepsiCo's performance. The impact of financial leverage on PepsiCo's ROE is illustrated in **Exhibit 5.4**. The height of each bar in the graph reflects PepsiCo's ROE for that year. Each bar is split into two components—ROA for the same year (the lower portion of each bar) and ROFL (the upper portion of each bar).

EXHIBIT 5.4 Contribution of Financial Leverage to PepsiCo's ROE

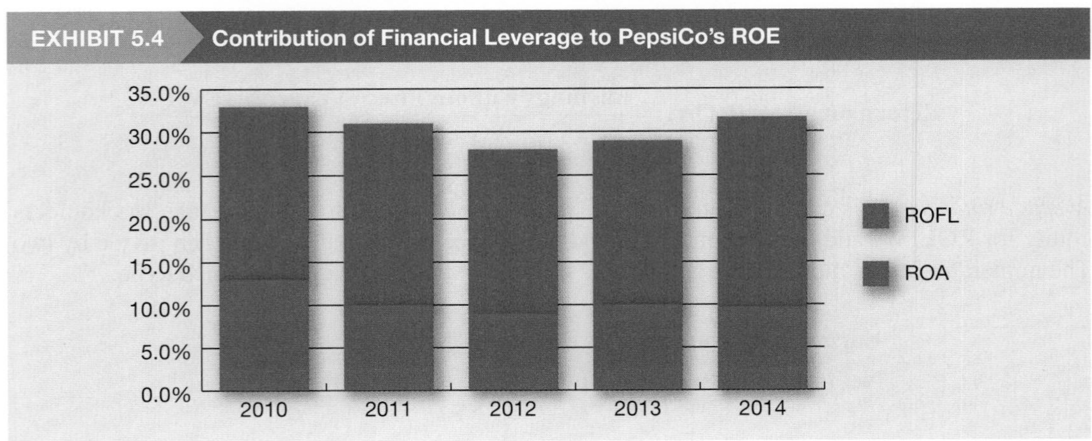

[1] The statutory federal tax rate for corporations is 35% (per U.S. tax code). In addition, many states tax corporate income, and those state taxes are deductible for federal tax purposes. Consequently, the net state tax rate is the statutory state tax rate less the federal tax benefit. Most companies provide both the federal tax rate and the state tax rate (net of the federal tax deduction) as percentages in the income tax footnote. If this information is available, the statutory tax rate is the sum of the two percentages. However, state tax rates (net of the federal tax deduction) vary from one company to the next and are typically small. Therefore, for purposes of illustration, we ignore state income taxes and use the federal statutory tax rate of 35% in these ratio calculations.

In **Exhibit 5.5**, we compare the ROE, ROA and ROFL of PepsiCo to that of several other companies featured in this text. As in **Exhibit 5.4**, the height of each bar represents the company's ROE for 2014. The lower portion of each bar is the company's ROA and the upper portion reflects the contribution of financial leverage (ROFL). The graph suggests that, with the possible exception of Verizon and Delta Air Lines, PepsiCo's ROE is influenced to a greater extent by financial leverage than the other companies.

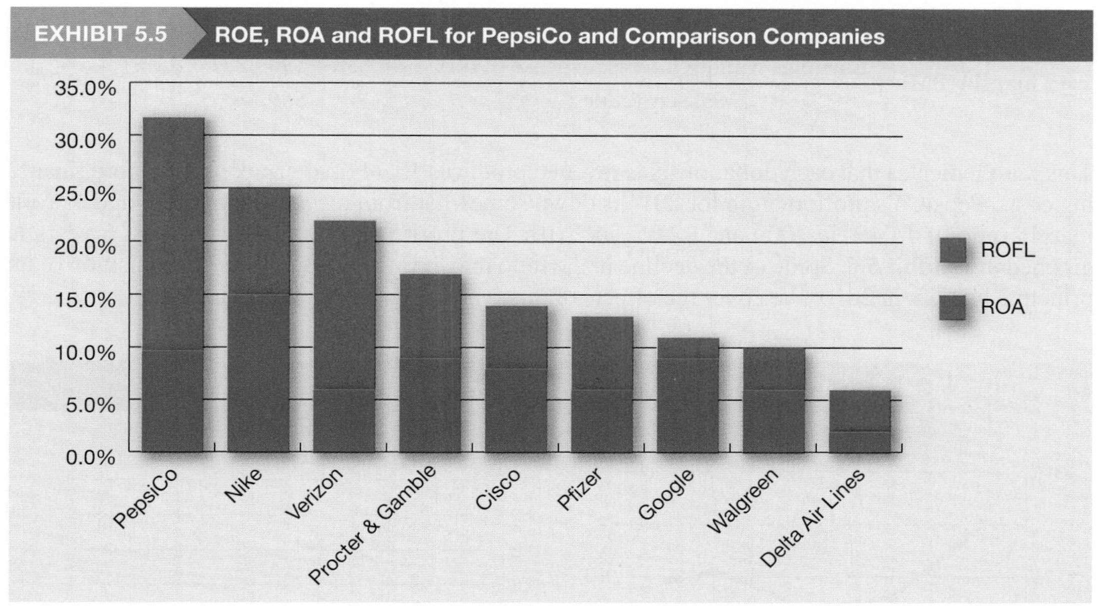

Later in this chapter, we examine the effects of financial leverage more closely and discuss several ratios that measure liquidity and solvency. These ratios help us to evaluate the risk associated with using financial leverage.

MID-CHAPTER REVIEW 2

Required

Refer to the financial statements for the **Coca-Cola Company** presented in Mid-Chapter Review 1 earlier in this chapter. Calculate Coca-Cola's ROE, ROA and ROFL for 2014.

GuidedExamples MBC

The solution to this review problem can be found on page 266.

Disaggregating ROA

LO3 Disaggregate ROA into profitability (profit margin) and efficiency (asset turnover) components.

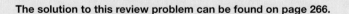

We can gain further insights into return on investment by disaggregating ROA into performance drivers that capture profitability and efficiency. ROA can be restated as the product of two ratios—profit margin and asset turnover—by simultaneously multiplying and dividing ROA by sales revenue:

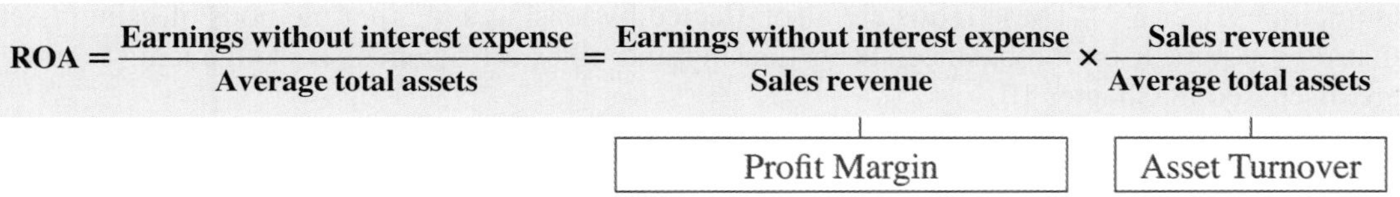

$$\text{ROA} = \frac{\textbf{Earnings without interest expense}}{\textbf{Average total assets}} = \frac{\textbf{Earnings without interest expense}}{\textbf{Sales revenue}} \times \frac{\textbf{Sales revenue}}{\textbf{Average total assets}}$$

The first ratio on the right-hand side of the above relationship is the **profit margin (PM)**. This ratio measures the profit, without interest expense, that is generated from each dollar of sales revenue. All other things being equal, a higher profit margin is preferable. Profit margin is affected by the level of gross profit that the company earns on its sales (sales revenue minus cost of goods sold), which depends on product prices and the cost of manufacturing or purchasing its product. It is also affected by operating expenses that are required to support sales of products or services. These include wages and salaries, marketing, research and development, as well as depreciation and other **capacity costs**. Finally, profit margin is affected by the level of competition, which affects product pricing, and by the company's operating strategy, which affects operating costs, especially discretionary costs such as advertising and research and development.

PepsiCo's profit margin ratio was 10.7% in 2014, computed as follows ($ millions):

$$\textbf{Profit margin (PM)} = \frac{\textbf{Earnings without interest expense (EWI)}}{\textbf{Sales revenue}} = \frac{\$6{,}558 + \$909 \times (1 - 35\%)}{\$66{,}683} = 10.7\%$$

This ratio indicates that each dollar of sales revenue produces 10.7¢ of after-tax profit before financing costs. PepsiCo's profit margin for 2014 is down somewhat from recent years. It reported a profit margin ratio of 14.4% in 2009 and 12.0% in 2010. The profit margin ratio for the past 5 years is graphed in **Exhibit 5.6**. Some of the decline in the ratio may be attributed to Pepsi's acquisition of its principal bottlers in 2010. We cover the effects of this type of transaction in Chapter 12.

EXHIBIT 5.6 PepsiCo's Profit Margin and Asset Turnover Ratios, 2010–2014

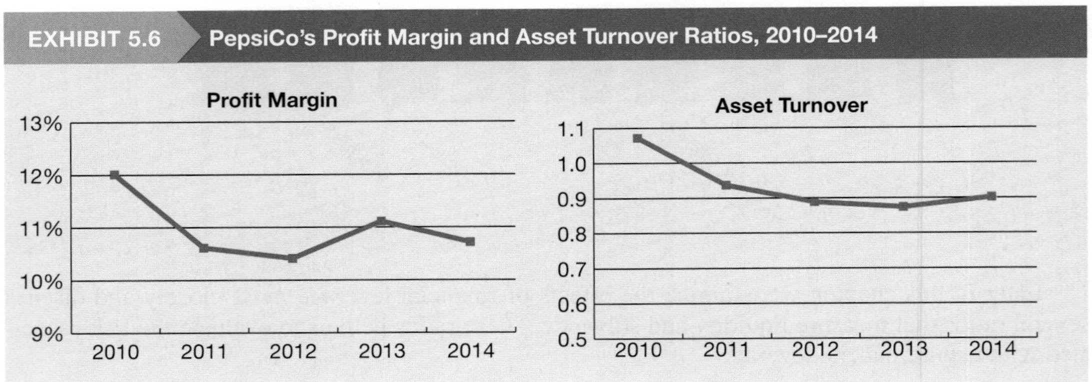

The **asset turnover (AT)** ratio reveals insights into a company's productivity and efficiency. This metric measures the level of sales generated by each dollar that a company invests in assets. A high asset turnover ratio suggests that assets are being used efficiently so, all other things being equal, a high asset turnover ratio is preferable. The ratio is affected by inventory management practices, credit policies, and most of all, the technology employed to produce a company's products or deliver its services.

The asset turnover ratio can be improved by increasing the level of sales for a given level of assets, or by efficiently managing assets. For many companies, efficiently managing working capital—primarily inventories and receivables—is the easiest way to limit investment in assets and increase turnover. On the other hand, it is usually more difficult to increase asset turnover by managing investment in long-term assets. Capital intensive companies, such as those in the telecommunications or energy production industries, tend to have lower asset turnover ratios (often less than 1.0) because the production technology employed by these firms requires a large investment in property, plant, and equipment. Retail companies, on the other hand, tend to have a relatively small investment in plant assets. As a result, they tend to have higher asset turnover ratios (sometimes over 3.0). These ratios are also affected by leasing and other methods of using assets that do not appear on the balance sheet. Leasing and other off-balance-sheet financing methods are discussed in Chapter 10.

PepsiCo's asset turnover ratio is computed as follows ($ millions):

$$\textbf{Asset turnover (AT)} = \frac{\textbf{Sales revenue}}{\textbf{Average total assets}} = \frac{\$66{,}683}{(\$77{,}478 + \$70{,}509)\,/\,2} = 0.901$$

The ratio indicates that each dollar of assets generates 90.1¢ in sales revenue each year. Over the past five years, PepsiCo's asset turnover has ranged from 0.87 in 2013 to 1.07 in 2010 as illustrated by the graphic in **Exhibit 5.6**.

YOU MAKE THE CALL

You are the Entrepreneur You are analyzing the performance of your start-up company. Your analysis of ROA reveals the following (industry benchmarks in parentheses): ROA is 16% (10%), PM is 18% (17%), and AT is 0.89 (0.59). What interpretations do you draw that are useful for managing your company? [Answer, page 250.]

Trade-Off Between Profit Margin and Asset Turnover ROA is the product of profit margin and asset turnover. By decomposing ROA in this way, we can identify the source of PepsiCo's decline in ROA between 2010 and 2014:

	ROA	=	Profit Margin	×	Asset Turnover
2010:	12.8%	=	11.97%	×	1.071
2014:	9.7%	=	10.72%	×	0.901

Between 2010 and 2014, PepsiCo's profit margin declined from 11.97% to 10.72% while, at the same time, asset turnover declined from 1.071 to 0.901. These changes are due in part to PepsiCo's acquisition of its principal bottlers, which contributed to a substantial increase in the company's reported assets (from $40 billion at the end of 2009 to $68 billion at the end of 2010). The usual cause of a decline in asset turnover is a decline in sales revenue, but PepsiCo's revenues increased substantially since 2010. As we saw earlier in the chapter when we examined PepsiCo's common-size income statement, a major cause of the profit margin decline was the increase in operating costs as a percentage of sales revenue. Because sales revenue appears to be increasing substantially, it is likely that management's best opportunity to increase ROA in the future would be to focus its efforts on increasing profitability.

Basic economics tells us that any successful business must earn an acceptable return on investment if it wants to attract capital from investors and survive. Yet, there are an infinite number of combinations of asset turnover and profit margin that will yield a given ROA. The trade-off between profit margin and asset turnover is heavily influenced by a company's business model. A company can attempt to increase its ROA by targeting higher profit margins, or by increasing its asset turnover. To an extent, this trade-off is the result of strategic decisions made by management. However, to a greater extent, the relative mix of margin and turnover is dictated by the industry in which the company operates. As mentioned earlier, one determinant of a company's profit margin is its competitive environment, while asset turnover is heavily influenced by the production technology employed. For this reason, companies in the same industry tend to exhibit similar combinations of margin and turnover while comparisons between industries can exhibit much greater variation. That is, within a given industry, differences in the mix of profit margin and asset turnover often reflect the specific strategy employed by each individual firm, while variations between industries are caused by differences in the competitive environment and production technology of each industry.

This trade-off is illustrated in **Exhibit 5.7**. The solid curved line represents the average ROA for all companies over the period from 2012 through 2014. Each point along that curve represents a combination of asset turnover and profit margin that yields the average ROA. Industries that are plotted near the upper left side of the graph are those that achieve their ROA targets by maintaining a high asset turnover. These industries are often characterized by intense competition and low profit margins. On the other hand, industries in the lower right-hand portion of the graph have lower asset turnover ratios because they typically employ capital-intensive production technologies. At the same time, the competitive environment within these industries allows companies to achieve higher profit margins to offset the lower turnover ratios.

EXHIBIT 5.7 Profit Margin and Turnover Across Industries

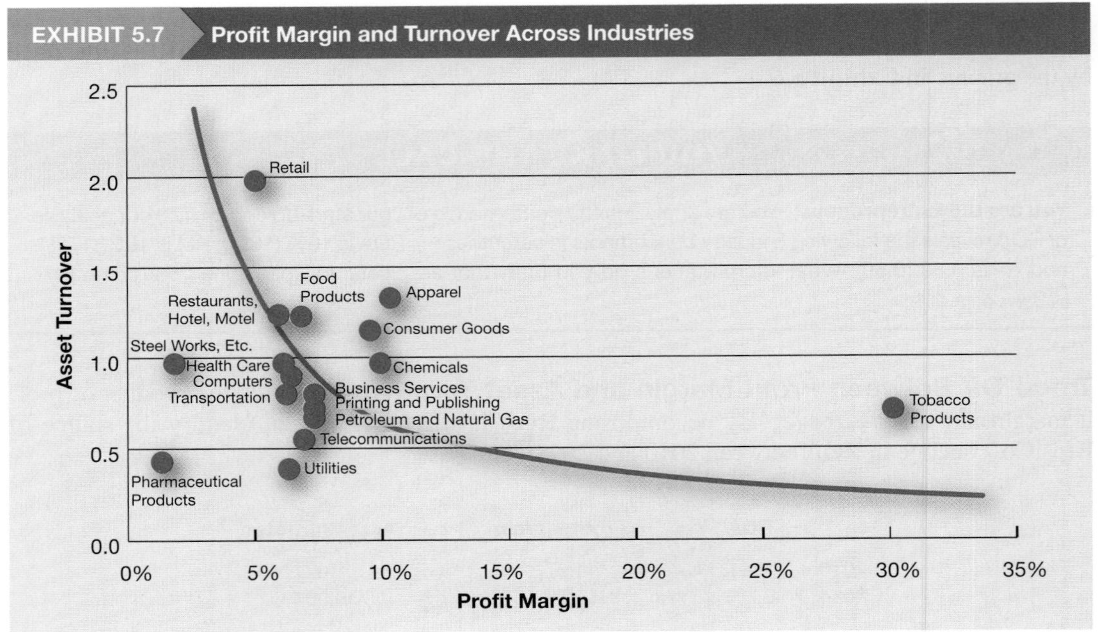

BUSINESS INSIGHT

The DuPont Model Disaggregation of return on equity (ROE) into three components—profitability, turnover, and financial leverage—was initially introduced by the **E.I. DuPont de Nemours and Company** to aid its managers in performance evaluation. DuPont realized that management's focus on profit alone was insufficient because profit can be increased simply by adding investments in low-yielding, but safe, assets. Further, DuPont wanted managers to think like investors and to manage their portfolio of activities using investment principles that allocate scarce investment capital to competing projects based on a goal of maximizing return on investment.

The basic DuPont model disaggregates ROE as the product of three ratios as follows:

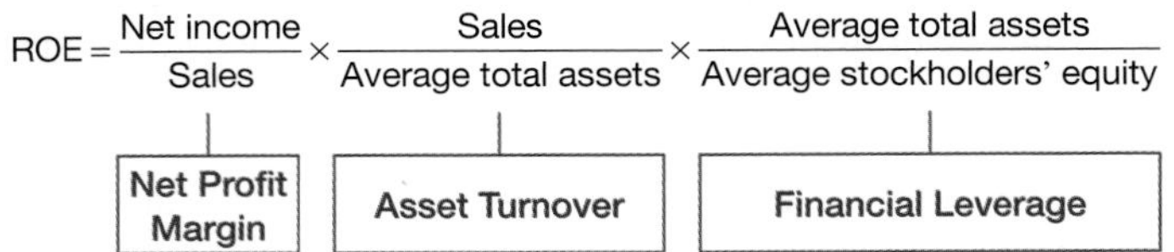

$$\text{ROE} = \frac{\text{Net income}}{\text{Sales}} \times \frac{\text{Sales}}{\text{Average total assets}} \times \frac{\text{Average total assets}}{\text{Average stockholders' equity}}$$

An important limitation of the DuPont model is that net profit margin is measured using net income in the numerator rather than earnings without interest expense (EWI). This means that this measure of profitability is affected by financial leverage—as financial leverage increases, interest expense increases and the net profit margin decreases. As a consequence, the model fails to adequately separate the effects of operating profitability on ROE from the effects of financial leverage. Despite this limitation, the DuPont model is widely used as a simple, straightforward way to disaggregate ROE.

Further Disaggregation of Profit Margin and Asset Turnover While disaggregation of ROA into profit margin and asset turnover yields useful insights into the factors driving company performance, analysts, investors, creditors, and managers often disaggregate these measures even further. The purpose of this analysis is to be more precise about the specific determinants of profitability and efficiency.

To disaggregate profit margin (PM), we examine gross profit on products sold and individual expense accounts that contribute to the total cost of operations. The key ratios include the gross profit margin and expense-to-sales ratios. **Gross profit margin (GPM)** is defined as:

$$\textbf{Gross profit margin (GPM)} = \frac{\textbf{Sales revenue} - \textbf{Cost of goods sold}}{\textbf{Sales revenue}}$$

PepsiCo's GPM is 53.7% ([\$66,683 million − \$30,884 million]/\$66,683 million). That is, just over half (53.7%) of every sales dollar is gross profit while slightly less than half (46.3%) goes to cover the cost of products sold.

Gross profit margin measures the percentage of each sales dollar that is left over after product costs are subtracted. It is easily determined by looking at the common-size income statement. This ratio is discussed in more detail in Chapter 7.

An **expense-to-sales (ETS)** ratio measures the percentage of each sales dollar that goes to cover a specific expense item and is computed by dividing the expense by sales revenue. Expense items that might be examined with ETS ratios include selling, general and administrative (SG&A) expenses, advertising expense, or research and development (R&D) expense, among others. Which specific ETS ratio is appropriate depends on the company being analyzed. For instance, advertising expense is an important expense item for a consumer products company, such as PepsiCo, while R&D expense is important for an R&D intensive pharmaceutical company, such as **Pfizer**. Analysts study trends in ETS ratios over time in an effort to uncover clues that might explain changes in profit margin and make predictions about future profitability.

PepsiCo's SG&A ETS ratio is computed by dividing selling, general and administrative expenses by net revenue. The resulting ETS ratio is 39.2% (\$26,126 million/\$66,683 million). This ratio indicates that 39.2¢ of every sales dollar goes to pay marketing and administrative costs. This ETS ratio is relatively high because this expense item includes PepsiCo's advertising expenditures.

To disaggregate asset turnover (AT), we examine individual asset accounts and compare them to sales or cost of goods sold. We focus on three specific turnover ratios—accounts receivable turnover (ART), inventory turnover (INVT), and property, plant, and equipment turnover (PPET).

Accounts receivable turnover (ART) is defined as follows:

$$\textbf{Accounts receivable turnover (ART)} = \frac{\textbf{Sales revenue}}{\textbf{Average accounts receivable}}$$

ART measures how many times receivables have been turned (collected) during the period. More turns indicate that accounts receivable are being collected more quickly, while low turnover often indicates difficulty with a company's credit policies. PepsiCo's ART is 9.8 times (\$66,683 million/[{\$6,954 million + \$6,651 million}/2]). ART is discussed in Chapter 6.

Inventory turnover (INVT) is defined as:

$$\textbf{Inventory turnover (INVT)} = \frac{\textbf{Cost of goods sold}}{\textbf{Average inventory}}$$

INVT measures the number of times during a period that total inventory is turned (sold). A high INVT indicates that inventory is managed efficiently. Retail companies, such as **Wal-Mart** and **Home Depot** focus a great deal of management attention on maintaining a high INVT ratio. PepsiCo's INVT is 9.4 times (\$30,884 million/[{\$3,409 million + \$3,143 million}/2]). This ratio is discussed further in Chapter 7.

Property, plant, and equipment turnover (PPET) measures the sales revenue produced for each dollar of investment in PP&E. It is computed as the ratio of sales to average PP&E assets:

$$\textbf{Property, plant, and equipment turnover (PPET)} = \frac{\textbf{Sales revenue}}{\textbf{Average PP \& E}}$$

PPET provides insights into asset utilization and how efficiently a company operates given its production technology. PepsiCo's PPET is 3.7 times (\$66,683 million/[{\$18,575 million + \$17,244 million}/2]). This ratio is revisited in Chapter 8.

In the next section, we examine ratios that focus on liquidity and solvency. These ratios help us evaluate the risk associated with debt financing and weigh the costs and benefits of financial leverage. **Exhibit 5.8** presents a schematic summary of the disaggregation of ROE. It identifies the two primary components of ROE—ROA and ROFL—and highlights the disaggregation of ROA into profit margin and asset turnover, along with the drivers of these ratios. In addition, the link between ROFL and liquidity and solvency analysis is highlighted.

EXHIBIT 5.8 ROE Disaggregation

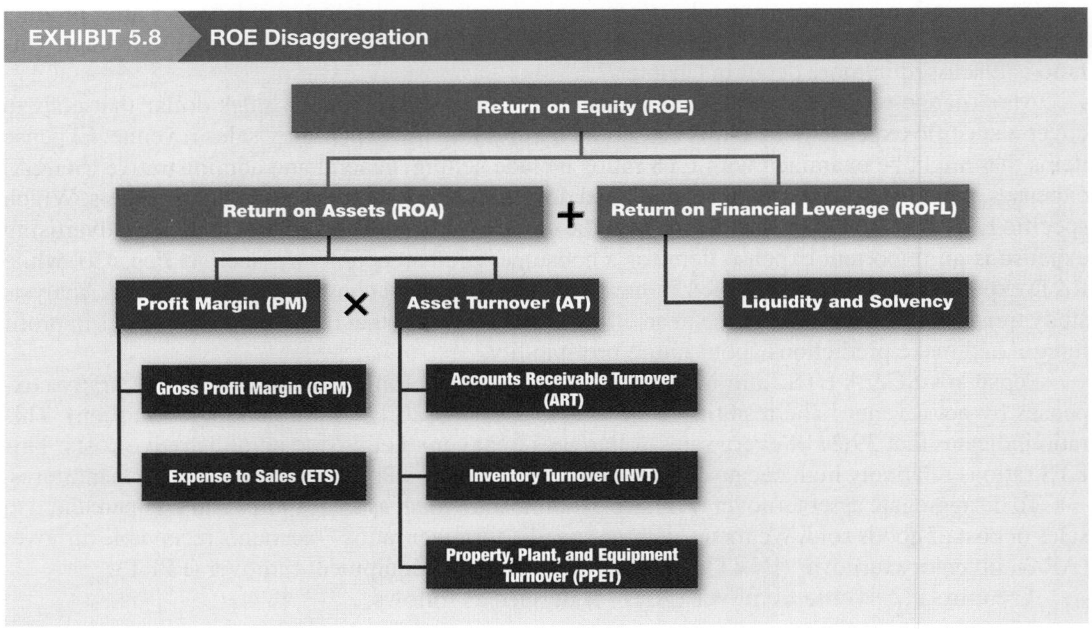

MID-CHAPTER REVIEW 3

Required

Refer to the financial statements for the **Coca-Cola Company** presented in Mid-Chapter Review 1 earlier in this chapter.

1. Calculate Coca-Cola's profit margin (PM) and asset turnover (AT) ratios for 2014.
2. Show that ROA = PM × AT using Coca-Cola's financial data.
3. Calculate Coca-Cola's gross profit margin (GPM), accounts receivable turnover (ART), inventory turnover (INVT), and property, plant, and equipment turnover (PPET) ratios for 2014.
4. Evaluate Coca-Cola's ratios in comparison to those of PepsiCo.

The solution to this review problem can be found on page 266.

4

LO4 Compute and interpret measures of liquidity and solvency.

LIQUIDITY AND SOLVENCY

Companies can use debt to increase financial leverage and boost ROE. The increase in ROE due to the use of debt is called *return on financial leverage (ROFL)*. The primary advantage of debt financing is that it is typically less costly than equity financing; the cost of debt financing is currently a little over 2%, while equity financing averages about 8%.[2]

[2] Equity financing is more costly than debt because, in the event that the firm fails, creditors collect their investment first, while stockholders collect the residual. Stockholders, therefore, demand a greater return on investment to compensate for assuming greater risk.

Exhibit 5.9 illustrates a comparison between two companies—one (Company A) is financed with 100% equity and the other (Company B) is financed with 50% debt and 50% equity. Both companies have $1,000 in (average) assets and EWI of $100, producing an ROA of 10% ($100/$1,000). Because Company A does not use debt financing, average equity equals average total assets. Also, it reports no interest expense in its income statement so net income equals EWI. Therefore, for Company A, ROE = ROA, and its ROFL = 0%.

EXHIBIT 5.9 The Effect of Debt Financing on ROE (ROA > interest rate)

	Company A	Company B
Assets (average)	$1,000	$1,000
EWI	100	100
ROA (EWI/Assets)	10%	10%
Equity (average)	$1,000	$ 500
Debt	0	500
Interest expense (4% of debt)	0	20
Net income (EWI – interest)	100	80
ROE (Net income/equity)	10%	16%
ROFL (ROE – ROA)	0%	6%

In contrast, Company B has $500 of equity financing and $500 of debt financing. It reports interest expense of $20 ($500 × 4%) leaving net income of $80 ($100 – $20). Company B's ROE is 16% ($80/$500), which means that its ROFL is 6% (16% – 10%). Company B has made effective use of debt financing to increase its ROE. As long as a company's ROA is greater than its cost of debt, its ROFL will be positive.[3]

We might further ask: If a higher ROE is desirable, why don't companies use as much debt financing as possible? The answer is that there are risks associated with debt financing. As the amount of debt in a company's balance sheet increases, so does the burden of interest costs on income and debt payments on cash flows. In the best of times, financial leverage increases returns to stockholders (ROE). In contrast, when earnings are depressed, financial leverage has the effect of making a bad year even worse. In the worst case, too much debt can lead to financial distress and even bankruptcy.

To illustrate how debt financing can reduce shareholder returns, **Exhibit 5.10** compares Company A and Company B in a year when reported profits are lower than in the previous example. Both companies have $1,000 in (average) assets and both report EWI of $30, producing an ROA of 3% ($30/$1,000). Company A does not use debt financing, so its ROE = 3%, and its ROFL = 0%. Because Company B has $500 of equity and $500 of debt, it reports interest expense of $20 ($500 × 4%) leaving net income of $10 ($30 – $20). Company B's ROE is 2% ($10/$500), which means that its ROFL is –1% (2% – 3%). That is, for Company B, the use of financial leverage has a negative effect on ROE. As this example illustrates, whenever ROA is less than the interest rate on the debt, debt financing reduces the return to shareholders.

EXHIBIT 5.10 The Effect of Debt Financing on ROE (ROA < interest rate)

	Company A	Company B
Assets (average)	$1,000	$1,000
EWI	30	30
ROA (EWI/Assets)	3%	3%
Equity (average)	$1,000	$ 500
Debt	0	500
Interest expense (4% of debt)	0	20
Net income (EWI – interest)	30	10
ROE (Net income/equity)	3%	2%
ROFL (ROE – ROA)	0%	–1%

[3] The interest cost on debt is tax deductible. Therefore, the relevant cost of debt to use to compare to ROA is the after-tax interest rate.

As a general rule, shareholders benefit from increased use of debt financing provided that the assets financed with the debt earn a return that exceeds the cost of the debt. However, increasing levels of debt result in successively higher interest rates charged by creditors. At some point, the cost of debt exceeds the return on assets that a company can expect from the debt financing. Thereafter, further debt financing does not make economic sense. The market, in essence, places a limit on the amount that a company can borrow.

In addition, creditors usually require a company to execute a loan agreement that places various restrictions on its operating activities. These restrictions, called **covenants**, help safeguard debtholders in the face of increased risk. This occurs because debtholders do not have a voice on the board of directors like stockholders do. These debt covenants impose a "cost" on the company beyond that of the interest rate, and these covenants are more stringent as a company increases its reliance on debt financing.

The median ratio of total liabilities to stockholders' equity, which measures the relative use of debt versus equity in a company's capital structure, is just over 1.0 for all publicly traded companies. This means that the typical company relies more on debt financing than on equity. However, the relative use of debt varies considerably across industries as illustrated in **Exhibit 5.11**.

EXHIBIT 5.11 Median Ratio of Liabilities to Equity for Selected Industries

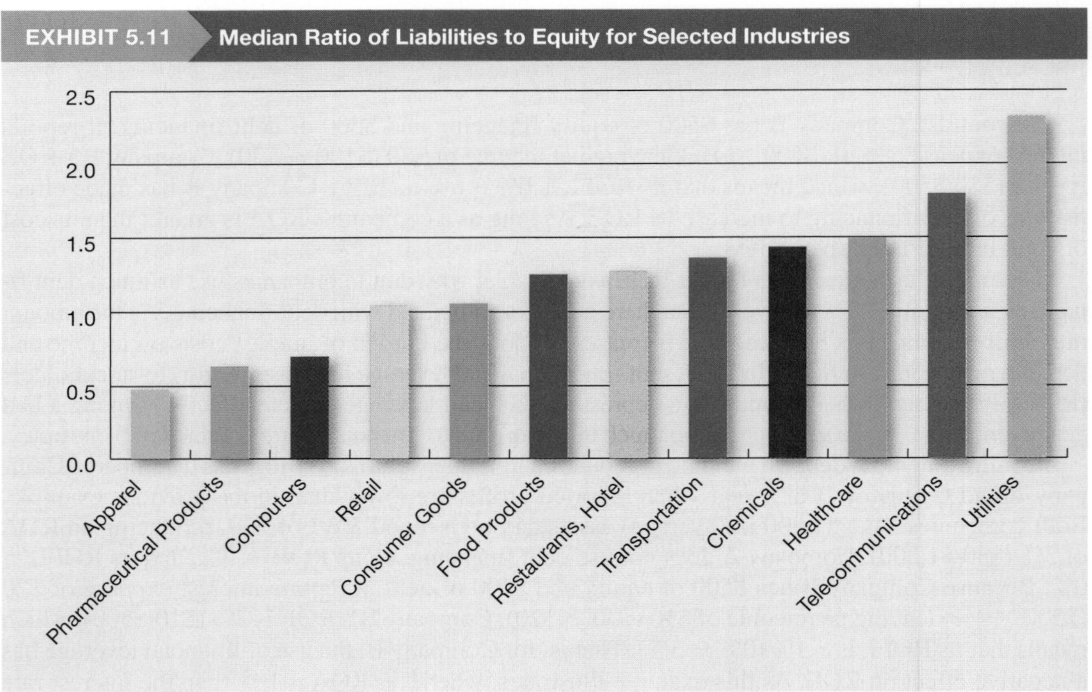

Companies in the utilities industry have relatively high proportions of debt. Because the utilities industry is regulated, profits and cash flows are relatively certain and stable and, as a result, utility companies can support a higher debt level. The healthcare and telecommunications industries also utilize a relatively high proportion of debt. These industries are not regulated, but their heavy investments in property, plant, and equipment require significant long-term debt. At the lower end of debt financing are pharmaceuticals and apparel companies. Historically, these industries have been characterized by relatively uncertain profits and cash flows. In addition, success in these industries depends heavily on intellectual property and human resources devoted to research and product development. These "assets" do not appear on the balance sheet and cannot be used as collateral when borrowing funds. Consequently, they use less debt in their capital structures.

To summarize, companies can effectively use debt to increase ROE. Although it reduces financing costs, debt increases **default risk**: the risk that the company will be unable to repay debt when it comes due. Because of this risk, analysts carefully examine a company's financial statements to determine if it is using debt financing effectively and judiciously.

The core of our analysis relating to debt is the examination of a company's ability to generate cash to *service* its debt (that is, to make required debt payments of both interest and principal).

Analysts, investors, and creditors are primarily concerned about whether the company has sufficient cash available or, alternatively, whether it is able to generate the required cash in the future to cover its debt obligations. The analysis of available cash is called **liquidity analysis**. The analysis of the company's ability to generate sufficient cash in the future is called **solvency analysis** (so named because a bankrupt company is said to be "insolvent").

Liquidity Analysis

Liquidity refers to cash availability: how much cash a company has, and how much it can raise on short notice. The most common ratios used to assess the degree of liquidity are the current ratio and the quick ratio, which were first introduced in Chapter 2, as well as the operating cash flow to current liabilities ratio, which was introduced in Chapter 4. Each of these ratios links required near-term payments to cash available in the near term.

Current Ratio *Current assets* are those assets that a company expects to convert into cash within the next operating cycle, which is typically a year. *Current liabilities* are those liabilities that come due within the next year. An excess of current assets over current liabilities (Current assets − Current liabilities), is known as *net working capital* or simply **working capital**. Positive working capital implies more expected cash inflows than cash outflows in the short run. The **current ratio** expresses working capital as a ratio and is computed as follows:

$$\textbf{Current ratio (CR)} = \frac{\textbf{Current assets}}{\textbf{Current liabilities}}$$

A current ratio greater than 1.0 implies positive working capital. Both working capital and the current ratio consider existing balance sheet data only and ignore cash inflows from future sales or other sources. The current ratio is more commonly used than working capital because ratios allow comparisons across companies of different sizes. Generally, companies prefer a higher current ratio; however, an excessively high current ratio indicates inefficient asset use. Furthermore, a current ratio less than 1.0 is not always problematic for at least two reasons:

1. A cash-and-carry company (like a grocery store) can have little or no receivables (and a low current ratio), but consistently large operating cash inflows ensure the company will be sufficiently liquid. A company can efficiently manage its working capital by minimizing receivables and inventories and maximizing payables. **The Kroger Company** and **Wal-Mart**, for example, use their buying power to exact extended credit terms from suppliers. Consequently, because both companies are essentially cash-and-carry companies, their current ratios are less than 1.0 and both are sufficiently liquid.
2. A service company will typically report little or no inventories among its current assets. In addition, some service companies do not report significant accounts receivable. If short-term borrowings and accrued expenses exceed cash and temporary investments, a current ratio of less than 1.0 would result. **United Continental Holdings, Inc.** is an example of such a firm.

The aim of current-ratio analysis is to discern if a company is having, or is likely to have, difficulty meeting its short-term obligations. If a company cannot cover its short-term debts with cash provided by operations, it may need to liquidate current assets to meet its obligations. **PepsiCo**'s current ratio was 1.14 ($20,663 million / $18,092 million) at December 31, 2014. At the end of 2013, its current ratio was 1.24 ($22,203 million / $17,839 million).

Quick Ratio The **quick ratio** is a variant of the current ratio. It focuses on quick assets, which are those assets likely to be converted to cash within a relatively short period of time, usually less than 90 days. Specifically, quick assets include cash, marketable securities, and accounts receivable; they exclude inventories and prepaid assets. The quick ratio is defined as follows:

$$\textbf{Quick ratio (QR)} = \frac{\textbf{Cash + Short-term securities + Accounts receivable}}{\textbf{Current liabilities}}$$

The quick ratio reflects on a company's ability to meet its current liabilities without liquidating inventories that could require markdowns. It is a more stringent test of liquidity than the current ratio and may provide more insight into company liquidity in some cases.

In 2014, PepsiCo's quick ratio was 0.85 ([$6,134 million + $2,592 million + $6,651 million]/$18,092 million), which was down from 0.93 in 2013 ([$9,375 million + $303 million + $6,954 million]/$17,839 million). While it is not uncommon for a company to report a quick ratio less than 1.0, PepsiCo's quick ratio has declined along with its current ratio.

Operating Cash Flow to Current Liabilities The **operating cash flow to current liabilities (OCFCL)** ratio was introduced in Chapter 4 and is defined as follows:

$$\textbf{Operating cash flow to current liabilities (OCFCL)} = \frac{\textbf{Cash flow from operations}}{\textbf{Average current liabilities}}$$

Cash flow from operations is taken directly from the statement of cash flows. It represents the net amount of cash derived from operating activities during the year. Ultimately the ability of a company to pay its debts is determined by whether its operations can generate enough cash to cover debt payments. Thus, a higher OCFCL ratio is generally preferred by analysts.

PepsiCo reported an OCFCL ratio of 0.58 in 2014 ($10,506 million / [($17,839 million + $18,092 million)/2]). Its 2013 OCFCL ratio was 0.55 ($9,688 million / [($17,089 million + $17,839 million)/2]). PepsiCo's OCFCL ratio has increased slightly over the past two years after a few years of decline. The increase in the OCFCL ratio, combined with the decline in the CR and QR suggests that PepsiCo's sources of liquidity should be examined further. Improvement in the ratio of cash flows to short-term obligations is generally a good sign, but this improvement appears to be the result of reducing the level of inventories and receivables from 2013 to 2014. In Chapter 4 we saw that reductions in inventory and receivables *increased* operating cash flows. As a consequence, the improvement may not be sustainable and continued improvement is certainly limited. **Exhibit 5.12** provides a plot of all three liquidity ratios over the past 5 years.

EXHIBIT 5.12 PepsiCo's Liquidity Ratios, 2010–2014

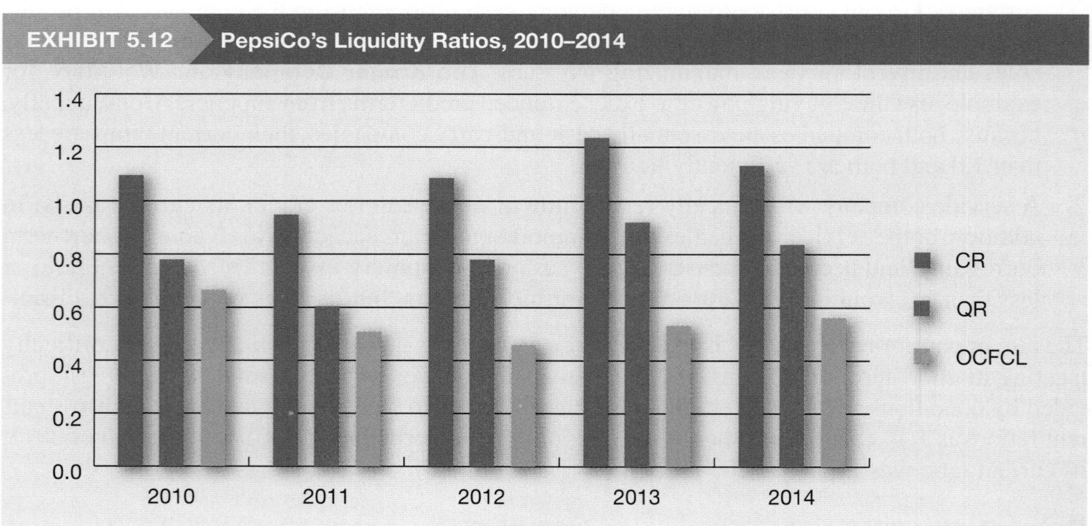

Solvency Analysis

Solvency refers to a company's ability to meet its debt obligations, including both periodic interest payments and the repayment of the principal amount borrowed. Solvency is crucial because an insolvent company is a failed company. There are two general approaches to measuring solvency. The first approach uses balance sheet data and assesses the proportion of capital raised from creditors. The second approach uses income statement data and assesses the profit generated relative to debt payment obligations. We discuss each approach in turn.

Debt-to-Equity The **debt-to-equity ratio**, which was introduced in Chapter 1, is a useful tool for the first type of solvency analysis. It is defined as follows:

$$\textbf{Debt-to-equity ratio} = \frac{\textbf{Total liabilities}}{\textbf{Total stockholders' equity}}$$

This ratio conveys how reliant a company is on creditor financing (which are fixed claims) compared with equity financing (which are flexible or residual claims). A higher ratio indicates less solvency, and more risk. PepsiCo's debt-to-equity ratio is 3.02 for 2014 ($52,961 million/$17,548 million). In 2013, its ratio was 2.18 ($53,089 million/$24,389 million). Between 2010 and 2013, PepsiCo's debt-to-equity ratio remained below 2.5 (see graph). The dramatic increase in 2014 was caused by a significant decrease in stockholders' equity from 2013 to 2014, and not by an increase in total liabilities. The decrease in stockholders' equity was due to negative foreign currency translation adjustments in 2014. Such adjustments are often beyond the ability of management to control. Nevertheless, the increase in the debt-to-equity ratio can have an impact on PepsiCo's ability to borrow at favorable interest rates. PepsiCo's debt-to-equity ratio is well above the average of approximately 1.2 for other companies in the food industry.

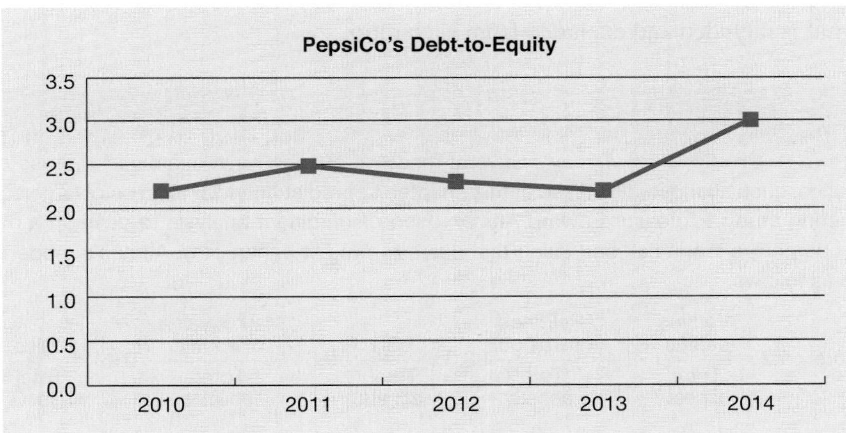

In practice, analysts use a variety of solvency measures that are similar to the debt-to-equity ratio. One variant of this ratio considers a company's *long-term* debt divided by equity. This approach assumes that current liabilities are repaid from current assets (so-called self-liquidating). Thus, it assumes that creditors and stockholders need only focus on the relative proportion of long-term capital.

Times Interest Earned The second type of solvency analysis compares profits to liabilities. This approach assesses how much operating profit is available to cover debt obligations. A common measure for this type of solvency analysis is the **times interest earned (TIE)** ratio (see Chapter 9) defined as follows:

$$\textbf{Times interest earned} = \frac{\textbf{Earnings before interest expense and taxes}}{\textbf{Interest expense}}$$

The times interest earned ratio reflects the operating income available to pay interest expense. The underlying assumption is that only interest needs to be paid because the principal will be refinanced. This ratio is sometimes abbreviated as EBIT/I. The numerator is similar to earnings without interest (EWI), but it is *pretax* instead of after tax.

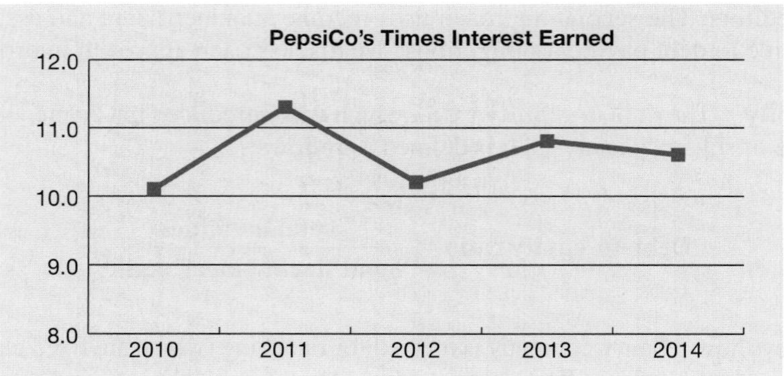

Management wants this ratio to be sufficiently high so that there is little risk of default. PepsiCo's TIE ratio was 10.63 times in 2014 ([\$8,757 million + \$909 million]/\$909 million), which is only slightly down from 10.76 times in 2013 ([\$8,891 million + \$911 million]/\$911 million). Over the 5-year period between 2010 and 2014, PepsiCo's TIE ratio has ranged from a low of 10.12 in 2010 to a high of 11.32 in 2011. The current level of this ratio suggests that PepsiCo is more than capable of earning income that is sufficient to cover its financing costs.

There are many variations of solvency and liquidity analysis and the ratios used. The basic idea is to construct measures that reflect a company's credit risk exposure. There is not one "best" financial leverage ratio. Instead, as financial statement users, we want to use measures that capture the risk we are most concerned with. It is also important to compute the ratios ourselves to ensure we know what is included and excluded from each ratio.

RESEARCH INSIGHT

Using Ratios to Predict Bankruptcy Several research studies have examined the use of various financial ratios, such as those discussed in this chapter, to predict financial distress of large companies. In a pioneering study, Professor Edward Altman used discriminant analysis to develop a method for scoring a company's credit risk and using that score to predict bankruptcy. Altman's model produced a **Z-score** as follows:

$$\text{Z-score} = 1.2 \times \frac{\text{Working capital}}{\text{Total assets}} + 1.4 \times \frac{\text{Retained earnings}}{\text{Total assets}} + 3.3 \times \frac{\text{EBIT}}{\text{Total assets}} + 0.6 \times \frac{\text{Market value of equity}}{\text{Total liabilities}} + 0.99 \times \frac{\text{Sales}}{\text{Total assets}}$$

The first variable is a measure of liquidity. The second and third variables measure long-term and short-term profitability. The fourth variable captures a company's financial leverage and the last variable is asset turnover. A Z-score greater than 3.0 indicates a healthy company, while a Z-score below 1.8 suggests a high potential for near-term bankruptcy. The model was 95% accurate at predicting bankruptcy one year in advance and 72% accurate two years in advance. Today, credit scoring models like Altman's Z-score are used by nearly all financial institutions and many other businesses to evaluate credit risk. (Altman, E., "Financial Ratios, Discriminant Analysis and the Prediction of Corporate Bankruptcy," *Journal of Finance*, September, 1968.)

Limitations of Ratio Analysis

The quality of financial statement analysis depends on the quality of financial information. We ought not blindly analyze numbers; doing so can lead to faulty conclusions and suboptimal decisions. Instead, we need to acknowledge that current accounting rules (GAAP) have limitations, and be fully aware of the company's environment, its competitive pressures, and any structural and strategic changes. **Exhibit 5.13** shows how ratios can differ significantly across industries, so comparisons to companies with similar customers, technologies and competitive pressures will be most meaningful. Even within industries, there may be differences in strategy that create big differences in ratio values. There can be other factors that limit the usefulness of financial accounting information for ratio analysis.

EXHIBIT 5.13 Industry Ratios: Medians of Companies with Market Capitalization > $500 Million (2012-2014)

	ROE	ROA	ROFL	PM	GPM	AT	ART	INVT	PPET	DE	TIE	CR	QR	OCFCL
Apparel	16.3%	9.5%	5.4%	10.3%	50.5%	1.34	9.79	3.20	7.87	0.48	32.36	2.84	1.54	0.75
Business Services	9.9%	5.0%	3.7%	7.3%	64.7%	0.81	5.64	28.30	10.52	0.83	9.22	1.80	1.62	0.48
Chemicals.	18.1%	8.1%	8.6%	9.9%	32.7%	0.98	6.53	5.17	3.13	1.43	8.95	2.18	1.24	0.54
Computers	9.8%	5.4%	4.0%	6.4%	52.5%	0.91	5.52	7.16	11.00	0.70	12.44	2.07	1.71	0.45
Consumer Goods.	13.9%	8.3%	6.7%	9.5%	47.8%	1.16	7.19	5.44	6.67	1.05	14.37	1.70	1.11	0.43
Food Products	13.3%	7.0%	5.9%	6.8%	32.4%	1.24	12.26	6.29	4.80	1.25	7.48	1.82	0.88	0.52
Healthcare	11.7%	5.9%	5.3%	6.1%	21.9%	0.98	7.39	44.73	4.74	1.49	4.39	1.52	1.16	0.60
Petroleum.	8.5%	5.3%	2.9%	7.3%	45.4%	0.68	6.83	15.94	0.44	1.13	3.87	1.26	0.84	1.10
Pharmaceutical.	-3.1%	-3.1%	-1.1%	1.3%	62.6%	0.44	5.85	2.39	4.48	0.63	3.50	4.14	3.50	0.11
Printing & Publishing . . .	12.5%	5.7%	7.1%	7.3%	55.5%	0.73	6.58	19.82	7.62	1.52	5.45	1.32	0.91	0.43
Restaurants, Hotel	14.5%	6.4%	6.7%	5.9%	26.0%	1.25	30.37	55.46	2.37	1.27	6.12	1.02	0.66	0.78
Retail	14.6%	7.5%	6.0%	5.0%	34.0%	1.99	46.25	5.40	6.77	1.04	9.75	1.70	0.63	0.51
Steel	5.6%	3.4%	1.4%	1.8%	17.5%	0.98	7.68	5.26	2.84	1.19	3.44	2.34	1.22	0.42
Telecommunications. . . .	12.1%	6.1%	5.2%	6.9%	51.2%	0.56	7.13	25.51	1.65	1.79	3.38	1.14	0.91	0.69
Tobacco	13.1%	14.2%	9.0%	30.1%	52.7%	0.72	40.01	3.34	7.84	2.15	9.36	1.02	0.49	0.49
Transportation	11.1%	5.5%	4.6%	6.2%	30.0%	0.81	10.24	32.27	1.00	1.36	4.22	1.33	1.09	0.69
Utilities	9.6%	4.1%	5.4%	6.3%	28.9%	0.40	7.47	13.55	0.46	2.32	3.12	0.93	0.59	0.66
Overall	11.0%	5.7%	5.3%	7.1%	34.6%	0.87	7.19	5.48	4.77	1.25	7.35	1.81	1.19	0.48

GAAP Limitations Several limitations in GAAP can distort financial ratios. Limitations include:

1. **Measurability**. Financial statements reflect what can be reliably measured. This results in nonrecognition of certain assets, often internally developed assets, the very assets that are most likely to confer a competitive advantage and create value. Examples are brand name, a superior management team, employee skills, and a reliable supply chain.
2. **Non-capitalized costs**. Related to the concept of measurability is the expensing of costs relating to "assets" that cannot be identified with enough precision to warrant capitalization. Examples are brand equity costs from advertising and other promotional activities, and research and development costs relating to future products.
3. **Historical costs**. Assets and liabilities are usually recorded at original acquisition or issuance costs. Subsequent increases in value are not recorded until realized, and declines in value are recognized only if deemed permanent.

Thus, GAAP balance sheets omit important and valuable assets. Our analysis of ROE, including that of liquidity and solvency, must consider that assets can be underreported and that ratios can be distorted. We discuss many of these limitations in more detail in later chapters.

Company Changes Many companies regularly undertake mergers, acquire new companies, and divest subsidiaries. Such major operational changes can impair the comparability of company ratios across time. Companies also change strategies, such as product pricing, R&D, and financing. We must understand the effects of such changes on ratios and exercise caution when we compare ratios from one period to the next. Companies also behave differently at different points in their life cycles. For instance, growth companies possess a different profile than do mature companies. Seasonal effects also markedly impact analysis of financial statements at different times of the year. Thus, we must consider life cycle and cyclicality when we compare ratios across companies and over time.

Conglomerate Effects Few companies are pure-play; instead, most companies operate in several businesses or industries. Most publicly traded companies consist of a parent company and multiple subsidiaries, often pursuing different lines of business. PepsiCo reports financial information for six separate business segments. Most heavy equipment manufacturers, for example, have finance subsidiaries (**Ford Credit Corporation** and **Cat Financial** are subsidiaries of **Ford** and **Caterpillar** respectively). Financial statements of such conglomerates are consolidated and include the financial statements of the parent and its subsidiaries. Consequently, such consolidated statements are challenging to analyze. Typically, analysts break the financials apart into their component businesses and separately analyze each component. Fortunately, companies must report financial information (albeit limited) for major business segments in their 10-Ks.

Means to an End Ratios reduce, to a single number, the myriad complexities of a company's operations. No one number can accurately capture the qualitative aspect of a company. Ratios cannot hope to capture the innumerable transactions and events that occur each day between a company and various parties. Ratios cannot meaningfully convey a company's marketing and management philosophies, its human resource activities, its financing activities, its strategic initiatives, and its product management. In our analysis we must learn to look through the numbers and ratios to better understand the operational factors that drive financial results. Successful analysis seeks to gain insight into what a company is really about and what the future portends. Our overriding purpose in analysis is to understand the past and present to better predict the future. Computing and examining ratios is just one step in that process.

CHAPTER-END REVIEW

Refer to the income statements and balance sheets for the **Coca-Cola Company** presented in Mid-Chapter Review 1 earlier in this chapter.

Required

Compute the following liquidity and solvency ratios for Coca-Cola and interpret your results in comparison to those of PepsiCo.

1. Current ratio
2. Quick ratio
3. Debt-to-equity ratio
4. Times interest earned

The solution to this review problem can be found on pages 266-267.

5

LO5 Measure and analyze the effect of operating activities on ROE.

APPENDIX 5A: Analyzing and Interpreting Core Operating Activities

In Chapter 4, we analyzed cash flows by grouping them into three categories—operating, investing, and financing. Similarly, the income statement and balance sheet can be formatted to distinguish between operating and nonoperating (investing and financing) activities. In this appendix, we consider the effect of operating activities on the return on investment. The distinction between returns earned from operating activities and those generated by nonoperating activities is important. Operations provide the primary value drivers for stockholders. It is for this reason that many analysts argue that operating activities must be executed successfully if a company expects to remain profitable in the long run.

Operating activities refer to the core transactions and events of a company. They consist of those activities required to deliver a company's products and services to its customers. A company is engaged in operating activities when it conducts research and development, establishes supply chains, assembles administrative support, produces and markets its products, and follows up with after-sale customer service. Although nonoperating activities, namely investing and financing activities, are important and must be managed well, they are not the primary value drivers for investors and creditors.

Operating returns are measured by the **return on net operating assets (RNOA)**. This return metric is defined as follows:

$$\text{RNOA} = \frac{\textbf{Net operating profit after taxes (NOPAT)}}{\textbf{Average net operating assets (NOA)}}$$

In order to calculate this ratio, we must first classify the income statement and balance sheet accounts into operating and nonoperating components so that we can assess each separately. First, we will consider operating components of the income statement and the calculation of NOPAT. Then, we consider operating and nonoperating components of the balance sheet and the calculation of NOA.

Reporting Operating Activities in the Income Statement The income statement reports operating activities through accounts such as sales revenue, cost of goods sold, selling, general and administrative (SG&A) expenses, depreciation, rent, insurance, wages, advertising, and R&D expenses. These activities create the most long-lasting effects on profitability and cash flows. Nonoperating items in the income statement include interest expense on borrowed funds and interest and dividend income on investments as well as gains and losses on those investments.

A commonly used measure of operating income is **net operating profit after taxes (NOPAT)**. NOPAT is calculated as:

NOPAT = Net income − [(Nonoperating revenues − Nonoperating expenses) × (1 − Marginal tax rate)]

NOPAT is an important measure of profitability. It is similar to net income except that NOPAT focuses exclusively on after-tax *operating* performance.

Computation of NOPAT requires that we separate nonoperating revenues and expenses from operating sources of income. Companies often report income from operations as a subtotal (before income taxes) within the income statement. These numbers should be interpreted with caution. Currently, there are no requirements within GAAP that specify which revenue and expense items should be included in operating income.[4] As a consequence, some nonoperating items may be included (as part of SG&A expense, for example). PepsiCo has investments in affiliated companies that distribute its snack foods in certain parts of the world. PepsiCo's income from these investments is included in its SG&A expense in the income statement, but the amount is not disclosed. While this income might appear to be nonoperating, most analysts would argue that this amount should be included in the calculation of NOPAT for PepsiCo, because these distribution operations are part of the core operating activities of the business.

The tax rate used to compute NOPAT is the **marginal tax rate**. This rate is the effective tax rate on nonoperating revenues and expenses. As we have done throughout this chapter, we use the federal statutory tax rate of 35% to approximate the marginal tax rate.[5] PepsiCo's NOPAT can be computed using this tax rate:

NOPAT = \$6,558 million − [(\$85 million − \$909 million) × (1 − 0.35)] = \$7,093.6 million

PepsiCo's NOPAT is greater than its net income of \$6,558 million in 2014. The difference between net income and NOPAT is the interest expense on its debt and interest income on its investments.

Reporting Operating Activities in the Balance Sheet The balance sheet also reflects both operating and nonoperating activities. The asset side of the balance sheet reports resources devoted to operating activities in accounts such as cash, receivables, inventories, property, plant, and equipment, and intangible assets. Among liabilities, accounts payable, accrued expenses, and some long-term liabilities such as deferred compensation and pension benefits arise out of operating activities. In addition, accrued and deferred income taxes are generally considered operating liabilities.

Investments in securities of other companies are usually considered nonoperating. The exception is that some equity-type investments are related to operations. PepsiCo's investment in its snack foods distributors is an example of this type of investment. Equity investments are discussed further in Chapter 12. Among a company's liabilities, short-term and long-term debt accounts are classified as nonoperating. These include accounts such as notes payable, interest payable, current maturities of long-term debt, capital leases, and long-term debt.

PepsiCo reports short-term investments of \$2,592 million in 2014 (\$303 million in 2013), which are nonoperating. It also reports long-term investments in non-controlled affiliates of \$2,689 in 2014 (\$2,623 in 2013). These long-term investments are the aforementioned equity investments in companies distributing PepsiCo's snack foods, and most analysts would consider them to be part of operations. PepsiCo's footnotes show that its noncurrent Other assets account includes nonoperating assets of \$447 million in 2014 (\$419 million in 2013). Its nonoperating liabilities include short-term debt obligations of \$5,076 million in 2014 (\$5,306 million in 2013) and long-term debt obligations of \$23,821 million in 2014 (\$24,333 million in 2013).

By subtracting total operating liabilities from total operating assets, we get **net operating assets (NOA)**.[6] PepsiCo's NOA for 2014 and 2013 is calculated as follows (\$ millions):

---

[4] The FASB recently released a preliminary draft of a proposal for presenting financial statements in a new format. Among other things, the objective is to better distinguish operating and nonoperating activities.

[5] As we argued earlier in this chapter, the federal statutory tax rate is a reasonable approximation of the marginal tax rate in many instances, including our analysis of PepsiCo. However, some nonoperating sources of revenue and expense are not taxed at this 35% rate. For example, most dividend income received from investments in the stock of other corporations is excluded from taxable income. A detailed analysis of marginal tax rates is beyond the scope of this text. Nevertheless, a thorough analysis of operating return would normally include a close examination of a company's income taxes.

[6] Total operating assets can be computed by subtracting nonoperating assets from total assets. Similarly, we can determine operating liabilities either by adding up the operating items or by subtracting the nonoperating items from total liabilities.

	2014	2013
Operating assets	\$70,509 − \$2,592 − \$447 = \$67,470	\$77,478 − \$303 − \$419 = \$76,756
Operating liabilities. . .	\$52,961 − \$5,076 − \$23,821 = \$24,064	\$53,089 − \$5,306 − \$24,333 = \$23,450
NOA	\$43,406	\$53,306

Given NOPAT and NOA we can compute PepsiCo's RNOA as follows:

$$\textbf{RNOA} = \frac{\textbf{NOPAT}}{\textbf{Average NOA}} = \frac{\textbf{\$7,093.6 million}}{\textbf{\$53,306 million + \$43,406 million) / 2}} = \textbf{14.7\%}$$

PepsiCo's ROE is 31.3% in 2014. Its RNOA is 14.7%, which represents less than half of the total return earned by stockholders.

Disaggregating RNOA

We gain further insights into operating returns by disaggregating RNOA into operating profit margin and asset turnover. RNOA can be presented as the product of net operating profit margin (NOPM) and net operating asset turnover (NOAT). We define **net operating profit margin (NOPM)** as the amount of operating profit produced as a percentage of each sales dollar. NOPM is similar to the profit margin (PM) ratio defined in the chapter, except that it excludes all nonoperating revenues and expenses from the calculation. PepsiCo's NOPM was 10.64% in 2014, computed as:

$$\textbf{NOPM} = \frac{\textbf{NOPAT}}{\textbf{Sales revenue}} = \frac{\textbf{\$7,093.6 million}}{\textbf{\$66,683 million}} = \textbf{10.64\%}$$

The ratio indicates that each dollar of sales revenue generated 10.6¢ of after-tax operating profit. PepsiCo's NOPAT is very close to PepsiCo's EWI because the primary nonoperating item in the company's income statement is interest expense. Thus its NOPM is almost identical to its profit margin of 10.7%.

Net operating asset turnover (NOAT) is defined as the ratio of sales revenue to average net operating assets (NOA). NOAT captures the amount of sales revenue generated by each dollar of net investment in operating assets. PepsiCo's NOAT is 1.38 times, computed as:

$$\textbf{NOAT} = \frac{\textbf{Sales revenue}}{\textbf{Average NOA}} = \frac{\textbf{\$66,683 million}}{\textbf{(\$53,306 million + \$43,406 million) / 2}} = \textbf{1.38}$$

This ratio suggests that each dollar of investment in net operating assets generates \$1.38 of sales revenue. This ratio is considerably higher than PepsiCo's asset turnover (AT) ratio of 0.901. This difference is caused by the difference between net operating assets (NOA) and total assets. NOAT is computed using average NOA in the denominator rather than average total assets. Thus, nonoperating assets are excluded, and operating assets are presented net of operating liabilities. The resulting denominator is, therefore, considerably smaller.

PepsiCo's RNOA is 14.7%. This return can be disaggregated into the product of NOPM and NOAT as follows:

$$\textbf{RNOA} = \textbf{NOPM} \times \textbf{NOAT}$$
$$\textbf{14.7\%} = \textbf{10.64\%} \times \textbf{1.38}$$

APPENDIX 5A REVIEW

Refer to the financial statements of the Coca-Cola Company presented in Mid-Chapter Review 1. Calculate Coca-Cola's return on net operating assets (RNOA) and then disaggregate RNOA into net operating profit margin (NOPM) and net operating asset turnover (NOAT).

The solution to this review problem can be found on page 267.

APPENDIX 5B: Pro Forma Financial Statements

6 **LO6** Prepare *pro forma* financial statements.

The ability to forecast future financial activities is an important aspect of many business decisions. We might, for example, wish to estimate the value of a company's common stock before purchasing its shares. Or, we might want to evaluate the creditworthiness of a prospective borrower. We might also be interested in comparing the financial impact of alternative business strategies or tactics. For each of these decision contexts, a forecast of future earnings and cash flows would be relevant to such an evaluation.

Pro forma financial statements are hypothetical statements prepared to reflect specific assumptions about the company and its transactions. The most common type of pro forma statements are those prepared for future periods based on assumptions about the future activities of a business.[7] By varying the assumptions, pro forma statements allow us to ask "what if" questions about the future activities of the company, the answers to which provide the necessary inputs underlying most business decisions.

In this appendix, we present a common, yet simple method for preparing pro forma financial statements. This method proceeds in seven steps:

1. Forecast sales revenue.
2. Forecast operating expenses, such as cost of goods sold and SG&A expenses.
3. Forecast operating assets and liabilities, including accounts receivable, inventory, property, plant, and equipment, accounts payable, and prepaid and accrued expenses.
4. Forecast nonoperating assets, liabilities, contributed capital, revenues and expenses.
5. Forecast net income, dividends and retained earnings.
6. Forecast the amount of cash required to balance the balance sheet.
7. Prepare a pro forma cash flow statement based on the pro forma income statement and balance sheet.

Step 1. Forecast Sales Revenue

The sales forecast is the crucial first step in the preparation of pro forma financial statements, because many of the accounts in the pro forma income statement and balance sheet depend on their relation to the sales forecast. The general method for forecasting sales is to assume a revenue growth rate and apply that rate to the current sales revenue amount:

Forecasted revenues = Current revenues × (1 + Revenue growth rate)

A good starting point for estimating the revenue growth rate is the historical rate of sales growth. This is obtained by using data from the horizontal analysis discussed earlier in the chapter. For example, over the past four years, PepsiCo has experienced an average sales growth rate of 3.6%. Once we have this historical rate as a starting point, we can then adjust the growth rate up or down based on other relevant information. For example, we might attempt to answer the following questions:

- How will future sales be affected by economic conditions? What will happen in the economy in the coming year? Do we expect economic growth or a recession? How will economic growth vary in various markets, such as the United States, Europe, Asia, and Latin America?
- What changes are expected from the company? Are there any new strategic initiatives planned? Is the company planning to open new stores, launch new products, new advertising campaigns, or new pricing tactics? Do we expect any acquisitions of other businesses?
- What changes in the competitive environment do we expect? Are new competitors entering the market? How will existing competitors respond to changes in the company's strategy? How will substitute products affect sales?

To answer each of the above questions, we rely on a variety of information sources, not the least of which is the management's discussion and analysis (MD&A) section of the company's 10-K report. We can also use publicly available information from competitors, suppliers, customers, industry organizations and government agencies to provide some insight into trends that can have an effect on future revenues. Our objective is to be able to adjust the historical growth rate up or down to reflect the insights we gain from reviewing this additional information. Using the historical growth rate of 3.6%, we forecast the 2015 revenue to be $69,084 million ($66,683 million × 1.036).

Step 2. Forecast Operating Expenses

Given our forecast of sales revenue, we then turn to forecasting operating expenses. We rely on the common-size income statement as a starting point to identify the relationship between operating expense items and sales revenue. That is, we use the expense-to-sales (ETS) ratio for each operating expense item to compute the forecasted expense:

Forecasted operating expense = Forecasted revenues × ETS ratio

[7] The term "pro forma financial statements" is a term that is also used to describe *current* period financial statements prepared under alternative assumptions. For example, management might use the term pro forma earnings when referring to earnings computed after excluding a major revenue or expense item, such as restructuring charges or income from discontinued operations. The term can also be used to describe financial statements prepared under a different set of accounting principles.

While historical ETS ratios provide a good place to start, we may want to adjust these ratios up or down based on observed trends or any additional information that we might have. For example, when we examined PepsiCo's common-size income statements, we learned that cost of goods sold decreased to 46.3% of sales in 2014, up from 47.0% in 2013. Will this trend continue into 2015? Or, alternatively, do we anticipate that this expense item will revert to historical levels in relation to sales? Has the company taken any steps to alter the trend in this ETS ratio? As was the case with the sales forecast, there are numerous sources of information that are potentially useful for making adjustments to the historical relationships.

For the purpose of illustration, we assume that the ETS ratios for all operating expense items remain the same in 2015 as they were in 2014. For example, we forecast PepsiCo's 2015 SG&A expense to be $27,081 million ($69,084 million × 39.2%).

Step 3. Forecast Operating Assets and Liabilities

The sales forecast can also be used to forecast operating assets and liabilities. The relationship between operating assets and revenues is based on asset turnover analysis. For example, when we compute accounts receivable turnover (ART), sales revenue is divided by average accounts receivable. When forecasting accounts receivable, we assume a relationship between sales revenue and year-end accounts receivable:

$$\textbf{Forecasted accounts receivable} = \frac{\textbf{Forecasted sales revenue} \times \textbf{Reported accounts receivable}}{\textbf{Reported sales revenue}}$$

PepsiCo reports accounts and notes receivable of $6,651 million in 2014, which is 9.97% of the reported sales revenue of $66,683 million. The forecasted accounts receivable for 2015 is, therefore, $6,888 million ($69,084 million × 9.97%).

The same procedure can be used to forecast other operating assets, such as inventories, prepaid expenses and property, plant, and equipment, as well as operating liabilities such as accounts payable and accrued expenses.

Step 4. Forecast Nonoperating Assets, Liabilities, Revenues and Expenses

While operating expenses, assets, and liabilities tend to be related to sales revenue, this is typically not the case for nonoperating items. Instead, nonoperating revenues, such as interest and dividend income, tend to be related to investments, while nonoperating expense, namely interest expense, is related to debt financing. As a starting point, we forecast each of these items by assuming no change from the current amounts. For example, PepsiCo reported long-term debt of $23,821 million in 2014 along with short-term obligations of $2,592 million. We forecast the same level of debt financing in 2015. Likewise, interest expense should remain the same at $909 million.

There may be information in the notes or in the MD&A section of the 10-K report to suggest other assumptions. For example, the notes typically reveal the amount of long-term debt that will come due in each of the next five years. This information can be used to adjust the balance in short-term obligations, because current maturities of long-term debt would be included under this item. Nevertheless, an assumption of no change is a good place to start.

Step 5. Forecast Net Income, Dividends, and Retained Earnings

Once we have forecasts of sales revenue (from step 1), operating expenses (step 2), and nonoperating revenues and expenses (step 4), we can calculate pretax earnings, income tax expense, and net income. Income tax expense is forecasted by multiplying pretax income by the effective tax rate:

$$\textbf{Forecasted income tax expense} = \textbf{Forecasted pretax income} \times \textbf{Effective tax rate}$$

The **effective tax rate** is the average tax rate applied to pretax earnings, and is computed by dividing reported income tax expense by reported pretax earnings. PepsiCo's effective tax rate was 25.1% in 2014 ($2,199 million/$8,757 million). Although this rate can be adjusted up or down based on additional information, we apply the 2014 effective tax rate to compute 2015 forecasted income taxes. This assumption results in forecasted income taxes of $2,284 million ($9,098 million × 25.1%) and forecasted net income of $6,814 million ($9,098 million − $2,284 million). PepsiCo's 2015 pro forma income statement is presented in **Exhibit 5B.1** alongside its 2014 reported income statement.

Our forecast of dividends relies on the **dividend payout ratio**, defined as dividend payments divided by net income.

$$\textbf{Forecasted dividends} = \textbf{Forecasted net income} \times \textbf{Dividend payout ratio}$$

PepsiCo paid cash dividends of $3,730 million in 2014, which is 56.9% of its net income of $6,558 million. Using this dividend payout ratio, we forecast 2015 dividends to be $3,877 million ($6,814 million × 56.9%).

Next, we can forecast retained earnings using the forecasts of net income and dividends:

$$\text{Forecasted retained earnings} = \text{Beginning retained earnings} + \text{Forecasted net income} - \text{Forecasted dividends}$$

Throughout this chapter, we have presented PepsiCo's stockholders' equity as a single amount, without separating retained earnings from contributed capital. Contributed capital increases when common stock is issued, and decreases when common stock is repurchased. PepsiCo has repurchased shares every year for the past five years and every indication is that they will continue to repurchase shares in 2015. Stock repurchases, net of common stock issued, have averaged 40% of net income over the past five years. If we assume that this rate will continue in 2015, we can estimate stock repurchases totaling \$2,726 million (\$6,814 million × 40%). Thus, total stockholders' equity in 2015 will equal \$17,759 computed as follows:

$$\text{Forecasted stockholders' equity} = \text{Beginning stockholders' equity} + \text{Forecasted net income} - \text{Forecasted dividends} - \text{Forecasted stock repurchases}$$

$$\$17{,}759 \text{ million} = \$17{,}548 \text{ million} + \$6{,}814 \text{ million} - \$3{,}877 \text{ million} - \$2{,}726 \text{ million}$$

EXHIBIT 5B.1 PepsiCo Pro Forma Income Statement

PEPSICO, INC.
2014 Income Statement and 2015 Pro Forma Income Statement

(\$ millions)	Pro forma 2015	As reported 2014
Net revenue (\$66,683 × 1.036)	\$69,084	\$66,683
Cost of sales (\$69,084 × 46.3%)	31,986	30,884
Selling, general and administrative expenses (\$69,084 × 39.2%)	27,081	26,126
Amortization of intangible assets (\$69,084 × 0.14%)	95	92
Operating profit	9,922	9,581
Interest expense (no change)	(909)	(909)
Interest income and other (no change)	85	85
Income before income taxes	9,098	8,757
Provision for income taxes (25.1% × pretax income)	2,284	2,199
Net income	\$ 6,814	\$ 6,558

Step 6. Forecast Cash

If the forecasts of all other components of the balance sheet are in place, we can then forecast the cash balance. This forecast is simply a "plug" amount that makes the balance sheet balance:

$$\text{Forecasted cash} = \text{Forecasted liabilities} + \text{Forecasted stockholders' equity} - \text{Forecasted noncash assets}$$

It is possible that the resulting forecast of cash will be negative or unreasonably small or large. If this occurs, we then revisit steps 4 and 5. If the cash forecast is negative or too low, we adjust our forecast of short-term debt and interest expense to reflect increased borrowing to cover cash needs. If the cash forecast is too large, we can assume that excess cash is invested in marketable securities and increase the amount of interest income. In either case, we then modify our forecast of income taxes, net income, dividends and retained earnings, before recalculating the cash forecast.

PepsiCo's 2015 pro forma balance sheet is presented in **Exhibit 5B.2**, alongside the company's 2014 actual balance sheet. The cash balance is forecasted to decrease slightly, from \$6,134 million in 2014 to \$6,081 million in 2015.

Step 7. Prepare the Pro Forma Cash Flow Statement

Once we have a pro forma income statement and balance sheet, we can prepare a pro forma cash flow statement using the methods illustrated in Chapter 4. To do so, we need a forecast of depreciation expense (if that

EXHIBIT 5B.2 PepsiCo Pro Forma Balance Sheet

PEPSICO, INC.
2014 Balance Sheet and 2015 Pro Forma Balance Sheet

($ millions)	Pro forma 2015	As reported 2014
Assets		
Cash and cash equivalents (plug to balance)	$ 6,081	$ 6,134
Short-term investment (no change)	2,592	2,592
Accounts and notes receivable, net ($69,084 × 9.97%)	6,888	6,651
Inventories ($69,084 × 4.71%)	3,254	3,143
Prepaid expenses and other current assets ($69,084 × 3.21%)	2,218	2,143
Total current assets	21,033	20,663
Property, plant, and equipment, net ($69,084 × 25.86%)	17,865	17,244
Amortizable intangible assets, net ($69,084 × 2.17%)	1,499	1,449
Goodwill (no change)	14,965	14,965
Other nonamortizable intangible assets (no change)	12,639	12,639
Investments in noncontrolled affiliates (no change)	2,689	2,689
Other assets ($69,084 × 1.29%)	891	860
Total assets	$71,581	$ 70,509
Liabilities and shareholders' equity		
Short-term obligations (no change)	$ 5,076	$ 5,076
Accounts payable and other current liabilities ($69,084 × 19.52%)	13,485	13,016
Total current liabilities	18,561	18,092
Long-term debt obligations (no change)	23,821	23,821
Other liabilities ($69,084 × 8.61%)	5,948	5,744
Deferred income taxes ($69,084 × 7.95%)	5,492	5,304
Total liabilities	53,822	52,961
Total equity ($17,548 + $6,814 − $3,877 − $2,726)	17,759	17,548
Total liabilities and equity	$71,581	$70,509

item is not explicitly listed as an operating expense in the income statement). The procedure for forecasting depreciation expense is the same as was used for other operating expenses—we simply use the depreciation ETS ratio.

PepsiCo reported depreciation and amortization expense of $2,625 million in 2014, which was 3.94% of sales revenue. Using this ETS ratio, we can forecast depreciation expense of $2,722 million in 2015 ($69,084 million × 3.94%). Using this forecast, along with other items forecasted earlier, we can prepare the pro forma cash flow statement, which is presented in **Exhibit 5B.3**.

Additional Considerations

Pro forma financial statements are based on a set of assumptions about the future. Any decisions that are based on pro forma statements are only as good as the quality of these assumptions. Therefore it is important that we appreciate the effect that each assumption has on the forecasted amounts. To this end, it is often helpful to use **sensitivity analysis** to examine the effect of alternative assumptions on the pro forma statements. For example, we might prepare three different pro forma income statements, one using our "most-likely" assumption for the sales forecast, and one each for the "best-case" and "worst-case" scenarios. In some situations, a change in the sales forecast can have a dramatic effect on net income and cash flows. Sensitivity analysis helps to identify these effects before a decision is made so that costly mistakes can be avoided.

It is also important to remember that these statements are predictions about the future and, as such, are bound to be wrong. That is, we expect that there will be **forecast errors**—differences between the forecasted and the actual amounts. The goal of a good forecast is accuracy, which means that we want the forecast errors to be as small as possible. Generating pro forma statements using a computer is relatively easy and the efficiency and precision of spreadsheet software can provide a false sense of confidence in the numbers. Spreadsheets routinely calculate forecasted amounts to the "nth" decimal place whether or not such precision is justified. However, an amount forecasted to the nearest penny may not be useful if the forecast is off by millions of dollars. It is better to be imprecisely accurate than to be precisely inaccurate.

EXHIBIT 5B.3 PepsiCo Pro Forma Cash Flow Statement

PEPSICO, INC. 2015 Pro Forma Cash Flow Statement ($ millions)	Pro forma 2015
Operations:	
Net income	$6,814
Adjustments:	
Depreciation and amortization ($69,084 × 3.94%)	2,722
Minus change in accounts and notes receivable	(237)
Minus change in inventories	(111)
Minus change in prepaid expenses and other current assets	(75)
Minus change in other assets	(31)
Plus change in accounts payable and other current liabilities	469
Plus change in other liabilities	204
Plus change in income taxes payable and deferred income taxes	188
Cash flow from operations	9,943
Investing activities:	
Investment in property, plant, and equipment, net and amortizable intangible assets	(3,393)
Cash used for investing activities	(3,393)
Financing activities:	
Cash dividends paid	(3,877)
Share repurchases, net	(2,726)
Cash used for financing activities	(6,603)
Net decrease in cash (10,785 − 4,534 − 3,423)	(53)
Cash and cash equivalents, 2014	6,134
Cash and cash equivalents, 2015	$6,081

APPENDIX 5B REVIEW

Refer to the income statements and balance sheets of the Coca-Cola Company presented in Mid-Chapter Review 1.

Required

Make the following assumptions:

- 2015 sales revenue is $50,000 million.
- Operating expenses increase in 2015 in proportion to sales revenue.
- Operating assets and liabilities increase based on their 2014 relation to sales revenue. Classify "Goodwill and other intangible assets," "Other assets," and "Other liabilities" as operating.
- Assume that nonoperating revenues, expenses, assets and liabilities do not change from 2014 to 2015.
- Dividend payout is 60% of net income.
- Assume 20% income tax rate.

Prepare a pro forma income statement and balance sheet for 2015.

The solution to this review problem can be found on pages 267–268.

SUMMARY

Prepare and analyze common-size financial statements. (p. 221) LO1

- Vertical analysis restates items in the income statement as a percentage of sales revenue and items in the balance sheet as a percentage of total assets.
- Horizontal analysis examines the percentage change from one year to the next for specific items in the income statement and balance sheet.

LO2 Compute and interpret measures of return on investment, including return on equity (ROE), return on assets (ROA), and return on financial leverage (ROFL). (p. 224)

- ROE is the primary measure of company performance. It captures the return earned by shareholder investment in the firm.
- ROA measures the return earned on the firm's investment in assets. It is not affected by the way those assets are financed.
- ROFL is the difference between ROE and ROA and measures the effect that financial leverage has on ROE.

LO3 Disaggregate ROA into profitability (profit margin) and efficiency (asset turnover) components. (p. 227)

- ROA can be disaggregated as the product of profit margin (PM) and asset turnover (AT).
- PM can be analyzed further by examining the gross profit margin and expense-to-sales ratios.
- AT can be analyzed further by examining accounts receivable turnover (ART), inventory turnover (INVT), and property, plant, and equipment turnover (PPET).
- The trade-off between PM and AT is determined by the company's strategy and its competitive environment.

LO4 Compute and interpret measures of liquidity and solvency. (p. 232)

- The current ratio (CR) and quick ratio (QR) measure short-term liquidity by comparing liquid assets to short-term obligations.
- The debt-to-equity ratio (D/E) and times interest earned ratio (TIE) measure long-term solvency by comparing sources of financing and the level of earnings to the cost of debt (interest).

LO5 Appendix 5A: Measure and analyze the effect of operating activities on ROE. (p. 240)

- Net operating profit after taxes (NOPAT) measures the portion of income that results from a business' core operating activities.
- Return on net operating assets (RNOA), defined as NOPAT/average net operating assets, measures the return on a company's net investment in operating assets.

LO6 Appendix 5B: Prepare *pro forma* financial statements. (p. 242)

- *Pro forma* financial statements are statements prepared for future periods based on assumptions about the future activities of the business.
- *Pro forma* statements can be used to evaluate the effects of alternative actions or assumptions on the financial statements.

KEY RATIOS

RETURN MEASURES

$$\text{Return on equity (ROE)} = \frac{\text{Net income}}{\text{Average stockholders' equity}}$$

$$\text{Earnings without interest expense (EWI)} = \text{Net income} + [\text{Interest expense} \times (1 - \text{Statutory tax rate})]$$

$$\text{Return on assets (ROA)} = \frac{\text{Earnings without interest expense (EWI)}}{\text{Average total assets}}$$

$$\text{Return on financial leverage (ROFL)} = \text{ROE} - \text{ROA}$$

PROFITABILITY RATIOS

$$\text{Profit margin (PM)} = \frac{\text{Earnings without interest expense (EWI)}}{\text{Sales revenue}}$$

$$\text{Gross profit margin (GPM)} = \frac{\text{Sales revenue} - \text{Cost of goods sold}}{\text{Sales revenue}}$$

$$\text{Expense-to-sales (ETS)} = \frac{\text{Individual expense items}}{\text{Sales revenue}}$$

TURNOVER RATIOS

$$\text{Asset turnover (AT)} = \frac{\text{Sales revenue}}{\text{Average total assets}}$$

$$\text{Accounts receivable turnover (ART)} = \frac{\text{Sales revenue}}{\text{Average accounts receivable}}$$

$$\text{Inventory turnover (INVT)} = \frac{\text{Cost of goods sold}}{\text{Average inventory}}$$

$$\text{Property, plant, and equipment turnover (PPET)} = \frac{\text{Sales revenue}}{\text{Average PP \& E}}$$

LIQUIDITY RATIOS

$$\text{Current ratio (CR)} = \frac{\text{Current assets}}{\text{Current liabilities}}$$

$$\text{Quick ratio (QR)} = \frac{\text{Cash} + \text{Short-term securities} + \text{Accounts receivable}}{\text{Current liabilities}}$$

$$\text{Operating cash flow to current liabilities (OCFCL)} = \frac{\text{Operating cash flow}}{\text{Average current liabilities}}$$

SOLVENCY RATIOS

$$\text{Times interest earned (TIE)} = \frac{\text{Earnings before interest expense and taxes (EBIT)}}{\text{Interest expense}}$$

$$\text{Debt-to-equity (DE)} = \frac{\text{Total liabilities}}{\text{Total stockholders' equity}}$$

KEY TERMS

Accounts receivable turnover (ART) (p. 231)
Asset turnover (AT) (p. 228)
Capacity costs (p. 228)
Common-size financial statements (p. 221)
Covenants (p. 234)
Current ratio (p. 235)
Debt-to-equity ratio (p. 237)
Default risk (p. 234)
Dividend payout ratio (p. 244)
Earnings without interest expense (EWI) (p. 225)
Effective tax rate (p. 244)
Expense-to-sales (ETS) (p. 231)
Financial leverage (p. 226)
Financial statement analysis (p. 220)
Forecast error (p. 246)
Gross profit margin (GPM) (p. 230)
Horizontal analysis (p. 223)
Inventory turnover (INVT) (p. 231)
Liquidity (p. 235)
Liquidity analysis (p. 235)
Marginal tax rate (p. 241)
Net operating assets (NOA) (p. 241)
Net operating asset turnover (NOAT) (p. 242)
Net operating profit after taxes (NOPAT) (p. 241)
Net operating profit margin (NOPM) (p. 242)
Operating cash flow to current liabilities (OCFCL) (p. 236)
Profit margin (PM) (p. 227)
Pro forma financial statements (p. 243)
Property, plant, and equipment turnover (PPET) (p. 231)
Quick ratio (p. 235)
Return on assets (ROA) (p. 225)
Return on equity (ROE) (p. 225)
Return on financial leverage (ROFL) (p. 226)
Return on net operating assets (RNOA) (p. 240)
Sensitivity analysis (p. 246)
Solvency (p. 236)
Solvency analysis (p. 235)
Times interest earned (TIE) (p. 237)
Vertical analysis (p. 221)
Working capital (p. 235)

Assignments with the logo in the margin are available in myBusinessCourse. See the Preface of the book for details.

MULTIPLE CHOICE

Multiple Choice Answers
1. c 2. b 3. b 4. b 5. b

1. Which of the following ratios would not be affected by an increase in cost of goods sold?
a. ROA
b. INVT
c. Quick ratio
d. PM

2. A company has the following values: PM = 0.07; EWI = $1,885; Average total assets = $37,400. AT equals
a. 0.05
b. 0.72
c. 0.36
d. AT is not determinable because its sales are not reported.

3. A company's current ratio is 2 and its quick ratio is 1. What can be said about the sum of the company's cash + marketable securities + accounts receivable?
a. The sum exceeds the current liabilities.
b. The sum is equal to the sum of the current liabilities.
c. The sum is equal to 1⁄2 of the total current liabilities.
d. None of the above is correct.

4. A company's interest expense is $500,000 and its net income is $14 million. If the company's effective tax rate is 30%, what is the company's times interest earned (TIE) ratio?
a. 90
b. 41
c. 32
d. 16

5. If a company's ROFL is negative, which of the following is *not* true?
a. ROA > ROE
b. The DE ratio is negative.
c. ROA < net interest rate
d. The company likely has a low TIE ratio.

GUIDANCE ANSWERS . . . YOU MAKE THE CALL

You are the Entrepreneur Your company is performing substantially better than its competitors. Namely, your ROA of 16% is markedly superior to competitors' ROA of 10%. However, ROA disaggregation shows that this is mainly attributed to your AT of 0.89 versus competitors' AT of 0.59. Your PM of 18% is essentially identical to competitors' PM of 17%. Accordingly, you will want to maintain your AT as further improvements are probably difficult to achieve. Importantly, you are likely to achieve the greatest benefit with efforts at improving your PM of 18%, which is only marginally better than the industry norm of 17%.

Superscript $^{A(B)}$ denotes assignments based on Appendix 5A (5B).

QUESTIONS

Q5-1. Explain in general terms the concept of return on investment. Why is this concept important in the analysis of financial performance?

Q5-2. (a) Explain how an increase in financial leverage can increase a company's ROE. (b) Given the potentially positive relation between financial leverage and ROE, why don't we see companies with 100% financial leverage (entirely nonowner financed)?

Q5-3. Gross profit margin [(Sales revenue − Cost of goods sold)/Sales revenue] is an important determinant of profit margin. Identify two factors that can cause gross profit margin to decline. Is a reduction in the gross profit margin always bad news? Explain.

Q5-4. Explain how a reduction in operating expenses as a percentage of sales can produce a short-term gain at the cost of long-term performance.

Q5-5. Describe the concept of asset turnover. What does the concept mean and why is it so important to understanding and interpreting financial performance?

Q5-6. Explain what it means when a company's ROE exceeds its ROA.

Q5-7. What are common-size financial statements? What role do they play in financial statement analysis?

Q5-8. How does a firm go about increasing its AT ratio? What strategies are likely to be most effective?

Q5-9.[A] What is meant by the term "net" in net operating assets (NOA)?

Q5-10. Why is it important to disaggregate ROA into profit margin (PM) and asset turnover (AT)?

Q5-11. What insights do we gain from the graphical relation between profit margin and asset turnover?

Q5-12. Explain the concept of liquidity and why it is crucial to company survival.

Q5-13. Identify at least two factors that limit the usefulness of ratio analysis.

MINI EXERCISES

M5-14. Return on Investment, DuPont Analysis and Financial Leverage LO2

The following table presents selected 2016 financial information for Sunder Company.

SUNDER COMPANY
Selected 2016 Financial Data

Balance Sheet:	
Average total assets	$1,000,000
Average total liabilities	500,000
Average stockholders' equity	500,000
Income statement:	
Sales revenue	$1,000,000
Earnings before interest (net of tax)	20,000
Interest expense (net of tax)	15,000
Net income	5,000

a. Compute Sunder's ROE, ROA and ROFL for 2016.

b. Use the DuPont analysis described in the Business Insight on page 230 to disaggregate ROE.

c. How did the use of financial leverage affect Sunder's ROE in 2016? Explain.

M5-15. Common-Size Balance Sheets LO1

Target Corporation
NYSE :: TGT

Following is the balance sheet for **Target Corporation**. Prepare Target's common-size balance sheets as of January 31, 2015 and February 1, 2014.

($ millions)	January 31, 2015	February 1, 2014
Assets		
Cash and cash equivalents	$ 2,210	$ 670
Inventory	8,790	8,278
Other current assets	3,087	2,625
Total current assets	14,087	11,573
Property and equipment, net	25,958	26,412
Other noncurrent assets	1,359	6,568
Total assets	$41,404	$44,553
Liabilities and shareholders' investment		
Accounts payable	$ 7,759	$ 7,335
Accrued and other current liabilities	3,886	4,299
Current portion of long-term debt and notes payable	91	1,143
Total current liabilities	11,736	12,777
Long-term debt	12,705	11,429
Deferred income taxes	1,321	1,349
Other noncurrent liabilities	1,645	2,767
Total shareholders' investment	13,997	16,231
Total liabilities and shareholders' investment	$41,404	$44,553

LO1 **M5-16. Common-Size Income Statements**

Target Corporation
NYSE :: TGT

Following is the income statement for **Target Corporation**. Prepare Target's common-size income statement for the fiscal year ended January 31, 2015.

($ millions)	Fiscal year ended January 31, 2015
Sales revenue	$72,618
Cost of sales	51,278
Selling, general and administrative expenses	14,676
Depreciation and amortization	2,129
Earnings from continuing operations before interest and income taxes	4,535
Net interest expense	882
Earnings from continuing operations before income taxes	3,653
Provision for income taxes	1,204
Net earnings from continuing operations	2,449
Discontinued operations, net of tax	(4,085)
Net earnings (loss)	$ (1,636)

LO2, 3 **M5-17. Compute ROA, Profit Margin, and Asset Turnover**

Target Corporation
NYSE :: TGT

Refer to the financial information for **Target Corporation**, presented in M5-15 and M5-16.

a. Compute its return on assets (ROA) for the fiscal year ending January 31, 2015. Compute two ROA measures, one using net earnings from continuing operations and one using net earnings.

b. Disaggregate ROA into profit margin (PM) and asset turnover (AT). Confirm that ROA = PM × AT.

LO4 **M5-18. Analysis and Interpretation of Liquidity and Solvency**

Homework MBC

Target Corporation
NYSE :: TGT

Refer to the financial information of **Target Corporation** in M5-15 and M5-16 to answer the following.

a. Compute Target's current ratio and quick ratio for January 2015 and February 2014. Comment on any observed trends.

b. Compute Target's times interest earned for the year ended January 31, 2015, and its debt-to-equity ratios for January 2015 and February 2014. Comment on any trends observed.

c. Summarize your findings in a conclusion about the company's liquidity and solvency. Do you have any concerns about Target's ability to meet its debt obligations?

LO1 **M5-19. Common-Size Balance Sheets**

3M Company
NYSE :: MMM

Following is the balance sheet for **3M Company**. Prepare common-size balance sheets for 2014 and 2013.

3M COMPANY AND SUBSIDIARIES		
December 31 ($ millions, except per share amount)	2014	2013
Assets		
Cash, cash equivalents and marketable securities	$ 2,523	$ 3,337
Accounts receivable	4,238	4,253
Total inventories	3,706	3,864
Other current assets	1,298	1,279
Total current assets	11,765	12,733
Investments	930	1,575
Property, plant, and equipment—net	8,489	8,652
Goodwill	7,050	7,345
Intangible assets—net	1,435	1,688
Other assets	1,600	1,557
Total assets	$31,269	$33,550

continued

continued from previous page

	2014	2013
Liabilities and Stockholders' Equity		
Short-term borrowings and current portion of long-term debt	$ 106	$ 1,683
Accounts payable	1,807	1,799
Accrued payroll	732	708
Accrued income taxes	435	417
Other current liabilities	2,918	2,891
Total current liabilities	5,998	7,498
Long-term debt	6,731	4,326
Other liabilities	5,398	3,778
Total liabilities	18,127	15,602
Stockholders' equity—net	13,142	17,948
Total liabilities and stockholders' equity	$31,269	$33,550

M5-20. Common-Size Income Statements

Following is the income statement for **3M Company**. Prepare common-size income statements for 2014 and 2013.

LO1

3M Company
NYSE :: MMM

3M COMPANY AND SUBSIDIARIES		
Year ended December 31 ($ millions)	**2014**	**2013**
Net sales	$31,821	$30,871
Operating expenses		
Cost of sales	16,447	16,106
Selling, general and administrative expenses	6,469	6,384
Research, development and related expenses	1,770	1,715
Operating income	7,135	6,666
Interest expense and income		
Interest expense	142	145
Interest income	(33)	(41)
Net interest	109	104
Income before income taxes and minority interest	7,026	6,562
Provision for income taxes	2,028	1,841
Net income	$ 4,998	$ 4,721

M5-21. Compute ROA, Profit Margin, and Asset Turnover

Refer to the balance sheet and income statement information for **3M Company**, presented in M5-19 and M5-20.

LO2, 3

3M Company
NYSE :: MMM

a. Compute 3M's 2014 return on assets (ROA).

b. Disaggregate ROA into profit margin (PM) and asset turnover (AT). Confirm that ROA = PM × AT.

M5-22. Compute ROA, Profit Margin and Asset Turnover for Competitors

Selected balance sheet and income statement information from **Urban Outfitters, Inc.** and **TJX Companies**, clothing retailers in the high-end and value-priced segments, respectively, follows.

LO2, 3

Urban Outfitters, Inc.
NASDAQ :: URBN
TJX Companies
NYSE :: TJX

Company ($ millions)	2014 Sales	2014 Earnings Without Interest Expense (EWI)	2014 Total Assets	2013 Total Assets
Urban Outfitters	$ 3,323	$ 232.4	$ 1,889	$ 2,221
TJX Companies	29,078	2,241.0	11,128	10,201

a. Compute the 2014 return on assets (ROA) for both companies.

b. Disaggregate ROA into profit margin (PM) and asset turnover (AT) for each company. Confirm that ROA = PM × AT.

c. Discuss differences observed with respect to PM and AT and interpret these differences in light of each company's business model.

LO4

Verizon Communications, Inc.
NYSE :: VZ

M5-23. Compute and Interpret Liquidity and Solvency Ratios

Selected balance sheet and income statement information from **Verizon Communications, Inc.**, follows.

($ millions)	2014	2013
Current assets	$ 29,623	$ 70,994
Current liabilities	28,064	27,050
Total liabilities	219,032	178,682
Equity	13,676	95,416
Earnings before interest and taxes	20,185	31,944
Interest expense	4,915	2,667
Net cash flow from operating activities	30,631	38,818

a. Compute the current ratio for each year and discuss any change in liquidity. How does Verizon's current ratio compare to the median for the telecommunications industry in **Exhibit 5.13**? What additional information about the numbers used to calculate this ratio might be useful in helping us assess liquidity? Explain.

b. Compute times interest earned, the debt-to-equity, and the operating cash flow to current liabilities ratios for each year and discuss any trends for each. (In 2012, current liabilities totaled $26,956 million.) Compare Verizon's ratios to those that are typical for its industry (refer to **Exhibit 5.13**). Do you have any concerns about the extent of Verizon's financial leverage and the company's ability to meet interest obligations? Explain.

c. Verizon's capital expenditures are expected to remain high as it seeks to respond to competitive pressures to upgrade the quality of its communication infrastructure. Assess Verizon's liquidity and solvency in light of this strategic direction.

LO2, 3

The Procter & Gamble Company
NYSE :: PG
CVS Health Corporation
NYSE :: CVS
Valero Energy Coporation
NYSE :: VLO

M5-24. Computing Turnover Ratios for Companies in Different Industries

Selected data from recent financial statements of **The Procter & Gamble Company**, **CVS Health Corporation**, and **Valero Energy Corporation** are presented below:

($ millions)	Procter & Gamble	CVS Health	Valero Energy
Sales	$ 83,062	$139,367	$130,844
Cost of sales	42,460	114,000	118,141
Average receivables	6,447	9,208	7,315
Average inventories	6,834	11,488	6,191
Average PP&E	21,985	8,729	34,933
Average total assets	141,765	72,889	46,405

a. Compute the asset turnover (AT) ratio for each company.

b. Compute the accounts receivable turnover (ART), inventory turnover (INVT), and PP&E turnover (PPET) for each company.

c. Discuss any differences across these three companies in the turnover ratios computed in *a* and *b*.

EXERCISES

LO2, 3

McDonald's Corporation
NYSE :: MCD
Yum! Brands, Inc.
NYSE :: YUM

E5-25. Compute and Interpret ROA, Profit Margin, and Asset Turnover of Competitors

Selected balance sheet and income statement information for **McDonald's Corporation** and **Yum! Brands, Inc.**, follows.

($ millions)	Sales Revenue	Interest Expense	Net Income	Average Total Assets
McDonald's	$27,441	$571	$4,758	$35,454
Yum! Brands	13,279	130	1,021	8,520

a. Compute the return on assets (ROA) for each company.

b. Disaggregate ROA into profit margin (PM) and asset turnover (AT) for each company.

c. Discuss any differences in these ratios for each company. Your interpretation should reflect the distinct business strategies of each company.

E5-26. Compute ROA, ROE and ROFL and Interpret the Effects of Leverage

LO2

Basic income statement and balance sheet information is given below for six different cases. For each case, the assets are financed with a mix of non-interest-bearing liabilities, 10% interest-bearing liability and stockholders' equity. In all cases, the income tax rate is 40%.

Case	A	B	C	D	E	F
Average assets	1,000	1,000	1,000	1,000	1,000	1,000
Non-interest-bearing liabilities	0	0	0	0	200	200
Interest-bearing liabilities	0	250	500	500	0	300
Average shareholders' equity	1,000	750	500	500	800	500
Earnings before interest and taxes (EBIT)	120	120	120	80	100	80

a. For each case, calculate the return on equity (ROE), return on assets (ROA) and return on financial leverage (ROFL).

b. Consider cases A, B and C. How does increasing leverage affect the three ratios? Why does the ROE grow from case A to case C?

c. Consider cases C and D. When does leverage work in favor of shareholders? Does that hold for case E?

d. Case F has two types of liabilities. How does ROA compare to the rate on interest-bearing liabilities? Does leverage work in favor of the shareholders? Why?

E5-27. Compute, Disaggregate, and Interpret Competitors' Rates of Return

LO2, 3

CVS Health Corporation
NYSE :: CVS
Walgreen Co.
NYSE :: WAG

Selected balance sheet and income statement information for the drug retailers **CVS Health Corporation** and **Walgreen Co.** follows.

($ millions)	CVS Health	Walgreen
Sales revenue—2014	$139,367	$76,392
Interest expense—2014	600	156
Net income—2014	4,644	2,031
Total assets—2014	74,252	37,182
Total assets—2013	71,526	35,481
Stockholders' equity—2014	37,963	20,561
Stockholders' equity—2013	37,938	19,454

a. Compute the 2014 return on assets (ROA) for each company.

b. Disaggregate ROA into profit margin (PM) and asset turnover (AT) for each company.

c. Compute the 2014 return on equity (ROE) and return on financial leverage (ROFL) for each company.

d. Discuss any differences in these ratios for each company. Identify the factor(s) that drives the differences in ROA observed from your analyses in parts *a* through *c*.

E5-28. Compute, Disaggregate, and Interpret ROE

LO2, 3

Intel Corporation
NASDAQ :: INTC

Selected fiscal year balance sheet and income statement information for the computer chip maker, **Intel Corporation**, follows ($ millions).

Balance sheet information ($ millions)	2014	2013	2012
Total assets	$91,956	$92,358	$84,351
Total shareholders' equity	55,865	58,256	51,203
Income statement information ($ millions)	**2014**	**2013**	**2012**
Sales revenue	$55,870	$52,708	$53,341
Interest expense	192	244	90
Net income	11,704	9,620	11,005

a. Calculate Intel's return on equity (ROE) for fiscal years 2014 and 2013.

b. Calculate Intel's return on assets (ROA) and return on financial leverage (ROFL) for each year. Is financial leverage working to the advantage of Intel's shareholders?

c. Use the DuPont formulation in the Business Insight on page 230 to analyze the variations in Intel's ROE over this period. How does this analysis differ from your answers to *a* and *b* above?

LO2, 3 Homework MBC

E5-29. Return on Investment, Financial Leverage, and DuPont Analysis

The following tables provide information from the recent annual reports of HD Rinker, AG.

Balance sheets ($ millions)	2016	2015	2014	2013
Total assets	€6,108	€6,451	€7,173	€6,972
Total liabilities	5,970	4,974	4,989	5,097
Total shareholders' equity	138	1,477	2,184	1,875

Income statements ($ millions) 52 weeks ended	2016	2015	2014
Sales revenue	€10,364	€9,613	€8,632
Earnings before interest and income taxes	1,473	1,459	887
Interest expense	246	208	237
Earnings before income taxes	1,227	1,251	650
Income tax expense	377	446	202
Net earnings	€ 850	€ 805	€ 448

a. Calculate HD Rinker's return on equity (ROE) for fiscal years 2016, 2015, and 2014.

b. Calculate HD Rinker's return on assets (ROA) and return on financial leverage (ROFL) for each year. Is financial leverage working to the advantage of HD Rinker's shareholders?

c. Use the DuPont formulation in the Business Insight on page 230 to analyze the variations in HD Rinker's ROE over this period. How does this analysis differ from your answers to *a* and *b* above?

LO2, 3 

Staples, Inc.
NASDAQ :: SPLS

E5-30. Compute, Disaggregate and Interpret ROE and ROA

Selected balance sheet and income statement information from **Staples, Inc.**, follows ($ millions).

Sales	Interest Expense	Net Income	Total Assets		Stockholders' Equity	
2014	2014	2014	2014	2013	2014	2013
$22,492	$49	$135	$10,314	$11,175	$5,313	$6,141

a. Compute the 2014 return on equity (ROE), return on assets (ROA), and return on financial leverage (ROFL).

b. Disaggregate ROA into profit margin (PM) and asset turnover (AT).

c. What inferences do we draw from PM compared to AT? How do these ratios compare to industry medians?

LO2, 3 

Intuit Inc.
NASDAQ :: INTU

E5-31. Compute, Disaggregate and Interpret ROE and ROA

Selected balance sheet and income statement information from the software company, **Intuit Inc.**, follows ($ millions).

Sales	Interest Expense	Net Income	Total Assets		Stockholders' Equity	
2014	2014	2014	2014	2013	2014	2013
$4,506	$31	$907	$5,201	$5,486	$3,078	$3,531

a. Compute the 2014 return on equity (ROE), return on assets (ROA), and return on financial leverage (ROFL).

b. Disaggregate the ROA from part *a* into profit margin (PM) and asset turnover (AT).

c. What can we learn by comparing PM to AT? What explanation can we offer for the relation between ROE and ROA observed and for Intuit's use of financial leverage?

LO4 

Comcast Corporation
NASDAQ :: CMCSA

E5-32. Compute and Interpret Liquidity and Solvency Ratios

Selected balance sheet and income statement information from **Comcast Corporation** for 2012 through 2014 follows ($ millions).

	Total Current Assets	Total Current Liabilities	Pretax Income	Interest Expense	Total Assets	Stockholders' Equity
2012	$19,991	$16,714	$11,609	$2,521	$164,971	$49,796
2013	14,075	18,912	11,115	2,574	158,813	51,058
2014	13,531	17,410	12,465	2,617	159,339	53,068

a. Compute the current ratio for each year and discuss any trend in liquidity. Do you believe the company is sufficiently liquid? Explain. What additional information about the accounting numbers comprising this ratio might be useful in helping you assess liquidity? Explain.

b. Compute times interest earned and the debt-to-equity ratio for each year and discuss any trends for each.

c. How do Comcast's ratios compare to the industry medians for the telecommunications industry in **Exhibit 5.13**?

d. What is your overall assessment of the company's liquidity and solvency from the analyses above? Explain.

E5-33. Compute and Interpret Liquidity and Solvency Ratios

LO4

Siemens AG
NYSE :: SI

Selected balance sheet and income statement information from **Siemens, AG**, for 2012 through 2014 follows (€ millions).

	Total Current Assets	Total Current Liabilities	Cash Flow from Operations	Pretax Income	Interest Expense	Total Liabilities	Stockholders' Equity
2012	€52,128	€42,627	€6,923	€6,636	€760	€77,396	€30,855
2013	46,937	37,868	7,186	5,813	784	73,825	28,111
2014	48,076	36,598	7,230	7,427	764	73,925	30,954

a. Compute the current ratio for each year and discuss any trend in liquidity. Also compute the operating cash flow to current liabilities (OCFCL) ratio for each year. (In 2011, current liabilities totaled €43,560 million.) Do you believe the company is sufficiently liquid? Explain. What additional information about the accounting numbers comprising this ratio might be useful in helping you assess liquidity? Explain.

b. Compute times interest earned and the debt-to-equity ratio for each year and discuss any trends for each.

c. What is your overall assessment of the company's liquidity and solvency from the analyses in *a* and *b*? Explain.

E5-34. Compute, Disaggregate and Interpret ROE and ROA

LO2, 3

The Gap, Inc.
NYSE :: GPS

Income statements for **The Gap, Inc.**, follow, along with selected balance sheet information ($ millions).

THE GAP, INC.
Consolidated Statement of Earnings

Fiscal year ended	Jan. 31, 2015	Feb. 1, 2014
Net sales.	$16,435	$16,148
Cost of goods sold and occupancy expenses.	10,146	9,855
Gross profit.	6,289	6,293
Operating expenses	4,206	4,144
Operating income.	2,083	2,149
Interest expense.	75	61
Interest income.	(5)	(5)
Income before income taxes	2,013	2,093
Income taxes	751	813
Net earnings.	$1,262	$1,280

THE GAP, INC.
Selected Balance Sheet Data

	Jan. 31, 2015	Feb. 1, 2014
Merchandise inventories	$1,889	$1,928
Total assets.	7,690	7,849
Total stockholders' equity	2,983	3,062

a. Compute the return on equity (ROE), return on assets (ROA), and return on financial leverage (ROFL) for the fiscal year ended January 31, 2015.

b. Disaggregate ROA into profit margin (PM) and asset turnover (AT).
c. Compute the gross profit margin (GPM) and inventory turnover (INVT) ratios for the fiscal year ended January 31, 2015.
d. Assess the Gap's performance. What are the most important drivers of the Gap's success?

LO1, 6 **E5-35.[B] Common-Size and Pro Forma Income Statements**

The Gap, Inc.
NYSE :: GPS

Refer to the income statements for **The Gap, Inc.**, presented in E5-34.

a. Prepare common-size income statements for fiscal years 2014 (ending January 31, 2015) and 2013 (ending February 1, 2014).
b. Prepare a pro forma income statement for the fiscal year 2015 (ending January 30, 2016), based on the following assumptions:
- Net sales total $15,000 million.
- Cost of goods sold and occupancy expenses are 64% of sales.
- Operating expenses total 26% of sales.
- Interest income and interest expense are unchanged from the 2014 amounts.
- The Gap's effective tax rate is 39%.

c. Given the Gap's business strategy, what are the factors that ultimately determine the accuracy of the pro forma statement prepared in *b*?

PROBLEMS

LO2, 3 **P5-36. Analysis and Interpretation of Return on Investment for Competitors**

Nike, Inc.
NYSE :: NKE
Adidas Group, AG
OTC :: ADDDF

Balance sheets and income statements for **Nike, Inc.**, and **Adidas Group** follow. Refer to these financial statements to answer the requirements.

	NIKE, INC. Balance Sheets ($ millions) May 31,		ADIDAS GROUP, AG Balance Sheets (€ millions) December 31,	
	2014	2013	2014	2013
Assets				
Cash and cash equivalents	$ 2,220	$ 3,337	€ 1,683	€ 1,587
Short-term investments	2,922	2,628	403	224
Accounts receivable	3,434	3,117	1,946	1,809
Inventories	3,947	3,484	2,526	2,634
Other current assets	1,173	1,064	789	603
Total current assets	13,696	13,630	7,347	6,857
Property, plant, and equipment	2,834	2,452	1,454	1,238
Intangible assets and goodwill	413	420	2,763	2,787
Long-term investments	—	—	171	150
Other noncurrent assets	1,651	1,043	682	567
Total assets	$18,594	$17,545	€12,417	€11,599
Liabilities and shareholders' equity				
Short-term debt	$ 174	$ 155	€ 288	€ 681
Accounts payable	1,930	1,669	1,652	1,825
Accrued expenses	2,491	2,036	1,249	1,147
Income taxes payable	432	84	294	240
Other current liabilities	—	18	894	839
Total current liabilities	5,027	3,962	4,378	4,732
Long-term debt	1,199	1,210	1,584	653
Other noncurrent liabilities	1,544	1,292	837	733
Total liabilities	7,770	6,464	6,799	6,118
Shareholders' equity	10,824	11,081	5,618	5,481
Total liabilities and shareholders' equity	$18,594	$17,545	€12,417	€11,599

	NIKE, INC. Income Sheets ($ millions) Year ended May 31,		ADIDAS GROUP, AG Income Sheets (€ millions) Year ended December 31,	
	2014	2013	2014	2013
Net sales	$27,799	$25,313	€14,534	€14,203
Cost of sales	15,353	14,279	7,610	7,202
Gross profit	12,446	11,034	6,924	7,001
Operating expenses, net	8,766	7,796	6,041	5,820
Operating profit	3,680	3,238	883	1,181
Interest and other income (expense)	(83)	38	19	26
Interest expense	53	20	67	94
Income before income taxes	3,544	3,256	835	1,113
Income taxes	851	805	271	340
Income from continuing operations	2,693	2,451	564	773
Gain (loss) from discontinued operations	—	21	(68)	17
Net income	$ 2,693	$ 2,472	€ 496	€ 790

REQUIRED

a. Compute return on equity (ROE), return on assets (ROA), and return on financial leverage (ROFL) for Nike and Adidas in 2014. The corporate tax rate in Germany, where Adidas is headquartered, is about 30%.

b. Disaggregate the ROA's computed into profit margin (PM) and asset turnover (AT) components. Which of these factors drives ROA for each company?

c. Compute the gross profit margin (GPM) and operating expense-to-sales ratios for each company. How do these companies' profitability measures compare?

d. Compute the accounts receivable turnover (ART), inventory turnover (INVT), and property, plant, and equipment turnover (PPET) for each company. How do these companies' turnover measures compare?

e. Nike's fiscal year ends on May 31, 2014, while Adidas's fiscal year ends on December 31, 2014 (a difference of seven months). How does this difference affect your analysis of ROE and ROA for these two companies?

f. Nike's financial statements are prepared in accordance with U.S. GAAP, while Adidas, a German company, follows IFRS rules. How does this difference in financial reporting standards affect your comparison of these companies' financial statements?

P5-37. Analysis and Interpretation of Liquidity and Solvency for Competitors

LO4

Nike, Inc.
NYSE :: NKE
Adidas Group, AG
OTC :: ADDDF

Refer to the financial statements of **Nike** and **Adidas** presented in P5-36.

REQUIRED

a. Compute each company's current ratio and quick ratio for each year. Comment on any changes that you observe.

b. Compute each company's times interest earned ratio and debt-to-equity ratio for each year. Comment on any observed changes.

c. Compare these two companies on the basis of liquidity and solvency. Do you have any concerns about either company's ability to meet its debt obligations?

P5-38. Analysis and Interpretation of Return on Investment for Competitors

LO2, 3

The Home Depot, Inc.
NYSE :: HD
Lowe's Companies, Inc.
NYSE :: LOW

Balance sheets and income statements for **The Home Depot, Inc.**, and **Lowe's Companies, Inc.**, follow. Refer to these financial statements to answer the requirements.

	HOME DEPOT, INC. Balance Sheets		LOWE'S COMPANIES Balance Sheets	
($ millions)	2014	2013	2014	2013
Assets				
Cash and cash equivalents	$ 1,723	$ 1,929	$ 466	$ 391
Short-term investments	—	—	125	185
Receivables, net	1,484	1,398		
Merchandise inventories	11,079	11,057	8,911	9,127
Other current assets	1,016	895	578	593
Total current assets	15,302	15,279	10,080	10,296
Property and equipment, net	22,720	23,348	20,034	20,834
Goodwill	1,353	1,289	—	—
Long-term investments	—	—	354	279
Other assets	571	602	1,359	1,323
Total assets	$39,946	$40,518	$31,827	$32,732
Liabilities and shareholders' equity				
Short-term debt and current maturities of long-term debt	$ 328	$ 33	$ 552	$ 435
Accounts payable	5,807	5,797	5,124	5,008
Accrued compensation and related expenses	1,391	1,428	773	785
Deferred revenue	1,468	1,337	979	892
Income taxes payable	35	12	—	—
Other current liabilities	2,240	2,142	1,920	1,756
Total current liabilities	11,269	10,749	9,348	8,876
Long-term debt, excluding current maturities	16,869	14,691	10,815	10,086
Deferred income taxes	642	514	97	291
Other long-term liabilities	1,844	2,042	1,599	1,626
Total liabilities	30,624	27,996	21,859	20,879
Total stockholders' equity	9,322	12,522	9,968	11,853
Total liabilities and shareholders' equity	$39,946	$40,518	$31,827	$32,732

	HOME DEPOT, INC. Income Statements		LOWE'S COMPANIES Income Statements	
($ millions)	2014	2013	2014	2013
Net sales	$83,176	$78,812	$56,223	$53,417
Cost of sales	54,222	51,422	36,665	34,941
Gross profit	28,954	27,390	19,558	18,476
Selling, general and administrative	16,834	16,597	13,281	12,865
Depreciation and amortization	1,651	1,627	1,485	1,462
Operating income	10,469	9,166	4,792	4,149
Investment and other income	337	12	6	4
Interest expense	830	711	522	480
Earnings before income taxes	9,976	8,467	4,276	3,673
Provision for income taxes	3,631	3,082	1,578	1,387
Net earnings	$ 6,345	$ 5,385	$ 2,698	$ 2,286

REQUIRED

a. Compute return on equity (ROE), return on assets (ROA), and return on financial leverage (ROFL) for each company in 2014.

b. Disaggregate the ROA's computed into profit margin (PM) and asset turnover (AT) components. Which of these factors drives ROA for each company?

c. Compute the gross profit margin (GPM) and operating expense-to-sales ratios for each company. How do these companies' profitability measures compare?

d. Compute the accounts receivable turnover (ART), inventory turnover (INVT), and property, plant, and equipment turnover (PPET) for each company. How do these companies' turnover measures compare?

e. Compare and evaluate these competitors' performance in 2014.

P5-39. Analysis and Interpretation of Liquidity and Solvency for Competitors

Refer to the financial statements of **Home Depot** and **Lowe's** presented in P5-38.

LO4
Home Depot, Inc.
NYSE :: HD
Lowe's Companies, Inc.
NYSE :: LOW

REQUIRED

a. Compute each company's current ratio and quick ratio for each year. Comment on any changes that you observe.

b. Compute each company's times interest earned ratio and debt-to-equity ratio for each year. Comment on any observed changes.

c. Compare these two companies on the basis of liquidity and solvency. Do you have any concerns about either company's ability to meet its debt obligations?

P5-40.[A] Analysis of the Effect of Operations on ROE

Refer to the financial statements of **Home Depot** and **Lowe's** presented in P5-38.

LO5
Home Depot, Inc.
NYSE :: HD
Lowe's Companies, Inc.
NYSE :: LOW

REQUIRED

a. Compute each company's net operating profit after taxes (NOPAT) for 2014 and net operating assets (NOA) for 2014 and 2013. Classify other assets and other liabilities (both current and noncurrent) as operating assets and liabilities in the balance sheet.

b. Compute each company's return on net operating assets (RNOA) for 2014.

c. Compute the 2014 net operating profit margin (NOPM) and net operating asset turnover (NOAT) for each company.

d. Compare operating returns for these two companies. How does RNOA compare to ROA? What insights are gained by focusing on operating returns?

P5-41. Analysis and Interpretation of Profitability

Balance sheets and income statements for **United Parcel Service, Inc., (UPS)** follow. Refer to these financial statements to answer the following requirements.

LO2, 3
United Parcel Service, Inc.
NYSE :: UPS

UNITED PARCEL SERVICE, INC.
Income Statement

Years Ended December 31 ($ millions)	2014	2013	2012
Revenue	$58,232	$55,438	$54,127
Compensation and benefits	32,045	28,557	33,102
Other operating expenses	21,219	19,847	19,682
Operating profit	4,968	7,034	1,343
Investment income	22	20	24
Interest expense	353	380	393
Income before income taxes	4,637	6,674	974
Income tax expense	1,605	2,302	167
Net income	$ 3,032	$ 4,372	$ 807

UNITED PARCEL SERVICE, INC.
Balance Sheet

December 31 ($ millions)	2014	2013	2012
Assets			
Cash and cash equivalents	$ 2,291	$ 4,665	$ 7,327
Marketable securities	992	580	597
Accounts receivable, net	6,661	6,502	6,111
Deferred income tax assets	590	684	583
Other current assets	1,274	956	973
Total current assets	11,808	13,387	15,591
Property, plant & equipment, net	18,281	17,961	17,894
Goodwill and other intangible assets, net	3,031	2,965	2,776
Noncurrent investments and restricted cash	489	444	307
Other noncurrent assets	1,862	1,455	2,295
Total assets	$35,471	$36,212	$38,863
Liabilities and shareowners' equity			
Current maturities of long-term debt and commercial paper	$ 923	$ 48	$ 1,781
Accounts payable	2,754	2,478	2,278
Accrued wages and withholdings	2,373	2,325	1,927
Self-insurance reserves, current portion	656	719	763
Other current liabilities	1,933	1,561	1,641
Total current liabilities	8,639	7,131	8,390
Long-term debt	9,864	10,824	11,089
Pension and postretirement benefit obligations	11,452	7,051	11,068
Deferred income tax liabilities	83	1,244	48
Self-insurance reserves	1,916	2,059	1,980
Other noncurrent liabilities	1,359	1,415	1,555
Total liabilities	33,313	29,724	34,130
Total shareowners' equity	2,158	6,488	4,733
Total liabilities and shareowners' equity	$35,471	$36,212	$38,863

REQUIRED

a. Compute ROA and disaggregate it into profit margin (PM) and asset turnover (AT) for 2014 and 2013. Comment on the drivers of the ROA.

b. Compute any expense to sales (ETS) ratios that you think might help explain UPS's profitability.

c. Compute return on equity (ROE) for 2014 and 2013.

d. Comment on the difference between ROE and ROA. What does this relation suggest about UPS's use of debt?

LO4
United Parcel Service
NYSE :: UPS

P5-42. Analysis and Interpretation of Liquidity and Solvency

Refer to the financial information of **United Parcel Service** in P5-41 to answer the following requirements.

REQUIRED

a. Compute its current ratio and quick ratio for 2014 and 2013. Comment on any observed trends.

b. Compute its times interest earned and its debt-to-equity ratios for 2014 and 2013. Comment on any trends observed.

c. Summarize your findings in a conclusion about the company's liquidity and solvency. Do you have any concerns about its ability to meet its debt obligations?

LO5
United Parcel Service
NYSE :: UPS

P5-43.[A] Computing and Analyzing Operating Returns

Refer to the financial statements of **United Parcel Service** in P5-41 to answer the following requirements.

REQUIRED

a. Compute net operating profit after taxes (NOPAT) for 2014 and net operating assets (NOA) for 2013 and 2014.

b. Compute the return on net operating assets (RNOA) for 2014. What percentage of UPS's ROE is generated by operations?

c. Decompose RNOA by computing net operating profit margin (NOPM) and net operating asset turnover (NOAT) for 2014.

d. What can be inferred about UPS from these ratios?

P5-44.[B] Preparing Pro Forma Financial Statements

LO6
United Parcel Service
NYSE :: UPS

Refer to the financial statements of **United Parcel Service** in P5-41 to answer the following requirements. The following assumptions should be useful:

- UPS's sales forecast for 2015 is $60,000 million.
- Operating expenses and operating profits increase in proportion to sales.
- Investment income and interest expense are unchanged in 2015.
- Income taxes are 35% of pretax earnings.
- Marketable securities and noncurrent investments are unchanged in 2015; all other assets (except cash) increase in proportion to sales.
- Long-term debt and current maturities of long-term debt are unchanged in 2015; all other liabilities increase in proportion to sales.
- Dividends are 50% of net income. Income and dividends are the only changes to stockholders' equity in 2015.

REQUIRED

a. Prepare a pro forma income statement for 2015.

b. Prepare a pro forma balance sheet for 2015.

P5-45. Comparing Profitability Ratios for Competitors

LO3

Abbott Laboratories
NYSE :: ABT
Bristol-Myers Squibb Company
NYSE :: BMY
Johnson & Johnson
NYSE :: JNJ
GlaxoSmithKline plc (ADR)
NYSE :: GSK
Pfizer Inc.
NYSE :: PFE

Selected income statement data for **Abbott Laboratories**, **Bristol-Myers Squibb Company**, **Johnson & Johnson**, **GlaxoSmithKline plc**, and **Pfizer, Inc.** is presented in the following table:

($ millions)	Abbott Laboratories	Bristol-Myers Squibb	Johnson & Johnson	Glaxo Smith Kline plc	Pfizer
Sales revenue	$20,247	$11,660	$74,331	$35,872	$49,605
Cost of sales	9,218	3,932	22,746	11,418	9,577
SG&A expense	6,530	4,822	21,954	13,466	14,097
R&D expense	1,345	4,534	8,494	5,379	8,393
Interest expense	150	203	533	1,134	1,360
Net income	2,284	2,029	16,323	4,297	9,168

REQUIRED

a. Compute the profit margin (PM) and gross profit margin (GPM) ratios for each company. (As a British company, GlaxoSmithKline plc has a statutory tax rate of 26.5% in 2014.)

b. Compute the research and development (R&D) expense to sales ratio and the selling, general and administrative (SG&A) expense to sales ratio for each company.

c. Compare the relative profitability of these pharmaceutical companies.

P5-46. Comparing Profitability and Turnover Ratios for Retail Companies

LO3

Best Buy Co., Inc.
NYSE :: BBY
The Kroger Co.
NYSE :: KR
Nordstrom, Inc.
NYSE :: JWN
Staples, Inc.
NASDAQ :: SPLS
Walgreen Co.
NYSE :: WAG

Selected financial statement data for **Best Buy Co., Inc.**, **The Kroger Co.**, **Nordstrom, Inc.**, **Staples, Inc.**, and **Walgreen Co.** is presented in the following table:

($ millions)	Best Buy	Kroger	Nordstrom	Staples	Walgreen
Sales revenue	$40,339	$108,465	$13,506	$22,492	$76,392
Cost of sales	31,292	85,512	8,406	16,691	54,823
Interest expense	90	488	138	49	156
Net income	1,233	1,728	720	135	1,932
Average receivables	1,294	1,191	2,489	1,883	2,925
Average inventories	5,275	5,670	1,632	2,236	6,464
Average PP&E	2,447	17,403	3,145	1,788	12,198
Average total assets	14,635	29,919	8,910	10,744	36,332

REQUIRED

a. Compute return on assets (ROA) profit margin (PM) and asset turnover (AT) for each company. Discuss the relative importance of PM and AT for each company.

b. Compute accounts receivable turnover (ART), inventory turnover (INVT) and property, plant, and equipment turnover (PPET) for each company. Discuss any difference that you observe.

c. Compute the gross profit margin (GPM) for each company. How does the GPM differ across companies? Does this difference seem to correlate with differences in ART or INVT? Explain.

CASES AND PROJECTS

LO3 **C5-47. Management Application: Gross Profit and Strategic Management**

One way to increase overall profitability is to increase gross profit. This can be accomplished by raising prices and/or by reducing manufacturing costs.

REQUIRED

a. Will raising prices and/or reducing manufacturing costs unambiguously increase gross profit? Explain.

b. What strategy might you develop as a manager to (i) yield a price increase for your product, or (ii) reduce product manufacturing cost?

LO3 **C5-48. Management Application: Asset Turnover and Strategic Management**

Increasing net operating asset turnover requires some combination of increasing sales and/or decreasing net operating assets. For the latter, many companies consider ways to reduce their investment in working capital (current assets less current liabilities). This can be accomplished by reducing the level of accounts receivable and inventories, or by increasing the level of accounts payable.

REQUIRED

a. Develop a list of suggested actions to achieve all three of these objectives as manager.

b. Examine the implications of each. That is, describe the marketing implications of reducing receivables and inventories, and the supplier implications of delaying payment. How can a company achieve working capital reduction without negatively impacting its performance?

LO2, 3, 4 **C5-49. Ethics and Governance: Earnings Management**

Companies are aware that analysts focus on profitability in evaluating financial performance. Managers have historically utilized a number of methods to improve reported profitability that are cosmetic in nature and do not affect "real" operating performance. These are typically subsumed under the general heading of "earnings management." Justification for such actions typically includes the following arguments:

- Increasing stock price by managing earnings benefits shareholders; thus, no one is hurt by these actions.
- Earnings management is a temporary fix; such actions will be curtailed once "real" profitability improves, as managers expect.

REQUIRED

a. Identify the affected parties in any scheme to manage profits to prop up stock price.

b. Do the ends (of earnings management) justify the means? Explain.

c. To what extent are the objectives of managers different from those of shareholders?

d. What governance structure can you envision that might prohibit earnings management?

SOLUTIONS TO REVIEW PROBLEMS

Mid-Chapter Review 1

SOLUTION

THE COCA-COLA COMPANY AND SUBSIDIARIES
Consolidated Statements of Income
($ millions)

Year ended December 31	2014	2013
Net operating revenues	100.0%	100.0%
Cost of goods sold	38.9%	39.3%
Gross profit	61.1%	60.7%
Selling, general and administrative expenses	37.4%	36.9%
Other operating charges	2.6%	1.9%
Operating income	21.1%	21.8%
Interest income	1.3%	1.1%
Interest expense	−1.1%	−1.0%
Other income (loss)—net	−1.1%	2.5%
Income before income taxes	20.3%	24.5%
Income taxes	4.8%	6.1%
Net income	15.5%	18.4%

THE COCA-COLA COMPANY AND SUBSIDIARIES
Common Size Balance Sheets

December 31,	2014	2013
Assets		
Cash and cash equivalents	9.7%	11.6%
Short-term investments and marketable securities	13.8%	10.9%
Trade accounts receivable	4.9%	5.4%
Inventories	3.4%	3.6%
Prepaid expenses and other current assets	4.1%	3.2%
Total current assets	35.8%	34.8%
Investments	14.8%	12.8%
Property, plant, and equipment, net	15.9%	16.6%
Goodwill and other intangible assets	28.7%	30.7%
Other assets	4.8%	5.2%
Total assets	100.0%	100.0%
Liabilities and Stockholders' Equity		
Accounts payable and accrued expenses	10.0%	10.6%
Loans and notes payable	20.9%	18.8%
Current maturities of long-term debt	3.9%	1.1%
Accrued income taxes	0.4%	0.3%
Total current liabilities	35.2%	30.9%
Long-term debt	20.7%	21.3%
Other liabilities	4.8%	3.9%
Deferred income taxes	6.1%	6.8%
Total liabilities	66.8%	62.9%
Total equity	33.2%	37.1%
Total liabilities and equity	100.0%	100.0%

Mid-Chapter Review 2

SOLUTION ($ MILLIONS)

$$\text{ROE} = \frac{\$7{,}124}{(\$33{,}440 + \$30{,}561)/2} = 22.26\%$$

$$\text{ROA} = \frac{\$7{,}124 + \$483 \times (1 - 0.35)}{(\$90{,}055 + \$92{,}023)/2} = 8.17\%$$

$$\text{ROFL} = 22.26\% - 8.12\% = 14.14\%$$

Mid-Chapter Review 3

SOLUTION ($ MILLIONS)

$$\text{PM} = \frac{\$7{,}124 + \$483 \times (1 - 0.35)}{\$45{,}998} = 16.17\%$$

$$\text{AT} = \frac{\$45{,}998}{(\$90{,}055 + \$92{,}023)/2} = 0.505 \text{ times}$$

$$16.17\% \times 0.505 = 8.17\%$$

$$\text{GPM} = \frac{\$45{,}998 - \$17{,}889}{\$45{,}998} = 61.11\%$$

$$\text{ART} = \frac{\$45{,}998}{(\$4{,}873 + \$4{,}466)/2} = 9.85 \text{ times}$$

$$\text{INVT} = \frac{\$17{,}889}{(\$3{,}277 + \$3{,}100)/2} = 5.61 \text{ times}$$

$$\text{PPET} = \frac{\$45{,}998}{(\$14{,}967 + \$14{,}633)/2} = 3.11 \text{ times}$$

PepsiCo and Coca-Cola have similar business models, and both companies achieve high returns on the capital invested by their shareholders. PepsiCo has a higher ROE, while the difference in ROA is much smaller (9.7% vs. 8.2%). Most of the difference in ROE is due to the fact that PepsiCo has a higher ROFL, caused by its higher use of liabilities as a source of financing. Coca-Cola has higher PM and GPM, while PepsiCo achieves a higher turnover of total assets. Closer analysis of turnover ratios reveals that ART is similar, implying that they employ similar credit policies. PepsiCo's inventory turns over significantly more quickly than Coca-Cola's inventory, perhaps reflecting differences in their product mix (e.g., PepsiCo's snack foods). This difference plays a significant role in PepsiCo's superior asset turnover.

Chapter-End Review

SOLUTION ($ MILLIONS)

$$\text{Current ratio} = \frac{\$32{,}986}{\$32{,}374} = 1.02$$

$$\text{Quick ratio} = \frac{\$8{,}958 + \$12{,}717 + \$4{,}466}{\$32{,}374} = 0.81$$

$$\text{Debt-to-equity ratio} = \frac{\$61{,}462}{\$30{,}561} = 2.01$$

$$\text{Times interest earned} = \frac{\$9{,}325 + \$483}{\$483} = 20.31$$

PepsiCo is slightly more liquid than Coca-Cola as indicated by a higher current ratio (1.14 vs. 1.02) and a higher quick ratio (0.85 vs. 0.81). In addition, PepsiCo has a much higher debt-to-equity ratio than Coke (3.02 vs. 2.01) suggesting that PepsiCo is relying more on debt financing. This is consistent with the higher ROFL ratio computed in Mid-Chapter Review 2. Nevertheless, neither company has significant issues related to solvency. Both report reasonably high times-interest-earned ratios (10.6 for PepsiCo and 20.3 for Coca-Cola).

Appendix 5A Review

SOLUTION ($ MILLIONS)

Operating assets:
2014: $92,023 − $3,678 − $12,717 = $75,628
2013: $90,055 − $1,119 − $9,854 = $79,082

Operating liabilities:
2014: $61,462 − $19,063 − $3,552 − $19,188 = $19,659
2013: $56,615 − $19,154 − $1,024 − $16,901 = $19,536

Net operating assets (NOA):
2014: $75,628 − $19,659 = $55,969
2013: $79,082 − $19,536 = $59,546

$$\text{NOPAT} = \$7{,}124 - [(\$594 - \$483 - \$494) \times (1 - 0.35)] = \$7{,}373.0$$

$$\text{RNOA} = \frac{\$7{,}373}{(\$55{,}969 + \$59{,}546)/2} = 12.8\%$$

$$\text{NOPM} = \frac{\$7{,}373}{\$45{,}998} = 16.0\%$$

$$\text{NOAT} = \frac{\$45{,}998}{(\$55{,}969 + \$59{,}546)/2} = 0.80$$

Appendix 5B Review

SOLUTION ($ MILLIONS)

THE COCA-COLA COMPANY AND SUBSIDIARIES
Pro Forma Statements of Income
($ millions)

Year ended December 31	2015
Net operating revenues	$50,000 (8.7% growth)
Cost of goods sold ($50,000 × 38.9%)	19,450
Gross profit	30,550
Selling, general and administrative expenses ($50,000 × 37.4%)	18,700
Other operating charges ($50,000 × 2.6%)	1,300
Operating income	10,550
Interest income	594
Interest expense	(483)
Other income (loss)—net	(494)
Income before income taxes	10,167
Income taxes ($10,170 × 20.0%)	2,033
Net income	$ 8,134

THE COCA-COLA COMPANY AND SUBSIDIARIES
Pro Forma Balance Sheet
($ millions)

December 31,	2015
Assets	
Cash and cash equivalents	$ 8,987
Marketable securities	12,717
Trade accounts receivable ($4,466 × 1.087)	4,855
Inventories ($3,100 × 1.087)	3,370
Prepaid expenses and other current assets ($3,745 × 1.087)	4,071
Total current assets	34,000
Investments	13,625
Property, plant, and equipment, net ($14,633 × 1.087)	15,906
Goodwill and other intangible assets ($26,372 × 1.087)	28,666
Other assets ($4,407 × 1.087)	4,790
Total assets	$96,987
Liabilities and Shareowners' Equity	
Accounts payable and accrued expenses ($9,234 × 1.087)	$10,037
Loans and notes payable	19,188
Current maturities of long-term debt	3,552
Accrued income taxes ($400 × 1.087)	435
Total current liabilities	33,212
Long-term debt	19,063
Other liabilities ($4,389 × 1.087)	4,771
Deferred income taxes ($5,636 × 1.087)	6,126
Total liabilities	63,172
Shareowners' equity ($30,561 + $8,134 − $4,880)	33,815
Total liabilities and shareowners' equity	$96,987

Reporting and Analyzing Revenues, Receivables, and Operating Income

LEARNING OBJECTIVES

1. Describe and apply the criteria for determining when revenue is recognized. (p. 274)
2. Illustrate revenue and expense recognition when the transaction involves future deliverables and/or multiple elements. (p. 275)
3. Illustrate revenue and expense recognition for long-term projects. (p. 279)
4. Estimate and account for uncollectible accounts receivable. (p. 282)
5. Calculate return on net operating assets, net operating profit after taxes, net operating profit margin, accounts receivable turnover, and average collection period. (p. 288)
6. Discuss earnings management and explain how it affects analysis and interpretation of financial statements. (p. 293)
7. Appendix 6A: Describe and illustrate the reporting for nonrecurring items. (p. 295)
8. Appendix 6B: Describe the new standard for revenue recognition and discuss its potential effects. (p. 298)

CISCO SYSTEMS
www.cisco.com

Cisco Systems, Inc., manufactures and sells networking and communication products for transporting data, voice, and video. It is the worldwide leader in networking for the Internet.

Its engineers have been prominent in the development of Internet Protocol (IP)-based networking technologies in the core areas of routing and switching, along with advancing technologies in areas such as IP telephony, wireless LAN, storage networking, and home networking. Its products are seemingly everywhere:

- Cisco routers and switches are a crucial component of all networks.
- Cisco wireless network and IP telephony products allow people to communicate freely and reduce the cost of long distance communications.
- Cisco wireless technology allows employees to connect to corporate networks over a virtual private network (VPN), and it has medical applications such as telerobotics that aid in surgery. Commercial applications include wireless displays on shopping carts, targeted advertisements, and quick checkout.
- Enterprise collaboration including enterprise content management, enterprise voice, and enterprise social networks is an area of recent growth for Cisco.
- Virtual classrooms, powered by Cisco's switching technology and web collaboration software, are part of the distance learning revolution.
- Cisco video kiosks serve customers, constituents, and students in the healthcare, transportation, retail, banking, and education sectors of the economy.
- Cisco offers the Unified Data Center platform designed to automate IT resulting in increased efficiency, more agile business responsiveness, and simplified IT operations.

After a decade of rapid annual growth, Cisco ran smack into the tech decline in 2001. The company reported a $1 billion loss after taking a massive $1.2 billion restructuring charge. The restructuring led to inventory write-downs and the severance of 6,000 employees and seemed to undermine Cisco's claims of cutting-edge e-efficiency. In 2011, Cisco announced a second restructuring costing $1.1 billion, mostly for early retirement and severance costs. Effectively, in less than a decade, Cisco spent over $3 billion to restructure its business from the ground up.

Cisco's then-CEO, John Chambers, commented to *BusinessWeek*, "success in the 1990s was often based on how fast you could get to market and how fast you could blow a product through your distribution [channels]. Our market changed dramatically in terms of what customers expected; we needed to have engineering and manufacturing and professional services and [sales] and customer support working together in a way that wasn't required before."

Profitability is the primary measure by which financial statement users gauge a company's success in efficiently offering products and services that receive a favorable response from customers. In this chapter, we focus on how companies report operating income. Operating income is determined by decisions about how and when to recognize revenues and expenses. In addition, the income statement also includes *nonrecurring* (or *transitory*) *items*, such as restructuring charges. Transitory items are often important events reflecting very large dollar amounts and are distinguished by the fact that they are unlikely to recur in subsequent years. Understanding how such nonrecurring items are reported is crucial to interpreting a company's profitability.

Cisco's performance cannot be measured by profits alone. In order to control costs and improve operating profits, Cisco has to effectively manage operating assets. For example, accounts receivable is an important operating asset at Cisco because all of its sales are on account. By extending credit to customers on favorable credit terms, Cisco stimulates sales. However, extending credit exposes the company to collectibility risk—the risk that some customers will not pay the amounts owed. In addition, accounts receivable do not earn interest, and involve administrative costs associated with billing and collection. Hence, management of receivables is critical to financial success. This chapter describes the reporting of receivables. The reporting of other operating assets is covered in subsequent chapters.

Cisco has named its new CEO who will succeed John Chambers in July of 2015. The company has done well over time but faces continual challenges in the fast-changing technology industry.

Sources: *Cisco Systems, Inc.,* 10-K Reports; www.Cisco.com; *The Wall Street Journal,* February 7, 2005; *BusinessWeek,* November/December 2003; *USA Today*, August 7, 2007; *Wall Street Journal*, June 2, 2009; *The Economist*, April 15, 2010; *The Wall Street Journal* May 4, 2015.

CHAPTER ORGANIZATION

Reporting and Analyzing Revenues, Receivables, and Operating Income

Reporting Operating Income	Reporting Receivables	Analyzing Financial Statements	Further Considerations
• Revenue Recognition • Accounting for Transactions with Future Deliverables • Accounting for Long-term Projects	• Allowance for Uncollectible Accounts • Footnote Disclosures and Interpretations	• Net Operating Profit After Taxes • Return on Net Operating Assets • Net Operating Profit Margin • Accounts Receivable Turnover • Average Collection Period	• Earnings Management • Reporting Nonrecurring Items (Appendix A) • New Standards for Revenue Recognition (Appendix B)

REPORTING OPERATING INCOME

The income statement is the primary source of information about recent company performance. This information is used to predict future performance for investment purposes and to assess the creditworthiness of a company. The income statement is also used to evaluate the quality of management.

This section describes the information reported in the income statement and its analysis implications. The central questions that the income statement attempts to answer are:

- How profitable has the company been recently?
- How did it achieve that profitability?
- Will the current profitability level persist?

To answer these three profitability questions, it is not enough to focus on a company's net income. Rather, we must use the various classifications within the income statement to see how profits were achieved and what the future prospects look like. **Exhibit 6.1** provides a schematic of the primary income statement classifications.

EXHIBIT 6.1 Income Statement Classifications

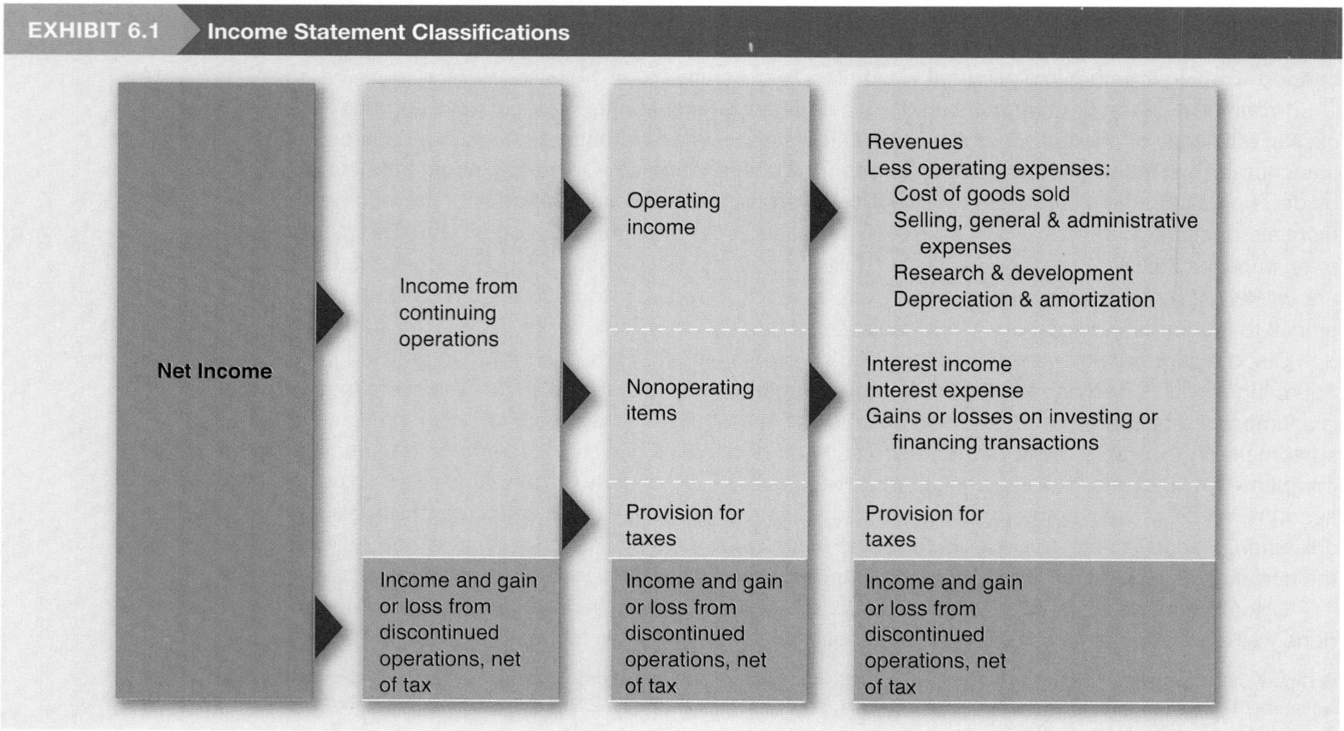

Operating activities refer to the primary transactions and events of a company. These include the purchase of goods from suppliers, the conversion of materials into finished products, the promotion and distribution of goods, the sale of goods and services to customers, and post-sale customer support. Operating activities are reported in the income statement under items such as sales, cost of goods sold, and selling, general, and administrative expenses. They represent a company's primary activities, which must be executed successfully for a company to remain consistently profitable.

Nonoperating activities relate to the financial (borrowing) and securities investment activities of a company. These activities are typically reported in the income statement under items such as interest income and expenses, dividend revenues, and gains and losses on sales of securities. Distinguishing income components by operating versus nonoperating is an important part of effective financial statement analysis because operating activities drive company performance. It is of interest, for example, to know whether company profitability results from operating activities, or whether poorly performing operating activities are being masked by income from nonoperating activities.

FYI When analyzing a company's income statement, it is important to distinguish operating activities from nonoperating activities and recurring activities from nonrecurring activities.

All the line items in income from continuing operations are presented before taxes, with the final line item being provision for income taxes, or tax expense. The accounting for income taxes is discussed more fully in Chapter 10.

If the company has income or loss items that qualify as discontinued operations, these will be presented after income from continuing operations. Discontinued operations are reported net of income tax expense or benefit. The appendix at the end of this chapter provides a detailed description of nonrecurring items. Finally, many large corporations report something called net income attributable to **noncontrolling interests**. Such an amount arises when a company consolidates a subsidiary that it controls, but for which it holds less than 100% ownership. This topic is covered in later chapters.

Exhibit 6.2 presents the 2014, 2013, and 2012 income statements (also called statements of operations) for Cisco Systems. Cisco has no discontinued operations during this time period, so

EXHIBIT 6.2 Distinguishing Operating and Nonoperating Sources of Income

CISCO SYSTEMS, INC.
Consolidated Statements of Operations
($ millions)

Year ended	July 26, 2014	July 27, 2013	July 28, 2012
Net sales:			
Product	$36,172	$38,029	$36,326
Service	10,970	10,578	9,735
Total net sales	47,142	48,607	46,061
Cost of sales:			
Product	15,641	15,541	14,505
Service	3,732	3,626	3,347
Total cost of sales	19,373	19,167	17,852
Gross Margin	27,769	29,440	28,209
Operating expenses:			
Research and development	6,294	5,942	5,488
Sales and marketing	9,503	9,538	9,647
General and administrative	1,934	2,264	2,322
Amortization of purchased intangible assets	275	395	383
Restructuring and other charges	418	105	304
Total operating expenses	18,424	18,244	18,144
Operating income	9,345	11,196	10,065
Interest income	691	654	650
Interest expense	(564)	(583)	(596)
Other income, net	243	(40)	40
Interest and other income, net	370	31	94
Income before provision for income taxes	9,715	11,227	10,159
Provision for income taxes	1,862	1,244	2,118
Net Income	$ 7,853	$ 9,983	$ 8,041

income from continuing operations is the same as net income. Like many companies, Cisco presents operating income as a subtotal in its income statement. Cisco's operating income is computed by subtracting its total operating expenses (including cost of sales, research and development, sales and marketing, general and administrative, amortization, and restructuring charges) from total sales revenues. Nonoperating income and expenses, such as interest income and expense, and other income and expense, are added to or deducted from the subtotal for operating income.

At this time, GAAP does not have specific rules for classifying revenue and expense items as either operating or nonoperating, so management must use judgment in reporting and financial statement users must be careful to examine each revenue and expense item to determine if it is appropriately listed as part of operating income. Specifically, sales, cost of goods sold, and most selling, general, and administrative expenses are categorized as operating activities. Alternatively, investment-related income from dividends and interest is nonoperating, as is interest expense. Gains and losses on debt retirements and sales of investments are also nonoperating.[1]

While we think of Cisco as a networking and communications company, it has more than $45 billion (43% of its assets) invested in financial instruments (mostly government and government-backed securities) at 2014 fiscal year-end. And these assets provided $691 million in interest income for 2014. So, making predictions about Cisco's profitability for 2015 would be improved by separating the results of its product and service operations from those of its investing activities. In addition, operating income is the normal focus of business unit managers in a company—financing activities and investments in financial instruments and tax administration are usually determined at the central corporate level.

Revenue Recognition

1 **LO1** Describe and apply the criteria for determining when revenue is recognized.

Revenue is one of the most important metrics of a company's operating success. The objective of almost all operating activities is to obtain a favorable response from customers, and revenue is a primary indicator of how customers view the company's product and service offerings. Companies can improve profits by reducing costs, but the effects of those improvements are limited unless revenues are increasing. Accordingly, growth in revenue is carefully monitored by management and by investors, as exemplified by the attention given to "same-store sales growth" in the retail industry.

BUSINESS INSIGHT

New Revenue Recognition Standards The FASB and the IASB issued new, converged accounting standards for revenue recognition in May of 2014. The new standard is intended to consolidate the guidance on revenue recognition into one standard in U.S. GAAP, eliminate inconsistencies that currently exist in applying revenue recognition to different transactions and in different industries, and align U.S. GAAP and IFRS on revenue recognition. The new standard generally employs many of the same broad concepts to revenue recognition as the current standards, but because the new standard is more principles based relative to the current U.S. rules, it will require management to exercise more judgment. Revenues will still have to be earned to be recognized, but the determination of when revenues are earned will change in some cases under the new standard. Collectibility is also important under the new standard, conceptually similar to the realized or realizable criterion under the current standard. The new standard is effective for publicly traded, calendar year-end companies starting January 1, 2018. Thus, because the effective date for the new standard is more than two years away at the time of this writing, we do not have examples of companies applying the new revenue standard. We provide an expanded discussion of the overriding principles of the new standard and conjecture about implications of the new standard in Appendix 6B at the end of this chapter. We discuss and provide examples of the current standards in the text of the chapter.

[1] To further complicate matters, the classification of some items in the income statement as nonoperating is not consistent with their classification in the cash flow statement. Specifically, interest and dividend income and interest expense are classified as operating in the cash flow statement and nonoperating in most income statements. Of course, the distinction between operating and nonoperating items depends on the company's business. For Cisco Systems, interest income and expense would be classified as nonoperating, but for a financial institution (e.g., a bank), those same items would be considered part of their operations. Purchases and sales of production equipment would be considered nonoperating for Cisco, but operating for a company in the business of buying and selling used equipment.

Revenue recognition refers to the timing and amount of revenue reported by the company. The decision of when to recognize revenue depends on certain criteria. Determining whether the criteria for revenue recognition are met is often subjective and requires judgment. Therefore, financial statement readers should pay careful attention to companies' revenue recognition, particularly when companies face market pressures to meet income targets. Indeed, many SEC enforcement actions against companies for inaccurate, and sometimes fraudulent financial reporting are for improper (usually premature) revenue recognition.

GAAP dictates two **revenue recognition criteria** that must be met for revenue to be recognized (and reported) on the income statement. Revenue must be (1) **realized or realizable**, and (2) **earned**. *Realized or realizable* means that the company's net assets increase. That is, it receives an asset or satisfies a liability as a result of a transaction or event. *Earned* means that the seller has executed its duties under the terms of the sales agreement and that the title has passed to the buyer.

Many companies recognize revenues when the product or service is delivered to the customer. For these companies, delivery occurs at the same time, or shortly after, the sale takes place. Revenue recognition complications arise if there is uncertainty about collectibility or when the sale is contingent on product performance, product approval, or similar contingencies. In some industries, it is standard practice to allow customers to return the product within a specified period of time. When the customer retains a **right of return**, it is sometimes inappropriate to recognize revenue at the time of delivery. For many companies, returns are either immaterial in amount or relatively easy to predict based on history of a large number of similar transactions. For these companies, revenue can be recognized when the product is delivered to the customer. The expected returns are estimated and deducted from revenue when reporting the sale in the income statement. However, if the amount of returns is difficult to estimate, revenues should not be recognized until the return period expires.

BUSINESS INSIGHT

Product Returns at Pfizer Following is an excerpt from **Pfizer Inc.**'s accounting policies as reported in its annual report.

> We record revenues from product sales when the goods are shipped and title passes to the customer. At the time of sale, we also record estimates for a variety of sales deductions, such as sales rebates, discounts and incentives, and product returns. When we cannot reasonably estimate the amount of future product returns, we record revenues when the risk of product return and/or additional sales deductions have been substantially eliminated.

Pfizer's policy regarding product returns is consistent with GAAP in that expected returns are estimated and deducted from sales at the time that the sale is recorded. If returns cannot be estimated, the sales revenue is deferred until the company is relatively certain that the product will not be returned.

The term "delivery" does not refer only to transportation to the customer's location, but also the transfer of title and the risks and rewards of ownership. In a **consignment** sale, a *consignor* delivers product to a *consignee*, but retains ownership until the consignee sells the product to the ultimate customer. As long as ownership remains with the consignor, a sale has not taken place. Only when the consignee sells the product should the consignor record the sales revenue.

LO2 Illustrate revenue and expense recognition when the transaction involves future deliverables and/or multiple elements.

2

Revenue Recognition Subsequent to Customer Purchase There are many businesses in which customers purchase a product or a service prior to its delivery. For instance, a customer may pay for a year's subscription to a periodical. The publisher receives the cash at the start of the subscription, but it earns revenue when it delivers the periodical to the subscriber. Or, a homeowner may pay for the upcoming year's casualty insurance, but the insurance company can only recognize revenue as it provides insurance coverage.

In settings where a company's customers pay for the product or service prior to its delivery, the company must recognize a liability (usually called **unearned revenue** or **deferred revenue**)[2] at the time of the customer's payment. Then this liability is reduced, and revenue recognized, as the product or service is delivered.

Suppose that on January 1, a subscriber pays $36 for an annual subscription to a monthly magazine. At the time of payment, the publisher would make the following entry:

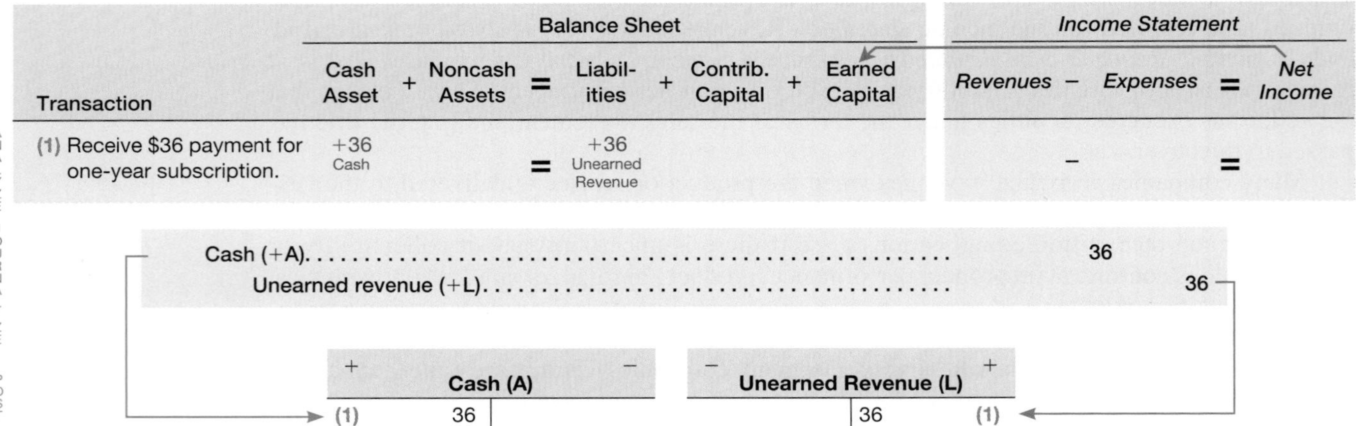

The unearned revenue liability represents the publisher's obligation—not to make a payment, but to provide the promised publication. Most liabilities reflect obligations to make a future payment, but unearned revenue is one of a handful of *deferred performance liabilities* that represent an obligation for future performance.

On March 31, at the end of its first quarter, the publisher would recognize that three magazines had been delivered to the subscriber, and the publisher has earned three times the monthly revenue of $3, or $9. The entry to recognize this revenue is the following.

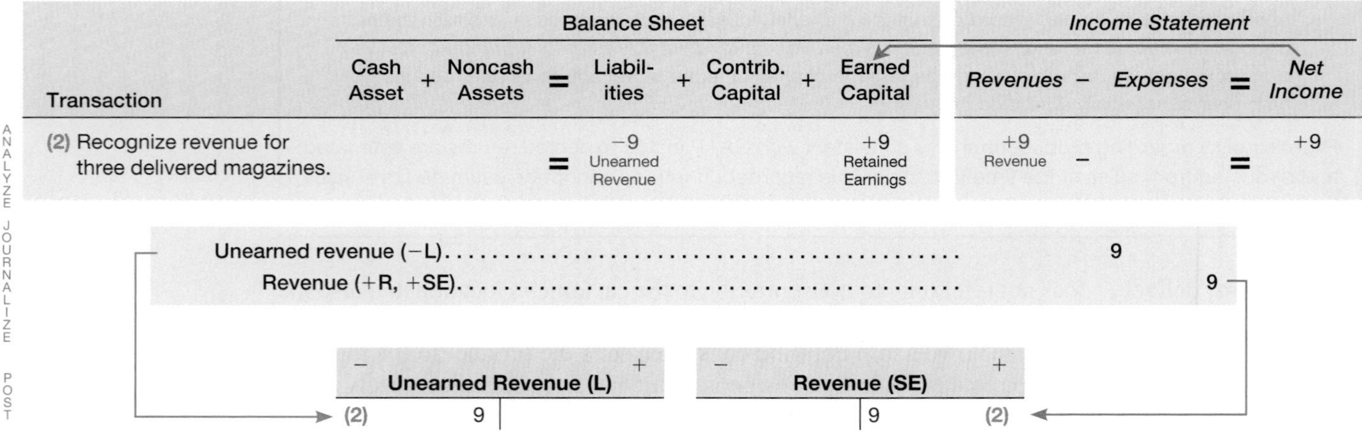

The same entries would be made until the subscription expired. In the March 31 balance sheet, the publisher would have a deferred revenue liability of $27, reflecting the remaining obligation for nine months of subscription delivery. And, the quarter's indirect method operating cash flows would include $9 in revenue (in net income) and the $27 increase in unearned revenue liability which, in total, reflect the $36 received from the customer.

[2] The term used for unearned revenue may be particular to the company's business. For instance, **Delta Air Lines** shows an Air Traffic Liability of $4,296 million at the end of 2014 which represents customers' purchases of tickets in advance of their flights. **The Allstate Corporation** uses the term *Unearned Premiums*. The new revenue recognition accounting standard uses the general term *contract liability*.

Unearned revenue is seen in a growing number of financial statements as companies increase their promises of future deliveries of products and service due to the changing nature of products and services in the economy and also in an effort to build a continuing relationship with their customers. From the point of view of a financial analyst, one implication of revenue deferral is that the change in revenue from one period to the next is not equal to the change in customer purchases over the same period. In the case of our publisher with one-year subscriptions, quarterly revenue is actually a composite of subscriber purchases over the current quarter plus the last three quarters and, therefore, not an ideal indicator of how current customers are responding to the publisher's offerings. Both the revenue and unearned revenue accounts need to be analyzed to obtain a complete picture.

A revenue recognition complication arises when two or more products or services are sold under the same sales agreement for one lump-sum price. These bundled sales are called **multiple element arrangements** and are commonplace in the software industry, where developers sell software, training, maintenance, and customer support in one transaction. In these circumstances, GAAP requires that the sales price be allocated among the various elements of the sale in proportion to their fair value. Revenue allocated to the elements that have not been delivered (such as maintenance and customer support) must be deferred and recognized as the service is rendered in future periods.

BUSINESS INSIGHT

Cisco's Revenue Recognition Following is an excerpt from Cisco Systems' policies on revenue recognition as reported in footnotes to its recent annual report.

> The Company recognizes revenue when persuasive evidence of an arrangement exists, delivery has occurred, the fee is fixed or determinable, and collectibility is reasonably assured. In instances where final acceptance of the product, system, or solution is specified by the customer, revenue is deferred until all acceptance criteria have been met. For hosting arrangements, the Company recognizes subscription revenue ratably over the subscription period, while usage revenue is recognized based on utilization. Software subscription revenue is deferred and recognized ratably over the subscription term upon delivery of the first product and commencement of the term. Technical support services revenue is deferred and recognized ratably over the period during which the services are to be performed, which is typically from one to three years.
>
> . . . The Company enters into revenue arrangements that may consist of multiple deliverables of its product and service offerings due to the needs of its customers. For example, a customer may purchase routing products along with a contract for technical support services. This arrangement would consist of multiple elements, with the products delivered in one reporting period and the technical support services delivered across multiple reporting periods . . .

Cisco goes on to discuss how it then allocates revenue among the various components of a multiple element contract using either vendor-specific objective evidence of price, third-party evidence of a selling price, or estimated selling prices. Cisco also states that it determines its price on which to allocate revenue based on the normal pricing practices for the specific product or service if that product or service is sold separately.

Cisco's criteria and methods of revenue recognition reflect current accounting standards and SEC guidance. In its recent 10-K, Cisco describes the new accounting standard and states that they are currently evaluating the impact of this accounting standard update on its financial reporting.

To illustrate revenue recognition for a multiple element arrangement (or bundled sale), assume that Software Innovations, Inc., develops marketing software designed to track customer questions and comments on the Internet and through social media. The software license sells for $125,000 and includes user training for up to 12 individuals and customer support for three years. Software Innovations estimates that the software, if licensed without training or customer support, would sell for $120,000. In addition, it estimates that the value of the user training services, if sold separately, would be $18,000 and the customer support would sell for $12,000. Software Innovations would allocate the $125,000 sales price as illustrated in **Exhibit 6.3**.

EXHIBIT 6.3 Allocation of the Sales Price in a Multiple Element Arrangement

Element	Estimated value	Percent of total value		Bundle sales price		Sales price allocated to each element
Software license	$120,000	80%	×	$125,000	=	$100,000
Training	18,000	12	×	125,000	=	15,000
Customer support	12,000	8	×	125,000	=	10,000
Total	$150,000	100%				$125,000

The sale would be recorded as revenue for the portion that was allocated to software and as deferred (or unearned) revenue for that portion that was allocated to training and customer support:

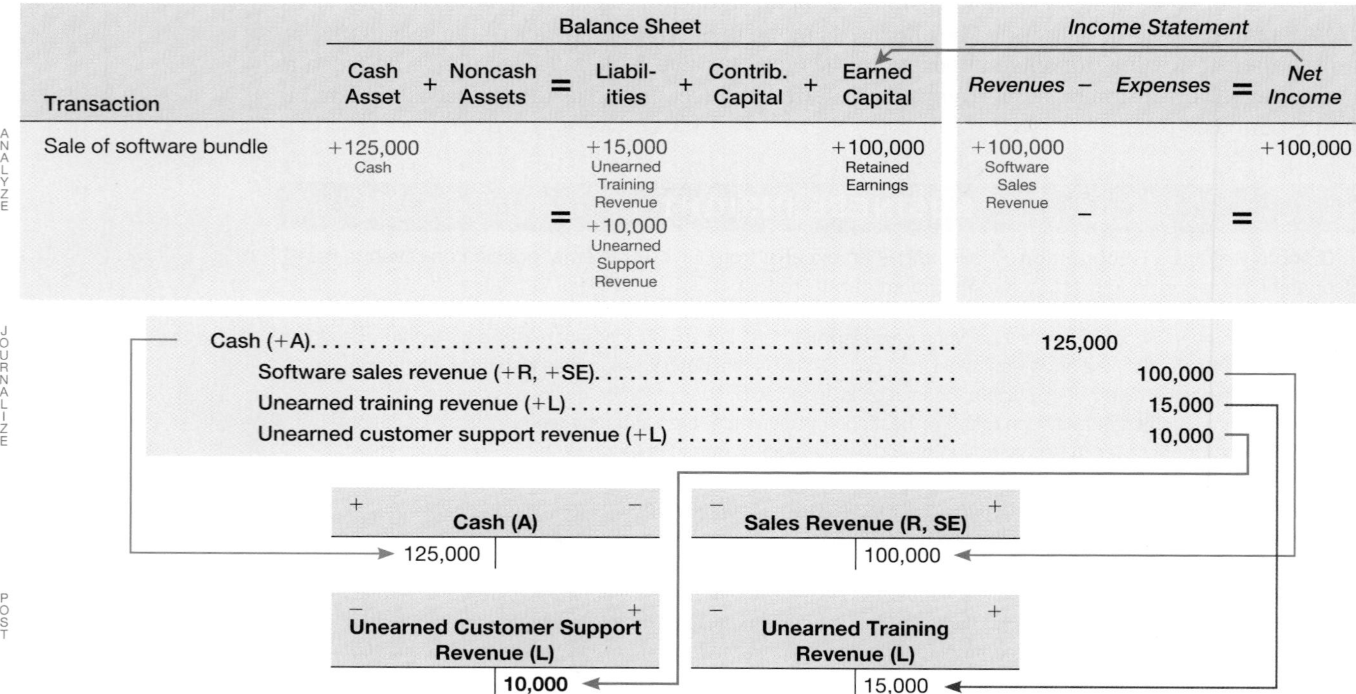

Transaction	Cash Asset	+ Noncash Assets	= Liabilities	+ Contrib. Capital	+ Earned Capital	Revenues	− Expenses	= Net Income
ANALYZE: Sale of software bundle	+125,000 Cash		= +15,000 Unearned Training Revenue; +10,000 Unearned Support Revenue		+100,000 Retained Earnings	+100,000 Software Sales Revenue	−	= +100,000

JOURNALIZE

	Dr.	Cr.
Cash (+A)	125,000	
Software sales revenue (+R, +SE)		100,000
Unearned training revenue (+L)		15,000
Unearned customer support revenue (+L)		10,000

POST

+ Cash (A) −	− Sales Revenue (R, SE) +	− Unearned Customer Support Revenue (L) +	− Unearned Training Revenue (L) +
125,000	100,000	10,000	15,000

The unearned training revenue would be recognized as training services are provided. Software Innovations might recognize 1/12 of the $15,000, or $1,250 for each individual trained. The unearned customer support revenue would be recognized over time ($10,000/3 = $3,333 each year).

MID-CHAPTER REVIEW 1

When **Microsoft Corporation** sells software, it recognizes part of the revenue at the time of customer purchase and defers the rest because it will deliver support and upgrades in the future. For instance, in its 2014 annual report, it states

> Revenue recognition for multiple-element arrangements requires judgment to determine if multiple elements exist, whether elements can be accounted for as separate units of accounting, and if so, the fair value for each of the elements. Where elements are delivered over different periods of time, and when allowed under U.S. GAAP, revenue is allocated to the respective elements based on their relative selling prices at the inception of the arrangement, and revenue is recognized as each element is delivered. . . . Technology guarantee programs are accounted for as multiple-element arrangements as customers receive free or significantly discounted rights to use upcoming new versions of a software product if they license existing versions of the product during the eligibility period. Revenue is allocated between the existing product and the new product, and revenue allocated to the new

product is deferred until that version is delivered . . . Software updates that will be provided free of charge are evaluated on a case-by-case basis to determine whether they meet the definition of an upgrade and create a multiple-element arrangement, which may require revenue to be deferred and recognized when the upgrade is delivered, or if it is determined that implied post-contract customer support ("PCS") is being provided, the arrangement is accounted for as a multiple-element arrangement and all revenue from the arrangement is deferred and recognized over the implied PCS term. If updates are determined to not meet the definition of an upgrade, revenue is generally recognized as products are shipped or made available.

In its income statement, Microsoft reports revenues for the past three years.

(in millions)	2014	2013	2012
Revenue	\$86,833	\$77,849	\$73,723

In its indirect-method operating cash flows, Microsoft makes many adjustments to its net income in arriving at cash from operations. Two of the adjustments are the following:

(in millions)	2014	2013	2012
Deferral of unearned revenue.	\$44,325	\$44,253	\$36,104
Recognition of unearned revenue	(41,739)	(41,921)	(33,347)

"Deferral of unearned revenue" provides the amount of customer purchases made during a year that were not recognized as revenue at the time of customer purchase. That is the amount that was put into the unearned revenue liability during the year. "Recognition of unearned revenue" refers to the amounts of revenue recognized during the year that derived from customer purchases made in earlier periods. This amount was taken out of the unearned revenue liability during the year and recognized as revenue on the income statement.

Required

1. Calculate the revenue growth rates for fiscal years 2013 and 2014.
2. From the information on revenues and on changes in the unearned revenue liability, determine the amount of customer purchases for fiscal years 2012, 2013, and 2014.
3. Calculate the growth rates in customer purchases for fiscal years 2013 and 2014. Why do these differ from those calculated in part 1?

The solution to this review problem can be found on page 321.

LO3 Illustrate revenue and expense recognition for long-term projects.

3

Revenue Recognition for Long-term Projects Challenges arise in determining revenue recognition for companies with long-term production processes (spanning more than one reporting period) such as consulting firms, construction companies, and defense contractors. For these companies, revenue is often recognized using the **percentage-of-completion method**, which recognizes revenue based on the costs incurred under the contract relative to its total expected costs.[3] In addition to determining when to recognize revenues to properly measure and report a company's performance, we must also decide when to recognize expenses. The idea of **expense recognition** was introduced in Chapter 2. Expenses are recognized when assets are diminished (or liabilities increased) as a result of earning revenue or supporting operations, even if there is no immediate decrease in cash. The following illustration demonstrates the appropriate recognition of revenues and expenses using the percentage-of-completion method.

PERCENTAGE-OF-COMPLETION METHOD To illustrate the percentage-of-completion method, assume that Built-Rite Construction signs a \$10 million contract to construct a building. The company estimates \$7.5 million in construction costs, yielding an expected gross profit of \$2.5 million. Further assume that Built-Rite incurs \$4.5 million in construction costs during the first year of construction, and the remaining \$3 million in costs during the second year. The amount of revenue and gross profit that Built-Rite would report each year is illustrated in **Exhibit 6.4**.

[3] In some circumstances, a company may use some other indicator of progress, like employee time or the achievement of customer-specified milestones.

EXHIBIT 6.4 Revenue Recognition Using the Percentage-of-Completion Method

Year	Percentage completed	Revenue recognized	Expense recognized	Gross profit
1.	$4,500,000/$7,500,000 = 60%	$10,000,000 × 60% = $ 6,000,000	$4,500,000	$1,500,000
2.	$3,000,000/$7,500,000 = 40%	$10,000,000 × 40% = 4,000,000	3,000,000	1,000,000
Totals	100%	$10,000,000	$7,500,000	$2,500,000

Using the percentage-of-completion method, Built-Rite would report $1.5 million in gross profit from this project in the first year and $1.0 million in the second year. The timing of revenue and gross profit coincides with the amount of work completed.

FYI GAAP requires use of the percentage-of-completion method for long-term contracts whenever management can reasonably estimate revenues and expenses.

The percentage-of-completion method of revenue recognition requires an estimate of total costs. This estimate is made at the beginning of the contract and is typically the one used to initially bid the contract. However, estimates are inherently prone to estimation error. If total construction costs are underestimated, the percentage of completion is overestimated (the denominator is too low) and too much revenue and gross profit are recognized in the early years of the project. The estimation process used in this method has the potential for inaccurate or, even, improper revenue recognition. Estimates of costs to complete projects are also difficult to verify for auditors. This uncertainty adds additional risk to financial statement analysis.

FYI Application of percentage-of-completion enhances earnings timeliness relative to the completed contract method. However, poor or biased estimates for applying percentage-of-completion can reduce or reverse the benefits of that more timely reporting.

To justify use of the percentage-of-completion method, a company must have a contract with the customer that specifies a fixed or determinable price. In addition, project costs must be reasonably estimable. When a long-term project fails to meet these criteria, all revenue should be deferred until the contract is complete. This approach is known as the **completed contract method**. **Exhibit 6.5** provides a comparison of the gross profit calculations using each of these two accounting methods for the Built-Rite Construction contract described earlier.

EXHIBIT 6.5 Comparison of the Percentage-of-Completion and Completed Contract Methods

Percentage-of-Completion Method			Completed Contract Method		
	Year 1	Year 2		Year 1	Year 2
Revenues	$6,000,000	$4,000,000	Revenues	$0	$10,000,000
Expenses	4,500,000	3,000,000	Expenses	0	7,500,000
Gross profit.	$1,500,000	$1,000,000	Gross profit.	$0	$ 2,500,000

The total revenue and gross profit are the same under either revenue recognition method. Likewise, there is no difference in the costs incurred to construct the building. The only difference between the percentage-of-completion method and the completed contract method is *when* the revenue and gross profit are reported in the income statement.

It is very likely that Built-Rite would have received some cash payments from the customer during the construction period. However, neither the percentage-of-completion method nor the completed contract method is affected by the schedule of cash payments from the customer. It would not make sense for Built-Rite to enter into this contract unless it had a high degree of confidence in the customer's ability and willingness to pay.

A GLOBAL PERSPECTIVE

Currently, International Financial Reporting Standards do not allow the completed contract method to be used for long-term contracts when percentage-of-completion is not appropriate. Instead, companies are required to use the **cost-recovery method**, in which revenues are recognized in an amount equal to the cost incurred (and expensed) in each period. The pattern of profit recognition is the same as (or very similar to) completed contract, but the revenues and expenses occur differently. IFRS will adopt the new converged revenue recognition standard as described briefly in the Business Insight Box on page 274 and in more detail in Appendix 6B and will recognize revenue either over time or at a point in time similar to the new standard in GAAP.

MID-CHAPTER REVIEW 2

GuidedExamples MBC

Following is a footnote from a recent annual report of Adler Corporation.

> **Note 2: Revenue Recognition**
> Revenue from long-term government contracts is recognized using the percentage-of-completion method of accounting. Production costs are capitalized by project and are expensed based on the ratio of current period costs to estimated total contract costs. Revenue from contracts with private organizations is recognized using the completed contract method.

Required

1. Speculate as to possible reasons why Adler Corporation uses different revenue recognition policies for long-term government contracts and for contracts with private organizations.
2. Assume that Adler signed a contract in 2016 for a long-term project at a contract price of $40,000,000. The project is estimated to take three years to complete and cost $30,000,000. The cost incurred in 2016 was $12,000,000, and projected costs in 2017 and 2018 are $13,500,000 and $4,500,000 respectively. Compute gross profit for each year assuming that the contract is reported using the
   a. percentage-of-completion method
   b. completed contract method
3. Assume that Adler Corporation overestimated the cost of the contract in question 2, such that the actual cost incurred in 2018 was $1,500,000 instead of $4,500,000. What effect would this overestimate have on income in each year?

The solution to this review problem can be found on page 321.

REPORTING ACCOUNTS RECEIVABLE

Receivables are usually a major part of operating working capital. They must be carefully managed as they represent a substantial asset for most companies. GAAP requires companies to report receivables at the amount they expect to collect, necessitating an estimation of uncollectible accounts. These estimates determine the amount of receivables reported on the balance sheet as well as revenues and expenses reported on the income statement. Accordingly, it is important that companies accurately assess uncollectible accounts and report them. It is also necessary that readers of financial reports understand management's accounting choices and the effects of those choices on reported balance sheets and income statements.

FYI The phrase *trade receivables* refers to accounts receivable from customers.

When companies sell to other companies, they usually do not expect cash upon delivery as is common with retail customers. Instead, they offer credit terms, and the resulting sales are called **credit sales** or *sales on account*.

FYI Receivables are claims held against customers and others for money, goods, or services.

Companies establish credit policies (to determine which customers receive credit) by weighing the expected losses from uncollectible accounts against the expected profits generated by offering credit. Sellers know that some buyers will be unable to pay their accounts when they become due. Buyers, for example, can suffer business downturns that are beyond their control and which limit their cash available to meet liabilities. They must, then, make choices concerning which of their liabilities to pay. Liabilities to the IRS, to banks, and to bondholders are usually paid, as those creditors have enforcement powers and can quickly seize assets and disrupt operations, leading to bankruptcy and eventual liquidation. Buyers also try to cover their payroll, as they cannot exist without employees. Then, if there is cash remaining, these customers will pay suppliers to ensure a continued flow of goods.

When a customer faces financial difficulties, suppliers are often the last creditors to receive payment and are often not paid in full. Consequently, there is risk in the collectibility of accounts receivable. This *collectibility risk* is crucial to analysis of accounts receivable.

Accounts receivable are reported on the balance sheet of the seller at **net realizable value**, which is the net amount that the seller expects to collect. Cisco reports $5,157 million of accounts receivable in the current asset section of its 2014 balance sheet. Its receivables are reported net of allowances for doubtful accounts of $265 million. This means that the total amount owed to Cisco by customers is $5,422 million ($5,157 million + $265 million), but the company *estimates* that $265 million of these receivables will be uncollectible. Thus, only the net amount that Cisco expects to collect is reported on the balance sheet.

FYI Receivables are classified into three types: (1) current or noncurrent, (2) trade or nontrade, (3) accounts receivable or notes receivable. **Notes receivable** and **notes payable** are discussed in Chapter 9.

We might ask why Cisco would sell to companies from whom they do not expect to collect the amounts owed. The answer is they would not *if* they knew beforehand who those companies were. That is, Cisco probably cannot identify those companies that constitute the $265 million in uncollectible accounts as of its statement date. Yet, Cisco knows from past experience that a certain portion of its receivables will prove uncollectible. GAAP requires a company to estimate the dollar amount of uncollectible accounts each time it issues its financial statements (even if it cannot identify specific accounts that are uncollectible), and to report its accounts receivable at the resulting *net realizable value* (total receivables less an **allowance for uncollectible accounts**).

4 **LO4** Estimate and account for uncollectible accounts receivable.

Determining the Allowance for Uncollectible Accounts

The amount of expected uncollectible accounts is usually estimated based on an **aging analysis**. When aging the accounts, an analysis of receivables is performed as of the balance sheet date. Specifically, each customer's account balance is categorized by the number of days or months that the related invoices are outstanding. Based on prior experience, assessment of current economic conditions, or on other available statistics, uncollectible (bad debt) percentages are applied to each of these categorized amounts, with larger percentages applied to older accounts. The result of this analysis is a dollar amount for the allowance for uncollectible accounts (also called allowance for doubtful accounts) at the balance sheet date.

To illustrate, **Exhibit 6.6** shows an aging analysis for a seller that began operations this year and is owed $100,000 of accounts receivable at year-end. Those accounts listed as current consist of those outstanding that are still within their original credit period. Accounts listed as 1–60 days past due are those 1 to 60 days past their due date. This classification would include an account that is 45 days outstanding for a net 30-day invoice. This same logic applies to all aged categories.

EXHIBIT 6.6 Aging of Accounts Receivable

Age of Accounts Receivable	Receivable Balance	Estimated Percent Uncollectible	Accounts Estimated Uncollectible
Current	$ 50,000	2%	$1,000
1–60 days past due	30,000	3	900
61–90 days past due	15,000	4	600
Over 90 days past due	5,000	8	400
Total	$100,000		$2,900

The calculation illustrated in **Exhibit 6.6** also reflects the seller's experience with uncollectible accounts, which manifests itself in the uncollectible percentages for each aged category. For example, on average, 3% of buyers' accounts that are 1–60 days past due prove uncollectible for this seller. Hence, it estimates a potential loss of $900 for those $30,000 in receivables for that aged category.

Another means of estimating uncollectible accounts is to use the **percentage of sales**. To illustrate, if our seller reports sales of $100,000 and estimates the uncollectible accounts at 3% of sales, estimated uncollectible accounts would be $3,000. The percentage of sales approach focuses on the amount of potentially uncollectible accounts among current-period sales, whereas the aging analysis is based on the current balance in accounts receivable. Thus, these two methods nearly always result in different estimates of uncollectible accounts. While the percentage of sales method is arguably simpler, an aging analysis generally provides more accurate estimates.

Reporting the Allowance for Uncollectible Accounts

How does the accounting system record this estimate? The amount that appears in the balance sheet as accounts receivable represents a collection of individual accounts—one or more receivables for each customer. Because we need to keep track of exactly how much each customer owes us, we cannot simply subtract estimated uncollectibles from accounts receivable.

In Chapter 3, we introduced contra-asset accounts to record accumulated depreciation. A contra-asset account is directly associated with an asset account, but serves to offset the balance of the asset account. To record the estimated uncollectible accounts without disturbing the balance in accounts receivable, we use another contra-asset—the allowance for uncollectible accounts.

To illustrate, we use the data from **Exhibit 6.6**. The summary journal entry to reflect credit sales follows.

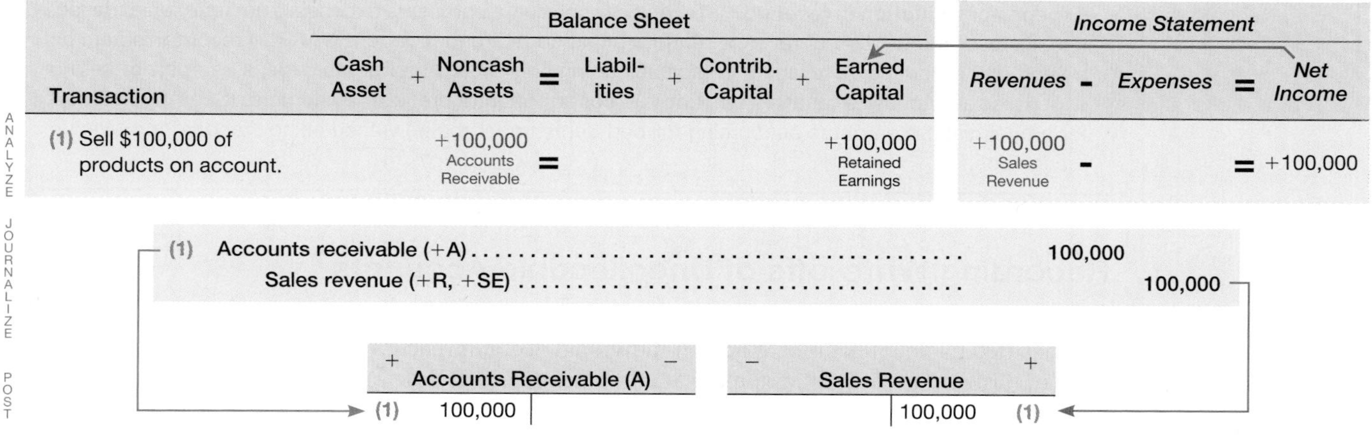

For an adjusting entry at year-end, uncollectible accounts are estimated and recorded as follows as **bad debts expense** (also called *provision for uncollectible accounts*). The allowance for uncollectible accounts is a contra-asset account. It offsets (reduces) accounts receivable.

FYI The term *provision* is sometimes used as a substitute for expense; often when the reported expense is an estimate.

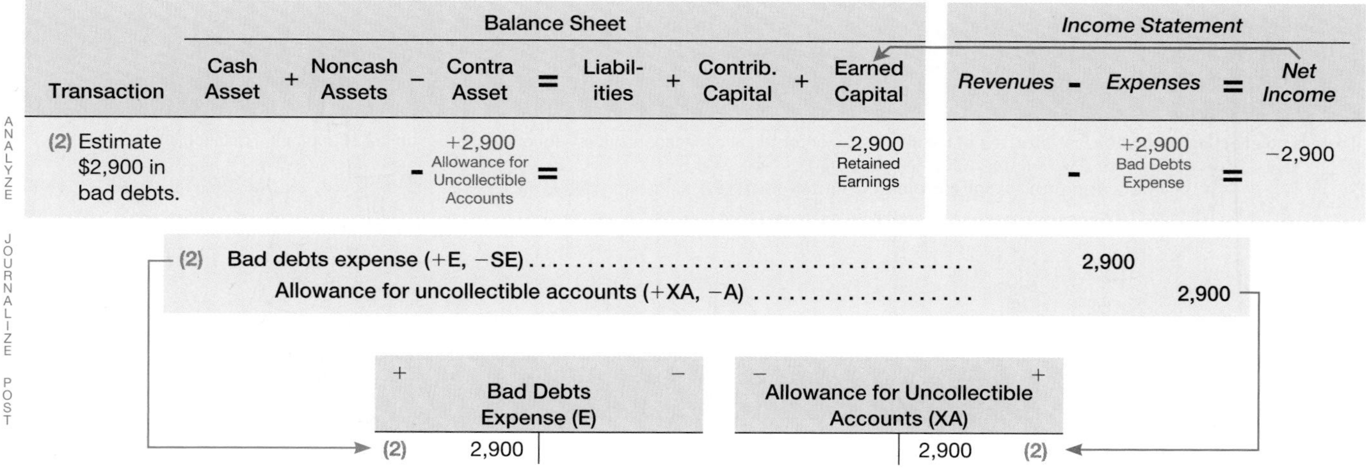

This accounting treatment serves three purposes. First, the balance in accounts receivable is reported in the balance sheet net of estimated uncollectible accounts as follows:

Accounts receivable, net of $2,900 in allowances	$97,100

The $97,100 is the net realizable value of the accounts receivable. Second, the original value of accounts receivable is preserved. The individual accounts that add up to the $100,000 in accounts receivable have not been altered. Third, bad debts expense of $2,900, which is part of the cost of offering credit to customers, is matched against the $100,000 sales generated on credit and reported in the income statement. Bad debts expense is usually included in SG&A expenses.

The allowance for uncollectible accounts is increased by bad debts expense (estimated provision for uncollectibles) and decreased when an account is written off. Because the allowance for uncollectible accounts is a contra-asset account, credit entries increase its balance. The greater the balance in the contra-asset account, the more the corresponding asset account is offset.

BUSINESS INSIGHT

Expense or reduction in revenue? Technically speaking, bad debts expense is not really an expense. It is, instead, a reduction of revenue. Although it is correct under current GAAP to record this item as a subtraction from sales revenue, companies commonly record bad debts expense as part of selling expenses to emphasize that this amount is a cost of offering credit to customers. (See Appendix 6B for a brief discussion of the accounting for bad debts under the new accounting standard for revenue recognition.)

Recording Write-offs of Uncollectible Accounts

Companies have collection processes and policies to determine when an overdue receivable should be classified as uncollectible. When an individual account reaches that classification, it is written off. To illustrate a write-off, assume that in the next period (Year 2), the company described above receives notice that one of its customers, owing $500 at the time, has declared bankruptcy. The seller's attorneys believe that the legal costs necessary to collect the amount would exceed the $500 owed. The seller could then decide to write off the account with the following entry.

ANALYZE

	Balance Sheet							Income Statement		
Transaction	Cash Asset	+ Noncash Assets	− Contra Asset	=	Liabil-ities	+ Contrib. Capital	+ Earned Capital	Revenues	− Expenses	= Net Income
(3) Write off $500 in accounts receivable.*		−500 Accounts Receivable	− −500 Allowance for Uncollectible Accounts	=					−	=

*There is no effect on accounts receivable, net of the allowance for uncollectible accounts. Consequently, there is no *net* effect on the balance sheet.

JOURNALIZE

(3) Allowance for uncollectible accounts (−XA, +A)	500	
Accounts receivable (−A).		500

POST

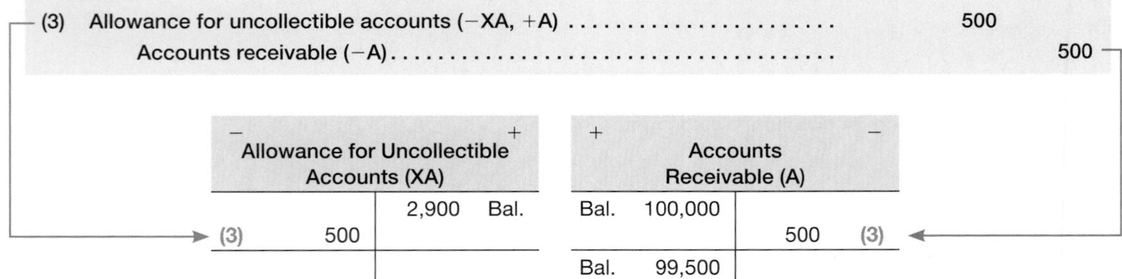

Exhibit 6.7 summarizes the effects of this write-off on the individual accounts.

EXHIBIT 6.7 Effects of an Accounts Receivable Write-Off

	Before Write-Off	Effects of Write-Off	After Write-Off
Accounts receivable.	$100,000	$ (500)	$99,500
Less: Allowance for uncollectible accounts	2,900	500	2,400
Accounts receivable, net of allowance.	$ 97,100		$97,100

The net amount of accounts receivable that is reported in the balance sheet after the write-off is the same amount that was reported before the write-off. This is always the case. The individual account receivable was reduced and the contra-asset was reduced by the same amount. Also, no entry was made to the income statement. The expense was estimated and recorded in the period when the credit sales were recorded.[4]

To complete the illustration, assume that management's aging of accounts at the end of Year 2 shows that the ending balance in the allowance account should be $3,000, so another $600 should be added to the allowance account at the end of Year 2. This $600 amount would reflect sales made in Year 2, as well as the seller's experience with collections during Year 2. The entry to record the Year 2 provision follows.

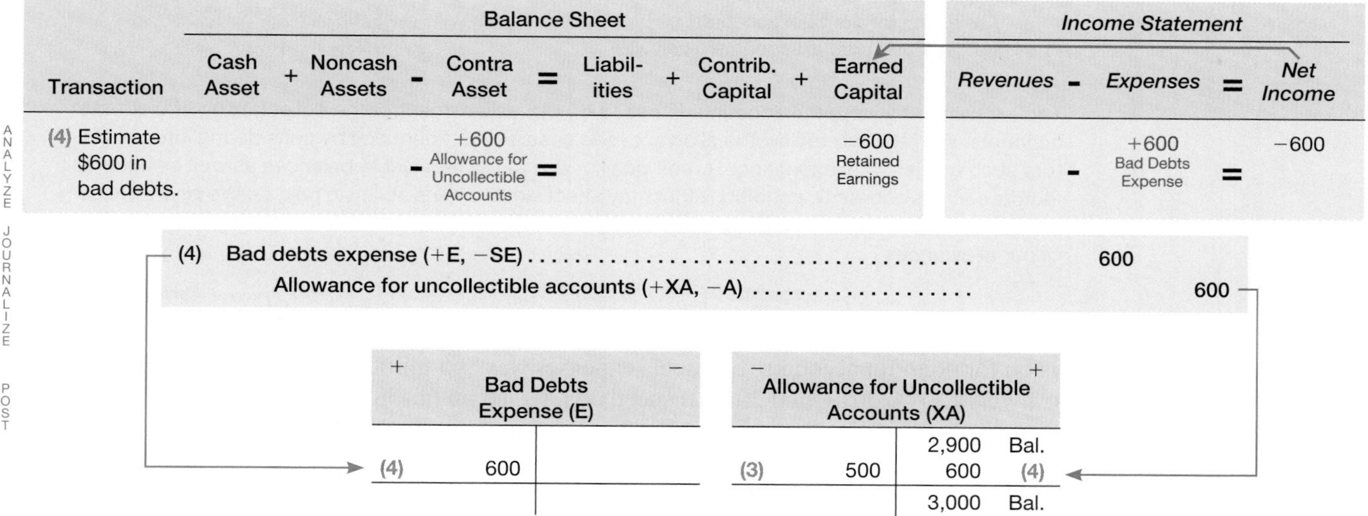

This entry is the same (albeit with a different dollar amount) as the entry made to record the estimate in Year 1. A reconciliation of allowance for uncollectible accounts for the two years follows.

	Year 1	Year 2
Allowance for uncollectible accounts, beginning balance	$ 0	$2,900
Add: provision for uncollectible accounts (bad debts expense estimate)	2,900	600
Subtract: write-offs of uncollectible accounts receivable	0	(500)
Allowance for uncollectible accounts, ending balance	$2,900	$3,000

To summarize, the *main balance sheet and income statement effects occur when the provision is made to the allowance for uncollectible accounts*. Accounts receivable (net) is reduced, and that reduction is reflected in the income statement as bad debts expense (usually part of selling, general, and administrative expenses). The net income reduction yields a corresponding equity reduction (via reduced retained earnings). Importantly, the main financial statement effects are at the point of *estimation*, not upon the event of *write-off*. In this way, the net accounts receivable reflects the most up-to-date judgments about future customer payments, and bad debts expense matches the current period's sales and incorporates any changes in management's assessment of the likelihood that customers will pay.

[4] Suppose a previously written off account is unexpectedly paid. If that occurs, the write-off entry (3) is reversed (reinstating the receivable and increasing the allowance), and the payment of this reinstated receivable is accounted for in the usual fashion.

Footnote Disclosures and Interpretations

In its balance sheets, Cisco reports Accounts receivables, net of allowance for doubtful accounts of $5,157 million at July 26, 2014, and $5,470 at July 27, 2013. In its MD&A (Management Discussion and Analysis), the company provides the following information.

Allowances for Receivables and Sales Returns

The allowances for receivables were as follows (in millions, except percentages):

	July 26, 2014	July 27, 2013
Allowance for doubtful accounts	$265	$228
Percentage of gross accounts receivable	4.9%	4.0%

The allowance for doubtful accounts is based on our assessment of the collectability of customer accounts. We regularly review the allowances to ensure their adequacy by considering internal factors such as historical experience, credit quality, age of the receivable balances as well as external factors such as economic conditions that may affect a customer's ability to pay. . . . We also consider the concentration of receivables outstanding with a particular customer in assessing the adequacy of our allowances . . .

In Cisco's 10-K report filed with the Securities and Exchange Commission, it discloses that its provision for doubtful accounts (bad debts expense) was $65 million, $33 million, and $19 million in fiscal years 2014, 2013, and 2012, respectively. Based on this information, we could construct a reconciliation of Cisco's allowance for doubtful accounts as presented in **Exhibit 6.8**.

EXHIBIT 6.8 Reconciliation of Cisco's Allowance for Doubtful Accounts

Allowance for Doubtful Accounts ($ millions)	
Balance at July 27, 2013	$228
Provision for doubtful accounts	65
Write-offs	(28)
Balance at July 26, 2014	$265

The footnotes may also disclose whether or not a company has *pledged* its accounts receivable as collateral for a short-term loan. If this is the case, a short-term loan is presented in the liabilities section of the balance sheet and a footnote explains the arrangement. As an alternative to borrowing, a company may *factor* (or sell) its accounts receivable to a bank or other financial institution. If the receivables have been factored, the bank or other financial institution accepts all responsibility for collection. Consequently, the receivables do not appear on the balance sheet of the selling company because they have been sold.

The reconciliation of Cisco's allowance account provides insight into the level of its annual provision (bad debts expense) relative to its write-offs. In 2014, Cisco wrote off $28 million in uncollectible accounts while recording a provision for doubtful accounts (bad debts expense) of $65 million. Because the provision exceeded the write-offs, the total allowance increased from $228 million in 2013 to $265 million in 2014.

Cisco's bad debts expense (or provision) has been volatile in recent years. It reported a provision for bad debts of $19 million in 2012 and $7 million in 2011. The changes in bad debts expense, both in absolute amount and as a percentage of sales revenue, could be caused by a number of factors. For example, the creditworthiness of Cisco's customers may have changed. These changes can be caused by changing economic conditions or changes in Cisco's credit policies (including collection efforts).

The magnitude of Cisco's uncollectible accounts relative to the company's overall size and profitability makes it an unlikely place for earnings management. But companies in other industries (banking, publishing, retail) often have receivables that require substantial adjustments for expected returns or uncollectible accounts. For instance, the publisher **John Wiley & Sons, Inc.**, reports accounts receivable of $149.7 million in its April 30, 2014, balance sheet, but this amount is net of an allowance for doubtful accounts of $7.9 million and an allowance for sales returns of $41.1 million. So, Wiley only expects to collect about 75% of the amounts it has billed customers. For such companies, modest changes in expectations of returns or collections can have a material effect on reported income.

Experience tells us that many companies have used the allowance for uncollectible accounts to shift income from one period into another. For instance, a company may overestimate its allowance in some years. Such an overestimation may have been unintentional, or it may have been an intentional attempt to manage earnings by building up a reserve (during good years) that can be drawn down in subsequent periods in order to increase reported income. Such a reserve is sometimes called a **cookie jar reserve**. Alternatively, a company may underestimate its provision in some years. This underestimation may be unintentional, or it may be an attempt to boost earnings to achieve some desired target. Looking at the patterns in the reconciliation of the allowance for uncollectible accounts may provide some indicators of this behavior.[5]

The MD&A section of a company's 10-K report often provides insights into changes in company policies, customers, or economic conditions to help explain changes in the allowance account. Further, the amount and timing of the uncollectible provision is largely controlled by management. Although external auditors assess the reasonableness of the allowance for uncollectible accounts, auditors do not possess the inside knowledge of management and are, therefore, at an information disadvantage, particularly if a dispute arises.

Some insight can be gained by comparing Cisco's allowance to those of its competitors. **Exhibit 6.9** illustrates that Cisco's allowance as a percentage of total receivables is significantly above that of its competitors, **F5 Networks, Inc.**, **Hewlett-Packard Company**, and **Juniper Networks, Inc.** This result suggests that Cisco is either more liberal in its credit policies or more conservative in its estimate of uncollectible accounts. In addition, Cisco increased the allowance as a percentage of receivables over this period, while none of its competitors did.

EXHIBIT 6.9 Allowance for Doubtful Accounts as a Percentage of Gross Receivables

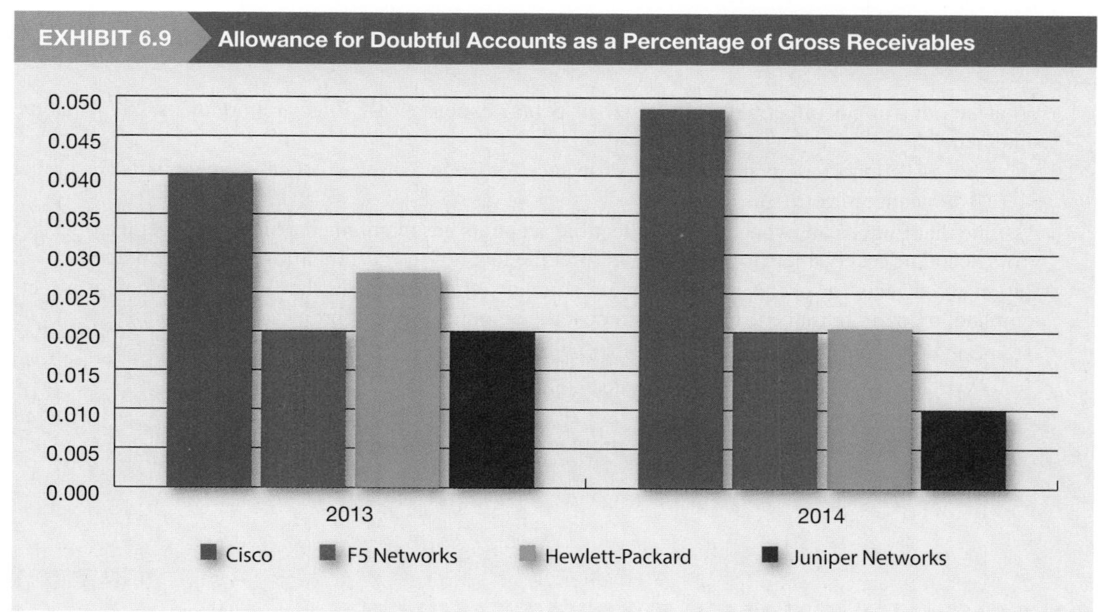

These companies do not have identical fiscal year-ends. Cisco's fiscal year ends in late July, F5 Networks on September 30, Hewlett-Packard on October 31, and Juniper Networks on December 31. The comparisons in this exhibit (and in those following) are based on the most recent financial statements for each company available prior to Cisco's statements.

Ultimately, a company makes two representations when reporting accounts receivable (net) in the current asset section of its balance sheet:

[5] See McNichols, Maureen and G. Peter Wilson, "Evidence of Earnings Management from the Provision for Bad Debts," *Journal of Accounting Research*, Supplement 1988.

1. It expects to collect the asset amount reported on the balance sheet (remember, accounts receivable are reported net of allowance for uncollectible accounts).
2. It expects to collect the asset amount within the next year (implied from its classification as a current asset).

From an analysis viewpoint, we scrutinize the adequacy of a company's provision for its uncollectible accounts. If the provision is inadequate, the cash ultimately collected will be less than what the company is reporting as net receivables.

The financial statement effects of uncollectible accounts are at the point of estimation, not at the time of a write-off. Nevertheless, it is important to remember that management sets the size of the allowance, albeit with auditor assurances.

MID-CHAPTER REVIEW 3

At December 31, 2016, Engel Company had a balance of $770,000 in its Accounts Receivable account and an unused balance of $7,000 in its Allowance for Uncollectible Accounts. The company then analyzed and aged its accounts receivable as follows:

Current	$468,000
1–60 days past due	244,000
61–180 days past due	38,000
Over 180 days past due	20,000
Total accounts receivable	$770,000

In the past, the company experienced losses as follows: 1% of current balances, 5% of balances 1–60 days past due, 15% of balances 61–180 days past due, and 40% of balances over 180 days past due. The company bases its provision for credit losses on the aging analysis.

Required

1. What amount of uncollectible accounts (bad debts) expense will Engel report in its 2016 income statement?
2. Show how Accounts Receivable and the Allowance for Uncollectible Accounts appear in its December 31, 2016, balance sheet.
3. Assume that Engel's allowance for uncollectible accounts has maintained a historical average of 2% of gross accounts receivable. How do you interpret the level of the current allowance percentage?
4. Report the effects for each of the following summary transactions in the financial statement effects template, prepare journal entries, and then post the amounts to the appropriate T-accounts.
   a. Bad debts expense estimated at $23,580.
   b. Write off $5,000 in customer accounts.

The solution to this review problem can be found on pages 322–323.

LO5 Calculate return on net operating assets, net operating profit after taxes, net operating profit margin, accounts receivable turnover, and average collection period.

5

ANALYZING FINANCIAL STATEMENTS

We began this chapter with a discussion of operating income and revenues and proceeded to examine receivables. We now introduce ratios that will aid in our analysis of income, revenue, and receivables. The first ratio is a measure of performance that relates the firm's operating achievements to the resources available. The next ratio, net operating profit margin, relates operating profit to sales. The last two ratios, accounts receivable turnover ratio and the average collection period, aid in the analysis of receivables. Before we discuss these ratios, we examine a commonly-used measure of operating profit first introduced in Chapter 5, net operating profit after taxes (NOPAT).

Net Operating Profit After Taxes (NOPAT)

Net operating profit after taxes (NOPAT) is a widely used measure of operating profitability. NOPAT is calculated as follows:

NOPAT = Net income − [(Nonoperating revenues − Nonoperating expenses) × (1 − Statutory tax rate)]

As described in Appendix A of Chapter 5, we assume that the applicable statutory tax rate on nonoperating revenues and expenses is equal to the federal statutory tax rate of 35%. To illustrate the calculation of NOPAT, refer to Cisco's income statement presented in **Exhibit 6.2**. Cisco reported net income of $7,853 million in 2014. It also reported net interest and other income of $370 million. Therefore, Cisco's NOPAT for 2014 is $7,613 million [$7,853 million − ($370 million × (1 − 0.35))]. In 2013, Cisco's NOPAT was $9,963 million [$9,983 million − ($31 million × (1 − 0.35))].

NOPAT is an important measure of profitability. It is similar to net income except that NOPAT focuses exclusively on after-tax operating performance, while net income measures the overall performance of the company and includes both operating and nonoperating components. NOPAT is used as a performance measure by management and analysts alike and it is also used in a number of ratios, such as the net operating profit margin.

Next, we examine two ratios that allow us to compare operating profitability across firms.

Analysis Objective

We want to gauge the profitability of a company's operations.

Analysis Tool

Return on net operating assets (RNOA).

$$\textbf{Return on net operating assets (RNOA)} = \frac{\textbf{NOPAT}}{\textbf{Average net operating assets}}$$

Applying the Ratio to Cisco Systems

$$\textbf{2013:}\ \text{RNOA} = \frac{\$9{,}963}{\$30{,}683} = 0.325 \text{ or } 32.5\%$$

$$\textbf{2014:}\ \text{RNOA} = \frac{\$7{,}613}{\$32{,}438} = 0.235 \text{ or } 23.5\%$$

Cisco's average total assets for fiscal 2014 total $103,162.5 million ([$105,134 million + $101,191 million]/2), but $44,016.5 of this amount represents average investments in marketable securities. So, average operating assets are $59,146 million. Cisco also reports average operating liabilities of $26,708 million. Subtracting this amount from average operating assets gives average net operating assets of $32,438 million.

BUSINESS INSIGHT

What constitutes "cash" and when is cash operating and when is it nonoperating? To compute RNOA in this book we make a simplifying assumption and consider marketable securities and other investments as nonoperating assets, but we consider cash to be an operating asset. This is a matter of judgment for the financial statement user when doing financial statement analysis. The categorization of investment securities as cash or as investments varies across firms. Some companies, such as Hewlett-Packard classify a significant amount of investments as cash equivalents, and thus include the amount in the cash balance on the balance sheet. Other companies include investments in a separate line item on the balance sheet (either in current, long-term assets, or some in each).

Guidance **Return on net operating assets (RNOA)** is conceptually similar to return on assets (ROA) except that it excludes all nonoperating components of income and investment from the calculation. The resulting ratio is a measure of how well the company is performing relative to its core objective. A company can use investments in securities and financial leverage to report a satisfactory level of profit and return overall, even when its primary operating activities are not performing well. RNOA can reveal weaknesses in a company's operating strategy that are not readily apparent from overall measures such as return on equity and return on assets.

A variation on RNOA is the **return on capital employed**. This ratio examines the return on net operating assets *before* income taxes and is often used to measure performance of business units and division managers within a large organization. Operating managers generally do not have responsibility for income taxes or financing activities. (These functions are typically the responsibility of central management.) Consequently, return on capital employed excludes income taxes and focuses exclusively on the resources made available to the unit manager.

Cisco does not provide enough information to calculate return on capital employed for individual business units, but we can do so for the company as a whole. From **Exhibit 6.2**, we see that pretax operating income is \$9,345 million. Average net operating assets, adjusted for income tax assets and liabilities, total \$31,701 million.[6] Thus, Cisco's return on capital employed is 29% (=\$9,345 million/\$31,701 million).

Cisco Systems in Context

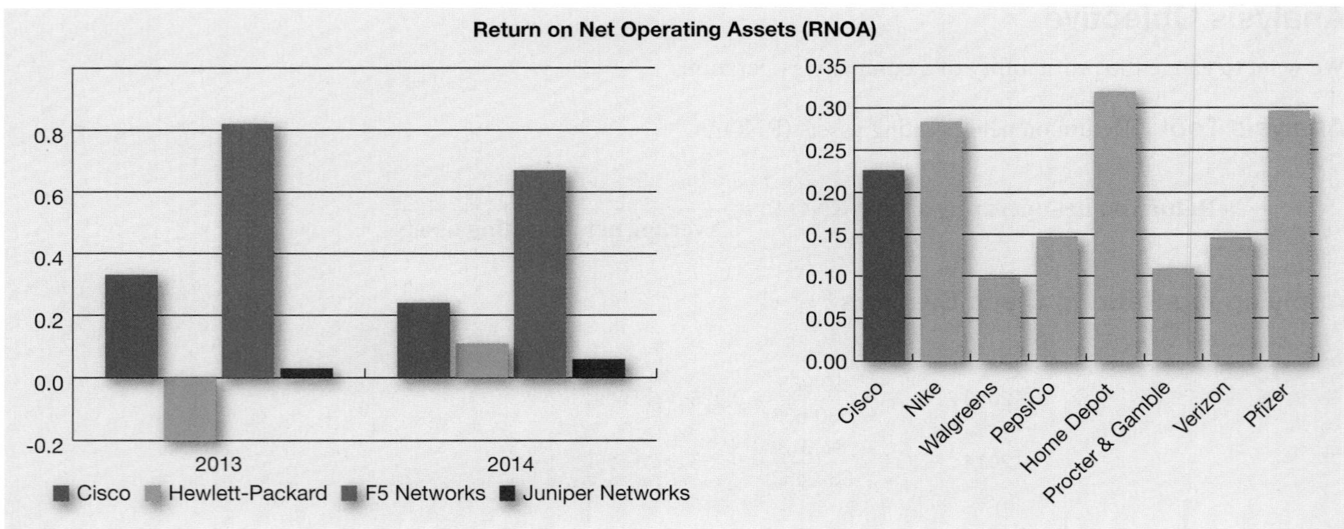

Analysis Tool Net operating profit margin (NOPM)

$$\textbf{Net operating profit margin (NOPM)} = \frac{\textbf{NOPAT}}{\textbf{Sales revenue}}$$

Applying the Ratio to Cisco Systems

$$\textbf{2013:}\ \text{NOPM} = \frac{\$9,963}{\$48,607} = 0.205 \text{ or } 20.5\%$$

$$\textbf{2014:}\ \text{NOPM} = \frac{\$7,613}{\$47,142} = 0.161 \text{ or } 16.1\%$$

[6] Because we use operating profit before taxes, accrued income taxes payable and deferred income taxes (assets and liabilities) should be excluded when computing net operating assets for this ratio. Cisco reported average deferred tax assets of \$2,712 million and income taxes payable of \$1,975 million. Thus, the average net operating assets used to calculate return on capital employed equals \$32,438 million − (\$2,712 million − \$1,975 million) = \$31,701 million.

Guidance Profit margins are commonly used to compare a company to its competitors and to evaluate the performance of business segments. **Net operating profit margin (NOPM)** is a useful summary measure that focuses on the overall operating profitability of the company relative to its sales revenue.

Cisco Systems in Context

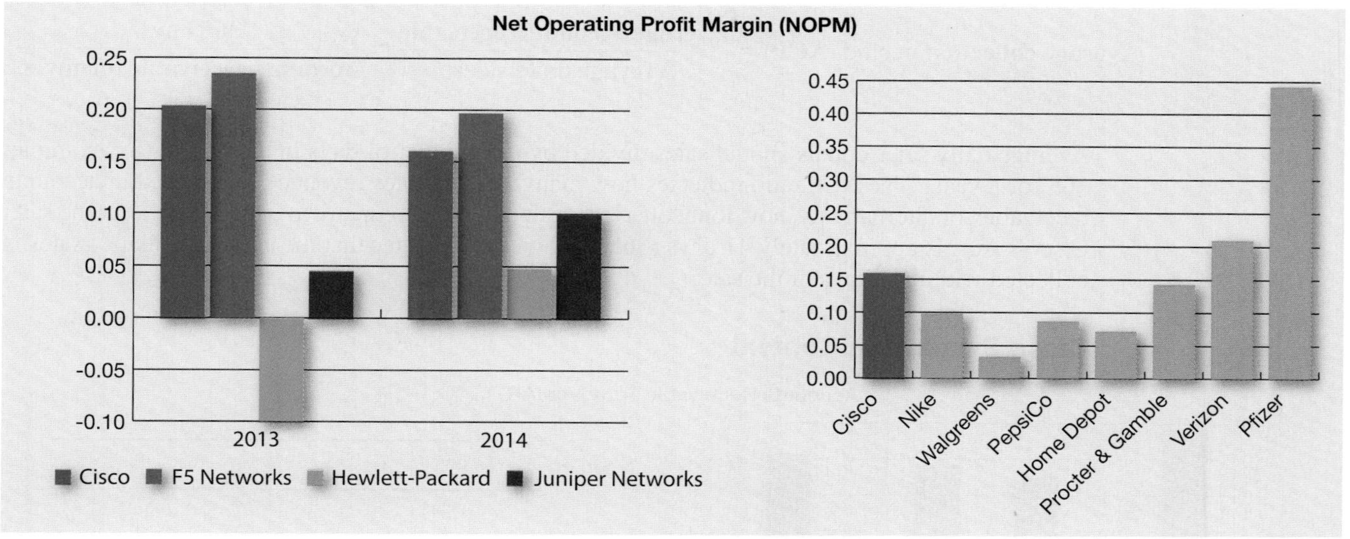

Takeaways Cisco's return on net operating assets and net operating profit margin are both within the range of the other companies we examine in this text. Retail businesses, such as **Walgreen Co.** and **Home Depot**, tend to have lower operating profit margins than companies in other industries. This does not necessarily translate into lower operating returns. Retail companies rely more heavily on turnover of operating assets to produce returns, relative to other industries.

Cisco's return on net operating assets is higher than two of its primary competitors, Hewlett-Packard and Juniper Networks, but has decreased slightly from 2013 to 2014. Only F5 Networks reported a higher return on net operating assets and operating profit margin than Cisco Systems. In sum, Cisco's operating performance appears to be relatively strong and it does not appear that the company relies too heavily on nonoperating sources of income to generate its returns. However, the decline in returns and margins from 2013 to 2014 may be cause for further investigation.

Analysis Objective

We want to evaluate a company's management of its receivables.

Analysis Tool Accounts receivable turnover (ART) and average collection period (ACP)

$$\textbf{Accounts receivable turnover (ART)} = \frac{\textbf{Sales revenue}}{\textbf{Average accounts receivable}}$$

Applying the Accounts Receivable Turnover Ratio to Cisco Systems

$$\textbf{2013:}\ \text{ART} = \frac{\$48{,}607}{(\$5{,}470 + \$4{,}369)/2} = 9.9\ \text{times}$$

$$\textbf{2014:}\ \text{ART} = \frac{\$47{,}142}{(\$5{,}157 + \$5{,}470)/2} = 8.9\ \text{times}$$

Guidance **Accounts receivable turnover** measures the number of times each year that accounts receivable is converted into cash. A high turnover ratio suggests that receivables are well managed and that sales revenue quickly leads to cash collected from customers.

A companion measure to accounts receivable turnover is the **average collection period**, also called *days sales outstanding* which is defined as:

$$\textbf{Average collection period (ACP)} = \frac{\textbf{Average accounts receivable}}{\textbf{Average daily sales}} = \frac{\textbf{365 days}}{\textbf{Accounts receivable turnover}}$$

Average daily sales equals annual sales divided by the number of days in the period (for example, 365 for a year). The ACP ratio indicates how many days of sales revenue are invested in accounts receivable, or alternatively, how long, on average, it takes the company to collect cash after the sale. Cisco's ACP is approximately 41 days (365/8.9), which indicates that the average dollar of sales is collected within 41 days of the sale.

Cisco Systems in Context

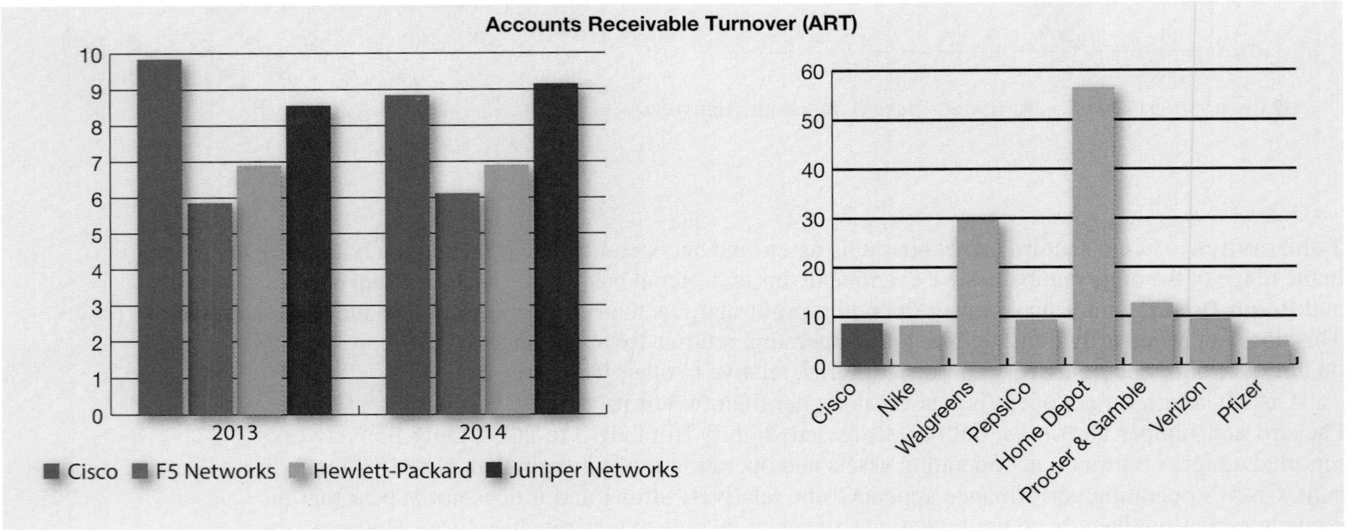

Takeaways The accounts receivable turnover and the average collection period yield valuable insights on at least two dimensions:

1. *Receivables quality.* A change in receivables turnover (and collection period) provides insight into accounts receivable quality. If turnover slows (collection period lengthens), the reason could be deterioration in collectibility of receivables. However, before reaching this conclusion, consider at least three alternative explanations:
   a. A seller can extend its credit terms. If the seller is attempting to enter new markets or take market share from competitors, it may extend credit terms to attract buyers.
   b. A seller can take on longer-paying customers. For example, facing increased competition, many computer and automobile companies began leasing their products, thus reducing the cash outlay for customers and stimulating sales. The change in mix away from cash sales and toward leasing had the effect of reducing receivables turnover and increasing the collection period.

c. The seller can increase the allowance provision. Receivables turnover is often computed using net receivables (after the allowance for uncollectible accounts). Overestimating the provision reduces net receivables and increases turnover.

2. *Asset utilization.* Asset turnover is an important measure of financial performance, both by managers for internal performance goals, as well as by the market in evaluating companies. High performing companies must be both efficient (controlling margins and operating expenses) and productive (getting the most out of their asset base). An increase in receivables ties up cash as the receivables must be financed, and slower-turning receivables carry increased risk of loss. One of the first "low-hanging fruits" that companies pursue in efforts to improve asset utilization is efficiency in receivables collection.

Other Considerations Accounts receivable are sometimes used by companies to obtain financing. This is done in one of two ways: (1) the company can use accounts receivable as collateral for a short-term loan in a transaction called *securitization*, or (2) the company can sell its receivables, which is referred to as *factoring*. A thorough discussion of these transactions is beyond the scope of this text. Nonetheless, if a firm uses securitization or factoring of receivables to obtain short-term financing, the amount of accounts receivable listed on the balance sheet is altered which, in turn, affects the ART ratio.

YOU MAKE THE CALL

You are the Receivables Manager You are analyzing your receivables turnover report for the period, and you are concerned that the average collection period is lengthening, causing a drop in cash flow from operations. What specific actions can you take to reduce the average collection period? [Answers on page 301]

EARNINGS MANAGEMENT

LO6 Discuss earnings management and explain how it affects analysis and interpretation of financial statements.

Management choices about transactions, accounting principles, estimates, disclosure, and presentation of income components are an inevitable part of financial reporting. Earnings management occurs when management uses this discretion to mask the underlying economic performance of a company.

There are many motives for earnings management, but these motives generally fall into one of two categories:

1. A desire to mislead some financial statement users about the financial performance of the company to gain economic advantage, or
2. A desire to influence legal contracts that use reported accounting numbers to specify contractual obligations and outcomes.[7]

Most earnings management practices relate to aggressive revenue or expense recognition practices. However, financial statement presentation can also be a concern. Below, we identify several examples of potentially misleading reporting.

FYI Earnings management involves earnings quality and management ethics. For the latter, management must consider both legal and personal ethical standards of conduct.

- *Overly optimistic (or overly pessimistic) estimates.* The use of estimates in accrual accounting is extensive. For instance, revenue recognition based on percentage of completion requires estimates of future construction costs. Depreciation expense depends on estimates of useful life, and bad debts expense depends on estimates of future customer payments. Although changes in estimates may be warranted by changes in business conditions, they can have a significant effect on reported net income and, thereby, may provide opportunities for managers to report income that is better (or worse) than it should be.

[7] See Healy, Paul M., and James M. Wahlen, "A Review of Earnings Management Literature and Its Implications for Standard Setting," *Accounting Horizons*, December 1999.

- *Channel stuffing.* **Channel stuffing** arises when a company uses its market power over customers or distributors to induce them to purchase more goods than necessary to meet their normal needs. Or, the seller may offer significant price reductions to encourage buyers to stock up on its products. Channel stuffing usually occurs immediately before the end of an accounting period and boosts the seller's revenue for that period (while increasing the buyer's inventory). The practice is not illegal and revenue may be recorded, as long as the transactions meet the necessary criteria for a sale.
- *Strategic timing and disclosure of transactions and nonrecurring gains and losses.* Management has some discretion over the timing of transactions that can affect financial statements. If management has an asset (e.g., a tract of land) with book value less than market value, it can choose when to sell the asset to recognize a gain and maintain steady improvements in net income. This practice is known as **income smoothing**. In some cases, these smoothing effects are reported in combination with other items, making it more difficult to separate recurring amounts from nonrecurring amounts. Or, a company could take a **big bath** by recording a nonrecurring loss in a period of already depressed income. Concentrating bad news in a single period reduces the amount of bad news recognized in other periods. Given adequate disclosure, the astute reader of the financial statements will separate nonrecurring income items from persistent operating income, making these income management tactics transparent.
- *Mischaracterizing transactions as arm's-length.* Transfers of inventories or other assets to related entities typically are not recorded until later **arm's-length** sales occur. Sometimes sales are disguised as being sold to unrelated entities to inflate income when (1) the buyer is a related party to the seller, or (2) financing is provided or guaranteed by the seller, or (3) the buyer is a special-purpose entity that fails to meet independence requirements. This financial reporting practice is not consistent with GAAP and may be fraudulent.

FYI An arm's-length transaction is any transaction between two unrelated parties.

BUSINESS INSIGHT

Sell-through Accounting at Cisco Following is an excerpt from Cisco System's revenue recognition policies from its annual report.

> Distributors hold inventory and typically sell to systems integrators, service providers, and other resellers. We refer to sales through distributors as our two-tier system of sales to the end customer. Revenue from distributors is recognized based on a sell-through method using information provided by them.

The "sell-through" method is essentially the same as the accounting for consignment arrangements. By not recognizing revenue until its distributors and retail partners sell its products to the final customer, Cisco greatly reduces the likelihood of any channel stuffing behavior.

The consequence of earnings management is that the usefulness of the information presented in the income statement is compromised. **Quality of earnings** is a term that analysts often use to describe the extent to which reported income reflects the underlying economic performance of a company. Financial statement users must be careful to examine the quality of a company's earnings before using that information to evaluate performance or value its securities.[8]

YOU MAKE THE CALL

You are the Controller While evaluating the performance of your sales staff, you notice that one of the salespeople consistently meets his quarterly sales quotas but never surpasses his goals by very much. You also discover that his customers often return an unusually large amount of product at the beginning of each quarter. What might be happening here? How would you investigate for potential abuse? [Answer on page 301]

[8] See Dechow, Patricia, Weili Ge, and Catherine Schrand, "Understanding Earnings Quality: A Review of the Proxies, their Determinants, and their Consequences," *Journal of Accounting and Economics*, December, 2010.

RESEARCH INSIGHT

Non-GAAP Income Nonrecurring items in income such as discontinued operations and restructuring charges make it difficult for investors to determine what portion of income is sustainable into the future. The past decade has seen more companies reporting **non-GAAP** or **pro forma income**, which purportedly excludes the effects of nonrecurring or noncash items that companies feel are unimportant for valuation purposes. Research, however, provides no evidence that more exclusions via pro forma income leads to more predictable future cash flows. More important, investors appear to be misled by the exclusions at the time of the non-GAAP income release. Research also finds that companies issuing pro forma income are more likely to be young companies concentrated in technology and business services. Too often, these companies are characterized by below-average sales and income when they choose to report pro forma income. Evidence also shows that the pro forma income can exceed GAAP income by as much as 20 percent.

Critics of non-GAAP income argue that the items excluded by managers from GAAP income are inconsistent across companies and time. They contend that a major motive for pro forma income is to mislead stakeholders. Legendary investor Warren Buffett puts pro forma in context (Berkshire Hathaway, Annual Report): "When companies or investment professionals use terms such as 'EBITDA' and 'pro forma,' they want you to unthinkingly accept concepts that are dangerously flawed."

CHAPTER-END REVIEW

The following data were taken from the 2014 10-K reports of **Comcast Corporation** and **Time Warner, Inc.**:

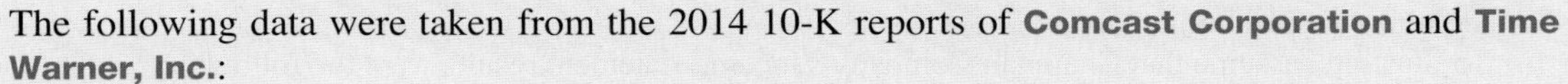

($ millions)	Comcast	Time Warner
Sales revenue	$68,775	$27,359
Net income	8,592	3,827
Nonoperating revenues	296	0
Nonoperating expenses	2,832	1,296
Accounts receivable, net (end-of-year)	6,321	7,720
Accounts receivable, net (beginning-of-year)	6,376	7,305
Operating assets (end-of-year)	155,602	60,933
Operating assets (beginning-of-year)	151,470	65,990
Operating liabilities (end-of-year)	56,971	16,289
Operating liabilities (beginning-of-year)	58,951	17,284

REQUIRED

1. Compute the following for each company:
   a. Net operating profit after taxes (NOPAT). Assume a 35% statutory tax rate.
   b. Return on net operating assets (RNOA).
   c. Net operating profit margin (NOPM).
   d. Accounts receivable turnover (ART).
   e. Average collection period (ACP).
2. Compare these two companies based on the ratios computed in (1). What inferences can you make about these competitors?

The solution to this review problem can be found on page 323.

APPENDIX 6A: Reporting Nonrecurring Items

LO7 Describe and illustrate the reporting for nonrecurring items.

In addition to categorizing income statement elements as either operating or nonoperating, it is also useful to separate **recurring** sources of income from those sources that are **nonrecurring**. Isolating nonrecurring earnings is useful for two reasons. First, to evaluate company performance or management quality, it is helpful to make comparisons of current performance with prior years and with other companies facing similar economic circumstances. It is easier to make these comparisons if we focus on recurring income components. Nonrecurring income components are likely to be specific to one company and one accounting period, making them irrelevant for comparative purposes. Second, estimation of company value involves forecasts of income and cash flows. Such forecasts are better when we can identify any nonrecurring effects in income and cash flows and then eliminate them from projections. Recurring earnings and cash flows are more **persistent** and, therefore, more useful in estimating company value.

FYI Previously, a third category, extraordinary items, existed that reported gains or losses from unusual and infrequent items. FASB has eliminated this third category effective for fiscal years beginning after December 15, 2015. The category was eliminated in an effort toward simplification. See Accounting Standards Update 2015-01.

Accounting standards attempt to distinguish some nonrecurring income components. Two of the most common nonrecurring items are:

- **Discontinued operations**—income related to business units that the company has discontinued and sold or plans to sell.
- **Restructuring charges**—expenses and losses related to significant reorganization of a company's operations.

Discontinued Operations

Discontinued operations refer to separately identifiable components of the company that management sells or intends to sell. Recent guidance for discontinued operations (ASU 2014-08) provides that only disposals representing a strategic shift in operations should be reported as discontinued operations. Examples include a disposal of a major geographical segment, a major line of business, or a major equity investment. The new guidance was issued because of concerns that too many disposals of small asset groups were being classified as discontinued operations.

The income or loss of the discontinued operations (net of tax), and the after-tax gain or loss on sale of the unit, are reported in the income statement below income from continuing operations. The segregation of discontinued operations means that its revenues and expenses are *not* reported with revenues and expenses from continuing operations.

To illustrate, assume that Chapman Company's income statement results were the following.

	Continuing Operations	Discontinued Operations	Total
Revenues	$10,000	$3,000	$13,000
Expenses	7,000	2,000	9,000
Pretax income	3,000	1,000	4,000
Tax expense (40%)	1,200	400	1,600
Net income	$ 1,800	$ 600	$ 2,400

The reported income statement would then appear with the separate disclosure for discontinued operations (shown in bold, separately net of any related taxes) as follows.

Revenues	$10,000
Expenses	7,000
Pretax income	3,000
Tax expense (40%)	1,200
Income from continuing operations	1,800
Income from discontinued operations, net of income taxes	**600**
Net income	$ 2,400

FYI Income, gains, and losses from discontinued operations are reported separately from other items to alert readers to their transitory nature.

Revenues and expenses reflect the continuing operations only, and the (persistent) income from continuing operations is reported after deducting the related tax expense. Results from the (transitory) discontinued operations are collapsed into one line item and reported separately net of any related taxes. The same is true for any gain or loss from sale of the discontinued operation's net assets. The net income figure is unchanged by this presentation, but our ability to evaluate and interpret income information is greatly improved.

Exit or Disposal Costs

Exit or disposal costs include but are not limited to **restructuring costs**. Exit and disposal costs typically include activities such as consolidating production facilities, reorganizing sales operations, outsourcing product lines, or discontinuing product lines within a business unit or that do not represent a strategic shift in operations. These costs should be separately disclosed if material, but if not material are not required to be shown as a separate line item on the income statement. Often these costs, such as restructuring costs, are material in nature and are shown as a separate line item or are detailed in the notes to the financial statements. These costs are considered transitory because many companies do not engage in restructuring activities every year. As such, these costs should be classified to a transitory category for analysis purposes even though the costs are included in income from continuing operations. Restructuring costs include, but are not limited to, the following types of costs:

1. Employee severance costs
2. Costs to consolidate and close facilities, including asset write-downs

The first of these, **employee severance costs**, represent accrued (estimated) costs for termination of employees as part of a restructuring program. The second part of restructuring costs consists of **asset write-downs**, also called *write-offs* or *charge-offs*. Restructuring activities usually involve closure or relocation of manufacturing or administrative facilities. This process can require the write-down of long-term assets (such as plant assets), and the write-down of inventories that are no longer salable at current carrying costs.

Cisco reported restructuring charges of $418 million in its fiscal 2014 income statement and $105 million (net) in its 2013 income statement. These charges were discussed in the footnotes.

FYI Management's ability to reduce income using restructuring charges and later reverse some of that charge (creating subsequent period income) reduces earnings quality. U.S. GAAP requires disclosures that enable a financial statement reader to track the restructuring activities and to identify any reversals that occur.

In August 2013, the Company announced a workforce reduction plan that would impact up to 4,000 employees, or 5% of the Company's global workforce. In connection with this restructuring action, the Company incurred charges of $418 million during fiscal 2014. The Company has completed the Fiscal 2014 restructuring and does not expect any remaining charges related to this action. The Fiscal 2011 Plans consist primarily of the realignment and restructuring of the Company's business announced in July 2011 and of certain consumer product lines as announced during April 2011. . . . The following table summarizes the activities related to the restructuring and other charges pursuant to the Company's Fiscal 2014 Plan and the Fiscal 2011 Plans related to the realignment and restructuring of the Company's business (in millions):

	Fiscal 2011 Plans	Employee Severance	Other	Total
Balance as of July 27, 2013	$28	$ 0	$ 0	$ 28
Gross charges in fiscal 2014		366	52	418
Cash payments	(22)	(326)	(4)	(352)
Non-cash items	(3)		(22)	(25)
Balance as of July 26, 2014	$ 3	$ 40	$26	$ 69

Most of Cisco's restructuring costs were in the form of severance pay to employees and payments to retirement programs as compensation to employees who elect to take early retirement. As of the end of fiscal 2014, Cisco had $69 million in restructuring charges that had been accrued but not yet paid.

RESEARCH INSIGHT

Restructuring Costs and Managerial Incentives Research has investigated the circumstances and effects of restructuring costs. Some research finds that stock prices increase upon announcement of a restructuring as if the market appreciates the company's candor. Research also finds that many companies that reduce income through restructuring costs later reverse those costs, resulting in a substantial income boost for the period of reversal. These reversals often occur when their absence would have yielded an earnings decline. Whether or not the market responds favorably to trimming the fat or simply disregards such transitory items as uninformative, managers have incentives to exclude such income-decreasing items from operating income. These incentives are contractually-based, extending from debt covenants and restrictions to managerial bonuses.

YOU MAKE THE CALL

You are the Financial Analyst You are analyzing the financial statements of a company that has reported a large restructuring cost, involving both employee severance and asset write-downs, in its income statement. How do you interpret and treat this cost in your analysis of its current and future period profitability? [Answer on page 301]

APPENDIX 6A REVIEW

On April 30, 2016, Singh Corporation decided to close its operations in Fiji. During the first four months of the year (January through April) these operations had reported a loss of $120,000. Singh paid its employees $12,000 in severance pay. The assets of this operation were sold at a loss of $18,000. The tax rate in Fiji is 30%.

REQUIRED

a. If this closure is recorded as discontinued operations, how should it be presented in Singh's income statement?
b. If this closure is classified as a restructuring charge, how would it be presented in Singh's income statement?
c. What would determine whether this event should be reported as discontinued operations or a restructuring charge?

The solution to this review problem can be found on page 324.

APPENDIX 6B: New Standards for Revenue Recognition

8 **LO8** Describe the new standard for revenue recognition and discuss its potential effects.

The FASB and the IASB issued new, converged accounting standards for revenue recognition in May of 2014.[9] The new standard is intended to develop a common revenue standard between U.S. GAAP and IFRS and to consolidate the guidance and rules for revenue recognition into one standard as opposed to the patchwork of standards and sources of guidance that had developed over time for various transactions and industries. In addition, the new standard aims to eliminate inconsistencies that exist across industries and transactions. The new standard is more principles based and will require management to exercise more judgment; however, it broadly employs many of the same overriding concepts to revenue recognition as the current standards. The standard setters intend for the new standards to improve comparability and disclosure for financial statement users.

In August 2015, FASB and IASB deferred the effective dates of the new standards by one year from the originally stated effective dates. The new effective dates are as follows. Public business entities, certain not-for-profit entities, and certain employee benefit plans are required to apply the guidance in Update 2014-09 to annual reporting periods beginning after December 15, 2017, including interim reporting periods within that reporting period. Thus, for calendar year-end companies, the required effective date is January 1, 2018.[10] All other entities, including private business entities, are required to apply the guidance in Update 2014-09 to annual reporting periods beginning after December 15, 2018, and interim reporting periods within annual reporting periods beginning after December 15, 2019.[11] Thus, the required effective dates are more than two years away at the time of the writing of this text. As a result, we do not have examples of companies applying the new standard and we cannot show any disclosures under the new standard. In this appendix, we discuss the overriding principles of the new standard and conjecture about potential implications of the new standard based on industry reports and company disclosures available at this time.

The new standard's core principle is that an entity should recognize revenue to depict the transfer of goods or services to customers in an amount that reflects the consideration to which the entity expects to be entitled in the exchange for those goods and services. FASB outlines the following five steps in the revenue recognition process:

Step 1. Identify the contract with a customer
Step 2. Identify the performance obligations in the contract
Step 3. Determine the transaction price
Step 4. Allocate the transaction price
Step 5. Recognize revenue when or as the entity satisfies a performance obligation

Collectibility of payment (broadly similar to the idea of realized or realizable discussed as part of the current accounting standards for revenue recognition) continues to be an important issue for revenue recognition. Under

---

[9] FASB issued Accounting Standards Update (ASU) 2014-09 and the IASB issued International Financial Reporting Standards 15, both entitled *Revenue from Contracts with Customers*. ASU 2014-09 creates Topic 606, *Revenue from Contracts with Customers*, in codified GAAP, which supersedes the revenue recognition requirements in Topic 605, *Revenue Recognition*, including most industry-specific revenue recognition guidance.

[10] Early adoption is permitted, but only as of annual reporting periods beginning after December 15, 2016, including interim reporting periods within that reporting period.

[11] Early adoption is also permitted for these entities, but only as early as annual reporting periods beginning after December 15, 2016, including interim reporting periods within that reporting period (or within annual reporting periods beginning one year after the annual reporting period in which the entity first applies the guidance in Update 2014-09).

the new standard, collectibility should be assessed in determining whether a contract exists (i.e., whether the entity has passed Step 1 of the 5-step revenue recognition process listed above).

In general, the new revenue recognition standard does not conceptually change the accounting for bad debts from the current rules. However, the new standard will require more judgment on the part of management in determining whether the expectation of partial payment on a sales contract is 1) evidence that the contract lacks collectibility in which case revenue cannot be recorded, 2) due to a price concession in which case revenue should be recorded but at the expected lower amount, or 3) a bad debt, in which case sales should be recognized in full but with bad debt provision recorded. The additional required judgment about collectibility could lead to uncertainty and potentially significant changes to revenue recognition for some entities. As firms apply the standard in future years, we will be able to observe and discuss more fully the consequences of these changes.

Long-Term Contracts

With respect to the accounting for long-term contracts, the new revenue recognition standard does not use the terms percentage-of-completion method, cost-recovery method, or completed contract method. All contracts fall under the 5-step process outlined above and revenue is recognized as performance obligations are satisfied, that is, when control of the good or service transfers to the customer. This can occur either at a point in time or over time. For most long-term contracts, revenue will be recognized over time. Under the new standard, measuring progress toward completion is done using either what is called the input method or the output method. It is likely that for many long-term contracts, such as construction contracts, most performance obligations will be measured over time using the input method. This method of revenue recognition is consistent with the percentage-of-completion method that is often applied under the current standard. Thus, the general overriding principles for revenue recognition are similar between the old and new standards for long-term contracts.

Disclosure

Significant changes in disclosure are required in the new standard. Companies will need to provide both qualitative and quantitative disclosure about contracts with customers including revenues recognized, disaggregation of revenues, contract balances, and performance obligations (including transaction prices allocated to remaining performance obligations). Additional disclosures will also be required about judgments and changes in judgments such as determining the timing of satisfaction of performance obligations (over time or at a point in time) and determining the transaction price and amounts allocated to performance obligations.

Potential Effects of Accounting Standards Update 2014-09 (Topic 606)

The effects of the new accounting standard for revenue recognition are not entirely clear at the time of this writing. The new standard calls for enhanced disclosure and additional documentation of internal controls over revenue recognition. In addition, while the overall spirit of the new standard is similar to current GAAP, it is likely the new standard will affect the reporting of revenues to some extent for many companies, especially those with multiple element contracts requiring revenue to be deferred and recognized across multiple periods. Some examples of potential and expected impacts are as follows.

- In **Microsoft**'s most recent annual report they state that they "*anticipate this standard will have a material impact on our consolidated financial statements and we are currently evaluating its impact.*"
- **Electronic Arts, Inc.** (see P6-47) states in its most recent annual report that ". . . *We recognize all of the revenue from bundled sales (i.e., online-enabled games that include updates on a when-and-if-available basis or a matchmaking service) on a deferred basis over an estimated offering period . . . We believe the current proposal by the FASB would require us to materially change the way we account for revenue by requiring us to recognize more revenue upon delivery of the primary product than we currently do under current accounting standards.*"
- A recent *Wall Street Journal* article (January 26, 2015) reports that **Ford Motor Co.** and **General Motors Co.** say that the new rules might force them to account separately for each car sold rather than allowing a grouping into comparable transactions.
- Airline companies may also be affected. It is likely that airlines will have to change the way they account for loyalty programs (e.g., frequent flier programs). For example, it appears likely that loyalty points will be treated as a revenue element and some portion of the transaction price will have to be allocated to the loyalty element based on the estimated standalone selling price of each performance obligation (Source: E&Y Technical Line, "The New Revenue Recognition Standard—Airlines").
- In a similar example as the airlines, companies that provide promotions or "free" goods may have to allocate revenues differently than they do currently. For example, when a wireless carrier sells a service contract and gives a free or discounted phone to the customer, it is likely that under the new standard

more revenue will likely be allocated to the sale of the phone, reducing margins on the service contracts. Even a simple retailer that offers a promotion such as buy three and get one free, will have to allocate revenue across the four products under the new standard.

- A panel of experts suggested that companies should be aware of changes to footnote disclosure requirements and should not regard those as an insignificant event. Lynne Triplett, a partner at Grant Thornton, said her greatest concern, "*is that companies aren't going to be prepared for the disclosures aspect*." (Source: Bloomberg BNA conference entitled, "Inside Revenue Recognition: A Deep Dive into Assessment & Implementation Under the New Revenue Recognition Standard" held on September 17, 2015, reported on in Bloomberg BNA on September 22, 2015).

At a high level, the new standard applies many of the same broad principles of revenue recognition as the current standard. However, there will likely be significant changes for many companies in terms of the timing of recognition, the allocation of revenue to transactions, and the disclosures about the revenue recognition process. These changes could have far reaching implications. For example, revenue recognition changes could affect operational decisions and outcomes such as the use of coupons, compensation in the form of sales commissions, and many others. As companies start to apply the standard, the standard setters may issue additional guidance or clarifications. In future editions of this text, we will incorporate examples from company disclosures as the new standard is applied and will discuss any future updates and guidance from the standard setters.

SUMMARY

LO1 Describe and apply the criteria for determining when revenue is recognized. (p. 274)

- Revenue is recognized when it is earned and realized (or realizable).

LO2 Illustrate revenue and expense recognition when the transaction involves future deliverables and/or multiple elements. (p. 275)

- When customers pay prior to the delivery of all elements of the product (or service) package, an unearned revenue liability must be recognized.
- When a company recognizes an unearned revenue liability, its reported revenue for a period does not coincide with the purchases made by customers in that period.

LO3 Illustrate revenue and expense recognition for long-term projects. (p. 279)

- Long-term contracts are recorded using the percentage-of-completion method when a signed contract exists with a fixed or determinable price, collection is reasonably assured, and the cost of completing the contract can be estimated.
- The completed contract method is used when the conditions for using percentage-of-completion are not met.

LO4 Estimate and account for uncollectible accounts receivable. (p. 282)

- Uncollectible accounts are usually estimated by aging the accounts receivable.
- Estimated uncollectible accounts are recorded as a contra-asset called allowance for uncollectible accounts.
- Write-offs of uncollectible accounts are deducted from accounts receivable and from the allowance account.

LO5 Calculate return on net operating assets, net operating profit after taxes, net operating profit margin, accounts receivable turnover, and average collection period. (p. 288)

- Net operating profit after taxes (NOPAT) and the net operating profit margin (NOPM) are measures of the profitability of operating activities.
- Return on net operating assets measures after-tax operating performance relative to available net operating assets; similarly, return on capital employed is a pretax measure that is used to evaluate business unit performance.
- Accounts receivable turnover (ART) and average collection period (ACP) measure the ability of the company to convert receivables into cash through collection.

LO6 Discuss earnings management and explain how it affects analysis and interpretation of financial statements. (p. 293)

- Earnings management occurs when management uses its discretion to mask the underlying economic performance of a company.
- The consequence of earnings management is that the usefulness of the information presented in the income statement is compromised.

Appendix 6A: Describe and illustrate the reporting for nonrecurring items. (p. 295) LO7

- Income or loss from discontinued operations is a transitory (nonrecurring) item that is reported net of income taxes after earnings from continuing operations.
- Restructuring charges include asset write-downs and employee severance costs. Even though these charges are typically reported among earnings from continuing operations, they are classified as transitory for analysis purposes.

Appendix 6B: Describe the new standard for revenue recognition and discuss its potential effects. (p. 298) LO8

- New standards for revenue recognition were issued to create a common revenue standard between IFRS and U.S. GAAP and to consolidate various rules and industry guidance into one standard.
- The effective date for calendar year companies that are publicly traded is January 1, 2018 and is January 1, 2019 for calendar year companies that are privately held
- The new revenue standard is, at a high level, conceptually similar to the current standard. However, the timing of revenue recognition will likely change for many companies, especially those with multiple element sales contracts. The new standard also requires much more disclosure about a company's revenue recognition process.

GUIDANCE ANSWERS . . . YOU MAKE THE CALL

You are the Receivables Manager First, you must realize that the extension of credit is an important tool in the marketing of your products, often as important as advertising and promotion. Given that receivables are necessary, there are some methods we can use to speed their collection. (1) We can better screen the customers to whom we extend credit. (2) We can negotiate advance or progress payments from customers. (3) We can use bank letters of credit or other automatic drafting prcedures so that billings need not be sent. (4) We can make sure products are sent as ordered to reduce disputes. (5) We can improve administration of past due accounts to provide for more timely notices of delinquencies and better collection procedures.

You are the Controller The salesperson may be channel stuffing or recording sales without a confirmed sales order. The unusual amount of returns suggests that sales revenues are most likely being recognized prematurely. To investigate, you could examine specific sales orders from customers who returned goods early in the following quarter, or contact customers directly. Most companies delay bonuses until after an appropriate return period expires and only credit the sales staff with net sales.

You are the Financial Analyst There are two usual components to a restructuring charge: asset write-downs (such as inventories, property, plant, and goodwill) and severance costs. Write-downs occur when the cash flow generating ability of an asset declines, thus reducing its current market value below its book value reported on the balance sheet. Arguably, this decline in cash flow generating ability did not occur solely in the current year and, most likely, has developed over several periods. Delays in loss recognition, such as write-downs of assets, are not uncommon. Thus, prior period income is arguably not as high as reported, and the current period loss is not as great as is reported. Turning to severance costs, their recognition can be viewed as an investment decision by the company that is expected to increase future cash flows (through decreased wages). If this cost accrual is capitalized on the balance sheet, current period income is increased and future period income would bear the amortization of this "asset" to match against future cash flow benefits from severance. This implies that current period income is not as low as reported; however, this adjustment is not GAAP as such severance costs cannot be capitalized. Yet, we can make such an adjustment in our analysis.

KEY RATIOS

Net operating profit after taxes (NOPAT)

$$\text{NOPAT} = \text{Net income} - [(\text{Nonoperating revenues} - \text{Nonoperating expenses}) \times (1 - \text{Statutory tax rate})]$$

Return on net operating assets (RNOA)

$$\text{RNOA} = \frac{\text{NOPAT}}{\text{Average net operating assets}}$$

Net operating profit margin (NOPM)

$$\text{NOPM} = \frac{\text{Net operating profit after taxes (NOPAT)}}{\text{Sales revenue}}$$

Accounts receivable turnover (ART)

$$\text{ART} = \frac{\text{Sales revenue}}{\text{Average accounts receivable}}$$

Average collection period (ACP)

$$\text{ACP} = \frac{\text{Average accounts receivable}}{\text{Average daily sales}} = \frac{365}{\text{Accounts receivable turnover (ART)}}$$

$$\text{Return on capital employed} = \frac{\text{Income from operations before taxes}}{\text{Average net operating assets}}$$

KEY TERMS

Accounts receivable turnover (p. 292)
Aging analysis (p. 282)
Allowance for uncollectible accounts (p. 282)
Arm's-length (p. 294)
Asset write-downs (p. 297)
Average collection period (p. 292)
Bad debts expense (p. 283)
Big bath (p. 294)
Channel stuffing (p. 294)
Completed contract method (p. 280)
Consignment (p. 275)
Cookie jar reserve (p. 287)
Cost-recovery method (p. 280)
Credit sales (p. 281)
Deferred revenue (p. 276)
Discontinued operations (p. 296)
Earned (p. 275)
Employee severance costs (p. 297)
Expense recognition (p. 279)
Income smoothing (p. 294)
Multiple element arrangements (p. 277)
Net operating profit after taxes (NOPAT) (p. 289)
Net operating profit margin (NOPM) (p. 291)
Net realizable value (p. 281)
Noncontrolling interest (p. 273)
Non-GAAP (p. 295)
Nonrecurring (p. 295)
Notes payable (p. 282)
Notes receivable (p. 282)
Percentage-of-completion method (p. 279)
Percentage of sales (p. 282)
Persistent (p. 296)
Pro forma income (p. 295)
Quality of earnings (p. 294)
Realized or realizable (p. 275)
Recurring (p. 295)
Restructuring charges (p. 296)
Restructuring costs (p. 296)
Return on capital employed (p. 290)
Return on net operating assets (RNOA) (p. 290)
Revenue recognition (p. 275)
Revenue recognition criteria (p. 275)
Right of return (p. 275)
Unearned revenue (p. 276)

Assignments with the MBC logo in the margin are available in myBusinessCourse. See the Preface of the book for details.

MULTIPLE CHOICE

Multiple Choice Answers
1.c 2.b 3.a 4.d 5.a 6.d

1. Which of the following best describes the condition(s) that must be present for the recognition of revenue?
a. Revenue must be earned and collected.
b. There are no uncertainties in measurement of income.
c. Revenue must be earned and realizable.
d. Expenses must be measurable and directly associated with the revenues.

2. When multiple products or services are bundled and sold for one price, the revenue should be
a. Recognized when the bundle of products is sold
b. Allocated among the different elements and recognized as each element is delivered to the customer
c. Deferred until all elements of the bundle are delivered to the customer.
d. Recognized when the customer pays cash for the products or services.

3. The percentage-of-completion method is preferable to the completed contract method and should be used unless:
a. There is a lack of dependable estimates or inherent hazards cause forecasts to be doubtful.
b. Completion rates are certain.
c. Profits are low.
d. Projects are more than five years to completion.

4. When management selectively excludes some revenues, expenses, gains, and losses from earnings calculated using generally accepted accounting principles, it is an example of
a. income smoothing.
b. big bath accounting.
c. cookie jar accounting.
d. pro forma earnings.

5. If bad debts expense is determined by estimating uncollectible accounts receivable, the entry to record the write-off of a specific uncollectible account would decrease
a. allowance for uncollectible accounts.
b. net income.

c. net book value of accounts receivable.
d. bad debts expense.

6. If management intentionally underestimates bad debts expense, then net income is

a. overstated and assets are understated.
b. understated and assets are overstated.
c. understated and asset are understated.
d. overstated and assets are overstated.

Superscript [A] denotes assignments based on Appendix 6A.

QUESTIONS

Q6-1. What are the criteria that guide firms in recognition of revenue? What does each of the criteria mean? How are the criteria met for a company like **Abercrombie & Fitch Co.**, a clothing retailer? How are the criteria met for a construction company that builds offices under long-term contracts with developers?

Abercrombie & Fitch
NYSE :: ANF

Q6-2. Why are discontinued operations reported separately from continuing operations in the income statement?

Q6-3. Identify the two typical categories of restructuring costs and their effects on the balance sheet and the income statement.

Q6-4. Explain the concept of a *big bath* and why restructuring costs are often identified with this event.

Q6-5. Why might companies want to manage earnings? Describe some of the tactics that some companies use to manage earnings.

Q6-6. What is the concept of *pro forma income* and why has this income measure been criticized?

Q6-7. Why does GAAP allow management to make estimates of amounts that are included in financial statements? Does this improve the usefulness of financial statements? Explain.

Q6-8. How might earnings forecasts that are published by financial analysts encourage companies to manage earnings?

Q6-9. Explain how management can shift income from one period into another by its estimation of uncollectible accounts.

Q6-10. During an examination of Wallace Company's financial statements, you notice that the allowance for uncollectible accounts has decreased as a percentage of accounts receivable. What are the possible explanations for this change?

Q6-11. Under what circumstances would it be correct to say that a company would be better off with more uncollectible accounts?

Q6-12. Estimating the bad debts expense by aging accounts receivable generally results in smaller errors than the percentage of credit sales approach. Can you explain why?

MINI EXERCISES

M6-13. Computing Percentage-of-Completion Revenues LO3

Bartov Corporation agreed to build a warehouse for $2,500,000. Expected (and actual) costs for the warehouse follow: 2016, $400,000; 2017, $1,000,000; and 2018, $500,000. The company completed the warehouse in 2018. Compute revenues, expenses, and income for each year 2016 through 2018 using the percentage-of-completion method.

M6-14. Assessing Revenue Recognition of Companies LO1
Identify and explain when each of the following companies should recognize revenue.

The GAP Inc.
NYSE :: GPS
Merck & Company Inc.
NYSE :: MRK
Deere & Company
NYSE :: DE

a. **The GAP Inc.**: The GAP is a retailer of clothing items for all ages.
b. **Merck & Company Inc.**: Merck engages in the development, manufacturing, and marketing of pharmaceutical products. It sells its drugs to retailers like **CVS Caremark Corporation** and **Walgreen Co.**
c. **Deere & Company**: Deere manufactures heavy equipment. It sells equipment to a network of independent distributors, who in turn sell the equipment to customers. Deere provides financing and insurance services both to distributors and customers.

Bank of America Corporation
NYSE :: BAC

d. **Bank of America Corporation**: Bank of America is a banking institution. It lends money to individuals and corporations and invests excess funds in marketable securities.

Johnson Controls, INC.
NYSE :: JCI

e. **Johnson Controls Inc.**: Johnson Controls manufactures products for the U.S. Government under long-term contracts.

Syngenta AG
NYSE :: SYT

f. **Syngenta AG**: Syngenta is a Swiss global agribusiness operating in crop protection, seeds, lawn and garden. Its products are consumed mainly by growers of diverse size and often sold through distributers. Some product return rates can be reliably estimated and some cannot be estimated.

LO1

M6-15. Estimating Revenue Recognition with Right of Return

The Unlimited Company offers an unconditional return policy for its retail clothing business. It normally expects 2% of sales at retail selling prices to be returned at some point prior to the expiration of the return period, and returned items cannot be resold. Assuming that it records total sales of $5 million for the current period, how much net revenue would it report for this period?

LO3

M6-16. Using Percentage-of-Completion and Completed Contract Methods

Halsey Building Company signed a contract to build an office building for $40,000,000. The scheduled construction costs follow.

Year	Cost
2016	$ 9,000,000
2017	15,000,000
2018	6,000,000
Total	$30,000,000

The building is completed in 2018.

For each year, compute the revenue, expense, and gross profit reported for this construction project using each of the following methods.

a. Percentage-of-completion method
b. Completed contract method

LO1, 2

M6-17. Explaining Revenue Recognition and Bundled Sales

A.J. Smith Electronics is a retail consumer electronics company that also sells extended warranty contracts for many of the products that it carries. The extended warranty provides coverage for three years beyond expiration of the manufacturer's warranty. In 2016, A.J. Smith sold extended warranties amounting to $1,700,000. The warranty coverage for all of these begins in 2017 and runs through 2019. The total expected cost of providing warranty services on these contracts is $500,000.

a. How should A.J. Smith recognize revenue on the extended warranty contracts?
b. Estimate the revenue, expense, and gross profit reported from these contracts in the year(s) that the revenue is recognized.
c. In 2017, as a special promotion, A.J. Smith sold a digital camera (retail price $300), a digital photograph printer (retail price $125), and an extended warranty contract for each (total retail price $75) as a package for a special price of $399. The extended warranty covers the period from 2018 through 2020. The company sold 200 of these camera–printer packages. Compute the revenue that A.J. Smith should recognize in each year from 2017 through 2020.

LO4

M6-18. Reporting Uncollectible Accounts and Accounts Receivables

Mohan Company estimates its uncollectible accounts by aging its accounts receivable and applying percentages to various aged categories of accounts. Mohan computes a total of $2,100 in estimated losses as of December 31, 2016. Its Accounts Receivable has a balance of $98,000, and its allowance for Uncollectible Accounts has an unused balance of $500 before adjustment at December 31, 2016.

a. What is the amount of bad debts expense that Mohan will report in 2016?
b. Determine the net amount of accounts receivable reported in current assets at December 31, 2016.
c. Set up T-accounts for both Bad Debt Expense and for Allowance for Uncollectible Accounts. Enter any beginning balances and effects from the information above (including your results from parts *a* and *b*). Explain the numbers for each of your T-accounts.

M6-19. Explaining the Allowance Method for Accounts Receivable LO4

At a recent board of directors meeting of Ascot, Inc., one of the directors expressed concern over the allowance for uncollectible accounts appearing in the company's balance sheet. "I don't understand this account," he said. "Why don't we just show accounts receivable at the amount owed to us and get rid of that allowance?" Respond to that director's question. Include in your response (a) an explanation of why the company has an allowance account, (b) what the balance sheet presentation of accounts receivable is intended to show, and (c) how the concept of expense recognition relates to the analysis and presentation of accounts receivable.

M6-20. Analyzing the Allowance for Uncollectible Accounts LO4, 5

Ralph Lauren Corporation
NYSE :: RL

Following is the current asset section from the **Ralph Lauren Corporation** balance sheet:

At March 29, 30 ($ millions)	2014	2013
Cash and cash equivalents	$ 797	$ 974
Short-term investments	488	325
Accounts receivable, net of allowances of $270 in 2014 and $245 in 2013	588	458
Inventories	1,020	896
Income tax receivable	62	29
Deferred tax assets	150	120
Prepaid expenses and other current assets	224	161
Total current assets	$3,329	$2,963

a. Compute the gross amount of accounts receivable for both 2014 and 2013. Compute the percentage of the allowance for uncollectible accounts relative to the gross amount of accounts receivable for each of these years.

b. How do you interpret the change in the percentage of the allowance for uncollectible accounts relative to total accounts receivable computed in part *a*?

c. Ralph Lauren reported net sales of $7,284 million in 2014. Compute its accounts receivable turnover and average collection period.

M6-21. Analyzing Accounts Receivable Changes LO4

The comparative balance sheets of Sloan Company reveal that accounts receivable (before deducting allowances) increased by $15,000 in 2016. During the same time period, the allowance for uncollectible accounts increased by $2,100. If sales revenue was $120,000 in 2016 and bad debts expense was 2% of sales, how much cash was collected from customers during the year?

M6-22. Evaluating Accounts Receivable Turnover for Competitors LO5

The Procter & Gamble Company
NYSE :: PG
Colgate-Palmolive Company
NYSE :: CL

The Procter & Gamble Company and **Colgate-Palmolive Company** report the following sales and accounts receivable balances ($ millions):

Procter & Gamble			Colgate-Palmolive		
Fiscal year	Sales	Accounts Receivable	Fiscal year	Sales	Accounts Receivable
June 30, 2014	$83,062	$6,386	December 31, 2013	$17,420	$1,636
June 30, 2013	82,581	6,508	December 31, 2012	17,085	1,668

a. Compute accounts receivable turnover and average collection period for both companies.

b. Identify and discuss a potential explanation for the difference between these competitors' accounts receivable turnover.

M6-23. Analyzing Accounts Receivable Changes LO4

In 2016, Grant Corporation recorded credit sales of $3,200,000 and bad debts expense of $42,000. Write-offs of uncollectible accounts totaled $39,000 and one account, worth $12,000, that had been written off in an earlier year was collected in 2016.

a. Prepare journal entries to record each of these transactions.

b. If net accounts receivable increased by $220,000, how much cash was collected from credit customers during the year? Prepare a journal entry to record cash collections.

c. Set up T-accounts and post each of the transactions in parts *a* and *b* to them.

d. Record each of the above transactions in the financial statement effects template to show the effect of these entries on the balance sheet and income statement.

LO2 **M6-24. Analyzing Unearned Revenue Changes**

Finn Publishing Corp. produces a monthly publication aimed at competitive swimmers, with articles profiling current stars of the sport, advice from coaches, and advertising by swimwear companies, training organizations and others. The magazine is distributed through newsstands and bookstores, and by mail to subscribers. The most common subscription is for twelve months. When Finn Publishing receives payment of an annual subscription, it records an Unearned Revenue liability that is reduced by 1/12th each month as publications are provided.

The table below provides four years of revenues from the income statement and unearned revenue from the balance sheet. (All amounts in $ thousands.)

Fiscal year	Revenue	Unearned revenue liability (end of year)
2015	$48,000	$20,000
2016	55,000	24,000
2017	62,000	26,000
2018	62,000	25,000

a. Calculate the growth in revenue from 2015 to 2016, 2016 to 2017, and from 2017 to 2018.

b. Calculate the amount of customer purchases in 2016, 2017, and 2018. Customer purchases are defined as sales made at newsstands and bookstores, plus the amount paid for new or renewal subscriptions. Again, calculate the growth rates from 2016 to 2017 and from 2017 to 2018.

c. Explain the differences in growth rates between parts *a* and *b* above.

LO2 **M6-25. Applying Revenue Recognition Criteria**

Commtech, Inc., designs and sells cellular phones. The company creates the technical specifications and the software for its products, though it outsources the production of the phones to an overseas contract manufacturer. Commtech has arrangements to sell its phones to the major wireless communications companies who, in turn, sell the phones to end customers packaged with calling plans.

The product life cycle for a phone model is about six months, and Commtech recognizes revenue at the time of delivery to the wireless communications company. The product team for the CD924 model has met to consider a possible modification to the phone. The software team has developed an improved global positioning application for a new phone model, and this application works in the CD924. It could be uploaded to existing phones through the wireless networks.

Marketing's analysis of focus groups and customer feedback is that further sales of the CD924 would be enhanced significantly if the new application were made available. The software engineers have demonstrated that the new GPS application can be successfully sent wirelessly to the CD924.

However, the finance manager points out that Commtech's financial statements have been based on the assumption that the company's phones do not involve "multiple deliverables," like upgrades. All revenue is recognized at the point of sale to the wireless communications companies. Like many communications hardware companies, Commtech has been under pressure to demonstrate its financial performance. Offering an upgrade to the CD924's navigation capabilities would probably be viewed as a significant deliverable in terms of customer value, and the finance manager says that "the accounting won't let us do it."

How should the product team proceed?

LO6 **M6-26. Earnings Management and the Allowance for Doubtful Accounts**

Verdi Co. builds and sells PC computers to customers. The company sells most of its products for immediate payment but also extends credit to some customers. The industry is competitive and in the most recent year many competitors showed declines in revenue. However, Verdi Co. showed stable revenues. It is later revealed that Verdi Co. made sales and extended credit to customers previously deemed to have credit scores too low for the company to extend credit. The company did not disclose this practice in its financial statements or elsewhere.

a. Explain how this practice would have enabled Verdi Co. to show stable sales.

b. How should Verdi Co. have accounted for these additional sales and related receivables in its financial statements?

c. How would the actions by Verdi Co. in the current period affect financial statements in future periods if the customers cannot pay for the computers they purchased on credit?

EXERCISES

E6-27. Assessing Revenue Recognition Timing

LO1, 2

Limited Brands, Inc. NYSE :: LTD
Boeing Company NYSE :: BA
Supervalu, Inc. NYSE :: SVU
Wells Fargo & Company NYSE :: WFC
Harley-Davidson, Inc. NYSE :: HOG
Time-Warner Inc. NYSE :: TWX

Discuss and justify when each of the following businesses should recognize revenues:

a. A clothing retailer like **Limited Brands, Inc.**
b. A contractor like **The Boeing Company** that performs work under long-term government contracts.
c. An operator of grocery stores like **SUPERVALU, INC.**
d. A producer of television shows, such as **MTV** that syndicates its content to television stations.
e. A residential real estate developer who constructs only speculative houses and later sells these houses to buyers.
f. A banking institution like **Wells Fargo & Company** that lends money for home mortgages.
g. A manufacturer like **Harley-Davidson, Inc.**
h. A publisher of magazines such as **Time-Warner Inc.**

E6-28. Assessing Revenue Recognition Timing and Income Measurement

LO1, 2

Discuss and justify when each of the following businesses should recognize revenue and identify any income measurement issues that are likely to arise.

a. **RealMoney.Com**, a division of **TheStreet.Com** provides investment advice to customers for an up-front fee. It provides these customers with password-protected access to its website where customers can download certain investment reports. Real Money has an obligation to provide updates on its website.

b. **Oracle Corporation** develops general ledger and other business application software that it sells to its customers. The customer pays an up-front fee to gain the right to use the software and a monthly fee for support services.

Oracle Corporation NASDAQ :: ORCL

c. **Intuit Inc.** develops tax preparation software that it sells to its customers for a flat fee. No further payment is required and the software cannot be returned, only exchanged if defective.

Intuit Inc. NASDAQ :: INTU

d. A developer of computer games sells its software with a 10-day right of return period during which the software can be returned for a full refund. After the 10-day period has expired, the software cannot be returned.

E6-29. Constructing and Assessing Income Statements Using Percentage of Completion

LO3

Homework

General Electric Company NYSE :: GE
Eversource Energy NYSE :: ES

Assume that **General Electric Company** agreed in February 2016 to construct an electricity generating facility for **Eversource Energy**, a utility serving the Boston area. The contract price of $500 million is to be paid as follows: $200 million at the time of signing; $100 million on December 31, 2016; and $200 million at completion in May 2017. General Electric incurred the following costs in constructing the power plant: $100 million in 2016, and $300 million in 2017.

a. Compute the amount of General Electric's revenue, expense, and income for both 2016 and 2017 under the percentage-of-completion revenue recognition method.
b. Compute the amount of GE's revenue, expense, and income for both 2016 and 2017 using the completed contract method.
c. Discuss whether you believe that the percentage-of-completion method or the completed contract method provides a good measure of GE's performance under the contract.

E6-30. Constructing and Assessing Income Statements Using Percentage of Completion

LO3

Homework

On March 15, 2017, Frankel Construction is contracted to build a shopping center at a contract price of $120 million. The schedule of expected (equals actual) cash collections and contract costs follows:

Year	Cash Collections	Cost Incurred
2017	$ 30 million	$15 million
2018	50 million	40 million
2019	40 million	30 million
Total	$120 million	$85 million

a. Calculate the amount of revenue, expense, and income for each of the three years 2017 through 2019 using (1) the percentage-of-completion method, and (2) the completed contract method. Which method more closely follows the cash flows produced by this project?

b. Discuss which method you believe provides the better measure of the construction company's performance under this contract.

LO2 **E6-31. Accounting for Multiple-Element Arrangements**

Amazon.com
NASDAQ :: AMZN

Amazon.com, Inc. provides the following description of its revenue recognition policies in its 2014 10-K report:

We recognize revenue from product sales or services rendered when the following four criteria are met: persuasive evidence of an arrangement exists, delivery has occurred or service has been rendered, the selling price is fixed or determinable, and collectability is reasonably assured. Revenue arrangements with multiple deliverables are divided into separate units and revenue is allocated using estimated selling prices if we do not have vendor-specific objective evidence or third-party evidence of the selling prices of the deliverables. We allocate the arrangement price to each of the elements based on the relative selling prices of each element. Estimated selling prices are management's best estimates of the prices that we would charge our customers if we were to sell the standalone elements separately and include considerations of customer demand, prices charged by us and others for similar deliverables, and the price if largely based on the cost of producing the product or service. Sales of our digital devices, including Kindle e-readers, Fire tablets, Fire TVs, Echo, and Fire phones, are considered arrangements with multiple deliverables, consisting of the device, undelivered software upgrades and/or undelivered non-software services such as cloud storage and free trial memberships to other services. The revenue allocated to the device, which is the substantial portion of the total sale price, and related costs are generally recognized upon delivery. Revenue related to undelivered software upgrades and/or undelivered non-software services is deferred and recognized generally on a straight-line basis over the estimated period the software upgrades and non-software services are expected to be provided for each of these devices. Sales of Amazon Prime memberships are also considered arrangements with multiple deliverables, including shipping benefits, Prime Instant Video, Prime Music, Prime Photo, and access to the Kindle Owners' Lending Library. The revenue related to the deliverables is amortized over the life of the membership based on the estimated delivery of services. Amazon Prime membership fees are allocated between product sales and service sales. Costs to deliver Amazon Prime benefits are recognized as cost of sales as incurred.

a. What is an "arrangement with multiple deliverables?" How are revenues recognized in such arrangements?

b. Assume that Amazon sells a Kindle with 3G wireless access and a commitment for future software upgrades for $190. Also assume that the device, if sold alone, would sell for $170 and that management estimates the selling price of the 3G access and software upgrades would be $30 if they were to be sold separately. What amount of revenue would Amazon recognize in the year of the sale? How would the remaining revenues be recognized?

c. Record the transaction described in part *b* using the financial statement effects template and in journal entry form.

LO5 **E6-32. Computing NOPAT, NOPM and RNOA**

GoPro, Inc.
NASDAQ :: GPRO

Selected information from the financial statements of **GoPro, Inc.** is provided below:

($ thousands)	2014	2013
Revenue	$1,394,205	$985,737
Operating income	187,035	98,703
Net interest expense and other nonoperating expense	6,060	7,374
Net income	128,088	60,578
Operating assets	815,364	439,671
Operating liabilities	276,487	254,227

a. Compute GoPro's net operating profit after taxes (NOPAT) for 2014 and 2013.

b. Compute GoPro's net operating profit margin (NOPM) for each year.

c. Compute GoPro's return on net operating assets (RNOA) for 2014.

LO1, 6 **E6-33. Applying Revenue Recognition Criteria**

Simpyl Technologies, Inc., manufactures electronic equipment used to facilitate control of production processes and tracking of assets using RFID and other technologies. Since its initial public offering in 1996, the company has shown consistent growth in revenue and earnings, and the stock price has reflected that impressive performance.

Operating in a very competitive environment, Simpyl Technologies provides significant bonus incentives to its sales representatives. These representatives sell the company's products directly to end customers, to value-added resellers, and to distributers.

Consider the four situations below. In each case, determine whether Simpyl Technologies can recognize revenue at this time. Describe the reasons for your judgment.

a. When selling directly to the end customer, Simpyl Technologies requires a sales contract with authorized signatures from the customer company. At the end of Simpyl's fiscal year, sales representative A asks to book revenue from a customer. The customer's purchasing manager has confirmed the intention to complete the purchase, but the contract has only one of the two required signatures. The second person is traveling and will return to the office in a few days (but after the end of Simpyl's fiscal year). The inventory to fulfill the order is sitting in Simpyl's warehouse. Can Simpyl recognize revenue at this time?

b. Sales representative B has an approved contract to deliver units that must be customized to meet the customer's specifications. Just prior to the end of the fiscal year, the uncustomized units are shipped to an intermediate staging area where they will be reconfigured to meet the customer's requirements. Can Simpyl recognize revenue on the basic, uncustomized units at this time?

c. Sales representative C has finalized an order from a value-added reseller who regularly purchases significant volumes of Simpyl's products. The products have been delivered to the customer at the beginning of the fiscal year, and Simpyl Technologies has no further responsibilities for the items. However, the sales representative (with the regional sales manager) is still conducting negotiations with the value-added reseller as to the volume discounts that will be offered for the current year. Can Simpyl recognize revenue on the items delivered to the customer?

d. Sales representative D has finalized an order from a distributor, and the items have been delivered. However, an examination of the distributor's financial condition shows that it does not have the resources to pay Simpyl for the items it has purchased. It needs to sell those items, so the resulting proceeds can be used to pay Simpyl. Can Simpyl recognize revenue on the items delivered to the distributor?

E6-34. Reporting Uncollectible Accounts and Accounts Receivable

LO4

Homework MBC

LaFond Company analyzes its accounts receivable at December 31, 2016, and arrives at the aged categories below along with the percentages that are estimated as uncollectible.

Age Group	Accounts Receivable	Estimated Loss %
Current (not past due)	$250,000	0.5%
1–30 days past due	90,000	1
31–60 days past due	20,000	2
61–120 days past due	11,000	5
121–180 days past due	6,000	10
Over 180 days past due	4,000	25
Total accounts receivable	$381,000	

At the beginning of the fourth quarter of 2016, there was a credit balance of $4,350 in the Allowance for Uncollectible Accounts. During the fourth quarter, LaFond Company wrote off $3,830 in receivables as uncollectible.

a. What amount of bad debts expense will LaFond report for 2016?

b. What is the balance of accounts receivable that it reports on its December 31, 2016, balance sheet?

c. Set up T-accounts for both Bad Debts Expense and for the Allowance for Uncollectible Accounts. Enter any unadjusted balances along with the dollar effects of the information described (including your results from parts *a* and *b*). Explain the numbers in each of the T-accounts.

E6-35. Analysis of Accounts Receivable and Allowance for Doubtful Accounts

LO4, 5

Steelcase, Inc.
NYSE :: SCS

Steelcase, Inc. reported the following amounts in its 2014 and 2013 10-K reports (years ended February 28, 2014 and February 22, 2013).

($ millions)	2014	2013
From the income statement:		
Net sales	$2,989	$2,869
From the balance sheet:		
Accounts receivable, net	306.8	287.3
Customer deposits	16.0	13.5
From the disclosure on allowance for doubtful accounts:		
Balance at beginning of period	14.5	19.6
Additions (reductions) charged to income	2.8	3.1
Adjustments or deductions	(4.3)	(8.2)
Balance at end of period	13.0	14.5

a. Prepare the journal entry to record accounts receivable written off as uncollectible in 2014. Also prepare the entry to record the provision for doubtful accounts (bad debts expense) for 2014. What effect did these entries have on Steelcase's income for that year?

b. Calculate Steelcase's gross receivables for the years given, and then determine the allowance for doubtful accounts as a percentage of the gross receivables.

c. Calculate Steelcase's accounts receivable turnover for 2014. (Use Accounts receivable, net for the calculation.)

d. How much cash did Steelcase receive from customers in 2014?

LO4 Homework MBC

E6-36. Analyzing and Reporting Receivable Transactions and Uncollectible Accounts (Using Percentage-of-Sales Method)

At the beginning of 2017, Penman Company had the following (normal) account balances in its financial records:

Accounts receivable	$122,000
Allowance for uncollectible accounts	7,900

During 2017, its credit sales were $1,173,000 and collections on credit sales were $1,150,000. The following additional transactions occurred during the year:

Feb. 17 Wrote off Nissim's account, $3,600.

May 28 Wrote off White's account, $2,400.

Dec. 15 Wrote off Ohlson's account, $900.

Dec. 31 Recorded the provision for uncollectible accounts at 0.8% of credit sales for the year. (*Hint*: The allowance account is increased by 0.8% of credit sales regardless of any prior write-offs.)

Compute and show how accounts receivable and the allowance for uncollectible accounts are reported in its December 31, 2017, balance sheet.

LO4 Homework

E6-37. Estimating Bad Debts Expense and Reporting of Receivables

At December 31, 2016, Sunil Company had a balance of $375,000 in its accounts receivable and an unused balance of $4,200 in its allowance for uncollectible accounts. The company then aged its accounts as follows:

Current	$304,000
0–60 days past due	44,000
61–180 days past due	18,000
Over 180 days past due	9,000
Total accounts receivable	$375,000

The company has experienced losses as follows: 1% of current balances, 5% of balances 0–60 days past due, 15% of balances 61–180 days past due, and 40% of balances over 180 days past due. The company continues to base its provision for credit losses on this aging analysis and percentages.

a. What amount of bad debts expense does Sunil report on its 2016 income statement?

b. Show how accounts receivable and the allowance for uncollectible accounts are reported in its December 31, 2016, balance sheet.

c. Set up T-accounts for both Bad Debts Expense and for the Allowance for Uncollectible Accounts. Enter any unadjusted balances along with the dollar effects of the information described (including your results from parts *a* and *b*). Explain the numbers in each of the T-accounts.

E6-38. Estimating Uncollectible Accounts and Reporting Receivables over Multiple Periods LO4

Homework MBC

Barth Company, which has been in business for three years, makes all of its sales on credit and does not offer cash discounts. Its credit sales, customer collections, and write-offs of uncollectible accounts for its first three years follow:

Year	Sales	Collections	Accounts Written Off
2015	$751,000	$733,000	$5,300
2016	876,000	864,000	5,800
2017	972,000	938,000	6,500

a. Barth uses the allowance method of recognizing credit losses that provides for such losses at the rate of 1% of sales. (This means the allowance account is increased by 1% of credit sales regardless of any write-offs and unused balances.) What amounts for accounts receivable and the allowance for uncollectible accounts are reported on its balance sheet at the end of 2017? What total amount of bad debts expense appears on its income statement for each of the three years?

b. Comment on the appropriateness of the 1% rate used to provide for bad debts based on your results in part *a*. (*Hint*: T-accounts can help with this analysis.)

E6-39.[A] Evaluating Business Segment Information LO5, 7

Hewlett-Packard
NYSE :: HPQ

Hewlett-Packard Company reports that its "organizational structure is based on a number of factors that management uses to evaluate, view and run its business operations." In its disclosures of segment information, there are seven segments—Personal Systems, Printing, Enterprise Group, Enterprise Services, Software, HP Financial Services, and Corporate Investments. The company provides the following information about these business segments:

($ millions)	2014	2013
Total net revenue:		
Personal systems	$34,303	$32,179
Printing	22,979	23,896
Enterprise group	27,814	28,081
Enterprise services	22,398	24,061
Software	3,933	4,021
HP financial services	3,498	3,629
Corporate investments	302	24
Earnings from operations:		
Personal systems	$ 1,270	$ 980
Printing	4,185	3,933
Enterprise group	4,008	4,259
Enterprise services	803	679
Software	872	868
HP financial services	389	399
Corporate investments	(199)	(316)
Total assets:		
Personal systems	$12,104	$11,690
Printing	10,063	11,088
Enterprise group	27,236	29,759
Enterprise services	13,472	16,217
Software	11,575	11,940
HP financial services	13,529	12,746
Corporate investments	34	105

a. Calculate the 2014 return on capital employed for each segment. (Base the calculation on total assets instead of net operating assets in the denominator—HP does not disclose operating liabilities by segment.)

b. Which segments are more profitable? Which are growing more quickly?

c. In 2014, HP reported restructuring charges of $1,619 million. Assume these charges are mostly attributable to the Enterprise Services segment. How should restructuring charges be reported in the income statement? How do these charges affect your interpretation of the return on capital employed by the Enterprise Services segment?

LO1, 2 **E6-40. Analyzing Unearned Revenue Liabilities**

The Lyric Opera of Chicago was founded in 1954 and is widely regarded as one of the world's greatest opera companies. Each year, The Lyric has an eight-opera season that extends from September to March, and its loyal subscribers (numbering more than 30,000) eagerly reserve their seats for coming performances. In fact, many subscribers purchase their tickets for the upcoming year before the close of The Lyric's fiscal year. For these ticket purchases, The Lyric recognizes a liability entitled Deferred Ticket and Other Revenue and defined in its footnotes as "Deferred ticket revenue relates to ticket sales for the following opera season."

Information about The Lyric Opera's ticket revenue and deferred ticket revenue liability is given below ($ thousands). Assume that the "Other" portion of deferred revenue is negligible.

Fiscal year ended	Ticket Sales (Revenue)	Deferred Ticket and Other Revenue (Year-end Liability)
2014	$28,878	$13,750
2013	26,671	14,525
2012	25,030	12,638
2011	23,775	12,711

a. What revenue recognition principle(s) drive The Lyric's deferral of advance ticket purchases?

b. Recreate the summary journal entries to recognize ticket sales revenue for The Lyric's fiscal year 2014 and advance sales for the fiscal year 2015 season.

c. The Lyric Opera's season changes every year, with a mixture of classical and contemporary operas. At the end of each fiscal year, management of The Lyric can observe the revenue generated by the season just concluded and also its subscribers' enthusiasm for the upcoming season. How might that information be used in managing the organization?

LO2 **E6-41. Accounting for Membership Fees and Rewards Program**

Costco Wholesale Corporation provides the following description of its revenue recognition policies for membership fees and rewards in its 10-K report dated August 31, 2014:

Costco Wholesale
NASDAQ :: COST

Membership fee revenue represents annual membership fees paid by substantially all of the Company's members. The Company accounts for membership fee revenue, net of estimated refunds, on a deferred basis, whereby revenue is recognized ratably over the one-year membership period. The Company's Executive Members qualify for a 2% reward (beginning November, 1, 2011 the reward increased from a maximum of $500 to $750 per year on qualified purchases), which can be redeemed at Costco warehouses. The Company accounts for this reward as a reduction in sales. The sales reduction and corresponding liability are computed after giving effect to the estimated impact of non-redemptions based on historical data. The net reduction in sales was $1,051, $970, and $900 in 2014, 2013, and 2012, respectively.

The following data were extracted from Costco's 2014 income statement and balance sheet:

($ millions)	2014	2013
Revenue		
Net sales	$110,212	$102,870
Membership fees	2,428	2,286
Total revenue	112,640	105,156
Current Liabilities		
Accounts payable	$ 8,491	$ 7,872
Accrued salaries and benefits	2,231	2,037
Accrued member rewards	773	710
Accrued sales and other taxes	442	382
Deferred membership fees	1,254	1,167
Other current liabilities	1,221	1,089
Total current liabilities	$14,412	$13,257

a. Explain Costco's accounting for membership fees and rewards programs.
b. Prepare journal entries to record (1) membership fees collected in cash in fiscal 2014 and (2) membership fee revenue recognized in 2014.
c. Prepare journal entries to record (1) member rewards earned by "executive members" in fiscal 2014 and (2) rewards redeemed during the year.

PROBLEMS

P6-42.[A] **Identifying Operating and Nonrecurring Income Components**

LO5, 7

The Dow Chemical Company
NYSE :: DOW

Following is the **The Dow Chemical Company** income statement.

($ millions) For Year Ended December 31	2014	2013
Net sales	$58,167	$57,080
Cost of sales	47,464	47,594
Research and development expenses	1,647	1,747
Selling, general, and administrative expenses	3,106	3,024
Amortization of intangibles	436	461
Goodwill and other intangible asset impairment losses	50	—
Restructuring charges (credits)	(3)	(22)
Asbestos-related charge	78	—
Equity in earnings of nonconsolidated affiliates	835	1,034
Sundry income (expense)—net	(27)	2,554
Interest income	51	41
Interest expense and amortization of debt discount	983	1,101
Income before income taxes	5,265	6,804
Provision for income taxes	1,426	1,988
Net income	$ 3,839	$ 4,816

REQUIRED

a. Identify the components in its statement that you would consider operating.
b. Identify those components that you would consider nonrecurring.
c. Compute net operating profit after taxes (NOPAT) and net operating profit margin (NOPM) for each year.

P6-43. Percentage-of-Completion and Completed Contract Methods

LO3

Philbrick Company signed a three-year contract to provide sales training to the employees of Elliot Company. The contract price is $1,200 per employee and the estimated number of employees to be trained is 400. The expected number to be trained in each year and the expected training costs follow.

	Number of employees	Training costs incurred
2016	125	$ 60,000
2017	200	75,000
2018	75	40,000
Total	400	$175,000

REQUIRED

a. For each year, compute the revenue, expense, and gross profit reported assuming revenue is recognized using the following method.
   1. Percentage-of-completion method, where percentage-of-completion is determined by the number of employees trained.
   2. Percentage-of-completion method, where percentage-of-completion is determined by the costs incurred.
   3. Completed contract method.

b. Which method do you believe is most appropriate in this situation? Explain.

LO6 **P6-44. Incentives for Earnings Management**

Harris Corporation pays senior management an annual bonus from a bonus pool. The size of the bonus pool is determined as follows.

Reported net income	Bonus pool
Less than or equal to $10 million	$0
Greater than $10 million, but less than or equal to $20 million	10% of income in excess of $10 million
Greater than $20 million	$1 million

REQUIRED

a. Assume that senior management expects current earnings to be $21 million and next year's earnings to be $18 million. What incentive does management of Harris Corporation have for managing earnings?

b. Assume that senior management expects current earnings to be $17 million and next year's earnings to be $24 million. What incentive does management of Harris Corporation have for managing earnings?

c. Assume that senior management expects current earnings to be $9.5 million and next year's earnings to be $12 million. What incentive does management of Harris Corporation have for managing earnings?

d. How might the bonus plan be structured to minimize the incentives for earnings management?

LO4 **P6-45. Interpreting Accounts Receivable and Uncollectible Accounts**

Nordstrom, Inc.
NYSE :: JWN

Nordstrom, Inc. provided the following information concerning its accounts receivable in note 3 of its 10-K report dated February 1, 2014 (fiscal year 2013):

NOTE 3: ACCOUNTS RECEIVABLE

The components of accounts receivable are as follows:

	2013	2012
Total credit card receivables	$2,184	$2,142
Allowance for credit losses	(80)	(85)
Credit card receivables, net	2,104	2,057
Other accounts receivable	73	72
Accounts receivable, net	$2,177	$2,129

Activity in the allowance for credit losses for the past two fiscal years is as follows:

Fiscal year	2013	2012
Allowance at beginning of year	$85	$115
Bad debt provision	52	42
Write-offs	(80)	(97)
Recoveries	23	25
Allowance at end of year	$80	$ 85

Credit Quality

The primary indicators of the credit quality of our credit card receivables are aging and delinquency, particularly the levels of account balances delinquent 30 days or more as these are the accounts most likely to be written off. The following table illustrates the aging and delinquency status of our credit card receivables:

	February 1, 2014		February 2, 2013	
	Balance	% of Total	Balance	% of Total
Current	$2,046	93.7%	$2,018	94.2%
1–29 days delinquent	99	4.5%	84	3.9%
30+ days delinquent:				
30–59 days delinquent	16	0.7%	15	0.7%
60–89 days delinquent	9	0.4%	10	0.5%
90 days or more delinquent	14	0.7%	15	0.7%
Total 30+ days delinquent	39	1.8%	40	1.9%
Total credit card receivables	$2,184	100.0%	$2,142	100.0%

REQUIRED

a. What amount did Nordstrom report as accounts receivable, net in its February 1, 2014 balance sheet?

b. Prepare journal entries to record the provision for bad debts, write-offs of uncollectible accounts, and recoveries in fiscal 2014. Post these entries to T-accounts. How should Nordstrom record recoveries?

c. Compute the ratio of allowance for credit losses to total credit card receivables for fiscal 2012 and 2013. Speculate as to what might be the cause of any change that you observe.

d. Nordstrom reported net sales of $12,166 million in fiscal 2013. Compute its accounts receivable turnover and average collection period for that year.

P6-46. Accounting for Product Returns

LO4

The GAP, Inc.
NYSE :: GPS

In its income statement for fiscal year 2013, **The Gap, Inc.**, reported net sales of $16,148 million and cost of goods sold and occupancy expenses of $9,855 million, resulting in a gross profit of $6,293 million. In its footnotes, The Gap reports that "Allowances for estimated returns are recorded based on estimated gross profit using our historical return patterns."

When The Gap accounts for estimated sales returns, it reduces sales revenue by the returns' expected sales price, reduces cost of goods sold by the returns' expected cost and recognizes a sales return allowance as a liability equal to the returns' expected gross profit.

A sales returns allowance of $26 million was reported among The Gap's liabilities at the end of fiscal year 2013, and the footnotes report that $896 million in allowance for returns was added to this liability during fiscal year 2013. Actual returns were reported at $897 million and subtracted from the liability.

REQUIRED

a. What was the balance in The Gap's sales returns allowance liability at the beginning of fiscal year 2013?

b. Suppose The Gap sells 100 units of an item for $50 each, and its gross profit on each unit is $20. Further, suppose The Gap expects that 10 of the units will be returned. What entries will be made to record the sale of 100 units (for cash) and the expected returns? What entry is made when ten customers subsequently return the items and receive a cash refund? Assume that the units are undamaged and can be sold to other customers.

c. Assume that the gross profit margin (gross profit divided by sales revenue) for returned items is the same as that for those that are not returned. Reconstruct the entry The Gap made to account for expected product returns in 2013. What were the 2013 gross sales for The Gap? What percentage of its sales does The Gap expect to be returned?

d. Suppose The Gap entered a new market in which it did not have the ability to predict product returns. How should it deal with the prospect of returns when it sells products to customers?

P6-47. Analyzing Unearned Revenue Changes

LO2

Electronic Arts Inc.
NASDAQ :: EA

Electronic Arts Inc. (EA) is a developer, marketer, publisher and distributor of video game software and content to be played on a variety of platforms. There is an increasing demand for the ability to play these games in an online environment, and EA has developed this capability in many of its products. In addition, EA maintains servers (or arranges for servers) for the online activities of its customers. When customers purchase online subscriptions, revenue is recognized ratably over the subscription period.

EA treats a significant portion of its software sales as "multiple-element arrangements" and—through fiscal 2007—deferred a portion of customer purchases based on the estimated value of the online services offered. Beginning in fiscal 2008, it was not possible to estimate the separate value of the software and the online services, so EA began to defer all such revenue over a six-month period. Starting July 1, 2013, based on an analysis by the company, revenue continues to be recognized over six months for games distributed online, but for physical games purchased at retailers revenue will be recognized over a nine-month period. EA's 2014 10-K states that U.S. GAAP requires the company to account for the consumer's right to receive unspecified updates or their matchmaking service for no additional fee as a "bundled" sale, or multiple-element arrangement.

Information from Electronic Arts' financial statements is given below. Prior to fiscal year 2006, no revenue was deferred. All amounts are in $ millions.

Fiscal year ending March 31	Net revenue	Deferred net revenue (liability)
2005	$3,129	$ 0
2006	2,951	9
2007	3,091	32
2008	3,665	387
2009	4,212	261
2010	3,654	766
2011	3,589	1,005
2012	4,143	1,048
2013	3,797	1,044
2014	3,575	1,490

REQUIRED

a. Calculate the growth rates in net revenue over the years in the table.

b. What are the purchases by customers in each of these years? What are the growth rates? Why do you think they differ from the growth rates in net revenue?

c. Would you predict a growth in 2015 revenue equal to that in 2014? Why?

CASES AND PROJECTS

LO1, 2 **C6-48. Revenue Recognition and Refunds**

Groupon, Inc.
NASDAQ :: GRPN

Groupon, Inc. is an internet-based marketing company which sells coupons (called "Groupons") for products and services offered by other merchants (merchant partners). Groupon offers a "daily deal" to subscribers. The daily deal provides significant savings on a variety of products and services provided that a minimum number of customers purchase the Groupon for each deal offered. This feature guarantees a sufficient volume of customers to ensure that the deal is profitable to the merchant partner.

When Groupon sells a coupon, it collects the proceeds from the customer (gross billings) and then remits a payment to the merchant partner. These payments are typically paid out over a 60-day period. Groupon's revenue recognition policy is described in its 10-K as follows:

Revenue Recognition

The Company recognizes revenue from Groupons when the following criteria are met: persuasive evidence of an arrangement exists; delivery has occurred; the selling price is fixed or determinable; and collectability is reasonably assured. These criteria are met when the number of customers who purchase the daily deal exceeds the predetermined threshold, the Groupon has been electronically delivered to the purchaser and a listing of Groupons sold has been made available to the merchant. At that time, the Company's obligations to the merchant, for which it is serving as an agent, are substantially complete. The Company's remaining obligations, which are limited to remitting payment to the merchant and continuing to make available on the Company's website the listing of Groupons previously provided to the merchant, are inconsequential or perfunctory. The Company records the net amount it retains from the sale of Groupons after paying an agreed upon percentage of the purchase price to the featured merchant excluding any applicable taxes. Revenue is recorded on a net basis because the Company is acting as an agent of the merchant in the transaction.

Groupon reported gross billings of $3,985.5 million in 2011, up from $745.3 million in 2010. Its net revenues were $1,610.4 million in 2011 and $312.9 million in 2010. Groupon also reported that it changed its method of revenue recognition during 2011:

The Company restated the Condensed Consolidated Statements of Operations for the three months ended March 31, 2011, included in the Form S-1 filed with the SEC on June 2, 2011, to correct for an error in its presentation of revenue. Most significantly, the Company restated its reporting of revenues from Groupons to be net of the amounts related to merchant fees. Historically, the Company reported the gross amounts billed to its subscribers as revenue. The Condensed Consolidated Statement of Operations for the three months ended March 31, 2011, was restated to show the net amount the Company retains after paying the merchant fees. The effect of the correction resulted in a reduction of previously reported revenues and corresponding reductions in cost of revenue in those periods. The change in presentation had no effect on pre-tax loss, net loss or any per share amounts for the period.

Groupon's refund policy is also described in its 2012 10-K report:

Our Groupon Promise states that we will provide our customers with a refund of the purchase price of a Groupon if they believe that we have let them down. . . . Our standard agreements with our merchant partners generally limit the time period during which we may seek reimbursement for customer refunds or claims. Our customers may make claims for refunds with respect to which we are unable to seek reimbursement from our merchant partners.

At the time revenue is recorded, we record an allowance for estimated customer refunds. We accrue costs associated with refunds in accrued expenses on the consolidated balance sheets. The cost of refunds where the amount payable to the merchant is recoverable is recorded in the consolidated statements of operations as a reduction to revenue. The cost of refunds when there is no amount recoverable from the merchant are presented as a cost of revenue.

To determine the amount of our refund reserve, we track refund patterns of prior deals, use that data to build a model and apply that model to current deals. Further analysis of our refund activity into 2012 indicated deviations from modeled refund behavior for deals featured in late 2011, particularly due to a shift in our fourth quarter deal mix and higher price point offers. Accordingly, we updated our refund model to reflect changes in the deal mix and price point of our deals over time and we believe this updated model will enable us to more accurately track and anticipate refund behavior.

REQUIRED

a. Assume that Groupon offers a daily deal that costs $200 per Groupon. It sells 600 of the Groupons and agrees to remit 50% of the gross revenue to the merchant within 60 days. Using journal entries, illustrate how Groupon would record the sale of this Groupon deal.

b. In the first quarter of 2011, Groupon changed its revenue recognition policy. How did this change affect its income statement?

c. Refer to the facts presented in part *a* above. Assume that Groupon expects that 10% of the Groupon customers will demand a refund within the first 60 days. How does Groupon record this estimate of returns? How are actual refunds recorded?

d. Now assume that an additional 5% of Groupon's customers demand refunds after the first 60 days. How are these refunds handled?

e. Given the uncertainty surrounding refunds, what alternative accounting approaches might Groupon consider for handling refunds?

C6-49. Interpreting Revenue Recognition Policies and Earnings Management

LO1, 2, 6
Dell Inc.
NASDAQ :: DELL

A *Wall Street Journal* article dated October 31, 2007, reported that an internal investigation at **Dell Inc.** had uncovered evidence of earnings management. The article states:

An internal investigation found that senior executives and other employees manipulated the company's financial statements to give the appearance of hitting quarterly performance goals.

One of the biggest problems uncovered in the investigation was the way Dell recognized revenue on software products it sells. Dell, a large reseller of other companies' software products, said it historically recognized revenue from software licenses at the time that the products were sold. . . . Based on its internal review, it should have deferred more revenue from software sales.

Another issue was product warranties. In some cases, Dell said it improperly recognized revenue associated with [extended] warranties over a shorter period of time than the duration of the contract.

The income statements from Dell's 2007 10-K report are presented below, along with the footnote outlining Dell's revenue recognition policies:

	Fiscal Year Ended		
	February 2, 2007	February 3, 2006 As Restated	January 28, 2005 As Restated
Net revenue	$57,420	$55,788	$49,121
Cost of net revenue	47,904	45,897	40,103
Gross margin	9,516	9,891	9,018
Operating expenses:			
Selling, general, and administrative	5,948	5,051	4,352
Research, development, and engineering	498	458	460
Total operating expenses	6,446	5,509	4,812
Operating income	3,070	4,382	4,206
Investment and other income, net	275	226	197
Income before income taxes	3,345	4,608	4,403
Income tax provision	762	1,006	1,385
Net income	$ 2,583	$ 3,602	$ 3,018

Revenue Recognition Net revenue includes sales of hardware, software and peripherals, and services (including extended service contracts and professional services). These products and services are sold either separately or as part of a multiple-element arrangement. Dell allocates revenue from multiple-element arrangements to the elements based on the relative fair value of each element, which is generally based on the relative sales price of each element when sold separately. The allocation of fair value for a multiple-element arrangement involving software is based on vendor specific objective evidence ("VSOE"), or in the absence of VSOE for delivered elements, the residual method. Under the residual method, Dell allocates revenue to software licenses at the inception of the license term when VSOE for all undelivered elements, such as Post Contract Customer Support ("PCS"), exists and all other revenue recognition criteria have been satisfied. In the absence of VSOE for undelivered elements, revenue is deferred and subsequently recognized over the term of the arrangement. For sales of extended warranties with a separate contract price, Dell defers revenue equal to the separately stated price. Revenue associated with undelivered elements is deferred and recorded when delivery occurs. Product revenue is recognized, net of an allowance for estimated returns, when both title and risk of loss transfer to the customer, provided that no significant obligations remain. Revenue from extended warranty and service contracts, for which Dell is obligated to perform, is recorded as deferred revenue and subsequently recognized over the term of the contract or when the service is completed. Revenue from sales of third-party extended warranty and service contracts or software PCS, for which Dell is not obligated to perform, and for which Dell does not meet the criteria for gross revenue recognition under EITF 99-19 is recognized on a net basis. All other revenue is recognized on a gross basis.

REQUIRED

a. Explain how Dell accounts for sales of other companies' software products. What are the potential risks of abuse of these accounting policies as a means to manage earnings?

b. Explain how Dell accounts for sales of extended warranty contracts. How did Dell employees manipulate these policies to manage earnings?

c. Discuss the incentives that exist to manage earnings to "give the appearance of hitting quarterly performance goals." How can a company such as Dell prevent earnings management in circumstances such as this?

LO2, 4, 5
John Wiley and Sons, Inc.
NYSE :: JW

C6-50. Accounting for Doubtful Accounts and Returns

John Wiley and Sons, Inc. publishes books, periodicals, software and other digital content. Its April 30, 2012 balance sheet reported the following amounts for accounts receivable ($ thousands):

April 30,	2012	2011
Accounts receivable	$171,561	$168,310

Wiley's income statement provided the following detail of operating income ($ thousands):

Year ended April 30	2012	2011
Revenue	$1,782,742	$1,742,551
Cost of sales	543,396	539,043
Operating and administrative expenses	922,177	910,847
Additional provision for doubtful accounts	—	9,290
Amortization of intangibles	36,750	35,223
Operating income	280,419	248,148

Wiley normally charges operating and administrative expenses for estimated doubtful accounts. However, in fiscal 2011, the company recorded an additional charge to reflect estimated losses from the **Borders Group, Inc.** bankruptcy. This was explained in note 9 of its financial statements:

Note 9—Additional Provision for Doubtful Trade Account
In fiscal year 2011, the Company recorded a pre-tax bad debt provision of $9.3 million, or $6.0 million after-tax ($0.10 per diluted share), related to the Company's customer, Borders Group, Inc. ("Borders"). The net charge was reflected in the Additional Provision for Doubtful Trade Account line item in the Consolidated Statements of Income and represented the difference between the Company's outstanding receivable with Borders, net of existing reserves and recoveries. There were no additional charges or bad debt expense with respect to this customer. On February 16, 2011, Borders filed a petition for reorganization relief under Chapter 11 of the U.S. Bankruptcy code.

Wiley provided the following supplemental information concerning doubtful accounts and returns in its footnotes ($ thousands):

	Balance at Beginning of Period	Charged to Costs and Expenses	Deductions from Reserve	Balance at End of Period
Year ended April 30, 2012				
Allowance for sales returns	$48,909	$82,901	$ 96,037	$35,773
Allowance for doubtful accounts	19,642	2,111	14,903	6,850
Year ended April 30, 2011				
Allowance for sales returns	55,311	96,841	103,243	48,909
Allowance for doubtful accounts	6,859	13,989	1,206	19,642

Net sales return reserves are reflected in the following accounts of the Consolidated Statements of Financial Position—increase (decrease):

April 30,	2012	2011
Accounts receivable	$(48,612)	$(65,664)
Inventory	7,246	9,485
Accounts and royalties payable	(5,593)	(7,270)
Decrease in net assets	$(35,773)	$(48,909)

REQUIRED

a. Prepare journal entries (and post to the related T-accounts) to record bad debts expense and accounts receivable write-offs for 2011 and 2012.

b. Compute the allowance for doubtful accounts as a percentage of accounts receivable. How does the "additional provision for doubtful accounts" affect your analysis of Wiley's accounts receivable?

c. Wiley has also established an allowance for returns. How do returns differ from doubtful accounts? Under what circumstances might this difference affect the accounting for returns?

d. Assume that Wiley accepted returns totaling $130 million in 2012 and that the inventory returned had a cost of $20 million. Moreover, assume that the returned merchandise was returned to inventory and can be resold. Prepare a journal entry to record estimated returns for 2012.

e. Calculate the accounts receivable turnover ratio and average collection period for 2012 using net accounts receivable.

LO7 DreamWorks AnimationSKG, Inc. NASDAQ :: DWA

C6-51.[A] **Interpreting Restructuring Charges**

The following is from the most recent 10-K of **DreamWorks Animation SKG, Inc.** for the year ended December 31, 2014.

In January 2015, we announced our 2015 Restructuring Plan involving the Company's core feature animation business intended to maximize our creative talent and resources, reduce costs and improve profitability. As a result, we recorded charges totaling approximately $210.1 million for the year ended December 31, 2014, including approximately $43.4 million relating to employee termination costs. . .

As of December 31, 2014, we employed approximately 2,700 people, many of whom were covered by employment agreements, which generally include non-disclosure agreements. In connection with the 2015 Restructuring Plan, we anticipate reducing our workforce by approximately 500 employees. . .

In connection with the 2015 Restructuring Plan, the Company has made changes in its senior leadership team and has also made changes based on its reevaluation of its feature film slate. The Company expects that the 2015 Restructuring Plan activities will result in charges related to employee-related costs resulting from headcount reductions, . . . costs were incurred during the three months ended December 31, 2014 . . . The Company expects that the remaining costs will be primarily incurred during the year ending December 31, 2015 and will result in total cash payments of approximately $76.0 million, primarily related to severance, benefits and contractual obligations. This excludes cash payments associated with anticipated excess labor costs as further described below. The actions associated with the restructuring plan are expected to be substantially completed during 2015.

The following tables summarizes the costs that we incurred during the year ended December 31, 2014, as well as the remaining costs we expect to incur in order to execute upon our 2015 Restructuring Plan:

	Year Ended December 31, 2014	Future Periods
Employee termination costs	$ 43.4	$12.3
Relocation and other employee-related costs	—	7.1
Lease obligations and related charges	—	6.7
Accelerated depreciation charges	—	19.3
Film and other inventory write-offs	155.5	—
Other contractual obligations	11.2	—
Additional labor and other excess costs	—	38.3
Total restructuring and related charges	$210.1	$83.7

Employee Termination Costs. Employee termination costs consist of severance and benefits (including stock-based compensation) which are accounted for based on the type of employment arrangement between the Company and the employee. Certain of these arrangements include obligations that are accounted for as non-retirement postemployment benefits. We also employ individuals under employment contracts. Charges related to non-retirement postemployment benefits and amounts due under employment contracts for employees who will no longer provide services are accrued when probable and estimable. Severance and benefits related to all other employees are accounted for in accordance with accounting guidance on costs associated with exit or disposal activities. Thus, such costs are recorded in the period in which the terms of the restructuring plan have been established, management with the appropriate authority commits to the plan and communication to employees has occurred.

Relocation and Other Employee-Related Costs. Relocation and other employee-related costs primarily consist of expected costs to relocate employees from our Northern California facility to our Southern California facility. Such costs are expensed as incurred and will be primarily incurred during the year ending December 31, 2015.

REQUIRED

a. Describe where on the income statement the above described restructuring charges are included.

b. Describe how an analyst of the company should treat the costs when doing financial statement analysis.

c. What incentives might management have to either overstate or understate the above described restructuring charges? Describe how future financial statements would be affected if the costs were overstated or understated when these charges were recorded in 2014.

SOLUTIONS TO REVIEW PROBLEMS

Mid-Chapter Review 1

SOLUTION

(All dollar amounts are in millions.)

1.

	2014	2013
Revenue growth rates	($86,833 − $77,849)/$77,849 = 11.5%	($77,849 − $73,723)/$73,723 = 5.6%

2. To determine the customer purchases during the year, we start with the revenue, then add the "Deferral of unearned revenue," then subtract the "Recognition of unearned revenue."

	2014	2013	2012
Revenue	$86,833	$77,849	$73,723
Plus "Deferral of unearned revenue"	44,325	44,253	36,104
Less "Recognition of unearned revenue".	41,739	41,921	33,347
Purchases made by customers	$89,419	$80,181	$76,480

3.

	2014	2013
Purchase growth rates	($89,419 − $80,181)/$80,181 = 11.5%	($80,181 − $76,480)/$76,480 = 4.8%

When a customer makes a purchase, Microsoft defers a substantial portion of the amount received and recognizes that portion over future periods. Therefore, revenue reported on the income statement is a combination of customer purchases in the current period, plus customer purchases in previous periods (up to three years ago). This has the effect of smoothing Microsoft's revenues over time.

Mid-Chapter Review 2

SOLUTION

1. The terms of the contract are likely different for government contracts and contracts with private organizations. To justify the use of the percentage-of-completion method, there must be a contract that specifies a fixed or determinable price. The contracts for private organizations might have more ambiguity as far as the pricing is concerned. Alternatively, Adler most likely has experience that would indicate that government contracts are less likely to be cancelled.
2. The percentage completed in each year is 40% in 2016 ($12,000,000/$30,000,000), 45% in 2017 ($13,500,000/$30,000,000), and 15% in 2018 ($4,500,000/$30,000,000).

   a. Percentage-of-completion method

	2016	2017	2018
Percentage completed.	40%	45%	15%
Contract revenue	$16,000,000	$18,000,000	$ 6,000,000
(Percentage completed × $40,000,000)			
Contract expense.	12,000,000	13,500,000	4,500,000
Gross profit.	$ 4,000,000	$ 4,500,000	$ 1,500,000

   b. Completed contract method

	2016	2017	2018
Contract revenue	$ 0	$ 0	$40,000,000
Contract expense.	0	0	30,000,000
Gross profit.	$ 0	$ 0	$10,000,000

3. Income would be understated in 2016 and 2017, but the difference would be made up in 2018 with higher than expected earnings. The gross profit in 2018 would be $6,000,000 − $1,500,000 = $4,500,000.

Mid-Chapter Review 3

SOLUTION

1. As of December 31, 2016,

Current	$468,000	×	1%	=	$ 4,680	
1–60 days past due	244,000	×	5%	=	12,200	
61–180 days past due	38,000	×	15%	=	5,700	
Over 180 days past due.	20,000	×	40%	=	8,000	
Amount required.					$30,580	
Unused allowance balance . . .					7,000	
Provision.					$23,580	2016 bad debts expense

2. Current assets section of balance sheet.

Accounts receivable, net of $30,580 in allowances.	$739,420

3. Engel Company has markedly increased the percentage of the allowance for uncollectible accounts to gross accounts receivable—from the historical 2% to the current 4% ($30,580/$770,000). There are at least two possible interpretations:
   a. The quality of Engel Company's receivables has declined. Possible causes include the following: (1) sales can stagnate and the company can feel compelled to sell to lower-quality accounts to maintain sales volume; (2) it may have introduced new products for which average credit losses are higher; and (3) its administration of accounts receivable can become lax.
   b. The company has intentionally increased its allowance account above the level needed for expected future losses so as to reduce current period income and "bank" that income for future periods (income shifting).
4. Transaction effects shown in the financial statement effects template.

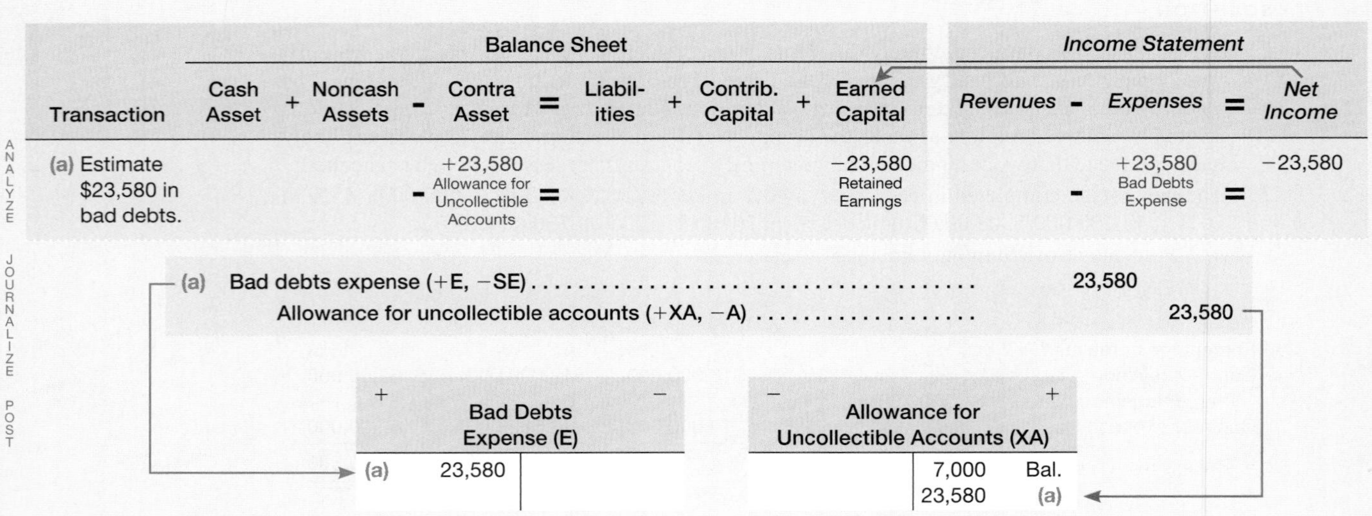

Transaction	Cash Asset	+	Noncash Assets	−	Contra Asset	=	Liabil-ities	+	Contrib. Capital	+	Earned Capital	Revenues	−	Expenses	=	Net Income
(a) Estimate $23,580 in bad debts.				−	+23,580 Allowance for Uncollectible Accounts	=					−23,580 Retained Earnings		−	+23,580 Bad Debts Expense	=	−23,580

(a) Bad debts expense (+E, −SE).	23,580	
Allowance for uncollectible accounts (+XA, −A)		23,580

ANALYZE

Transaction	Cash Asset	+	Noncash Assets	-	Contra Asset	=	Liabil-ities	+	Contrib. Capital	+	Earned Capital	Revenues	-	Expenses	=	Net Income
(b) Write off $5,000 in accounts receivable.*			−5,000 Accounts Receivable	-	−5,000 Allowance for Uncollectible Accounts	=							-		=	

(Balance Sheet: Transaction through Earned Capital; Income Statement: Revenues − Expenses = Net Income)

* There is no effect on net accounts receivable.

JOURNALIZE

POST

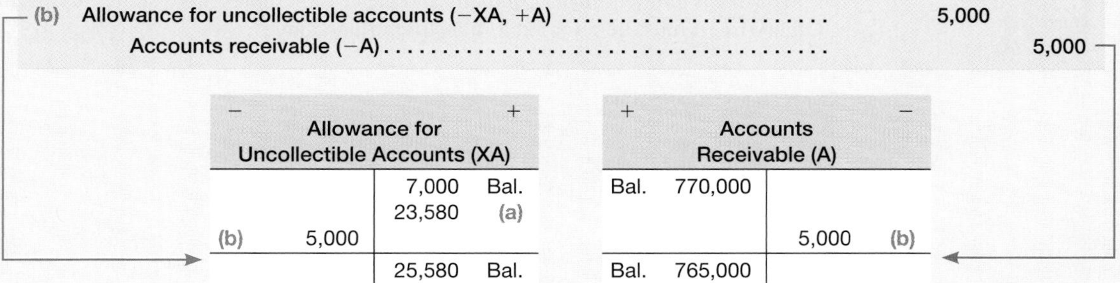

(b) Allowance for uncollectible accounts (−XA, +A) 5,000
Accounts receivable (−A).. 5,000
− Allowance for Uncollectible Accounts (XA) +
7,000 Bal.
23,580 (a)
(b) 5,000
25,580 Bal.
+ Accounts Receivable (A) −
Bal. 770,000
5,000 (b)
Bal. 765,000

Chapter-End Review

SOLUTION

1.

($ millions)	Comcast	Time Warner
NOPAT	$8,592 − [($296 − $2,832) × (1 − 0.35)] = $10,240.4	$3,827 − [($0 − $1,296) × (1 − 0.35)] = $4,669.4
Average net operating assets	[($155,602 − $56,971) + ($151,470 − $58,951)]/2 = $95,575	[($60,933 - $16,289) + ($65,990 − $17,284)]/2 = $46,675
Return on net operating assets	$10,240.4/$95,575 = 0.107	$4,669.4/$46,675 = 0.100
Net operating profit margin.............	$10,240.4/$68,775 = 0.149	$4,669.4/$27,359 = 0.171
Accounts receivable turnover............	$68,775/[($6,321 + $6,376)/2] = 10.8	$27,359/[($7,720 + $7,305)/2] = 3.64
Average collection period	= 365/10.8 = 33.8 days	= 365/3.64 = 100.3 days

2. These two companies are similar in their performance ratios. Comcast reports a 10.7% return on net operating assets and a 14.9% net operating profit margin while Time Warner reports a 10.0% RNOA and a 17.1% NOPM. Thus, these companies generate nearly identical returns on their assets, but Time Warner appears to control costs better per dollar of revenue as shown in their higher margins.

However, there is a significant difference between these two competitors when it comes to accounts receivable. Time Warner turns its receivables 3.64 times per year, for an average collection period (ACP) of 100.3 days. Comcast, on the other hand, has an accounts receivable turnover of 10.8 times and an ACP of 33.8 days. Thus, Comcast collects receivables nearly three times faster than Time Warner.

Appendix 6A Review

SOLUTION

a. A loss from discontinued operations of $105,000 would be reported below income from continuing operations. The loss is net of tax and is calculated as follows: $105,000 = ($120,000 + $12,000 + $18,000) × (1 − 30%).

b. A restructuring charge of $30,000 ($12,000 + $18,000) would be reported as part of operating income. The loss is before taxes. The tax effect of the restructuring charge would be included in the provision for income taxes (income tax expense).

c. Singh could report this loss as discontinued operations only if the closure represented a separate business unit within the company and the closure represents a strategic shift in operations. Otherwise, it must be reported as a restructuring charge.

7 Reporting and Analyzing Inventory

LEARNING OBJECTIVES

1. Interpret disclosures of information concerning operating expenses, including manufacturing and retail inventory costs. (p. 328)
2. Account for inventory and cost of goods sold using different costing methods. (p. 332)
3. Apply the lower of cost or market rule to value inventory. (p. 337)
4. Evaluate how inventory costing affects management decisions and outsiders' interpretations of financial statements. (p. 341)
5. Define and interpret gross profit margin and inventory turnover ratios. Use inventory footnote information to make appropriate adjustments to ratios. (p. 345)
6. Appendix 7A: Analyze LIFO liquidations and the impact they have on the financial statements. (p. 351)

HOME DEPOT
www.HomeDepot.com

The Home Depot, Inc. is the world's largest home improvement retailer and the second largest specialty retailer in the United States. At February 1, 2015, the company operated 2,269 retail stores worldwide, and reported sales of $83 billion. This performance represents a fifth year of increasing revenues.

Management of The Home Depot has focused in recent years on "improving the performance of our existing stores,"[1] with less emphasis on expansion. Indeed, their stated strategic framework consists of three key initiatives—1) customer service, 2) product authority, and 3) disciplined capital allocation, productivity, and efficiency. The Home Depot's net operating profit margin (net operating profit divided by sales revenue) has increased significantly between 2011 and 2014, reflecting a combination of management's attention to costs and an improving economy. The company has performed very well in recent years.

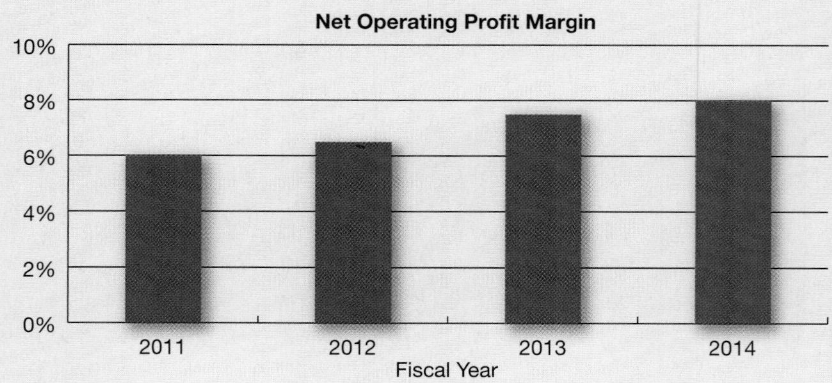

[1] Home Depot CEO Frank Blake in an interview with Rachel Tobin Blake published in *The Atlantic Journal-Constitution*, February 1, 2009.

A key element of Home Depot's operating strategy is inventory management. Inventory represents one of the largest assets on Home Depot's balance sheet. A typical Home Depot store carries 30,000 to 40,000 products during the year, ranging from garden supplies to hardware and lumber to household appliances. These stores are stocked through a sophisticated logistics program designed to ensure product availability for customers and low supply chain costs. The fiscal 2014 annual report states that the company "continued to focus on optimizing our supply chain network and improving our inventory, transportation and distribution productivity." As of February 1, 2015, the company operated 34 bulk distribution centers, 21 stocking distribution centers, 10 specialty distribution centers, and 19 Rapid Deployment Centers (RDCs) where merchandise from manufacturers is received and prepared for immediate delivery to stores. The company also utilizes its retail stores as a network of locations for customers who shop online.

In this chapter, we examine the reporting of inventory and cost of goods sold. For most retail and manufacturing businesses, cost of goods sold and the related inventory management costs represent the largest source of expenses in the income statement. Carrying large stocks of inventory is costly for any business. The more that a business can minimize the amount of resources tied up in merchandise or materials, while still meeting customer demand, the more profitable it will be. Moreover, excessive inventory balances can indicate poor inventory management, obsolete products, and weakening sales. We explore accounting methods designed to measure inventory costs and determine cost of goods sold. We also look at measures that help us assess the effectiveness of inventory management practices for companies such as The Home Depot.

Sources: *Fortune*, May 2012; The Home Depot, Inc. 2010-2014 10-K reports; The Home Depot does not end its fiscal year on December 31, but rather on the Sunday closest to January 31. So, "Fiscal Year 2014" actually ended on February 1, 2015. One interesting aspect of this practice is that most of The Home Depot's fiscal years have 52 weeks, but periodically a fiscal year will have 53 weeks. (Fiscal Year 2012 was the most recent year of this event.)

CHAPTER ORGANIZATION

Reporting and Analyzing Inventory

Reporting Operating Expenses	Inventory Costing Methods	Financial Statement Effects and Disclosure	Analyzing Financial Statements
• Expense Recognition • Recording and Reporting Inventory Costs • Manufacturing Inventory	• FIFO • LIFO • Average Cost • Lower of Cost or Market	• Footnote Disclosures • Income Statement Effects • Balance Sheet Effects • Cash Flow Effects	• Gross Profit Analysis • Inventory Turnover • LIFO Liquidation (Appendix 7A)

REPORTING OPERATING EXPENSES

1

LO1 Interpret disclosures of information concerning operating expenses, including manufacturing and retail inventory costs.

In Chapter 6, we introduced the concept of operating income and discussed issues surrounding revenue recognition and how best to measure and report a company's performance. But the amount of revenue from customers must be interpreted relative to the resources that were required to achieve it. Operating expenses include the costs of acquiring the products (and services) that customers purchase, plus the costs of selling efforts, administrative functions, and any other activities that support the operations of the company. Careful examination of these costs allows financial statement users to judge management's performance, to identify emerging problems, and to make predictions of future performance. For instance, we may address the following questions.

- Are the company's costs of providing products increasing or decreasing?
- Is the company able to maintain its margins in the face of changes in costs or competition?
- Does management's ability to judge customer tastes and preferences allow it to avoid overstocks of unpopular inventory and the resulting price discounts that reduce margins?

In this chapter, we begin our examination of operating expenses by studying inventory and cost of goods sold. The reporting of inventory and cost of goods sold is important for three reasons. First, cost of goods sold is often the largest single expense in a company's income statement, and inventory may be one of the largest assets in the balance sheet. Consequently, information about inventory and cost of goods sold is critical for interpreting the financial statements. Second, in order to effectively manage operations and resources, management needs accurate and timely information about inventory quantities and costs. Finally, alternative methods of accounting for inventory and cost of goods sold can distort interpretations of margins and turnovers unless the information in the financial statement footnotes is used.

Expense Recognition Principles

In addition to determining when to recognize revenues to properly measure and report a company's performance, we must also determine when to recognize expenses. In general, expenses are recognized when assets are diminished (or liabilities increased) as a result of earning revenue or supporting operations, even if there is no immediate decrease in cash. Expense recognition can be generally divided into the following three approaches.

- **Direct association.** Any cost that can be *directly* associated with a specific source of revenue should be recognized as an expense at the same time that the related revenue is recognized. For a merchandising company (a retailer or a wholesaler), an example of direct association is recognizing cost of goods sold and sales revenue when the product is delivered to the customer. The cost of acquiring the inventory is recorded in the inventory asset account where it remains until the item is sold. At that point, the inventory cost is removed from the inventory asset and transferred to expenses. The future costs of any obligations arising from current revenues should also be estimated and recognized as liabilities and matched as expenses against those revenues. An example of such an expense is expected warranty costs, a topic covered in Chapter 9.

  For a manufacturing company, the accounting system distinguishes between *product costs* and *period costs*. Product costs are incurred to benefit the company's manufacturing activities and include raw materials, production workers and supervisors, depreciation on equipment and facilities, utilities, and so on. Even though some of these costs cannot be directly associated with a unit of production, the accounting system accumulates product costs and assigns them to inventory assets until the unit is sold. All costs not classified as product costs are considered period costs.

- **Immediate recognition.** Many period costs are necessary for generating revenues and income but cannot be directly associated with specific revenues. Some costs can be associated with all of the revenues of an accounting period, but not with any specific sales transaction that occurred during that period. Examples include most administrative and marketing costs. These costs are recognized as expenses in the period when the costs are incurred. Other expense items, such as research and development (R&D) expense, are recognized immediately because of U.S. GAAP requirements.
- **Systematic allocation.** Costs that benefit more than one accounting period and cannot be associated with specific revenues or assigned to a specific period must be allocated across all of the periods benefited. The most common example is depreciation expense. When an asset is purchased, it is capitalized (recorded in an asset account). The asset cost is then converted into an expense over the duration of its useful life according to a depreciation formula or schedule established by management. Depreciation of long-term assets is discussed in Chapter 8.

Inventory and cost of goods sold expense are important for product companies—manufacturers, wholesalers, and retailers. But before turning to an examination of these accounts at The Home Depot, we should recognize that cost of sales expense is also a critical performance component for many service companies, particularly those who engage in projects for their clients and customers. For fiscal 2014, the consulting firm **Accenture PLC** reports revenues of $31.9 billion and cost of services of $22.2 billion; the professional staffing company **Kelly Services, Inc.** reported net service revenues of $5.6 billion and direct costs of services of $4.7 billion; and **Google Inc.** reported revenue of $66 billion and cost of sales of $25.7 billion. While these companies report no inventory, the relationship of revenues to costs of revenues remains important.

Reporting Inventory Costs in the Financial Statements

To help frame our discussion of inventory, **Exhibits 7.1** and **7.2** present information from the current asset section of the balance sheet and the continuing operations section of the income statement for The Home Depot. We highlight merchandise inventories in the balance sheet as well as cost of goods sold in the income statement.

When inventory is purchased or produced, it is capitalized and carried on the balance sheet as an asset until it is sold, at which time its cost is transferred from the balance sheet to the income statement as an expense (cost of goods sold). Cost of goods sold (COGS) is then subtracted from sales revenue to yield **gross profit**:

Gross profit = Sales revenue − Cost of goods sold

The manner in which inventory costs are transferred from the balance sheet to the income statement affects both the level of inventories reported on the balance sheet and the amount of gross profit (and net income) reported on the income statement.

EXHIBIT 7.1 Balance Sheets (Current Assets Only)

THE HOME DEPOT, INC.
Consolidated Balance Sheets

($ millions)	February 1, 2015	February 2, 2014
Assets		
Current assets:		
Cash and cash equivalents	$ 1,723	$ 1,929
Receivables, net	1,484	1,398
Merchandise inventories	11,079	11,057
Other current assets	1,016	895
Total current assets	$15,302	$15,279

EXHIBIT 7.2 Income Statement (Continuing Operations Only)

THE HOME DEPOT, INC. Consolidated Statement of Earnings ($ millions)	Fiscal year 2014
Net sales	$83,176
Cost of sales	54,222
Gross profit	28,954
Total operating expenses	18,485
Operating income	10,469
Interest and other, net	493
Earnings from continuing operations before provision for income taxes	9,976
Provision for income taxes	3,631
Earnings from continuing operations	$ 6,345

Recording Inventory Costs in the Financial Statements

To illustrate the inventory purchasing and selling cycle, assume that a start-up company purchases 800 units of merchandise inventory at a cost of $4 cash per unit. We account for this transaction as follows:

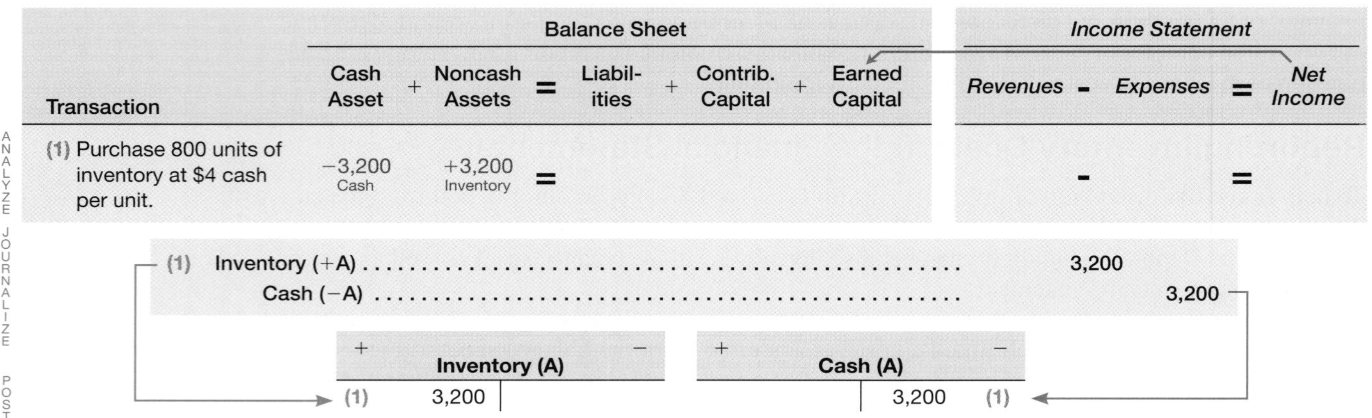

Next, assume this company sells 500 of those units for $7 cash per unit. The two following entries are required to record (a) the sales revenue and (b) the expense for the cost of the inventory sold.

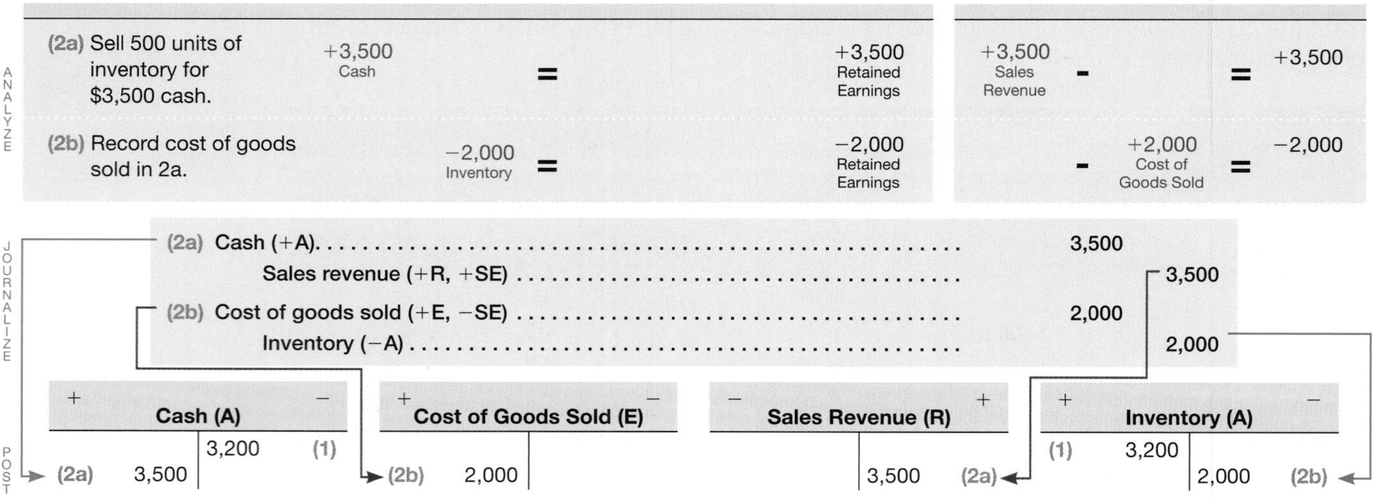

The gross profit from this sale is $1,500 ($3,500 − $2,000). Also, $1,200 worth of merchandise remains in inventory (300 units × $4 per unit).

Inventory and the Cost of Acquisition

In general, a company should recognize all inventories to which it holds legal title, and that inventory should be recognized at the cost of acquiring the inventory. On occasion, that means that the company will recognize items in inventory that are not on its premises. For instance, if a company purchases inventory from a supplier on an "FOB shipping point" basis, meaning that the purchasing company receives title to the goods as soon as they are shipped by the supplier, the purchasing company should recognize the inventory as soon as it receives notice that the goods have been shipped. A similar situation occurs when a company ships its own products to a customer, but has not yet fulfilled the requirements for recognizing revenue on the shipment. In this case, the cost of the products remains in the selling company's inventory account until revenue (and cost of goods sold) can be recognized.

FYI The term **FOB ("free on board") shipping point** means that title passes to the purchaser as soon as it is shipped by the seller. **FOB destination** means that the seller retains title until the item arrives at the purchaser's location.

It is also possible for a company to have physical possession of inventory items, but not to have legal title. **Target Corporation**, for example, reports the following in a recent 10-K.

> We routinely enter into arrangements with certain vendors whereby we do not purchase or pay for merchandise until the merchandise is ultimately sold to a guest. Activity under this program is included in sales and cost of sales in the Consolidated Statements of Operations, but the merchandise received under the program is not included in inventory in our Consolidated Statements of Financial Position because of the virtually simultaneous purchase and sale of this inventory.

Inventory is reported in the balance sheet at its cost, including any cost to acquire, transport, and prepare goods for sale. In some cases, determining the cost of inventory requires accounting for various incentives that suppliers offer to purchase more or to pay promptly. If a company qualifies for a supplier's volume discount or rebate, it should immediately recognize the effective reduction in the cost of inventory and cost of goods sold. Or, if the company purchases inventory on credit, suppliers often grant **cash discounts** to buyers if payment is made within a specified time period. Cash discounts are usually established as part of the credit terms and stated as a percentage of the purchase price. For example, credit terms of 1/10, n/30 (one-ten, net-thirty) indicate that a 1% cash discount is allowed if the payment is made within 10 days. If the cash discount is not taken, the full purchase price is due in 30 days. Cash discounts are discussed in greater detail in Chapter 9.

Inventory Reporting by Manufacturing Firms

Retail and wholesale businesses purchase merchandise for resale to customers. In contrast, a manufacturing firm produces the goods it sells. Its inventory reporting is designed to reflect this difference in the nature of its operations.

FYI Only one inventory account appears in the financial statements of a merchandiser. A manufacturer normally has three inventory accounts: Raw Materials, Work-in-Process, and Finished Goods.

Manufacturing firms typically report three categories of inventory account:

- **Raw materials inventory**—the cost of parts and materials purchased from suppliers for use in the production process. When raw materials are used in the production process, the cost of the materials used is transferred from raw materials inventory into the work-in-process inventory account.
- **Work-in-process inventory**—the cost of the inventory of partially completed goods. Work-in-process (abbreviated WIP) includes the materials used in the production of the product as well as labor cost and overhead cost. (Methods by which labor and overhead costs are assigned to products in the WIP account is a *managerial accounting* topic.) When the production process is completed, the cost of goods produced is transferred from WIP into the finished goods inventory account.
- **Finished goods inventory**—the cost of the stock of completed product ready for delivery to customers. When finished goods are sold, cost of goods sold is debited and finished goods inventory is credited, much the same as in a retail business.

EXHIBIT 7.3 Components of Inventory for Cisco Systems, Inc.

	July 26, 2014
Inventories ($ millions):	
Raw materials	$ 77
Work in process	5
Finished goods	
Distributor inventory and deferred cost of sales	595
Manufactured finished goods	606
Total finished goods	1,201
Service-related spares	273
Demonstration systems	35
Total	$1,591

A complete illustration of the accounting process for a manufacturing business is beyond the scope of this text. However, it is useful to understand how these inventory accounts are presented in the financial statements of manufacturing firms. In some cases, each of the three categories of inventory is presented in the balance sheet. Usually, however, the balance sheet only presents the combined total of the three accounts, leaving the detail to be presented in the footnotes. **Cisco Systems** reported inventory of $1,591 million in its balance sheet dated July 26, 2014. **Exhibit 7.3** details the components of Cisco's inventory balance as presented in its 10-K report. It shows that finished goods inventory represented the largest portion of the total inventory balance and that almost half of these finished goods are held by Cisco's distributors. (Cisco's "sell-through" revenue recognition was described in Chapter 6.) Cisco reports two additional categories of inventory—spare parts and systems used in product demonstrations. **Exhibit 7.3** is representative of the footnote disclosure provided by many manufacturing companies.

BUSINESS INSIGHT

If a manufacturing company has an unexpected buildup of inventory, the interpretation depends on the type of inventory. A larger-than-normal buildup of finished goods would imply that the company was having difficulty getting customers to purchase its products. However, if the buildup is in work-in-process inventory, it might imply a problem with manufacturing processes, particularly if accompanied by a decrease in finished goods inventory.

2 **LO2** Account for inventory and cost of goods sold using different costing methods.

INVENTORY COSTING METHODS

The computation of cost of goods sold is important and is shown in **Exhibit 7.4**.

EXHIBIT 7.4 Cost of Goods Sold Computation

	Beginning inventory value (prior period ending balance sheet)
+	Cost of inventory purchases and/or production
	Cost of goods available for sale
−	Ending inventory value (current period balance sheet)
	Cost of goods sold (current income statement)

The cost of inventory available at the beginning of a period is a carryover from the ending inventory balance of the prior period. The costs of current period purchases of inventory (or costs of newly manufactured inventories) are added to the costs of beginning inventory on the balance sheet, yielding the total cost of goods (inventory) available for sale. Then, the total cost of goods available either ends up in cost of goods sold for the period (reported on the income statement) or is carried forward as inventory to start the next period (reported on the ending balance sheet). This cost flow is schematically shown in **Exhibit 7.5**.

Understanding the flow of inventory costs is important. If the beginning inventory plus all inventory purchased or manufactured during the period is sold, then COGS is equal to the cost of the goods available for sale. However, when inventory remains at the end of a period, companies must identify the cost of those inventories that have been sold and the cost of those inventories that remain.

EXHIBIT 7.5 Inventory Cost Flows to Financial Statements

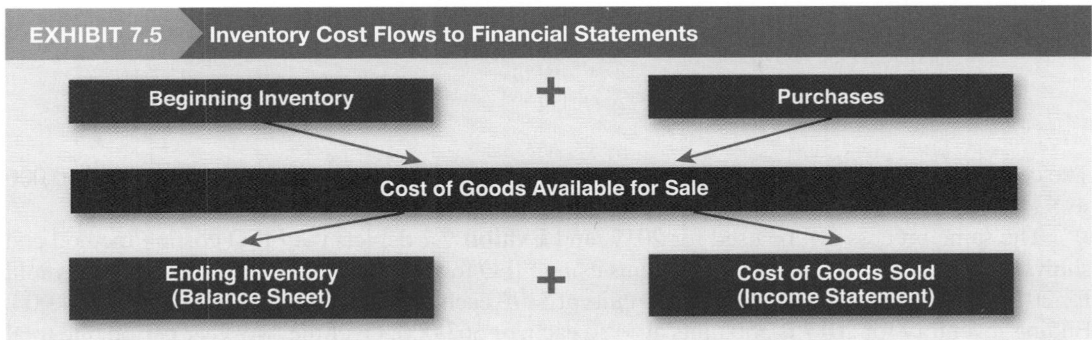

Most companies will organize the physical flow of their inventories to keep the cost of inventory management low, while minimizing the likelihood of spoilage or obsolescence. However, the accounting for inventory and cost of goods sold does not have to follow the physical flow of the units of inventory, so companies may report using a **cost flow assumption** that does not conform to the actual movement of product through the firm. (For instance, many grocery chains use last-in, first-out to account for inventory costs, but that doesn't mean that they put the newest produce out to sell while keeping the older produce back in the storeroom.)

Illustration To illustrate the possible cost flow assumptions that companies can adopt, assume that **Exhibit 7.6** reflects the inventory records of Butler Company.

EXHIBIT 7.6 Summary Inventory Records for Butler Company

		Number of Units	Cost per Unit	Total Cost	Number of Units	Price per Unit	Total Revenue
January 1, 2016	Beginning inventory	500	$100	$ 50,000			
2016	Inventory purchased.	200	170	34,000			
	Inventory sold.				450	$250	$112,500
2017	Inventory purchased.	600	180	108,000			
	Inventory sold.				500	255	127,500

Butler Company began the period with inventory consisting of 500 units it purchased at a total cost of $50,000 ($100 each). During the two-year period, the company purchased an additional 200 units costing $34,000 and 600 units costing $108,000. The total cost of goods available for sale for this two-year period equals $192,000.

Tracking the number of units available for sale each year and in inventory at the end of each year is simple. However, the changing cost per unit makes it more complicated to determine the cost of goods sold and the ending inventory. The relationships depicted in **Exhibit 7.5** can hold in multiple ways, depending on the cost flow assumption chosen. Three inventory costing methods are acceptable under U.S. GAAP (though only two are permitted under IFRS, as we discuss later).[2]

First-In, First-Out (FIFO)

The **first-in, first-out (FIFO)** inventory costing method transfers costs from inventory in the order that they were initially recorded. That is, FIFO assumes that the first costs recorded in inventory (first-in) are the first costs transferred from inventory (first-out) to cost of goods sold. Conversely, the costs of the last units purchased are the costs that remain in inventory at year-end. Applying FIFO to the data in **Exhibit 7.6** means that the costs relating to the 450 units sold

FYI First-in, first-out (FIFO) assumes that goods are used in the order in which they are purchased; the inventory remaining represents the most recent purchases.

[2] Of the firms in the Standard and Poor's 500 Index as of December 31, 2013, 17.2% have a LIFO reserve reported on Compustat (database of annual reports). A few additional firms may be on LIFO but have a zero reserve. (An example is Hollyfrontier Corporation. It reported a zero LIFO reserve in 2014 caused by the large decline in oil prices during 2014.)

are all taken from its *beginning* inventory, which consists of 500 units. The company's 2016 cost of goods sold and gross profit, using FIFO, is computed as follows:

Sales	$112,500
COGS (450 @ $100 each)	45,000
Gross profit	$ 67,500

The cost remaining in inventory and reported on its 2016 year-end balance sheet is $39,000 ($50,000 + $34,000 − $45,000; also computed 50 × $100 + 200 × $170).

The same process can be used for 2017, and **Exhibit 7.7** depicts the FIFO costing method and shows the resulting financial statement items using FIFO for 2016 and 2017. FIFO cost of goods sold for 2017 is 50 units at $100 each plus 200 units at $170 each plus 250 units at $180 each, or $84,000. Ending inventory for 2017 is 350 units at $180 each, or $63,000. Over the two-year period, the total cost of goods available for sale of $192,000 is either recognized as cost of goods sold ($45,000 + $84,000 = $129,000) or remains in ending inventory ($63,000).

EXHIBIT 7.7 Butler Company using FIFO Inventory Costing

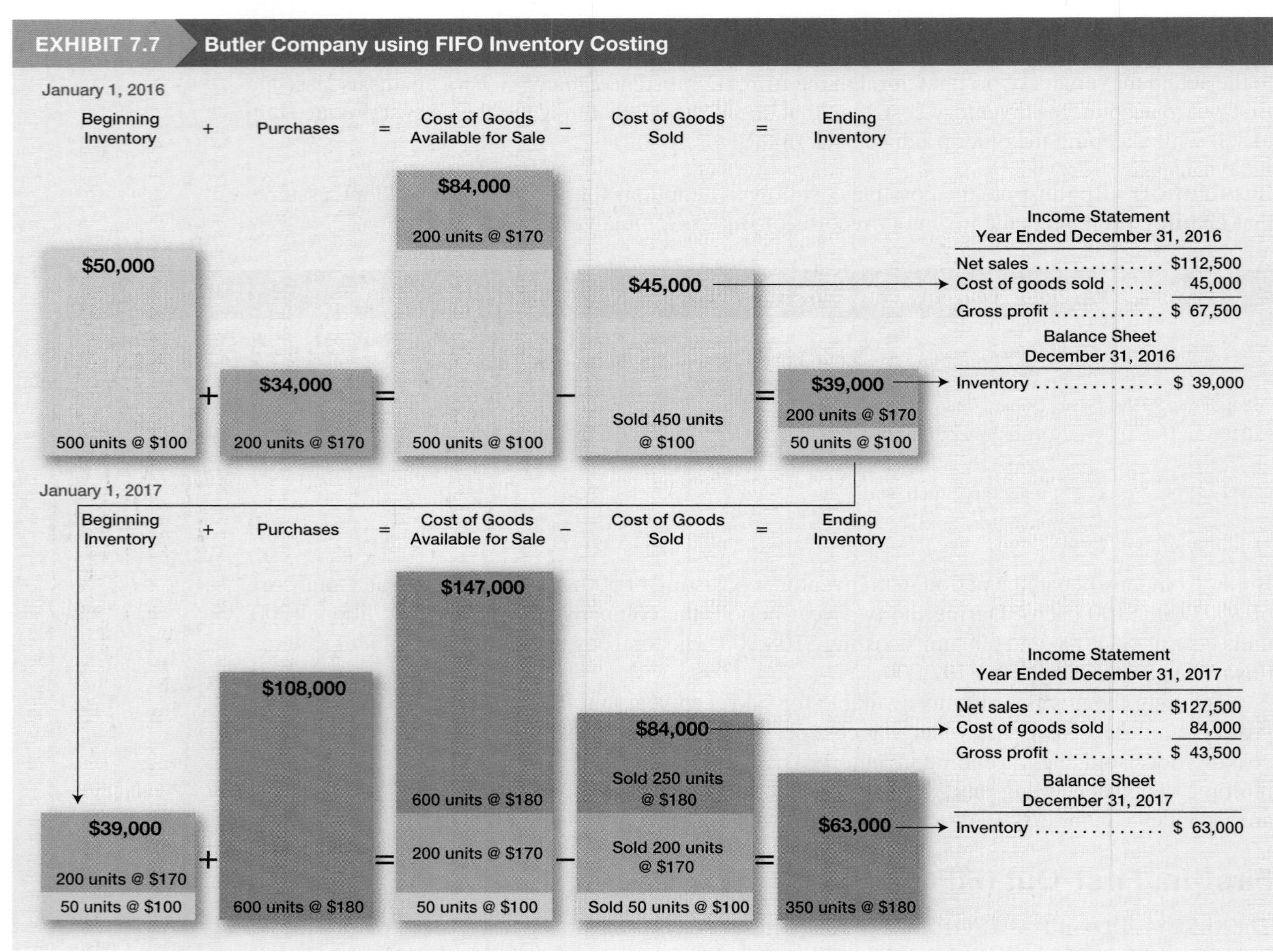

Last-In, First-Out (LIFO)

FYI Last-in, first-out (LIFO) matches the cost of the last goods purchased against revenue.

The **last-in, first-out (LIFO)** inventory costing method transfers to cost of goods sold the most recent costs that were recorded in inventory. That is, we assume that the most recent costs recorded in inventory (last-in) are the first costs transferred from inventory (first-out). Conversely, the costs of the first units purchased are the costs that remain in inventory at year-end. Butler Company's 2016 cost of goods sold and gross profit, using LIFO, are computed as follows:

Sales.	$112,500
COGS: (200 @ $170 each = $34,000)	
(250 @ $100 each = $25,000).	59,000
Gross profit.	$ 53,500

The cost remaining in inventory and reported on its 2016 balance sheet is $25,000 ($50,000 + $34,000 − $59,000; also computed 250 × $100).

The same process can be used for 2017, and **Exhibit 7.8** depicts the LIFO costing method and shows the resulting financial statement values using LIFO for both years. LIFO cost of goods sold for 2017 is 500 units at $180 each, or $90,000. Ending inventory is 250 units at $100 each plus 100 units at $180 each, or $43,000. Again, the two-year total cost of goods available for sale of $192,000 is either recognized as cost of goods sold ($59,000 + $90,000 = $149,000) or remains in inventory ($43,000).

EXHIBIT 7.8 Butler Company using LIFO Inventory Costing

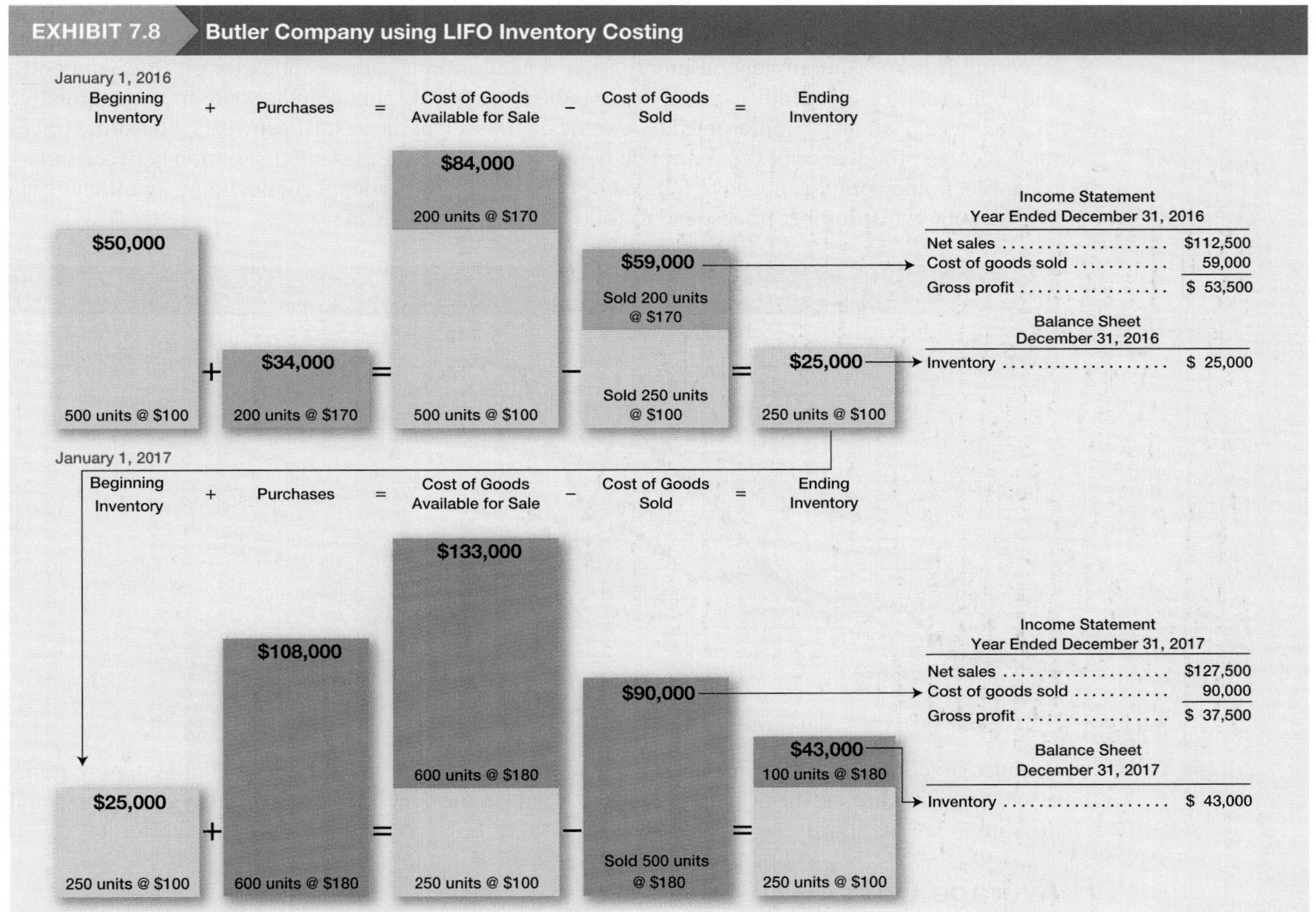

The exhibit shows that **LIFO layers** of inventories added in each year are kept separately. So, the ending inventory in 2017 consists of a pre-2016 layer of 250 units at $100 each plus a 2017 layer of 100 units at $180 each. When unit sales exceed purchases (as we discuss in the appendix), the first costs carried to cost of goods sold are those purchased in the current year, followed by the most recent layer of LIFO inventory and working down to the oldest layers. So, the 2016 beginning inventory value of $100 per unit remains in LIFO inventory as long as there are 250 units remaining at the end of the year. One aspect of this flow assumption is that reported LIFO inventory values can be significantly lower than the current cost of acquiring the same inventory.

LIFO inventory costing is always applied on a periodic, annual basis. This means that Butler's cost of goods sold and ending inventory for 2017 do not depend on the timing of the sales and purchases within the year. Inventory levels might be drawn down below 250 units *during* the year, but the 250 unit LIFO layer at $100 each remains in ending inventory as long as inventory is built up to 250 units by the *end* of the year.

Inventory Costing and Price Changes

There are several important aspects of inventory costing that are illustrated by the Butler Company example. First, both LIFO and FIFO are historical cost methods, though they allocate the costs of inventory differently. All costs are accounted for, but in different ways.

Second, the differences between LIFO and FIFO arise when the costs of inventory change over time. In general, LIFO puts more recent costs into cost of goods sold expense, so LIFO cost of goods sold is higher than FIFO cost of goods sold (and gross profit correspondingly lower) when the costs of inventory are rising over time. This phenomenon can be seen in years 2016 and 2017 for Butler Company. If the costs of inventory are falling, then FIFO cost of goods sold exceeds LIFO cost of goods sold.

One place where we can observe the cost trends of acquiring inventory is in the U.S. Bureau of Labor Statistics' Producer Price Indices. These indices track the costs of producing a wide variety of products in the United States. **Exhibit 7.9** shows the recent trends (and fluctuations) in the Consumer Price Index (a measure of general inflation), a general Producer Price Index for all finished goods, and four Producer Price Indices for specific industries. (These annual indices are measured relative to 1982 prices, which are represented by a value of 100.) Over the past fifteen years, consumer prices (and average producer prices) have trended upward, but there is substantial variation between industries. Electronic components have trended down, gasoline has fluctuated, declining significantly in the last year, while lumber prices tend to follow construction trends.

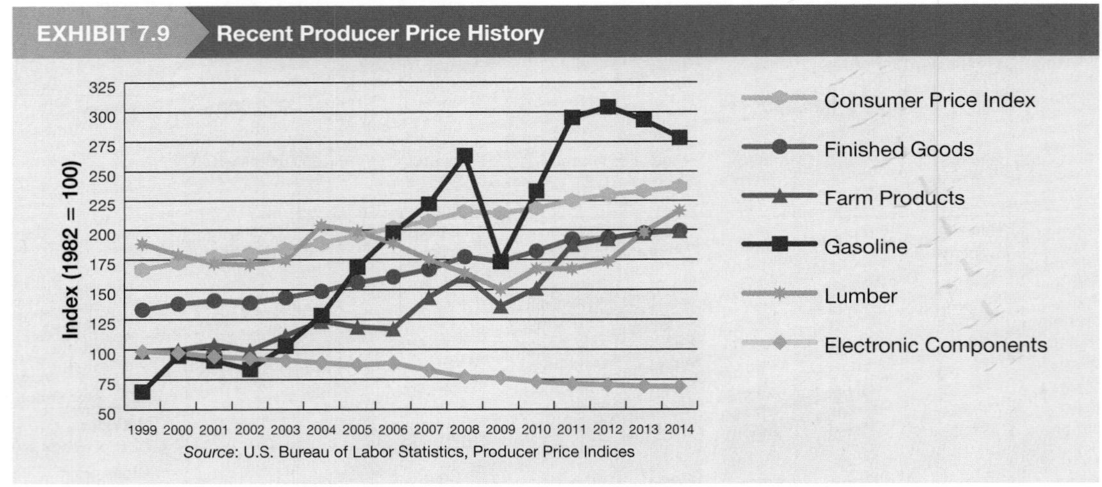

Source: U.S. Bureau of Labor Statistics, Producer Price Indices

Because inventories are so important for many companies, the financial reporting system requires disclosures that are useful in interpreting financial performance. We turn to those disclosures and their implications shortly.

Average Cost (AC)

FYI Average cost values inventory on the basis of the average cost of all similar goods available during the period.

The **average cost (AC)** method computes the 2016 cost of goods sold as an average of the cost to purchase all of the inventories that were available for sale during the period as follows:

Sales	$112,500
COGS (450 @ $120 [{$50,000 + $34,000}/700 units] each)	54,000
Gross profit	$ 58,500

The average cost of $120 per unit is determined from the total cost of goods available for sale divided by the number of units available for sale ($84,000/700 units). The cost remaining in inventory and reported on its 2016 balance sheet is $30,000 ($84,000 − $54,000; also computed 250 × $120).

When average cost is applied to the future years, the beginning inventory balance's average cost is again averaged with the inventory acquisitions made during the year. This new average is used to assign costs to that year's ending inventory and cost of goods sold. For the Butler Company, the average cost is $120 for 2016 and $162.35 (rounded) for 2017. The average cost for 2017 is the opening inventory balance plus the period's purchases ($30,000 + $108,000) divided by the total number of units available for sale (250 + 600). So, 2017 cost of goods sold is 500 units at $162.35 each, and ending inventory is 350 units at that same average cost. **Exhibit 7.10** depicts the average cost method and shows the resulting financial statement values using average cost for both years.

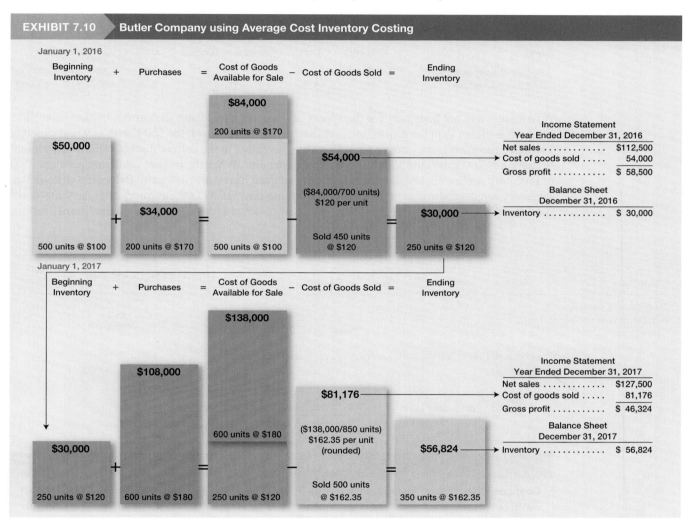

EXHIBIT 7.10 **Butler Company using Average Cost Inventory Costing**

January 1, 2016

Beginning Inventory + Purchases = Cost of Goods Available for Sale − Cost of Goods Sold = Ending Inventory

$50,000 (500 units @ $100) + $34,000 (200 units @ $170) = $84,000 (200 units @ $170; 500 units @ $100) − $54,000 (($84,000/700 units) $120 per unit; Sold 450 units @ $120) = $30,000 (250 units @ $120)

Income Statement
Year Ended December 31, 2016

Net sales	$112,500
Cost of goods sold	54,000
Gross profit	$ 58,500

Balance Sheet
December 31, 2016

Inventory	$ 30,000

January 1, 2017

Beginning Inventory + Purchases = Cost of Goods Available for Sale − Cost of Goods Sold = Ending Inventory

$30,000 (250 units @ $120) + $108,000 (600 units @ $180) = $138,000 (600 units @ $180; 250 units @ $120) − $81,176 (($138,000/850 units) $162.35 per unit (rounded); Sold 500 units @ $162.35) = $56,824 (350 units @ $162.35)

Income Statement
Year Ended December 31, 2017

Net sales	$127,500
Cost of goods sold	81,176
Gross profit	$ 46,324

Balance Sheet
December 31, 2017

Inventory	$ 56,824

Lower of Cost or Market

LO3 Apply the lower of cost or market rule to value inventory.

Companies are required to write down the carrying amount of inventories on the balance sheet, *if* the reported cost (using FIFO, for example) exceeds the market value. This process is called reporting inventories at the **lower of cost or market (LCM)**. Should the market value be less than reported cost, the inventories must be written down from cost to market value, resulting in the following financial statement effects.

- Inventory book value is written down to current market value, reducing total assets.
- Inventory write-down is reflected as an expense (part of cost of goods sold) on the income statement, reducing current period gross profit, income, and equity.

The most common occurrence of inventory write-downs is in connection with restructuring activities. These write-downs are either included in cost of goods sold or on a separate line in the income statement.

FYI If inventory declines in value below its original cost, for whatever reason, the inventory is written down to reflect this loss.

The write-down of inventories can potentially shift income from one period to another. If, for example, inventories were written down below current replacement cost (too conservative), future gross profit would be increased as lower future costs would be reflected in cost of goods sold. GAAP anticipates this possibility by requiring that inventories not be written down below a floor that is equal to net realizable value less a normal markup. Although this does allow some discretion (and the ability to manage income), the net realizable value and markup values must be confirmed by the company's auditors.[3]

FYI Standards require the consistent application of costing methods from one period to another.

Illustration To illustrate the lower of cost or market rule, assume Home Depot has the following items in its current period ending inventory:

Item	Quantity	Cost per Unit	Market Value (replacement cost)	LCM per Unit	Total LCM
Spools of copper wire	250	$10	$15	$10	250 × $10 = $2,500
Sheets of wood paneling	500	$ 8	$ 6	$ 6	500 × $ 6 = $3,000

A write-down is not necessary for the spools of copper wire because the current market value ($15 per unit) is higher than the acquisition cost ($10 per unit). However, the 500 sheets of wood paneling should be recorded in the current period's ending inventory at the current market value of $6 per unit because it is lower than the acquisition cost of $8 per unit. When the market value (replacement cost) of inventory declines below its acquisition cost, we must record a write-down. Before the write-down, inventory is recorded at cost of $6,500. With the write-down of $1,000, inventory after the write-down is recorded at LCM of $5,500. The effects of this write-down and corresponding journal entries follow:

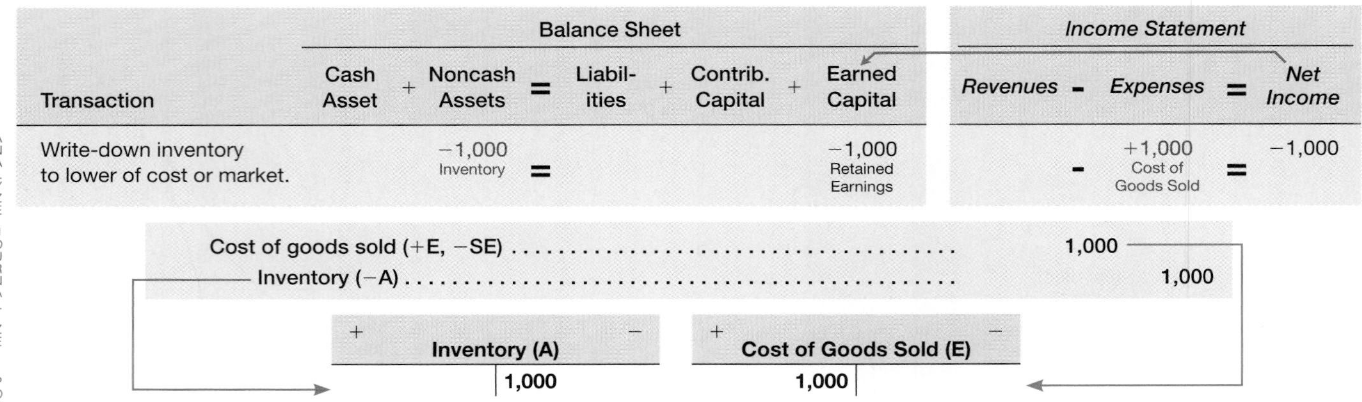

Transaction	Cash Asset	+ Noncash Assets	= Liabilities	+ Contrib. Capital	+ Earned Capital	Revenues	− Expenses	= Net Income
Write-down inventory to lower of cost or market.		−1,000 Inventory			−1,000 Retained Earnings		+1,000 Cost of Goods Sold	−1,000

Balance Sheet / Income Statement

Cost of goods sold (+E, −SE)	1,000	
Inventory (−A)		1,000

+ Inventory (A) −	
	1,000

+ Cost of Goods Sold (E) −	
1,000	

ANALYZE JOURNALIZE POST

BUSINESS INSIGHT

Changes to Inventory Costing In July of 2015, FASB issued an Accounting Standards Update (ASU) 2015-11 that requires companies (other than those using LIFO or the retail inventory method) to apply the lower of cost or net realizable value (LCNRV) rather than the lower of cost or market. Net realizable value (NRV) is the estimated selling price less costs to complete the sale. This ASU essentially provides a narrower definition of "market" and aligns U.S. GAAP more closely with IFRS. The new rules are effective for fiscal years beginning after December 15, 2016.

A GLOBAL PERSPECTIVE

Under U.S. GAAP, inventory that has been written down cannot be revalued later at higher levels even if the market value of that inventory increases. IFRS, on the other hand, does allow companies to reverse the write-down of the inventory up to the acquisition cost if market values warrant. The revaluation results in a debit to Inventory and a credit to Cost of Goods Sold. The option to revalue inventory after a write-down differs across countries.

[3] Recall Cisco's inventory write-down discussed in the opening pages of Chapter 6.

MID-CHAPTER REVIEW

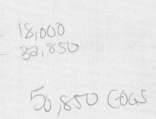

PART 1

At the beginning of the current period, Hutton Company holds 1,000 units of its only product with a per-unit cost of $18. A summary of purchases during the current period follows:

	Units	Unit Cost	Cost
Beginning Inventory	1,000	$18.00	$18,000
Purchases: #1	1,800	18.25	32,850
#2	800	18.50	14,800
#3	1,200	19.00	22,800
Goods available for sale	4,800		$88,450

During the current period, Hutton sells 2,800 units.

Required

1. Assume that Hutton uses the first-in, first-out (FIFO) method. Compute the cost of goods sold for the current period and the ending inventory balance.
2. Assume that Hutton uses the last-in, first-out (LIFO) method. Compute the cost of goods sold for the current period and the ending inventory balance.
3. Assume that Hutton uses the average cost (AC) method. Compute the cost of goods sold for the current period and the ending inventory balance.
4. As manager, which one of these three inventory costing methods would you choose:
   a. To reflect what is probably the physical flow of goods? Explain.
   b. To minimize income taxes for the period? Explain.
5. Assume that Hutton utilizes the LIFO method and instead of purchasing lot #3, the company allows its inventory level to decline and delays purchasing lot #3 until the next period. Compute cost of goods sold under this scenario and discuss the effect of end-of-year purchases under LIFO.
6. Record the effects of each of the following summary transactions *a* and *b* in the financial statement effects template, prepare journal entries, set up T-accounts for each of the accounts used, and post the journal entries to those T-accounts.
   a. Purchased inventory for $70,450 cash.
   b. Sold $50,850 of inventory for $85,000 cash.

PART 2

Venner Company had the following inventory at December 31, 2017.

	Quantity	Unit Price Cost	Market
Fans			
Model X1	300	$18	$19
Model X2	250	22	24
Model X3	400	29	26
Heaters			
Model B7	500	24	28
Model B8	290	35	32
Model B9	100	41	38

Required

1. Determine ending inventory by applying the lower of cost or market rule to
   a. Each item of inventory.
   b. Each major category of inventory.
   c. Total inventory.
2. Which of the LCM procedures from requirement 1 results in the lowest net income for 2017? Explain.

The solution to this review problem can be found on pages 367–369.

FINANCIAL STATEMENT EFFECTS AND DISCLOSURE

FYI Standards require financial statement disclosure of (1) the composition of the inventory (in the balance sheet or a separate schedule in the notes), (2) significant or unusual inventory financing arrangements, and (3) inventory costing methods employed (which can differ for different types of inventory).

The notes to the financial statements describe, at least in general terms, the inventory accounting method used by a company. To illustrate, The Home Depot reports $11,079 million in merchandise inventory on its February 1, 2015, balance sheet as a current asset. The following note was taken from that 10-K report:

Merchandise Inventories

Our Merchandise Inventories are stated at the lower of cost (first-in, first-out) or market, with approximately 74% valued under the retail inventory method and the remainder under a cost method. Retailers like us, with many different types of merchandise at low unit cost and a large number of transactions, frequently use the retail inventory method. Under the retail inventory method, Merchandise Inventories are stated at cost, which is determined by applying a cost-to-retail ratio to the ending retail value of inventories. As our inventory retail value is adjusted regularly to reflect market conditions, our inventory valued under the retail method approximates the lower of cost or market. We evaluate our inventory valued under a cost method at the end of each quarter to ensure that it is carried at the lower of cost or market. The valuation allowance for Merchandise Inventories valued under a cost method was not material to our Consolidated Financial Statements as of the end of fiscal 2014 or 2013.

Independent physical inventory counts or cycle counts are taken on a regular basis in each store and distribution center to ensure that amounts reflected in the accompanying Consolidated Financial Statements for Merchandise Inventories are properly stated. During the period between physical inventory counts in our stores, we accrue for estimated losses related to shrink on a store-by-store basis. Shrink (or in the case of excess inventory, "swell") is the difference between the recorded amount of inventory and the physical inventory. Shrink may occur due to theft, loss, inaccurate records for the receipt of inventory or deterioration of goods, among other things. We estimate shrink as a percent of Net Sales using the average shrink results from the previous two physical inventories. The estimates are evaluated quarterly and adjusted based on recent shrink results and current trends in the business. Actual shrink results did not vary materially from estimated amounts for fiscal 2014, 2013 or 2012.

This note includes several items that would be of interest to financial statement users:

1. The Home Depot uses the FIFO method to determine the cost of its inventory suggesting several methods are likely to be in use.
2. Inventory is reported at the lower of cost or market value, and the amount of write-down (the valuation allowance) was not material at the financial statement date.
3. The company periodically takes a physical count of inventory to identify "shrink." Shrink refers to the loss of inventory due to theft, breakage or damage, spoilage (for perishable goods), or other losses, as well as inaccurate records.

When businesses adjust inventory balances for shrink, the loss is debited to cost of goods sold. Hence, cost of goods sold expense on the income statement includes the actual cost of products sold during the period plus the loss due to shrink as well as losses resulting from lower of cost or market adjustments and discounts lost.

Another illustration of inventory disclosure is taken from the notes of **Kaiser Aluminum Corporation**. Kaiser reports an inventory of $214.7 million on its December 31, 2014, balance sheet. The following note was taken from its 2014 10-K report ($ millions):

Inventories. Inventories are stated at the lower of cost or market value. Finished products, work-in-process and raw material inventories are stated on the last-in, first-out ("LIFO") basis. The excesses of current cost over the stated LIFO value of inventory at December 31, 2014 and December 31, 2013 were $37.6 and $0.4, respectively. Other inventories, principally operating supplies and repair and maintenance parts, are stated at average cost. Inventory costs consist of material, labor and manufacturing overhead, including depreciation.

There are several interesting items disclosed in Kaiser's note:

1. Kaiser uses LIFO to report the cost of its raw materials, work in process, and finished goods inventory, but uses average cost for supplies and other. Neither U.S. GAAP nor tax authorities such as the IRS require the use of a single inventory costing method. That is, companies are allowed to, and frequently do, use different inventory costing methods for different categories of inventory. In addition, multinational companies may use one costing method in the United States and a different method for foreign inventory stocks.
2. Although Kaiser reports inventory costs at the lower of cost or market, the market value of its inventory (indicated by its current or FIFO cost) is significantly higher than its cost based on LIFO accounting. In fact, the note reports that current cost exceeded the \$214.7 million LIFO cost by \$37.6 million. That means that the replacement cost of its inventory was \$252.3 million (\$214.7 + \$37.6). Companies using LIFO are required to report the difference between the LIFO cost and current value—determined either as market value or replacement cost or as the FIFO cost. The difference between the ending inventory's FIFO cost (or current cost) and its LIFO cost is called the **LIFO reserve**.

Why do companies disclose such details on inventory, and why is so much attention paid to inventory in financial statement analysis? First, the magnitude of a company's investment in inventory is often large—impacting both balance sheets and income statements. Second, risks of inventory losses are often high, as they are tied to technical obsolescence and consumer tastes. Third, it can provide insight into future performance—both good and bad. Fourth, high inventory levels result in substantial costs for the company, such as:

- Financing costs to purchase inventories (when not purchased on credit)
- Storage costs of inventories (such as warehousing and related facilities)
- Handling costs of inventories (including wages)
- Insurance costs of inventories

Consequently, companies seek to keep inventories at levels that balance these costs against the cost of insufficient inventory (stock-out and resulting lost sales and delays in production, as machines and employees sit idle awaiting inventories to process).

Next, we turn our focus on the effects of the different inventory costing assumptions on the financial statements.

Financial Statement Effects of Inventory Costing

LO4 Evaluate how inventory costing affects management decisions and outsiders' interpretations of financial statements.

The three inventory costing methods described a few pages earlier yield differing levels of gross profit for our illustrative example, as shown in **Exhibit 7.11**.

We emphasize that, even though the various methods produce different financial statements, the underlying events are the same. That is, different accounting methods can make similar situations seem more different than they really are.

FYI If ending inventory is misstated, then (1) the inventory, retained earnings, working capital, and current ratio in the balance sheet are misstated, and (2) the cost of goods sold and net income in the income statement are misstated.

LIFO Reserve **Exhibit 7.11** demonstrates one of the income statement/balance sheet links that proves useful in analyzing financial statements. In the beginning inventory for 2016, LIFO and FIFO start from the same point—500 units at \$100 each. But during 2016, FIFO would record cost of goods sold that is \$14,000 less than LIFO (\$45,000 versus \$59,000). During 2016, LIFO put \$14,000 more into cost of goods sold than FIFO did, but that also means that LIFO put \$14,000 less into ending inventory. We can see that the LIFO reserve has grown from zero to \$14,000, the same amount. This relationship continues in 2017: the LIFO reserve increased by \$6,000 (from \$14,000 to \$20,000), and the LIFO cost of goods sold was \$6,000 greater than the FIFO cost of goods sold (\$90,000 versus \$84,000). The LIFO reserve equals the ending inventory's FIFO cost less LIFO cost, but it is also the *cumulative* difference between LIFO and FIFO cost of goods sold. The *change* in the LIFO reserve is the difference between LIFO and FIFO cost of goods sold for the current period.

So, if Butler Company chose to report using LIFO, we could estimate what the company's FIFO cost of goods sold would have been by seeing how the LIFO reserve changed.

FIFO cost of goods sold = LIFO cost of goods sold − Change in the LIFO reserve

EXHIBIT 7.11 Financial Statement Effects of Inventory Costing Methods for Butler Company

		FIFO	LIFO	Average Cost
January 1, 2016	**Balance Sheet**			
	Beginning inventory	$ 50,000	$ 50,000	$ 50,000
	LIFO Reserve	—	—	—
Year Ended 2016	**Income Statement**			
	Revenue	$112,500	$112,500	$112,500
	Cost of goods sold:			
	Beginning inventory	50,000	50,000	50,000
	Add: Purchases	34,000	34,000	34,000
	Goods available for sale	84,000	84,000	84,000
	Subtract: Ending inventory	39,000	25,000	30,000
	Cost of goods sold	45,000	59,000	54,000
	Gross profit	67,500	53,500	58,500
	Selling, general and administrative expenses (assumed number)	10,000	10,000	10,000
	Income before income taxes	57,500	43,500	48,500
	Income tax expense (35%)	20,125	15,225	16,975
	Net income	$ 37,375	$ 28,275	$ 31,525
December 31, 2016	**Balance Sheet**			
	Ending inventory	$ 39,000	$ 25,000	$ 30,000
	LIFO Reserve	—	$ 14,000	—
Year Ended 2017	**Income Statement**			
	Revenue	$127,500	$127,500	$127,500
	Cost of goods sold:			
	Beginning inventory	39,000	25,000	30,000
	Add: Purchases	108,000	108,000	108,000
	Goods available for sale	147,000	133,000	138,000
	Subtract: Ending inventory	63,000	43,000	56,824
	Cost of goods sold	84,000	90,000	81,176
	Gross profit	43,500	37,500	46,324
	Selling, general and administrative expenses (assumed number)	10,000	10,000	10,000
	Income before income taxes	33,500	27,500	36,324
	Income tax expense (35%)	11,725	9,625	12,713
	Net income	$ 21,775	$ 17,875	$ 23,611
December 31, 2017	**Balance Sheet**			
	Ending inventory	63,000	43,000	56,824
	LIFO Reserve	—	20,000	—

That relationship proves useful if we want to compare Butler Company's gross profit to that of another company using FIFO. Changes in the LIFO reserve also give a rough indication of how a company's inventory costs changed over the period. If costs increase, the LIFO reserve increases; if costs decrease, the LIFO reserve decreases.

Income Statement Effects The income differences between inventory accounting methods are a function of two factors. First is the speed and direction of inventory cost changes. For Butler Company, inventory costs have increased from $100 per unit to $180 per unit in a two-year period. If costs increased more slowly, the difference between LIFO and FIFO would decrease. And, if costs decreased, the differences would reverse: FIFO cost of goods sold would be greater than LIFO cost of goods sold.

The second factor determining the differences is the length of time inventory is held by the company. If Butler Company were able to operate with zero inventory (or at least begin and end the reporting period with zero inventory), the three inventory accounting methods would yield exactly the same cost of goods sold. On the other hand, if inventory must be held for a long period, the differences would increase.

Effects of Changing Costs When the cost of a company's products is changing, management usually makes corresponding changes in the prices it charges for those products. If costs are declining, competitive pressures are likely to push down the prices customers are willing to pay. If costs are increasing, the company will try to increase prices to recover at least some of the greater cost. When costs fluctuate (for example, for a commodity), management may act to cause its prices to fluctuate in an effort to maintain its target profit margin.[4]

If costs and prices are rising, then FIFO reports a higher gross margin, because the costs of older, lower-cost inventory are being matched against current selling prices. For tax purposes, the company would prefer to use LIFO because it would decrease gross profit and decrease taxable income. If Butler Company were subject to a 35% income tax rate, the use of LIFO rather than FIFO reduces taxes by $4,900 in 2016 ($20,125 − $15,225 in **Exhibit 7.11**, or 35% of the $14,000 difference in 2016 cost of goods sold) and by $2,100 in 2017 ($11,725 − $9,625 in **Exhibit 7.11**, or 35% of the $6,000 difference in 2017 cost of goods sold). In total over the two years, using LIFO (rather than FIFO) would reduce Butler's tax bill by $7,000 (which equals 35% of the $20,000 LIFO reserve at the end of 2017).

In the United States, LIFO is a popular tax method for accounting for inventories that have an upward trend in costs. But, the Internal Revenue Service has imposed a LIFO conformity requirement. If Butler Company is using LIFO for tax reporting, it must use LIFO for reporting to its shareholders. For inventories with a decreasing trend in costs, FIFO reduces the amount of taxes paid. FIFO is allowed by the Internal Revenue Service, but there is no corresponding conformity requirement for firms that use FIFO.

FYI When a company adopts LIFO in its tax filings, the company is required to use LIFO for reporting to its shareholders (in its 10-K). This requirement is known as the LIFO conformity rule.

Balance Sheet Effects The ending inventory using LIFO for our illustration is less than that reported using FIFO. In prolonged periods of rising costs, using LIFO yields ending inventories that are markedly lower than FIFO. As a result, balance sheets using LIFO do not accurately represent the cost that a company would incur to replace its current investment in inventories.

Kaiser, for example, reported that the current value of its inventory was $37.6 million higher than the LIFO cost at the end of 2014. That is, the amount presented in its balance sheet was understated (relative to current value) by more than $37 million. For purposes of analysis, the value of the LIFO reserve can be viewed as an **unrealized holding gain**—a gain resulting from holding inventory as prices are rising. That is, there is a holding gain due to rising inventory costs that has not been recorded in the financial statements. This gain is not recognized until the inventory is sold. In its December 31, 2014, balance sheet, Kaiser reported current assets of $825.2 million and current liabilities of $426.4 million, for a current ratio of $825.2 ÷ $426.4, or about 1.94. However, Kaiser's inventory is not reported at an up-to-date amount, while the accounts payable would reflect the current prices owed to suppliers. Therefore, an improved measure of the current ratio would be [$825.2 + $37.6] ÷ $426.4, or about 2.02.

In contrast, by assigning the most recently purchased inventory items to ending inventory, FIFO costing tends to approximate current value in the balance sheet. Hence, companies using FIFO tend not to have large unrealized inventory holding gains. However, if prices fall, companies using FIFO are more likely to adjust inventory values to the lower of cost or market.

FYI Some companies highlight this in their disclosures. For example, another company that uses LIFO, Chevron Corporation, mentions the current ratio effect in the notes to their statements saying "The current ratio was adversely affected by the fact that Chevron's inventories are valued on a last-in, first-out basis."

Cash Flow Effects The increased gross profit using FIFO results in higher pretax income and, consequently, higher taxes payable (assuming FIFO is also used for tax reporting). Conversely, the use of LIFO in an inflationary environment results in a lower tax liability.

Use of LIFO has reduced the dollar amount of Kaiser inventories by $37.6 million, resulting in a cumulative increase in cost of goods sold and a cumulative decrease in gross profit and pretax profit of that same amount.[5] The decrease in cumulative pretax profits has lowered Kaiser's tax bill over the life of the company by roughly $13.2 million ($37.6 million × 35% assumed corpo-

[4] LIFO has a reporting advantage when inventory costs fluctuate, in that it matches current period costs against current period revenues. For a company that holds one quarter's worth of inventory, FIFO matches the costs from three months ago against current period revenues. Such a "mismatch" might make it difficult for management to convey its success in maintaining its current profit margin.

[5] Cost of Goods Sold = Beginning Inventories + Purchases − Ending Inventories. Thus, as ending inventories decrease, cost of goods sold increases.

rate tax rate), which has increased Kaiser's cumulative operating cash flow by that same amount. The increased cash flow from tax savings is often cited as a compelling reason for management to adopt LIFO.

Adjusting the Balance Sheet to FIFO For analysis purposes, we can use the LIFO reserve to adjust the balance sheet and income statement to achieve comparability between companies that utilize different inventory costing methods. For example, if we wanted to compare Kaiser with another company using FIFO, we add the LIFO reserve to its LIFO inventory. As explained above, this \$37.6 million increase in 2014 inventories increases its cumulative pretax profits by \$37.6 million and taxes by \$13.2 million. Thus, the balance sheet adjustments involve increasing inventories by \$37.6 million, tax liabilities by \$13.2 million, and retained earnings by the remaining after-tax amount of \$24.4 million (computed as \$37.6 million − \$13.2 million).

A GLOBAL PERSPECTIVE

One of the important differences in inventory accounting between U.S. GAAP and IFRS is that the latter does not allow the use of last-in, first-out (LIFO) accounting. Only FIFO and Average Cost are allowed for companies reporting under IFRS.

An analyst comparing a U.S. GAAP company to an IFRS company would need to keep an eye on these inventory differences and, when necessary, do the conversions described in the preceding paragraphs. While FIFO firms are not required to disclose what they would have looked like under LIFO, LIFO firms must disclose enough information to do a rough approximation of what they would have looked like under FIFO—making for an improved comparison with an IFRS company.

The fact that IFRS does not allow LIFO—combined with the U.S. Internal Revenue Service's conformity requirement—creates a dilemma if the United States were to adopt IFRS. For instance, if Kaiser were to have adopted IFRS for fiscal year 2014, reporting FIFO inventory and cost of goods sold in subsequent financial reports, the IRS would consider that Kaiser had given up its LIFO election and would require payment of the \$13.2 million in taxes that had been deferred by the use of LIFO. This concern often appears in companies' comment letters to the Securities and Exchange Commission on the proposed move to IFRS in the United States.

It is also worth noting that when comparing companies in the same industry, accounting choices can differ. For example, GM and Ford use LIFO while Honda, a Japanese firm, uses FIFO.

Adjusting the Income Statement to FIFO To adjust the income statement from LIFO to FIFO, we use the *change* in the LIFO reserve. For Kaiser, the LIFO reserve changed from \$0.4 million in 2013 to \$37.6 million in 2014, an increase of \$37.2 million. To adjust the income statement to FIFO, we subtract \$37.2 from the cost of goods sold (reported using LIFO) and add the same amount to gross profit and pretax income. To estimate net income, we need to adjust for income taxes. Assuming a corporate tax rate of 35%, the use of LIFO provides Kaiser with tax savings of \$13 million (\$37.2 million × 0.35). Thus, 2014 net income using FIFO would be higher by \$24.2 million (\$37.2 million − \$13 million).

RESEARCH INSIGHT

LIFO and Stock Prices The value-relevance of inventory disclosures depends at least partly on whether investors rely more on the income statement or the balance sheet to assess future cash flows. Under LIFO, cost of goods sold reflects current costs, whereas FIFO ending inventory reflects current costs. This implies that LIFO enhances the usefulness of the income statement to the detriment of the balance sheet. This trade-off partly motivates the required LIFO reserve disclosure (the adjustment necessary to restate LIFO ending inventory and cost of good sold to FIFO).

Research suggests that LIFO-based income statements better reflect stock prices than do pro forma FIFO income statements that are constructed using the LIFO reserve. Research also shows a negative relation between stock prices and LIFO reserve—meaning that higher magnitudes of LIFO reserve are associated with lower stock prices. This is consistent with the LIFO reserve being viewed as an inflation indicator (for either current or future inventory costs) detrimental to company value.

ANALYZING FINANCIAL STATEMENTS

Analysis Objective

LO5 Define and interpret gross profit margin and inventory turnover ratios. Use inventory footnote information to make appropriate adjustments to ratios.

We are trying to determine whether Home Depot's sales provide sufficient revenues to cover its operation costs, primarily selling and administrative expenses, after allowing for the costs of manufacturing.

Analysis Tool Gross Profit Margin (GPM) Ratio

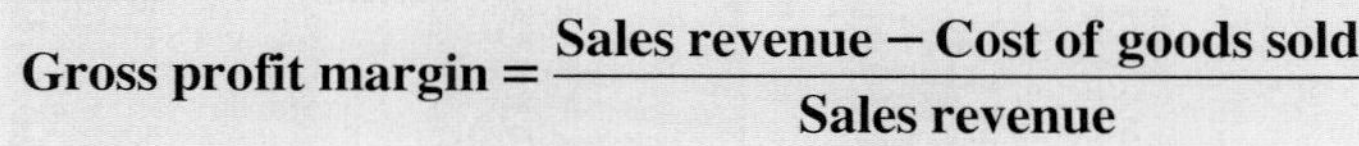

$$\textbf{Gross profit margin} = \frac{\textbf{Sales revenue} - \textbf{Cost of goods sold}}{\textbf{Sales revenue}}$$

Applying the Gross Profit Margin Ratio to Home Depot

$$\textbf{2012:}\quad \frac{(\$74{,}754 - \$48{,}912)}{\$74{,}754} = 0.346 \text{ or } 34.6\%$$

$$\textbf{2013:}\quad \frac{(\$78{,}812 - \$51{,}422)}{\$78{,}812} = 0.348 \text{ or } 34.8\%$$

$$\textbf{2014:}\quad \frac{(\$83{,}176 - \$54{,}222)}{\$83{,}176} = 0.348 \text{ or } 34.8\%$$

Guidance The gross profit margin is commonly used instead of the dollar amount of gross profit as it allows for comparisons across companies and over time. A decline in GPM is usually cause for concern because it indicates that the company has less ability to pass on to customers increased costs in its products. Because companies try to charge the highest price the market will bear, a decline in GPM is often the result of market forces beyond the company's control. Some possible reasons for a GPM decline are:

- Product line is stale. Perhaps it is out of fashion and the company must resort to markdowns to reduce overstocked inventories. Or, perhaps the product lines have lost their technological edge, yielding reduced demand.
- A change in product mix resulting from a change in buyers' behavior (more generic brands, more necessities, fewer big-ticket items).
- New competitors enter the market. Perhaps substitute products or new technologies are now available from competitors, yielding increased pressure to reduce selling prices.
- General decline in economic activity. Perhaps an economic downturn reduces product demand. The weak housing market during the latter half of the decade likely affected the gross profits of home improvement companies.
- Inventory is overstocked. Perhaps the company overproduced goods and finds itself in an overstock position. This can require reduced selling prices to move inventory.

Takeaways The Home Depot's sales revenue has increased from fiscal year 2012 to fiscal year 2014. The company was successful in maintaining its gross profit margin. However, to properly evaluate gross profit margin, it is useful to make comparisons with other companies in the same industry. **Exhibit 7.12** graphically compares The Home Depot's gross profit margin with that of its largest (but smaller) competitor, **Lowe's Companies, Inc.**

As the bar graph illustrates, The Home Depot and Lowe's have reported nearly identical, and very stable, gross profit margins in the last three years. In addition, in 2014 The Home Depot's sales revenue increased by 5.5%, while Lowe's revenues increased by 5.3%.

To gain further insights, **Exhibit 7.13** compares the gross profit margin of The Home Depot with that of several other retailers: **Target Corporation**, a national chain of retail variety stores; **Staples, Inc.**, a retail office supply store; and **Whole Foods Market Inc.**, a retail specialty grocery store chain. The graph illustrates that the highest gross profit margin belongs to Whole Foods, the specialty grocery store, while the lowest was that of Staples. Also, while the percentages fluctuate

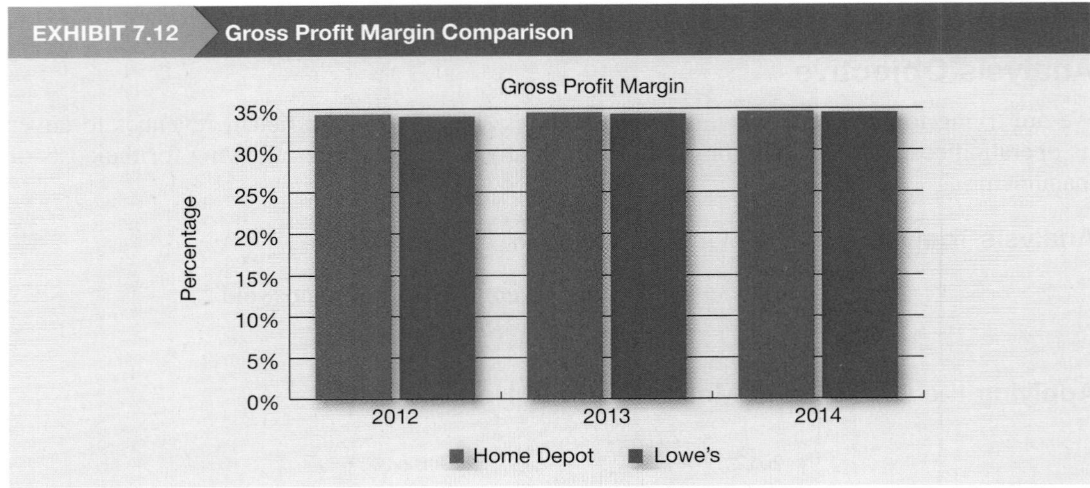

slightly from year to year, the *relative* level of gross profit percentage remains the same over time, reflecting the fact that the industry or type of business is a major determinant of gross profit margin.

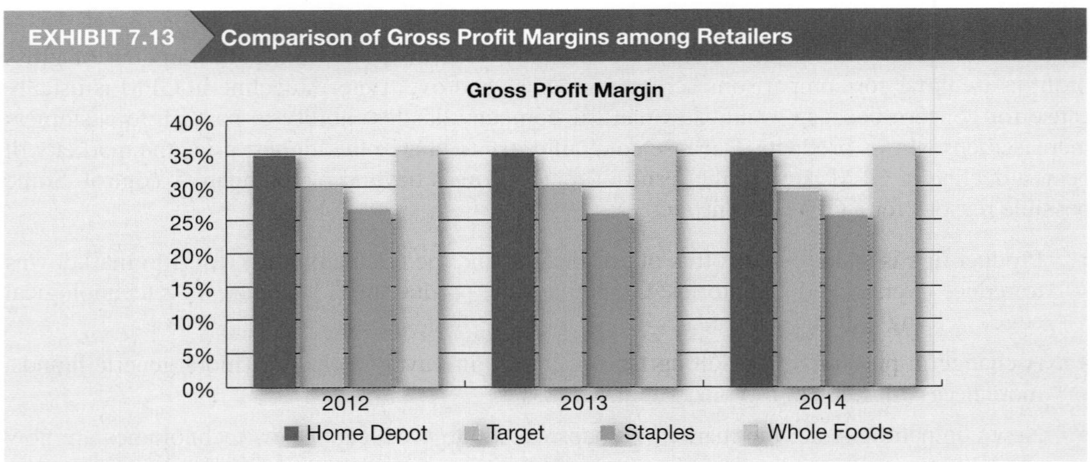

Because of competitive pressures, companies rarely have the opportunity to affect gross margin with price increases. (Of course, an astute choice of product offerings is likely to reduce pricing discounts and improve the gross profit margin.) Most improvements in gross margin that we witness are the result of better management of supply chains, production processes, or distribution networks. Similarly, a decline in gross profit margin suggests problems or inefficiencies in these processes. Companies that succeed typically do so because of better performance on basic business processes. This is one of The Home Depot's primary objectives.

Comparison of gross profit margins across selected focus companies:

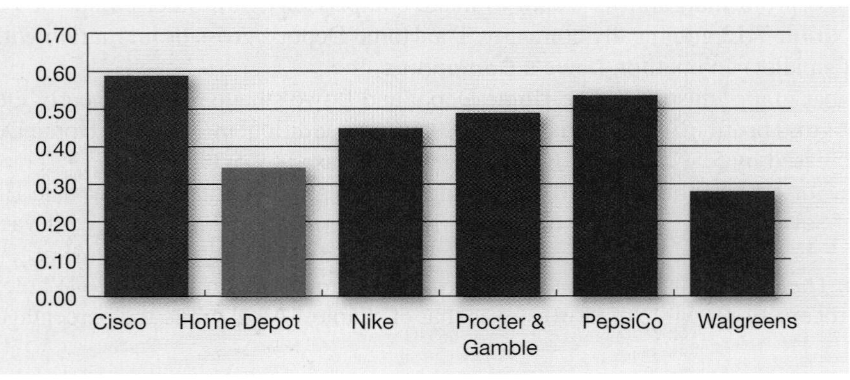

Analysis Objective

We wish to determine how quickly inventory passes through the production process and results in sales.

Analysis Tool Inventory Turnover (INVT) Ratio

$$\textbf{Inventory turnover} = \frac{\textbf{Cost of goods sold}}{\textbf{Average inventory}}$$

Applying Inventory Turnover Ratio to Home Depot

2012:	\$48,912/[(\$10,710 + \$10,325)/2] = 4.7 Times per year
2013:	\$51,422/[(\$11,057 + \$10,710)/2] = 4.7 Times per year
2014:	\$54,222/[(\$11,079 + \$11,057)/2] = 4.9 Times per year

Home Depot in Context

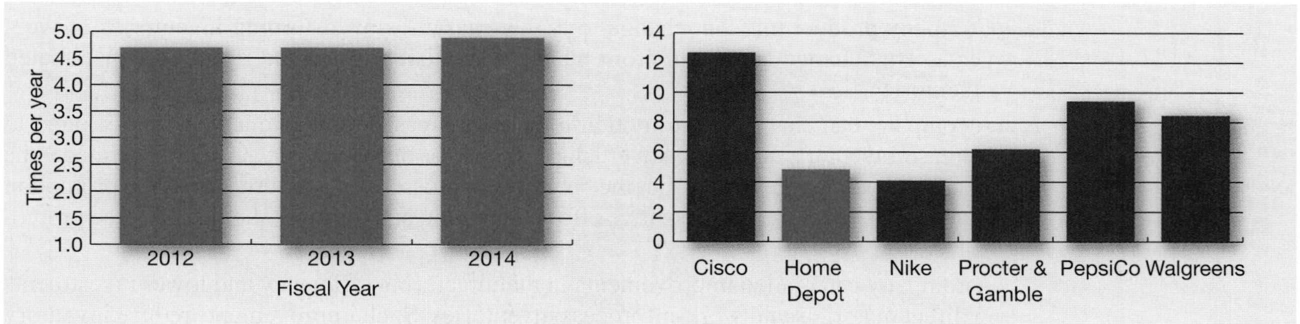

Cost of goods sold is in the numerator because inventory is reported at cost. The denominator is the average of beginning inventory and ending inventory to recognize growth (or decline) in the company's investment in inventory over the period. Inventory turnover indicates how many times inventory turns (is sold) during a period. More turns indicate that inventory is being sold more quickly.

Analysis Tool Average inventory days outstanding (AIDO), also called *days inventory outstanding*:

$$\textbf{Average inventory days outstanding} = \frac{\textbf{Average inventory}}{\textbf{Average daily cost of goods sold}}$$

Applying Average Inventory Days Outstanding Ratio to Home Depot

2012:	[(\$10,710 + \$10,325)/2]/[\$48,912/365] = 78 Days
2013:	[(\$11,057 + \$10,710)/2]/[\$51,422/365] = 77 Days
2014:	[(\$11,079 + \$11,057)/2]/[\$54,222/365] = 75 Days

Home Depot in Context

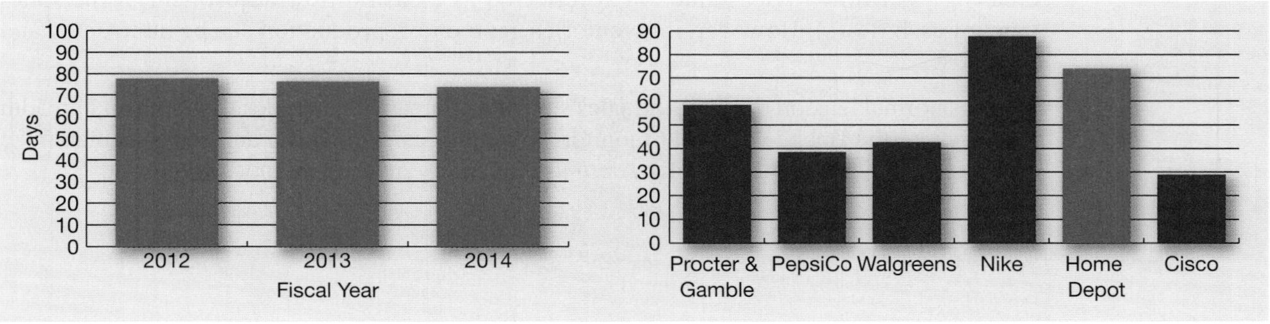

The average daily cost of goods sold equals cost of goods sold divided by the number of days in the period (for our example, 365 for a year).

Average inventory days outstanding indicates how long, on average, inventories are on the shelves or in production before being sold. For example, if a retailer's annual cost of goods sold is $1,200 and average inventories are $300, inventories are turning four times and are on the shelves 91.25 days [$300/($1,200/365)] on average. This performance might be an acceptable turnover for the retail fashion industry where it needs to sell out its inventories each retail selling season, but it would not be acceptable for the grocery industry.

Guidance Analysis of inventory turnover is important for at least two reasons:

1. *Inventory quality*. Inventory turnover can be compared with those of prior periods and competitors. Higher turnover is viewed favorably, implying that products are salable, preferably without undue discounting of selling prices, or that production processes are functioning smoothly. Conversely, lower turnover implies that inventory is on the shelves for a longer period of time, perhaps from excessive purchases or production, missed fashion trends or technological advances, increased competition, and so forth. Our conclusions about higher or lower turnover must consider alternative explanations including:

   a. Company product mix can change to higher-margin, slower-turning inventories or vice-versa. This change can occur from business acquisitions and the resulting consolidated inventories.

   b. A company can change its promotion policies. Increased, effective advertising is likely to increase inventory turnover. Advertising expense is in SG&A, not COGS. Therefore, the cost is in operating expenses, but the benefit is in gross profit and turnover. If the promotion campaign is successful, the positive effects in margin and turnover should offset the promotion cost in SG&A.

   c. A company can realize improvements in manufacturing efficiency and lower investments in direct materials and work-in-process inventories. Such improvements reduce inventory and, consequently, increase inventory turnover. Although positive, such improvements do not yield any information about the desirability of a company's product line.

2. *Asset utilization*. Companies strive to optimize their inventory investment. Carrying too much inventory is expensive, and too little inventory risks stock-outs and lost sales (current and future). There are operational changes that companies can make to reduce inventory including:

   a. Improved manufacturing processes can eliminate bottlenecks and the consequent build-up of work-in-process inventories.

   b. Just-in-time (JIT) deliveries from suppliers that provide raw materials to the production line when needed can reduce the level of raw materials required.

   c. Demand-pull production, in which raw materials are released into the production process when final goods are demanded by customers instead of producing for estimated demand, can reduce inventory levels. **Dell Inc.** was founded on a business model that produced for actual, rather than estimated, demand; many of its computers are manufactured after the customer order is received.

   Reducing inventories reduces inventory carrying costs, thus improving profitability and increasing cash flow (asset reduction is reflected as a cash inflow adjustment in the statement of cash flows). However, if inventories get too low, production can be interrupted and sales lost.

There is normal tension between the sales side of a company that argues for depth and breadth of inventory and the finance side that monitors inventory carrying costs and seeks to maximize cash flow. Companies, therefore, seek to *optimize* inventory investment, not *minimize* it.

RESEARCH INSIGHT

In a recent *Wall Street Journal* article, it was reported that in 2013, companies reported deficiencies in their procedures to account for inventory and cost of sales, i.e., internal control weaknesses, so numerous that the category ranked number two in areas with such deficiencies.[6] Recent academic research suggests these deficiencies are important. According to a study of companies over 2004–2009, the evidence is consistent with firms that have inventory-related material weaknesses having systematically lower inventory turnover ratios and being more likely to report inventory impairments relative to firms with effective internal control. In addition, the study shows that firms that fix their internal control weaknesses show improvements in inventory turnover rates.[7]

Takeaways **Exhibit 7.14** compares inventory turnover for The Home Depot with that of its chief rival, Lowe's. Both Home Depot's and Lowe's inventory turnover and AIDO improved over the period 2012–2014. Lowe's inventory turnover decreased, but increases in inventories probably helped it to maintain revenues and gross profit in the changing economic climate.

EXHIBIT 7.14 **Inventory Turnover Comparison**

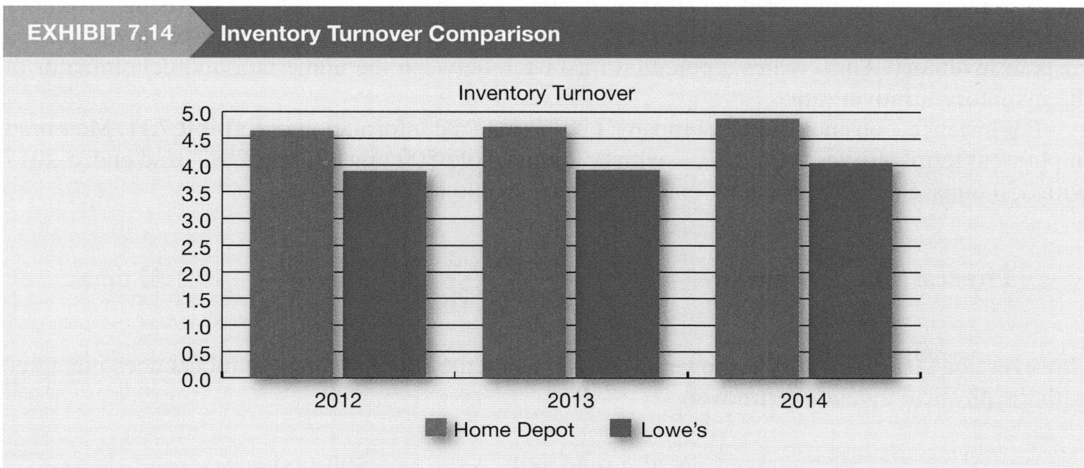

It is also instructive to compare the home improvement retail industry, represented by The Home Depot, with other retailers as illustrated in **Exhibit 7.15**.

EXHIBIT 7.15 **Inventory Turnover for Various Retail Companies**

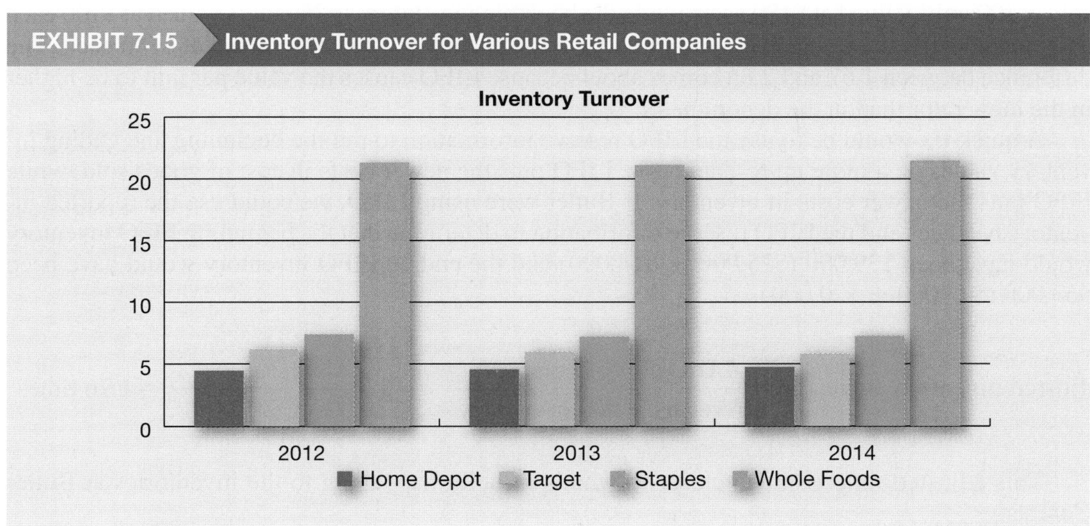

[6] "More Accounting Deficiencies Linked to Inventory," *Wall Street Journal* August 26, 2014.

[7] See Feng, Mei, Chan Li, Sarah E. McVay, and Hollis Skaife, "Does Ineffective Internal Control over Financial Reporting affect a Firm's Operations? Evidence from Firms' Inventory Management." The Accounting Review, March 2015.

In the retail grocery industry, high inventory turnover is a necessity given that a significant portion of a grocer's inventory is perishable. Whole Foods' high turnover is typical of what we might expect from retail grocers. The Home Depot's turnover is lower than any of the comparison companies. Target's turnover is lower than that of Staples, the consumer office products retailer, despite the fact that part of Target's sales is food related. The small portion of food product sales as a percentage of total sales explains why Target's turnover is not comparable to that of Whole Foods.

YOU MAKE THE CALL

You are the Plant Manager You are analyzing your inventory turnover report for the month and are concerned that the average inventory days outstanding is lengthening. What actions can you take to reduce average inventory days outstanding? [Answer on page 354]

Adjusting Turnover Ratios For a company using the last-in, first-out (LIFO) inventory method, it is advisable to make an adjustment before calculating the inventory turnover ratio. LIFO is most commonly used when management has experienced a trend of rising inventory costs. As a result, LIFO puts higher (newer) costs into cost of goods sold and leaves lower (older) costs in inventory. This creates a potential mismatch between the numerator and denominator of the inventory turnover ratio.

For instance, consider Butler Company's 2017 financial information in **Exhibit 7.11**. Measured in physical terms, Butler started 2017 with 250 units, sold 500 units during 2017, and ended 2017 with 350 units. So, the physical inventory turnover would be

$$\textbf{Physical inventory turnover} = \frac{\textbf{Units sold}}{\textbf{Average units held}} = \frac{500}{(250 + 350)/2} = 1.67 \text{ times}$$

However, the 2017 inventory turnover calculated using the LIFO reported numbers does not agree with the physical inventory turnover.

$$\textbf{LIFO inventory turnover} = \frac{\textbf{Cost of goods sold}}{\textbf{Average inventory}} = \frac{\$90{,}000}{(\$25{,}000 + \$43{,}000)/2} = 2.65 \text{ times}$$

Why is the LIFO inventory turnover higher? The distortion occurs because the LIFO cost of goods sold is 500 units valued at $180 each, while the beginning inventory is 250 units valued at $100 each and the ending inventory is 250 units valued at $100 each plus 100 units valued at $180 each. The difference between 1.67 and 2.65 comes about because LIFO causes the value per unit to be higher in the numerator than in the denominator.

A quick fix would be to use the LIFO reserve information to put the beginning and ending inventory values on a more up-to-date basis. LIFO puts the newer costs in cost of goods sold, while FIFO puts the newer costs in inventory. If Butler were using LIFO, we could use the reported inventory balances and the LIFO reserve information to determine that the beginning FIFO inventory would have been $39,000 ($25,000 + $14,000) and the ending FIFO inventory would have been $63,000 ($43,000 + $20,000).

$$\textbf{Adjusted inventory turnover} = \frac{\textbf{LIFO cost of good sold}}{\textbf{Average FIFO inventory}} = \frac{\$90{,}000}{(\$39{,}000 + \$63{,}000)/2} = 1.76 \text{ times}$$

This adjusted ratio is much closer to what's actually happening to the inventories at Butler Company.

The magnitude of this adjustment can be significant. For instance, **Chevron Corporation** in its 2014 annual report states that its 2014 expense for "Purchased crude oil and products" was $119,671 million. Chevron's balance sheet totals for inventories were $6,380 million at the end of 2013 and $6,505 million at the end of 2014, for an average of $6,442.5 million. These numbers would give an inventory turnover ratio of $119,671 million ÷ $6,442.5 million, or 18.6 times, implying that inventory is held less than 20 days on average.

However, we know that the LIFO inventory balances are out of date. Chevron's LIFO reserve disclosure says that the replacement cost of inventories was higher than the reported amounts by $9,150 million at the end of 2013 and $8,135 million at the end of 2014, making the replacement cost of inventories equal to $15,530 million at the end of 2013 and $14,640 million at the end of 2014. The adjusted inventory turnover ratio would be $119,671/[($15,530 + $14,640)/2] = 7.9, implying that inventory is held about 46 days.

Following a similar line of analysis, it would be possible to construct a FIFO inventory turnover for Chevron, which could be useful in making comparisons to another company that uses IFRS in its financial reports.

CHAPTER-END REVIEW

GuidedExamples MBC

Publix Super Markets Inc. reports inventory and cost of goods sold using the last-in, first-out (LIFO) costing method for a "significant portion" of U.S. inventory. The table below presents financial information from its 2012, 2013, and 2014 10-K reports.

($ millions)	2014	2013	2012
Revenue	$30,560	$28,917	$27,485
Cost of goods sold	22,233	20,937	19,911
Gross profit	$ 8,327	$ 7,980	$ 7,574
Balance Sheet:			
Inventory	$ 1,598	$ 1,507	$ 1,409
Notes to financial statements			
LIFO reserve	$ 421	$ 390	$ 375

REQUIRED

1. Compute the gross profit margin for each year, 2012 through 2014, and the inventory turnover ratio for 2013 and 2014.
2. What amount for cost of goods sold and gross profit would Publix report in 2013 and 2014 if FIFO were used to assign costs to inventory and cost of goods sold? (Assume that FIFO cost is equal to the current value of Publix's inventory.)
3. Recalculate Publix's inventory turnover ratio for 2013 and 2014 assuming that FIFO had been used to value inventory.

The solution to this review problem can be found on page 369.

APPENDIX 7A: LIFO Liquidation

LO6 Analyze LIFO liquidations and the impact they have on the financial statements. 6

When companies use LIFO inventory costing, the most recent costs of purchasing inventory are transferred to cost of goods sold, while older costs remain in ending inventory. Each time inventory is purchased at a different price, a new *layer* (also called a **LIFO layer**) is added to the inventory balance. As long as a year's purchases equal or exceed the quantity sold, older cost layers remain in inventory—sometimes for several years. On the other hand, when the quantity sold exceeds the quantity purchased, inventory costs from these older cost layers are transferred to cost of goods sold. This situation is called **LIFO liquidation**. Because these older costs are usually much lower than current replacement costs, LIFO liquidation normally yields a boost to current gross profit as these older costs are matched against current revenues.

To illustrate the effects of LIFO liquidation, we return to the example of Butler Company in **Exhibit 7.6** and add an additional year. At the end of 2017, Butler has 350 units in inventory, 250 at $100 each and 100 at $180 each. Suppose that during 2018, the company purchases 500 units at $190 and sells 650 units. At the end of 2018, Butler will have only 200 units remaining in inventory and, under LIFO, those units will be assigned a cost of $100 each. The determination of cost of goods sold and ending inventory for 2018 can be seen in **Exhibit 7A.1**.

EXHIBIT 7A.1 Calculation of 2018 LIFO Inventory and Cost of Goods Sold

Beginning Inventory	250 units at $100 each plus 100 units at $180 each	$ 43,000
Purchases.	500 units at $190 each	95,000
Cost of goods available for sale.		138,000
Ending inventory.	200 units at $100 each	20,000
Cost of goods sold.	500 units at $190 each plus 100 units at $180 each plus 50 units at $100 each	$118,000

Exhibit 7A.2 portrays graphically that the inventory reduction in 2018 eliminated the LIFO layer added in 2017 and reduced the original LIFO layer from the start of 2016.

EXHIBIT 7A.2 Butler Company LIFO Inventory Flows

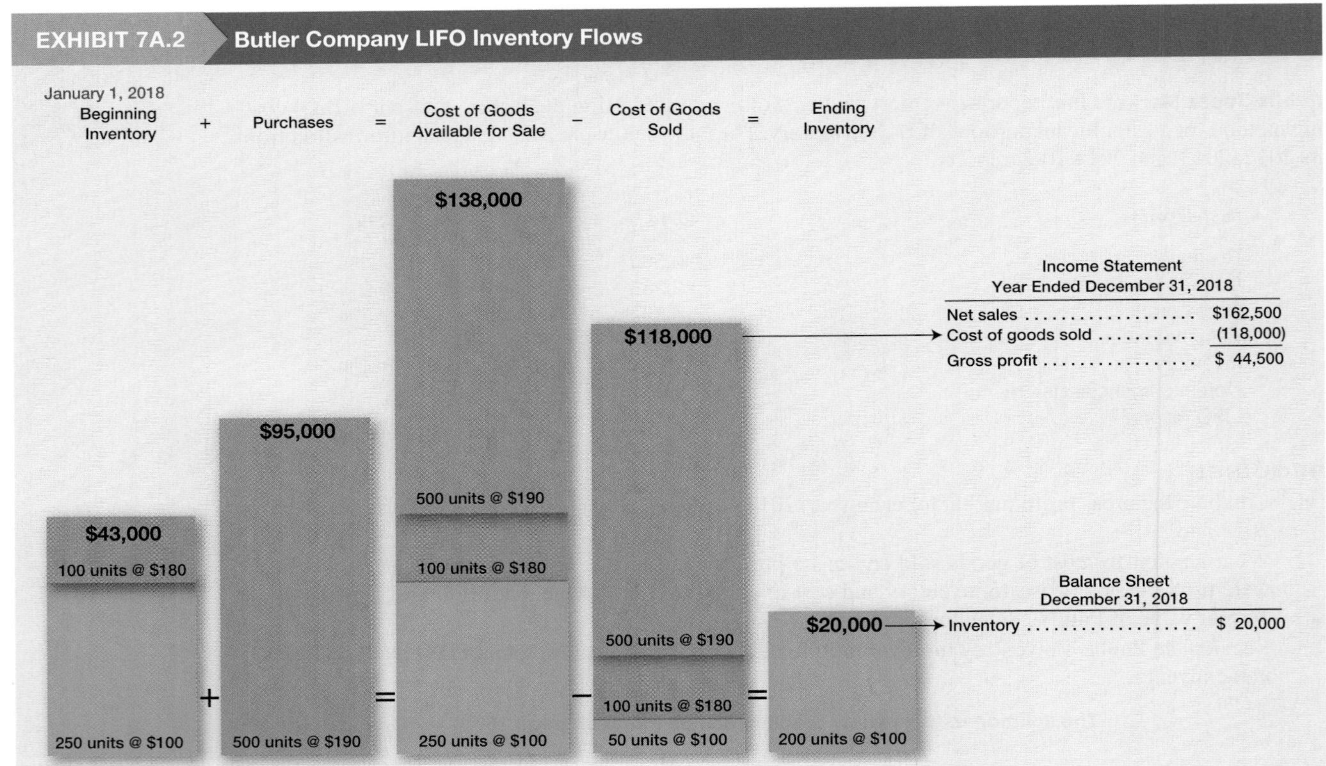

What would have happened if Butler had purchased 650 units at $190 in 2018? The ending inventory would have been identical to the beginning inventory. And, the cost of goods sold would have been $123,500 (650 units at $190 each), higher than the $118,000 cost of goods sold in **Exhibit 7A.1**. This difference can be attributed to the differences between the current unit cost of inventory ($190) and the old unit costs ($180 and $100) that had been in inventory but are now in cost of goods sold.

Thus, Butler's cost of goods sold has been *reduced* by $5,500 due to the LIFO liquidation, and its gross profit and income before tax have been *increased* by the same amount. If Butler's tax rate were 35%, the net income would be increased by $3,575. This **LIFO liquidation gain** must be disclosed in the company's footnotes.

The effect of LIFO liquidation is evident in the following footnote information from Notes A and G to **Alcoa Inc.**'s 2014 annual report.

Notes A and G: Inventories

Inventory Valuation. Inventories are carried at the lower of cost or market, with cost for a substantial portion of U.S. and Canadian inventories determined under the last-in, first-out (LIFO) method. The cost of other inventories is principally determined under the average-cost method.

Note G: (dollars in millions) At December 31, 2014 and 2013, the total amount of inventories valued on a LIFO basis was $1,514 and $1,169, respectively. If valued on an average-cost basis, total inventories would have been $767 and $691 higher at December 31, 2014 and 2013, respectively. During 2013 and 2012, reductions in LIFO inventory quantities caused partial liquidations of the lower cost LIFO inventory base. These liquidations resulted in the recognition of income of $26 ($17 after-tax) in 2013 and $1 ($1 after-tax) in 2012.

Alcoa reports that reductions in inventory quantities led to the sale (at current selling prices) of products that carried costs from prior years that were less than current costs. As a result of these inventory reductions, pretax income increased by $26 million in 2013 and by $1 million in 2012.

Analysis Implications

LIFO liquidation boosts gross profit when older, lower costs are matched against revenues based on current sales prices. This increase in gross profit is transitory. Once an old LIFO layer is liquidated, it can only be replaced at current prices. The transitory boost in gross profit temporarily distorts the gross profit margin (GPM) ratio.

It is important that we ask why the LIFO liquidation happened. Involuntary LIFO liquidations result from circumstances beyond the company's control, such as disruptions in supply due to a natural disaster. Voluntary LIFO liquidations are the result of a management decision to reduce inventory levels. While this result is sometimes the result of efforts to lower costs and improve efficiency, it can also be the consequence of earnings management.

If a voluntary LIFO liquidation is the result of earnings management, we should remember that the extra gross profit that is reported is taxable. These tax consequences provide an incentive for companies to *avoid* LIFO liquidations by maintaining ending inventories at levels equal to or greater than beginning inventory quantities. Maintaining these inventory levels can be inefficient, leading to higher inventory holding costs. However, in the short run, the tax savings can be greater than the costs.

On one hand, management could liquidate LIFO inventories to report higher earnings. On the other hand, management may hold too much inventory to avoid paying extra taxes. A careful evaluation of future cash flows usually identifies the preferred course of action.

APPENDIX 7A REVIEW

Dickhaut Corporation imports and sells a product that is produced in the Dominican Republic. In the summer of 2016, a hurricane disrupted production and affected Dickhaut's supply of this product. Dickhaut uses LIFO to determine the cost of its inventory and cost of goods sold. On January 1, 2016, Dickhaut's inventory of this product consisted of the following:

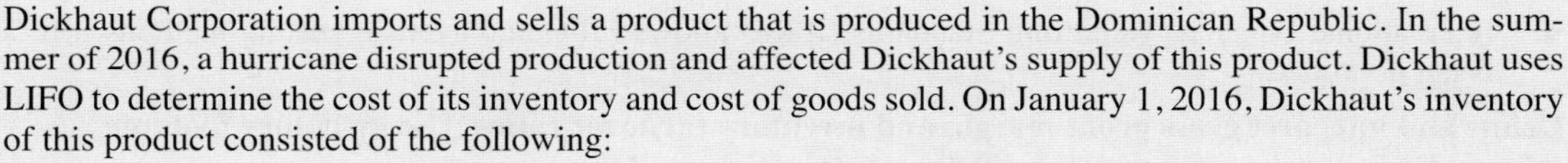

Year Purchased	Quantity (units)	Cost Per Unit	Total Cost
2014	2,000	$20	$ 40,000
2015	3,000	30	90,000
Total	5,000		$130,000

Through mid-December, purchases were limited to 7,000 units, because the cost had increased to $70 per unit. Dickhaut sold 11,500 units during 2016 at a price of $65 per unit, which significantly depleted its inventory. However, the cost was expected to drop to $55 per unit by early January 2017.

Required

a. Assume that Dickhaut makes no further purchases during 2016. Compute its gross profit for 2016.
b. Assume that Dickhaut purchases 4,500 units for $70 per unit before the end of December 2016, so that it maintains its balance of inventory at 5,000 units. Compute its gross profit for 2016.
c. How should Dickhaut disclose the LIFO liquidation if it chooses not to make a year-end purchase?
d. If Dickhaut's corporate tax rate is 35%, should it make a year-end purchase? If so, how many units should the company purchase before December 31, 2016? Assume that the management of Dickhaut believes it is efficient (in the long run) to carry 5,000 units in inventory.

The solution to this review problem can be found on page 370.

SUMMARY

Interpret disclosures of information concerning operating expenses, including manufacturing and retail inventory costs. (p. 328) LO1

- Inventory is reported in the balance sheet at its cost, including any cost to acquire, transport and prepare goods for sale.

- Manufacturing inventory consists of raw materials, work in process and finished goods. The cost of manufacturing inventory includes the cost of materials and labor used to produce goods, as well as overhead cost.

LO2 Account for inventory and cost of goods sold using different costing methods. (p. 332)

- FIFO places the cost of the most recent purchases in ending inventory and older costs in the cost of goods sold.
- LIFO places the cost of the most recent purchases in cost of goods sold and older costs in inventory.
- The average cost method computes an average unit cost, which is used to value inventories *and* cost of goods sold.

LO3 Apply the lower of cost or market rule to value inventory. (p. 337)

- If the market value of inventory falls below its cost, the inventory is written down to market value, thereby reducing total assets.
- The loss is added to cost of goods sold and reported in the income statement (unless it is large enough to warrant separate disclosure).

LO4 Evaluate how inventory costing affects management decisions and outsiders' interpretations of financial statements. (p. 341)

- When inventory costs are rising, LIFO costing reports higher cost of goods sold and lower income than either FIFO or average costing.
- If LIFO is used for tax reporting, it must be used for financial reporting.
- Companies that use LIFO have an incentive to hold inventories to avoid LIFO *liquidation* and the resulting higher income taxes.
- LIFO distorts the inventory turnover ratio because inventories are often severely undervalued (relative to current cost of goods sold). Management can boost earnings by liquidating these undervalued inventories.
- International Financial Reporting Standards (IFRS) allows FIFO and average costing methods. LIFO is not permitted.

LO5 Define and interpret gross profit margin and inventory turnover ratios. Use inventory footnote information to make appropriate adjustments to ratios. (p. 345)

- Gross profit margin (GPM)—a measure of profitability that focuses on the amount of revenue in excess of cost of goods sold as a percentage of revenue
- Gross profit margin is defined as Gross profit/Sales revenue.
- Inventory turnover (INVT)—a measure of the frequency at which the average balance in inventory is sold each year
- Inventory turnover is defined as Cost of goods sold/Average inventory.
- These ratios provide insight into how efficiently the company is managing inventory.
- Footnote disclosures enable a financial statement reader to determine the up-to-date costs of LIFO inventories, to estimate what cost of goods sold would have been under FIFO, and to compute an inventory turnover ratio that is not subject to the distortions noted above in LO4.

LO6 Appendix 7A: Analyze LIFO liquidations and the impact they have on the financial statements. (p. 351)

- LIFO liquidation is the result of selling and not replenishing inventory stocks purchased in previous accounting periods.
- When inventory costs are increasing, LIFO liquidation results in higher net income as the unrealized holding gains from LIFO are realized.

GUIDANCE ANSWERS . . . YOU MAKE THE CALL

You are the Plant Manager Companies need inventories to avoid lost sales opportunities; however, there are several ways to minimize inventory needs. (1) We can reduce product costs by improving product design to eliminate costly features not valued by customers. (2) We can use more cost-efficient suppliers, possibly including production in lower wage-rate parts of the world. (3) We can reduce raw material inventories with just-in-time delivery from suppliers. (4) We can eliminate bottlenecks in the production process that increase work-in-process inventories. (5) We can manufacture for orders rather than for estimates of demand to reduce finished goods inventories. (6) We can improve warehousing and distribution to reduce duplicate inventories. (7) We can monitor product sales and adjust product mix as demand changes to reduce finished goods inventories.

KEY RATIOS

Gross profit (GP)

$$GP = \text{Sales revenue} - \text{Cost of goods sold}$$

Gross profit margin (GPM)

$$\text{Gross profit margin} = \frac{\text{Sales revenue} - \text{Cost of goods sold}}{\text{Sales revenue}}$$

Inventory turnover (INVT)

$$INVT = \frac{\text{Cost of goods sold}}{\text{Average inventory}}$$

Average inventory days outstanding (AIDO)

$$AIDO = \frac{\text{Average inventory}}{\text{Average daily cost of goods sold}}$$

KEY TERMS

Average cost (AC) (p. 336)
Cash discounts (p. 331)
Cost flow assumption (p. 333)
Direct association (p. 328)
Finished goods inventory (p. 331)
First-in, first-out (FIFO) (p. 333)
FOB destination (p. 331)
FOB shipping point (p. 331)
Gross profit (p. 329)
Immediate recognition (p. 329)
Last-in, first-out (LIFO) (p. 334)
LIFO layer (p. 351)
LIFO layers (p. 335)
LIFO liquidation (p. 351)
LIFO liquidation gain (p. 352)
LIFO reserve (p. 341)
Lower of cost or market (LCM) (p. 337)
Raw materials inventory (p. 331)
Systematic allocation (p. 329)
Unrealized holding gain (p. 343)
Work-in-process inventory (p. 331)

Assignments with the logo in the margin are available in myBusinessCourse.
See the Preface of the book for details.

MULTIPLE CHOICE

Multiple Choice Answers
1. c 2. c 3. a 4. d 5. b

1. Which of the following is not normally reported as part of total manufacturing inventory cost? 
   a. work-in-process
   b. finished goods
   c. property, plant, and equipment
   d. raw materials

2. When the current year's ending inventory amount is overstated, then the  
   a. current year's cost of goods sold is overstated.
   b. current year's total assets are understated.
   c. current year's net income is overstated.
   d. next year's income is overstated.

3. In a period of rising prices, the inventory cost allocation method that tends to result in the lowest reported net income is  
   a. LIFO.
   b. FIFO.
   c. average cost.
   d. specific identification.

4. Assume that Beyer Corporation has the following initial balance and subsequent purchase of inventory: 

Beginning inventory, 2017	2,000 units @ $50 each	$100,000
Inventory purchased in 2017	5,000 units @ $75 each	$375,000
Cost of goods available for sale in 2017	7,000 units	$475,000

During 2017, Beyer Corporation sold 6,000 units. Which of the following is not true?

a. FIFO cost of goods sold would be $400,000.
b. FIFO ending inventory would be $75,000.
c. LIFO cost of goods sold would be $425,000.
d. LIFO ending inventory would be $75,000.

5. Sletten Industries uses the last-in, first-out (LIFO) method of accounting for the inventories of its single product. For fiscal year 2017, the company reported sales revenue of $200 million and cost of goods sold of $135 million. The following table was reported in the financial statement footnotes.

($ millions)	January 1, 2017	December 31, 2017
Inventory value at LIFO	$25	$28
LIFO Reserve	14	22
Inventory value at FIFO	$39	$50

If Sletten Industries had used FIFO to account for its inventory, its 2017 gross profit would be

a. $87 million.
b. $73 million.
c. $57 million.
d. $65 million.

Superscript A denotes assignments based on Appendix 7A.

QUESTIONS

Q7-1. Under what circumstances is it justified to include transportation costs in the value of the inventory purchased?

Q7-2. Why do relatively stable inventory costs reduce the importance of management's choice of an inventory costing method?

Q7-3. What is one explanation for increased gross profit during periods of rising inventory costs when FIFO is used?

Q7-4. If inventory costs are rising, which inventory costing method—first-in, first-out; last-in, first-out; or average cost—yields the (a) lowest ending inventory? (b) lowest net income? (c) largest ending inventory? (d) largest net income? (e) greatest cash flow assuming that method is used for tax purposes?

Q7-5. Even though it does not reflect their physical flow of goods, why might companies adopt last-in, first-out inventory costing in periods when costs are consistently rising?

Kaiser Aluminum Corporation
NASDAQ :: KALU

Q7-6. In a recent annual report, **Kaiser Aluminum Corporation** made the following statement in reference to its inventories: "The Company recorded pretax charges of approximately $19.4 million because of a reduction in the carrying values of its inventories caused principally by prevailing lower prices for alumina, primary aluminum, and fabricated products." What basic accounting principle caused Kaiser Aluminum to record this $19.4 million pretax charge? Briefly describe the rationale for this principle.

Q7-7. Under what conditions would each of the inventory costing methods discussed in the chapter produce the same results?

Q7-8. What is inventory "shrink?" How does a company determine the amount of inventory shrink that may have occurred?

Q7-9. What is a LIFO reserve? How is the LIFO reserve related to unrealized holding gains?

Q7-10. Analysts claim that it is more difficult to forecast net income for a company that uses LIFO. Why might this be true?

Q7-11.^{A} LIFO liquidation may be involuntary—that is beyond the control of management. Suggest two situations that might lead to involuntary LIFO liquidation.

Q7-12.^{A} LIFO liquidation is often discretionary. What motives might management have to liquidate LIFO inventory?

MINI EXERCISES

M7-13. Recording an Inventory Purchase LO1

Shields Company has purchased inventories incurring the following costs: (a) the invoice amount of $500, (b) shipping charges of $30, (c) interest of $10 on the $500 borrowed to finance the purchase, and (d) $5 for the cost of moving the inventory to the company's warehouse.

REQUIRED

Determine the cost to be assigned to the inventory and record the purchase using "T" accounts.

M7-14. Recording Inventory Costs LO1

Schrand Inc., a merchandiser, is requesting help in determining what costs ought to be considered as costs when incurred or treated as inventory costs, which are expensed as COGS. The costs include: sales persons wages, utilities such as heat and light in the store, the floor supervisor's salary, the cost of merchandise to be sold, costs of packaging and shipping to buyers.

REQUIRED

Determine the items above that should be included in inventory.

M7-15. Determining Cost of Goods Sold for a Manufacturing Company LO1

Ybarra Products began operations in 2017. During its first year, the company purchased raw materials costing $84,000 and used $63,000 of those materials in the production of its products. The company's manufacturing operations also incurred labor costs of $58,000 and overhead costs of $28,000. At year end 2017, Ybarra had $19,000 of partially completed product in work-in-process inventory and $35,000 in finished goods inventory. What was Ybarra Company's cost of goods sold in 2017?

M7-16. Calculating Gross Profit Margin LO5

Homework MBC

Johnson & Johnson
NYSE :: JNJ

Johnson & Johnson reported the following revenue and cost of goods sold information in its 10-K report for 2014, 2013, and 2012.

($ millions)	2014	2013	2012
Sales to customers.	$74,331	$71,312	$67,224
Cost of products sold.	22,746	22,342	21,658

Compute Johnson & Johnson's gross profit margin for each year.

M7-17. Calculating Effect of Inventory Errors LO1

For each of the following scenarios, determine the effect of the error on income in the current period and in the subsequent period. To answer these questions, rely on the inventory equation:

Beginning inventory + Purchases − Cost of goods sold = Ending inventory

a. Porter Company received a shipment of merchandise costing $32,000 near the end of the fiscal year. The shipment was mistakenly recorded at a cost of $23,000.

b. Chiu, Inc., purchased merchandise costing $16,000. When the shipment was received, it was determined that the merchandise was damaged in shipment. The goods were returned to the supplier, but the accounting department was not notified and the invoice was paid.

c. After taking a physical count of its inventory, Murray Corporation determined that it had "shrink" of $12,500, and the books were adjusted accordingly. However, inventory costing $5,000 was never counted.

M7-18. Calculating LIFO, FIFO, Income and Cash Flows LO2, 4

An acquaintance has proposed the following business plan to you. A local company requires a consistent quantity of a commodity and is looking for a reliable supplier. You could become that reliable supplier.

The cost of the commodity is expected to rise steadily over the foreseeable future, but the company is willing to pay more than the price that is current at the time. All you would need to do is make an investment, purchase the inventory and then deliver inventory to the company over the following year. One complication is that the commodity is available for purchase only seasonally, so at the end of every year you would need to purchase the supply for the following year. The customer pays promptly on delivery.

An initial cash investment of $62,000 would be used to purchase $50,000 of inventory in December 2016. The remaining cash would be held for liquidity needs. In the following year, you would deliver this inventory to the customer. Inventory costs are expected to increase by $10,000 per year, and the customer agrees to pay $15,000 more than the current cost of inventory. So, during 2017, you would deliver inventory that originally cost $50,000, receive payment of $75,000 and pay $60,000 to purchase inventory for the current year. This pattern would continue in future years, but with annually increasing costs of inventory and corresponding increases in the price charged the customer.

If you accept this proposal, your objective would be to receive $9,000 in dividends (about a 15% return on the $62,000 investment) at the end of each year. Assume your business would have an income tax rate of 40%.

a. Construct a projected balance sheet as of the end of December 2016.
b. Construct financial forecasts of income statements, cash flows (direct method) and balance sheets for the next three years (through 2019). Assume that your business would operate in a tax jurisdiction that requires the use of FIFO for inventory. Would this opportunity meet your financial objective?
c. Suppose that your business would operate in a tax jurisdiction that allowed the use of LIFO for inventory. Would this opportunity meet your financial objective? Why?

LO2 **M7-19. Computing Cost of Goods Sold and Ending Inventory Under FIFO, LIFO, and Average Cost**

Assume that Gode Company reports the following initial balance and subsequent purchase of inventory:

Beginning inventory, 2017	1,000 units @ $100 each	$100,000
Inventory purchased in 2017	2,000 units @ $150 each	300,000
Cost of goods available for sale in 2017	3,000 units	$400,000

Assume that 1,700 units are sold during 2017. Compute the cost of goods sold for 2017 and the balance reported as ending inventory on its 2017 balance sheet under the following inventory costing methods:

a. FIFO
b. LIFO
c. Average Cost

LO2 **M7-20. Inferring Purchases Using Cost of Goods Sold and Inventory Balances**

Geiger Corporation, a retail company, reported inventories of $1,320,000 in 2016 and $1,460,000 in 2017. The 2017 income statement reported cost of goods sold of $6,980,000.

a. Compute the amount of inventory purchased during 2017.
b. Prepare journal entries to record (1) purchases, and (2) cost of goods sold.
c. Post the journal entries in part *b* to their respective T-accounts.
d. Record each of the transactions in part *b* in the financial statement effects template to show the effect of these entries on the balance sheet and income statement.

LO2 **M7-21. Computing Cost of Goods Sold and Ending Inventory**

Bartov Corporation reports the following beginning inventory and purchases for 2017:

Beginning inventory, 2017	400 units @ $10 each	$ 4,000
Inventory purchased in 2017	700 units @ $12 each	8,400
Cost of goods available for sale in 2017	1,100 units	$12,400

Bartov sells 600 of these units in 2017. Compute its cost of goods sold for 2017 and the ending inventory reported on its 2017 balance sheet under each of the following inventory costing methods:

a. FIFO
b. LIFO
c. Average cost

M7-22. Computing and Evaluating Inventory Turnover

LO5

Wal-Mart Stores, Inc. NYSE :: WMT
Target Corporation NYSE :: TGT

Wal-Mart Stores, Inc., and **Target Corporation** reported the following in their financial reports:

($ billions)	Wal-Mart			Target		
Fiscal Year	Sales	COGS	Inventory	Sales	COGS	Inventory
2014	$476	$358	$44.9	$72.6	$51.3	$8.79
2013	469	352	43.8	71.3	50.0	8.28
2012	447	335	40.7	72.0	50.6	7.90

a. Compute the 2014 and 2013 inventory turnovers for each of these two retailers.

b. Discuss any changes that are evident in inventory turnover across years and companies from part *a*.

c. Describe ways in which a retailer can improve its inventory turnover. Are there ways to increase inventory turnover that are not beneficial to the company's long-term interests?

M7-23. Inferring Purchases Using Cost of Goods Sold and Inventory Balances

LO2

Penno Company reported ending inventories of $23,560,000 in 2017 and $25,790,000 in 2016. Cost of goods sold totaled $142,790,000 in 2017.

a. Prepare the journal entry to record cost of goods sold.

b. Set up a T-account for inventory and post the cost of goods sold entry from part *a* to this account.

c. Using the T-account from *b*, determine the amount of inventory that was purchased in 2017. Prepare a journal entry to record those purchases.

d. Using the financial statement effects template, show the effects of the entries in parts *a* and *c* on the balance sheet and income statement.

M7-24. Determining Lower of Cost or Market

LO3

The following data refer to Froning Company's ending inventory.

Item Code	Quantity	Unit Cost	Unit Market
LXC.	60	$45	$48
KWT	210	38	34
MOR.	300	22	20
NES	100	27	32

Determine the ending inventory amount by applying the lower of cost or market rule to (*a*) each item of inventory and (*b*) the total inventory.

EXERCISES

E7-25. Analyzing Inventory and Margin in a Seasonal Business

LO5

West Marine, Inc. NASDAQ :: WMAR

West Marine, Inc., opened its first boating supply store in 1975. Since that time, the company has grown to be one of the largest boating supply companies in the world, with fiscal year 2014 revenues in excess of $675 million. The accompanying table provides financial information for two recent years. West Marine's fiscal year is closely aligned with the calendar year. All amounts are in millions.

Time Period	Net Revenues	Cost of Goods Sold	Ending Inventory
Fiscal year 2012	—	—	**$189**
First quarter 2013	$114	$ 89	238
Second quarter 2013	237	149	237
Third quarter 2013	193	136	217
Fourth quarter 2013	119	98	203
Fiscal year 2013	**663**	**472**	**203**
First quarter 2014	113	88	245
Second quarter 2014	236	154	244
Third quarter 2014	197	138	215
Fourth quarter 2014	130	103	214
Fiscal year 2014	**676**	**483**	**214**

a. Using the fiscal year (annual) information for 2013 and 2014, calculate the gross profit margin and the inventory turnover ratio.

b. West Marine is in a seasonal business, in which the sales total for the second and third quarters is substantially higher than the sales total for the first and fourth quarters. Calculate the company's gross profit margin by quarter. What do you learn from the seasonal pattern in the gross profit margin?

c. What is the seasonal pattern in inventory balances? What effect does West Marine's choice of fiscal year-end have on the inventory turnover ratio calculated in *a*?

d. Recalculate West Marine's inventory turnover ratios for 2013 and 2014 using a weighted average of the company's inventory investment over the year.

LO2, 4 **E7-26. Applying and Analyzing Inventory Costing Methods**

At the beginning of the current period, Chen carried 1,000 units of its product with a unit cost of $20. A summary of purchases during the current period follows:

	Units	Unit Cost	Cost
Beginning Inventory	1,000	$20	$20,000
Purchases: #1	1,800	22	39,600
#2	800	26	20,800
#3	1,200	29	34,800

During the current period, Chen sold 2,800 units.

a. Assume that Chen uses the first-in, first-out method. Compute its cost of goods sold for the current period and the ending inventory balance.

b. Assume that Chen uses the last-in, first-out method. Compute its cost of goods sold for the current period and the ending inventory balance.

c. Assume that Chen uses the average cost method. Compute its cost of goods sold for the current period and the ending inventory balance.

d. Which of these three inventory costing methods would you choose to:
1. Reflect what is probably the physical flow of goods? Explain.
2. Minimize income taxes for the period? Explain.
3. Report the largest amount of income for the period? Explain.

LO2 **E7-27. Computing Cost of Sales and Ending Inventory**

Stocken Company has the following financial records for the current period:

	Units	Unit Cost
Beginning inventory	100	$46
Purchases: #1	650	42
#2	550	38
#3	200	36

Ending inventory at the end of this period is 350 units. Compute the ending inventory and the cost of goods sold for the current period using (*a*) first-in, first-out, (*b*) average cost, and (*c*) last-in, first-out.

LO3 **E7-28. Determining Lower of Cost or Market**

Crane Company had the following inventory at December 31, 2017.

		Unit Price	
	Quantity	Cost	Market
Desks			
Model 9001	70	$190	$210
Model 9002	45	280	268
Model 9003	20	350	360
Cabinets			
Model 7001	120	60	64
Model 7002	80	95	88
Model 7003	50	130	126

a. Determine the ending inventory amount by applying the lower of cost or market rule to
   1. Each item of inventory.
   2. Each major category of inventory.
   3. Total inventory.

b. Which of the LCM procedures from requirement *a* results in the lowest net income for 2017? Explain.

E7-29. Analyzing Inventory Footnote Disclosure

LO2, 4

General Motors
NYSE :: GM

General Motors Corporation reported the following information in its 10-K report:

Inventories at December 31 ($ millions)	2008	2007
Productive material, work in process, and supplies	$ 4,849	$ 6,267
Finished product, service parts, etc.	9,426	10,095
Total inventories at FIFO	14,275	16,362
Less LIFO allowance	(1,233)	(1,423)
Total automotive and other inventories, less allowances	$13,042	$14,939

The company reports its inventory using the LIFO costing method during 2007 and 2008.

a. At what dollar amount are inventories reported on its 2008 balance sheet?

b. At what dollar amount would inventories have been reported in 2008 if FIFO inventory costing had been used?

c. What cumulative effect has the use of LIFO had, as of year-end 2008, on GM's pretax income, compared to the pretax income that would have been reported using the FIFO costing method?

d. Assuming a 35% income tax rate, what is the cumulative effect on GM's tax liability as of year-end 2008?

e. In July 2009, GM changed its inventory accounting to FIFO costs. Why do you suppose GM made that choice?

E7-30. Analyzing of Inventory and Footnote Disclosure

LO2, 4

Deere & Company
NYSE :: DE

The inventory footnote from **Deere & Company**'s 2013 10-K follows ($ millions).

15. INVENTORIES

Most inventories owned by Deere & Company and its US equipment subsidiaries are valued at cost, on the "last-in, first-out" (LIFO) basis. Remaining inventories are generally valued at the lower of cost, on the "first-in, first-out" (FIFO) basis, or market. The value of gross inventories on the LIFO basis represented 63 percent and 61 percent of worldwide gross inventories at FIFO value on October 31, 2013 and 2012, respectively. If all inventories had been valued on a FIFO basis, estimated inventories by major classification at October 31 in millions of dollars would have been as follows:

	2013	2012
Raw materials and supplies	$1,954	$1,874
Work-in-process	753	652
Finished goods and parts	3,757	4,065
Total FIFO value	6,464	6,591
Less adjustment to LIFO value	(1,529)	(1,421)
Inventories	$4,935	$5,170

We note that not all of Deere's inventories are reported using the same inventory costing method (companies can use different inventory costing methods for different inventory pools).

a. At what dollar amount are Deere's inventories reported on its 2013 balance sheet?

b. At what dollar amount would inventories have been reported on Deere's 2013 balance sheet had it used FIFO inventory costing?

c. What *cumulative* effect has the use of LIFO inventory costing had, as of year-end 2013, on its pretax income compared with the pretax income it would have reported had it used FIFO inventory costing? Explain.

d. Assuming a 35% income tax rate, by what *cumulative* dollar amount has Deere's tax liability been affected by use of LIFO inventory costing as of year-end 2013? Has the use of LIFO inventory costing increased or decreased its cumulative tax liability?

e. What effect has the use of LIFO inventory costing had on Deere's pretax income and tax liability for 2013 (assume a 35% income tax rate)?

f. Deere's 2014 annual report has similar disclosures but also states: "The pretax favorable income effect from the liquidation of LIFO inventory during 2014 was approximately $13 million." Explain what happened in 2014 with respect to Deere's inventory and why there was a favorable income effect.

LO2, 4, 5

E7-31. Analyzing Inventories Using LIFO Inventory Footnote

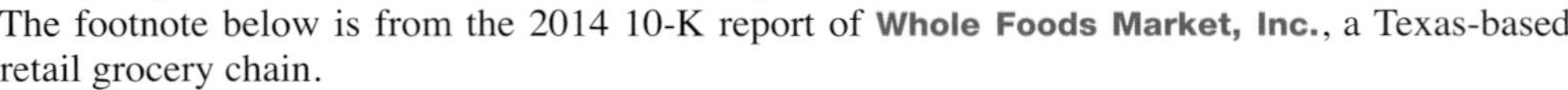

Whole Foods
NASDAQ :: WFMI

The footnote below is from the 2014 10-K report of **Whole Foods Market, Inc.**, a Texas-based retail grocery chain.

Inventories

The Company values inventories at the lower of cost or market. Cost was determined using the dollar value retail last-in, first-out ("LIFO") method for approximately 93.5% and 92.8% of inventories in fiscal years 2014 and 2013, respectively. Under the LIFO method, the cost assigned to items sold is based on the cost of the most recent items purchased. As a result, the costs of the first items purchased remain in inventory and are used to value ending inventory. The excess of estimated current costs over LIFO carrying value, or LIFO reserve, was approximately $48 million and $32 million at September 28, 2014 and September 29, 2013, respectively. Costs for remaining inventories are determined by the first-in, first-out method. Cost before the LIFO adjustment is principally determined using the item cost method, which is calculated by counting each item in inventory, assigning costs to each of these items based on the actual purchase cost (net of vendor allowances) of each item and recording the actual cost of items sold.

Whole Foods operates the world's largest chain of natural and organic food stores. In 2014, Whole Foods reported sales revenue of $14,194 million and cost of goods sold of $9,150 million. The following information was extracted from the company's 2014 and 2013 balance sheets:

($ millions)	2014	2013
Merchandise inventories	$441	$414

a. Calculate the amount of inventories purchased by Whole Foods in 2014.

b. What amount of gross profit would Whole Foods have reported if the FIFO method had been used to value all inventories?

c. Calculate the gross profit margin (GPM) as reported and assuming that the FIFO method had been used to value all inventories.

LO5

E7-32. Calculating Gross Profit Margin and Inventory Turnover

MBC

Tiffany & Co.
NYSE :: TIF
Zale Corporation
NYSE :: ZLC
Blue Nile, Inc.
NASDAQ :: NILE

The following table presents sales revenue, cost of goods sold, and inventory amounts for three retailers of fine jewelry, **Tiffany & Co.**, **Zale Corporation**, and **Blue Nile, Inc.** (an Internet retailer).

($ millions)	2013	2012
Tiffany & Co.		
Revenues	$4,031	$3,794
Cost of goods sold	1,691	1,631
Inventory	2,327	2,234
Zale Corporation		
Revenues	$1,888	$1,867
Cost of goods sold	904	906
Inventory	768	742
Blue Nile, Inc.		
Revenues	$ 450	$ 400
Cost of goods sold	366	325
Inventory	35	33

a. Compute the gross profit margin (GPM) for each of these companies for 2013 and 2012.

b. Compute the inventory turnover ratio and the average inventory days outstanding for 2013 for each company.

c. What factors might determine the differences among these three companies' ratios?

d. Zale reports that as of July 31, 2013 its LIFO reserve totaled $63 million while at July 31, 2012 it totaled $58.3 million. Using a 35% tax rate, how much money did Zale save in fiscal 2013 using LIFO and how much has Zale saved since it began using LIFO to value its inventories?

PROBLEMS

P7-33. Analyzing Inventory and Its Footnote Disclosure

LO2, 4, 5
Caterpillar, Inc.
NYSE :: CAT
Komatsu Ltd. (ADR)
OTC :: KMTUY

Caterpillar Inc. and **Komatsu Ltd.** are international manufacturers of industrial and construction equipment. Caterpillar's headquarters is in the United States, while Komatsu's headquarters is in Japan. The following information comes from their recent financial statements.

Caterpillar—fiscal year ending December 31, 2013 ($ millions)	
Cost of goods sold	$40,727
Beginning inventory	15,547
Ending inventory	12,625
Komatsu—fiscal year ending March 31, 2014 (¥ millions)	
Cost of goods sold	¥1,393,048
Beginning inventory	633,647
Ending inventory	625,077

In its footnotes, Caterpillar also provides the following information (assume no LIFO liquidation):

Inventories
Inventories are stated at the lower of cost or market. Cost is principally determined using the last-in, first-out (LIFO) method. The value of inventories on the LIFO basis represented about 60 percent of total inventories at December 31, 2013 and 2012, and about 65 percent at December 31, 2011. If the FIFO (first-in, first-out) method had been in use, inventories would have been $2,504 million, $2,750 million and $2,422 million higher than reported at December 31, 2013, 2012 and 2011, respectively.

REQUIRED

a. Calculate the inventory turnover ratios for Caterpillar and Komatsu using the information reported in their financial statements. Describe some operational reasons that companies might have differing inventory turnover ratios, even if they are in the same industry.

b. Did the cost of Caterpillar's acquiring (i.e., producing) products go up or down in 2013?

c. Assuming a 35% income tax rate, by what cumulative dollar amount has Caterpillar's tax liability been affected by use of LIFO inventory costing as of fiscal year-end 2013? Has the use of LIFO inventory costing increased or decreased its cumulative tax liability?

d. What effect has the use of LIFO inventory costing had on Caterpillar's pretax income and tax liability for fiscal year 2013? (Assume a 35% tax rate.)

e. In its footnotes, Komatsu reports that it "determines cost of work in process and finished products using the specific identification method based on actual costs accumulated under a job-order cost system. The cost of finished parts is determined principally using the first-in, first-out method." What effect does this footnote have on your interpretation in question *a* above? Use the information available to make a more appropriate comparison of the two companies' inventory turnover.

P7-34. Analyzing Inventory Disclosure Comparing LIFO and FIFO

LO2, 4, 5

Kroger
NYSE :: KR

The current asset section of the 2014 and 2013 fiscal year end balance sheets of **The Kroger Co.** are presented in the accompanying table:

($ millions)	January 31, 2015	February 1, 2014
Current assets		
Cash and temporary cash investments	$ 268	$ 401
Deposits in-transit	988	958
Receivables	1,266	1,116
FIFO inventory	6,933	6,801
LIFO credit	(1,245)	(1,150)
Prepaid and other current assets	701	704
Total current assets	$8,911	$8,830

In addition, Kroger provides the following footnote describing its inventory accounting policy (assume the following is their complete disclosure):

Inventories are stated at the lower of cost (principally on a LIFO basis) or market. In total, approximately 95% of inventories in 2014 and 2013 were valued using the LIFO method. Cost for the balance of the inventories, including substantially all fuel inventories, was determined using the FIFO method. Replacement cost was higher than the carrying amount by $1,245 million at January 31, 2015 and $1,150 million at February 1, 2014. We follow the Link-Chain, Dollar-Value LIFO method for purposes of calculating our LIFO charge or credit.

REQUIRED

a. At what dollar amount does Kroger report its inventory in its January 31, 2015, balance sheet?

b. What is the cumulative effect (through January 31, 2015) of the use of LIFO on Kroger's pretax earnings?

c. Assuming a 35% tax rate, what is the cumulative (through January 31, 2015) tax effect of the use of LIFO to determine inventory costs?

d. Kroger reported net earnings of $1,728 million in its fiscal year 2014 income statement. Assuming a 35% tax rate, what amount of net earnings would Kroger report if the company used the FIFO inventory costing method?

e. Kroger reported merchandise costs (cost of goods sold) of $85,512 million in fiscal year 2014. Compute its inventory turnover for the year.

f. How would the inventory turnover ratio differ if the FIFO costing method had been used?

LO5 Homework MBC

Samsung Electronics Co. Ltd. KRX: 005930
Hewlett-Packard and Company NYSE :: HPQ
Apple Inc. NASDAQ :: AAPL

P7-35. Calculating Gross Profit and Inventory Turnover

The following table presents sales revenue, cost of goods sold, and inventory amounts for three computer/electronics companies, **Samsung Electronics Co.**, **Hewlett-Packard Company**, and **Apple Inc.**

($ millions)		Fiscal year ending	
Samsung Electronics Co. Ltd. (S. Korean won)	Dec. 31, 2014	Dec. 31, 2013	Dec. 31, 2012
Revenues	206,205,987	228,692,667	201,103,613
Cost of goods sold	128,278,800	137,696,309	126,651,931
Inventory	17,317,504	19,134,868	17,747,413
Hewlett-Packard Company (US dollar)	Oct. 31, 2014	Oct. 31, 2013	Oct. 31, 2012
Revenues (products only)	73,726	72,398	77,887
Cost of goods sold	56,469	55,632	59,468
Inventory	6,415	6,046	6,317
Apple Inc. (US dollar)	Sep. 27, 2014	Sep. 28, 2013	Sep. 29, 2012
Revenues	182,795	170,910	156,508
Cost of goods sold	112,258	106,606	87,846
Inventory	2,111	1,764	791

REQUIRED

a. Compute the gross profit margin (GPM) for each of these companies for all three fiscal years.

b. Compute the inventory turnover ratio and the average inventory days outstanding for each company for the last two fiscal years. (All three firms use FIFO inventory costing.)

c. What factors might determine the differences among these three companies' ratios?

LO2, 4, 6

Seneca Foods Corporation NASDAQ :: SENEA

P7-36.[A] Analyzing and Interpreting Inventories and Its Related Ratios and Disclosures

The current asset section from **Seneca Foods Corporation**, a low-cost producer and distributor of quality fruits and vegetables, March 31, 2014 annual report follows:

($ thousands)	March 31, 2014	March 31, 2013
Current Assets		
Cash and cash equivalents	$ 13,839	$ 14,104
Accounts receivable, net	76,964	78,240
Inventories	451,250	479,730
Deferred income taxes	8,412	9,400
Other current assets	33,594	25,299
Total current assets	$584,059	$606,773

Seneca reports the following related to its gross profit:

($ thousands)	Years Ended 2014	2013
Net sales	$1,340,208	$1,276,297
Cost of sales	1,249,245	1,134,985
Gross profit	$ 90,963	$ 141,312

Seneca further reports the following footnote:

11. Inventories
Effective December 30, 2007 (beginning of 4th quarter of Fiscal Year 2008), the Company changed its inventory valuation method from the lower of cost, determined under the FIFO method, or market to the lower of cost, determined under the LIFO method, or market. In the high inflation environment that the Company was experiencing, the Company believed that the LIFO inventory method was preferable over the FIFO method because it better compares the cost of current production to current revenue. The effect of LIFO was to reduce net earnings by $13.2 million in 2014, increase net earnings by $2.7 million in 2013 and reduce net earnings by $30.8 million in 2012, compared to what would have been reported using the FIFO inventory method. The reduction in earnings per share was $1.19 ($1.19 diluted) in 2014, increase in earnings per share was $0.24 ($0.24 diluted) in 2013, and the reduction in earnings per share was $2.53 ($2.52 diluted) in 2012. During 2014 and 2012, certain inventory quantities accounted for on the LIFO method were reduced, resulting in the liquidation of certain quantities carried at costs prevailing in prior years. The impact on net earnings of these liquidations was an increase of $4.8 million and $2.9 million during 2014 and 2012, respectively. The excess of FIFO cost of inventory over the LIFO cost of inventory was $153 million in 2014 and $133 million in 2013.

In prior financial statements, Seneca has stated that it "manages the Company for cash, not reported earnings" and that the "decision to switch to LIFO has turned out to be a very prudent one of the last five years."

a. Compute the ratio of inventories to total current assets for both 2014 and 2013. Is the change observed for the ratio a positive development for a company such as Seneca? Explain.

b. Compute inventory turnover for both 2014 and 2013 (2012 ending inventories were $432,433). Interpret and explain the change in inventory turnover as positive or negative for the company.

c. What inventory costing method does Seneca use? What effect has the use of this method (relative to FIFO or LIFO) had on its reported income for 2014? Was the result an increase or decrease? Explain.

d. Seneca claims that it manages its company for cash flow. Does its inventory reporting help the Company to do so? How much in taxes has Seneca saved, assuming a 35% tax rate, by the inventory approach it adopted?

CASES AND PROJECTS

C7-37.[A] Analyzing Effects of LIFO on Inventory Turnover Ratios

LO2, 4, 5, 6

Exxon Mobil Corp.
NYSE :: XOM
BP, p.l.c.
NYSE :: BP

The current assets of **Exxon Mobil Corporation** follow:

($ millions)	2014	2013
Current assets		
Cash and cash equivalents	$ 4,658	$ 4,913
Notes and accounts receivable, less estimated doubtful amounts	28,009	33,152
Inventories:		
Crude oil, products and merchandise	12,384	12,117
Materials and supplies	4,294	4,018
Other current assets	3,565	5,108
Total current assets	$52,910	$59,308

In addition, the following note was provided in its 2014 10-K report:

Inventories. Crude oil, products and merchandise inventories are carried at the lower of current market value or cost (generally determined under the last-in, first-out method—LIFO). Inventory costs include expenditures and other charges (including depreciation) directly and indirectly incurred in bringing the inventory to its existing condition and location. Selling expenses and general and administrative expenses are reported as period costs and excluded from inventory cost. Inventories of materials and supplies are valued at cost or less.

In 2014, 2013 and 2012, net income included gains of $187 million, $282 million and $328 million, respectively, attributable to the combined effects of LIFO inventory accumulations and drawdowns. The aggregate replacement cost of inventories was estimated to exceed their LIFO carrying values by $10.6 billion and $21.2 billion at December 31, 2014, and 2013, respectively.

REQUIRED

a. Exxon Mobil reported pretax earnings of $51,630 million in 2014. What amount of pretax earnings would have been reported by the company if inventory had been reported using the FIFO costing method?

b. Exxon Mobil reported cost of goods sold of $225,972 million in 2014. Compute its inventory turnover ratio for 2014 using total inventories.

c. **BP, p.l.c.** (BP) reports its financial information using IFRS. For fiscal year 2014, BP reported cost of goods sold of $281,907 million, beginning inventory of $29,231 million and ending inventory of $18,373 million. Compute BP's inventory turnover ratio for fiscal year 2014.

d. Compare your answers in parts *b* and *c*. BP can't use LIFO to report under IFRS, so revise your calculations in such a way as to find out which company has faster inventory turnover.

e. What is meant by the statement that "2014 net income included gains of $187 million attributable to the combined effects of LIFO inventory accumulations and draw-downs"?

LO2, 4
Virco Manufacturing Corp.
NASDAQ :: VIRC

C7-38. Analyzing Effects of Change from LIFO to FIFO Inventory Costing

Virco Manufacturing Corp. provided the following note in its annual report for the year ended January 31, 2011:

On January 31, 2011, the Company elected to change its costing method for the material component of raw materials, work in process, and finished goods inventory to the lower of cost or market using the first-in first-out ("FIFO") method, from the lower of cost or market using the last-in first out ("LIFO") method. The labor and overhead components of inventory have historically been valued on a FIFO basis. The Company believes that the FIFO method for the material component of inventory is preferable as it conforms the inventory costing methods for all components of inventory into a single costing method and better reflects current acquisition costs of those inventories on our consolidated balance sheets. Additionally, presentation of inventory at FIFO aligns the financial reporting with the Company's borrowing base under its line of credit (see Note 3 for further discussion of the line of credit). Further, this change will promote greater comparability with companies that have adopted International Financial Reporting Standards, which does not recognize LIFO as an acceptable accounting method. In accordance with FASB ASC Topic 250, "Accounting Changes and Error Corrections," all prior periods presented have been adjusted to apply the new accounting method retrospectively. In addition, as an indirect effect of the change in our inventory costing method from LIFO to FIFO, the Company recorded additional inventory lower of cost or market expenses and changes in deferred tax assets and income tax expense. The retroactive effect of the change in our inventory costing method...increased the February 1, 2008, opening retained earnings balance by $4.1 million, and increased our inventory and retained earnings balances by $8.5 million and $5.4 million as of January 31, 2009, by $6.9 million and $4.3 million as of January 31, 2010, and by $7.6 million and $4.7 million as of January 31, 2011, respectively.

REQUIRED

a. What do the stated changes in inventory in each year represent (e.g., the $7.6 million in 2011)? Equity? What is the difference between the two?

b. What were Virco's stated reasons for the change to FIFO?

c. In the Annual Report for the year ended January 2010, Virco states the following: "Inventories are stated at the lower of cost or market. Cost is determined using the last-in, first-out ("LIFO") method of valuation for the material content of inventories and the first-in, first-out ("FIFO") method for labor and overhead. The Company uses LIFO as it results in a better matching of costs and revenues." What are some possible motivations behind why Virco changed to the FIFO method of accounting beyond those listed by management?

SOLUTIONS TO REVIEW PROBLEMS

Mid-Chapter Review Part 1

SOLUTION

Preliminary computation: Units in ending inventory = 4,800 available − 2,800 sold = 2,000

1. First-in, first-out (FIFO)

Cost of goods sold computation:	**Units**		**Cost**		**Total**
	1,000	@	$18.00	=	$18,000
	1,800	@	$18.25	=	32,850
	2,800				**$50,850**
Cost of goods available for sale		$88,450			
Less: Cost of goods sold		50,850			
Ending inventory ($22,800 + $14,800)		**$37,600**			

2. Last-in, first-out (LIFO)

Cost of goods sold computation:	**Units**		**Cost**		**Total**
	1,200	@	$19.00	=	$22,800
	800	@	$18.50	=	14,800
	800	@	$18.25	=	14,600
	2,800				**$52,200**
Cost of goods available for sale		$88,450			
Less: Cost of goods sold		52,200			
Ending inventory [$18,000 + (1,000 × $18.25)]		**$36,250**			

3. Average cost (AC)

Average unit cost	= $88,450/4,800	= $18.427
Cost of goods sold	= 2,800 × $18.427	= $51,596
Ending inventory	= 2,000 × $18.427	= $36,854

4. *a.* FIFO in most circumstances reflects physical flow. For example, FIFO would apply to the physical flow of perishables and to situations where the earlier items acquired are moved out first because of risk of deterioration or obsolescence.

   b. LIFO results in the lowest ending inventory amount during periods of rising costs, which in turn yields the lowest net income and the lowest income taxes.

5. Last-in, first-out with LIFO liquidation

Cost of goods sold computation:	**Units**		**Cost**		**Total**
	800	@	$18.50	=	$14,800
	1,800	@	$18.25	=	32,850
	200	@	$18.00	=	3,600
	2,800				**$51,250**
Cost of goods available for sale		$65,650			
Less: Cost of goods sold		51,250			
Ending inventory (800 × $18)		**$14,400**			

The company's LIFO gross profit has increased by $950 ($52,200 − $51,250). This increase is from LIFO liquidation, which is the reduction of inventory quantities that results in matching older (lower) cost layers against current selling prices. The company has, in effect, dipped into lower-cost layers to boost current period profit—all from a simple delay of inventory purchases.

6. Transaction effects shown in the financial statement effects template, journal entries, and T-accounts.

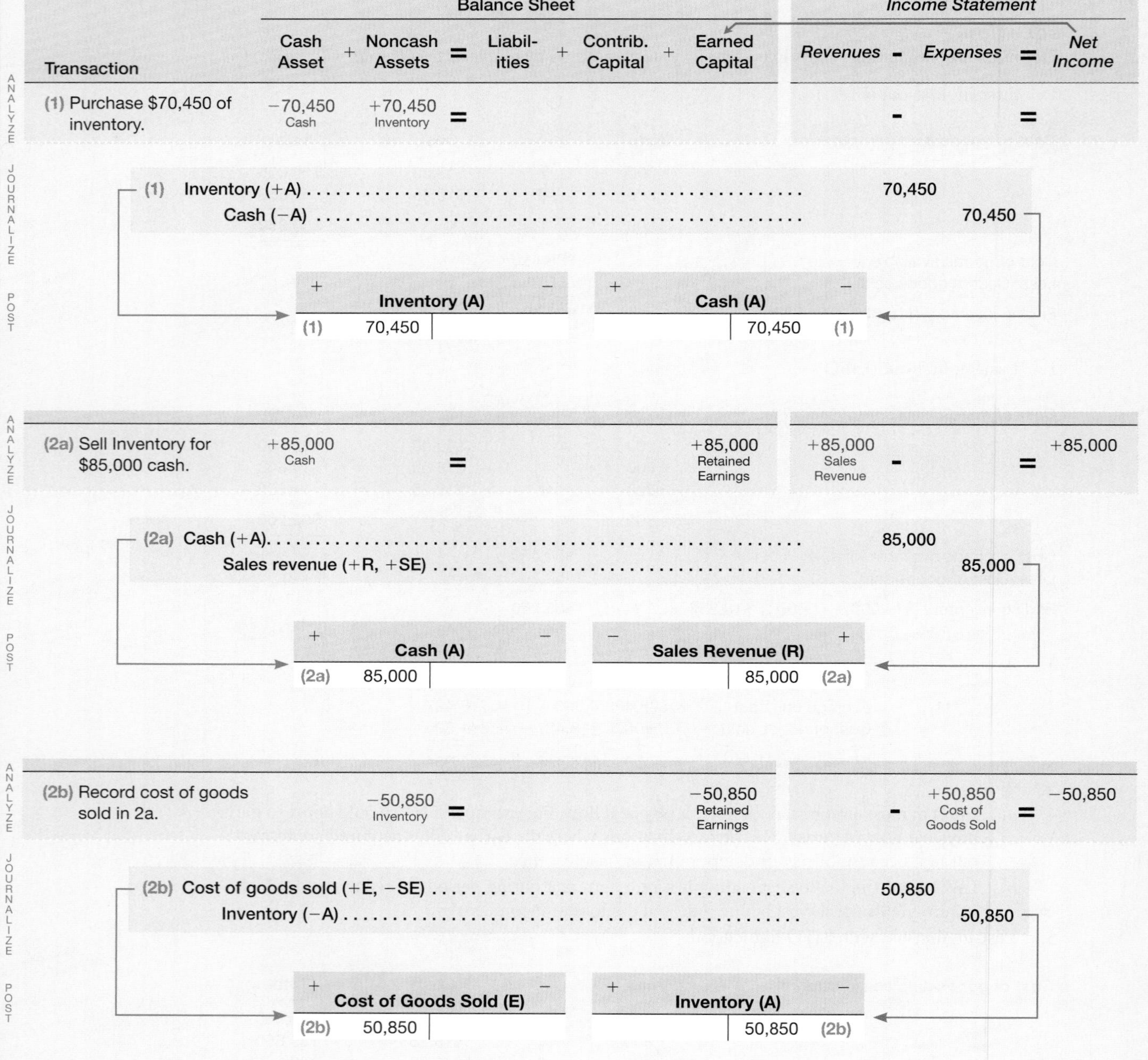

Mid-Chapter Review Part 2

SOLUTION

1.

Item	Quantity	Cost	Market	Inventory Amounts Cost	Market	LCM (by Item)
Fans						
Model X1	300	$18	$19	$ 5,400	$ 5,700	$ 5,400
Model X2	250	22	24	5,500	6,000	5,500
Model X3	400	29	26	11,600	10,400	10,400
Totals				$22,500	$22,100	$21,300
Heaters						
Model B7	500	24	28	$12,000	$14,000	$12,000
Model B8	290	35	32	10,150	9,280	9,280
Model B9	100	41	38	4,100	3,800	3,800
Totals				26,250	27,080	25,080
Totals				$48,750	$49,180	$46,380

a. As shown in this schedule, applying the lower of cost or market rule to each item of the inventory results in an ending inventory amount of $46,380.

b. Applying the lower of cost or market rule to each major category of the inventory results in an ending inventory amount of $48,350, calculated as follows:

Fans	$22,100
Heaters.	26,250
	$48,350

c. As shown in this schedule, applying the lower of cost or market rule to the total inventory results in an ending inventory amount of $48,750.

2. The LCM procedure that results in the lowest ending inventory amount also results in the lowest net income for the year (the lower the ending inventory amount, the higher the cost of goods sold). Applying the lower of cost or market rule to each item of the inventory results in the lowest net income for the year.

Chapter-End Review

SOLUTION

1. The gross profit margin is calculated as follows:

Gross profit margin:		
2012:	$7,574/$27,485 =	0.276 (or 27.6%)
2013:	$7,980/$28,917 =	0.276 (or 27.6%)
2014:	$8,327/$30,560 =	0.272 (or 27.2%)
Inventory turnover:		
2013:	$20,937/[($1,507 + $1,409)/2] =	14.4 times
2014:	$22,233/[($1,598 + $1,507)/2] =	14.3 times

2. Cost of goods sold and gross profit must be adjusted by the change in the LIFO reserve to convert to FIFO.

Cost of goods sold		
2013:	$20,937 − ($390 − $375) =	$20,922
2014:	$22,233 − ($421 − $390) =	$22,202
Gross profit		
2013:	$7,980 + ($390 − $375) =	$ 7,995
2014:	$8,327 + ($421 − $390) =	$ 8,358

The use of LIFO resulted in a higher cost of goods sold and a lower gross profit for both years.

3. Restated inventory turnover calculations:

2013:	$20,922/[($1,897 + $1,784)/2] =	11.4 times
2014:	$22,202/[($2,019 + $1,897)/2] =	11.3 times

Because inventory values are higher and cost of goods sold is lower under FIFO, the inventory turnover ratio is slightly lower when FIFO numbers are used.

Appendix 7A Review

SOLUTION

a.

Sales revenue	
(11,500 × $65)	$747,500
Cost of goods sold	
(7,000 × $70) + (3,000 × $30) + (1,500 × $20)	610,000
Gross profit.	$137,500

b.

Sales revenue	
(11,500 × $65)	$747,500
Cost of goods sold	
(11,500 × $70)	805,000
Gross profit.	$ (57,500)

c. Dickhaut should report in its footnotes that gross profit was increased by $195,000 [$137,500 − $(57,500)] due to LIFO liquidation. It's worth noting that Dickhaut could report any gross profit between $(57,500) and $137,500 by adjusting its end-of-year purchases.

d. The replenishment decision should depend on the cash flows from each alternative over the planning period (until the point where inventory could be replenished next year at $55). The following table looks at three alternatives—no year-end purchase, a year-end purchase of 4,500 units, and a year-end purchase of 1,500 units. The second alternative would retain all the LIFO layers that were in the beginning inventory, while the third alternative would retain only the 2014 layer at $20 per unit. For this last alternative, cost of goods sold would be $685,000 (8,500 units at $70 each plus 3,000 units at $30 each).

As the table shows, the second alternative is preferred to the first, but the third alternative is preferred over the other two. (Of course, this analysis is based on the assumption that 5,000 units will be held in inventory for the entire planning horizon. If Dickhaut anticipates future inventory reductions, e.g., due to product changes, end-of-year purchases would only defer the payment of taxes and their relative advantage would decrease.)

	No purchase		Purchase 4,500 units		Purchase 1,500 units	
	Income	**Cash Flows**	**Income**	**Cash Flows**	**Income**	**Cash Flows**
Revenue	$747,500	$747,500	$747,500	$747,500	$747,500	$747,500
COGS.	610,000		805,000		685,000	
Gross profit.	137,500		(57,500)		62,500	
Tax (35%)	(48,125)	(48,125)	20,125	20,125	(21,875)	(21,875)
Year-end purchases				(315,000)		(105,000)
2017 purchases		(247,500)				(165,000)
Total cash flows		$451,875		$452,625		$455,625

Reporting and Analyzing Long-Term Operating Assets

LEARNING OBJECTIVES

1. Describe and distinguish between tangible and intangible assets. (p. 374)
2. Determine which costs to capitalize and report as assets and which costs to expense. (p. 375)
3. Apply different depreciation methods to allocate the cost of assets over time. (p. 377)
4. Determine the effects of asset sales and impairments on financial statements. (p. 381)
5. Describe the accounting and reporting for intangible assets. (p. 388)
6. Analyze the effects of tangible and intangible assets on key performance measures. (p. 393)

PROCTER & GAMBLE

www.pg.com

The Procter & Gamble Company (P&G) has successfully reinvented itself . . . again. Founded in 1837 by William Procter and James Gamble, P&G is the largest consumer products company in the world today. P&G markets its products in more than 180 countries and its annual sales now are in excess of $83 billion, which far exceeds competitors such as **Colgate-Palmolive Company** and **Kimberly-Clark Corporation**. P&G has focused on its higher-margin products such as those in beauty care. P&G's advertising budget is 11% of sales, which is slightly larger than Colgate's and more than twice as large as Kimberly-Clark's.

P&G's financial performance has been impressive. Its return on equity (ROE) in 2014 was 17%. Although more financially leveraged than the average publicly traded company, there is little need for concern because P&G generates almost $14 billion in operating cash flow, which is more than sufficient to cover its $700 million in interest payments. P&G also paid almost $7 billion in dividends and repurchased more than $6 billion of its own shares in 2014. (Stock repurchases are covered more fully in Chapter 11.)

P&G has made divesting underperforming brands a strategic goal. For example, P&G recently sold off its pet care business to Mars, Inc. and Spectrum Brands Holdings, Inc. In addition, P&G agreed to divest its Duracell batteries business to Berkshire Hathaway, Inc. and has entered into deals to exit Vicks VapoStream, Camay and Zest bar soap brands, and several skin care and fragrance brands.

P&G's remaining product stable consists of numerous well-recognized household brands. Surveys in the business press show that the company is widely admired. A partial listing follows by business segment, including some "Billion Dollar Brands" in each segment:

- **Baby and Family Care**—Bounty, Charmin, Pampers
- **Beauty**— CoverGirl, Head & Shoulders, Olay, Pantene, Wella
- **Fabric and Home Care**—Ace, Febreze, Cascade, Cheer, Dawn, Downy, Gain, Tide
- **Grooming**—Braun, Gillette, Mach3
- **Health Care**—Always, Crest, Oral-B

However, substantial risks exist. In the fiscal 2014 annual report, management states that "Our business model relies on continued growth and success of existing brands and products, as well as the creation of new products. The markets and industry segments in which we offer our products are highly competitive. . . Achieving our business results depends, in part, on the successful development, introduction, and marketing of new products and improvements to our equipment and manufacturing processes." External risks also exist. For example, in recent years commodity costs have risen rapidly and significantly, and cautious consumers have made it difficult for P&G to increase prices and maintain margins. In the last year, the strength of the dollar also hurt P&G. Around 60% of the company's business is generated outside North America. Lower consumption in several countries due to pricing actions taken to offset the effects of currency changes negatively affected sales.

In this chapter, we explore the reporting and analysis of long-term operating assets. In order to maintain growth in sales, income, and cash flows, capital-intensive companies like P&G must be diligent in managing long-term operating assets. As is the case with P&G, many companies have made large investments in innovation and brand value. These investments are not always reflected adequately in the balance sheet. Management's choices and GAAP rules concerning the reporting of long-term operating assets can have a marked impact on the analysis and interpretation of financial statements.

Sources: *Procter & Gamble* 2014 Annual Report and 10-K.

CHAPTER ORGANIZATION

Reporting and Analyzing Long-Term Operating Assets		
Property, Plant, and Equipment	**Analyzing Financial Statements**	**Intangible Assets**
• Determining Costs to Capitalize • Depreciation Methods • Changes in Accounting Estimates • Asset Sales and Impairments • Footnote Disclosures	• PPE Turnover • Percent Depreciated Ratio • Cash Flow Effects	• Research and Development Costs • Patents, Trademarks, and Franchises • Amortization and Impairment • Goodwill • Footnote Disclosures • Analysis Implications

1

LO1 Describe and distinguish between tangible and intangible assets.

INTRODUCTION

Investments in long-term operating assets often represent the largest component of a company's balance sheet. Effectively managing long-term operating assets is crucial, because these investments affect company performance for several years and are frequently irreversible. To evaluate how well a company is managing operating assets, we need to understand how they are measured and reported.

This chapter describes the accounting, reporting, and analysis of long-term operating assets including tangible and intangible assets. **Tangible assets** are assets that have physical substance. They are frequently included in the balance sheet as *property, plant, and equipment*, and include land, buildings, machinery, fixtures, and equipment. **Intangible assets**, such as trademarks and patents, do not have physical substance, but provide the owner with specific rights and privileges.

Long-term operating assets have two common characteristics. First, unlike inventory, these assets are not acquired for resale. Instead, they are necessary to produce and deliver the products and services that generate revenues for the company. Second, these assets help produce revenues for multiple accounting periods. Consequently, accountants focus considerable attention on how they are reported in the balance sheet and how these costs are transferred over time to the income statement as expenses.

To illustrate the size and importance of long-term operating assets, the asset section (only) of P&G's balance sheet is reproduced in **Exhibit 8.1**. We can see as of June 30, 2014, the end of P&G's fiscal year, P&G's net investment in property, plant, and equipment totaled approximately \$22.3 billion and its intangible assets represent an \$84.5 billion investment. Together, these two categories of assets make up almost three-fourths of P&G's total assets.

This chapter is divided into two main sections. The first section focuses on accounting for tangible property, plant, and equipment and the related depreciation expense that is reported each period in the income statement. The second section examines the measurement and reporting of intangible assets.

PROPERTY, PLANT, AND EQUIPMENT (PPE)

For many companies, the largest category of operating assets is its long-term property, plant, and equipment (PPE) assets. The size and duration of this asset category raises several important questions, including:

- Which costs should be **capitalized** on the balance sheet as assets? Which should be expensed?
- How should capitalized costs be allocated to the accounting periods that benefited from the asset?
- How should asset sales or significant changes in assets' fair values be reported?

This section explains the accounting, reporting, and analysis of PPE assets and related items.

EXHIBIT 8.1 Procter & Gamble Balance Sheet (assets only)

($ millions)	June 30 2014	2013
Assets		
Current assets		
Cash and cash equivalents	$ 8,558	$ 5,947
Available-for-sale investment securities	2,128	—
Accounts receivable	6,386	6,508
Inventories		
Materials and supplies	1,742	1,704
Work in process	684	722
Finished goods	4,333	4,483
Total inventories	6,759	6,909
Deferred income taxes	1,092	948
Prepaid expenses and other current assets	3,845	3,678
Assets held for sale	2,849	—
Total current assets	31,617	23,990
Property, plant, and equipment		
Buildings	8,022	7,829
Machinery and equipment	32,398	31,070
Land	893	878
Construction in progress	3,114	3,235
	44,427	43,012
Accumulated depreciation	(22,123)	(21,346)
Net property, plant, and equipment	22,304	21,666
Goodwill and other intangible assets		
Goodwill	53,704	55,188
Trademarks and other intangible assets, net	30,843	31,572
Net goodwill and other intangible assets	84,547	86,760
Other noncurrent assets	5,798	6,847
Total assets	$ 144,266	$ 139,263

LO2 Determine which costs to capitalize and report as assets and which costs to expense.

Determining Costs to Capitalize

When a company acquires an asset, it must first decide which portion of the cost should be included among the expenses of the current period and which costs should be capitalized as part of the asset and reported in the balance sheet. Outlays to acquire PPE are called **capital expenditures**. Expenditures that are recorded as an asset must possess each of the following two characteristics:

1. The asset is owned or controlled by the company.
2. The asset is expected to provide future benefits.

All normal costs incurred to acquire an asset and prepare it for its intended use should be capitalized and reported in the balance sheet. These costs would include the purchase price of the asset plus any of the following: installation costs, taxes, shipping costs, legal fees, and setup or calibration costs. If owning an asset carries legal obligations at the end of the asset's life (for example, to remove the asset or to perform environmental remediation), the current cost of those obligations should be included in the asset's cost and recognized as a liability at the time the asset is acquired. This cost will be included in the subsequent depreciation of the asset.

Determining the specific costs that should be capitalized requires judgment. There are two important considerations to address when deciding which costs to capitalize. First, companies can only capitalize costs that are *directly linked* to future benefits. Incidental costs or costs that would be incurred regardless of whether the asset is purchased should not be capitalized. Second, the costs capitalized as an asset can be no greater than the expected future benefits to be derived from use of the asset. This requirement means that if a company reports a $200 asset, we can reasonably expect that it will derive at least $200 in expected future cash inflows from the use and ultimate disposition of the asset.

Sometimes, companies construct assets for their own use rather than purchasing a similar asset from another company. In this case, all of the costs incurred to construct the asset—including materials, labor, and a reasonable amount of overhead—should be included in the cost that is capitalized. In addition, in many cases, a portion of the interest expense incurred during the construction period should also be capitalized as part of the asset's cost. This interest is called **capitalized interest**. Capitalizing some of a company's interest cost as part of the cost of a self-constructed asset reduces interest expense in the current period and increases depreciation expense in future periods when the asset is placed in service.

Once an asset is placed in service, additional costs are often incurred to maintain and improve the asset. Routine repairs and maintenance costs are necessary to realize the full potential benefits of ownership of the asset and should be treated as expenses of the period in which the maintenance is performed. However, if the cost can be considered an *improvement or betterment* of the asset, the cost should be capitalized. An improvement or betterment is an outlay that either enhances the usefulness of the asset or extends the asset's useful life beyond the original expectation.

YOU MAKE THE CALL

You are the Company Accountant Your company has just purchased a plot of land as a building site for an office building. After the purchase, you discover that the building site was once the site of an oil well. Before construction can commence, your company must spend $40,000 to properly cap the oil well and prepare the site to meet current environmental standards. How should you account for the $40,000 cleanup cost? [Answers on page 395]

Depreciation

FYI Depreciation is a systematic allocation of asset cost over the useful life—not a measure of the change in fair value.

Once an asset has been recorded in the balance sheet, the cost must be transferred over time from the balance sheet to the income statement and reported as an expense. The nature of long-term operating assets is that they benefit more than one period. As a consequence, it is impossible to match a specific portion of the cost *directly* to the revenues of a particular period. Accounting principles require that this expense be recognized as equitably as possible over the asset's useful economic life. Therefore, we rely on a *systematic allocation* to assign a portion of the asset's cost to each period benefited. This systematic allocation of cost is called **depreciation**.

The concept of systematic allocation of an asset's cost is important. When depreciation expense is recorded, the reported value of the asset (also called the *book value* or *carrying value*) is reduced. Naturally, it is tempting to infer that the fair value of the asset is lower as a result. However, this reported value does not reflect the fair value of the asset. The fair value of the asset may decline by more or less than the amount of depreciation expense, and can even increase in some periods. Depreciation expense should only be interpreted as an assignment of costs to an accounting period and not a measure of the decline in fair value of the asset.

The amount of cost that is allocated to a given period is recorded as depreciation expense in the income statement with a balancing entry in **accumulated depreciation** in the balance sheet. Accumulated depreciation is a contra-asset account (denoted "XA" in the journal entry). Like all contra-asset accounts, it offsets the balance in the corresponding asset account. To illustrate, assume that Dehning Company purchases a heavy-duty delivery truck for $100,000 and decides to record $18,000 of depreciation expense in the first year of operation. The following entries would be recorded with a cash outflow reflected in the investing section of the statement of cash flows.

The asset would be presented in the balance sheet at period-end at its net book value.

Truck, at cost	$100,000	
Less accumulated depreciation	18,000	
Truck, net	$ 82,000	(Book Value)

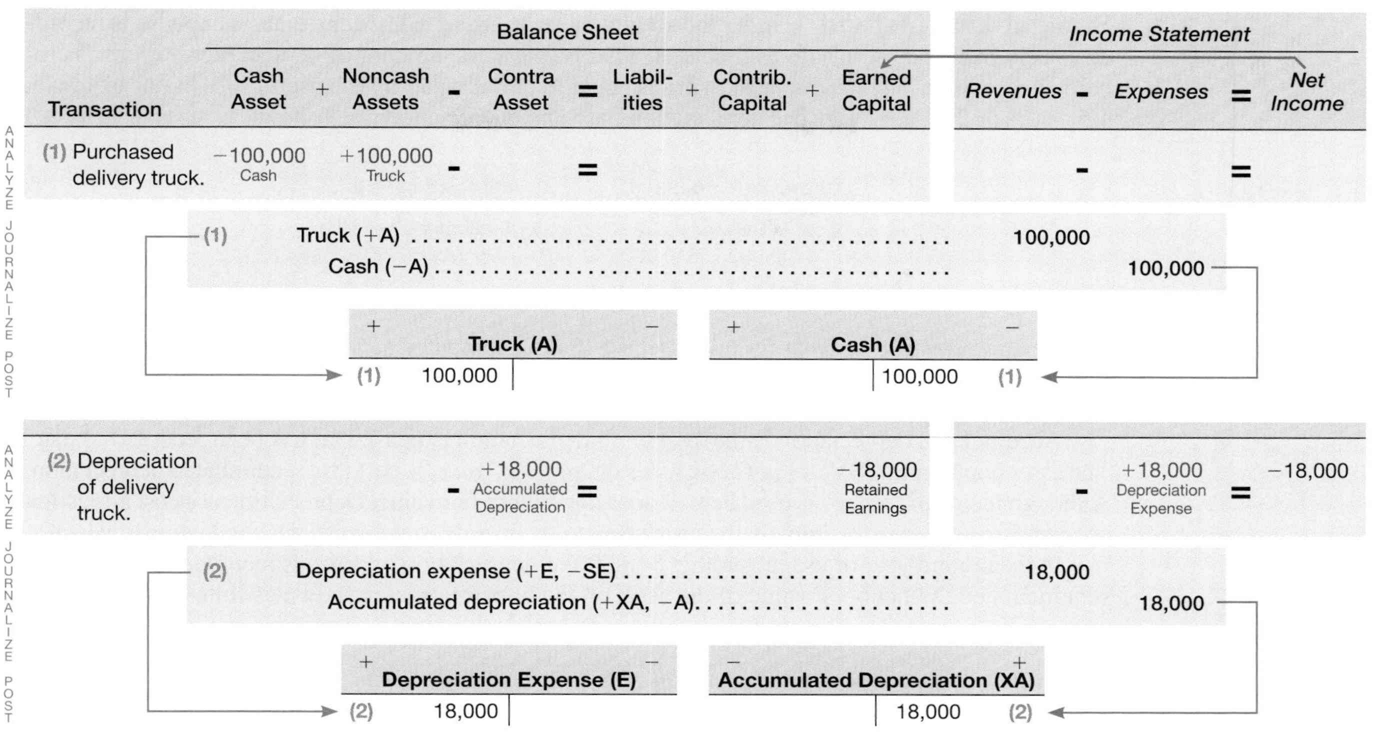

By presenting the information using a contra-asset account, the original acquisition cost of the asset is preserved in the asset account. The net book value of the asset reflects the acquisition cost less the balance in the accumulated depreciation account. The balance in the accumulated depreciation account is the sum of the depreciation expense that has been recorded to date. In **Exhibit 8.1**, Procter & Gamble reports that the original cost of its property, plant, and equipment is $44,427 million and the depreciation accumulated as of June 30, 2014 is $22,123 million. The result is a net book value of $22,304 million.

Depreciation Methods

LO3 Apply different depreciation methods to allocate the cost of assets over time.

Two estimates are required to compute the amount of depreciation expense to record each period.

1. **Useful life**. The useful life is the period of time over which the asset is expected to provide economic benefits to the company. The useful life is not the same as the physical life of the asset. An asset may or may not provide economic benefits to the company for its entire physical life. This useful life should not exceed the period of time that the company intends to use the asset. For example, if a company has a policy of replacing automobiles every two years, the useful life should be set at no longer than two years, even if the automobiles physically last three years or more.
2. **Residual (or salvage) value**. The residual value is the expected realizable value of the asset at the end of its useful life. This value may be the disposal or scrap value, or it may be an estimated resale value for a used asset.

These factors must be estimated when the asset is acquired. The **depreciation base**, also called the *nonrecoverable cost*, is the portion of the cost that is depreciated. The depreciation base is the capitalized cost of the asset less the estimated residual value. This amount is allocated over the useful life of the asset according to the *depreciation method* that the company has selected.

To illustrate alternative depreciation methods, we return to the example presented earlier. Assume that Dehning Company purchases a delivery truck for $100,000. The company expects the truck to last five years and estimates a residual value of $10,000. The depreciation base is $90,000 ($100,000 – $10,000). We illustrate the three most common depreciation methods:

1. Straight-line method
2. Double-declining-balance method
3. Units-of-production method

Straight-Line Method Under the **straight-line method (SL)**, depreciation expense is recorded evenly over the useful life of the asset. That is, the same amount of depreciation expense is recorded each year. The **depreciation rate** is equal to one divided by the useful life. In our example, 1/5 = 0.2 or 20% per year. The depreciation base and depreciation rate follow.

Depreciation Base	Depreciation Rate
Cost − Salvage value = $100,000 − $10,000 = $90,000	1/Estimated useful life = 1/5 years = 20%

Depreciation expense per year for this asset is $18,000, computed as $90,000 × 20%. For the asset's first full year of usage, $18,000 of depreciation expense is reported in the income statement. At the end of that first year the asset is reported on the balance sheet as shown earlier in the chapter.

Accumulated depreciation is the sum of all depreciation expense that has been recorded to date. The asset **book value (BV)**, or *net book value* or *carrying value,* is cost less accumulated depreciation. Although the word "value" is used here, it does not refer to fair value. Depreciation is a cost allocation concept (transfer of costs from the balance sheet to the income statement), not a valuation concept.

In the second year of usage, another $18,000 of depreciation expense is recorded in the income statement and the net book value of the asset on the balance sheet is shown as follows:

Truck, at cost	$100,000
Less accumulated depreciation	36,000
Truck, net	$ 64,000

Accumulated depreciation now includes the sum of the first and second years' depreciation ($36,000), and the net book value of the asset is now reduced to $64,000. After the fifth year, a total of $90,000 of accumulated depreciation will be recorded, yielding a net book value for the truck of $10,000, its estimated salvage value.

Double-Declining-Balance Method GAAP allows companies to use **accelerated depreciation** methods. Accelerated depreciation methods record more depreciation expense in the early years of an asset's useful life and less expense in the later years. The total depreciation expense recorded *over the entire useful life* of the asset is the same as with straight-line depreciation. The only difference is in the amount of depreciation recorded for *any given year*.

The **double-declining-balance (DDB) method** is an accelerated depreciation method that computes the depreciation rate as twice the straight-line rate. This double rate is then multiplied by the net book value of the asset, which declines each period as accumulated depreciation increases. For Dehning Company, the depreciation base and the depreciation rate are computed as follows:

Depreciation Base	Depreciation Rate
Net Book Value = Cost − Accumulated Depreciation	2 × SL rate = 2 × 20% = 40%

FYI When calculating DDB depreciation, the depreciation rate is multiplied by the book value; residual value is not subtracted from book value.

The depreciation expense for the first year of usage for this asset is $40,000, computed as $100,000 × 40%. At the end of the first full year, $40,000 of depreciation expense is reported on the income statement (compared with $18,000 under the SL method), and the asset is reported on the balance sheet as follows:

Truck, at cost	$100,000
Less accumulated depreciation	40,000
Truck, net	$ 60,000

In the second year, $24,000 ($60,000 × 40%) of depreciation expense is reported in the income statement and the net book value of the asset on the balance sheet is shown as follows:

Truck, at cost	$100,000
Less accumulated depreciation	64,000
Truck, net	$ 36,000

The double-declining-balance method continues to record depreciation expense in this manner until the salvage amount is reached, at which point the depreciation process is discontinued. This leaves a net book value equal to the salvage value as with the straight-line method. The DDB depreciation schedule for the life of this asset is illustrated in **Exhibit 8.2**.

EXHIBIT 8.2 Double-Declining-Balance Depreciation Schedule

Year	Book Value at Beginning of Year	Depreciation Expense	Book Value at End of Year
1	$100,000	100,000 × 40% = $40,000	$60,000
2	60,000	60,000 × 40% = 24,000	36,000
3	36,000	36,000 × 40% = 14,400	21,600
4	21,600	21,600 × 40% = 8,640	12,960
5	12,960	12,960 − 10,000 = 2,960*	10,000

*The depreciation expense in the fifth year is not calculated as 40% × $12,960 because the resulting depreciation would reduce the net book value below the $10,000 residual value. Instead, the residual value ($10,000) is subtracted from the remaining book value ($12,960), resulting in depreciation expense of $2,960.

Exhibit 8.3 compares the depreciation expense and net book value for both the SL and DDB methods. During the first two years, the DDB method yields higher depreciation expense in comparison with the SL method. Beginning in the third year, this pattern reverses and the SL method produces higher depreciation expense. Over the asset's life, the same $90,000 in total depreciation expense is recorded, leaving a residual value of $10,000 on the balance sheet under both methods.

EXHIBIT 8.3 Comparison of Straight-Line and Double-Declining-Balance Depreciation

	Straight-Line		Double-Declining-Balance	
Year	Depreciation Expense	Book Value at End of Year	Depreciation Expense	Book Value at End of Year
1	$18,000	$82,000	$40,000	$60,000
2	18,000	64,000	24,000	36,000
3	18,000	46,000	14,400	21,600
4	18,000	28,000	8,640	12,960
5	18,000	10,000	2,960	10,000
	$90,000		$90,000	

All depreciation methods yield the same salvage value

Total depreciation over asset life is identical for all methods

Units-of-Production Method Under the **units-of-production method**, the useful life of the asset is defined in terms of the number of units of service provided by the asset. For instance, this could be the number of units produced, the number of hours that a machine is operated, or, as with Dehning Company's delivery truck, the number of miles driven. To illustrate, assume that Dehning Company estimates that the delivery truck will provide 150,000 miles of service before it is sold for its residual value of $10,000. The depreciation rate is expressed in terms of a cost per mile driven, computed as follows:

$$\frac{\$100{,}000 - \$10{,}000}{150{,}000 \text{ miles}} = \$0.60 \text{ per mile}$$

If the delivery truck is driven 35,000 miles in year 1, the depreciation expense for that year would be $21,000 (35,000 × $0.60). This method produces an amount of depreciation that varies from year to year as the use of the asset varies.

The units-of-production method is used by companies with natural resources such as oil reserves, mineral deposits, or timberlands. These assets are often referred to as **wasting assets**, because the asset is consumed as it is used. The acquisition cost of a natural resource, plus any costs incurred to prepare the asset for its intended use, should be capitalized and reported among PPE assets in the balance sheet.

When the natural resource is used or extracted, inventory is created. The cost of the resource is transferred from the long-term asset account into inventory and, once the inventory is sold, to the income statement as cost of goods sold. The process of transferring costs from the resource account into inventory is called **depletion**.

Depletion is very much like depreciation of tangible operating assets, except that the amount of depletion recorded each period should reflect the amount of the resource that was actually extracted or used up during that period. As a result, depletion is usually calculated using the units-of-production method. The depletion rate is calculated as follows:

$$\textbf{Depletion rate per unit consumed} = \frac{\textbf{Acquisition cost} - \textbf{Residual value}}{\textbf{Estimated quantity of resource available}}$$

The calculation requires an estimate of the quantity of the resource available, which usually requires the assistance of experts, such as geologists or engineers, who are trained to make these determinations.

Depreciation for Tax Purposes Most companies use the straight-line method for financial reporting purposes and an accelerated depreciation method for tax returns.[1] Governments allow accelerated depreciation, in part, to provide incentives for taxpayers to invest. As a result of the differing depreciation methods used for financial accounting and tax purposes, lower depreciation expense (and higher income) is reported for financial accounting purposes early in the life of an asset relative to tax purposes. Even though this difference reverses in later years, companies prefer to defer the tax payments so that the cash savings can be invested to produce earnings. Further, even with the reversal in the later years of an asset's life, if total depreciable assets are growing at a fast enough rate, the additional first-year depreciation on newly acquired assets more than offsets the lower depreciation expense on older assets, yielding a continuing deferral of taxable income and taxes paid. There are other differences between financial reporting and tax reporting that create issues in determining a company's tax expense. In Chapter 10, we explore these differences further and examine deferred tax liabilities and deferred tax assets.

Changes in Accounting Estimates

The estimates required in the depreciation process are made when the asset is acquired. When necessary, companies can, and do, change these estimates during the useful lives of assets. When either the useful life or residual value estimates change, the change is applied prospectively. That is, companies use the new estimates from the date of the change going forward and do not restate the financial statements of prior periods.

To illustrate, assume that, after three years of straight-line depreciation, Dehning Company decided to extend the useful life of its truck from 5 years to 6 years. From **Exhibit 8.3**, the book value of the delivery truck at the end of the third year is \$46,000. The change in estimated useful life would not require a formal accounting entry. Instead, depreciation expense would be recalculated for the remaining three years of the truck's useful life:

$$\frac{\$46,000 - \$10,000}{3 \text{ years}} = \$12,000 \text{ per year}$$

Thus, beginning in year four, depreciation expense of \$12,000 (instead of \$18,000) would be recorded each year.

[1] The IRS mandates the use of MACRS (Modified Accelerated Cost Recovery System) for tax purposes. This method fixes the useful life for various classes of assets, assumes no salvage value, and generally produces depreciation amounts consistent with the double-rate, double-declining-balance method. When a declining balance method is used with zero salvage, the depreciation schedule must switch after the midpoint of the asset's life to straight-line depreciation of the remaining balance over the remaining life.

Asset Sales and Impairments

This section discusses gains and losses from asset sales and computation and disclosure of asset impairments.

LO4 Determine the effects of asset sales and impairments on financial statements.

Gains and Losses on Asset Sales The gain or loss on the sale (disposition) of a long-term asset is computed as follows:

Gain or loss on asset sale = Proceeds from sale − Book value of asset sold

The book (carrying) value of an asset is its acquisition cost less accumulated depreciation. When an asset is sold, its acquisition cost and related accumulated depreciation are removed from the balance sheet and any gain or loss is reported in income from continuing operations. To illustrate such a transaction, assume that Dehning Company decided to sell the delivery truck after four years of straight-line depreciation. From **Exhibit 8.3**, we know that the book value of the truck is $28,000 ($100,000 − $72,000). If the truck is sold for $30,000, the entry to record the sale follows.

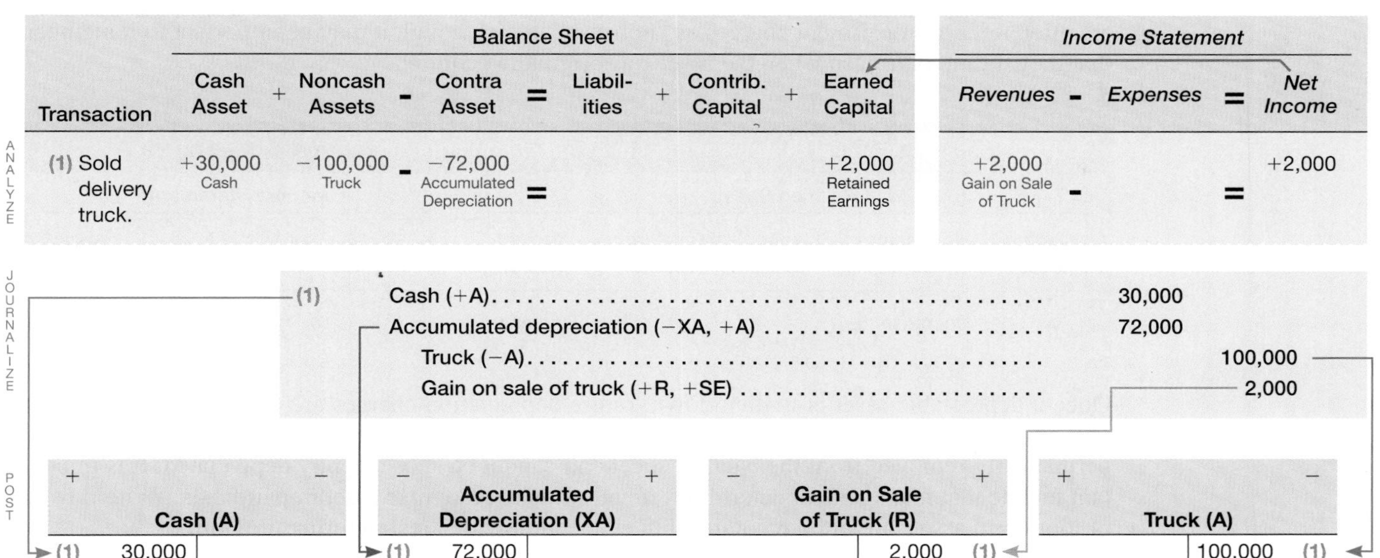

	Balance Sheet													Income Statement				
Transaction	Cash Asset	+	Noncash Assets	−	Contra Asset	=	Liabil-ities	+	Contrib. Capital	+	Earned Capital			Revenues	−	Expenses	=	Net Income
(1) Sold delivery truck.	+30,000 Cash		−100,000 Truck	−	−72,000 Accumulated Depreciation	=					+2,000 Retained Earnings			+2,000 Gain on Sale of Truck	−		=	+2,000

ANALYZE

JOURNALIZE

		Debit	Credit
(1)	Cash (+A)	30,000	
	Accumulated depreciation (−XA, +A)	72,000	
	Truck (−A)		100,000
	Gain on sale of truck (+R, +SE)		2,000

POST

+ Cash (A) −	− Accumulated Depreciation (XA) +	− Gain on Sale of Truck (R) +	+ Truck (A) −
(1) 30,000	(1) 72,000	2,000 (1)	100,000 (1)

Gains and losses on asset sales can be large, and analysts must be aware of these nonrecurring operating income components. Further, if the gains are deemed immaterial, companies often include such gains and losses in general line items of the income statement—often as a component of selling, general and administrative expenses. As described in Chapter 4, the $30,000 increase in cash is an investing cash inflow in the statement of cash flows, and the $2,000 gain would be subtracted from net income in an indirect-method statement of cash flows from operating activities.

Asset Impairments Property, plant, and equipment assets are reported at their net book values (original cost less accumulated depreciation). This is the case even if fair values of these assets increase subsequent to acquisition. As a result, there can be unrecognized gains hidden in the balance sheet.

However, if fair values of PPE assets subsequently decrease—and it can be determined that the asset value is permanently impaired—then companies must recognize losses on those assets. **Impairment** of PPE assets is determined by comparing the sum of *expected* future (undiscounted) cash flows from the asset with its net book value. If these expected cash flows are greater than net book value, no impairment is deemed to exist. However, if the sum of expected cash flows is less than net book value, the asset is deemed impaired and it is written down to its current fair value (generally, the discounted present value of those expected cash flows). **Exhibit 8.4** depicts this impairment analysis.

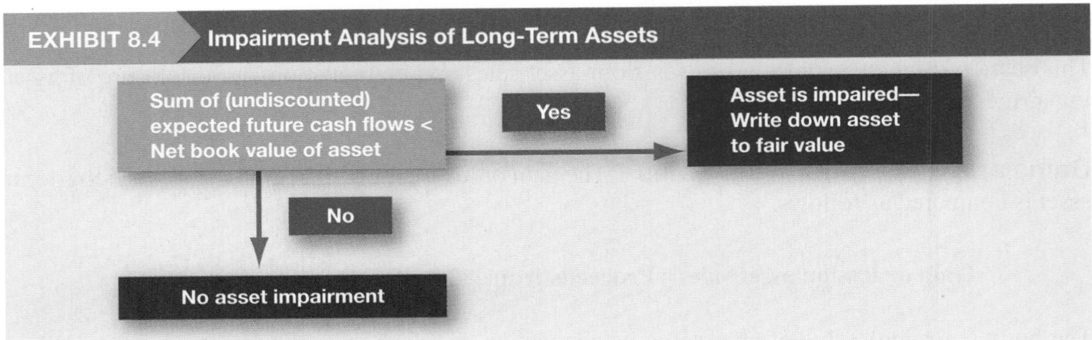

EXHIBIT 8.4 Impairment Analysis of Long-Term Assets

When a company records an impairment charge, assets are reduced by the amount of the write-down and the loss is recognized in the income statement, which reduces current period income. These effects are illustrated in **Exhibit 8.5**. Impairment charges are often included as part of **restructuring costs** along with future costs of workforce reductions. The entry in **Exhibit 8.5** reduces net income, but does not affect current cash flows, so the impairment charges would be added back to net income when reporting an indirect-method cash flows from operating activities. Managers often refer to impairment charges as "noncash" items, though it may be important to remember that they did involve cash when the asset was originally acquired.

EXHIBIT 8.5 Financial Statement Effects of Asset Impairment

Balance Sheet							*Income Statement*				
Cash Asset +	Noncash Assets	=	Liabil-ities +	Contrib. Capital +	Earned Capital		*Revenues*	-	*Expenses*	=	*Net Income*
	Decrease	=			Decrease			-	Increase	=	Decrease

Once a depreciable asset is written down, future depreciation charges are reduced by the amount of the write-down. This result occurs because that portion of the asset's cost that is written down is permanently removed from the balance sheet and cannot be subsequently depreciated. It is important to note that management determines if and when to recognize asset impairments. Write-downs of long-term assets are often recognized in connection with a restructuring program.

Analysis of asset write-downs presents two potential challenges:

1. *Insufficient write-down*. Assets sometimes are impaired to a larger degree than is recognized. This situation can arise if management is overly optimistic about future prospects or is reluctant to recognize the full loss in income. Underestimation of an impairment causes current income to be overstated and income in future years to be lower relative to income that would have been reported had the impairment been correctly recorded.
2. *Aggressive write-down*. This *big bath* scenario can arise if income is currently and severely depressed by recognizing a larger impairment charge than the actual costs. Management's view is that the market will not penalize the firm for an extra write-off, and that doing so purges the balance sheet of costs that would otherwise reduce future years' income. This leads to income being overstated for several years after the write-down.

Neither of these cases is condoned under GAAP. Yet, because management is estimating future cash flows for the impairment test and such estimates are difficult to verify, it has some degree of latitude over the timing and amount of the write-off and can use that discretion to manage reported income.

Footnote Disclosure

Procter & Gamble provides the following information in footnote 1 of its 2014 Annual Report to describe its accounting for PPE assets.

Property, plant, and equipment
Property, plant, and equipment is recorded at cost reduced by accumulated depreciation. Depreciation expense is recognized over the assets' estimated useful lives using the straight-line method.

Machinery and equipment includes office furniture and fixtures (15-year life), computer equipment and capitalized software (3- to 5-year lives) and manufacturing equipment (3- to 20-year lives). Buildings are depreciated over an estimated useful life of 40 years. Estimated useful lives are periodically reviewed and, where appropriate, changes are made prospectively. Where certain events or changes in operating conditions occur, asset lives may be adjusted and an impairment assessment may be performed on the recoverability of the carrying amounts.

The note details P&G's depreciation method (straight-line) and the estimated useful lives of various classes of PPE assets. Later in the notes, the company reports "asset-related costs" included in its restructuring charges of $179 million for the year ended June 30, 2014. The company describes these costs as follows:

Asset-related costs
Asset-related costs consist of both asset write-downs and accelerated depreciation. Asset write-downs relate to the establishment of a new fair value basis for assets held-for-sale or disposal. These assets were written down to the lower of their current carrying basis or amounts expected to be realized upon disposal, less minor disposal costs. Charges for accelerated depreciation relate to long-lived assets that will be taken out of service prior to the end of their normal service period. These assets related primarily to manufacturing consolidations and technology standardization. The asset-related charges will not have a significant impact on future depreciation charges.

Based on other disclosures in the statements, most of the assets held for sale noted above are related to the goodwill and other intangible assets of Pet Care, a business Procter & Gamble is in the process of selling.

A GLOBAL PERSPECTIVE

International Financial Reporting Standards (IFRS) are very similar to U.S. GAAP in the recognition of asset values when acquired and in the depreciation methods allowed. However, IFRS requires that companies recognize depreciation separately on the significant components of an asset. So, a U.S. company that acquires a building might recognize a single asset and depreciate it over the expected useful life of the building. An IFRS company would be required to recognize a bundle of assets like the structure, the roof, the elevators, the HVAC system, etc. Each of these components would be depreciated separately over its expected useful life, generally producing a more accelerated depreciation expense.

One implication of this difference is that subsequent expenditures might be dealt with differently. The U.S. company that replaces the HVAC system after its expected fifteen-year life would classify the expenditure as a maintenance expense. But the IFRS company would have fully depreciated the original HVAC system, and the new system would be treated as a capital expenditure, creating a new asset.

International Financial Reporting Standards for changes in long-term operating asset values have significant differences from U.S. GAAP. IFRS allows companies to report their property, plant, and equipment on a revalued basis. That is, companies may choose to conduct regular appraisals of their property, plant, and equipment and to adjust their balance sheet amounts to those appraised values. Depreciation expense is also adjusted for changes in values. While this option is allowed under IFRS, it appears that the vast majority of companies use historical cost to account for property, plant, and equipment. (IFRS also has provisions for companies operating in hyperinflationary environments.)

For IFRS companies using historical cost, impairment is a single-step process in which an asset's book value is compared to the larger of its value in use (present value of future cash flows) and its net selling price (fair value less cost to sell). If the book value is higher, an impairment is reported. Unlike U.S. GAAP, if an impairment is subsequently recovered, an IFRS company may increase the asset's value to what it would have been without the prior impairment.

RESEARCH INSIGHT

Recent research provides evidence that while IFRS provides a free choice between fair value and historical cost for non-financial assets, most companies using IFRS commit to historical cost accounting for plant and equipment. The evidence is consistent with market demands leading managers to utilize historical cost when the reliability of fair value is lower and when costs of estimating fair value are higher.[2]

ANALYZING FINANCIAL STATEMENTS

Most companies produce their financial performance with their long-term operating assets like property, plant, and equipment and with their intellectual property. Effective use of these assets represents one of the key components of success for companies. In addition, these assets are acquired with the anticipation that they will provide benefits for an extended period of time. They are often expensive relative to their annual benefit, and most of these assets require replenishment on an ongoing basis.

Analysis Objective

We are trying to gauge the effectiveness of Procter & Gamble's use of its physical productive assets.

Analysis Tool PPE Turnover (PPET)

$$\textbf{Turnover (PPET)} = \frac{\textbf{Sales revenue}}{\textbf{Average PPE, net}}$$

Applying the PPE Turnover Ratio to Procter & Gamble

$$2012: \frac{\$83{,}680}{\$20{,}835} = 4.02$$

$$2013: \frac{\$84{,}167}{\$21{,}021.5} = 4.00$$

$$2014: \frac{\$83{,}062}{\$21{,}985} = 3.78$$

Guidance Property, plant, and equipment turnovers vary greatly by industry and are affected by companies' manufacturing strategies, so it is difficult to give specific guidance. In general, a higher ratio is preferred, as it is one significant component of the company's return on assets.

Procter & Gamble in Context

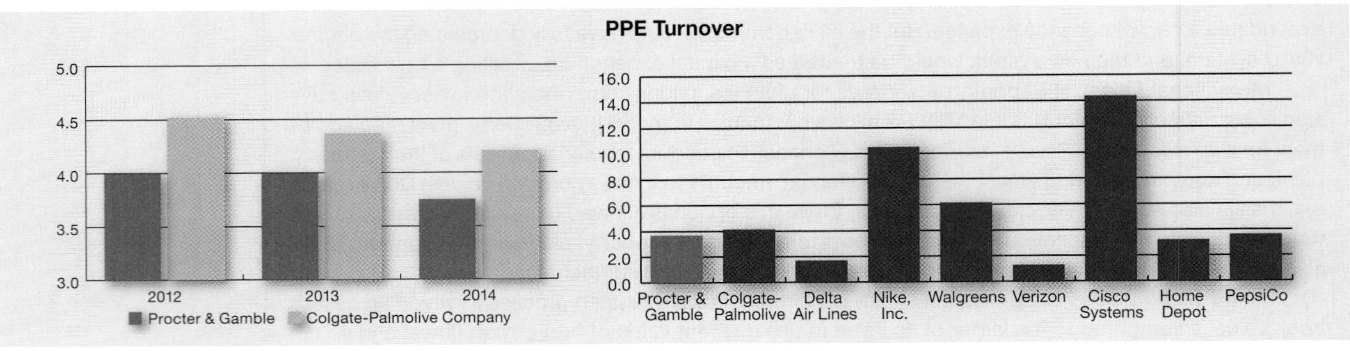

These companies do not have identical fiscal year-ends. Procter & Gamble's year end is June 30, 2014. For the other companies we used financial statements ending as follows: Colgate-Palmolive, Delta, Verizon Communications, and PepsiCo—all December 2014; Nike—May 2014; Walgreens—August 2014; Cisco—July 2014; Home Depot—February 2014.

[2] See Christensen, Hans B., and Valeri V. Nikolaev, "Does fair value accounting for non-financial assets pass the market test?" *Review of Accounting Studies*, September 2013.

Takeaways P&G's fiscal 2014 and 2013 PPET decreased from the value in 2012. Companies prefer that PPET be higher rather than lower, because it implies a lower level of capital investment is required to achieve a given level of sales revenue. P&G's PPET is lower than Colgate-Palmolive, though it is higher than some others in its industry. We can also see that PPET differs considerably by industry—capital-intensive businesses with long-lived assets like Delta Air Lines and Verizon Communications have a low ratio.

Other Considerations Besides effectiveness of asset usage, PPET depends on a number of factors that affect the denominator and that should be taken into account in interpreting the numbers. First, it reflects the company's manufacturing strategy; a company that outsources its production will have a very high PPET, like Nike. Or, a company that has assets that are more fully depreciated will also report a high PPET. In Chapter 12, we discuss how ratios mixing income statement and balance sheet information can be affected by acquisitions of other companies. Finally, we find in Chapter 10 that there are (at the time of this writing) ways for a company to acquire the use of productive resources that do not appear among its assets (e.g., operating leases), increasing the ratio.

Analysis Objective

We are trying to gauge the age of P&G's long-term tangible operating assets relative to their expected useful lives.

Analysis Tool Percent Depreciated

$$\textbf{Percent depreciated} = \frac{\textbf{Accumulated depreciation}}{\textbf{Cost of depreciable assets}}$$

Applying the Percent Depreciated Ratio to Procter & Gamble Accumulated depreciation can be seen in the balance sheet or footnotes. The original cost of depreciable assets can be found in the same places. (See **Exhibit 8.1** for P&G's presentation.) Two types of property, plant, and equipment are not depreciated. Land is one type, and the other is construction in progress. Land is not depreciated because it has an indefinite life, and construction in progress is not depreciated until the constructed asset is placed in service. For P&G, the \$44,427 million original cost of property, plant, and equipment includes \$893 million for land and \$3,114 for construction in progress, which must be removed from the denominator.

$$2012: \frac{\$19{,}856}{(\$40{,}233 - \$2{,}687)} = 54.2\%$$

$$2013: \frac{\$21{,}346}{(\$43{,}012 - \$878 - \$3{,}235)} = 54.9\%$$

$$2014: \frac{\$22{,}123}{(\$44{,}427 - \$893 - \$3{,}114)} = 54.7\%$$

Guidance Percent depreciated depends on a company's age and on the occurrence of disruptive technological shifts in products and production methods. A new company will have a lower ratio, as will a company that has just made substantial investments in new productive facilities. A high ratio could mean that a company's productive resources are nearing the end of their useful lives and that substantial investments will be required in the near future.[3]

[3] Some companies do not provide complete disclosure for this computation. For example, Cisco Systems combines land and buildings in one line item and thus, an external reader of the statements cannot subtract the book value of land from the denominator to compute the percent depreciated accurately.

Procter & Gamble in Context

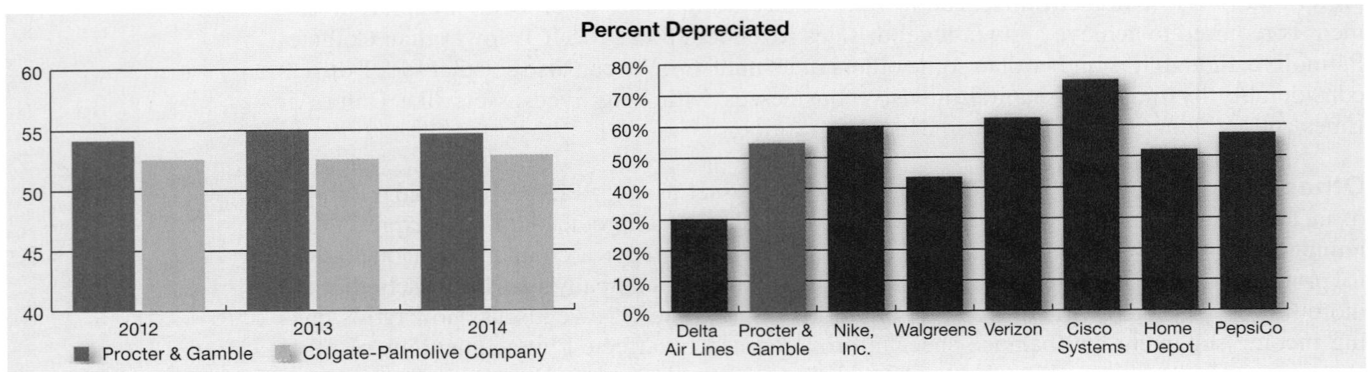

Takeaways Both Procter & Gamble and Colgate-Palmolive are mature companies experiencing long-term steady growth. They acquire assets on a continuing basis and, as a result, they have some assets that are brand-new and others that are reaching the end of their productive lives. The net result is that the percent depreciated ratio is approximately 50% to 55% for both companies.

Other Considerations Companies' percent depreciated ratio may differ because they are using different depreciation methods (straight-line or accelerated) or because they have chosen different useful lives for their assets. For instance, one airline depreciates its aircraft over twenty-five years to zero salvage value, while another depreciates its aircraft over fifteen years to ten percent salvage. A percent depreciated ratio of 50% for the first company would mean its average aircraft is 12.5 years old, while the same 50% ratio would imply aircraft that was 8.3 years old for the second company. As a result, it is always advisable to check companies' footnotes to make sure that the ratios are interpreted correctly.

BUSINESS INSIGHT

Federal authorities arrested **WorldCom, Inc.**'s CEO, Bernie Ebbers, and chief financial officer, Scott Sullivan, in August 2002 for allegedly conspiring to alter the telecommunications giant's financial statements to meet analyst expectations. They were accused of *cooking the books* so the company would not show a loss for 2001 and subsequent quarters.

Specifically, WorldCom incurred large costs in anticipation of an increase in Internet-related business that did not materialize. The executives shifted these costs to the balance sheet and recorded them as PPE, thereby inflating current profitability. By capitalizing these costs (moving them from the income statement to the balance sheet), WorldCom was able to disguise these costs as an asset to be allocated as future costs. Contrary to WorldCom's usual practices and prevailing accounting principles, no support existed for capitalization.

Although the WorldCom case also involved alleged fraud, an astute analyst would have suspected something was amiss from analysis of WorldCom's property, plant, and equipment turnover (Sales/Average property, plant, and equipment) as shown below. The decline in turnover reveals that its assets constituted an ever-increasing percent of total sales during 1995 to 2002, by quarter. This finding does not, in itself, imply fraud. It does, however, raise serious questions that should have been answered by WorldCom executives in meetings with analysts.

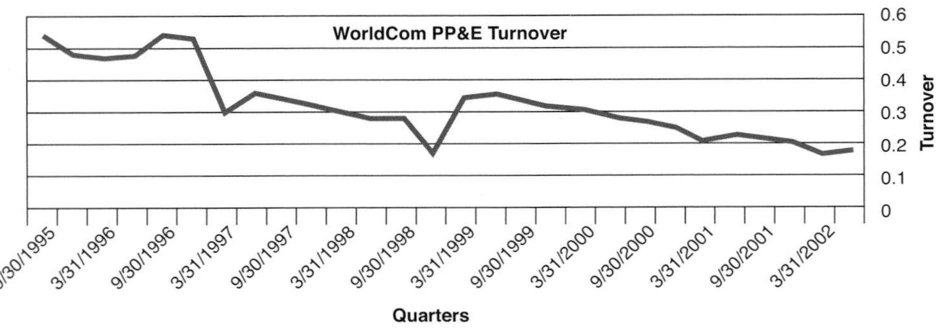

Cash Flow Effects

When cash is involved in the acquisition of plant or equipment, the cash amount is reported as a use of cash in the investment section of the statement of cash flows as discussed in Chapter 4. Any cash received from asset sales is reported as a source of cash. The investing section of Procter & Gamble's 2014 annual report is shown below.

($ millions)	2014	2013	2012
Investing activities			
Capital expenditures	$(3,848)	$(4,008)	$(3,964)
Proceeds from asset sales	570	584	2,893
Acquisitions, net of cash acquired	(24)	(1,145)	(134)
Purchase of available-for-sale investment securities	(568)	(1,605)	—
Proceeds from sales of available-for-sale investment securities	24	—	—
Change in investments	(261)	(121)	112
Total investing activities	$(4,107)	$(6,295)	$(1,093)

In 2014, P&G paid cash of $3,848 million to acquire plant assets and received cash of $570 million on the disposal of plant and equipment. Losses (gains) on these disposal transactions would be added (subtracted) as adjustments in the operating section. Acquisitions of other companies was small in terms of cash outlays in 2014 but in the year ended June 2013 constituted 18% of P&G's net investing activities.

For the Dehning Company delivery truck sale described earlier in this chapter, the investing section of the cash flow statement would show $30,000 of cash proceeds. The gain on the sale would be subtracted from net income in the operating section. No receivable was involved in the sale.

YOU MAKE THE CALL

You are the Division Manager You are the division manager for a main operating division of your company. You are concerned that a declining PPE turnover is adversely affecting your division's profitability. What specific actions can you take to increase PPE turnover? [Answers on page 395]

MID-CHAPTER REVIEW

GuidedExamples MBC

On January 2, Lev Company purchases equipment for use in fabrication of a part for one of its key products. The equipment costs $95,000, and its estimated useful life is five years, after which it is expected to be sold for $10,000.

REQUIRED

1. Compute depreciation expense for each year of the equipment's useful life for each of the following depreciation methods:
   a. Straight-line
   b. Double-declining-balance
2. Assume that Lev Company uses the straight-line depreciation method. Show the effects of these entries on the balance sheet and the income statement using the financial statement effects template. Prepare journal entries to record the initial purchase of the equipment on January 2 and the year-end depreciation adjustment on December 31, and post the journal entries to T-accounts.
3. Show how the equipment is reported on Lev's balance sheet at the end of the third year assuming straight-line depreciation.
4. Assume that this is the only depreciable asset the company owns and that it uses straight-line depreciation. Using the depreciation expense computed in 1*a* and the balance sheet presentation from *3*, estimate the percent depreciated for this asset at the end of the third year.

The solution to this review problem can be found on pages 409–410.

INTANGIBLE ASSETS

5

LO5 Describe the accounting and reporting for intangible assets.

Intangible assets are assets that lack physical substance but provide future benefits to the owner in the form of specific property rights or legal rights. For many companies, these assets have become an important source of competitive advantage and company value.

For financial accounting purposes, intangible assets are classified as either *separately transferable or not separately transferable*. *Separately transferable* intangible assets generally fall into one of two categories. The first category is assets that are the product of contractual or other legal rights. These intangibles include patents, trademarks, copyrights, franchises, license agreements, broadcast rights, mineral rights, and noncompetition agreements. The second category of separately transferable intangible assets includes benefits that are not contractually or legally defined, but can be separated from the company and sold, transferred, or exchanged. Examples include customer lists, unpatented technology, formulas, processes, and databases. There are also intangible assets that are not separately transferable, primarily goodwill. Procter & Gamble reports its intangible assets on its 2014 balance sheet in just two categories ($ in millions): Goodwill $53,704; Trademarks and Other Intangible Assets $30,843. The majority of these assets resulted from the acquisition of **The Gillette Company**.

The issues involved in reporting intangible assets are conceptually similar to those of accounting for property, plant, and equipment. We must first decide which costs to capitalize and then we need to determine how and when those costs will be transferred to the income statement. However, intangible assets often pose a particularly difficult problem for accountants. This problem arises because the benefits provided by these assets are often uncertain and difficult to quantify. In addition, the useful life of an intangible asset is often impossible to estimate with confidence.

As was the case with property, plant, and equipment, intangible assets are either purchased from another individual or company or internally developed. Like PPE assets, the cost of purchased intangible assets is capitalized. Unlike PPE assets, though, we generally do not capitalize the cost of internally developed intangible assets. Research and development (R&D) costs, and the patents and technologies that are created as a result of R&D, serve as useful examples.

Research and Development Costs

R&D activities are a major expenditure for most companies, especially for those in technology and pharmaceutical industries where R&D expenses can exceed 10% of revenues. These expenses include employment costs for R&D personnel, R&D-related contract services, and R&D plant asset costs.

Companies invest millions of dollars in R&D because they expect that the future benefits resulting from these activities will eventually exceed the costs. Successful R&D activities create new products that can be sold and new technologies that can be utilized to create and sustain a competitive advantage. Unfortunately, only a fraction of R&D projects reach commercial production, and it is difficult to predict which projects will be successful. Moreover, it is often difficult to predict when the benefits will be realized, even if the project is successful.

Because of the uncertainty surrounding the benefits of R&D, accounting for R&D activities follows a uniform method—*immediate recognition as an expense*. This approach applies to all R&D costs incurred prior to the start of commercial production, including the salaries and wages of personnel engaged in R&D activities, the cost of materials and supplies, and the equipment and facilities used in the project. Should any of the R&D activities prove successful, the benefits should result in higher net income in future periods. Costs incurred internally to develop new software products do not satisfy the capitalization requirement of providing expected future profits until the technological feasibility of the product is established. Therefore, until the feasibility requirement can be met, these costs are expensed.

If equipment and facilities are purchased for a specific R&D project, and have no other use, their cost is expensed immediately even though their useful life would typically extend beyond the current period. The expensing of R&D equipment and facilities is in stark contrast to the capitalization-and-depreciation of non-R&D plant assets. The expensing of R&D plant assets is mandated unless those assets have alternative future uses (in other R&D projects or otherwise). For example, a general research facility housing multi-use lab equipment should be capitalized and depreciated like any other depreciable asset. However, project-directed research buildings and equipment with no alternate uses must be expensed.

BUSINESS INSIGHT

R&D Costs at Cisco Systems Cisco spends between $5 billion and $6.5 billion annually for R&D compared with its revenues of around $45–$50 billion, or about 12%–14%. This level reflects a high percent of revenues devoted to R&D in comparison with nontechnology companies, but typifies companies that compete in the high-tech arena. Following is the R&D-expense-to-sales ratio (also called *R&D Intensity*) for Cisco and some related companies.

	2014	2013	2012
Cisco Systems, Inc.	13.4%	12.2%	11.9%
Juniper Networks, Inc.	21.7%	22.3%	25.2%
Telefonaktiebolaget LM Ericsson	15.9%	14.2%	14.4%
Alcatel Lucent SA	16.8%	16.4%	16.1%
Hewlett-Packard Company	3.1%	2.8%	2.8%

RESEARCH INSIGHT

Research has provided evidence consistent with managers reducing R&D spending when trying to meet certain earnings targets or other earnings goals. Part of this is due to the accounting—research and development costs are expensed immediately reducing reported earnings in the current period. Thus, although the research and development spending should provide better future performance, it harms current performance leading "myopic" managers to cut back.[4] Recent research also suggests that some firms do not disclose research spending even when it appears that they must have such costs. One theory is that these firms do not want to disclose their research and development spending in order to hide the extent of their costs from their competitors.[5]

Patents

Successful research and development activity often leads a company to obtain a **patent** for its discoveries. A patent is an exclusive right to produce a product or use a technology. Patents are granted to protect the inventor of the new product or technology by preventing other companies from copying the innovation. The fair value of a patent depends on the commercial success of the product or technology. For example, a patent on the formula for a new drug to treat diabetes could be worth billions of dollars.

If a patent is purchased from the inventor, the purchase price is capitalized and reported in the balance sheet as an intangible asset. On the other hand, if the patent is developed internally, only the legal costs and registration fees are capitalized. The R&D cost to develop the new product or technology is expensed as incurred. This accounting illustrates the marked difference between purchased and internally created intangible assets.

Copyrights

A copyright is an exclusive right granted by the government to an individual author, composer, play writer, or similar individual for the life of the creator plus 70 years. Corporations can also obtain a copyright for varying periods set by law. Copyrights, like patents, can be acquired. The acquisition cost would be capitalized and amortized over the expected remaining economic life.

Trademarks

A **trademark** is a registered name, logo, package design, image, jingle, or slogan that is associated with a product. Many trademarks are easily recognizable, such as the **Nike** "swoosh," the shape of a **Coca-Cola** bottle, **McDonald's** golden arches, and the musical tones played in computer advertisements featuring **Intel** computer chips. Companies spend millions of dollars developing and

[4] See Bushee, Brian, "The Influence of Institutional Investors on Myopic R&D Investment Behavior." *Accounting Review*, 1998; Graham, John R., Cam Harvey and Shiva Rajgopal, "The Economic Implications of Corporate Financial Reporting." *Journal of Accounting and Economics*, 2005; and Sloan, Richard and P. Dechow. "Executive Incentives and the Horizon Problem: An Empirical Investigation," *Journal of Accounting and Economics*, 1991, for examples of research on this topic.

[5] See Koh, P.S., and D. M. Reeb. "Missing R&D". *Journal of Accounting and Economics*, Forthcoming.

protecting trademarks and their value is enhanced by advertising programs that increase their recognition. If a trademark is purchased from another company, the purchase price is capitalized. However, the cost of internally developed trademarks is expensed as incurred. Likewise, all advertising costs are expensed immediately, even if the value of a trademark is enhanced by the advertisement. For these reasons, many trademarks are not presented in the balance sheet.

BUSINESS INSIGHT

Trademarks and Patents at P&G Procter & Gamble has acquired many of the products it currently markets to consumers. Others were developed internally. The following paragraph from the Management Discussion and Analysis section of P&G's 2014 annual report emphasizes the importance of these intangible assets to the company.

> ***Ability to Achieve Business Plans.*** We are a consumer products company and rely on continued demand for our brands and products. To achieve business goals, we must develop and sell products that appeal to consumers and retail trade customers. Our continued success is dependent on innovation with respect to both products and operations and on the continued positive reputations of our brands. This means we must be able to obtain and maintain patents and trademarks and respond to technological advances and patents granted to competition. Our success is also dependent on effective sales, advertising and marketing programs in a more fast-paced and rapidly changing environment.

Franchise Rights

A **franchise** is a contractual agreement that gives a company the right to operate a particular business in an area for a particular period of time. For example, a franchise may give the owner the right to operate a number of fast-food restaurants in a particular geographic region for twenty years. *Operating rights* and *licenses* are similar to franchise rights, except that they are typically granted by government agencies. Most franchise rights are purchased and, as a result, the purchase price should be capitalized and presented as an intangible asset in the balance sheet.

Amortization and Impairment of Identifiable Intangible Assets

When intangible assets are acquired and capitalized, a determination must be made as to whether the asset has a **definite life**. Examples of intangible assets with definite lives include patents and franchise rights. An intangible asset with a definite life must be *amortized* over the expected useful life of the asset. **Amortization** is the systematic allocation of the cost of an intangible asset to the periods benefited, similar to depreciation of tangible assets.

Amortization expense is generally recorded using the straight-line method. The expense is included in the income statement as a component of operating income, and is often included among selling, general and administrative expenses. The cost of the intangible asset is presented in the balance sheet net of accumulated amortization.

Amortization To illustrate, assume that Landsman Company spent $100,000 in early 2016 to purchase a patent. The entry to record the capitalization of this cost follows.

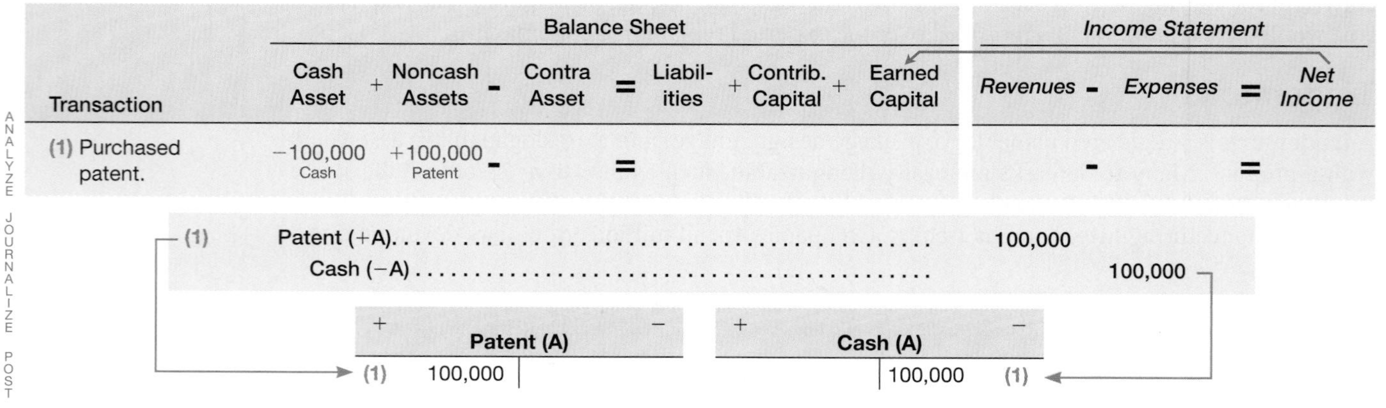

Transaction	Cash Asset	+	Noncash Assets	−	Contra Asset	=	Liabilities	+	Contrib. Capital	+	Earned Capital	Revenues	−	Expenses	=	Net Income
(1) Purchased patent.	−100,000 Cash		+100,000 Patent	−		=							−		=	

ANALYZE

JOURNALIZE

		Dr.	Cr.
(1)	Patent (+A)	100,000	
	Cash (−A)		100,000

POST

+ Patent (A) −		+ Cash (A) −	
(1) 100,000			100,000 (1)

Although the patent had a remaining legal life of 12 years, Landsman estimated that the useful life of the patent was 5 years. Thus the intangible asset has a definite life. The entry to record the annual amortization expense at the end of 2016 follows.

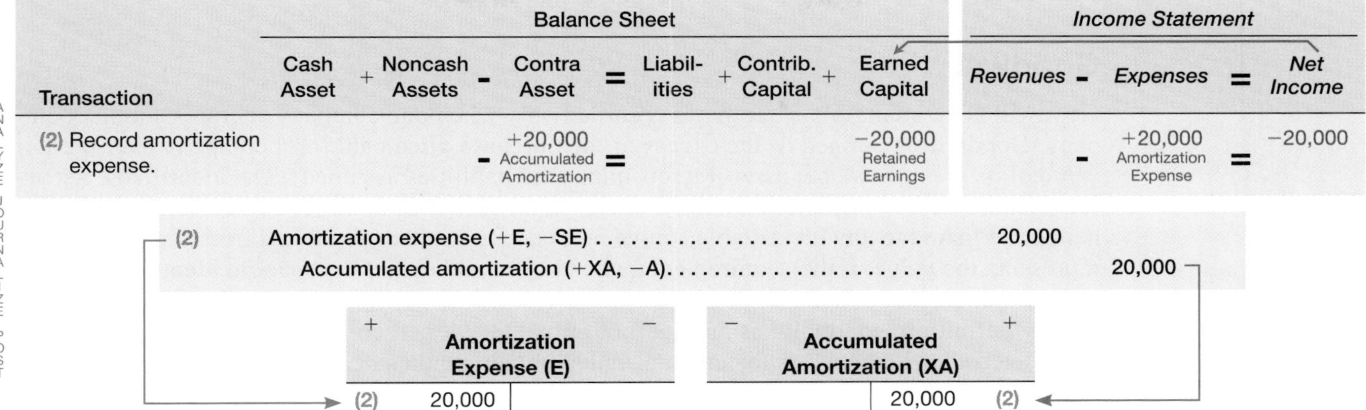

Transaction	Cash Asset	+ Noncash Assets	− Contra Asset	= Liabilities	+ Contrib. Capital	+ Earned Capital	Revenues	− Expenses	= Net Income
(2) Record amortization expense.			+20,000 Accumulated Amortization			−20,000 Retained Earnings		+20,000 Amortization Expense	−20,000

		Debit	Credit
(2)	Amortization expense (+E, −SE)	20,000	
	Accumulated amortization (+XA, −A)		20,000

Amortization Expense (E): (2) 20,000 (debit)

Accumulated Amortization (XA): 20,000 (2) (credit)

Impairment Some transferable intangible assets, such as some trademarks, have indefinite lives. For these assets, the expected useful life extends far enough into the future that it is impossible for management to estimate a useful life. An intangible asset with an indefinite life should not be amortized until the useful life of the asset can be specified. That is, no expense is recorded until management can reasonably estimate the useful life of the asset.

Although intangible assets with indefinite lives are not subject to amortization, they must be tested annually to determine if their value has been impaired. The impairment test for intangibles is slightly different from the impairment test used to evaluate PPE assets. The intangible asset is impaired if the book value of the asset exceeds its fair value and the write-down is equal to the difference between the book value and the fair value.

To illustrate, assume that Norell Company purchased a trademark in 2014 for $240,000 and determined that the intangible asset had an indefinite life. The entry to record the purchase of the trademark follows.

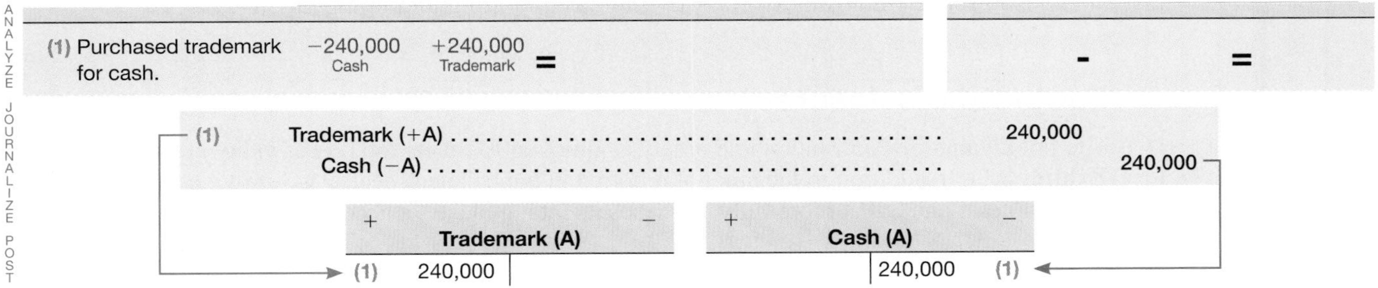

Transaction	Cash Asset	+ Noncash Assets	− Contra Asset	= Liabilities	+ Contrib. Capital	+ Earned Capital	Revenues	− Expenses	= Net Income
(1) Purchased trademark for cash.	−240,000 Cash	+240,000 Trademark							

		Debit	Credit
(1)	Trademark (+A)	240,000	
	Cash (−A)		240,000

Trademark (A): (1) 240,000 (debit)

Cash (A): 240,000 (1) (credit)

In 2017, changes in regulations caused Norell to conclude that the value of the trademark had been impaired. They estimated the current fair value was $100,000, resulting in a loss of $140,000 ($240,000 – $100,000). The entry to record the impairment of the trademark would be as follows.

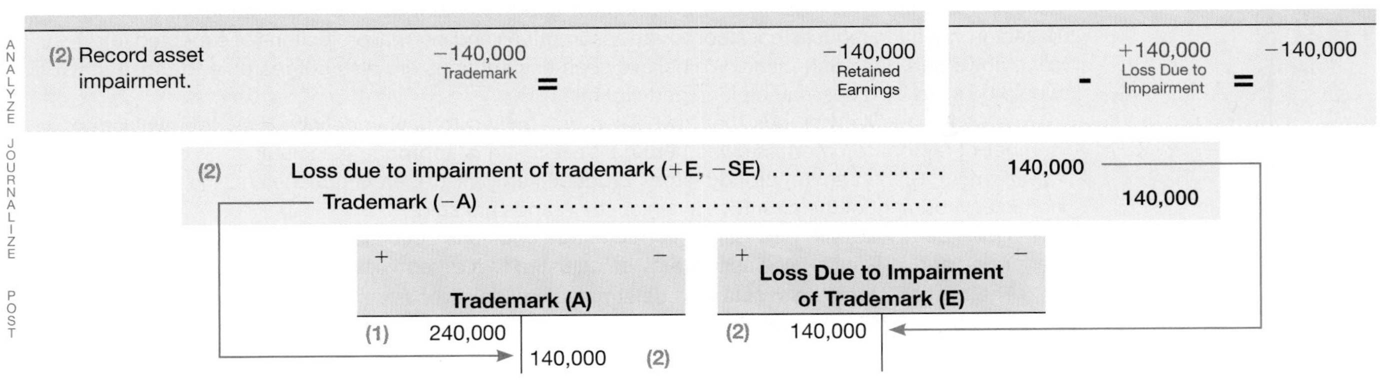

Transaction	Cash Asset	+ Noncash Assets	− Contra Asset	= Liabilities	+ Contrib. Capital	+ Earned Capital	Revenues	− Expenses	= Net Income
(2) Record asset impairment.		−140,000 Trademark				−140,000 Retained Earnings		+140,000 Loss Due to Impairment	−140,000

		Debit	Credit
(2)	Loss due to impairment of trademark (+E, −SE)	140,000	
	Trademark (−A)		140,000

Trademark (A): (1) 240,000 (debit); 140,000 (2) (credit)

Loss Due to Impairment of Trademark (E): (2) 140,000 (debit)

If the value of the trademark subsequently decreases further, additional impairment losses would be recorded. However, increases in the fair value of the asset would not be recorded. Furthermore, if, at any time, Norell determined that the trademark had a definite life, the company would begin amortizing the remaining value over the remaining estimated life.

Goodwill

Goodwill is an intangible asset that is recorded only when one company acquires another company. **Goodwill** is defined as the excess of the purchase price paid for a company over the fair value of its *identifiable* net assets (assets minus the liabilities assumed). The identifiable net assets include any *identifiable intangible assets* acquired in the purchase. Therefore, goodwill can neither be linked to any identifiable source, nor can it be sold or separated from the company. It represents the value of the acquired company above and beyond the specific identifiable assets listed on the balance sheet.

By definition, goodwill has an indefinite life. Once it is recorded in the balance sheet, it is not amortized. Instead, it is subject to an annual impairment test. Goodwill is impaired when the fair value of the acquired business (more specifically, any testable reporting unit) is less than the recorded book value. If this occurs, goodwill is written down to an imputed value. The goodwill write-down (also called a goodwill write-off) results in the immediate transfer of some or all of a company's goodwill book value from the balance sheet to the income statement as an expense. The book value of goodwill is immediately reduced and a corresponding expense is reported in the income statement. Like the impairment write-down of tangible assets, the write-down of goodwill is a discretionary expense whose amount and timing are largely determined by management (with auditor acceptance).

It is commonplace to see goodwill impairment write-downs related to unsuccessful acquisitions, particularly those from the acquisition boom of the late 1990s and the recent recession of 2008–2009. Goodwill write-downs usually represent material amounts. For example, **Time Warner Inc.** wrote off $54 billion of goodwill in the second quarter of 2002, which arose from the $106 billion merger of AOL and Time-Warner. This write-off exceeded the *total revenues* of 483 of the Fortune 500 companies (*Fortune*, 2002). Goodwill write-downs are usually nonrecurring, but are typically reported by companies in income from continuing operations. For analysis purpose we normally classify them as operating and nonrecurring.

Footnote Disclosures

The book value of P&G intangible assets is almost 60% of its total asset value in 2014 (refer to **Exhibit 8.1**). In addition to the amount reported in the balance sheet, P&G provides the following in footnotes 1 and 2 that more fully describes its intangible asset accounting.

Note 1: Summary of Significant Accounting Policies—
Goodwill and Other Intangible Assets

Goodwill and indefinite-lived intangible assets are not amortized, but are evaluated for impairment annually or more often if indicators of a potential impairment are present. Our annual impairment testing of goodwill is performed separately from our impairment testing of indefinite-lived intangible assets. The annual evaluation for impairment of goodwill and indefinite-lived intangible assets is based on valuation models that incorporate assumptions and internal projections of expected future cash flows and operating plans. We believe such assumptions are also comparable to those that would be used by other marketplace participants.

We have acquired brands that have been determined to have indefinite lives. We evaluate a number of factors to determine whether an indefinite life is appropriate, including the competitive environment, market share, brand history, product life cycles, operating plans and the macroeconomic environment of the countries in which the brands are sold.

When certain events or changes in operating conditions occur, an impairment assessment is performed and indefinite-lived assets may be adjusted to a determinable life.

The cost of intangible assets with determinable useful lives is amortized to reflect the pattern of economic benefits consumed, either on a straight-line or accelerated basis over the estimated periods benefited. Patents, technology and other intangible assets with contractual terms are generally amortized over their respective legal or contractual lives. Customer relationships, brands and other non-contractual intangible assets with determinable lives are amortized over periods generally ranging from 5 to 30 years. When certain events or changes in operating conditions occur, an impairment assessment is performed and remaining lives of intangible assets with determinable lives may be adjusted.

Procter & Gamble's largest intangible is goodwill ($53.7 billion). The acquisition of Gillette in 2006 resulted in the recognition of $35.3 billion of goodwill, some of which remains as part of goodwill currently on the balance sheet. P&G paid $53.4 billion for Gillette upon acquisition in 2006, and at the time allocated $29.7 billion to other intangibles.

Note 2: Goodwill and Intangible Assets
Identifiable intangible assets were comprised of:

	2014		2013	
	Gross Carrying Amount	**Accumulated Depreciation**	**Gross Carrying Amount**	**Accumulated Depreciation**
Intangible assets with determinable lives				
Brands	$ 4,154	$(2,205)	$ 4,251	$(2,020)
Patents and technology	2,850	(2,082)	2,976	(2,032)
Customer relationships	2,002	(763)	2,118	(703)
Other.	355	(164)	348	(168)
Total	9,361	(5,214)	9,693	(4,923)
Brands with indefinite lives. . . .	26,696	—	26,802	—
Total	$36,057	$(5,214)	$36,495	$(4,923)

There are two observations that we can make from the above disclosures. First, P&G has purchased a significant amount of intangible assets by acquiring other companies. We can infer this from the large amount of goodwill assets reported in the balance sheet ($53.7 billion). Second, most of P&G's identifiable intangible assets are trademarks and most have indefinite lives. Hence, we might expect that the amount of amortization expense in any given year would be small, as indicated by the total in the above table. However, goodwill impairment write-offs could be substantial in any given year.

Analysis Implications

LO6 Analyze the effects of tangible and intangible assets on key performance measures.

6

Because internally generated intangible assets are not capitalized, an important component of a company's assets is potentially hidden from users of the financial statements. Moreover, differential treatment of purchased and internally created assets makes it difficult to compare companies. If one company generates its patents and trademarks internally, while another company purchases these intangibles, their balance sheets can differ dramatically, even if the two companies are otherwise very similar.

These hidden intangible assets can distort our analysis of the financial statements. For example, when a company expenses R&D costs, especially R&D equipment and facilities that can potentially benefit more than one period, both the income statement and balance sheet are distorted. Net income, assets, and stockholders' equity are all understated.

The income statement effects may be small if a company regularly purchases R&D assets and the amount of purchases is relatively constant from year to year. Specifically, after the average useful life is reached, say in 5 to 10 years, the expensing of current-year purchases will be approximately the same as the depreciation that would have been reported had the assets been capitalized. Thus, the income statement effect is mitigated. However, the recorded assets and equity are still understated. This accounting produces an upward bias in asset turnover ratios and ROE.

Finally, the statement of cash flows is also affected by the manner in which a company acquires its intellectual assets. A company that generates its patents and trademarks internally recognizes the expenditures as part of cash flow from operating activities. However, a company that purchases its patents and trademarks from an independent party or through acquisitions recognizes the expenditures as part of cash flow from investing activities.

A GLOBAL PERSPECTIVE

Under International Financial Reporting Standards, development costs can be capitalized as intangible assets when specific criteria are met. For instance, the company must be able to demonstrate that it has the ability and the intention to complete the development process and to produce an intangible asset that will generate future benefits through use or sale.

Here is an example from GlaxoSmithKline plc's footnotes:

> **Research and development**
> Research and development expenditure is charged to the income statement in the period in which it is incurred. Development expenditure is capitalised when the criteria for recognising an asset are met, usually when a regulatory filing has been made in a major market and approval is considered highly probable. Property, plant, and equipment used for research and development is capitalised and depreciated in accordance with the Group's policy.

Under IFRS, similar to under U.S. GAAP, goodwill must be periodically evaluated for impairment. The overall concepts are very similar between IFRS and GAAP but the details differ. For example, under IFRS companies are required to compare the recoverable amount (defined as the higher of the fair value or value-in-use) of a cash-generating unit to the carrying value of that unit to determine an impairment loss. Just as under U.S. GAAP, once impaired, goodwill cannot be revalued upward. Although, note that this is different from the treatment of PPE under IFRS, as discussed earlier in the chapter.

CHAPTER-END REVIEW

In 2016, Bowen Company's R&D department developed a new production process that significantly reduced the time and cost required to manufacture its product. R&D costs were $120,000. The process was patented on July 1, 2016. Legal costs and fees to acquire the patent totalled $12,500. Bowen estimated the useful life of the patent at 10 years.

On July 1, 2018, Bowen sold the nonexclusive right to use the new process to Kennedy Company for $90,000. Because Bowen retained the patent, the agreement allows Kennedy to use, but not sell, the new technology for a period of 5 years. Both Bowen Company and Kennedy Company have December 31 fiscal years.

On July 1, 2020, another competitor obtained a patent on a new process that made Bowen's patent obsolete.

Required

1. How should Bowen Company account for the R&D costs and legal costs incurred to obtain the patent? Show the effects of these entries using the financial statement effects template, prepare the appropriate journal entries necessary to account for the costs incurred in 2016, and post the entries to T-accounts.
2. What amount of amortization expense would Bowen record each year? Show the effects of these transactions using the financial statement effects template, prepare a journal entry to record amortization expense on December 31, 2016, and post the entries to T-accounts.
3. How would Kennedy Company record the acquisition of the rights to use the new technology? Show the effects of this transaction using the financial statement effects template, prepare a journal entry to record the purchase of the technology rights, and post the entry to T-accounts.
4. What effect would the new patent registered by the other competitor have on Bowen Company? On Kennedy Company? Show the effects of this transaction using the financial statement effects template, prepare a journal entry to record the impairment loss for Kennedy Company, and post the entry to T-accounts.

The solution to this review problem can be found on pages 410–411.

SUMMARY

Describe and distinguish between tangible and intangible assets. (p. 374) LO1

- Tangible assets, including land, buildings, machinery, and equipment are assets with physical substance and are usually classified as property, plant, and equipment.
- Intangible assets are long-term assets lacking in physical substance, such as patents, trademarks, franchise rights and goodwill.

Determine which costs to capitalize and report as assets and which costs to expense. (p. 375) LO2

- All costs incurred to acquire an asset and prepare it for its intended use should be capitalized and reported in the balance sheet.
- The cost of self-constructed assets should include all costs incurred during construction, including the interest cost of financing the construction.

Apply different depreciation methods to allocate the cost of assets over time. (p. 377) LO3

- Depreciation methods generally fall into three categories:
  (1) Straight-line depreciation
  (2) Accelerated depreciation, such as the double-declining-balance method
  (3) Units-of-production method

Determine the effects of asset sales and impairments on financial statements. (p. 381) LO4

- The sale of a long-term asset will result in a gain or loss if the proceeds from the sale are greater than or less than the book value of the asset.
- If the expected benefits (undiscounted cash flows) derived from an asset fall below its book value, the asset is impaired and should be written down to fair value.

Describe the accounting and reporting for intangible assets. (p. 388) LO5

- For the most part, internally generated intangible assets are not recognized in the balance sheet.
- Intangible assets purchased from other companies are capitalized and presented separately in the balance sheet.
- Intangible assets with definite lives are amortized using the straight-line method.
- Intangible assets with indefinite lives are not amortized.

Analyze the effects of tangible and intangible assets on key performance measures. (p. 393) LO6

- PPE turnover and long-term asset turnover ratios provide insights into the capital intensity of a company and how efficiently the company is utilizing these investments.
- The ratio of accumulated depreciation divided by the cost of depreciable assets measures the percent depreciated.

GUIDANCE ANSWERS . . . YOU MAKE THE CALL

You are the Company Accountant Any cost that is necessary in order to bring an asset into service should be capitalized as a part of the cost of the asset. In this case, your company cannot build an office building on this property until the oil well is properly capped. Therefore, the $40,000 cost of capping the oil well should be capitalized as part of the cost of the land.

You are the Division Manager To increase PPE turnover one must either increase sales or reduce PPE assets. The first step is to identify unproductive or inefficiently utilized assets. Unnecessary assets can be sold, and some processes can be outsourced. Also, by reducing down time, effective maintenance practices will increase asset productivity.

KEY RATIOS

$$\text{PPE Turnover (PPET)} = \frac{\text{Sales revenue}}{\text{Average PP \& E, net}} \qquad \text{Percent depreciated} = \frac{\text{Accumulated depreciation}}{\text{Cost of depreciable asset}}$$

KEY TERMS

Accelerated depreciation (p. 378)
Accumulated depreciation (p. 376)
Amortization (p. 390)
Book value (BV) (p. 378)
Capital expenditures (p. 375)
Capitalized (p. 374)
Capitalized interest (p. 376)
Definite life (p. 390)
Depletion (p. 380)
Depreciation (p. 376)
Depreciation base (p. 377)
Depreciation rate (p. 378)
Double-declining-balance (DDB) method (p. 378)
Franchise (p. 390)
Goodwill (p. 392)
Impairment (p. 381)
Intangible assets (p. 374)
Patent (p. 389)
Residual (or salvage) value (p. 377)
Restructuring costs (p. 382)
Straight-line method (p. 378)
Straight-line method (SL) (p. 378)
Tangible assets (p. 374)
Trademark (p. 389)
Units-of-production method (p. 379)
Useful life (p. 377)
Wasting assets (p. 380)

Assignments with the MBC logo in the margin are available in myBusinessCourse. See the Preface of the book for details.

MULTIPLE CHOICE

Multiple Choice Answers
1. a 2. b 3. c 4. d 5. c 6. b

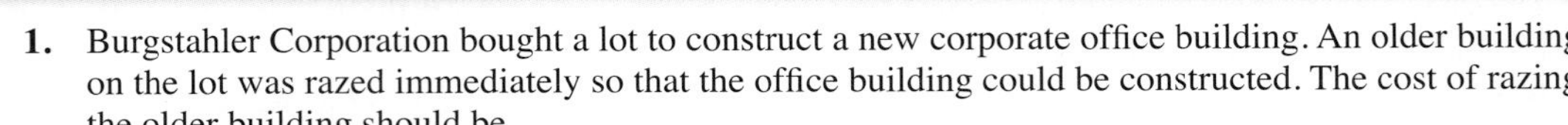

1. Burgstahler Corporation bought a lot to construct a new corporate office building. An older building on the lot was razed immediately so that the office building could be constructed. The cost of razing the older building should be
   a. recorded as part of the cost of the land.
   b. written off as a loss in the year of purchase.
   c. written off as an extraordinary item in the year of purchase.
   d. recorded as part of the cost of the new building.

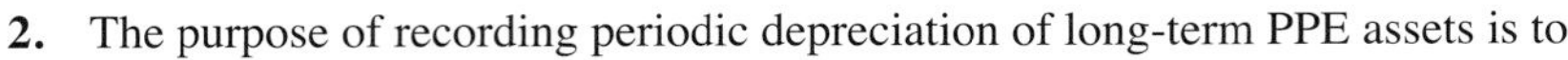

2. The purpose of recording periodic depreciation of long-term PPE assets is to
   a. report declining asset values on the balance sheet.
   b. allocate asset costs over the periods benefited by use of the assets.
   c. account for costs to reflect the change in general price levels.
   d. set aside funds to replace assets when their economic usefulness expires.

3. When the estimate of an asset's useful life is changed,
   a. depreciation expense for all past periods must be recalculated.
   b. there is no change in the amount of depreciation expense recorded for future years.
   c. only depreciation expense for current and future years is affected.
   d. only depreciation expense in the current year is affected.

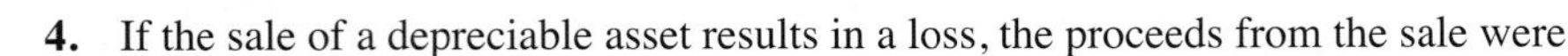

4. If the sale of a depreciable asset results in a loss, the proceeds from the sale were
   a. less than current fair value.
   b. greater than cost.
   c. greater than book value.
   d. less than book value.

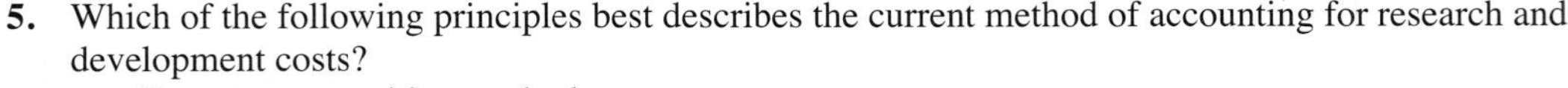

5. Which of the following principles best describes the current method of accounting for research and development costs?
   a. Revenue recognition method
   b. Systematic and rational allocation
   c. Immediate recognition as an expense
   d. Income tax minimization

6. Goodwill should be recorded in the balance sheet as an intangible asset only when
   a. it is sold to another company.
   b. it is acquired through the purchase of another business.
   c. a company reports above-normal earnings for five or more consecutive years.
   d. it can be established that a definite benefit or advantage has resulted from some item such as an excellent reputation for service.

QUESTIONS

Q8-1. How should companies account for costs, such as maintenance or improvements, which are incurred after an asset is acquired?

Q8-2. What is the effect of capitalized interest on the income statement in the period that an asset is constructed? What is the effect in future periods?

Q8-3. Why is the recognition of depreciation expense necessary for proper expense recognition?

Q8-4. Why do companies use accelerated depreciation for income tax purposes, when the total depreciation taken over the asset's useful life is identical to straight-line depreciation?

Q8-5. How should a company treat a change in an asset's estimated useful life or residual value? Which period(s)—past, present, or future—is affected by this change?

Q8-6. What factors determine the gain or loss from the sale of a long-term operating asset?

Q8-7. When is a PPE asset considered to be impaired? How is the impairment loss determined?

Q8-8. What is the proper accounting treatment for research and development costs? Why are R&D costs not capitalized under GAAP?

Q8-9. Why are some intangible assets amortized while others are not? What is meant by an intangible asset with an "indefinite life"?

Q8-10. Under what circumstances should a company report goodwill in its balance sheet? What is the effect of goodwill on the income statement?

MINI EXERCISES

M8-11. Determining Whether to Capitalize or Expense LO2

Homework MBC

For each of the following items, indicate whether the cost should be capitalized or expensed immediately:

a. Paid $1,200 for routine maintenance of machinery
b. Paid $5,400 to rent equipment for two years
c. Paid $2,000 to equip the production line with new instruments that measure quality
d. Paid $20,000 to repair the roof on the building
e. Paid $1,600 to refurbish a machine, thereby extending its useful life
f. Purchased a patent for $5,000

M8-12. Computing Depreciation Under Straight-Line and Double-Declining-Balance LO3

A delivery van costing $18,000 is expected to have a $1,500 salvage value at the end of its useful life of 5 years. Assume that the truck was purchased on January 1, 2016. Compute the depreciation expense for 2017 (its second year) under each of the following depreciation methods:

a. Straight-line
b. Double-declining-balance

M8-13. Computing Depreciation Under Alternative Methods LO3

Equipment costing $130,000 is expected to have a residual value of $10,000 at the end of its six-year useful life. The equipment is metered so that the number of units processed is counted. The equipment is designed to process 1,000,000 units in its lifetime. In 2016 and 2017, the equipment processed 180,000 units and 140,000 units respectively. Calculate the depreciation expense for 2016 and 2017 using each of the following methods:

a. Straight-line
b. Double-declining-balance
c. Units of production

M8-14. Recording the Sale of PPE Assets LO4

As part of a renovation of its showroom, O'Keefe Auto Dealership sold furniture and fixtures that were eight years old for $3,500 in cash. The assets had been purchased for $40,000 and had been depreciated using the straight-line method with no residual value and a useful life of ten years.

a. Prepare a journal entry to record this transaction.
b. Show how the sale of the furniture and fixtures affects the balance sheet and income statement using the financial statement effects template.

LO4 

M8-15. Recording the Sale of PPE Assets

Gaver Company sold machinery that had originally cost $75,000 for $25,000 in cash. The machinery was three years old and had been depreciated using the double-declining-balance method assuming a five-year useful life and a residual value of $5,000.

a. Prepare a journal entry to record this sale.
b. Using the financial statement effects template, show how the sale of the machinery affects the balance sheet and income statement.

LO3 

M8-16. Computing Depreciation Under Straight-Line and Double-Declining-Balance for Partial Years

A machine costing $145,800 is purchased on May 1, 2016. The machine is expected to be obsolete after three years (36 months) and, thereafter, no longer useful to the company. The estimated salvage value is $5,400. Compute depreciation expense for both 2016 and 2017 under each of the following depreciation methods:

a. Straight-line
b. Double-declining-balance

LO1, 2, 5

Siemens AG
NYSE :: SI

M8-17. Accounting for Research and Development Under IFRS

The following information on **Siemens AG**'s treatment of research and development is extracted from its 2014 financial statements. Siemens AG is an integrated technology company with activities in the fields of industry, energy and healthcare. The company is incorporated under the laws of Germany and reports using International Financial Reporting Standards (IFRS).

Research and development costs—Costs of research activities undertaken with the prospect of gaining new scientific or technical knowledge and understanding are expensed as incurred.

Costs for development activities, whereby research findings are applied to a plan or design for the production of new or substantially improved products and processes, are capitalized if (1) development costs can be measured reliably, the product or process is (2) technically and (3) commercially feasible, (4) future economic benefits are probable and (5) Siemens intends, and (6) has sufficient resources, to complete development and to use or sell the asset. The costs capitalized include the cost of materials, direct labour and other directly attributable expenditure that serves to prepare the asset for use. Such capitalized costs are included in line item Other intangible assets as software and other internally generated intangible assets. Other development costs are expensed as incurred. Capitalized development costs are stated at cost less accumulated amortization and impairment losses with an amortization period of generally three to five years.

a. How does the reporting under IFRS differ from reporting under U.S. GAAP for research and development?
b. At year-end September 30, 2014 Siemens had a gross carrying amount of Other Intangible Assets of 10.8 billion Euros and accumulated amortization and impairment related to those assets of 6.3 billion Euros. Should the amounts capitalized be tested annually for impairment?

LO3 

M8-18. Computing Double-Declining-Balance Depreciation

DeFond Company purchased equipment for $50,000. For each of the following sets of assumptions, prepare a depreciation schedule (all years) for this equipment assuming that DeFond uses the double-declining-balance depreciation method.

Useful life	Residual value
a. Four years	$8,000
b. Five years.	$3,000
c. Ten years	$1,000

LO3 

M8-19. Computing and Recording Depletion Expense

The Nelson Oil Company estimated that the oil reserve that it acquired in 2016 would produce 4 million barrels of oil. The company extracted 300,000 barrels the first year, 500,000 barrels in 2017, and 600,000 barrels in 2018. Nelson paid $32,000,000 for the oil reserve.

a. Compute the depletion expense for each year—2016, 2017, and 2018.
b. Prepare the journal entries to record (i) the acquisition of the oil reserve, and (ii) the depletion for 2016.
c. Open T-accounts and post the entries from part *b* in the accounts.

LO6 

Texas Instruments Incorporated
NYSE :: TXN
Intel Corporation
NASDAQ :: INTC

M8-20. Computing and Comparing PPE Turnover for Two Companies

Texas Instruments Incorporated and **Intel Corporation** report the following information:

	Texas Instruments		Intel Corp	
($ millions)	Sales	PPE, net	Sales	PPE, net
2014	$13,045	$2,840	$55,870	$33,238
2013	12,205	3,399	52,708	31,428

a. Compute the 2014 PPE turnover for both companies. Comment on any difference you observe.

b. Discuss ways in which high-tech manufacturing companies like these can increase their PPE turnover.

M8-21. Assessing Research and Development Expenses

LO5, 6

Abbott Laboratories
NYSE :: ABT

Abbott Laboratories reports the following income statement (in partial form):

Year Ended December 31 ($ millions)	2014
Net sales.	$20,247
Cost of products sold.	9,218
Amortization of intangible assets.	555
Research and development*	1,345
Selling, general and administrative	6,530
Total operating cost and expenses	17,648
Operating earnings.	$ 2,599

* including acquired in-process and collaborations R&D

a. Compute the percent of net sales that Abbott Laboratories spends on research and development (R&D). How would you assess the appropriateness of its R&D expense level?

b. Using the financial statement effects template, describe how the accounting for R&D expenditures affects Abbot Laboratories' balance sheet and income statement.

EXERCISES

E8-22. Recording Asset Acquisition, Depreciation, and Disposal

LO2, 3, 4

On January 2, 2016, Verdi Company acquired a machine for $85,000. In addition to the purchase price, Verdi spent $2,000 for shipping and installation, and $2,500 to calibrate the machine prior to use. The company estimates that the machine has a useful life of five years and residual value of $7,000.

a. Prepare journal entries to record the acquisition costs.

b. Calculate the annual depreciation expense using straight-line depreciation and prepare a journal entry to record depreciation expense for 2016.

c. On December 31, 2019, Verdi sold the machine to another company for $12,000. Prepare the necessary journal entry to record the sale.

E8-23. Computing Straight-Line and Double-Declining-Balance Depreciation

LO3

On January 2, Haskins Company purchases a laser cutting machine for use in fabrication of a part for one of its key products. The machine cost $80,000, and its estimated useful life is five years, after which the expected salvage value is $5,000. Compute depreciation expense for each year of the machine's useful life under each of the following depreciation methods:

a. Straight-line

b. Double-declining-balance

E8-24. Computing Depreciation, Asset Book Value, and Gain or Loss on Asset Sale

LO3, 4

Sloan Company uses its own executive charter plane that originally cost $800,000. It has recorded straight-line depreciation on the plane for six full years, with an $80,000 expected salvage value at the end of its estimated 10-year useful life. Sloan disposes of the plane at the end of the sixth year.

a. At the disposal date, what is the (1) accumulated depreciation and (2) net book value of the plane?

b. Prepare a journal entry to record the disposal of the plane assuming that the sales price is

1. Cash equal to the book value of the plane.
2. $195,000 cash.
3. $600,000 cash.

LO3 

E8-25. Computing Straight-Line and Double-Declining-Balance Depreciation

On January 2, 2016, Dechow Company purchases a machine to help manufacture a part for one of its key products. The machine cost $218,700 and is estimated to have a useful life of six years, with an expected salvage value of $23,400.

Compute each year's depreciation expense for 2016 and 2017 for each of the following depreciation methods.

a. Straight-line
b. Double-declining-balance

LO3, 4 

E8-26. Computing Depreciation, Asset Book Value, and Gain or Loss on Asset Sale

Palepu Company owns and operates a delivery van that originally cost $27,200. Straight-line depreciation on the van has been recorded for three years, with a $2,000 expected salvage value at the end of its estimated six-year useful life. Depreciation was last recorded at the end of the third year, at which time Palepu disposes of this van.

a. Compute the net book value of the van on the sale date.
b. Compute the gain or loss on sale of the van if its sales price is for:
   1. Cash equal to book value of van.
   2. $15,000 cash.
   3. $12,000 cash.

LO3 

E8-27. Computing Depreciation and Accounting for a Change of Estimate

Lambert Company acquired machinery costing $110,000 on January 2, 2016. At that time, Lambert estimated that the useful life of the equipment was 6 years and that the residual value would be $15,000 at the end of its useful life. Compute depreciation expense for this asset for 2016, 2017, and 2018 using the

a. straight-line method.
b. double-declining-balance method.
c. Assume that on January 2, 2018, Lambert revised its estimate of the useful life to 7 years and changed its estimate of the residual value to $10,000. What effect would this have on depreciation expense in 2018 for each of the above depreciation methods?

LO3 

E8-28. Computing Depreciation and Accounting for a Change of Estimate

In January 2016, Rankine Company paid $8,500,000 for land and a building. An appraisal estimated that the land had a fair value of $2,500,000 and the building was worth $6,000,000. Rankine estimated that the useful life of the building was 30 years, with no residual value.

a. Calculate annual depreciation expense using the straight-line method.
b. Calculate depreciation for 2016 and 2017 using the double-declining-balance method.
c. Assume that in 2018, Rankine changed its estimate of the useful life of the building to 25 years. If the company is using the double-declining-balance method of depreciation, what amount of depreciation expense would Rankine record in 2018?

LO6 

E8-29. Estimating the Percent Depreciated

The property and equipment footnote from the **Deere & Company** balance sheet follows ($ millions):

Deere & Company
NYSE :: DE

PROPERTY AND DEPRECIATION

A summary of property and equipment at October 31, 2014, in millions of dollars follows:

	2014
Land	$ 124
Buildings and building equipment	3,108
Machinery and equipment	5,089
Dies, patterns, tools, etc.	1,552
All other	926
Construction in progress	530
Total at cost	11,329
Less accumulated depreciation	5,751
Property and equipment—net	$ 5,578

During 2014, the company reported $696 million of depreciation expense.

Estimate the percent depreciated of Deere's depreciable assets. How do you interpret this figure?

E8-30. Computing and Evaluating Receivables, Inventory, and PPE Turnovers

LO6

3M Company
NYSE :: MMM

3M Company reports the following financial statement amounts in its 10-K report:

($ millions)	Sales	Cost of Sales	Receivables	Inventories	PPE, net
2014	$31,821	$16,447	$4,238	$3,706	$8,489
2013	30,871	16,106	4,253	3,864	8,652
2012	29,904	15,685	4,061	3,837	8,378

a. Compute the receivables, inventory, and PPE turnover ratios for both 2014 and 2013. (Receivables turnover and inventory turnover are discussed in Chapters 6 and 7, respectively.)

b. What changes are evident in the turnover rates of 3M for these years? Discuss ways in which a company such as 3M can improve its turnover within each of these three areas.

E8-31. Identifying and Accounting for Intangible Assets

LO1, 5

On the first day of 2016, Holthausen Company acquired the assets of Leftwich Company including several intangible assets. These include a patent on Leftwich's primary product, a device called a plentiscope. Leftwich carried the patent on its books for $1,500, but Holthausen believes that the fair value is $200,000. The patent expires in seven years, but competitors can be expected to develop competing patents within three years. Holthausen believes that, with expected technological improvements, the product is marketable for at least 20 years.

The registration of the trademark for the Leftwich name is scheduled to expire in 15 years. However, the Leftwich brand name, which Holthausen believes is worth $500,000, could be applied to related products for many years beyond that.

As part of the acquisition, Leftwich's principal researcher left the company. As part of the acquisition, he signed a five-year noncompetition agreement that prevents him from developing competing products. Holthausen paid the scientist $300,000 to sign the agreement.

a. What amount should be capitalized for each of the identifiable intangible assets?

b. What amount of amortization expense should Holthausen record in 2016 for each asset?

E8-32. Computing and Recording Depletion Expense

LO3

In 2016, Eldenburg Mining Company purchased land for $7,200,000 that had a natural resource reserve estimated to be 500,000 tons. Development and road construction costs on the land were $420,000, and a building was constructed at a cost of $50,000. When the natural resources are completely extracted, the land has an estimated residual value of $1,200,000. In addition, the cost to restore the property to comply with environmental regulations is estimated to be $800,000. Production in 2016 and 2017 was 60,000 tons and 85,000 tons, respectively.

a. Compute the depletion charge for 2016 and 2017. (You should include depreciation on the building, if any, as part of the depletion charge.)

b. Prepare a journal entry to record each year's depletion expense as determined in part *a*.

E8-33. Computing and Interpreting Percent Depreciated and PPE Turnover

LO6

Adams Golf, Inc.
NASDAQ :: ADGF

The following footnote is from Note 4 to the 2011 10-K of **Adams Golf, Inc.**, a Texas-based manufacturer of golf equipment ($ thousands):

Property and Equipment, net		
Property and equipment consist of the following at December 31	2011	2010
Equipment	$ 2,691	$ 2,629
Computers and software	8,011	7,854
Furniture and fixtures	1,117	993
Leaseholds improvements	447	328
Accumulated depreciation and amortization	(11,320)	(10,925)
	$ 946	$ 879

a. Calculate the percent depreciated ratio for each year.

b. Sales revenue totaled $96,504 in 2011 (all values are in $ thousands). Calculate the PPE turnover ratio (PPET).

c. Comment on these ratios. Do you notice anything unusual?

LO5

Callaway Golf Co.
NYSE :: ELY
Apple, Inc.
NASDAQ :: AAPL
Samsung Electronics Co., Ltd
KS :: 005930
Intel Corporation
NASDAQ :: INTC
Microsoft Corporation
NASDAQ :: MSFT
Baxter International, Inc.
NYSE :: BAX
Pfizer, Inc.
NYSE :: PFE
Merck & Co., Inc
NYSE :: MRK
Monsanto Co.
NYSE :: MON
Syngenta AG
NYSE :: SYT
Deere & Co.
NYSE :: DE

E8-34. Evaluating R&D Expenditures of Companies

R&D intensity is measured by the ratio of research and development expense to sales revenue. The following table compares the R&D intensity for various companies.

Company	R&D Intensity
Callaway Golf Co.	3.53%
Samsung Electronics Co., Ltd (Korea)	6.46%
Apple, Inc.	3.30%
Intel Corporation	20.65%
Microsoft Corporation	13.11%
Baxter International, Inc.	8.52%
Pfizer, Inc.	16.90%
Merck & Co., Inc.	17.00%
Monsanto Co.	10.88%
Syngenta AG (Switzerland)	9.45%
Deere & Company	4.03%

a. Comment on the differences among these companies. To what extent are the differences related to industry affiliation?

b. What other factors (besides industry affiliation) might determine a company's R&D intensity?

LO4 Homework MBC

E8-35. Computing and Assessing Plant Asset Impairment

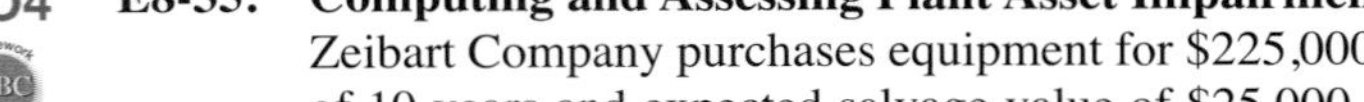

Zeibart Company purchases equipment for $225,000 on July 1, 2012, with an estimated useful life of 10 years and expected salvage value of $25,000. Straight-line depreciation is used. On July 1, 2016, economic factors cause the fair value of the equipment to decline to $90,000. On this date, Zeibart examines the equipment for impairment and estimates $125,000 in future cash inflows related to use of this equipment.

a. Is the equipment impaired at July 1, 2016? Explain.

b. If the equipment is impaired on July 1, 2016, compute the impairment loss and prepare a journal entry to record the loss.

c. What amount of depreciation expense would Zeibart record for the 12 months from July 1, 2016 through June 30, 2017? Prepare a journal entry to record this depreciation expense. (*Hint:* Assume no change in salvage value.)

d. Using the financial statement effects template, show how the entries in parts *b* and *c* affect Zeibart Company's balance sheet and income statement.

PROBLEMS

LO4 Homework MBC

Golden Enterprises, Inc.
NASDAQ :: GLDC

P8-36. Computing and Recording Gain or Loss on Asset Sale

The following information was provided in the 2014 10-K report of **Golden Enterprises, Inc.**

Note 10: Land, Buildings and Equipment

	May 30, 2014	May 31, 2013
Property, plant, and equipment, Gross, Total	$95,174,198	$93,022,443
Less: Accumulated depreciation	69,502,854	65,927,389
Property, plant, and equipment, Net, Total	$25,671,344	$27,095,054

The company's statement of cash flows, including the reconciliation of net income to cash from operations, provided the following information for the year ended May 30, 2014:

- Depreciation expense was $3,778,563.
- Purchases of property, plant, and equipment were $2,380,287.
- Proceeds from the sale of property, plant, and equipment were $48,125.

REQUIRED

Using this information, prepare a journal entry to record the sale of property, plant, and equipment.

LO5 Homework MBC

Agilent Technologies, Inc.
NYSE :: A
Hewlett-Packard Company
NYSE :: HPQ

P8-37. Analyzing and Assessing Research and Development Expenses

Agilent Technologies, Inc., the high-tech spin-off from **Hewlett-Packard Company**, reports the following operating profit for 2014 in its 10-K ($ millions):

Net revenue	
Products	$5,686
Services and other	1,295
Total net revenue	6,981
Costs and expenses	
Cost of products	2,673
Cost of services and other	715
Total costs	3,388
Research and development	719
Selling, general and administrative	2,043
Total costs and expenses	6,150
Income from operations	$ 831

REQUIRED

a. What percentage of its total net revenue is Agilent spending on research and development?

b. How are its balance sheet and income statement affected by the accounting for R&D costs?

c. In 2003, Agilent's spending on R&D was $1,051 million—17.4% of its total net revenue. What are some possible ways that the company might have reduced its R&D intensity from 2003 to 2014? What are some of the possible implications for the company?

P8-38. Analyzing PPE Accounts and Recording PPE Transactions, Including Discontinued Operations LO4

Target Corporation
NYSE :: TGT

The 2014 and 2013 income statements and balance sheets (asset section only) for **Target Corporation** follow, along with its footnote describing Target's accounting for property and equipment. Target's cash flow statement for fiscal 2014 reported capital expenditures of $1,786 million and disposal proceeds for property and equipment of $95 million. No gain or loss was reported on property and equipment disposals. In addition, Target acquired property and equipment through non-cash acquisitions not reported on the statement of cash flows. ***(Note some numbers were added to make the disclosure complete.)***

Consolidated Statements of Operations

($ millions)	2014	2013	2012
Sales	$72,618	$71,279	$71,960
Credit card revenues	—	—	1,341
Total revenues	72,618	71,279	73,301
Cost of sales	51,278	50,039	50,568
Selling, general and administrative expenses	14,676	14,465	14,643
Credit card expenses	—	—	467
Depreciation and amortization	2,129	1,996	2,044
Gain on receivables transaction	—	(391)	(161)
Earnings from continuing operations before interest expense and income taxes	4,535	5,170	5,740
Net interest expense	882	1,049	684
Earnings from continuing operations before income taxes	3,653	4,121	5,056
Provision for income taxes	1,204	1,427	1,741
Net earnings from continuing operations	2,449	2,694	3,315
Discontinued operations, net of tax	(4,085)	(723)	(316)
Net (loss)/earnings	$ (1,636)	$ 1,971	$ 2,999

Consolidated Statements of Financial Position (Asset Section Only) ($ millions)	January 31, 2015	February 1, 2014
Assets		
Cash and cash equivalents, including short-term investments of $1,520 and $3	$ 2,210	$ 670
Inventory	8,790	8,278
Assets of discontinued operations	1,333	793
Other current assets	1,754	1,832
Total current assets	14,087	11,573
Property and equipment		
Land	6,127	6,143
Buildings and improvements	26,614	25,984
Fixtures and equipment	5,346	5,199
Computer hardware and software	2,553	2,395
Construction-in-progress	424	757
Accumulated depreciation	(15,106)	(14,066)
Property and equipment, net	25,958	26,412
Noncurrent assets of discontinued operations	442	5,461
Other noncurrent assets	917	1,107
Total assets	$41,404	$44,553

12. Property and Equipment

Property and equipment is depreciated using the straight-line method over estimated useful lives or lease terms if shorter. We amortize leasehold improvements purchased after the beginning of the initial lease term over the shorter of the assets' useful lives or a term that includes the original lease term, plus any renewals that are reasonably assured at the date the leasehold improvements are acquired. Depreciation expense for 2014, 2013 and 2012 was $2,108 million, $1,975 million and $2,027 million, respectively. For income tax purposes, accelerated depreciation methods are generally used. Repair and maintenance costs are expensed as incurred ***and were $715 million in 2014, $643 million in 2013, and $650 in 2012.*** Facility pre-opening costs, including supplies and payroll, are expensed as incurred.

Estimated Useful Lives	Life (in years)
Buildings and improvements	8-39
Fixtures and equipment	2-15
Computer hardware and software	2-7

Long-lived assets are reviewed for impairment when events or changes in circumstances, such as a decision to relocate or close a store or make significant software changes, indicate that the asset's carrying value may not be recoverable. For asset groups classified as held for sale, the carrying value is compared to the fair value less cost to sell. We estimate fair value by obtaining market appraisals, valuations from third party brokers or other valuation techniques.

Impairments ($ millions)	2014	2013	2012
Impairments included in segment SG&A	$108	$58	$37
Unallocated impairments	16	19	—
Total impairments	$124	$77	$37

REQUIRED

a. Prepare journal entries to record the following for 2014:
   i. Depreciation expense
   ii. Capital expenditures
   iii. Disposal of property, plant, and equipment
   iv. Repair and maintenance costs
   v. Impairments and write-downs (Assume that impairments and write-downs reduce the property and equipment account, rather than increasing accumulated depreciation.)

b. Estimate the amount of property and equipment that was acquired through non-cash transactions.

P8-39. Reporting PPE Transactions and Asset Impairment

LO4
Williams-Sonoma
NYSE :: WSM

Note B from the fiscal 2010 10-K report of **Williams-Sonoma, Inc.**, (January 30, 2011) follows. Its cash flow statement reported that the company made capital expenditures of $61,906,000 during fiscal 2010, impaired assets of $5,453,000 and recorded depreciation expense of $144,630,000. In addition, the company reported a gain on the disposal of property and equipment of $1,139,000.

Note B: Property and Equipment

Property and equipment consists of the following:

($ thousands)	Jan. 30, 2011	Jan. 31, 2010
Leasehold improvements	$ 809,239	$ 831,757
Fixtures and equipment	572,155	576,488
Capitalized software	292,424	267,724
Land and buildings	126,061	135,692
Corporate systems projects in progress	56,602	65,989
Construction in progress	1,568	14,905
Corporate aircraft (held for sale)	0	10,029
Total	1,858,049	1,902,584
Accumulated depreciation and amortization	(1,127,493)	(1,073,557)
Property and equipment—net	$ 730,556	$ 829,027

We review the carrying value of all long-lived assets for impairment, primarily at a store level, whenever events or changes in circumstances indicate that the carrying value of an asset may not be recoverable. We review for impairment all stores for which current or projected cash flows from operations are not sufficient to recover the carrying value of the assets. Impairment results when the carrying value of the assets exceeds the estimated undiscounted future cash flows over the remaining life of the lease. Our estimate of undiscounted future cash flows over the store lease term (generally 5 to 22 years) is based upon our experience, historical operations of the stores and estimates of future store profitability and economic conditions. The future estimates of store profitability and economic conditions require estimating such factors as sales growth, gross margin, employment rates, lease escalations, inflation on operating expenses and the overall economics of the retail industry, and are therefore subject to variability and difficult to predict. If a long-lived asset is found to be impaired, the amount recognized for impairment is equal to the difference between the net carrying value and the asset's fair value.

REQUIRED

Prepare journal entries to record the following for fiscal 2010:

a. Depreciation expense
b. Capital expenditures
c. Impairment of property and equipment (Assume that impairments and write-downs reduce the property and equipment account, rather than increasing accumulated depreciation.)
d. Disposal of property and equipment

CASES AND PROJECTS

C8-40. Interpreting and Reporting Property, Plant, and Equipment (PPE) Expenditures

LO4, 6
General Mills, Inc.
NYSE :: GIS

General Mills, Inc. is a global consumer foods company. The firm manufactures and sells a wide range of branded products and is a major supplier to the foodservice and baking industries. The company's core product areas are ready-to-eat cereal, super-premium ice cream, convenient meal solutions, and healthy snacking. The following data are taken from the company's 2014 annual report. From the balance sheet:

($ millions)	May 25, 2014	May 26, 2013
Land, buildings, and equipment:		
Land	$ 106.9	$ 101.2
Buildings	2,228.4	2,168.3
Buildings under capital lease	0.3	0.3
Equipment	5,979.7	5,731.1
Equipment under capital lease	9.0	9.0
Capitalized software	468.0	427.9
Construction in progress	600.8	495.1
Total land, buildings, and equipment	9,393.1	8,932.9
Less accumulated depreciation	(5,451.2)	(5,054.8)
Total	$3,941.9	$3,878.1

From the income statement ($ millions):

	2014	2013
Net sales	$17,909.6	$ 17,774.1

REQUIRED

a. Compute the PPE turnover for 2014. Assuming an average PPE turnover of 4.0 for the company's closest competitors, does General Mills appear to be capital intensive?

b. Calculate the percentage depreciated of General Mills' depreciable assets at the end of fiscal year 2014. What implications might the result suggest for the company's future cash flows?

c. General Mills reports depreciation expense of approximately $585 million in 2014. Estimate the average useful life of its depreciable assets by dividing average depreciable assets by depreciation expense.

d. During 2014, General Mills purchased $664 million of land, buildings and equipment for cash. Create the necessary journal entries to reflect the asset purchases and the year's depreciation charge.

LO6 **C8-41. Managing Operating Assets to Improve Performance. A Management Application**
Return on a company's net operating assets is commonly used to evaluate financial performance. One way to increase performance is to focus on operating assets.

REQUIRED

Indicate how this might be done in relation to the following asset categories. Indicate also any potential problems a given action might create.

a. Receivables

b. Inventories

c. Property, plant, and equipment

d. Intangibles

LO4, 5, 6 **C8-42. Determining the Effects of Capitalizing Versus Expensing Software Development Costs**

Take-Two Interactive Software, Inc.
NASDAQ ::TTWO

The following excerpts are taken from the March 31, 2014 annual report of **Take-Two Interactive Software, Inc.**, a maker and distributor of video games. All amounts are in thousands of U.S dollars.

Income Statement Information:	2014	2013
Net sales	$2,350,568	$1,214,483
Cost of goods sold	1,414,327	715,837
Operating expenses	520,985	493,407
Income (loss) from operations	$ 415,256	$ 5,239

Information from the Management Discussion, Balance Sheet and Note 8:

Software Development Costs and Licenses
Capitalized software development costs include direct costs incurred for internally developed titles and payments made to third-party software developers under development agreements. We capitalize internal software development costs (including stock-based compensation, specifically identifiable employee payroll expense and incentive compensation costs related to the completion and release of titles), third-party production and other content costs, subsequent to establishing technological feasibility of a software title.

Technological feasibility of a product includes the completion of both technical design documentation and game design documentation. Significant management judgments and estimates are utilized in the assessment of when technological feasibility is established. For products where proven technology exists, this may occur early in the development cycle. Technological feasibility is evaluated on a product by product basis. Amortization of capitalized software development costs and licenses commences when a product is released and is recorded on a title-by-title basis in cost of goods sold. For capitalized software development costs, amortization is calculated using (1) the proportion of current year revenues to the total revenues expected to be recorded over the life of the title or (2) the straight-line method over the remaining estimated useful life of the title, whichever is greater. For capitalized licenses, amortization is calculated as a ratio of (1) current period revenues to the total revenues expected to be recorded over the remaining life of the title or (2) the contractual royalty rate based on actual net product sales as defined in the licensing agreement, whichever is greater. ...We evaluate the future recoverability of capitalized software development costs and licenses on a quarterly basis. Recoverability is primarily assessed based on the actual title's performance. For products that are scheduled to be released in the future, recoverability is evaluated based on the expected performance of the specific products to which the cost or license relates. We utilize a number of criteria in evaluating expected product performance, including: historical performance of comparable products developed with comparable technology; market performance of comparable titles; orders for the product prior to its release; general market conditions; and, past performance of the franchise. When management determines that the value of the title is unlikely to be recovered by product sales, capitalized costs are charged to cost of goods sold in the period in which such determination is made.

Capitalized Software Development Costs and Licenses	2014	2013
Beginning balance	$294,196	$315,979
Additions	197,046	208,965
Amortization and write-downs	(265,533)	(230,748)
Ending balance	$225,709	$294,196

Assume an income tax rate of 35% where necessary.

REQUIRED

a. You wish to compare the performance of Take-Two with one of its competitors, **Electronic Arts, Inc.** However, Electronic Arts does not capitalize any significant amounts of its software development costs. Estimate Take-Two's 2014 Income from operations if it did not capitalize any software development costs. *Briefly* explain your adjustment(s).

b. Is there any indication that Take-Two might have changed its software amortization estimates from 2013 to 2014? Explain *briefly*.

C8-43. Analyzing Impairment Charges

LO4

DreamWorks Animation SKG Inc.
NASDAQ :: DWA

In the last quarter of 2014, **DreamWorks Animation SKG Inc.** recorded a loss. Part of this loss was due to impairment charges. In their annual report the company stated:

We are required to amortize capitalized production costs over the expected revenue streams as we recognize revenue from the associated films or other projects. The amount of production costs that will be amortized each quarter depends on, among other things, how much future revenue we expect to receive from each project. Unamortized production costs are evaluated for impairment each reporting period on a project-by-project basis. If estimated remaining revenue is not sufficient to recover the unamortized production costs, the unamortized production costs will be written down to fair value. In any given quarter, if we lower our previous forecast with respect to total anticipated revenue from any individual feature film or other project, we may be required to accelerate amortization or record impairment charges with respect to the unamortized costs, even if we have previously recorded impairment charges for such film or other project. For instance, in the quarter ended December 31, 2013, we incurred a write-down of $13.5 million for our film *Turbo* and in the year ended December 31, 2014, we incurred write-downs of $66.5 million for our film *Mr. Peabody and Sherman* and $30.3 million for our film *The Penguins of Madagascar*. Such impairment charges adversely impacted our business, operating results and financial condition.

REQUIRED

a. DreamWorks reported an $86.2 million pre-tax loss for the year 2014. What would pre-tax income or loss have been without the above described impairment charges?

b. DreamWorks is in the film production/media industry. From the paragraph above, describe how companies in this industry account for their film production costs – when incurred and over time.

c. Show the journal entry for 2014 to record the impairment charges related to *Mr. Peabody and Sherman* and *The Penguins of Madagascar*.

LO4, 5, 6
Vodafone Public Limited Company
NASDAQ :: VOD

C8-44. Goodwill Impairment Under IFRS

Vodafone Group Public Limited Company's (UK) Annual Report reports the following information (year ended March 31, 2014):

	2014 £m
Revenue	$38,346
Cost of sales	(27,942)
Gross profit	10,404
Selling and distribution expenses	(3,033)
Administrative expenses	(4,245)
Share of results of equity accounted associates and joint ventures	278
Impairment losses	(6,600)
Other income and expense	(717)
Operating (loss)/profit	(3,913)
Non-operating income and expense	(149)
Investment income	346
Financing costs	(1,554)
(Loss)/profit before taxation	(5,270)
Income tax credit/(expense)	16,582
Profit/(loss) for the financial year from continuing operations	11,312
Profit for the financial year from discontinued operations	48,108
Profit for the financial year	$59,420

The company also provides the following disclosures in the notes to their financial statements:

Impairment reviews

IFRS requires management to perform impairment tests annually for indefinite lived assets and, for finite lived assets, if events or changes in circumstances indicate that their carrying amounts may not be recoverable. Impairment testing requires management to judge whether the carrying value of assets can be supported by the net present value of future cash flows that they generate. Calculating the net present value of the future cash flows requires assumptions to be made in respect of highly uncertain matters . . .

Accounting Policies—Goodwill

Goodwill is not subject to amortisation but is tested for impairment annually or whenever there is an indication that the asset may be impaired. For the purpose of impairment testing, assets are grouped at the lowest levels for which there are separately identifiable cash flows, known as cash-generating units. If the recoverable amount of the cash-generating unit is less than the carrying amount of the unit, the impairment loss is allocated first to reduce the carrying amount of any goodwill allocated to the unit and then to other assets of the unit pro-rata on the basis of the carrying amount of each asset in the unit. Impairment losses recognised for goodwill are not reversible in subsequent periods. The recoverable amount is the higher of fair value less costs to sell and value in use. In assessing value in use, the estimated future cash flows are discounted to their present value using a pre-tax discount rate that reflects current market assessments of the time value of money and the risks specific to the asset for which the estimates of future cash flows have not been adjusted.

Assets

Goodwill and other intangible assets

Our total intangible assets increased to £46.7 billion from £44.1 billion. The increase primarily arose as a result of £11.5 billion additions as a result of the Group's acquisitions . . . partially offset by £6.6 billion of goodwill impairments, reductions of £2.6 billion as a result of unfavourable movements in foreign exchange rates and £3.5 billion of amortisation.

REQUIRED

a. Briefly describe the general goodwill impairment rules that Vodafone used relative to those that would apply under U.S. GAAP. Are they very different?

b. How would you treat the goodwill impairment if you were a financial analyst evaluating the company? How did the charge affect pre-tax income for Vodafone?

c. How does such an impairment charge affect the cash flows of the company?

SOLUTIONS TO REVIEW PROBLEMS

Mid-Chapter Review

SOLUTION

1*a*. Straight-line Depreciation expense = ($95,000 − $10,000)/5 years = $17,000 per year

1*b*. Double-declining-balance (twice straight-line rate = 2 × (1/5) = 40%

Year	Book Value × Rate	Depreciation Expense
1	$95,000 × 0.40 =	$38,000
2	($95,000 − $38,000) × 0.40 =	22,800
3	($95,000 − $60,800) × 0.40 =	13,680
4	($95,000 − $74,480) × 0.40 =	8,208
5	($95,000 − $82,688) × 0.40 =	2,312*

*The formula value of $4,925 is not reported because it would depreciate the asset below residual value. Only the $2,312 needed to reach residual value is depreciated.

2.

	Balance Sheet						Income Statement		
Transaction	Cash Asset +	Noncash Assets −	Contra Asset =	Liabil-ities +	Contrib. Capital +	Earned Capital	Revenues −	Expenses =	Net Income
ANALYZE (a) Purchased equipment.	−95,000 Cash	+95,000 Equipment							
ANALYZE (b) Recorded annual depreciation.			+17,000 Accumulated Depreciation			−17,000 Retained Earnings		+17,000 Depreciation Expense	−17,000

JOURNALIZE

(a)	Equipment (+A)	95,000	
	Cash (−A)		95,000

POST

+ Equipment (A) −		+ Cash (A) −	
(a) 95,000			95,000 (a)

JOURNALIZE

(b)	Depreciation expense (+E, −SE)	17,000	
	Accumulated depreciation (+XA, −A)		17,000

POST

+ Depreciation—Expense (E) −		− Accumulated Depreciation (XA) +	
(b) 17,000			17,000 (b)

3.

Equipment, cost	$95,000
Less accumulated depreciation	51,000
Equipment, net	$44,000

Equipment is reported on Lev's balance sheet at its net book value of $44,000.

4. The percent depreciated is computed as: Accumulated Depreciation/Depreciable Asset Cost = $51,000/$95,000 = 53.7%. The equipment is more than one-half depreciated at the end of the third year. Again, the lack of knowledge of salvage value has resulted in an underestimate of the percent depreciated. Still, this estimate is useful in that we know that the company's asset

is over one-half depreciated and is likely to require replacement in about 2 years (less than one-half of its useful life of 5 years). This replacement will become a cash outflow or financing need when it arises and should be considered in our projections of future cash flows.

Chapter-End Review

SOLUTION

1. Bowen Company would expense the $120,000 in R&D costs in 2016. The $12,500 in legal fees to obtain the patent would be capitalized. As a result, the book value of the patent would be $12,500 on July 1, 2016. The entries to record these costs would be:

ANALYZE

	Balance Sheet													Income Statement				
Transaction	Cash Asset	+	Noncash Assets	-	Contra Asset	=	Liabil-ities	+	Contrib. Capital	+	Earned Capital		Revenues	-	Expenses	=	Net Income
(a) Record R&D costs as R&D expense.	−120,000 Cash			-		=					−120,000 Retained Earnings			-	+120,000 R&D Expense	=	−120,000
(b) Record acquisition of patent.	−12,500 Cash		+12,500 Patent	-		=								-		=	

JOURNALIZE

(a) R&D expense (+E, −SE) 120,000
Cash (−A) 120,000

POST

+ Research & Development Expense (E)	−
(a) 120,000	

+ Cash (A)	−
	120,000 (a)

JOURNALIZE

(b) Patent (+A) 12,500
Cash (−A) 12,500

POST

+ Patent (A)	−
(b) 12,500	

+ Cash (A)	−
	120,000 (a)
	12,500 (b)

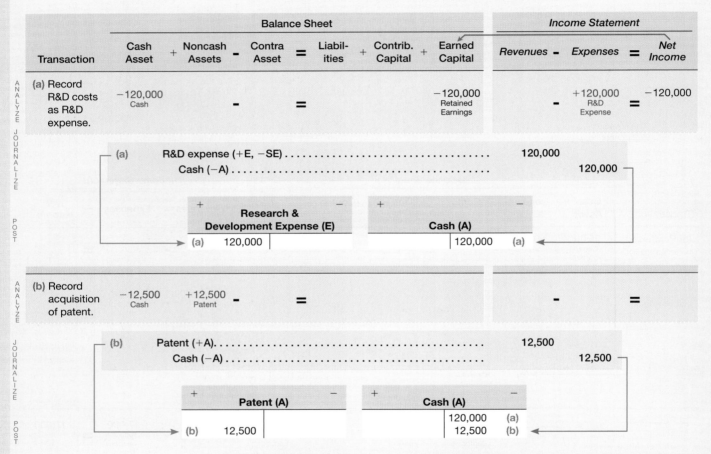

2. Each year, beginning on July 1, 2016, Bowen would record amortization expense of $1,250 ($12,500/10). For 2016, six months of amortization expense, or $625, would be recorded ($1,250/2). The journal entry would be:

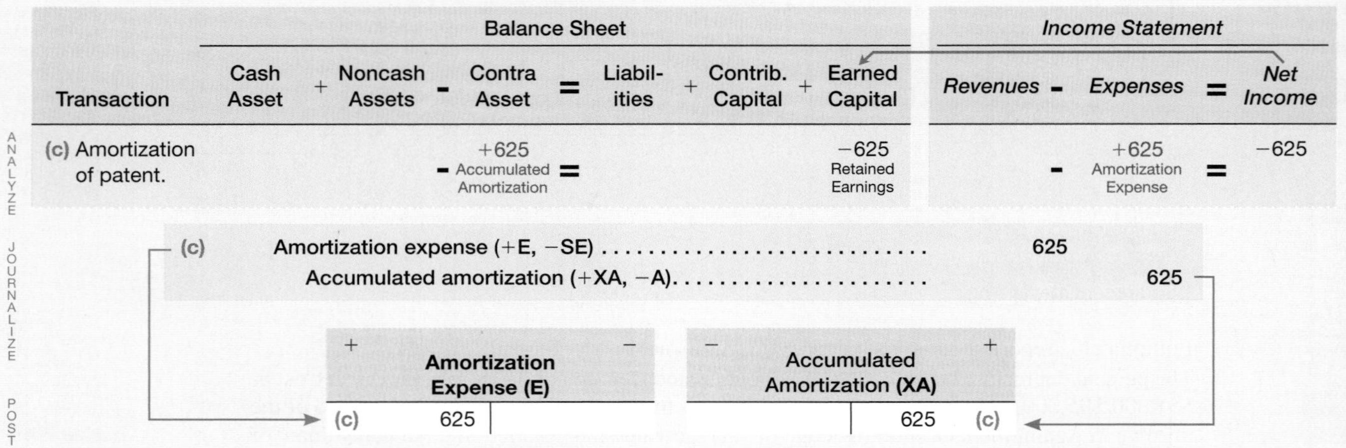

ANALYZE

	Balance Sheet													Income Statement				
Transaction	Cash Asset	+	Noncash Assets	-	Contra Asset	=	Liabil-ities	+	Contrib. Capital	+	Earned Capital		Revenues	-	Expenses	=	Net Income
(c) Amortization of patent.				-	+625 Accumulated Amortization	=					−625 Retained Earnings			-	+625 Amortization Expense	=	−625

JOURNALIZE

(c) Amortization expense (+E, −SE) 625
Accumulated amortization (+XA, −A) 625

POST

+ Amortization Expense (E)	−
(c) 625	

− Accumulated Amortization (XA)	+
	625 (c)

3. Because Kennedy purchased the right to use the technology, the purchase price can be capitalized as an intangible asset and amortized over the five-year length of the agreement. Kennedy would record amortization expense of $18,000 ($90,000/5) each year, beginning July 1, 2018. (Bowen would recognize the $90,000 as revenue.) The journal entry that Kennedy Company would need to record the acquisition of the technology rights would be as follows:

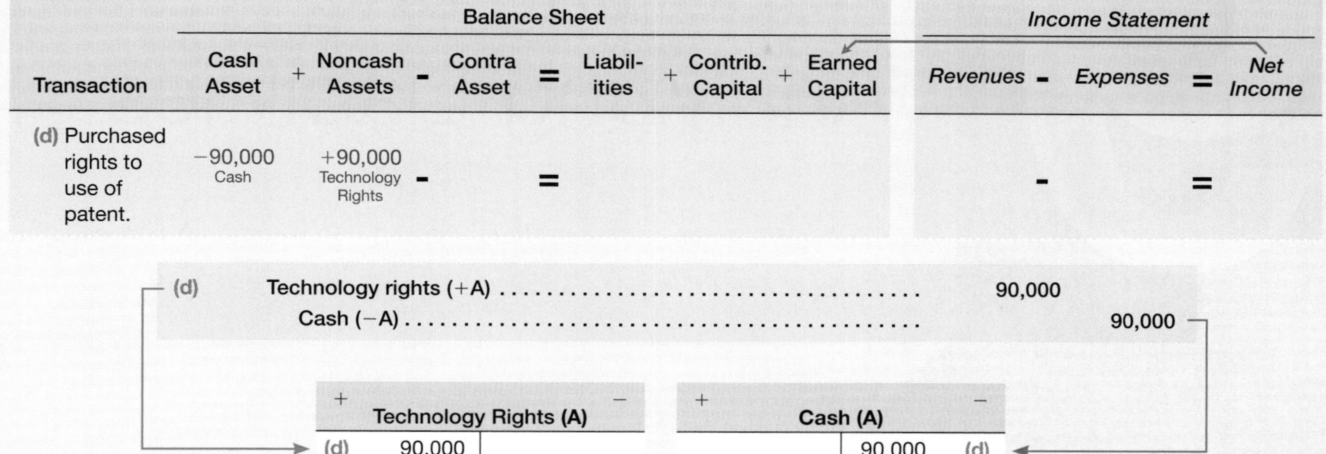

4. Given that the patent is obsolete, both Bowen Company and Kennedy Company would record impairment losses. Bowen would write off the unamortized balance in the patent account, resulting in a loss of $7,500 [$12,500 − ($1,250 × 4)]. Kennedy Company would write off the remaining value of the technology agreement, recording an impairment loss of $54,000 [$90,000 − ($18,000 × 2)]. Kennedy's journal entry would be:

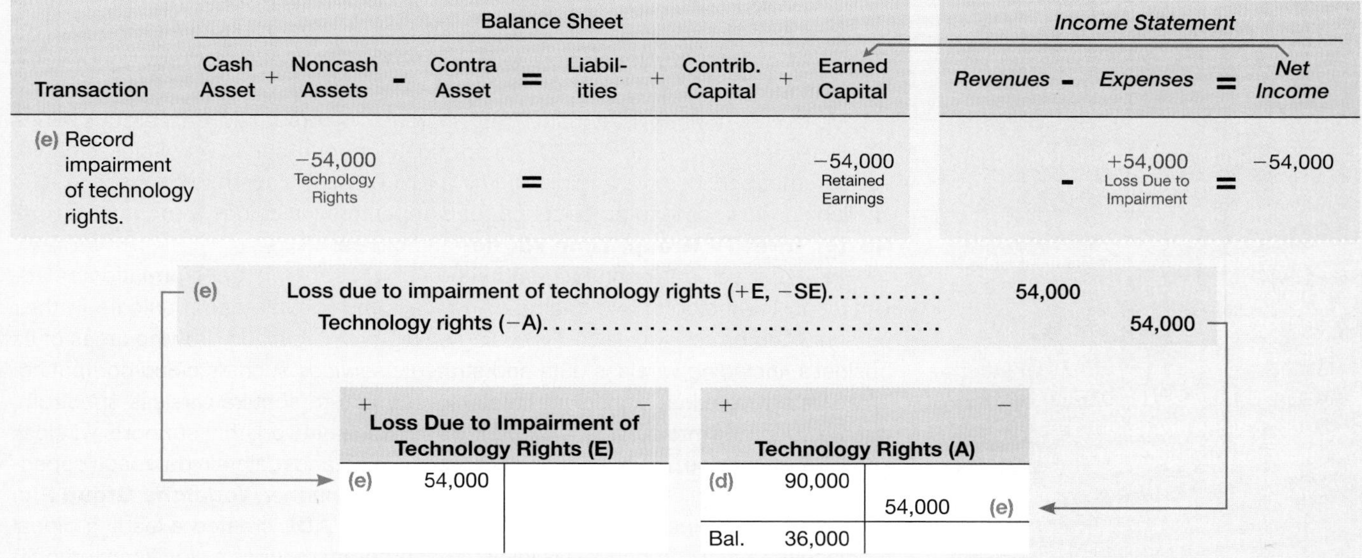

Reporting and Analyzing Liabilities

LEARNING OBJECTIVES

1. Identify and account for current operating liabilities. (p. 415)
2. Describe and account for current nonoperating (financial) liabilities. (p. 422)
3. Explain and illustrate the pricing of long-term nonoperating liabilities. (p. 427)
4. Analyze and account for financial statement effects of long-term nonoperating liabilities. (p. 430)
5. Explain how solvency ratios and debt ratings are determined and how they impact the cost of debt. (p. 437)

VERIZON

www.verizon.com

In 2000, **Bell Atlantic Corporation** merged with **GTE** to form **Verizon Communications**. After its 2006 acquisition of **MCI Communications Corp.** and subsequent acquisition of **Alltel Corporation** in 2008, the corporation became the world's largest provider of communications services.

Verizon's industry is experiencing increasing competition as product lines blur between wireline (or POTS—plain old telephone service), wireless, cable, and Internet services. Lowell McAdam, Verizon's CEO since mid-2011, faces the challenging task of fending off a host of competitors including **Comcast**, **Sprint-Nextel**, **DirecTV Group**, **Time Warner** and others.

In recent years Verizon has embarked upon a strategic transformation as advances in technology have changed the ways that people communicate in their personal and professional lives, focusing on higher margin and growing areas of its business, including wireless data and strategic services such as cloud computing. This strategy requires significant capital investment to acquire wireless spectrum, put the spectrum into service, expand the fiber optic network that supports wireless and wireline service, maintain networks and develop and maintain database capacity. In 2014, Verizon bought out the 45% interest of a partner (**Vodafone Group Plc**) in its wireless business, and its 2015 acquisition of **AOL** created a leading global media technology company. This investment program requires a significant amount of cash at a time when the company is faced with more than $110.5 billion in debt and $33.3 billion in employee benefit obligations. Fortunately, Verizon's operating cash flow remains strong at $30.6 billion in 2014.

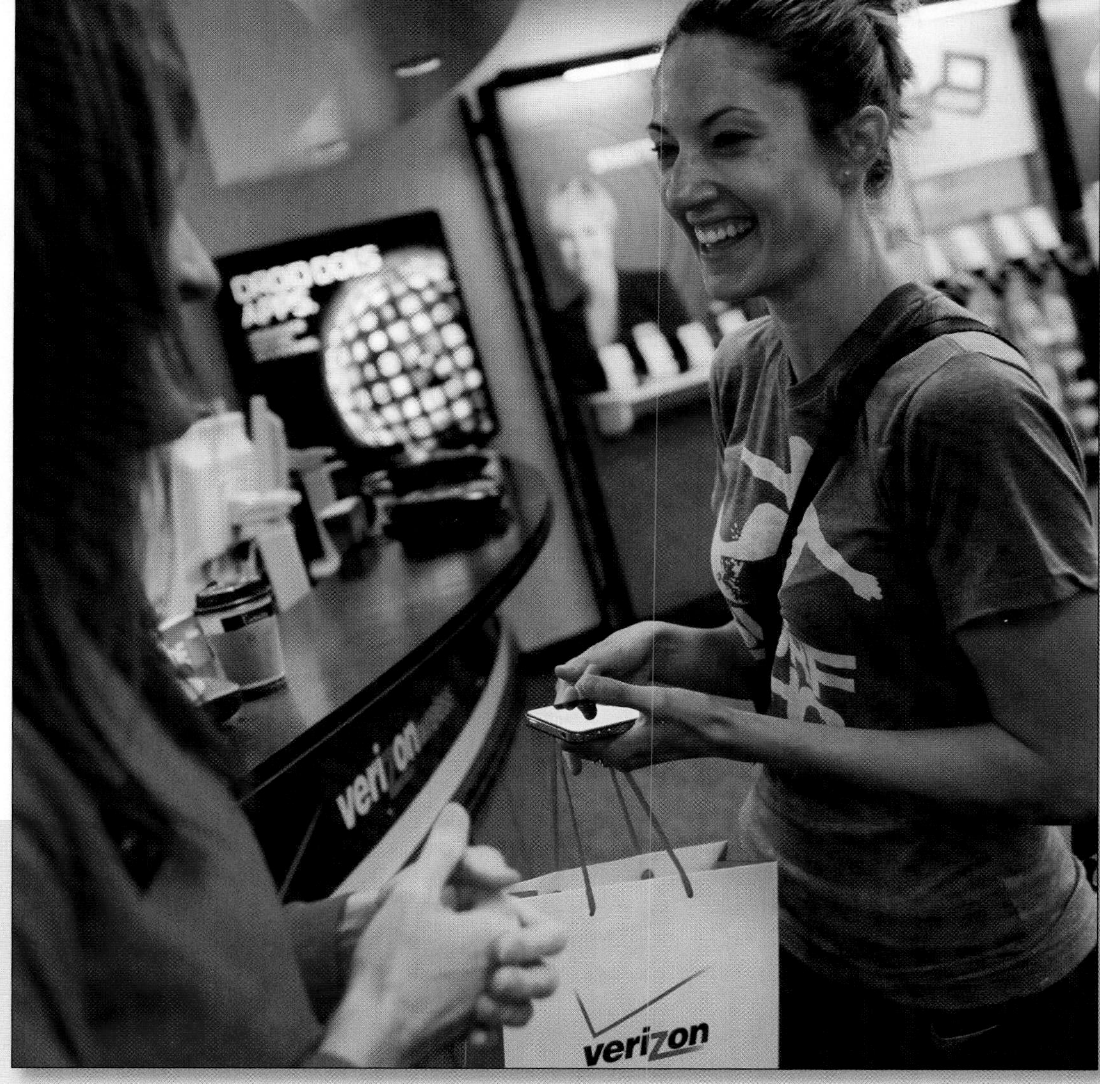

Previous chapters focused on the reporting of operating assets, including receivables, inventories, property, plant, and equipment, and intangible assets, along with the related expenses. We now turn our attention to the other side of the balance sheet. Chapter 9 examines how we value liabilities and how debt financing along with the subsequent payment of interest and principal affect the financial statements. We also discuss the required disclosures that enable us to effectively analyze a company's ability to make its liability payments as they mature. Chapter 10 focuses on the reporting for three specific types of liabilities, and Chapter 11 examines the reporting of stockholders' equity.

As Verizon faces increased competition from other telecom companies, cable, and Internet providers, it must continue to innovate in order to maintain its position as the industry leader. This objective will require large investments in technology and infrastructure, only part of which will come from its operating cash flow. To be successful, McAdam will need to manage Verizon's increased debt burden and efficiently allocate cash resources between strategic investments and debt payments.

Sources: *The Wall Street Journal* 5/2011; *Verizon* 2014 10-K.

CHAPTER ORGANIZATION

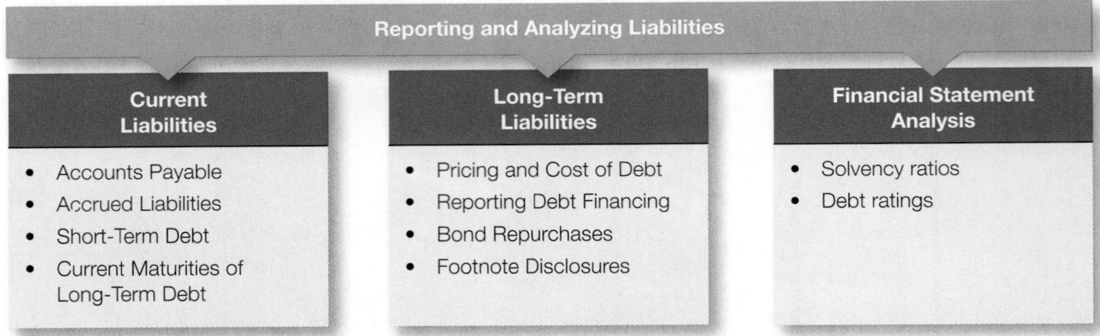

INTRODUCTION

Just as asset disclosures provide us with information on where a company invests its funds, the disclosures concerning liabilities and equity inform us as to how those assets are financed. To be successful, a company must not only invest funds wisely, but must also be astute in the manner in which it finances those investments.

Companies hope to finance their assets at the lowest possible cost. The cost of financing assets with liabilities is the interest charged by the lender. While many liabilities bear explicit interest rates, many other liabilities (such as accounts payable and accrued liabilities) are non-interest-bearing. This fact does not mean that these liabilities are cost-free. For example, while a supplier may appear to offer interest-free credit terms, the cost of that credit is implicitly included in the price it charges for the goods or services it sells.

Verizon's liabilities and equity, as taken from its 2014 10-K report, are presented in **Exhibit 9.1**. Just as assets are classified as either current or noncurrent, so are liabilities presented in the balance sheet as either current or noncurrent.

Current liabilities, as the name implies, are short-term in nature, generally requiring payment within the coming year. As a result, they are not a suitable source of funding for long-term assets that generate cash flows over several years. Instead, companies often finance long-term assets with long-term liabilities that require payments over several years, so that the cash outflows required by the financing source match the cash inflows produced by the assets to which they relate.

EXHIBIT 9.1 Verizon Communications' Liabilities and Equity

At December 31 ($ millions)	2014	2013
Current liabilities		
Debt maturing within one year	$ 2,735	$ 3,933
Accounts payable and accrued liabilities	16,680	16,453
Other	8,649	6,664
Total current liabilities	28,064	27,050
Long-term debt	110,536	89,658
Employee benefit obligations	33,280	27,682
Deferred income taxes	41,578	28,639
Other liabilities	5,574	5,653
Total liabilities	219,032	178,682
Total equity	13,676	95,416
Total liabilities and equity	$232,708	$274,098

When a company acquires assets, and finances them with liabilities, its **financial leverage** increases. Because the magnitude of required liability payments increases with the level of liability financing, those larger payments increase the chance of default should a downturn in business occur. Increasing levels of liabilities make the company riskier to creditors who, consequently, demand a higher return on the financing they provide to the company. The assessment of default risk is part of liquidity and solvency analysis.

This chapter, along with Chapter 10, focuses on liabilities that are reported on the balance sheet and the corresponding interest costs reported in the income statement. All such liabilities represent probable, nondiscretionary, future obligations that are the result of events that have already occurred. Chapter 10 also addresses *off-balance sheet financing*, which encompasses future obligations that are reported in the notes, but not on the face of the balance sheet. An understanding of both on-balance-sheet and off-balance-sheet financing is central to evaluating a company's financial condition and assessing its risk of default.

CURRENT LIABILITIES

Liabilities are separated on the balance sheet into current and noncurrent (long-term). We first focus our attention on current liabilities, which are obligations that must be met (paid) within one year. Most current liabilities such as those related to utilities, wages, insurance, rent, and taxes, generate a corresponding impact on operating expenses.

Verizon reports three categories of current liabilities: (1) debt maturing within one year, which includes short-term borrowings as well as long-term obligations that are scheduled for payment in the upcoming year, (2) accounts payable and accrued liabilities, and (3) other current liabilities, which consist mainly of customer deposits, dividends declared but not yet paid, and miscellaneous short-term obligations too small to list separately.

It is helpful to separate current liabilities into operating and nonoperating components. These two components primarily consist of:

1. Current operating liabilities
    - **Accounts payable** Obligations to others for amounts owed on purchases of goods and services. These are usually non-interest-bearing.
    - **Accrued liabilities** Obligations for expenses incurred that have not been paid as of the end of the current period. These include, for example, accruals for employee wages earned but yet unpaid, accruals for taxes (usually quarterly) on payroll and current-period profits, and accruals for other liabilities such as rent, utilities, interest, and insurance. Accruals are made to properly reflect the liabilities owed as of the statement date and the expenses incurred in the period. Each one is journalized by a debit to an expense account and a credit to a related liability.
    - **Deferred performance liabilities** Obligations that will be satisfied, not by paying cash, but instead, by providing products or services to customers. Examples of deferred performance liabilities include customer deposits, unearned gift card revenues for retail companies, and liabilities for frequent flier programs offered by airlines.
2. Current nonoperating liabilities
    - **Short-term interest-bearing debt** Short-term bank borrowings and notes expected to mature in whole or in part during the upcoming year.
    - **Current maturities of long-term debt** Long-term borrowings that are scheduled to mature in whole or in part during the upcoming year.

The remainder of this section describes current liabilities.

Accounts Payable

LO1 Identify and account for current operating liabilities.

1

Accounts payable, which are part of current operating liabilities, arise from the purchase of goods and services from others on credit. Verizon reports $16,680 million in accounts payable and accrued liabilities as of December 31, 2014. Its accounts payable represent $5,598 million, or 34%, of this total amount.

Accounts payable are a non-interest-bearing source of financing. Increased payables reduce the amount of net working capital, because these payables are deducted from current assets in the computation of net working capital. Also, increased payables improves operating cash flow (because inventories were purchased without using cash). An increase in accounts payable also increases profitability because it causes a reduction in the level of interest-bearing debt that is required to finance operating assets. ROE increases when companies make use of this low-cost financing source.

However, management must be careful to avoid excessive "**leaning on the trade**" because short-term income and cash flow gains can result in long-term costs such as damaged supply channels.[1]

When a company purchases goods or services on credit, suppliers often grant **cash discounts** to buyers if payment is made within a specified time period. Cash discounts are usually established as part of the credit terms and stated as a percentage of the purchase price. For example, credit terms of 1/10, n/30 (one-ten, net-thirty) indicate that a 1% cash discount is allowed if the payment is made within 10 days. If the cash discount is not taken, the full purchase price is due in 30 days.

Net-of-Discount Method To illustrate a cash discount, assume that a company purchases 1,000 units of merchandise at $4 per unit on terms of 1/10, n/30. The total purchase price is 1,000 × $4 = $4,000. However, if payment is made within 10 days, the net purchase price would then be $3,960 ($4,000 − $40). While this difference seems like a small amount, consider the cost of not taking the discount. If the discount is missed, the buyer is afforded an extra 20 days to pay for the merchandise, for which it pays a penalty of $40, or $2 per day. Two dollars per day is the equivalent of $730 dollars per year which, in turn, is equivalent to paying interest at an annual rate of 18.4% ($730/$3,960).[2]

When cash discounts are offered, the inventory purchase should be recorded at its cost using the **net-of-discount method**. When the net-of-discount method is used, inventory is capitalized at the net cost, assuming that the discount will be taken by the buyer. Continuing with our example, the following entry would be recorded by the buyer at the time of purchase:

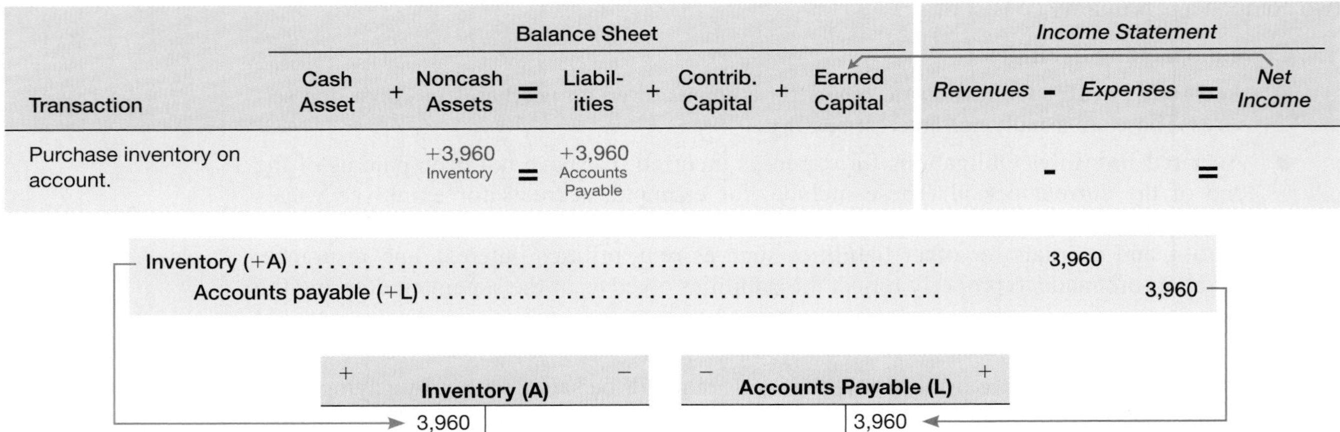

Transaction	Cash Asset	+	Noncash Assets	=	Liabilities	+	Contrib. Capital	+	Earned Capital	Revenues	−	Expenses	=	Net Income
Purchase inventory on account.			+3,960 Inventory	=	+3,960 Accounts Payable						−		=	

ANALYZE JOURNALIZE POST

	Dr.	Cr.
Inventory (+A)	3,960	
Accounts payable (+L)		3,960

+ Inventory (A) −	− Accounts Payable (L) +
3,960	3,960

When payment is made within the 10-day discount period, accounts payable is debited and cash is credited:

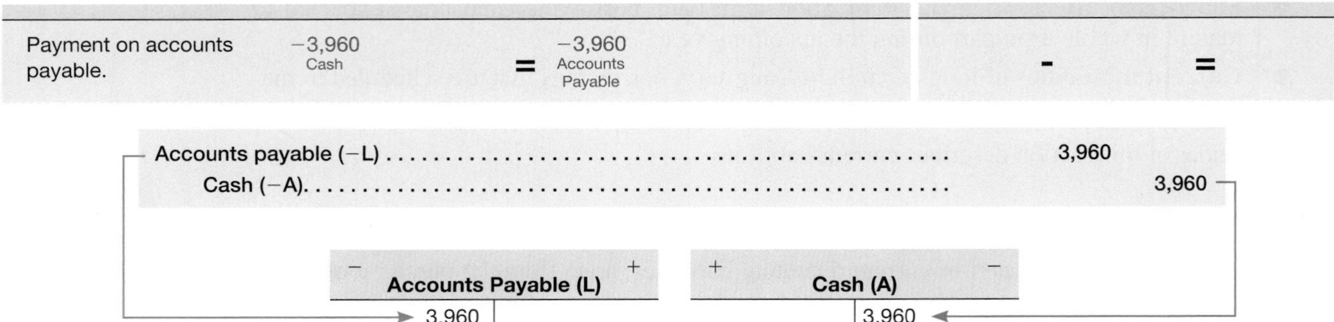

Transaction	Cash Asset	+	Noncash Assets	=	Liabilities	+	Contrib. Capital	+	Earned Capital	Revenues	−	Expenses	=	Net Income
Payment on accounts payable.	−3,960 Cash			=	−3,960 Accounts Payable						−		=	

ANALYZE JOURNALIZE POST

	Dr.	Cr.
Accounts payable (−L)	3,960	
Cash (−A)		3,960

− Accounts Payable (L) +	+ Cash (A) −
3,960	3,960

However, when a discount is missed, the lost discount must be recorded. For example, if full payment is made after the 10-day discount period, the payment is recorded as follows:

[1] One must be careful, because excessive delays in the payment of payables can result in suppliers charging a higher price for their goods or, ultimately, refusing to sell to certain buyers. This situation is a hidden "financing" cost that, even though it is not interest, is a real cost.

[2] Compound interest methods (introduced in Appendix A) would arrive at a slightly higher annual rate of interest, about 19.6%.

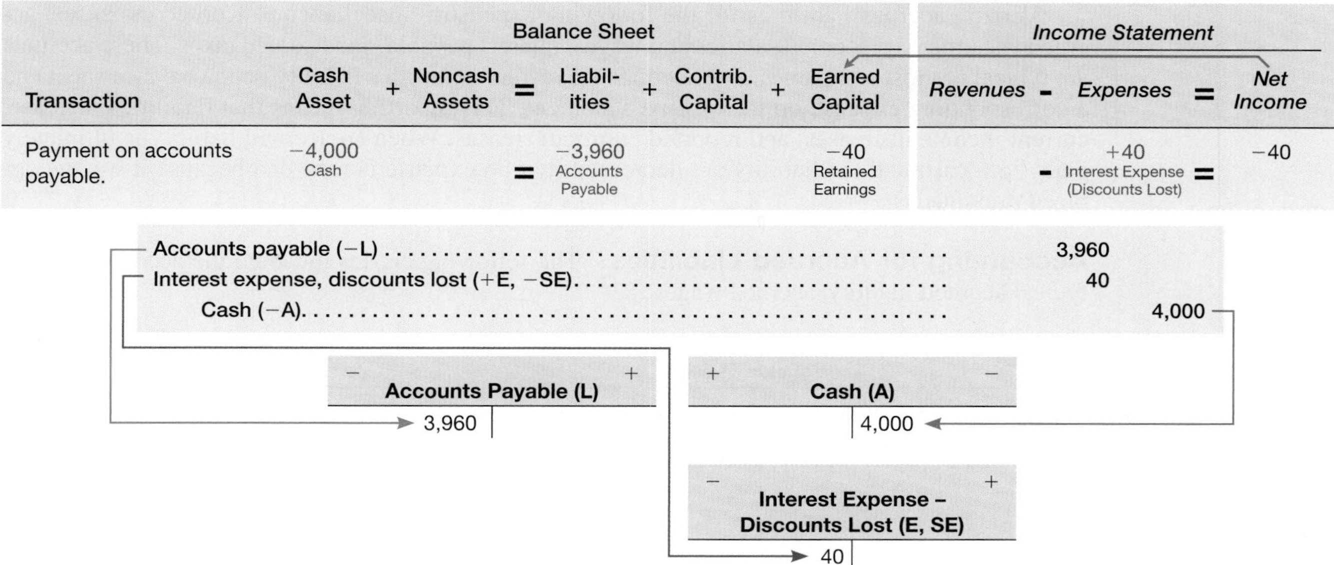

The missed discount is an expense in the period when the discount is lost. This serves two purposes. First, discounts lost are not capitalized as part of inventory and are not added to cost of goods sold. Instead, the lost discounts are treated like a finance charge and recorded as an expense of the period when the discount is missed. Second, the net-of-discount method highlights late payments by explicitly keeping a record of lost discounts. Given the high cost of missed cash discounts, most businesses would likely want to minimize the amount of discounts lost. Thus, keeping a record of discounts lost is useful when it comes to managing cash and accounts payable.

MID-CHAPTER REVIEW 1

On April 12, Waymire Corporation purchased raw materials costing $29,000 on credit. The credit terms were 2/10, n/30.

a. If Waymire paid for the materials on April 19, how much would it pay?
b. Compute the cost of a lost discount as an annual percentage interest rate.

The solution to this review problem can be found on page 456.

Accrued Liabilities

Accrued liabilities are identified at the end of an accounting period to reflect liabilities and expenses that have been incurred during the period but are not yet paid.[3] **Verizon** reports details of its $16,680 million accounts payable and accrued liabilities, including its $5,598 accounts payable, in footnote 16 to its 2014 10-K report:

December 31 ($ millions)	2014	2013
Accounts payable	$ 5,598	$ 4,954
Accrued expenses	4,016	3,954
Accrued vacation pay, salaries and wages	4,131	4,790
Interest payable	1,478	1,199
Taxes payable	1,457	1,556
Total	$16,680	$16,453

[3] Accruals can also be made for recognition of revenue and a corresponding receivable. An example of this situation would be revenue recognition on a long-term contract that has reached a particular milestone, or for interest earned but not received on an investment in bonds that is still outstanding at period-end.

Verizon accrues liabilities for the following expenses: miscellaneous accrued expenses, accrued vacation pay, accrued salaries and wages, interest payable, and accrued taxes. These accruals are typical of most companies. The accruals are recognized with a liability on the balance sheet and a corresponding expense on the income statement. This reporting means that liabilities increase, current income decreases, and reported equity decreases. When an accrued liability is ultimately paid, both cash and the liability are decreased (but no expense is recorded because it was recognized previously).

Accounting for Accrued Liabilities The following entries illustrate the accounting for a typical accrued liability, accrued wages:

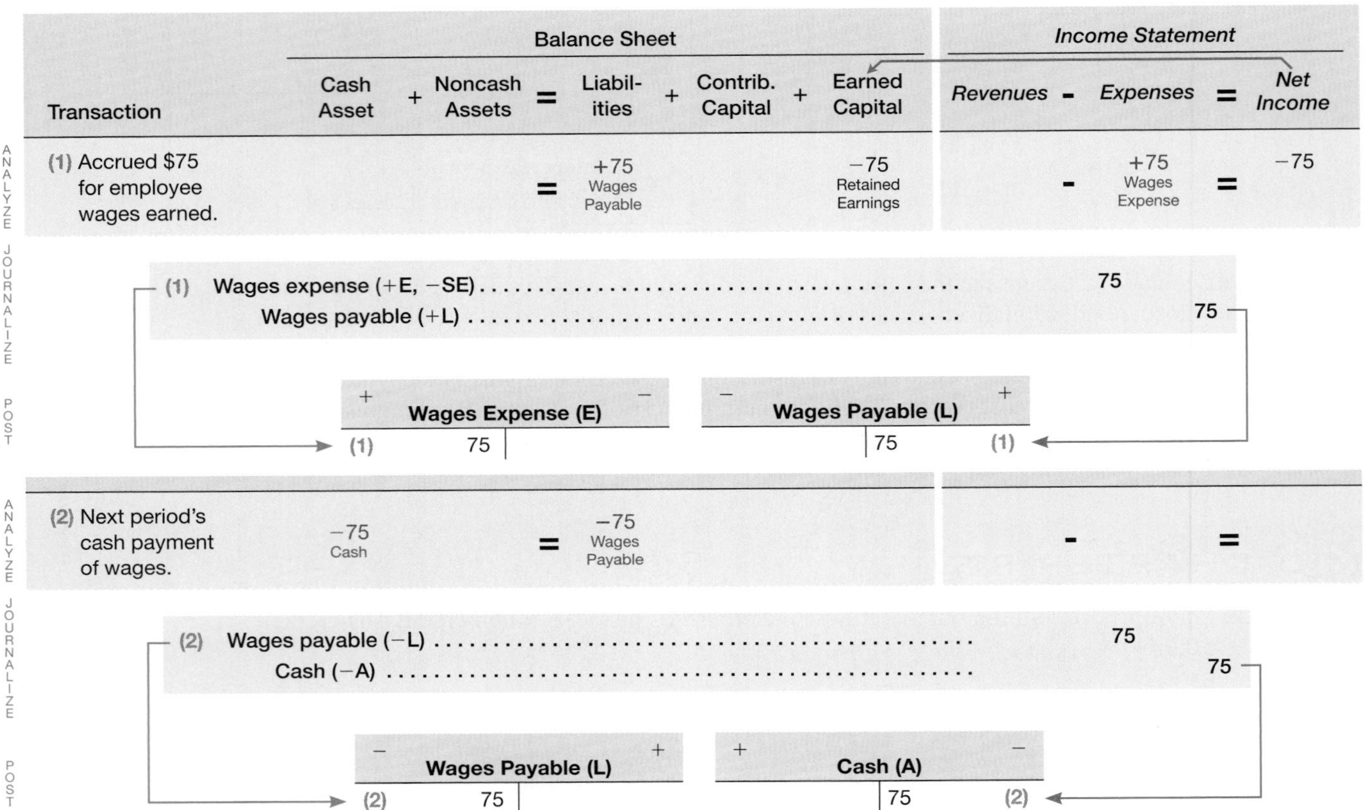

The following financial statement effects result from this accrual of employee wages:

- Employees have worked during a period and have not yet been paid. The effect of this accrual is to increase wages payable on the balance sheet and to recognize wages expense on the income statement. Failure to recognize this liability and associated expense would understate liabilities on the balance sheet and overstate income.
- Employees are paid in the following period, resulting in a cash decrease and a reduction in wages payable. This payment does not result in expense because the expense was recognized in the prior period when incurred.

Contingent Liabilities The accrued wages illustration relates to events that are fairly certain. We know, for example, when wages are incurred but not paid. Other examples of such accruals are rental costs, insurance premiums due but not yet paid, and taxes owed.

Some accrued liabilities, however, are less certain than others. Consider a company facing a lawsuit. Should it record the possible liability and related expense? The answer depends on the likelihood of occurrence and the ability to estimate the obligation. Specifically, if the obligation is *probable* **and** the amount *estimable,* then a company will recognize this obligation, called a **contingent liability**, with a corresponding charge to income. If an obligation is only *reasonably possible,* regardless of the company's ability to estimate the amount, the contingent liability is not reported on the balance sheet and is merely disclosed in the footnotes. All other contingent liabilities that are less than reasonably possible are not accrued—disclosure in a note is permitted but not required.

A GLOBAL PERSPECTIVE

Reporting Contingent Liabilities U.S. GAAP and IFRS are similar with respect to reporting accrued liabilities. The one exception is contingencies. IFRS uses the term *provisions* to refer to contingent liabilities that are accrued and reported on the balance sheet while an obligation that is disclosed in the notes is labeled *contingent liability*. Both GAAP and IFRS require accrual of the "best estimate" of the liability. However, if the best estimate of the future payments required to settle the obligation is a range of values, IFRS requires that the midpoint of the range be used as the estimated value of the contingent liability or provision. In the same situation, U.S. GAAP requires that the low end of the range be used, with disclosure of the maximum.

Warranties The new revenue recognition standard discussed in Chapter 6 has implications for the accounting for warranty obligations. When a company delivers a product with a warranty, is the warranty simply assurance that the product will function as intended, or should it be considered a separate performance obligation? If it is considered a separate performance obligation, then the company would allocate the purchase price between the product and the warranty and recognize an unearned revenue liability at the time of purchase, as shown in Chapter 6.[4] However, if the warranty is not a separate performance obligation (e.g., it cannot be purchased separately from the product and is intended as assurance that the product will perform as expected), a liability accrual for the warranty obligation must be made at the time of purchase.

The expected cost of the warranty commitment usually is reasonably estimated at the time of sale based on past experience. GAAP requires manufacturers to record the expected cost of warranties as a liability, and to record the related expected warranty expense in the income statement to match against the sales revenue reported for that period.

To illustrate, the effects of an accrual of a $1,000 warranty liability are:

	Balance Sheet									Income Statement				
Transaction	Cash Asset	+	Noncash Assets	=	Liabilities	+	Contrib. Capital	+	Earned Capital	Revenues	−	Expenses	=	Net Income
(1) Accrued $1,000 of expected warranty costs on goods sold this period.				=	+1,000 Warranty Liability				−1,000 Retained Earnings		−	+1,000 Warranty Expense	=	−1,000

ANALYZE

JOURNALIZE

(1) Warranty expense (+E, −SE)	1,000	
Warranty liability (+L)		1,000

POST

+ Warranty Expense (E) −	
(1) 1,000	

− Warranty Liability (L) +	
	1,000 (1)

[4] Under current GAAP, deferral of revenue is required for extended warranties that are purchased separately from the product.

	Balance Sheet					Income Statement		
Transaction	Cash Asset	+ Noncash Assets	= Liabil-ities	+ Contrib. Capital	+ Earned Capital	Revenues	− Expenses	= Net Income
(2) Next period's costs (sent $950 in replacement products) to cover failures under warranty.		−950 Inventory	= −950 Warranty Liability				−	=

ANALYZE / JOURNALIZE / POST

(2) Warranty liability (−L)	950	
Inventory (−A)		950

− Warranty Liability (L) +	
(2) 950	

+ Inventory (A) −	
	950 (2)

Reporting of warranty liabilities has the same effect on financial statements as does the accrual of wages expense in the previous section. That is, a liability is recorded on the balance sheet and an expense is reported in the income statement, reducing income by the warranty accrual. When the defective product is later replaced (or repaired), the liability is reduced together with the cost of the inventory (or other assets) spent to satisfy the claim. (Only a portion of the products estimated to fail does so in the current period; we expect other product failures in future periods. Using methods similar to the aging of accounts in Chapter 6, management monitors this estimate and adjusts it if failure is higher or lower than expected.) As in the accrual of wages, the expense is reported when it is incurred and the liability is estimated at that time, not when payments are made.

Apple Inc. reports $4,159 million of warranty liability in its 2014 balance sheet. The footnotes reveal the following additional information:

Accrued Warranty and Indemnification The Company offers a basic limited parts and labor warranty on its hardware products. The basic warranty period for hardware products is typically one year from the date of purchase by the end-user. The Company also offers a 90-day basic warranty for its service parts used to repair the Company's hardware products. The Company provides currently for the estimated cost that may be incurred under its basic limited product warranties at the time related revenue is recognized. Factors considered in determining appropriate accruals for product warranty obligations include the size of the installed base of products subject to warranty protection, historical and projected warranty claim rates, historical and projected cost-per-claim and knowledge of specific product failures that are outside of the Company's typical experience. The Company assesses the adequacy of its preexisting warranty liabilities and adjusts the amounts as necessary based on actual experience and changes in future estimates.

The following table shows changes in the Company's accrued warranties and related costs for 2014, 2013 and 2012 (in millions):

	2014	2013	2012
Beginning accrued warranty and related costs	$2,967	$1,638	$1,240
Cost of warranty claims	(3,760)	(3,703)	(1,786)
Accruals for product warranty	4,952	5,032	2,184
Ending accrued warranty and related costs	$4,159	$2,967	$1,638

In 2014, Apple incurred $3,760 million in cost to replace or repair defective products during the year, reducing the liability by this amount. This cost can be in the form of cash paid to customers or to employees as wages, and in the form of parts used for repairs. The company accrued an additional $4,952 million in new warranty liabilities in 2014. It is important to realize that only the increase in the liability resulting from additional accruals affects the income statement, reducing income through the additional warranty expense. Warranty payments reduce the warranty liability but have no impact on the income statement.

U.S. GAAP requires that the warranty liability reflect the estimated amount of cost that the company expects to incur as a result of warranty claims. This amount is often difficult to estimate and is prone to error. There is also the possibility that a company might intentionally underestimate its warranty liability to report higher current income, or overestimate it so as to depress current income and create an additional liability on the balance sheet that can be used to absorb future warranty costs without the need to record additional expense. Doing so would shift income from the current period to one or more future periods. Warranty liabilities should be compared with sales levels. Any deviations from the historical relation of the warranty liability to sales may indicate a change in product quality or, alternatively, it may reveal earnings management.

All accrued liabilities result in a liability on the balance sheet and an expense on the income statement. Management has some latitude in determining the amount and timing for accruals. This latitude can lead to misreporting of income and liabilities (unintentional or otherwise). For example, if accruals are underestimated, then liabilities are underestimated, income is overestimated, and retained earnings are overestimated. In subsequent periods when an understated accrued liability is reversed (it is recognized in the account), reported income is lower than it should be; this is because prior period income was higher than it should have been. (The reverse holds for overestimated accruals.) The over- and under-reporting of accruals, therefore, results in the shifting of income from one period into another.

Experience tells us that some accrued liabilities are more prone to misstatement than others. Estimated accruals that are linked with restructuring programs, including severance accruals and accruals for asset write-downs, are often overstated, as are estimated environmental liabilities. Companies sometimes overestimate these "one-time" accruals, resulting in early recognition of expenses (as "nonrecurring items") and a corresponding reduction in current period income. This choice, in turn, boosts income in future years when management decides that the accrual can be reversed because it was initially too large. This may suggest that management is conservative and wants to avoid understating liabilities. It can also reflect a desire by management to show earnings growth in the future by shifting current income to future periods. Accrued liabilities set up to smooth income over future periods are called "**cookie jar reserves**." The terms "clearing the decks" and "taking a big bath" have also been applied to such accounting practices.

YOU MAKE THE CALL

You are the Analyst **Dow Chemical Company** reported accrued environmental liabilities in excess of $706 million in its 2014 balance sheet. What conditions needed to be met before these liabilities could be reported? The company also indicated in a footnote that actual environmental liabilities could be twice this amount. How does this uncertainty potentially affect Dow's balance sheet? [Answers on page 443]

MID-CHAPTER REVIEW 2

The **Toro Company** reported warranty liabilities of $72,177,000 in its October 31, 2013 balance sheet. On its October 31, 2014 balance sheet, it reported a liability of $71,080,000. It recognized $37,471,000 in net warranty expenses during fiscal year 2014, ending October 31, 2014. What amount of cost did Toro incur to cover warranty claims in 2014? How would the fulfillment of these claims be recorded?

The solution to this review problem can be found on pages 456–457.

2

LO2 Describe and account for current nonoperating (financial) liabilities.

Current Nonoperating (Financial) Liabilities

Current nonoperating (financial) liabilities include short-term bank loans, the accrual of interest on those loans, and the current maturities of long-term debt. Companies generally try to structure their financing so that debt service requirements (payments) of those financing obligations coincide with the cash inflows from the assets financed. This strategy means that current assets are usually financed with current liabilities, and that long-term assets are financed with long-term liability (and equity) sources.

The use of short-term financing is particularly important for companies that have seasonal sales. To illustrate, a seasonal company's investment in current assets tends to fluctuate during the year as depicted in the graphic below:

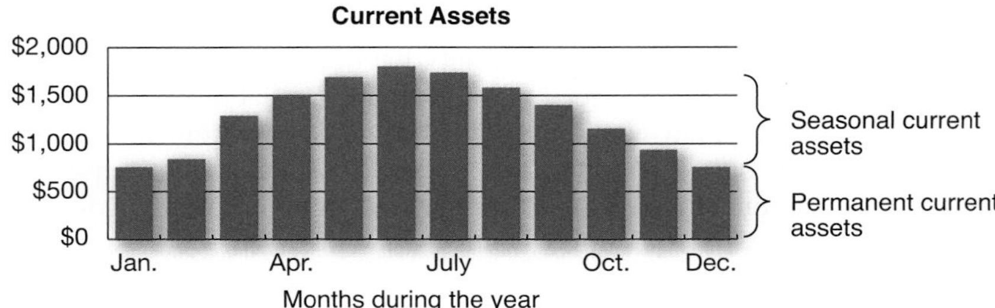

This particular company does most of its selling in the summer months. More inventory is purchased and manufactured in the early spring than at any other time of the year. Sales of the company's manufactured goods are also greater during the summer months, giving rise to accounts receivable that are higher than normal during the summer and fall. The peak working capital level is reached at the height of the selling season and is lowest when the business slows in the off-season. There is a permanent level of working capital required for this business (about $750), and a seasonal component (maximum of about $1,000). Businesses differ in their working capital requirements, but many have permanent and seasonal components.

If a company's working capital needs fluctuate from one season to the next, then the financing needs of the company are also seasonal. Some assets can be financed with short-term operating liabilities. For example, seasonal increases in inventory balances are typically financed with increased levels of accounts payable. However, operating liabilities are unlikely to meet all of the financing needs of a company. Additional financing is provided by short-term interest-bearing debt.

This section focuses on short-term nonoperating liabilities. These include short-term debt and interest as well as current maturities of long-term liabilities.

Short-Term Interest-Bearing Debt Seasonal swings in working capital are often financed with a bank line of credit (short-term debt). In this case the bank provides a commitment to lend up to a given level with the understanding that the amounts borrowed are repaid in full sometime during the year. An interest-bearing note is evidence of such borrowing.

When these short-term funds are borrowed, the cash received is reported on the balance sheet together with an increase in liabilities (notes payable). The note is reported as a current liability because the expectation is that it will be paid within a year. This borrowing transaction has no effect on income or equity, but there will be a financing cash inflow on the statement of cash flows. The borrower incurs (and the lender earns) interest on the note as time passes. U.S. GAAP requires the borrower to accrue the interest liability and the related interest expense each time financial statements are issued.

To illustrate, assume that Verizon borrows $1,000 cash from 1st Bank on January 1. The note bears interest at a 12% annual (3% quarterly) rate, and the interest is payable on the first of each subsequent quarter (April 1, July 1, October 1, January 1). Assuming that Verizon issues calendar-quarter financial statements, this borrowing results in the following financial statement effects for the period January 1 through April 1:

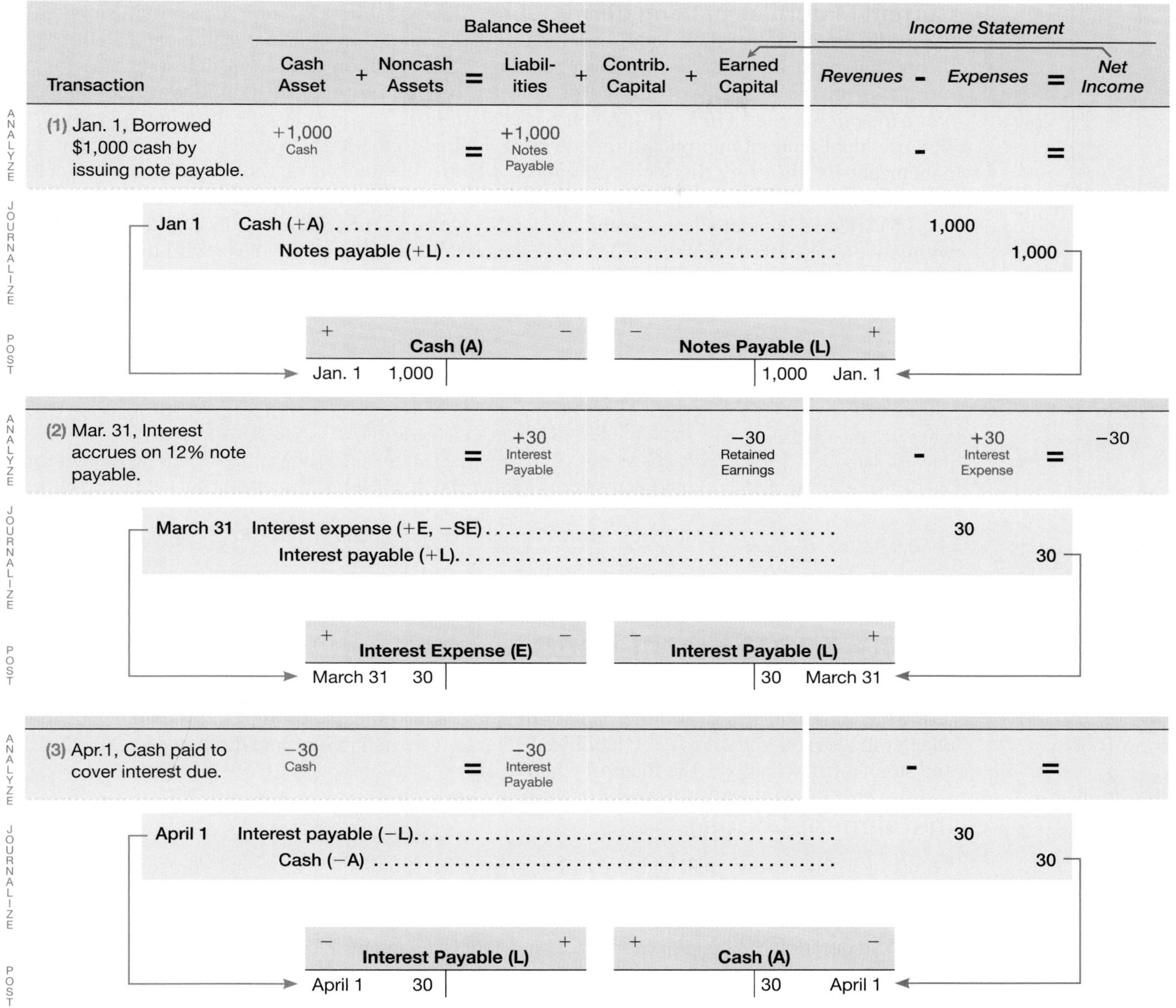

The January 1 borrowing is reflected by an increase in cash and in notes payable. On March 31, this company issues its quarterly financial statements. Although interest is not paid until April 1, the company has incurred three months' interest obligation as of March 31. Failure to recognize this liability and the expense incurred would not fairly present the financial condition of the company. Accordingly, the quarterly accrued interest is computed as follows:

Interest Expense	=	**Principal**	×	**Annual Rate**	×	**Portion of Year Outstanding**
\$30	=	**\$1,000**	×	**12%**	×	**3/12**

The subsequent interest payment on April 1 is reflected in the financial statements as a reduction of cash and a reduction of the interest payable liability accrued on March 31. There is no expense reported on April 1, because it was recorded the previous day (March 31) when the financial statements were prepared, however the payment of interest would be an operating cash outflow in the statement of cash flows for the quarter beginning April 1. (For fixed-maturity borrowings specified in days, such as a 90-day note, we use a 365-day year for interest accrual computations, see Mid-Chapter Review 3.)

Current Maturities of Long-Term Debt All companies are required to provide a schedule of the maturities of their long-term debt in the footnotes to financial statements. Debt payments that must be made during the upcoming 12 months on long-term debt (such as for a mortgage) or the maturity of a bond or note are reported as current liabilities called *current maturities of long-term debt*. This change is accomplished by a reclassification in the accounts. The principal amount approaching maturity is debited to the long-term debt account (reducing noncurrent liabilities by that amount) and credited to the current maturities of long-term debt account (increasing current liabilities by that amount).

In Verizon's balance sheet, the current liability section shows $2,735 million in debt maturing within one year of the December 31, 2014, balance sheet date. The footnotes reveal that $338 million of this amount represents short-term debt, and the remaining $2,397 million is long-term debt that must be repaid or refinanced sometime during 2015.

MID-CHAPTER REVIEW 3

Gigler Company borrowed $10,000 on a 90-day, 6% note payable dated January 15. The bank accrues interest daily based on a 365-day year. Use journal entries, T-accounts, and the financial statement effects template to show the implications (amounts and accounts) of the January 31 month-end interest accrual.

The solution to this review problem can be found on page 457.

LONG-TERM LIABILITIES

Companies generally try to fund long-term investments in assets with long-term financing. Long-term financing consists of long-term liabilities and stockholders' equity. The remainder of this chapter focuses on long-term debt liabilities. Other long-term liabilities are discussed in Chapter 10 and stockholders' equity is the focus of Chapter 11.

Installment Loans

Companies can borrow small amounts of long-term debt from banks, insurance companies, or other financial institutions. These liabilities are often designed as installment loans and may be secured by specific assets called **collateral**. Installment loans are loans that require a fixed periodic payment for a fixed duration of time. For example, assume that a company decides to finance an office building with a 15-year mortgage requiring 180 equal monthly payments (180 payments = 15 years × 12 months). The fixed payment on an installment loan includes a portion of the principal (i.e., the amount borrowed) plus any interest that has accrued on the loan.

To illustrate the accounting for installment loans, assume that Shevlin Company borrowed $40,000 from 1st Bank on July 1, 2015. The terms of the loan require that Shevlin repay the loan in 12 equal quarterly payments over a three-year period and require 8% interest per year. The quarterly payment is $3,782 and can be calculated using the Table A3 (page 639) present value factor for 12 periods (3 years × 4 quarters) and 2% interest (8% per year ÷ 4 quarters) as follows:

$$\text{Present Value} = \text{Payment} \times \text{Present Value Factor}$$

$$\frac{\text{Present Value}}{\text{Present Value Factor}} = \text{Payment}$$

$$\frac{\$40{,}000}{10.57534} = \$3{,}782$$

Using a financial calculator, we can compute the payment by letting N be the number of quarters and setting I/Yr equal to the interest rate per quarter. The payment can then be calculated as follows: N = 12; I/Yr = 2; PV = 40,000; FV = 0:

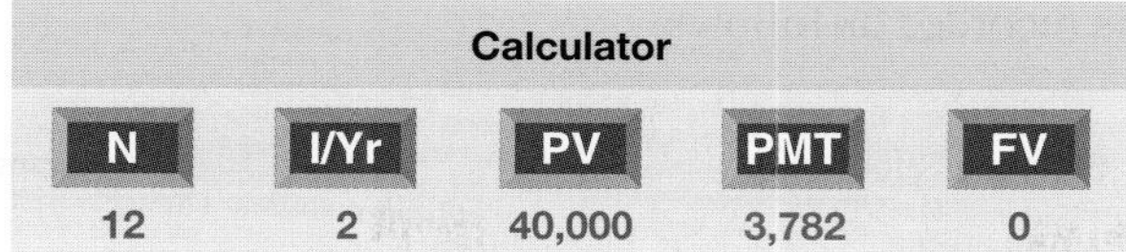

When Shevlin Company agrees to the loan terms, it receives the loan amount, $40,000 in cash, and incurs a $40,000 liability (installment loan payable). The loan is recorded on July 1 as follows:

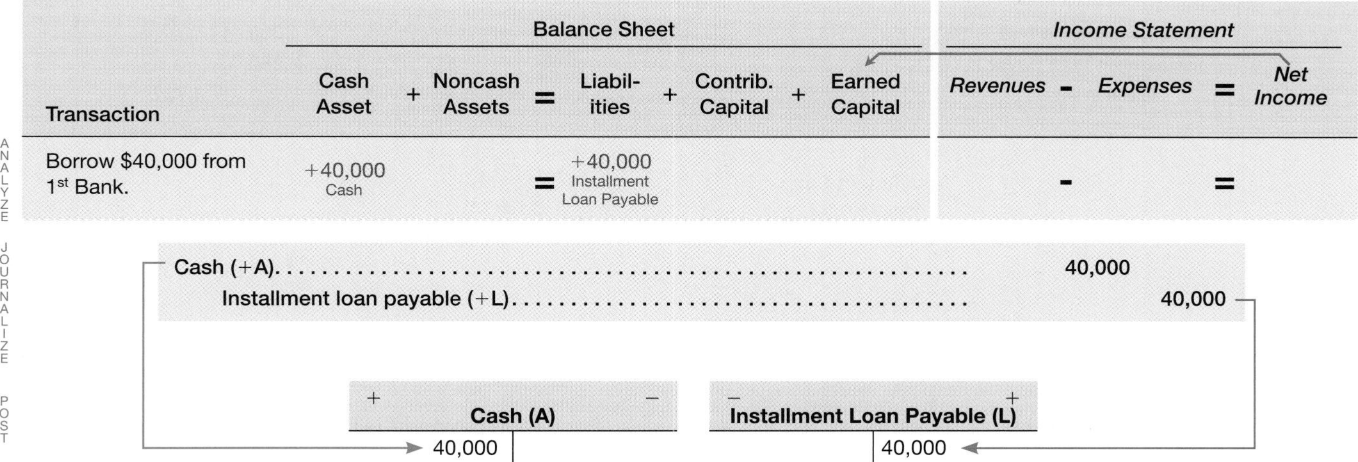

ANALYZE

Transaction	Cash Asset	+	Noncash Assets	=	Liabil-ities	+	Contrib. Capital	+	Earned Capital	Revenues	−	Expenses	=	Net Income
Borrow $40,000 from 1st Bank.	+40,000 Cash			=	+40,000 Installment Loan Payable						−		=	

JOURNALIZE

Cash (+A)	40,000	
Installment loan payable (+L)		40,000

POST

+ Cash (A) −	
40,000	

− Installment Loan Payable (L) +	
	40,000

On October 1, 2015, the first payment of $3,782 is due. The payment includes both interest for the three months from July 1 through September 30, and some portion of the original loan amount (the **principal**). The division of the payment between interest and principal is best illustrated using a **loan amortization table**, like the one in **Exhibit 9.2**. (Pages 624–634 in Appendix A demonstrate the use of Excel to calculate the required payment and the amortization table.)

Each payment includes interest and principal. The first loan payment, due on October 1, 2015, is summarized in the second row of the table. Column [B] is the quarterly loan payment. Column [C] is the interest expense, computed by multiplying column [A] by the interest rate (2 percent per quarter). Column [D] is the principal portion of the payment, which is the cash payment (column [B]) less the interest (column [C]). The remaining balance on the loan is in column [E], which is equal to the beginning balance in column [A] less the principal payment from column [D]. The loan balance decreases with each payment until the loan is paid off on July 1, 2018.

EXHIBIT 9.2 Loan Amortization Table

Date	[A] Beginning Balance	[B] Cash Payment	[C] ([A] × interest %) Interest	[D] ([B] − [C]) Principal	[E] ([A] − [D]) Balance
07/01/15					40,000
10/01/15	40,000	3,782	800	2,982	37,018
01/01/16	37,018	3,782	740	3,042	33,976
04/01/16	33,976	3,782	679	3,103	30,873
07/01/16	30,873	3,782	617	3,165	27,708
10/01/16	27,708	3,782	554	3,228	24,480
01/01/17	24,480	3,782	489	3,293	21,187
04/01/17	21,187	3,782	423	3,359	17,828
07/01/17	17,828	3,782	356	3,426	14,402
10/01/17	14,402	3,782	288	3,494	10,908
01/01/18	10,908	3,782	218	3,564	7,344
04/01/18	7,344	3,782	146	3,636	3,708
07/01/18	3,708	3,782	74	3,708	0

The first payment is recorded as follows:

	Balance Sheet									Income Statement				
Transaction	Cash Asset	+	Noncash Assets	=	Liabil-ities	+	Contrib. Capital	+	Earned Capital	Revenues	-	Expenses	=	Net Income
Record first payment on installment loan.	−3,782 Cash			=	−2,982 Installment Loan Payable				−800 Retained Earnings		-	+800 Interest Expense	=	−800

ANALYZE

JOURNALIZE

Interest expense (+E, −SE)	800	
Installment loan payable (−L)	2,982	
Cash (−A)		3,782

POST

− Installment Loan Payable (L) +	
2,982	

+ Cash (A) −	
	3,782

+ Interest Expense (E, SE) −	
800	

Subsequent payments are recorded similarly. Each loan payment is the same amount, quarter after quarter. And each period's interest expense is equal to the beginning loan balance times the periodic interest rate. Any difference between the payment and the interest expense affects the loan balance. In **Exhibit 9.2**, each payment contains some portion of interest expense and some portion of principal repayment, and the amounts change over time. As principal is repaid, the loan balance decreases, reducing the subsequent periods' interest expense and increasing the subsequent periods' principal repayment.

Bonds

Sometimes the amount or duration of financing required by a company is greater than the amount that a bank or insurance company can provide. Companies can borrow larger amounts of money by issuing bonds (or notes) in the capital markets. Bonds and notes are debt securities issued by companies and traded in the bond markets. When a company issues bonds, it is borrowing money. The investors who buy the bonds are lending money to the issuing company. That is, the bondholders are the company's creditors. Because the bond markets provide companies with access to large amounts of capital, bonds represent a very common, cost-effective source of long-term debt financing.

Bonds and notes are structured like any other borrowing. The borrower receives cash and agrees to pay it back with interest. Generally, the entire **face amount** (principal) of the bond or note is repaid at maturity and interest payments are made (usually semiannually) in the interim.

Companies wishing to raise funds in the bond market normally work with an underwriter (e.g., **Goldman Sachs**) to set the terms of the bond issue. The underwriter sells individual bonds (usually in $1,000 denominations) from this general bond issue to its retail clients, corporations and professional portfolio managers (e.g., **The Vanguard Group**), and it receives a fee for underwriting the bond issue.

Once issued, the bonds can be traded in the secondary market between investors just like stocks. Market prices of bonds fluctuate daily despite the fact that the company's obligation for payment of principal and interest remains fixed throughout the life of the bond. This occurs because of fluctuations in the general level of interest rates and changes in the financial condition of the borrowing company.

The following sections analyze and interpret the reporting for bonds. We first examine the mechanics of bond pricing. In a subsequent section, we address the accounting for and reporting of bonds.

LO3 Explain and illustrate the pricing of long-term nonoperating liabilities.

3

Pricing of Bonds

Two different interest rates are crucial for understanding how a bond is priced.

- **Coupon (contract or stated) rate** The coupon rate of interest is stated in the bond contract. It is used to compute the dollar amount of (semiannual) interest payments that are paid to bondholders during the life of the bond issue.
- **Market (yield) rate** The market rate is the interest rate that investors expect to earn on the investment for this debt security. This rate is used to price the bond issue.

The coupon (contract) rate is used to compute interest payments and the market (yield) rate is used to price the bond. The coupon rate and the market rate are nearly always different. The coupon rate is fixed prior to issuance of the bond and remains so throughout its life (unless the interest rate "floats" with market rates). Market rates of interest, on the other hand, fluctuate continually with the supply and demand for bonds in the marketplace, general macroeconomic conditions, and the financial condition of borrowers.

The bond price equals the **present value** of the expected cash flows to the bondholder. Specifically, bondholders normally expect to receive two different cash flows:

1. **Periodic interest payments** (usually semiannual) during the bond's life. These cash flows are typically in the form of equal payments at periodic intervals, called an **annuity**.
2. **Single payment** of the face (principal) amount of the bond at maturity.

The bond price equals the present value of the periodic interest payments plus the present value of the principal payment at maturity. We next illustrate the issuance of bonds at three different prices: at par, at a discount, and at a premium.

Bonds Issued at Par When a bond is issued at par, its coupon rate is identical to the market rate. Under this condition, a $1,000 bond sells for $1,000 in the market. To illustrate bond pricing, assume that investors wish to value a bond issue with a face amount of $100,000, a 6% annual coupon rate with interest payable semiannually (3% semiannual rate), and a maturity of 4 years.[5] Investors purchasing this issue receive the following cash flows:

	Number of Payments	Dollars per Payment	Total Cash Flows
Semiannual interest payments	4 years × 2 = 8	$100,000 × 3% = $ 3,000	$ 24,000
Principal payment at maturity.	1	$100,000	100,000
			$124,000

Specifically, the bond agreement dictates that the borrower makes 8 semiannual payments of $3,000 each, computed as $100,000 × (6%/2), plus the $100,000 face amount at maturity, for a total of $124,000 in cash flows. Each $1,000 bond in this bond issue provides the bondholder with an annuity of 8 payments of $30 and a principal payment of $1,000 at maturity. For an individual bond, the cash flows total $1,240 (= $30 × 8 + $1,000).

When pricing bonds, the number of periods used for computing the present value is the number of interest (coupon) payments required by the bond. In this case, there are 8 semiannual interest payments required, so we use 8, six-month periods to value the bond. The market interest rate (yield) is 6% per year, which is 3% per six-month period.

The bond price is the present value of the interest annuity plus the present value of the principal payment. Assuming that investors desire a 6% annual market rate (yield), the bond sells for exactly $100,000, which is computed as follows:

[5] Semiannual interest payments are typical for bonds. With semiannual interest payments, the issuer pays bondholders two interest payments per year. The semiannual interest rate is the annual rate divided by two.

	Payment	Present Value Factor[a]	Present Value
Interest	$ 3,000	7.01969[b]	$ 21,059
Principal	$100,000	0.78941[c]	78,941
			$100,000

[a] Mechanics of using tables to compute present values are explained in Appendix A at the end of the text. Present value factors are taken from tables provided in Appendix A.

[b] Present value of ordinary annuity for 8 periods discounted at 3% per period.

[c] Present value of single payment in 8 periods hence discounted at 3% per period.

Because the bond contract pays investors a 6% annual rate when investors demand a 6% market rate, investors purchase these bonds at the **par (face) value** of $1,000 per bond, or $100,000 in total.[6] Using a financial calculator, we can compute the bond value as follows: N = 8; I/Yr = 3; PMT = 3,000; FV = 100,000:

Calculator				
N	I/Yr	PV	PMT	FV
8	3	100,000	3,000	100,000

Bonds Issued at a Discount As a second illustration, assume that market conditions are such that investors demand an 8% annual yield (4% semiannual) for the 6% coupon bond, while all other details remain the same. The bond now sells for $93,267, computed as follows:

	Payment	Present Value Factor	Present Value
Interest	$ 3,000	6.73274[a]	$20,198
Principal	$100,000	0.73069[b]	73,069
			$93,267

[a] Present value of ordinary annuity for 8 periods discounted at 4% per period.

[b] Present value of single payment in 8 periods hence discounted at 4% per period.

Using a financial calculator, the bond is priced as follows: N = 8; I/Yr = 4; PMT = 3,000; FV = 100,000:

Calculator				
N	I/Yr	PV	PMT	FV
8	4	93,267	3,000	100,000

The market price of the bond issue is, therefore, $93,267. The price of each bond in the bond issue is $932.67 (= $93,267/100).

Because the bond carries a coupon rate *lower* than that which investors demand, the bond is less desirable and sells at a **discount**. In general, bonds sell at a discount whenever the coupon rate is less than the market rate.[7]

Bonds Issued at a Premium As a third illustration, assume that investors in the bond market demand a 4% annual yield (2% semiannual) for the 6% coupon bonds, while all other details remain the same. The bond issue now sells for $107,325, computed as follows:

[6] If we purchase a bond after the semiannual interest date, we must pay accrued interest in addition to the purchase price. This interest is returned to us in the regular interest payment. (This procedure makes the bookkeeping easier for the issuer/underwriter.)

[7] Bond prices are often stated in percent form. For example, a bond sold at par is said to be sold at 100 (that is, 100% of its face value, par). The bond sold at $932.67 is said to be sold at 93.267 (93.267% of par, computed as $932.67/$1,000).

	Payment	Present Value Factor	Present Value
Interest	$ 3,000	7.32548[a]	$ 21,976
Principal	$100,000	0.85349[b]	85,349
			$107,325

[a] Present value of ordinary annuity for 8 periods discounted at 2% per period.

[b] Present value of single payment in 8 periods hence discounted at 2% per period.

Using a financial calculator, the bond is priced as follows: N = 8; I/Yr = 2; PMT = 3,000; FV = 100,000:

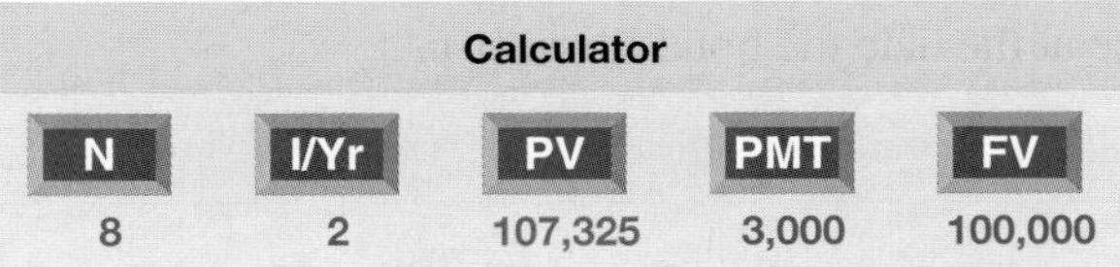

Calculator				
N	I/Yr	PV	PMT	FV
8	2	107,325	3,000	100,000

The market price of the bond issue is, therefore, $107,325. The price of each bond in the bond issue is $1,073.25 (= $107,325/100).

Because the bond carries a coupon rate higher than that which investors demand, the bond is more desirable and sells at a **premium**. In general, bonds sell at a premium whenever the coupon rate is greater than the market rate. **Exhibit 9.3** summarizes this relation for bond pricing.

EXHIBIT 9.3 Coupon Rate, Market Rate, and Bond Pricing

Coupon rate > market rate	→	Bond sells at a **premium** (above face amount)
Coupon rate = market rate	→	Bond sells at **par** (at face amount)
Coupon rate < market rate	→	Bond sells at a **discount** (below face amount)

Effective Cost of Debt

When a bond sells for par, the cost to the issuing company is the cash interest paid. In our first illustration where the bond is issued at par, the *effective cost* of the bond is the 6% interest paid by the issuer.

When a bond sells at a discount, the issuer's effective cost consists of two parts: (1) the cash interest paid and (2) the discount incurred. The discount, which is the difference between par and the lower issue price, is a cost that must eventually be reflected in the issuer's income statement as an expense. This fact means that the effective cost of a discount bond is greater than if the bond had sold at par. A discount is a cost and, like any other cost, must eventually be transferred from the balance sheet to the income statement as an expense. In the previous section's discount example, the economic substance is that the bond issuer has not borrowed $100,000 at 6%, but rather $93,267 at 8%.

When a bond sells at a premium, the issuer's effective cost consists of (1) the cash interest paid and (2) a cost reduction due to the premium received. The premium is a benefit that must eventually find its way from the balance sheet to the income statement as a *reduction* of interest expense. As a result of the premium, the effective cost of a premium bond is less than if the bond had sold at par. Effectively, the bond issuer has borrowed $107,325 at 4% in the premium example above.

Bonds are priced to yield the return (market rate) demanded by investors in the bond market, which results in the effective interest rate of a bond *always* equaling the yield (market) rate, regardless of the coupon (stated) rate of the bond. Bond prices are set by the market so as to always yield the rate required by investors based on the terms and qualities of the bond. Companies cannot influence the effective cost of debt by raising or lowering the coupon rate. We discuss the factors affecting the market yield later in the chapter.

The effective cost of debt is ultimately reflected in the amount reported in the issuer's income statement as interest expense. This amount can be, and usually is, different from the cash interest paid. The two are the same only for a bond issued at par. The next section discusses how management reports bonds on the balance sheet and interest expense on the income statement.

LO4 Analyze and account for financial statement effects of long-term nonoperating liabilities.

4

Reporting of Bond Financing

This section identifies and describes the financial statement effects of bond transactions.

Bonds Issued at Par When a bond sells at par, the issuing company receives the cash proceeds and accepts an obligation to make payments per the bond contract. Specifically, cash is increased and a liability (bonds payable) is increased by the same amount. Using the facts from our earlier illustration, the issuance of bonds at par has the following financial statement effects (there is no revenue or expense at the date the bond is issued):

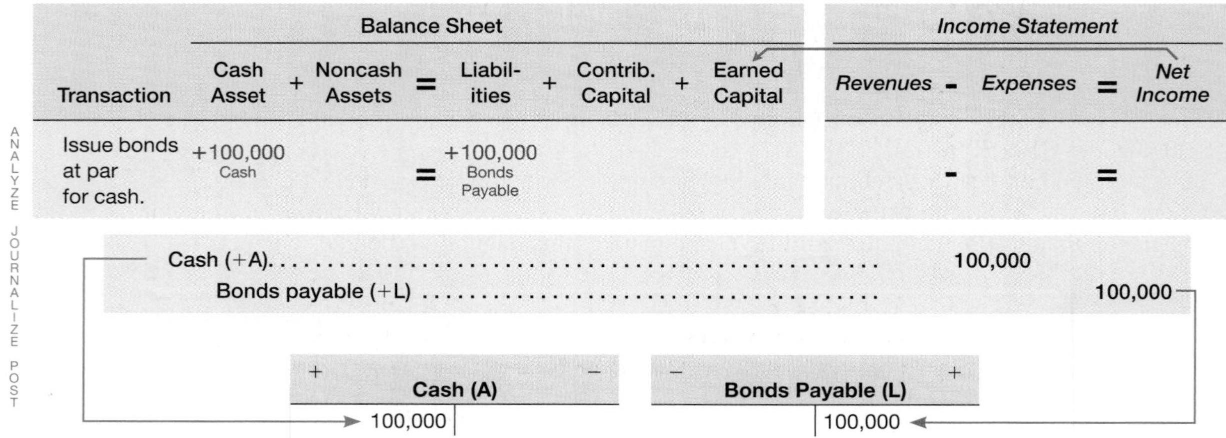

	Balance Sheet									Income Statement				
Transaction	Cash Asset	+	Noncash Assets	=	Liabilities	+	Contrib. Capital	+	Earned Capital	*Revenues*	-	*Expenses*	=	*Net Income*
Issue bonds at par for cash.	+100,000 Cash			=	+100,000 Bonds Payable						-		=	

Cash (+A)	100,000	
Bonds payable (+L)		100,000

+ Cash (A) −		− Bonds Payable (L) +	
100,000			100,000

Bonds Issued at a Discount For the discount bond case, cash is increased by the proceeds from the sale of the bonds, and the liability increases by the same amount. However, the net liability consisting of the two components shown below (including a bond discount contra liability) is reported on the balance sheet.

FYI "Bonds Payable, Net" is a common title reflecting the face value of the bond less the unamortized discount.

Bonds payable, face	$100,000
Less bond discount	(6,733)
Bonds payable, net	$ 93,267

Using the facts above from our bond discount illustration, the financial statement effects follow:

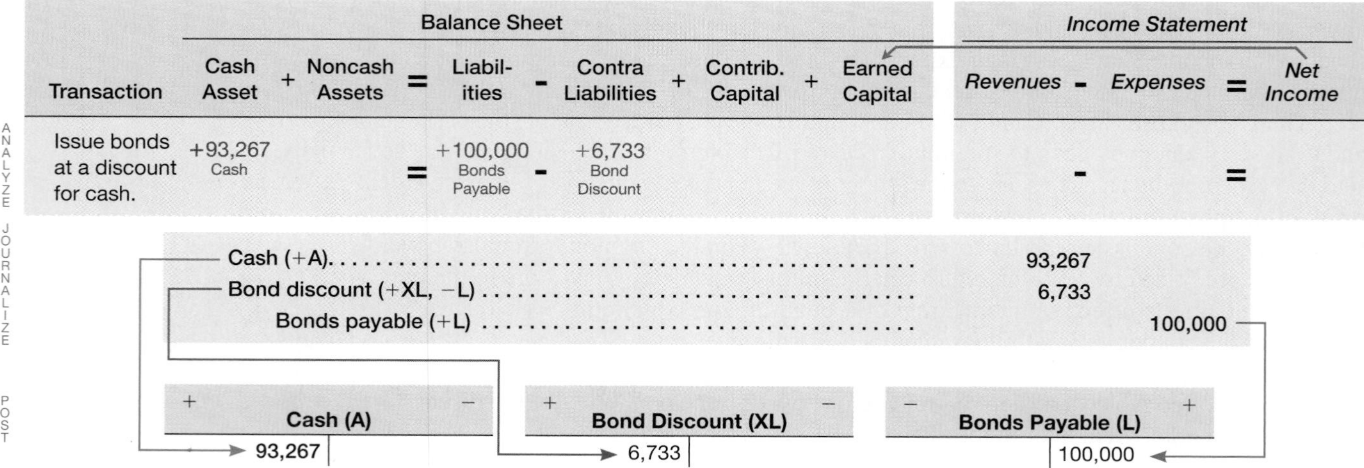

	Balance Sheet											Income Statement				
Transaction	Cash Asset	+	Noncash Assets	=	Liabilities	-	Contra Liabilities	+	Contrib. Capital	+	Earned Capital	*Revenues*	-	*Expenses*	=	*Net Income*
Issue bonds at a discount for cash.	+93,267 Cash			=	+100,000 Bonds Payable	-	+6,733 Bond Discount						-		=	

Cash (+A)	93,267	
Bond discount (+XL, −L)	6,733	
Bonds payable (+L)		100,000

+ Cash (A) −		+ Bond Discount (XL) −		− Bonds Payable (L) +	
93,267		6,733			100,000

Bonds are reported on the balance sheet net of any discount (or plus any premium). When the bond matures, however, the company is obligated to repay $100,000. Accordingly, at maturity, the bond liability must read $100,000, the amount that is owed. Therefore, between the bond issuance and its maturity, the discount must decline to zero. This reduction of the discount over the life of the bond is called **amortization**. This amortization causes the effective interest expense to be greater than the periodic cash interest payments based on the coupon rate.

BUSINESS INSIGHT

Zeros and Strips Zero coupon bonds and notes, called *zeros*, do not carry an explicit coupon rate. However, the pricing of these bonds and notes is done in the same manner as those with coupon rates—the exception is the absence of an interest annuity. This omission means that the price is the present value of just the principal payment at maturity; hence the bond is sold at a *deep discount*. For example, consider a 4-year, $100,000 zero coupon bond, priced to yield a market rate of 6%. The only payment would be the return of principal 4 years away. We already know that the present value of this single payment is $78,941. This "zero" would initially sell for $78,941 resulting in a substantial discount of $21,059.

Another interesting variation on traditional bonds is a *strip*, which is short for ***S**eparately **TR**aded **I**nterest and **P**rincipal*. Initially, a strip is priced and sold just like an ordinary bond. Subsequently, the two payment components—the periodic coupon payments and the *balloon* payment of principal which is due when the bond matures—are sold separately. A 4-year, $100,000 bond priced at $100,000 to yield 6% would be separated into two securities: 1) a zero, selling for $78,941, representing the present value of this single payment, and, 2) another security, priced at $21,059, representing the present value of the coupon payments.

Bonds Issued at a Premium When a bond is sold at a premium, the cash proceeds and net bond liability are recorded at the amount of the proceeds received (not the face amount of the bond). Again, using the facts above from our premium bond illustration, the financial statement effects are:

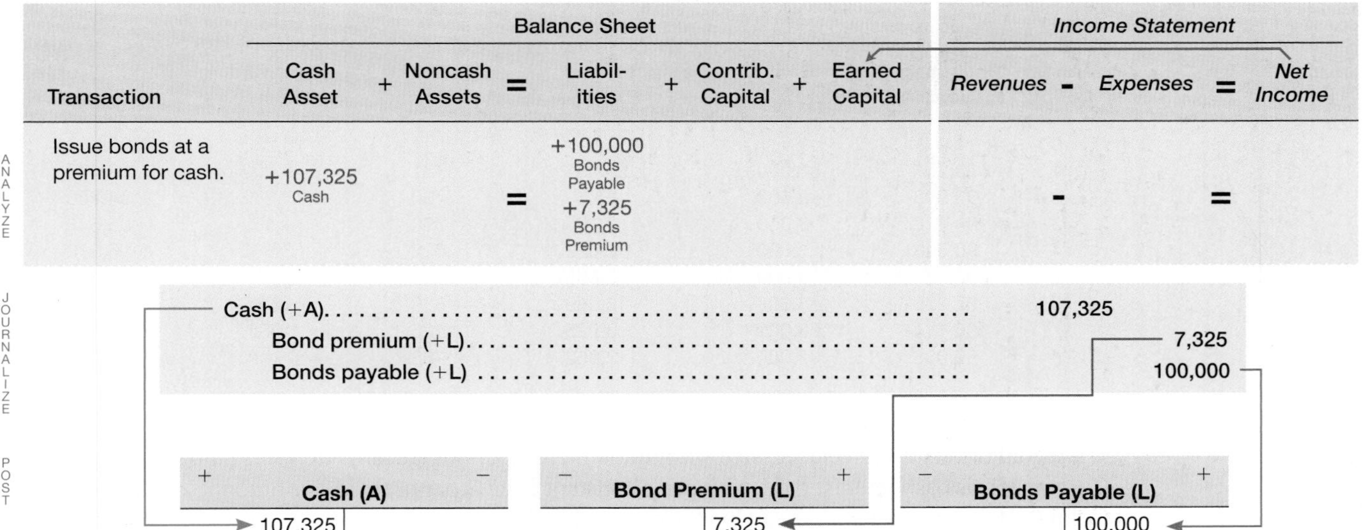

ANALYZE

Transaction	Cash Asset	+ Noncash Assets	= Liabilities	+ Contrib. Capital	+ Earned Capital	Revenues	− Expenses	= Net Income
Issue bonds at a premium for cash.	+107,325 Cash		= +100,000 Bonds Payable; +7,325 Bonds Premium				−	=

JOURNALIZE

	Debit	Credit
Cash (+A)	107,325	
Bond premium (+L)		7,325
Bonds payable (+L)		100,000

POST

+ Cash (A) −	− Bond Premium (L) +	− Bonds Payable (L) +
107,325	7,325	100,000

The net bond liability amount reported on the balance sheet, again, consists of two parts:

Bonds payable, face	$100,000
Add bond premium	7,325
Bonds payable, net	$107,325

The $100,000 must be repaid at maturity, and the premium is amortized to zero over the life of the bond. The premium represents a *benefit*, which yields a *reduction* in interest expense on the income statement.

Effects of Discount and Premium Amortization

The amount of interest expense that is reported on the income statement always equals the loan balance at the beginning of the period (bonds payable, net of discount or premium) times the market interest rate at the time of issue. For bonds issued at par, interest expense equals the cash interest payment. However, for bonds issued at a discount or premium, interest expense reported on the income statement equals interest paid adjusted for the amortization of the discount or premium:

	Cash interest paid			Cash interest paid
+	Amortization of discount	or	−	Amortization of premium
	Interest expense			Interest expense

Specifically, periodic amortization of a discount is added to the cash interest paid to get interest expense for a discount bond. Amortization of the discount reflects the additional cost the issuer incurs from issuance of the bonds at a discount and its recognition, via amortization, as an increase to interest expense. For a premium bond, the premium is a benefit the issuer receives at issuance. Amortization of the premium reduces interest expense over the debt term. Consequently, interest expense on the income statement represents the *effective cost* of debt (the *nominal cost* of debt is the cash interest paid). This is true whether the bonds are issued at par, at a discount, or at a premium.

Companies amortize discounts and premiums using the effective interest method. To illustrate, recall the assumptions of the discount bond above—face amount of $100,000, a 6% annual coupon rate payable semiannually (3% semiannual rate), a maturity of 4 years, and a market (yield) rate of 8% annual (4% semiannual). These facts resulted in a bond issue price of $932.67 per bond or $93,267 for the entire bond issue. **Exhibit 9.4** illustrates a bond discount amortization table for this bond.

EXHIBIT 9.4 Bond Discount Amortization Table

Semi-Annual Period	[A] Beginning Balance	[B] *(Face × coupon%)* Cash Interest Paid	[C] *([A] × market%)* Interest Expense	[D] *([C] − [B])* Discount Amortization	[E] *(Prior bal − [D])* Discount Balance	[F] *(Face − [E])* Bond Payable Net
0					$6,733	$ 93,267
1	$93,267	$3,000	$3,731	$731	6,002	93,998
2	93,998	3,000	3,760	760	5,242	94,758
3	94,758	3,000	3,790	790	4,452	95,548
4	95,548	3,000	3,822	822	3,630	96,370
5	96,370	3,000	3,855	855	2,775	97,225
6	97,225	3,000	3,889	889	1,886	98,114
7	98,114	3,000	3,925	925	962	99,038
8	99,038	3,000	3,962	962	0	100,000

The interest period is denoted in the left-most column. Period 0 is the point in time at which the bond is issued. Periods 1–8 are successive six-month interest periods (recall, interest is paid semiannually). Column [B] is cash interest paid, which is a constant $3,000 per period (face amount × coupon rate). Column [C] is interest expense, which is reported in the income statement. This column is computed as the carrying amount of the bond at the beginning of the period (column [A]) multiplied by the 4% semiannual yield rate used to compute the bond issue price. Column [D] is discount amortization, which is the difference between interest expense and cash interest paid. Column [E] is the discount balance, which is the previous balance of the discount less the discount amortization in column [D]. Column [F] is the net bond payable, which is the $100,000 face amount less the unamortized discount from column [E]. Column [A] is the value from the previous period's column [F].

The amortization process continues until period 8, at which time the discount balance is $0 and the net bond payable is $100,000 (the maturity value). An amortization table reveals the financial statement effects of the bond for its duration. Specifically, we see the cash effects in column [B], the income statement effects in column [C], and the balance sheet effects in columns [D], [E], and [F].

To record the interest payment at the end of period 1, we use the values in row 1 of the amortization table. The resulting entry is recorded as follows:

	Balance Sheet						Income Statement		
Transaction	Cash Asset	+ Noncash Assets	= Liabilities	− Contra Liabilities	+ Contrib. Capital	+ Earned Capital	Revenues	− Expenses	= Net Income
Record interest payment and interest expense on bond.	−3,000 Cash		=	− −731 Bond Discount		−3,731 Retained Earnings		− +3,731 Interest Expense	= −3,731

ANALYZE

JOURNALIZE

Interest expense (+E, −SE)	3,731	
Cash (−A)		3,000
Bond discount (−XL, +L)		731

POST

+ Interest Expense (E) −		+ Cash (A) −		+ Bond Discount (XL) −	
3,731			3,000		731

To illustrate amortization of a premium bond, we use the assumptions of the premium bond above—$100,000 face value, a 6% annual coupon rate payable semiannually (3% semiannual rate), a maturity of 4 years, and a 4% annual market (yield) rate (2% semiannual). These parameters resulted in a bond issue price of $1,073.25 per bond or $107,325 for the entire bond issue. **Exhibit 9.5** shows the bond premium amortization table for this bond.

EXHIBIT 9.5 Bond Premium Amortization Table

Semi-Annual Period	[A] Beginning Balance	[B] *(Face × coupon%)* Cash Interest Paid	[C] *([A] × market%)* Interest Expense	[D] *([B] − [C])* Premium Amortization	[E] *(Prior bal − [D])* Premium Balance	[F] *(Face + [E])* Bond Payable Net
0					$7,325	$107,325
1	$107,325	$3,000	$2,147	$853	6,472	106,472
2	106,472	3,000	2,129	871	5,601	105,601
3	105,601	3,000	2,112	888	4,713	104,713
4	104,713	3,000	2,094	906	3,807	103,807
5	103,807	3,000	2,076	924	2,883	102,883
6	102,883	3,000	2,058	942	1,941	101,941
7	101,941	3,000	2,039	961	980	100,980
8	100,980	3,000	2,020	980	0	100,000

Interest expense is computed using the same process that we used for discount bonds. The difference is that the yield rate is 4% (2% semiannual) in the premium case. Cash interest paid follows from the bond contract (face amount × coupon rate), and the other columns' computations reflect the premium amortization. After period 8, the premium is fully amortized (equals zero) and the net bond payable balance is $100,000, the amount owed at maturity. The book value of bonds issued at a discount starts below the face value and, over time, increases. The book value of bonds issued at a premium starts above the bonds' face value and, over time, decreases. At maturity, the book value of both types of bonds equals the face value that must be paid to the bondholders. Again, an amortization table reveals the financial statement effects of the bond—the cash effects in column [B], the income statement effects in column [C], and the balance sheet effects in columns [D], [E], and [F].

To record the interest payment at the end of period 1, we, again, use the values in row 1 of the amortization table. The resulting entry is recorded as follows:

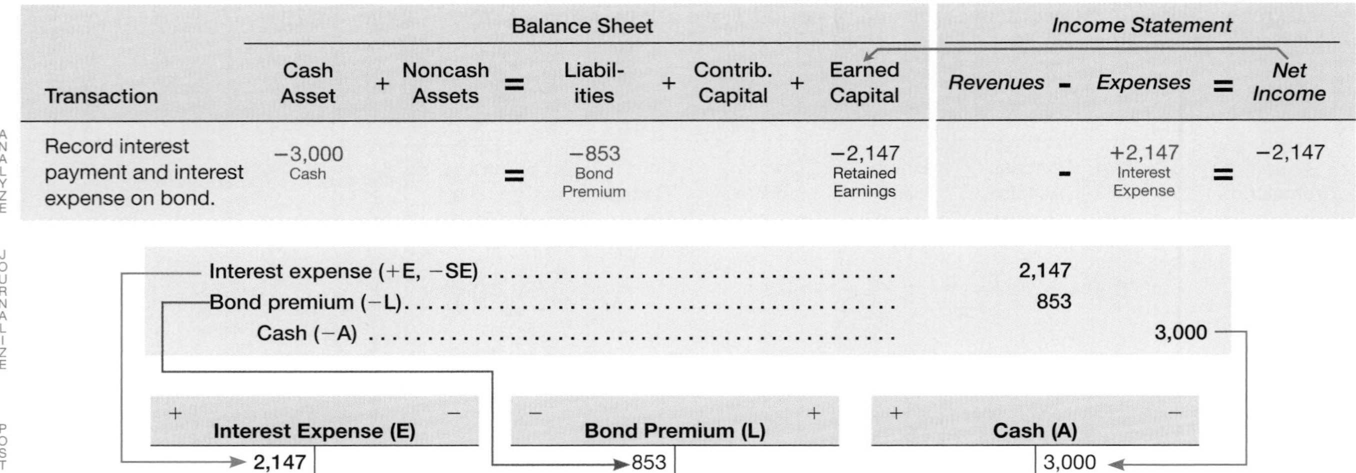

The Fair Value Option

Thus far, we have described the reporting of liabilities at *historical cost*. This means that all financial statement relationships are established on the date that the liability is created and do not subsequently change. For example, the interest rate used to value a bond is the market rate of interest on the date that the bond is issued and the reported value of the bond is the face value plus the unamortized premium or minus the unamortized discount. Yet, once issued, bonds can be traded in secondary markets. Market interest rates fluctuate and, as a consequence, the market value of a bond is likely to change after the bond is issued.

As an alternative to historical cost, a company may elect to report some or all of its financial liabilities at *fair value*. Moreover, a company may choose to report some of its liabilities at historical cost and others at fair value. It must make this choice at the inception of the liability (e.g., at the time that a bond is issued) and cannot subsequently switch between fair value and historical cost for that liability. If a company elects to report a liability at fair value in its balance sheet, then any changes in fair value are reported as a gain or loss in its income statement. If a liability is to be reported at historical cost, then its fair value is disclosed in the notes.

To illustrate how we report a liability at fair value, we refer to our example of a 4-year, 6% bond issued at a discount to yield 8%. The issue price of this bond is $93,267 and we assume that the bond is issued on June 30, 2015. Six months later, on December 31, the issuing company pays the first of eight coupon payments of $3,000. From **Exhibit 9.4**, we know that after this coupon payment, the bond payable, net of the discount, is equal to $93,998. Now assume that the market value of the bond has increased to $96,943. (This price increase is consistent with a market interest rate that has decreased to 7%.) The bond would now be reported on the balance sheet at a value of $96,943:

Bonds payable	$100,000
Less, unamortized discount	6,002
Bond payable, net (historical cost)	$ 93,998
Plus, fair value adjustment	2,945
Bond payable, net (fair value)	$ 96,943

The increase in the bond's fair value must be added to an account that adjusts the bond payable liability. The balancing entry is included as a loss in the income statement, and ends up in retained earnings. The fair value adjustment would be recorded as follows:

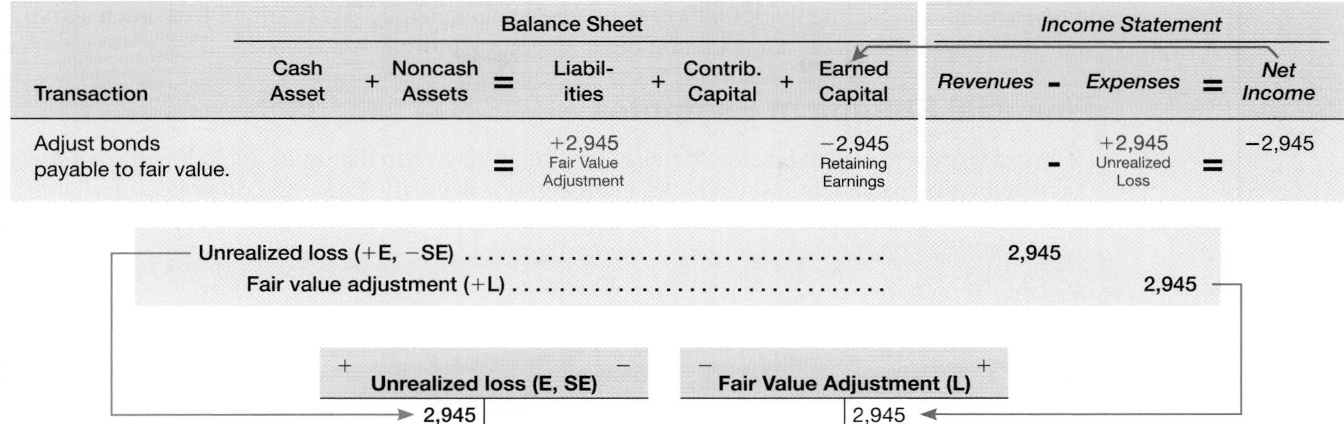

Transaction	Cash Asset	+ Noncash Assets	=	Liabil-ities	+ Contrib. Capital	+ Earned Capital	Revenues	−	Expenses	=	Net Income
Adjust bonds payable to fair value.			=	+2,945 Fair Value Adjustment		−2,945 Retaining Earnings		−	+2,945 Unrealized Loss	=	−2,945

	Debit	Credit
Unrealized loss (+E, −SE)	2,945	
Fair value adjustment (+L)		2,945

The fair value computation does not affect the calculation of interest expense or the amortization of the bond discount in this or any subsequent period. The unrealized loss does have an effect on the income statement. For this illustration, the total effect on income for 2015 is $6,676, which is computed as:

Coupon payment, July 1—December 31	$3,000
Amortization of the bond discount	731
Interest expense	$3,731
Unrealized loss	2,945
Total effect (decrease) on earnings	$6,676

If the fair value of this bond decreases (e.g., because interest rates increase), the fair value adjustment account would be debited and an unrealized gain would be credited and reported in the income statement. We discuss the fair value option further in Chapter 12.[8]

Effects of Bond Repurchase

Companies can and sometimes do repurchase (also called *redeem*) their bonds prior to maturity. The bond indenture (contract agreement) often includes a **call provision** giving the company the right to repurchase its bond by paying a small premium above face value. Alternatively, the company can repurchase bonds in the open market. When a company uses historical cost to account for its bonds, a bond repurchase usually results in a gain or loss, and is computed as follows:

Gain or loss on bond repurchase = Book value of the bond − Repurchase payment

The *book (carrying) value of the bond* is the net amount reported on the balance sheet. If the issuer pays more to retire the bonds than the amount carried on its balance sheet, a loss is reported on its income statement, usually called *loss on bond retirement*. The issuer reports a *gain on bond retirement* if the repurchase price is less than the book value of the bond.

GAAP dictates that any gains or losses on bond repurchases be reported as part of ordinary income unless they meet the criteria for treatment as part of discontinued operations. Relatively few debt retirements meet these criteria and, hence, most gains and losses on bond repurchases are reported as part of income from continuing operations.

The question arises as to how gains and losses on the redemption of bonds should affect our analysis of a company's profitability. Because bonds and notes payable represent nonoperating

[8] At the time of this textbook writing, the FASB is considering a change in the fair value accounting for companies' own debt. When a company's credit standing deteriorates under current fair value accounting, the fair value of its debt decreases and produces a gain on the company's income statement. Likewise, when a company's credit standing improves, the company reports a loss from the increased fair value of its debt. Many investors find these effects counter-intuitive. It is projected that the FASB will require these gains and losses to be reported in Other Comprehensive Income (discussed in Chapter 12) and have no effect on Net Income until the company's debt is redeemed.

items, activities including the refunding of bonds and any gain or loss resulting from such activity should be omitted from our computation of net operating profit.

Financial Statement Footnotes

Companies are required to disclose details about their long-term liabilities, including the amounts borrowed under each debt issuance, the interest rates, maturity dates, and other key provisions. Following is Verizon's disclosure in note 8 to its 2014 10-K for its long-term debt ($ millions):

Long-Term Debt

Outstanding long-term obligations are as follows:

At December 31	Interest Rates %	Maturities	(dollars in millions) 2014	2013
Verizon Communications—notes payable and other	0.30—3.85	2015—2042	$ 27,617	$20,416
	4.15—5.50	2018—2054	40,701	20,226
	5.85—6.90	2018—2054	24,341	31,965
	7.35—8.95	2018—2039	2,264	5,023
	Floating	2015—2025	14,600	5,500
Verizon Wireless—notes payable and other	8.75—8.88	2015—2018	676	3,931
Verizon—Alltel assumed notes	6.80—7.88	2029—2032	686	1,300
Telephone subsidiaries—debentures	5.13—6.86	2027—2033	1,075	1,075
	7.38—7.88	2022—2032	1,099	1,099
	8.00—8.75	2019—2031	880	880
Other subsidiaries—debentures and other	6.84—8.75	2018—2028	1,432	1,700
Capital lease obligations (average rate of 4.0% and 8.1% in 2014 and 2013, respectively)			516	293
Unamortized discount, net of premium			(2,954)	(264)
Total long-term debt, including current maturities			112,933	93,144
Less long-term debt maturing within one year			2,397	3,486
Total long-term debt			$110,536	$89,658

Verizon reports a book value for long-term debt of $112,933 million at year-end 2014. Of this amount, $2,397 million matures in the next year, hence its classification as a current liability (current maturities of long-term debt) and the remainder matures after 2015. Verizon also reports $2,954 million in unamortized discount (net of unamortized premium) on this debt.

In addition to amounts, rates, and due dates on its long-term debt, Verizon also reports aggregate maturities for the 5 years subsequent to its balance sheet date:

Maturities of Long-Term Debt

Maturities of long-term debt outstanding at December 31, 2014, are as follows ($ millions):

2015	$ 2,397
2016	6,114
2017	3,911
2018	6,529
2019	6,088
Thereafter	87,894

This reporting reveals that Verizon is required to make principal payments of $25,039 million between 2015 and 2019, and $87,894 million thereafter. Such maturities are important as a company must meet its required payments, negotiate a rescheduling of the indebtedness, or refinance the debt to avoid default. The latter (default) usually has severe consequences as debt holders have legal remedies available to them, which can result in bankruptcy of the company.

Verizon's disclosure on the fair value of its total debt follows:

The fair value of our debt is determined using various methods, including quoted prices for identical terms and maturities . . . as well as quoted prices for similar terms and maturities in inactive markets and future cash flows discounted at current rates. . . The fair value of our short-term and long-term debt, excluding capital leases, was as follows ($ millions):

	2014		2013	
At December 31,	Carrying Amount	Fair Value	Carrying Amount	Fair Value
Short-term and long-term debt, excluding capital leases.	$112,755	$126,549	$93,298	$103,527

As of December 31, 2014, indebtedness with a book value of $112,755 million had a fair value of $126,549 million, resulting in an unrecognized liability (and loss if the debt is redeemed) of $13,794 million (due mainly to a decline in interest rates subsequent to bond issuance). The justification for not recognizing unrealized gains and losses on the balance sheet and income statement is that such amounts can reverse with future fluctuations in interest rates. Further, because only the face amount of debt is repaid at maturity, unrealized gains and losses that arise during intervening years are not necessarily relevant. (This same logic is used to justify the nonrecognition of gains and losses on held-to-maturity investments in debt securities, a topic covered in Chapter 12.) At this time, Verizon, like most U.S. companies, has elected to report liabilities at historical cost in the financial statements and disclose fair values in the footnotes.

Interest and the Statement of Cash Flows

GAAP requires that interest payments (and receipts) be included in cash flows from operating activities. For companies using the indirect method for operating cash flows, net income already includes interest expense. Because interest expense does not equal interest payments, the reconciliation of net income to cash flows from operating activities should include an adjustment for any amortization of bond discounts or premiums.

However, interest income and interest expense are typically related to nonoperating assets (investments in securities) and nonoperating liabilities (interest-bearing bonds and notes), respectively. As such, they should be omitted from all computations of net operating profit (as in Appendix A to Chapter 5) and also separated from other cash flows when analyzing a company's operations, even though it sometimes requires some digging in the financial statements to determine their magnitudes.

ANALYZING FINANCIAL STATEMENTS

LO5 Explain how solvency ratios and debt ratings are determined and how they impact the cost of debt.

5

A major concern of managers and analysts is the solvency of the corporation. In this chapter we revisit two ratios discussed in previous chapters, both of which are designed to measure a firm's solvency. The first ratio is the debt-to-equity ratio (D/E), first introduced in Chapter 1. It measures the extent to which a company relies on debt financing, also known as financial leverage. The second ratio is times-interest-earned (TIE), which measures the ability of current operations to cover interest costs.

Analysis Objective

We want to gauge the ability of a company to satisfy its long-term debt obligations and remain solvent.

Analysis Tool Debt-to-Equity Ratio

$$\textbf{Debt-to-equity ratio (D/E)} = \frac{\textbf{Total liabilities}}{\textbf{Total stockholders' equity}}$$

Applying the Ratio to Verizon

$$\textbf{2012:} \frac{\$139,689}{\$85,533} = 1.63 \text{ or } 163\%$$

$$\textbf{2013:} \frac{\$178,682}{\$95,416} = 1.87 \text{ or } 187\%$$

$$\textbf{2014:} \frac{\$219,032}{\$13,676} = 16.02 \text{ or } 1602\%$$

Guidance A debt-to-equity ratio equal to 1.0 implies that the company is relying on debt and equity financing in equal amounts. As a company's reliance on debt increases and the company's long-term solvency becomes more of a concern, this ratio increases. A debt-to-equity ratio of about 1.5 is about average, though **Exhibit 5.13** (in Chapter 5) shows that the ratio varies by industry.

Verizon in Context

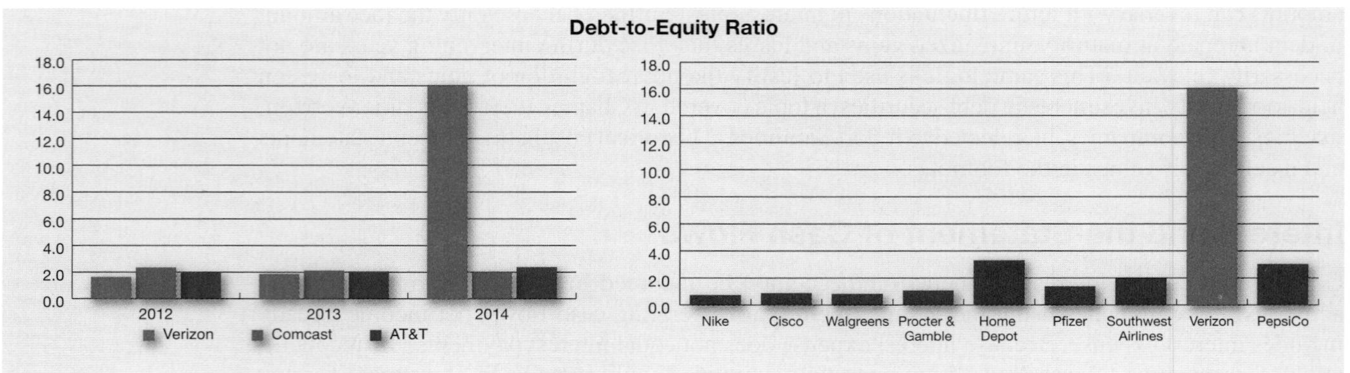

Analysis Tool Times Interest Earned

$$\textbf{Times interest earned (TIE)} = \frac{\textbf{Earnings before interest and taxes}}{\textbf{Interest expense}}$$

Applying the Ratio to Verizon

$$\textbf{2012:} \frac{\$12,468}{\$2,571} = 4.85 \text{ times}$$

$$\textbf{2013:} \frac{\$31,944}{\$2,667} = 11.98 \text{ times}$$

$$\textbf{2014:} \frac{\$20,185}{\$4,915} = 4.11 \text{ times}$$

Guidance When a company relies on debt financing, it assumes the burden of paying the interest on the debt. The times interest earned ratio measures the burden of interest costs by comparing earnings before interest and taxes (EBIT) to annual interest expense. A high TIE ratio indicates that a company is able to meet its interest costs without adversely affecting profitability.

Verizon in Context

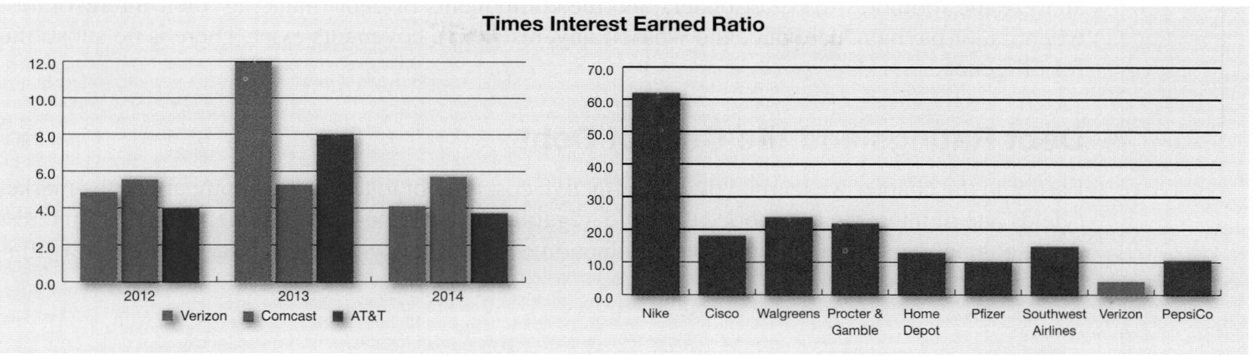

Takeaways Before 2014, Verizon's debt-to-equity ratio was lower than either Comcast or AT&T, two of its competitors. In 2014, Verizon engaged in a transaction to buy out the 45% equity interest of its wireless partner (Vodafone Group Plc) that had the effect of reducing its cash and reducing its shareholders equity by a substantial amount. Verizon's debt-to equity ratio has been higher than most of the companies we have looked at in this text, and in 2014, it is substantially higher. Its times interest earned ratio is lower than many companies, though it remains higher than its competitor, AT&T. The size of this ratio is driven by two factors—the amount of debt financing, which in turn determines interest expense, as well as profitability. We should also take into account that Verizon's depreciation and amortization expense is almost as large as its earnings before interest and taxes. Therefore, its cash from operating activities may be able to support a higher debt load.

In sum, Verizon appears to be a company with a very high level of financial leverage, as indicated by a debt-to-equity ratio that is much higher than average and a lower than average times interest earned ratio. However, we must also recognize that financial reports do not recognize the values of many company resources, particularly opportunities for future growth. At the time of this writing, the total market value of Verizon's common stock is more than $193.7 billion, while the book value of shareholders' equity at the end of 2014 was $13.7 billion.

Other Considerations In Chapter 5 we learned that debt financing is a double-edged sword. When used effectively, financial leverage increases return on equity because debt financing is generally less costly than equity financing. However, debt carries with it the risk of **default**, which is the risk that the company will be unable to pay its obligations when they come due (insolvency). To provide some protection against default risk, creditors usually require a company to execute a loan agreement that places restrictions on the company's activities. These restrictions, called covenants, impose indirect costs on a firm beyond the explicit cost of interest, and these indirect costs tend to increase as a company increases its reliance on debt financing. When a company's solvency ratios are close to the limits specified by its covenants, management is more likely to pass up profitable investment opportunities or engage in counterproductive earnings management activities to avoid violating these restrictions.

Walgreen Co. has two lines of credit totaling $1.35 billion as of the end of its 2014 fiscal year. In its footnotes, Walgreens reports:

> The Company's ability to access these facilities is subject to compliance with the terms and conditions of the credit facilities, including financial covenants. The covenants require the Company to maintain certain financial ratios related to minimum net worth and priority debt, along with limitations on the sale of assets and purchases of investments. At August 31, 2014, the Company was in compliance with all such covenants.

There are several variations on the ratios that we have discussed here and there is no single ratio that can be described as the best measure of company solvency. As with all ratios, solvency measures can be distorted by uncertain, inappropriate or inaccurate data. It is always helpful to analyze the footnotes to better understand the components of debt financing, their interest rates, when major payments are due, and what, if any, restrictive covenants exist. There is no substitute for diligence.

Debt Ratings and the Cost of Debt

Earlier in the chapter we learned that the effective cost of debt to the issuing company is the market (yield) rate of interest used to price the bond, regardless of the bond coupon rate. The rate of interest that a company must pay on its debt is a function of the maturity of that debt and the creditworthiness of the issuing company.

RESEARCH INSIGHT

Accounting Conservatism and Cost of Debt Research indicates that companies applying more conservative accounting methods incur a lower cost of debt. Research also suggests that while accounting conservatism can lead to lower-quality accounting income (because such income does not fully reflect economic reality), creditors are more confident in the numbers and view them as more credible. Evidence also implies that companies can lower the required return demanded by creditors (the risk premium) by issuing high-quality financial reports that include enhanced footnote disclosures and detailed supplemental reports.

A company's debt rating, also referred to as credit quality and creditworthiness, is related to default risk. Companies seeking to obtain bond financing from the capital markets, normally first seek a rating on their proposed debt issuance from one of several rating agencies such as **Standard & Poor's**, **Moody's Investors Service**, or **Fitch**. The aim of rating agencies is to rate debt so that its default risk is more accurately determined and priced by the market. Such debt issuances carry debt ratings from one or more of the three large rating agencies as shown in **Exhibit 9.6**. This exhibit includes the general description attached to the debt for each rating class—for example, AAA is assigned to debt of prime maximum safety (maximum creditworthiness). Bonds with credit ratings below investment grade (below Baa or BBB) are referred to as "high yield" bonds or, more pejoratively, "junk bonds," which may not be purchased by many professionally managed portfolios.

EXHIBIT 9.6 Corporate Debt Ratings and Descriptions

Moody's	S&P	Fitch	Description
Aaa	AAA	AAA	Prime Maximum Safety
Aa	AA	AA	High Grade, High Quality
A	A	A	Upper-Medium Grade
Baa	BBB	BBB	Lower-Medium Grade
Ba	BB	BB	Non-Investment Grade
B	B	B	Speculative
Caa	CCC	CCC	Substantial Risk
Ca	CC	CC	Extremely Speculative
C	C	C	Exceptionally High Risk
	D		Default

YOU MAKE THE CALL

You are the Vice President of Finance Your company is currently rated BB by credit rating agencies. You are considering possible financial and other restructurings of the company to increase your credit rating. What types of restructurings might you consider? What benefits will your company receive from those restructurings? What costs will your company incur to implement such restructurings? [Answers on page 443]

Verizon bonds are rated A− according to Fitch, and BBB+ according to S&P, as of 2015.[9] It is this rating that, in conjunction with the maturity of its bonds, establishes the market interest rate and consequent selling price. There are a number of considerations that affect the rating of a bond. **Standard & Poor's** lists the following factors among its credit rating criteria:

Business Risk
- Industry characteristics
- Competitive position (e.g., marketing, technology, efficiency, regulation)
- Management

Financial Risk
- Financial characteristics
- Financial policy
- Profitability
- Capital structure
- Cash flow protection
- Financial flexibility

Rating agencies use a number of accounting ratios to help establish creditworthiness, including measures of liquidity, solvency and profitability. These ratios are variants of the ratios we describe in Chapter 5 and in this chapter, especially those used to assess solvency.

There are other relevant factors in setting debt ratings, including the following:

- **Collateral** Companies can provide security for debt in the form of mortgages on assets. To the extent debt is secured, the debt holder is in a preferred position vis-à-vis other creditors.
- **Covenants** Debt agreements (indentures) can contain restrictions on the issuing company to protect debt holders. Examples are restrictions on excessive dividend payment, on other company acquisitions, on further borrowing, and on maintaining minimum levels for key liquidity and solvency ratios. These covenants provide debt holders some means of control over the issuer's operations because, unlike equity investors, they do not have voting rights.
- **Options** Debt obligations involve contracts between the borrowing company and debt holders. Options are sometimes written into debt contracts. Examples are options to convert debt into stock (so that debt holders have a stake in value creation) and options allowing the issuing company to repurchase its debt before maturity (usually at a premium).

CHAPTER-END REVIEW

GuidedExamples MBC

On January 1, 2016, Givoly Company issues $300,000 of 15-year, 10% bonds payable for $351,876, yielding an effective interest rate of 8%. Interest is payable semiannually on June 30 and December 31. (1) Show computations to confirm the issue price of $351,876, and (2) provide Givoly's journal entries, T-accounts, and complete financial statement effects template for (a) bond issuance, (b) semiannual interest payment and premium amortization on June 30, 2016, and (c) semiannual interest payment and premium amortization on December 31, 2016.

The solution to this review problem can be found on pages 457-458.

[9] Standard & Poor's reports that ratings "may be modified by the addition of a plus (+) or minus (-) sign to show relative standing within the major rating categories."

SUMMARY

LO1 Identify and account for current operating liabilities. (p. 415)

- Current liabilities are short-term and generally non-interest-bearing; accordingly, firms try to maximize the financing of their assets using these sources of funds.
- ROE increases when firms make use of accounts payable increases to finance operating assets; a firm must avoid excessive "leaning on the trade" for short-term gains that can damage long-term supplier relationships.
- When cash discounts are offered by creditors, companies use the net of discount method to report accounts payable information.
- Accrued liabilities reflect amounts that have been recognized as expenses in the current (or a prior) period, but not yet paid.
- While all accruals result in a liability on the balance sheet and an expense on the income statement, management has latitude in determining (in some cases, estimating) their amount and timing; this discretion offers the opportunity for managing earnings.

LO2 Describe and account for current nonoperating (financial) liabilities. (p. 422)

- Management will generally try to assure that the debt service on financial (nonoperating) liabilities coincides with the cash flows from the assets financed.
- When large amounts of financing are required for, say, plant and equipment, firms find that bonds, notes, and other forms of long-term financing provide a cost-efficient means of raising capital.

LO3 Explain and illustrate the pricing of long-term nonoperating liabilities. (p. 427)

- The coupon rate indicated on a bond contract determines the periodic interest payment. The required return on any bond called the market (yield or effective) rate is determined by market conditions and rarely equals the coupon (contract) rate. The market rate is used to price the bond and determines the effective cost of the debt to the issuer.
- If the market rate is below the coupon rate, the bond will sell at a premium to its face value, assuring that the owner of the bond earns only the market rate of interest. If the market rate exceeds the coupon rate, the bond will sell at a discount so that the bond is issued at less than its face value.

LO4 Analyze and account for financial statement effects of long-term nonoperating liabilities. (p. 430)

- A discount for a bond selling below its face value represents additional interest expense over time to the issuer because the issuer received less than face value upon issuance, but must pay the holder the face value at the bond's maturity; this discount represents additional interest beyond the coupon payment to the holder. The premium on a bond selling above its face value lowers the interest cost to the issuer.
- Companies may choose to report liabilities at fair value; if the fair value option is elected, changes in fair value are reported as gains and losses in the income statement.[10]
- Gains and losses on bonds repurchased must be reported in operating income, unless they are part of discontinued operations. Such transactions do not represent operating activities, and gains/losses should be removed when determining cash from operations with the indirect method.

LO5 Explain how solvency ratios and debt ratings are determined and how they impact the cost of debt. (p. 437)

- Two debt-related ratios that are particularly useful in evaluating a company's solvency include the debt-to-equity ratio and the times interest earned ratio.
- The market rate of interest to a firm reflects the creditworthiness of the particular issuer. Credit agencies play an important role in this process by issuing debt ratings.
- Borrowing is typically secured by collateral that places the lender in a superior position to other creditors and covenants that put restrictions on the borrower's activities; bonds can also contain options including those for conversion or repurchase.

[10] A projected change in accounting standards may result in these gains and losses being reported in other comprehensive income—described in Chapter 12—until the debt is retired.

GUIDANCE ANSWERS . . . YOU MAKE THE CALL

You are the Analyst Accrued liabilities must be probable and estimable before they can be reported in the balance sheet. If Dow's environmental costs turn out to be higher than management estimates, it may be understating its liabilities (and overstating equity). As an analyst, if you suspect that Dow's estimate is too low, you should add an additional estimated liability to the company's balance sheet.

You are the Vice President of Finance The types of restructurings you might consider are those yielding a strengthening of the financial ratios typically used to assess liquidity and solvency by the rating agencies. Such restructurings include inventory reduction to generate cash, the reallocation of cash outflows from investing activities (PPE or intangible assets) to debt reduction, and reducing the cash outflows for repurchases of the company's stock (treasury stock). These actions increase liquidity or reduce financial leverage and, thus, should yield an improved debt rating. An improved debt rating gives the company access to more debt holders, as the current debt rating is below investment grade and is not a suitable investment for many professionally managed portfolios. An improved debt rating also yields a lower interest rate on debt. Offsetting these benefits are costs such as the following: (1) potential loss of sales from inventory stock-outs; (2) potential future cash flow reductions and loss of market power from reduced investing in PPE and intangibles; and (3) possible reductions in share price if shareholders were expecting more cash to be returned in the form of dividends and stock buybacks. All cost and benefits must be assessed before you pursue any restructurings.

KEY RATIOS

$$\text{Debt-to-equity (D / E)} = \frac{\text{Total liabilities}}{\text{Total stockholders' equity}}$$

$$\text{Times interest earned (TIE)} = \frac{\text{Earnings before interest and taxes}}{\text{Interest}}$$

KEY TERMS

Accounts payable (p. 415)
Accrued liabilities (p. 415)
Amortization (p. 431)
Annuity (p. 427)
Call provision (p. 435)
Cash discounts (p. 416)
Collateral (p. 424, 441)
Contingent liability (p. 419)
Cookie jar reserves (p. 421)
Coupon (contract or stated) rate (p. 427)
Covenants (p. 441)
Current maturities of long-term debt (p. 415)
Default (p. 439)
Deferred performance liabilities (p. 415)
Discount (p. 428)
Face amount (p. 426)
Financial leverage (p. 414)
Leaning on the trade (p. 416)
Loan amortization table (p. 425)
Market (yield) rate (p. 427)
Net-of-discount method (p. 416)
Options (p. 441)
Par (face) value (p. 428)
Periodic interest payments (p. 427)
Premium (p. 429)
Present value (p. 427)
Principal (p. 425)
Short-term interest-bearing debt (p. 415)
Single payment (p. 427)

Assignments with the MBC logo in the margin are available in myBusinessCourse.
See the Preface of the book for details.

MULTIPLE CHOICE

1. Which of the following statements is correct? A decrease in accrued wages liability:

a. decreases cash flows from operations.
b. decreases working capital.
c. increases net income.
d. increases net nonoperating (financial) assets.

Multiple Choice Answers
1. a 2. b 3. b
4. c 5. a, b, and d

2. On April 1, 2015, a firm borrows $12,000 at an annual interest rate of 10% with payments required semiannually on September 30 and March 31. How much interest payable and how much interest expense should appear on the firm's annual report at the end of the firm's fiscal year, December 31, 2015?
   a. $900 payable and $300 expense.
   b. $300 payable and $900 expense.
   c. $600 payable and $600 expense.
   d. $900 payable and $600 expense.

3. A firm issues $30,000,000 of 10-year bonds and receives $29.5 million in cash. Which of the following statements is correct?
   a. The bonds do not have a coupon rate because they are zeros.
   b. The market rate exceeds the coupon rate.
   c. The contract rate exceeds the market rate.
   d. The bonds were issued at par.

4. A firm issues $5 million of 10-year, 6% notes with interest paid semiannually. At issuance the firm received $5,817,565 cash reflecting a 4% yield. What is the amount of premium written off against interest expense in the first year the notes are outstanding?
   a. $48,318
   b. $24,527
   c. $67,971
   d. $33,649

5. On May 1, 2016, Wild, Inc. makes an early repayment of long-term debt due to mature on June 1, 2018. Which of the following ratios for the year 2016 is (are) decreased by this repayment?
   a. Current Ratio
   b. Quick Ratio
   c. Times Interest Earned
   d. Debt-to-Equity

QUESTIONS

Q9-1. What does the term *current liabilities* mean? What assets are usually used to settle current liabilities?

Q9-2. What is the justification for using the net-of-discount method to record inventory purchases when cash discounts are offered?

Q9-3. What is an accrual? How do accruals impact the balance sheet and the income statement?

Q9-4. What is the difference between a bond coupon rate and its market interest rate (yield)?

Q9-5. How does issuing a bond at a premium or discount affect the bond's *effective* interest rate vis-à-vis the coupon (stated) rate?

Q9-6. Why do companies report a gain or loss on the repurchase of their bonds (assuming the repurchase price is different from bond book value)?

Q9-7. How do debt ratings affect the cost of borrowing for a company?

Q9-8. How would you interpret a company's reported gain or loss on the repurchase of its bonds?

Q9-9. What do the following terms mean? (a) bonds payable, (b) call provision, (c) face value, (d) coupon, (e) bond discount, (f) bond premium, and (g) amortization of bond premium or discount.

Q9-10. What are the advantages and disadvantages of issuing bonds rather than common stock?

Q9-11. A $3,000,000 issue of 10-year, 9% bonds was sold at 98 plus accrued interest three months after the bonds were dated. What net amount of cash is received?

Q9-12. How does issuing bonds at a premium or discount "adjust the contract rate to the applicable market rate of interest"?

Q9-13. Regardless of whether premium or discount is involved, what generalization can be made about the change in the book value of bonds payable during the period in which they are outstanding?

Q9-14. If the effective interest amortization method is used for bonds payable, how does the periodic interest expense change over the life of the bonds when they are issued (a) at a discount and (b) at a premium?

Q9-15. How should premium and discount on bonds payable be presented in the balance sheet?

Q9-16. On April 30, 2016, one year before maturity, Weber Company retired $200,000 of 9% bonds payable at 101. The book value of the bonds on April 30 was $197,600. Bond interest was last paid on April 30, 2016. What is the gain or loss on the retirement of the bonds?

Q9-17. Brownlee Company borrowed money by issuing a 20-year mortgage note payable. The note will be repaid in equal monthly installments. The interest expense component of each payment decreases with each payment. Why?

MINI EXERCISES

M9-18. Recording Cash Discounts

LO1

On November 15, 2015, Shields Company purchased inventory costing $6,200 on credit. The credit terms were 2/10, n/30.

a. Assume that Shields Company paid the invoice on November 23, 2015. Prepare journal entries to record the purchase of this inventory and the cash payment to the supplier using the net-of-discount method.

b. Set up the necessary T-accounts and post the journal entries from question *a* to the accounts.

c. Compute the cost of a lost discount as an annual percentage rate.

M9-19. Recording Cash Discounts

LO1

Schrand Corporation purchases materials from a supplier that offers credit terms of 2/15, n/60. It purchased $12,500 of merchandise inventory from that supplier on January 20, 2016.

a. Assume that Schrand Corporation paid the invoice on February 15, 2016. Prepare journal entries to record the purchase of this inventory and the cash payment to the supplier using the net-of-discount method.

b. Set up the necessary T-accounts and post the journal entries from question *a* to the accounts.

c. Compute the cost of a lost discount as an annual percentage rate.

M9-20. Analyzing and Computing Financial Statement Effects of Loan Interest

LO2

Huddart Company gave a creditor a 90-day, 8% note payable for $7,200 on December 16.

a. Prepare the journal entry to record the year-end December 31st accounting adjustment Huddart must make.

b. Post the journal entries from part *a* to their respective T-accounts.

c. Record the transaction from part *a* in the financial statement effects template.

	Balance Sheet										*Income Statement*				
Transaction	Cash Asset	+	Noncash Assets	=	Liabil-ities	+	Contrib. Capital	+	Earned Capital		*Revenues*	-	*Expenses*	=	*Net Income*

M9-21. Analyzing and Determining the Amount of a Liability

LO1, 2

For each of the following situations, indicate the liability amount, if any, which is reported on the balance sheet of Hirst, Inc., at December 31, 2015.

a. Hirst owes $110,000 at year-end 2015 for its inventory purchases.

b. Hirst agreed to purchase a $28,000 drill press in January 2016.

c. During November and December of 2015, Hirst sold products to a firm with a 90-day warranty against product failure. Estimated 2016 costs of honoring this warranty are $2,200.

d. Hirst provides a profit-sharing bonus for its executives equal to 5% of its reported pretax annual income. The estimated pretax income for 2015 is $600,000. Bonuses are not paid until January of the following year.

M9-22. Interpreting Relations Between Bond Price, Coupon, Yield, and Rating

LO3, 5

Microsoft Corporation
NASDAQ :: MSFT

In early February 2015, **Microsoft Corporation** issued a series of corporate bonds with maturities ranging from 5 years to 40 years. The bond issue was rated AAA by Standard & Poor's and Aaa by Moody's. Two of the bond offerings are described below.

Amount: $2.25 billion; Maturity: February 12, 2025; Coupon: 2.7%; Price: 99.37; Yield: 2.772%.
Amount: $2.25 billion; Maturity: February 12, 2055; Coupon: 4.0%; Price: 98.76; Yield: 4.063%.

a. Discuss the relation between the coupon rate, issuance price, and yield for the 2025 issue.

b. Compare the yields on the two bond issues. Why are the yields different when the bond ratings are the same?

LO4 

M9-23. Determining Gain or Loss on Bond Redemption

On January 1, 2016, two years before maturity, Easton Company retires $400,000 of its 8.5% bonds payable at the current market price of 102 (102% of the bond face amount, or $400,000 × 1.02 = $408,000). The bond book value on January 1, 2016 is $397,000 reflecting an unamortized discount of $3,000. Bond interest is presently fully paid and recorded up to the date of retirement. What is the gain or loss on retirement of these bonds?

LO4

Pfizer, Inc.
NYSE :: PFE

M9-24. Interpreting Bond Footnote

In its 2014 balance sheet, **Pfizer, Inc.** reports a value of $3,011 million as current portion of long-term debt. In addition, Pfizer reports the following maturity schedule for its remaining $31,481 million in long-term debt outstanding:

($ millions)	2016	2017	2018	2019	After 2019
Maturities	$3,990	$3,963	$2,339	$4,771	$16,418

a. Why does the table not include 2015? How much long-term debt is due in 2015?
b. What implications does the payment schedule have for your evaluation of Pfizer's liquidity and solvency?

LO1 

M9-25. Classifying Debt Accounts into the Balance Sheet or Income Statement

Indicate the proper financial statement classification (balance sheet or income statement) for each of the following accounts:

a. Gain on Bond Retirement
b. Discount on Bonds Payable
c. Mortgage Notes Payable
d. Bonds Payable
e. Bond Interest Expense
f. Bond Interest Payable (due next period)
g. Premium on Bonds Payable
h. Loss on Bond Retirement

LO4

Cencosud SA
NYSE :: CNCO

M9-26. Interpreting Bond Footnote Disclosures

Cencosud SA is a leading Latin American retailer, with approximately US$3.34 billion in short- and long-term debt outstanding as of December 31, 2013. In its 20-F filing with the Securities and Exchange Commission, Cencosud reports the following:

Our loan agreements and outstanding bonds contain a number of covenants requiring us to comply with certain financial ratios and other tests. The most restrictive financial covenants under these loan agreements and bonds require us to maintain:

- a ratio of consolidated Net Financial Debt to consolidated net worth not exceeding 1.2 to 1;
- a ratio of consolidated Net Financial Debt to EBITDA (as defined in the relevant credit agreements) for the most recent four consecutive fiscal quarters for such period of less than 5.25 to 1;
- unencumbered assets in an amount equal to at least 120% of the outstanding principal amount of total liabilities;
- minimum consolidated assets of at least UF 50.5 million[11]; and
- minimum consolidated net worth of at least UF 28.0 million.

As of the date of this annual report, we are in compliance with all of our loan and debt instruments.

a. Why do creditors impose restrictive covenants on borrowers?
b. How might restrictive covenants such as these affect management decisions?
c. What implications do these restrictions have on an analysis of the company and its solvency?

LO4 

M9-27. Analyzing Financial Statement Effects of Bond Redemption

Holthausen Corporation issued $400,000 of 11%, 20-year bonds at 108 on January 1, 2010. Interest is payable semiannually on June 30 and December 31. Through January 1, 2016, Holthausen amortized $4,191 of the bond premium. On January 1, 2016, Holthausen retires the bonds at 103.

a. Prepare journal entries to record the issue and retirement of these bonds.
b. Post the journal entries from part *a* to their respective T-accounts.
c. Record each of the transactions from part *a* in the financial statement effects template.

[11] "UF" refers to *Unidades de Fomento*. The UF is an inflation-indexed Chilean monetary unit with a value in Chilean pesos that is adjusted daily to reflect changes in the official Consumer Price Index ("CPI").

M9-28. Analyzing Financial Statement Effects of Bond Redemption

LO4

Dechow, Inc., issued $250,000 of 8%, 15-year bonds at 96 on July 1, 2009. Interest is payable semiannually on December 31 and June 30. Through June 30, 2016, Dechow amortized $3,186 of the bond discount. On July 1, 2016, Dechow retired the bonds at 101.

a. Prepare journal entries to record the issue and retirement of these bonds. (Assume the June interest expense has already been recorded.)

b. Post the journal entries from part *a* to their respective T-accounts.

c. Record each of the transactions from part *a* in the financial statement effects template.

M9-29. Analyzing and Computing Accrued Interest on Notes

LO4

Compute any interest accrued for each of the following notes payable owed by Penman, Inc., as of December 31, 2015 (use a 365-day year):

Lender	Issuance Date	Principal	Interest Rate (%)	Term
Nissim.	11/21/15	$18,000	10%	120 days
Klein	12/13/15	14,000	9	90 days
Bildersee.	12/19/15	16,000	12	60 days

M9-30. Debt Ratings and Capital Structure

LO5

General Mills, Inc.
NYSE :: GIS

General Mills, Inc. reports the following information in the Management Discussion & Analysis section of its 2014 10-K report:

Cash Flows from Financing Activities ($ millions)	2014
Change in notes payable	$ 572.9
Issuance of long-term debt	1,673.0
Payment of long-term debt	(1,444.8)
Proceeds from common stock issued on exercised options, including tax benefit.	177.4
Purchases of common stock for treasury	(1,745.3)
Dividends paid	(983.3)
Dividends to noncontrolling interests and other, net	(74.0)
Net cash used by financing activities.	$(1,824.1)

a. General Mills reported net income of $1,861.3 million in 2014. What effect did these financing cash flows have on General Mills solvency measures in 2014? Explain.

b. Would the changes in financing tend to lower or increase the firm's debt rating? (Currently General Mills long-term debt is rated at upper medium grade.)

M9-31. Computing Bond Issue Price

LO3

Bushman, Inc., issues $500,000 of 9% bonds that pay interest semiannually and mature in 10 years. Compute the bond issue price assuming that the bonds' market rate is:

a. 8% per year compounded semiannually.

b. 10% per year compounded semiannually.

M9-32. Computing Issue Price for Zero-Coupon Bonds

LO3

Baiman, Inc., issues $500,000 of zero-coupon bonds that mature in 10 years. Compute the bond issue price assuming that the bonds' market rate is:

a. 8% per year compounded semiannually.

b. 10% per year compounded semiannually.

c. If prior to the debt issue at 10%, the firm had total assets of $3 million and total equity of $1 million, what would be the effect of the new borrowing on the financial leverage of the firm?

M9-33. Financial Statement Effects of Accounts Payable Transactions

LO1

Petroni Company engages in the following sequence of transactions every month:

1. Purchases $300 of inventory on credit.
2. Sells $300 of inventory for $420 on credit.
3. Pays other operating expenses of $110 in cash.
4. Collects $420 in cash from customers.
5. Pays supplier of inventory $300.

a. Create a monthly income statement and statement of operating cash flow (direct method) for four consecutive months.

b. The CFO is disappointed with the cash flows from the business. They do not provide the support for investment and growth that she wants. She proposes delaying supplier payments by a month. That is, each month's inventory purchase will be paid for in the following month. How would this change the monthly income statements and operating cash flows in part *a*? Would it provide the steady flow of cash that the CFO is looking for? Why?

LO3, 4

M9-34. Computing Bond Issue Price and Preparing an Amortization Table in Excel

On December 31, 2015, Kaplan, Inc., issues $500,000 of 9% bonds that pay interest semiannually and mature in 10 years (December 31, 2025).

a. Using the Excel PV worksheet function, compute the issue price assuming that the bonds' market rate is 8% per year compounded semiannually. (Refer to Appendix A for illustration.)

b. Prepare an amortization table in Excel to demonstrate the amortization of the book (carrying) value to the $500,000 maturity value at the end of the 20th semiannual period. (Refer to Appendix A for illustration.)

LO4

M9-35. Classifying Bond-Related Accounts

Indicate the proper financial statement classification for each of the following accounts:

Gain on Bond Retirement (material amount)
Discount on Bonds Payable
Mortgage Notes Payable
Bonds Payable
Bond Interest Expense
Bond Interest Payable
Premium on Bonds Payable

LO3, 4

M9-36. Recording and Assessing the Effects of Installment Loans

On December 31, 2015, Thomas, Inc., borrowed $700,000 on a 12%, 15-year mortgage note payable. The note is to be repaid in equal semiannual installments of $50,854 (payable on June 30 and December 31).

a. Prepare journal entries to record (1) the issuance of the mortgage note payable, (2) the payment of the first installment on June 30, 2016, and (3) the payment of the second installment on December 31, 2016. Round amounts to the nearest dollar.

b. Post the journal entries from part *a* to their respective T-accounts.

c. Record each of the transactions from part *a* in the financial statement effects template.

LO3

M9-37. Determining Bond Prices

Lunar, Inc., plans to issue $900,000 of 10% bonds that will pay interest semiannually and mature in 5 years. Assume that the effective interest rate is 12% per year compounded semiannually. Compute the selling price of the bonds. Use Tables 2 and 3 in Appendix A near the end of the book.

EXERCISES

LO1

E9-38. Analyzing and Computing Accrued Warranty Liability and Expense

Waymire Company sells a motor that carries a 60-day unconditional warranty against product failure. Waymire estimates that between the sale and lapse of the product warranty, 2% of the 69,000 units sold this period will require repair at an average cost of $50 per unit. The warranty liability for this product had a beginning-of-period balance of $30,000, and $27,000 has already been spent on warranty repairs and replacements during the period.

a. How much warranty expense must Waymire report in its income statement and what amount of warranty liability must it report on its balance sheet for this year?

b. What analysis issues do we need to consider with respect to the amount of reported warranty liability?

c. What solvency ratios are increased if warranty liabilities rise?

E9-39. Analyzing Contingencies and Assessing Liabilities LO1

The following independent situations represent various types of liabilities. Analyze each situation and indicate which of the following is the proper accounting treatment for each company: (1) record in accounts, (2) disclose in a financial statement footnote, or (3) neither record nor disclose.

a. A stockholder has filed a lawsuit against Clinch Corporation. Clinch's attorneys have reviewed the facts of the case. Their review revealed that similar lawsuits have never resulted in a cash award and it is highly unlikely that this lawsuit will either.

b. Foster Company signed a 60-day, 10% note when it purchased (and received) items from another company.

c. The Department of Environment Protection notifies Shevlin Company that a state where it has a plant is filing a lawsuit for groundwater pollution against Shevlin and another company that has a plant adjacent to Shevlin's plant. Test results have not identified the exact source of the pollution. Shevlin's manufacturing process often produces by-products that can pollute groundwater.

d. Sloan Company manufactured and sold products to a retailer that sold the products to consumers. The Sloan Company warranty offers replacement of the product if it is found to be defective within 90 days of the sale to the consumer. Historically, 1.2% of the products are returned for replacement.

E9-40. Analyzing and Computing Accrued Wages Liability and Expense LO1

Demski Company pays its employees on the 1st and 15th of each month. It is March 31 and Demski is preparing financial statements for this quarter. Its employees have earned $25,000 since the 15th of this month and have not yet been paid. How will Demski's balance sheet and income statement change to reflect the accrual of wages that must be made at March 31? What balance sheet and income statement accounts would be incorrectly reported if Demski failed to make this accrual (for each account indicate whether it would be overstated or understated)?

E9-41. Analyzing and Reporting Financial Statement Effects of Bond Transactions LO3, 4

On January 1, 2016, Hutton Corp. issued $300,000 of 15-year, 11% bonds payable for $377,814, yielding an effective interest rate of 8%. Interest is payable semiannually on June 30 and December 31.

a. Show computations to confirm the issue price of $377,814.

b. Prepare journal entries to record the bond issuance, semiannual interest payment and premium amortization on June 30, 2016, and semiannual interest payment and premium amortization on December 31, 2016. Use the effective interest rate method.

c. Post the journal entries from part *b* to their respective T-accounts.

d. Record each of the transactions from part *b* in the financial statement effects template.

E9-42. Computing the Bond Issue Price LO3

D'Souza, Inc., issues $900,000 of 11% bonds that pay interest semiannually and mature in seven years. Assume that the market interest (yield) rate is 12% per year compounded semiannually. Compute the bond issue price.

E9-43. Interpreting Warranty Liability Disclosures LO1

The following disclosures were provided by **Siemens AG** in its 2014 annual report:

Siemens AG
OTCMKTS :: SIEGY

Product-related expenses

Provisions for estimated costs related to product warranties are recorded in line item Cost of sales at the time the related sale is recognized, and are established on an individual basis, except for the standard product business. The estimates reflect historic experience of warranty costs, as well as information regarding product failure experienced during construction, installation or testing of products. In the case of new products, expert opinions and industry data are also taken into consideration in estimating product warranty provisions.

Note 23 Provisions

	Provision for Warranties Year ended September 30	
(in millions of €)	**2014**	**2013**
Beginning balance	€3,350	€3,405
Additions	1,776	1,544
Usage	(771)	(828)
Reversals	(657)	(683)
Translation differences and other	23	(88)
Ending balance	€3,721	€3,350

a. The Provision that Siemens reports is an estimated warranty liability. What would constitute "additions" to the provision? Prepare a journal entry to record this addition.

b. What constitutes "usage" of the provision? Besides the provision, what other accounts are likely to be affected by usage? Prepare a journal entry to record usage of €771 million.

c. "Reversals" are corrections of previous estimates of warranty obligations. Why would it be useful to report reversals separately from additions?

d. Siemens reported sales revenue of €71,920 million in 2014 and €73,445 in 2013. Calculate the ratio of warranty expense to sales for each year.

LO4 **E9-44. Reporting Financial Statement Effects of Bond Transactions**

Lundholm, Inc., which reports financial statements each December 31, is authorized to issue $500,000 of 9%, 15-year bonds dated May 1, 2015, with interest payments on October 31 and April 30. Assume the bonds are issued at par on May 1, 2015.

a. Prepare journal entries to record the bond issuance, payment of the first semiannual period's interest, and retirement of $300,000 of the bonds at 101 on November 1, 2016.

b. Post the journal entries from part *a* to their respective T-accounts.

c. Record each of the transactions from part *a* in the financial statement effects template.

LO3, 4 **E9-45. Reporting Financial Statement Effects of Bond Transactions**

On January 1, 2016, McKeown, Inc., issued $250,000 of 8%, 9-year bonds for $220,776, yielding a market (yield) rate of 10%. Semiannual interest is payable on June 30 and December 31 of each year.

a. Show computations to confirm the bond issue price.

b. Prepare journal entries to record the bond issuance, semiannual interest payment and discount amortization on June 30, 2016, and semiannual interest payment and discount amortization on December 31, 2016. Use the effective interest rate.

c. Post the journal entries from part *b* to their respective T-accounts.

d. Record each of the transactions from part *b* in the financial statement effects template.

LO3, 4 **E9-46. Reporting Financial Statement Effects of Bond Transactions**

On January 1, 2016, Shields, Inc., issued $800,000 of 9%, 20-year bonds for $879,172, yielding a market (yield) rate of 8%. Semiannual interest is payable on June 30 and December 31 of each year.

a. Show computations to confirm the bond issue price.

b. Prepare journal entries to record the bond issuance, semiannual interest payment and premium amortization on June 30, 2016, and semiannual interest payment and premium amortization on December 31, 2016. Use the effective interest rate method.

c. Post the journal entries from part *b* to their respective T-accounts.

d. Record each of the transactions from part *b* in the financial statement effects template.

LO3, 4 **E9-47. Analyzing Bond Pricing, Interest Rates, and Financial Statement Effect of a Bond Issue**

Deere & Company
NYSE :: DE

Following is a price quote for $200 million of 6.55% coupon bonds issued by **Deere & Company** that mature in October 2028:

Ratings/Industry	Issue/Call Information	Coupon/Maturity	Price/YTM
A2/A	**Deere & Company**.	6.550	123.962
Industrial.	Non Callable, NYBE, DE. . . .	10-01-2028	4.178

This quote indicates that, on this day, Deere's bonds have a market price of 123.962 (123.962% of face value), resulting in a yield of 4.178%.

a. Assuming that these bonds were originally issued at or close to par value, what does the above market price reveal about the direction that interest rates have changed since Deere issued its bonds? (Assume that Deere's debt rating has remained the same.)

b. Does the change in interest rates since the issuance of these bonds affect the amount of interest expense that Deere is reporting in its income statement? Explain.

c. If Deere were to repurchase its bonds at the above market price of 123.962, how would the repurchase affect its current income? Assume that the bonds were issued at face value (100).

d. Assuming that the bonds remain outstanding until their maturity, at what market price will the bonds sell on their due date of October 1, 2028?

E9-48. Analyzing and Reporting Financial Statement Effects of Bond Transactions LO3, 4

On January 1, 2016, Trueman Corp. issued $600,000 of 20-year, 11% bonds for $554,860, yielding a market (yield) rate of 12%. Interest is payable semiannually on June 30 and December 31.

a. Confirm the bond issue price.

b. Prepare journal entries to record the bond issuance, semiannual interest payment and discount amortization on June 30, 2016, and semiannual interest payment and discount amortization on December 31, 2016. Use the effective interest rate method.

c. Post the journal entries from part *b* to their respective T-accounts.

d. Trueman elected to report these bonds in its financial statements at fair value. On December 31, 2016, these bonds were listed in the bond market at a price of 101 (or 101% of par value). What entry is required to adjust the reported value of these bonds to fair value?

e. Prepare a table summarizing the effect of these bonds on earnings for 2016.

E9-49. Reporting and Interpreting Bond Disclosures

LO2, 4

The adjusted trial balance for the Hass Corporation at the end of 2015 contains the following accounts:

$ 25,000	Bond Interest Payable
600,000	9% Bonds Payable due 2017
500,000	10% Bonds Payable due 2016
19,000	Discount on 9% Bonds Payable
2,000	Premium on 8% Bonds Payable
170,500	Zero-Coupon Bonds Payable due 2018
100,000	8% Bonds Payable due 2020

Prepare the long-term liabilities section of the balance sheet. Indicate the proper balance sheet classification for accounts listed above that do not belong in the long-term liabilities section.

E9-50. Recording and Assessing the Effects of Installment Loans LO3, 4

On December 31, 2015, Dehning, Inc., borrowed $500,000 on an 8%, 10-year mortgage note payable. The note is to be repaid in equal quarterly installments of $18,278 (beginning March 31, 2016).

a. Prepare journal entries to reflect (1) the issuance of the mortgage note payable, (2) the payment of the first installment on March 31, 2016, and (3) the payment of the second installment on June 30, 2016. Round amounts to the nearest dollar.

b. Post the journal entries from part *a* to their respective T-accounts.

c. Record each of the transactions from part *a* in the financial statement effects template.

PROBLEMS

P9-51. Interpreting Warranty Liability Disclosures LO1

Hewlett-Packard
NYSE :: HPQ
Cisco Systems, Inc.
NASDAQ :: CSCO

The following information was extracted from the 2014 10-K reports of **Hewlett-Packard Company** and **Cisco Systems, Inc.**

	Hewlett-Packard		Cisco Systems, Inc.	
($ millions)	2014	2013	2014	2013
Revenue from product sales	$73,726	$72,398	$36,172	$38,029
Warranty expense.	1,840	2,007	704	649
Accrued warranty liability.	1,956	2,031	446	402

REQUIRED

a. Compute the amount of warranty costs incurred in 2014 for each company. (That is, what amount was spent for warranty repairs and settlements in 2014?)

b. Compare these two companies on the basis of the ratio of warranty expense to sales. What factors might explain any difference that you observe?

P9-52. Recording and Assessing the Effects of Bond Financing (with Accrued Interest) LO3, 4

Eskew, Inc., which closes its books on December 31, is authorized to issue $500,000 of 9%, 15-year bonds dated May 1, 2015, with interest payments on November 1 and May 1.

REQUIRED

Assuming that the bonds were sold at 100 plus accrued interest on October 1, 2015, prepare the necessary journal entries for items *a.–f.* below.

a. The bond issuance.

b. Payment of the first semiannual period's interest on November 1, 2015.

c. Accrual of bond interest expense at December 31, 2015.

d. The adjustment to fair value on December 31, 2015 assuming that Eskew, Inc. elected to use the fair value option. On that date, the bond traded at a price of 99 (99% of par value) in the bond market.

e. Payment of the semiannual interest on May 1, 2016. (The firm does not make reversing entries.)

f. Retirement of $300,000 of the bonds at 101 on May 1, 2020 (immediately after the interest payment on that date). Assume that the fair value adjustment account for the entire issue has a debit balance of $15,000 as of that date. *Hint:* Sixty percent of the outstanding bonds were retired in this transaction.

g. Suppose fair value adjustments of bond values were not posted to net income, but rather to other comprehensive income. How would Eskew, Inc.'s December 31, 2015 financial statements change?

LO3, 4 CVS Health Corp. NYSE :: CVS

P9-53. Interpreting Debt Footnotes on Interest Rates and Expense

CVS Health Corp. discloses the following footnote in its 10-K relating to its debt:

BORROWING AND CREDIT AGREEMENTS

Following is a summary of the Company's borrowings as reported in note 5 to the firm's 10-K.

In millions	2014	2013
Commercial paper	$ 685	$ —
4.875% senior notes due 2014	—	550
3.25% senior notes due 2015	550	550
6.125% senior notes due 2016	421	421
1.2% senior notes due 2016	750	750
5.75% senior notes due 2017	1,080	1,310
2.25% senior notes due 2018	1,250	1,250
6.6% senior notes due 2019	394	394
2.25% senior notes due 2019	850	—
4.75% senior notes due 2020	450	450
4.125% senior notes due 2021	550	550
2.75% senior notes due 2022	1,250	1,250
4.0% senior notes due 2023	1,250	1,250
3.375% senior notes due 2024	650	—
6.25% senior notes due 2027	453	1,000
6.125% senior notes due 2039	734	1,500
5.75% senior notes due 2041	493	950
5.3% senior notes due 2043	750	750
Capital lease obligations	391	390
Other	4	87
	12,955	13,402
Less:		
Short-term debt (commercial paper)	(685)	—
Current portion of long-term debt	(575)	(561)
Long-term debt	$11,695	$12,841

CVS also discloses that its interest expense was $615 million in 2014, after deducting capitalized interest of $19 million. It paid interest of $647 million.

REQUIRED

a. What was the average interest rate on CVS debt in 2014?

b. Does your computation in part *a* seem reasonable given the disclosure relating to specific bond issues? Explain.

c. Why can the amount of interest paid be different from the amount of interest expense recorded in the income statement?

P9-54. Recording and Assessing the Effects of Bond Financing (with Accrued Interest) LO3, 4

Petroni, Inc., which closes its books on December 31, is authorized to issue $800,000 of 9%, 20-year bonds dated March 1, 2016, with interest payments on September 1 and March 1.

REQUIRED

Assuming that the bonds were sold at 100 plus accrued interest on July 1, 2016, prepare the necessary journal entries, post the journal entries to their respective T-accounts, and record each transaction in the financial statement effects template.

a. The bond issuance.
b. Payment of the semiannual interest on September 1, 2016.
c. Accrual of bond interest expense at December 31, 2016.
d. Payment of the semiannual interest on March 1, 2017. (The firm does not make reversing entries.)
e. Retirement of $200,000 of the bonds at 101 on March 1, 2017 (immediately after the interest payment on that date).

P9-55. Preparing an Amortization Schedule and Recording the Effects of Bonds LO3, 4

On December 31, 2015, Kasznik, Inc., issued $720,000 of 11%, 10-year bonds for $678,708, yielding an effective interest rate of 12%. Semiannual interest is payable on June 30 and December 31 each year. The firm uses the effective interest method to amortize the discount.

REQUIRED

a. Prepare an amortization schedule showing the necessary information for the first two interest periods. Round amounts to the nearest dollar.
b. Prepare the journal entries for (1) the bond issuance on December 31, 2015, (2) to record bond interest expense and discount amortization at June 30, 2016, and (3) to record bond interest expense and discount amortization at December 31, 2016.
c. Post the journal entries from part *b* to their respective T-accounts.
d. Record each of the transactions from part *b* in the financial statement effects template.

P9-56. Preparing an Amortization Schedule and Recording the Effects of Bonds LO3, 4

On April 30, 2016, Cheng, Inc., issued $250,000 of 6%, 15-year bonds for $206,770, yielding an effective interest rate of 8%. Semiannual interest is payable on October 31 and April 30 each year. The firm uses the effective interest method to amortize the discount.

REQUIRED

a. Prepare an amortization schedule showing the necessary information for the first two interest periods. Round amounts to the nearest dollar.
b. Prepare the journal entries (1) for the bond issuance on April 30, 2016, (2) to record the bond interest payment and discount amortization at October 31, 2016, (3) the adjusting entry to record bond interest expense and discount amortization at December 31, 2016, the close of the firm's accounting year, and (4) to record the bond interest payment and discount amortization at April 30, 2017.
c. Post the journal entries from part *b* to their respective T-accounts.
d. Record each of the transactions from part *b* in the financial statement effects template.

P9-57. Recording and Assessing the Effects of Installment Loans: Semiannual Installments LO3, 4

On December 31, 2015, Wasley Corporation borrowed $500,000 on a 10%, 10-year mortgage note payable. The note is to be repaid with equal semiannual installments, beginning June 30, 2016.

REQUIRED

a. Compute the amount of the semiannual installment payment. Use the appropriate table (in Appendix A near the end of the book) or a financial calculator, and round amount to the nearest dollar.
b. Prepare the journal entry (1) to record Wasley's borrowing of funds on December 31, 2015, (2) to record Wasley's installment payment on June 30, 2016, and (3) to record Wasley's installment payment on December 31, 2016. (Round amounts to the nearest dollar.)
c. Post the journal entries from part *b* to their respective T-accounts.
d. Record each of the transactions from part *b* in the financial statement effects template.

P9-58. Recording and Assessing the Effects of Installment Loans: Quarterly Installments LO3, 4

On December 31, 2015, Watts Corporation borrowed $950,000 on an 8%, 5-year mortgage note payable. The note is to be repaid with equal quarterly installments, beginning March 31, 2016.

REQUIRED

a. Compute the amount of the quarterly installment payment. Use the appropriate table (in Appendix A near the end of the book) or a financial calculator, and round amount to the nearest dollar.

b. Prepare the journal entries (1) to record the borrowing of funds by Watts Corporation on December 31, 2015, (2) to record the installment payment by Watts Corporation on March 31, 2016, and (3) to record the installment payment by Watts Corporation on June 30, 2016.

c. Post the journal entries from part *b* to their respective T-accounts.

d. Record each of the transactions from part *b* in the financial statement effects template.

LO1 **P9-59. Contingent Liabilities**

BP, PLC
NYSE :: BP

BP operates off-shore oil drilling platforms including rigs in the Gulf of Mexico. In April 2010, explosions and a fire on the Deepwater Horizon rig led to the death of 11 crew members and a 200-million-gallon oil spill in the Gulf of Mexico. BP's 2010 annual report included the following description of its contingent liabilities (provision) related to this accident:

In estimating the amount of the provision, BP has determined a range of possible outcomes for Individual and Business Claims, and State and Local Claims.... BP has concluded that a reasonable range of possible outcomes for the amount of the provision at December 31, 2010, is $6 billion to $13 billion. BP believes that the provision recorded at December 31, 2010, of $9.2 billion represents a reliable best estimate from within this range of possible outcomes.

REQUIRED

a. BP prepares its financial statements in accordance with IFRS. How did BP report the $9.2 billion estimate in its 2010 financial statements?

b. How would the accounting for this provision differ if BP prepared its financial statements in accordance with U.S. GAAP?

CASES AND PROJECTS

LO3, 4, 5 **C9-60. Interpreting Debt Disclosures**

Comcast
NASDAQ :: CMCSA

Comcast Corporation's 2014 income statement and partial balance sheet (liabilities and equity, only) are presented below. In addition, footnote 10 pertaining to Comcast's long-term debt obligations is provided. All $ amounts are presented in millions.

Summarized Consolidated Statement of Income

Year ended December 31 (in millions)	2014	2013
Revenue	$68,775	$64,657
Costs and expenses:		
Programming and production	20,912	19,670
Other operating and administrative	19,862	18,584
Advertising, marketing and promotion	5,078	4,969
Depreciation and amortization	8,019	7,871
	53,871	51,094
Operating income	14,904	13,563
Other income (expense)		
Interest expense	(2,617)	(2,574)
Other	178	126
	(2,439)	(2,448)
Income before income taxes	12,465	11,115
Income tax expense	(3,873)	(3,980)
Net income	$ 8,592	$ 7,135

Summarized Consolidated Balance Sheet (Liabilities and Equity only) December 31 (in millions)	2014	2013
Current liabilities:		
Accounts payable and accrued expenses related to trade creditors	$ 5,638	$ 5,528
Accrued participations and residuals	1,347	1,239
Deferred revenue	915	898
Accrued expenses and other current liabilities	5,293	7,967
Current portion of long-term debt	4,217	3,280
Total current liabilities	17,410	18,912
Long-term debt, less current portion	44,017	44,567
Deferred income taxes	32,959	31,935
Other noncurrent liabilities	11,885	12,341
Total liabilities	106,271	107,755
Total equity	53,068	51,058
Total liabilities and equity	$159,339	$158,813

Note 10: Long-term Debt

Long-term Debt Outstanding December 31 (in millions)	Weighted-Average Interest Rate as of December 31, 2014	2014	2013
Commercial paper	0.373%	$ 845	$ 1,350
Revolving bank credit facilities	—%	—	1,250
Senior notes with maturities of 5 years or less	4.642%	15,334	15,080
Senior notes with maturities between 5 and 10 years	4.822%	10,527	11,533
Senior notes with maturities greater than 10 years[(a)]	5.737%	20,937	18,010
Other, including capital lease obligations	—%	591	624
Total debt	4.95%[(b)]	48,234	47,847
Less: Current portion		4,217	3,280
Long-term debt		$44,017	$44,567

[(a)] The December 31, 2014 and 2013 amounts include £625 million of 5.50% notes due 2029 translated at $974 million and $1 billion, respectively, using the exchange rates at these dates.

[(b)] Includes the effects of our derivative financial instruments.

As of December 31, 2014 and 2013, our debt had an estimated fair value of $55.3 billion and $51.8 billion, respectively. The estimated fair value of our publicly traded debt is primarily based on Level 1 inputs that use the quoted market values for the debt. The estimated fair value of debt for which there are no quoted market prices is based on Level 2 inputs that use interest rates available to us for debt with similar terms and remaining maturities. See Note 20 for additional information on our cross-guarantee structure.

Debt Maturities (in millions)	Weighted-Average Interest Rate as of December 31, 2014	
2015	4.990%	$ 4,217
2016	4.158%	3,530
2017	6.973%	2,558
2018	4.124%	4,117
2019	3.159%	2,205
Thereafter	5.425%	31,607

REQUIRED

a. Comcast provided cash flow information revealing that the company paid interest equal to $2,389 million in 2014. Explain why this amount is different from the amount of interest expense reported in its 2014 income statement.

b. Comcast reports its debt using historical cost. What would be the impact on the financial statements if the company elected to report all of its debt at fair value? Be specific.

c. The financial ratios specified in Comcast's loan agreements include the solvency measures described in this chapter. Calculate Comcast's debt-to-equity ratio and times-interest-earned for 2014. Explain why creditors might include these ratios in the restrictive covenants of loan agreements.

d. Violation of debt covenants can be a serious event that can impose substantial costs on a company. What actions might management take to avoid violating debt covenants if the company's ratios are near the covenant limits?

LO3, 4, 5 **C9-61. Assessing Debt Financing, Company Interests, and Managerial Ethics**

Foster Corporation is in the third quarter of the current year, and projections are that net income will be down about $600,000 from the previous year. Foster's return on assets is also projected to decline from its usual 15% to approximately 13%. If earnings do decline, this year will be the second consecutive year of decline. Foster's president is quite concerned about these projections (and his job) and has called a meeting of the firm's officers for next week to consider ways to "turn things around—and fast."

Margot Barth, treasurer of Foster Corporation, has received a memorandum from her assistant, Lorie McNichols. Barth had asked McNichols if she had any suggestions as to how Foster might improve its earnings performance for the current year. McNichols' memo reads as follows:

> As you know, we have $3,000,000 of 4%, 20-year bonds payable outstanding. We issued these bonds 10 years ago at face value, so they have 10 years left to maturity. When they mature, we would probably replace them with other bonds. The economy is expecting a period of greater inflation, and interest rates have increased to about 8%. My proposal is to replace these bonds right now. More specifically, I propose:
>
> 1. Immediately issue $3,000,000 of 20-year, 8% bonds payable. These bonds will be issued at face value.
> 2. Use the proceeds from the new bonds to buy back and retire our outstanding 4% bonds. Because of the current high rates of interest, these bonds are trading in the market at about $2,200,000.
> 3. The benefits to Foster are that (a) the retirement of the old bonds will generate an $800,000 gain for the income statement and (b) there will be an extra $800,000 of cash available for other uses.

Barth is intrigued by the possibility of generating an $800,000 gain for the income statement. However, she is not sure this proposal is in the best long-run interests of the firm and its stockholders.

REQUIRED

a. How is the $800,000 gain calculated from the retirement of the old bonds? Where would this gain be reported in Foster's income statement?

b. Why might this proposal not be in the best long-run interests of the firm and its stockholders?

c. What possible ethical conflict is present in this proposal?

SOLUTIONS TO REVIEW PROBLEMS

Mid-Chapter Review 1

SOLUTION

a. The discount would be $580 ($29,000 × 0.02). Thus, Waymire would pay $28,420 ($29,000 − $580).

b. The cost of the lost discount is $29 per day ($580/20) or $10,585 per year (simple interest). The implicit financing cost of the lost discount is 37.24% ($10,585/$28,420).

Mid-Chapter Review 2

SOLUTION

Toro Company incurred $38,568 thousand in warranty claims in 2014 ($000):

$72,177 + $37,471 − warranty claims = $71,080. Warranty claims = $38,568.

This cost would be recorded as follows:

	Balance Sheet									Income Statement				
Transaction	Cash Asset	+	Noncash Assets	=	Liabil-ities	+	Contrib. Capital	+	Earned Capital	Revenues	-	Expenses	=	Net Income
Payment to satisfy warranty claims.	−38,568 Cash			=	−38,568 Warranty Liability						-		=	

ANALYZE JOURNALIZE POST

Warranty liability (−L)	38,568	
Cash (−A)		38,568

− Warranty Liability (L) +	
38,568	

+ Cash (A) −	
	38,568

The credit entry to cash assumes that cash was paid to satisfy the warranty claims. Toro could also have credited wages payable, or parts inventory as needed.

Mid-Chapter Review 3

SOLUTION

The related journal entry to recognize the accrual of interest is:

	Balance Sheet									Income Statement				
Transaction	Cash Asset	+	Noncash Assets	=	Liabil-ities	+	Contrib. Capital	+	Earned Capital	Revenues	-	Expenses	=	Net Income
Accrued $26 of interest as of January 31*.				=	+26 Interest Payable				−26 Retained Earnings		-	+26 Interest Expense	=	−26

ANALYZE JOURNALIZE POST

Interest expense (+E, −SE)	26	
Interest payable (+L)		26

+ Interest Expense (E) −	
26	

− Interest Payable (L) +	
	26

*Accrued interest for a 16-day period at January 31 = $10,000 × 0.06 × 16/365 = $26.

Chapter-End Review

SOLUTION

1. Issue price for $300,000, 15-year, 10% semiannual bonds discounted at 8%:

Present value of principal payment ($300,000 × 0.30832)	$ 92,496
Present value of semiannual interest payments ($15,000 × 17.29203)	259,380
Issue price of bonds	$351,876

2.

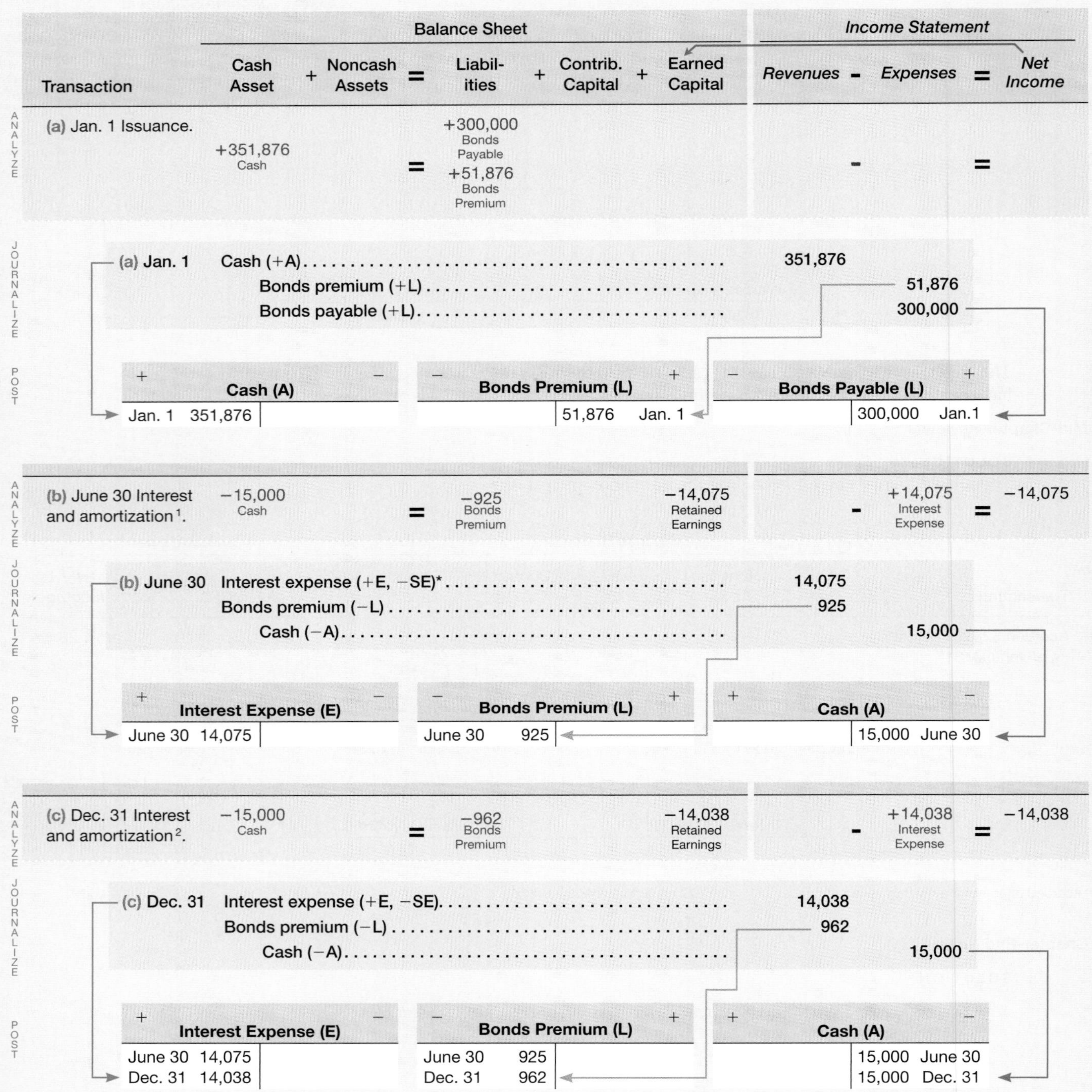

[1] $300,000 × 0.10 × 6/12 = $15,000 cash payment; 0.04 × $351,876 = $14,075 interest expense; the difference is the bond premium amortization, a reduction of the net bond carrying amount.

[2] 0.04 × ($351,876 − $925) = $14,038 interest expense. The difference between this amount and the $15,000 cash payment is the premium amortization, a reduction of the net bond carrying amount.

10 Reporting and Analyzing Leases, Pensions, and Income Taxes

LEARNING OBJECTIVES

1. Define off-balance-sheet financing and explain its effects on financial analysis. (p. 462)
2. Account for leases using the operating lease method and the capital lease method. (p. 463)
3. Convert off-balance-sheet operating leases to the capital lease method. (p. 469)
4. Explain and interpret the reporting for pension plans. (p. 475)
5. Analyze and interpret pension footnote disclosures. (p. 478)
6. Describe and interpret accounting for income taxes. (p. 484)

DELTA AIR LINES
www.delta.com

Delta Air Lines confronts competing demands for its available cash flow as a result of a heavy debt load that includes borrowed money, aircraft leases, and pension and other postemployment obligations. The magnitude of obligations arising from aircraft leases often surprises those outside the industry. Many airlines do not own all the planes that they fly. The airlines often lease a significant portion of their planes from commercial leasing companies rather than own the planes themselves.

In many cases, neither the leased planes (the assets) nor the lease obligations (the liabilities) would be on Delta's balance sheet. That omission can alter investors' perceptions of the capital investment Delta needs to operate its business as well as the level of debt it carries. Methods that companies apply to avoid reporting potential liabilities (and related expenses), are commonly referred to as *off-balance-sheet financing*.

We describe an analytical procedure that provides an alternative view of the company's investing and financing activities. The analytical adjustment increases the liability on Delta's balance sheet. We estimate that Delta has lease payment obligations not recorded on the balance sheet of nearly $9 billion in 2014, which is

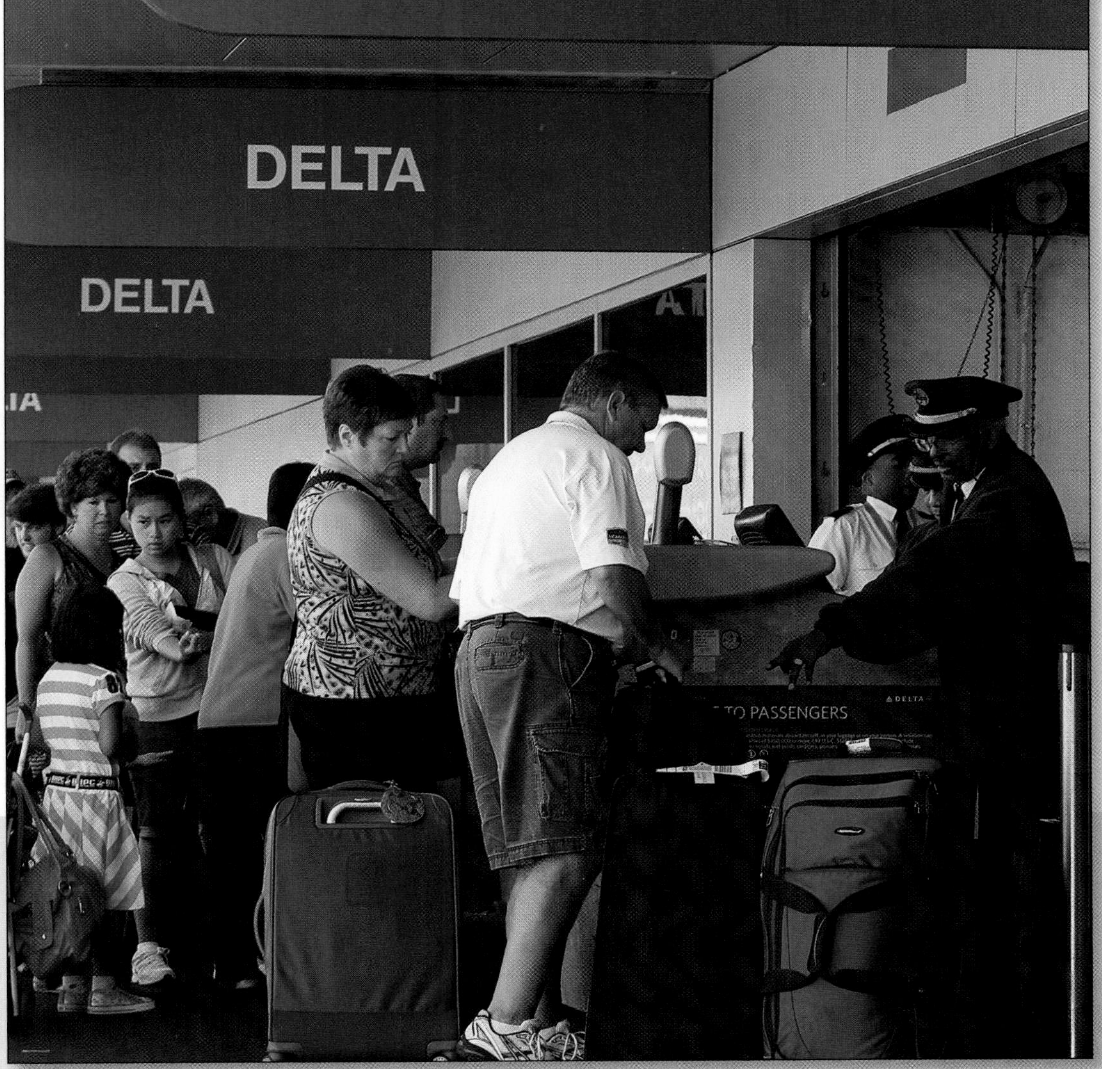

a significant amount when compared to the company's reported noncurrent liabilities of $28 billion. This chapter discusses the accounting for leases, explains the analytical adjustment, and illustrates how to apply the adjustment.

Pensions and deferred income taxes are major liabilities or assets reported in many firm's financial statements, including Delta Air Lines. In this chapter, we will explore the reporting of leases, pensions, and income taxes, along with the various assumptions that underlie the reported figures. We also examine the impact that these items have on reported earnings and cash flows, and how they affect the company's financial position and performance. Understanding this information is essential if we are to assess the future potential of Delta Air Lines and other companies.

Sources: Delta Air Lines 2014 Annual Report

CHAPTER ORGANIZATION

Reporting and Analyzing Leases, Pensions, and Income Taxes

Leases	Pensions	Income Taxes
• Lessee Reporting of Leases • Footnote Disclosures • Capitalization of Operating Leases • Analyzing Financial Statements	• Reporting of Defined Benefit Pension Plans • Footnote Disclosures • Other Postretirement Benefits	• Reporting Tax Expense • Footnote Disclosures • Book-Tax Differences • Computation and Analysis

INTRODUCTION

1 **LO1** Define off-balance-sheet financing and explain its effects on financial analysis.

Investors, creditors, and other users of financial statements assess the composition of a company's balance sheet and its relation to the income statement. Chapter 6 introduced the concept of earnings quality to refer to the extent to which reported income reflects the underlying economic performance of a company. Similarly, the quality of the balance sheet refers to the extent to which the assets and liabilities of a company are reported in a manner that accurately reflects its economic resources and obligations. For example, in previous chapters, we highlighted the reporting of LIFO inventories and noncapitalized intangible assets to illustrate how some assets can be undervalued or even excluded from the balance sheet. This chapter focuses on the reporting of liabilities that can often only be found in the notes to the financial statements.

Financial managers are keenly aware of the importance that financial markets place on the quality of balance sheets. This importance creates pressure on companies to *window dress* their financial statements in order to report their financial condition and performance in the best possible light. One means of improving the perceived financial condition of the company is by keeping debt off the

BUSINESS INSIGHT

Nike's Off-Balance-Sheet Obligations Lebron James, Maria Sharapova, and Tom Brady are just some of the marquee athletes who endorse **Nike, Inc.** products. These athletes sign long-term, multimillion dollar contracts to use and promote Nike shoes, apparel, and accessories. These long-term endorsement contracts are just one of Nike's off-balance-sheet obligations. Consider the following note from Nike's 10-K report.

Contractual Obligations

Our significant long-term contractual obligations as of May 31, 2014, and significant endorsement contracts entered into through the date of this report are as follows ($ millions):

	Cash Payments Due During the Year Ended May 31,						
Description of Commitment	**2015**	**2016**	**2017**	**2018**	**2019**	**Thereafter**	**Total**
Operating leases	$ 427	$ 399	$ 366	$311	$251	$1,050	$ 2,804
Capital leases	36	35	1	1	1	—	74
Long-term debt	46	145	79	56	37	1,488	1,851
Endorsement contracts	991	787	672	524	349	1,381	4,704
Product purchase obligations	3,688	—	—	—	—	—	3,688
Other	309	108	78	7	3	12	517
Total	$5,497	$1,474	$1,196	$899	$641	$3,931	$13,638

Of these obligations disclosed, only its long-term debt is included in the balance sheet. If the other obligations were presented in the balance sheet at their present values (ignoring any related off-balance-sheet assets that might also need to be capitalized), Nike's debt-to-equity ratio would increase in 2014 by 135% from 0.72 to 1.69.

balance sheet. **Off-balance-sheet financing** refers to financial obligations of a company that are not reported as liabilities in the balance sheet.

Off-balance-sheet financing reduces the amount of debt reported on the balance sheet, thereby lowering the company's financial leverage ratios. Additionally, many off-balance-sheet financing techniques (e.g., operating leases and contract manufacturing) remove assets from the balance sheet, along with the liabilities, without reducing revenues or markedly affecting net income. Such techniques cause operation ratios, such as return on assets (ROA), to appear stronger than they are.

FYI Off-balance-sheet financing usually requires off-balance-sheet assets—this means the off-balance-sheet remains balanced!

This chapter focuses on three common financial obligations that companies report in their financial statements—leases, pensions, and income taxes. The liability section of Delta Air Lines' balance sheet is presented in **Exhibit 10.1**. The amounts reported on Delta's balance sheet related to leases and pensions are highlighted. Delta reports a deferred asset related to income taxes for 2013 and 2014; we discuss what this means later in the chapter.

EXHIBIT 10.1 Delta Air Lines Balance Sheet (Liabilities Only)

($ millions)	2014	2013
Current Liabilities:		
Current maturities of long-term debt and capital leases	$1,216	$1,547
Air traffic liability	4,296	4,122
Accounts payable	2,622	2,300
Accrued salaries and related benefits	2,266	1,926
Hedge derivatives liability	2,772	146
Frequent flyer deferred revenue	1,580	1,861
Other accrued liabilities	2,127	2,250
Total current liabilities	16,879	14,152
Noncurrent Liabilities:		
Long-term debt and capital leases	8,561	9,795
Pension, postretirement and related benefits	15,138	12,392
Frequent flyer deferred revenue	2,602	2,559
Other noncurrent liabilities	2,128	1,711
Total noncurrent liabilities	28,429	26,457
Total liabilities	$45,308	$40,609

In addition to the obligations presented in its balance sheet, Delta reports most of its leases in its footnotes and not on its balance sheet. Whether they are reported in the footnotes or on the balance sheet, management enjoys considerable discretion in determining the value of these obligations and how they are presented. Understanding the information in these disclosures enables us to analyze the impact of these obligations on the financial condition of the company.

LEASES

LO2 Account for leases using the operating lease method and the capital lease method.

2

A lease is a contract between the owner of an asset (the **lessor**) and the party desiring to use that asset (the **lessee**). Because this is a private contract between two willing parties, it is governed only by applicable commercial law, and can include whatever provisions are negotiated between the parties. The lessor and lessee can be any legal form of organization, including private individuals, corporations, partnerships, and joint ventures.

Leases generally contain the following terms:

- The lessor allows the lessee the unrestricted right to use the asset during the lease term.
- The lessee agrees to make periodic payments to the lessor and to maintain the asset.
- The legal title to the asset remains with the lessor. At the end of the lease, either the lessor takes physical possession of the asset, or the lessee purchases the asset from the lessor at a price specified in the lease contract.

From the lessor's standpoint, lease payments are set at an amount that yields an acceptable return on investment, commensurate with the credit standing of the lessee. The lessor, thus, obtains a quality investment, and the lessee gains use of the asset.

From the lessee's perspective, the lease serves as a financing vehicle, similar to an intermediate-term secured bank loan. However, there are several advantages to leasing over bank financing:

- Leases often require less equity investment than bank financing. That is, banks often only lend a portion of the asset's cost and require the borrower to make up the difference from its available cash.
- Leases often require payments to be made at the beginning of the period (e.g., the first of the month). However, because leases are contracts between two parties, their terms can be structured in any way to meet their respective needs. For example, a lease can allow variable payments to match seasonal cash inflows of the lessee, or have graduated payments for companies in their start-up phase.
- If the lessee requires the use of the asset for only a part of its useful life, leasing avoids the need to sell a used asset.
- Because the lessor retains ownership of the asset, leases provide the lessor with tax benefits such as accelerated depreciation deductions. This fact can lead to lower payments for lessees.
- According to current U.S. GAAP, if the lease is properly structured, neither the leased asset nor the lease liability is reported on the lessee's balance sheet. Accordingly, leasing can be a form of off-balance-sheet financing.

FYI New standards are forthcoming that will put almost all leases on the balance sheet. We discuss this new treatment below.

Lessee Reporting of Leases

GAAP identifies two different approaches for the reporting of leases by the lessee:

- **Capital lease method**. This method requires that both the leased asset and the lease liability be reported on the balance sheet. The leased asset is depreciated like any other long-term asset. The lease liability is amortized like debt, where lease payments are separated into interest expense and principal repayment.
- **Operating lease method**. Under this method, neither the leased asset nor the lease liability is on the balance sheet. Lease payments are recorded as rent expense by the lessee when paid.

To illustrate the two approaches to lease accounting, assume that Richardson Electronics agrees to lease retail store space in a shopping center. The lease is a 5-year lease with annual payments of $10,000 due at each year-end. (Most leases require payments at the beginning of each period; we use year-end payments here for simplification.) Using a 7% interest rate, the present value of the five annual lease payments equals $41,002, computed as $10,000 × 4.10020 (Appendix A, Table A.3). This amount is used for valuing the lease under the capital lease method.

Using a calculator, the present value of the annual lease payments is computed as follows:[1]

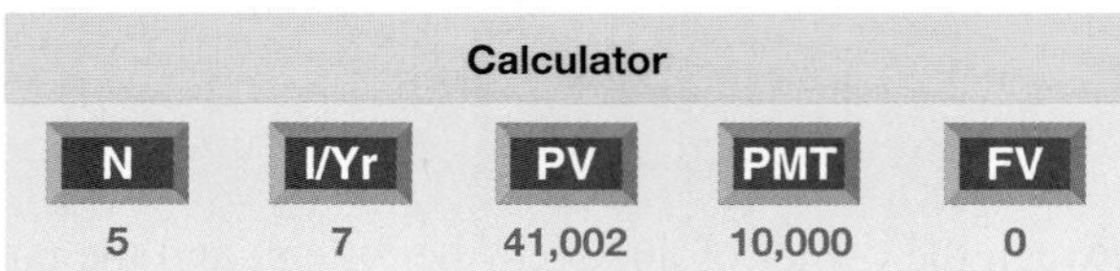

Operating Leases When the operating lease method is used, leased assets and lease liabilities are not recorded in the balance sheet. No accounting entry is recorded when the lease

[1] The result produced by the financial calculator is actually −41,002. The present value will always have the opposite sign from the payment. So, if the payment is positive, the present value will be negative. **Appendix A** illustrates the use of a financial calculator to compute present values. In this calculation, it is important to set the payments per year (period) to 1 and make sure that the payments are set to occur at the end of each period.

agreement is signed. At each year-end, Richardson would record the rent payment as rent expense as follows.

Rent expense (+E, −SE)	10,000	
Cash (−A)		10,000

Because no asset or liability is reported, the only time an operating lease affects the balance sheet is if rent is prepaid (resulting in prepaid rent in current assets) or if unpaid rent is accrued (resulting in accrued rent payable, a current liability). The income statement reports the lease payment as rent expense. The existence and key details of the lease agreement are disclosed in a footnote.

Capital Leases When the capital lease method is applied, the lessee records an asset and a liability at the time that the lease agreement is signed. Both the asset and the liability are valued using the present value of the lease payments. The entry that would be recorded when Richardson Electronics signs its lease is:

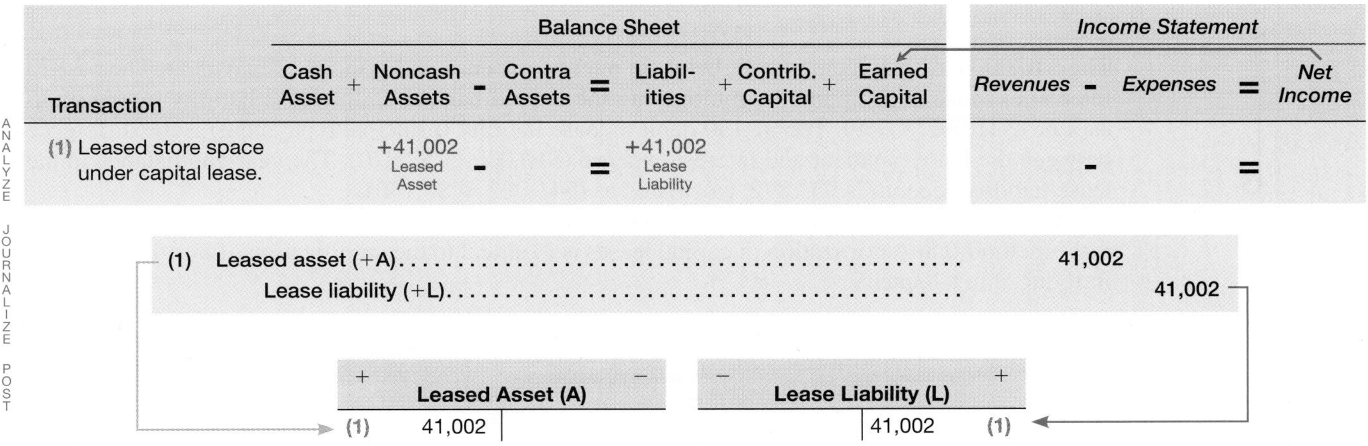

The asset is reported among long-term (PPE) assets in the balance sheet and the liability is reported in long-term debt.

At the end of the first year, two entries are required, one to account for the asset and the other to account for the lease payment. Like other long-term assets, the leased asset must be depreciated. The entry to depreciate Richardson's leased asset (assuming straight-line depreciation, a useful life of 5 years, and zero residual value [$41,002/5 = $8,200]) is:

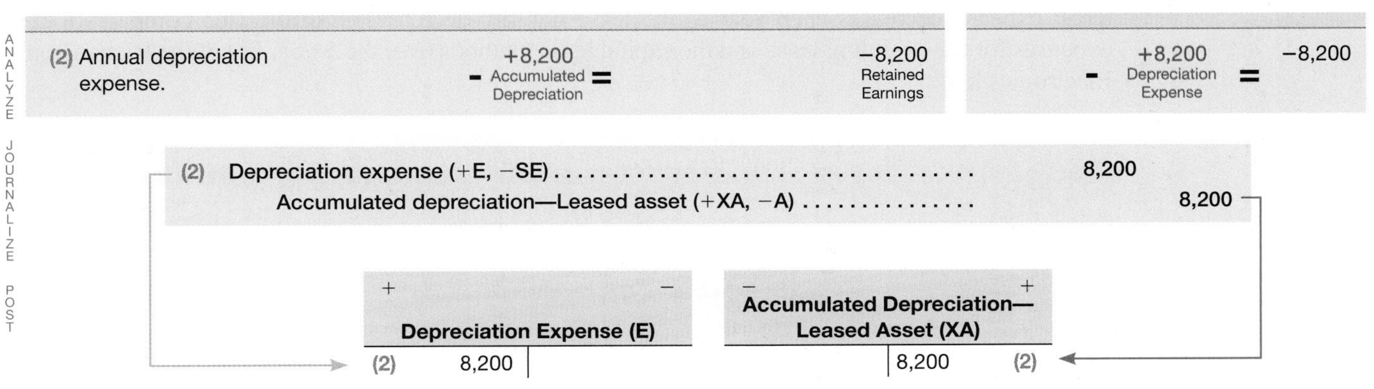

The financial statement effects and related entry to record the annual lease payment are:

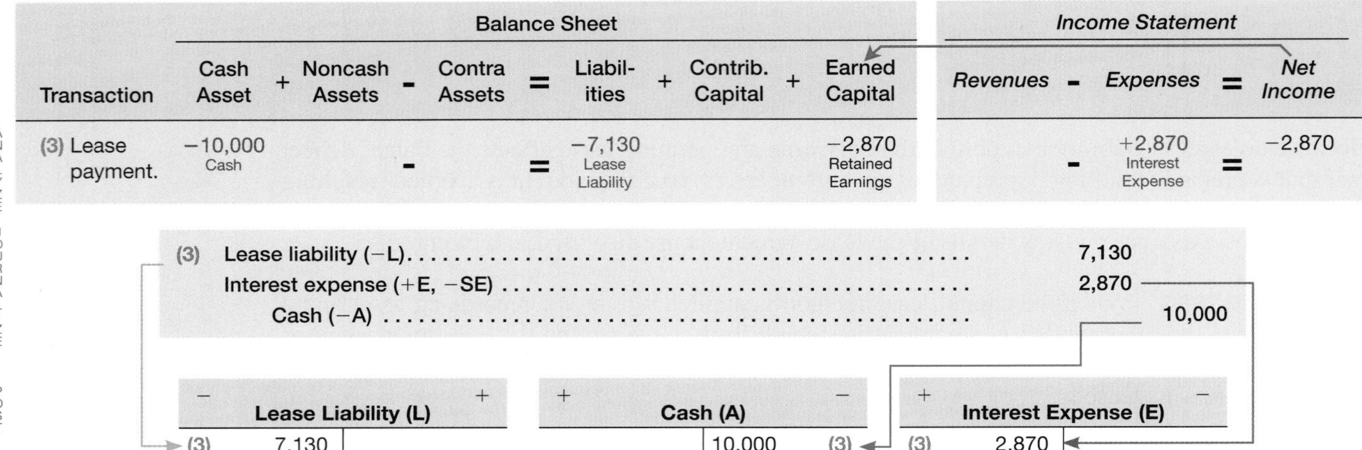

The $10,000 cash payment is split between interest expense and principal repayment. The $2,870 interest expense is computed by multiplying the unpaid balance in the lease liability by the interest rate ($41,002 × 7%). The $7,130 debit to lease liability (principal repayment) is the difference between the lease payment and interest expense ($10,000 − $2,870). The year-end balance in the lease liability account is $33,872, calculated as ($41,002 − $7,130).

Exhibit 10.2 presents the amortization table for Richardson's lease liability under the capital lease method. The amortization of capital leases is identical to the amortization of installment loans introduced in Chapter 9.

EXHIBIT 10.2 Amortization Table for a Capital Lease Liability

A Year	B Beginning-year Lease Liability	C Interest Expense (B × 7%)	D Payment	E Principal Repayment (D − C)	F Ending-year Lease Liability (B − E)
1	$41,002	$2,870	$10,000	$7,130	$33,872
2	33,872	2,371	10,000	7,629	26,243
3	26,243	1,837	10,000	8,163	18,080
4	18,080	1,266	10,000	8,734	9,346
5	9,346	654	10,000	9,346	0

Comparing Operating Lease and Capital Lease Methods In **Exhibit 10.2**, the interest expense decreases each year as the lease liability decreases. **Exhibit 10.3** compares total expenses for the operating lease and the capital lease methods over the 5-year life of the Richardson Electronics lease.

EXHIBIT 10.3 Comparison of Expenses Under Alternative Lease Accounting Methods

	Capital Lease Method			Operating Lease Method
Year	Interest Expense	Depreciation Expense	Total Expense	Rent Expense
1	$2,870	$ 8,200	$11,070	$10,000
2	2,371	8,200	10,571	10,000
3	1,837	8,200	10,037	10,000
4	1,266	8,201	9,467	10,000
5	654	8,201	8,855	10,000
Total	$8,998	$41,002	$50,000	$50,000

Exhibit 10.3 shows how the capital lease method reports a higher total expense (depreciation plus interest) in the early years of the lease and a lower total expense in the later years. Total expense over the 5-year life of the lease is the same under both methods and is equal to the total of the lease payments ($50,000).

The effects of these two accounting methods on the lessee's financial statements are summarized in **Exhibit 10.4**.

EXHIBIT 10.4 Financial Statement Effects of Lease Methods for the Lessee

Lease Type	Assets	Liabilities	Expenses	Cash Flows
Capital	Leased asset reported	Lease liability reported	Depreciation and interest expense	Interest is operating cash flow; principal is financing
Operating	Leased asset not reported	Lease liability not reported	Rent expense	Payment is operating cash flow

U.S. GAAP defines four criteria to determine the classification of a lease as capital or operating. FASB considers meeting one or more of these criteria as an indication that the benefits and risks of ownership are effectively transferred to the lessee. The lessee *must* capitalize the lease *if one or more* of these criteria are met:

1. The lease automatically transfers ownership of the leased asset to the lessee at the lease-end.
2. The lease agreement allows the lessee to purchase the asset at a discounted price (say $1) at the lease-end; this is called a bargain purchase option.
3. The lease term is at least 75% of the economic useful life of the asset.
4. The present value of the lease payments is at least 90% of the asset's fair value.

BUSINESS INSIGHT

The Financial Accounting Standards Board has been working on new standards for leases for several years. Much of this time was spent on a convergence project with the International Accounting Standards Board on the topic. The Boards could not come to agreement on the treatment of leases in the income statement, and thus differences will remain between GAAP and IFRS with regard to leases.

U.S. GAAP will change significantly, however. The proposed change to the lease standard will require that all leases be recorded by the lessee as an asset and a liability, except very short-term rental agreements (less than twelve months). Recognizing that a lease represents the right to use an asset for a specified period of time, the proposed standard refers to the leased asset as a right-of-use asset to be capitalized on a company's balance sheet. Thus, once the new standard is effective, both an asset and a liability will be recorded and the concept of operating leases being off-balance-sheet will no longer apply (unless the lease is short term in duration). The income statement, however, will continue to reflect different treatment between the two types of leases—operating and capital (or finance). The finance type leases (capital leases) will require a recording of interest expense and depreciation, consistent with how current capital leases are accounted for under existing leases guidance. The operating type leases will be expensed on a straight-line basis (rather than high interest costs early in the term of the lease), which is consistent with how current operating leases are accounted for under the exisiting guidance for leases. The FASB does not have a defined effective date for the new standards at the current time.

A GLOBAL PERSPECTIVE

IFRS accounting for leases will also change significantly. The International Accounting Standards Board has proposed a single lease model for IFRS. All leases will be recorded in the same manner on the balance sheet and on the income statement in a manner similar to the capital lease method under U.S. GAAP. In contrast, as described in the Business Insight box above, U.S. GAAP retained a dual model because the income statement treatment varies between the types of leases. In addition to the short-term lease exception that is proposed under U.S. GAAP, there will also be an exception under IFRS if the lease is for a small asset defined in terms of asset value.

Accounting for leases using the operating lease method offers several reporting benefits to the lessee:

- The leased asset is not reported on the balance sheet. This reporting means that asset turnover ratios are higher because reported operating assets are lower and revenues are unaffected.
- The lease liability is not reported on the balance sheet. This means that common balance sheet measures of leverage (such as liabilities divided by equity) are improved. Consequently, many managers believe the company would then command a better debt rating and a lower interest rate on borrowed funds.
- For the early years of the lease term, rent expense reported for an operating lease is less than the sum of depreciation and interest expense reported for a capital lease. This reporting means that net income is higher in those early years with an operating lease. (However, the corporation's net *operating* profit after taxes is *lower* for an operating lease because rent expense is an operating expense whereas only depreciation expense [not interest expense] is considered an operating expense for a capital lease.)

The benefits of using the operating method to account for leases are quite clear to managers, leading them to avoid lease capitalization if possible. Furthermore, the lease accounting standard is structured around rigid requirements relating to capitalization. Whenever accounting standards are rigidly defined, clever managers that are so inclined can structure lease contracts to meet the letter of the standard to achieve a desired accounting result even though the essence of the transaction would suggest a different accounting treatment.

Footnote Disclosures of Leases

Disclosures of expected payments for leases are required under both operating and capital lease methods. Delta Air Lines provides a typical disclosure from its 2014 annual report:

Note 9: Lease Obligations

We lease aircraft, airport terminals, maintenance facilities, ticket offices and other property and equipment from third parties. Rental expense for operating leases, which is recorded on a straight-line basis over the life of the lease term, totaled $1.2 billion for the year ended December 31, 2014 and $1.1 billion for the years ended December 31, 2013 and 2012. Amounts due under capital leases are recorded as liabilities, while assets acquired under capital leases are recorded as property and equipment. Amortization of assets recorded under capital leases is included in depreciation and amortization expense.

The following tables summarize, as of December 31, 2014, our minimum rental commitments under capital leases and noncancelable operating leases (including certain aircraft flown by Contract Carriers) with initial or remaining terms in excess of one year:

Year Ending December 31 ($ millions)	Operating Leases	Capital Leases
2015	$ 1,707	$ 157
2016	1,493	139
2017	1,323	97
2018	1,120	51
2019	929	33
Thereafter	6,169	42
Total minimum lease payments	$12,741	519
Less: amount representing interest		(121)
Present value of future minimum lease payments		398
Less: current obligations under capital leases		(107)
Long-term capital lease obligations		$ 291

Delta Air Lines' footnote disclosure reports minimum contractual lease payment obligations for each of the next five years (2015 through 2019) and the total lease payment obligations that come due in 2020 and beyond. This presentation is similar to disclosures of future maturities for long-term debt. The company also must provide separate disclosures for operating leases and capital leases (Delta has both operating and capital leases outstanding).

The purpose of this lease disclosure is to provide information concerning current and future payment obligations. These contractual obligations are similar to debt payments. While the obligations under capital leases are reported in long-term debt, the operating lease obligations are not reported in the balance sheet. However, the operating lease obligations must be considered in our evaluation of the company's financial condition.

Capital Leases and the Cash Flow Statement A capital lease results in an increase to long-term operating assets and an increase in long-term liabilities. However, in many cases, there is no effect on cash flows at the inception of the lease—see entry (1) on page 463. As a consequence, the initial inception of the lease should be reported as a material noncash transaction and not presented in the cash flow statement under either investing or financing cash flows. Subsequently, the depreciation of the leased asset is added (in an indirect method cash flow statement) to cash flow from operations (an expense that does not require a cash outlay) and the principal portion of the lease payment is treated as debt repayment under cash flows from financing activities.

YOU MAKE THE CALL

You are the Division President You are the president of an operating division. Your CFO recommends operating lease treatment for asset acquisitions to reduce reported assets and liabilities on your balance sheet. To achieve this classification, you must negotiate leases with terms that you feel are not advantageous to your company. What is your response? [Answer on page 493]

Capitalization of Operating Leases

LO3 Convert off-balance-sheet operating leases to the capital lease method.

3

When a company uses the operating lease method to report its leases, it can have significant resources that are not recognized as assets and significant obligations that are not recognized as liabilities on its balance sheet. As a result, there are distortions in many important measures of financial condition and performance.

- Return on assets (ROA) and asset turnover ratios are overstated due to nonreporting of leased assets.
- Financial leverage ratios are understated by the nonreporting of lease liabilities.
- Net operating profit margin (NOPM) is understated. Although, over the life of the lease, rent expense under operating leases equals depreciation plus interest expense under capital leases, only depreciation expense is included in net operating profit after tax (NOPAT)—interest is a nonoperating expense.
- While cash payments are the same whether the lease is classified as operating or capital, cash flow from operations is higher for capital leases because part of the lease payment (the principal) is treated as a financing cash outflow.

When operating leases are not capitalized, the balance sheet neither reflects all of the assets that are used in the business, nor the nonoperating obligations for which the company is liable. Such noncapitalization of leases makes ROE appear to be of higher quality. This result is, of course, an important reason why managers want to exclude leases from the balance sheet.

Despite structuring leases to achieve off-balance-sheet financing, required lease disclosures allow us to capitalize operating leases for analysis purposes. This capitalization process involves four steps (these are the same steps that the company would follow to record the asset and liability on the balance sheet if the leases had been classified as capital leases):

1. Estimate the discount rate.
2. Estimate the future payments required under operating leases.
3. Compute the present value of future operating lease payments.
4. Adjust the financial statements to include the present value from Step 3 as both a leased asset and a lease liability.

Step 1. There are at least two approaches to determine the appropriate discount rate for our analysis: (1) If the company discloses capital leases, we can impute (infer) an implicit rate of return: a rate that yields the present value computed by the company given the future capital lease payments (see the Business Insight box later in this section for an illustration). (2) Use the rate that corresponds to the company's credit rating or the rate from any recent borrowings involving intermediate-term secured obligations. Companies typically disclose these details in their long-term debt footnote. To illustrate the capitalization of operating leases, we use the Delta Air Lines lease footnote (page 466). For this illustration, we assume a discount rate of 7%, which is approximately equal to the average rate of interest on Delta's debt.

BUSINESS INSIGHT

Imputed Discount Rate Computation for Leases When companies report both operating and capital leases, the average rate used to discount capital leases can be imputed (inferred) from disclosures in the leasing footnote. **Southwest Airlines** presents the following table in the footnotes to its 2014 10-K report:

($ millions)	Capital Leases	Operating Leases, Net
2015	$ 33	$ 684
2016	42	636
2017	45	592
2018	44	496
2019	43	430
Thereafter	202	2,317
Total minimum lease payments	409	$5,155
Less amount representing interest	75	
Present value of minimum lease payments	334	
Less current portion	23	
Long-term portion	$311	

The note reports that the total of the minimum lease payments under capital leases is $409 million and the present value of those payments is $334 million. Using Excel, we estimate the discount rate that Southwest used for its capital lease computations with the IRR function (=**IRR(values)**) as shown in the following spreadsheet. The entries in cells B2 through G2 are taken from Southwest's reported schedule of lease maturities, and those in cells H2 through L2 assume a continuation of the $43 million in capital lease payments in 2020 until the $202 million of estimated payments after 2019 is accounted for. The spreadsheet method yields an estimate of 4% for the discount rate that Southwest implicitly used for capitalization of its capital leases in its 2014 balance sheet.

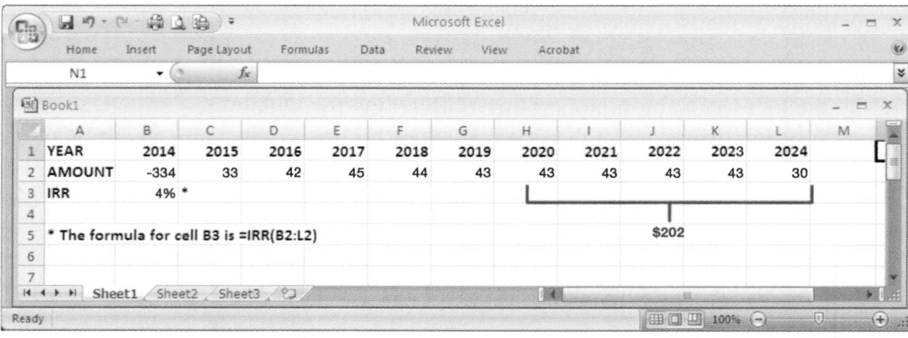

	A	B	C	D	E	F	G	H	I	J	K	L
1	YEAR	2014	2015	2016	2017	2018	2019	2020	2021	2022	2023	2024
2	AMOUNT	-334	33	42	45	44	43	43	43	43	43	30
3	IRR	4% *										
4										$202		
5	* The formula for cell B3 is =IRR(B2:L2)											

Step 2. The future payments required under operating leases are detailed in Delta's footnotes. The leases footnote typically provides the required cash payment for each of the next five years and then an amount representing total payments for all years after that. In Delta's 2014 10-K report, it reported cash payments for operating leases due each year from 2015 through 2019. In addition, it reports that scheduled lease payments after 2019 total $6,169 million.

One limitation of the footnote disclosure is that the information about the lease payments occurring after the next five years (in 2020 and later) is presented as a lump sum instead of specific payment amounts for each year. Unless we have detailed information about operating leases beyond that which is presented in the footnotes, we are limited to making an assumption about these cash payments. One approach is to assume that the lease payment that we know is due in 2019 ($929 million) is repeated in 2020 and each subsequent year until the total amount of lease payments is reached. This usually requires that we assume a smaller, residual lease payment in the last year to reach the total payments exactly. Using this assumption, Delta's operating lease payments would be $929 million each year from 2020 through 2025, and $595 million in 2026.[2]

Step 3. Once we have a discount rate from Step 1 and a series of cash flows from Step 2, we are ready to compute the present value of the cash flows. Because the lease payments vary from year to year, we cannot compute the present value as an ordinary annuity. One approach is to compute the present value of each payment and then total the present values. This approach is presented in **Exhibit 10.5** using present value factors from **Table A.2** in Appendix A.

EXHIBIT 10.5 Present Value of Delta Air Lines, Inc. Operating Lease Payments ($ millions)

	Year	Operating Lease Payment	Present Value Factor (Table A.2, 7%)	Present Value (Payment × PV Factor)
1	2015	$ 1,707	0.93458	$1,595
2	2016	1,493	0.87344	1,304
3	2017	1,323	0.81630	1,080
4	2018	1,120	0.76290	854
5	2019	929	0.71299	662
6	2020	929	0.66634	619
7	2021	929	0.62275	579
8	2022	929	0.58201	541
9	2023	929	0.54393	505
10	2024	929	0.50835	472
11	2025	929	0.47509	441
12	2026	595	0.44401	264
		$12,741		$8,918*

* Rounded total rather than the sum of the rounded present values.

As an alternative to using the present value tables from Appendix A, we can use the NPV function in Excel to compute the present value.[3] This approach is illustrated in the spreadsheet below:

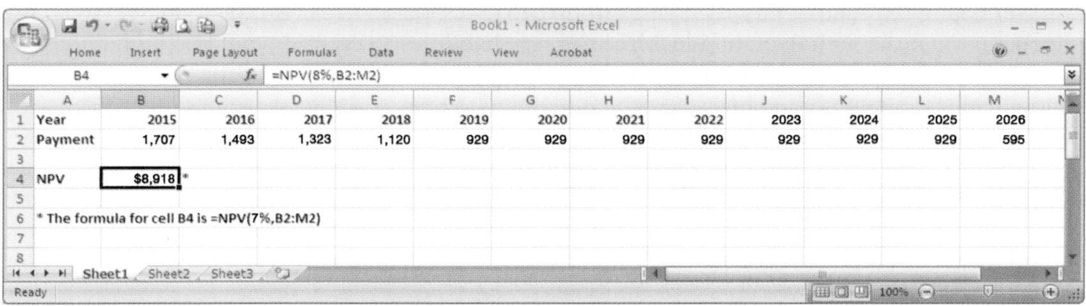

Book1 - Microsoft Excel

B4 =NPV(8%,B2:M2)

	A	B	C	D	E	F	G	H	I	J	K	L	M
1	Year	2015	2016	2017	2018	2019	2020	2021	2022	2023	2024	2025	2026
2	Payment	1,707	1,493	1,323	1,120	929	929	929	929	929	929	929	595
3													
4	NPV	$8,918*											
5													
6	* The formula for cell B4 is =NPV(7%,B2:M2)												

---

[2] There are other reasonable assumptions that we could make that would be consistent with the facts presented in the footnotes. As outsiders analyzing the financial statements, we are limited to estimating the present value of a company's operating leases and to do that, some assumptions are unavoidable.

[3] The NPV function is also available on most financial calculators.

Step 4. Once we've computed the present value of the operating lease payments, we can use the computed amount to adjust the balance sheet and income statement as we illustrate in **Exhibit 10.6**.

EXHIBIT 10.6 Analytical Adjustments from Capitalization of Delta Air Lines' Operating Leases

($ millions)	Reported	Adjustments	Adjusted	Percent Increase
Assets	$54,121	$8,918	$63,039	16.5%
Liabilities	45,308	8,918	54,226	19.7%
Equity	8,813		8,813	—

By adding the present value of the operating lease payments to both the assets and the liabilities in the balance sheet, we are, in effect, treating these leases as capital leases. If this is the first year of the leases, the initial entry the company would use to record the leases if they were capital leases (and the entry we will use to adjust the balance sheet to be "as if" the leases are capital leases) would be as shown in the following financial statement effects template.[4]

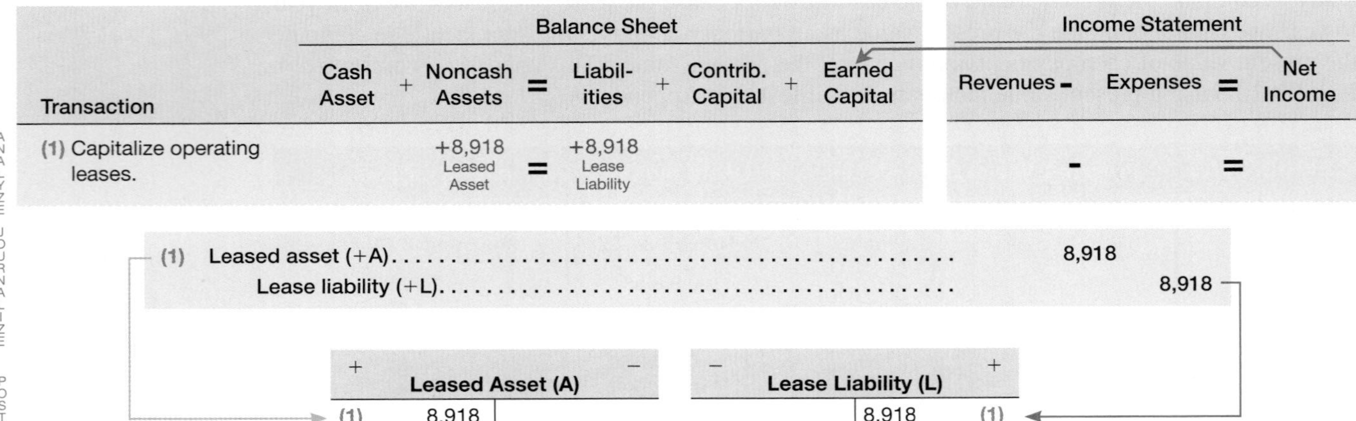

Operating Leases and Financial Ratios An asset acquired under an operating lease will not appear in the company balance sheet and the related liability will not appear among the liabilities. The omission also affects the income statement, although to a lesser extent. Depreciation is understated but the rent expense offsets the understatement. However, as we have seen, it is possible to estimate the capitalized value of the assets and the size of the associated obligation, which can then be considered in an analysis of the firm using the ratios we have previously introduced.

The capitalization of operating leases has a marked impact on Delta's balance sheet. For the airline and retailing industries, in particular, leased assets (airplanes and real estate) comprise a large portion of net operating assets and these leases are usually classified as operating.

Using the year-end data presented in **Exhibit 10.6** and given revenues of $40,362 million, asset turnover (using year-end figures) decreases from 0.75 ($40,362/$54,121) to 0.64 ($40,362/$63,039). In general for firms with operating leases, leverage (liabilities to equity) would be higher than we would infer from reported financial statements. The adjusted assets and liabilities arguably present a more realistic picture of the invested capital required to operate Delta as well as other firms with significant operating lease commitments.

It is important to consider operating lease commitments that do not appear on the balance sheet as payments that must be satisfied with cash, just as is the case with the other fixed commitments such as interest on outstanding debt. Other off-balance-sheet commitment items, such as purchase commitments, should also be included. The impact of these commitments can be gauged using the ratio of operating cash flow to fixed commitments.

[4] For simplicity, we assume the initial year of the lease. Realistically, the leases will be at various stages in their terms. Thus, to consider what the financial statements would look like if the leases were capital, we need to think about how the asset and liability change over time. Generally, depreciation of the asset will be straight-line. On the liability side, early in lease life, most of the lease payments will be interest, not principal. As a result, the balance of the asset will decline faster than the balance of the liability. Thus, we would have to adjust the asset and liability by different amounts. See pages 463-464 and Mid-Chapter Review 1 for examples.

ANALYZING FINANCIAL STATEMENTS

Analysis Objective

We want to assess the effect of financial obligations, including off-balance-sheet commitments, on financial solvency and liquidity.

Analysis Tool Fixed Commitments Ratio

$$\textbf{Fixed commitments ratio} = \frac{\textbf{Operating cash flow before fixed commitments}}{\textbf{Fixed commitments}}$$

Applying the Fixed Commitments Ratio to Delta Air Lines Some fixed commitments, such as operating lease payments and purchase commitments, are cash outflows that are classified as operating activities in the cash flow statement. Others (for example, payments due on long-term debt) are classified as financing cash flows and some can be classified as investing (for example, commitments to purchase plant assets). Delta reports total fixed commitments of $8,504 million in its 10-K report. Of these, $1,219 million is for non-interest payments on long-term debt and capital leases (financing) and $1,480 million is for aircraft purchase commitments (investing). Subtracting these amounts leaves the amount of fixed commitments that are part of operating cash flows ($8,504 million − $1,219 million − $1,480 million = $5,805 million). To compute the **fixed commitments ratio**, we start with operating cash flows, add back the fixed commitments that are classified as operating and then divide by the total amount of fixed commitments.[5]

$$\textbf{2012:}\ 1.00 = \frac{\$2,467 + \$6,317}{\$8,793}$$

$$\textbf{2013:}\ 1.14 = \frac{\$4,504 + \$5,649}{\$8,890}$$

$$\textbf{2014:}\ 1.26 = \frac{\$4,947 + \$5,805}{\$8,504}$$

Guidance A fixed commitments ratio less than 1.0 indicates that a company is generating insufficient cash flows from operations to meet its contractual obligations. Some commitments may be met by selling assets, or by raising additional financing. For example, when long-term debt comes due, it can be refinanced with new debt if the company is otherwise in sound financial health.

Delta Air Lines in Context

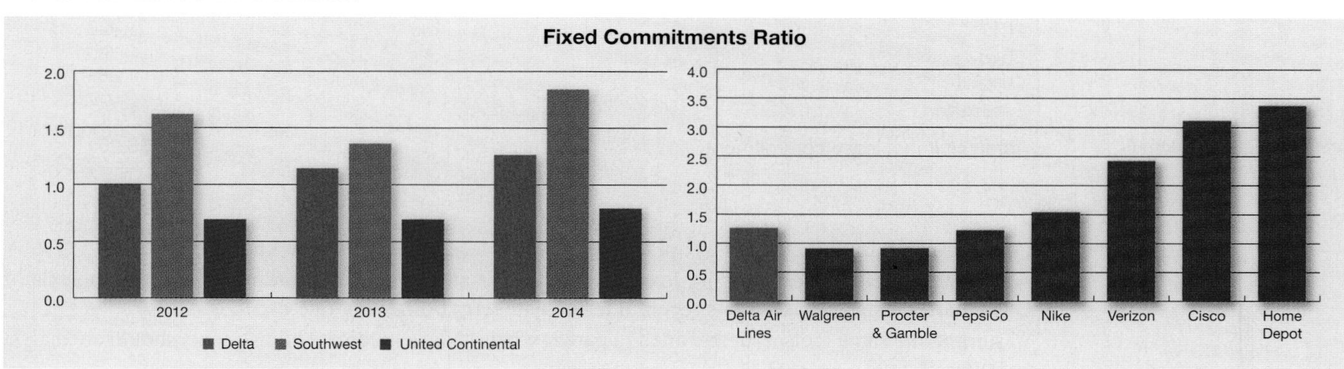

[5] Companies often disclose future fixed commitments by year. For ease of computation in our examples, we use cash flows from 2014 and fixed commitments for 2015 to compute the 2014 ratio. Thus, we are making an implicit assumption that the fixed commitments for the next year are similar to those for the current year.

Takeaways There is a range of values across firms within an industry and across industries. In our set of companies above for 2014, the ratio ranges from 0.80 for United Continental to 3.37 for Home Depot. Historically, airlines have had relatively low ratios due to large amounts of operating leases, pension commitments, and other obligations. Southwest has always been an exception and now that Delta has improved its performance and cash flows, their ratio is near the middle of the companies we display above. The key takeaway is that off-balance-sheet obligations can have a significant impact on our analysis and understanding of a company's solvency and liquidity.

Other Considerations The fixed commitments ratio is but one measure of financial solvency and liquidity. It should be used in conjunction with other ratios, such as the debt-to-equity ratio and the current ratio in an effort to gauge the ability of the firm to meet its financial obligations.

MID-CHAPTER REVIEW 1

PART A

Assume that **The Gap Inc.** leased a vacant retail space with the intention of opening another store. The lease calls for annual lease payments of $32,000, due at the end of each of the next ten years. Assume the appropriate discount rate is 7%.

1. If the lease is treated as a capital lease, what journal entry(ies) would Gap make to record the initial signing of the lease agreement?
2. How would Gap record depreciation expense and the first lease payment at the end of the first year of the lease?
3. If this lease is accounted for as an operating lease, what entry(ies) would be necessary during the first year?

PART B

Following is the leasing footnote disclosure from note 12 in **The Gap Inc.**'s 2014 10-K report.

> We lease most of our store premises and some of our corporate facilities and distribution centers. These operating leases expire at various dates through 2030. Most store leases are for a five-year base period and include options that allow us to extend the lease term beyond the initial base period, subject to terms agreed upon at lease inception. Some leases also include early termination options, which can be exercised under specific conditions. The aggregate minimum non-cancelable annual lease payments under leases in effect on January 31, 2015, are:

Fiscal Year	(in millions)
2015	$1,136
2016	1,096
2017	920
2018	760
2019	638
Thereafter	1,701
Total minimum lease commitment	$6,251

1. Does Gap classify these leases as operating or capital leases? How do you know?
2. Assuming its leases are operating leases, compute the adjustments that are necessary for analysis of Gap's balance sheet. (Use Gap's recent intermediate term borrowing rate of 5%.)
3. Assuming the same facts as determined in part 2, what income statement adjustments should an analyst consider, if any?

The solution to this review problem can be found on pages 513-514.

PENSIONS

LO4 Explain and interpret the reporting for pension plans.

4

Companies frequently offer retirement or pension plans as a benefit for their employees. There are two general types of pension plans:

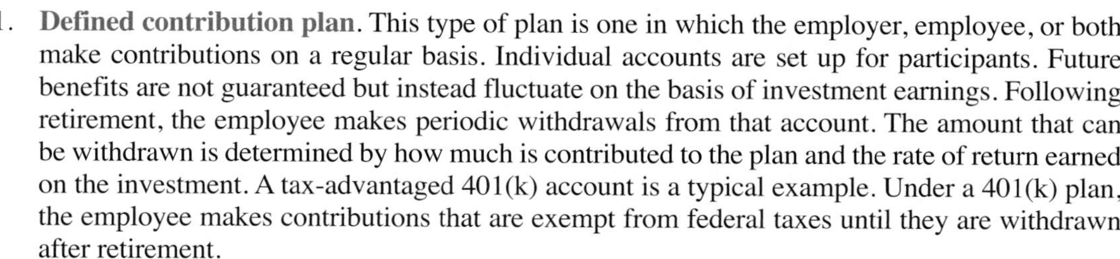

1. **Defined contribution plan.** This type of plan is one in which the employer, employee, or both make contributions on a regular basis. Individual accounts are set up for participants. Future benefits are not guaranteed but instead fluctuate on the basis of investment earnings. Following retirement, the employee makes periodic withdrawals from that account. The amount that can be withdrawn is determined by how much is contributed to the plan and the rate of return earned on the investment. A tax-advantaged 401(k) account is a typical example. Under a 401(k) plan, the employee makes contributions that are exempt from federal taxes until they are withdrawn after retirement.

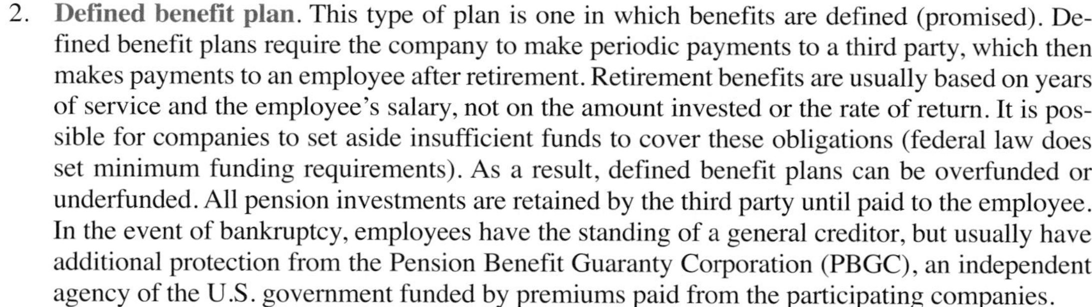

2. **Defined benefit plan.** This type of plan is one in which benefits are defined (promised). Defined benefit plans require the company to make periodic payments to a third party, which then makes payments to an employee after retirement. Retirement benefits are usually based on years of service and the employee's salary, not on the amount invested or the rate of return. It is possible for companies to set aside insufficient funds to cover these obligations (federal law does set minimum funding requirements). As a result, defined benefit plans can be overfunded or underfunded. All pension investments are retained by the third party until paid to the employee. In the event of bankruptcy, employees have the standing of a general creditor, but usually have additional protection from the Pension Benefit Guaranty Corporation (PBGC), an independent agency of the U.S. government funded by premiums paid from the participating companies.

For a defined contribution plan, the company contribution is recorded as an expense in the income statement when the cash is paid or the liability accrued. A defined benefit plan is more complex. Although the company contributes cash or securities to the pension investment account, the pension obligation is not satisfied until the employee receives pension benefits, which may be many years into the future. This section focuses on how a defined benefit plan is reported in the financial statements, and how we assess company performance and financial condition when such a plan exists.

Balance Sheet Effects of Defined Benefit Pension Plans

Pension plan assets are primarily investments in stocks and bonds (mostly of other companies, but it is not uncommon for companies to invest pension funds in their own stock). Pension liabilities (called the **projected benefit obligation** or **PBO**) are the company's obligations to pay current and former employees. The difference between the fair value of the pension plan assets and the projected benefit obligation is called the **funded status** of the pension plan. If the PBO exceeds the pension plan assets, the pension is **underfunded**. Conversely, if pension plan assets exceed the PBO, the pension plan is **overfunded**. Under current U.S. GAAP, companies are required to record only the funded status on their balance sheets (that is, the *net* amount, not the pension plan assets and PBO separately), either as an asset if the plan is overfunded, or as a liability if it is underfunded.

Pension plan assets consist of stocks and bonds whose value changes each period in three ways. First, the value of the investments increases or decreases as a result of interest, dividends, and gains or losses on the stocks and bonds held. Second, the pension plan assets increase when the company contributes additional cash or stock to the investment account. Third, the pension plan assets decrease by the amount of benefits paid to retirees during the period. These three changes in the pension plan assets are articulated below.

	Pension Plan Assets
	Pension plan assets, beginning balance
+	Actual returns on investments (interest, dividends, gains and losses)
+	Company contributions to pension plan
−	Benefits paid to retirees
=	Pension plan assets, ending balance

The pension liability, or PBO (projected benefit obligation), is computed as the present value of the expected future benefit payments to employees. The future payments depend on the number of years the employee is expected to work (years of service) and the employee's salary level at retirement. Consequently, companies must estimate future wage increases, as well as the number of employees expected to reach retirement age (or the vesting requirement) with the company. In addition, in order to compute the present value of benefit payments, the company has to estimate how long the plan participants are likely to receive pension benefits following retirement (that is, how long the employee—and often surviving spouse—will live). Once the future retiree pool is determined and the expected future payments under the plan are estimated, the expected payments are then discounted to arrive at the present value of the pension obligation. This is the PBO. A reconciliation of the PBO from beginning balance to year-end balance follows.

	Projected Benefit Obligation
	Projected benefit obligation, beginning balance
+	Service cost
+	Interest cost
+/−	Actuarial losses (gains)
−	Benefits paid to retirees
=	Projected benefit obligation, ending balance

As this reconciliation shows, the balance in the PBO changes during the period for four reasons.

- First, as employees continue to work for the company, their pension benefits increase. The annual **service cost** represents the additional (future) pension benefits earned by employees during the current year.
- Second, **interest cost** accrues on the outstanding pension liability, just as it would with any other long-term liability (see the accounting for bond liabilities in Chapter 9). Because there are no scheduled interest payments on the PBO, the interest cost accrues each year, that is, interest is added to the existing liability.
- Third, the PBO can increase (or decrease) due to **actuarial losses (and gains)**, which arise when companies make changes in their pension plans or make *changes in actuarial assumptions* (including assumptions that are used to estimate the PBO, such as the rate of wage inflation, termination and mortality rates, and the discount rate used to compute the present value of future obligations). For example, if a company increases the discount rate used to compute the present value of future pension plan payments from, say, 8% to 9%, the present value of future benefit payments declines (just like bond prices) and the company records a gain. Conversely, if the discount rate is reduced to 7%, the present value of the PBO increases and a loss is recorded. Other assumptions used to estimate the pension liability (such as the expected wage inflation rate or the expected life span of current and former employees) can create similar actuarial losses or gains.
- Fourth, pension benefit payments to retirees reduce the PBO (that portion of the liability is now paid).

Finally, the net pension liability (or asset) that is reported in a company's balance sheet, then, is computed as follows:

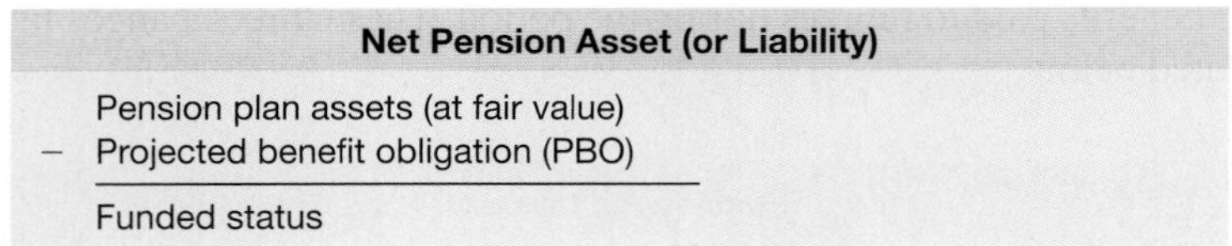

	Net Pension Asset (or Liability)
	Pension plan assets (at fair value)
−	Projected benefit obligation (PBO)
	Funded status

If the funded status is positive (assets exceed liabilities), the overfunded pension plan is reported on the balance sheet as an asset, typically called prepaid pension cost. If the funded status is negative (liabilities exceed assets), it is reported as a liability.[6] During the early 2000s, long-term interest

[6] Companies that have a defined benefit plan typically maintain many pension plans. Some are overfunded and others are underfunded. Current U.S. GAAP requires companies to group all of the overfunded and underfunded plans together, and to present a net asset for the overfunded plans and a net liability for the underfunded plans.

rates declined drastically and many companies lowered their discount rate for computing the present value of future pension payments. Lower discount rates meant higher PBO values. This period also witnessed two bear markets—the "dot com crash" in 2000–2001 and the financial crisis of 2008–2010—and pension plan assets declined in value. The combined effect of the increase in PBO and the decrease in asset values caused many pension funds to become severely underfunded. They have not fully recovered. Of the 1,500 largest U.S companies reporting pension plans (pension plan data available on the Compustat database) in 2014, 81% reported pension plans that were underfunded. Delta Air Lines reported an underfunded pension obligation of $12.5 billion in 2014. This amount was equal to 23 percent of its total assets. Many companies with a defined benefit plan report that their plans are underfunded. The underfunded liability as a percent of total assets for Delta and several other companies is reported in the graphic below.[7]

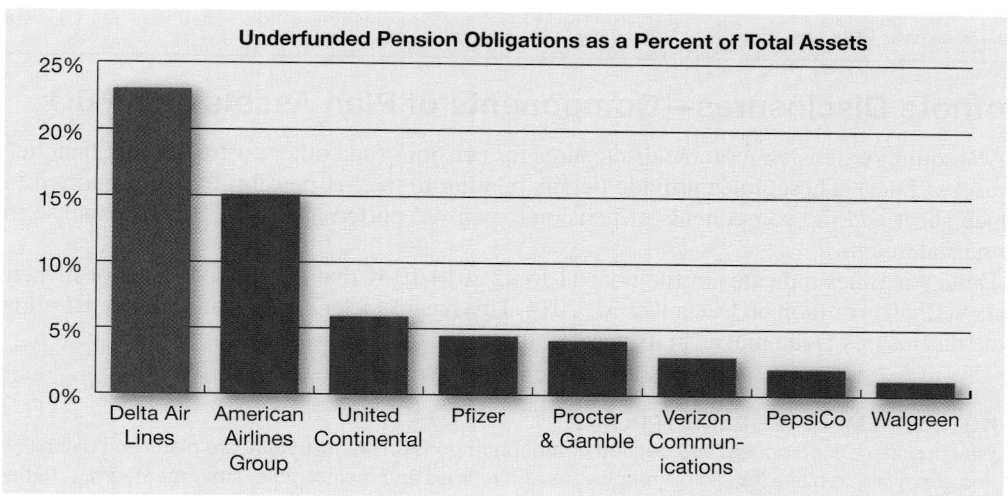

Income Statement Effects of Defined Benefit Pension Plans

In a defined benefit plan, pension expense is not determined by the company's contribution to the pension fund. Instead, net pension expense is computed as follows.

	Net Pension Expense
	Service cost
+	Interest cost
−	*Expected* return on pension plan assets
±	Amortization of deferred amounts
	Net pension expense

The net pension expense is rarely reported separately on the income statement. Instead, it is included with other forms of compensation expense in selling, general and administrative (SG&A) expenses. However, pension expense is disclosed separately in footnotes.

The net pension expense has four components. The previous section about the PBO described the first two components: service costs and interest costs. The third component of pension expense relates to the return on pension plan assets, which *reduces* total pension expense. To compute this component, companies use the long-term *expected* rate of return on the pension plan assets, rather than the *actual* return, and multiply that expected rate by the balance in the pension plan assets account. Use of the expected return rather than actual return is an important distinction. Company CEOs and CFOs dislike income variability because they believe that stockholders react negatively to it, so company executives intensely (and successfully) lobbied the FASB to use the more stable expected long-term investment return, rather than the actual return, in computing pension expense. Thus, the pension plan assets' expected return is subtracted to compute net pension expense.

Any difference between the expected and the actual return is accumulated, together with other deferred amounts, off-balance-sheet and reported in the footnotes. Other deferred amounts include

[7] Southwest Airlines does not offer a defined benefit plan, but does offer a defined contribution plan.

changes in PBO resulting from changes in estimates used to compute the PBO and from amendments to the pension plans made by the company. However, if the deferred amounts exceed certain limits, the excess is recognized on-balance-sheet with a corresponding amount recognized as amortization in the income statement.[8] This amortization is the fourth component of pension expense and can be either a positive or negative amount depending on the sign of the difference between expected and actual return on plan assets.

YOU MAKE THE CALL

You are a Consultant to the FASB The Board has asked your input on whether the assets in the pension fund should be netted against Pension Benefit Obligation (PBO) or whether the pension asset and the pension obligation should be reported separately. How would you advise the Board? [Answer on page 493]

Footnote Disclosures—Components of Plan Assets and PBO

5 **LO5** Analyze and interpret pension footnote disclosures.

GAAP requires extensive footnote disclosures for pensions (and other postretirement benefits that we discuss later). These notes provide details relating to the net pension liability reported in the balance sheet and the components of pension expense reported as part of SG&A expense in the income statement.

Delta Air Lines indicates in footnote 11 to its 2014 10-K that the funded status of its pension plan is $(12,501) million on December 31, 2014. This means Delta's plan is underfunded. Following are the disclosures Delta makes in its pension footnote.

NOTE 11—EMPLOYEE BENEFIT PLANS

We sponsor defined benefit and defined contribution pension plans, healthcare plans and disability and survivorship plans for eligible employees and retirees and their eligible family members. . . . The defined benefit plans are closed to new entrants and frozen for future benefit accruals. The Pension Protection Act of 2006 allows commercial airlines to elect alternative funding rules . . . under which the unfunded liability for a frozen defined benefit plan may be amortized over a 17-year period. . . . We estimate that the funding requirements under these plans will total at least $950 million in 2015.

Benefit Obligations, Fair Value of Plan Assets and Funded Status ($ millions):	2014	2013
Benefit obligation at beginning of period	$19,060	$21,489
Service cost	—	—
Interest cost	928	861
Actuarial loss (gain)	2,923	(2,212)
Benefits paid, including lump sums and annuities	(1,055)	(1,078)
Participant contributions	—	—
Benefit obligation at end of period	$21,856	$19,060
Fair value of plan assets at beginning of period	$8,937	$8,196
Actual gain on plan assets	556	905
Employer contributions	917	914
Participant contributions	—	—
Benefits paid, including lump sums and annuities	(1,055)	(1,078)
Fair value of plan assets at end of period	$9,355	$8,937
Funded status at end of period	$(12,501)	$(10,123)

[8] To avoid amortization, the deferred amounts must be less than 10% of the PBO or pension investments, whichever is less. The excess, if any, is amortized until no further excess remains. When the excess is eliminated (by investment returns or company contributions, for example), the amortization ceases.

Delta's PBO began 2014 with a balance of $19,060 million. It increased by the accrual of $928 million in interest cost. During the year, Delta also realized an actuarial loss of $2,923 million, which increased the pension liability. The PBO decreased as a result of $1,055 million in benefits paid to retirees, leaving a balance of $21,856 million at year-end.

Pension plan assets began the year with a fair value of $8,937 million, which increased by $556 million from investment returns (gains) and increased by $917 million from company contributions. The company drew down its investments to make pension payments of $1,055 million to retirees, leaving the pension plan assets with a year-end balance of $9,355 million. The funded status of Delta's pension plan at year-end is $(12,501) million ($21,856 million − $9,355 million). The negative balance indicates that its pension plan is underfunded. The PBO and pension plan assets accounts cannot be separated into operating and nonoperating components; thus, most analysts treat the entire funded status as an operating item (either asset or liability).

Footnote Disclosures—Components of Pension Expense

Delta Air Lines incurred $784 million of pension expense in 2014. This is not broken out separately in its income statement. Instead, it is included in SG&A expense. Details of this expense are found in its pension footnote. Delta reported $551 million in pension cost related to defined contribution plans. In addition, Delta reported its expense related to its defined benefit plans as follows ($ millions):

	2014	2013
Service cost	$ —	$ —
Interest cost	928	861
Expected return on assets	(829)	(734)
Recognized net actuarial loss	134	221
Net periodic cost for defined benefit plans	$233	$354

Most analysts consider the service cost portion of pension expense to be an operating expense, similar to salaries and other benefits. However, the interest cost component is generally viewed as a financing cost. Similarly, the expected return on plan assets is not considered operating. Because Delta's defined benefit pension plan is closed and further accrual of benefits is frozen, it reported no service cost in 2014 and the entire $233 million of defined benefit pension cost would be treated as nonoperating for analysis purposes. The costs related to the defined contribution plan are considered operating expenses.

RESEARCH INSIGHT

Valuation of Pension Footnote Disclosures The FASB requires footnote disclosure of the major components of pension cost presumably because it is useful for investors. Pension-related research has examined whether investors assign different valuation multiples to the components of pension cost when assessing company market value. Research finds that the market does, indeed, attach different interpretation to pension components, reflecting differences in information about recurring vs. nonrecurring expenses.

Interest cost is the product of the PBO and the discount rate. This discount rate is set by the company. The expected dollar return on pension assets is the product of the pension plan asset balance and the expected long-run rate of return on the investment portfolio. This rate is also set by the company. Further, the PBO is affected by the expected rate of wage inflation, termination and mortality rates, all of which are estimated by the company.

U.S. GAAP requires disclosure of several rates used by the company in its estimation of PBO and the related pension expense. Delta Air Lines discloses the following table in its pension footnote:

	2014	2013
Weighted-average assumptions used to determine net periodic benefit cost for the years ended December 31		
Discount rate	4.99%	4.10%
Expected long-term rate of return on plan assets	8.94	8.94

During 2014, Delta increased its assumed discount rate, which is used to compute the present value of the PBO and determine interest cost component of pension expense. The expected rate of return on plan assets remained constant.

Changes in these assumptions have the following general effects on pension expense and, thus, profitability. This table summarizes the effects of increases in the various rates. Decreases have the exact opposite effects of increases.

Estimate change	Probable effect on pension expense	Reason for effect
Discount rate increase	Increases	While the higher discount rate reduces the PBO, the lower PBO is multiplied by a higher interest rate. The rate effect is generally larger than the discount effect, resulting in increased pension expense.
Investment return increase	Decreases	The dollar amount of expected return on plan assets is the product of the plan assets balance and the expected long-term rate of return. Increasing the return increases the expected return on plan assets, thus reducing pension expense.
Wage inflation increase	Increases	The expected rate of wage inflation affects future wage levels that determine expected pension payments. An increase, thus, increases PBO, which increases both the service and interest cost components of pension expense.

In the case of Delta Air Lines, for example, a higher discount rate increased interest cost in 2014 relative to 2013. However, Delta recorded a higher expected return on plan assets (the expected rate was constant but the base must have changed) and a lower amount of recognized net actuarial loss in 2014 compared to 2013. Thus, the net cost in 2014 is lower. It is often the case that companies reduce the expected investment returns with a lag, but increase them without a lag, to favorably impact profitability. We must be aware of the impact of these changes in assumptions in our evaluation of company profitability.

BUSINESS INSIGHT

Pension Buyout at GM **General Motors**' pension obligation was at one time the largest of any company in the world. In 2011, its defined benefit plans were underfunded by $25.4 billion. Because pension fund assets are invested in securities, the underfunded balance can increase if the stock market falls. Analysts argued that the size, risk, and long duration of these obligations depressed GM's credit rating and its stock price.

In an effort to remove some of the projected obligations from its balance sheet, GM offered to buy out the pensions of 42,000 retirees in 2012. The pensions of an additional 76,000 retirees were transferred to **Prudential Financial** who will make the annuity payments to the retirees. Although the buyout required an immediate cash payment, the move removed approximately $26 billion of pension obligations from GM's 2012 balance sheet, thus improving solvency ratios. In addition, the reduced obligation means that future income statements will reflect lower pension expense due to reduced interest costs. GM's 2014 financial statement shows that the defined benefit pension plans are still underfunded by $24.1 billion. The related pension expense included in the income statement for 2014 was $151 million, considerably less than the pension expense in 2012 of $2.9 billion.

Footnote Disclosures and Future Cash Flows

The net periodic pension cost (expense) of $233 million is considerably less than the $917 million in cash that Delta contributed to its defined benefit plans. In addition, Delta paid $551 million into its defined contribution plans. Thus, its total pension expense for 2014 was $784 million ($233 million + $551 million) and its cash contributions totaled $1,468 million ($917 million + $551 million).

BUSINESS INSIGHT

How Pensions Confound Income Analysis Overfunded pension plans and boom markets can inflate income. Specifically, when the stock market is booming, pension investments realize large gains that flow to income (via reduced pension expense). Although pension plan assets do not belong to shareholders (as they are the legal entitlement of current and future retirees), the gains and losses from those plan assets are reported in income. The following graph plots the funded status of **General Electric Company**'s pension plan together with pension expense (revenue) that GE reported from 2000 to 2014.

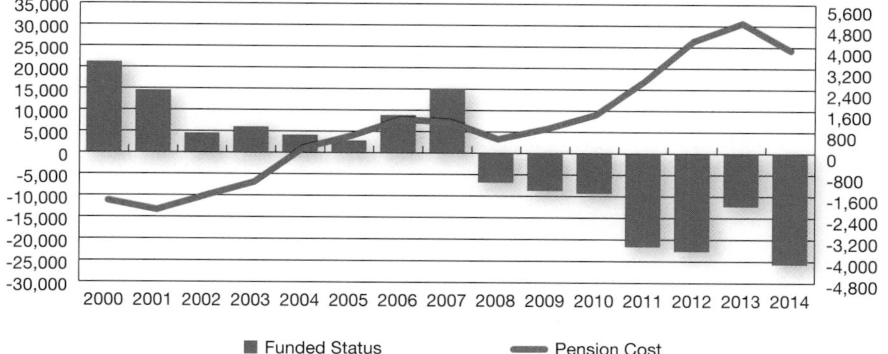

GE's funded status was consistently positive (indicating an overfunded plan) until 2008. The degree of overfunding peaked in 1999 at the height of the stock market, and began to decline during the bear market of the early 2000s. GE reported pension *revenue* (not expense) during this period. In 2001, GE's reported pension *revenue* was $2,095 million (10.6% of its pretax income). Because of the plan's overfunded status, the expected return and amortization of deferred gains components of pension expense amounted to $5,288 million, far in excess of the service and interest costs of $3,193 million. Since 2004, GE has recorded pension expense (rather than revenue) as the pension plan's overfunding and expected long-term rates of return declined, and in 2008 the funded status turned negative. In 2014, GE reported an unfunded liability of $25.7 billion and a pension expense of $4.0 billion.

Companies use their pension plan assets to pay pension benefits to retirees. When markets are booming, as was true during the 1990s, pension plan assets can grow rapidly. However, when markets reverse, as in the bear market of the early 2000s and in 2008–2009, the value of pension plan assets can decline. The company's annual pension plan contribution is an investment decision influenced, in part, by market conditions and minimum required contributions specified by law.[9] Companies' cash contributions come from borrowed funds or operating cash flows.

RESEARCH INSIGHT

Why Do Companies Offer Pensions? Research examines why companies choose to offer pension benefits. It finds that deferred compensation plans and pensions help align the long-term interests of owners and employees. Research also examines the composition of pension investments. It finds that a large portion of pension fund assets are invested in fixed-income securities, which are of lower risk than other investment securities. This implies that pension assets are less risky than nonpension assets. However, in severe economic downturns, some corporations curtail their pension plan contributions in order to protect cash flow.

Delta Air Lines paid $1,055 million in pension benefits to retirees in 2014, yet it contributed only $917 million to pension assets that year. The remaining amount was paid out of available funds in the investment account. Cash contributions to the pension plan assets are the relevant amounts for an analysis of projected cash flows. Benefits paid in relation to the pension liability balance

[9] The Pension Protection Act of 2006 tightens funding requirements so employers make greater cash contributions to pension funds, closes loopholes that allow companies with underfunded plans to skip cash pension payments, prohibits employers and union leaders from promising extra benefits if pension plans are markedly underfunded, and strengthens disclosure rules to give workers and retirees more information about the status of their pension plan.

can provide a clue about the need for *future* cash contributions. Companies are required to disclose the expected benefit payments for five years after the statement date and the remaining obligations thereafter. Following is Delta's benefit disclosure statement:

The following table summarizes the benefit payments that are scheduled to be paid in the years ending December 31 ($ millions):

	Pension Benefits
2015	$1,124
2016	1,133
2017	1,153
2018	1,173
2019	1,191
2020–2024	6,229

Delta's unfunded pension amount grew by over $2 billion from 2013 to 2014. The company was, however, able to contribute $917 million and the plan assets had an actual return of $556 million. Thus, the company was able to cover its current year cash outflows of $1,055 million from these sources, which has not always been the case for Delta. The reason for the growth in the net unfunded balance in its pension plan is from increases in the pension liability. In general for pension plans, and as is true at Delta, life expectancies are getting longer but retirement ages are not increasing. Thus, pension payments are expected to be paid for a longer period of time, increasing the liability. In addition, market rates of interest are low requiring discount rates used to value the liabilities to be (somewhat) low, which makes the liability higher.

One application of the pension footnote is to assess the likelihood that the company will be required to increase its cash contributions to the pension plan. This estimate is made by examining the funded status of the pension plan and the projected payments to retirees. For severely underfunded plans, the projected payments to retirees will not be covered by existing pension assets and current negative investment returns. When this occurs, the company will need to divert operating cash flow from other prospective projects to cover its pension plan. Alternatively, if operating cash flows will not be sufficient, it will likely need to borrow to fund those payments. This decision can be especially troublesome as the debt service payments include interest, thus, effectively increasing the cost of the pension contribution.

Other Post-Employment Benefits

In addition to pension benefits, many companies provide health care and insurance benefits to retired employees. These benefits are referred to as **other post-employment benefits (OPEB)**. These benefits present reporting challenges similar to pension accounting. However, companies most often provide these benefits on a "pay-as-you-go" basis and it is rare for companies to make contributions in advance for OPEB. As a result, this liability, known as the **accumulated post-employment benefit obligation (APBO)**, is largely, if not totally, unfunded. GAAP requires that the unfunded APBO liability, net of any unrecognized amounts, be reported in the balance sheet and the annual service costs and interest costs be accrued as expenses each year. This requirement is controversial for two reasons. First, future health care costs are especially difficult to estimate, so the value of the resulting APBO (the present value of the future benefits) is fraught with error. Second, these benefits are provided at the discretion of the employer and can be altered or terminated at any time. Consequently, employers argue that without a legal obligation to pay these benefits, the liability should not be reported in the balance sheet.

Other post-employment benefits can produce large liabilities. For example, Delta Air Lines reports an underfunded health care obligation of $2,505 million and a related expense of $101 million in 2014. Our analysis of cash flows related to pension obligations can be extended to other post-employment benefit obligations. For example, in addition to its pension payments, Delta also discloses that it is obligated to make health care payments to retirees totaling $2,633 million over the next 10 years. Our analysis of projected cash flows must consider this potential cash outflow.

RESEARCH INSIGHT

Valuation of Nonpension Post-Employment Benefits The FASB requires employers to accrue the costs of all nonpension post-employment benefits; known as *accumulated post-employment benefit obligation* (APBO). These benefits consist primarily of health care and insurance. This requirement is controversial due to concerns about the reliability of the liability estimate. Research finds that the APBO (alone) is associated with company value. However, when other pension-related variables are included in the research, the APBO liability is no longer useful in explaining company value. Research concludes that the pension-related variables do a better job at conveying value-relevant information than the APBO number alone, which implies that the APBO number is less reliable.

A GLOBAL PERSPECTIVE

Pension Fund Status IFRS and U.S. GAAP require companies to report the funded status of their defined benefit pension plans on the balance sheet. IFRS, however, calculates pension expense differently. First, unlike U.S. GAAP, IFRS requires that the expected return on pension assets must be the same rate as the discount rate used to value the PBO. In addition, IFRS recognizes the cost of plan amendments in the income statement immediately, rather than amortizing those costs over the service life of employees. There are still other differences that make direct comparison across IFRS and U.S. GAAP firms difficult.

MID-CHAPTER REVIEW 2

The following pension data is taken from footnote 8 of **United Continental Holdings, Inc.**, 10-K report.

($ millions)	2014
Change in Benefit Obligation	
Projected benefit obligation at beginning of year	$4,000
Service cost	98
Interest cost	201
Actuarial (gains) losses	807
Gross benefits paid and settlements	(281)
Other	(22)
Projected benefit obligation at end of year	$4,803
Change in Plan Assets	
Fair value of plan assets at beginning of year	$2,397
Actual gains (losses) on plan assets	151
Employer contributions	307
Gross benefits paid and settlements	(281)
Other	(12)
Fair value of plan assets at end of year	$2,562
Funded status of the plans	$(2,241)

Following is United Continental's footnote for its pension cost as reported in its income statement.

Components of Net Periodic Benefit Cost	Defined Benefit Pension 2014
Service cost	$ 98
Interest cost	201
Expected return on plan assets	(180)
Amortization and other	13
Net periodic benefit cost	$132

Required

1. In general, what factors impact a company's pension benefit obligation during a period?
2. In general, what factors impact a company's pension plan investments during a period?
3. What amount is reported on the balance sheet relating to the United Continental pension plan?
4. How does the expected return on plan assets affect pension cost?
5. How does United Continental's expected return on plan assets compare with its actual return (in $s) for 2014?
6. How much net pension cost is reflected in United Continental's 2014 income statement?
7. Assess United Continental's ability to meet payment obligations to retirees.

The solution to this review problem can be found on pages 514-515.

ACCOUNTING FOR INCOME TAXES

6 **LO6** Describe and interpret accounting for income taxes.

Companies maintain two sets of books, one for reporting to their shareholders and creditors and one to report to tax authorities. This is not unethical or illegal. In fact, it is often required. Companies with publicly traded securities compute and report financial accounting income under the rules (e.g., GAAP or IFRS) provided by the financial accounting standards setters (e.g., FASB in the United States). As we have discussed, this income computation is done on the accrual basis, and it is meant to provide information about firm performance to outside stakeholders, such as investors and creditors.[10] Companies must also compute taxable income and report the amount on their tax return(s) filed with the tax authorities in the jurisdictions in which they are required to file (e.g., the Internal Revenue Service and state tax authorities in the United States). Taxable income is determined under the rules promulgated by the government of the taxing jurisdiction (e.g., the Internal Revenue Code in the United States). Tax authorities have different objectives from financial accounting standard setters. The tax rules are set in order to raise money to fund government activities, to encourage or discourage certain behaviors, and (hopefully) based on some sense of fairness and equity. In contrast, financial accounting income is meant to provide information about firm performance to investors, creditors, and other stakeholders so that these parties can make informed decisions about investments and loans. The rules and objectives are very different for the two income measures, and as a result, the two resulting income numbers for a company can be very different.

Our objective here is to learn how to determine a corporation's income tax expense that is reported on the income statement for financial accounting purposes. Financial accounting uses accrual accounting, thus, income tax expense is determined using accrual accounting just like all other expenses. As a result, income tax expense on the income statement is not the cash taxes paid for the reporting period. Instead, it is the accrual-based expense measure, meaning it is the total income tax expense related to the financial accounting income reported in the period regardless of whether those income taxes are paid in the current period or in the future. Furthermore, because it is accrual-based, there will be resulting assets and liabilities that need to be accounted for on the balance sheet. These include what are called deferred tax liabilities and deferred tax assets.

Book-Tax Differences

There are two general types of differences between taxable income and financial accounting income, also known as book-tax differences—permanent differences and temporary differences.

A permanent difference is an item of income or expense that is accounted for differently for book and tax purposes in the current year and never reverses in a future year. A simple example of a permanent difference is interest income on municipal bonds. Municipal bond interest income is included in financial accounting income. However, municipal bond interest is tax exempt at the federal level, meaning it is not included in taxable income. Thus, if a company has municipal bond interest income, its financial accounting income will be higher than its taxable income by the amount of municipal bond interest. This difference will not reverse in the future

[10] All companies have to report to tax authorities but many privately held companies do not have to comply with GAAP.

because the municipal bond interest is never included in taxable income. The accounting for income tax with respect to a permanent difference is straightforward; no deferred tax assets or liabilities are created. Income tax expense is lower (in this case) in the current year as a result of the taxes saved by investing in municipal bonds.

A temporary difference is an item of income or expense that is different between book and taxable income in the current year, but will reverse in a future year such that the same amount is included in taxable income and book income over time. Temporary differences are:

1. created by using accrual accounting for book and cash accounting for tax, and/or
2. created by using different rules for determining the accrual amount for book than for tax.

FYI We use the term book income to refer to income before income taxes, as reported in financial statements. Taxable income refers to income reported in the income tax return.

A common example of a temporary difference is depreciation. For financial accounting purposes companies often use straight-line depreciation as discussed in Chapter 8. For U.S. tax purposes, however, companies use an accelerated method of depreciation (the Modified Accelerated Cost Recovery System (MACRS)). Thus, early in an asset's life, tax depreciation will be greater than book depreciation. However, over the life of the asset the same amount of depreciation will be recorded for book and tax (assuming zero salvage value). This is a temporary difference because tax depreciation is higher earlier on but will be equal to or less than book depreciation in later years in the asset's life. In other words, the book-tax difference will reverse. The computation of the income tax expense is more difficult in this case. We need to account for the taxes due on taxable income (the cash taxes) *and* an accrual of taxes that are known to be due in a future period when the depreciation difference reverses. In other words, our total income tax expense is the tax expense related to financial accounting income for the period regardless of whether the taxes are actually paid this year. The accrual for the portion not yet paid creates a **deferred tax liability**—the book-tax difference in this period will lead to higher taxable income relative to book income in the future. This higher relative taxable income means higher cash taxes to be paid in the future—that is, a liability.

Example Assume Clark Corporation is in its first year of business. It purchases a piece of equipment that costs $200,000 with a useful life of 4 years and no net salvage value. The firm uses straight-line depreciation for financial reporting purposes and accelerated depreciation under MACRS for tax purposes (we will use double declining balance depreciation as an approximation for our example). Comparing the depreciation schedules reveals the following information:

FYI Income tax expense is also titled **provision for income tax**.

	Tax Reporting	Financial Reporting		
Year	DDB Depreciation	Straight-Line Depreciation	Tax vs. Book Difference	Cumulative Tax-Book Difference
1	$100,000	$50,000	$50,000	$50,000
2	50,000	50,000	0	50,000
3	25,000	50,000	(25,000)	25,000
4	25,000	50,000	(25,000)	0

Assume the corporate statutory tax rate is 40%, we expect the tax rate to stay at 40% for the entire 4 years, and that depreciation is the only book-tax difference for the Clark Corporation. The deferred tax liability at the end of each year is the cumulative book-tax difference times the tax rate. The tax rate to be used is the tax rate expected to be in effect when the book-tax difference reverses. The deferred tax expense each period is the current year book-tax difference (which is the change in the cumulative book-tax difference) times the tax rate. The deferred tax liability at the end of each year and the deferred tax expense for each year for Clark Corporation would be:

Year	Cumulative Tax-Book Difference	Tax Rate	Deferred Tax Liability, End of Year	Deferred Tax Expense
1	$50,000	40%	$20,000	$20,000
2	50,000	40%	20,000	0
3	25,000	40%	10,000	(10,000)
4	0	40%	0	(10,000)

Now assume for illustration that financial accounting earnings each year before depreciation and taxes are $125,000 and there are no other book-tax differences. The yearly calculation of financial reporting and taxable income along with the income tax expense is as follows:

	Tax			
Year	**1**	**2**	**3**	**4**
Earnings before depreciation	$125,000	$125,000	$125,000	$125,000
Depreciation deduction	(100,000)	(50,000)	(25,000)	(25,000)
Taxable income	25,000	75,000	100,000	100,000
Tax due on the tax return (@ 40%)	10,000	30,000	40,000	40,000

	Financial Reporting			
Year	**1**	**2**	**3**	**4**
Earnings before depreciation	$125,000	$125,000	$125,000	$125,000
Depreciation expense	(50,000)	(50,000)	(50,000)	(50,000)
Earnings before tax	75,000	75,000	75,000	75,000
Tax expense	30,000	30,000	30,000	30,000

The entry to record income tax expense in Year 1 follows using the financial statement effects template and journal entry form:

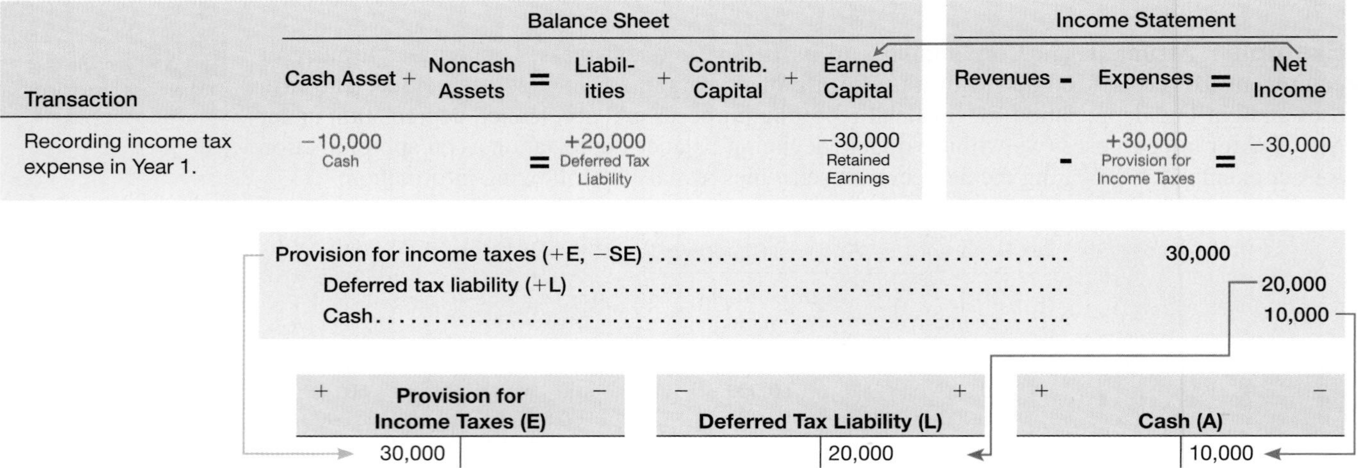

In Year 4, Clark Corporation records its income tax expense. The entry is recorded as follows:

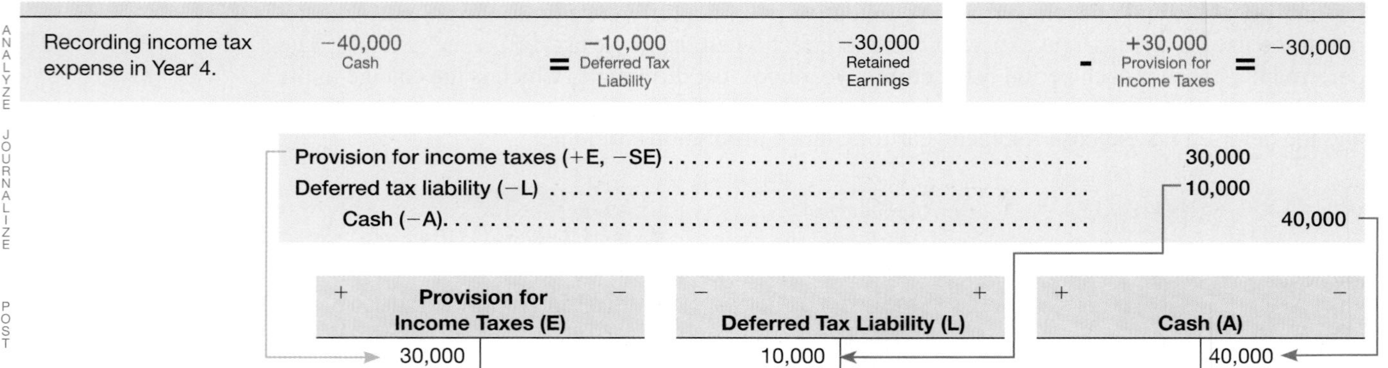

The analysis highlights several facts:

1. Over the 4 years, tax payments to the IRS total $120,000 = $10,000 + $30,000 + $40,000 + $40,000. Total tax expense on the books for the 4 years also equals $120,000 = 4 × $30,000.
2. The timing of the tax payments differs from the tax expense recognized on the books.
3. The deferred tax liability created in the first year because the tax code allows a larger deduction for depreciation, is reduced to zero in the 4th year when the useful life of the asset is over and the timing of the depreciation deductions reverse.
4. The cash flow takes place consistent with the tax code. The accounting expense amount is an accrual-basis measure.
5. In year 1, the corporation's provision for income tax consists of current income tax expense of $10,000 and deferred income tax expense of $20,000 for the total income tax expense of $30,000. In year 4, the corporation has current income tax expense of $40,000 and deferred income tax expense of $(10,000) for a total income tax expense of $30,000. The total income tax expense is shown on the income statement and the more detailed breakout into current and deferred expense is disclosed in the notes to the financial statements.

Depreciation generally will lead to a deferred tax liability because tax depreciation is usually faster than book depreciation. There are also transactions that generate the necessity to record a **deferred tax asset**. For example, bad debts, warranty expense, and many other accrued expenses usually require an associated deferred tax asset to be recorded. For financial accounting purposes, bad debt expense and warranty expense are expensed using management estimates before the receivable actually goes bad and before the warranty costs are actually paid. Again, this is because financial accounting is done on the accrual method and expenses that are associated with the revenue recorded generally are estimated and accrued before they are paid in cash. This is the conservative nature of financial reporting. For tax purposes, these expenses cannot be estimated but instead are deductible generally only when paid. This difference in timing between tax reporting and financial accounting leads to temporary differences where the tax deduction is later in time than the financial accounting expense (opposite of what we just illustrated for depreciation). Because in this case a tax deduction will occur in the future due to a transaction or event in the current period, the company has a deferred tax asset (future benefit) that needs to be recorded.

Temporary book-tax differences also occur with items of revenue. Take for example, unearned revenue we described in Chapter 6. If a company receives cash in advance of being able to recognize revenue, the company will record unearned revenue (a liability) until the revenue is earned and can be recognized. For tax purposes, however, the cash received is generally recorded as income in the period it is received. Thus, there is a book-tax difference. In this case, the revenue is recorded for tax in an earlier period than for financial accounting, meaning that in some future year(s) taxable income will be less than financial accounting income when the revenue is recognized according to the GAAP rules. That means the company has a deferred tax asset to record in the year the cash is received because in a future period taxable income will be lower than book income because of the unearned revenue recorded in the current year.

As a brief example, let's say that the corporation Josie's Jewelry, Inc. makes sales of $100,000 in the current period and estimates and records a bad debt expense of $5,000. This is an expense for financial reporting purposes but there is no deduction allowed for tax purposes in the current period. The tax deduction is not allowed until the receivable actually goes bad (i.e., is deemed to be uncollectible). Using a tax rate of 40%, Josie's Jewelry would report an increase in a deferred tax asset in the current period of $2,000 ($5,000 × 40%) and a corresponding deferred tax benefit (i.e., a negative deferred tax expense) on the income statement. When the receivable is deemed uncollectible and written off in a future period and the deduction is taken for tax purposes, the corporation will reverse the deferred tax asset to zero (assuming the full $5,000 is the amount that eventually is deducted for tax purposes) and record a $2,000 deferred tax expense. Notice that in this future period, the deduction is taken for tax purposes so the actual tax paid is lower and thus, current tax expense is lower by $2,000. In addition, because of the deferred tax asset reversal, deferred tax expense is increased. Thus, the net effect on income in the future period is zero. This is correct because the tax benefit was accrued in the first period when the revenue was earned, bad debt expense was recorded, and deferred tax asset was established.[11]

BUSINESS INSIGHT

The United States has a worldwide tax system, meaning the United States taxes multinational corporations incorporated in the United States on their worldwide earnings. Operating earnings earned by a subsidiary in a foreign jurisdiction, however, are not taxed in the United States when earned, but are taxed in the United States when repatriated to the U.S. parent company as a dividend (tax credits for foreign income taxes paid are allowed to mitigate double taxation). Because the United States has a high corporate statutory tax rate, many U.S. corporations do not repatriate earnings from their foreign subsidiaries in order to avoid (defer) the U.S. tax on those earnings. As of the time of this writing, most estimates are that there is in excess of $2 trillion of unremitted earnings in foreign subsidiaries of U.S. multinational corporations (the estimates of how much of this is in cash versus reinvested in property, plant, and equipment vary).

How do companies account for the current and future taxes on these unremitted foreign earnings? The earnings of the foreign subsidiaries are included in financial accounting income in the same manner as earnings from domestic subsidiaries. But, as just described, the operating earnings of the foreign subsidiaries are not included in taxable income until repatriated to the United States. Thus, a temporary book-tax difference exists. This temporary book-tax difference creates a deferred tax liability (because future taxable income will be greater than future financial accounting income when the earnings are repatriated) in the amount of unremitted earnings times the U.S. tax rate (less foreign tax credits). However, the accounting standards allow for an exception to normal deferred tax accounting if management expects to leave the earnings in the foreign subsidiaries and not return the earnings to the U.S. parent. In such a case the foreign earnings are called indefinitely reinvested (also known as permanently reinvested) and the corporation does not have to accrue the expected U.S. income taxes but can instead treat the book-tax difference related to unremitted foreign earnings as a permanent difference. As a result, the company's effective tax rate can be significantly reduced, and accounting earnings increased.

An example of a company with a substantial amount of offshore earnings and cash is Apple, Inc. In its 2014 10-K, Apple provides very good disclosure about its income tax expense and the effect of U.S. taxation of its foreign earnings. Apple reports that the company has $69.7 billion of unremitted foreign earnings on which it has not accrued any U.S. income tax expense. The company reports that it estimates that the U.S. income tax associated with those earnings would be $23.3 billion. Thus, Apple has not recorded $23.3 billion in income tax expense over the life of the company that it otherwise would have had to record if the exception to deferred tax accounting did not exist. This has increased earnings by $23.3 billion over the life of the company. In 2014, the company's effective tax rate is 26% (not the statutory federal rate of 35%) almost entirely because of foreign earnings in lower taxed jurisdictions on which Apple does not accrue U.S. income taxes. The United States is currently contemplating corporate tax reform, particularly with respect to how the United States taxes the foreign earnings of U.S. corporations. Whether any legislation will pass remains to be seen, but if successful there could be significant financial statement effects.

Net Operating Losses Another book-tax difference is a net operating loss carryover. For tax purposes, corporations can carryover operating losses to future years.[12] Financial accounting does not have such a rule; if a corporation has a loss for financial reporting, the loss is recorded and the corporation starts the next year with a clean slate and measures income for that next year only. Thus, the net operating loss carryover is a temporary book-tax difference. Because the loss carryover represents future deductions for tax purposes, the company has and must record an increase to deferred tax assets and a deferred tax benefit (i.e., negative deferred tax expense) in the

[11] When a company has both deferred tax assets and deferred tax liabilities, the assets and liabilities are first separated into current and long-term amounts. The current deferred tax assets and current deferred tax liabilities are then reported net in the balance sheet under current assets or current liabilities, whichever is greater. Long-term amounts are treated similarly. It is not uncommon, therefore to see a company report deferred tax assets under current assets in the balance sheet, while reporting deferred tax liabilities under long-term liabilities. The FASB in 2015 issued a proposed Accounting Standard Update to change this accounting, however, such that all deferred tax assets and liabilities would be reported as long-term.

[12] Under current rules, corporations can carry net operating losses back two years for tax purposes and forward for 20 years. In essence, allowing loss carryovers for tax purposes approximates an averaging of income over time so companies with volatile income are not required to pay high taxes in years with high income and then get no relief in years with losses. We ignore the carryback in our discussion for simplicity (and because it does not create a deferred tax asset).

amount of the loss carryover times the tax rate (the tax rate expected to be in effect when the loss carryover will be used to offset taxes). Thus, even though the corporation is not getting the cash benefits of the deduction yet, the accounting rules require the company to accrue the benefit to the current period.

Valuation Allowance After a corporation computes its income tax expense and records its deferred tax assets and liabilities, the corporation has yet another step to complete. The corporation must evaluate the realizability of the deferred tax assets. This means that management must estimate whether the company will have sufficient future taxable income to offset the future deductions represented by the deferred tax assets. If management does not think the company will have enough future taxable income to be able to use all the deferred tax assets (i.e., future deductions), then a reserve (i.e., a contra-asset) must be established against the deferred tax assets. Thus, the deferred tax assets on the balance sheet will not be overstated. As an analogy, recall that when a company has accounts receivables it must evaluate the collectability of those receivables and establish an allowance for doubtful accounts to ensure the accounts receivable asset is not overstated. In addition, inventory is valued at lower of cost or market (or soon to be lower of cost or net realizable value) so that inventory is not overstated on the balance sheet. Again, this is the conservative nature of the financial accounting rules. Similarly, if a corporation has deferred tax assets (i.e., future tax deductions) that management does not expect to be able to use to offset future taxable income, then the company must record a **valuation allowance**. When the contra-asset is recorded, deferred tax expense is increased which decreases accounting income (and if a valuation allowance is reduced, deferred tax expense is reduced, increasing income). A more detailed discussion is beyond the scope of this text, but net operating losses and associated valuation allowances have been an important part of many companies', including Delta's, accounting for income taxes as we will see below.

RESEARCH INSIGHT

Recent research has examined how important the exception to deferred tax accounting is to managers when making "real" decisions such as whether to operate outside the United States and whether to repatriate cash to the United States. While the importance of cash tax savings is well known, the evidence in the studies suggests that lowering income tax expense for financial accounting purposes is statistically just as important as saving the cash taxes.[13] This suggests that the numbers reported as financial accounting income are extremely important to managers.

Income Tax Disclosures

Delta Air Lines reported income before income taxes of $1,072 million in 2014. Delta reported an income tax expense of $413 million in 2014. In 2013, Delta reported income before income taxes of $2,527 million and income tax benefit (the opposite of an income tax expense) of $8,013 million.

To fully understand how income tax expense (or benefit) is determined, we refer to the footnotes. Note 13 to Delta's 2014 10-K report contains the table shown in **Exhibit 10.7**.

EXHIBIT 10.7 Delta Air Lines Income Tax Expense

Year ended December 31 ($ millions)	2014	2013
Current income tax (provision) benefit	$ 1	$ 22
Deferred tax (provision) benefit net of valuation allowance	(414)	7,991
Income tax (provision) benefit	$(413)	$8,013

The income tax expense or benefit reported in the income statement consists of two primary components:

[13] See John Graham, Michelle Hanlon, Terry Shevlin, "Real Effects of Accounting Rules: Evidence from Multinational Firms' Investment Location and Repatriation Decisions," *Journal of Accounting Research*, March 2011.

Current tax expense—this can be thought of for our purposes as the amount that has been paid or is payable to tax authorities in the current period (it also usually contains the income effects of some tax accruals that are beyond the scope of this text).

Deferred tax expense—this is the effect on tax expense due to changes in deferred tax liabilities and assets. It is the result of temporary differences between the reported income statement and the tax return.

Based on the table shown in **Exhibit 10.7**, Delta reported a tax benefit of $1 million for current taxes. This tax benefit potentially suggests that Delta reported a loss on its tax return in 2014 and potentially expects tax refunds of $1 million. It also reported a net deferred tax expense of $414 million.

Companies must also disclose the components of deferred tax assets and liabilities. The components of Delta's deferred tax assets and liabilities are presented in **Exhibit 10.8**.

EXHIBIT 10.8 Components of Delta Air Lines' Deferred Income Taxes

December 31 ($ millions)	2014	2013
Deferred tax assets:		
Net operating loss carryforwards	$ 4,782	$ 6,024
Pension, postretirement and other benefits	6,033	4,982
Fuel derivatives MTM adjustments	777	0
AMT credit carryforwards	357	378
Deferred revenue	1,824	1,965
Other	659	698
Valuation allowance	(46)	(177)
Total deferred tax assets, net of valuation allowance	$14,386	$13,870
Deferred tax liabilities:		
Depreciation	$ 4,663	$ 4,799
Intangible assets	1,684	1,704
Other	444	639
Total deferred tax liabilities	$ 6,791	$ 7,142
Deferred tax assets, net	$ 7,595	$ 6,728

Delta's deferred tax assets were greater than its deferred tax liabilities in both 2014 and 2013. Notice that Delta has a large deferred tax liability for depreciation. We would expect this for a capital intensive company like an airline (assuming not all planes are leased via operating leases). Notice also that Delta has a large deferred tax asset for pensions and other postretirement benefits. As we discussed earlier in the chapter, Delta has a large unfunded pension liability. The company has to record the liability and a pension expense for financial accounting on the accrual basis but does not get a tax deduction until funds are contributed to the plan. Thus, larger expenses have been recorded for book relative to the deductions taken for tax. In the future, this will reverse (assuming Delta eventually funds its pension) and the deductions for tax will be greater than the expenses for book. Finally, note that Delta's other large deferred tax asset is for net operating loss carryforwards. In prior years, as recent as 2011 and 2012, Delta established a large valuation allowance against its deferred tax assets indicating that management did not think the company would have enough future taxable income to be able to offset the net operating loss carryovers. However, starting in 2012 and to a large degree in 2013, Delta decreased the valuation allowance (by $8 billion in 2013) indicating that management thinks that taxable income will be high enough in the future to use all the tax loss carryforwards. In the 2014 10-K, management states that "During 2014 we continued our trend of sustained profitability, recording pre-tax profit of $1.1 billion for the year. After considering all available positive and negative evidence, we released additional valuation allowance related to net operating losses . . . " As Delta reduces the valuation allowance, more of the deferred tax assets related to the net operating loss carryovers are recognized on the balance sheet. Analysts sometimes consider management's assessment and changes in valuation allowances an indicator of future prospects for the company. In addition, one has to consider large increases to net income from changes in the valuation allowance (like Delta had in 2013) and understand that such large changes will not happen every year; the income from the valuation allowance release is nonrecurring.

Companies also report in the footnotes a reconciliation of differences between the statutory U.S. tax rate (currently 35%) and the tax expense reported in the income statement. The **effective tax rate** is determined by dividing the provision for income taxes (tax expense) by the income before income taxes. Delta's effective tax rate for 2014 was 38.5% ($413 million/$1,072 million). Effective tax rates can vary considerably from one company to another due to permanent differences, tax credits, and other factors. A comparison of the effective tax rate for several companies is presented in **Exhibit 10.9**. The exhibit also splits the tax expense into current and deferred amounts. For example, the highest effective tax rates were reported by **Walgreen**, **Delta**, **Southwest Airlines**, and **Chevron Corporation**. Each of their effective tax rates are greater than the U.S. statutory rate of 35%. However, most of Chevron's and Walgreen's taxes are current while the airlines' taxes are largely deferred. On the other extreme, **Cisco**, **Procter & Gamble**, and **Verizon** reported effective tax rates around 20%.

EXHIBIT 10.9 Comparison of Effective Tax Rates

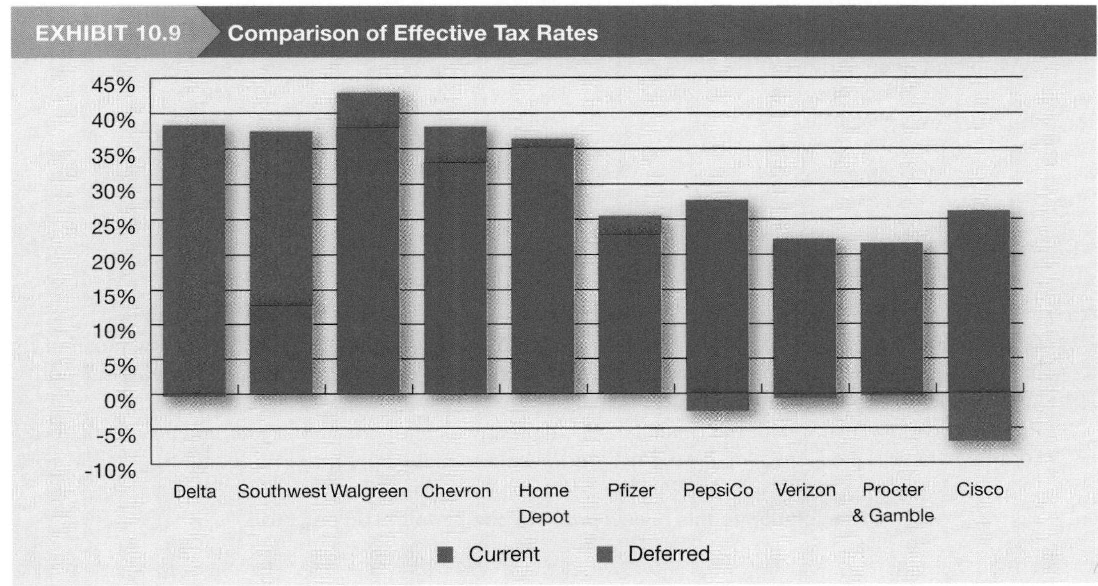

Deferred Taxes in the Cash Flow Statement

Income taxes, including deferred income taxes, are reported in the operating section of the cash flow statement. When the cash flow statement is prepared using the direct method, deferred income taxes are excluded from taxes paid in cash. When the indirect (or reconciliation) method is used, the deferred portion of the income tax expense must be added back to net income as an expense not requiring the use of cash. The amount of income taxes paid in cash is then reported at the bottom of the cash flow statement or in the footnotes.

Computation and Analysis of Taxes

An analysis of deferred taxes can yield useful insights. An increase in deferred tax liabilities indicates that a company is reporting higher profits in its income statement than in its tax return. The difference between reported corporate profits and taxable income increased substantially in the late 1990s, just prior to the stock market decline.

Although an increase in deferred tax liabilities can be the result of legitimate differences between financial reporting standards and tax rules, we must be aware of the possibility that such differences can also be caused by tax avoidance or by earnings management, improper revenue recognition, or other questionable accounting practices. More advanced courses cover the accounting for income taxes in more depth.

RESEARCH INSIGHT

Recent research has studied the accounting for income tax. Several papers have examined whether the overall difference between a company's taxable income and its financial accounting income contains any information about earnings quality. The idea is that if managers use accruals to manage financial accounting earnings upward, taxable income would not likely be similarly managed because there are fewer accruals for tax purposes (e.g., allowance for doubtful accounts, warranty reserves, etc.). The evidence is generally consistent with this hypothesis.[14]

CHAPTER-END REVIEW

The following footnote is from the 2016 annual report of Adler Corporation.

Note 9: Income Taxes
The provision for income taxes includes the following

($ thousands)	2016
Current provision	
Domestic	$1,342
Foreign	146
Deferred provision (credit)	
Domestic	960
Foreign	(58)
Total	$2,390

Required

1. (a) What is the amount of income tax expense reported on its income statement? (b) How much of its income tax expense is payable in cash? (c) Assuming that its deferred tax liability increased, identify an example that could account for such a change.
2. Prepare the entry, using both the financial statement effects template and in journal entry form, to record its income tax expense for 2016. Post journal entries to the appropriate T-accounts.

The solution to this review problem can be found on page 515.

SUMMARY

LO1 Define off-balance-sheet financing and explain its effects on financial analysis. (p. 462)

- Off-balance-sheet financing refers to financial obligations of the company that are not recognized as liabilities in the balance sheet. Recognizing these obligations often requires recognizing off-balance-sheet assets.
- Off-balance-sheet financing improves financial leverage ratios and its corresponding unrecognized assets improve performance measures.

LO2 Account for leases using the operating lease method and the capital lease method. (p. 463)

- Operating lease payments are treated as ordinary rent expense. No asset or liability is recorded.
- A capital lease records an asset and a liability equal to the present value of the minimum lease payments. The income statement reports interest expense on the liability and depreciation on the asset.

LO3 Convert off-balance-sheet operating leases to the capital lease method. (p. 469)

- Compute the present value of future cash payments required under operating leases. These cash obligations are disclosed in footnotes.
- Add a leased asset and a lease liability to the balance sheet equal to the present value of the future cash payments.

[14] See the following studies: 1) Phillips, John, Mort Pincus, and Sonja Rego, "Earnings Management: New Evidence Based on Deferred Tax Expense." *The Accounting Review*, 1999, 2) Lev, Baruch and Doron Nissim, "Taxable Income, Future Earnings, and Equity Values," *The Accounting Review*, October 2004, and 3) Hanlon, Michelle, "The Persistence and Pricing of Earnings, Accruals, and Cash Flows When Firms Have Large Book-Tax Differences," *The Accounting Review*, January 2005.

Explain and interpret the reporting for pension plans. (p. 475) LO4

- Pension and other postretirement obligations represent one of the largest obligations for most companies.
- The projected benefit obligation is the present value of the estimated future benefits that a company expects to pay retired employees.
- The net liability that a company reports on the balance sheet is the projected benefit obligation offset by the plan assets.

Analyze and interpret pension footnote disclosures. (p. 478) LO5

- Pension footnotes provide detailed information about changes in pension obligations, changes in plan assets, and the determinants of pension expense.
- Pension footnotes provide information allowing us to interpret pension expenses and cash flows.

Describe and interpret accounting for income taxes. (p. 484) LO6

- While income tax expense is reported below income from operations, it is an operating expense. The initial item in an indirect cash flow statement is net income, which reflects the deduction of the tax expense.
- Income tax expense is determined as the sum of the tax computed as due to the government and the net change in deferred taxes.
- Deferred taxes occur because of differences between U.S. GAAP reporting and the tax due based on the rules of the tax authority. The former are based on accrual accounting while the latter are often based on a cash-based accounting system.

GUIDANCE ANSWERS . . . YOU MAKE THE CALL

You are the Division President You must take care in accepting lease terms that are not advantageous to your company merely to achieve off-balance-sheet financing. Long-term shareholder value is created by managing your operation well, including negotiating leases with acceptable terms. Lease footnote disclosures also provide sufficient information for skilled analysts to undo the operating lease treatment. This means that you can end up with effective capitalization of a lease with lease terms that are not in the best interests of your company and with few benefits from off-balance-sheet financing. There is also the potential for lost credibility with stakeholders.

You are a Consultant to the FASB This issue is one of the questions confronting the FASB. Normally accountants do not favor offsetting liabilities against the related assets as is currently the reporting practice required under GAAP. However, because the pension fund is a separate legal entity, there is a problem with reporting the pension plan assets among the firm's assets. A company does not have unilateral control over a pension trust. It can put assets into the trust but can not easily get them out of the trust. For this reason, the pension assets do not meet the criteria we normally require for recognition. While we do not know how the FASB will resolve this matter, we suspect the reporting of the net asset or liability will continue to be required.

KEY RATIOS

$$\text{Fixed commitments ratio} = \frac{\text{Operating cash flow before fixed commitments}}{\text{Fixed commitments}}$$

$$\text{Effective tax rate} = \frac{\text{Provision for income taxes (expense)}}{\text{Income before income taxes}}$$

KEY TERMS

Accumulated post-employment benefit obligation (APBO) (p. 482)
Actuarial losses and gains (p. 476)
Capital lease method (p. 464)
Deferred tax asset (p. 487)
Deferred tax liability (p. 485)
Defined benefit plan (p. 475)
Defined contribution plan (p. 475)
Effective tax rate (p. 491)
Fixed commitments ratio (p. 473)
Funded status (p. 475)
Interest cost (p. 476)
Lessee (p. 463)
Lessor (p. 463)

Assignments with the MBC logo in the margin are available in myBusinessCourse. See the Preface of the book for details.

MULTIPLE CHOICE

Multiple Choice Answers
1. a 2. d 3. d 4. b 5. d 6. c

1. U.S. GAAP requires that certain leases be accounted for as *capital leases*. The reason for this treatment is that this type of lease
a. conveys the benefits and risks of ownership of the asset.
b. is an example of form over substance.
c. provides the use of the leased asset to the lessee for a limited period of time.
d. is an example of off-balance-sheet financing.

2. For a lease that is accounted for as an operating lease by the lessee, the monthly rental payments should be
a. allocated between interest expense and depreciation expense.
b. allocated between a reduction in the liability for leased assets and interest expense.
c. recorded as a reduction in the liability for leased assets.
d. recorded as rent expense.

3. The balance sheet liability for a capital lease would be reduced each period by the
a. lease payment.
b. lease payment plus the amortization of the related asset.
c. lease payment less the amortization of the related asset.
d. lease payment less the periodic interest expense.

4. Which of the following statements characterizes defined benefit pension plans?
a. The employer's obligation is satisfied by making the necessary periodic contribution.
b. Retirement benefits are based on the plan's benefit formula.
c. Retirement benefits depend on how well pension fund assets have been managed.
d. Contributions are made in equal amounts by employer and employees.

5. When the value of pension plan assets is greater than the projected benefit obligation,
a. the difference is added to pension expense.
b. the difference is reported as deferred pension cost.
c. the difference is reported as a contra equity adjustment.
d. the pension plan is overfunded.

6. Which of the following is *not* a component of net pension expense?
a. Interest cost
b. Expected return on plan assets
c. Benefits paid to retirees
d. Amortization of actuarial gains or losses

QUESTIONS

Q10-1. What are the financial reporting differences between an operating lease and a capital lease? Explain.

Q10-2. Are footnote disclosures sufficient to overcome nonrecognition on the balance sheet of assets and related liabilities for operating leases? Explain.

Q10-3. Is the expense of a lease over its entire life the same whether or not it is capitalized? Explain.

Q10-4. What are the economic and accounting differences between a defined contribution plan and a defined benefit plan?

Q10-5. Under what circumstances will a company report a net pension asset? A net pension liability?

Q10-6. What are the components of pension expense that is reported in the income statement?

Q10-7. What effect does the use of expected returns on pension investments and the deferral of unexpected gains and losses on those investments have on income?

Q10-8. How is the initial valuation determined for the asset and the liability with a capital lease?

Q10-9. Over what time period should the cost of providing retirement benefits to employees be expensed?

Q10-10. What is the conceptual reason why income tax expense on the income statement is not equal to cash taxes paid?

Q10-11. Under what circumstances would a tax payment be made that also requires the recording of a deferred tax asset or liability?

MINI EXERCISES

M10-12. Accounting for Leases LO2

On January 3, 2017, Hanna Corporation signed a lease on a machine for its manufacturing operation. The lease requires Hanna to make six annual lease payments of $12,000 with the first payment due December 31, 2017. Hanna could have financed the machine by borrowing the purchase price at an interest rate of 7%.

a. Prepare the journal entries that Hanna Corporation would make on January 3 and December 31, 2017, to record this lease assuming
   i. the lease is reported as an operating lease.
   ii. the lease is reported as a capital lease.

b. Assuming that the lease is treated as a capital lease, post the journal entries of part *a* to the appropriate T-accounts.

c. Show how the entries posted in part *b* would affect the financial statements using the financial statement effects template.

M10-13. Accounting for Leases LO2

On July 1, 2017, Shroff Company leased a warehouse building under a 10-year lease agreement. The lease requires quarterly lease payments of $4,500. The first lease payment is due on September 30, 2017. The lease was reported as a capital lease using an 8% annual interest rate.

a. Prepare the journal entry to record the initial signing of the lease on July 1, 2017.

b. Prepare the journal entries that would be necessary on September 30 and December 31, 2017.

c. Post the entries from parts *a* and *b* in their appropriate T-accounts.

d. Prepare a financial statement effects template to show the effects of the entries from parts *a* and *b* on the balance sheet and income statement.

e. Redo parts *a* and *b* assuming that the lease is reported as an operating lease. Is the expense recognized in 2017 under the operating lease method higher or lower than under the capital lease method? Explain.

M10-14. Accounting for Operating and Capital Leases LO2, 3

On January 1, 2017, Weber, Inc., entered into two lease contracts. The first lease contract was a six-year lease for computer equipment with $15,000 annual lease payments due at the end of each year. Weber took possession of the equipment on January 1, 2017. The second lease contract was a six-month lease, beginning January 1, 2017, for warehouse storage space with $1,000 monthly lease payments due the first of each month. Weber made the first month's payment on January 1, 2017. The present value of the lease payments under the first contract is $74,520. The present value of the lease payments under the second contract is $5,853.

REQUIRED

a. Assume that the first lease contract is a capital lease. Prepare the appropriate journal entry for this lease on January 1, 2017.

b. Assume the second lease contract is an operating lease. Prepare the proper journal entry for this lease on January 1, 2017.

M10-15. Analyzing and Interpreting Leasing Footnote Disclosures LO2

YUM! Brands
NYSE :: YUM

YUM! Brands, Inc., reports the following information related to non-cancelable leases in Note 11 of its 2014 10-K.

At December 27, 2014, we operated nearly 8,700 restaurants, leasing the underlying land and/or building in approximately 7,775 of those restaurants with the vast majority of our commitments expiring within 20 years from the inception of the lease. In addition, the Company leases or subleases approximately 875 units to franchises principally in the United States, UK, China, and Mexico. We also lease office space for headquarters and support functions, as well as certain office and restaurant equipment. We do not consider any of these individual leases material to our operations. Most leases require us to pay related executory costs, which include property taxes, maintenance, and insurance.

a. Yum has both capital and operating leases. In general, what effects does each of these lease types have on Yum's balance sheet and its income statement?

b. What types of adjustments might you consider to Yum's balance sheet for analysis purposes?

LO3

YUM! Brands
NYSE :: YUM

M10-16. Analyzing and Capitalizing Operating Lease Payments Disclosed in Footnotes

YUM! Brands, Inc. discloses the following in Note 11 to its 2014 10-K report relating to its lease commitments:

(In millions)	Capital Leases	Operating Leases
2015	$ 20	$ 709
2016	21	661
2017	20	609
2018	20	555
2019	20	501
Thereafter	181	2,444
Total minimum lease payments	$282	$5,479

At December 27, 2014, the present value of minimum payments under capital leases was $175 million.

Operating leases are not reflected on-balance-sheet. In our analysis of a company, we often desire to capitalize these operating leases, that is, add the present value of these lease payments to both the reported assets and liabilities.

a. What is the implied interest rate in the capital leases?

b. Compute the present value of Yum!'s operating lease payments assuming a discount rate equal to the rate computed in part *a*.

c. What effect does capitalization of Yum!'s operating leases have on its total liabilities (it reported total liabilities of $6,732 million for 2014)?

LO4

M10-17. Accounting for Pension Benefits

Bartov Corporation has a defined contribution pension plan for its employees. Each year, Bartov contributes to the plan an amount equal to 4% of the employee payroll for the year. Bartov's 2016 payroll was $400,000. Bartov also provides a life insurance benefit that pays a $50,000 death benefit to the beneficiaries of retired employees. At the end of 2016, Bartov estimates that its liability under the life insurance program is $625,000. Bartov has assets with a fair value of $175,000 in a trust fund that are available to meet the death benefit payments.

REQUIRED

a. Prepare the journal entry at December 31, 2016, to record Bartov's 2016 defined contribution to a pension trustee who will manage the pension funds for the firm's employees.

b. What amount of liability for death benefit payments must Bartov report in its December 31, 2016, balance sheet? Explain.

LO4, 5

Exxon Mobil Corporation
NYSE :: XOM

M10-18. Analyzing and Interpreting Pension Disclosures—Expenses and Returns

Exxon Mobil Corporation discloses the following information in footnote 17 in its 10-K report:

(In millions)	2014
Service cost	$1,267
Interest cost	1,945
Expected return on plan assets	(1,992)
Amortization of actuarial loss (gain)	1,037
Net pension enhancement and curtailment/settlement cost	276
Amortization of prior service cost	128
Net periodic pension benefit cost	$2,661

a. How much pension expense does Exxon Mobil Corporation report in its 2014 income statement?
b. What effect does its "expected return on plan assets" have on its reported pension expense? Explain.
c. Explain use of the word *expected* as it relates to results of pension plan investments.

M10-19. Analyzing and Interpreting Pension Disclosures—Expenses and Returns LO4, 5

YUM! Brands
NYSE :: YUM

YUM! Brands, Inc., discloses the following pension footnote in its 10-K report:

	Pension Benefits	
(In millions)	**2014**	**2013**
Service cost	$17	$21
Interest cost	54	54
Amortization of prior service cost	1	2
Expected return on plan assets	(56)	(59)
Amortization of net loss	17	48
Net periodic benefit cost	$33	$66

a. How much pension expense does Yum report in its 2014 income statement?
b. What effect does its "expected return on plan assets" have on its reported pension expense? Explain.
c. Explain use of the word *expected* as it relates to results of pension plan investments.

M10-20. Analyzing and Interpreting Retirement Benefit Footnote LO4, 5

Abercrombie & Fitch
NYSE :: ANF

Abercrombie & Fitch Co. discloses the following footnote relating to its retirement plans in its 2014 10-K report:

15. RETIREMENT BENEFITS The Company maintains the Abercombie & Fitch Co. Savings & Retirement Plan, a qualified plan. All U.S. associates are eligible to participate in this plan if they are at least 21 years of age and have completed a year of employment with 1,000 or more hours of service. In addition, the Company maintains the Abercrombie & Fitch Nonqualified Savings and Supplemental Retirement Plan. . . Participation in these plans is based on service and compensation. The Company's contributions are based on a percentage of associates' eligible annual compensation. The cost of the Company's contributions to these plans was $13.8 million, $18.3 million, and $21.1 million in fiscal 2014, 2013, and 2012, respectively.

a. Does Abercrombie have a defined contribution or defined benefit pension plan? Explain.
b. How does Abercrombie account for its contributions to its retirement plan?
c. How is Abercrombie's obligation to its retirement plan reported on its balance sheet?

M10-21. Analyzing and Interpreting Footnote on Contract Manufacturers LO1

Nike
NYSE :: NKE

Nike, Inc. reports the following information relating to its manufacturing activities in the footnotes to its 2014 10-K report:

MANUFACTURING Virtually all of our footwear is manufactured outside of the United States by independent contract manufacturers who often operate multiple factories. In fiscal 2014, contract factories in Vietnam, China, and Indonesia manufactured approximately 43%, 28%, and 25% of total NIKE Brand footwear, respectively. We also have manufacturing agreements with independent factories in Argentina, Brazil, India, and Mexico to manufacture footwear for sale primarily within those countries. In fiscal 2014, five footwear contract manufacturers each accounted for greater than 10% of fiscal 2014 footwear production, and in aggregate accounted for approximately 67% of NIKE Brand footwear production in fiscal 2014.

a. What effect does the use of contract manufacturers have on Nike's balance sheet?
b. Nike executes purchase contracts with its contract manufacturers to purchase their output. How are executory contracts reported under GAAP? Does your answer suggest a possible motivation for the use of contract manufacturing?

M10-22. Computing and Reporting Deferred Income Taxes LO6

Fisk, Inc., purchased $600,000 of construction equipment on January 1, 2014. The equipment is being depreciated on a straight-line basis over six years with no expected salvage value. MACRS depreciation is being used on the firm's tax returns. At December 31, 2016, the equipment's book value is $300,000 and its tax basis is $173,000 (this is Fisk's only temporary difference). Over the next three years, straight-line depreciation will exceed MACRS depreciation by $31,000 in 2017, $31,000 in 2018, and $65,000 in 2019. Assume that the income tax rate in effect for all years is 40%.

a. What amount of deferred tax liability should appear in Fisk's December 31, 2016, balance sheet?
b. What amount of deferred tax liability should appear in Fisk's December 31, 2017, balance sheet?
c. What amount of deferred tax liability should appear in Fisk's December 31, 2018, balance sheet?
d. Where should the deferred tax liability accounts be classified in Fisk's 2016, 2017, and 2018 year-end balance sheets?

EXERCISES

LO2, 3

Homework MBC

Target NYSE :: TGT

E10-23. Analyzing and Interpreting Leasing Footnote
The 2014 10-K report of **Target Corporation** provides the following footnote ($ thousands).

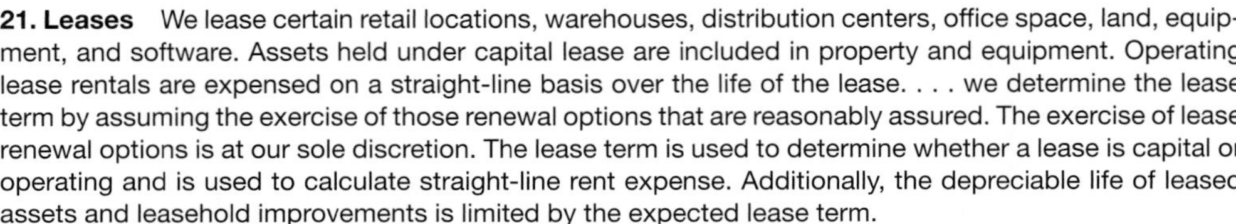

21. Leases We lease certain retail locations, warehouses, distribution centers, office space, land, equipment, and software. Assets held under capital lease are included in property and equipment. Operating lease rentals are expensed on a straight-line basis over the life of the lease. . . . we determine the lease term by assuming the exercise of those renewal options that are reasonably assured. The exercise of lease renewal options is at our sole discretion. The lease term is used to determine whether a lease is capital or operating and is used to calculate straight-line rent expense. Additionally, the depreciable life of leased assets and leasehold improvements is limited by the expected lease term.

Rent expense is included in SG&A. Some of our lease agreements include rental payments based on a percentage of retail sales over contractual levels . . . Certain leases require us to pay real estate taxes, insurance, maintenance, and other operating expenses associated with the leased premises. These expenses are classified in SG&A consistent with similar costs for owned locations.

Most long-term leases include one or more options to renew, with renewal terms that can extend the lease term from one to more than fifty years. Certain leases also include options to purchase the leased property.

Future Minimum Lease Payments (millions)	Operating Leases	Capital Leases
2015	$ 186	$ 123
2016	178	94
2017	170	58
2018	165	55
2019	154	54
After 2019	2,974	1,019
Total future minimum lease payments	$3,827	1,403
Less: Interest		614
Present value of future minimum capital lease payments		$ 789

a. Compute the present value of Target's operating leases. Assume a 5% discount rate.
b. If the operating leases are classified as capital leases, indicate how the amount in part *a* would be reported in Target's balance sheet using the financial statement effects template.
c. Would recognition of the operating leases affect the current ratio? Explain.
d. Prepare journal entries to record the capitalization of Target's operating leases at the end of fiscal 2014. Enter them in the appropriate T-accounts.
e. Do these leases represent a substantial fixed commitment to Target given Target's operating cash flow of $4,439 million in 2014?

LO4, 5

Target NYSE :: TGT

E10-24. Analyzing and Interpreting Pension Plan Benefit Footnote
Target Corporation provides the following footnote relating to its retirement plans in its 2014 10-K report:

Defined Contribution Plans Team members who meet eligibility requirements can participate in a defined contribution 401(k) plan by investing up to 80 percent of their compensation, as limited by statute or regulation. Generally, we match 100 percent of each team member's contribution up to 5 percent of total compensation. Company match contributions are made to funds designated by the participant. Benefits expense related to these matching contributions was $220 million, $229 million, and $218 million in 2014, 2013, and 2012, respectively.

a. Does Target have a defined contribution or defined benefit pension plan? Explain.
b. How would Target account for its contributions to its retirement plan?
c. How is Target's obligation to its retirement plan reported on its balance sheet?
d. Do you see any problems for employees in Target's plan?

E10-25. Analyzing and Interpreting Leasing Footnote
The Home Depot, Inc. included the following footnote in its fiscal 2014 10-K report:

LO2, 3

The Home Depot
NYSE :: HD

The approximate future minimum lease payments under capital and all other leases at February 1, 2015 were as follows (amounts in millions):

Fiscal year	Capital Leases	Operating Leases
2015	$ 113	$ 893
2016	111	817
2017	108	737
2018	101	638
2019	97	561
Thereafter	880	4,059
Total minimum lease payments	1,410	$7,705
Less imputed interest	726	
Present value of minimum lease payments	684	
Amount included in current liabilities	36	
Long-term lease obligations excluding current installments	$ 648	

The assets under capital leases recorded in Property and Equipment, net of amortization, totaled $557 million and $374 million at February 1, 2015 and February 2, 2014, respectively.

The Home Depot reported stockholders' equity of $9,322 million and total assets of $39,946 million in its fiscal 2014 balance sheet.

a. What was the total amount of capital lease obligations reported in The Home Depot's fiscal 2014 balance sheet? Why is this amount not equal to the $557 million that it reported for assets under capital leases on that date?
b. Using a 4% discount rate, compute the present value of Home Depot's scheduled operating lease payments.
c. Estimate the effect that capitalizing operating leases would have on The Home Depot's debt-to-equity ratio.

E10-26. Analyzing and Interpreting Footnote on Both Operating and Capital Leases
Verizon Communications Inc. provides the following footnote relating to its leasing activities in its 10-K report.

LO2, 3

Verizon
NYSE :: VZ

The aggregate minimum rental commitments under noncancelable leases for the periods shown at December 31, 2014, are:

Years (dollars in millions)	Capital Leases	Operating Leases
2015	$181	$ 2,499
2016	137	2,245
2017	113	1,960
2018	68	1,660
2019	39	1,369
Thereafter	60	4,670
Total minimum rental commitments	598	$14,403
Less interest and executory costs	82	
Present value of minimum lease payments	516	
Less current installments	158	
Long-term obligation at December 31, 2014	$358	

a. Assuming that this is the only available information relating to its leasing activities, what amount does Verizon report on its balance sheet for its lease obligations? Does this amount represent its total obligation to lessors? How do you know?

b. What effect has its lease classification as capital or operating had on Verizon's balance sheet? Over the life of its leases, what effect does this lease classification have on its net income?

c. Based on the information provided by Verizon in this footnote, what amount of interest expense will it report on capital leases in 2015? (Hint: prepare a journal entry to record the 2015 lease payment.)

d. Estimate the present value of Verizon's operating leases using a 5% discount rate. What would be the effect on Verizon's balance sheet if these leases were reported as capital leases?

LO2, 3

Walgreen Co.
NASDAQ :: WAG

E10-27. Analyzing, Interpreting, and Capitalizing Operating Leases

Walgreen Co. provided the following information in footnote 3 of its 2014 10-K report ($ millions):

Future minimum rental payments under operating leases with remaining noncancelable terms in excess of one year are as follows:

(in millions)	Operating
2015	$ 2,569
2016	2,533
2017	2,493
2018	2,407
2019	2,295
Thereafter	22,168
Total	$34,465

a. Assuming a 5% discount rate, what adjustments to Walgreen's balance sheet would be necessary to convert these operating leases into capital leases?

b. If the leases were reported as capital leases instead of operating leases, what would be the effect on Walgreen's 2015 income statement (assuming no other changes)?

LO2, 3

Nike
NYSE :: NKE

E10-28. Analyzing, Interpreting, and Capitalizing Operating Leases

Nike, Inc. reports the following data concerning leases in its 2014 10-K.

Note 14—Commitments and Contingencies

The Company leases space for certain of its offices, warehouses and retail stores under leases expiring from 1 to 20 years after May 31, 2014. . . . Amounts of minimum future annual rental commitments under noncancelable operating leases in each of the five years ending May 31, 2015 through 2019 are $427 million, $399 million, $366 million, $311 million, $251 million, respectively, and $1,050 million in later years.

a. What adjustment(s) might you consider to Nike's balance sheet given this information and assuming that Nike's discount rate is 4%? Explain.

b. Show how the amount computed in part *a* would be reported in the balance sheet using the financial statement effects template.

c. Prepare journal entries to record the capitalization of these operating leases at the end of fiscal 2014. What journal entries would be required to record lease payments and lease related expenses in 2015 if these leases were accounted for as capital leases? Assume straight-line depreciation and a ten-year life.

d. Post the journal entries from part *c* to the appropriate T-accounts.

LO4, 5

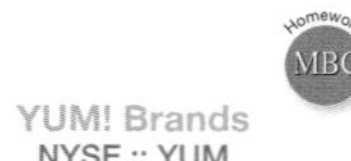

YUM! Brands
NYSE :: YUM

E10-29. Analyzing and Interpreting Pension Footnote—Funded and Reported Amounts

YUM! Brands, Inc., reports the following pension footnote in Note 13 of its 10-K report.

December 27 (in millions)	Pension Benefits 2014
Change in benefit obligation	
Projected benefit obligation at beginning of year	$1,025
Service cost	17
Interest cost	54
Curtailments	(2)
Plan amendments	1
Special termination benefits	3
Benefits paid	(65)
Settlements	(17)
Actuarial (gain) loss	290
Administrative expenses	(5)
Projected benefit obligation at end of year	$1,301
Change in plan assets	
Fair value of plan assets at beginning of year	$ 933
Actual return on plan assets	124
Employer contributions	21
Benefits paid	(65)
Settlements	(17)
Administrative expenses	(5)
Fair value of plan assets at end of year	$ 991
Funded status—end of year	$ (310)

a. Describe what is meant by *service cost* and *interest cost*.
b. What is the source of funds to make payments to retirees?
c. Show the computation of the 2014 funded status for Yum.
d. What net pension amount is reported on its 2014 balance sheet?

E10-30. Analyzing and Interpreting Pension Footnote—Funded and Reported Amounts LO4, 5

Verizon Communications Inc. reports the following pension data in Note 12 to its 2014 10-K report.

Verizon
NYSE :: VZ

At December 31 ($ millions)	Pension 2014
Change in Benefit Obligations	
Beginning of year	$23,032
Service cost	327
Interest cost	1,035
Plan amendments	(89)
Actuarial loss (gain), net	2,977
Benefits paid and settlements	(1,973)
Curtailment and termination benefits	11
End of year	25,320
Change in Plan Assets	
Beginning of year	17,111
Actual return on plan assets	1,778
Company contributions	1,632
Benefits paid and settlements	(1,973)
End of year	18,548
Funded Status	
End of year	$ (6,772)

a. Describe what is meant by *service cost* and *interest cost*.
b. What is the source of funds to make payments to retirees?
c. Show the computation of Verizon's 2014 funded status.
d. What net pension amount is reported on its 2014 balance sheet?

LO6 

E10-31. Computing and Reporting Deferred Income Taxes

Early in January 2016, Oler, Inc., purchased equipment costing $16,000. The equipment had a 2-year useful life and was depreciated in the amount of $8,000 in 2016 and 2017. Oler deducted the entire $16,000 on its tax return in 2016. This difference was the only one between its tax return and its financial statements. Oler's income before depreciation expense and income taxes was $236,000 in 2016 and $245,000 in 2017. The tax rate in each year was 40%.

REQUIRED

a. What amount of deferred tax liability should Oler report in 2016 and 2017?
b. Prepare the journal entries to record income taxes for 2016 and 2017.
c. Repeat requirement *b* if the tax rate in 2016 was only 35%.

LO6 

E10-32. Calculating and Reporting Deferred Income Taxes

Bens' Corporation paid $12,000 on December 31, 2016, for equipment with a three-year useful life. The equipment will be depreciated in the amount of $4,000 each year. Bens' took the entire $12,000 as an expense in its tax return in 2016. Assume this is the only timing difference between the firm's books and its tax return. Bens' tax rate is 40%.

REQUIRED

a. What amount of deferred tax liability should appear in Bens' 12/31/2016 balance sheet?
b. Where in the balance sheet should the deferred tax liability appear?
c. What amount of deferred tax liability should appear in Bens' 12/31/2017 balance sheet?

LO6 

Nike
NYSE :: NKE

E10-33. Recording Income Tax Expense

Nike, Inc., reports the following tax information in Note 9 to its 2014 financial report.

Income before income taxes is as follows:

Year Ended May 31 (In millions)	2014	2013	2012
Income before income taxes:			
United States	$3,066	$1,231	$ 799
Foreign	478	2,025	2,212
	$3,544	$3,256	$3,011

The provision for income taxes is as follows:

Year Ended May 31 (In millions)	2014	2013	2012
Current:			
United States			
Federal	$371	$432	$286
State	93	69	51
Foreign	398	398	488
	862	899	825
Deferred:			
United States			
Federal	8	0	(47)
State	(3)	(4)	5
Foreign	(16)	(90)	(29)
	(11)	(94)	(71)
	$851	$805	$754

a. Record Nike's provision for income taxes for 2014 using the financial statement effects template.
b. Record Nike's provision for income taxes for 2014 using journal entries.
c. Explain how the provision for income taxes affects Nike's financial statements.
d. Calculate and compare Nike's effective tax rate for 2014, 2013 and 2012.

LO6 

Boeing
NYSE :: BA

E10-34. Recording Income Tax Expense

The Boeing Company reports the following tax information in Note 4 to its 2014 financial report.

Year ended December 31,	2014	2013	2012
Current tax expense			
U.S. federal.	$ 676	$ (82)	$ 657
Non-U.S..	91	76	52
U.S. state	69	11	19
	836	5	728
Deferred tax expense			
U.S. federal.	828	1,531	1,209
Non-U.S..	34	41	(13)
U.S. state	(7)	69	83
	855	1,641	1,279
Total income tax expense.	$1,691	$1,646	$2,007

a. Record Boeing's provision for income taxes for 2014 using the financial statement effects template.

b. Record Boeing's provision for income taxes for 2014 using journal entries.

c. Explain how the provision for income affects Boeing's financial statements.

PROBLEMS

P10-35. Analyzing, Interpreting, and Capitalizing Operating Leases

LO2, 3

Staples, Inc.
NASDAQ :: SPLS

Staples, Inc., reports the following footnote relating to its capital and operating leases in its fiscal 2014 10-K report ($ thousands).

Future minimum lease commitments due for retail distribution, fulfillment, and support facilities (including restructured facilities and lease commitments for 11 retail stores not yet opened at January 31, 2015) and equipment leases under noncancellable operating leases are as follows (in thousands):

Fiscal Year	Total
2015	$ 703,905
2016	599,304
2017	479,441
2018	348,146
2019	254,085
Thereafter	545,640
	$2,930,521

Rent expense was approximately $767.5 million, $801.4 million, and $838.9 million for 2014, 2013, and 2012, respectively.

a. What dollar adjustment(s) might you consider to Staples' balance sheet given this information and assuming that Staples intermediate-term borrowing rate is 5%? Explain. (Staples reported total liabilities of $5 billion for 2014.) Round the average life to the nearest year.

b. Show how the amount computed in part *a* would be reported in the balance sheet using the financial statement effects template.

c. Prepare journal entries to record the capitalization of these operating leases at the end of fiscal 2014. What journal entries would be required to record lease payments and lease related expenses in 2015 if these leases were accounted for as capital leases? Assume leased assets are depreciated over a 9-year life using the straight-line method.

d. Post the journal entries from part *c* to the appropriate T-accounts.

P10-36. Capitalizing Operating Leases

LO2, 3

CVS Health Corporation
NYSE :: CVS

The 2014 10-K report of **CVS Health Corporation** included the following footnote.

Leases

The Company leases most of its retail and mail order locations, ten of its distribution centers and certain corporate offices under noncancelable operating leases, typically with initial terms of 15 to 25 years and with options that permit renewals for additional periods. The Company also leases certain equipment and other assets under noncancelable operating leases, typically with initial terms of 3 to 10 years. Minimum rent is expensed on a straight-line basis over the term of the lease. In addition to minimum rental payments, certain leases require additional payments based on sales volume, as well as reimbursement for real estate taxes, common area maintenance and insurance, which are expensed when incurred.

The following table is a summary of the Company's net rental expense for operating leases for the years ended December 31:

(in millions)	2014	2013	2012
Minimum rentals	$2,320	$2,210	$2,165

The following table is a summary of the future minimum lease payments under capital and operating leases as of December 31, 2014:

(in millions)	Capital Leases	Operating Leases
2015	$ 47	$ 2,279
2016	47	2,220
2017	47	2,121
2018	48	2,007
2019	48	1,861
Thereafter	573	16,794
Total future lease payments	810	$27,282
Less: imputed interest	(419)	
Present value of capital lease obligations	$391	

The Company finances a portion of its store development program through sale-leaseback transactions. The properties are generally sold at net book value, which generally approximates fair value, and the resulting leases generally qualify and are accounted for as operating leases. The operating leases that resulted from these transactions are included in the above table. The Company does not have any retained or contingent interests in the stores and does not provide any guarantees, other than a guarantee of lease payments, in connection with the sale-leaseback transactions. Proceeds from sale-leaseback transactions totaled $515 million in 2014, $600 million in 2013 and $529 million in 2012.

REQUIRED

a. Prepare the journal entry to record CVS's rent expense under operating leases on December 31, 2014. Assume that this expense was paid in cash and none of this expense was prepaid or accrued in other years.

b. Assume that CVS reclassified its operating leases as capital leases and that the appropriate discount rate is 4%. What amount would CVS report as a lease liability in its December 31, 2014 balance sheet?

c. If these leases are treated as capital leases instead of operating leases, what would be the effect on CVS's 2014 income statement? Its 2015 income statement? The assets are depreciated on a straight-line basis over 10 years.

d. Show the results of capitalization using the financial statement effects template.

e. If these leases had been treated as capital leases instead of operating leases, what would be the effect on CVS's 2014 statement of cash flows?

f. Briefly, describe the effects of CVS's sale-leaseback transaction on the company's balance sheet.

LO2, 3 **P10-37. Analyzing, Interpreting, and Capitalizing Leasing Disclosures**

Best Buy
NYSE :: BBY

The **Best Buy Co., Inc.**, 10-K report has the following footnote (8) related to its leasing activities.

The future minimum lease payments under our capital, financing, and operating leases by fiscal year (not including contingent rentals) at January 31, 2015, were as follows ($ millions):

Fiscal Year	Capital Leases	Financing Leases	Operating Leases
2016	$22	$24	$ 873
2017	11	18	771
2018	7	14	641
2019	4	9	499
2020	2	6	365
Thereafter	15	9	727
Subtotal	61	80	$3,876
Less: imputed interest	(9)	(11)	
Present value	$52	$69	

REQUIRED

a. What does Best Buy report on its balance sheet in regard to its leases?

b. What is the general effect that capitalization of Best Buy's operating leases would have on its balance sheet? Over the life of the lease, what effect does this classification have on its net income?

c. Using a 7% discount rate, estimate the assets and liabilities that it fails to report as a result of its off-balance-sheet lease financing.

d. Using the financial statement effects template, show how capitalizing these operating leases would affect the balance sheet and income statement. Assume straight-line depreciation over a 10-year life.

e. Prepare journal entries to record the capitalization of these operating leases at January 31, 2015. What journal entries would be required to record the operating lease and lease related expenses in the year ended January, 2016 if these leases were accounted for as capital leases?

f. Post the journal entries from part *e* to the appropriate T-accounts.

g. What impact would capitalization of the company's operating leases have on analyzing Best Buy? What ratios might be affected?

P10-38. Analyzing and Interpreting Pension Disclosures LO4, 5

Hoopes Corporation's December 31, 2015, 10-K report has the following disclosures related to its retirement plans.

The following table provides a reconciliation of the changes in the pension and postretirement healthcare plans' benefit obligations and fair value of assets over the two-year period ended December 31, 2015, and a statement of the funded status as of December 31, 2015 and 2014 (in millions):

	Pension Plans	
(in millions)	**2015**	**2014**
Changes in Projected Benefit Obligation ("PBO")		
PBO at beginning of year	$14,484	$11,050
Service cost	521	417
Interest cost	900	823
Actuarial (gain) loss	1,875	2,607
Benefits paid	(468)	(391)
Other	60	(22)
PBO at end of year	$17,372	$14,484
Change in Plan Assets		
Fair value of plan assets at beginning of year	$13,295	$10,812
Actual return on plan assets	2,425	1,994
Company contributions	557	900
Benefits paid	(468)	(391)
Other	32	(20)
Fair value of plan assets at end of year	$15,841	$13,295

Net periodic benefit cost for the three years ended December 31 were as follows (in millions):

	Pension Plans		
(in millions)	**2015**	**2014**	**2013**
Service cost	$ 521	$417	$ 499
Interest cost	900	823	798
Expected return on plan assets	(1,062)	(955)	(1,059)
Recognized actuarial (gains) losses and other	184	23	(61)
Net periodic benefit cost	$ 543	$308	$ 177

Weighted-average actuarial assumptions for our primary U.S. pension plans, which represent substantially all of our PBO, are as follows:

	Pension Plans		
(in millions)	**2015**	**2014**	**2013**
Discount rate used to determine benefit obligation	5.76%	6.37%	7.68%
Rate of increase in future compensation levels used to determine benefit obligation	4.58	4.63	4.42
Expected long-term rate of return on assets	8.00	8.00	8.50

REQUIRED

a. How much pension expense (revenue) does Hoopes report in its 2015 income statement?

b. Hoopes reports a $1,062 million expected return on plan assets as an offset to 2015 pension expense. Approximately, how is this amount computed? What is the actual gain or loss realized on its 2015 plan assets? What is the purpose of using this estimated amount instead of the actual gain or loss?

c. What factors affected its 2015 pension liability? What factors affected its 2015 plan assets?

d. What does the term *funded status* mean? What is the funded status of the 2015 Hoopes retirement plans? What amount of asset or liability does Hoopes report on its 2015 balance sheet relating to its retirement plans?

e. Hoopes decreased its discount rate from 6.37% to 5.76% in 2015. What effect(s) does this have on its balance sheet and its income statement?

f. Hoopes changed its estimate of expected annual wage increases used to determine its defined benefit obligation in 2015. What effect(s) does this change have on its financial statements? In general, how does such a change affect income?

LO4, 5 **P10-39. Analyzing and Interpreting Pension Footnote—Funded and Reported Amounts**

Johnson and Johnson
NYSE :: JNJ

Johnson and Johnson reports the following pension footnote as part of its 2014 10-K report.

(in millions)	**Pension Benefits 2014**
Change in Benefit Obligation	
Projected benefit obligation—beginning of year	$21,488
Service cost	882
Interest cost	1,018
Plan participant contributions	59
Amendments	(60)
Actuarial (gains) losses	5,395
Divestitures and acquisitions	(121)
Curtailments, settlements and restructuring	(53)
Benefits paid from plan	(813)
Effect of exchange rates	(906)
Projected benefit obligation—end of year	$26,889

continued

continued from previous page

(in millions)	2014
Change in Plan Assets	
Plan assets at fair value—beginning of year	$20,901
Actual return on plan assets	2,078
Company contributions	1,176
Plan participant contributions	59
Settlements	(40)
Divestitures and acquisitions	(109)
Benefits paid from plan assets	(813)
Effect of exchange rates	(677)
Plan assets at fair value—end of year	$22,575
Funded status—end of year	$ (4,314)

a. Describe what is meant by *service cost* and *interest cost*.
b. What is the actual return on pension investments in 2014?
c. Provide an example under which an "actuarial loss," such as the $5,395 million loss that Johnson and Johnson reports in 2014, might arise.
d. What is the source of funds to make payments to retirees?
e. How much cash did Johnson and Johnson contribute to its pension plans in 2014?
f. How much cash did the company pay to retirees in 2014?
g. Show the computation of its 2014 funded status.
h. What net pension amount is reported on its 2014 balance sheet?

P10-40. Interpreting the Income Tax Expense Footnote

LO6
General Electric
NYSE :: GE

General Electric Company reports the following tax information in its 2014 financial report.

($ millions)	2014	2013	2012
Earnings before provision for income taxes	$17,229	$16,151	$17,381
Provision for income taxes:			
Current tax expense	2,958	3,971	3,686
Deferred tax expense (benefit)	(1,186)	(3,295)	(1,152)
Total provision (benefit) for income taxes	$ 1,772	$ 676	$ 2,534

REQUIRED

a. What amount of tax expense is reported in GE's 2014 income statement? In 2013? In 2012? How much of each year's income tax expense is current tax expense and how much is deferred tax expense?
b. Compute GE's effective tax rate for each year.
c. Assume that GE's deferred tax benefit in 2014 is due to a decrease in deferred tax liabilities. Provide an example that would be consistent with this situation.
d. Assume that GE's deferred tax benefit in 2014 is due to an increase in a deferred tax asset. Explain how temporary differences would create a deferred tax asset. What would cause this asset to increase in value?

P10-41. Calculating and Reporting Income Tax Expense

LO6

Lynch Company began operations in 2016. The company reported $24,000 of depreciation expense on its income statement in 2016 and $26,000 in 2017. On its tax returns, Lynch deducted $32,000 for depreciation in 2016 and $37,000 in 2017. The 2017 tax return shows a tax obligation (liability) of $19,200 based on a 40% tax rate.

REQUIRED

a. Determine the temporary difference between the book value of depreciable assets and the tax basis of these assets at the end of 2016 and 2017.
b. Calculate the deferred tax liability for each year.
c. Calculate the income tax expense for 2017.
d. Prepare a journal entry to record income tax expense and post the entry to the appropriate T-accounts for 2017.

LO6 **P10-42. Calculating and Reporting Income Tax Expense**
Carter Inc. began operations in 2016. The company reported $130,000 of depreciation expense on its 2016 income statement and $128,000 in 2017. Carter Inc. deducted $140,000 for depreciation on its tax return in 2016 and $122,000 in 2017. The company reports a tax obligation of $45,150 for 2017 based on a tax rate of 35%.

REQUIRED

a. Determine the temporary difference between the book value of depreciable assets and the tax basis of these assets at the end of 2016 and 2017.
b. Calculate the deferred tax liability at the end of each year.
c. Calculate the income tax expense for 2017.
d. Prepare a journal entry to record income tax for 2017 and post the entry to the appropriate T-accounts.

LO6 **P10-43. Computing and Reporting Deferred Income Taxes**
Robinson Inc. paid $12,000 on December 31, 2016, for equipment with a two-year useful life. The equipment was depreciated for book purposes at $6,000 in 2017 and 2018. Robinson deducted the entire amount on its 2016 tax return. Assume this was the firm's only depreciable asset and that the firm's tax rate was 35% for 2016 and 2017 and 40% for 2018. The tax rate increase is not known until 2018. Assume, further, that Robinson's income before depreciation and taxes was $320,000 in 2016, $400,000 in 2017, and $420,000 in 2018.

REQUIRED

a. Calculate the book value of the asset on 12/31 for 2016, 2017, and 2018.
b. Calculate the tax basis of the asset on 12/31 for 2016, 2017, and 2018.
c. What deferred tax liability should be reported for 2016, 2017, and 2018?
d. Prepare journal entries to record income taxes for 2016, 2017, and 2018.

CASES AND PROJECTS

LO4, 5 **C10-44. Analyzing and Interpreting Pension Disclosures**

Dow Chemical
NYSE :: DOW

The Dow Chemical Company provides the following footnote disclosures in its 10-K report relating to its pension plans.

	Defined Benefit Pension Plans	
(in millions)	**2014**	**2013**
Service cost	$ 411	$ 471
Interest cost	1,096	1,012
Expected return on plan assets	(1,322)	(1,248)
Amortization of prior service cost	22	25
Amortization of unrecognized loss (gain)	500	788
Curtailment/settlement/other	(2)	5
Net periodic cost	$ 705	$ 1,053
Change in projected benefit obligation		
Benefit obligation at beginning of year	$25,027	$26,840
Service cost	411	471
Interest cost	1,096	1,012
Plan participants' contributions	21	17
Amendments	(500)	0
Actuarial changes in assumptions and experience	4,096	(2,029)
Acquisition/divestiture/other activity	(1)	0
Benefits paid	(1,316)	(1,322)
Currency impact	(779)	123
Termination benefits/curtailment cost	(76)	(85)
Benefit obligation at end of year	$27,979	$25,027

continued

continued from previous page

	2014	2013
Fair value of plan assets at beginning of year	$18,827	$17,725
Actual return on plan assets	1,961	1,548
Currency impact	(593)	85
Employer contributions	815	865
Plan participants' contributions	21	17
Acquisition/divestiture/other activity	(86)	(91)
Benefits paid	(1,316)	(1,322)
Fair value of plan assets at end of year	$19,629	$18,827

	Benefit Obligations at December 31	
Weighted Average Assumptions for All Pension Plans	**2014**	**2013**
Discount rate	3.60%	4.54%
Rate of increase in future compensation levels	4.13%	4.15%
Expected long-term rate of return on plan assets	—	—

REQUIRED

a. How much pension expense (revenue) does Dow Chemical report in its 2014 income statement?

b. Dow reports a $1,322 million expected return on plan assets as an offset to 2014 pension expense. Estimate the rate of return Dow expected to earn on its plan assets in 2014.

c. What factors affected its 2014 pension liability? What factors affected its 2014 plan assets?

d. What does the term *funded status* mean? What is the funded status of the 2014 Dow retirement plans at the end of 2014? What amount of asset or liability should Dow report on its 2014 balance sheet relating to its retirement plans?

e. Dow changed its discount rate from 4.54% to 3.60% in 2014. What effect(s) does this change have on its balance sheet and its income statement?

f. Suppose Dow increased its estimate of expected returns on plan assets in 2015. What effect(s) would this increase have on its income statement? Explain.

g. Dow provides us with its weighted-average discount rate. The company operates with manufacturing facilities in over 201 sites in 35 countries. Would you expect that the discount rate differed in the United States from the average rate outside the United States? Explain. What would you expect for future compensation levels?

C10-45. Interpreting Capital and Operating Leases

LO1, 2, 3
JetBlue Airways Corporation
NASDAQ: JBLU

JetBlue Airways Corporation reports the following leasing information in its 2014 10-K.

Excerpt from Note 2—Long-term Debt, Short-term Borrowings and Capital Lease Obligations

As of December 31, 2014, four capital leased Airbus A320 aircraft and two capital leased Airbus A321 aircraft were included in property and equipment at a cost of $253 million with accumulated amortization of $40 million. As of December 31, 2013, four capital leased Airbus A320 aircraft were included in property and equipment at a cost of $152 million with accumulated amortization of $33 million. The future minimum lease payments under these noncancelable leases are $23 million in 2015, $23 million in 2016, $23 million in 2017, $23 million in 2018, $23 million in 2019 and $98 million in the years thereafter. Included in the future minimum lease payments is $43 million representing interest, resulting in a present value of capital leases of $170 million with a current portion of $15 million and a long-term portion of $155 million.

Note 3—Operating Leases

We lease aircraft, all of our facilities at the airports we serve, office space and other equipment. These leases have varying terms and conditions, with some having early termination clauses which we determine to be the lease expiration date. The length of the lease depends upon the type of asset being leased, with the latest lease expiring in 2035. Total rental expense for all operating leases was $298 million in 2014, $295 million in 2013 and $284 million in 2012. As of December 31, 2014, 60 of the 203 aircraft in our fleet were leased under operating leases, with lease expiration dates ranging from 2016 to 2026. . . . Our aircraft lease agreements contain termination provisions which include standard maintenance and return conditions. Our policy is to record these lease return conditions when they are probable and the costs can be estimated.

Future minimum lease payments under noncancelable operating leases, including those described above, with initial or remaining terms in excess of one year at December 31, 2014, are as follows (in millions):

	Aircraft	Other	Total
2015	$150	$ 85	$ 235
2016	90	80	170
2017	75	65	140
2018	75	60	135
2019	58	57	115
Thereafter	213	487	700
Total minimum operating lease payments	$661	$834	$1,495

In the past we have entered into sale-leaseback arrangements with a third party lender for 45 of our operating aircraft. The sale-leasebacks occurred simultaneously with the delivery of the related aircraft to us from their manufacturers. Each sale-leaseback transaction was structured with a separate trust set up by the third party lender, the assets of which consist of the one aircraft initially transferred to it following the sale by us and the subsequent lease arrangement with us. Because of their limited capitalization and the potential need for additional financial support, these trusts are VIEs as defined in the *Consolidations* topic of the Codification and must be considered for consolidation in our financial statements. Our assessment of each trust considers both quantitative and qualitative factors, including whether we have the power to direct the activities and to what extent we participate in the sharing of benefits and losses of the trusts. JetBlue does not retain any equity interests in any of these trusts and our obligations to them are limited to the fixed rental payments we are required to make to them. These were approximately $585 million as of December 31, 2014 and are reflected in the future minimum lease payments in the table above. Our only interest in these entities is the purchase options to acquire the aircraft as specified above. Since there are no other arrangements, either implicit or explicit, between us and the individual trusts that would result in our absorbing additional variability from the trusts, we concluded we are not the primary beneficiary of these trusts. We account for these leases as operating leases, following the appropriate lease guidance as required by the *Leases* topic in the Codification.

REQUIRED

a. What entry did JetBlue make to record rent payments on operating leases in 2014? What entry will be required in 2015?

b. What is the total liability for leases that JetBlue reports in its 2014 balance sheet? How much of this liability is current? Noncurrent? Is this (total liability) amount representative of its obligations? Explain.

c. JetBlue reported that it operated four aircraft under capital leases at the end of 2013. Assume that all these leases were still in effect at the end of 2014. Prepare journal entries to record (i) new capital lease agreements signed during 2014, and (ii) depreciation of leased assets in 2014. Post your entries to T-accounts.

d. Based on the information above, prepare the entry that JetBlue would make in 2015 to record lease payments on capital leases. Record your entry in the financial statement effects template and in journal entry form. Post your entry to T-accounts.

e. Using a 4% discount rate, estimate the asset and liability that JetBlue would report if it capitalized all of its operating leases. JetBlue reports long-term debt of $1,968 million in its 2014 balance sheet. Would this amount be affected substantially if operating leases were capitalized?

f. Based on your calculations in part *e*, what journal entry would be necessary to record lease payments in 2015 if all of JetBlue's operating leases are capitalized at the end of 2014?

LO6 Williams-Sonoma NYSE :: WSM

C10-46. Interpreting Income Tax Footnotes

The following information is taken from **Williams-Sonoma, Inc.**'s 10-K ($ thousands).

Note D: Income Taxes

The components of earnings before income taxes, by tax jurisdiction, are as follows:

	Fiscal Year Ended		
(in thousands)	Feb. 1, 2015 (52 Weeks)	Feb. 2, 2014 (52 Weeks)	Feb. 3, 2013 (53 Weeks)
United States	$482,739	$448,764	$401,542
Foreign	19,464	3,918	8,414
Total earnings before income taxes	$502,203	$452,682	$409,956

The provision for income taxes consists of the following:

	Fiscal Year Ended		
(in thousands)	Feb. 1, 2015 (52 Weeks)	Feb. 2, 2014 (52 Weeks)	Feb. 3, 2013 (53 Weeks)
Current			
Federal	$157,227	$173,686	$136,742
State	31,959	25,748	22,072
Foreign	4,411	2,690	3,441
Total current	193,597	202,124	162,255
Deferred			
Federal	2,719	(26,324)	(7,827)
State	(2,547)	(1,277)	(1,202)
Foreign	(420)	(743)	(0)
Total deferred	(248)	(28,344)	(9,029)
Total provision	$193,349	$173,780	$153,226

We have historically elected not to provide for U.S. income taxes with respect to the undistributed earnings of our foreign subsidiaries as we intended to utilize those earnings in our foreign operations for an indefinite period of time. As of February 1, 2015 the accumulated undistributed earnings of all foreign subsidiaries were approximately $43,300,000 and are sufficient to support our anticipated future cash needs for our foreign operations. We currently intend to utilize those undistributed earnings for an indefinite period of time and will only repatriate such earnings when it is tax effective to do so. It is currently not practical to estimate the tax liability that might be payable if these foreign earnings were to be repatriated.

Significant components of our deferred tax accounts are as follows:

(in thousands)	Feb. 1, 2015	Feb. 2, 2014
Current:		
Compensation	$ 15,968	$ 14,378
Merchandise inventories	30,328	27,337
Accrued liabilities	28,866	26,461
Customer deposits	60,989	58,479
Prepaid catalog expenses	(12,753)	(12,576)
Other	7,220	7,407
Total current	130,618	121,486
Non-current:		
Depreciation	(9,888)	(4,216)
Deferred rent	18,925	17,500
Deferred lease incentives	(37,098)	(33,065)
Stock-based compensation	19,857	28,948
Executive deferral plan	5,437	5,699
Uncertainties	7,061	4,378
Valuation allowance	(1,568)	(1,048)
Other	1,539	(4,372)
Total non-current	4,265	13,824
Total deferred tax assets, net	$134,883	$135,310

REQUIRED

a. What amount of income tax expense did Williams-Sonoma report for the year ended February 1, 2015?

b. Calculate Williams-Sonoma's effective tax rate for each year reported. In addition, calculate the rate of U.S. federal taxes on U.S. income in the fiscal year ended February 1, 2015.

c. Williams-Sonoma reported income taxes payable of $32,488 thousand in its February 1, 2015 balance sheet, and $49,365 thousand at February 2, 2014. What amount of income taxes did it pay in cash during the fiscal year ended February 1, 2015?[15]

d. Prepare a journal entry to record income tax expense for the fiscal year ended February 1, 2015.

e. The company reported a net book value of property, plant, and equipment of $883,012 thousand on February 1, 2015. Given a tax rate of 35%, what is an estimate of the tax basis of these assets on that date?

f. The company reported prepaid catalog expense of $33,942 thousand as a current asset in its February 1, 2015, balance sheet. The company provided the following explanation of this asset in footnote A to its 10-K:

Advertising and Prepaid Catalog Expenses
Advertising expenses consist of media and production costs related to catalog mailings, e-commerce advertising and other direct marketing activities. All advertising costs are expensed as incurred, or upon the release of the initial advertisement, with the exception of prepaid catalog expenses. Prepaid catalog expenses consist primarily of third party incremental direct costs, including creative design, paper, printing, postage and mailing costs for all of our direct response catalogs. Such costs are capitalized as prepaid catalog expenses and are amortized over their expected period of future benefit. . . . Each catalog is generally fully amortized over a six to nine month period, with the majority of the amortization occurring within the first four to five months.

Explain how this expense results in a temporary difference between tax and financial reporting. Did the item create a current or long-term deferred tax asset or a liability and in what amount?

g. How much in unremitted foreign earnings on which no U.S. tax has been accrued (i.e., indefinitely reinvested earnings) does the company have in its foreign subsidiaries? If the company were required to estimate and record an accrual for the amount of U.S. tax on those earnings, how would accounting earnings be affected?

h. Williams-Sonoma has a valuation allowance listed in its schedule of deferred tax assets and liabilities. Briefly and in general explain what a valuation allowance is and how it affects deferred taxes and reported income.

LO6 **C10-47. Interpreting Income Tax Disclosures**

Google Inc.
NASDAQ :: GOOG

Google Inc. reported the following in note 14 to its 2014 10-K report:

Note 14. Income Taxes
Income from continuing operations before income taxes included income from domestic operations of $6,447 million, $7,044 million, and $7,936 million for the years ended December 31, 2012, 2013, and 2014, and income from foreign operations of $8,021 million, $8,855 million, and $9,323 million for the years ended December 31, 2012, 2013, and 2014.

The provision for income taxes consists of the following (in millions):

	Year Ended December 31,		
	2012	2013	2014
Current:			
Federal	$2,484	$2,217	$2,424
State	169	117	140
Foreign	312	711	774
Total	2,965	3,045	3,338
Deferred:			
Federal	(109)	(421)	29
State	5	0	7
Foreign	55	(72)	(43)
Total	(49)	(493)	(7)
Provision for income taxes	$2,916	$2,552	$3,331

[15] For this problem, assume a simple case. The complicating factors that would change the answer are beyond the scope of this text. For those readers aware of these complicating factors, assume there are no acquisitions of other companies during the year and that Williams-Sonoma has no unrecognized tax benefits.

We have not provided U.S. income taxes and foreign withholding taxes on the undistributed earnings of foreign subsidiaries as of December 31, 2014 because we intend to permanently reinvest such earnings outside the U.S. If these foreign earnings were to be repatriated in the future, the related U.S. tax liability may be reduced by any foreign income taxes previously paid on these earnings. As of December 31, 2014, the cumulative amount of earnings upon which U.S. income taxes have not been provided is approximately $47.4 billion. Determination of the amount of unrecognized deferred tax liability related to these earnings is not practicable.

REQUIRED

a. Compute Google's effective tax rate for each year presented. Also, compute Google's domestic tax rate (federal plus state) and its tax rate on income from foreign operations.

b. Explain what is meant by the disclosure in the final paragraph of the footnote regarding the "undistributed earnings of foreign subsidiaries."

c. Estimate the amount of taxes that Google might owe if all of the undistributed earnings were repatriated to the United States. Why is it "not practicable" to determine an amount of deferred income taxes on these undistributed earnings?

SOLUTIONS TO REVIEW PROBLEMS

Mid-Chapter Review 1

SOLUTION TO PART A

1. The present value of the lease payments is $224,755, computed as $32,000 × 7.02358.

ANALYZE

	Balance Sheet													Income Statement				
Transaction	Cash Asset	+	Noncash Assets	-	Contra Assets	=	Liabilities	+	Contrib. Capital	+	Earned Capital		Revenues	-	Expenses	=	Net Income
(1) Leased store under capital lease.			+224,755 Leased Asset	-		=	+224,755 Lease Liability							-		=	

JOURNALIZE

(1) Leased asset (+A)	224,755	
Lease liability (+L)		224,755

POST

+ Leased Asset (A) −	
(1) 224,755	

− Lease Liability (L) +	
	224,755 (1)

2. At the first year-end, Gap would record depreciation expense of $22,476 ($224,755/10) and interest expense of $15,733 ($224,755 × .07).

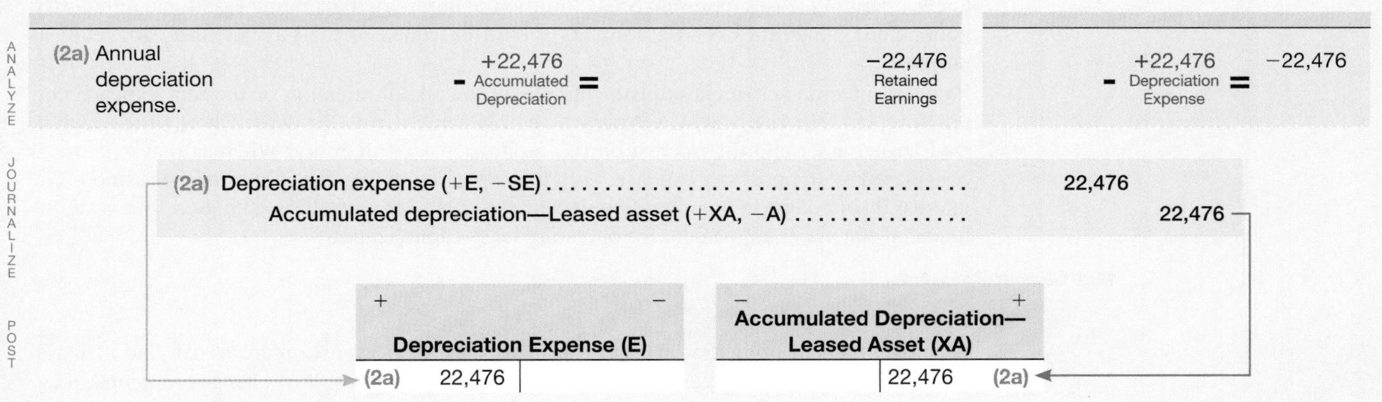

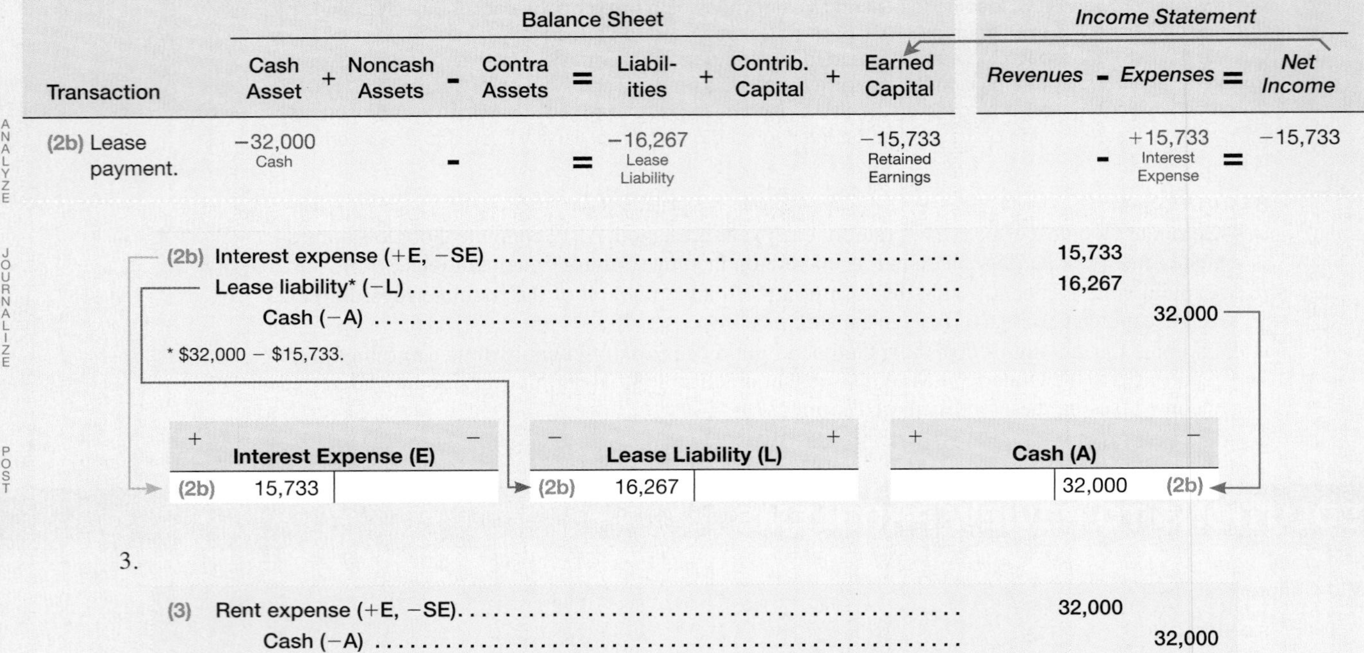

3.

(3) Rent expense (+E, −SE) 32,000
Cash (−A) 32,000

SOLUTION TO PART B

1. Gap's leases are classified as operating leases—see footnote. Also, since there are no disclosures in the leasing footnote related to capital leases, we know that all of the leases are classified as operating.
2. Using a 5% discount rate, the present value of its operating leases follows ($ millions):

	Year	Operating Lease Payment	Present Value Factor (Table A.2, 5%)	Present Value (Payment × PV Factor)
1	2015	$1,136	0.95238	$1,082
2	2016	1,096	0.90703	994
3	2017	920	0.86384	795
4	2018	760	0.82270	625
5	2019	638	0.78353	500
6	2020	638	0.74622	476
7	2021	638	0.71068	453
8	2022	425	0.67684	288
Total		$6,251		$5,213

Gap's operating leases represent $5,213 million of unreported operating assets and unreported nonoperating liabilities. These amounts should be added to the balance sheet for analysis purposes.

3. Potential income statement adjustments would include elimination of the rent expense currently reported in Gap's SG&A expenses and replacing it with the depreciation of the capitalized leased asset and the interest on the capitalized lease liability. Whereas rent expense is considered as an operating expense, only the depreciation expense is similarly classified. The interest is, of course, a nonoperating expense. NOPAT, as a result, is increased following the financial statement adjustment for operating lease capitalization.

Mid-Chaper Review 2

SOLUTION

1. A pension benefit obligation increases primarily by service cost, interest cost, and actuarial losses. The latter are increases in the pension liability as a result of changes in actuarial assumptions. The pension benefit obligation is decreased by the payment of benefits to retirees and by actuarial gains.

2. Pension investments increase through positive investment returns for the period and by cash contributions made by the company. Investments decrease by payments made to retirees and investment losses.
3. United Continental's funded status is $(2,241) million ($4,803 million PBO − $2,562 million pension assets) as of 2014. The negative amount indicates that the plan is underfunded. Therefore, this amount is reported as a liability on the company's balance sheet.
4. Expected return on plan assets acts as an offset to service cost and interest cost in computing the net pension cost. As the expected return increases (decreases), net pension cost decreases (increases).
5. United Continental's expected return of $180 million exceeded its actual return of $151 million in 2014.
6. United Continental reports net pension expense of $132 million in 2014.
7. United Continental's funded status is negative, indicating an underfunded plan. The company contributed $307 million to the pension plan in 2014. It is likely that the company will need to increase its future funding levels to cover the plan's requirements. This action is likely to have negative consequences for its ability to fund other operating needs, and could damage its competitive position in the future.

Chapter-End Review

SOLUTION

1. *a.* $2,390.
   b. $1,488 = $1,342 + $146 is currently payable or has already been paid in 2016.
   c. The most obvious example would be depreciation allowed in 2016 by the tax code exceeded that calculated by the straight-line method.

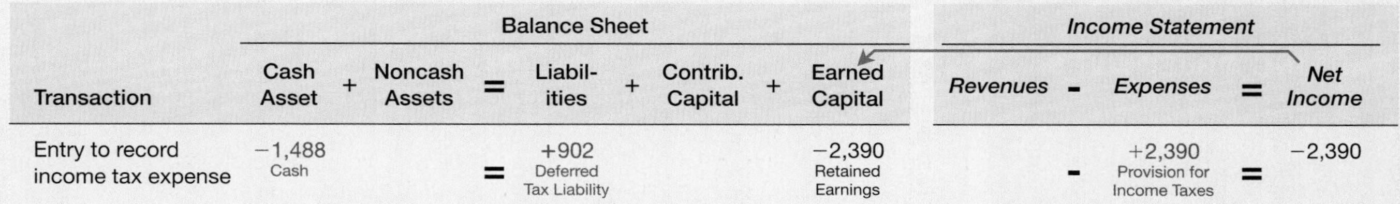

	Balance Sheet									Income Statement				
Transaction	Cash Asset	+	Noncash Assets	=	Liabilities	+	Contrib. Capital	+	Earned Capital	Revenues	−	Expenses	=	Net Income
Entry to record income tax expense	−1,488 Cash			=	+902 Deferred Tax Liability				−2,390 Retained Earnings		−	+2,390 Provision for Income Taxes	=	−2,390

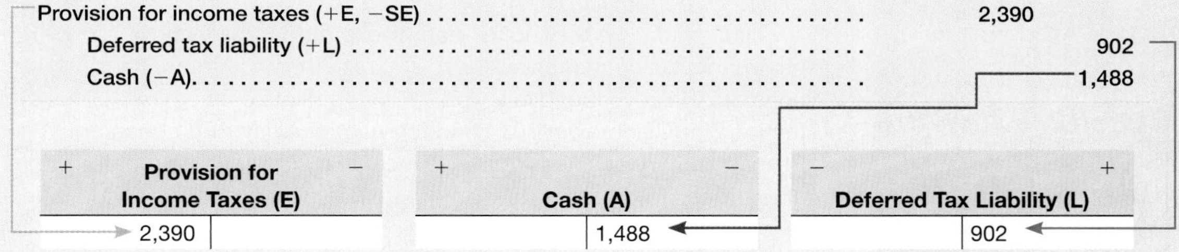

Provision for income taxes (+E, −SE)	2,390	
Deferred tax liability (+L)		902
Cash (−A)		1,488

11 Reporting and Analyzing Stockholders' Equity

LEARNING OBJECTIVES

1. Describe business financing through stock issuances. (p. 518)
2. Explain and account for the issuance and repurchase of stock. (p. 521)
3. Describe how operations increase the equity of a business. (p. 525)
4. Explain and account for dividends and stock splits. (p. 525)
5. Define and illustrate comprehensive income. (p. 530)
6. Describe and illustrate the basic and diluted earnings per share computations. (p. 533)
7. Appendix 11A: Analyze the accounting for convertible securities, stock rights, and stock options. (p. 535)

PFIZER

www.pfizer.com

Pfizer Inc. is a research-based, global pharmaceutical company that discovers, develops, manufactures, and markets prescription medicines. Pfizer's 2014 revenues were almost $50 billion, down from almost $55 billion just two years earlier. Although Lyrica led the company with 10% of sales, Enbrel, Celebrex, Lipitor, and Viagra also contributed substantially to Pfizer's bottom line.

Unfortunately, the Lipitor patent expired in 2011 and many of Pfizer's other pharmaceutical patents are due to expire in the near future, causing Pfizer's projections of 2015 revenue to fall by 8%. Of immediate concern is the loss of patent protections for Celebrex in 2014 and for Viagra in major European and Asian markets. Pfizer's primary business activities include discovering and marketing new, patentable drugs. To discover new drugs, Pfizer spends sizeable amounts each year on research and development: $6.7 billion in 2013 and $8.4 billion in 2014.

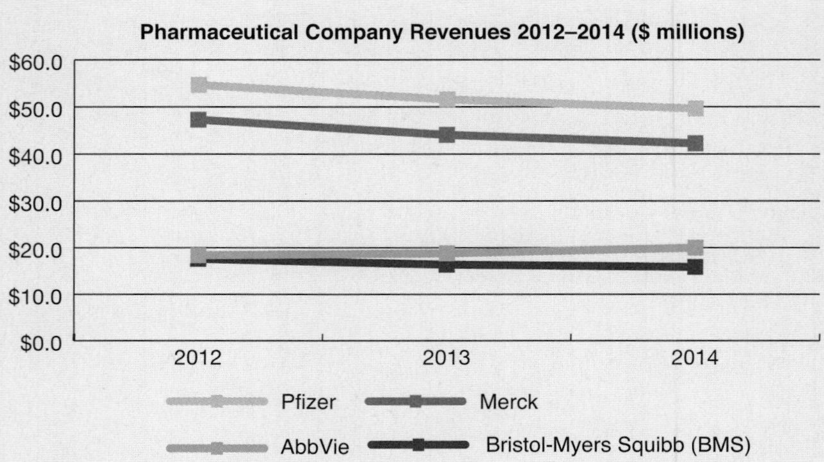

Pfizer faces increased competition from its major rivals, **Merck & Co., Inc.**, **AbbVie Inc.**, and **Bristol-Myers Squibb**, and also from generic manufacturers. In addition,

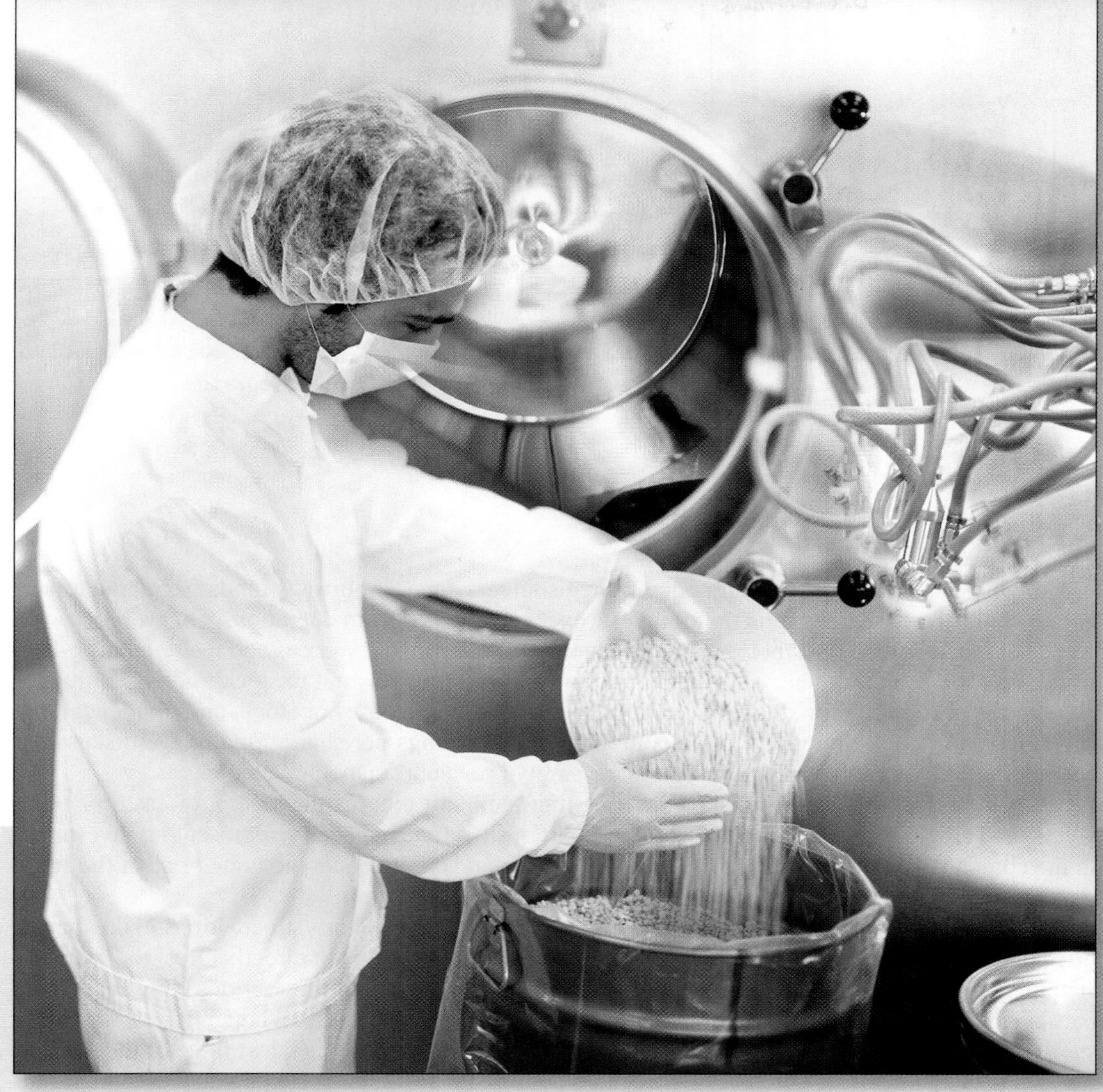

Pfizer reports that the "Patient Protection and Affordable Care Act" of 2010 cost the company almost $1 billion in 2014 and will continue to affect the company in future years.

One critical component of Pfizer's recent strategy has been to spread its high overhead costs across a broader sales base and to rationalize its production and sales activities. In 2000, Pfizer merged with **Warner-Lambert Company**, and in 2003 it acquired **Pharmacia**. The merger with Warner-Lambert and acquisition of Pharmacia made Pfizer the largest pharmaceutical company in the world. Since 2003, Pfizer has continued to acquire other companies, including **Esperion Therapeutics, Inc.** (2004), **Vicuron Pharmaceuticals, Inc.** (2005), **BioRexis Pharmaceuticals Corporation** (2007), **Coley Pharmaceutical Group** (2008), **Wyeth** (2009), and **King Pharmaceuticals, Inc.** in 2011. In 2014, Pfizer made an unsuccessful $119 billion bid to acquire **AstraZeneca plc**, which has $26 billion in revenues. Pfizer divested its animal health business in 2013 and its nutrition business in 2012 to focus more on its core businesses.

Pfizer must balance the capital needs of its acquisition strategy and its heavy commitment to research and development with the expectations of shareholders. From 2012 through 2014, the company reports $51 billion of net cash flow from operating activities, but it also paid $49 billion in cash to shareholders in the form of dividends and share repurchases. Other transactions involving shareholders' equity included share-based compensation for employees and conversions of one form of shareholders' equity to another.

This chapter describes the reporting and analysis of equity transactions, including sales and repurchases of stock, dividends, comprehensive income, and convertible securities.

Sources: *The Wall Street Journal* (January 27, 2009; May 21, 2009; April 21, 2015), *New York Times* (January 27, 2009; May 27, 2014), *Business Week* (April and June, 2009), *Fortune* (August, 2009), and Pfizer 2014 10-K Report.

CHAPTER ORGANIZATION

Reporting and Analyzing Stockholders' Equity

Contributed Capital	Earned Capital	Earnings per Share	Further Considerations (Appendix 11A)
• Classes of Stock • Accounting for Stock	• Cash Dividends • Stock Dividends and Splits • Comprehensive Income	• Basic EPS • Diluted EPS	• Convertible Securities • Stock Rights • Stock Options

1 **LO1** Describe business financing through stock issuances.

INTRODUCTION

A company finances its assets from one of three sources: either it borrows funds from creditors, it obtains funds from shareholders or it reinvests excess cash flow from operations. On average, companies obtain about 60% of their external financing from borrowed sources and the remaining 40% from shareholder investment. This chapter describes the issues relating to stockholders' equity, including the accounting for stock transactions (issues and repurchases of stock, and dividends), the accounting for stock options, and the computation of earnings per share. Finally, we discuss the accounting for convertible securities, an increasingly prevalent financing vehicle.

When a company issues stock to the investing public, it records the receipt of cash (or other assets) and an increase in contributed capital, a part of stockholders' equity, representing investment in the company by shareholders. The increases in cash and equity equal the issue price of the stock on the issue date multiplied by the number of shares sold.

Contributed capital is accounted for at *historical cost*. Consequently, fluctuations in the market price of the issuer's stock subsequent to the initial public offering do not directly affect the financial statements of the issuing company. These fluctuations are the result of transactions between outside parties not involving the issuer. When and if stock is repurchased and subsequently resold, the issuer's contributed capital decreases (increases) by the current purchase (sales) price of the shares.

FYI Corporations never record gains or losses resulting from transactions between the company and its owners.

There is an important difference between accounting for stockholders' equity and accounting for transactions involving assets and liabilities: *there is never any gain or loss reported on the purchase and sale of stock or the payment of dividends*. Instead, these "gains and losses" are reflected as increases and decreases in the contributed capital component of the issuing company's stockholders' equity.

This chapter focuses on the two broad categories of shareholder investment: contributed capital and earned capital. **Exhibit 11.1** provides an illustration of this breakdown using Pfizer's stockholders' equity as of December 31, 2014.

EXHIBIT 11.1 Stockholders' Equity from Pfizer's Balance Sheet

	Shareholders' Equity (millions except preferred stock issued and per common share data)	Dec. 31, 2014
Contributed capital	Preferred stock, no par value, at stated value; 27 shares authorized; issued: 2014—717	$ 29
	Common stock, $0.05 par value; 12,000 shares authorized; issued: 2014—9,110	455
	Additional paid-in capital	78,977
	Treasury stock, shares at cost: 2014—2,819	(73,021)
Earned capital	Retained earnings	72,176
	Accumulated other comprehensive income (loss)	(7,316)
	Total Pfizer Inc. shareholders' equity	71,301
	Equity attributable to noncontrolling interests	321
	Total equity	$71,622

Pfizer, like other companies, has two broad categories of stockholders' equity:

1. **Contributed capital** This section reports the proceeds received by the issuing company from original stock issuances. Contributed capital often includes common stock, preferred stock, and additional paid-in capital. Netted against these capital accounts is treasury stock, the amounts

paid to repurchase shares of the issuer's stock from its investors less the proceeds from the resale of such shares. Collectively, these accounts are generically referred to as contributed capital (or *paid-in capital*).

2. **Earned capital** This section consists of (a) retained earnings (or accumulated deficit, if negative), which represent the cumulative income and losses of the company less any dividends to shareholders, and (b) accumulated other comprehensive income (AOCI), which includes changes to equity that are not included in income and are, therefore, not reflected in retained earnings. For Pfizer, AOCI includes foreign currency translation adjustments, changes in market values of derivatives, unrecognized gains and losses on available-for-sale securities, and pension adjustments.

Before turning to a discussion of contributed capital and earned capital, we note one other item in **Exhibit 11.1**—Equity attributable to **noncontrolling interests**. This amount results from the practice of consolidating subsidiaries that are controlled, but not wholly owned, and it represents neither capital contributed to Pfizer nor capital earned by Pfizer's shareholders. Chapter 12 provides a brief introduction to this topic.

CONTRIBUTED CAPITAL

We begin our discussion with contributed capital. Contributed capital represents the cumulative cash inflow that the company has received from the sale of various classes of stock, less the net cash that it has paid out to repurchase its stock from the market.

Pfizer's contributed capital consists of preferred and common stock, additional paid-in capital, less costs of treasury stock (repurchased shares).

Classes of Stock

There are two general classes of stock: preferred and common. The difference between the two lies in the respective legal rights conferred upon each class.

Common Stock Shares of **common stock** represent the primary ownership unit in a corporation. Common stockholders have voting rights which allow them to participate in the governance of the corporation. The total number of common shares is usually presented on the face of the balance sheet. There are three numbers of shares to be aware of:

- The number of **shares authorized** represents the upper limit on the number of shares that the corporation can issue. This number is established in the *articles of incorporation* and can only be increased by an affirmative shareholder vote.
- The number of **shares issued** is the actual number of shares that have been sold to stockholders by the corporation.
- The number of **shares outstanding** is the number of issued shares less the number of shares repurchased as treasury stock.

Pfizer's common stock is described as follows in its 2014 balance sheet (shares in millions):

Common stock, $0.05 par value; 12,000 shares authorized; issued: 2014—9,110

The Pfizer common stock has the following important characteristics:

- Pfizer common stock has a par value of $0.05 per share. The **par value** is an arbitrary amount set by company organizers at the time of formation. Generally, par value has no substance from a financial reporting or statement analysis perspective (there are some legal implications, which are usually minor). Its main impact is in specifying the allocation of proceeds from stock issuances between the two contributed capital accounts on the balance sheet: common stock and additional paid-in capital.
- Pfizer has authorized the issuance of 12,000 million shares. As of December 31, 2014, 9,110 million shares are issued yielding a total par value of $455 million = $0.05 × 9,110 million shares. When shares are first issued, the number of shares outstanding equals those issued. Any

shares subsequently repurchased as treasury stock are subtracted from issued shares to derive outstanding shares.

Some corporations issue multiple classes of stock, with differential voting rights. For instance, **Google Inc.** has Class A common stock with one vote per share, Class B common stock with ten votes per share, and Class C capital stock with no voting rights at all. All shares participate equally in dividends, but this structure has allowed the original management team to raise capital while retaining voting control over the corporation.

Preferred Stock **Preferred stock** generally has some preference, or priority, with respect to common stock but does not have voting rights. Two typical preferences are:

1. **Dividend preference** Preferred shareholders receive dividends on their shares before common shareholders do. If dividends are not paid in a given year, those dividends are normally forgone. However, some preferred stock contracts include a *cumulative provision* stipulating that any forgone dividends must first be paid to preferred shareholders, together with the current year's dividends, before any dividends are paid to common shareholders.
2. **Liquidation preference** If a company fails, its assets are sold (liquidated) and the proceeds are paid to the creditors and shareholders, in that order. Shareholders, therefore, have a greater risk of loss than do creditors. Among shareholders, the preferred shareholders receive payment in full before any proceeds are paid to common shareholders. This liquidation preference makes preferred shares less risky than common shares. Any liquidation payment to preferred shares is normally at its par value, although it is sometimes specified in excess of par, called a **liquidating value**.

The preferred stock of Pfizer is described in Note 12 to its 2014 10-K:

The Series A convertible perpetual preferred stock is held by an Employee Stock Ownership Plan "Preferred ESOP" Trust and provides dividends at the rate of 6.25%, which are accumulated and paid quarterly. The per-share stated value is $40,300 and the preferred stock ranks senior to our common stock as to dividends and liquidation rights. Each share is convertible, at the holder's option, into 2,574.87 shares of our common stock with equal voting rights. The conversion option is indexed to our common stock and requires share settlement, and therefore, is reported at the fair value at the date of issuance. We may redeem the preferred stock at any time or upon termination of the Preferred ESOP, at our option, in cash, in shares of common stock or a combination of both at a price of $40,300 per share.

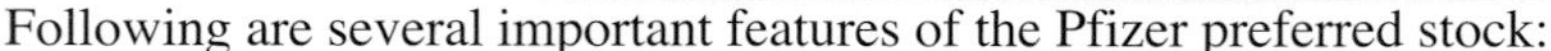

Following are several important features of the Pfizer preferred stock:

- There are 27 million preferred shares authorized, of which 717 shares are issued as of December 31, 2014. The articles of incorporation set the number of shares authorized for issuance. Once that limit is reached, shareholders must approve any increase in authorized shares.
- Pfizer preferred stock has a preference with respect to dividends and liquidation; meaning that preferred shareholders are paid before common shareholders.
- Pfizer preferred stock pays a dividend of 6.25% of its par (stated) value of $40,300. This feature means that each preferred share is entitled to annual dividends of $2,518.75 ($40,300 × 6.25%), payable quarterly.
- Pfizer preferred stock is convertible into common stock at the option of the holder and at a predetermined exchange rate. A preferred share is convertible, at the holder's option, into 2,574.87 common shares.
- Pfizer can redeem (repurchase) its preferred stock at any time in cash, common stock, or both.

Pfizer's cumulative preferred shares carry a dividend yield of 6.25%. This dividend yield compares favorably with the $1.04 per share (3.47% yield on a $30 average share price) paid to its common shareholders. Generally, preferred stock can be an attractive investment for shareholders seeking higher dividend yields, especially when tax laws wholly or partially exempt such dividends from taxation.

There are three additional features sometimes seen in preferred stock agreements:

1. **Call feature** The call feature provides the issuer with the right, but not the obligation, to repurchase the preferred shares at a specified price. This price can vary according to a specified time. A decline in the market rate of interest is one event that can lead to the firm exercising

the call provision. While of value to the issuer of the preferred stock, the call provision makes the issue less attractive to potential investors. The result is a lower offering price per share.

2. **Conversion feature** The yield on preferred stock, especially when coupled with a cumulative feature, is similar to the interest rate on a bond or note. Further limited protection is offered because preferred shareholders receive the par value at liquidation like debtholders receive face value. The fixed yield and liquidation value for the preferred stock limit the upside potential return of preferred shareholders. This constraint can be overcome by inclusion of a *conversion feature* that allows preferred stockholders to convert their shares into common shares at their option at a predetermined conversion ratio. Some preferred contracts give the company an option to force conversion.

   The conversion feature causes the shares to be more attractive to potential investors because the preferred stockholders now have the opportunity to share in the fruits of a successful company with the common stockholders. Indeed, the market price of preferred stock tends to reflect the added value of the conversion feature.

3. **Participation feature** Preferred shares sometimes carry a *participation feature* that allows preferred shareholders to share ratably with common stockholders in dividends. The dividend preference over common shares can be a benefit when dividend payments are meager, but a fixed dividend yield limits upside potential if the company performs exceptionally well. This limitation can be overcome with a participation feature.

A GLOBAL PERSPECTIVE

Under IFRS, convertible debt securities are termed compound financial instruments because the conversion feature has a value even if it is not legally detachable for sale. IFRS (but not GAAP) splits the convertible bonds' value into the separate debt and equity values for reporting purposes.

Accounting for Stock Transactions

LO2 Explain and account for the issuance and repurchase of stock.

2

We cover the accounting for stock transactions in this section, including the accounting for stock issuances and for stock repurchases.

Stock Issuance Stock issuances, whether common or preferred, yield an increase in both assets and stockholders' equity. Companies use stock issuances to obtain cash and other assets for use in their business.

Stock issuances increase assets (cash) by the number of shares sold multiplied by the issuance price of the stock on the issue date. Equity increases by the same amount, which is reflected in contributed capital accounts. Specifically, assuming the issuance of common stock, the common stock account increases by the number of shares sold multiplied by its par value and the additional paid-in capital account is increased for the remainder of the purchase price.[1]

BUSINESS INSIGHT

Alibaba's IPO In September of 2014, **Alibaba Group** offered its shares to the general public for the first time. The first public sale of common stock by a corporation is called an initial public offering, or IPO for short. After the IPO, any offering of stock to the public is called a seasoned equity offering.

At the time, Alibaba's IPO was the largest in history, raising approximately $25 billion. The common stock had a par value of $0.000025, but was offered to the public for $68 per share. Within a couple of months after the stock opened for trade on the New York Stock Exchange, the price increased to almost $120 per share, but then began to fall. By the company's fiscal year end in March 2015, Alibaba's shares were trading for just over $83 per share, about 20% greater than their original offer price and almost 50 times their earnings per share.

[1] Companies who offer their shares for sale to the general public are called *public corporations*. In a *private company*, ownership is limited to a smaller number of investors and the stock is not available to the general public. The distinction between public and private corporations should not be confused with media references to the public sector and the private sector. The *public sector* refers to government entities. Virtually all business entities, including public corporations, are considered part of the *private sector*.

To illustrate, assume that Davis Company issues 10,000 shares of $1 par value common stock at a market price of $43 cash per share. The financial statement effects and entries for this stock issuance follow.

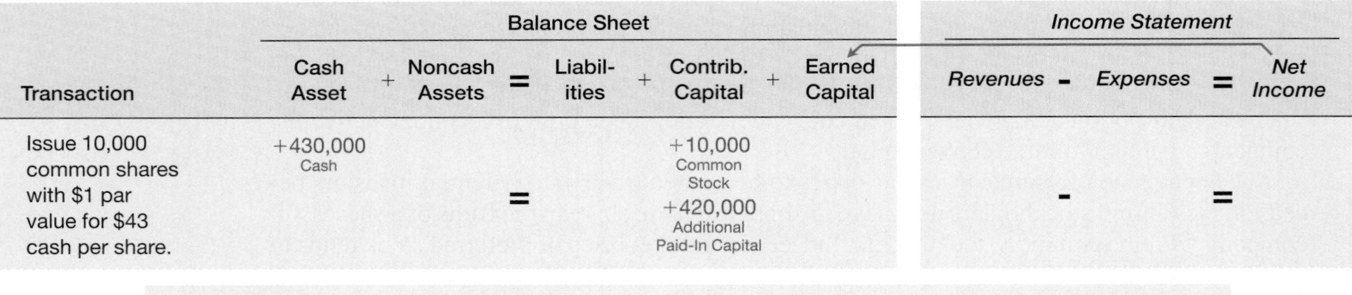

Transaction	Cash Asset	+ Noncash Assets	= Liabil-ities	+ Contrib. Capital	+ Earned Capital	Revenues	− Expenses	= Net Income
Issue 10,000 common shares with $1 par value for $43 cash per share.	+430,000 Cash		=	+10,000 Common Stock +420,000 Additional Paid-In Capital			−	=

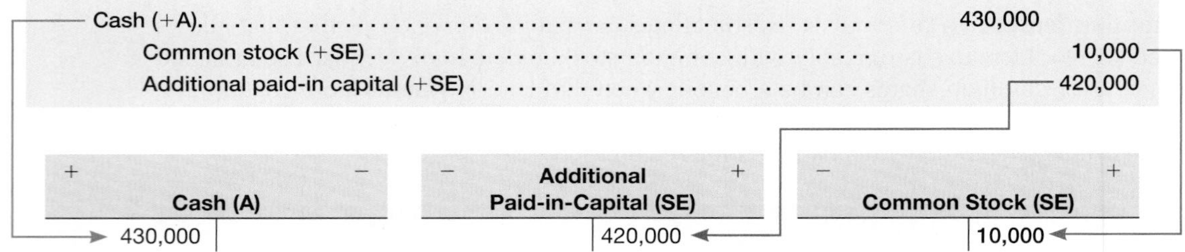

Cash (+A)	430,000	
Common stock (+SE)		10,000
Additional paid-in capital (+SE)		420,000

+ Cash (A) −	− Additional Paid-in-Capital (SE) +	− Common Stock (SE) +
430,000	420,000	10,000

Specifically, the following financial statement effects of the stock issuance are:

1. Cash increases by $430,000 (10,000 shares × $43 per share) and is reported as a cash inflow from financing activities on the statement of cash flows.
2. Common stock increases by the $10,000 par value of shares sold (10,000 shares × $1 par value).[2]
3. Additional paid-in capital increases by the $420,000 difference between the issue price and par value ($430,000 − $10,000).

FYI Stock issuance affects the balance sheet, the statement of cash flows and the statement of stockholders' equity. There is never any revenue or gain from stock issuance reported in the income statement.

Once shares are issued, they are freely traded in the market among investors. The proceeds of those sales and any gains and losses on those sales do not affect the issuing company and are not recorded in its accounting records. Further, fluctuations in the issuing company's stock price subsequent to issuance do not directly affect its financial statements. Hence, the equity section of the balance sheet cannot be used to determine the current market value of the company. The market value (or market capitalization) is given by the product of the number of common shares outstanding times the current per-share price of the stock.

Pfizer's outstanding common shares, repeated from **Exhibit 11.1** are (in millions):

Common stock, $0.05 par value; 12,000 shares authorized; issued: 2014—9,110	$ 455
Additional paid-in capital	78,977

Pfizer's common stock, in the amount of $455 million, equals the number of shares issued multiplied by the common stock's par value: 9,110 million × $0.05 = $455 million.[3] The balance of the proceeds from stock issuances ($78,977 million) is included in the additional paid-in capital account. Total proceeds from stock issuances are $79,432 million, or $8.72 per share ($79,432 million/9,110 million shares).

[2] Common stock can also be issued as "no par" or as "no par with a stated value." For no par stock, the common stock account is increased by the entire proceeds of the sale and no amount is assigned to additional paid-in capital. For no par stock with a stated value, the stated value is treated just like par value; that is, common stock is increased by the number of shares multiplied by the stated value, and the remainder is assigned to the additional paid-in capital account.

[3] The number of shares issued and the par value of those shares are both rounded to the nearest million.

RESEARCH INSIGHT

Stock Issuance and Stock Returns Seasoned equity offerings are issuances of common stock by firms that already have outstanding shares. On average, stock price declines when a company announces that it will issue additional shares of common stock. Investors infer that issuing common stock rather than debt is an indication that management believes the stock is overvalued in the market, making it a more attractive form of financing. In addition, research has found that companies engage in earnings management around seasoned equity offerings, using both accrual estimates (e.g., underestimating bad debt expense or warranty expense) and real transactions (e.g., cutting R&D or accelerating sales). As a result, both earnings and stock returns decline in subsequent periods.

Stock Repurchase Pfizer provides the following description of its stock repurchase program in notes to its 10-K report.

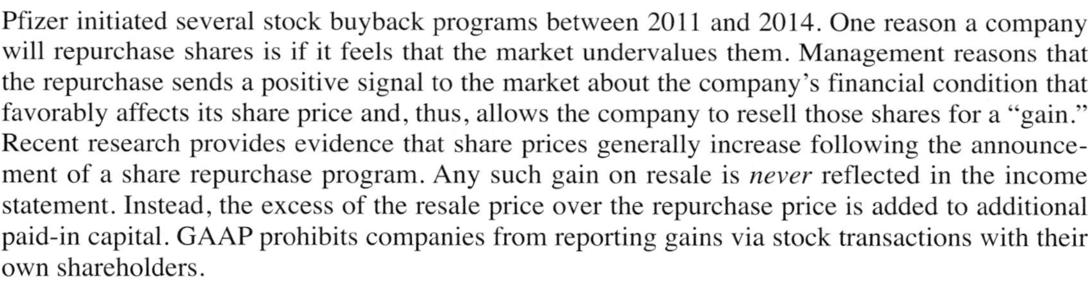

Our December 2011 $10 billion share-purchase plan was exhausted in the first quarter of 2013. Our November 2012 $10 billion share-purchase plan was exhausted in the fourth quarter of 2013. On June 27, 2013, we announced that the Board of Directors had authorized an additional $10 billion share-purchase plan, and share purchases commenced thereunder in October 2013. On October 23, 2014, we announced that the Board of Directors had authorized an additional $11 billion share-purchase plan . . . After giving effect to share purchases through year-end 2014, our remaining share-purchase authorization was approximately $11.5 billion at December 31, 2014.

Pfizer initiated several stock buyback programs between 2011 and 2014. One reason a company will repurchase shares is if it feels that the market undervalues them. Management reasons that the repurchase sends a positive signal to the market about the company's financial condition that favorably affects its share price and, thus, allows the company to resell those shares for a "gain." Recent research provides evidence that share prices generally increase following the announcement of a share repurchase program. Any such gain on resale is *never* reflected in the income statement. Instead, the excess of the resale price over the repurchase price is added to additional paid-in capital. GAAP prohibits companies from reporting gains via stock transactions with their own shareholders.

Another reason shares are repurchased is to offset the dilutive effects of an employee stock option program. When an employee exercises stock options, the number of shares outstanding increases. These additional shares reduce earnings per share and are, therefore, viewed as *dilutive*. In response, many companies repurchase an equivalent number of shares in a desire to keep outstanding shares constant. Corporations also buy back their own shares in order to concentrate ownership to avoid an unwelcome takeover action. Repurchased shares do not participate in dividends or in shareholder votes.

A GLOBAL PERSPECTIVE

The accounting for share repurchases under IFRS is similar to GAAP. IFRS allows the repurchase also to be recorded as a decrease to the common equity, additional paid-in capital, and retained earnings or some combination.

A stock repurchase has the opposite financial statement effects from a stock issuance. That is, cash is reduced by the price of the shares repurchased (number of shares repurchased multiplied by the purchase price per share) and stockholders' equity is reduced by the same amount. The reduction in equity is achieved by increasing a contra equity account called **treasury stock**. *A contra equity account is a negative equity account with a debit balance,* which reduces stockholders' equity. Thus, when a contra equity account increases, total equity decreases.

Any subsequent reissuance of treasury stock does not yield a gain or loss. Instead, the difference between the proceeds received and the repurchase price of the treasury stock is reflected as an increase or decease to additional paid-in capital.

To illustrate, assume that 3,000 common shares of Davis Company stock previously issued for $43 are later repurchased for $40. The financial statement effects and entries for this stock repurchase follow.

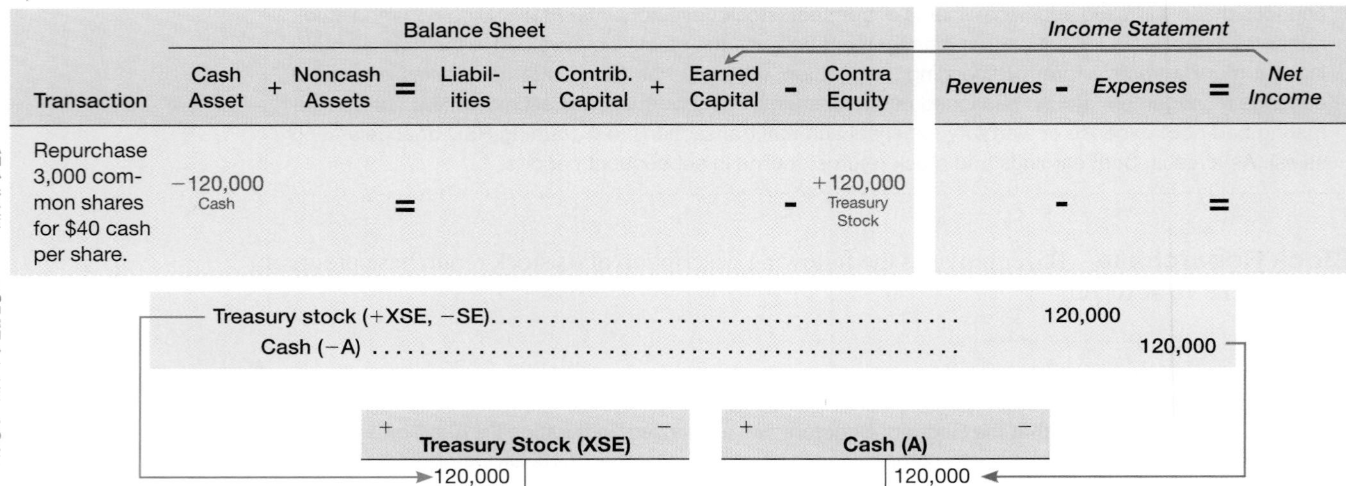

Assets (cash) and equity both decrease. Treasury stock (a contra equity account) increases by $120,000, which reduces stockholders' equity by that same amount.

Assume that these 3,000 shares are then subsequently resold for $42 cash per share. The financial statement effects and entries for this treasury stock sale follow.

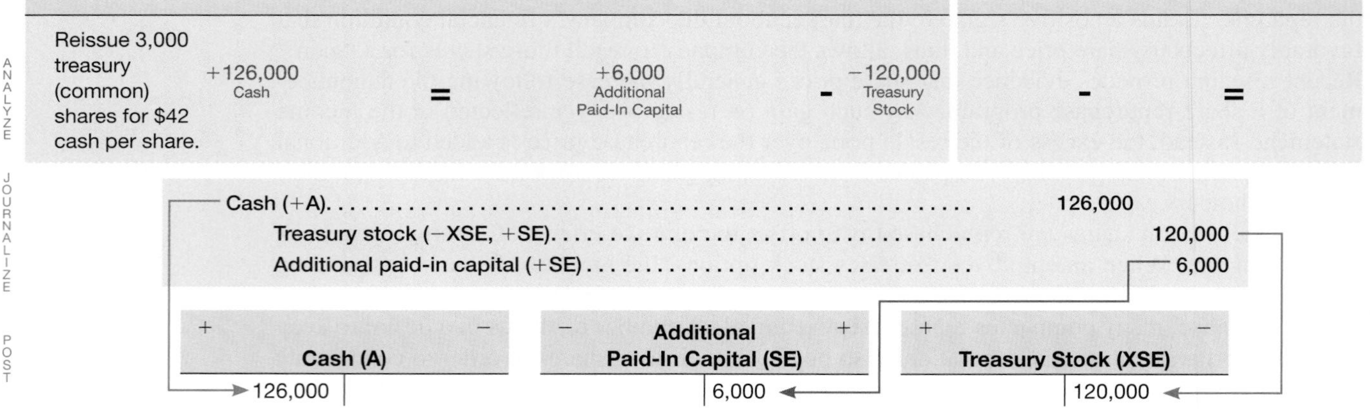

Cash assets increase by $126,000 (3,000 shares × $42 per share), the treasury stock account is reduced by the $120,000 cost of the treasury shares issued, and the $6,000 excess (3,000 shares × $2 per share) is reported as an increase in additional paid-in capital.[4] Again, there is no effect on the income statement—companies are prohibited from reporting gains and losses from repurchases and reissuances of their own stock.

The treasury stock section of Pfizer's 2014 balance sheet is reproduced below.

At December 31 (millions)	2014
Treasury stock, shares at cost: 2014—2,819	$(73,021)

Pfizer has repurchased a cumulative total of 2,819 million shares of its common stock for $73,021 million, an average repurchase price of $25.90 per share. This compares with total contributed

[4] If the reissue price is below the repurchase price, then additional paid-in capital is reduced until it reaches a zero balance, after which retained earnings is reduced.

capital of $79,461 million ($29 million + $455 million + $78,977 million). Although some of Pfizer's treasury purchases were to offset increases in shares outstanding due to the exercise of stock options, it appears that most of these purchases are motivated by a perceived low stock price by Pfizer management. When there have been several repurchases and sales of treasury stock, a question arises as to which shares were sold. Typically the solution is to assume a flow such as the first shares repurchased are the first ones assumed to be sold (first-in, first-out).

YOU MAKE THE CALL

You are the Chief Financial Officer You believe that your company's stock price is lower than its real value. You are considering various alternatives to increase that price, including the repurchase of company stock in the market. What are some considerations relating to this decision? [Answer on page 540]

MID-CHAPTER REVIEW 1

GuidedExamples MBC

Plesko Corporation reported the following transactions relating to its stock accounts in 2015.

Jan.	15	Issued 10,000 shares of $5 par value common stock at $17 cash per share.
Mar.	31	Purchased 2,000 shares of its own common stock at $15 cash per share.
June	25	Reissued 1,000 shares of its treasury stock at $20 cash per share.

Show the financial impact of each transaction using the financial statement effects template, provide the appropriate journal entry for each transaction, and post the journal entries to the related T-accounts.

The solution to this review problem can be found on page 558.

eLectures MBC

EARNED CAPITAL

LO3 Describe how operations increase the equity of a business. 3

We now turn our attention to the earned capital portion of stockholders' equity. Earned capital represents the cumulative profit that has been retained by the company. Recall that earned capital is increased by income earned and decreased by any losses incurred. Earned capital is also decreased by dividends paid to shareholders. Not all dividends are paid in the form of cash, however. In fact, companies can pay dividends in many forms, including property (such as land, for example) or additional shares of stock. We cover both cash and stock dividends in this section. Earned capital also includes the positive or negative effects of accumulated other comprehensive income (AOCI). The earned capital of Pfizer is highlighted in the following graphic:

Shareholders' Equity (millions, except preferred shares issued and par value)	Dec. 31, 2014
Preferred stock, no par value, at stated value; 27 shares authorized; issued: 2014—717	$ 29
Common stock, $0.05 par value; 12,000 shares authorized; issued: 2014—9,110	455
Additional paid-in capital	78,977
Treasury stock, shares at cost: 2014—2,819	(73,021)
Retained earnings	72,176
Accumulated other comprehensive income (loss)	(7,316)
Total Pfizer Inc. shareholders' equity	71,301
Equity attributable to noncontrolling interests	321
Total equity	$71,622

Cash Dividends

LO4 Explain and account for dividends and stock splits. 4

Many companies, but not all, pay dividends. Their reasons for dividend payments are varied. Most dividends are paid in cash on a quarterly basis. The following is a description of Pfizer's dividend policy from its 2014 10-K.

Dividends on Common Stock

We paid dividends on our common stock of $6.6 billion in 2014, $6.6 billion in 2013 and $6.5 billion in 2012. In December 2014, our Board of Directors declared a first-quarter 2015 dividend of $0.28 per share, payable on March 3, 2015, to shareholders of record at the close of business on February 6, 2015. The first-quarter 2015 cash dividend will be our 305th consecutive quarterly dividend.

Our current and projected dividends provide a return to shareholders while maintaining sufficient capital to invest in growing our businesses and to seek to increase shareholder value. Our dividends are not restricted by debt covenants. While the dividend level remains a decision of Pfizer's Board of Directors and will continue to be evaluated in the context of future business performance, we currently believe that we can support future annual dividend increases, barring significant unforeseen events.

Outsiders closely monitor dividend payments. It is generally perceived that the level of dividend payments is related to the expected long-term core income. Accordingly, dividend increases are usually accompanied by stock price increases, and companies rarely reduce their dividends unless absolutely necessary. Dividend reductions are, therefore, met with substantial stock-price declines.

Financial Effects of Cash Dividends Cash dividends reduce both cash and retained earnings by the amount of the cash dividends paid. To illustrate, Pfizer paid $6.6 billion in 2014 cash dividends on its common and preferred shares. The financial statement effects of this cash dividend payment are reflected as a reduction in assets (cash) and a reduction in retained earnings as follows.

($ billions)	Balance Sheet									Income Statement				
Transaction	Cash Asset	+	Noncash Assets	=	Liabil-ities	+	Contrib. Capital	+	Earned Capital	*Revenues*	-	*Expenses*	=	*Net Income*
ANALYZE: Paid $6.6 billion cash dividends on common and preferred shares.	−6.6 Cash			=					−6.6 Retained Earnings		-		=	

JOURNALIZE

	Dr.	Cr.
Retained earnings (−SE)	6.6	
Cash (−A)		6.6

POST

− Retained Earnings (SE) +	
6.6	

+ Cash (A) −	
	6.6

Dividend payments have no effect on profitability. They are a direct reduction to retained earnings and bypass the income statement.

BUSINESS INSIGHT

While many technology companies appear to have ample financial resources to pay dividends, the tax strategies described in Chapter 10 make it costly to use those resources. For instance, **Apple Inc.** reported end-of-fiscal year 2014 cash and financial investments of $155 billion, 67% of the company's total assets. However, $137 billion of this amount was held by Apple's foreign subsidiaries and had not yet been subject to U.S. taxation. If Apple repatriated some portion of these resources to pay dividends to its shareholders, it would have to pay approximately one-third of the amount to U.S. tax authorities. As a result, Apple borrowed a total of $35 billion in fiscal years 2013 and 2014, at least in part to return cash to shareholders in the form of dividends and repurchases of common stock.

Preferred stock dividends have priority over those for common shares, including unpaid prior years' preferred dividends (dividends in arrears) when preferred stock is cumulative. To illustrate, assume that Hanna Company has 15,000 shares of $50 par value, 8% preferred stock outstanding and 50,000 shares of $5 par value common stock outstanding. During its first three years in business, assume that Hanna declares $20,000 dividends in the first year, $260,000 of dividends in the second year, and $60,000 of dividends in the third year. If the preferred stock is cumulative, the total amount of dividends paid to each class of stock in each of the three years would be:

	Preferred Stock	Common Stock
Year 1		
Current-year dividend ($15,000 × $50 × 8%; but only $20,000 is paid, leaving $40,000 in arrears).	$20,000	
Balance to common.		$ 0
Year 2		
Arrearage from Year 1 [($15,000 × $50 × 8%) − $20,000]. . . .	40,000	
Current-year dividend ($15,000 × $50 × 8%).	60,000	
Balance to common [$260,000 − ($40,000 + $60,000)].		160,000
Year 3		
Current-year dividend ($15,000 × $50 × 8%).	60,000	
Balance to common.		0

MID-CHAPTER REVIEW 2

Finn Corporation has outstanding 10,000 shares of $100 par value, 5% preferred stock and 50,000 shares of $5 par value common stock. During its first three years in business, Finn declared no dividends in the first year, $300,000 of cash dividends in the second year, and $80,000 of cash dividends in the third year.

a. If the preferred stock is cumulative, determine the total amount of dividends paid to each class of stock for each of the three years.

b. If the preferred stock is not cumulative, determine the total amount of dividends paid to each class of stock for each of the three years.

The solution to this review problem can be found on page 559.

Stock Dividends and Splits

Dividends need not be paid in cash. Many companies pay **stock dividends**, that is dividends in the form of additional shares of stock. Companies can also distribute additional shares to their stockholders with a stock split. We cover both of these distributions in this section.

Stock Dividends When dividends are paid in the form of the company's stock, retained earnings are reduced and contributed capital is increased. However, the amount by which retained earnings are reduced depends on the proportion of the outstanding shares distributed to the total outstanding shares on the issue date. **Exhibit 11.2** illustrates two possibilities depending on whether a stock dividend is classified as either a small stock dividend or a large stock dividend. When the additional number of shares issued as a stock dividend is so great that it is likely to have a negative impact on the market price per share of the stock, the dividend must be treated as a large stock dividend. Dividends of less than 20%–25% of the outstanding shares are considered to be small stock dividends, while dividends of more than 20%–25% are classified as large stock dividends.

EXHIBIT 11.2 Analysis of Stock Dividend Effects

Percentage of Outstanding Shares Distributed	Retained Earnings	Contributed Capital
Less than 20%–25% *(small stock dividend)*	Reduce by **market value** of shares distributed	Common stock increased by par value of shares distributed; additional paid-in capital increased for the balance
More than 20%–25% *(large stock dividend)*	Reduce by **par value** of shares distributed	Common stock increased by par value of shares distributed

For *small stock dividends,* retained earnings are reduced by the *market* value of the shares distributed (dividend shares × market price per share) and contributed capital is increased by the same amount. For the contributed capital increase, the common stock is increased by the par value of the shares distributed and the remainder [dividend shares × (market value per share − par value per share)] increases additional paid-in capital. For *large stock dividends,* retained earnings are reduced by the *par* value of the shares distributed (dividend shares × par value per share), and common stock is increased by the same amount (no change to additional paid-in capital).

To illustrate the financial statement effects of dividends, assume that a company has 1 million shares of $5 par common stock outstanding. It then declares a small stock dividend of 15% of the outstanding shares (1,000,000 shares × 15% = 150,000 shares) when the market price of the stock is $30 per share. This small stock dividend has the following financial statement effects:

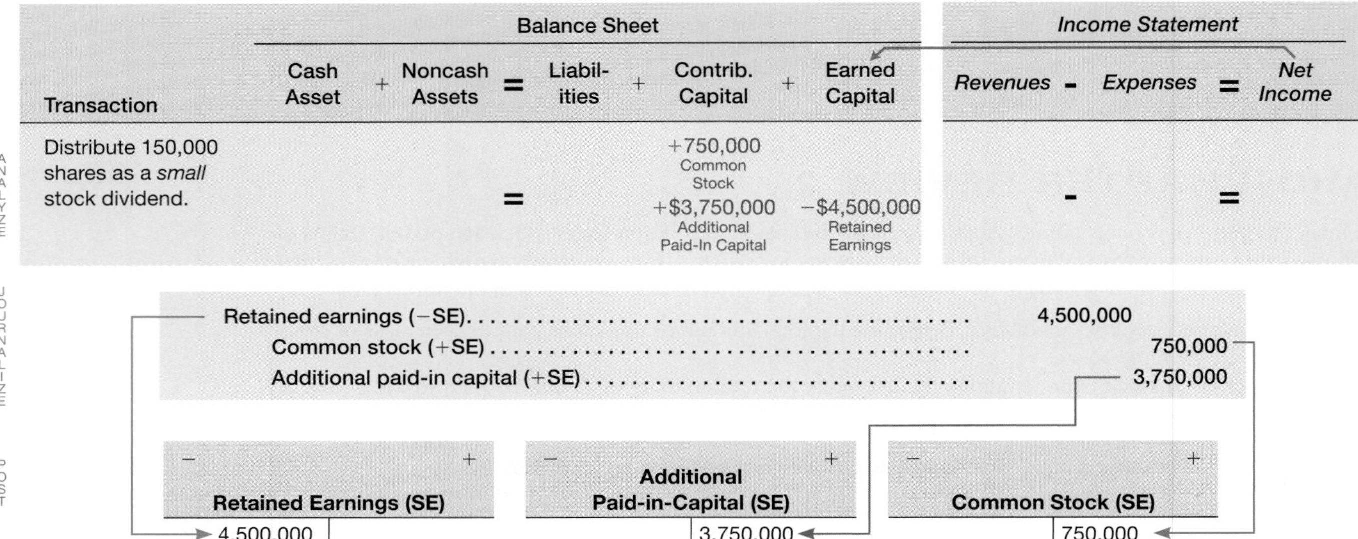

Retained earnings are reduced by $4,500,000, which equals the market value of the small stock dividend (150,000 shares × $30 market price per share). The increase in contributed capital is treated as follows: common stock is increased by the par value of $750,000 (150,000 shares × $5 par value), and the remainder of $3,750,000 increases additional paid-in capital. Similar to cash dividend payments, the stock dividends, whether large or small, never impact income. But unlike cash dividends, stock dividends do not affect the cash flows from financing activities.

Next, assume instead that a company declares a large stock dividend of 70% of the 1 million outstanding common ($5 par) shares when the market price of the stock is $30 per share. This large stock dividend has the following financial statement effects and related entries:

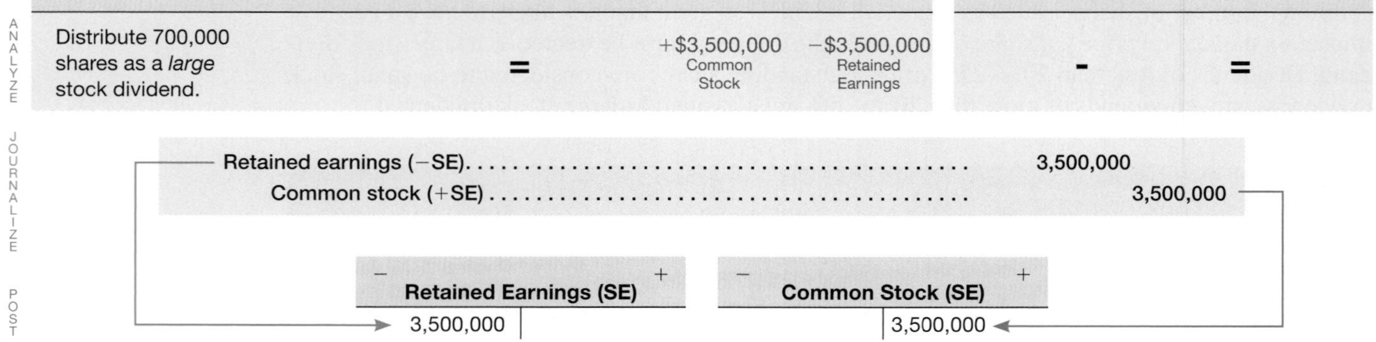

Retained earnings are reduced by $3,500,000, which equals the par value of the large stock dividend (700,000 shares × $5 par value per share). Common stock is increased by the par value of $3,500,000. There is no effect on additional paid-in capital because the dividend is reported at par value.

For both large and small stock dividends, companies are required to show comparable shares outstanding for all prior periods for which earnings per share (EPS) is reported in the statements. The reasoning is that a stock dividend has no effect on the ownership percentage of each common stockholder. As such, to show a dilution in reported EPS would erroneously suggest a decline in profitability when it is simply due to an increase in shares outstanding.

Stock Splits A **stock split** is a proportionate distribution of shares and, as such, is similar in substance to a stock dividend. A typical stock split is 2-for-1, which means that the company distributes one additional share for each share owned by a shareholder. Following the distribution, each investor owns twice as many shares, yet their percentage ownership in the company is unchanged.

A stock split is not a monetary transaction and, as such, there are no financial statement effects. However, companies must disclose the new number of shares outstanding for all periods presented in the financial statements. Further, many states require that the par value of shares be proportionately adjusted as well (for example, halved for a 2-for-1 split).[5]

Stock Transactions and the Cash Flows Statement

The issuance of common stock, the acquisition of treasury stock, and cash (but not stock) dividends affect the financing section of the cash flow statement as follows:

Transaction	Effect on Cash Flow from Financing Activities
Issuance of Common Stock	Increase
Acquisition of Treasury Stock	Decrease
Sale of Treasury Stock	Increase
Cash Dividends Paid	Decrease

Stock splits and stock dividends do not influence the cash flows statement and are often used when cash is short but the continuation of a dividend is considered necessary.

MID-CHAPTER REVIEW 3

The stockholders' equity of Zhang Corporation at December 31, 2014, follows.

5% preferred stock, $100 par value, 10,000 shares authorized; 4,000 shares issued and outstanding	$ 400,000
Common stock, $5 par value, 200,000 shares authorized; 50,000 shares issued and outstanding	250,000
Paid-in capital in excess of par value—Preferred stock	40,000
Paid-in capital in excess of par value—Common stock	300,000
Retained earnings	656,000
Total stockholders' equity	$1,646,000

The following transactions occurred during 2015. Show the financial impact of each transaction using the financial statement effects template, provide the appropriate journal entry for each transaction, and post the journal entries to the related T-accounts.

Apr. 1 Declared and issued a 100% stock dividend on all outstanding shares of common stock when the market value of the stock was $11 per share.

Dec. 7 Declared and issued a 3% stock dividend on all outstanding shares of common stock when the market value of the stock was $7 per share.

Dec. 31 Declared and paid a cash dividend of $1.20 per share on all outstanding common shares.

The solution to this review problem can be found on pages 559–560.

[5] If state law requires that par value not be reduced for a stock split, this event should be described as a *stock split effected in the form of a dividend*.

5

LO5 Define and illustrate comprehensive income.

Comprehensive Income

Comprehensive income is a more inclusive notion of company performance than net income. It includes all recognized changes in equity that occur during a period except those resulting from contributions by and distributions to owners.

Specifically, comprehensive income includes net income *plus* additional gains and losses not included in the income statement. These additional gains and losses are called *other comprehensive income* and include, for example, foreign currency adjustments, unrealized gains or losses on available-for-sale securities and derivatives, and adjustments to pension and other benefit plans. Comprehensive income includes the effects on a company of some economic events that are often outside of management's control. Accordingly, some observers assert that net income is a measure of management's performance, while comprehensive income is a measure of company performance.

Comprehensive income can be reported by firms in one of two ways. The first reporting method is to present a statement of comprehensive income that combines net income and other comprehensive income in one statement. Such a statement begins much like any income statement, with revenues, cost of goods sold, operating expenses and so forth. However, in the statement of comprehensive income, net income is a subtotal, followed by the gains and losses that are classified as other comprehensive income. The second reporting approach presents other comprehensive income in a separate statement immediately following the income statement. Pfizer follows the second reporting approach. Its statement of comprehensive income is presented in **Exhibit 11.3**.

EXHIBIT 11.3 Pfizer's 2014 Abridged Consolidated Statement of Comprehensive Income ($ millions)

Net income		$9,168
Other comprehensive income:		
Foreign currency translation adjustments, net	(2,054)	
Unrealized holding gains on derivative financial instruments, net	501	
Unrealized holding gains/(losses) on available-for-sale securities, net	(418)	
Benefit plans: actuarial gains/(losses), net	(3,690)	
Benefit plans: prior service credit and other, net	672	
Tax benefit/(provision) on other comprehensive income/(loss)	946	
Total other comprehensive income/(loss)		(4,042)
Comprehensive income before allocation to noncontrolling interests		$5,126
Less: Comprehensive income attributable to noncontrolling interests		36
Comprehensive income attributable to Pfizer Inc.		$5,090

Unlike net income, other comprehensive income is not closed to retained earnings at the end of each accounting period. Instead, other comprehensive income is closed to a separate earned capital account called **accumulated other comprehensive income** (abbreviated AOCI).

In its 2014 balance sheet, Pfizer reports accumulated other comprehensive income of $(7,316), compared to $(3,271) in 2013. The $4,045 decrease from 2013 to 2014 is (almost) equal to the $(4,042) other comprehensive income for 2014 that Pfizer reported in its statement of comprehensive income (**Exhibit 11.3**). (The $3 million "slippage" is due to noncontrolling interests' share of other comprehensive income items.)

A GLOBAL PERSPECTIVE

As with U.S. GAAP, companies reporting under IFRS have a choice of presenting a single statement including components of profit and loss and other comprehensive income or presenting two statements—one for profit and loss (the income statement) and one that begins with profit or loss and then provides other comprehensive income components.

Summary of Stockholders' Equity

A summary of transactions that affect stockholders' equity is included in the statement of stockholders' equity. This statement reports a reconciliation of the beginning and ending balances of important stockholders' equity accounts. Pfizer's statement of stockholders' equity is shown in **Exhibit 11.4**. Pfizer's statement of shareholders' equity reveals the following key transactions for 2014:

- Total comprehensive income increased shareholders' equity by $5,090 million (net income of $9,135 million less other comprehensive loss of $4,045 million).
- Dividends to preferred and common shareholders decreased stockholders' equity by $6,692 million ($2 million + $6,690 million).
- Employee share-based compensation increased equity by $1,597 million.
- Common stock repurchases decreased equity by $5,000 million.
- Conversion of preferred stock into common stock and redemptions decreased the preferred stock account, for a net decrease in stockholders' equity of $8 million.

EXHIBIT 11.4 Pfizer's Stockholders' Equity (December 31, 2014)

(Millions, Except Preferred Shares)	Preferred Stock Shares	Preferred Stock Stated Value	Common Stock Shares	Common Stock Par Value	Additional Paid-In Capital	Treasury Stock Shares	Treasury Stock Cost	Retained Earnings	Accum. Other Comp. Loss	Share-holders Equity	Non-controlling Interests	Total Equity
Balance December 31, 2013	829	$33	9,051	$453	$77,283	(2,652)	$(67,923)	$69,732	$(3,271)	$76,307	$313	$76,620
Net income								9,135		9,135	32	9,168
Other comprehensive income/(loss), net of tax									(4,045)	(4,045)	3	(4,042)
Cash dividends declared:												
Common stock								(6,690)		(6,690)		(6,690)
Preferred stock								(2)		(2)		(2)
Noncontrolling interests											(6)	(6)
Share-based payment transactions			59	3	1,693	(2)	(100)			1,597		1,597
Purchases of common stock						(165)	(5,000)			(5,000)		(5,000)
Preferred stock conversions and redemptions	(112)	(4)			(4)	—	1			(8)		(8)
Other	—	—	—	(1)	5	—	—	—	—	5	(22)	(17)
Balance December 31, 2014	717	$29	9,110	$455	$78,977	(2,819)	$(73,021)	$72,176	$(7,316)	$71,301	$321	$71,622

ANALYZING FINANCIAL STATEMENTS

Analysis Objective

We want to measure the return on investment by common shareholders.

Before getting to the specifics of the performance ratio, we must address a complexity introduced when a company (like Pfizer) has a subsidiary that is not 100% owned. Suppose Company A owns 85% of the common stock of Company B. The remaining 15% of B's shareholders are called a "non-controlling interest." Company A would be required to incorporate the assets, liabilities, revenues and expenses of Company B in its reports. As a result, Company A's reported net income would include all the income from both A and B. But then there is an adjustment in which 15% of B's income is subtracted (as "net income attributable to noncontrolling interests"), and the resulting number is "net income attributable to common shareholders." We use this information to develop the following measure of profit that can be attributed to common shareholders of the reporting company.

Net income available for common shareholders =
Net income − Net income attributable to noncontrolling interests − Preferred dividends

A similar adjustment is required on the balance sheet, where total equity consists of "equity attributable to noncontrolling interests" plus "common shareholders' equity" (as can be seen in **Exhibit 11.4**).

Analysis Tool Return on Common Equity (ROCE)

$$\text{Return on Common Equity (ROCE)} = \frac{\text{Net income available for common shareholders}}{\text{Average common shareholders' equity}}$$

Applying the Ratio to Pfizer

$$2013\ \text{ROCE} = \frac{\$22{,}072 - \$69 - \$2}{[(\$76{,}620 - \$313) + (\$81{,}678 - \$418)]/2} = 0.279, \text{ or } 27.9\%$$

$$2014\ \text{ROCE} = \frac{\$9{,}168 - \$32 - \$2}{[(\$71{,}622 - \$321) + (\$76{,}620 - \$313)]/2} = 0.124, \text{ or } 12.4\%$$

Guidance ROCE is similar to ROE except that when we compute ROCE, we remove the effect of noncontrolling interests and preferred stock from both the numerator and denominator.

Pfizer in Context

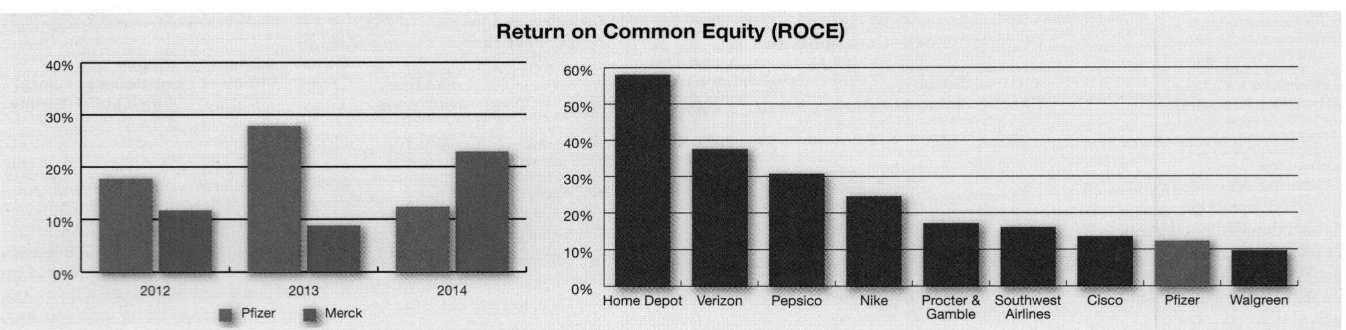

Takeaways Neither Pfizer's nor Merck's ROCE has been stable for the past few years. The large values in 2013 for Pfizer and in 2014 for Merck reflect unusual gains from the sale of discontinued businesses. Such items are not likely to recur on a regular basis. Relative to other focus companies in this text, Pfizer's ROCE is low. It is about the same as that of Cisco and higher than Walgreens.

Many companies have little or no preferred stock or noncontrolling interests. So the difference between return on common equity (ROCE) and return on equity (ROE) will be immaterial for these firms. When preferred stock is present, ROCE is a more accurate measure of return to common shareholders.

Other Considerations In Chapter 5, we learned that ROE can be decomposed into two components: return on assets and return on financial leverage. Differences between firms may reflect a difference in performance, or a difference in the reliance on debt financing. A similar division can be done with ROCE with the caveat that ROCE essentially treats preferred stock as debt rather than equity.

One final point: the financial press sometimes refers to a measure called **book value per share**. This amount is the net book value of the company that is available to common shareholders, defined as: stockholders' equity less preferred stock less equity attributable to noncontrolling interest divided by the number of common shares outstanding (issued common shares less treasury shares). Pfizer's 2014 book value per share is computed as: ($71,622 million − $29 million − $321 million)/(9,110 million shares − 2,819 million shares) = $11.33 book value per common share.

MID-CHAPTER REVIEW 4

The stockholders' equity of Sloan Corporation at December 31, 2014, follows.

Common stock, $5 par value, 400,000 shares authorized; 160,000 shares issued and outstanding . . .	$800,000
Paid-in capital in excess of par value . . .	920,000
Retained earnings . . .	513,000

During 2015, the following transactions occurred:

June 28 Declared and issued a 10% common stock dividend when the market value is $11 per share.
Dec. 5 Declared and paid a cash dividend of $1.25 per share.
Dec. 31 Updated retained earnings for net income of $412,000.

Compute the year-ending balance of retained earnings for 2015.

The solution to this review problem can be found on page 560.

eLectures MBC

EARNINGS PER SHARE

LO6 Describe and illustrate the basic and diluted earnings per share computations.

The income statement reports at least one, and potentially two, earnings per share (EPS) numbers: basic and diluted. The difference between the two measures is illustrated as follows:

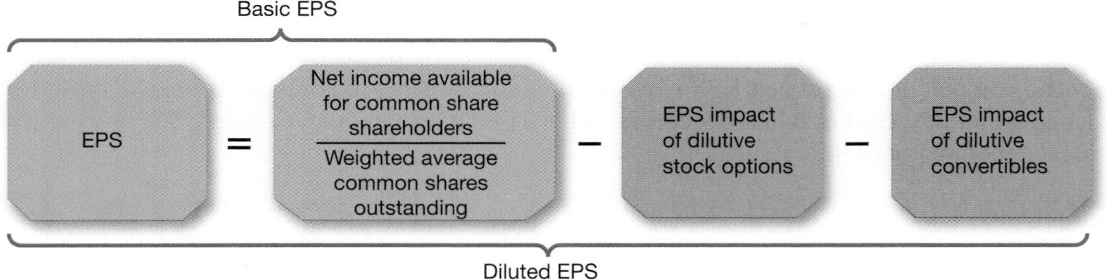

All public companies are required to report basic EPS. If the company has a complex capital structure, it is also required to report diluted EPS. A company is said to have a **complex capital structure** if it has certain *dilutive securities* outstanding. **Dilutive securities** are securities that can be converted into shares of common stock and would therefore reduce (or dilute) the earnings per share upon conversion. The three primary types of dilutive securities are:

- Stock options
- Convertible debt
- Convertible preferred stock

The Appendix at the end of this chapter details the accounting for these securities. A company with none of these dilutive securities outstanding is said to have a **simple capital structure**.

Basic EPS (BEPS) is computed as earnings available for common shareholders (net income less net income attributable to noncontrolling interests and preferred dividends) divided by the weighted average number of common shares outstanding for the year. (The number of shares is "weighted" by the amount of time each share was outstanding during the year.) The subtraction of net income attributable to noncontrolling interests and preferred stock dividends yields the income per common share available for dividend payments to common shareholders. The preferred dividends are subtracted because this portion of net income does not accrue to the common stockholders.

Computation of **Diluted EPS (DEPS)** reflects the added shares that would have been issued if all "in the money" stock options and other convertible securities had been exercised at the beginning of the year. When DEPS is calculated, the corporation needs to consider the maximum potential reduction (dilution) of its BEPS that could occur if the conversion of these securities took place. To do so means that any of these securities that do not reduce BEPS upon conversion are not to be considered converted. The result must be a figure that is lower than BEPS. The actual calculation can be quite complex. This does not detract from the importance of the DEPS value. The diluted earnings per share figure is favored by analysts as a better indicator of performance compared to basic earnings per share. Because reported DEPS never exceeds reported BEPS, the calculation is considered conservative.

Computation and Analysis of EPS

The computation of basic EPS is relatively straightforward, particularly when the firm neither issues nor buys any of its shares during the year. The formula is:

$$\textbf{Basic EPS (BEPS)} = \frac{\textbf{Net income available for common shareholders}}{\textbf{Weighted average number of common shares outstanding}}$$

To illustrate this calculation, assume that United Bridge Corporation reported net income of $200,000 in 2015 and paid $24,000 in preferred dividends. At the beginning of the year, the company had 44,000 shares of common stock outstanding. On June 30 (exactly the midpoint of the year) United Bridge purchased 8,000 shares of stock as treasury stock. Thus, the number of shares outstanding for the first six months of 2015 was 44,000 and, for the second half of the year, the company had 36,000 shares outstanding. The weighted average number of shares outstanding was, therefore, 40,000 [(44,000 + 36,000)/2]. Basic EPS would be calculated as follows:

$$\textbf{Basic EPS} = \frac{\$200{,}000 - \$24{,}000}{40{,}000 \text{ shares}} = \$4.40 \text{ per share}$$

The computation of diluted EPS is more complex in that it requires adjusting the basic EPS calculation for the effect of dilutive securities. This will typically require adjusting both the numerator and denominator of the calculation.

Diluted earnings per share (DEPS) =

$$\frac{\textbf{Net income available for common shareholders + Add-backs}}{\textbf{Weighted average number of common shares + Shares of convertible securities and stock options assumed to be converted}}$$

To illustrate, assume that United Bridge Corporation's preferred stock is convertible into 8,000 shares of common stock. To calculate diluted EPS, we must assume that the convertible preferred shares were converted at the beginning of the year. If this had occurred, two things would have been different for United Bridge. First, the weighted average number of shares outstanding would be higher by 8,000 shares. Second, the company would not have paid preferred dividends of $24,000. The resulting calculation would be:

$$\textbf{Diluted EPS} = \frac{\$200{,}000}{48{,}000 \text{ shares}} = \$4.17 \text{ per share}$$

A full description of the procedures for calculating diluted EPS is beyond the scope of this text. However, as the calculation above illustrates, diluted EPS adjusts basic EPS for the effect of dilutive securities. Reported DEPS must be no larger than BEPS to reflect its conservative message.

Pfizer reports both basic and diluted EPS. The table below, drawn from Pfizer's 2014 consolidated income statement, presents its basic and diluted EPS figures.

Year Ended December 31	2014	2013
Earnings per common share—basic		
Income from continuing operations attributable to Pfizer Inc. common shareholders.	$1.43	$1.67
Discontinued operations—net of tax.	0.01	1.56
Net income attributable to Pfizer Inc. common shareholders.	$1.44	$3.23
Earnings per common share—diluted		
Income from continuing operations attributable to Pfizer Inc. common shareholders.	$1.41	$1.65
Discontinued operations—net of tax.	0.01	1.54
Net income attributable to Pfizer Inc. common shareholders.	$1.42	$3.19
Weighted average shares—basic (millions)	6.346	6,813
Weighted average shares—diluted (millions)	6,424	6,895

Several observations should be made regarding Pfizer's EPS disclosures:

1. Pfizer reports basic EPS of $1.44 in 2014 and $3.23 in 2013. Diluted EPS is $0.02 lower and $0.04 lower in 2014 and 2013, respectively. The difference between basic and diluted EPS is caused by the effect of dilutive securities. Specifically, Pfizer has outstanding stock options and convertible preferred stock. Most publicly traded companies have at least one type of dilutive security outstanding. However, the dilutive effect of these securities on Pfizer's EPS is negligible.
2. The income statement further separates these EPS figures into EPS from continuing operations and EPS from discontinued operations. In 2014, discontinued operations increased Pfizer's EPS by $0.01 per share, but the effects of discontinued operations were much larger in 2013. GAAP requires separate reporting of the effects of nonrecurring items on EPS, including discontinued operations (see Chapter 6).

3. Pfizer used weighted average shares outstanding of 6,346 million shares to calculate basic EPS. This number is not the same as the number of shares outstanding in its December 31, 2014 balance sheet. Nor is it the simple average of the beginning and ending numbers of shares outstanding. The precise number of shares used in the EPS calculations requires knowing exactly when common stock and treasury stock transactions occurred during the year so that the weighted average number of shares outstanding can be calculated. Such detailed information is seldom available in a company's 10-K report.

EPS figures are sometimes used as a method of comparing operating results for companies of different sizes under the assumption that the number of shares outstanding is proportional to the income level (that is, a company twice the size of another will report double the income and will have double the common shares outstanding, leaving EPS approximately equal for the two companies). This assumption is erroneous. Management controls the number of common shares outstanding. Different companies also have different philosophies regarding share issuance and repurchase. For example, consider that most companies report annual EPS of less than $5, while **Berkshire Hathaway Inc.** reported EPS of $12,092 for 2014! The large amount occurs because Berkshire Hathaway has so few common shares outstanding, not necessarily because it has stellar profits.

Most analysts prefer to concentrate their attention on diluted EPS versus basic EPS as the more important measure, but the value of the EPS number is influenced by a number of factors including the number of common shares outstanding. For this reason, comparisons are more useful over time than across firms, but a careful reader should differentiate between EPS growth that comes from increases in the numerator and EPS growth that comes from decreases in the denominator. For these reasons, EPS may be of limited use in evaluating a firm's operational performance.

BUSINESS INSIGHT

From 2012 to 2014, **International Business Machines Corp.**'s Basic EPS from continuing operations increased by 5.4%. However, the company's income from continuing operations fell by 7.3% over the same period. The reason for these differing directions is IBM's repurchases of its own stock. The weighted-average number of basic common shares outstanding fell by 12.1% from 2012 to 2014.

CHAPTER-END REVIEW

GuidedExamples MBC

Petroni Corporation reported net income of $1,750 million in 2015. The weighted average number of common shares outstanding during 2015 was 760 million shares. Petroni paid $40 million in dividends on preferred stock, which was convertible into 10 million shares of common stock.

1. Calculate Petroni's basic earnings per share for 2015.
2. Calculate Petroni's diluted earnings per share for 2015.
3. What EPS numbers should Petroni report on its 2015 income statement?

The solution to this review problem can be found on page 561.

APPENDIX 11A: Dilutive Securities: Further Considerations

Convertible Securities

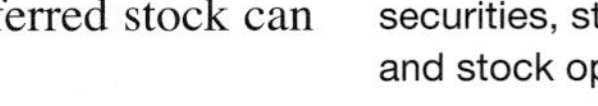

LO7 Analyze the accounting for convertible securities, stock rights, and stock options.

Convertible securities are debt and equity securities that provide the holder with an option to convert those securities into other securities. Convertible debentures, for example, are debt securities that give the holder the option to convert the debt into common stock at a predetermined conversion price. Preferred stock can also contain a conversion privilege.

To illustrate, assume 5,000 shares of preferred stock were issued at a stated value of $100 per share, with each share convertible into 12 shares of $5 par value common stock. The appropriate journal entry would be:

Cash (+A)	500,000	
Preferred stock (stated value) (+SE)		500,000

Now assume that 2,000 shares are converted to (2,000 × 12) = 24,000 shares of common stock. The appropriate journal entry is:

Preferred stock (stated value) (−SE)	200,000	
Common stock (par $5) (+SE)		10,000
Additional paid-in capital (+SE)		190,000

Conversion privileges offer an additional benefit to the holder of a security. That is, debtholders and preferred stockholders carry senior positions as claimants in bankruptcy, and carry a fixed-interest or dividend yield. With a conversion privilege, they can enjoy the residual benefits of common shareholders should the company perform well.

A conversion option is valuable and yields a higher price for the securities than they would otherwise command. However, conversion privileges impose a cost on common shareholders. That is, the higher market price received for convertible securities is offset by the cost imposed on the subordinate (common) securities. Conversion of these securities into common shares dilutes the ownership percentage of existing holders of the firm's common stock.

Accounting for the issuance of a convertible security is straightforward: the conversion option is *not* valued on the balance sheet unless it is detachable from the security (and, thus, separately saleable). Instead, the convertible preferred stock or convertible debt is recorded just like preferred stock or debt that does not have a conversion feature.

When securities are converted, the book value of the converted security is removed from the balance sheet and a corresponding increase is made to contributed capital. To illustrate the most commonly used method, assume that a company has convertible bonds with a face value of $1,000 and an unamortized premium of $100. Its holders convert them into 20 shares of $10 par value common stock. The financial statement effects and related entries of this conversion would be:

ANALYZE

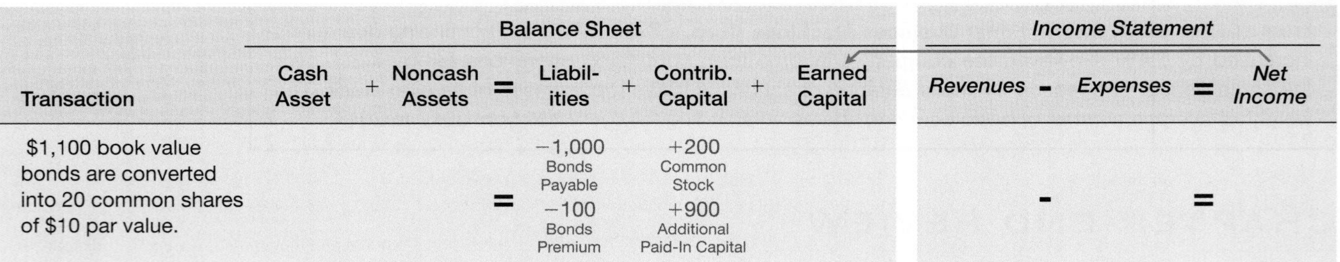

	Balance Sheet					Income Statement		
Transaction	Cash Asset	+ Noncash Assets	= Liabilities	+ Contrib. Capital	+ Earned Capital	Revenues	− Expenses	= Net Income
$1,100 book value bonds are converted into 20 common shares of $10 par value.			= −1,000 Bonds Payable −100 Bonds Premium	+200 Common Stock +900 Additional Paid-In Capital			−	=

JOURNALIZE

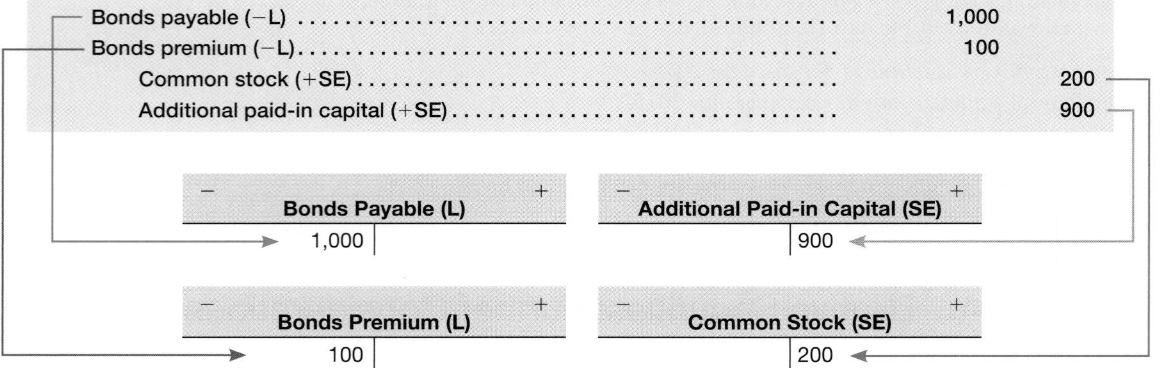

Bonds payable (−L)	1,000	
Bonds premium (−L)	100	
Common stock (+SE)		200
Additional paid-in capital (+SE)		900

POST

The key financial statement effects of this transaction are:

- The bond's face value ($1,000) and unamortized premium ($100) of the bonds are removed from the balance sheet.
- Common stock increases by the par value of the shares issued (20 shares × $10 par = $200) and additional paid-in capital increases for the balance ($900).
- There is no effect on income from this conversion unless an interest accrual is required.

One final note: the potentially dilutive effect of convertible securities is taken into account in the computation of diluted earnings per share (DEPS). Specifically, the diluted EPS computation assumes conversion at the beginning of the year (or when the security is issued if during the year). The earnings available to common shares in the numerator are increased by any forgone after-tax interest expense or preferred dividends, and the additional shares to be issued in the conversion increase the shares outstanding in the denominator.

Stock Rights

Corporations often issue **stock rights** that give the holder an option to acquire a specified number of shares of capital stock under prescribed conditions and within a stated period. The evidence of stock rights is a certificate called a **stock warrant**. Stock rights are issued for several reasons that include the following:

- To compensate outside parties (such as underwriters, promoters, board members, and other professionals) for services provided to the company;
- As a preemptive right that gives existing stockholders the first chance to buy additional shares when the corporation decides to raise additional equity capital through share issuances;
- To compensate officers and other employees of the corporation (rights in this form are referred to as **stock options**);
- To enhance the marketability of other securities issued by the company (an example is issuing rights to purchase common stock with convertible bonds).

Stock rights or warrants specify the:

- Number of rights represented by the warrant
- Option price per share (which can be zero)
- Number of rights needed to obtain a share of the stock
- Expiration date of the rights
- Instructions for the exercise of rights

Accounting for stock rights is complex. The goals of this discussion are to understand the essence of (1) stock rights issued to current stockholders and (2) stock options issued to employees and others.

Stock rights issued to current stockholders have three important dates: (1) Announcement date of the rights offering; (2) Issuance date of the rights; and (3) Expiration date of the rights. Between the announcement date and the issuance date, the price of the stock will reflect the value of the rights. After the issuance date, the shares and the rights trade separately. Shareholders can exercise their rights, sell their stock, or allow the rights to lapse.

To illustrate, assume on December 10, 2014, a company announces the issue of rights to purchase one additional share of its $5 par value common stock for every 10 shares currently held on January 1, 2015. The exercise price per share is $20 and the rights expire September 1, 2015. Assume further that 7,000 of the rights are exercised.

- No recognition is required at the announcement date and at the issuance date.
- The first entry is made when the first stock right is exercised. We give only the summary entry that would be appropriate after September 1, 2015.

Sept 1: To record the issuance of 7,000 shares of common stock on exercise of stock rights:
The financial statement effects and related entries would be (amounts in millions):

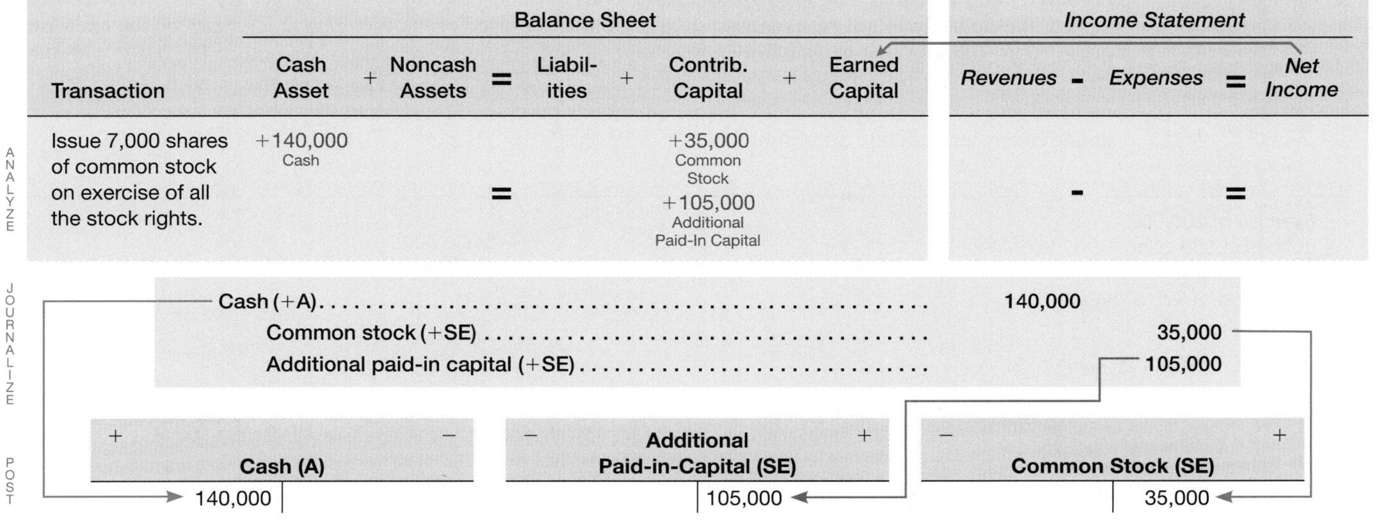

	Balance Sheet									Income Statement				
Transaction	Cash Asset	+	Noncash Assets	=	Liabilities	+	Contrib. Capital	+	Earned Capital	Revenues	−	Expenses	=	Net Income
Issue 7,000 shares of common stock on exercise of all the stock rights.	+140,000 Cash			=			+35,000 Common Stock +105,000 Additional Paid-In Capital				−		=	

ANALYZE

JOURNALIZE

	Dr.	Cr.
Cash (+A)	140,000	
Common stock (+SE)		35,000
Additional paid-in capital (+SE)		105,000

POST

+ Cash (A) −		− Additional Paid-in-Capital (SE) +		− Common Stock (SE) +	
140,000			105,000		35,000

Stock Options

Accounting for stock options has been a contentious issue for a number of years. Accounting standard setters, on the one hand, argue that the options to purchase a corporation's stock at a discount (or even without a discount) are valuable. They point to the willingness of senior management and others to accept stock options instead of cash in payment for services rendered as evidence of their value. Thus, the FASB concluded that the fair value of each stock option award must be recognized as an expense on the firm's income statement.

However, senior managements of start-up firms typically argue that it is necessary in the face of cash shortages to compensate those providing service at least partly using stock options. If these option grants are treated as an expense, it will cause their firms to appear less profitable, thereby stifling investment and business growth. Those arguing against recognizing an expense also point to the difficulties in obtaining precise values for these options.

These difficulties are real, but methods of valuing options do exist that provide reasonable estimates of option values. The FASB decided that such awards are expenses and the expense must be reported at the fair value of the option grant. For example, in Note 13 to its 2014 10-K report, Pfizer reports the fair value of stock option grants to be \$196.2 million (44.6 million options granted × \$4.40 per option).

Stock option grants normally require a vesting period. The **vesting period** is a period of time during which the employee is not allowed to exercise the stock option. For example, a stock option may expire in 5 years and vest over a period of 3 years. Such an option would be exercisable in the fourth or fifth year of its life. Rather than recognizing the entire option value as compensation expense at the time that the option grant is awarded, GAAP requires that the fair value of the option be recorded ratably over the vesting period.

To illustrate stock option accounting, suppose that on January 1, 2015, a company grants options to purchase 200,000 shares to senior management as part of its performance bonus plan. The options are granted with an exercise price of \$30 (the current price), and can be exercised after vesting in 2 years. The firm uses an accepted valuation method (not discussed here) to obtain a fair value of \$10 per option. The accounting and financial statement effects and related entries for 2015 would be:

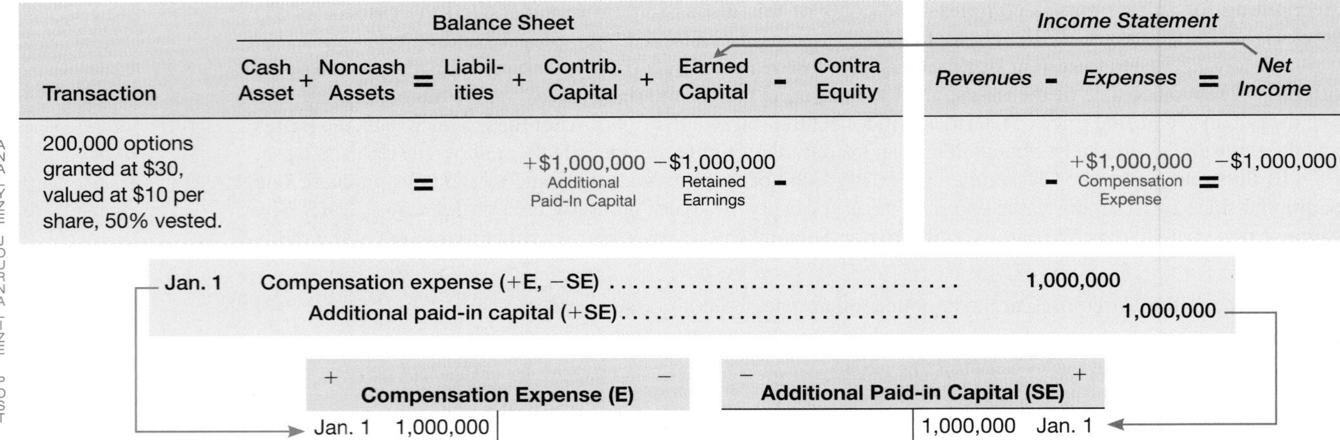

A similar entry is required in 2016, bringing the total stock-based compensation expense to \$2 million. Once vested, the option will not be exercised unless the market price of the common stock exceeds the exercise price. Next, suppose that its stock price rises and all options are exercised on November 15, 2017, with the stock being issued from treasury shares purchased previously at \$25. The accounting and financial statement effects follow. In effect, senior management has purchased these shares by contributing \$2 million in employment services and \$6 million in cash.

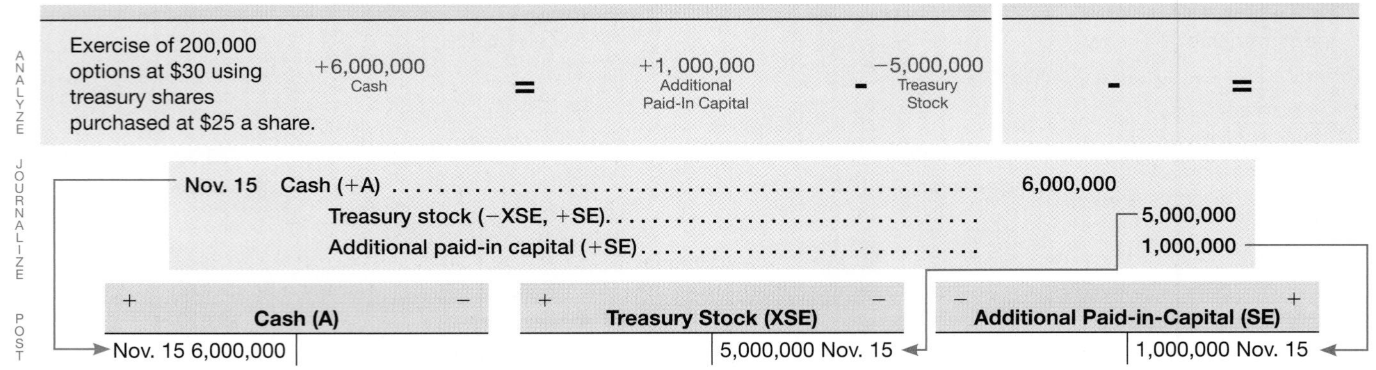

APPENDIX 11A REVIEW

Kallapur, Inc. has issued convertible debentures: each $1,000 bond is convertible into 200 shares of $1 par common stock. Assume that the bonds were sold at a discount, and that each bond has a current unamortized discount equal to $150.

REQUIRED

1. Using the financial statement effects template, illustrate the effects of the conversion of one of its bonds.
2. Prepare journal entries for the transaction assuming conversion of one bond.
3. Post the journal entries to the related T-accounts.

The solution to this review problem can be found on page 561.

SUMMARY

Describe business financing through stock issuances. (p. 518) LO1

- Contributed capital represents the cumulative cash (or other asset) inflow that the company has received from the sale of various classes of stock, preferred and common.
- Preferred stock receives preference in terms of dividends before common and, if cumulative, receives all dividends not paid in the past before common dividends can be paid. Preferred stock can also be designated as convertible into common stock at the holder's option and at a predetermined conversion ratio. Voting privileges reside only with the common stock.

Explain and account for the issuance and repurchase of stock. (p. 521) LO2

- Common stock is often repurchased by the firm for use in stock award programs or to signal management confidence in the company or simply to return cash to shareholders. Repurchased stock is either cancelled or held for reissue. The repurchase is debited to a contra equity account titled treasury stock.

Describe how operations increase the equity of a business. (p. 525) LO3

- Earned capital includes retained earnings, which represents the cumulative profit that has been retained by the company. Earned capital is increased by income earned and decreased by losses and dividends declared by the firm. Earned capital also includes the effects of items included in other comprehensive income.

Explain and account for dividends and stock splits. (p. 525) LO4

- Dividends in the form of stock decrease retained earnings and increase contributed capital by an equivalent amount.
- A stock split is a proportionate distribution similar in substance to a stock dividend. The new number of shares outstanding must be disclosed. Otherwise, no further accounting is required unless the state of incorporation requires that the par value be proportionally adjusted.

Define and illustrate comprehensive income. (p. 530) LO5

- Comprehensive income includes several additional items not recognized in net income including: adjustments for changes in foreign exchange rates, unrealized changes in available-for-sale securities, and pension liability adjustments. The concept is designed to highlight impacts on net assets that are beyond management's control.

Describe and illustrate the basic and diluted earnings per share computations. (p. 533) LO6

- Earnings per share is a closely watched number reported for all publicly traded firms. Basic EPS is computed as the ratio of net income (less preferred dividends and noncontrolling interests) to the weighted average number of outstanding shares for the period. The value of this performance metric is subject to all the difficulties in measuring net income including the fact that net income can increase due to an acquisition or divestiture that can have no impact on the number of outstanding shares.
- Most analysts are more interested in what is termed diluted earnings per share. This conservative calculation, which, if reported, never exceeds basic EPS, reflects the maximum reduction in basic EPS possible assuming conversion of the convertible securities.
- Stock options that are "in the money" are always dilutive.
- Convertible securities that would be antidilutive are treated as if they were not converted.

LO7 Appendix 11A: Analyze the accounting for convertible securities, stock rights, and stock options. (p. 535)

- Convertible securities are debt and equity instruments, including stock rights, that allow these securities to be exchanged for other securities, typically common stock. The convertible feature adds value to the security to which it is attached.
- Stock options, one form of stock right, allow the holders to exchange them at a specified (strike) price for common stock. This right is valuable and should create an expense when granted to an employee or other individual. Expense recognition is appropriate, using the value obtained by applying an options-pricing model, even though the calculation is not precise. The option will not be exercised unless the market price of the common stock exceeds the strike price.
- Convertible preferred stock and convertible debt securities need to be considered in the calculation of DEPS to the extent conversion reduces reported BEPS.

GUIDANCE ANSWERS . . . YOU MAKE THE CALL

You are the Chief Financial Officer Several points must be considered. (1) Treasury shares are likely to prop up earnings per share (EPS). While the numerator (earnings) is likely dampened by the use of cash for the stock repurchase, EPS is likely to increase because of the reduced shares in the denominator. (2) If the shares are sufficiently undervalued (in management's opinion), the stock repurchase and subsequent resale can provide a better return than some alternative investments. (3) Stock repurchases send a strong signal to the market that management feels its stock is undervalued. This is more credible than merely making that argument with analysts. On the other hand, company cash is diverted from other investments. This is bothersome if such investments are mutually exclusive either now or in the future.

KEY RATIOS

Net income available for common shareholders =
Net income − Net income attributable to noncontrolling interests − Preferred dividends

$$\text{Return on Common Equity (ROCE)} = \frac{\text{Net income available for common shareholders}}{\text{Average common shareholders' equity}}$$

$$\text{Basic earnings per share (BEPS)} = \frac{\text{Net income available for common shareholders}}{\text{Weighted average number of common shares outstanding}}$$

Diluted earnings per share (DEPS) =

$$\frac{\text{Net income available for common shareholders + Add-backs}}{\text{Weighted average number of common shares + Shares of convertible securities and stock options assumed to be converted}}$$

KEY TERMS

Accumulated other comprehensive income (p. 530)
Basic EPS (p. 533)
Book value per share (p. 532)
Call feature (p. 520)
Common stock (p. 519)
Complex capital structure (p. 533)
Comprehensive income (p. 530)
Contributed capital (p. 518)
Conversion feature (p. 521)
Convertible securities (p. 535)
Diluted EPS (p. 533)
Dilutive securities (p. 533)
Dividend preference (p. 520)
Earned capital (p. 519)
Liquidating value (p. 520)
Liquidation preference (p. 520)
Noncontrolling interest (p. 519)
Participation feature (p. 521)
Par value (p. 519)

Preferred stock (p. 520)
Shares authorized (p. 519)
Shares issued (p. 519)
Shares outstanding (p. 519)
Simple capital structure (p. 533)
Stock dividends (p. 527)
Stock options (p. 537)
Stock rights (p. 537)
Stock split (p. 529)
Stock warrant (p. 537)
Treasury stock (p. 523)
Vesting period (p. 538)

Assignments with the MBC logo in the margin are available in myBusinessCourse. See the Preface of the book for details.

MULTIPLE CHOICE

Multiple Choice Answers
1. d 2. a 3. a 4. d 5. d

1. Suppose Pfizer issues 100,000 shares of its common stock, $0.05 par value, to obtain a warehouse and the accompanying land when the price of the stock is $22.00. Which one of the following statements is not true? 
   a. The newly acquired assets will increase total assets by $2.2 million.
   b. Retained earnings are unaffected.
   c. The common stock account increases by $5,000.
   d. Total shareholders' equity increases by $2,195,000.

2. Assume Pfizer resells 10,000 shares of its stock that were purchased when the market price of the stock was $25. If the shares are resold for $22, which one of the following statements holds? 
   a. Additional paid-in capital decreases by $30,000.
   b. The treasury stock account increases by $30,000.
   c. Additional paid-in capital increases by $30,000.
   d. The treasury stock account decreases by $30,000.

3. Suppose Pfizer declares a 200,000 common stock dividend (par $0.05) when the market value of a share is $20.00. Which one of the following statements is true? 
   a. The common stock account increases by $10,000.
   b. Additional paid-in capital decreases by $3.99 million.
   c. Retained earnings increases by $4 million.
   d. Additional paid-in capital increases by $4 million.

4. Which of the following statements is true? 
   a. When a *large stock dividend* is paid, retained earnings are reduced by the market value of the shares distributed.
   b. Neither stock dividends nor stock splits affect basic earnings per share calculations.
   c. A three-for-one stock split increases the total outstanding shares by 300%.
   d. A stock split has no financial statement effects because it is not a monetary transaction.

5. Which of the following statements is not true in relation to diluted EPS (DEPS)?
   a. Stock options that are in the money will always cause DEPS to be less than basic EPS.
   b. Convertible bonds, if dilutive, will cause changes in both the numerator and the denominator of DEPS.
   c. Stock analysts tend to concentrate their attention on DEPS instead of basic EPS.
   d. A company's only equity contract that can lead to dilution is stock options.

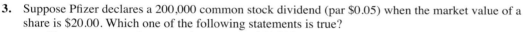

QUESTIONS

Q11-1. Define *par value stock*. What is the significance of a stock's par value from an accounting and analysis perspective?

Q11-2. What are the basic differences between preferred stock and common stock? What are the typical features of preferred stock?

Q11-3. What features make preferred stock similar to debt? Similar to common stock?

Q11-4. What is meant by dividend arrearage on preferred stock? If dividends are two years in arrears on $500,000 of 6% preferred stock, and dividends are declared at the end of this year, what amount of total dividends must preferred shareholders receive before any distributions are made to common shareholders?

Q11-5. Distinguish between authorized stock and issued stock. Why might the number of shares issued be more than the number of shares outstanding?

Q11-6. Describe the difference between contributed capital and earned capital. Specifically, how can earned capital be considered as an investment by the company's shareholders?

Q11-7. How does the account "additional paid-in capital" (APIC) arise? What inferences, if any, can you draw from the amount of APIC as reported on the balance sheet relative to the common stock amount in relation to the financial condition of the company?

Q11-8. Define *stock split*. What are the major reasons for a stock split?

Q11-9. Define *treasury stock*. Why might a corporation acquire treasury stock? How is treasury stock reported in the balance sheet?

Q11-10. If a corporation purchases 600 shares of its own common stock at $10 per share and resells them at $14 per share, where would the $2,400 increase in capital be reported in the financial statements? Why is no gain reported?

Q11-11. A corporation has total stockholders' equity of $4,628,000 and one class of $2 par value common stock. The corporation has 500,000 shares authorized; 300,000 shares issued; 260,000 shares outstanding; and 40,000 shares as treasury stock. What is its book value per share?

Q11-12. What is a stock dividend? How does a common stock dividend distributed to common shareholders affect their respective ownership interests?

Q11-13. What is the difference between the accounting for a small stock dividend and the accounting for a large stock dividend?

Q11-14. Employee stock options have a potentially dilutive effect on earnings per share (EPS) that is recognized in the diluted EPS computation. What can companies do to offset these dilutive effects and how might this action affect the balance sheet?

Q11-15. What information is reported in a statement of stockholders' equity?

Q11-16. What items are typically reported under the stockholders' equity category of other comprehensive income (OCI)?

Q11-17. What is a stock option vesting period? How does the vesting period affect the recognition of compensation expense for stock options?

Q11-18. Describe the accounting for a convertible bond. Would this accounting ever result in the recognition of a gain in the income statement?

MINI EXERCISES

LO1 **M11-19. Analyzing and Identifying Financial Statement Effects of Stock Issuances**

On June 1, Beatty Corp. issues (*a*) 8,000 shares of $50 par value preferred stock at $68 cash per share and it issues (*b*) 12,000 shares of $1 par value common stock at $10 cash per share.

a. Do these transactions increase contributed capital or earned capital?

b. What is the effect of these transactions on Beatty Corp.'s income statement?

c. What are the differences between the preferred stock and the common stock issued by Beatty Corp.?

LO2 **M11-20. Analyzing and Identifying Financial Statement Effects of Stock Issuances**

On September 1, Magliolo, Inc., (*a*) issues 18,000 shares of $10 par value preferred stock at $48 cash per share and (*b*) issues 120,000 shares of $2 par value common stock at $37 cash per share.

a. Using the financial statement effects template, illustrate the effects of these two issuances.

b. Prepare the journal entries for the two issuances.

c. Post the journal entries from *b* to the related T-accounts.

LO2 **M11-21. Distinguishing between Common Stock and Additional Paid-in Capital**

Cisco Systems
NASDAQ :: CSCO

Following is the stockholders' equity section from the **Cisco Systems, Inc.**, balance sheet (in millions, except par value).

Shareholders' equity	July 26, 2014
Preferred stock, no par value: 5 shares authorized; none issued and outstanding	$ —
Common stock and additional paid-in capital, $0.001 par value: 20,000 shares authorized; 5,107 shares issued and outstanding	41,884
Retained earnings	14,093
Accumulated other comprehensive income	677
Total Cisco shareholders' equity	56,654
Noncontrolling interests	7
Total equity	$56,661

For the $41,884 million reported as "common stock and additional paid-in capital," what portion is common stock and what portion is additional paid-in capital? Explain.

M11-22. Identifying and Analyzing Financial Statement Effects of Stock Issuance and Repurchase

LO2

On January 1, 2016, Bartov Company issues 5,000 shares of $100 par value preferred stock at $250 cash per share. On March 1, the company repurchases 5,000 shares of previously issued $1 par value common stock at $83 cash per share.

a. Using the financial statement effects template, illustrate the effects of these two transactions.
b. Prepare the journal entries for the two transactions.
c. Post the journal entries from *b* to the related T-accounts.

M11-23. Assessing the Financial Statement Effects of a Stock Split

LO4

Starbucks Corporation
NASDAQ :: SBUX

In its second quarter 2015 10-Q, **Starbucks Corporation** included the following information:

On April 9, 2015, we effected a two-for-one stock split of our $0.001 par value common stock for shareholders of record as of March 30, 2015. All share and per-share data in our consolidated financial statements and notes has been retroactively adjusted to reflect this stock split.

Starbucks effected this stock split as a large stock dividend. What changes has Starbucks made to its balance sheet as a result of this action?

M11-24. Computing Basic and Diluted Earnings per Share

LO2, 6

Zeller Corporation began 2015 with 120,000 shares of common stock and 16,000 shares of convertible preferred stock outstanding. On March 1 an additional 10,000 shares of common stock were issued. On August 1, another 16,000 shares of common stock were issued. On November 1, 6,000 shares of common stock were acquired for the treasury. The preferred stock has a $2 per-share dividend rate, and each share may be converted into one share of common stock. Zeller Corporation's 2015 net income is $501,000.

a. Compute basic earnings per share for 2015.
b. Compute diluted earnings per share for 2015.
c. If the preferred stock were not convertible, Zeller Corporation would have a simple capital structure. How would this change Zeller's earnings per share presentation?

M11-25. Assessing Common Stock and Treasury Stock Balances

LO2, 6

Toyota Motor Corporation (ADR)
NYSE :: TM

Following is the stockholders' equity section from the **Toyota Motor Corporation**'s balance sheet for the 2015 fiscal year, which ended on March 31, 2015.

Toyota Motor Corporation Shareholders' Equity (Millions of Yen)	March 31, 2015
Common stock, no par value: authorized 10,000,000,000 shares, issued 3,417,997,492 shares at March 31, 2015	¥ 397,050
Additional paid-in capital	547,054
Retained earnings	15,591,947
Accumulated other comprehensive income (loss)	1,477,545
Treasury stock, at cost: 271,183,861 shares at March 31, 2015	(1,225,465)
Total Toyota Motor Corporation shareholders' equity	¥16,788,131

a. Toyota has repurchased 271,183,861 shares that comprise its March 31, 2015 treasury stock account. Compute the number of outstanding shares as of March 31, 2015.
b. Assume that all of this treasury stock had been acquired in one purchase on July 1, 2014. What would have been the effect on the denominator of the basic EPS calculation?

LO4

M11-26. Identifying and Analyzing Financial Statement Effects of Cash Dividends

Freid Corp. has outstanding 6,000 shares of $50 par value, 6% preferred stock, and 40,000 shares of $1 par value common stock. The company has $328,000 of retained earnings. At year-end, the company declares and pays the regular $3 per share cash dividend on preferred stock and a $2.20 per share cash dividend on common stock.

a. Using the financial statement effects template, illustrate the effects of these two dividend payments.
b. Prepare the journal entries for the two dividend payments.
c. Post the journal entries from *b* to the related T-accounts.

LO4

M11-27. Analyzing and Identifying Financial Statement Effects of Stock Dividends

Dutta Corp. has outstanding 70,000 shares of $5 par value common stock. At year-end, the company declares and issues a 4% common stock dividend when the market price of the stock is $21 per share.

a. Using the financial statement effects template, illustrate the effects of this dividend declaration and payment.
b. Prepare the journal entries for the stock dividend declaration and payment.
c. Post the journal entries from *b* to the related T-accounts.

LO4

M11-28. Analyzing, Identifying, and Explaining the Effects of a Stock Split

On September 1, Weiss Company has 250,000 shares of $15 par value ($165 market value) common stock that are issued and outstanding. Its balance sheet on that date shows the following account balances relating to the common stock.

Common stock.	$3,750,000
Paid-in capital in excess of par value.	2,250,000

On September 2, Weiss splits its stock 3-for-2 and reduces the par value to $10 per share.

a. How many shares of common stock are issued and outstanding immediately after the stock split?
b. What is the dollar balance of the common stock account immediately after the stock split?
c. What is the likely reason that Weiss Company split its stock?

LO4

M11-29. Distributing Cash Dividends to Preferred and Common Shareholders

Dechow Company has outstanding 20,000 shares of $50 par value, 6% cumulative preferred stock, and 80,000 shares of $10 par value common stock. The company declares and pays cash dividends amounting to $160,000.

a. If no arrearage on the preferred stock exists, how much in total dividends, and in dividends per share, is paid to each class of stock?
b. If one year's dividend arrearage on the preferred stock exists, how much in total dividends, and in dividends per share, is paid to each class of stock?

LO3, 4

M11-30. Analyzing and Preparing a Retained Earnings Reconciliation

Use the following data to prepare the 2015 retained earnings reconciliation for Bamber Company.

Total retained earnings, December 31, 2014	$347,000
Stock dividends declared and paid in 2015.	28,000
Cash dividends declared and paid in 2015	35,000
Net income for 2015.	94,000

LO4

M11-31. Accounting for Large Stock Dividend and Stock Split

Watts Corporation has 40,000 shares of $10 par value common stock outstanding and retained earnings of $820,000. The company declares a 100% stock dividend. The market price at the declaration is $17 per share.

a. Prepare the general journal entry for the stock dividend.
b. Assume that the company splits its stock two shares for one share and reduces the par value from $10 to $5 rather than declaring a 100% stock dividend. How does the accounting for the stock split differ from the accounting for the 100% stock dividend?

M11-32. Computing Basic and Diluted Earnings per Share

LO6

During 2015, Park Corporation had 50,000 shares of $10 par value common stock and 10,000 shares of 8%, $50 par value convertible preferred stock outstanding. Each share of preferred stock may be converted into three shares of common stock. Park Corporation's 2015 net income was $440,000.

a. Compute the basic earnings per share for 2015.
b. Compute the diluted earnings per share for 2015.

M11-33. Computing Earnings per Share

LO6

Kingery Corporation began the calendar (and fiscal) year with a simple structure consisting of 38,000 shares of common stock outstanding. On May 1, 10,000 additional shares were issued, and another 1,000 shares were issued on September 1. The company had a net income for the year of $234,000.

a. Compute the earnings per share of common stock.
b. Assume that the company also had 6,000 shares of 6%, $50 par value cumulative preferred stock outstanding throughout the year. Compute the basic earnings per share of common stock.

M11-34. Defining and Computing Earnings per Share

LO6

Siemens AG (ADR)
OTCMKTS :: SIEGY

Siemens AG reports the following basic and diluted earnings per share in its 2014 annual report.

	Year Ended September 30,	
(shares in thousands; earnings per share in €)	2014	2013
Income from continuing operations attributable to shareholders of Siemens AG . . .	€ 5,267	€ 4,059
Weighted average shares outstanding—basic.	843,449	843,819
Effect of dilutive share-based payment	8,485	8,433
Weighted average shares outstanding—diluted	€851,934	€852,252
Basic earnings per share (from continuing operations)	€ 6.24	€ 4.81
Diluted earnings per share (from continuing operations)	€ 6.18	€ 4.76

a. Describe the accounting definitions for basic and diluted earnings per share.
b. Identify the Siemens numbers that make up both EPS computations.
c. What calculation limits the reported value of diluted EPS?

M11-35. Analyzing Stock Option Expense for Income

LO7

Merck & Co.
NYSE :: MRK

Merck & Co., Inc., reported net income attributable to Merck & Co., Inc. of $11,920 million for the 2014 fiscal year. Its 2014 10-K report contained the following information regarding its stock options.

Employee stock options are granted to purchase shares of Company stock at the fair market value at the time of grant. These awards generally vest one-third each year over a three-year period, with a contractual term of 7-10 years . . . The weighted average exercise price of options granted in 2014 was $58.14 per option . . . The weighted average fair value of options granted in 2014 was $6.79 per option.

a. Merck granted 4,872,000 options to employees in 2014. Using a journal entry, show how the stock option grants would be recorded in 2014. (Assume all grants took place on January 1, 2014.)
b. How does the granting of stock options affect EPS?
c. Merck employees exercised 39,293,000 options in 2014, paying a total of $1,560 million in cash to the company. Using a summary journal entry, show how these option exercises would be recorded in 2014.
d. How does the exercise of stock options affect EPS?

M11-36. Examining the Effect of Stock Transactions

LO2, 4, 6

Year 1: Noreen Company issues 10,000 shares of its no-par common stock for $30/share in cash.
Year 2: Noreen Company buys 1,000 shares of its no-par common stock for $28/share in cash.
Year 3: Noreen Company declares but has not yet paid a dividend on its no-par common stock of $2 per share. The company's basic earnings per share were $10 in the third year.

Indicate the effect (increase, decrease, no effect) of each of these stock decisions for each year on the items listed.

Year	Total Assets	Total Liabilities	Total Stockholders' Equity	EPS	Operating Income
1					
2					
3					

LO1, 2, 3, 6

M11-37. Reporting Stockholders' Equity

Bonner Company began business this year and immediately sold 600,000 common shares for $18,000,000 cash and paid $1,000,000 in common dividends. At midyear, the firm bought back some of its own shares. The company reports the following additional information at year-end:

Net income	$5,000,000
Common stock, at par	$6,000,000
Retained earnings beginning of year	$ 0
Common shares authorized:	1,000,000
Common shares outstanding at year's end:.	550,000

a. What was the average sales price of a common share when issued?
b. What is the par value of the common?
c. How much is in the Additional paid-in capital account at the end of the year?
d. Determine the retained earnings amount at the end of the year.
e. How many shares of stock are in the treasury at the end of the year?
f. Compute BEPS.

LO6

JetBlue
NASDAQ :: JBLU

M11-38. Analyzing Earnings Per Share Effects of Convertible Securities

JetBlue Airways Corporation reports the following data in its 2014 10-K. The data relate to the corporation's computation of its earnings per share calculations. (Dollar and share data are in millions.)

Numerator:	**2014**
Net income	$401
Effect of dilutive securities:	
Interest on convertible debt, net of income taxes and profit sharing	7
Net income applicable to common stockholders after assumed conversions for diluted earnings per share	$408
Denominator:	
Weighted average shares outstanding for basic earnings per share	294.7
Effect of dilutive securities:	
Employee stock options and restricted stock units	2.4
Convertible debt	46.2
Adjusted weighted average shares outstanding and assumed conversions for diluted earnings per share	343.3

REQUIRED

a. What is the objective behind the calculation of diluted EPS?
b. Calculate JetBlue's basic EPS.
c. Calculate JetBlue's diluted EPS.
d. JetBlue excluded 6.9 million stock options from the computation of diluted EPS. Under what circumstances would this be appropriate?

EXERCISES

E11-39. Identifying and Analyzing Financial Statement Effects of Stock Transactions LO2

Lipe Company reports the following transactions relating to its stock accounts.

Feb. 20 Issued 10,000 shares of $1 par value common stock at $25 cash per share.
Feb. 21 Issued 15,000 shares of $100 par value, 8% preferred stock at $275 cash per share.
Jun. 30 Purchased 2,000 shares of its own common stock at $15 cash per share.
Sep. 25 Sold 1,000 shares of the treasury stock at $21 cash per share.

a. Using the financial statement effects template, illustrate the effects of these transactions.
b. Prepare the journal entries for these transactions.
c. Post the journal entries from *b* to the related T-accounts.

E11-40. Analyzing and Identifying Financial Statement Effects of Stock Transactions LO2

McNichols Corp. reports the following transactions relating to its stock accounts.

Jan. 15 Issued 25,000 shares of $5 par value common stock at $17 cash per share.
Jan. 20 Issued 6,000 shares of $50 par value, 8% preferred stock at $78 cash per share.
Mar. 31 Purchased 3,000 shares of its own common stock at $20 cash per share.
June 25 Sold 2,000 shares of the treasury stock at $26 cash per share.
July 15 Sold the remaining 1,000 shares of treasury stock at $19 cash per share.

a. Using the financial statement effects template, illustrate the effects of these transactions.
b. Prepare the journal entries for these transactions.
c. Post the journal entries from *b* to the related T-accounts.

E11-41. Analyzing and Computing Average Issue Price and Treasury Stock Cost LO1, 2, 6

The Coca-Cola Company
NYSE :: KO

Following is the stockholders' equity section from the **The Coca-Cola Company** 2014 balance sheet. (All amounts in millions except par value.)

The Coca-Cola Company Shareowners' Equity	December 31, 2014
Common stock—$0.25 par value; authorized—11,200 shares; issued—7,040 shares. . . .	$ 1,760
Capital surplus	13,154
Reinvested earnings. . . .	63,408
Accumulated other comprehensive income (loss)	(5,777)
Treasury stock, at cost—2,674 shares. . . .	(42,225)
Equity attributable to shareowners of The Coca-Cola Company	$30,320

a. Compute the number of shares outstanding.
b. At what average price were the Coca-Cola shares issued?
c. At what average cost were the Coca-Cola treasury stock shares purchased?
d. How should treasury stock be treated in calculating EPS?

E11-42. Analyzing and Distributing Cash Dividends to Preferred and Common Stocks LO4

Moser Company began business on March 1, 2015. At that time, it issued 20,000 shares of $60 par value, 7% cumulative preferred stock and 100,000 shares of $5 par value common stock. Through the end of 2017, there has been no change in the number of preferred and common shares outstanding.

a. Assume that Moser declared and paid cash dividends of $0 in 2015, $183,000 in 2016, and $200,000 in 2017. Compute the total cash dividends and the dividends per share paid to each class of stock in 2015, 2016, and 2017.
b. Assume that Moser declared and paid cash dividends of $0 in 2015, $84,000 in 2016, and $150,000 in 2017. Compute the total cash dividends and the dividends per share paid to each class of stock in 2015, 2016, and 2017.

E11-43. Computing Basic and Diluted Earnings per Share LO6

Nichols Corporation began the year 2015 with 25,000 shares of common stock and 5,000 shares of convertible preferred stock outstanding. On May 1, an additional 9,000 shares of common stock were issued. On July 1, 6,000 shares of common stock were acquired for the treasury. On September 1, the 6,000 treasury shares of common stock were reissued. The preferred stock has a $4 per-share dividend rate, and each share may be converted into two shares of common stock. Nichols Corporation's 2015 net income is $230,000.

a. Compute earnings per share for 2015.
b. Compute diluted earnings per share for 2015.
c. If the preferred stock were not convertible, Nichols Corporation would have a simple capital structure. How would this change Nichols's earnings per share presentation?

LO4, 6 

E11-44. Analyzing and Distributing Cash Dividends to Preferred and Common Stocks
Potter Company has outstanding 15,000 shares of $50 par value, 8% preferred stock and 50,000 shares of $5 par value common stock. During its first three years in business, it declared and paid no cash dividends in the first year, $280,000 in the second year, and $60,000 in the third year.

a. If the preferred stock is cumulative, determine the total amount of cash dividends paid to each class of stock in each of the three years.
b. If the preferred stock is noncumulative, determine the total amount of cash dividends paid to each class of stock in each of the three years.
c. How should each type of preferred dividends be treated in calculating EPS?

LO1, 2 Homework MBC

Chipotle Mexican Grill
NYSE :: CMG

E11-45. Analyzing and Computing Issue Price, Treasury Stock Cost, and Shares Outstanding
The following is the stockholders' equity section from **Chipotle Mexican Grill, Inc.**'s balance sheet (in thousands, except per share data).

Shareholders' Equity	December 31, 2014
Preferred stock, $0.01 par value, 600,000 shares authorized, no shares issued as of December 31, 2014	$ —
Common stock, $0.01 par value, 230,000 shares authorized, and 35,394 shares issued as of December 31, 2014	354
Additional paid-in capital	1,038,932
Treasury stock, at cost, 4,367 common shares at December 31, 2014	(748,759)
Accumulated other comprehensive income	(429)
Retained earnings	1,722,271
Total shareholders' equity	$2,012,369

a. Show the computation to derive the $354 thousand for common stock.
b. At what average price has Chipotle issued its common stock?
c. How many shares of Chipotle common stock are outstanding as of December 31, 2014?
d. At what average cost has Chipotle repurchased its treasury stock as of December 31, 2014?
e. Give three reasons why a company such as Chipotle would want to repurchase almost $750 million of its common stock.

LO4 

E11-46. Analyzing and Distributing Cash Dividends to Preferred and Common Stocks
Skinner Company began business on June 30, 2015. At that time, it issued 18,000 shares of $50 par value, 6% cumulative preferred stock and 90,000 shares of $10 par value common stock. Through the end of 2017, there has been no change in the number of preferred and common shares outstanding.

a. Assume that Skinner declared and paid cash dividends of $63,000 in 2015, $0 in 2016, and $378,000 in 2017. Compute the total cash dividends and the dividends per share paid to each class of stock in 2015, 2016, and 2017.
b. Assume that Skinner declared and paid cash dividends of $0 in 2015, $108,000 in 2016, and $189,000 in 2017. Compute the total cash dividends and the dividends per share paid to each class of stock in 2015, 2016, and 2017.

LO4 

E11-47. Analyzing and Identifying Financial Statement Effects of Dividends
Chaney Company has outstanding 25,000 shares of $10 par value common stock. It also has $405,000 of retained earnings. Near the current year-end, the company declares and pays a cash dividend of $1.90 per share and declares and issues a 4% stock dividend. The market price of the stock at the declaration date is $35 per share.

a. Using the financial statement effects template, illustrate the effects of these two separate dividends.
b. Prepare the journal entries for these two separate dividend transactions.
c. Post the journal entries from *b* to the related T-accounts.

E11-48. Identifying and Analyzing Financial Statement Effects of Dividends LO3, 4

The stockholders' equity of Palepu Company at December 31, 2015, appears below.

Common stock, $10 par value, 200,000 shares authorized; 80,000 shares issued and outstanding	$800,000
Paid-in capital in excess of par value	480,000
Retained earnings	305,000

During 2016, the following transactions occurred:

May 12 Declared and issued a 7% stock dividend; the common stock market value was $18 per share.

Dec. 31 Declared and paid a cash dividend of 75 cents per share.

a. Using the financial statement effects template, illustrate the effects of these transactions.
b. Prepare the journal entries for these transactions.
c. Post the journal entries from *b* to the related T-accounts.
d. Prepare a retained earnings reconciliation for 2016 assuming that the company reports 2016 net income of $283,000.

E11-49. Analyzing and Identifying Financial Statement Effects of Dividends LO3, 4

The stockholders' equity of Kinney Company at December 31, 2015, is shown below:

5% preferred stock, $100 par value, 10,000 shares authorized; 4,000 shares issued and outstanding	$ 400,000
Common stock, $5 par value, 200,000 shares authorized; 50,000 shares issued and outstanding	250,000
Paid-in capital in excess of par value—preferred stock	40,000
Paid-in capital in excess of par value—common stock	300,000
Retained earnings	656,000
Total stockholders' equity	$1,646,000

The following transactions, among others, occurred during 2016.

Apr. 1 Declared and issued a 100% stock dividend on all outstanding shares of common stock. The market value of the stock was $11 per share.

Dec. 7 Declared and issued a 3% stock dividend on all outstanding shares of common stock. The market value of the stock was $14 per share.

Dec. 20 Declared and paid (1) the annual cash dividend on the preferred stock and (2) a cash dividend of 80 cents per common share.

a. Using the financial statement effects template, illustrate the effects of these transactions.
b. Prepare the journal entries for these transactions.
c. Post the journal entries from *b* to the related T-accounts.
d. Prepare a 2016 retained earnings reconciliation assuming that the company reports 2016 net income of $253,000.

E11-50. Analyzing, Identifying, and Explaining the Effects of a Stock Split LO4, 6

On March 1 of the current year, Xie Company has 400,000 shares of $20 par value common stock that are issued and outstanding. Its balance sheet shows the following account balances relating to common stock.

Common stock	$8,000,000
Paid-in capital in excess of par value	3,400,000

On March 2, Xie Company splits its common stock 2-for-1 and reduces the par value to $10 per share.

a. How many shares of common stock are issued and outstanding immediately after the stock split?
b. What is the dollar balance in its common stock account immediately after the stock split?
c. What is the dollar balance in its paid-in capital in excess of par value account immediately after the stock split?
d. What is the effect of a stock split on the calculation of EPS?

LO3, 4

Intuit Inc.
NASDAQ :: INTU

E11-51. Analyzing and Computing Dividends and Effect of Options Exercises
Following is the stockholders' equity section of the **Intuit Inc.** balance sheet (dollars in millions, except par value; shares in thousands). Changes in the company's outstanding shares are due to (1) treasury share purchases by the company and (2) issues of treasury shares for employee stock options.

Stockholders' Equity ($ millions)	July 31, 2014	July 31, 2013
Preferred stock, $0.01 par value		
Authorized—1,345 shares total; 145 shares designated Series A;		
250 shares designated Series B Junior Participating		
Issued and outstanding—none.	$ —	$ —
Common stock, $0.01 par value		
Authorized—750,000 shares		
Outstanding—284,950 shares at July 31, 2014 and 299,503 shares at		
July 31, 2013.	3	3
Additional paid-in capital	3,558	3,198
Treasury stock, at cost.	(6,430)	(4,952)
Accumulated other comprehensive income (loss)	(2)	20
Retained earnings	5,949	5,262
Total stockholders' equity	**$3,078**	**$3,531**

a. In the fiscal year ended July 31, 2014, Intuit reported net income of $907 million. How much did Intuit pay in dividends to its common shareholders?

b. In the fiscal year ended January 31, 2014, Intuit repurchased 22,467 thousand of its common shares. How many shares were issued to employees under stock option plans?

c. Intuit's issuance of shares for stock option plans increased the Additional paid-in capital balance by $74 million. Was the (average) option exercise price greater or less than the (average) amount Intuit paid to acquire the treasury shares that were reissued?

LO2

Merck & Co.
NYSE :: MRK

E11-52. Analyzing and Computing Issue Price, Treasury Stock Cost, and Shares Outstanding
Following is the stockholders' equity section of the **Merck & Co., Inc.**, balance sheet.

Merck & Co., Inc. Stockholders' Equity ($ millions)	Dec. 31, 2014	Dec. 31, 2013
Common stock, $0.50 par value		
Authorized—6,500,000,000 shares		
Issued—3,577,103,522 shares in 2014 and 2013.	$ 1,788	$ 1,788
Other paid-in capital	40,423	40,508
Retained earnings	46,021	39,257
Accumulated other comprehensive loss	(4,323)	(2,197)
	83,909	79,356
Less treasury stock, at cost:		
738,963,326 shares in 2014 and 649,576,808 shares in 2013 . . .	35,262	29,591
Total Merck & Co., Inc. stockholders' equity	$48,647	$49,765

a. Explain the derivation of the $1,788 million in the common stock account.

b. Using December 31, 2014 balances, at what average issue price were the Merck common shares issued?

c. At what average cost was the Merck treasury stock as of December 31, 2014?

d. How many common shares are outstanding as of December 31, 2014?

LO7

McKesson Corporation
NYSE :: MCK

E11-53. Assessing Effects of Employee Stock Options for Income and EPS
The following data is taken from the March 31, 2015, income statement of **McKesson Corporation** (millions, except for per share amounts). McKesson has neither preferred stock nor convertible securities outstanding.

Earnings (Loss) Per Common Share Attributable to McKesson Corporation	
Diluted	
Continuing operations	$ 7.54
Discontinued operations	(1.27)
Total	$ 6.27
Basic	
Continuing operations	$ 7.66
Discontinued operations	(1.29)
Total	$ 6.37
Weighted average common shares	
Diluted	235
Basic	232

a. Estimate McKesson's loss from discontinued operations in the year ended March 31, 2015. Is the amount you calculated before or after tax?

b. Estimate McKesson's net earnings from continuing operations for fiscal year 2015.

c. McKesson reports diluted earnings per share of $6.27 in 2015. What might have caused the dilution?

E11-54. Interpreting Information in the Statement of Shareholders' Equity

LO2, 4

Walt Disney Co.
NYSE :: DIS

The 2014 statement of stockholders' equity for **Walt Disney Co.** is presented below. (Disney includes both par value and additional paid-in capital under the heading "Common Stock." Noncontrolling interests have been excluded for simplicity. All amounts in millions.)

	Equity Attributable to Disney					
	Shares	Common Stock	Retained Earnings	Accumulated Other Comprehensive Income (Loss)	Treasury Stock	Total Disney Equity
Balance at September 28, 2013	1,773	$33,440	$47,758	$(1,187)	$(34,582)	$45,429
Comprehensive income	—	—	7,501	(781)	—	6,720
Equity compensation activity	18	844	—	—	—	844
Common stock repurchases	(84)	—	—	—	(6,527)	(6,527)
Dividends	—	17	(1,525)	—	—	(1,508)
Contributions	—	—	—	—	—	—
Distributions and other	—	—	—	—	—	—
Balance at September 27, 2014	1,707	$34,301	$53,734	$(1,968)	$(41,109)	$44,958

REQUIRED

a. Did Disney issue any additional common shares in fiscal year 2014 (ending on September 27, 2014)?

b. What was Disney's total comprehensive income in 2014?

c. Show how Disney recorded the purchase of treasury shares in 2014 using the financial statement effects template. Prepare the journal entry and post to the related T-accounts.

d. According to its statement of cash flows, Disney paid common dividends of $1,508 million in fiscal year 2014. What might be a possible explanation for the fact that dividends reduced retained earnings by $1,525 million?

PROBLEMS

LO2, 3, 6

P11-55. Analyzing and Identifying Financial Statement Effects of Stock Transactions
The stockholders' equity section of Gupta Company at December 31, 2014, follows.

8% preferred stock, $25 par value, 50,000 shares authorized; 6,800 shares issued and outstanding	$170,000
Common stock, $10 par value, 200,000 shares authorized; 50,000 shares issued and outstanding	500,000
Paid-in capital in excess of par value—preferred stock	68,000
Paid-in capital in excess of par value—common stock	200,000
Retained earnings	270,000

During 2015, the following transactions occurred:

Jan. 10 Issued 28,000 shares of common stock for $17 cash per share.
Jan. 23 Purchased 8,000 shares of common stock for the treasury at $19 cash per share.
Mar. 14 Sold one-half of the treasury shares acquired January 23 for $21 cash per share.
July 15 Issued 3,200 shares of preferred stock for $128,000 cash.
Nov. 15 Sold 1,000 of the treasury shares acquired January 23 for $24 cash per share.

REQUIRED

a. Using the financial statement effects template, illustrate the effects of each transaction.
b. Prepare the journal entries for these transactions.
c. Post the journal entries from *b* to the related T-accounts.
d. Indicate the impact of each transaction on the calculation of basic EPS.
e. Prepare the December 31, 2015, stockholders' equity section of the balance sheet assuming the company reports 2015 net income of $59,000.

LO2, 3, 4, 5, 6

P11-56. Analyzing and Identifying Financial Statement Effects of Stock Transactions
The stockholders' equity of Sougiannis Company at December 31, 2014, follows.

7% Preferred stock, $100 par value, 20,000 shares authorized; 5,000 shares issued and outstanding	$ 500,000
Common stock, $15 par value, 100,000 shares authorized; 40,000 shares issued and outstanding	600,000
Paid-in capital in excess of par value—preferred stock	24,000
Paid-in capital in excess of par value—common stock	360,000
Retained earnings	325,000
Total stockholders' equity	$1,809,000

The following transactions, among others, occurred during 2015.

Jan. 12 Announced a 3-for-1 common stock split, reducing the par value of the common stock to $5 per share. The authorized shares were increased to 300,000 shares.
Sept. 1 Acquired 10,000 shares of common stock for the treasury at $10 cash per share.
Oct. 12 Sold 1,500 treasury shares acquired September 1 at $12 cash per share.
Nov. 21 Issued 5,000 shares of common stock at $11 cash per share.
Dec. 28 Sold 1,200 treasury shares acquired September 1 at $9 cash per share.

REQUIRED

a. Using the financial statement effects template, illustrate the effects of each transaction.
b. Prepare the journal entries for these transactions.
c. Post the journal entries from *b* to the related T-accounts.
d. Indicate the impact of each transaction on the calculation of basic EPS.
e. Prepare the December 31, 2015, stockholders' equity section of the balance sheet assuming that the company reports 2015 net income of $83,000.
f. Compute return on common equity for 2015.

P11-57. Identifying and Analyzing Financial Statement Effects of Stock Transactions LO2, 3, 6

The stockholders' equity of Verrecchia Company at December 31, 2014, follows.

Common stock, $5 par value, 350,000 shares authorized; 150,000 shares issued and outstanding	$750,000
Paid-in capital in excess of par value	600,000
Retained earnings	346,000

During 2015, the following transactions occurred.

- Jan. 5 Issued 10,000 shares of common stock for $12 cash per share.
- Jan. 18 Purchased 4,000 shares of common stock for the treasury at $14 cash per share.
- Mar. 12 Sold one-fourth of the treasury shares acquired January 18 for $17 cash per share.
- July 17 Sold 500 shares of the remaining treasury stock for $13 cash per share.
- Oct. 1 Issued 5,000 shares of 8%, $25 par value preferred stock for $35 cash per share. This is the first issuance of preferred shares from 50,000 authorized shares.

REQUIRED

a. Using the financial statement effects template, illustrate the effects of each transaction.
b. Prepare the journal entries for these transactions.
c. Post the journal entries from *b* to the related T-accounts.
d. Prepare the December 31, 2015, stockholders' equity section of the balance sheet assuming that the company reports net income of $72,500 for the year.
e. How will each transaction affect the calculation of basic EPS?

P11-58. Identifying and Analyzing Financial Statement Effects of Stock Transactions LO2, 4

Following is the stockholders' equity of Dennis Corporation at December 31, 2014.

8% preferred stock, $50 par value, 10,000 shares authorized; 7,000 shares issued and outstanding	$ 350,000
Common stock, $20 par value, 50,000 shares authorized; 25,000 shares issued and outstanding	500,000
Paid-in capital in excess of par value—preferred stock	70,000
Paid-in capital in excess of par value—common stock	385,000
Retained earnings	238,000
Total stockholders' equity	$1,543,000

The following transactions, among others, occurred during 2015.

- Jan. 15 Issued 1,000 shares of preferred stock for $62 cash per share.
- Jan. 20 Issued 4,000 shares of common stock at $36 cash per share.
- May 18 Announced a 2-for-1 common stock split, reducing the par value of the common stock to $10 per share. The authorization was increased to 100,000 shares.
- June 1 Issued 2,000 shares of common stock for $60,000 cash.
- Sept. 1 Purchased 2,500 shares of common stock for the treasury at $18 cash per share.
- Oct. 12 Sold 900 treasury shares at $21 cash per share.
- Dec. 22 Issued 500 shares of preferred stock for $59 cash per share.

REQUIRED

a. Using the financial statement effects template, illustrate the effects of each transaction.
b. Prepare the journal entries for these transactions.
c. Post the journal entries from *b* to the related T-accounts.

P11-59. Analyzing and Interpreting Stockholders' Equity and EPS LO1, 2, 5, 7

Procter & Gamble
NYSE :: PG

Following is the stockholders' equity section of the balance sheet for **The Procter & Gamble Company** along with selected earnings and dividend data. For simplicity, balances for noncontrolling interests have been left out of income and shareholders' equity information.

($ millions except per share amounts)	2014	2013
Net earnings attributable to Procter & Gamble shareholders	$11,643	$11,312
Common dividends	6,658	6,275
Preferred dividends	253	244
Basic net earnings per common share	$ 4.19	$ 4.04
Diluted net earnings per common share	$ 4.01	$ 3.86
Shareholders' equity:		
Convertible class A preferred stock, stated value $1 per share	$ 1,111	$ 1,137
Common stock, stated value $1 per share	4,009	4,009
Additional paid-in capital	63,911	63,538
Treasury stock, at cost (shares held: 2014—1,298.4, 2013—1,266.9)	(75,805)	(71,966)
Retained earnings	84,990	80,197
Accumulated other comprehensive income/(loss)	(7,662)	(7,499)
Other	(1,340)	(1,352)
Shareholders' equity attributable to Procter & Gamble shareholders	$69,214	$68,064

a. Compute the number of shares outstanding at the end of each fiscal year. Estimate the average number of shares outstanding during 2014. How do these two computations compare?

b. Calculate the average cost per share of the shares held as treasury stock at the end of each fiscal year.

c. In 2014, preferred shareholders elected to convert 3.2 million shares of preferred stock ($26 million book value) into common stock. Rather than issue new shares, the company granted to the preferred shareholders 3.2 million common shares held in treasury stock with a total cost of $22 million. Prepare a journal entry to illustrate how this transaction would have been recorded.

d. P&G has no convertible debt outstanding. What could explain the reported diluted EPS?

e. Calculate P&G's return on common equity (ROCE) for fiscal 2014.

LO5, 7 **P11-60. Analyzing and Interpreting Equity Accounts and Comprehensive Income**

Google Inc.
NASDAQ :: GOOG

The 2012 and 2013 statements of stockholders' equity for **Google Inc.** are presented below along with portions on Note 12 relating to stockholders' equity.

GOOGLE INC.
Consolidated Statements of Stockholders' Equity
(In millions, except for share amounts which are reflected in thousands)

($ millions)	Class A and Class B Common Stock and Additional Paid-in Capital: Shares	Amount	Accumulated Other Comprehensive Income	Retained Earnings	Total Stock-holders' Equity
Balance at Dec. 31, 2011	324,895	$20,264	$276	$37,605	$58,145
Common stock issued	5,084	736	0	0	736
Stock-based compensation expense		2,692	0	0	2,692
Stock-based compensation tax benefits		166	0	0	166
Tax withholding related to vesting of restricted stock units		(1,023)	0	0	(1,023)
Net income		0	0	10,737	10,737
Other comprehensive income		0	262	0	262
Balance at Dec. 31, 2012	329,979	22,835	538	48,342	71,715
Common stock issued	5,853	1,174	0	0	1,174
Stock-based compensation expense		3,343	0	0	3,343
Stock-based compensation tax benefits		449	0	0	449
Tax withholding related to vesting of restricted stock units		(1,879)	0	0	(1,879)
Net income		0	0	12,920	12,920
Other comprehensive income		0	(413)	0	(413)
Balance at Dec. 31, 2013	335,832	$25,922	$125	$61,262	$87,309

Note 12: Stockholders' Equity

Class A and Class B Common Stock

Our board of directors has authorized two classes of common stock, Class A and Class B. At December 31, 2013, there were 9,000,000,000 and 3,000,000,000 shares authorized and there were 279,325,564 and 56,506,728 shares outstanding of Class A and Class B common stock, $0.001 par value. The rights of the holders of Class A and Class B common stock are identical, except with respect to voting. Each share of Class A common stock is entitled to one vote per share. Each share of Class B common stock is entitled to 10 votes per share. Shares of Class B common stock may be converted at any time at the option of the stockholder and automatically convert upon sale or transfer to Class A common stock. We refer to Class A and Class B common stock as common stock throughout the notes to these financial statements, unless otherwise noted.

Stock Plans

We maintain the 1998 Stock Plan, the 2000 Stock Plan, the 2003 Stock Plan, the 2003 Stock Plan (No. 2), the 2003 Stock Plan (No. 3), the 2004 Stock Plan, the 2012 Stock Plan, and plans assumed through acquisitions, all of which are collectively referred to as the "Stock Plans." Under our Stock Plans, incentive and non-qualified stock options or rights to purchase common stock may be granted to eligible participants. Options are generally granted for a term of 10 years. Under the Stock Plans, we have also issued RSUs. An RSU award is an agreement to issue shares of our stock at the time the award vests. Except for options granted pursuant to our stock option exchange program completed in March 2009 (the Exchange), options granted and RSUs issued to participants under the Stock Plans generally vest over four years contingent upon employment or service with us on the vesting date.

We estimated the fair value of each option award on the date of grant using the BSM option pricing model. Our assumptions about stock-price volatility have been based exclusively on the implied volatilities of publicly traded options to buy our stock with contractual terms closest to the expected life of options granted to our employees. We estimate the expected term based upon the historical exercise behavior of our employees. The risk-free interest rate for periods within the contractual life of the award is based on the U.S. Treasury yield curve in effect at the time of grant.

The following table summarizes the activities for our options for the year ended December 31, 2013:

	Number of Shares	Weighted-Average Exercise Price	Aggregate Intrinsic Value ($ millions)
Balance at December 31, 2012	8,551,395	$405.98	
Granted	1,571	$723.25	
Exercised	(3,299,276)	$355.56	
Forfeited/canceled	(220,827)	$595.92	
Balance at December 31, 2013	5,032,863	$431.00	$3,470

The aggregate intrinsic value is calculated as the difference between the exercise price of the underlying awards and the closing stock price of $1,120.71 of our Class A common stock on December 31, 2013. The weighted-average estimated fair value of options granted during 2013 was $214.39 per share.

REQUIRED

a. What is the difference between Google's Class A common stock and its Class B common stock? Why do they have two different classes of common stock? In fiscal year 2014, Google created shares of Class C capital stock, which participate in any common dividends, but have no voting rights. What might be the purpose of the Class C stock?

b. Google granted 1,571 stock options in 2013. Compute the aggregate fair value of the options that Google granted to employees in 2013.

c. Prepare a journal entry to record the 2013 option grants. Assuming a four-year vesting period, what impact did these grants have on Google's earnings before income taxes in 2013?

d. Google refers to the fair value of options granted as well as the *intrinsic* value of the options. Calculate the aggregate intrinsic value of options granted in 2013. Why is this amount different from the fair value of those options?

e. Google reported net income of $12,920 million in 2013 and basic EPS of $38.82 per share. Estimate the weighted average number of shares used to calculate basic EPS.

f. If all outstanding stock options were exercised in 2013, what would be the impact on Google's basic EPS?

g. Google reported diluted EPS of $38.13 in 2013. Why is this amount different from the answer that you gave in *f*?

CASES AND PROJECTS

LO7

Northrop Grumman
NYSE :: NOC

C11-61. Interpreting Disclosure on Convertible Preferred Securities

Northrop Grumman Corporation reports the following in footnote 4 to its 2008 10-K related to its convertible preferred stock.

Conversion of Preferred Stock – On February 20, 2008, the company's board of directors approved the redemption of the 3.5 million shares of mandatorily redeemable convertible preferred stock on April 4, 2008. Prior to the redemption date, substantially all of the preferred shares were converted into common stock at the election of shareholders. All remaining unconverted preferred shares were redeemed by the company on the redemption date. As a result of the conversion and redemption, the company issued approximately 6.4 million shares of common stock.

REQUIRED

a. What do you believe is meant by the terms "mandatorily redeemable" prior to the words "preferred stock"?

b. Northrop's balance sheet at December 31, 2007, shows preferred stock of $350 million and $0 million on December 31, 2008. Northrop originally sold the preferred shares at par. What was the preferred par value per share?

c. The fair market value of a preferred share, as reported by Northrop on December 31, 2008, was $146. What could account for the substantial increase in the value per share?

d. How should preferred stock be treated in an analysis of a company?

e. Discuss the general effects of the April 4th conversion on Northrop Grumman's balance sheet.

LO1, 2

C11-62. Identifying Corporate Takeover, Stock Ownership, and Managerial Ethics

Ron King, chairperson of the board of directors and chief executive officer of Image, Inc., is pondering a recommendation to make to the firm's board of directors in response to actions taken by Jack Hatcher. Hatcher recently informed King and other board members that he (Hatcher) had purchased 15% of the voting stock of Image at $12 per share and is considering an attempt to take control of the company. His effort to take control would include offering $16 per share to stockholders to induce them to sell shares to him. Hatcher also indicated that he would abandon his takeover plans if the company would buy back his stock at a price 50% over its current market price of $13 per share.

King views the proposed takeover by Hatcher as a hostile maneuver. Hatcher has a reputation of identifying companies that are undervalued (that is, their underlying net assets are worth more than the price of the outstanding stock), buying enough stock to take control of such a company, replacing top management, and, on occasion, breaking up the company (that is, selling off the various divisions to the highest bidder). The process has proven profitable to Hatcher and his financial backers. Stockholders of the companies taken over also benefited because Hatcher paid them attractive prices to buy their stock.

King recognizes that Image is currently undervalued by the stock market but believes that eventually the company will significantly improve its financial performance to the long-run benefit of its stockholders.

REQUIRED

What are the ethical issues that King should consider in arriving at a recommendation to make to the board of directors regarding Hatcher's offer to be "bought out" of his takeover plans?

LO1, 2, 3

C11-63. Understanding Shareholders' Meeting, Managerial Communications, and Financial Interpretations

The stockholders' equity section of Pillar Corporation's comparative balance sheet at the end of 2014 and 2015 is presented below. It is part of the financial data just reviewed at a stockholders' meeting.

	December 31, 2015	December 31, 2014
Common stock, $10 par value, 600,000 shares authorized; issued at December 31, 2015, 275,000 shares; 2014, 250,000 shares	$ 2,750,000	$2,500,000
Paid-in capital in excess of par	4,575,000	4,125,000
Retained earnings (see Note)	2,960,000	2,825,000
Total stockholders' equity	$10,285,000	$9,450,000

Note: Availability of retained earnings for cash dividends is restricted by $2,000,000 due to a planned plant expansion.

The following items were also disclosed at the stockholders' meeting: net income for 2015 was $1,220,000; a 10% stock dividend was issued December 14, 2015; when the stock dividend was declared, the market value was $28 per share; the market value per share at December 31, 2015, was $26; management plans to borrow $500,000 to help finance a new plant addition, which is expected to cost a total of $2,300,000; and the customary $1.54 per share cash dividend had been revised to $1.40 when declared and issued the last week of December 2015. As part of its investor relations program, during the stockholders' meeting management asked stockholders to write any questions they might have concerning the firm's operations or finances. As assistant controller, you are given the stockholders' questions.

REQUIRED

Prepare brief but reasonably complete answers to the following questions:

a. What did Pillar do with the cash proceeds from the stock dividend issued in December?

b. What was my book value per share at the end of 2014 and 2015?

c. I owned 7,500 shares of Pillar in 2014 and have not sold any shares. How much more or less of the corporation do I own at December 31, 2015 and what happened to the market value of my interest in the company?

d. I heard someone say that stock dividends don't give me anything I didn't already have. Why did you issue one? Are you trying to fool us?

e. Instead of a stock dividend, why didn't you declare a cash dividend and let us buy the new shares that were issued?

f. Why are you cutting back on the dividends I receive?

g. If you have $2,000,000 put aside in retained earnings for the new plant addition, which will cost $2,300,000, why are you borrowing $500,000 instead of just the $300,000 needed?

C11-64. Assessing Stock Buybacks, Corporate Accountability, and Managerial Ethics LO2, 3, 6

Liz Plummer, vice president and general counsel, chairs the Executive Compensation Committee for Sunlight Corporation. Four and one-half years ago, the compensation committee designed a performance bonus plan for top management that was approved by the board of directors. The plan provides an attractive bonus for top management if the firm's earnings per share grows each year over a five-year period. The plan is now in its fifth year; for the past four years, earnings per share has grown each year. Last year, earnings per share was $1.95 (net income was $7,800,000 and the weighted average common shares outstanding was 4,000,000). Sunlight Corporation has no preferred stock and has had 4,000,000 common shares outstanding for several years. Plummer has recently seen an estimate that Sunlight's net income this year will decrease about 5% from last year because of a slight recession in the economy.

Plummer is disturbed by an item on the agenda for the board of directors meeting on June 20 and an accompanying note from Rob Lundy. Lundy is vice president and chief financial officer for Sunlight. Lundy is proposing to the board that Sunlight buy back 600,000 shares of its own common stock on July 1. Lundy's explanation is that the firm's stock is undervalued now and that Sunlight has excess cash available. When the stock subsequently recovers in value, Lundy notes, Sunlight will reissue the shares and generate a nice increase in contributed capital.

Lundy's note to Plummer merely states, "Look forward to your support of my proposal at the board meeting."

REQUIRED

Why is Plummer disturbed by Lundy's proposal and note? What possible ethical problem does Plummer face when Lundy's proposal is up for a vote at the board meeting?

SOLUTIONS TO REVIEW PROBLEMS

Mid-Chapter Review 1

SOLUTION

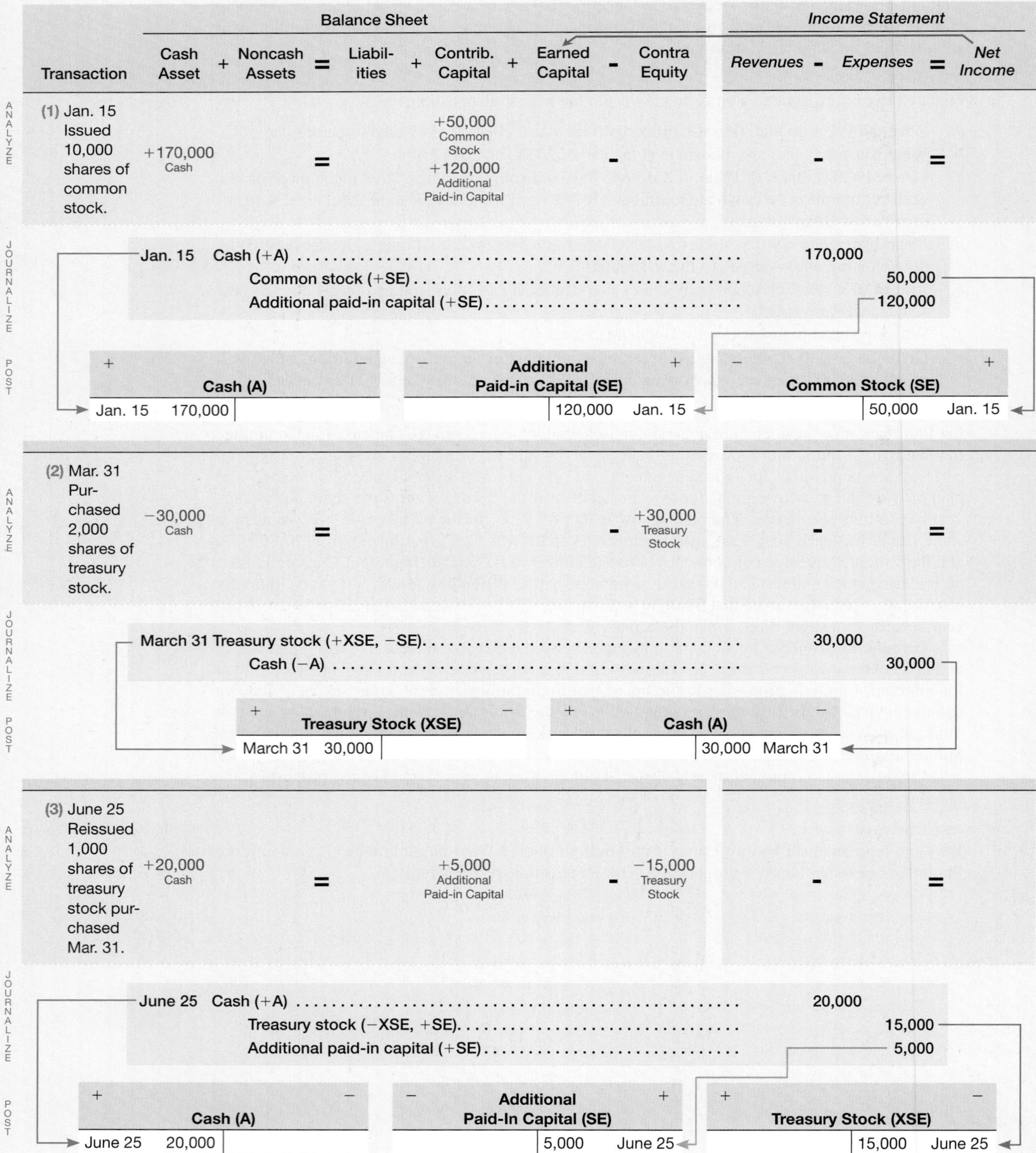

Transaction	Cash Asset	+ Noncash Assets	= Liabil-ities	+ Contrib. Capital	+ Earned Capital	− Contra Equity	Revenues	− Expenses	= Net Income
(1) Jan. 15 Issued 10,000 shares of common stock.	+170,000 Cash		=	+50,000 Common Stock; +120,000 Additional Paid-in Capital		−		−	=
(2) Mar. 31 Purchased 2,000 shares of treasury stock.	−30,000 Cash		=			− +30,000 Treasury Stock		−	=
(3) June 25 Reissued 1,000 shares of treasury stock purchased Mar. 31.	+20,000 Cash		=	+5,000 Additional Paid-in Capital		− −15,000 Treasury Stock		−	=

Date	Account	Debit	Credit
Jan. 15	Cash (+A)	170,000	
	Common stock (+SE)		50,000
	Additional paid-in capital (+SE)		120,000
March 31	Treasury stock (+XSE, −SE)	30,000	
	Cash (−A)		30,000
June 25	Cash (+A)	20,000	
	Treasury stock (−XSE, +SE)		15,000
	Additional paid-in capital (+SE)		5,000

Mid-Chapter Review 2

SOLUTION

a.

	Preferred Stock	Common Stock
Year 1	$ 0	$ 0
Year 2		
Arrearage from Year 1 ($1,000,000 × 5%)	50,000	
Current-year dividend ($1,000,000 × 5%)	50,000	
Balance to common		200,000
Year 3		
Current-year dividend ($1,000,000 × 5%)	50,000	
Balance to common		30,000

b.

	Preferred Stock	Common Stock
Year 1	$ 0	$ 0
Year 2		
Current-year dividend ($1,000,000 × 5%)	50,000	
Balance to common		250,000
Year 3		
Current-year dividend ($1,000,000 × 5%)	50,000	
Balance to common		30,000

Mid-Chapter Review 3

SOLUTION

ANALYZE

Transaction	Balance Sheet: Cash Asset	+ Noncash Assets	= Liabilities	+ Contrib. Capital	+ Earned Capital	Income Statement: Revenues	− Expenses	= Net Income
(1) Apr. 1 Declared a 100% stock dividend.			=	+250,000 Common Stock	−250,000[1] Retained Earnings		−	=

JOURNALIZE

(1) April 1	Retained earnings (−SE)	250,000	
	Common stock (+SE)		250,000

POST

− Retained Earnings (SE) +	
April 1 250,000	

− Common Stock (SE) +	
	250,000 April 1

1 This large stock dividend reduces retained earnings at the par value of shares distributed (50,000 shares × 100% × $5 par value = $250,000). Contributed capital (common stock) increases by the same amount.

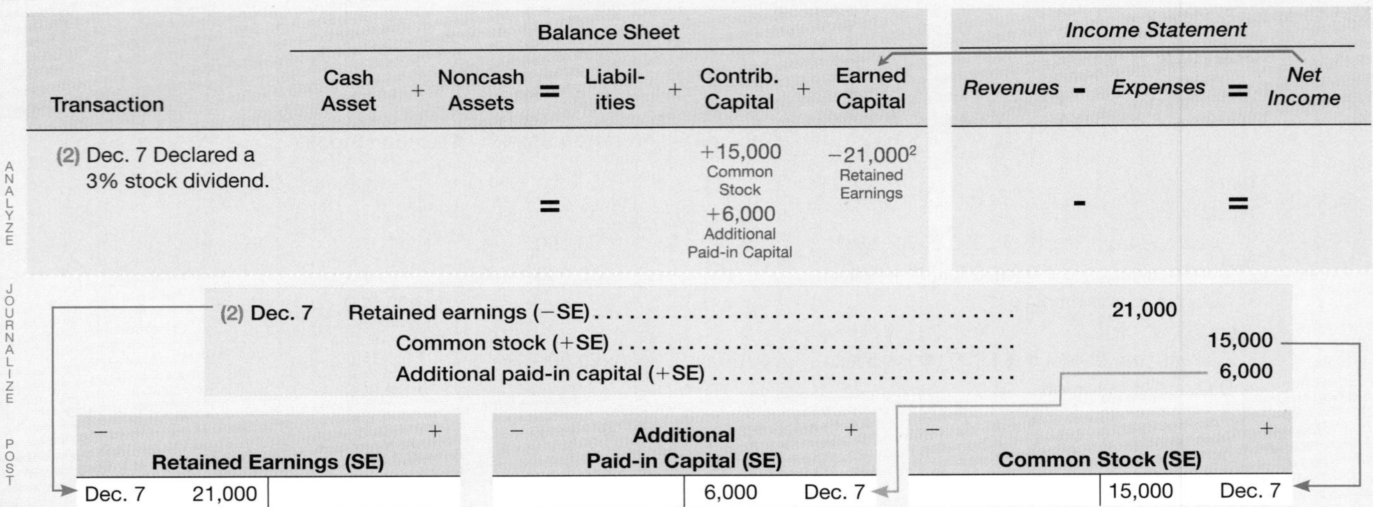

2 This small stock dividend reduces retained earnings at the market value of shares distributed (3% × 100,000 shares × $7 per share = $21,000). Contributed capital increases by the same amount ($15,000 to common stock and $6,000 to paid-in capital).

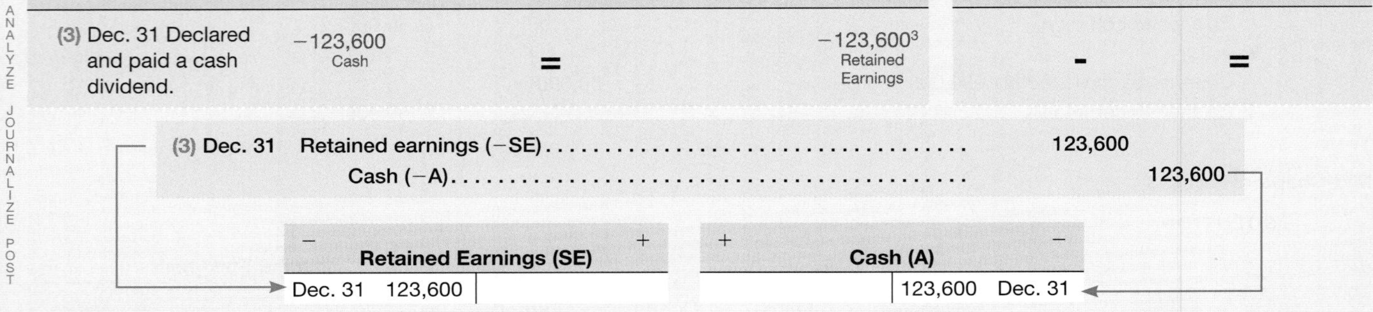

ANALYZE
(3) Dec. 31 Declared and paid a cash dividend.
−123,600 Cash
−123,600³ Retained Earnings
JOURNALIZE
(3) Dec. 31 Retained earnings (−SE) 123,600
Cash (−A) 123,600
POST
Retained Earnings (SE)
Dec. 31 123,600
Cash (A)
123,600 Dec. 31

3 At the time of the cash dividend, there are 103,000 shares outstanding. The cash paid is, therefore, 103,000 shares × $1.20 per share = $123,600.

Mid-Chapter Review 4

SOLUTION

Retained Earnings Reconciliation For Year Ended December 31, 2015		
Retained earnings, December 31, 2014		$513,000
Add: Net income		412,000
		925,000
Less: Cash dividends declared $1.25 × [160,000 + (0.10 × 160,000)]	$220,000	
Stock dividends declared $11 × (160,000 × 0.10)	176,000	396,000
Retained earnings, December 31, 2015		$529,000

Chapter-End Review

SOLUTION

1. Basic EPS would be calculated as follows (millions, except per share amount):

$$\text{Basic EPS} = \frac{\$1{,}750 - \$40}{760 \text{ shares}} = \$2.25 \text{ per share}$$

2. Diluted EPS is calculated as follows (millions, except per share amounts):

$$\text{Diluted EPS} = \frac{\$1{,}750}{770 \text{ shares}} = \$2.27 \text{ per share}$$

3. Petroni would only report basic EPS on its income statement. Diluted EPS, as calculated in requirement 2, is actually higher than basic EPS because the convertible preferred stock is anti-dilutive. GAAP requires that reported diluted EPS must be lower than basic EPS. Consequently, Petroni would not report the diluted EPS number.

Apendix 11A Review

SOLUTION

ANALYZE

	Balance Sheet						*Income Statement*		
Transaction	Cash Asset +	Noncash Assets =	Liabil-ities -	Contra Liabilities +	Contrib. Capital +	Earned Capital	*Revenues* -	*Expenses* =	*Net Income*
Conversion of an \$850 book-value bond into 200 common shares of \$1 par value.		=	−1,000 Bonds Payable -	−150 Bond Discount	+200 Common Stock +650 Additional Paid-In Capital		-	=	

JOURNALIZE / POST

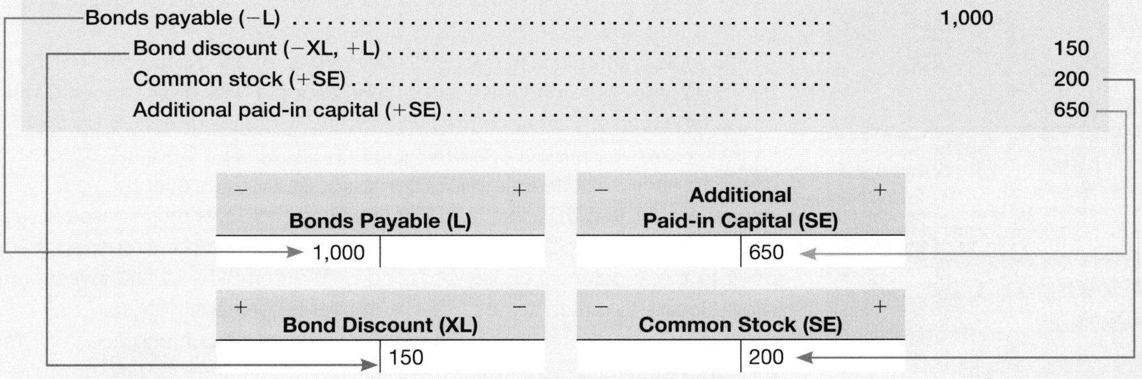

Bonds payable (−L)	1,000	
Bond discount (−XL, +L)		150
Common stock (+SE)		200
Additional paid-in capital (+SE)		650

12 Reporting and Analyzing Financial Investments

LEARNING OBJECTIVES

1. Explain and interpret the three levels of investor influence over an investee—passive, significant, and controlling. (p. 564)
2. Describe the term "fair value" and the fair value hierarchy. (p. 566)
3. Describe and analyze accounting for passive investments. (p. 567)
4. Explain and analyze accounting for investments with significant influence. (p. 575)
5. Describe and analyze accounting for investments with control. (p. 579)
6. Appendix 12A: Illustrate and analyze accounting mechanics for equity method investments. (p. 589)
7. Appendix 12B: Apply consolidation accounting mechanics. (p. 590)
8. Appendix 12C: Discuss the reporting of derivative securities. (p. 591)

GOOGLE
www.google.com

When Sergey Brin and Larry Page, Stanford computer science students, started **Google Inc.**, in September, 1998, they were probably unaware that their fortune would be made in the advertising field that now generates nearly all its revenue.

Google went public in August, 2004, with an offering price below $100 a share. By mid-2012, the share price exceeded $630! Google "has created more investor wealth in less time than any other company in history." Google currently is up over 500% since its IPO. However, the accompanying graph shows that Google's spectacular returns occurred early in its life as a public company, and returns over the past five years have been more in line with market and industry averages. Over these past five years, Google has met investor expectations (which are high), but has not exceeded them. Analysts point to the substantial challenge faced by the company to find investments that will allow Google to match its past returns of over 50 percent.

Google faces competition in general purpose search engines from **Yahoo, Inc.** and **Microsoft Corporation**, in vertical search engines and e-commerce websites from **Kayak.com**, **Monster Worldwide, Inc.**, **Amazon.com, Inc.** and others, in social networks from **Facebook, Inc.** and **Twitter, Inc.** The company also competes fiercely with **Apple Inc.** in the mobile applications market. In addition, the company faces legal challenges from competitors and anti-trust investigations in the United States and other countries. Google faces substantial competition as it attempts to build its presence in the second largest Internet market, China.

Google addresses these growth challenges in several ways. More than one-third of Google's employees engage in research and development to advance the company's provision of cutting-edge products and services to its users. In addition, Google acquires companies with technology that the company can leverage. Most of these acquisitions are small, but Google acquired **YouTube, Inc.** in 2006 for $1.19 billion, **DoubleClick, Inc.** in 2008 for $3.19 billion, **Motorola Mobility Holdings, Inc.** in 2012 for $12.4 billion and **Nest Labs, Inc.** in 2014 for $2.7 billion. In addition to these investments for operating growth, Google's 2014 balance sheet shows that approximately 50% of its reported assets are cash and securities.

As we discuss in this chapter, the accounting method used to report investments depends on the investor company's purpose in making the investment and on the

COMPARISON OF 5 YEAR CUMULATIVE TOTAL RETURN*
Among Google Inc., the S&P 500 Index, the
NASDAQ Composite Index, and the RDG Internet Composite Index

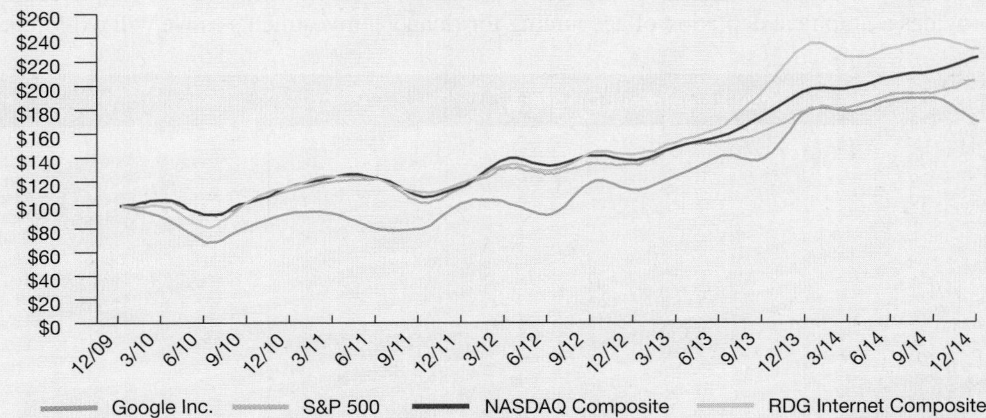

*$100 invested on 12/31/09 in stock or index, including reinvestment of dividends. Fiscal year ending December 31.

degree of influence or control that the investor company can exert over the investee company (the company whose securities are being purchased). One consequence of these accounting methods is that small changes in the amount invested can produce significant changes in the investor's financial statements. (Note: In August, 2015, Google formed a holding company called Alphabet, Inc., the largest subsidiary of which is Google.)

Sources: Google 2014 10-K report, *Wall Street Journal*, Aug. 10, 2015.

CHAPTER ORGANIZATION

Reporting and Analyzing Financial Investments

Passive Investments	Investments with Significant Influence	Investments with Control	Further Considerations
• Trading Securities • Available-for-Sale Securities • Held-to-Maturity Securities	• Accounting and Reporting • Equity Method and Effects on Ratios	• Accounting and Reporting • Acquired Assets and Liabilities • Accounting for Goodwill • Noncontrolling Interest	• Equity Method Mechanics (Appendix 12A) • Consolidation Accounting Mechanics (Appendix 12B) • Reporting Derivative Securities (Appendix 12C)

INTRODUCTION

1

LO1 Explain and interpret the three levels of investor influence over an investee—passive, significant, and controlling.

Most companies invest in government securities or the securities of other companies. These investments often have the following strategic goals:

- **Short-term investment of excess cash.** Companies often generate excess cash for investment either during slow times of the year (after receivables are collected and before seasonal production begins) or for liquidity needs (such as to counter strategic moves by competitors or to quickly respond to acquisition opportunities).[1]
- **Alliances for strategic purposes.** Companies often acquire an equity interest in other companies for strategic purposes, such as gaining access to their research and development activities, to supply or distribution markets, or to their production and marketing expertise.
- **Market penetration or expansion.** Acquisitions of controlling interests in other companies can achieve vertical or horizontal integration in existing markets or can be avenues to penetrate new and growing markets.

Investments in government securities and in the securities of other companies are usually referred to as **financial investments**. Firms make these investments for different purposes, so accounting for the investments can follow one of five different methods, each of which affects the balance sheet and the income statement differently. To help assimilate the materials in this chapter, **Exhibit 12.1** provides a graphical depiction of accounting for financial investments as we will explore it.

EXHIBIT 12.1 Financial Investment Diagram

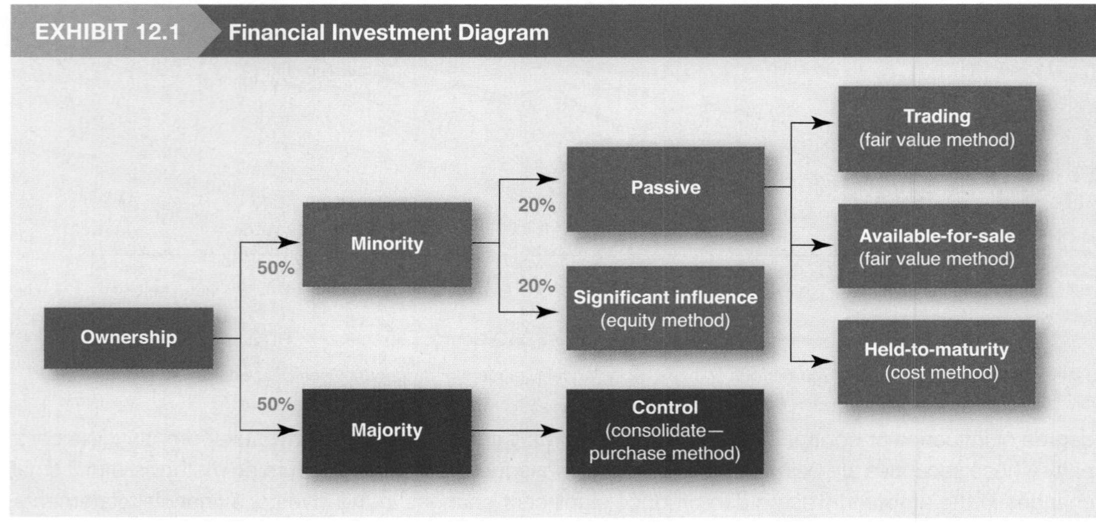

[1] Many U.S. firms operate subsidiaries in foreign countries with lower tax rates. The income earned by those subsidiaries is subject to U.S. income tax only when the income is repatriated in the form of dividends. The desire to delay those tax payments results in a cash build-up in the subsidiaries.

The degree of influence or control that the investor company (purchaser) can exert over the investee organization (the company or government whose securities are being purchased) determines the accounting method. U.S. GAAP identifies three levels of influence/control:

1. **Passive influence**. In this case, the purchasing company is merely an investor and cannot exert influence over the investee organization. The purchaser's goal for this investment is to realize dividends and capital gains. Generally, passive investor status is presumed if the investor company owns less than 20% of the outstanding voting stock of the investee. Investments in debt securities, such as bonds or notes of other organizations, are also classified as passive investments.
2. **Significant influence**. An investor company can sometimes exert significant influence over, but not control, the activities of an investee company. This level of influence can result from the percentage of voting stock owned. It also can result from legal agreements, such as a license to use technology, a formula, or a trade secret like production know-how. It also can occur when the investor company is the sole supplier or customer of the investee. Generally, significant influence is presumed if the investor company owns 20% to 50% of the voting stock of the investee.
3. **Controlling influence**. When a company has control over another, it has the ability to elect a majority of the board of directors and, as a result, the ability to determine its strategic direction and hiring of executive management. Control is generally presumed if the investor company owns more than 50% of the outstanding voting stock of the investee company. Control can sometimes occur at less than 50% stock ownership by virtue of legal agreements, technology licensing, or other contractual means.

Once the level of influence/control is determined, the appropriate accounting method is applied as outlined in **Exhibit 12.2**.

EXHIBIT 12.2 Investment Type, Accounting Treatment, and Financial Statement Effects

	Accounting	Balance Sheet Effects	Income Statement Effects	Cash Flow Effects
Passive	Trading	Investment balance reported as end-of-period fair value	Dividend payments from investee are included in income Capital gain/loss recognized in the period in which it occurs	Purchase/sale of investee yields investing cash flows Dividend payments received from investee are operating cash inflows
	Available-for-Sale	Investment balance reported as end-of-period fair value	Dividend payments from investee are included in income Capital gain/loss recognized when investment sold; interim gain/loss reported as AOCI*	Purchase/sale of investee yields investing cash flows Dividend payments received from investee are operating cash inflows
	Held-to-Maturity	Investment balance reported at acquisition cost	Dividend payments from investee are included in income Capital gain/loss recognized when investment sold	Purchase/sale of investee yields investing cash flows Dividend payments received from investee are operating cash inflows
Significant Influence	Equity Method	Investment balance reflects purchase price and subsequent changes in proportion owned of investee's equity	Investor reports income equal to percent owned of investee income Sale of investee yields gains/losses	Purchase/sale of investee yields investing cash flows Dividend payments received from investee are operating cash inflows
Control	Consolidation	Balance sheets of investor and investee are presented as if one entity	Income statements of investor and investee are presented as if one entity Sale of investee yields gains/losses	Purchase/sale of investee yields investing cash flows Cash flows of investor and investee are presented as if one entity

*AOCI is defined on page 528 and discussed further in the following pages.

There are two basic reporting issues with investments: (1) how investment income should be recognized and (2) at what amount (cost or fair value) the investment should be reported on the balance sheet. We next discuss both of these issues under each of the three investment types.

FAIR VALUE: AN INTRODUCTION

2 **LO2** Describe the term "fair value" and the fair value hierarchy.

The term **fair value** is finding increasing use in the language of accounting, but it is particularly prevalent in the accounting for financial investments. When an investor purchases a security for $100, the relevance of that acquisition cost fades rather quickly. If the investor considers selling the security a year later, the original $100 cost is much less meaningful than the current price for the security in the markets. Or, if we were to look at the balance sheet of a company, it would be useful to know how much its investments are worth today, rather than what was paid for them at various points in the past.

When accounting requires the use of fair value, U.S. GAAP defines fair value as the amount that an independent buyer would be willing to pay for an asset (or the amount that would need to be paid to discharge a liability) in an orderly transaction. For an asset that is actively traded on financial markets, fair value is the amount that we would receive by selling that asset at the balance sheet date. But fair value is also used when there is no active market for the asset. When Google accounts for its acquisition of Motorola, it must report the fair value of the patent portfolio that it obtained in that transaction. In such cases, fair value is not "mark-to-market," but rather "mark-to-model." For instance, fair value might be determined by a discounted cash flow analysis as in Chapter 9. U.S. GAAP allows various methods to be used in determining the "most representative" fair value at the appropriate date.

While fair values are often deemed to be more relevant than historical cost, they are also viewed as more subjective—particularly when fair value is determined by reference to a model rather than a liquid market. For this reason, U.S. GAAP requires that firms disclose the methods used to determine fair value for their assets using a **fair value hierarchy**.

Level 1: Values based on quoted prices in active markets for identical assets/liabilities. An example would be a common share of a company traded on an active exchange. For instance, Google's class A common stock closed at a price of $530.66 per share on December 31, 2014. That price would be used to determine the fair value of another company's investment in Google stock.

Level 2: Values based on observable inputs other than Level 1 (e.g., quoted prices for similar assets/liabilities or interest rates or yield curves). An example would be a bond that is infrequently traded, but that is similar to bonds that are actively traded. Moody's rates Google bonds at Aa2. Other bonds with that rating would likely have a similar yield, which could be used to compute the present value of the bond payments to estimate the fair value of a bond investment.

Level 3: Values based on inputs observable only to the reporting entity (e.g., management estimates or assumptions). An example would be an operating asset that is judged to be impaired.

Google's use of fair value to report its investments is presented in the coming pages. The purpose of the classification is to provide an assessment of the subjectivity that underlies the numbers in the balance sheet (and sometimes, the income statement), with Level 1 being the most reliable and Level 3 being the most subjective.

In addition, companies have a **fair value option** that provides them with the *option* of using fair value to measure the value of most financial assets and liabilities. This option extends the use of fair value to a wide range of financial assets and liabilities, including accounts and notes receivable, accounts and notes payable, and bonds payable. This standard is optional, however, and thus far its application has been limited mostly to financial institutions such as banks and insurance companies.[2]

[2] Other assets that *must* be reported at fair value include (1) derivative securities, such as options, futures and forward contracts, that are purchased to hedge price, interest rate, or foreign exchange rate fluctuations, (2) long-term assets that are impaired, and (3) inventories that have been written down to fair value based on the lower-of-cost-or-market rule. In addition, U.S. GAAP provides companies with the *option* of using fair value to measure the value of most financial assets and liabilities.

PASSIVE INVESTMENTS

LO3 Describe and analyze accounting for passive investments.

The term "passive" refers to the investor's role in trying to influence the operations of the investee organization. So, short-term investments of excess cash are typically passive investments, usually in liquid securities. In addition, investors seeking trading profits from short-term capital gains would be considered passive investors, even though their trading style may be active. Passive investments can involve either equity or debt securities. Debt securities have no ownership interest, so they are always passive. Equity investments are passive when the ownership level is not sufficient to influence or control the investee. Passive investments can be broadly grouped into two categories: those reported at cost and those reported at fair value. Furthermore, there are two methods for reporting investments at fair value. These alternative treatments are discussed below.

Acquisition and Sale

When an investment is acquired, regardless of the amount of shares purchased or the percentage of outstanding shares acquired, the investment is initially recorded on the balance sheet at its fair value, that is, its price on the date of purchase. This accounting is the same as that for the acquisition of other assets such as inventories or plant assets. Subsequent to acquisition, investments are carried on the balance sheet as current or long-term assets, depending on management's expectations about their ultimate holding period (the assets are reported as current assets if management expects to dispose of them within one year).

When investments are sold, any recognized gain or loss on sale usually is equal to the difference between the proceeds received and the book (carrying) value of the investment on the balance sheet. However, there is one passive investment method where that is not true.

To illustrate the simplest acquisition and sale of a passive investment, assume that Pownall Company purchases an investment in King Company consisting of 1,000 shares for $20 cash per share (the acquisition price includes transaction costs such as brokerage fees). Later in the same reporting period, Pownall sells 400 of the 1,000 shares for $30 cash per share. The financial statement effects of these transactions and their related entries for Pownall follow:

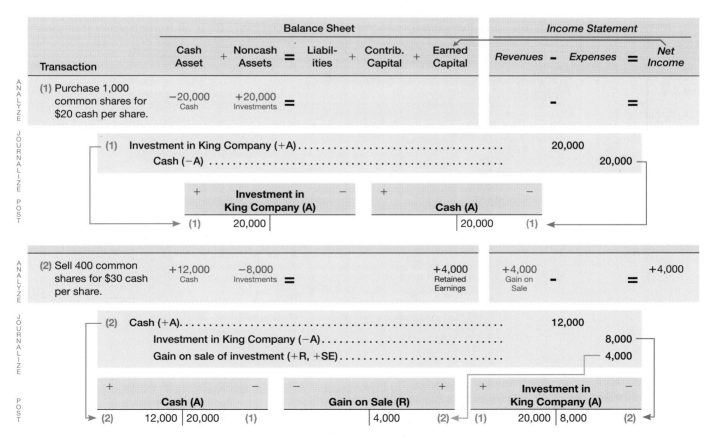

Transaction	Cash Asset	+ Noncash Assets	= Liabilities	+ Contrib. Capital	+ Earned Capital	Revenues	− Expenses	= Net Income
(1) Purchase 1,000 common shares for $20 cash per share.	−20,000 Cash	+20,000 Investments						
(2) Sell 400 common shares for $30 cash per share.	+12,000 Cash	−8,000 Investments			+4,000 Retained Earnings	+4,000 Gain on Sale		+4,000

ANALYZE / JOURNALIZE / POST

(1) Investment in King Company (+A) 20,000
  Cash (−A) 20,000

+ Investment in King Company (A) −	
(1) 20,000	

+ Cash (A) −	
	20,000 (1)

(2) Cash (+A) 12,000
  Investment in King Company (−A) 8,000
  Gain on sale of investment (+R, +SE) 4,000

+ Cash (A) −	
(2) 12,000	20,000 (1)

− Gain on Sale (R) +	
	4,000 (2)

+ Investment in King Company (A) −	
(1) 20,000	8,000 (2)

The gain or loss on sale is reported as a component of *other income,* which is commonly commingled with interest and dividend revenue in the income statement.

On the statement of cash flows, the $20,000 purchase (transaction 1) would be an investing cash outflow, and the $12,000 proceeds (transaction 2) would be an investing cash inflow. If Pownall Company presents its cash flows from operating activities using the indirect method, we would see a subtraction of the $4,000 gain on sale among the adjustments from net income to cash from operations.

Accounting for the purchase and sale of investments is similar to any other asset. Further, there is no difference in accounting for purchases and sales across the different types of passive investments when those purchases and sales occur in the same reporting period.

However, as Pownall Company reaches the end of its fiscal reporting period (a quarter- or year-end), we can see that there are different ways in which we might determine the balance sheet value of the 600 shares of King Company that Pownall Company still owns. And, that balance sheet value will be the asset's book value going forward, affecting gains and losses now and when the shares are ultimately sold.

Investments Marked to Fair Value

The following two classifications of marketable securities require the investment to be reported on the balance sheet at current fair value:

1. **Trading (T) securities**. These are investments in securities that management intends to actively buy and sell for trading profits as market prices fluctuate.
2. **Available-for-sale (AFS) securities**. These are investments in securities that management intends to hold for capital gains and dividend revenue; although it may sell them if the price is right or if the organization needs cash.

Investments in both equity and debt securities qualify for these classifications. Management's assignment of securities between these two classifications depends on the degree of turnover (transaction volume) it expects in the investment portfolio, which reflects its intent to actively trade the securities or not. Available-for-sale portfolios exhibit less turnover than do trading portfolios. Once that classification is established, reporting for a portfolio follows procedures detailed in **Exhibit 12.3**.

FYI GAAP permits companies to have multiple portfolios, each with a different classification. Management can change portfolio classification provided it adheres to strict disclosure and reporting requirements if its expectations of turnover change.

EXHIBIT 12.3 Accounting Treatment for Trading and Available-for-Sale Investments

Investment Classification	Reporting of Fair Value Changes	Reporting Gains and Losses on Sale	Reporting Dividends Received
Trading (T)	Balance sheet values are updated to reflect fair value changes; unrealized gains and losses are reported as investment income; affects equity via retained earnings	Gain or loss on sale equals proceeds minus the most recent book (fair) value	Reported as investment income in income statement
Available-for-Sale (AFS)	Balance sheet values are updated to reflect fair value changes; unrealized gains and losses bypass the income statement and are reported directly in accumulated other comprehensive income (AOCI), a component of equity; these changes are reported in the statement of shareholders' equity	Gain or loss on sale equals proceeds minus the original acquisition cost of the investment; any unrealized gains or losses in accumulated other comprehensive income must be eliminated	Reported as investment income in income statement

Both trading (T) and available-for-sale (AFS) investments are reported at fair values on the statement date. Whether the change in fair value affects current income depends on the investment classification: available-for-sale securities have no immediate income effect; trading securities have an income effect. The impact on equity is similar for both classifications, with the only difference being whether the change is reflected in retained earnings or in accumulated other comprehensive income (AOCI) in equity. Dividends and any gains or losses on security sales are reported in the investment income section of the income statement for both classifications.[3]

FYI When trading securities are marked-to-fair value, the unrealized gain is recorded as income and reported in the income statement. For available-for-sale investments, unrealized gains are reported as other comprehensive income.

Fair Value Adjustments To illustrate the accounting for changes in fair value subsequent to purchase (and before sale), assume that Pownall's investment in King Co. (600 remaining shares purchased for $20 per share) could be sold for $25 per share at year-end. The investment must be marked to fair value in an adjusting entry to reflect the $3,000 unrealized gain ($5 per share increase for 600 shares).

If the investment is classified as trading securities (T) the entry would be:

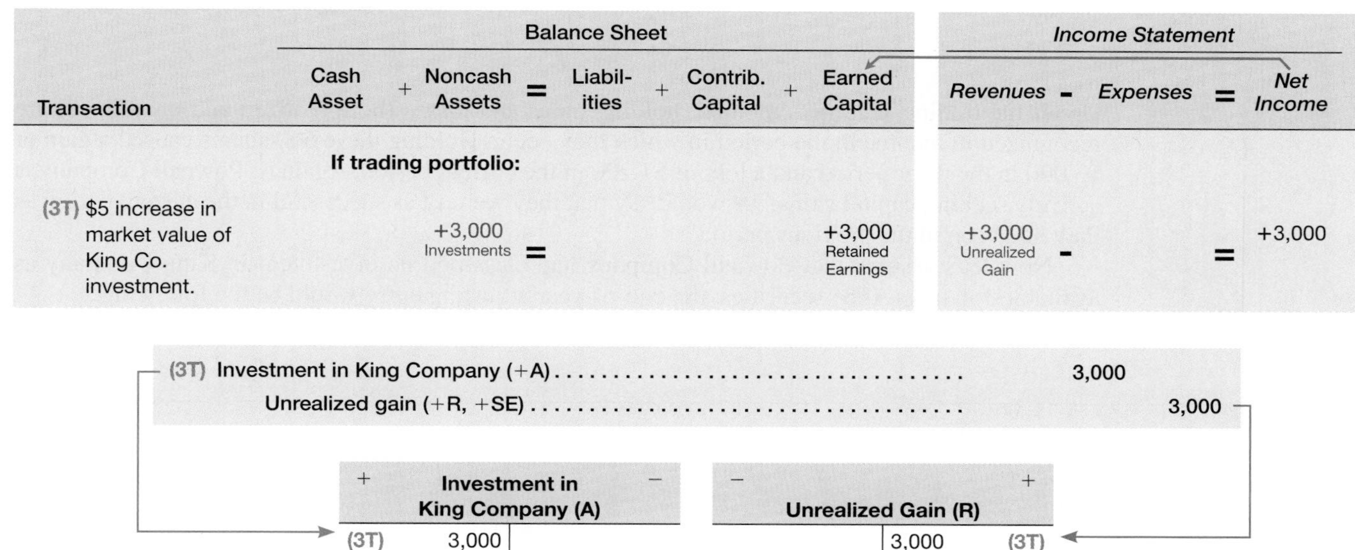

The investment account is increased by $3,000, making the end-of-year book value of Pownall's investment equal to $15,000, its fair value. Total investment income reported on Pownall's income statement would be $7,000, consisting of $4,000 in realized holding gains and $3,000 in unrealized holding gains. If Pownall is actively trading to achieve capital gains, then this approach seems like the correct way to "keep score."

This entry to adjust the balance sheet to reflect the fair value of the securities is an adjusting entry. It would need to be made at the end of every fiscal period as financial reports are being prepared.

What happens when the securities are subsequently sold? Assume that Pownall Company sells its 600 shares of King Company for $23 per share shortly after the end of the last reporting period. Pownall receives $13,800 in cash, and it no longer owns the shares of King Company. When the trading method is used, the accounting for the sale of shares is relatively simple:

[3] At the time of this textbook writing, the FASB is considering a change in the fair value accounting for investments in equity securities. The proposal would force companies to report changes in fair value for all securities on the income statement as unrealized gains or losses. Unrealized gains and losses on available-for-sale securities would no longer be recorded in AOCI. This change, if implemented, would effectively eliminate the distinction between trading securities and available-for-sale securities.

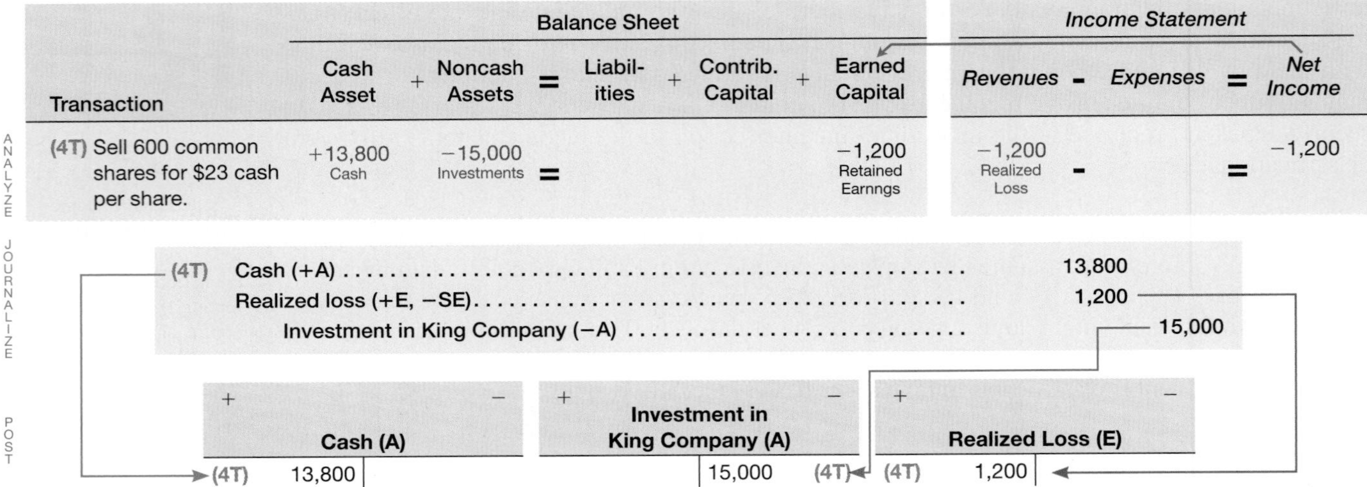

Under the trading securities method, holding gains and losses (both realized and unrealized) are recognized in income in the period in which they occur. Holding these 600 shares caused a gain of $3,000 in the prior period and a loss of $1,200 in the current period. Again, if Pownall Company is actively seeking capital gains, we would say that they weren't as successful in the current period as they had been in the previous period.

Now let's assume that Pownall Company had classified its investment in King Company as available-for-sale (AFS) securities; the end-of-year adjusting entry would be the following:

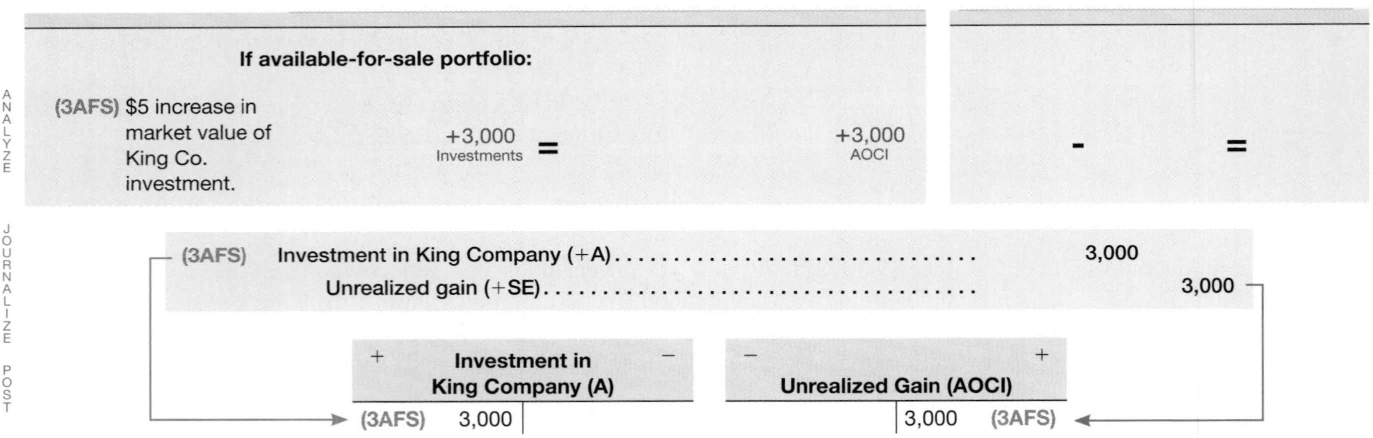

As under the trading method, the investment account is increased by $3,000 to reflect the increase in fair value of the shares owned. However, when accounted for as an AFS security, the unrealized gain (or loss) is recorded as an increase in accumulated other comprehensive income (AOCI), a separate component of shareholders' equity. Therefore, the increase in the investment does not result in an immediate income statement effect. Under AFS, Pownall Company's investment income for this period would reflect only the $4,000 realized gain from the sale of 400 shares. The $3,000 unrealized gain is reflected in stockholders' equity, but not reported on the income statement. In a sense, the balance sheet has been updated to reflect the current values, but the income statement has been left out of the picture for the time being.

When Pownall Company sells the 600 shares for $13,800 in the subsequent period, the entry under AFS would be the following:

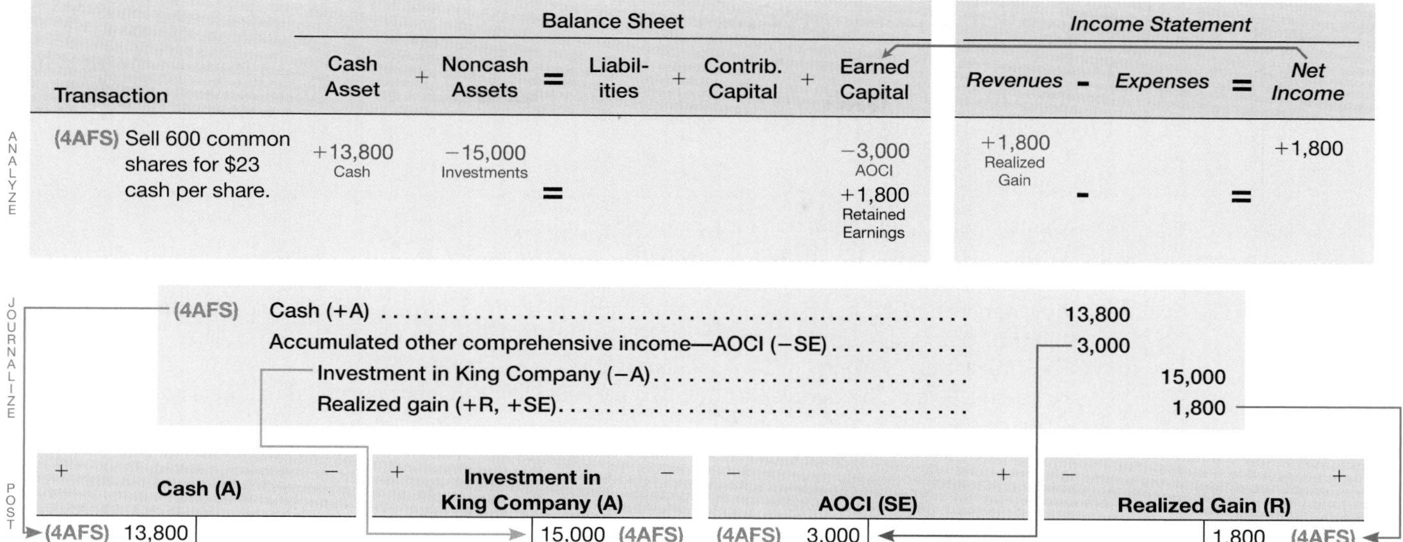

Under AFS, the realized gain (loss) goes into income when the security is sold, and the amount is determined by comparing the amount received when the shares are sold ($23 per share) to the amount paid for the shares when originally purchased ($20 per share). When the investment is sold, the entry must delete the investment (which was valued at $25 per share at the end of last period) *and* the unrealized holding gain ($5 per share) that was put into accumulated other comprehensive income when those shares were revalued. Both the Investment in King Company account and the AOCI for King Company have zero balances after this transaction.

The principal difference between trading and available-for-sale accounting is in the income statement. Under the trading security method, Pownall Company records income of $7,000 ($4,000 as a realized gain + $3,000 as an unrealized gain) in the first period and a loss of $1,200 in the second period. Under available-for-sale, Pownall Company records income of $4,000 in the first period and income of $1,800 in the second period. The total income from the investment in King Company is the same, but the timing is different. These differences are summarized in the following table:

	Income reported in income statement from investment in 1,000 shares at a cost of $20 per share	
	Trading	**Available-for-sale**
Period 1:		
Sell 400 shares at $30 per share	$4,000	$4,000
Adjust remaining 600 shares to fair value of $25 per share	3,000	—
Total period 1 income	$7,000	$4,000
Period 2:		
Sell 600 shares at $23 per share	($1,200)	$1,800
Total period 2 income (loss)	($1,200)	$1,800
Total income – period 1 plus period 2	$5,800	$5,800

Because of the difference in the way unrealized gains and losses are reported, the classification of investments as either trading or available-for-sale will have an effect on key ratios that might be used to evaluate the performance of a company. Ratios that use net income in the calculation are affected. Return on equity (ROE), return on assets (ROA) and profit margin (PM) are among the ratios affected. Return on net operating assets (RNOA), which is discussed in Appendix A at the end of Chapter 5, would not be affected by this classification because passive investments would be considered nonoperating assets and excluded from the calculation of net operating assets and the gains and losses would be excluded from net operating profit after taxes (NOPAT).

Financial Statement Disclosures

Companies are required to disclose cost and fair value information on their investment portfolios in footnotes to financial statements. **Google** reports its accounting policies for its investments in note 1 to its 2014 10-K report:

Cash, Cash Equivalents, and Marketable Securities

We invest our excess cash primarily in time deposits, money market and other funds, including cash collateral received related to our securities lending program, highly liquid debt instruments of the U.S. government and its agencies, debt instruments issued by foreign governments and municipalities in the U.S., corporate securities, mortgage-backed securities, and asset-backed securities.

We classify all highly liquid investments with stated maturities of three months or less from date of purchase as cash equivalents and all highly liquid investments with stated maturities of greater than three months as marketable securities.

We determine the appropriate classification of our investments in marketable securities at the time of purchase and reevaluate such designation at each balance sheet date. We have classified and accounted for our marketable securities as available-for-sale. We may or may not hold securities with stated maturities greater than 12 months until maturity. After consideration of our risk versus reward objectives, as well as our liquidity requirements, we may sell these securities prior to their stated maturities. As we view these securities as available to support current operations, we classify securities with maturities beyond 12 months as current assets under the caption marketable securities in the accompanying Consolidated Balance Sheets. We carry these securities at fair value, and report the unrealized gains and losses, net of taxes, as a component of stockholders' equity, except for unrealized losses determined to be other-than-temporary, which we record within interest and other income, net. We determine any realized gains or losses on the sale of marketable securities on a specific identification method, and we record such gains and losses as a component of interest and other income, net.

This footnote reveals that Google reports investments with maturities of three months or less as cash equivalents. These investments are most likely treated as trading securities and any changes in their fair value would result in a gain or loss that would be reported in the income statement. Because of the short maturity of these investments, the gains and losses due to changes in fair value are generally very small. Those investments with longer maturities are reported as marketable securities and classified as available-for-sale. Consistent with this accounting treatment, Google notes that its marketable securities are carried in the balance sheet at fair value and it reports the "unrealized gains and losses, net of taxes, as a component of stockholders' equity." The cash, cash equivalents, and marketable securities are presented under current assets in the balance sheet:

December 31 ($ millions)	2014
Cash and cash equivalents	$18,347
Marketable securities	46,048
Total cash, cash equivalents, and marketable securities	64,395

In note 2 to its 10-K, Google provides further information about the composition of its investment portfolio:

Cash, Cash Equivalents, and Marketable Securities

The following tables summarize our cash, cash equivalents and marketable securities by significant investment categories (in millions):

	As of December 31, 2014					
	Adjusted Cost	Gross Unrealized Gains	Gross Unrealized Losses	Fair Value	Cash and Cash Equivalents	Marketable Securities
Cash	$ 9,863	$ 0	$ 0	$ 9,863	$ 9,863	$ 0
Level 1:						
Money market and other funds	2,532	0	0	2,532	2,532	0
U.S. government notes	15,320	37	(4)	15,353	1,128	14,225
Marketable equity securities	988	428	(64)	1,352	0	1,352
	18,840	465	(68)	19,237	3,660	15,577
Level 2:						
Time deposits	2,409	0	0	2,409	2,309	100
Money market and other funds	1,762	0	0	1,762	1,762	0
Fixed-income bond funds	385	0	(38)	347	0	347
U.S. government agencies	2,327	8	(1)	2,334	750	1,584
Foreign government bonds	1,828	22	(10)	1,840	0	1,840
Municipal securities	3,370	33	(6)	3,397	3	3,394
Corporate debt securities	11,499	114	(122)	11,491	0	11,491
Agency residential mortgage-backed securities	8,196	109	(42)	8,263	0	8,263
Asset-backed securities	3,456	1	(5)	3,452	0	3,452
	35,232	287	(224)	35,295	4,824	30,471
Total	$63,935	$752	$(292)	$64,395	$18,347	$46,048

A large portion of Google's investment in marketable securities is in government debt securities, including U.S. government debt, foreign government bonds, and municipal securities. The various types of securities are divided into two groups, labeled "Level 1" and "Level 2." These labels refer to the method used to determine the fair value of each investment. The fair values of the investments listed as Level 1 are determined by looking at quoted prices in active markets. For most of Google's marketable securities, fair value is determined by a "mark-to-model" approach where the model uses information from publicly available sources (Level 2). None of Google's investments are listed as Level 3.

For each type of investment, Google reports its cost, its fair value, and the gross unrealized gains and losses; the latter equaling the difference between the cost and fair value. Google reports the cost of its cash and investments at $63,935 million and its fair value at $64,395 million. The fair value total is then divided into cash and cash equivalents of $18,347 million and marketable securities of $46,048 million.

The note reports gross unrealized gains of $752 million and gross unrealized losses of $292 million. These gains and losses can be almost entirely attributed to the portfolio of marketable securities, which are classified as available-for-sale investments. The net gain of $460 million ($752 million − $292 million) is reported net of tax in accumulated other comprehensive income (AOCI), which is included in the stockholders' equity section of the balance sheet.

Potential for Earnings Management

The difference between available-for-sale investments and trading securities—as far as the way changes in fair value are reported—creates the potential for earnings management. For example, if management wishes to report higher net income, investments that have increased in value could be classified as trading securities while investments that have declined in value could be classified as available-for-sale securities. This classification would mean that the unrealized gains on the trading securities would be reported on the income statement, while the unrealized losses on available-for-sale securities would bypass the income statement and be subtracted from AOCI. In addition, management is free to reclassify investments if it sees fit to do so.

Because of the potential for earnings management, the FASB requires that investments be measured at fair value at the time that a security is reclassified from one category to another. If trading securities are reclassified as available-for-sale securities, for example, any unrealized gain or loss must be recognized as income at the time of the reclassification. This prevents management from moving investments between categories to hide a loss in AOCI.

Nevertheless, available-for-sale securities offer the opportunity for earnings management, because management can decide when to recognize the unrealized gain (or loss) in the income statement. When investments are classified as available-for-sale securities, any unrealized gain or loss is recorded directly in stockholders' equity as AOCI until one of two things happens: (1) management decides to sell the securities, or (2) management decides to reclassify the investment as trading securities. In either case, the unrealized gain or loss is immediately recognized in the income statement and thus transferred from AOCI to retained earnings.

Google's footnote allows us to observe how a firm might use its investments in marketable securities to manage its net income for the year. Suppose, for example, that Google wanted to increase net income for the 2014 reporting year. Google reports gross unrealized gains of $752 million on its marketable securities. Because these securities are classified as available-for-sale, these gains have not been reported previously in Google's income statement. So, if Google decided to reclassify these available-for-sale securities as trading securities, it could immediately recognize the $752 million unrealized gain and report it on its 2014 income statement.

Instead of reclassifying the investments, Google could sell the securities and recognize the gain. (The unrealized gain would now be realized.) In fact, Google could sell the investment to record the gain and then immediately buy back similar securities at the same price (or very near to it). The company would incur some transaction costs, but it would be able to increase its income without changing its portfolio or reclassifying its investments.

One way to determine whether a company is selling and buying available-for-sale securities to manage earnings is to examine the cash flow statement. Under the heading of investing activities, companies are required to report cash flows from buying and selling investments separately. During 2014, Google reported that cash proceeds from the sale or maturity of marketable securities totaled $51,315 million, while cash spent to buy marketable securities totaled $56,310 million. These two cash flow numbers were, by far, the largest cash flows reported in Google's cash flow statement. Of course, we cannot automatically conclude that these transactions were the result of earnings management. Realized gains and losses on available-for-sale investments should be disclosed in a company's footnotes, and Google's footnotes report realized gains of $238 million and realized losses of $85 million for 2014. In addition, we could look at the adjustments to net income in the indirect method cash from operations to identify gains and losses from investing activities.

Investments Reported at Cost

Investments for which fair value cannot be determined must be accounted for using the cost method. Under the **cost method**, the investment is continually reported at its historical cost, and any cash dividends and interest received are recognized in current income. Gains or losses on investments carried at cost are only recorded when an investment is sold and the resulting gain or loss is realized.

Debt securities that management intends to hold to maturity are also reported using the cost method. These debt securities are classified as **held-to-maturity (HTM)**. **Exhibit 12.4** summarizes the reporting of these securities.

EXHIBIT 12.4 Accounting Treatment for Held-to-Maturity Investments

Investment Classification	Reporting of Fair Value Changes	Reporting Interest Received and Gains and Losses on Sale
Held-to-Maturity (HTM)	Fair value changes are not reported in either the balance sheet or income statement	Reported as other income in income statement

Fluctuations in fair value are not reflected on either the balance sheet or the income statement. The presumption is that these investments are held to maturity, at which time they are settled at their face value. Fluctuations in fair value, as a result, are less relevant for this investment classification. Any interest received, and gains and losses on the sale of these investments, are recorded in current income.

MID-CHAPTER REVIEW 1

PART 1: AVAILABLE-FOR-SALE SECURITIES

Show the effects (amount and account) of the following four transactions involving investments in marketable securities classified as available-for-sale in the financial statement effects template, prepare the journal entries, and post the journal entries to the appropriate T-accounts.

1. Purchased 1,000 shares of Pincus common stock for $15 cash per share.
2. Received cash dividend of $2 per share on Pincus common stock.
3. Year-end market price of Pincus common stock is $18 per share.
4. Sold all 1,000 shares of Pincus common stock for $19,000 cash.

PART 2: TRADING SECURITIES

Using the same transaction information 1 through 4 from part 1, enter the effects (amount and account) relating to these transactions in the financial statement effects template, prepare the journal entries and post the journal entries to the related T-accounts assuming that the investments are classified as trading securities.

The solution to this review problem can be found on pages 613–615.

INVESTMENTS WITH SIGNIFICANT INFLUENCE

LO4 Explain and analyze accounting for investments with significant influence.

4

Many companies make investments in other companies that yield them significant influence over those other companies. These intercorporate investments are usually made for strategic reasons including:

- **Prelude to acquisition.** Significant ownership can allow the investor company to gain a seat on the board of directors from which it can learn much about the investee company, its products, and its industry.
- **Strategic alliance.** One example of a strategic alliance is an investment in a company that provides inputs for the investor's production process. This relationship is closer than the usual supplier-buyer relationship, often because the investor company provides trade secrets or technical know-how of its production process.
- **Pursuit of research and development.** Many research activities in the pharmaceutical, software, and oil and gas industries are conducted jointly. The common motivation is to reduce risk or the amount of capital invested by the investor. The investor company's equity investment often carries an option to purchase additional shares or the entire company, which it can exercise if the research activities are fruitful.

A crucial feature in each of these investments is that the investor company has ownership sufficient to exert *significant influence* over the investee company. GAAP requires that such investments be accounted for using the *equity method*.

Significant influence is the ability of the investor to affect the financing or operating policies of the investee. Ownership levels of 20% to 50% of the outstanding common stock of the investee presume significant influence. Significant influence can also exist when ownership is less than 20%. Evidence of such influence can be that the investor company is able to gain a seat on the board of directors of the investee by virtue of its equity investment, or the investor controls technical know-how or patents that are used by the investee, or the investor is able to exert significant influence by virtue of legal contracts between it and the investee. There is growing pressure for determining significant influence by the facts and circumstances of the investment instead of the strict ownership percentage rule reflected in current corporate reporting.

Accounting for Investments with Significant Influence

Investments with significant influence must be accounted for using the **equity method**. The equity method of accounting for investments reports the investment on the balance sheet at an amount equal to the proportion of the investee's equity owned by the investor; hence the name equity method. (This accounting assumes acquisition at book value. Acquisition at an amount greater than book value is covered in Appendix 12A.) Contrary to passive investments that are reported at fair value, equity method investments increase (decrease) with increases (decreases) in the equity of the investee.

Equity method accounting is summarized as follows:

- Investments are initially recorded at their purchase cost.
- Dividends received are treated as a recovery of the investment and, thus, reduce the investment balance (unlike passive investments, dividends are *not* reported as income).
- The investor reports income equal to its proportionate share of the reported income of the investee; the investment account is increased by that income or decreased by its share of any loss.
- The investment is *not* reported at fair value as is the case with most passive investments.

To illustrate the accounting for investments using the equity method, consider the following scenario: Assume that Google acquires a 30% interest in Mitel Networks, a company seeking to develop a new technology in a strategic alliance with Google. At acquisition, Mitel reports $1,000 of stockholders' equity, and Google purchases its 30% stake for $300. At the first year-end, Mitel reports profits of $100 and pays $20 in cash dividends to its shareholders ($6 to Google). Following are the financial statement effects for Google (the investor company) for this investment using the equity method:

Transaction	Balance Sheet: Cash Asset	+	Noncash Assets	=	Liabil-ities	+	Contrib. Capital	+	Earned Capital	Income Statement: Revenues	-	Expenses	=	Net Income
(1) Purchased 30% investment in Mitel for $300 cash.	−300 Cash		+300 Investment in Mitel	=							-		=	
(2) Mitel reports $100 income.			+30 Investment in Mitel	=					+30 Retained Earnings	+30 Investment Income	-		=	+30
(3) Mitel pays $20 cash dividends, $6 to Google.	+6 Cash		−6 Investment in Mitel	=							-		=	
Ending balance of Google's investment account.			324											

The related journal entries and T-accounts are:

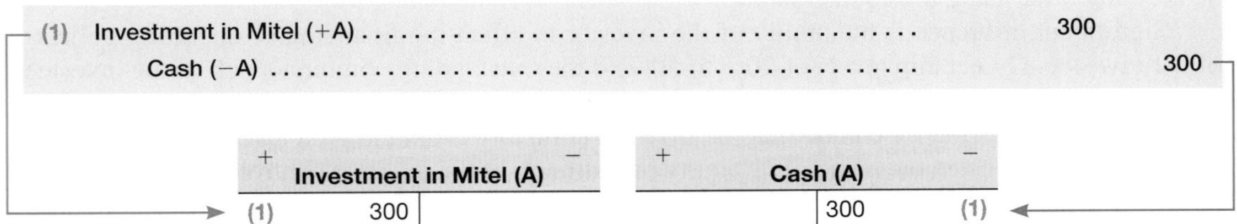

		Dr.	Cr.
(1)	Investment in Mitel (+A)	300	
	Cash (−A)		300

+ Investment in Mitel (A) −	
(1) 300	

+ Cash (A) −	
	300 (1)

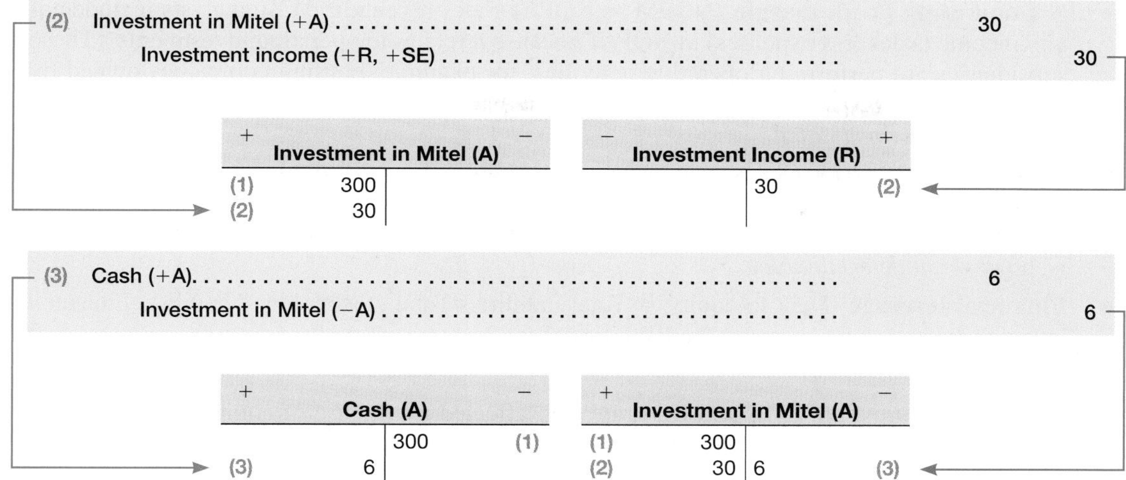

The investment is initially reported on Google's balance sheet at its purchase price of $300, representing a 30% interest in Mitel's equity of $1,000. During the year, Mitel's equity increases to $1,080 ($1,000 plus $100 income and less $20 dividends). Likewise, Google's investment increases by $30 to reflect its 30% share of Mitel's $100 income and decreases by $6 from Mitel's $20 of dividends (30% × $20). After these transactions, Google's investment in Mitel is reported on Google's balance sheet at 30% of $1,080, or $324. Appendix 12A covers the case in which Google might have paid a premium over 30% of the fair value of Mitel's net assets.

On the statement of cash flows, the original investment in Mitel would be seen as a $300 investing cash outflow. The $6 dividend received would be an operating cash inflow. However, the indirect method presentation would start with net income, which includes $30 in income from Mitel. Therefore, a negative $24 adjustment would be necessary (entitled something like "excess of equity income over dividends received") to arrive at the correct operating cash inflow.

Two final points about equity method accounting: First, just as the equity of a company is different from its fair value, so is the balance of the equity investment account different from its fair value. Indeed, there can be a substantial difference between the book value of an investment and its fair value. Second, if the investee company reports income, the investor company also reports income. Recognition of equity income by the investor, however, does not mean that it has received that income in cash. Cash is only received if the investee's directors declare a dividend payment.

FYI Investee dividend-paying ability can be (a) restricted by regulatory agencies or foreign governments, (b) prohibited under debt agreements for highly leveraged borrowers, and/or (c) influenced by directors that the investor does not control.

RESEARCH INSIGHT

Equity Income and Stock Prices The equity method of accounting for investments does not recognize any dividends received from the investee or any fair value changes for the investee in the investor's income until the investment is sold. However, research has found a positive relation between investors' and investees' stock prices at the time of investees' earnings and dividend announcements. This relation suggests that the fair value includes information regarding investees' earnings and dividends when assessing the stock prices of investor companies. This finding implies the market looks beyond the book value of the investment account in determining stock prices of investor companies. The finding also reflects the fact that the earnings from the operations of subsidiaries are considered earnings of the parent corporation.

Equity Method Accounting and Effects on Ratios

Under equity method accounting, only the net equity owned is reported on the balance sheet (not the assets and liabilities to which the investment relates), and only the net equity in earnings is reported in the income statement (not the investee's sales and expenses). Both the balance sheet and income statements are, therefore, markedly affected. Further, because the gross assets and liabilities are left off the balance sheet, and because the sales and expenses are omitted from the income statement, several financial ratios are also affected. Some important examples are highlighted:

- **Net operating profit margin** (NOPM = NOPAT/Sales revenue). Most analysts include equity income (sales less expenses) in NOPAT because it relates to operating investments. (These subsidiaries are performing operating activities, for example, bottling companies owned by Coca-Cola.) However, the investee's sales are omitted from the investor's sales. The reported NOPM is, thus, *overstated*.
- **Asset turnover ratios** (Sales revenue/Average assets). Because the investee's sales and its assets are omitted from the investor's financial statements, asset turnover ratios such as inventory turnover, receivables turnover, and PPE turnover are affected. The direction of the effect is, however, *indeterminable*.
- **Financial leverage** (Debt-to-equity = Total liabilities/Total stockholders' equity). Financial leverage is *understated* because the liabilities of the investee are omitted from the numerator of the debt-to-equity ratio.

Profitability ratios like ROE and ROA are also affected by the use of equity method investments, though the exact direction would require a careful analysis of the noncontrolling interests described on page 583. Analysts frequently adjust reported financial statements for equity investments before conducting their analysis. One approach to adjusting the reported financial statements would be to consolidate the equity method investee with the investor company.

Financial Statement Disclosures

Coca-Cola Company reports its interest in three of its international affiliates using the equity method. It reported the following amounts in its 2014 and 2013 financial statements:

Coca-Cola—Financial Statement Effects of Equity Investments

($ millions)	2014	2013
Balance sheet:		
Equity method investments	$9,947	$10,393
Income statement:		
Equity income—net	$ 769	$ 602
Cash flow statement:		
Equity income, net of dividends	$ 371	$ 201

Coca-Cola's equity method investment of $9,947 million represents 10.8% of its total assets of $92,023 million. Its equity income of $769 million is (coincidentally) 10.8% of its consolidated net income of $7,124 million. Pertinent portions of note 6 from Coca-Cola's 2014 10-K report are presented below:

The Company's equity method investments include our ownership interests in Coca-Cola FEMSA, Coca-Cola Hellenic and Coca-Cola Amatil. As of December 31, 2014, we owned 28 percent, 23 percent and 29 percent, respectively, of these companies' outstanding shares. As of December 31, 2014, our investment in our equity method investees in the aggregate exceeded our proportionate share of the net assets of these equity method investees by $1,671 million. This difference is not amortized.

A summary of financial information for our equity method investees in the aggregate is as follows (in millions):

Year ended December 31,	2014
Net operating revenues	$52,627
Cost of goods sold	31,810
Gross profit	20,817
Operating income	4,489
Consolidated net income	$ 2,440
Less: Net income attributable to noncontrolling interests	74
Net income attributable to common shareowners	$ 2,366
Equity income (loss)—net	$ 769

December 31,	2014
Current assets	$16,184
Noncurrent assets	40,080
Total assets	$56,264
Current liabilities	12,477
Noncurrent liabilities	16,657
Total liabilities	$29,134
Equity attributable to shareowners of investees	26,363
Equity attributable to noncontrolling interests	767
Total equity	27,130
Company equity investment	$ 9,947

YOU MAKE THE CALL

You are the Chief Financial Officer A substantial percentage of your company's sales are made through a key downstream producer, who combines your product with other materials to make the product that is ultimately purchased by consumers. In the last two years, this downstream producer has been branching out into other products that limit the capacity that can be devoted to your product. As a result, the growth prospects for your company have been diminished. What potential courses of action can you consider? Explain. (Answer on page 536.)

MID-CHAPTER REVIEW 2

Show the effects (amount and account) relating to the following four transactions involving investments in marketable securities accounted for using the equity method in the financial statement effects template, prepare the journal entries, and post the journal entries to the related T-accounts.

1. Purchased 5,000 shares of Hribar common stock at $10 cash per share. These shares reflect 30% ownership of Hribar.
2. Received a $2 per share cash dividend on Hribar common stock.
3. Made an adjustment to reflect $100,000 income reported by Hribar.
4. Sold all 5,000 shares of Hribar common stock for $90,000.

The solution to this review problem can be found on pages 615–616.

INVESTMENTS WITH CONTROL

LO5 Describe and analyze accounting for investments with control.

5

If the investor company owns enough of the voting stock of the investee company such that it can exercise control over the investee, it must report **consolidated financial statements**. For example, in footnote 1 to its 2014 10-K describing its accounting policies, Google reports:

Basis of Consolidation The Consolidated Financial Statements include the accounts of Google and our subsidiaries. All intercompany balances and transactions have been eliminated.

This statement means that Google's financial statements are an aggregation of those of the parent company and all its subsidiary companies to create the financial statements of the total economic entity. This process involves adding up the separate financial statements, while being careful to remove the effect of transactions between the separate entities.

Accounting for Investments with Control

Accounting for business combinations (acquisitions) involves one additional step to equity method accounting. Under the equity method, the investment balance represents the proportion of the investee's equity owned by the investor, and the investor company income statement includes its proportionate share of the investee's income. Consolidation accounting (1) replaces the investment balance with the investee's assets and liabilities to which it relates, and (2) replaces the equity income reported by the investor with the investee's sales and expenses to which it relates. Specifically, the consolidated balance sheet includes the gross assets and liabilities of the investee company, and the income statement includes the gross sales and expenses of the investee.

To illustrate, consider the following scenario. Penman Company acquires all of the common stock of Nissim Company by exchanging $3,000 cash for all of Nissim's common stock. In this case, the $3,000 purchase price is equal to the book value of Nissim's stockholders' equity (contributed capital of $2,000 and retained earnings of $1,000), and we assume that the fair values of Nissim's assets and liabilities are the same as their book values. On Penman's balance sheet, the investment in Nissim Co. appears as a financial investment (GAAP only requires consolidation for financial statements issued to the public, not for the internal financial records of the separate companies). Penman records an initial balance in the investment account of $3,000, which equals the purchase price. The balance sheets for Penman and Nissim immediately after the acquisition, together with the required consolidating adjustments (or eliminations), and the consolidated balance sheet that the two companies report are shown in **Exhibit 12.5**.

EXHIBIT 12.5 Mechanics of Consolidation Accounting (Purchased at Book Value, where Book Values = Fair Values)

	Penman Company	Nissim Company	Consolidating Adjustments*	Consolidated
Current assets	$ 5,000	$1,000		$ 6,000
Investment in Nissim	3,000	0	$(3,000)	0
PPE, net	10,000	4,000		14,000
Total assets	$18,000	$5,000		$20,000
Liabilities	$ 5,000	$2,000		$ 7,000
Contributed capital	10,000	2,000	(2,000)	10,000
Retained earnings	3,000	1,000	(1,000)	3,000
Total liabilities and equity	$18,000	$5,000		$20,000

*The accounting equation remains in balance with these adjustments.

Penman controls the activities of Nissim, so GAAP requires consolidation of the two balance sheets. That is, Penman must report a balance sheet as if the two companies were one economic entity. For the most part, this process involves adding together the companies' resources and obligations. However, if one company has a claim on the other (e.g., a receivable) and the other company has an obligation to the first (e.g., a payable), the consolidation process must eliminate both the claim and the obligation. In the case of Penman Company and Nissim Company, the consolidated balances for current assets, PPE, and liabilities are the sum of those accounts on each balance sheet. Penman's asset investment in Nissim represents a claim on Nissim Company, and Nissim's stockholders' equity accounts represent an obligation that is held by Penman, and this intercompany claim/obligation must be eliminated to complete the consolidation. This elimination is accomplished by removing the financial investment of $3,000, and removing Nissim's equity to which that investment relates.

The consolidated balance sheet is shown in the far right column of **Exhibit 12.5**. It shows total assets of $20,000, total liabilities of $7,000, and stockholders' equity of $13,000. Consolidated equity equals that of the parent company—this is always the case when the parent owns 100% of the subsidiary's shares.

Comparing the left and right columns of **Exhibit 12.5** demonstrates the difference between the equity method and consolidation. In the left column, it appears that Penman spent $3,000 to acquire a financial asset. However, in the right column, it appears that Penman spent $3,000 to acquire a "bundle" of assets and liabilities consisting of $1,000 in cash plus $4,000 in PPE minus $2,000 in liabilities. The purchase of the financial asset was the means by which this bundle was acquired. The net value of this bundle is $3,000, so the net assets don't change. But the financial statement reader gets more information about what was acquired.

Penman Company's statement of cash flows would show an investing cash outflow for the acquisition of Nissim Company. However, the outflow is shown net of the cash received in the acquisition, which was $1,000. Therefore, the investing section would have a line item showing something like "Cash paid for acquisitions, net of cash acquired" with an outflow of $2,000.

In addition, the changes in Penman's operating assets and liabilities on this year's balance sheet from last year's balance sheet will no longer match the adjustments for operating assets and liabilities on the indirect method statement of cash flows from operations. For instance, the change in Penman's receivables will be changes due to its own operations (including Nissim after the acquisition) plus any receivables acquired in the Nissim acquisition.

The illustration above assumes that the purchase price of the acquisition equals book value and the fair values of the acquired company's assets and liabilities are equal to their book values. What changes, if any, occur when the purchase price and book value are different? To explore this case, consider an acquisition where purchase price exceeds book value (the typical scenario). This situation might arise, for example, if an investor company believes it is acquiring something of value that is not reported on the investee's balance sheet—such as tangible assets whose fair values have risen above book value, or unrecorded intangible assets like patents or corporate synergies. If an acquisition is made at a price in excess of book value, all net assets acquired (both tangible and intangible) must be recognized on the consolidated balance sheet.

To illustrate an acquisition where purchase price exceeds book value, assume that Penman Company acquires 100% of Nissim Company for $4,000 instead of the $3,000 purchase price we used in the previous illustration. Also assume that in determining its purchase price, Penman feels that the additional $1,000 ($4,000 vs. $3,000) is justified because (1) Nissim's PPE is worth $300 more than its book value, and (2) Penman expects to realize $700 in additional value from corporate synergies.

The $4,000 investment account reflects two components: the book value acquired of $3,000 (as before) and an additional $1,000 of newly acquired assets. The post-acquisition balance sheets of the two companies, together with the consolidating adjustments and the consolidated balance sheet, are shown in **Exhibit 12.6**.

EXHIBIT 12.6 Mechanics of Consolidation Accounting (Purchased above Book Value)

	Penman Company	Nissim Company	Consolidating Adjustments	Consolidated
Current assets	$ 4,000	$1,000		$ 5,000
Investment in Nissim	4,000	0	$(4,000)	0
PPE, net	10,000	4,000	300	14,300
Goodwill			700	700
Total assets	$18,000	$5,000		$20,000
Liabilities	$ 5,000	$2,000		$ 7,000
Contributed capital	10,000	2,000	(2,000)	10,000
Retained earnings	3,000	1,000	(1,000)	3,000
Total liabilities and equity	$18,000	$5,000		$20,000

The consolidated balances for current assets, PPE, and liabilities are the sum of those accounts on each company's balance sheet. The investment account, however, includes newly acquired assets that must be reported on the consolidated balance sheet. The consolidation process in this case has two steps. First, the $3,000 equity of Nissim Company is eliminated against the investment account as before. Then, the remaining $1,000 of the investment account is eliminated through the adjustments for newly acquired assets on the consolidated balance sheet ($300 of

PPE and $700 of goodwill not reported on Nissim's balance sheet). Thus, the consolidated balance sheet reflects the book value of Penman and the *fair value* (book value plus the excess of Nissim's fair value over book value) for Nissim Company at the acquisition date.

Reporting of Acquired Assets and Liabilities

Acquisitions are often made at a purchase price in excess of the book value of the investee company's equity. The excess purchase price must be allocated to all of the assets and liabilities acquired, including those that do not currently appear on the balance sheet of the investee. This allocation can be done in three steps:

Step 1: Adjust the book value of all tangible assets acquired and all liabilities assumed to fair value. This adjustment addresses the issue of misvalued assets and liabilities on the investee firm's balance sheet.

Step 2: Assign a fair value to any identifiable intangible assets. Recall from Chapter 8 that intangible assets are only reported on the balance sheet if they are purchased; internally created intangible assets are not capitalized. This step allows the acquiring firm to assign a value to the investee's intangible assets, even if those assets are not reported on the investee firm's balance sheet.

Step 3: Assign the residual amount to goodwill. Goodwill is the excess of the acquisition price over the fair value of identifiable net assets acquired. That is, whatever value cannot be assigned to identifiable tangible and intangible assets is considered goodwill.[4]

The acquiring company is required to disclose relevant information about the allocation of the purchase price in its footnotes.

For example, consider Google's reported allocation of its total $2.6 billion purchase price in February 2014 for Nest Labs, Inc. as reported in Note 5 to its 2014 10-K report:

Note 5. Acquisitions

In February 2014, we completed the acquisition of Nest Labs, Inc. (Nest), a company whose mission is to reinvent devices in the home such as thermostats and smoke alarms. Prior to this transaction, we had an approximately 12% ownership interest in Nest. The acquisition is expected to enhance Google's suite of products and services and allow Nest to continue to innovate upon devices in the home, making them more useful, intuitive, and thoughtful, and to reach more users in more countries.

Of the total $2.6 billion purchase price and the fair value of our previously held equity interest of $152 million, $51 million was cash acquired, $430 million was attributed to intangible assets, $2.3 billion was attributed to goodwill, and $84 million was attributed to net liabilities assumed. The goodwill of $2.3 billion is primarily attributable to synergies expected to arise after the acquisition. Goodwill is not expected to be deductible for tax purposes. . . .

For all acquisitions completed during the year ended December 31, 2014, patents and developed technology have a weighted-average useful life of 5.1 years, customer relationships have a weighted-average useful life of 4.5 years, and trade names and other have a weighted-average useful life of 6.9 years.

Of the total acquisition price of $2.7 billion, Google assigned $2.3 billion to goodwill. The remaining (approximately) $400 million includes $51 million in cash plus $430 million in intangible assets, less $84 million in liabilities. The $430 million in intangible assets and the $84 million in liabilities were recorded at fair value at the time of the acquisition.

Google reports its aggregated goodwill separately on its balance sheet, but combines its other intangible assets in its balance sheet under the title "Intangible assets, net." Goodwill can only be recognized as an asset in an acquisition and only then in the amount by which the purchase price exceeds the fair value of the net assets acquired, including all identifiable intangible assets.

[4] What happens if goodwill is negative? Such a "bargain purchase" is uncommon, because it implies that the "whole" of the acquired company is worth less than the sum of its parts. Therefore, when an acquirer believes that it has made a bargain purchase, it must carefully check its valuation of all the components of the goodwill calculation. If that review confirms that the acquirer has made a bargain purchase, then it recognizes a gain in its income from continuing operations.

For the acquisitions it made in 2014, Google estimates customer relationships have a weighted average useful life of 4.5 years. Patents and developed technology have a weighted average useful life of 5.1 years. Tradenames and other intangibles have a weighted average useful life of 6.9 years. The majority of these assets are not deductible for tax purposes. These estimated lives determine the annual amortization expense associated with these assets on the firm's financial books. Goodwill is not amortized under GAAP although it is subject to impairment write-down. The effect of this accounting treatment is to relieve the income statement of the annual amortization expense. The SEC is sufficiently concerned with the impact on the income statement that it scrutinizes acquisition accounting for excessive goodwill capitalization.

Reporting of Goodwill GAAP requires companies to test goodwill annually for impairment just like any other asset. The impairment test is a two-step process:

1. The fair value of the investee company (the reporting unit) is compared with the book value of the investor's investment account.[5]
2. If the fair value is less than the investment balance, the investment is deemed impaired. The company must then estimate the goodwill value as if the subsidiary were acquired for its current fair value, and the imputed balance for goodwill becomes the amount at which it is recorded. If this imputed amount is less than its book value, goodwill must be written down, resulting in an impairment loss that is reported in the consolidated income statement.

To illustrate the impairment computation, assume that an investment, currently reported at $1 million on the investor's balance sheet, has a current fair value of $900,000. The consolidated balance sheet reports net assets (absent goodwill) at $700,000 and goodwill at $300,000. Analysis reveals that the current fair value of the net assets of the investee company (absent goodwill) is $700,000. This analysis indicates goodwill is impaired by $100,000, which is computed as follows.

Fair value of investee company	$ 900,000
Fair value of net assets (absent goodwill)	(700,000)
Implied goodwill	200,000
Current goodwill balance	(300,000)
Impairment loss	$(100,000)

The financial statement effects and related journal entry and T-accounts are:

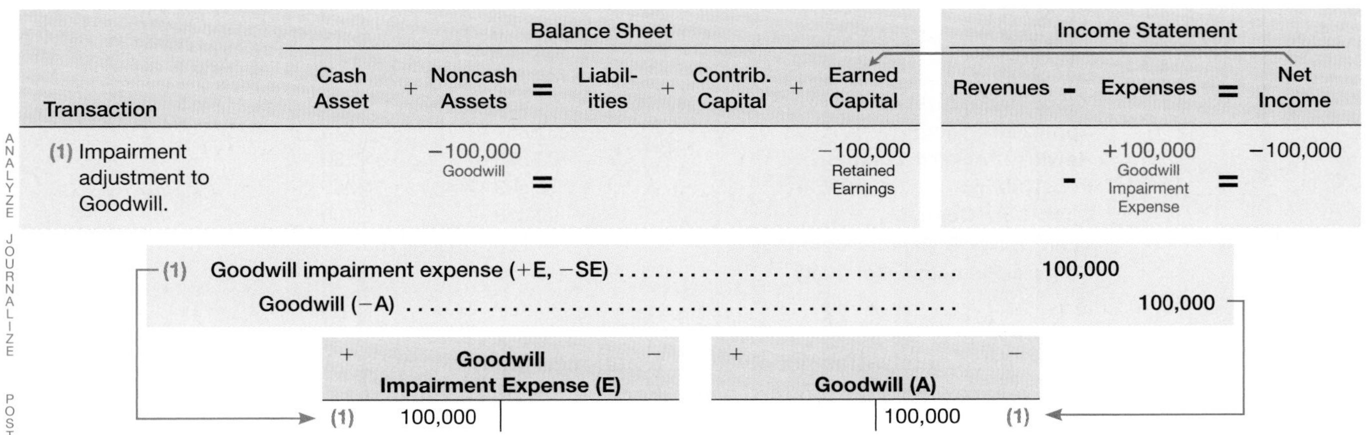

	Balance Sheet									Income Statement				
Transaction	Cash Asset	+	Noncash Assets	=	Liabil-ities	+	Contrib. Capital	+	Earned Capital	Revenues	-	Expenses	=	Net Income
(1) Impairment adjustment to Goodwill.			−100,000 Goodwill	=					−100,000 Retained Earnings		-	+100,000 Goodwill Impairment Expense	=	−100,000

(1) Goodwill impairment expense (+E, −SE)	100,000	
Goodwill (−A)		100,000

+ Goodwill Impairment Expense (E) −		+ Goodwill (A) −	
(1) 100,000			100,000 (1)

This analysis of investee company implies that goodwill must be written down by $100,000. The impairment loss is reported as a separate line item in the consolidated income statement. The related footnote disclosure describes the reasons for the write-down.

Yahoo! Inc. reports the following goodwill impairment in excerpts from note 5 of its 2014 10-K:

[5] The fair value of the investee company can be determined using market comparables or another valuation method (such as the discounted cash flow model, residual operating income model, or P/E multiples).

The changes in the carrying amount of goodwill for the year ended December 31, 2014 were as follows (in thousands):

	Americas	EMEA	Asia Pacific	Total
Net balance as of December 31, 2013......	$3,802,334	$546,856	$330,458	$4,679,648
Acquisitions and other..................	533,894	110,203	(607)	643,490
Goodwill impairment charge		(79,135)	(9,279)	(88,414)
Foreign currency translation adjustments ...	(2,271)	(46,109)	(22,690)	(71,070)
Net balance as of December 31, 2014......	$4,333,957	$531,815	$297,882	$5,163,654

In 2014, as a result of the annual goodwill impairment test, the Company concluded that the carrying value of the Middle East reporting unit, included in the EMEA reportable segment, and the carrying value of the India & Southeast Asia reporting unit included in the Asia Pacific reportable segment both exceeded their respective fair values. As required by the second step of the impairment test, the Company performed an allocation of the fair value to all the assets and liabilities of the reporting unit, including identifiable intangible assets, based on their estimated fair values, to determine the implied fair value of goodwill. Accordingly, the Company recorded a goodwill impairment charge related to the Middle East and India & Southeast Asia reporting units of $79 million and $9 million, respectively, during the quarter ended December 31, 2014 for the difference between the carrying value of the goodwill in the reporting unit and its implied fair value with no goodwill remaining in either reporting unit. The impairment resulted from a decline in business conditions in the Middle East and India & Southeast Asia during the latter half of 2014.

At the end of 2014, Yahoo had a goodwill balance of $5,164 million. The goodwill balance represented 8.3% of its total assets and 13.3% of its stockholders' equity. The $88.4 million impairment charge in 2014 was 61.9% of its operating income. Yahoo's disclosures hint at the complexity of the process that a company follows to determine goodwill impairment charges.

Reported goodwill across companies differs widely in total and as a percentage of company assets as the following fiscal 2014 figures indicate ($ millions).

Company	Total Assets	Reported Goodwill	Goodwill Percentage
Google, Inc.	$131,133	$15,599	11.9%
Yahoo! Inc.	61,960	5,164	8.3%
Apple, Inc.	231,839	4,616	2.0%
Hewlett-Packard Company	103,206	31,139	30.2%
PepsiCo, Inc.	70,509	14,965	21.2%
Coca-Cola Company......................	92,023	12,100	13.1%
The Procter & Gamble Company	144,266	53,704	37.2%
Colgate-Palmolive Company..............	13,459	2,307	17.1%

Reported goodwill is not always a useful measure of the asset's value, particularly when the actual value exceeds the reported value. For example, the value of the Coca-Cola brand name alone exceeds the reported total asset value of the firm, yet its reported goodwill is only 13.1% of total assets.

BUSINESS INSIGHT

In competitive bidding situations, the winning bidder is likely to be the one who most overvalued the item, a phenomenon known as the "winner's curse." Therefore, acquisition goodwill is viewed with some skepticism by financial analysts. Does the goodwill represent synergies like future cost savings or business opportunities that are available only to the combined companies? Or, does it represent an overpayment?

A *Wall Street Journal* article described multi-billion dollar goodwill impairment charges by Hewlett-Packard, Microsoft and Boston Scientific and ascribes these charges to acquisitions that did not "pan out." The article identified more companies whose goodwill assets exceeded their total market value.

When companies record a goodwill impairment charge, they often emphasize that the impairment was a "non-cash charge," implying that it is therefore less important. That statement is true as far as the current period is concerned, but acquisitions involve cash or some other item of value. In Hewlett-Packard's case, its $8 billion goodwill impairment in the third quarter of 2012 was primarily related to its acquisition of EDS, which required a cash outflow of more than $13 billion when the deal closed in 2008 and resulted in about $10.4 billion in goodwill. Goodwill impairment requires no *current* cash outflows, but it does reflect on the wisdom of *past* cash outflows.

Source: Scott Thurm, "Buyers Beware: The Goodwill Games," *Wall Street Journal*, August 14, 2012.

Noncontrolling Interest

Noncontrolling interest represents the equity of shareholders who own a minority of the shares of one or more of the subsidiaries in a consolidated entity. When a company acquires a controlling interest in a company, it must consolidate the subsidiary when preparing its financial statements by reporting all of the subsidiary's assets and liabilities in the consolidated balance sheet and all of the subsidiary's revenues and expenses in the consolidated income statement. This is true even when the controlling parent company acquires less than 100% of the subsidiary. When less than 100% of the subsidiary's shares are acquired, there are two groups of shareholders: the parent company's shareholders and the noncontrolling shareholders who own a minority of the subsidiary's shares. These noncontrolling shareholders have a claim on the net assets and the earnings of the subsidiary company.

To illustrate the reporting of noncontrolling interest, assume that Penman Company acquires 80% of Nissim Company for $2,400 (80% of $3,000). Because Penman must consolidate 100% of the assets and liabilities of Nissim, Penman's equity must increase to maintain the accounting equation. A new equity account titled noncontrolling interests is added to Penman's stockholders' equity. The consolidation worksheet is presented in **Exhibit 12.7**.

EXHIBIT 12.7 Mechanics of Consolidation Accounting (Less than 100% of Subsidiary Shares Purchased at Book Value)

	Penman Company	Nissim Company	Consolidating Adjustments	Consolidated
Current assets	$ 5,600	$1,000		$ 6,600
Investment in Nissim	2,400	0	$(2,400)	0
PPE, net	10,000	4,000		14,000
Total assets	$18,000	$5,000		$20,600
Liabilities	$ 5,000	$2,000		$ 7,000
Contributed capital	10,000	2,000	(2,000)	10,000
Retained earnings	3,000	1,000	(1,000)	3,000
Penman shareholders' equity	13,000			13,000
Noncontrolling interests			600	600
Total equity	13,000			13,600
Total liabilities and equity	$18,000	$5,000		$20,600

The contributed capital of the consolidated entity (common stock, additional paid-in capital, treasury stock, etc.) refers to the parent company's shareholders' equity (in this example, Penman Company). The net assets owned by the noncontrolling shareholders are represented in one account, labeled noncontrolling interests. Each period, the noncontrolling interests equity account is increased by the noncontrolling shareholders' share of the subsidiary's net income, and decreased by any dividends paid to those shareholders.

The consolidated income statement lists total consolidated revenues and expenses and consolidated net income. After net income is computed, the portion of net income that is attributed to noncontrolling interests is subtracted. If the noncontrolling shareholders own 20% of the subsidiary's shares, then 20% of the earnings of the subsidiary are subtracted from the consolidated entity's income statement. (This is not 20% of the consolidated company's earnings, only 20% of the subsidiary's earnings.)

The stockholders' equity section of Yahoo!'s 2014 balance sheet is shown as an illustration of the presentation of noncontrolling interests in the balance sheet:

Yahoo! Inc. Consolidated Balance Sheet (Stockholders' equity section only)	
($ thousands)	**December 31, 2014**
Preferred stock, $0.001 par value	—
Common stock, $0.001 par value	$ 945
Additional paid-in capital	8,496,683
Treasury stock, at cost	(712,455)
Retained earnings	8,937,036
Accumulated other comprehensive income	22,019,628
Total Yahoo! Inc. stockholders' equity	38,741,837
Noncontrolling interests	43,755
Total equity	$38,785,592

Total Yahoo! Inc. stockholders' equity is listed at $38,741.8 million. This is the equity claim of those investors who own shares in Yahoo!. Next, the $43.8 million of noncontrolling interests is listed. This amount represents the share of Yahoo! subsidiaries' net assets that is owned by minority shareholders. The final line lists the total equity, which is the sum of Yahoo!'s stockholders' equity and the noncontrolling interests. Yahoo!'s income statement presents noncontrolling interests as follows:

Yahoo! Inc. Consolidated Income Statement (excerpts)	
($ thousands)	**Year ended December 31, 2014**
Income before income taxes and earnings in equity interests	$10,512,381
Provision for income taxes	(4,038,102)
Earnings in equity interests, net of tax	1,057,863
Net income	7,532,142
Net income attributable to noncontrolling interests	(10,411)
Net income attributable to Yahoo! Inc.	$ 7,521,731

Yahoo! presents its earnings in equity method investments after the provision for income taxes so these earnings are presented net of income taxes. Yahoo! then presents net income of $7,532.1 million. This is income for the consolidated entity, including the share of income for Yahoo!'s shareholders as well as that portion that is for the noncontrolling interests. Next, the income attributable to noncontrolling interests ($10.4 million) is subtracted, leaving net income attributable to Yahoo!'s shareholders ($7,521.7 million).

A GLOBAL PERSPECTIVE

U.S. GAAP and IFRS are very similar in their treatment of the accounting for investments as covered in this chapter. IFRS defines the term fair value in the same way and requires disclosure of fair values according to their determination as Level 1, Level 2 or Level 3. Passive investments are classified as being for trading purposes or as being held-to-maturity, with all other passive investments accounted as available-for-sale.

GAAP uses the term "equity" or "affiliate" to describe an investment involving significant influence (usually between 20% and 50%). IFRS uses the term "associate" to describe such an investment, with the same 20% threshold. The investment balance is equal to the investor's cost plus the proportionate share of changes in the investee's net assets since the date of investment. If the investor's cost exceeds the proportionate book value, the excess is attributed to individual assets (including goodwill) and liabilities and subsequent earnings will include the appropriate amortizations of those value adjustments.

The process of accounting for an acquisition and issuing subsequent consolidated financial statements is very similar to that described in the previous section.

Under proposed International Financial Reporting Standards (IFRS), trading, available-for-sale, and held-to-maturity portfolios are accounted for similarly to GAAP.

Limitations of Consolidation Reporting Consolidation of financial statements is meant to present a financial picture of the entire set of companies under control of the parent. Because investors typically purchase stock in the parent company and not in the subsidiaries, the view is more relevant than would be one of the parent company's own balance sheet with subsidiaries reported as equity investments. Still, we must be aware of certain limitations that the consolidation process entails:

1. Consolidated income does not imply that cash is received by the parent company and is available for subsidiaries. The parent can only receive cash via dividend payments, and dividend payments may trigger tax obligations. It is readily possible, therefore, for an individual subsidiary to experience cash flow problems even though the consolidated group has strong cash flows. Likewise, debts of a subsidiary are not obligations of the consolidated group. Thus, even if the consolidated balance sheet is strong, creditors of a failing subsidiary are often unable to sue the parent or other subsidiaries to recoup losses.
2. Consolidated balance sheets and income statements are a mix of the subsidiaries, often from different industries. Comparisons across companies, even if in similar industries, are often complicated by the different mix of subsidiary companies. Companies are required to report some financial results for their business segments. For instance, **General Electric** reports revenues, operating profits and assets for each of its six operating segments—Energy Infrastructure, Aviation, Healthcare, Transportation, Home & Business Solutions, and GE Capital.
3. Segment disclosures on individual subsidiaries are affected by intercorporate transfer-pricing policies that can artificially inflate the profitability of one segment at the expense of another. Companies also have considerable discretion in the allocation of corporate overhead to subsidiaries, which can markedly affect segment and subsidiary profitability.

FINANCIAL STATEMENT ANALYSIS

This section introduces no new ratios, but the topics covered in Chapter 12 do have implications for ratios covered in other chapters. For instance, gains and losses on available-for-sale securities are not recognized in income until those securities are sold. Therefore, management can increase net income by selling securities on which it has gains or decrease net income by selling securities on which it has losses. As a result, management may have a means to smooth the variations in income over time, using gains and losses from previous periods that have nothing to do with current performance. As careful financial statement users, we can read the footnotes to find the realized gains and losses included in income for the period.

Financial ratio comparisons are also affected by the percentage ownership of affiliated companies. For instance, suppose Naughton Group has 50% ownership in the company that distributes its products. Chapman Enterprises, a competitor of Naughton, owns 55% of the shares of the company that distributes its products. While the difference between 50% and 55% ownership probably has little economic significance, the accounting reports for Naughton and Chapman will look very different. Naughton's income statement will report only its own revenues and expenses, while Chapman's income statement will report its own revenues and expenses *and* the revenues and expenses of the distribution company (less any intercompany adjustments). Naughton's balance sheet will report its own assets, including its 50% equity in the distributor, while Chapman's balance sheet will report its own assets *plus* the assets of the distribution company. Financial statement readers should interpret comparisons of ratios like PPE Turnover in light of these effects.

A similar "quantum" change in accounting occurs at 20% ownership. There may appear to be little economic difference between owning 19% of a company's shares and owning 20% of those shares. But there is a significant difference in the accounting for those two alternatives, and this difference sometimes affects the choice between a 19% investment and a 20% investment. If the investee is a start-up earning losses, a 20% investment would require the investor to recognize 20% of those losses in its own income. A 19% investment would not recognize any share of the losses.

Finally, acquisitions disrupt the usual relationships between income statement and balance sheet items. When one company acquires another, the acquirer consolidates the acquired company as of the date that the deal closes. At that point, it includes the acquired company's assets and liabilities on the consolidated balance sheet, and it begins to report the acquired company's revenues and expenses from that time forward. So, if Hoskin Corp. acquires 100% of Lynch, Inc. on December 31, 2016, how will the inventory turnover ratio be affected? The 2016 cost of goods sold for Hoskin will reflect a year of Hoskin's COGS plus one day of Lynch's COGS. The beginning-of-year inventory will be 100% of Hoskin's inventory at that time, but the end-of-year inventory will be 100% of Hoskin's inventory *plus* 100% of Lynch's inventory. The inventory turnover ratio is likely to decrease significantly, but that decrease is due to the acquisition, not necessarily a decline in Hoskin's performance. A careful reader of the financial statements should try to separate out the effects of the acquisition from the ongoing performance of the company.

CHAPTER-END REVIEW

On January 1 of the current year, Bradshaw Company purchased all of the common shares of Dukes Company for $600,000 cash—this is $200,000 in excess of Dukes's book value of its equity. The balance sheets of the two firms immediately after the acquisition follow:

	Bradshaw (Parent)	Dukes (Subsidiary)	Consolidating Adjustments	Consolidated
Current assets	$1,000,000	$100,000		
Investment in Dukes	600,000	—		
PPE, net	3,000,000	400,000		
Goodwill	—	—		
Total assets	$4,600,000	$500,000		
Liabilities	$1,000,000	$100,000		
Contributed capital	2,000,000	200,000		
Retained earnings	1,600,000	200,000		
Total liabilities and equity	$4,600,000	$500,000		

During purchase negotiations, Dukes's PPE was appraised at $500,000, and all of Dukes's remaining assets and liabilities were appraised at values approximating their book values. Also, Bradshaw concluded that payment of an additional $100,000 was warranted because of anticipated corporate synergies. Show the impact of the transaction in the financial statement effects template, prepare the appropriate journal entry, post the journal entry to the related T-accounts, and prepare the consolidated balance sheet at acquisition.

The solution to this review problem can be found on page 617.

APPENDIX 12A: Equity Method Mechanics

LO6 Illustrate and analyze accounting mechanics for equity method investments.

The appendix provides a comprehensive example of accounting for an equity method investment. Assume that Petroni Company acquires a 30% interest in the outstanding voting shares of Wahlen Company on January 1, 2016, for $234,000 in cash. On that date, Wahlen's book value of equity is $560,000. Petroni agrees to pay $234,000 for a company with a book value of equity equivalent to $168,000 ($560,000 × 30%) because it feels that (1) Wahlen's balance sheet is undervalued by $140,000 (Petroni estimates PPE is undervalued by $50,000 and that Wahlen has unrecorded patents valued at $90,000) and (2) the investment is expected to yield intangible benefits valued at $24,000. (The $140,000 by which the balance sheet is undervalued translates into an investment equivalent of $42,000 [$140,000 × 30%]. This, plus the intangible benefits valued at $24,000, comprises the $66,000 difference between the purchase price [$234,000] and the book value equivalent [$168,000].)

The effect of the investment on Petroni's books is to reduce cash by $234,000 and to report the investment in Wahlen for $234,000. The investment is reported at its fair value at acquisition, just like all other asset acquisitions, and it is reported as a noncurrent asset because the expected holding period of equity method investments is in excess of one year. Subsequent to this purchase there are three main aspects of equity method accounting:

1. Dividends received from the investee are treated as a return *of* the investment rather than a return *on* the investment (investor company records an increase in cash received and a decrease in the investment account).
2. When the investee company reports net income for a period, the investor company reports its proportionate ownership of that income. This amount is usually reported in the investment income section of its income statement. Thus, both income and the investment account increase from equity method income. If the investee company reports a net *loss* for the period, income of the investor company is reduced as well as its investment account by its proportionate share.
3. The investment balance is not marked-to-fair value (market) as with passive investments. Instead, it is recorded at its historical cost and is increased (decreased) by the investor company's proportionate share of investee income (loss) and decreased by any cash dividends received. Unrecognized gains (losses) can, therefore, occur if the fair value of the investment differs from this adjusted cost. (If a decline in value is deemed "other than temporary," then the investment would be written down.)

To illustrate these mechanics, let's return to our illustration and assume that subsequent to acquisition, Wahlen reports net income of $50,000 and pays $10,000 cash dividends. Petroni would reflect these events in the FSET as follows:

	Balance Sheet										Income Statement				
Transaction	Cash Asset	+	Noncash Assets	=	Liabil-ities	+	Contrib. Capital	+	Earned Capital		Revenues	-	Expenses	=	Net Income
(1) Purchase 30% of Wahlen Co. stock.	−234,000 Cash		+234,000 Investment in Wahlen	=								-		=	
(2) Recognize 30% of Wahlen net income.			+15,000 Investment in Wahlen						+15,000 Retained Earnings		+15,000 Investment Income				+15,000
(3) Receive 30% of Wahlen dividends.	+3,000 Cash		−3,000 Investment in Wahlen												

After these entries, the investment balance is $246,000. Petroni has an investing cash outflow of $234,000 and an operating cash inflow of $3,000. Retained earnings increase by $15,000 from recognizing the 30% share of Wahlen's net income.

However, Petroni must also account for the differential values that accounted for the purchase premium. If Wahlen's PPE is undervalued by $50,000 and has an expected remaining life of twenty years, Petroni must depreciate $750 (= 30%*$50,000/20 years) in value for each of the next twenty years. And, if the unrecorded patents have an expected useful life of nine years, Petroni must amortize $3,000 (= 30%*$90,000/9 years) of the investment's value for each of the coming nine years. These amortizations are deducted from the investment income recognized by Petroni. The entries are the following:

Transaction	Cash Asset	+	Noncash Assets	=	Liabilities	+	Contrib. Capital	+	Earned Capital		Revenues	-	Expenses	=	Net Income
(4) Depreciate additional PPE value.			−750 Investment in Wahlen	=					−750 Retained Earnings		−750 Investment Income	-		=	−750
(5) Amortize additional patent assets.			−3,000 Investment in Wahlen						−3,000 Retained Earnings		−3,000 Investment Income				−3,000

A part of the premium paid by Petroni is attributed to items that have definite lives (PPE and patents), and we must account for those amounts in judging the investment's performance. In this case, Petroni records income of $11,250 on its $234,000 investment − $15,000 for its share of Wahlen's income, minus the $3,750 amortization of the premiium paid for PPE and patents. The Investment in Wahlen asset has a value of $242,250 ($234,000 + 15,000 − 3,000 − 750 − 3,000) after all entries.

The amount attributed to goodwill is tested for impairment annually, but it is not subject to periodic amortization.

APPENDIX 12B: Consolidation Accounting Mechanics

7 **LO7** Apply consolidation accounting mechanics.

This appendix is a continuation of the example we introduced in Appendix 12A, extended to the consolidation of a parent company and one wholly owned subsidiary. Assume that Petroni Company acquires 100% (rather than 30% as in Appendix 12A) of the outstanding voting shares of Wahlen Company on January 1, 2016. To obtain these shares, Petroni pays $420,000 cash and issues 20,000 shares of its $10 par value common stock. On this date, Petroni's stock has a fair value of $18 per share, and Wahlen's book value of equity is $560,000. Petroni is willing to pay $780,000 ($420,000 plus 20,000 shares at $18 per share) for this company with a book value of equity of $560,000 because it believes Wahlen's balance sheet is understated by $140,000 (its PPE is undervalued by $50,000 and it has unrecorded patents valued at $90,000). The remaining $80,000 of the purchase price excess over book value is ascribed to corporate synergies and other unidentifiable intangible assets (goodwill). Thus, the purchase price consists of the following three components:

Investment ($780,000)
- Book value of Wahlen ($560,000)
- Excess fair value over book ($140,000)
- Goodwill ($80,000)

The investment in Wahlen appears as a financial asset on Petroni's books. This means that at acquisition, Petroni's assets increase by $360,000 (cash decreases by $420,000 and the investments account increases by $780,000) and its equity (contributed capital) increases by the same amount.

The balance sheets of Petroni and Wahlen at acquisition follow, including the adjustments that occur in the consolidation process and the ultimate consolidated balance sheet.

Accounts	Petroni Company	Wahlen Company	Consolidation Adjustments*		Consolidated Balance Sheet
			Entry S	Entry A	
Cash	$ 168,000	$ 80,000			$ 248,000
Receivables, net	320,000	180,000			500,000
Inventory	440,000	260,000			700,000
Investment in Wahlen	780,000	0	$(560,000)	$(220,000)	0
Land	200,000	120,000			320,000
PPE, net	1,040,000	320,000		50,000	1,410,000
Patents	0	0		90,000	90,000
Goodwill	0	0		80,000	80,000
Totals	$2,948,000	$960,000			$3,348,000
Accounts payable	$ 320,000	$ 60,000			$ 380,000
Long-term liabilities	760,000	340,000			1,100,000
Contributed capital	1,148,000	80,000	(80,000)		1,148,000
Retained earnings	720,000	480,000	(480,000)		720,000
Totals	$2,948,000	$960,000			$3,348,000

*Entry S refers to elimination of subsidiary stockholders' equity, and Entry A refers to adjustment of assets and liabilities acquired.

The initial balance of the investment account at acquisition ($780,000) reflects the $700,000 fair value of Wahlen's net tangible assets and patents ($560,000 book value + $140,000 undervaluation of assets) plus the goodwill ($80,000) acquired. Goodwill is the excess of the purchase price over the fair value of the net assets acquired. It does not appear on Petroni's balance sheet as an explicit asset at this point. It is, however, included in the investment balance and will emerge as a separate asset during consolidation.

The process of completing the initial consolidated balance sheet involves eliminating Petroni's investment account and replacing it with the assets and liabilities of Wahlen Company to which it relates. Recall the investment account consists of three items: the book value of Wahlen ($560,000), the excess of net asset fair value over book value ($140,000), and goodwill ($80,000). The consolidation process eliminates each item as follows:

Entry S: Elimination of Wahlen's book value of equity: Investment account is reduced by the $560,000 book value of Wahlen, and each of the components of Wahlen's equity ($80,000 common stock and $480,000 retained earnings) are eliminated.

Entry A: Elimination of the excess of purchase price over book value: Investment account is reduced by $220,000 to zero. The remaining adjustments increase assets (A) by the additional purchase price paid. PPE is written up by $50,000, and a $90,000 patent asset and an $80,000 goodwill asset are reported.

Stepping back from the consolidation process, we can see its effects by comparing the Petroni Company (parent) balance sheet to the consolidated balance sheet. The Petroni Company balance sheet shows a financial asset valued at $780,000. Consolidation gives us a different perspective. Rather than viewing this as a financial investment, consolidation views the financial investment as the *means* by which Petroni Company acquired a bundle of assets and liabilities. That is, the financial asset of $780,000 has been replaced by Cash ($80,000), Receivables ($180,000), Inventory ($260,000), Land ($120,000), PPE – net ($370,000), Patent ($90,000), Goodwill ($80,000), Payables ($60,000) and Long-term liabilities ($340,000). This bundle has a net value equal to the $780,000, but it provides much more detail about the transaction in which Petroni engaged.

The one part of the balance sheet that is not changed by the consolidation is the shareholders' equity section. The consolidated shareholders' equity accounts are the same as the parent company shareholders' equity accounts when the parent owns 100% of the subsidiary.

Consolidation is similar in successive periods. To the extent that the excess purchase price has been assigned to depreciable assets, or identifiable intangible assets that are amortized over their useful lives, the new assets recognized initially are depreciated. If the PPE value adjustment has an estimated life of 20 years, then the consolidated income statement would include depreciation of 1/20 of this $50,000 each year. Amortization of the $90,000 patent would also appear in the consolidated income statement. Finally, because goodwill is not amortized under GAAP, it remains at its carrying amount of $80,000 on the consolidated balance sheet unless and until it is impaired and written down.

APPENDIX 12C: Accounting for Investments in Derivatives

LO8 Discuss the reporting of derivative securities.

8

Derivatives refer to financial instruments that are utilized by companies to reduce various kinds of risks. Some examples follow:

- A company expects to purchase raw materials for its production process and wants to reduce the risk that the purchase price increases prior to the purchase.
- A company has an accounts receivable on its books that is payable in a foreign currency and wants to reduce the risk that exchange rates move unfavorably prior to collection.
- A company borrows funds on a floating rate of interest (such as linked to the prime rate) and wants to convert the loan to a fixed rate of interest.

Companies are commonly exposed to these and many similar types of risk. Although companies are generally willing to assume the normal market risks that are inherent in their business, many of these financial-type risks can add variability to income and are uncontrollable. Fortunately, commodities, currencies, and interest rates are all traded on various markets and, further, securities have been developed to manage all of these risks. These securities fall under the label of derivatives. They include forward contracts, futures contracts, option contracts, and swap agreements.

Companies use derivatives to manage many of these financial risks. The reduction of risk comes at a price: the fee that another party (called the counterparty) is charging to assume that risk. Most counterparties are financial institutions, and managing financial risk is their business and a source of their profits. Although derivatives can be used effectively to manage financial risk, they can also be used for speculation with potentially disastrous results. It is for this reason that regulators passed standards regarding their disclosure in financial statements.

Reporting of Derivatives Derivatives work by offsetting the gain or loss for the asset or liability to which they relate. Derivatives thus shelter the company from such fluctuations. For example, if a hedged receivable denominated in a foreign currency declines in value (due to a strengthening of the $US), the derivative security will increase in value by an offsetting amount, at least in theory. As a result, net equity remains unaffected and no gain or loss arises, nor is a loss reported in income.[6]

Although accounting for derivatives is complex, it essentially boils down to this: the derivative contract, and the asset or liability to which it relates, are both reported on the balance sheet at fair value. The asset and liability are offsetting *if* the hedge is effective and, thus, net equity is unaffected. Likewise, the related gains and losses are largely offsetting, leaving income unaffected. Income is impacted only to the extent that the hedging activities are ineffective or result from speculative activities. It is this latter activity, in particular, that regulators were concerned about in formulating accounting standards for derivatives.

Disclosure of Derivatives Companies are required to disclose both qualitative and quantitative information about derivatives in notes to their financial statements and elsewhere (usually in Management's Discussion and Analysis section). The aim of these disclosures is to inform outsiders about potential risks underlying derivative securities.

Following is **Southwest Airlines Co.**'s disclosures from note 1 to its 2014 10-K report relating to its use of derivatives.

Financial Derivative Instruments

The Company accounts for financial derivative instruments at fair value and applies hedge accounting rules where appropriate. The Company utilizes various derivative instruments, including crude oil, unleaded gasoline, and heating oil-based derivatives, to attempt to reduce the risk of its exposure to jet fuel price increases. These instruments consist primarily of purchased call options, collar structures, call spreads, put spreads, and fixed-price swap agreements, and upon proper qualification are accounted for as cash-flow hedges. The Company also has interest rate swap agreements to convert a portion of its fixed-rate debt to floating rates and has swap agreements that convert certain floating-rate debt to a fixed-rate. These interest rate hedges are appropriately designated as either fair value hedges or as cash flow hedges.

Since the majority of the Company's financial derivative instruments are not traded on a market exchange, the Company estimates their fair values. Depending on the type of instrument, the values are determined by the use of present value methods or option value models with assumptions about commodity prices based on those observed in underlying markets. Also, since there is not a reliable forward market for jet fuel, the Company must estimate the future prices of jet fuel in order to measure the effectiveness of the hedging instruments in offsetting changes to those prices. Forward jet fuel prices are estimated through utilization of a statistical-based regression equation with data from market forward prices of like commodities. This equation is then adjusted for certain items, such as transportation costs, that are stated in the Company's fuel purchasing contracts with its vendors.

For the effective portion of settled fuel hedges, the Company records the associated gains or losses as a component of Fuel and oil expense in the Consolidated Statement of Income. For amounts representing ineffectiveness, as defined, or changes in fair value of derivative instruments for which hedge accounting is not applied, the Company records any gains or losses as a component of Other (gains) losses, net, in the Consolidated Statement of Income. Amounts that are paid or received in connection with the purchase or sale of financial derivative instruments (i.e., premium costs of option contracts) are classified as a component of Other (gains) losses, net, in the Consolidated Statement of Income in the period in which the instrument settles or expires. All cash flows associated with purchasing and selling derivatives are classified as operating cash flows in the Consolidated Statement of Cash Flows, within Changes in certain assets and liabilities.

Southwest Airlines' derivative use is mainly to hedge against fuel cost. Those hedges act to place a ceiling on fuel cost. For 2014, these instruments covered 34% of the company's fuel requirements.

From a reporting standpoint, unrealized gains and losses on these option contracts are accumulated in the Accumulated Other Comprehensive Income (AOCI) portion of its stockholders' equity until the fuel is purchased. Once that fuel is purchased, those unrealized gains and losses are removed from AOCI and the gain (loss) on the option is used to offset the loss (gain) on fuel. While the effect of fuel hedging on Southwest Airlines' profitability was minor in 2014, it has had a much bigger impact in previous years.

Although the fair value of derivatives and their related assets or liabilities can be substantial, the net effect on earnings and stockholders' equity is usually minor because companies are mainly using them as

[6] Unrealized gains and losses on derivatives classified as effective *cash flow hedges* (such as those relating to planned purchases of commodities) are accumulated in other comprehensive income (OCI) and are not recognized in current income until the transaction is complete (such as when both the purchase and sale of inventory occurs). Unrealized gains and losses on derivatives classified as *fair value hedges* (such as those relating to interest rate hedges and swaps, and the hedging of asset values such as relating to securities) as well as the changes in value of the hedged asset (liability) are recorded in current income.

hedges and not as speculative securities. The accounting standards for derivative instruments were enacted in response to a concern that speculative activities were not adequately disclosed. Subsequent to its passage, the financial effects have often appeared modest (with occasional exceptions such as **JP Morgan Chase**'s "London Whale"). Either these companies were not speculating to the extent expected, or they have since reduced their level of speculation in response to increased scrutiny from better disclosures.

SUMMARY

Explain and interpret the three levels of investor influence over an investee–passive, significant, and controlling. (p. 564) LO1

- Ownership of 20% or less in another corporation is treated as a passive investment by the investor.
- Significant influence is assumed to be available to the investor corporation if it owns more than 20% but not over 50% of the outstanding voting stock of the investee corporation.
- Control is generally presumed if the investing firm owns more than 50% of the outstanding voting stock of the investee corporation.

Describe the term "fair value" and the fair value hierarchy. (p. 566) LO2

- Fair value is the amount that an independent buyer would be willing to pay for an asset (or the amount that would need to be paid to discharge a liability) in an orderly transaction.
- Fair value can be determined by reference to a market price when available, but it may also be determined by other methods (discounted cash flow analysis, pricing of comparable assets, etc.). GAAP defines three levels of fair value determination:
  - Level 1: Values based on quoted prices in active markets for identical assets/liabilities
  - Level 2: Values based on observable inputs other than Level 1 (e.g., quoted prices for similar assets/liabilities or interest rates or yield curves)
  - Level 3: Values based on inputs observable only to the reporting entity (e.g., management estimates or assumptions.)
- GAAP requires that companies disclose their fair value determinations in the footnotes of their financial statements.

Describe and analyze accounting for passive investments. (p. 567) LO3

- Ownership of 20% or less in another corporation is treated as a passive investment by the investor. Investing for returns is the objective rather than influencing another corporation's decisions. The investment is reported as a long-term asset only if the intention is to retain the asset for longer than a year. Passive investments are segregated into two types, called trading securities or securities available-for-sale.
- Trading securities are securities that will be converted into cash in a very short period of time. Any trading securities held at the end of an accounting period are marked to their fair value. The value change is recognized as an unrealized gain (or loss) in the income statement.
- Available-for-sale securities are held for long-term capital gains or dividends. Any securities held at the end of an accounting period are also marked to their fair value. However, the value change bypasses the income statement to become part of retained earnings called other comprehensive income.
- Gains and losses realized on sale, and dividends on passive investments are reported as other income in the income statement.
- Debt securities that management intends to hold to maturity are carried at cost unless their value is considered impaired in which case the security is written down. Otherwise changes in fair value are not recognized on the balance sheet or the income statement.

Explain and analyze accounting for investments with significant influence. (p. 575) LO4

- Significant influence is assumed to be available to the investor corporation if it owns more than 20% but not over 50% of the outstanding voting stock of the investee corporation. Typically, the investment is initially recorded as a long-term asset at the purchase price.
- In the case of significant influence, the equity method of reporting is followed.
- Under the equity method, the investor recognizes its proportionate share of the investee's net income as income and an increase in the investment account. Any dividends received by the investor are treated as a recovery of the investment and reduce the investment balance.

LO5 Describe and analyze accounting for investments with control. (p. 579)

- If a corporation is considered to have control of another corporation, the financial statements of both firms are consolidated and reported as though they were a single entity.
- Control means that the investor has the ability to affect the strategic direction of the investee. Control is generally presumed if the investing firm owns more than 50% of the outstanding voting stock of the investee corporation.
- At the time of the acquisition, acquired assets and liabilities are restated at fair value in the consolidated balance sheet.
- If the purchase price exceeds the fair value of acquired assets, the remainder is labeled "goodwill." Goodwill is not amortized, but tested for impairment annually.

LO6 Appendix 12A: Illustrate and analyze accounting mechanics for equity method investments. (p. 589)

- Under the equity method of accounting, neither the investee's assets nor its liabilities are reported on the investor's balance sheet. Only the proportionate investment is reported. Further, only the investor's net equity is reported in income; and the investee's sales and expenses are omitted.
- The result is that revenues and expenses, but not NOPAT, are understated; NOPM (NOPAT/Sales) is overstated; and net operating assets (NOA) are understated. Also, financial leverage is understated. ROE remains unaffected.

LO7 Appendix 12B: Apply consolidation accounting mechanics. (p. 590)

- Identifiable intangible assets (such as patents, trademarks, customer lists) often result from the acquisition of one corporation by another. This is a situation in which the acquirer will have control and consolidation accounting is required.
- Intangibles are valued at the purchase date and then amortized over their economic life. Any remaining purchase price not allocated to tangible or identifiable intangible assets is treated as goodwill.
- Goodwill is not amortized but is written down when and if considered impaired. The write-down is an expense of the period.
- Reports of consolidated corporations are often difficult to understand because they commingle the assets, liabilities, revenues, expenses, and cash flows of several businesses that can be very different. General Electric and its subsidiary provide an example.

LO8 Appendix 12C: Discuss the reporting of derivative securities. (p. 591)

- Derivatives refer to financial instruments that are utilized by companies to reduce various kinds of risks.
- Derivatives work by offsetting the gain or loss for the asset or liability to which they relate.
- The accounting for derivatives boils down to this: the derivative contract and the asset or liability to which it relates are both reported on the balance sheet at fair value. The asset and liability are offsetting if the hedge is effective. Likewise, the related gains and losses are largely offsetting, leaving income unaffected.

GUIDANCE ANSWERS . . . YOU MAKE THE CALL

You are the Chief Financial Officer When a key component of a company's distribution process begins to turn its attention to other products, it can have a detrimental effect of the prospects for future growth. For instance, the soft-drink companies depend heavily on their bottling companies to get the product to the consumer. In these circumstances, companies may purchase enough shares in the distribution company to exert significant influence (or even control) over the key distributor.

KEY TERMS

Asset turnover ratios (p. 578)
Available-for-sale (AFS) securities (p. 568)
Consolidated financial statements (p. 579)
Controlling influence (p. 565)
Cost method (p. 574)
Derivatives (p. 591)
Equity method (p. 576)
Fair value (p. 566)
Fair value hierarchy (p. 566)
Fair value option (p. 566)
Financial investments (p. 564)
Financial leverage (p. 578)
Held-to-maturity (HTM) (p. 574)
Net operating profit margin (p. 578)
Passive influence (p. 565)
Significant influence (p. 565)
Trading (T) securities (p. 568)

Assignments with the MBC logo in the margin are available in myBusinessCourse. See the Preface of the book for details.

MULTIPLE CHOICE

Multiple Choice Answers
1. c 2. e 3. a 4. b

1. Corporation A owns 50% of corporation B. This is a case where:
a. Corporation A controls corporation B.
b. Corporation A does not control corporation B.
c. Corporation A has significant influence on corporation B.
d. Corporation A does not have a significant influence on corporation B.
e. Both *a* and *c* are correct.

2. In accounting for available-for-sale securities, the:
a. Securities are reported at their fair value, along with their fair value adjustment from cost.
b. Securities are reported at cost.
c. Increases in fair value are reported in income.
d. Increases in fair value are not reported in income.
e. Both *a* and *d* are correct.

3. Which of the following statements is true of investments accounted for under the equity method?
a. Investor reports its percentage share of the investee's income in its operating income.
b. Investor reports dividends received from the investee in its operating income.
c. Investment is reported at its fair value.
d. Investment is reported at cost plus any dividends received from the investee.
e. Investment is reported at fair value less any dividends received from the investee.

4. Which of the following statements is true about goodwill?
a. Current reporting standards require that goodwill be amortized over its economic life.
b. Goodwill is written down when the fair value of the investee implies a goodwill value below the investor's goodwill account.
c. Goodwill can be recognized only when the acquisition price does not exceed the value of the tangible and identifiable intangible assets acquired.
d. The recording of goodwill can be based on the acquisition of assets such as patents and trademarks.
e. Goodwill equals retained earnings.

Superscript $^{A (B, C)}$ denotes assignments based on Appendix 12A (12B, 12C).

QUESTIONS

Q12-1. What measure (fair value or amortized cost) is used for the balance sheet to report (a) trading securities, (b) available-for-sale securities, and (c) held-to-maturity securities?

Q12-2. What is an unrealized holding gain (loss)? Explain.

Q12-3. Where are unrealized holding gains and losses related to trading securities reported in the financial statements? Where are unrealized holding gains and losses related to available-for-sale securities reported in the financial statements?

Q12-4. What does *significant influence* imply regarding financial investments? Describe the accounting procedures used for such investments.

Q12-5. On January 1 of the current year, Yetman Company purchases 40% of the common stock of Livnat Company for $250,000 cash. During the year, Livnat reports $80,000 of net income and pays $60,000 in cash dividends. At year-end, what amount should appear in Yetman's balance sheet for its investment in Livnat?

Q12-6. What accounting method is used when a stock investment represents more than 50% of the investee company's voting stock? Explain.

Q12-7. What is the underlying objective of consolidated financial statements?

Q12-8. Finn Company purchases all of the common stock of Murray Company for $750,000 when Murray Company has $300,000 of common stock and $450,000 of retained earnings. If a consolidated balance sheet is prepared immediately after the acquisition, what amounts are eliminated in preparing it? Explain.

Q12-9.[B] Bradshaw Company owns 100% of Dee Company. At year-end, Dee owes Bradshaw $75,000. If a consolidated balance sheet is prepared at year-end, how is the $75,000 handled? Explain.

Q12-10. What are some limitations of consolidated financial statements?

MINI EXERCISES

LO1

M12-11. Classifying Investments as Passive, Significant or Controlling

For each of the situations below, determine if the investment should be reported as a passive investment (P), an investment reflecting significant influence (SI), or a controlling interest (C).

a. ______ Griffin Company purchased 25% of the common stock of Wright, Inc. Griffin is one of several suppliers that Wright, Inc. relies on to supply subcomponents.

b. ______ Dye Corporation purchased 20% of the 2016 $40 million bond issue offered by Glover Company.

c. ______ Zhao, Inc. purchased 2,000 shares of Google, Inc. common stock, paying $1.1 million.

d. ______ Watts Corporation purchased 65% of the common stock of Zimmerman, Inc. common stock for cash. Watts and Zimmerman had been engaged in several strategic alliances prior to the purchase.

e. ______ Shevlin, Inc. purchased 15% of Bowen Company's common stock. Shevlin is Bowen Company's largest customer, buying more than 60% of its output.

LO3

M12-12. Interpreting Disclosures of Available-for-Sale Securities

Cisco Systems, Inc.
NASDAQ :: CSCO

Use the following year-end footnote information from **Cisco Systems, Inc.**'s 10-K report to answer parts *a* and *b*.

($ millions)	2014
Cost of available-for-sale investments securities	$44,619
Gross unrealized gains	759
Gross unrealized losses	(30)
Fair value of available-for-sale investments securities	$45,348

a. At what amount is its available-for-sale investments reported on Cisco's 2014 balance sheet? Explain.

b. How is its net unrealized gain of $729 million ($759 million − $30 million) reported by Cisco in its financial statements?

LO3

M12-13. Accounting for Available-for-Sale and Trading Securities

Assume that Wasley Company purchases 6,000 common shares of Pincus Company for $12 cash per share. During the year, Wasley receives a cash dividend of $1.10 per common share from Pincus, and the year-end market price of Pincus common stock is $13 per share. How much income does Wasley report relating to this investment for the year if it accounts for the investment as:

a. Available-for-sale investment?

b. Trading investment?

LO2

M12-14. Analyzing Disclosures of Investment Securities

Cisco Systems, Inc.
NASDAQ :: CSCO

On its July 26, 2014 balance sheet, **Cisco Systems, Inc.** reports available-for-sale investments with a value of $45,348 million. As available-for-sale securities, these investments are reported at their fair value, and Cisco provides the following information in its footnotes.

	July 26, 2014 Fair Value Measurements			
	Level 1	Level 2	Level 3	Total Balance
Available-for-sale investments:				
U.S. government securities	$ —	$31,734	$ —	$31,734
U.S. government agency securities	—	1,063	—	1,063
Non-U.S. government and agency securities	—	861	—	861
Corporate debt securities.	—	9,159	—	9,159
Mortgage-backed securities	—	579	—	579
Publicly traded equity securities	$1,952	—	—	$ 1,952

a. Explain the differences between the three columns labeled Level 1, Level 2 and Level 3.

b. Are all of these investments "marked-to-fair value"? If not, which ones are not marked-to-fair value? Which investment values do you regard as most subjective? Least subjective?

c. If Cisco needed to raise cash to take advantage of an investment opportunity, which of these investments do you regard as most liquid (i.e., most easily turned into cash)? Least liquid?

M12-15. Analyzing and Interpreting Equity Method Investments LO4

Stober Company purchases an investment in Lang Company at a purchase price of $1 million cash, representing 30% of the book value of Lang. During the year, Lang reports net income of $100,000 and pays cash dividends of $40,000. At the end of the year, the fair value of Stober's investment is $1.2 million.

a. At what amount is the investment reported on Stober's balance sheet at year-end?

b. What amount of income from investments does Stober report? Explain.

c. Stober's $200,000 unrealized gain in investment fair value (choose one and explain):
   (1) Is not reflected on either its income statement or balance sheet.
   (2) Is reported in its current income.
   (3) Is reported on its balance sheet only.
   (4) Is reported in its other comprehensive income.

d. Prepare journal entries to record the transactions and events above.

e. Post the journal entries from *d* to their respective T-accounts.

f. Record each of the transactions from *d* in the financial statement effects template.

M12-16. Calculating Income for Equity Method Investments LO4

Kross Company purchases an equity investment in Penno Company at a purchase price of $5 million, representing 40% of the book value of Penno. During the current year, Penno reports net income of $600,000 and pays cash dividends of $200,000. At the end of the year, the market value of Kross's investment is $5.3 million. What amount of income does Kross report relating to this investment in Penno for the year? Explain.

M12-17. Computing Consolidating Adjustments and Noncontrolling Interest LO5

Philipich Company purchases 80% of Hirst Company's common stock for $600,000 cash when Hirst Company has $300,000 of common stock and $450,000 of retained earnings. If a consolidated balance sheet is prepared immediately after the acquisition, what amounts are eliminated when preparing that statement? What amount of noncontrolling interest appears in the consolidated balance sheet?

M12-18. Computing Consolidated Net Income LO5

Benartzi Company purchased a 90% interest in Liang Company on January 1 of the current year. Benartzi Company had $600,000 net income for the current year *before* recognizing its share of Liang Company's net income. If Liang Company had net income of $150,000 for the year, what is the consolidated net income for the year?

M12-19. Effect of Investing on Ratios LO4, 5

DeFond Company wishes to secure a reliable supply of a key component for its production processes, and its management is considering two alternative investments. Verduzco Company produces exactly the supply that DeFond needs, so DeFond could use cash to purchase 100% of the common stock of Verduzco. Lin Company produces twice as much of the component that DeFond needs, but DeFond could form a joint venture with another company where each would purchase 50% of Lin Company's common stock and each take 50% of Lin Company's output.

The table that follows gives the balance sheet information for all three companies prior to any investment by DeFond. For the questions below, assume that DeFond would be able to purchase shares at the investee companies' book values and that the investee companies' assets and liabilities have fair values equal to their book values.

	DeFond Company	Verduzco Company	Lin Company
Cash	$ 800	$ 100	$ 200
Investment	—	—	—
Noncash assets	2,000	900	1,800
Liabilities	2,200	700	1,400
Shareholders' Equity	600	300	600

a. Suppose that DeFond purchases 100% of Verduzco's common stock for $300. Produce the consolidated balance sheet for DeFond immediately after the acquisition.

b. Suppose that DeFond purchases 50% of Lin's common stock for $300. Produce the balance sheet for DeFond immediately after the investment (using the equity method).

c. From a business perspective, either of these investments will accomplish the objective of obtaining a reliable supply of components. How will the financial ratios differ between the two alternatives?

LO3 **M12-20. Reporting of and Analyzing Financial Effects of Trading (Debt) Securities**

Hartgraves Company had the following transactions and adjustments related to a bond investment that is a trading security.

2015

Oct. 1 Purchased $500,000 face value of Skyline, Inc.'s 7% bonds at 97 plus a brokerage commission of $1,000. The bonds pay interest on September 30 and March 31 and mature in 20 years. Hartgraves Company expects to sell the bonds in the near future.

Dec. 31 Made the adjusting entry to record interest earned on investment in the Skyline bonds.

31 Made the adjusting entry to record the current fair value of the Skyline bonds. At December 31, 2015, the fair value of the Skyline bonds was $490,000.

2016

Mar. 31 Received the semiannual interest payment on investment in the Skyline bonds.

Apr. 1 Sold the Skyline bond investment for $492,300 cash.

a. Prepare journal entries to record these transactions.

b. Post the journal entries from *a* to their respective T-accounts.

c. Record each of the transactions in the financial statement effects template.

LO3 **M12-21. Reporting of and Analyzing Financial Effects of Trading (Equity) Securities**

Blouin Company had the following transactions and adjustment related to a stock investment that is a trading security.

2015

Nov. 15 Purchased 10,000 shares of Lane, Inc.'s common stock at $17 per share plus a brokerage commission of $1,200. Blouin expects to sell the stock in the near future.

Dec. 22 Received a cash dividend of $1.00 per share of common stock from Lane.

31 Made the adjusting entry to reflect year-end fair value of the stock investment in Lane. The year-end fair value of the Lane common stock is $15.50 per share.

2016

Jan. 20 Sold all 10,000 shares of the Lane common stock for $150,000.

a. Prepare journal entries to record these transactions.

b. Post the journal entries from *a* to their respective T-accounts.

c. Record each of the transactions in the financial statement effects template.

LO3 **M12-22. Reporting of and Analyzing Financial Effects of Available-for-Sale (Equity) Securities**

Refer to the data for Blouin Company in Mini Exercise 12-21. Assume that when the shares were purchased, management did not intend to sell the stock in the near future. Record the transactions and adjustments for Blouin Company as an available-for-sale security.

M12-23. Computing Stockholders' Equity in Consolidation LO5

On January 1 of the current year, Halen Company purchased all of the common shares of Jolson Company for $575,000 cash. On this date, the stockholders' equity of Halen Company consisted of $600,000 in common stock and $310,000 in retained earnings. Jolson Company had $350,000 in common stock and $225,000 in retained earnings. What amount of total stockholders' equity appears on the consolidated balance sheet?

EXERCISES

E12-24. Assessing Financial Statement Effects of Trading and Available-for-Sale Securities LO1, 3

Four transactions involving investments in marketable securities classified as trading follow.

(1) Purchased 6,000 common shares of Liu, Inc., for $12 cash per share.
(2) Received a cash dividend of $1.10 per common share from Liu.
(3) Year-end market price of Liu common stock is $11.25 per share.
(4) Sold all 6,000 common shares of Liu for $66,900.

a. Prepare journal entries to record the four transactions.
b. Post the journal entries from *a* to their respective T-accounts.
c. Record each of the transactions from *a* in the financial statement effects template.
d. Using the same transaction information as above and assuming the investments in marketable securities are classified as available-for-sale, (i) prepare journal entries to record the transactions, (ii) post the journal entries to their respective T-accounts, and (iii) record each of the transactions in the financial statement effects template.

E12-25. Assessing Financial Statement Effects of Trading and Available-for-Sale Securities LO1, 3

For the following transactions involving investments in marketable securities, assume that:

a. Investments are classified as trading.
(1) Ohlson Co. purchases 5,000 common shares of Freeman Co. at $16 cash per share.
(2) Ohlson Co. receives a cash dividend of $1.25 per common share from Freeman.
(3) Year-end market price of Freeman common stock is $17.50 per share.
(4) Ohlson Co. sells all 5,000 common shares of Freeman for $86,400 cash.
(i) prepare journal entries to record the four transactions, (ii) post the journal entries to their respective T-accounts, and (iii) record each of the transactions in the financial statement effects template.

b. Investments are classified as available-for-sale (for same four transactions from *a*).
(i) prepare journal entries to record the transactions, (ii) post the journal entries to their respective T-accounts, and (iii) record each of the transactions in the financial statement effects template.

E12-26. Interpreting Footnotes on Security Investments LO1, 3, 4

SunTrust Banks, Inc.
NYSE :: STI
The Coca-Cola Company
NYSE :: KO

SunTrust Banks, Inc. is a bank holding company based in Atlanta, Georgia. Founded in 1891 as the Commercial Travelers' Savings Bank, the organization underwrote **The Coca-Cola Company**'s initial public offering in 1919, receiving Coca-Cola stock in lieu of underwriting fees. Over the ensuing 91 years, the SunTrust organization has maintained a close relationship with Coca-Cola. Robert Woodruff, Coca-Cola's president from 1923 to 1954, was the son of long-time SunTrust president, Ernest Woodruff. The original copy of the famous Coca-Cola formula is stored in a safe deposit box at one of SunTrust's Atlanta branches.

The financial crisis of 2007-2009 put pressure on most large American financial institutions, including SunTrust. Although the company did not suffer the spectacular drops in asset values that made headlines at other banks, its exposure to property markets and securities connected to these markets caused the bank's regulatory capital to decline.

The following information is taken from Note 5 of SunTrust's 2006 annual report:

Note 5: Securities Available for Sale
Securities available for sale at December 31 were as follows:

	2006			
($ thousands)	**Amortized Cost**	**Unrealized Gains**	**Unrealized Losses**	**Fair Value**
U.S. Treasury and other U.S. government agencies and corporations	$ 1,607,999	$ 8,602	$ 16,144	$ 1,600,457
States and political subdivisions	1,032,247	13,515	4,639	1,041,123
Asset-backed securities	1,128,032	1,891	17,584	1,112,339
Mortgage-backed securities	17,337,311	37,365	243,762	17,130,914
Corporate bonds	468,855	1,477	7,521	462,811
Common stock of The Coca-Cola Company	110	2,324,716	—	2,324,826
Other securities	1,423,799	5,446	—	1,429,245
Total securities available for sale	$22,998,353	$2,393,012	$289,650	$25,101,715

a. On December 31, 2006, SunTrust owned 48.183 million shares of Coca-Cola stock. What was the amortized cost of this investment? (This is the value imputed to the underwriting services provided in 1919 plus the historical value of any dividends reinvested in Coca-Cola stock over the ensuing 87 years.) What was the fair value of SunTrust's investment in Coca-Cola on December 31, 2006?

b. What is the maximum amount by which SunTrust Banks, Inc. could have increased its retained earnings by sales of Coca-Cola stock on December 31, 2006? Assume a 35% tax rate would be applied to gains from disposal of available-for-sale securities. Also, assume that taxes would be paid in cash immediately, i.e., on December 31.

c. Beginning in 2007, the pressures of the financial crisis caused SunTrust to use its investment in Coca-Cola to boost its required capital. SunTrust sold 4.605 million shares of Coca-Cola's stock in 2007 for a price of $51 per share. Assume that the sale took place early in the year. Provide a journal entry for this transaction (ignore taxes).

LO1, 3

E12-27. Reporting of and Analyzing Financial Effects of Trading (Debt) Securities
Barclay, Inc., had the following transactions and adjustments related to a bond investment that is classified as a trading security.

2015

Nov. 1 Purchased $300,000 face value of Joos, Inc.'s 9% bonds at 102 plus a brokerage commission of $900. The bonds pay interest on October 31 and April 30 and mature in 15 years. Barclay expects to sell the bonds in the near future.

Dec. 31 Made the adjusting entry to record interest earned on investment in the Joos bonds.

31 Made the adjusting entry to record the current fair value of the Joos bonds. At December 31, 2015, the fair value of the Joos bonds was $301,500.

2016

Apr. 30 Received the semiannual interest payment on investment in the Joos bonds.

May 1 Sold the Joos bond investment for $300,900 cash.

a. Prepare journal entries to record these transactions.

b. Post the journal entries from *a* to their respective T-accounts.

c. Record each of the transactions in the financial statement effects template.

LO5

E12-28. Reporting of Stockholders' Equity in Consolidation
Baylor Company purchased 75% of the common stock of Reed Company for $600,000 in cash when the stockholders' equity of Reed Company consisted of $500,000 in common stock and $300,000 in retained earnings. On the acquisition date, the stockholders' equity of Baylor Company consisted of $900,000 in common stock and $440,000 in retained earnings. Prepare the stockholders' equity section in the consolidated balance sheet as of the acquisition date.

LO3

CNA Financial Corporation
NYSE :: CNA

E12-29. Interpreting Footnote Disclosures for Investments
CNA Financial Corporation provides the following information from its 2014 10-K report:

Valuation of investments: The Company classifies its fixed maturity securities and its equity securities as either available-for-sale or trading, and as such, they are carried at fair value. Changes in fair value of trading securities are reported within Net investment income on the Consolidated Statements of Operations. Changes in fair value related to available-for-sale securities are reported as a component of Other comprehensive income. The cost of fixed maturity securities classified as available-for-sale is adjusted for amortization of premiums and accretion of discounts to maturity, which are included in Net investment income on the Consolidated Statements of Operations. Losses may be recognized within Net realized investment gains (losses) on the Consolidated Statements of Operations when a decline in value is determined by the Company to be other-than-temporary.

Summary of Fixed Maturity and Equity Securities

December 31, 2014 ($ millions)	Cost or Amortized Cost	Gross Unrealized Gains	Gross Unrealized Losses	Estimated Fair Value
Fixed maturity securities available-for-sale:				
Corporate and other bonds	$17,210	$1,721	$61	$18,870
States, municipalities and political subdivisions	11,285	1,463	8	12,740
Asset-backed				
Residential mortgage-backed	5,028	218	13	5,233
Commercial mortgage-backed	2,056	93	5	2,144
Other asset-backed	1,234	11	10	1,235
Total asset-backed	8,318	322	28	8,612
U.S. Treasury and obligations of government-sponsored enterprises	26	5	—	31
Foreign government	438	16	—	454
Redeemable preferred stock	39	3	—	42
Total fixed maturity securities available-for-sale	37,316	3,530	97	40,749
Total fixed maturity securities trading	19	—	—	19
Equity securities available-for-sale:				
Common stock	38	9	—	47
Preferred stock	172	5	2	175
Total equity securities available-for-sale	210	14	2	222
Total	$37,545	$3,544	$99	$40,990

a. At what amount is its investment portfolio reflected on its balance sheet? In your answer identify its fair value, cost, and any unrealized gains and losses.

b. How are its unrealized gains and/or losses reflected in CNA's balance sheet and income statement?

c. How are any impairment losses and the gains and losses realized from the sale of securities reflected in CNA's balance sheet and income statement?

E12-30. Assessing Financial Statement Effects of Equity Method Securities LO4

The following transactions involve investments in marketable securities and are accounted for using the equity method.

(1) Purchased 12,000 common shares of Barth Co. at $9 cash per share; the shares represent 30% ownership in Barth.
(2) Received a cash dividend of $1.25 per common share from Barth.
(3) Recorded income from Barth stock investment when Barth's net income is $80,000.
(4) Sold all 12,000 common shares of Barth for $120,500.

a. Prepare journal entries to record these four transactions.

b. Post the journal entries from *a* to their respective T-accounts.

c. Record each of the transactions in the financial statement effects template.

E12-31. Assessing Financial Statement Effects of Equity Method Securities LO4

The following transactions involve investments in marketable securities and are accounted for using the equity method.

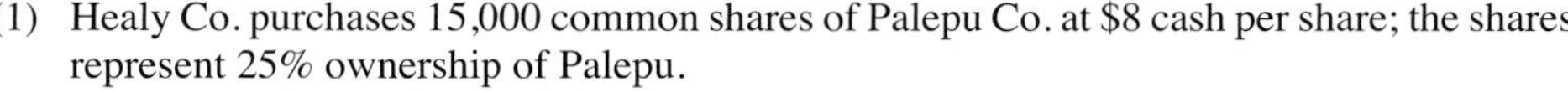

(1) Healy Co. purchases 15,000 common shares of Palepu Co. at $8 cash per share; the shares represent 25% ownership of Palepu.
(2) Healy receives a cash dividend of $0.80 per common share from Palepu.
(3) Palepu reports annual net income of $120,000.
(4) Healy sells all 15,000 common shares of Palepu for $140,000 cash.

a. Prepare journal entries to record these four transactions.
b. Post the journal entries from *a* to their respective T-accounts.
c. Record each of the transactions in the financial statement effects template.

LO1, 3, 4 **E12-32. Assessing Financial Statement Effects of Passive and Equity Method Investments**

On January 1, 2016, Ball Corporation purchased, as a stock investment, 10,000 shares of Leftwich Company common stock for $15 cash per share. On December 31, 2016, Leftwich announced net income of $80,000 for the year and paid a cash dividend of $1.10 per share. At December 31, 2016, the market value of Leftwich's stock was $19 per share.

a. Assume that the stock acquired by Ball represents 15% of Leftwich's voting stock and that Ball classifies it as available-for-sale. For the following transactions, (1) prepare journal entries, (2) post those journal entries to their respective T-accounts, and (3) record each of the transactions in the financial statement effects template.
   (1) Ball purchased 10,000 common shares of Leftwich at $15 cash per share; the shares represent a 15% ownership in Leftwich.
   (2) Leftwich reported annual net income of $80,000.
   (3) Received a cash dividend of $1.10 per common share from Leftwich.
   (4) Year-end market price of Leftwich common stock is $19 per share.

b. Assume that the stock acquired by Ball represents 30% of Leftwich's voting stock and that Ball accounts for this investment using the equity method since it is able to exert significant influence. For the same four transactions as above, (1) prepare journal entries, (2) post those journal entries to their respective T-accounts, and (3) record each of the transactions in the financial statement effects template.

LO1, 3 **E12-33. Reporting Passive Investments**

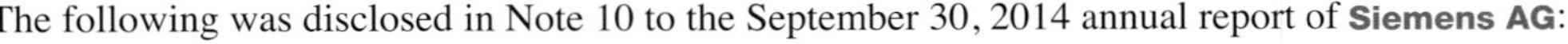

The following was disclosed in Note 10 to the September 30, 2014 annual report of **Siemens AG**:

Siemens AG
NYSE :: SI

Available-for-sale financial assets

The following tables summarize the current portion of the Company's investment in available-for-sale financial assets:

	September 30, 2014			
(€ millions)	**Cost**	**Fair Value**	**Unrealized Gain**	**Unrealized Loss**
Equity instruments	€ 1	€ 1	€ —	€—
Debt instruments	693	702	9	—
Fund shares	194	222	28	—
	€888	€925	€37	€—

	September 30, 2013			
(€ millions)	**Cost**	**Fair Value**	**Unrealized Gain**	**Unrealized Loss**
Equity instruments	€ 6	€ 8	€ 2	€—
Debt instruments	379	382	3	—
Fund shares	195	211	16	(1)
	€580	€601	€21	€ (1)

Noncurrent available-for-sale financial assets, which are included in line item Other financial assets are measured at fair value, if reliably measurable. They primarily consist of equity instruments, including shares in AtoS and in OSRAM. As of September 30, 2014 and 2013 non-current available-for-sale financial assets measured at cost amount to €192 million and €167 million, respectively; noncurrent available-for-sale financial assets measured at fair value amount to €1,611 million and €1,394 million, respectively.

a. What was the total amount that was reported for available-for-sale securities in Siemens' 2014 balance sheet? Where are the unrealized gains and losses reported?

b. In fiscal 2014, Siemens purchased short-term (current) available-for-sale securities costing €613 million and sold short-term (current) available-for-sale securities for €317 in cash. What amount of gain or loss was realized on the sale of these securities? Where was this gain or loss reported?

c. What amount of gain or loss would Siemens report in its 2014 income statement if the current portion of available-for-sale securities were classified as trading securities?

E12-34. Allocation of Acquisition Purchase Price

LO5

Medtronic, PLC
NYSE :: MDT

On January 26, 2015, Medtronic completed the acquisition of Covidien plc in a cash and stock transaction valued at approximately $50 billion. In connection with the transaction, Medtronic, Inc., a Minnesota corporation (Medtronic, Inc.), and Covidien were combined under and became subsidiaries of **Medtronic plc**, a public limited company organized under the laws of Ireland. Medtronic plc reported the allocation of the $50 billion purchase price to various assets and liabilities acquired in its April 2015 10-K as presented below ($ billions):

Current assets	$ 6.5
Property, plant and equipment	2.4
Intangible assets	26.3
Goodwill	?
Other assets	0.7
Current liabilities	3.3
Long-term liabilities, net	12.2

a. How are the values in the above table determined?

b. How much goodwill would Medtronic recognize from this acquisition? How will that goodwill be treated in subsequent periods?

c. Do you think Medtronic's shareholders would prefer to see an allocation that gives a lot of value to separately-identifiable assets or an allocation where most of the acquistion price goes to goodwill? Why?

E12-35. Reporting of and Analyzing Financial Effects of Trading (Equity) Securities

LO1, 3

Guay Company had the following transactions and adjustment related to a stock investment classified as a trading security.

2015

Nov. 15 Purchased 5,000 shares of Core, Inc.'s common stock at $16 per share plus a brokerage commission of $900. Guay Company expects to sell the stock in the near future.

Dec. 22 Received a cash dividend of $1.25 per share of common stock from Core.

31 Made the adjusting entry to reflect year-end fair value of the stock investment in Core. The year-end market price of the Core common stock is $17.50 per share.

2016

Jan. 20 Sold all 5,000 shares of the Core common stock for $86,400.

a. Prepare journal entries to record these transactions.

b. Post the journal entries from *a* to their respective T-accounts.

c. Record each of the transactions in the financial statement effects template.

E12-36. Reporting of and Analyzing Financial Effects of Available-for-Sale (Equity) Securities

LO1, 3

Refer to the data for Guay Company in Exercise 12-35. Assume that when the shares were purchased, management did not intend to sell the stock in the near future. Record the transactions and adjustments for Guay Company under this assumption.

E12-37. Reporting and Interpreting Stock Investment Performance

LO1, 3, 4

Kasznik Company began operations in 2016 and, by year-end (December 31), had made six stock investments. Year-end information on these stock investments follows.

Company	Cost or Equity Basis (as appropriate)	Year-End Fair Value	Investment Classification
Barth, Inc.	$ 68,000	$ 65,300	Trading
Foster, Inc.	162,500	160,000	Trading
McNichols, Inc.	197,000	192,000	Available-for-sale
Patell, Inc.	157,000	154,700	Available-for-sale
Ertimur, Inc.	100,000	102,400	Equity method
Soliman, Inc.	136,000	133,200	Equity method

a. At what total amount are the trading stock investments reported at in the December 31, 2016, balance sheet?

b. At what total amount are the available-for-sale stock investments reported at in the December 31, 2016, balance sheet?

c. At what total amount are the equity method stock investments reported at in the December 31, 2016, balance sheet?

d. What total amount of unrealized holding gains or unrealized holding losses related to stock investments appears in the 2016 income statement?

e. What total amount of unrealized holding gains or unrealized holding losses related to stock investments appears in the stockholders' equity section of the December 31, 2016, balance sheet?

f. What total amount of fair value adjustment to stock investments appears in the December 31, 2016, balance sheet? Which category of stock investments does the fair value adjustment relate to? Does the fair value adjustment increase or decrease the financial statement presentation of these stock investments?

LO1, 4

E12-38. Analyzing Equity Method Investment Footnotes

Merck & Co., Inc.
NYSE :: MRK

Merck & Co., Inc. reports a December 31, 2013 balance of $1.6 billion in "Investments in affiliates accounted for using the equity method" ("Investments in affiliates"). Provide the entries for the following events for fiscal year 2014:

a. Merck's share of income from its affiliates was $257 million.

b. Merck received dividends and distributions from its affiliates of $185 million during fiscal year 2014.

c. During fiscal year 2014, Merck divested its $1.4 billion investment in AstraZeneca LP, recognizing a gain of $650 million.

d. After these events, what should be the balance in Merck's investments in affiliates account at December 31, 2014? The actual balance was $337 million. What might explain any differences between these two values?

LO7

Homework MBC

E12-39.[B] Constructing the Consolidated Balance Sheet at Acquisition

On January 1 of the current year, Healy Company purchased all of the common shares of Miller Company for $500,000 cash. Balance sheets of the two firms at acquisition follow.

	Healy Company	Miller Company	Consolidating Adjustments	Consolidated
Current assets	$1,700,000	$120,000		
Investment in Miller	500,000	—		
Plant assets, net	3,000,000	410,000		
Goodwill	—	—		
Total assets	$5,200,000	$530,000		
Liabilities	$ 700,000	$ 90,000		
Contributed capital	3,500,000	400,000		
Retained earnings	1,000,000	40,000		
Total liabilities and equity	$5,200,000	$530,000		

During purchase negotiations, Miller's plant assets were appraised at $425,000; and, all of its remaining assets and liabilities were appraised at values approximating their book values. Healy also concluded that an additional $45,000 (in goodwill) demanded by Miller's shareholders was warranted because Miller's earning power was better than the industry average. (1) Prepare the consolidating adjustments, (2) Prepare the consolidated balance sheet at acquisition, (3) Prepare journal entries to record the transactions, (4) Post the journal entries to their respective T-accounts, and (5) Record each of the transactions in the financial statement effects template.

LO7

Homework MBC

E12-40.[B] Constructing the Consolidated Balance Sheet at Acquisition

Rayburn Company purchased all of Kanodia Company's common stock for cash on January 1, at which time the separate balance sheets of the two corporations appeared as follows:

	Rayburn Company	Kanodia Company	Consolidating Adjustments	Consolidated
Investment in Kanodia	$ 600,000	—		
Other assets	2,300,000	$700,000		
Goodwill	—	—		
Total assets	$2,900,000	$700,000		
Liabilities	$ 900,000	$160,000		
Contributed capital	1,400,000	300,000		
Retained earnings	600,000	240,000		
Total liabilities and equity	$2,900,000	$700,000		

During purchase negotiations, Rayburn determined that the appraised value of Kanodia's other assets was $720,000; and, all of its remaining assets and liabilities were appraised at values approximating their book values. The remaining $40,000 of the purchase price was ascribed to goodwill. (1) Prepare the consolidating adjustments, (2) Prepare the consolidated balance sheet at acquisition, (3) Prepare journal entries to record the transactions, (4) Post the journal entries to their respective T-accounts, and (5) Record each of the transactions in the financial statement effects template.

E12-41. Assessing Goodwill Impairment LO5

On January 1, 2016, Engel Company purchases 100% of Ball Company for $16.8 million. At the time of acquisition, Ball's stockholders' equity is reported at $16.2 million. Engel ascribes the excess of $600,000 to goodwill. Assume that the fair value of Ball declines to $12.5 million and that the fair value of Ball's tangible net assets is estimated at $12.3 million as of December 31, 2016.

a. Provide computations to determine if the goodwill has become impaired and, if so, the amount of the impairment.

b. What impact does the impairment of goodwill have on Engel's financial statements?

E12-42.[B] Constructing the Consolidated Balance Sheet at Acquisition LO5, 7

Easton Company acquires 100 percent of the outstanding voting shares of Harris Company on January 1, 2016. To obtain these shares, Easton pays $210,000 in cash and issues 5,000 of its $10 par value common stock. On this date, Easton's stock has a fair value of $36 per share, and Harris's book value of stockholders' equity is $280,000. Easton is willing to pay $390,000 for a company with a book value for equity of $280,000 because it believes that (1) Harris buildings are undervalued by $40,000, and (2) Harris has an unrecorded patent that Easton values at $30,000. Easton considers the remaining balance sheet items to be fairly valued (no book-to-fair value difference). The remaining $40,000 of the purchase price excess over book value is ascribed to corporate synergies and other general unidentifiable intangible assets (goodwill). The January 1, 2016, balance sheets at the acquisition date follow:

	Easton Company	Harris Company	Consolidating Adjustments	Consolidated
Cash	$ 84,000	$ 40,000		
Receivables	160,000	90,000		
Inventory	220,000	130,000		
Investment in Harris	390,000	—		
Land	100,000	60,000		
Buildings, net	400,000	110,000		
Equipment, net	120,000	50,000		
Total assets	$1,474,000	$480,000		
Accounts payable	$ 160,000	$ 30,000		
Long-term liabilities	380,000	170,000		
Common stock	500,000	40,000		
Additional paid-in capital	74,000	—		
Retained earnings	360,000	240,000		
Total liabilities & equity	$1,474,000	$480,000		

a. Show the breakdown of the investment into the book value acquired, the excess of fair value over book value, and the portion of the investment representing goodwill.

b. Prepare the consolidating adjustments and the consolidated balance sheet. Identify the adjustments by whether they relate to the elimination of stockholders' equity [S] or the excess of purchase price over book value [A].

c. How will the excess of the purchase price over book value acquired be treated in years subsequent to the acquisition?

LO6 **E12-43.[A] Accounting for Equity Method Investments**

Refer to the Easton Company acquisition described in E12-42. Instead of a 100% acquisition, assume that Easton purchased 40% of the outstanding shares of Harris Company on January 1, 2016, for $156,000 in cash. Also assume that the undervalued buildings have an estimated remaining useful life of 20 years and the unrecorded patent has a useful life of 5 years.

During 2016, Harris reported net income of $80,000 and paid cash dividends to shareholders totaling $40,000.

a. Prepare journal entries to record Easton Company's equity in the earnings of Harris Company, including any amortization of the excess of fair value over book value of assets acquired.

b. What is the value of the investment in Harris Company reported on Easton Company's balance sheet as of December 31, 2016?

LO8 **E12-44.[C] Reporting and Analyzing Derivatives**

Hewlett-Packard Company
NYSE :: HPQ

Hewlett-Packard Company reports the following information on its cash-flow hedges (derivatives) in comprehensive income (net income plus other comprehensive income) in its 2014 10-K report:

($ millions)	Total
Net earnings	$5,013
Net unrealized gain on available-for-sale securities	6
Net unrealized gain on cash flow hedges	488
Net unrealized components of defined benefit pension plans	(2,446)
Net cumulative translation adjustment	(85)
Provision for income taxes	(66)
Comprehensive income	$2,910

a. Identify and describe the usual applications for derivatives.

b. How are derivatives and their related assets (and/or liabilities) reported on the balance sheet?

c. By what amount has the unrealized gain or loss on the HP derivatives affected its current income? What are the analysis implications?

PROBLEMS

LO1, 2, 3 **P12-45. Analyzing and Interpreting Available-for-Sale Securities Disclosures**

Metlife Inc.
NYSE :: MET

Following is a portion of the investments footnote 8 from **MetLife Inc.**'s 2014 10-K report. Investment earnings are a crucial component of the financial performance of insurance companies such as MetLife, and investments comprise a large part of its assets. MetLife accounts for its bond investments as available-for-sale securities.

Fixed Maturity Securities Available-for-Sale

The following tables present the fixed maturity securities AFS by sector.

(in millions)	Cost or Amortized Cost	Gains	Temporary Losses	OTTI Losses	Estimated Fair Value
	December 31, 2014				
		Gross Unrealized			
Fixed Maturity Securities:					
U.S. corporate	$ 96,235	$10,343	$ 624	$ —	$105,954
Foreign corporate	57,695	4,651	664	7	61,675
U.S. Treasury and agency	54,654	6,892	30	—	61,516
Foreign government	47,327	5,500	161	—	52,666
RMBS	38,064	2,102	214	106	39,846
State and political subdivision	12,922	2,291	26	—	15,187
CMBS	13,762	615	46	(1)	14,332
ABS	14,121	240	112	—	14,249
Total fixed maturity securities	$334,780	$32,634	$1,877	$112	$365,425

(in millions)	Cost or Amortized Cost	Gains	Temporary Losses	OTTI Losses	Estimated Fair Value
	December 31, 2013				
		Gross Unrealized			
Fixed Maturity Securities:					
U.S. corporate	$100,203	$ 7,495	$1,229	$ —	$106,469
Foreign corporate	59,778	3,939	565	—	63,152
U.S. Treasury and agency	43,928	2,251	1,056	—	45,123
Foreign government	50,717	4,107	387	—	54,437
RMBS	34,167	1,584	490	206	35,055
State and political subdivision	13,233	903	306	—	13,830
CMBS	16,115	605	170	—	16,550
ABS	15,458	296	171	12	15,571
Total fixed maturity securities	$333,599	$21,180	$4,374	$218	$350,187

REQUIRED

a. At what amount does MetLife report its bond investments on its balance sheets for 2014 and 2013?

b. What are its net unrealized gains (losses) for 2014 and 2013? By what amount did these unrealized gains (losses) affect its reported income?

c. What is the difference between *realized* and *unrealized* gains and losses? Are realized gains and losses treated differently in the income statement than unrealized gains and losses? MetLife's 2014 pre-tax income was $8,804 million. What is the maximum amount MetLife could have increased pre-tax income by selling available-for-sale securities on the last day of 2014?

d. Many analysts compute a *mark-to-market investment return* as follows: Net investment income + Realized gains and losses + Change in unrealized gains and losses. Do you think that this metric provides insights into the performance of MetLife's investment portfolio beyond that which is included in GAAP income statements? Explain.

P12-46.[B] Preparing the Consolidated Balance Sheet LO5, 7

On January 1, 2016, Gem Company purchased for $392,000 cash a 70% stock interest in Alpine, Inc., which then had common stock of $420,000 and retained earnings of $140,000. Balance sheets of the two companies immediately after the acquisition were as follows:

	Gem	Alpine
Current assets	$258,000	$160,000
Stock investment—Controlling (Alpine)	392,000	—
Plant and equipment (net)	265,000	460,000
Total assets	$915,000	$620,000

continued

continued from previous page

	Gem	Alpine
Liabilities	$ 50,000	$ 60,000
Common stock	700,000	420,000
Retained earnings	165,000	140,000
Total liabilities and stockholders' equity	$915,000	$620,000

At the time of Gem's investment, the fair values of Alpine's assets and liabilities were equal to their book values.

REQUIRED

Prepare the consolidated balance sheet on the acquisition date; include a column for consolidating adjustments (see **Exhibit 12.7** for guidance).

LO1, 2, 3, 4, 5 **P12-47. Analyzing and Reporting Debt Investment Performance**

Columbia Company began operations in 2016 and by year-end (December 31) had made six bond investments. Year-end information on these bond investments follows.

Company	Face Value	Cost or Amortized Cost	Year-End Fair Value	Classification
Ling, Inc.	$100,000	$102,400	$105,300	Trading
Wren, Inc.	$250,000	$262,500	$270,000	Trading
Olanamic, Inc.	$200,000	$197,000	$199,000	Available for sale
Fossil, Inc.	$150,000	$154,000	$160,000	Available for sale
Meander, Inc.	$100,000	$101,200	$102,400	Held to maturity
Resin, Inc.	$140,000	$136,000	$137,000	Held to maturity

REQUIRED

a. At what total amount will the trading bond investments be reported in the December 31, 2016, balance sheet?

b. At what total amount will the available-for-sale bond investments be reported in the December 31, 2016, balance sheet?

c. At what total amount will the held-to-maturity bond investments be reported in the December 31, 2016, balance sheet?

d. What total amount of unrealized holding gains or unrealized holding losses related to bond investments will appear in the 2016 income statement?

e. What total amount of unrealized holding gains or unrealized holding losses related to bond investments will appear in the stockholders' equity section of the December 31, 2016, balance sheet?

f. What total amount of fair value adjustment to bond investments will appear in the December 31, 2016, balance sheet? Which category of bond investments does the fair value adjustment relate to? Does the fair value adjustment increase or decrease the financial statement presentation of these bond investments?

LO1, 4, 5, 6, 7 **P12-48.[A, B] Analyzing and Interpreting Disclosures on Consolidations**

Caterpillar Inc.
NYSE :: CAT

Caterpillar Inc. consists of two business units: the manufacturing company (parent corporation) and a wholly owned finance subsidiary. These two units are consolidated in Caterpillar's 2014 10-K report. Following is a supplemental disclosure that Caterpillar includes in its 10-K report that shows the separate balance sheets of the parent and its subsidiary, as well as consolidating adjustments and the consolidated balance sheet presented to shareholders. This supplemental disclosure is not mandated under GAAP, but is voluntarily reported by Caterpillar as useful information for investors and creditors.

	Supplemental Consolidating Data			
	Consolidated	Machinery, Energy & Transportation	Financial Products	Consolidating Adjustments
Assets				
Current assets				
Cash and short-term investments	$ 7,341	$ 6,317	$ 1,024	$ —
Receivables—trade and other	7,737	4,215	300	3,222
Receivables—finance	9,027	—	13,458	(4,431)
Deferred and refundable income taxes	1,739	1,644	95	—
Prepaid expenses and other current assets	818	399	432	(13)
Inventories	12,205	12,205	—	—
Total current assets	38,867	24,780	15,309	(1,222)
Property, plant and equipment—net	16,577	12,392	4,185	—
Long-term receivables—trade and other	1,364	154	268	942
Long-term receivables—finance	14,644	—	15,618	(974)
Investments in unconsolidated affiliated companies	257	257	—	—
Investments in Financial Products subsidiaries	—	4,488	—	(4,488)
Noncurrent deferred and refundable income taxes	1,404	1,980	98	(674)
Intangible assets	3,076	3,069	7	—
Goodwill	6,694	6,677	17	—
Other assets	1,798	391	1,407	—
Total assets	$84,681	$54,188	$36,909	$(6,416)
Liabilities				
Current liabilities				
Short-term borrowings	$ 4,708	$ 9	$ 5,807	$(1,108)
Accounts payable	6,515	6,436	180	(101)
Accrued expenses	3,548	3,273	288	(13)
Accrued wages, salaries and employee benefits	2,438	2,396	42	—
Customer advances	1,697	1,697	—	—
Dividends payable	424	424	—	—
Other current liabilities	1,754	1,361	402	(9)
Long-term debt due within one year	6,793	510	6,283	—
Total current liabilities	27,877	16,106	13,002	(1,231)
Long-term debt due after one year	27,784	9,525	18,291	(32)
Liability for postemployment benefits	8,963	8,963	—	—
Other liabilities	3,231	2,768	1,128	(665)
Total liabilities	67,855	37,362	32,421	(1,928)
Stockholders' equity				
Common stock	5,016	5,016	911	(911)
Treasury stock	(15,726)	(15,726)	—	—
Profit employed in the business	33,887	33,887	3,756	(3,756)
Accumulated other comprehensive income (loss)	(6,431)	(6,431)	(311)	311
Noncontrolling interests	80	80	132	(132)
Total stockholders' equity	16,826	16,826	4,488	(4,488)
Total liabilities and stockholders' equity	$84,681	$54,188	$36,909	$(6,416)

REQUIRED

a. Does each individual company (unit) maintain its own financial statements? Explain. Why does GAAP require consolidation instead of providing the financial statements of individual companies (units)?

b. What is the balance of Investments in Financial Products Subsidiaries as of December 31, 2014, on the parent's balance sheet (Machinery, Energy & Transportation)? What is the equity balance of the financial products subsidiary to which this relates as of December 31, 2014? Do you see a relation? Will this relation always exist?

c. Refer to your answer for *a*. How does the equity method of accounting for the investment in the subsidiary company obscure the actual financial condition of the parent company that is revealed in the consolidated financial statements?

d. Refer to the Consolidating Adjustments column reported—it is used to prepare the consolidated balance sheet. Generally, what do these adjustments accomplish?

e. Compare the consolidated balance of stockholders' equity with the stockholders' equity of the parent company (Machinery, Energy & Transportation). Will the relation that is evident always hold? Explain.

f. Recall that the parent company uses the equity method of accounting for its investment in the subsidiary, and that this account is eliminated in the consolidation process. What is the relation between consolidated net income and the net income of the parent company? Explain.

g. What do you believe is the implication for the consolidated balance sheet if the fair value of the Financial Products subsidiary is greater than the book value of its stockholders' equity?

CASES AND PROJECTS

LO1, 3, 4

Yahoo! Inc.
NASDAQ :: YHOO
Alibaba Group
NYSE :: BABA

C12-49. Effect of Investment Accounting on Performance Ratios

Since 2005, **Yahoo! Inc.** has held a significant investment in **Alibaba Group**. In September, 2014, Alibaba Group closed its initial public offering (IPO) of American Depository Shares (shares). Yahoo! sold 140 million shares in the IPO realizing a pretax gain of $10.3 billion. Following completion of the IPO, Yahoo! retained 383.6 million shares of Alibaba Group representing approximately 15% of the outstanding shares. Note 2 to Yahoo!'s 2014 10-K report details its remaining investment in Alibaba.

($ thousands)	Cost Basis	Fair Value
Alibaba Group equity securities	$ 2,713,484	$39,867,789

Yahoo! reported the following (abridged) income statements in its 2014 10-K report ($ thousands):

Year Ended December 31,	2014	2013
Revenue	$4,618,133	$4,680,380
Operating expenses	4,475,191	4,090,454
Income from operations	142,942	589,926
Other income, net	10,369,439	43,357
Income before income taxes and earnings in equity interests	10,512,381	633,283
Provision for income taxes	(4,038,102)	(153,392)
Earnings in equity interests, net of tax	1,057,863	896,675
Net income	$7,532,142	$1,376,566

The following is from Yahoo!'s balance sheets as presented in its 2014 and 2013 10-K reports ($ thousands):

As of December 31,	2014	2013	2012
Total assets	$61,960,344	$16,804,959	$17,103,253
Net operating assets (operating assets – operating liabilities)	$11,416,323	$11,144,097	$10,961,873

REQUIRED

a. At the end of 2013, Yahoo! owned 24% of the shares in Alibaba Group and reported its investment as an equity method investment. Describe the impact of the Alibaba Group IPO on Yahoo!'s financial statements. What method does Yahoo! appear to be using to report its investment in Alibaba in 2014?

b. Compute Yahoo!'s return on assets (ROA) for 2014 and 2013.

c. Compute Yahoo!'s 2014 and 2013 net operating profit after taxes (NOPAT) and its return on net operating assets (RNOA = NOPAT ÷ average net operating assets; refer to Appendix A at the end of Chapter 5 for further discussion). How does this ratio compare to the ROA ratios computed in *b*?

d. Yahoo! is using the available-for-sale accounting method to report its investment in Alibaba Group at the end of 2014. What amount is reported in Yahoo!'s 2014 balance sheet for this investment? What is reported in Yahoo!'s income statement related to this investment?

e. What would be the effect on Yahoo!'s ROA and RNOA ratios if it had classified its investment in Alibaba Group as trading securities?

f. If, in 2014, Yahoo! continued to use the equity method to report its investment in Alibaba, what would be the impact on Yahoo!'s ROA and RNOA? (Do not attempt to calculate ROA or RNOA under the equity method.)

C12-50. Analyzing Financial Statement Effects of Passive and Equity Investments **LO1, 3, 4**

On January 2, 2016, Magee, Inc., purchased, as a stock investment, 20,000 shares of Dye, Inc.'s common stock for $21 per share, including commissions and taxes. On December 31, 2016, Dye announced a net income of $280,000 for the year and declared a dividend of 80 cents per share, payable January 15, 2017, to stockholders of record on January 5, 2017. At December 31, 2016, the market value of Dye's stock was $18 per share. Magee received its dividend on January 18, 2017.

REQUIRED

a. Assume that the stock acquired by Magee represents 10% of Dye's voting stock and is classified in the trading category. Prepare all journal entries appropriate for this investment, beginning with the purchase on January 2, 2016, and ending with the receipt of the dividend on January 18, 2017. (Magee recognizes dividend income when received.)

b. Post the journal entries from part *a* to their respective T-accounts.

c. Record each of the transactions from part *a* in the financial statement effects template.

d. Assume that the stock acquired by Magee represents 40% of Dye's voting stock. Prepare all journal entries appropriate for this investment, beginning with the purchase on January 2, 2016, and ending with the receipt of the dividend on January 18, 2017.

e. Post the journal entries from part *d* to their respective T-accounts.

f. Record each of the transactions from part *d* in the financial statement effects template.

C12-51. Assessing Management Interpretation of Consolidated Financial Statements **LO1, 2, 3, 4, 5**

Demski, Inc., manufactures heating and cooling systems. It has a 75% interest in Asare Company, which manufactures thermostats, switches, and other controls for heating and cooling products. It also has a 100% interest in Demski Finance Company, created by the parent company to finance sales of its products to contractors and other consumers. The parent company's only other investment is a 25% interest in the common stock of Knechel, Inc., which produces certain circuits used by Demski, Inc. A condensed consolidated balance sheet of the entity for the current year follows.

DEMSKI, INC., AND SUBSIDIARIES
Consolidated Balance Sheet
December 31, 2016

Assets		
Current assets		$19,300,000
Stock investment—Influential (Knechel)		2,600,000
Other assets		71,400,000
Excess of cost over equity acquired in net assets of Asare Company		1,700,000
Total assets		$95,000,000
Liabilities and shareholders' equity		
Current liabilities		$10,300,000
Long-term liabilities		14,200,000
Shareholders' equity		
Common stock	$50,000,000	
Retained earnings	16,700,000	
Demski, Inc. shareholders' equity	66,700,000	
Noncontrolling interests	3,800,000	
Total shareholders' equity		70,500,000
Total liabilities and shareholders' equity		$95,000,000

This balance sheet, along with other financial statements, was furnished to shareholders before their annual meeting, and all shareholders were invited to submit questions to be answered at the meeting. As chief financial officer of Demski, you have been appointed to respond to the questions at the meeting.

REQUIRED

Answer the following shareholder questions.

a. What is meant by *consolidated* financial statements?

b. Why is the investment in Knechel shown on the consolidated balance sheet, but the investments in Asare and Demski Finance are omitted?

c. Explain the meaning of the asset Excess of Cost over Equity Acquired in Net Assets of Asare Company.

d. What is meant by *noncontrolling interest* and to what company is this account related?

LO1, 2, 3, 4 **C12-52. Understanding Intercorporate Investments, Accounting Practices, and Managerial Ethics** Doug Stevens, controller of Nexgen, Inc., has asked his assistant, Gayle Sayres, for suggestions as to how the company can improve its financial performance for the year. The company is in the last quarter of the year and projections to the end of the year show the company will have a net loss of about $400,000.

"My suggestion," said Sayres, "is that we sell 1,000 of the 200,000 common shares of Heflin Company that we own. The 200,000 shares gives us a 20% ownership of Heflin, and we have been using the equity method to account for this investment. We have owned this stock a long time and the current market value of the 200,000 shares is about $750,000 above our book value for the stock."

"That sale will only generate a gain of about $3,750," replied Stevens.

"The rest of the story," continued Sayres, "is that once we sell the 1,000 shares, we will own less than 20% of Heflin. We can then reclassify the remaining 199,000 shares from the influential category to the trading category. Once in the trading category, we value the stocks at their current fair value, include the rest of the $750,000 gain in this year's income statement, and finish the year with a healthy net income."

"But," responded Stevens, "we aren't going to sell all the Heflin stock; 1,000 shares maybe, but certainly not any more. We own that stock because they are a long-term supplier of ours. Indeed, we even have representation on their board of directors. The 199,000 shares do not belong in the trading category."

Sayres rolled her eyes and continued, "The classification of an investment as trading or not depends on management's intent. This year-end we claim it was our intent to sell the stock. Next year we change our minds and take the stock out of the trading category. Generally accepted accounting principles can't legislate management intent, nor can our outside auditors read our minds. Besides, why shouldn't we take advantage of the flexibility in GAAP to avoid reporting a net loss for this year?"

REQUIRED

a. Should generally accepted accounting principles permit management's intent to influence accounting classifications and measurements?

b. Is it ethical for Doug Stevens to implement the recommendation of Gayle Sayres?

SOLUTIONS TO REVIEW PROBLEMS

Mid-Chapter Review 1

SOLUTION TO PART 1

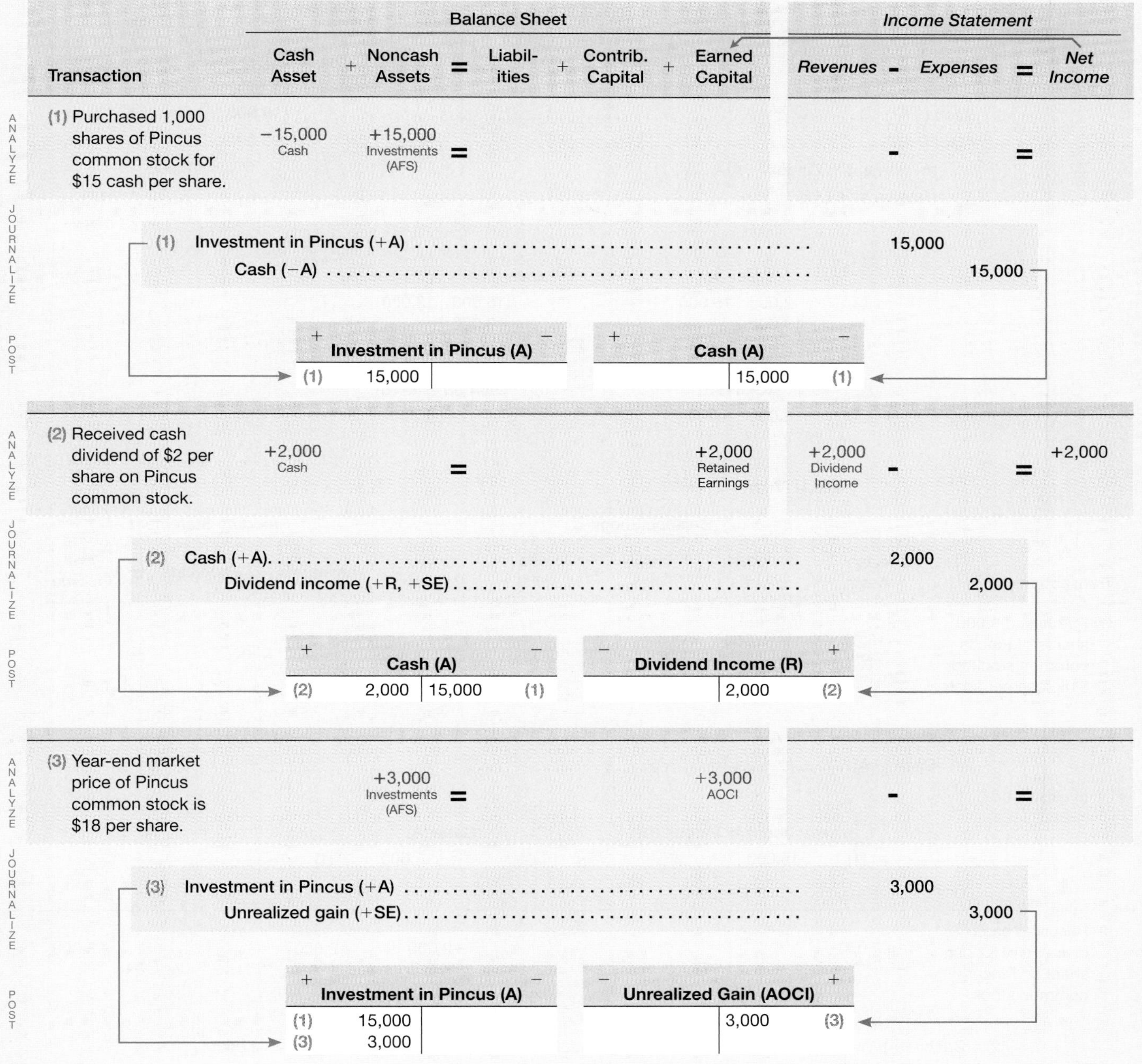

Transaction	Cash Asset	+ Noncash Assets	= Liabil-ities	+ Contrib. Capital	+ Earned Capital	Revenues	− Expenses	= Net Income
(1) Purchased 1,000 shares of Pincus common stock for $15 cash per share.	−15,000 Cash	+15,000 Investments (AFS)						
(2) Received cash dividend of $2 per share on Pincus common stock.	+2,000 Cash				+2,000 Retained Earnings	+2,000 Dividend Income		+2,000
(3) Year-end market price of Pincus common stock is $18 per share.		+3,000 Investments (AFS)			+3,000 AOCI			

(1) Investment in Pincus (+A) 15,000
Cash (−A) 15,000

Investment in Pincus (A)	
+	−
(1) 15,000	

Cash (A)	
+	−
	15,000 (1)

(2) Cash (+A) 2,000
Dividend income (+R, +SE) 2,000

Cash (A)	
+	−
(2) 2,000	15,000 (1)

Dividend Income (R)	
−	+
	2,000 (2)

(3) Investment in Pincus (+A) 3,000
Unrealized gain (+SE) 3,000

Investment in Pincus (A)	
+	−
(1) 15,000	
(3) 3,000	

Unrealized Gain (AOCI)	
−	+
	3,000 (3)

continued

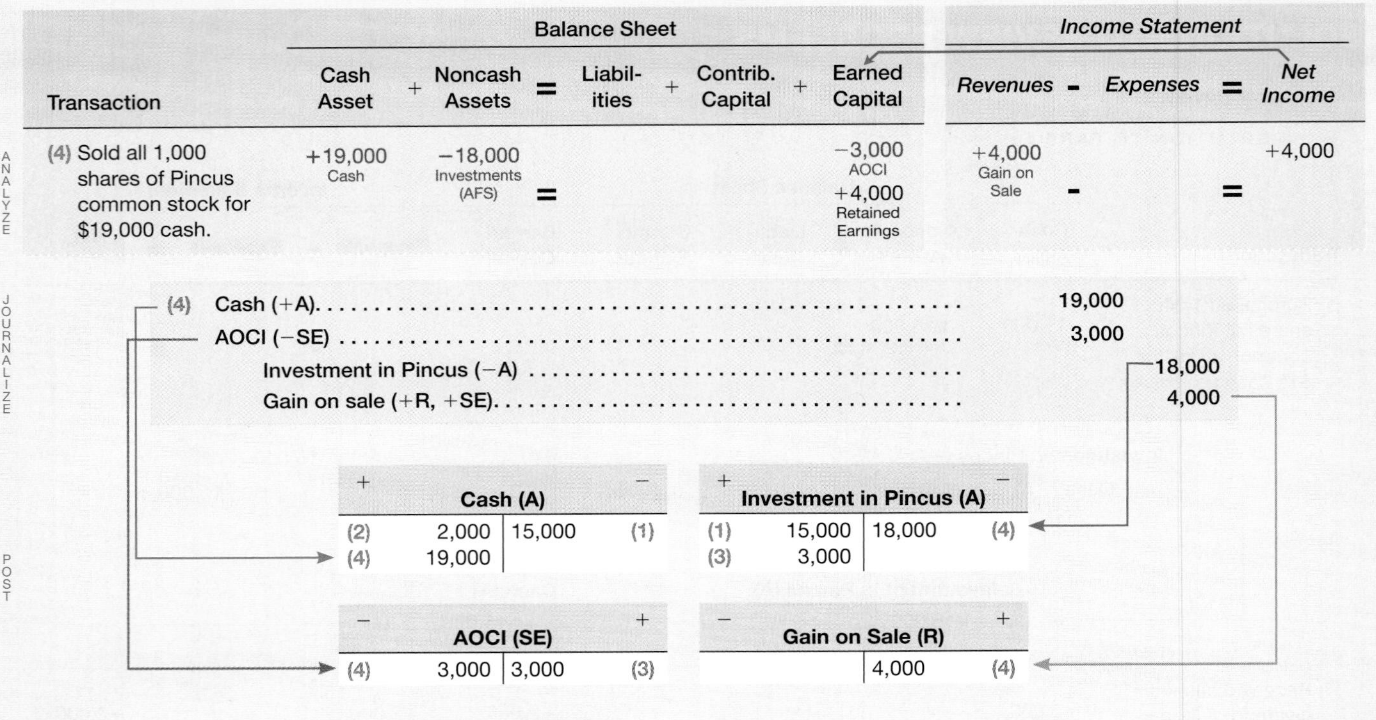

Transaction	Cash Asset	+	Noncash Assets	=	Liabilities	+	Contrib. Capital	+	Earned Capital	Revenues	−	Expenses	=	Net Income
(4) Sold all 1,000 shares of Pincus common stock for $19,000 cash.	+19,000 Cash		−18,000 Investments (AFS)	=					−3,000 AOCI +4,000 Retained Earnings	+4,000 Gain on Sale	−		=	+4,000

(4) Cash (+A) 19,000
AOCI (−SE) 3,000
Investment in Pincus (−A) 18,000
Gain on sale (+R, +SE) 4,000

SOLUTION TO PART 2

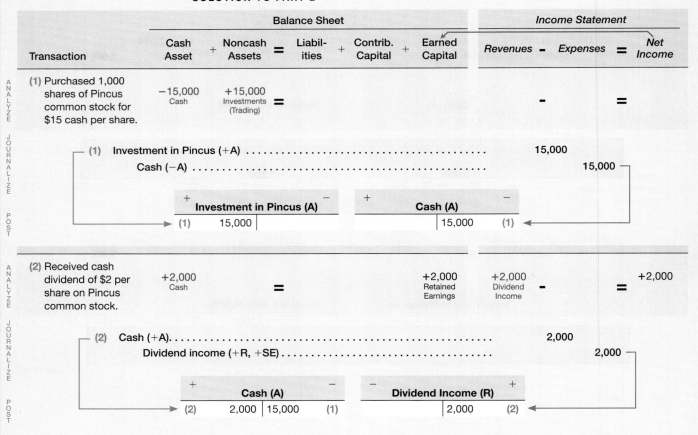

	Balance Sheet									Income Statement				
Transaction	Cash Asset	+	Noncash Assets	=	Liabilities	+	Contrib. Capital	+	Earned Capital	Revenues	−	Expenses	=	Net Income
(1) Purchased 1,000 shares of Pincus common stock for $15 cash per share.	−15,000 Cash		+15,000 Investments (Trading)	=							−		=	
(2) Received cash dividend of $2 per share on Pincus common stock.	+2,000 Cash			=					+2,000 Retained Earnings	+2,000 Dividend Income	−		=	+2,000

Journalize (1):

(1) Investment in Pincus (+A) 15,000
Cash (−A) 15,000

Post (1):

+ Investment in Pincus (A) −	
(1) 15,000	

+ Cash (A) −	
	15,000 (1)

Journalize (2):

(2) Cash (+A) 2,000
Dividend income (+R, +SE) 2,000

Post (2):

+ Cash (A) −	
(2) 2,000	15,000 (1)

− Dividend Income (R) +	
	2,000 (2)

continued

	Balance Sheet										Income Statement				
Transaction	Cash Asset	+	Noncash Assets	=	Liabil-ities	+	Contrib. Capital	+	Earned Capital		Revenues	-	Expenses	=	Net Income
ANALYZE (3) Year-end market price of Pincus common stock is $18 per share.			+3,000 Investments (Trading)	=					+3,000 Retained Earnings		+3,000 Unrealized Gain	-		=	+3,000

JOURNALIZE

	Dr.	Cr.
(3) Investment in Pincus (+A)	3,000	
Unrealized gain (+R, +SE)		3,000

POST

Investment in Pincus (A)

+		−
(1) 15,000		
(3) 3,000		

Unrealized Gain (R)

−	+	
	3,000	(3)

	Cash Asset	+	Noncash Assets	=	Liabil-ities	+	Contrib. Capital	+	Earned Capital		Revenues	-	Expenses	=	Net Income
ANALYZE (4) Sold all 1,000 shares of Pincus common stock for $19,000 cash.	+19,000 Cash		−18,000 Investments (Trading)	=					+1,000 Retained Earnings		+1,000 Gain on Sale	-		=	+1,000

JOURNALIZE

	Dr.	Cr.
(4) Cash (+A)	19,000	
Investment in Pincus (−A)		18,000
Gain on sale (+R, +SE)		1,000

POST

Cash (A)

+		−	
(2)	2,000	15,000	(1)
(4)	19,000		

Gain on Sale (R)

−	+	
	1,000	(4)

Investment in Pincus (A)

+		−	
(1)	15,000	18,000	(4)
(3)	3,000		

Mid-Chapter Review 2

SOLUTION

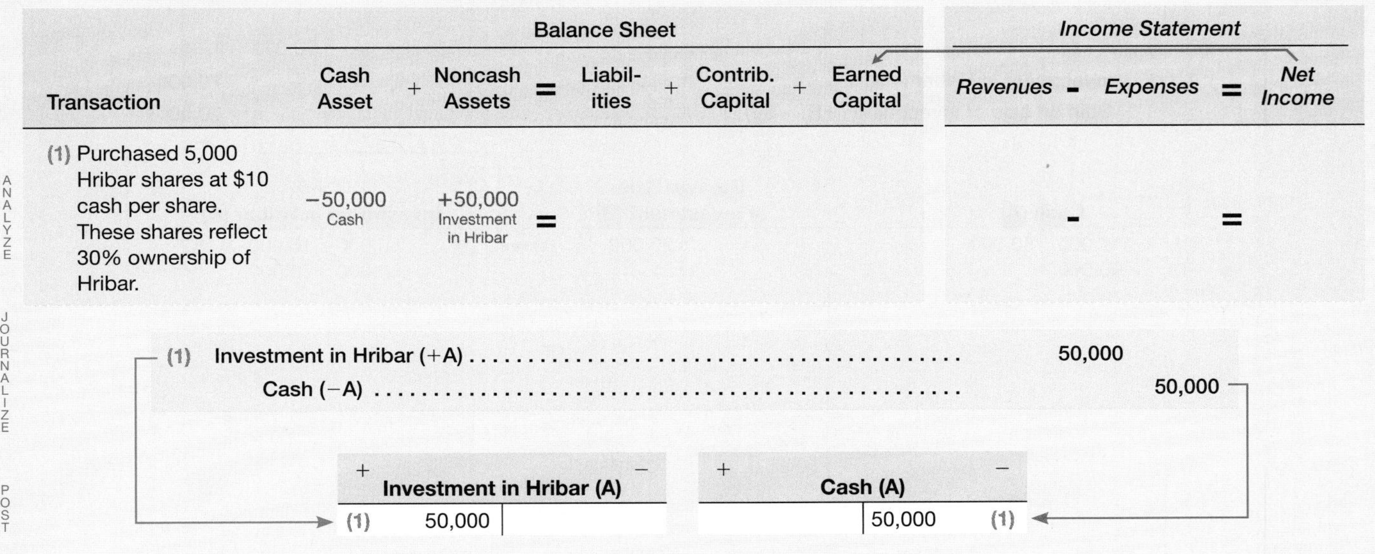

	Balance Sheet										Income Statement				
Transaction	Cash Asset	+	Noncash Assets	=	Liabil-ities	+	Contrib. Capital	+	Earned Capital		Revenues	-	Expenses	=	Net Income
ANALYZE (1) Purchased 5,000 Hribar shares at $10 cash per share. These shares reflect 30% ownership of Hribar.	−50,000 Cash		+50,000 Investment in Hribar	=								-		=	

JOURNALIZE

	Dr.	Cr.
(1) Investment in Hribar (+A)	50,000	
Cash (−A)		50,000

POST

Investment in Hribar (A)

+		−
(1)	50,000	

Cash (A)

+	−	
	50,000	(1)

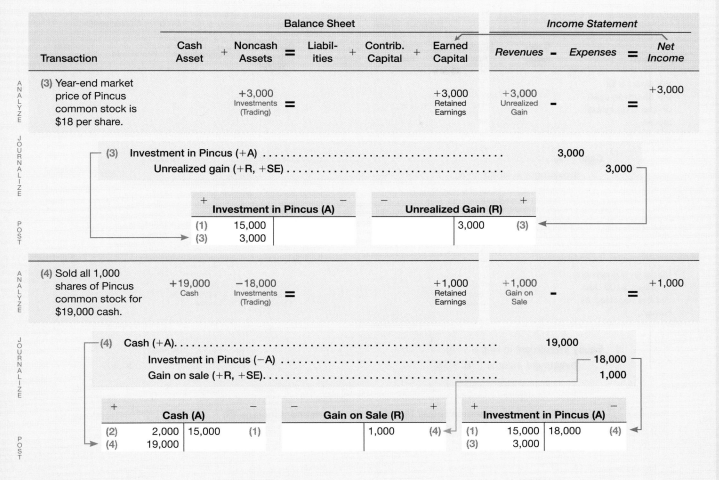

continued

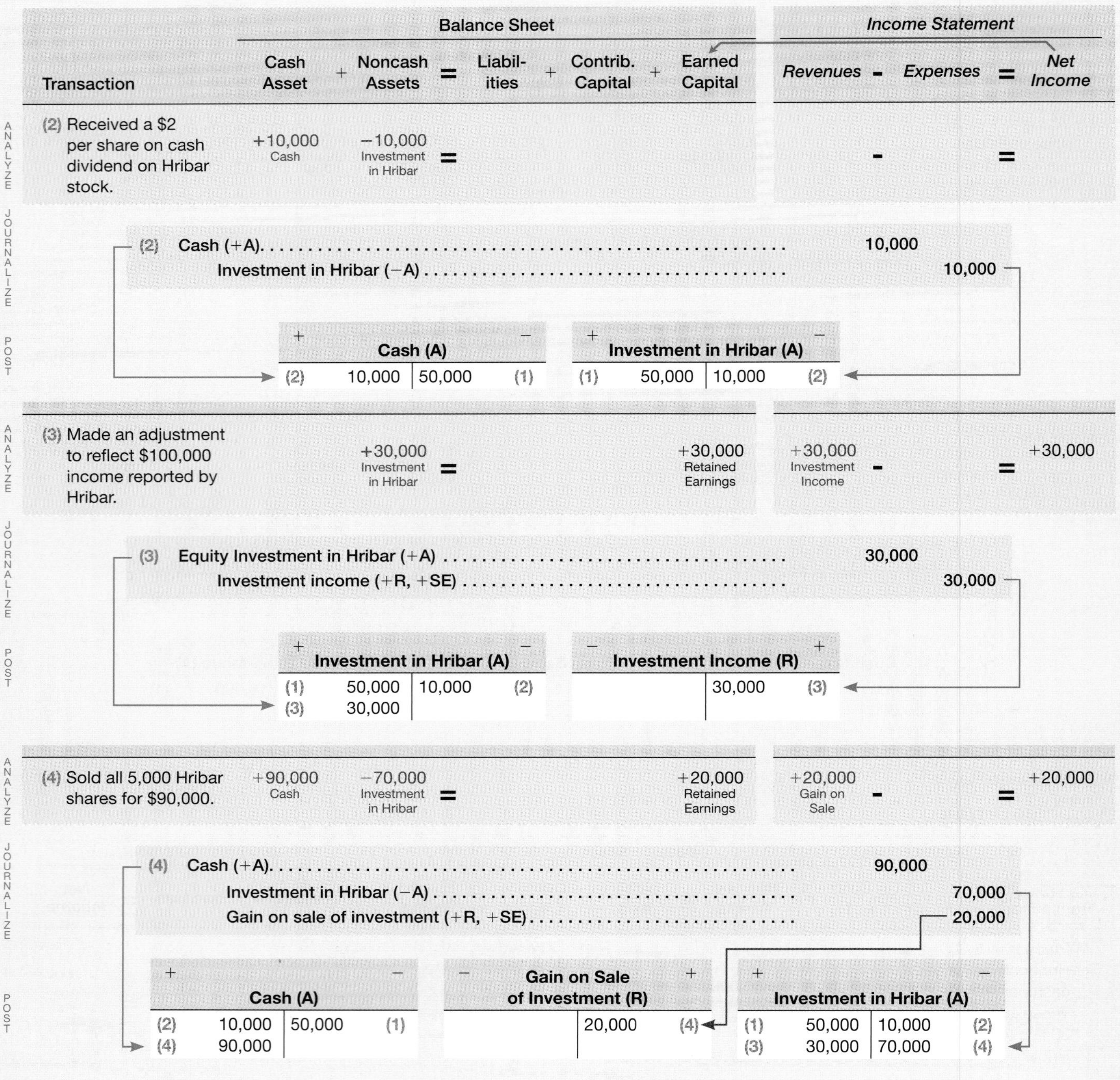
Balance Sheet
Income Statement
Transaction
Cash Asset + Noncash Assets = Liabil-ities + Contrib. Capital + Earned Capital
Revenues - Expenses = Net Income
ANALYZE
(2) Received a $2 per share on cash dividend on Hribar stock.
+10,000 Cash
−10,000 Investment in Hribar
JOURNALIZE
(2) Cash (+A) 10,000
Investment in Hribar (−A) 10,000
POST
Cash (A)
(2) 10,000 | 50,000 (1)
Investment in Hribar (A)
(1) 50,000 | 10,000 (2)
ANALYZE
(3) Made an adjustment to reflect $100,000 income reported by Hribar.
+30,000 Investment in Hribar
+30,000 Retained Earnings
+30,000 Investment Income
+30,000
JOURNALIZE
(3) Equity Investment in Hribar (+A) 30,000
Investment income (+R, +SE) 30,000
POST
Investment in Hribar (A)
(1) 50,000 | 10,000 (2)
(3) 30,000
Investment Income (R)
30,000 (3)
ANALYZE
(4) Sold all 5,000 Hribar shares for $90,000.
+90,000 Cash
−70,000 Investment in Hribar
+20,000 Retained Earnings
+20,000 Gain on Sale
+20,000
JOURNALIZE
(4) Cash (+A) 90,000
Investment in Hribar (−A) 70,000
Gain on sale of investment (+R, +SE) 20,000
POST
Cash (A)
(2) 10,000 | 50,000 (1)
(4) 90,000
Gain on Sale of Investment (R)
20,000 (4)
Investment in Hribar (A)
(1) 50,000 | 10,000 (2)
(3) 30,000 | 70,000 (4)

Chapter-End Review

SOLUTION

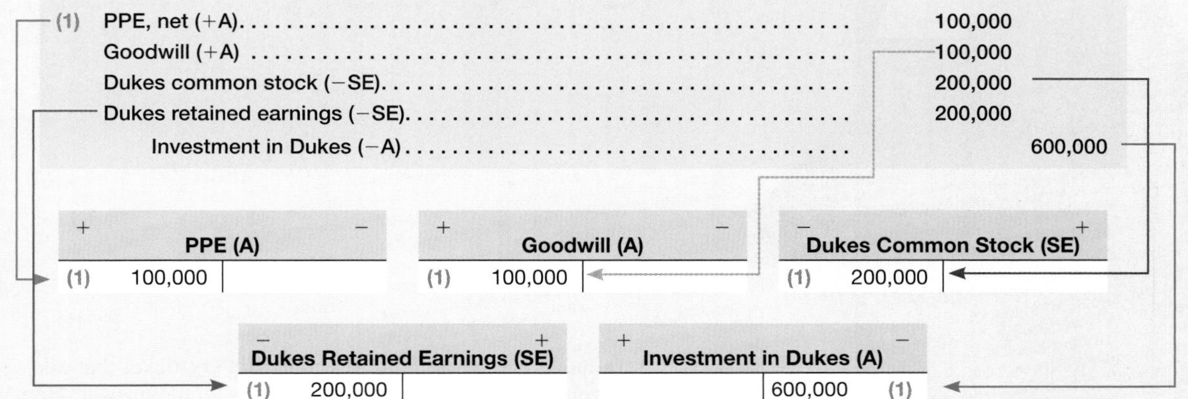

	Bradshaw (Parent)	Dukes (Subsidiary)	Consolidating Adjustments	Consolidated
Current assets	$1,000,000	$100,000		$1,100,000
Investment in Dukes	600,000	—	$(600,000)	
PPE, net	3,000,000	400,000	100,000	3,500,000
Goodwill	—	—	100,000	100,000
Total assets	$4,600,000	$500,000		$4,700,000
Liabilities	$1,000,000	$100,000		$1,100,000
Contributed capital	2,000,000	200,000	(200,000)	2,000,000
Retained earnings	1,600,000	200,000	(200,000)	1,600,000
Total liabilities and equity	$4,600,000	$500,000		$4,700,000

Notes: The $600,000 investment account is eliminated together with the $400,000 book value of Dukes's equity to which it mainly relates. The remaining $200,000 consists of the additional $100,000 in PPE assets and the $100,000 in goodwill from expected corporate synergies. Following these adjustments, the balance sheet items are summed to yield the consolidated balance sheet.

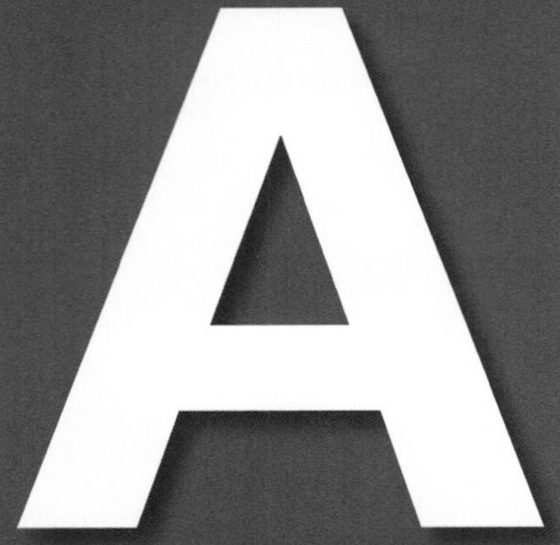

Compound Interest and the Time-Value of Money

Suppose you were lucky enough to hold a winning lottery ticket that allowed you to choose when you would receive your prize. Most of us would answer: Now! But let's say this ticket gave you the option of receiving \$20,000 now, or \$24,000 two years from now. Which would you choose?

Of course, \$24,000 is better than \$20,000. But the choice is not that simple. If you take the \$20,000 today, you can buy a new car, pay next semester's tuition, or invest the money in the stock market. If you wait, you'll receive the larger prize, but you may have to take the bus for the next two years, postpone your college studies, or pass up on a great investment opportunity.

This is the essence of what is called the **time-value of money**. A dollar received today is worth more than a dollar received two years in the future. Having cash in our possession gives us the opportunity to spend or invest that cash today. Cash received in the future cannot be spent or invested today.[1]

The easiest way to illustrate the time-value of money is to assume that we collect the \$20,000 cash prize today and invest it in a money-market account that guarantees a 10% return on your investment. In one year, the investment would be worth \$22,000—which is the original \$20,000 investment plus \$2,000 interest (\$20,000 × 10%). At the end of two years, the investment would be worth \$24,200 [= \$22,000 + (\$22,000 × 10%) = \$22,000 × 1.10].

In the second year, the investment earns a return of \$2,200, which is \$22,000 × 10%. The interest earned in the second year is greater than the interest earned in year one because the interest earned in the first year earns interest in year two. This interest earned on interest is called **compound interest**. As interest accumulates on an investment, both the original investment and the accumulated interest will earn a return in subsequent periods. Interest calculated on the original investment, but not on interest accrued in prior periods, is called **simple interest**.

This Appendix explains and illustrates the concepts of time-value of money and compound interest. It is divided into three sections. The first two address future value concepts and present value concepts, respectively. In the last section, we illustrate the use of spreadsheet software to compute present and future values.

---

[1] The time value of money is primarily due to lost opportunities. However, the risk associated with some future cash flows will influence our assessment of their time value. That is, there may be some uncertainty associated with a future payment. For instance, in our lottery ticket example, there may be a possibility that the payer could default on the \$24,000 payment. Risk is reflected in time value calculations by using higher interest rates for risky cash flows.

FUTURE VALUE CONCEPTS

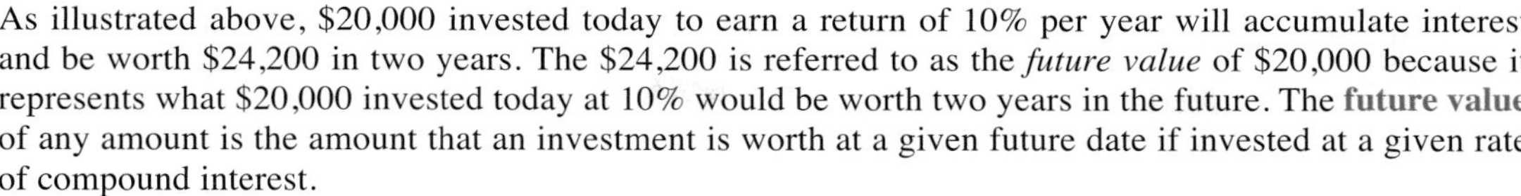

As illustrated above, \$20,000 invested today to earn a return of 10% per year will accumulate interest and be worth \$24,200 in two years. The \$24,200 is referred to as the *future value* of \$20,000 because it represents what \$20,000 invested today at 10% would be worth two years in the future. The **future value** of any amount is the amount that an investment is worth at a given future date if invested at a given rate of compound interest.

Assume that we allow our \$20,000 investment to continue to earn interest for three years. The interest will continue to compound and the future value will continue to grow. This is illustrated in **Exhibit A.1**.

EXHIBIT A.1 Future Value of \$20,000

Initial investment.	\$20,000
Interest earned in year 1 (initial investment × 10%)	2,000
Investment plus accumulated interest (future value) in 1 year	22,000
Interest earned in year 2 (year 1 amount × 10%)	2,200
Investment plus accumulated interest (future value) in 2 years	24,200
Interest earned in year 3 (year 2 amount × 10%)	2,420
Investment plus accumulated interest (future value) in 3 years	\$26,620

As **Exhibit A.1** illustrates, the future value of \$20,000 invested for three years at 10% per year is \$26,620. This can be calculated as $\$26,620 = \$20,000 \times 1.10 \times 1.10 \times 1.10 = \$20,000 \times (1.10)^3$. Similarly, if the interest rate is 8%, the future value is $\$25,194 = \$20,000 \times (1.08)^3$. That is, to determine the future value of an amount n periods in the future, we multiply the present value by one plus the interest rate, raised to the nth power:

$$\textbf{Future Value} = \textbf{Present Value} \times (1 + \textbf{interest rate})^n$$

The future value of any amount depends on two factors: time and rate. That is, how many periods (e.g., years or months) into the future do we want to project the future value and what rate of return (or interest rate) do we use? There are two simple methods that we can use to obtain future values. The first method uses tables presented at the end of this Appendix. **Table A.1** presents the future value of a single amount. To use the table, move across the top of the table to choose the appropriate interest rate and then move down the column to choose the number of periods in the future. **Table A.1** shows that future value increases in the number of periods and in the interest rate.

For example, if we move across the top to the 10% column and then down to period 3, **Table A.1** provides a value of 1.33100. This is the future value of \$1 in three periods at 10% interest per period and is called the **future value factor**. If we want to calculate the future value of \$20,000, we multiply the *future value factor* from **Table A.1** by \$20,000:

Initial Amount	×	Future Value Factor	=	Future Value
\$20,000	×	**1.33100**	=	**\$26,620**

The future value can also be calculated using a financial calculator. Financial calculators require four inputs to calculate a fifth value, which is the solution. We illustrate the use of a calculator with the following graphic:

Calculator

N	I/Yr	PV	PMT	FV
3	10	20,000	0	26,620

On the financial calculator, N is the number of periods (3), I/Yr is the interest rate per period (10), PV is the current, or present, value (\$20,000), PMT refers to a periodic payment (0 in our example) and FV is the future value. Because we are calculating the future value in this illustration, that value is highlighted in red as the solution.[2]

Whether we use the tables at the end of the Appendix or a financial calculator, it is important to recognize that these computations are based on an interest rate *per period*. Most interest rates are stated on an annual, or *per year*, basis. However, for compound interest calculations, a period need not be equal to a year.

[2] Actually, most calculators return a solution of −26,620. The calculator interprets the PV as an investment (cash out) and FV as the return (cash in). So, if PV is entered as a positive amount, then FV will come back negative, and vice versa.

Therefore, we must always be careful to adjust our interest rate *per year* to the appropriate interest rate *per period* and use the corresponding number of time periods in our calculations.

To illustrate, assume that our $20,000 investment paid 8% annual interest, *compounded quarterly*. Although the interest rate is quoted as 8% *per year*, the rate is actually 2% every three-month *period* (=8%/4). Hence, in three years, we would have twelve periods. To determine the future value, we would go down the 2% column in **Table A.1** to the 12-period row to get a future value factor of 1.26824.

Initial Amount	×	Future Value Factor	=	Future Value
$20,000	×	**1.26824**	=	**$25,365**

Alternatively, using the financial calculator:

Calculator				
N	I/Yr	PV	PMT	FV
12	2	20,000	0	25,365

That is, the future value of $20,000 invested for three years at 8%, compounded quarterly, is $25,365.

PRESENT VALUE CONCEPTS

The concept of *present value* is the inverse of future value. Rather than determining how much an amount today is worth in the future, present value determines how much a future amount is worth today. The **present value** of an amount is the value *today* of a cash flow occurring at a future date given a rate of compound interest. As was the case with future value, present values depend on two factors: time and rate.

Present value is a particularly useful concept because it allows us to compare cash flows occurring at different times in the future. We can do this because we can calculate the value of each cash flow at a common point in time—today. For example, let's say we want to compare two investments. Investment A pays $15,000 in two years. Investment B pays $16,000 in three years. We cannot compare these two investments directly, because the payoffs occur in different amounts at different times in the future.[3] However, we can determine how much each payoff is worth today. If the appropriate interest rate is 8%, the present value of Investment A is $12,860 and the present value of Investment B is $12,701. (We demonstrate how to compute these amounts below.) Hence, Investment A is worth more today than Investment B. By determining the value of each cash payoff at the same point in time (today) we can easily compare the alternatives.

Present Value of a Single Amount

To determine the present value of a single cash payment occurring one period in the future, we simply divide the future cash flow by one plus the interest rate (the interest rate is also called the **discount rate**):[4]

$$\textbf{Present Value} = \frac{\textbf{Future Value}}{\textbf{(1 + discount rate)}}$$

If the cash flow occurs n periods in the future, we rearrange the equation from the previous page and divide by one plus the discount rate raised to the nth power:

$$\textbf{Present Value} = \frac{\textbf{Future Value}}{\textbf{(1 + discount rate)}^{n}}$$

[3] The reason that this comparison is difficult is that Investment A pays a return in two years while Investment B doesn't pay a return until year 3. One way to understand this complexity is to ask: What will happen to the cash earned on Investment A during the third year? Or, alternatively, if we invest the return on Investment A for an additional year, how much would we earn after three years? By comparing present values, we are implicitly assuming that any cash payoffs from either investment could be reinvested at the rate of return used to calculate the present value.

[4] The term "discount rate" is often used when referring to present values. This is because when future cash flows are valued using present value calculations, the present value is always less than the future cash amount. Hence, we say that the future value is "discounted" to the present value using the "discount rate."

There are two simple methods for obtaining the present value of a single cash flow occurring at any date in the future. The first method relies on **Table A.2** at the end of this Appendix. We use **Table A.2** in the same way we used **Table A.1** to calculate future values. First, we choose the column representing the appropriate discount rate, and then we move down the column to select the number of periods in the future. The value in the table is the **present value factor**, which decreases in the number of periods and the interest rate. We then multiply the future amount by the *present value factor* to get the present value.

For example, consider Investment A. From **Table A.2**, the present value factor for 8% and two periods is 0.85734. The present value of $15,000 received in two years, discounted at 8% per year is calculated as follows:

Future Amount	×	**Present Value Factor**	=	**Present Value**
$15,000	×	**0.85734**	=	**$12,860**

The present value can also be computed using a financial calculator. In this case, N=2; I/Yr = 8; PMT = 0; FV = 15,000 and PV is our answer (highlighted in red).

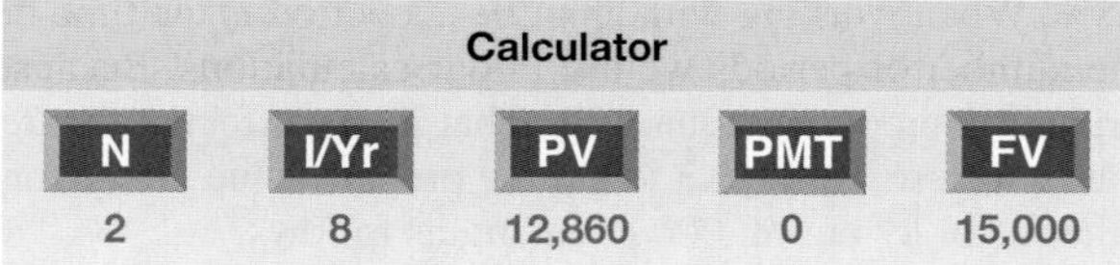

By similar means we can compute the present value of Investment B. The present value factor for 8%, and three periods is 0.79383. The present value of $16,000 received in three years, discounted at 8% per year is:

Future Amount	×	**Present Value Factor**	=	**Present Value**
$16,000	×	**0.79383**	=	**$12,701**

Or, using the financial calculator, we get the same answer as follows:

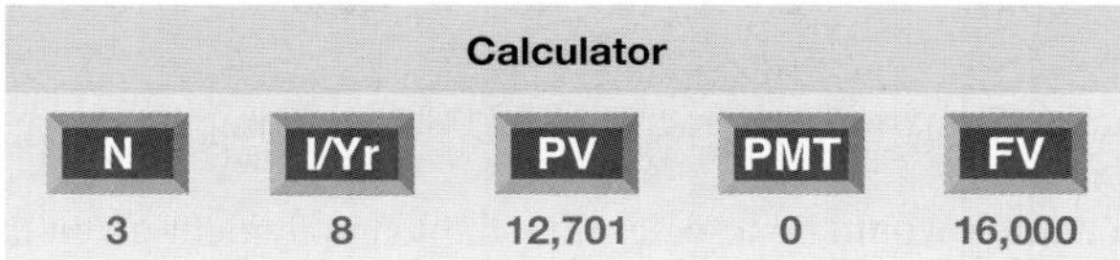

Present Value of an Annuity

Sometimes, we are faced with determining the present value of a series of regular, equal payments, called an **annuity**. For example, let's say we have an investment that pays $7,000 each year for the next three years. We can calculate the present value of each payment and then sum the results to get the present value of the entire annuity. Assume the appropriate discount rate is 6% per year. From **Table A.2**, the present value factors for a 6% discount rate are 0.94340 for one period, 0.89000 for two periods, and 0.83962 for three periods. The calculation of the present value is presented in **Exhibit A.2** (rounded to the nearest whole dollar):

EXHIBIT A.2 Present Value of an Annuity of 3 Payments of $7,000 Discounted at 6%

	Future Payment	×	Present Value Factor	=	Present Value
1	$7,000		0.94340		6,604
2	7,000		0.89000		6,230
3	7,000		0.83962		5,877
					$18,711

While this method of computing the present value of an annuity is accurate, it can be tedious for annuities with many cash payments. **Table A.3** at the end of this Appendix presents present value factors for annuities of various lengths. This table is used in the same way as **Table A.2**: first we choose the column reflecting our discount rate, and then we choose the row representing the number of payments. From **Table A.3**, the present value factor for an annuity of three payments discounted at 6% is 2.67301. To calculate the present value of an annuity, we multiply the periodic payment by the present value factor:

Payment	×	**Present Value Factor**	=	**Present Value**
$7,000	×	**2.67301**	=	**$18,711**

Or alternatively, using a financial calculator, we enter N=3, I/Yr=6, PMT=7,000, FV=0, and the solution is the PV, highlighted in red:

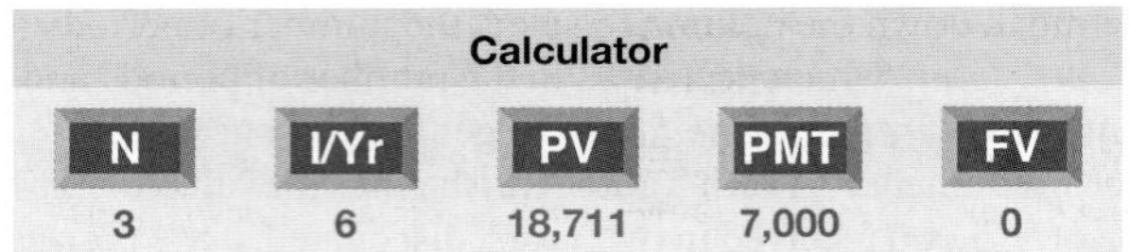

Calculator				
N	I/Yr	PV	PMT	FV
3	6	18,711	7,000	0

Installment Loans

One useful application of the present value of an annuity is to value an *installment loan*. An **installment loan** is a loan that requires a series of equal payments, or installments, each of which includes interest and some of the original principal. Assume that we take out a bank loan requiring 12 quarterly payments of $2,000 and an annual interest rate of 8%. When working with annuities, a period is the time between payments and the number of payments is the number of periods we use in our calculations. Because the payments are made quarterly, the 8% annual rate is compounded quarterly. That is, the effective interest rate is 2% per quarter. To calculate the loan amount, we use **Table A.3** to get the present value factor for 12 payments discounted at 2%, and then multiply the factor by our $2,000 payment, as follows:

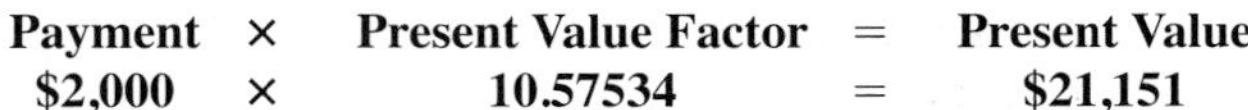

Payment	×	Present Value Factor	=	Present Value
$2,000	×	**10.57534**	=	**$21,151**

Calculator				
N	I/Yr	PV	PMT	FV
12	2	21,151	2,000	0

That is, if we agreed to make 12 quarterly payments of $2,000, including an interest charge of 2% per quarter, we could borrow $21,151.

A more common calculation would be to determine the loan payment given the amount borrowed. For example, if we borrow $30,000 and agree to repay the loan in 24 equal monthly payments at a 12% annual interest rate (1% per month), what monthly payment would we need to make to repay the loan plus interest? To compute the payment, we divide the present value (the loan amount) by the present value factor from **Table A.3** (1%, 24 periods) as follows:

Present Value	÷	Present Value Factor	=	Payment
$30,000	÷	**21.24339**	=	**$1,412.20**

Using a financial calculator, we can calculate the payment (PMT) directly, given the other inputs:

Calculator				
N	I/Yr	PV	PMT	FV
24	1	30,000	1,412.20	0

Bond Valuation

From Chapter 9, we know that a typical corporate bond has a face value of $1,000 and pays periodic interest payments every six months based on the stated (or coupon) interest rate. That is, the face value and the stated rate of a bond allow us to lay out the cash flows that will be paid to the bondholder. We also know that bonds are valued using the market interest rate, which may be different from the stated rate.

Bonds represent a combination of an annuity of the periodic interest payments and a single future payment of the face value, or principal payment, sometimes called a **balloon payment**. In order to value a bond, we must calculate the present value of each of these two components. Let's assume that we wish to value a $1,000, 5-year, 7% bond that pays a semi-annual coupon payment. The face value is $1,000 and the semi-annual payment is $35 (= $1,000 × 7%/2). Let's assume a market interest rate (yield) of 8% (which is 4% every six months). The bond is valued as the sum of two parts:

1. Use **Table A.2** to compute the value of the principal (balloon) payment.
2. Use **Table A.3** to compute the value of the annuity of interest (coupon) payments.

This calculation is illustrated in **Exhibit A.3**:

EXHIBIT A.3 Calculating a Bond Value Using Present Value Tables (4%, 10 periods)

	Cash Flow	×	Present Value Factor	=	Present Value
Face value: 1 payment of $1,000 at the end of 5 years (**Table A.2**—4%, 10 periods)	$1,000	×	0.67556	=	675.56
Semi-annual coupon payments: 10-payment annuity of $35 every six months (**Table A.3**—4%, 10 periods)	$35	×	8.11090	=	283.88
					$959.44

The bond value can also be calculated using a financial calculator, with the following inputs: N=10; I/Yr=4; PMT=35; FV=1,000. The solution is the PV:

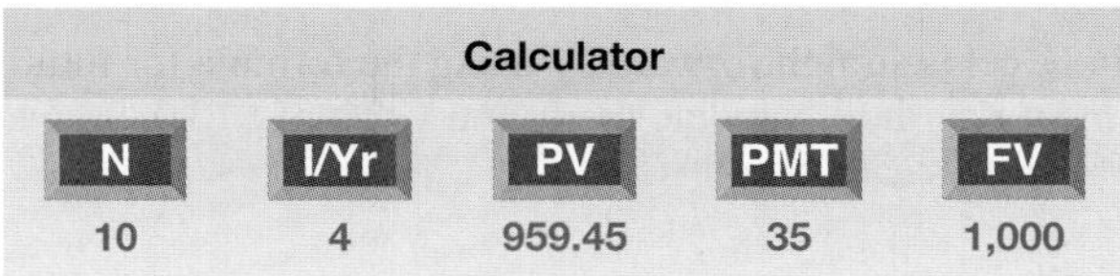

The calculator automatically adds the present value of the annuity (10 payments of $35) to the present value of the single amount ($1,000 principal value) to get the bond value. That is, the market is willing to invest $959.45 in a $1,000, 5-year, 7% bond that pays interest semi-annually, and this amount is what would be received in proceeds from issuing the bond. The difference between $1,000 and $959.45 can be attributed to the difference between the 7% coupon rate of interest and the 8% required by investors.

Calculating Bond Yields

Sometimes we know the future cash payments and the present value of those payments, but not the discount rate used to compute the present value. This would be useful, for example, if we knew the price of a bond but wanted to determine the yield.

To illustrate the calculation of a bond yield, assume that we have a $1,000, 8-year, 5% bond that is currently priced at 104 (104% of par value or $1,040). The semiannual interest payment is $25 (= $1,000 × 5%/2) and the principal amount of $1,000 is due in 8 years (16 semiannual periods). We input the following values: N=16; PV=1,040; PMT=25; FV=1,000. The solution is returned by pressing the I/Yr button:

Calculator

N	I/Yr	PV	PMT	FV
16	2.20	1,040	25	1,000

In this case, the calculator returns a solution of 2.20%. This is the interest rate *per period* that discounts the future payments on the bond to the present value of $1,040. Because each period is six months, we must double this rate to get the bond yield (or market rate of interest), which is always quoted on an annual basis. Thus, the yield on this bond is 4.4% (= 2.2% × 2).[5]

Future Value of Annuities

On occasion, we may have a future funding target that will be met by making period payments. For instance, we may wish to accumulate a down payment for a residence or accumulate a retirement balance to draw upon in future years. For this analysis, we must examine the future value created by an annuity, i.e., a series of payments.

Suppose we wish to accumulate a down payment by making quarterly payments into an account that earns 4% per year (1% per quarter). Payments of $2,000 would be made at the beginning of each quarter

[5] Technically, in order to obtain the result illustrated here, the amounts for PMT and FV must be entered with the same sign, but the PV amount must be entered with the opposite sign. For example, if we enter PV = −1,040, PMT = 25 and FV = 1,000, we would get the result above.

and would continue for five years. How much would accumulate over the five years? The future value of each payment can be determined using **Table A.1**, but **Table A.4** accumulates the amounts in a convenient format. An annuity of $2,000 per quarter for 20 quarters at 1% per period would produce a future value of:

Payment	×	**Future Value Factor**	=	**Future Value**
$2,000	×	**22.2392**	=	**$44,478.40**

This analysis would also allow for testing the sensitivity of the amount to various factors. For instance, making payments for 6 years, would increase the balance to $54,486.40. Investing in an account that provided 2% interest per quarter would accumulate $49,566.60 after five years.

USING EXCEL TO COMPUTE TIME VALUE

Spreadsheet software, such as Microsoft Excel© is extremely useful for performing a variety of time-value calculations. In this section, we illustrate a few of the features of Excel.

Future Value Calculations

Calculating future value in Excel is straightforward by using the formula for future value or using the function wizard feature. Assume we wish to compute the future value of $12,000 invested today at 6% interest for four years. The formula for this calculation is:

=12000*1.06^4

Excel returns the value 15149.72. An alternative method of making this calculation is by using the function wizard. The function wizard is accessed by clicking on the *fx* icon in the formula bar at the top of the spreadsheet.

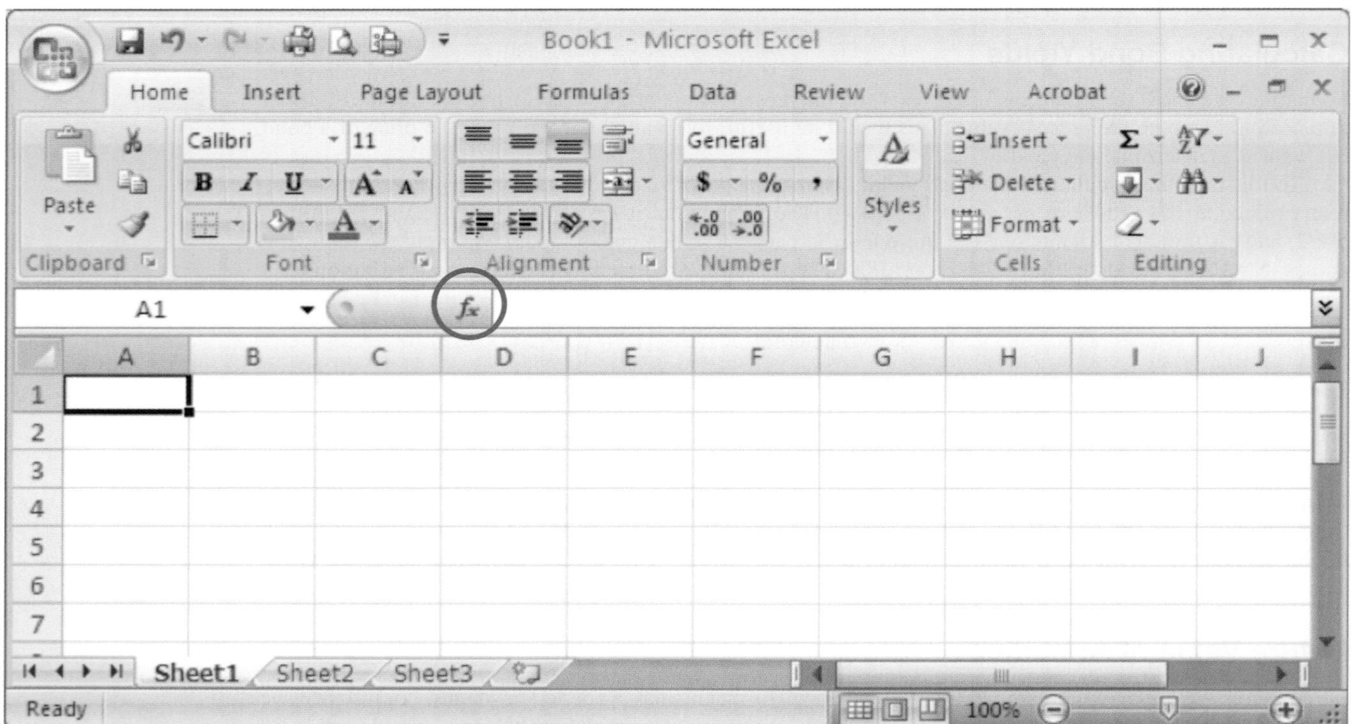

Clicking on the *fx* icon opens a dialog box that offers a variety of built-in functions. The dialog box appears as follows:

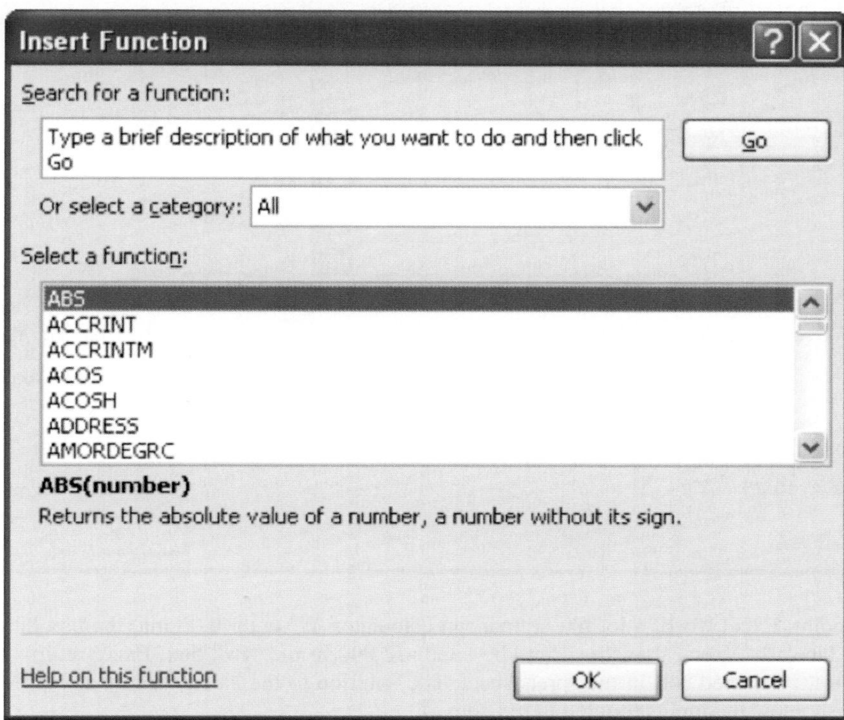

Now, the user can scroll through the long list of built-in Excel functions or customize the search by selecting a category of functions. In the screen shot below, the category of functions described as "Financial" is selected. Scrolling through the list, we select the FV function (for future value).

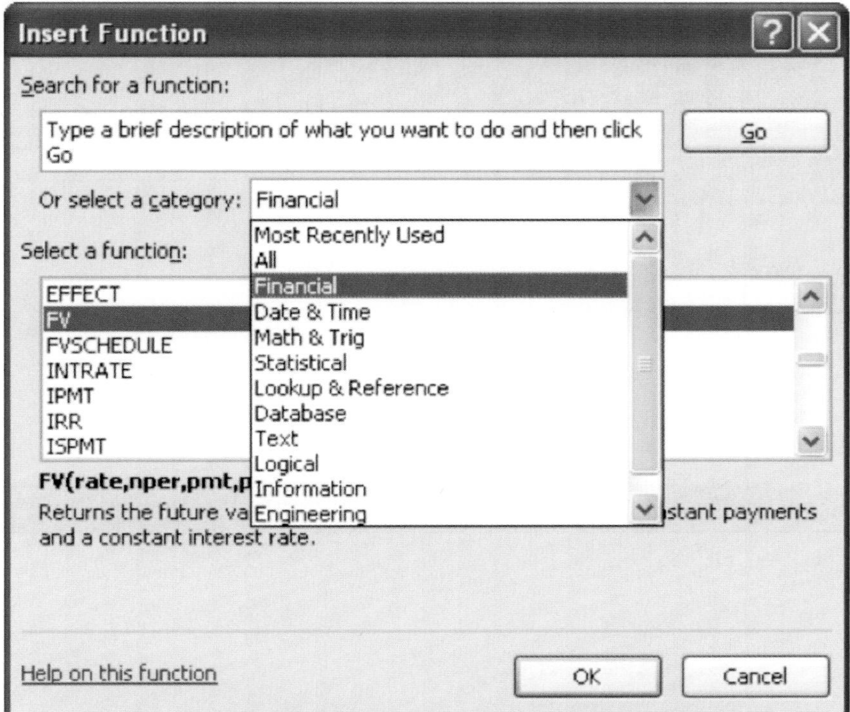

Once the FV function is selected, a new dialog box appears:

Function Arguments

FV

Rate	.06	=	0.06
Nper	4	=	4
Pmt	0	=	0
Pv	-12000	=	-12000
Type		=	number

= 15149.72352

Returns the future value of an investment based on periodic, constant payments and a constant interest rate.

Pv is the present value, or the lump-sum amount that a series of future payments is worth now. If omitted, Pv = 0.

Formula result = 15149.72352

Help on this function

OK Cancel

At this point, Excel works a lot like a financial calculator. We enter 0.06 into the box labeled "Rate," 4 in the box labeled "Nper," 0 in the "Pmt" box and -12,000 in the "Pv" box. Excel returns the value of $15,149.72 in the selected cell in the spreadsheet. The solution to the calculation is also presented in the dialog box just below the inputs (circled in red above).

One advantage of Excel, is that it allows the user to enter cell locations as function arguments in the dialog box. This can be useful if we wish to gauge the impact of changing an argument. For instance, we could enter the following in a spreadsheet:

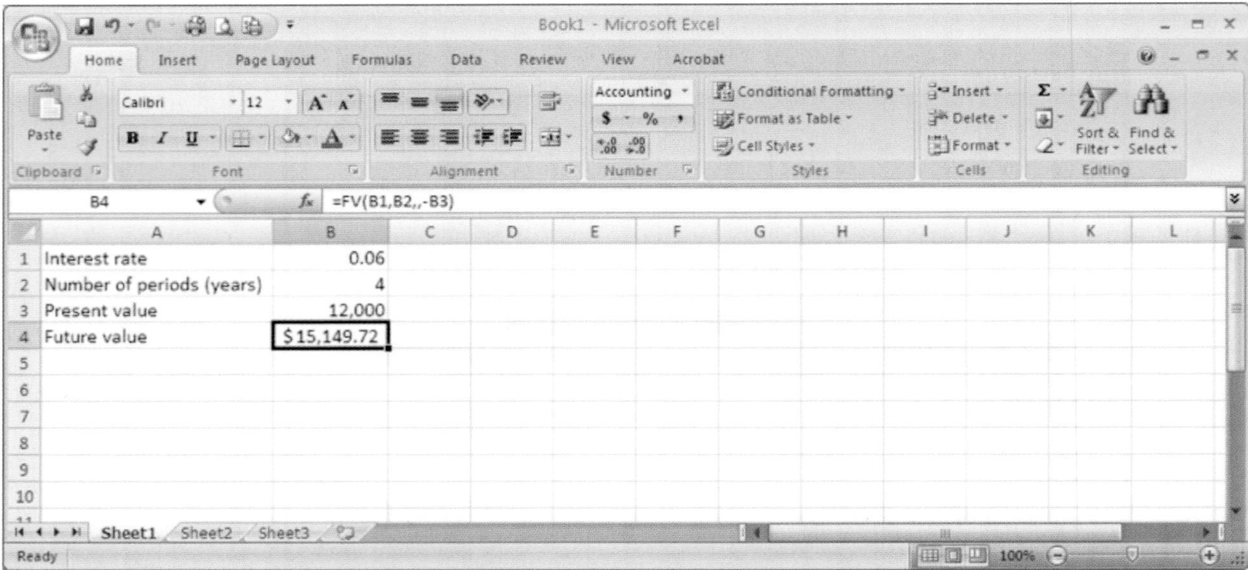

The amount presented as the "Future value" is actually returned by the dialog box below:

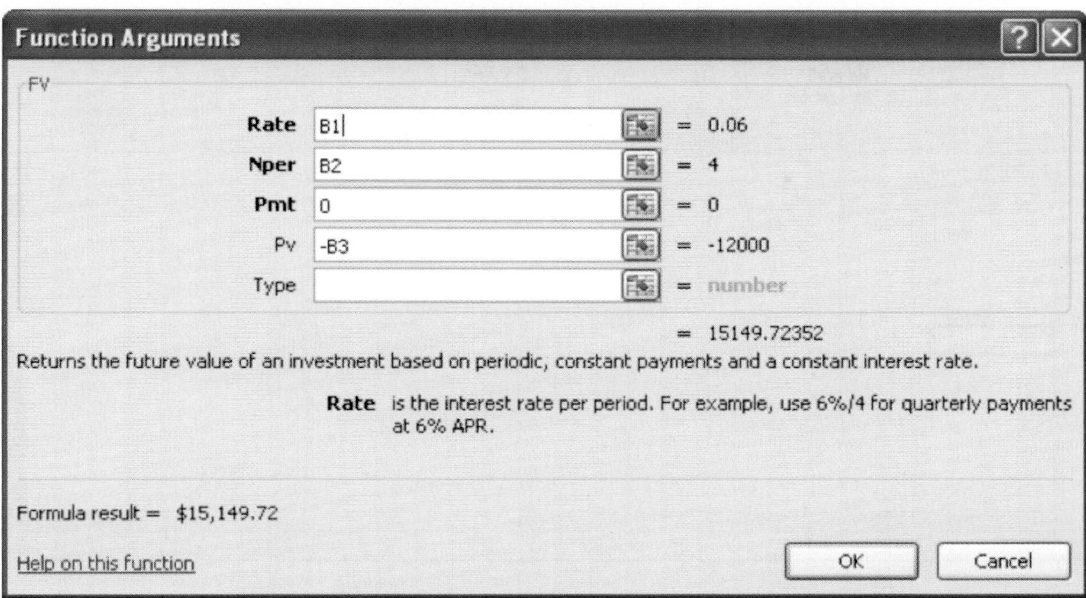

When we enter cell locations (e.g. "B1") in the boxes for function arguments, the function wizard uses the value in that cell as the argument. The benefit of this is that we can now change an argument and recalculate the future value without revisiting the function wizard dialog box. For example, let's say we wish to determine what the future value of our investment would be if we held our investment for five years instead of four years. We simply replace the "4" in cell B2 with a "5" as follows:

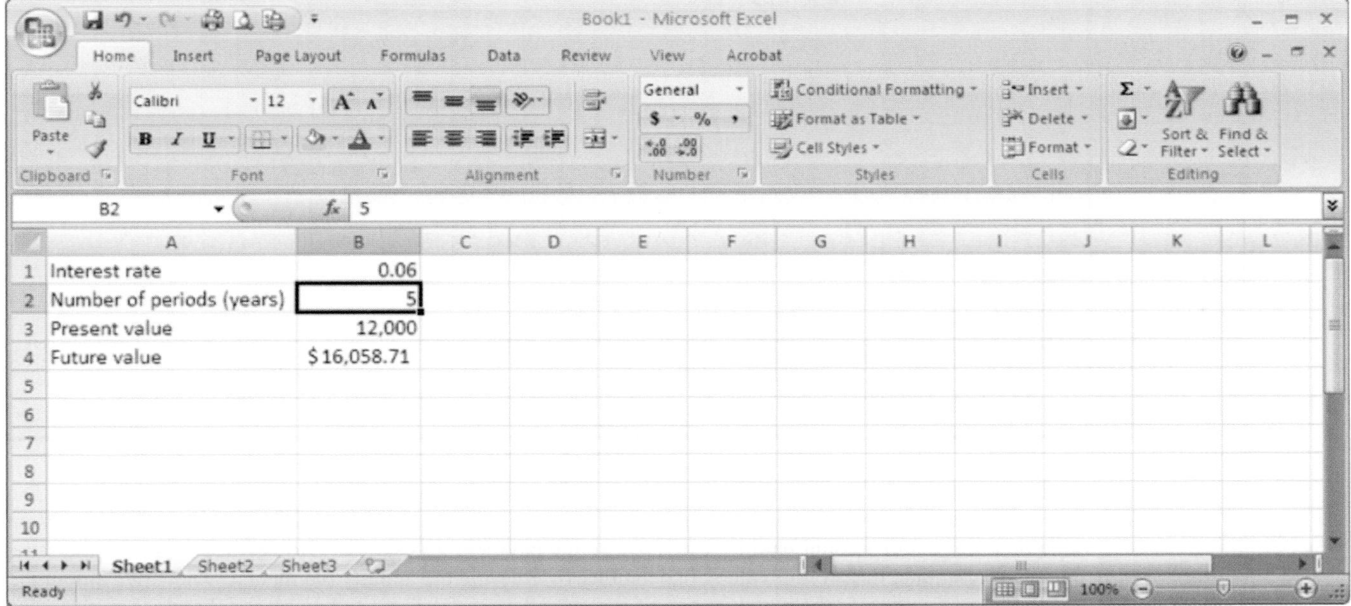

Excel automatically returns the value of $16,058.71 as the future value (cell B4).

Present Value Calculations

Computing present value is as straightforward as future value. The function to use is "PV" for present value. Let's assume we wish to calculate the present value of $15,000 that we expect to receive in two years discounted at 8% per year. Earlier, we determined that the present value is $12,860. To make this calculation using Excel, we enter each of the arguments in the spreadsheet as follows:

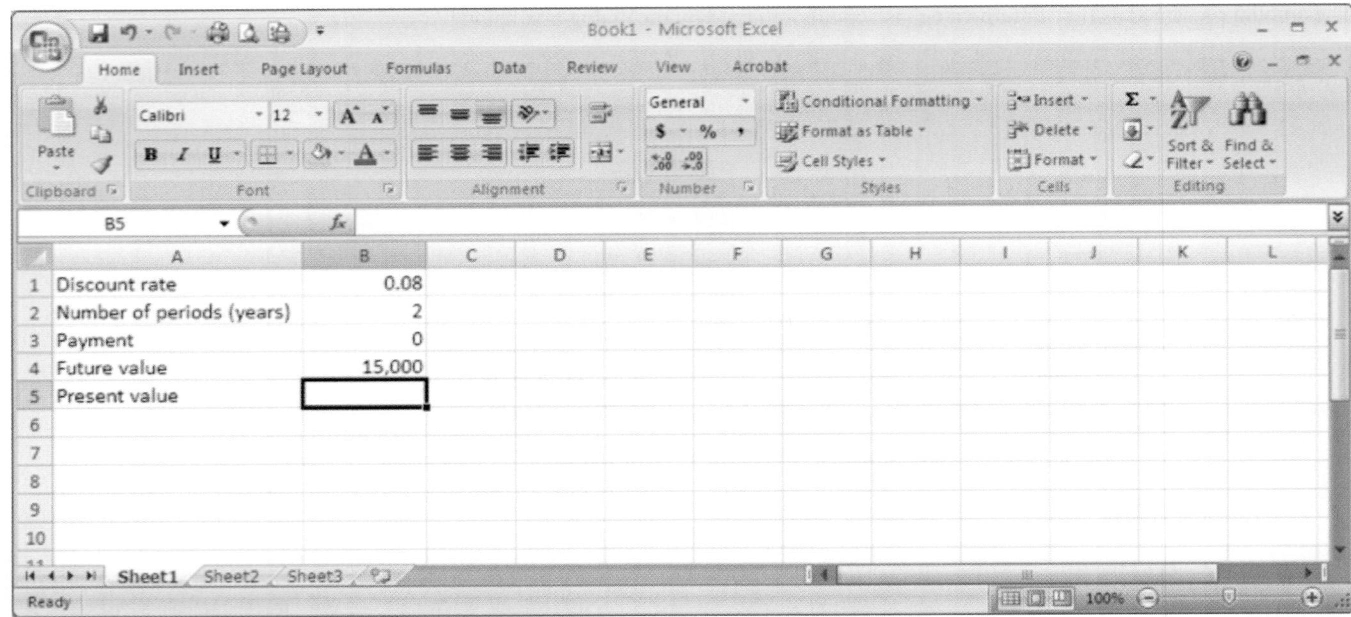

We then use the function wizard to access the "PV" function:

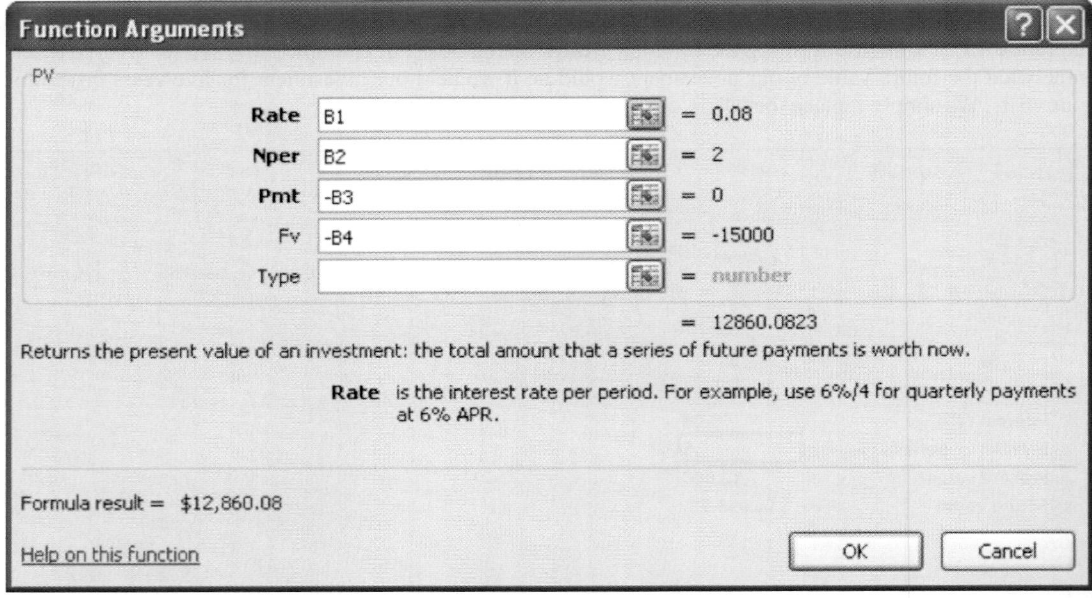

The PV function is similar to the FV function. The amount returned is the present value of $12,860.08. The "Pmt" argument in the PV function is used for annuity payments. In this example, we wanted the present value of a lump-sum amount paid in two years, so the payment was set to 0. However, we can use the same function to compute the present value of an annuity by entering the annuity payment as a negative amount in the "Pmt" argument or in the payment cell of our spreadsheet. Earlier, we determined that the present value of a series of $7,000 payments received annually for three years and discounted at 6% is $18,711. To compute this amount using Excel, we list the payment (Pmt) as 7,000 and the future value (FV) as 0:

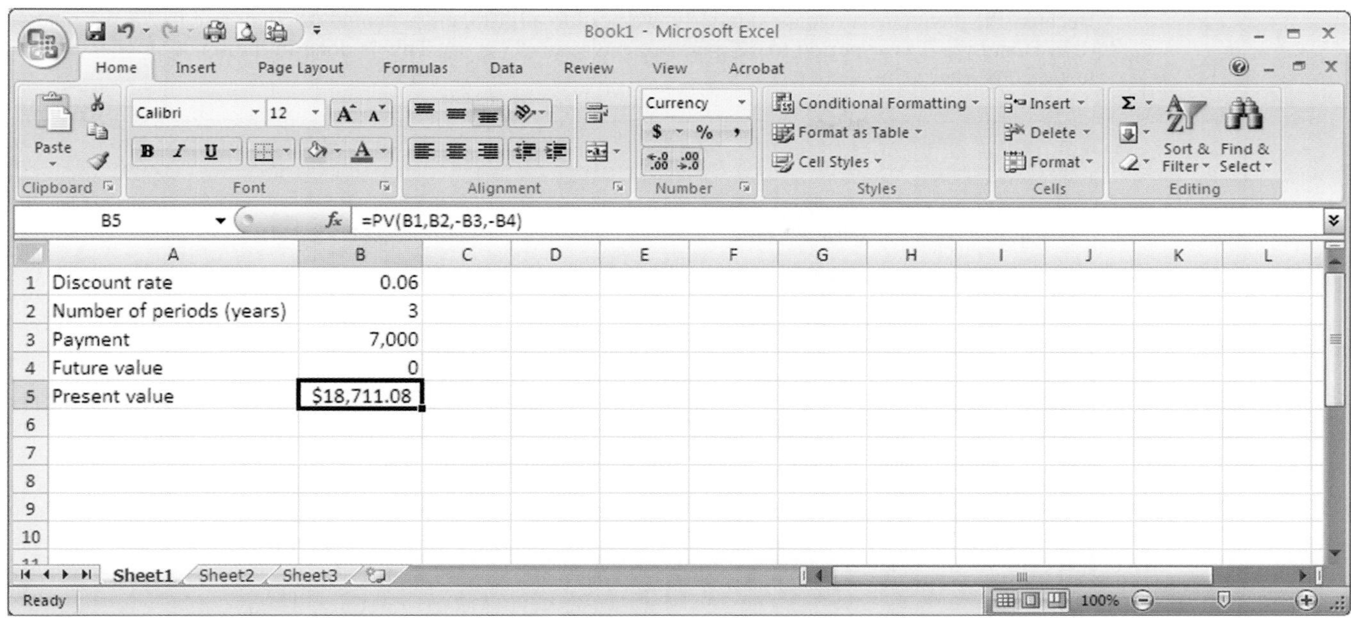

Similarly, our installment loan that requires 12 quarterly payments of $2,000 at 8% interest per year (2% per quarter) would have a present value of $21,150.68, which is computed as follows:

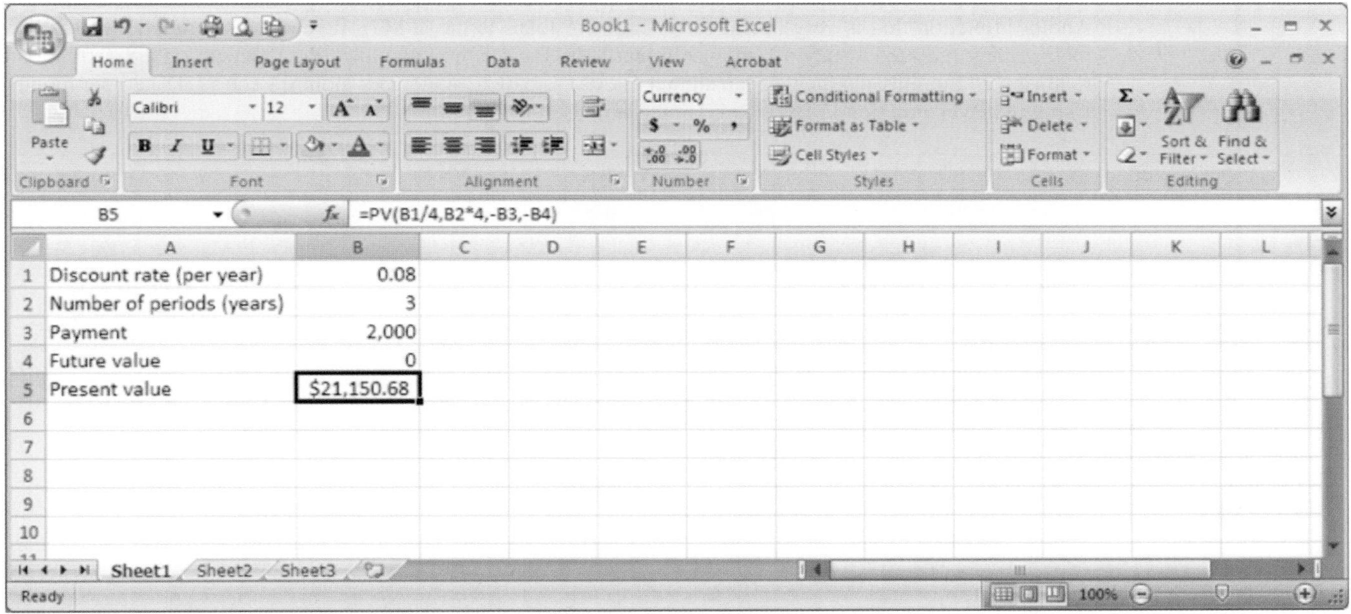

Because the payments are made quarterly, we need to adjust the 8% annual discount rate to 2% per quarter (8%/4) and the 3 year period to 12 quarterly payments (3 × 4). This is done in the function wizard as illustrated below:

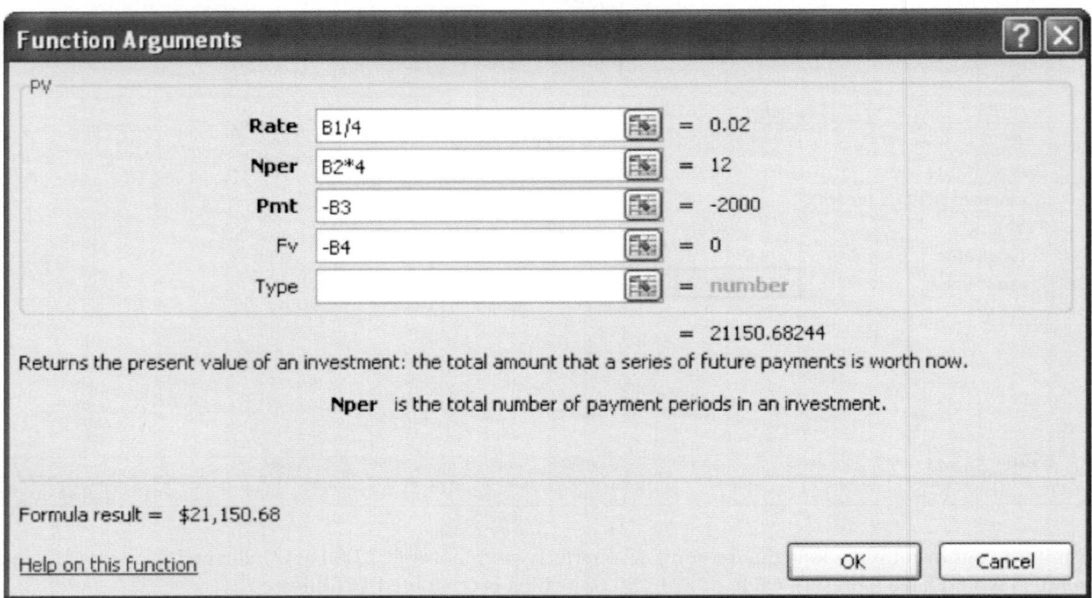

Another function that is very useful for installment loans is the "PMT" function. This function calculates the payment required to pay off an installment loan. Earlier, we calculated the payment on a $30,000 loan requiring 24 monthly payments at an annual interest rate of 12% (1% per month) to be $1,412.20 per month. Using the PMT function in Excel, we get the same result:

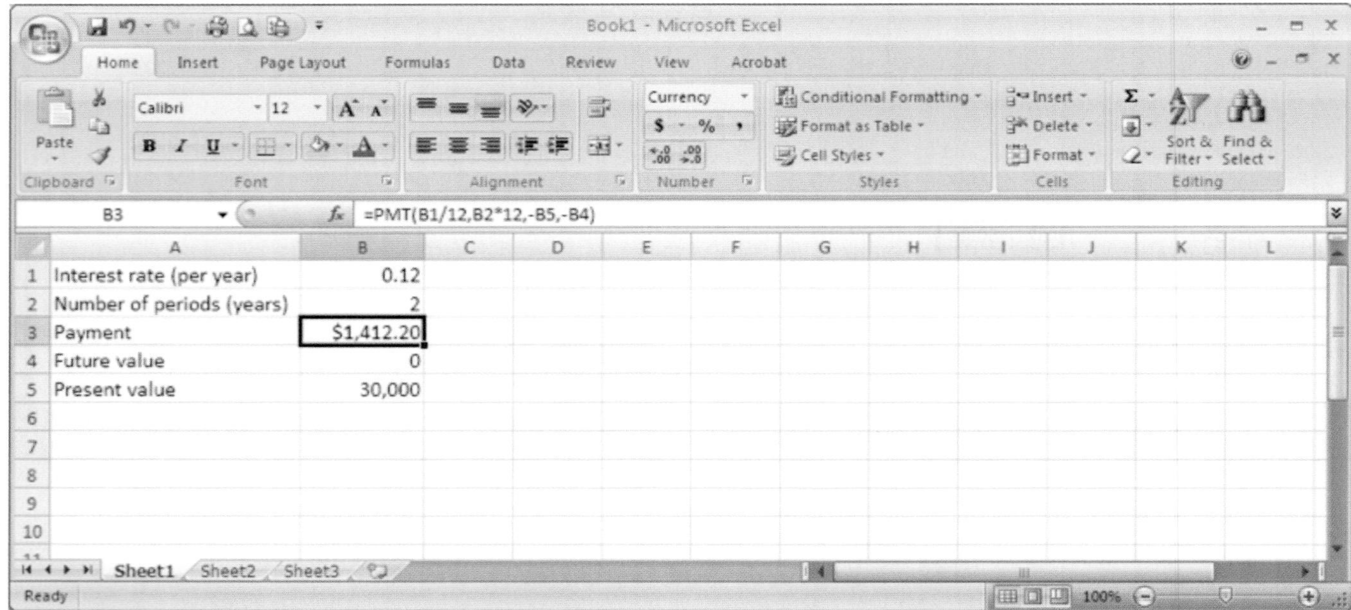

Here we need to divide the annual interest rate by 12 and multiply the number of years by 12 in order to allow for monthly compounding.

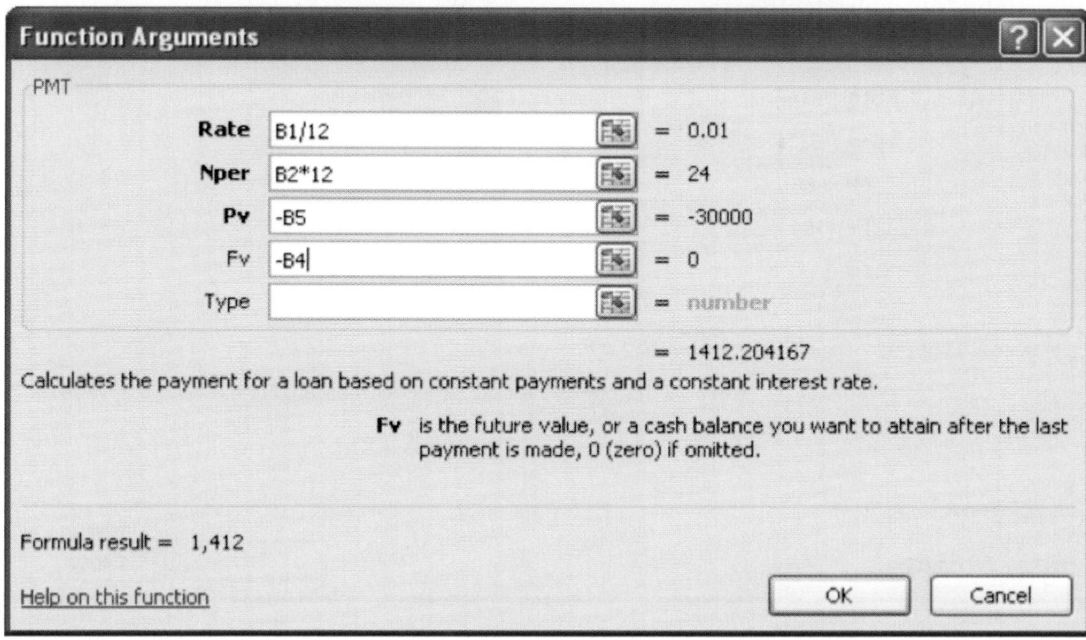

Excel is very useful for setting up loan amortization tables. These tables lay out the loan payments and calculate the interest and principal included in each payment. To illustrate, assume we borrow $5,000 at 4% annual interest, and agree to repay the loan in 8 quarterly payments (four payments per year for two years). The quarterly payment is $653.45 calculated as follows:

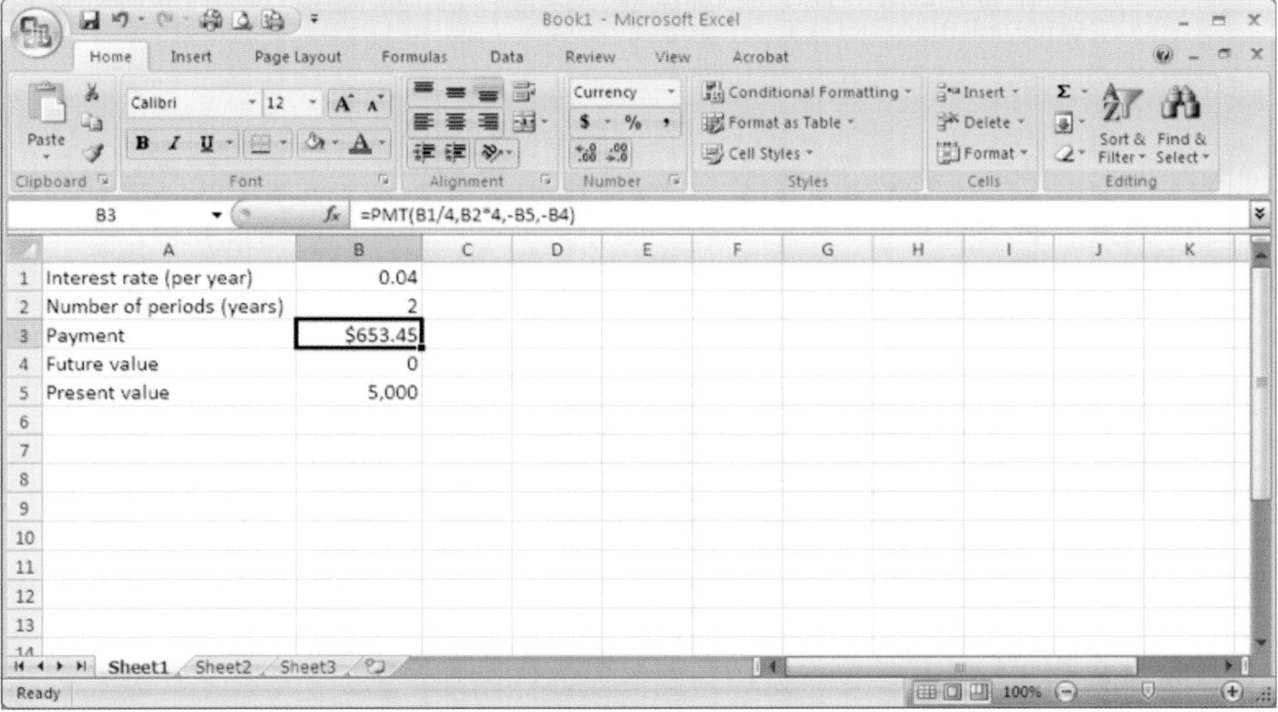

The function box appears as follows:

Function Arguments

PMT

Rate	B1/4	=	0.01
Nper	B2*4	=	8
Pv	-B5	=	-5000
Fv	-B4	=	0
Type		=	number

= 653.4514602

Calculates the payment for a loan based on constant payments and a constant interest rate.

Rate is the interest rate per period for the loan. For example, use 6%/4 for quarterly payments at 6% APR.

Formula result = $653.45

Help on this function

OK Cancel

The loan amortization table can be set up on the same worksheet or in a separate sheet linked to the payment calculation. Here we use the same worksheet.

The first column [D] lists the period (1 through 8). In the second column [E], we list the loan balance at the beginning of each period. For the first period, the beginning balance is the loan amount of $5,000. Thereafter, the beginning balance is set equal to the ending balance from the previous period, which is in column [I]. Column [F] lists the quarterly payment of $653.45. In column [G], we compute the interest each quarter. This amount is equal to the loan balance at the beginning of the period (Column [E]) times the interest rate (cell B1) divided by 4.

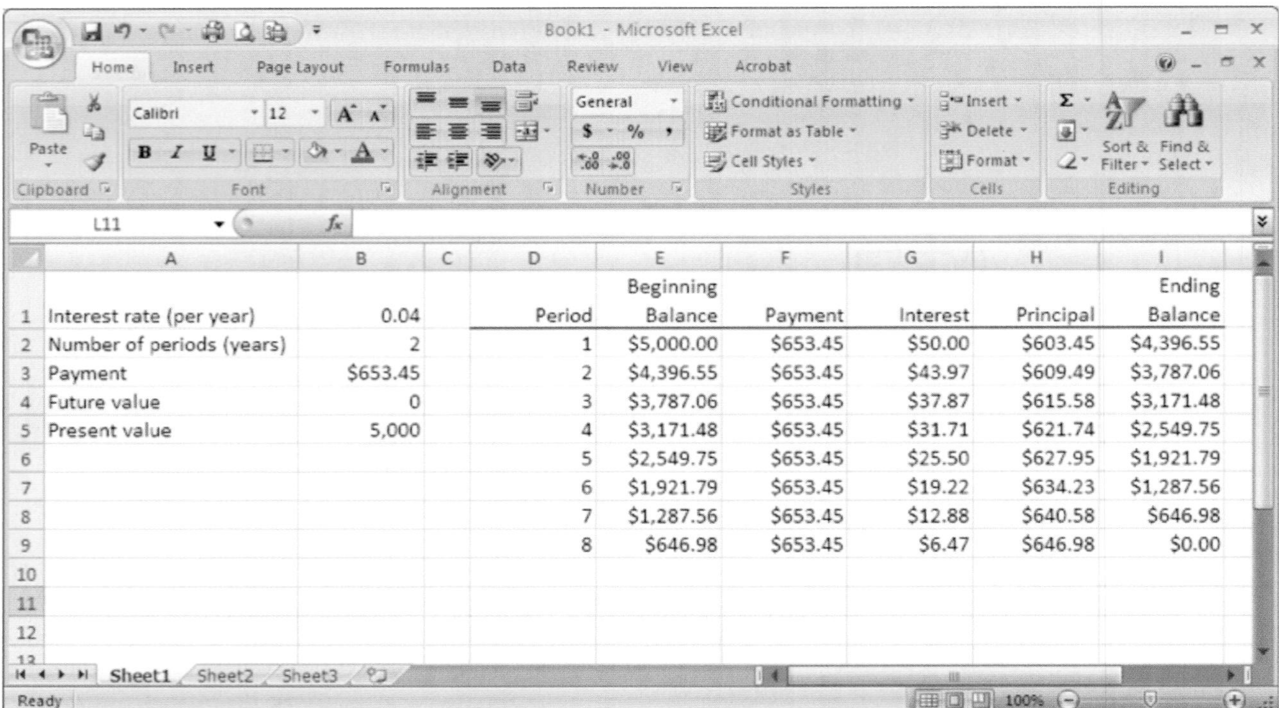

	A	B	C	D	E	F	G	H	I
1	Interest rate (per year)	0.04		Period	Beginning Balance	Payment	Interest	Principal	Ending Balance
2	Number of periods (years)	2		1	$5,000.00	$653.45	$50.00	$603.45	$4,396.55
3	Payment	$653.45		2	$4,396.55	$653.45	$43.97	$609.49	$3,787.06
4	Future value	0		3	$3,787.06	$653.45	$37.87	$615.58	$3,171.48
5	Present value	5,000		4	$3,171.48	$653.45	$31.71	$621.74	$2,549.75
6				5	$2,549.75	$653.45	$25.50	$627.95	$1,921.79
7				6	$1,921.79	$653.45	$19.22	$634.23	$1,287.56
8				7	$1,287.56	$653.45	$12.88	$640.58	$646.98
9				8	$646.98	$653.45	$6.47	$646.98	$0.00

In column [H] we compute the principal component of each payment. This amount is the payment (column [F]) minus the interest (column [G]). Finally, the ending balance (column [I]) is the beginning balance (column [E]) minus the principal (column [H]). Note that the ending balance in period 8 is $0 (the loan has been completely paid off).

Loan amortization tables are especially useful for accountants because the table computes the amounts we enter for each payment. To illustrate, to record the original $5,000 loan, we make the following journal entry:

Cash (+A)	5,000.00	
Loan payable (+L)		5,000.00

Now, each period, we make a loan payment of $653.45 and that payment is part interest expense and part loan principal. To determine the split between interest and principal, we consult the loan amortization table. For instance, in period 1, the payment is split as $50.00 of interest and $603.45 of principal. To record this payment, we would make the following journal entry:

Interest expense (+E, −SE)	50.00	
Loan payable (−L)	603.45	
Cash (−A)		653.45

Finally, Excel allows us to easily compute the present value of a series of irregular cash flows. To do this we use the NPV function. (NPV stands for *Net Present Value*.) To compute NPV we need a series of cash flows at regular time intervals, such as one payment per year. If we skip a period, we must enter a 0 for that period. The cash flows can be a mixture of positive and negative cash flows (for instance receipts and payments). In the following spreadsheet, we present a series of seven cash flows and calculate the present value of these payments discounted at 5% using the NPV function.

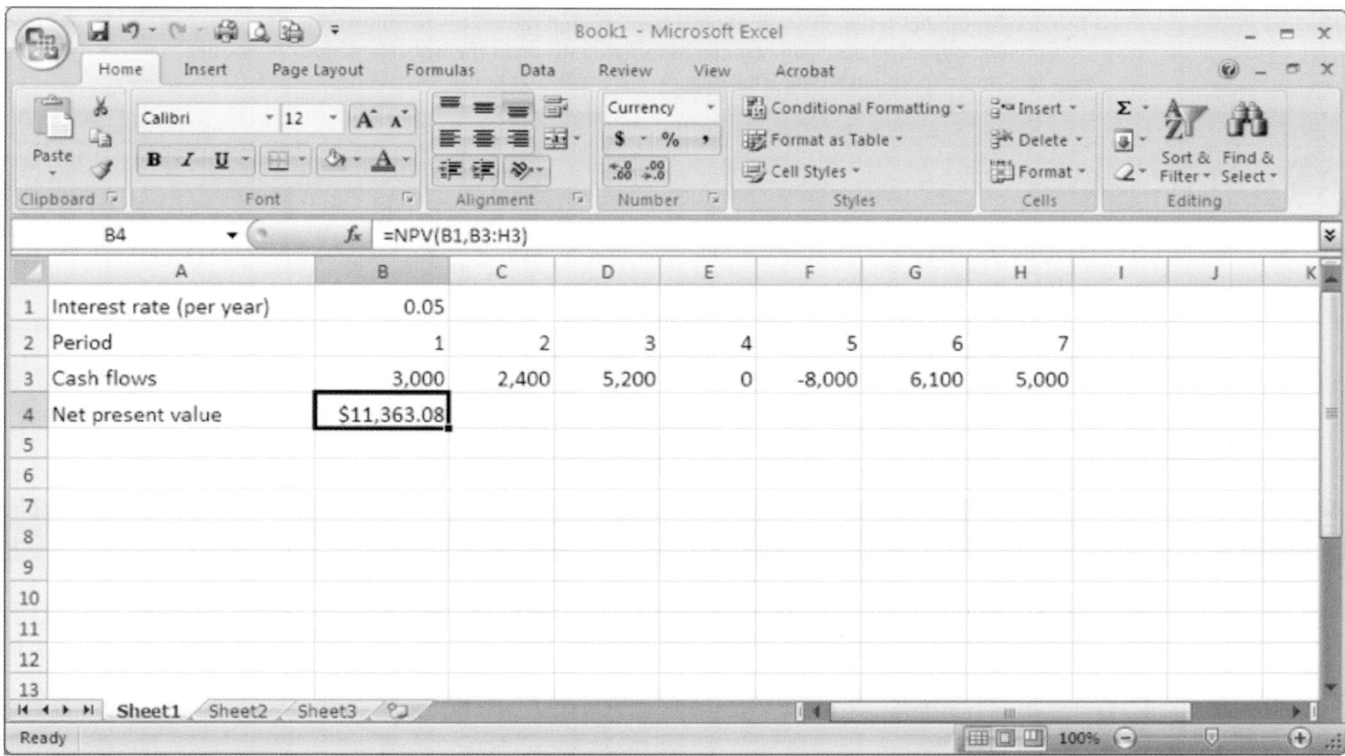

	A	B	C	D	E	F	G	H
1	Interest rate (per year)	0.05						
2	Period	1	2	3	4	5	6	7
3	Cash flows	3,000	2,400	5,200	0	-8,000	6,100	5,000
4	Net present value	$11,363.08						

The spreadsheet shows a net present value of $11,363.08. The function wizard dialog box for the NPV function is presented below:

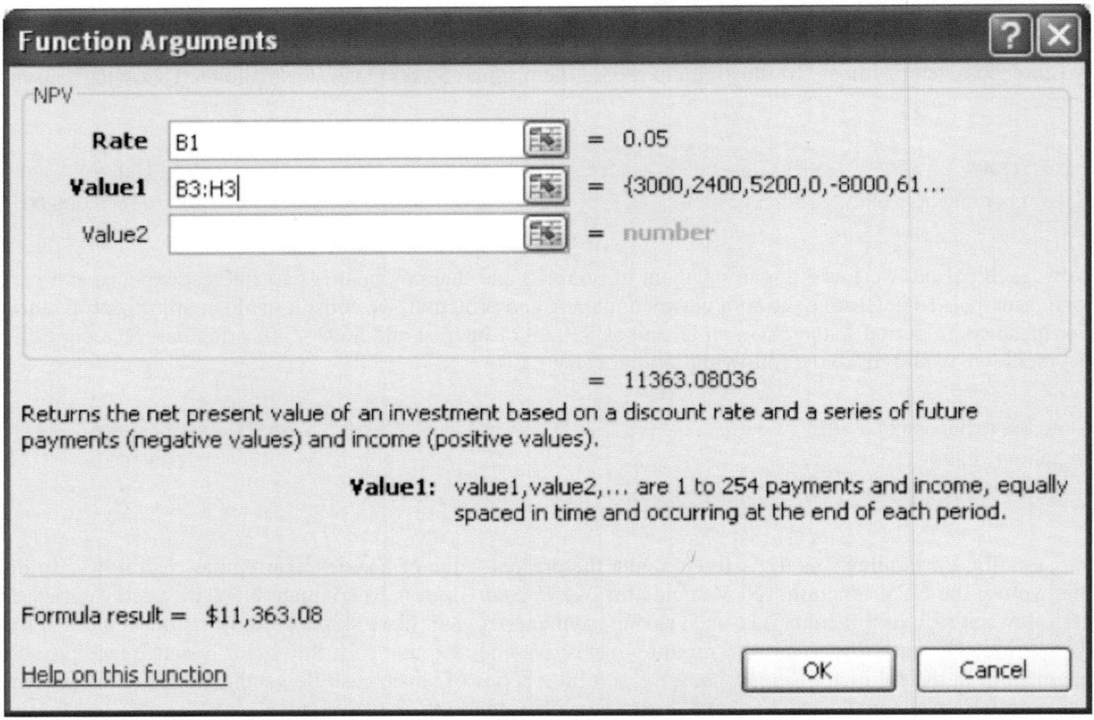
Function Arguments
NPV
Rate B1 = 0.05
Value1 B3:H3 = {3000,2400,5200,0,-8000,61...
Value2 = number
= 11363.08036
Returns the net present value of an investment based on a discount rate and a series of future payments (negative values) and income (positive values).
Value1: value1,value2,... are 1 to 254 payments and income, equally spaced in time and occurring at the end of each period.
Formula result = $11,363.08
Help on this function
OK
Cancel

The first argument in the NPV function is the discount rate. This is followed by the series of cash flows that is being discounted. These can be entered individually in in the box for "Value1," "Value2," etc. or by referring to a range of values in the spreadsheet, such as B3:H3, as shown above.

KEY TERMS

Annuity (p. 621)
Balloon payment (p. 622)
Compound interest (p. 618)
Discount rate (p. 620)
Future value (p. 619)
Future value factor (p. 619)
Installment loan (p. 622)
Present value (p. 620)
Present value factor (p. 621)
Simple interest (p. 618)
Time-value of money (p. 618)

Assignments with the logo in the margin are available in myBusinessCourse. See the Preface of the book for details.

EXERCISES

EA-1. Dawn Riley deposited $4,000 in a money market account on January 2, 2016. How much will her savings be worth on January 2, 2022 if the money market account earns a return of

a. 4%?
b. 6%?
c. 8%?

EA-2. Jason Shields invested $7,500 in an account that pays a 12% return. How much will the account be worth in four years if the interest is compounded

a. annually?
b. quarterly?
c. monthly?

EA-3. Leslie Porter is planning a trip to Europe upon graduation in two years. She anticipates that her trip will cost $14,000. She would like to set aside an amount now to save for the trip. How much should she set aside if her savings earns 4% interest compounded quarterly?

EA-4. Matt Wilson has an investment opportunity that promises to pay him $24,000 in four years. He could earn 6% if he invested his money elsewhere. What is the maximum amount that he should be willing to invest in this opportunity?

EA-5. Robert Smith purchased a used car for $14,000. To pay for his purchase, he borrowed $12,500 from a local bank at 12%. The loan requires that Robert repay the loan by making 36 monthly payments. How much will Robert have to pay each month to repay the loan?

EA-6. Refer to Exercise EA-5. How much interest will Robert Smith pay as part of his first monthly payment?

EA-7. Sandy Nguyen just graduated from college and has $40,000 in student loans. The loans bear interest at a rate of 8% and require quarterly payments.

a. What amount should Sandy pay each quarter if she wishes to pay off her student loans in six years?

b. Sandy can only afford to pay $1,500 per quarter. How long will it take Sandy to repay these loans ?

EA-8. In 2015, Cart Inc. adopted a plan to accumulate funds for environmental remediation beginning July 2, 2020 at an estimated cost of $20 million. Cart plans to make five equal annual payments into a fund earning 6% interest compounded annually. The first deposit is scheduled for July 1, 2015. Determine the amount of the required annual deposit.

EA-9. On May 1, 2015, Ott, Inc. sold merchandise to Fox Inc. Fox signed a noninterest bearing note requiring payment of $60,000 annually for 7 years. The first payment is due May 1, 2016. The prevailing rate for similar notes on that date is 9%. What amount should Ott, Inc. report as revenue in 2015 and 2016?

EA-10. Rex Corporation accepted a $10,000, 5% interest bearing note from Brooks Inc. on December 1, 2015 in exchange for machinery with a list sales price of $9,500. The note is payable on December 1, 2018. If the prevailing interest rate is 8%, what revenues should Rex report in its income statement for the year ended December 31, 2015?

EA-11. Rye Company is considering purchasing a new machine with a useful life of ten years, at which time its salvage value is estimated to be $50,000. Management estimates a net increase in operating cash inflow due to the new machine at $200,000 per year. What is the maximum amount the company should be willing to pay for the machine if the relevant cost of capital associated with this type of investment is 12%?

EA-12. Debra Wilcox won $7 million in the California lottery. She must choose how she wants the prize to be paid to her. First, Debra can elect to receive 26 annual payments, with the first payment due immediately. Second, she can elect to receive a single payment immediately for the entire amount. However, if she elects the single payment option, the winning prize is reduced to one-half the winnings ($3.5 million). Which option should Debra choose if her cost of capital (discount rate) is

a. 8%?

b. 4%?

c. What rate would make Debra indifferent between these two options?

EA-13. Linda Reed, an executive at VIP Inc. has earned a performance bonus. She has the option of accepting $60,000 now or $100,000 5 years from now. What would you advise her to do? Explain and support with calculations.

EA-14. On September 1, 2015, Luft, Inc. deposited $400,000 in a debt retirement fund. The company needs $955,000 cash to settle a maturing debt September 1, 2023. What is the minimal rate of compound interest required to assure the debt will be paid when due?

EA-15. Wolf Inc. establishes a construction fund on July 1, 2015, by making a single deposit of $360,000. At the end of each year, Wolf will deposit an additional $60,000. The fund guarantees a 12% return each year. How much will be in the fund on June 30, 2019?

EA-16. Sylvia Owen, owner of I-Haul Trucking is considering expanding operations from Seattle to the Portland area. Expansion is estimated to cost $10 million including the required new facilities and

additional trucks. Owen has elected to finance the expansion by borrowing from her local bank at a yearly interest rate of 10%. She has agreed to repay the loan in twenty equal payments over a 10-year period to begin in one year. (Payments will be made at the end of every half-year period.)

a. What will Ms. Owen's periodic payments be?
b. How much of her first payment will be interest expense?
c. Assume that after five years, Ms. Owen decided to pay off the loan early. How much would she owe at that time?

Homework MBC **EA-17.** On November 1, 2015, Ybarra Construction Company issued $200,000 of 5-year bonds that pay interest at an annual rate of 5%. The interest payments are due every six months (that is, the interest is compounded semi-annually). At the end of the five-year period, Ybarra must pay the bond holders a balloon payment of $200,000.

a. What would the issue price of the bonds be if the prevailing interest rate is (i) 4%? (ii) 6%?
b. Compute the market price of these bonds on November 1, 2017 assuming that the prevailing market interest rate at that time is 8%.

Homework MBC **EA-18.** On August 1, 2015, Paradise Airlines agreed to lease a passenger jet from Boeing Corporation. The 20-year lease requires an annual payment of $450,000. If Paradise were to purchase the jet, it could borrow the necessary funds at a 9% interest rate.

a. What is the present value of the lease payments if the first payment is due on August 1, 2016?
b. What is the present value of the lease payments if the first payment is due on August 1, 2015?

Homework MBC **EA-19.** Burnham Corporation is comparing two alternatives for leasing a machine.

Alternative A is a lease that requires six annual payments of $8,000 with the first payment due immediately.
Alternative B is a lease that requires two payments of $11,000 and three payments of $9,000 with the first payment due one year from now.

a. Which alternative should Burnham choose if the relevant discount rate is 5%?
b. Which alternative should Burnham choose if the relevant interest rate is 7%?

Homework MBC **EA-20.** On January 2, 2016, DeSantis Company is comparing two alternatives for leasing a machine.

Alternative A is a lease that requires 24 quarterly payments of $3,000 with the first payment due on March 31, 2016.
Alternative B is a lease that requires five annual payments of $14,300 with the first payment due on December 31, 2016.

Which alternative should DeSantis choose if the appropriate discount rate is 8% compounded quarterly?

Homework MBC **EA-21.** Despite his relative youth, Samuel Hunter has started planning for his retirement. At present, he has $2,400 he can invest, and he believes that he will be able to invest that amount each year for the next 39 years—40 contributions in total.

a. If his investment earns 4% per year for the 40 years, how much will Samuel have accumulated at the end of 40 years?
b. If Samuel delays investing for 10 years, how will that affect the balance accumulated at the end of 40 years?
c. If Samuel begins investing now and finds an investment earning 5% per year for 40 years, how much more will he have accumulated than if he earns 4%?

Homework MBC **EA-22.** Janice Utley is saving for a real estate investment. If she invests $1,000 now and then at the beginning of each of the next 35 months (36 months in total) at an interest rate of 1% per month, what will be the investment balance at the end of month 36?

TABLE A.1 Future Value of Single Amount $f = (1 + i)^t$

	Interest Rate											
Period	**0.01**	**0.02**	**0.03**	**0.04**	**0.05**	**0.06**	**0.07**	**0.08**	**0.09**	**0.10**	**0.11**	**0.12**
1	1.01000	1.02000	1.03000	1.04000	1.05000	1.06000	1.07000	1.08000	1.09000	1.10000	1.11000	1.12000
2	1.02010	1.04040	1.06090	1.08160	1.10250	1.12360	1.14490	1.16640	1.18810	1.21000	1.23210	1.25440
3	1.03030	1.06121	1.09273	1.12486	1.15763	1.19102	1.22504	1.25971	1.29503	1.33100	1.36763	1.40493
4	1.04060	1.08243	1.12551	1.16986	1.21551	1.26248	1.31080	1.36049	1.41158	1.46410	1.51807	1.57352
5	1.05101	1.10408	1.15927	1.21665	1.27628	1.33823	1.40255	1.46933	1.53862	1.61051	1.68506	1.76234
6	1.06152	1.12616	1.19405	1.26532	1.34010	1.41852	1.50073	1.58687	1.67710	1.77156	1.87041	1.97382
7	1.07214	1.14869	1.22987	1.31593	1.40710	1.50363	1.60578	1.71382	1.82804	1.94872	2.07616	2.21068
8	1.08286	1.17166	1.26677	1.36857	1.47746	1.59385	1.71819	1.85093	1.99256	2.14359	2.30454	2.47596
9	1.09369	1.19509	1.30477	1.42331	1.55133	1.68948	1.83846	1.99900	2.17189	2.35795	2.55804	2.77308
10	1.10462	1.21899	1.34392	1.48024	1.62889	1.79085	1.96715	2.15892	2.36736	2.59374	2.83942	3.10585
11	1.11567	1.24337	1.38423	1.53945	1.71034	1.89830	2.10485	2.33164	2.58043	2.85312	3.15176	3.47855
12	1.12683	1.26824	1.42576	1.60103	1.79586	2.01220	2.25219	2.51817	2.81266	3.13843	3.49845	3.89598
13	1.13809	1.29361	1.46853	1.66507	1.88565	2.13293	2.40985	2.71962	3.06580	3.45227	3.88328	4.36349
14	1.14947	1.31948	1.51259	1.73168	1.97993	2.26090	2.57853	2.93719	3.34173	3.79750	4.31044	4.88711
15	1.16097	1.34587	1.55797	1.80094	2.07893	2.39656	2.75903	3.17217	3.64248	4.17725	4.78459	5.47357
16	1.17258	1.37279	1.60471	1.87298	2.18287	2.54035	2.95216	3.42594	3.97031	4.59497	5.31089	6.13039
17	1.18430	1.40024	1.65285	1.94790	2.29202	2.69277	3.15882	3.70002	4.32763	5.05447	5.89509	6.86604
18	1.19615	1.42825	1.70243	2.02582	2.40662	2.85434	3.37993	3.99602	4.71712	5.55992	6.54355	7.68997
19	1.20811	1.45681	1.75351	2.10685	2.52695	3.02560	3.61653	4.31570	5.14166	6.11591	7.26334	8.61276
20	1.22019	1.48595	1.80611	2.19112	2.65330	3.20714	3.86968	4.66096	5.60441	6.72750	8.06231	9.64629
21	1.23239	1.51567	1.86029	2.27877	2.78596	3.39956	4.14056	5.03383	6.10881	7.40025	8.94917	10.80385
22	1.24472	1.54598	1.91610	2.36992	2.92526	3.60354	4.43040	5.43654	6.65860	8.14027	9.93357	12.10031
23	1.25716	1.57690	1.97359	2.46472	3.07152	3.81975	4.74053	5.87146	7.25787	8.95430	11.02627	13.55235
24	1.26973	1.60844	2.03279	2.56330	3.22510	4.04893	5.07237	6.34118	7.91108	9.84973	12.23916	15.17863
25	1.28243	1.64061	2.09378	2.66584	3.38635	4.29187	5.42743	6.84848	8.62308	10.83471	13.58546	17.00006
26	1.29526	1.67342	2.15659	2.77247	3.55567	4.54938	5.80735	7.39635	9.39916	11.91818	15.07986	19.04007
27	1.30821	1.70689	2.22129	2.88337	3.73346	4.82235	6.21387	7.98806	10.24508	13.10999	16.73865	21.32488
28	1.32129	1.74102	2.28793	2.99870	3.92013	5.11169	6.64884	8.62711	11.16714	14.42099	18.57990	23.88387
29	1.33450	1.77584	2.35657	3.11865	4.11614	5.41839	7.11426	9.31727	12.17218	15.86309	20.62369	26.74993
30	1.34785	1.81136	2.42726	3.24340	4.32194	5.74349	7.61226	10.06266	13.26768	17.44940	22.89230	29.95992
31	1.36133	1.84759	2.50008	3.37313	4.53804	6.08810	8.14511	10.86767	14.46177	19.19434	25.41045	33.55511
32	1.37494	1.88454	2.57508	3.50806	4.76494	6.45339	8.71527	11.73708	15.76333	21.11378	28.20560	37.58173
33	1.38869	1.92223	2.65234	3.64838	5.00319	6.84059	9.32534	12.67605	17.18203	23.22515	31.30821	42.09153
34	1.40258	1.96068	2.73191	3.79432	5.25335	7.25103	9.97811	13.69013	18.72841	25.54767	34.75212	47.14252
35	1.41660	1.99989	2.81386	3.94609	5.51602	7.68609	10.67658	14.78534	20.41397	28.10244	38.57485	52.79962
36	1.43077	2.03989	2.89828	4.10393	5.79182	8.14725	11.42394	15.96817	22.25123	30.91268	42.81808	59.13557
37	1.44508	2.08069	2.98523	4.26809	6.08141	8.63609	12.22362	17.24563	24.25384	34.00395	47.52807	66.23184
38	1.45953	2.12230	3.07478	4.43881	6.38548	9.15425	13.07927	18.62528	26.43668	37.40434	52.75616	74.17966
39	1.47412	2.16474	3.16703	4.61637	6.70475	9.70351	13.99482	20.11530	28.81598	41.14478	58.55934	83.08122
40	1.48886	2.20804	3.26204	4.80102	7.03999	10.28572	14.97446	21.72452	31.40942	45.25926	65.00087	93.05097

TABLE A.2 Present Value of Single Amount $p = 1/(1+i)^t$

	Interest Rate											
Period	**0.01**	**0.02**	**0.03**	**0.04**	**0.05**	**0.06**	**0.07**	**0.08**	**0.09**	**0.10**	**0.11**	**0.12**
1	0.99010	0.98039	0.97087	0.96154	0.95238	0.94340	0.93458	0.92593	0.91743	0.90909	0.90090	0.89286
2	0.98030	0.96117	0.94260	0.92456	0.90703	0.89000	0.87344	0.85734	0.84168	0.82645	0.81162	0.79719
3	0.97059	0.94232	0.91514	0.88900	0.86384	0.83962	0.81630	0.79383	0.77218	0.75131	0.73119	0.71178
4	0.96098	0.92385	0.88849	0.85480	0.82270	0.79209	0.76290	0.73503	0.70843	0.68301	0.65873	0.63552
5	0.95147	0.90573	0.86261	0.82193	0.78353	0.74726	0.71299	0.68058	0.64993	0.62092	0.59345	0.56743
6	0.94205	0.88797	0.83748	0.79031	0.74622	0.70496	0.66634	0.63017	0.59627	0.56447	0.53464	0.50663
7	0.93272	0.87056	0.81309	0.75992	0.71068	0.66506	0.62275	0.58349	0.54703	0.51316	0.48166	0.45235
8	0.92348	0.85349	0.78941	0.73069	0.67684	0.62741	0.58201	0.54027	0.50187	0.46651	0.43393	0.40388
9	0.91434	0.83676	0.76642	0.70259	0.64461	0.59190	0.54393	0.50025	0.46043	0.42410	0.39092	0.36061
10	0.90529	0.82035	0.74409	0.67556	0.61391	0.55839	0.50835	0.46319	0.42241	0.38554	0.35218	0.32197
11	0.89632	0.80426	0.72242	0.64958	0.58468	0.52679	0.47509	0.42888	0.38753	0.35049	0.31728	0.28748
12	0.88745	0.78849	0.70138	0.62460	0.55684	0.49697	0.44401	0.39711	0.35553	0.31863	0.28584	0.25668
13	0.87866	0.77303	0.68095	0.60057	0.53032	0.46884	0.41496	0.36770	0.32618	0.28966	0.25751	0.22917
14	0.86996	0.75788	0.66112	0.57748	0.50507	0.44230	0.38782	0.34046	0.29925	0.26333	0.23199	0.20462
15	0.86135	0.74301	0.64186	0.55526	0.48102	0.41727	0.36245	0.31524	0.27454	0.23939	0.20900	0.18270
16	0.85282	0.72845	0.62317	0.53391	0.45811	0.39365	0.33873	0.29189	0.25187	0.21763	0.18829	0.16312
17	0.84438	0.71416	0.60502	0.51337	0.43630	0.37136	0.31657	0.27027	0.23107	0.19784	0.16963	0.14564
18	0.83602	0.70016	0.58739	0.49363	0.41552	0.35034	0.29586	0.25025	0.21199	0.17986	0.15282	0.13004
19	0.82774	0.68643	0.57029	0.47464	0.39573	0.33051	0.27651	0.23171	0.19449	0.16351	0.13768	0.11611
20	0.81954	0.67297	0.55368	0.45639	0.37689	0.31180	0.25842	0.21455	0.17843	0.14864	0.12403	0.10367
21	0.81143	0.65978	0.53755	0.43883	0.35894	0.29416	0.24151	0.19866	0.16370	0.13513	0.11174	0.09256
22	0.80340	0.64684	0.52189	0.42196	0.34185	0.27751	0.22571	0.18394	0.15018	0.12285	0.10067	0.08264
23	0.79544	0.63416	0.50669	0.40573	0.32557	0.26180	0.21095	0.17032	0.13778	0.11168	0.09069	0.07379
24	0.78757	0.62172	0.49193	0.39012	0.31007	0.24698	0.19715	0.15770	0.12640	0.10153	0.08170	0.06588
25	0.77977	0.60953	0.47761	0.37512	0.29530	0.23300	0.18425	0.14602	0.11597	0.09230	0.07361	0.05882
26	0.77205	0.59758	0.46369	0.36069	0.28124	0.21981	0.17220	0.13520	0.10639	0.08391	0.06631	0.05252
27	0.76440	0.58586	0.45019	0.34682	0.26785	0.20737	0.16093	0.12519	0.09761	0.07628	0.05974	0.04689
28	0.75684	0.57437	0.43708	0.33348	0.25509	0.19563	0.15040	0.11591	0.08955	0.06934	0.05382	0.04187
29	0.74934	0.56311	0.42435	0.32065	0.24295	0.18456	0.14056	0.10733	0.08215	0.06304	0.04849	0.03738
30	0.74192	0.55207	0.41199	0.30832	0.23138	0.17411	0.13137	0.09938	0.07537	0.05731	0.04368	0.03338
31	0.73458	0.54125	0.39999	0.29646	0.22036	0.16425	0.12277	0.09202	0.06915	0.05210	0.03935	0.02980
32	0.72730	0.53063	0.38834	0.28506	0.20987	0.15496	0.11474	0.08520	0.06344	0.04736	0.03545	0.02661
33	0.72010	0.52023	0.37703	0.27409	0.19987	0.14619	0.10723	0.07889	0.05820	0.04306	0.03194	0.02376
34	0.71297	0.51003	0.36604	0.26355	0.19035	0.13791	0.10022	0.07305	0.05339	0.03914	0.02878	0.02121
35	0.70591	0.50003	0.35538	0.25342	0.18129	0.13011	0.09366	0.06763	0.04899	0.03558	0.02592	0.01894
36	0.69892	0.49022	0.34503	0.24367	0.17266	0.12274	0.08754	0.06262	0.04494	0.03235	0.02335	0.01691
37	0.69200	0.48061	0.33498	0.23430	0.16444	0.11579	0.08181	0.05799	0.04123	0.02941	0.02104	0.01510
38	0.68515	0.47119	0.32523	0.22529	0.15661	0.10924	0.07646	0.05369	0.03783	0.02673	0.01896	0.01348
39	0.67837	0.46195	0.31575	0.21662	0.14915	0.10306	0.07146	0.04971	0.03470	0.02430	0.01708	0.01204
40	0.67165	0.45289	0.30656	0.20829	0.14205	0.09722	0.06678	0.04603	0.03184	0.02209	0.01538	0.01075

TABLE A.3 Present Value of Ordinary Annuity $p = \{1 - [1/(1+i)^t]\}/i$

	Interest Rate											
Period	**0.01**	**0.02**	**0.03**	**0.04**	**0.05**	**0.06**	**0.07**	**0.08**	**0.09**	**0.10**	**0.11**	**0.12**
1	0.99010	0.98039	0.97087	0.96154	0.95238	0.94340	0.93458	0.92593	0.91743	0.90909	0.90090	0.89286
2	1.97040	1.94156	1.91347	1.88609	1.85941	1.83339	1.80802	1.78326	1.75911	1.73554	1.71252	1.69005
3	2.94099	2.88388	2.82861	2.77509	2.72325	2.67301	2.62432	2.57710	2.53129	2.48685	2.44371	2.40183
4	3.90197	3.80773	3.71710	3.62990	3.54595	3.46511	3.38721	3.31213	3.23972	3.16987	3.10245	3.03735
5	4.85343	4.71346	4.57971	4.45182	4.32948	4.21236	4.10020	3.99271	3.88965	3.79079	3.69590	3.60478
6	5.79548	5.60143	5.41719	5.24214	5.07569	4.91732	4.76654	4.62288	4.48592	4.35526	4.23054	4.11141
7	6.72819	6.47199	6.23028	6.00205	5.78637	5.58238	5.38929	5.20637	5.03295	4.86842	4.71220	4.56376
8	7.65168	7.32548	7.01969	6.73274	6.46321	6.20979	5.97130	5.74664	5.53482	5.33493	5.14612	4.96764
9	8.56602	8.16224	7.78611	7.43533	7.10782	6.80169	6.51523	6.24689	5.99525	5.75902	5.53705	5.32825
10	9.47130	8.98259	8.53020	8.11090	7.72173	7.36009	7.02358	6.71008	6.41766	6.14457	5.88923	5.65022
11	10.36763	9.78685	9.25262	8.76048	8.30641	7.88687	7.49867	7.13896	6.80519	6.49506	6.20652	5.93770
12	11.25508	10.57534	9.95400	9.38507	8.86325	8.38384	7.94269	7.53608	7.16073	6.81369	6.49236	6.19437
13	12.13374	11.34837	10.63496	9.98565	9.39357	8.85268	8.35765	7.90378	7.48690	7.10336	6.74987	6.42355
14	13.00370	12.10625	11.29607	10.56312	9.89864	9.29498	8.74547	8.24424	7.78615	7.36669	6.98187	6.62817
15	13.86505	12.84926	11.93794	11.11839	10.37966	9.71225	9.10791	8.55948	8.06069	7.60608	7.19087	6.81086
16	14.71787	13.57771	12.56110	11.65230	10.83777	10.10590	9.44665	8.85137	8.31256	7.82371	7.37916	6.97399
17	15.56225	14.29187	13.16612	12.16567	11.27407	10.47726	9.76322	9.12164	8.54363	8.02155	7.54879	7.11963
18	16.39827	14.99203	13.75351	12.65930	11.68959	10.82760	10.05909	9.37189	8.75563	8.20141	7.70162	7.24967
19	17.22601	15.67846	14.32380	13.13394	12.08532	11.15812	10.33560	9.60360	8.95011	8.36492	7.83929	7.36578
20	18.04555	16.35143	14.87747	13.59033	12.46221	11.46992	10.59401	9.81815	9.12855	8.51356	7.96333	7.46944
21	18.85698	17.01121	15.41502	14.02916	12.82115	11.76408	10.83553	10.01680	9.29224	8.64869	8.07507	7.56200
22	19.66038	17.65805	15.93692	14.45112	13.16300	12.04158	11.06124	10.20074	9.44243	8.77154	8.17574	7.64465
23	20.45582	18.29220	16.44361	14.85684	13.48857	12.30338	11.27219	10.37106	9.58021	8.88322	8.26643	7.71843
24	21.24339	18.91393	16.93554	15.24696	13.79864	12.55036	11.46933	10.52876	9.70661	8.98474	8.34814	7.78432
25	22.02316	19.52346	17.41315	15.62208	14.09394	12.78336	11.65358	10.67478	9.82258	9.07704	8.42174	7.84314
26	22.79520	20.12104	17.87684	15.98277	14.37519	13.00317	11.82578	10.80998	9.92897	9.16095	8.48806	7.89566
27	23.55961	20.70690	18.32703	16.32959	14.64303	13.21053	11.98671	10.93516	10.02658	9.23722	8.54780	7.94255
28	24.31644	21.28127	18.76411	16.66306	14.89813	13.40616	12.13711	11.05108	10.11613	9.30657	8.60162	7.98442
29	25.06579	21.84438	19.18845	16.98371	15.14107	13.59072	12.27767	11.15841	10.19828	9.36961	8.65011	8.02181
30	25.80771	22.39646	19.60044	17.29203	15.37245	13.76483	12.40904	11.25778	10.27365	9.42691	8.69379	8.05518
31	26.54229	22.93770	20.00043	17.58849	15.59281	13.92909	12.53181	11.34980	10.34280	9.47901	8.73315	8.08499
32	27.26959	23.46833	20.38877	17.87355	15.80268	14.08404	12.64656	11.43500	10.40624	9.52638	8.76860	8.11159
33	27.98969	23.98856	20.76579	18.14765	16.00255	14.23023	12.75379	11.51389	10.46444	9.56943	8.80054	8.13535
34	28.70267	24.49859	21.13184	18.41120	16.19290	14.36814	12.85401	11.58693	10.51784	9.60857	8.82932	8.15656
35	29.40858	24.99862	21.48722	18.66461	16.37419	14.49825	12.94767	11.65457	10.56682	9.64416	8.85524	8.17550
36	30.10751	25.48884	21.83225	18.90828	16.54685	14.62099	13.03521	11.71719	10.61176	9.67651	8.87859	8.19241
37	30.79951	25.96945	22.16724	19.14258	16.71129	14.73678	13.11702	11.77518	10.65299	9.70592	8.89963	8.20751
38	31.48466	26.44064	22.49246	19.36786	16.86789	14.84602	13.19347	11.82887	10.69082	9.73265	8.91859	8.22099
39	32.16303	26.90259	22.80822	19.58448	17.01704	14.94907	13.26493	11.87858	10.72552	9.75696	8.93567	8.23303
40	32.83469	27.35548	23.11477	19.79277	17.15909	15.04630	13.33171	11.92461	10.75736	9.77905	8.95105	8.24378

TABLE A.4 Future Value of Annuity Paid at Beginning of Period

	Interest Rate											
Period	**0.01**	**0.02**	**0.03**	**0.04**	**0.05**	**0.06**	**0.07**	**0.08**	**0.09**	**0.10**	**0.11**	**0.12**
1	1.0100	1.0200	1.0300	1.0400	1.0500	1.0600	1.0700	1.0800	1.0900	1.1000	1.1100	1.1200
2	2.0301	2.0604	2.0909	2.1216	2.1525	2.1836	2.2149	2.2464	2.2781	2.3100	2.3421	2.3744
3	3.0604	3.1216	3.1836	3.2465	3.3101	3.3746	3.4399	3.5061	3.5731	3.6410	3.7097	3.7793
4	4.1010	4.2040	4.3091	4.4163	4.5256	4.6371	4.7507	4.8666	4.9847	5.1051	5.2278	5.3528
5	5.1520	5.3081	5.4684	5.6330	5.8019	5.9753	6.1533	6.3359	6.5233	6.7156	6.9129	7.1152
6	6.2135	6.4343	6.6625	6.8983	7.1420	7.3938	7.6540	7.9228	8.2004	8.4872	8.7833	9.0890
7	7.2857	7.5830	7.8923	8.2142	8.5491	8.8975	9.2598	9.6366	10.0285	10.4359	10.8594	11.2997
8	8.3685	8.7546	9.1591	9.5828	10.0266	10.4913	10.9780	11.4876	12.0210	12.5795	13.1640	13.7757
9	9.4622	9.9497	10.4639	11.0061	11.5779	12.1808	12.8164	13.4866	14.1929	14.9374	15.7220	16.5487
10	10.5668	11.1687	11.8078	12.4864	13.2068	13.9716	14.7836	15.6455	16.5603	17.5312	18.5614	19.6546
11	11.6825	12.4121	13.1920	14.0258	14.9171	15.8699	16.8885	17.9771	19.1407	20.3843	21.7132	23.1331
12	12.8093	13.6803	14.6178	15.6268	16.7130	17.8821	19.1406	20.4953	21.9534	23.5227	25.2116	27.0291
13	13.9474	14.9739	16.0863	17.2919	18.5986	20.0151	21.5505	23.2149	25.0192	26.9750	29.0949	31.3926
14	15.0969	16.2934	17.5989	19.0236	20.5786	22.2760	24.1290	26.1521	28.3609	30.7725	33.4054	36.2797
15	16.2579	17.6393	19.1569	20.8245	22.6575	24.6725	26.8881	29.3243	32.0034	34.9497	38.1899	41.7533
16	17.4304	19.0121	20.7616	22.6975	24.8404	27.2129	29.8402	32.7502	35.9737	39.5447	43.5008	47.8837
17	18.6147	20.4123	22.4144	24.6454	27.1324	29.9057	32.9990	36.4502	40.3013	44.5992	49.3959	54.7497
18	19.8109	21.8406	24.1169	26.6712	29.5390	32.7600	36.3790	40.4463	45.0185	50.1591	55.9395	62.4397
19	21.0190	23.2974	25.8704	28.7781	32.0660	35.7856	39.9955	44.7620	50.1601	56.2750	63.2028	71.0524
20	22.2392	24.7833	27.6765	30.9692	34.7193	38.9927	43.8652	49.4229	55.7645	63.0025	71.2651	80.6987
21	23.4716	26.2990	29.5368	33.2480	37.5052	42.3923	48.0057	54.4568	61.8733	70.4027	80.2143	91.5026
22	24.7163	27.8450	31.4529	35.6179	40.4305	45.9958	52.4361	59.8933	68.5319	78.5430	90.1479	103.6029
23	25.9735	29.4219	33.4265	38.0826	43.5020	49.8156	57.1767	65.7648	75.7898	87.4973	101.1742	117.1552
24	27.2432	31.0303	35.4593	40.6459	46.7271	53.8645	62.2490	72.1059	83.7009	97.3471	113.4133	132.3339
25	28.5256	32.6709	37.5530	43.3117	50.1135	58.1564	67.6765	78.9544	92.3240	108.1818	126.9988	149.3339
26	29.8209	34.3443	39.7096	46.0842	53.6691	62.7058	73.4838	86.3508	101.7231	120.0999	142.0786	168.3740
27	31.1291	36.0512	41.9309	48.9676	57.4026	67.5281	79.6977	94.3388	111.9682	133.2099	158.8173	189.6989
28	32.4504	37.7922	44.2189	51.9663	61.3227	72.6398	86.3465	102.9659	123.1354	147.6309	177.3972	213.5828
29	33.7849	39.5681	46.5754	55.0849	65.4388	78.0582	93.4608	112.2832	135.3075	163.4940	198.0209	240.3327
30	35.1327	41.3794	49.0027	58.3283	69.7608	83.8017	101.0730	122.3459	148.5752	180.9434	220.9132	270.2926
31	36.4941	43.2270	51.5028	61.7015	74.2988	89.8898	109.2182	133.2135	163.0370	200.1378	246.3236	303.8477
32	37.8690	45.1116	54.0778	65.2095	79.0638	96.3432	117.9334	144.9506	178.8003	221.2515	274.5292	341.4294
33	39.2577	47.0338	56.7302	68.8579	84.0670	103.1838	127.2588	157.6267	195.9823	244.4767	305.8374	383.5210
34	40.6603	48.9945	59.4621	72.6522	89.3203	110.4348	137.2369	171.3168	214.7108	270.0244	340.5896	430.6635
35	42.0769	50.9944	62.2759	76.5983	94.8363	118.1209	147.9135	186.1021	235.1247	298.1268	379.1644	483.4631
36	43.5076	53.0343	65.1742	80.7022	100.6281	126.2681	159.3374	202.0703	257.3759	329.0395	421.9825	542.5987
37	44.9527	55.1149	68.1594	84.9703	106.7095	134.9042	171.5610	219.3159	281.6298	363.0434	469.5106	608.8305
38	46.4123	57.2372	71.2342	89.4091	113.0950	144.0585	184.6403	237.9412	308.0665	400.4478	522.2667	683.0102
39	47.8864	59.4020	74.4013	94.0255	119.7998	153.7620	198.6351	258.0565	336.8824	441.5926	580.8261	766.0914
40	49.3752	61.6100	77.6633	98.8265	126.8398	164.0477	213.6096	279.7810	368.2919	486.8518	645.8269	859.1424

Glossary

A

accelerated depreciation Depreciation method in which more depreciation expense is recorded early in an asset's useful life and less in its later life

account An individual record of increases and decreases for an item in the accounting system

accounting The process of identifying, measuring, and communicating financial information to help people make economic decisions

accounting cycle The sequence of activities used to accumulate and report financial statements during a fiscal year

accounting equation The basic financial relationship that investing equals financing, commonly expressed as assets = liabilities + equity

accounts payable Amounts owed to suppliers for goods and services purchased on credit

accounts payable turnover Ratio defined as cost of goods sold divided by average accounts payable

accounts receivable Amounts due to a company from customers arising from the sale of products on credit

accounts receivable turnover (ART) Annual net sales divided by average accounts receivable (net)

accrual accounting The recognition of revenue when earned and the matching of expenses when incurred

accruals Adjustments that reflect revenues earned but not received or recorded and expenses incurred but not paid or recorded

accrued expense An expense incurred before payment is made, such as wages, utilities, and taxes; recognized with an adjusting entry

accrued income Any revenues or income for an accounting period that have been earned and realized, but are not received or billed

accrued liabilities Obligations for expenses that have been recognized and recorded but not yet paid

accrued revenue The value of services provided that have not as yet been billed or paid for by a client

accumulated depreciation A contra asset reported in the balance sheet; reflects the total depreciation recorded for an asset up to the balance sheet date

accumulated other comprehensive income or loss Accumulated changes in equity that are not reported in the income statement

accumulated postretirement obligation (APBO) A liability for benefits, such as health care benefits, to be paid after an employee retires

additional paid-in capital Amounts received from the primary owners of a company in addition to the par or stated value of common stock

adjusting entries Journal entries made at the end of an accounting period to reflect accrual accounting; rarely involve cash; usually affect a balance sheet account (an asset or liability account) and an income statement account (an expense or revenue account)

adjusted trial balance A listing of all general ledger account balances prepared after adjustments are recorded and posted

aging analysis Estimate of expected uncollectible accounts based on the number of days past invoices are outstanding

allowance for uncollectible accounts An estimate of the receivables that a company will be unable to collect; reported as a contra-asset

American Institute of Certified Public Accountants (AICPA) Professional organization of CPAs in the United States

amortization The systematic allocation of an account balance to expense; usually refers to the periodic writing off of an intangible asset

annuity A pattern of cash flows in which equal amounts are spaced equally over a number of periods

arm's length Any transaction between two unrelated parties

articulation The linkage of financial statements within and across accounting periods

asset a resource owned by the company that is expected to provide the company future economic benefits

asset turnover The sales to average assets ratio, which reflects effectiveness in generating sales from assets; also called *total asset turnover*

asset utilization The efficiency a company has in turning over assets

asset write-downs Restructuring activity where long-term assets or unsalable inventory is reduced in value in the company financial reports; also called *write-offs* or *charge-offs*

audited Financial statements that have been reviewed by an *independent party (such as an audit firm);* financial statements that *present fairly* and *in all material respects* the company's financial condition and the results of its operations

available-for-sale (AFS) Investments in securities that management intends to hold for capital gains and dividend revenue

average cash cycle (ACC) The average period of time from when cash is invested in inventories until they are sold; the addition of the average collection period and modified average inventory days outstanding less the modified average payable days outstanding

average collection period (ACP) A measure related to accounts receivable turnover, which is defined as average accounts receivable divided by average daily sales

average cost (AC) Inventory costing method that views cost of goods sold as an average of the cost to purchase all inventories available for sale during a particular period

average inventory days outstanding (AIDO) A companion measure to inventory turnover computed as average inventory divided by average daily cost of goods sold; also called *days inventory outstanding*

average payable days outstanding A ratio defined as average accounts payable divided by average daily cost of goods sold

B

bad debt expense The cost of uncollectible accounts; also called *provision for uncollectible accounts*

balance sheet A financial report based on the accounting equation that lists a company's assets, liabilities, and equity at a certain point in time

balloon payment A lump sum payment due when a bond or other loan matures

bank reconciliation A schedule that accounts for all differences between the ending balance on the bank statement and the ending balance of the general ledger's cash account, as well as determining the reconciled cash balance at the end of the month

basic EPS Earnings per share, defined as net income less dividends on preferred stock divided by weighted average of common shares outstanding for the year

big bath Situation where a company recognizes large write-offs in a period of already depressed income

board of directors Governing body of a corporation; elected by the shareholders to represent shareholder interests and oversee management

book value The dollar amount carried in the accounts of a particular item; the value of an item less its accumulated depreciation; also called *net book value* or *carrying value*

book value per share The net book value of a company available to common shareholders, defined as stockholders' equity less preferred stock divided by the number of common shares outstanding

bundled sales Two or more products sold together under one lump-sum price

C

calendar year A fiscal year that runs from January 1 to December 31

call provision A company's right to repurchase its own bond

capacity costs Operating expenses related to providing the ability to produce and sell products and provide services to customers; includes costs such as depreciation, rent, utilities, insurance and other related costs

capital The assets that provide value to the company

capital expenditures Financial outlays to acquire property, plant, and equipment

capital lease method Method of reporting leases that requires both the lease asset and lease liability to be reported on the balance sheet

capital markets Financing sources that often involve a company's issuance of securities (stocks, bonds, and notes)

capitalization The recording of an asset's cost as an asset on the balance sheet rather than as an expense on the income statement; these costs are transferred to expense as the asset is used up

capitalized To include a portion of an asset's cost on the balance sheet

capitalized interest Interest incurred during construction that is recorded as a part of the cost of a self-constructed (rather than purchased) asset

cash Currency, bank deposits, certificates of deposit, and other cash equivalents

cash accounting Accounting method where revenues are only recognized when received in cash and expenses are only recognized when paid in cash

cash and cash equivalents A balance sheet account that combines cash with certain short-term, highly liquid investments

cash discounts A price reduction offered by suppliers to buyers if payment is made within a specified time period; usually established as part of the credit terms and stated as a percentage of the purchase price

cash equivalents Short-term, highly liquid investments that are easily convertible into a known cash amount and are relatively unaffected by interest rate changes

cash flow from operations divided by net income An objective performance measure; the higher this ratio, the higher the quality of income

change in accounting estimate Adjustment in a generally accepted accounting principle, such as varying the time period an item is depreciated, that is applied prospectively from the date of change

change in accounting principle Adoption of a generally accepted accounting principle that differs from one previously used for reporting purposes

channel stuffing When a company uses its market power over customers or distributors to induce them to purchase more goods than necessary to meet their normal needs

chart of accounts Form that facilitates transaction analysis and the preparation of general ledger entries

check A written order directing a particular bank to pay a specified amount of money to a person named on the check

closing procedures Part of the accounting cycle in which the balances of temporary accounts are transferred into permanent accounts

collateral Mortgages on assets a company owns as security for debt financing

collectibility risk The chance that items sold on credit will not be paid in full

common-size comparative financial statement A financial statement in which each item is presented as a percentage of a key figure such as sales or total assets

common stock The basic ownership class of corporate capital stock, carrying the rights to vote, share in earnings, participate in future stock issues, and share in any liquidation proceeds after prior claims have been settled

comparative balance sheet Financial statement that compares the assets, liabilities, and equity of a company over several distinct periods

comparative financial statements A frequently encountered form of horizontal analysis that compares dollar and percentage changes for important items and classification totals

comparative income statement Financial statement that compares the revenues and expenses of a company over several distinct periods

compensating balance A minimum amount that a bank requires a firm to maintain in a bank account as part of a borrowing arrangement

completed contract method Revenue recognition method in which revenue is deferred until the contract is complete

complex capital structure Stockholders' equity that includes *dilutive securities* outstanding; required to report diluted EPS (earnings per share)

compound interest Interest that accrues on outstanding interest

compound journal entry A journal entry that involves more than two accounts

conceptual framework Guidelines developed by the FASB to provide a structure for considering future standards, as well as to guide accountants in areas where standards do not currently exist

consignment A type of sale in which a *consignor* delivers product to a *consignee*, but retains ownership until the consignee sells the product to the ultimate customer

consolidated financial statements An aggregation (an adding up) of financial statements of the parent company and all its subsidiary companies, less any intercompany activities

contingent liability A potential obligation, the eventual occurrence of which usually depends on some future event beyond the control of the firm; contingent liabilities may originate with such events as lawsuits, credit guarantees, and environmental damages

contra accounts Accounts used to record reductions in or offsets to a related account

contra-asset account A means to offset an asset account without directly reducing that account

contributed capital The net funding that a company receives from issuing and reacquiring its equity shares; the difference between what the company receives from issuing shares and the cost it takes to buy them back

controlling influence When a company owns a majority of another company's voting stock, such that it has the ability to elect a majority of the board of directors and, as a result, the ability to affect its strategic direction and hiring of executive management

conversion feature Contract provision that allows bondholders or preferred shareholders to convert their shares into common stock at a predetermined conversion ratio

convertible securities Debt and equity securities that provide the holder with an option to convert those securities into other securities

cookie jar reserve Accounting method in which income is shifted from the current period to a future period

core (persistent) components Elements of income that are most likely to persist and are most relevant for projecting future financial performance

corporation A form of business organization that is a separate legal entity from its owners; characterized by a large number of owners who own shares of equity and who are not involved in managing the day-to-day operations of the company

cost flow assumption One of several alternative methods used to account for inventory and cost of goods sold when input prices change

cost method Accounting method in which investment is continually reported at its historical cost, and cash dividends and interest are recognized in current income

cost of goods sold An expense reflecting the cost of merchandise or manufactured products sold to customers

coupon (contract or stated) rate The interest rate stated in the bond contract; used to compute interest payments during the bond's life

covenants Contractual requirements that the loan recipient maintain minimum levels of capital to safeguard lenders

credit entry An entry on the right-hand side of an account; used to record decreases in assets and increases in liabilities and stockholders' equity

credit sales A business transaction between companies where no cash immediately changes hands; also called *sales on account*

creditors Those to whom a company owes money; those who provide debt financing

currency translation adjustment The unrecognized gain or loss on assets and liabilities denominated in foreign currencies

current assets The most liquid assets, which can be converted into cash within one year or one operating cycle

current liabilities Obligations such as accounts payable, accrued liabilities, unearned revenues, short-term notes payable, and current maturities of long-term debt that are due within one year

current maturities of long-term debt Long-term borrowings that are scheduled to mature in whole or in part during the upcoming year, including accrued interest

current ratio Measure of liquidity defined as current assets divided by current liabilities; a ratio greater than 1.0 implies positive net working capital

D

debit entry An entry on the left-hand side of an account; used to record increases in assets and decreases in liabilities and stockholders' equity

debt-to-equity (DE) A common measure of financial leverage, defined as total liabilities divided by stockholder's equity

default The nonpayment of interest and principal or the failure to adhere to various terms and conditions of an investment

deferral An accounting adjustment in which assets and revenues received in advance of a certain accounting period are allocated as expenses and revenues during that period

deferred income taxes The difference between income tax expense as reported in the income statement and income taxes due to taxing authorities; reported in the balance sheet as either an asset or liability

deferred performance liabilities Obligations that will be satisfied, not by paying cash, but instead, by providing products or services to customers

deferred revenue See *unearned revenue*

deferred tax asset Situation when tax reporting income is less than financial reporting income; the deferred tax asset expires when the temporary difference reverses

deferred tax liability Taxes to be paid in the future when taxable income is higher than financial reporting income; also called *deferred taxes*

defined benefit plan Pension plan in which the company makes periodic payments to an employee after retirement, generally based on years of service and employee's age

defined contribution plan Pension plan in which a company makes periodic contributions to a current employee's account, which the employee may drawn upon following retirement; many plans require an employee matching contribution

definite life A determinable period of time that an intangible asset, such as a patent or franchise right, exists

depletion The process of transferring costs from the resource account into inventory as resources are used up

deposits in transit Deposits not yet recorded by the bank

depreciation The decline in value of equipment and assets due to wear, deterioration, and obsolescence; process of allocating costs of equipment, vehicles, and buildings to the periods benefiting from their use

depreciation and amortization expenses Write-offs of previously recorded assets added to net income as it is converted to net operating cash flow

depreciation base The capitalized cost of an asset less the estimated residual value

depreciation method Means of calculating the reduction in an asset's value over its useful life

depreciation rate Method of depreciation equal to one divided by the item's useful life

derivatives Financial instruments that are utilized by companies to reduce various kinds of risk

detection control An internal control a company adopts to discover problems soon after they arise

diluted EPS Earnings per share that includes stock options and convertible securities in the calculations

dilutive securities Securities that can be converted into shares of common stock and would therefore reduce (or dilute) the earnings per share upon conversion

direct association Recognizing a cost directly associated with a specific source of revenue at the same time the related revenue is recognized

direct method Accounting method that presents net cash flow from operating activities by showing the major categories of operating cash receipts and payments

disclosure The act of providing financial and nonfinancial information to external users

discontinued operations Any separately identifiable component of a company that management abandons, sells or intends to sell

discount Situation where a bond's coupon rate is less than market rate

discount rate The interest rate used in present value calculations

dividend payout ratio Dividend payments divided by net income

dividend preference The order in which shareholders receive dividends; preferred shareholders take precedence over common shareholders

double declining balance (DDB) method An accelerated depreciation method that computes the depreciation rate as twice the straight-line rate times the remaining balance of the asset

double entry accounting system The dual effects where, in order to maintain the equality of the accounting equation, each transaction must affect at least two accounts

E

earned capital The cumulative net income (losses) retained by the company; income not paid to shareholders as dividends

earned income Income in which the seller has executed its duties under the terms of the sales agreement and the title has passed to the buyer

earnings before interest (EBI) Measures the income generated by a firm before taking into account any of its financing costs; computed as Net income + [Interest expense × (1 − Statutory tax rate)]

earnings before interest and taxes (EBIT) Measures the income generated by a firm before interest expense and income taxes

earnings management Discretionary choices management makes that mask the underlying economic performance of a company

earnings quality A measure of earnings in terms of sustainability, the ability for income to persist in future periods

economic consequences Issues resulting from accounting changes

economic value added (EVA) Net operating profits after tax less a charge for the use of capital equal to beginning capital utilized in the business multiplied by the weighted average cost of capital

EDGAR Database maintained by the SEC where financial statements are available for download

effective cost The cost to a bond's issuing company for offering the bond, generally as cash interest paid plus the discount or premium incurred

effective tax rate The average tax rate applied to pretax earnings; computed by dividing reported income tax expense by reported pretax earnings

employee severance costs Accrued (estimated) costs for termination of employees as part of a restructuring program

equity Capital provided by the company's owners, including stock, retained earnings, and additional paid-in capital; the owners' claim in the company

equity carve outs Corporate divestitures that are generally motivated by the belief that consolidated financial statements obscure the performance of individual business units

equity method Accounting method that reports investment on the balance sheet at an amount equal to the percentage of the investee's equity owned by the investor

equity valuation model A means of defining the value of an equity security in terms of the present value of future forecasted amounts

executory contract Situation such as a purchase order where a future sacrifice is probable and the amount of the sacrifice can be reasonably estimated, but the transaction that caused the obligation has not yet occurred

expense Outflow or use of assets, including costs of products and services sold, operating costs, and interest on debt, to generate revenue

expense to sales (ETS) A ratio measuring the percentage of each sales dollar that goes to cover a specific expense item; computed by dividing the expense by sales revenue

expensed Situation when a cost is recorded in the income statement and labeled as an expense

extraordinary items Material gains or losses that are not related to normal business operations; must be both unusual in nature and infrequent in occurrence

F

face amount The principal amount of a bond, which is repaid at maturity

fair value The value of an asset based on current rates in the general public

fair value option Provides companies with the option of using fair value to measure the value of most financial assets and liabilities

feedback value A characteristic of information that enables users to confirm or correct prior expectations

financial accounting The process of recording, summarizing, and analyzing financial transactions designed primarily for decision makers outside of the company

Financial Accounting Standards Board (FASB) Standard-setting organization which publishes accounting standards governing the preparation of financial reports

financial leverage The proportionate use of borrowed funds in the capital structure

financial statement analysis Identifying and examining relationships between numbers within the financial statements and trends in these relationships from one period to the next

financial statement effects template Form that captures each transaction and its financial statement effects on the balance sheet and income statement

financing activities Methods companies use to fund investment resources

finished goods Inventory account that records completed manufactured items waiting to be sold

first-in first-out (FIFO) Inventory costing method that transfers costs from inventory in the order they were initially recorded

fiscal year The annual (one year) accounting period adopted by a company for its financial activities

fixed commitments ratio The ratio of operating cash flow to fixed commitments; computed as operating cash flow divided by fixed commitments

fixed costs Expenses that do not change with changes in sales volume (over a reasonable range)

forecast error Differences between amounts reported in the financial statements and amounts forecasted in pro forma financial statements

franchise A contractual agreement that gives a company the right to operate a particular business in an area for a particular period of time

free cash flow The net cash flow from operations less capital expenditures and dividends

fundamental analysis Method of using a company's financial information to estimate its value, which is used in buy-sell strategies

funded status The difference between a company's pension plan assets and the projected benefit obligation

future benefits Revenues or some other compensation a company expects to receive in a later period

future value The amount that a specific investment is worth at a future date if invested at a given rate of compound interest

future value factor A value that is multiplied by a current amount to obtain its equivalent value at a future date; the value of $1 invested for a number of periods at a specified interest rate

G

gain on bond retirement Situation where the repurchase price of a bond is less than the net bonds payable

general journal A flexible journal that allows any type of business transaction to be included

generally accepted accounting principles (GAAP) An overall set of standards and procedures accountants have developed that apply to the preparation of financial statements

goodwill An intangible asset recorded when a company acquires another company, consisting of the value of a company above and beyond the fair value of its specific assets

gross profit The difference between revenues (at selling prices) and cost of goods sold (at purchasing price or manufacturing cost)

gross profit margin (GPM) A measure that reflects the net impact of sales on profitability, defined as gross profit divided by net sales

H

held-to-maturity (HTM) Debt securities that management holds on to for their full term

historical cost The original acquisition cost, less the portion that that has expired or been transferred to the income statement

horizontal analysis An examination of data across two or more consecutive time periods, which assists in analyzing company performance and predicting future performance

I

immediate recognition Costs recognized as expenses in a period when they were incurred, even though they cannot be directly linked to specific revenues

impairment Loss of property, plant, and equipment value determined by comparing the sum of expected future cash flows to the asset's net book value

income Also called *net income*, equals revenue minus expense, and is the increase in net assets (equity) resulting from the company's operations

income smoothing The discretionary management practice of choosing the timing of transactions in order to minimize fluctuations and maintain steady improvements in net income

income statement A financial report on operating activities that lists revenues less expenses over a period of time, yielding a company's net income

indefinite lives Situation where an intangible asset's expected useful life extends far enough into the future that it is practically impossible to accurately determine

indirect method Accounting method for preparing the statement of cash flows in which the operating section begins with net income and converts it to cash flows from operations

in-process research and development An intangible asset whose cost must be written off immediately upon purchase

installment loan Loan that requires a fixed periodic payment for a fixed duration of time

insufficient write-down Impairment of assets to a larger degree than is recognized

intangible assets Assets such as trademarks and patents that supply the owner rights rather than physical objects

intercorporate investments Investments in the securities of other companies

interest cost Interest accrued on outstanding pension liability, which is added to the liability each year

internal auditing A company function that provides independent appraisals of the company's financial statements, its internal controls, and its operations

internal controls Policies and procedures used to protect assets, ensure reliable accounting, promote efficient operations, and urge adherence to company policies

International Accounting Standards Board (IASB) The governing body established to develop acceptable accounting standards on a worldwide basis

International Financial Reporting Standards (IFRS) Guidelines developed by the IASB with the intention of unifying all public companies under one global set of reporting standards

inventory Goods purchased or produced for sale to customers

inventory quality The rate at which inventory is turned over; the faster the turnover, the higher the quality

inventory turnover (INVT) Measure of inventory management computed as cost of goods sold divided by average inventory

investing activities Methods companies use to acquire and dispose of assets in the course of production and sales

J

journal A tabular record in which business activities are analyzed in terms of debits and credits and recorded in chronological order before they are entered in the general ledger; also called *book of original entry*

journal entries An accounting entry in a company's financial records that accountants use to represent individual transactions

L

last-in, first-out (LIFO) Inventory costing method that transfers the most recent costs from inventory first

leaning on the trade An increase in accounts payable, which results in an increase in net cash flows from operating activities

lease asset The value of a leased item

lease liability The payments required to lease an item

lessee A party to a lease who wishes to use the asset

lessor The owner of an asset

liability A probable future economic sacrifice resulting from a past or current event

licenses See *operating rights*

LIFO layer New layer added to inventory at an updated price each time inventory is purchased in companies using LIFO inventory costing; the most recent costs are transferred to cost of goods sold

LIFO liquidation Situation when, in companies using LIFO inventory costing, quantity of inventory sold exceeds that purchased, in which case the costs of older inventory is transferred to cost of good sold

LIFO reserve The difference between the cost of inventories using FIFO and the cost using LIFO

liquidation preference In the event of a company's failure, preferred shareholders are reimbursed in full before common shareholders are paid

liquidity The ease of converting noncash assets into cash

long-term debt Amounts borrowed from creditors that are scheduled to be repaid more than one year into the future

long-term debt-to-equity A common measure of leverage that focuses on long-term financing, defined as long-term debt divided by stockholders' equity

long-term investments Investments that the company does not intend to sell in the near future

long-term operating asset turnover The rate that reflects capital intensity relative to sales, defined as net sales divided by average long-term operating assets

loss on bond retirement Situation if a bond's issuer pays more to retire the bonds than the amount carried on its balance sheet

lower of cost or market (LCM) Process of reporting inventories at the lower of its cost or its current market value

M

maker Owner of a checking account

managerial accounting The process of recording, summarizing, and analyzing financial transactions designed primarily for decision makers within the company

manufacturing costs Expenses associated with product production, including materials, labor, and overhead

marginal tax rate The tax rate that applies to the marginal dollar of income; the tax rate generally applied to nonoperating revenues and expenses

mark-to-market Method of valuing assets that results in an adjustment of an asset's carrying amount to its fair value

market rate The interest rate that investors expect to earn on their debt security investment; used to price the bond; also called *yield rate*

market value Company value computed by multiplying the number of outstanding shares of common stock by the market price per share

marketable securities Short-term investments that can be quickly sold to raise cash

markup The difference between an item's selling price and the cost incurred to produce it

matching Recognizing expenses in the same period that the associated revenue is recognized

minority interest An ownership in a company that is less than a majority or controlling interest

N

net assets Assets minus liabilities

net financial expense Net operating profit after tax less net income

net financial obligations (NFO) The difference between financial (nonoperating) obligations and financial (nonoperating) assets; positive if obligations exceed assets

net financial rate Net financial expense divided by average net financial obligations

net income The difference between revenues and expenses when revenues exceed expenses

net interest rate (NIR) The average interest rate after taxes on total liabilities; calculated as [Interest expense × (1 − Statutory tax rate)]/Average total liabilities

net loss The difference between revenues and expenses when expenses exceed revenues

net-of-discount method Inventory capitalized at the net cost, assuming that a cash discount will be taken by the buyer

net operating assets (NOA) Current and long-term operating assets less current and long-term operating liabilities

net operating assets turnover (NOAT) A measure of turnover defined as sales divided by average net operating assets

net operating profit margin (NOPM) The amount of operating profit produced as a percentage of each sales dollar; excludes all nonoperating revenues and expenses; calculated as Net operating profit after tax (NOPAT) divided by Sales revenue

net operating profit after tax (NOPAT) Sales less operating expenses (including taxes)

net operating working capital (NOWC) Operating current assets less operating current liabilities

net operating working capital turnover (NOWCT) Management's effectiveness in using operating working capital, defined as net sales divided by average net operating working capital

net profit margin The income to sales ratio, which reflects the profitability of sales; also called simply *profit margin*

net realizable value The value of a company's receivables, less an allowance for uncollectible accounts

net working capital The difference between current assets and current liabilities; also called *working capital*

neutrality A characteristic of information that is free of any bias intended to attain a predetermined result or to induce a particular mode of behavior

nominal cost Cash interest paid on a debt

non pro rata distribution A case where stockholders can accept or reject the distribution of shares

noncash investing and financing activities Significant financial events that do not affect current cash flows, such as issuance of stocks and bonds in exchange for property, plant, and equipment

noncurrent assets Assets not used up or converted to cash in one year; include Long-term financial investments, Property, plant, and equipment (PPE), and Intangible and other assets

noncurrent liabilities Obligations such as long-term debt and other long-term liabilities that are to be paid after one year

non-operating revenues and expenses Costs related to the company's financing and investing activities, including interest revenue and interest expense

nonrecurring Revenues and expenses that are unlikely to arise in the future and are largely irrelevant to predictions of future performance

notes payable Account assigned to a company's financial borrowings

notes receivable Receivables that are based on a formal written promise to pay a specified amount and a predetermined date

O

off-balance-sheet financing A company's financial obligations that are not reported as liabilities in the balance sheet

on-balance-sheet financing The reporting of financing effects, namely current and noncurrent liabilities, on the balance sheet

operating activities Methods companies use to produce, promote, and sell its products and services

operating cash flow to capital expenditures ratio A measure that helps assess a firm's ability to replace its property, plant, and equipment, or expand as needed; calculated as operating cash flows from operating activities divided by annual capital expenditures

operating cash flow to current liabilities ratio A measure of the ability to liquidate current liabilities, calculated as net cash flow from operating activities divided by average current liabilities

operating cash flow to liabilities (OCFL) A method to compare operating flows to liabilities, defined as net cash flow from operations divided by total liabilities

operating cycle The time between paying cash for goods or employee services and receiving cash from customers

operating expense The usual and customary costs a company incurs to support its main business activities, including cost of goods sold, selling expenses, depreciation expenses, amortization expenses, and research and development expenses

operating expense margin (OEM) The ratio obtained by dividing any operating expense category by sales

operating lease method Method of reporting leases where neither the lease asset nor the lease liability is on the balance sheet

operating rights A contractual agreement similar to franchise rights, but typically granted by government agencies

options See stock options

ordinary annuity A series of fixed payments made at the end of each period over a specified time period

other long-term liabilities Various obligations, such as pension liabilities and long-term tax liabilities, that will be satisfied at least one year in the future

other post-employment benefits (OPEB) Benefits, other than pension benefits, such as health care and insurance benefits, provided by a company to retired employees

other postretirement benefits Items such as health care and insurance benefits offered to retired employees

outstanding checks Checks not yet recorded by the bank

overfunded Situation where pension plan assets exceed pension liabilities

P

par value Face value of a bond; in stocks, an arbitrary amount set by company organizers at the time of formation

participation feature Contract provision that allows preferred shareholders to share ratably with common shareholders in dividends

partnership A form of business entity characterized by two or more owners who are also usually involved in managing the business

passive influence Indicating lack of control of, or active participation in, the affairs of an investee company.

patent An exclusive right to produce a product or use a technology

payee The person named on a check who will receive compensation

payer The bank that will compensate the recipient of a check

percent change Financial statement adjustment computed by dollar change (analysis period amount less base period amount) divided by base period amount, with the result multiplied by 100

percentage-of-completion method Revenue recognition method which recognizes revenue by determining the costs incurred under the contract relative to its total expected costs

percentage of sales A means to estimate uncollectible accounts that computes bad debts expense as a percentage of total sales

periodic interest payment Interest payments made in the form of equal cash flows at periodic intervals

permanent account An account used to prepare the balance sheet; that is, asset, liability, and equity capital (capital stock and retained earnings) accounts; any balance in a permanent account at the end of an accounting period is carried forward to the next period

permanent difference A difference in amount between two financial statements that does not reverse in time

persistent An amount that is expected to be maintained in future periods; see also recurring

plan assets The assets of a pension plan that involve investments in stocks and bonds

planning activities The process of identifying a company's goals, and the strategies adopted to reach those goals

post-closing trial balance Accounting balance prepared after closing entries are recorded and posted to verify the equality between debits and credits in the general ledger after the adjusting and closing process

posting The transfer of debit and credit entries from the journal to their related general ledger accounts

predictive value A characteristic of information referring to its ability to increase the accuracy of a forecast

preferred stock Stock that possesses priority over common stock, such as first right to dividends or liquidation payout

premium When a bond's coupon rate is greater than the market rate

prepaid expenses Costs paid in advance for rent, insurance, or other services

present value The amount of money a stock or bond is worth at the current time

present value factor A value that is multiplied by a future amount to obtain its equivalent value at the current date; the value of $1 received in the future discounted for a number of periods at a specified discount rate

prevention control An internal control companies adopt to deter problems before they arise

profit margin (PM) A ratio measuring profit, before interest expense, that is generated from each dollar of sales revenue; calculated as Earnings before interest (EBI) divided by Sales revenue

profitability The ability of a company to generate net income

pro forma financial statements Hypothetical statements prepared to reflect specific assumptions about a company and its transactions; often referring to forecasted financial statements

pro forma income GAAP income from continuing operations (excluding discontinued operations and extraordinary items), less transitory items

pro rata distribution Shares distributed to stockholders on a pro rata basis

projected benefit obligation (PBO) Pension liabilities that represent future obligations to current and former employees

property, plant, and equipment (PPE) Tangible assets recorded on a balance sheet, including land, factory buildings, warehouses, office buildings, office equipment, and other items used in the operation of a business

provision for income tax Income tax expense

Public Company Accounting Oversight Board (PCAOB) Board established by the Sarbanes-Oxley Act to approve auditing standards and monitor the quality of financial statements and audits

purchase method The prescribed method of accounting for business combinations; under the purchase method, assets and liabilities of the acquired company are recorded at fair value, together with identifiable intangible assets; the balance is ascribed to goodwill

Q

quality of earnings The extent to which reported income reflects the underlying economic performance of a company

quick ratio (QR) A ratio that reflects a company's ability to meet its current liabilities without liquidating inventories

R

raw materials and supplies Inventory account that records items used in production processes

realized or realizable income Income in which the company's net assets increase

receivables quality The likelihood of collecting on a receivables account, which a company can change by extending credit terms, taking on longer-paying customers, and increasing the allowance provision

reconciled cash balance A company's cash balance after accounting for deposits in transit and outstanding checks

recurring An amount that is expected to be reported again in future periods; see also persistent

redeem Company repurchasing their bonds prior to maturity

relevance The usefulness of information to those who use financial statements in decision making

reliability The ability to objectively determine and accurately measure a value, such as historical cost

representational faithfulness A characteristic of accounting information referring to the degree with which it reflects the underlying economic events it purports to measure

residual (or salvage) value The expected realizable value of an asset at the end of its useful life

restructuring costs Expenses typically associated with activities such as consolidating production facilities, reorganizing sales operations, outsourcing activities, or discontinuing product lines

retained earnings Earned capital, the cumulative net income and loss, of the company (from its inception) that has not been paid to shareholders as dividends

return The amount of money earned on an investment, often expressed as investment income divided by the amount invested; also called *yield*

return on assets (ROA) A computation of net income divided by average total assets; also called *return on invested capital*

return on equity (ROE) The ultimate measure of performance from the shareholders' perspective, computed as net income divided by average equity

return on financial leverage (ROFL) A measure of the effect that financial leverage has on Return on equity (ROE); calculated as Return on equity (ROE) minus Return on assets (ROA)

return on net operating assets (RNOA) A measure of operating returns; calculated as Net operating profit after taxes (NOPAT) divided by Average net operating assets (NOA)

return on sales An overall test of operating efficiency defined as net income divided by net sales revenue; Increase in net assets (assets less liabilities) as a result of business activities

revenue The increase in equity resulting from the sale of goods and services to customers

revenue recognition The timing and amount of revenue reported by a company

revenue recognition criteria Requirements that must be met for income to be recognized on the income statement; according to GAAP, revenue must be realized/realizable and earned

revenue recognition principle Accounting rule that requires revenue to be recognized (recorded) only when earned

right of return The allowance for a customer to return a product within a specified period of time

risk The uncertainty of expected return, which is an intrinsic part of each investment

risk-free rate The market rate of interest defined as the yield on U.S. Government borrowings, computed as yield rate less spread

S

Sarbanes-Oxley Act Act passed in 2002 which requires a company's CEO and CFO to personally sign a statement attesting to the accuracy and completeness of financial statements

Securities and Exchange Commision (SEC) Commision created by the 1934 Securities Act to regulate the issuance and trading of securities

security valuation A determination of the value of equity securities

sell-off The outright sale of a business unit

sensitivity analysis The process of examining the effect of alternative assumptions on the pro forma statements; helps to identify these effects before a decision is made so that costly mistakes can be avoided

service cost The additional pension benefits earned by employees each year

shareholders' equity See *equity*

shares authorized The number of shares that a corporation can issue without amending its corporate charter

shares issued The actual number of shares that have been sold to stockholders by a corporation

shares outstanding The number of issued shares less the number of shares repurchased as treasury stock

short term borrowings Debt payable to banks or other creditors that is due within one year or within one operating cycle

short-term interest-bearing debt Short-term bank borrowings and notes expected to mature in whole or in part during the upcoming year

short-term notes payable Short-term debt payable to banks or other creditors

significant influence The ability of an investor to affect an investee's financing or operating policies

simple capital structure Stockholders' equity with no *dilutive securities* outstanding

sole proprietorship A form of business characterized by a single owner who typically manages the daily operations

solvency A company's ability to meet its obligations, mainly to creditors

solvency analysis A review of a company's ability to meet its financial obligations, which is aided by financial leverage ratios

spin-off A form of equity carve out in which a company distributes subsidiary shares it owns as dividends to its shareholders, making shareholders owners of the subsidiary

spread The difference between the net financial return (NFR) and the return on net operating activities (RNOA); also called *risk premium*

statement of cash flows A financial report that identifies net cash flows into and out of a company from operating, investing, and financing activities over a period of time

statement of responsibility Form included with each financial statement of a publicly traded company assuring management is responsible for the statements, they have been prepared using GAAP, and they are audited by an outside organization

statement of stockholders' equity A financial statement that reports on changes in key equity accounts over a period of time; also called a *statement of equity*

stock option A stock right giving the holder the right to acquire a share of stock at a preset price within a specified period of time; used to compensate officers and other employees

stock rights A stockholder's option to acquire a specified number of shares of capital stock under prescribed conditions and within a stated period

stock split A distribution (or increase in the number) of shares of common stock accompanied by a proportionate decrease in the par value

stock warrant A certificate that provides the holder with stock rights

stockholders Owners of a corporation; holders of shares of stock in a corporation

stockholders' equity See *equity*

straight-line depreciation Determination of annual depreciation expense by dividing the asset's cost by its estimated useful life

suppliers Providers of merchandise for resale or materials needed for operating activities

systematic allocation Costs that benefit more than one accounting period and cannot be associated with specific revenues

T

T-account A graphic representation of an account, shaped like a large T, which uses one side to record increases to the account and the other side to record decreases

tangible assets Assets that have physical substance, such as property, plant, and equipment

temporary account An account used to gather information for an accounting period; at the end of the period, the balance is transferred to a permanent owners' equity account; revenue, expense, and dividends accounts are temporary accounts

temporary difference A difference in amount between two financial statements that reverses in time

timeliness A characteristic of information that is received by decision makers before it loses its capacity to influence decisions

times interest earned (TIE) A determination of how much income is available to service debt, defined as earnings before interest and taxes divided by interest expense

time value of money The recognition that the value of an amount of money depends on when the money is received;

tombstone An announcement of debt offered to the public

trade credit The financing used to purchase inventories on credit from other companies

trademark A registered name, logo, package design, image, jingle, or slogan associated with a product

trading securities Investments in securities that management intends to actively buy and sell for trading profits as market prices fluctuate

transitory components Elements of income that are not recurring; financial projections are improved if these are excluded from them

treasury stock Shares of outstanding stock that have been acquired by the issuing corporation; a contra equity account

trend analysis A type of horizontal analysis in which a base period is chosen and all subsequent period amounts are defined relative to the base

trend percentages A comparison of the same financial item over two or more years, stated as a percentage of a base-year amount

U

unadjusted trial balance Account balances before any adjustments are made

underfunded Situation where pension liabilities exceed pension plan assets

unearned revenue Cash received for products or services to be provided at a later time

units-of-production method A common depreciation method in which the useful life of the asset is defined in terms of the number of units of service provided by the asset

unrealized holding gain A gain resulting from holding an asset such as inventory as prices are rising

unrecognized prior service cost An accounting adjustment to a pension that represents the portion of the liability earned by employees prior to the plan's inception or a plan amendment

useful life The period of time over which the asset in expected to provide economic benefits to the company

V

variable costs Expenses that change in proportion to changes in sales volume

verifiability A characteristic of accounting information referring to the ability of an independent auditor to reproduce the accounting information by examining the underlying economic events and transactions

vertical analysis A means of overcoming size differences among companies by expressing income statement items as a percentage of net sales and all balance sheet items as a percentage of total assets

vesting period A period of time during which the employee is not allowed to exercise a stock option; also refers to a period after which an employee retains his or her pension benefits even if employment is terminated

W

wasting assets Assets consumed as they are used, including natural resources such as oil reserves, mineral deposits, or timberland

weighted average cost of capital (WACC) The discount rate where the weights are the relative percentages of debt and equity in the capital structure and are applied to the expected returns on debt and equity, respectively

work in process Inventory account that tracks the value of items currently being produced

working capital Current assets less current liabilities

Index

A

B

C

D

E

F

G

J

P

S

T

X

Z